FOR REFERENCE

NOT TO BE TAKEN FROM THIS ROOM

HANDBOOK
OF
TRANSPORT AND
THE ENVIRONMENT

HANDBOOKS IN TRANSPORT

4

Series Editors

DAVID A. HENSHER

KENNETH J. BUTTON

HANDBOOK OF TRANSPORT AND THE ENVIRONMENT

Edited by

DAVID A. HENSHER
*Institute of Transport Studies,
University of Sydney*

KENNETH J. BUTTON
*The School of Public Policy,
George Mason University*

ELSEVIER
2003
Amsterdam – Boston – Heidelberg – London – New York – Oxford
Paris – San Diego – San Francisco – Singapore – Sydney – Tokyo

ELSEVIER B.V.	ELSEVIER Inc.	**ELSEVIER Ltd**	ELSEVIER Ltd
Sara Burgerhartstraat 25	525 B Street, Suite 1900	**The Boulevard, Langford Lane**	84 Theobalds Road
P.O. Box 211, 1000 AE Amsterdam	San Diego, CA 92101-4495	**Kidlington, Oxford OX5 1GB**	London WC1X 8RR
The Netherlands	USA	**UK**	UK

© 2003 Elsevier Ltd. All rights reserved.

This work is protected under copyright by Elsevier Ltd, and the following terms and conditions apply to its use:

Photocopying
Single photocopies of single chapters may be made for personal use as allowed by national copyright laws. Permission of the Publisher and payment of a fee is required for all other photocopying, including multiple or systematic copying, copying for advertising or promotional purposes, resale, and all forms of document delivery. Special rates are available for educational institutions that wish to make photocopies for non-profit educational classroom use.

Permissions may be sought directly from Elsevier's Rights Department in Oxford, UK: phone (+44) 1865 843830, fax (+44) 1865 853333, e-mail: permissions@elsevier.com. Requests may also be completed on-line via the Elsevier homepage (http://www.elsevier.com/locate/permissions).

In the USA, users may clear permissions and make payments through the Copyright Clearance Center, Inc., 222 Rosewood Drive, Danvers, MA 01923, USA; phone: (+1) (978) 7508400, fax: (+1) (978) 7504744, and in the UK through the Copyright Licensing Agency Rapid Clearance Service (CLARCS), 90 Tottenham Court Road, London W1P 0LP, UK; phone: (+44) 20 7631 5555; fax: (+44) 20 7631 5500. Other countries may have a local reprographic rights agency for payments.

Derivative Works
Tables of contents may be reproduced for internal circulation, but permission of the Publisher is required for external resale or distribution of such material. Permission of the Publisher is required for all other derivative works, including compilations and translations.

Electronic Storage or Usage
Permission of the Publisher is required to store or use electronically any material contained in this work, including any chapter or part of a chapter.

Except as outlined above, no part of this work may be reproduced, stored in a retrieval system or transmitted in any form or by any means, electronic, mechanical, photocopying, recording or otherwise, without prior written permission of the Publisher. Address permissions requests to: Elsevier's Rights Department, at the fax and e-mail addresses noted above.

Notice
No responsibility is assumed by the Publisher for any injury and/or damage to persons or property as a matter of products liability, negligence or otherwise, or from any use or operation of any methods, products, instructions or ideas contained in the material herein. Because of rapid advances in the medical sciences, in particular, independent verification of diagnoses and drug dosages should be made.

First edition 2003

Library of Congress Cataloging in Publication Data: A catalog record is available from the Library of Congress.
British Library Cataloguing in Publication Data: A catalogue record is available from the British Library.

ISBN: 0-08-044103-3
Series ISSN: 1472-7889

♾ The paper used in this publication meets the requirements of ANSI/NISO Z39.48-1992 (Permanence of Paper).
Printed in The Netherlands.

INTRODUCTION TO THE SERIES

Transportation and logistics research has now reached maturity, with a solid foundation of established methodology for professionals to turn to and for future researchers and practitioners to build on. Elsevier is marking this stage in the life of the subject by launching a landmark series of reference works: *Elsevier's Handbooks in Transport*. Comprising specially commissioned chapters from the leading experts of their topics, each title in the series will encapsulate the essential knowledge of a major area within transportation and logistics. To practitioners, researchers and students alike, these books will be authoritative, accessible and invaluable.

David A. Hensher
Kenneth J. Button

CONTENTS

Introduction to the series v

Chapter 1
Introduction
DAVID A. HENSHER and KENNETH J. BUTTON 1

1. Introduction 1
2. Transport and the environment 3
3. The Handbook 5

Chapter 2
Environmental Concepts – Physical and Economic
WERNER ROTHENGATTER 9

1. Introduction 9
2. Physical basis of environmental impacts 13
   2.1. The choice of indicators 13
   2.2. Physical measurement and the responsibility of the transport sector ... 18
3. Treatment of environmental risk by physical (hard) constraints ... 21
   3.1. The principles of ecological economics 21
   3.2. Safe minimum standards 22
   3.3. Environmental legacy 22
4. Economic concepts for the evaluation of environmental impacts ... 24
   4.1. The welfare maximization approach 24
   4.2. Risk approach 27
5. A sustainable development of the transport system 30
6. Conclusions 33
References 34

Chapter 3
Climate Change
MANFRED LENZEN, CHRISTOPHER DEY and CLIVE HAMILTON ... 37

1. Introduction 37
   1.1. The greenhouse effect and the radiative forcing of climate ... 38
   1.2. Sources of greenhouse gas emissions 42
   1.3. Equity and sustainability in the context of climate change ... 42
   1.4. History of greenhouse gas emissions 45
   1.5. International negotiations 48
2. Transport and greenhouse gas emissions 52

	2.1. Mobile sources	52
	2.2. History of emissions	53
3.	Conclusions: the role of transport in future abatement efforts	55
References		58

Chapter 4

Air Quality
BRITT A. HOLMÉN and DEBBIE A. NIEMEIER · 61

1.	Introduction	61
2.	Mobile source emissions overview	64
	2.1. On-road sources	65
	2.2. Off-road sources	68
3.	Important issues facing us	72
	3.1. Fine particles	72
	3.2. Toxics	74
References		76

Chapter 5

The Economics of Noise
DAVID GILLEN · 81

1.	Introduction	81
2.	The economics of noise	83
3.	Externalities and social cost	83
4.	Social cost and strategy choice	84
	4.1. Property rights for noise	87
5.	Airport noise measures	87
	5.1. Assessing the costs of noise management strategies	88
	5.2. Assessing the benefits of noise management strategies	89
6.	Summary	93
References		95

Chapter 6

Safety
IAN SAVAGE · 97

1.	Introduction	97
2.	Estimating the risks	97
	2.1. The big picture	97
	2.2. Health risks versus environmental risks	99
	2.3. Quantitative risk assessment	100
3.	Risk assessment	102
	3.1. Intolerable and negligible risks	102
	3.2. ALARP risks	103

4.	Market forces and failures	105
	4.1. Market failures	105
	4.2. The law and economics of externalities	106
5.	Is liability sufficient?	108
	5.1. Some types of financial harm are ineligible for compensation	108
	5.2. Emergency response costs are borne by the public	109
	5.3. Non-pecuniary losses	109
	5.4. Liability is not accurately reflected in pricing	110
	5.5. Bystanders prefer zero risk	110
	5.6. Risk perceptions may differ from reality	111
	5.7. Liability is an "after the fact" remedy	112
6.	Public policy	113
7.	Summary	115
	References	116

Chapter 7

Amenity and Severance
SUSAN HANDY — 117

1.	Introduction	117
2.	Defining the concepts	118
	2.1. Amenity	118
	2.2. Severance	120
	2.3. The connection between amenity and severance	122
3.	Techniques for assessing amenity and severance	123
	3.1. Assessing amenity	124
	3.2. Measuring severance	128
	3.3. Incorporating amenity and severance into composite measures	130
4.	Policies to improve amenity and reduce severance	131
	4.1. Improving amenity	131
	4.2. Reducing severance	134
5.	Conclusions	138
	References	139

Chapter 8

Transportation Fuels – A System Perspective
BENGT JOHANSSON — 141

1.	Introduction	141
2.	Fuel chains – an introduction	142
3.	Primary energy sources for transportation fuels	143
4.	Conventional fuels in ICEVs	144
5.	Alternative fuels – technologies and emissions	146
	5.1. Methane gas	146

		5.2. Biodiesel	146
		5.3. Ethanol	146
		5.4. Methanol and dimethyl ether (DME)	147
		5.5. Hydrogen	147
		5.6. Electricity	148
		5.7. The use of alternative fuels in HEVs and FCEVs	148
	6.	Fuel cycle emissions	148
	7.	Environmental and resource aspects of renewable energy technologies	150
	8.	Economic issues – a focus on alternatives	152
	9.	Discussion	155
	References		156

Chapter 9

Fuel Options
MUKESH KHARE and PRATEEK SHARMA — 159

1.	Introduction	159
2.	Types of fuels	160
	2.1. Gasoline	160
	2.2. Gasoline fuel properties and their effects on emissions	161
	2.3. Diesel	161
	2.4. Type and effect of emissions from conventional fuel-driven vehicles	164
3.	Alternative fuels	165
	3.1. What are AFs?	166
	3.2. Why are AFs important?	166
	3.3. AF characteristics	167
4.	Types of AFs	168
	4.1. Compressed natural gas	168
	4.2. Liquefied petroleum gas	170
	4.3. Methanol	172
	4.4. Ethanol	173
	4.5. Biodiesel	174
	4.6. Hydrogen	175
	4.7. Electricity	177
5.	Greenhouse gas emissions	178
6.	Factors influencing the large-scale use of AFs	179
	6.1. Cost	179
	6.2. End use considerations	180
	6.3. Life cycle emissions	180
7.	Conclusions	181
Acknowledgments		182
References		182

Chapter 10

Cleaner Vehicles
DANIEL SPERLING 185

1. Introduction 185
2. Recent history of alternative fuels 185
3. Internal combustion engines 187
    3.1. Spark ignition (gasoline) engines 187
    3.2. Diesel engines 188
4. Toward electric-drive vehicle technology 189
    4.1. Battery electric vehicles 190
    4.2. Hybrid electric vehicles 191
    4.3. Fuel cell vehicles and hydrogen 193
5. Conclusions 198
References 198

Chapter 11

Carbon Dioxide Emissions from Transportation: Trends, Driving Factors, and Forces for Change
LEE J. SCHIPPER and LEWIS FULTON 203

1. The CO_2 problem: the policy imperative after Kyoto 203
2. Underlying factors affecting CO_2 emissions for travel and freight .. 204
    2.1. Passenger transport 206
    2.2. Freight transport 212
    2.3. Non-IEA countries 216
3. The future 219
    3.1. Technology 219
    3.2. Policies under development 222
References 224

Chapter 12

Transport Energy and Emissions: Buses
JOHN STANLEY and PAUL WATKISS 227

1. Scope 227
2. Air pollution 228
    2.1. Choice of pollutants and impacts 228
    2.2. Criteria emissions from heavy-duty motor vehicles 229
    2.3. Diesel 232
    2.4. Alternative fuels 233
    2.5. Quantifying and valuing air pollution effects 236
3. Climate change 238
    3.1. Emissions 238

		3.2. Putting a cost on greenhouse gas emissions	239

      3.2. Putting a cost on greenhouse gas emissions   239
      3.3. Charges per litre   241
  4. Public and private transport   242
  5. Conclusions   244
  References   244

Chapter 13

Transport Energy and Emissions: Urban Public Transport
STEPHEN POTTER   247

  1. Urban public transport and energy use   247
  2. Measuring vehicle energy and emissions   248
  3. Air quality emissions   248
  4. Climate change emissions   251
  5. Improving energy and emissions from public transport   256
  6. Energy and emissions at the systems level   259
  7. Conclusions   261
  References   261

Chapter 14

Transport Energy and Emissions: Aviation
HUGH SOMERVILLE   263

  1. Background   263
      1.1. The industry   263
      1.2. Aviation and sustainable development   264
  2. Emissions   266
      2.1. Local air quality   266
      2.2. Global impact   268
      2.3. Aviation and global warming   269
      2.4. Regulatory controls   272
      2.5. Market-based measures   272
      2.6. Voluntary measures   274
      2.7. Inefficiencies   275
      2.8. What are airlines doing   275
  3. The future   276
  4. Conclusion   277
  References   277

Chapter 15

Environmental Impacts of Shipping
WAYNE K. TALLEY   279

  1. Introduction   279
  2. Vessel oil spills   279

3.	Ballast water disposal	285
4.	Air pollution	287
5.	Anti-fouling pollution (tributyltin)	287
6.	Dredging	288
7.	Vessel scrapping	289
8.	Waste disposal at sea	289
9.	Summary	290
	References	290

Chapter 16
Transport Energy and Emissions: Rail
ALAIN BONNAFOUS and CHARLES RAUX — 293

1.	Introduction	293
2.	The historical association between rail and energy efficiency	293
	2.1 From the first rails …	294
	2.2. … to spatial expansion	294
3.	Energy use and pollution: some orders of magnitude	295
	3.1. The energy problem	295
	3.2. The problem of negative impacts	297
4.	From average values to realities in the field	298
	4.1. Varied energy balance sheets	299
	4.2. Negative impacts and carbon dioxide emissions	300
5.	So what is the optimum policy?	301
	5.1. Should we attract travelers to trains?	301
	5.2. A very topical example for freight	304
	5.3. Evaluation still remains to be done	306
6.	Conclusion	306
	References	307

Chapter 17
Environmental Impact Assessment for Sustainable Transport
SUNDER L. DHINGRA, K.V.K. RAO and V.M. TOM — 309

1.	Introduction	309
2.	The environmental impact assessment process	311
3.	The transport model	311
4.	Air pollution	312
5.	Noise impact assessment	314
6.	Ecological impacts	316
7.	Social and economic impacts	318
8.	Travel impacts	320
	8.1. Transport congestion indicator	321
	8.2. Transport efficiency index	321

9.	Implementation of EIA	322
10.	A case study	322
	10.1. The Mumbai Urban Transport Project	322
	10.2. The EIA process	323
	10.3. Transport modeling	324
	10.4. Air quality impacts	324
	10.5. Noise impacts	325
	10.6. Ecological impacts	325
	10.7. Social impacts	325
	10.8. Travel impacts	326
	10.9. EIA evaluation	326
	10.10. Inferences	328
11.	Conclusion	328
	References	329

Chapter 18

Transport Investment Appraisal and the Environment
PETER NIJKAMP, BARRY UBBELS and ERIK VERHOEF   333

1.	Introduction	333
2.	Transport infrastructure investment and appraisal methods	334
3.	CBA in transport: some issues relevant for environmental appraisal	336
	3.1. Welfare measurement in applied CBAs: social surplus	337
	3.2. CBA under various "second-best" conditions	337
	3.3. Discounting	341
	3.4. Spatial scope of CBAs	343
	3.5. Transport appraisal and environmental sustainability	344
4.	The valuation of environmental effects from transport	347
	4.1. Environmental effects of transport	347
	4.2. The valuation of environmental externalities	348
	4.3. Some recent estimates of environmental external costs of transport	351
5.	Conclusion	353
	Acknowledgments	354
	References	354

Chapter 19

Evaluation of Environmental Impacts
EMILE QUINET   357

1.	Introduction	357
2.	The scope of the analysis	357
3.	The objectives of the evaluation	358

4.	Methodological issues	359
5.	Evaluation by type of impact	362
	5.1. Non-quantifiable impacts	362
	5.2. Quantifiable impacts which are non-monetizable or monetizable only with difficulty	363
	5.3. Quantifiable and monetizable impacts	365
6.	The presentation in perspective and results of the studies	369
7.	Conclusions	371
	References	373

Chapter 20

Valuation of Environmental Externalities
WIKTOR ADAMOWICZ — 375

1.	Introduction	375
2.	The damage function approach	377
3.	Value and valuation techniques	378
	3.1. Change in consumer and producer surplus	379
	3.2. Avoided costs	379
	3.3. Averting behavior	379
	3.4. Hedonic price methods	379
	3.5. Contingent valuation	380
	3.6. Choice experiments	380
	3.7. Travel cost models	381
4.	Valuation of non-health end-points	381
	4.1. Valuation of agricultural and forest impacts	381
	4.2. Valuation of recreation impacts	383
	4.3. Valuation of other non-health impacts	385
	4.4. Passive use values	386
5.	Examples of non-health values	387
6.	Conclusions	387
	Acknowledgment	388
	References	388

Chapter 21

Valuation Case Studies
JUAN DE DIOS ORTÚZAR and LUIS IGNACIO RIZZI — 391

1.	Introduction	391
2.	Random utility and SP methods	392
3.	First case study: interurban road accidents	394
	3.1. The choice context	396
	3.2. Discrete choice modeling	396
	3.3. Introduction of socio-economic variables	399

4.	Second case study: valuation of local air pollution		400
	4.1.	Definition of the air quality attribute	400
	4.2.	Identification of attributes and selection of measurement units	401
	4.3.	Data collection strategy	402
	4.4.	Modeling results	402
5.	Third case study: valuation of noise		404
6.	Summary		407
Acknowledgments			408
References			408

Chapter 22

The Health Effects of Motor Vehicle-related Air Pollution
DONALD R. McCUBBIN and MARK A. DELUCCHI — 411

1.	Introduction		411
2.	Air emissions from motor vehicle use		412
3.	Exposure to ambient air pollution related to motor vehicle use		413
4.	Health effects of exposure to motor vehicle air pollution		414
	4.1.	Particulate matter	415
	4.2.	Ozone	418
	4.3.	Carbon monoxide	418
	4.4.	Nitrogen dioxide	419
	4.5.	Sulfur dioxide	419
	4.6.	Toxic air pollutants	420
5.	Valuing the health effects of motor vehicle air pollution		421
	5.1.	Valuing health effects using damage function approach	421
6.	Analyses of the social cost of the health effects of motor vehicle air pollution		423
7.	Unanswered questions		424
References			425

Chapter 23

Environmental Externalities of Motor Vehicle Use
MARK A. DELUCCHI — 429

1.	Introduction		429
2.	Definitions and scope		430
	2.1.	What is an externality?	430
	2.2.	Scope of the chapter	431
3.	External environmental costs of motor vehicle use		432
	3.1.	General method	432
	3.2.	Air pollution: health effects	433
	3.3.	Air pollution: reduced visibility	434

		3.4.	Air pollution: crop losses	437
		3.5.	Air pollution: material damage	438
		3.6.	Air pollution: forest damage	439
		3.7.	Climate change	440
		3.8.	Noise	441
		3.9.	Water pollution: large oil spills	444
		3.10.	Water pollution: other	444
		3.11.	Other external environmental costs of motor vehicle use	445
		3.12.	Summary of environmental external costs of motor vehicle use	445
	4.	Some applications		445
		4.1.	Evaluating alternative fuels	445
		4.2.	Mode choice	446
		4.3.	Trade-offs between urban air pollution and climate change	447
		4.4.	Motor vehicle pricing, land use, and transit	447
		4.5.	Optimal pricing, taxation, and investment	447
	5.	Conclusion		448
	References			448

Chapter 24

Valuation of Safety
MICHAEL JONES-LEE and GRAHAM LOOMES   451

1.	Introduction	451
2.	Valuing safety: issues of principle	452
3.	Empirical estimates of WTP-based values of safety	455
4.	WTP-based values of road safety	456
5.	WTP-based values of rail safety	457
6.	The valuation of safety by Railtrack	458
7.	Summary and conclusion	460
References		462

Chapter 25

Location Externalities: Effects on Modeling, Infrastructure Provision and Optimal Planning
FRANCISCO MARTÍNEZ   463

1.	Introduction		463
2.	The land use theoretical model		465
3.	An operational model		468
4.	Scenarios and benefits		469
5.	Optimal planning		471
	5.1.	Social prices for land expropriation	472
	5.2.	Optimal land pricing	475
6.	Summary		477

Acknowledgments	477
References	478

Chapter 26

Macroeconomic Policies and the Environment
STEIN HANSEN   481

1. Introduction	481
2. Do we need a "green GDP"?	481
3. Environmental impacts of macroeconomic policies	485
4. Macro-impacts of environmental policies and technological progress	491
5. Mainstreaming environmental impacts into macroeconomic analyses	493
References	494

Chapter 27

History of Environmental Legislation
PETER R. STOPHER   497

1. Introduction	497
2. The emergence of modern environmental legislation	499
3. US legislation on transport and the environment	502
3.1. The National Environmental Protection Act of 1969	502
3.2. Subsequent US federal legislation	505
3.3. Other legislation in the USA	509
4. Legislation on transport and the environment in other countries	509
5. Australian legislation on transport and the environment	510
6. Conclusions	513
References	513

Chapter 28

International Coordination of Environmental Policies and Multilateral Environmental Agreements
JEROEN C.J.M. VAN DEN BERGH and NURIA CASTELLS   515

1. The need for international coordination of environmental policies	515
2. Environmental policy theory: from a national to an international perspective	516
3. Theories of multilateral environmental agreements	518
4. MEAs in practice	521
5. Conclusions	526
Acknowledgment	526
References	526

Chapter 29
Environmental Pricing in Transport
EDWARD CALTHROP and STEF PROOST — 529

1. Introduction — 529
2. Rationale for environmental taxes — 529
   - 2.1. Efficient outcome — 530
   - 2.2. Choice of instruments — 531
   - 2.3. No intervention — 532
   - 2.4. Emissions tax — 532
   - 2.5. Emissions subsidy — 533
   - 2.6. A product tax (or kilometer tax) — 534
   - 2.7. Technological standard — 535
   - 2.8. Comparing instruments — 535
3. Implementation issues — 538
   - 3.1. Unavailability of emissions tax — 538
   - 3.2. Variability in air pollution damage — 539
4. Comparison with multiple distortions — 540
   - 4.1. Road congestion and air pollution — 540
   - 4.2. Interactions between transport markets and distorted labor markets — 542
   - 4.3. Equity impacts and institutional issues — 543
5. Conclusions — 543

Acknowledgements — 544
References — 544

Chapter 30
Planning for Sustainable Environmental Futures
DAVID GILLINGWATER and STEPHEN ISON — 547

1. Introduction — 547
2. Planning and sustainable development – principles — 547
3. Planning sustainable environmental futures — 552
   - 3.1. Case study – local transport plans and planning policy guidance — 554
   - 3.2. Case study – new settlement plans — 558
4. Conclusions — 561

References — 562

Chapter 31
Environmental Justice Applications in Transport: The International Perspective
RAHAF ALSNIH and PETER R. STOPHER — 565

1. Introduction — 565
2. Background — 566
   - 2.1. Definition — 568

3. Legislation — 569
4. The need to address environmental justice in transport planning — 570
5. Transport and land use interrelationships — 572
6. Transport and environmental justice: current practices — 573
7. Data issues and model estimates — 575
   7.1. Data limitations and recommendations — 577
8. International applications for environmental justice — 579
9. Conclusion — 580
Appendix. Assessing Title VI capability – review questions: an attachment to the Federal Highway Administration and Federal Transit Administration memorandum *Implementing Title VI Requirements in Metropolitan and Statewide Planning*, October 1999 — 581
References — 583

Chapter 32

Winners and losers in Transport Policy: on Efficiency, Equity, and Compensation
PIET RIETVELD — 585

1. Introduction — 585
2. A politico-economic model of transport policy — 586
3. Compensation in transport policy. — 591
4. A joint framework for equity and efficiency in transport policy — 593
5. Equity concepts — 595
6. Conclusion — 599
References — 600

Chapter 33

Unintended Effects of Polices
PHIL GOODWIN — 603

1. Background — 603
2. Examples of problems — 604
   2.1. Does road building to divert traffic from environmentally sensitive areas result in an overall increase in traffic? — 604
   2.2. Does town center pedestrianization reduce trade? — 606
   2.3. Does transport investment discourage economic growth and regeneration? — 607
   2.4. Do park-and-ride schemes divert people from public transport? — 609
   2.5. Does reallocating road space for environmental improvements cause traffic chaos in neighboring areas? — 610
3. Conclusions — 611
References — 612

Chapter 34

Global Warming and Emission Trading
TRUONG PHUOC TRUONG — 615

1. Introduction — 615
2. Global warming as a technological and climate change issue — 617
3. Global warming as an economic issue — 618
4. Emission trading as an instrument for coordinating GHG emission reduction activities — 619
   - 4.1. Determination of the initial volume of permits — 620
   - 4.2. Distribution of emission permits — 623
   - 4.3. Emission trading and efficiency gains — 624
   - 4.4. Other issues relating to emission trading — 626
   - 4.5. Free trade in goods and free trade in emission permits — 629
- References — 631

Chapter 35

Travel, Tourism, and the Environment
KENNETH J. BUTTON — 633

1. Introduction — 633
2. Background — 634
   - 2.1. The history — 634
   - 2.2. The magnitude — 635
   - 2.3. Transportation — 637
3. Transportation–tourism–environmental linkages — 637
4. The environmental implications — 639
   - 4.1. The consumption effect — 639
   - 4.2. The access effect — 640
   - 4.3. The tourist effect — 640
   - 4.4. Ecotourism — 643
5. Policy responses — 644
6. Conclusions — 645
- References — 645

Chapter 36

Gender, Transportation, and the Environment
AMANDA ROOT and LAURIE SCHINTLER — 647

1. Introduction — 647
2. Women and transport — 648
   - 2.1. Distance traveled — 649
   - 2.2. Licensing and auto ownership — 650
   - 2.3. Mode of transportation — 651

		2.4.	Trip purpose and complexity of trip-making	652

	3.	Women and environmentalism	653
		3.1. Mobility needs of women	654
		3.2. Women and traffic management	656
	4.	Transportation planning and modeling	658
	5.	Policy implications and conclusions	660
		References	662

Chapter 37

Logistics and the Environment
ALAN C. McKINNON — 665

1.	Introduction	665
2.	Reducing transport intensity	667
	2.1. Reconfiguring production and distribution systems	670
	2.2. Pattern of sourcing	671
	2.3. Vehicle routing	672
3.	Transferring freight to less environmentally damaging modes	673
4.	Improving vehicle utilization	674
	4.1. Empty running	674
	4.2. Load factors on laden trips	675
	4.3. Legal limits on vehicle size and weight	679
5.	City logistics	680
6.	Conclusion	682
	References	683

Chapter 38

Reverse Logistics: An Overview and a Causal Model
SHAMS RAHMAN — 687

1.	Introduction	687
2.	Motivation for reverse logistics	688
	2.1. Environmental considerations	689
	2.2. Government policy and legislation	689
	2.3. Economic considerations	690
	2.4. Shift toward buying sets of services	690
3.	Characteristics of reverse logistics	690
	3.1. Supply–demand balance	692
	3.2. Accumulation and shortage of parts	692
	3.3. Logistical network	692
	3.4. Transportation	693
4.	Recovery processes and its hierarchy	693
5.	Modeling reverse logistics systems	695
	5.1. Network models for reuse	696

	5.2.	Network models for remanufacturing	697
	5.3.	Network models for recycling	698
6.	An effective reverse logistics system		700
7.	Conclusion		704
	References		704

Chapter 39

Transportation of Hazardous Goods and Materials
WILLIAM G. WATERS II — 707

1. Introduction — 707
2. Hazardous materials and transportation — 707
   - 2.1. Regulatory obligations and incident reporting — 708
   - 2.2. Rationales for regulation — 709
3. Hazmat studies — 710
   - 3.1. Aggregate studies of hazmat incidents and their costs — 710
   - 3.2. QRA of hazmat shipments and regulations — 715
   - 3.3. Reducing risks or their consequences — 721
4. Challenges in risk analysis of hazmat transportation — 722
5. Conclusions — 723
   Acknowledgements — 724
   References — 724

Chapter 40

Public Attitudes
TOMMY GÄRLING, PETER LOUKOPOULOS and MARTIN LEE-GOSSELIN — 725

1. Introduction — 725
2. Attitude concepts — 725
3. Environmental values — 728
4. Changing public attitudes related to travel behavior — 730
5. Summary and conclusions — 735
   References — 735

Chapter 41

Travel Behavior Change through Individual Engagement
GEOFF ROSE and ELIZABETH AMPT — 739

1. Introduction — 739
2. Evolution of travel behavior change programs — 740
3. The nature of existing travel behavior change programs — 743
   - 3.1. IndiMark — 743
   - 3.2. Travel Blending — 745
4. Impacts of travel behavior change programs — 747
   - 4.1. At the level of the individual — 748

	4.2. Aggregate changes	748
	4.3. Financial and economic evaluation	751
5.	What remains to be learned	753
6.	Conclusions	754
	References	754

Chapter 42

Packaging Policies to Address Environmental Concerns
ERAN FEITELSON — 757

1.	Introduction	757
2.	Generating effective packages	759
	2.1. Single-goal packages	759
	2.2. Multiple-goal policy packages	761
3.	Politically acceptable packages	762
4.	Institutional, temporal and spatial considerations	764
	4.1. Spatial scale and time horizons	765
	4.2. Institutional aspects	766
5.	Conclusions	768
	References	769

Chapter 43

The Street: Integrating Transport and Urban Environment
STEPHEN MARSHALL — 771

1.	Introduction	771
2.	The street as a microcosm	772
3.	Recognition and prioritization of street users	773
	3.1. Recognition	774
	3.2. Prioritization	777
	3.3. Provision of road space	778
	3.4. Provision for people	779
4.	Street typology and road hierarchy	780
	4.1. Conventional road hierarchy	780
	4.2. Contemporary evolution	781
5.	Toward the sustainable street	782
6.	Conclusions	783
	References	785

Chapter 44

Integrated Transport Models for Environmental Assessment
DAVID A. HENSHER — 787

1.	Introduction	787

2.	Some key building blocks for ILUTMSs and IMSM systems for passenger travel	789
	2.1. Policy relevance	789
	2.2. Behavioral response relevance	790
	2.3. Spatial detail relevance	790
	2.4. Decision-maker relevance	791
	2.5. Output relevance	792
3.	The profile of two ILUTMSs	793
	3.1. TRESIS	793
	3.2. IRPUD	799
4.	Conclusions	803
	Acknowledgments	803
	References	804

Chapter 45
Transportation Demand Management and "Win–win" Transportation Solutions
TODD A. LITMAN   805

1.	What is transportation demand management?	805
2.	Consumer impacts of TDM	806
3.	TDM evaluation and planning	807
4.	Market distortions and reforms	809
5.	Win–win transportation solutions	809
6.	Examples of win–win solutions	811
	6.1. Federal	811
	6.2. Regional and local	812
7.	Conclusions	814
	References	814

Author Index	815
Subject Index	823

Chapter 1

INTRODUCTION

DAVID A. HENSHER
University of Sydney

KENNETH J. BUTTON
George Mason University, Fairfax, VA

1. Introduction

The community has always viewed transport with mixed feelings. The Romans banned traffic in cities at night to reduce noise, and Britain made some unfortunate walk in front of early cars to give warning of their approach. Our concern withtraffic has perhaps become more acute in the modern era – indeed, some commentators have likened modern transport to "industry on wheels." One reason for this is that the long-standing concerns with the impact of transport on the local environment have extended to more global concerns as technology has developed.

The trouble is that transport provides the technological means to facilitate movement of people and goods, and people not surprisingly like that. But it is also at the center of growing concerns about environmental degradation in the form of air pollution, global warming, noise, and safety. Combined with traffic congestionin major conurbations at seaports, at airports, and on the roads, the environmental effects of transportation are regularly cited in surveys as major contributors to the ills of twenty-first century society. Roads in particular, which provide the infrastructure for moving cars and trucks, have come under increasing criticism on environmental grounds. The question of whether they are the servants of technology has been raised, rather than whether they offer a positive opportunity to mould the environment.

Transport systems provide the mechanistic infrastructure used to facilitate movement; they also have a broader and socially valuable role in contributing to the economic, social, and environmental fabric of civilization; they act as the lubricant of the modern socio-economic system. What would a nation look like and how would it function in the absence of streets and roads, airports, and docks? Transport systems today are key elements in the global economic system, components in a society's amenity infrastructure, and settings of mounting economic, environmental, and social challenges.

The emphasis on outcomes (e.g. accessibility, mobility, clean air, and safety) rather than means of delivery (e.g. cars, buses, trains, trucks, aircraft, and ships) is increasingly important. The traditional emphasis on transport modes fails to accommodate institutionally the widening set of media available for "moving" information and to reflect people's contributions to a nation's activity. Setting constraints on particular forms of transport to achieve desirable environmental outcomes must be evaluated within a broader set of ways to satisfy opportunities offered by "high-tech" and "high-touch" industries. This contrasts with the traditional approach of imposing *a priori* beliefs that only improvements in particular modes of transport will solve the ills of society.

An environmental goal emphasizes quality of life and environmental aspects, under the broad umbrella of sustainability. Some control or direction of traditional economic activity is likely to be required as a trade-off with sustainability. Enhancement and preservation of environmental quality means implementing policies to mitigate environmental degradation and conserve the biology of ecosystems, as well as linking preventative environmental protection, pollution control mechanisms, and the protection of public health.

The initial volume in this series – *Handbook of Transport Modelling* – contains contributions largely concerned with looking at how models can be developed to assist in public and private decision-making. Volume 1 emphasized the theoretical aspects of transport models with more limited attention on the working and institutions of the transport system. These are of immense importance in policy formulation but they say little about the ways transport systems are developed, planned, managed, and regulated. They take as axiomatic that policy instruments are available and may be deployed to influence future events.

A second volume – *Transport Logistics and Supply-chain Management* – is concerned with how those operating transport services, and in particular freight transport services, make use of transport systems. There have been significant changes in the way freight transport is now treated as the result of technical developments in transport, new information systems becoming available, reformed institutional structures, and enhanced management techniques. These changes have mainly been seen in the private sector. Consequently, while there is some limited information of the public sectors' role, this is not a primary focus.

A third handbook deals with *Transport Systems and Traffic Control*, and focuses on the broader nature of transport systems and the implementation of public policy across transport systems. It looks at transport systems more directly. It is much more public sector focused in the sense that it is government and government agencies that provide much of the key underlying infrastructure that allows transport systems to operate, and that control access to that infrastructure and the ways in which it is used. These are no small issues at a time when problems such as urban traffic congestion, environmental intrusion, transport safety, and budgetary constraints are exercising the minds of policy makers.

This volume focuses on transport themes with an environmental emphasis. As one of the most, if not the primary, challenging issue facing the transport sector – and some would say civilization – the need for an entire handbook volume on the environment was inevitable. Although environmental impacts, policies, and assessment protocols were addressed in all previous handbooks given the strong links to modeling, logistics, and traffic systems, a much fuller treatment is justified herein.

2. Transport and the environment

The environment pervades our very existence, and is arguably the most important long-term issue that will dictate the way that transport policy, planning and decision-making will be executed. In launching Part D (*Transport and Environment*) of *Transportation Research* in 1996, the editor-in-chief states in the preface that: "The environment is one of those topics which refuses to go away. Meanwhile there is mounting concern that with the current rapid expansion of traffic, sustainable development will not be possible without major changes in transport policy and technology."

Many of the environmental problems that are both real and sensitive community issues stem from the use of transport infrastructure by passenger and freight vehicles. Automobiles, airplanes and trucks are major sources of local pollutants, such as lead, carbon monoxide, and noise. Traffic congestion exacerbates these problems, and also imposes direct economic and health costs on users and non-users in the form of wasted time and money, stress, and other illnesses. Transport systems also make a significant contribution to global warming through emissions of carbon dioxide (CO_2) and other greenhouse gases.

The main environmental issues associated with the transport sector are air quality, enhanced greenhouse gas emissions (mainly CO_2), noise, impact on biodiversity, and land use. Emissions from transport – primarily road and air traffic – represent a very high share of the overall emissions: about 90% of all lead emissions, about 50% of all nitrogen oxides (NO_x) emissions and about 30% of all volatile organic compound (VOC) emissions. Twenty-two percent of the total CO_2 emissions are from the transport sector. Of this, about 80% of the emissions arise from road transport, with more than 55% from the private car alone.

The main components of transport emissions include CO_2, carbon monoxide (CO), hydrocarbons (HCs), VOCs, NO_x, sulfur dioxide (SO_2), particulate matter (PM), lead, and other combustion by-products. Some exhaust emissions from road transport also produce secondary pollution, such as photochemical oxidants. Apart from the use and depletion of non-renewable resources as well as the main emissions problem, other environmental issues linked to transportation include operational pollution, land intrusion, and water pollution.

Land use and biodiversity have recently received major consideration in the sustainable transportation debate. The main problem seems to be landscape fragmentation by transport infrastructure. The construction and use of roads, railways, and canals creates several negative effects on the biodiversity of land. It has direct effects, such as loss and disturbance of habitats and species, as well as the long-term influence of partitioning and isolating ecosystems and species population. Transport infrastructure covers an increasing amount of land to the virtual exclusion of other uses, cuts through ecosystems, and spoils the view of natural scenery and historic monuments.

As the observed level of wealth in industrial society increases, and the demand for transport use grows, society faces real and special challenges to contain and reverse the trends within the wide range of negative impacts of greater mobility. Communities are not expressing blanket concern about transport *per se*; rather, they are concerned about specific issues – principally freeways, toll roads, and the location of seaports and airports – and about the "failure" of governments to do something about the harmful outcomes from these specific investments. Governments, however, although aware of the need for appropriate actions to help stem the desire for mobility, especially by implementing a range of pricing instruments, often lack the political will to execute such policies. The emphasis on physical incentives and disincentives to achieve change relative to financial opportunities continues to be a major constraint on containing the environmental costs of transport systems.

These problems will inevitable become much more acute in the future as economic development takes place outside of existing centers.

Poor countries have low levels of car ownership and make limited use of air transport. That said, the environmental emissions of many of the vehicles in these countries are high because of their age and poor maintenance, and weak environmental codes, but this is generally offset by their small number in terms of global and local effects. As incomes rise, the requirements for economic efficiency on the part of the production sector, and the aspirations of the population for mobility and the prestige that goes with car ownership, will push up traffic volumes.

Despite the concerns about adverse environmental effects, it cannot be overlooked that there are very many positive features of transport. The challenge is to manage the benefits of transportation better so that the broad set of environmental impacts is reduced to acceptable levels while ensuring acceptable outcomes in terms of economic performance and equity. Civic pride embellished in the design of transport systems is increasingly seen as in need of being given a center stage in the deliberations. A challenge of sustainable transport will require careful consideration of technological innovation and increasing consumer awareness.

In preparing the structure and content of the current volume we undertook a meta-analysis of the contributions to *Transportation Research D* as a useful way of listing the key themes that this volume would have to address. A further search through other key transport and planning journals, in particular, provided a mechanism for refining the initial list. The outcome was the contents of this handbook. The chapters cover environmental concepts (physical and economic); key environmental concerns (global warming, air quality, noise, safety, amenity, and severance); the role of fuel sources and vehicle technology (including intelligent transport systems) as means of reducing environmental externalities; appraisal, valuation, and impacts of externalities; institutional and political settings and policies designed to combat growing environmental concerns; and the role of environmental legislation.

A number of chapters highlight specific key themes that cut across many of the topic areas listed above – for example, travel and tourism, gender, public attitudes, and greening of the local environment. Early in the Handbook there are chapters that give an overview of the contribution of each main transport sector to the consumption of energy and the creation of emissions. While there are strong arguments for avoiding modal segmentation and to tie transport *per se* to environmental matters, the reality of the situation is still that public policy, public administrations, and, indeed, public perception is modally based.

3. The Handbook

Transport and the Environment is the fourth in the series *Handbooks in Transport*. The earlier volumes, as we noted, have been concerned with transport modeling, with transport logistics and supply chain management, and with transport systems and traffic control. The coverage of these handbooks is meant to be neither comprehensive nor always excessively deep; they are neither textbooks nor research monographs. Each chapter is designed to be read by those new to a transport field as well as by those who are already familiar with the area. As such, each chapter has been written in a way that readers will gain an overview and useful insights. At the same time, those readers who are already practitioners in that field will gain knowledge through the presentation of advanced and/or updated tools and new materials and state-of-the-art developments.

The *Oxford Dictionary* definition of a handbook is that it is a "guidebook" or a "manual." In other words it is a practical tool to help its readers carry through particular activities or operations. It is not a textbook. A textbook is, again deferring to the *Oxford Dictionary*, a "manual of instruction," because it goes beyond a simple pedagogic device. It is also not a monograph, which offers a "separate treatise on a single subject or class of subjects." A handbook contains information and concepts that are useful and offered in a concise fashion; indeed, that is where the term derives from – it can be carried in the hand.

The current handbook may be useful in some contexts for instruction, but its main aim is to help those involved in transport with a focus on the environment to perform their tasks effectively and efficiently. As anyone using a handbook knows, there is always the problem of level. The key thing about a handbook is that it should be accessible to those who need to consult it.

The coverage in this volume reflects what are generally seen as key subject areas. In this case, since the handbook is part of a more extensive series, some topics have been allocated to other volumes simply because they also have as much right to be there as in this book. When designing the framework for the volume it was decided to be as contemporary as possible and to bias the contributions towards discourses that reflect the current state of the art rather than to simply set down what is often the current practice. This has the limitation that the handbook moves a little away from being a strict "manual," but it does offer what we feel will be a more enduring range of subjects as a result.

Although any classification of themes is to some degree inevitably arbitrary, we have divided the book into a series of topic areas. These represent our effort to typify what researchers and practitioners see as the foci of any structured study in which the environment is a central input. There has been no effort to completely standardize the different contributions. This would destroy the individuality of the authors and also artificially disguise the fact that there is no consensus as to how the environment and a growing theme in transport should be viewed – the subject is a fluid one and methodologies quite correctly change as new information emerges and new thoughts are stirred. Indeed, the material set out in this introduction is largely subjective and there are others who would take a somewhat different approach to the topics covered herein. The common denominator to the approaches adopted is the deployment of a mixture of a synthesis of methods and case studies.

Part 1

CONCEPTS

Chapter 2

ENVIRONMENTAL CONCEPTS – PHYSICAL AND ECONOMIC

WERNER ROTHENGATTER
University of Karlsruhe

1. Introduction

The quality of the environment is influenced by the economic activities of production, energy use, consumption, and transport. During the early stages of industrial development, industrial activity was the main cause of environmental damage; now, in most developed countries the transport sector is the predominant source of environmental harm (Figure 1) and the transport sector is still very dynamic. Passenger transport in most countries is growing at rates equal to GDP. Air traffic

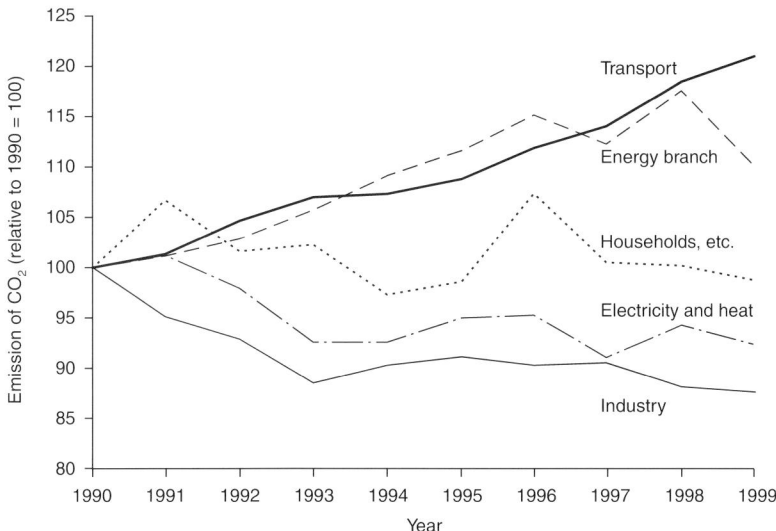

Figure 1. Trends in carbon dioxide emissions from fossil fuels in the EU by sector. The contribution from transport in 1999 was 29%, of which was 24% from road, 4% from air, and 1% from inland navigation and railways. (Source: EUROSTAT.)

Handbook of Transport and the Environment, Edited by D.A. Hensher and K.J. Button
© *2003, Elsevier Ltd*

is growing much faster, at rates often double or triple of the GDP growth rate. Freight transport has de-coupled from GDP in some countries in an environmentally undesired direction. In particular the tonne and vehicle kilometers of road transport are growing much faster than GDP. The development of logistics is supporting this trend. As shippers prefer high flexibility and perfect control of transport to integrate freight movements into the supply chains the freight modal split in many countries is changing in favor of the road.

Table 1 compares the impact of different modes of transport on the environment for the EU (EU 15), the USA, Japan, China, and Russia for 1999.

The future will likely see the dynamics of growth being driven more by countries in transition (Central and East European countries, CEECs), developing countries, and countries which are at the threshold of industrial development (China and Russia). In these countries the growth of motorization is significantly above that of the current industrial powers, with car use – in particular in cities – causing increasingly serious environmental problems. Also, air traffic and the road freight industry are developing rapidly. Figure 2 gives an example of this development in CEECs. It shows that within two decades international road passenger transport is projected to grow by a factor of between 2 and 4. In these sectors rising congestion is likely to multiply the negative effects of the individual environmental problems, as capacity extension usually cannot keep up with the pace of demand. Potentially environmentally more-friendly transport modes such as railways, coaches, inland waterways, or coastal shipping could gain a considerable share of the transport market and its growth; however, as the environmental advantage is not reflected economically by environmental cost differentials – in the absence of internalization of external costs – environmentally cleaner transport may not be commercially

Table 1
Overview of international transport figures, including CO_2 emissions

	Country				
	EU 15	USA	Japan	China	Russia
Passenger cars (millions)	169.0	131.8	51.2	4.2	19.7
Motorization (cars/1000 persons)	451	488	406	3	135
Mode of travel (billion pkm)					
Car	3676	6216	723	NR	NR
Air (domestic)	260	767	76	80	56
Rail	281	23	389	370	81
Transportation of goods (billion tkm)					
Truck	1254	1499	301	548	140
Inland waterways	121	521	0	NR	66
Transport CO_2 emissions	872	1771	278	219	137

Key: pkm, person kilometers; tkm, tonne kilometers; NR, not reported.

Ch. 2: Environmental Concepts – Physical and Economic 11

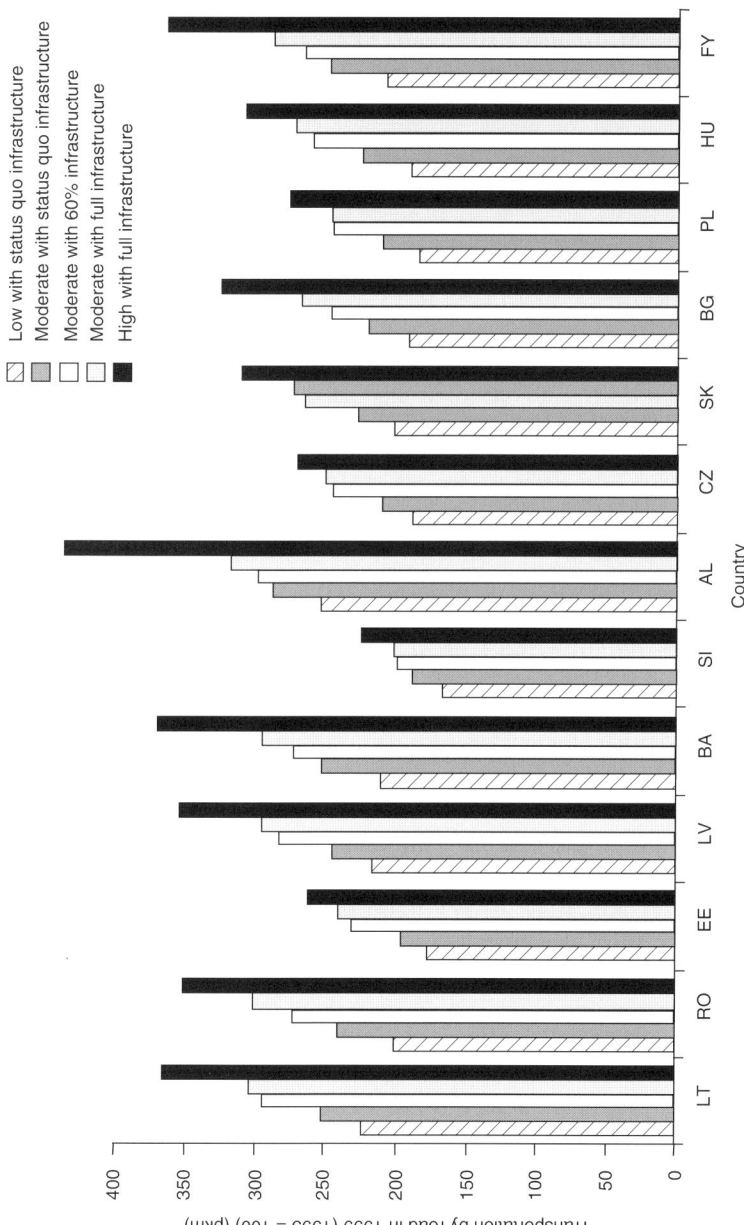

Figure 2. Road passenger traffic trends in CEECs. LT, Lithuania; RO, Romania; EE, Estonia; LV, Latvia; BA, Bosnia; SI, Slovenia; AL, Albania; CZ, Czech Republic; SK, Slovak Republic; BG, Bulgaria; PL, Poland; HU, Hungary; FY, Former Republic of Macedonia. (Data are from a large study on transport development in 13 CEEC countries prepared by NEA, INRETS and IWW on behalf of the EC in 1999.)

viable. Therefore, the market shares of environmentally more benign modes in CEECs is likely to drop dramatically in a competitive market regime. For example, railway freight transport, which had about 70% of the market of land-borne freight transport in CEECs before the political changes at the end of the 1980s, is expected to drop to below 25% by 2015, assuming a high economic growth combined with low transport regulation scenario.

In addition to the problems generated by transport demand there are also considerable risks to the environment arising from provision of transport infrastructure, e.g. reducing biodiversity or adversely affecting rare species. These risks may be especially acute in developing countries. In the developed countries these risks are often given a high priority, either in the legal system or through less formal civil actions.

Given this background, transport policy is confronted with a range of challenges in controlling the undesired effects of transport on the environment. A clear understanding of the environmental phenomena in the physical sense is important in doing this, i.e. by analyzing the impact chain, beginning with the production of effects, their physical distribution, eventual accompaniment by synergy and accumulation effects, their concentration at particular locations, and their influence on man, materials, and nature. This physical impact chain has also an economic dimension insofar as impacts have to be evaluated to inform us of the best strategies for environmental policy. Of course, an economic evaluation cannot be done without information from other disciplines on the environmental impacts of transport.

This chapter starts by defining environmental indicators and their measurement, and the analysis of impact chains. At any stage of the impact chain, the transport sector will not be the only cause of environmental problems; thus, the allocation of responsibility to individual causes of environmental risk in a reliable way also needs to be considered. In this context it should be added that although transport is usually a major cause of environmental risk with respect to the main indicators, it often contributes no more than 20–30% to the total. As we see later, in a number of cases the damage produced by environmental effects is so evident to policy makers that they have decided on regulatory solutions without taking into account explicit economic evaluations.

Section 4 offers explicit evaluation possibilities are presented, focusing on economic concepts. The economic valuation has to follow the chain of impacts (bottom-up analysis) to satisfy the principles of precaution and of causality. It will be shown that the environment needs different treatment in different contexts either based on the precaution principle, which starts from safe minimum standards for environmental quality, or on the polluter pays principle, which can be based on standard economic evaluations such as willingness-to-pay estimators or hedonic prices. Section 5 brings together the information from the two evaluation principles to sketch out a development of the transport system oriented toward safe minimum impact levels for the environment and controlled by economic instruments (soft constraints) as well as regulation (hard constraints).

The chapter does not give a complete overview of worldwide transport development and aggregate figures on environmental indicators, nor give general figures for environmental impacts or on the effectiveness of public policy. Rather, the aim is to focus on prototype approaches to solving environmental problems that are linked to planning and policy making.

2. Physical basis of environmental impacts

2.1. The choice of indicators

The environment is the non-productive natural base of human activities. Environmental resources play different roles in the economy. They can be used in production (e.g. 300 000 liters of water are required to produce an automobile), for consumption (e.g. a picnic in the woods), or as deposits for waste (e.g. air pollution). The level of the impacts can be local (e.g. noise), regional (e.g. disturbance of biodiversity), or global (e.g. greenhouse gases). The first problem when analyzing environmental impacts is to define which indicators to use to study environmental quality. Starting from a broad viewpoint, one can identify many of the so-called external costs of transport as detrimental to environmental quality. Usually the following impacts are mentioned in the literature (INFRAS/IWW, 2000): noise; air pollution; climate change; disturbance to nature, the landscape, and water and ground sealing; separation in urban areas; scarcity of space in urban areas; reduction in natural visibility; accidents; and additional effects from upstream/downstream processes.

For each indicator there exist critical values that indicate human life is endangered either directly or indirectly. Below these critical values there can occur negative impacts on human well-being, that reflect in complaints of affected people and decreasing land values for affected areas.

Noise

Transport noise not only causes undesirable social disturbances but it also affects our wellbeing, that can lead to damage to physical and psychological health. Hearing defects can be caused by noise levels above 85 dB(A), while lower levels, above 60 dB(A), may cause nervous stress reactions, such as an increase in the heart rate, an increase in blood pressure, and hormonal changes. A number of studies have looked at the link between transport noise and health. Maschke and Ising (1997) reviewed studies on the effects of night-time traffic noise on public health, and concluded that such noise causes stress and thus increases the risk of gastrointestinal and cardiovascular diseases.

At least two studies give empirical evidence for an increase in mortality owing to transport noise. Babisch et al. (1993) investigated the effects of transport noise (65–70 dB(A)) using two representative samples of 4860 men in Caerphilly and Speedwell (UK). They showed that the risk of cardiac infarctions increases by 20% if individuals are exposed to outdoor transport noise above 65 dB(A). In another study, Babisch et al. (1994) questioned 645 male patients in Berlin hospitals who had suffered from heart attacks, and compared the results with a representative sample of 3390 men. The research confirmed the results from the previous study in the UK for transport noise in the 70–75 dB(A) bracket, and revealed increasing risks for transport noise above 75 dB(A). The results of the studies are summarized in Table 2.

Ising et al. (1998) conducted a review of studies on the health risks due to noise exposure, and confirmed that the experimental and epidemiological studies are consistent. They concluded that a reduction in transport noise to below 65 dB(A) during the day and 55 dB(A) during the night would decrease cardiac fatalities in Germany by 3%.

Traffic noise lower than these critical levels will still disturb people. However, the degree of perceived disturbance varies markedly by region and social group. For example, it was recently stated in the context of a public consultation for plans to build an additional runway at Frankfurt airport that people in the Frankfurt area seem to have a particular sensitivity to noise. Another example is the preference of Italian people to have dinner at noisy places in cities. This implies that the results of regional studies on willingness to pay for noise reduction below the critical values cannot be transferred to other regions.

Air pollution

Air pollution is measured by the emission and concentrations of lead (Pb), carbon monoxide (CO), sulfur dioxide (SO_2), nitrogen oxides (NO_x), benzene and volatile

Table 2
Increased percentage risk of cardiac infarctions due to transport noise

		Sound level (dB(A))		
Source	Location	65–70	70–75	75–80
Babisch et al. (1993)	Caerphilly, Speedwell	+20%	–	–
Babisch et al. (1994)	Berlin	–	+20%	+70%
Values used by INFRAS/IWW		+20%	+30%	

Table 3
Particle emissions from vehicle exhausts and non-exhaust sources

Mode of transport	Non-exhaust PM_{10} (g/vehicle km or g/train km)	Mean percentage of exhaust PM_{10}	Mean percentage of non-exhaust PM_{10}
Car	0.12	12%	88%
Bus	1.2	37%	63%
LDV	0.21	56%	43%
HDV	1.2	31%	69%
Rail (passenger)	2	49%	51%
Rail (freight)	2	61%	39%

Source: INFRAS (1999a).

components (C_mH_n), and particulate matter (soot, dust). Air pollution can cause damage to, for example: human health; materials and buildings; agricultural crops; and forests.

Historically, a series of leading indicators have been developed, beginning with lead, followed by carbon dioxide, and then nitrogen oxides. Each leading indicator reflects the most challenging environmental problem at a given time.

The negative impact of air pollution on health is relatively well documented. However, its impacts on and monetary damage to materials and buildings or to the biosphere are less well investigated. In Europe there is only one study available (INFRAS, 1992), where damage to buildings has been estimated in enough detail (for Switzerland) that generalizations are possible. The impact on crop losses (especially due to high ozone levels) is easier to evaluate, and several studies have estimated the potential damages to agricultural crops. In earlier studies, other impacts (especially acid rain and damage to forests) were also considered. Recent scientific studies, however, are not able to draw concrete conclusions on the impact of transport emissions. Some estimations for Sweden are available, where acid rain, caused by nitric acid and, to some extent, sulfuric acid, is considered, but for the most important pollutant (NO_x), recent European values on production and regional concentrations are not available.

A very important assumption in a World Health Organisation (WHO) study from 1999 is the use of particle emission (PM_{10}) as a leading indicator for impact measurement and cost allocation. It should be noted that not all the particle emissions are from vehicle exhausts: significant emissions are caused by road abrasion, tire and clutch abrasion, as well as re-suspension (for both road and rail transport). INFRAS (1999a) indicates that about 80% of road PM_{10} is due to non-exhaust sources (Table 3). A reduction in emission factors for the 2010 forecast does not affect the non-exhaust PM_{10} emissions, which will take a larger share in future. This effect is not important for air and waterways transport.

Climate change

Greenhouse gases concentrate in the atmosphere and contribute to a change in the earth's climate. According to studies by the Intergovernmental Panel for Climate Change (IPCC), the world's temperature is increasing as a consequence of anthropogeneous emissions. Estimations are between 1.4 and 5.8°C in 100 years (Intergovernmental Panel for Climate Change, 2001). Furthermore, chlorofluorocarbon emissions are lowering the concentration of atmospheric ozone at the poles, causing ozone holes with the associated risks from ultraviolet rays. Greenhouse gases consist of carbon dioxide, methane, tropospheric ozone, halocarbons, and N_2O. Particulates (e.g. polycyclic aromatics, metals, and carbon) also contribute to the greenhouse effect.

Carbon dioxide is the best-known greenhouse gas, but only accounts for about 50% of the total but about 25% of this is contributed by transport. Methane is produced by natural processes and by agriculture. Older types of refrigeration and air-conditioning units release halocarbons. There is a lively debate concerning the extent to which global warming is also caused by fossil fuel particulate black carbon and by organic matter. This latter effect is not covered by the Kyoto Protocol, and as a consequence not in the reduction strategies that have been agreed on (the US government has retracted its agreement to the protocol). If the research results of Jacobson (2002) are confirmed, then the theories on greenhouse gas reduction will have to be redefined. In particular, diesel engines, which produce less carbon dioxide but much more particulate matter than Otto (gasoline) engines, would have to be treated differently in environmental policy.

Disturbance to nature, the landscape, and water and ground sealing

The effects on nature, the landscape, and species predominantly arise from the provision of transport infrastructure rather than from traffic itself. An estimation of the severity of this type of environmental impact depends significantly on the individual's or society's perception and are thus usually difficult to measure.[a] This because they are widely irreversible[b] in nature and occur as interdependent processes over a long time horizon.

One can distinguish two kinds of effect:

(1) Effects which are caused by the provision of infrastructure (roads, rail tracks, dams, bridges, airports, etc.):

---

[a]It is important to state that air pollution and climate change will also harm the biosphere. However, these effects are included in the cost of air pollution and climate change discussed earlier.

[b]With regard to existing infrastructure, the costs of disturbing the landscape, biodiversity, etc., are sunk and there is little scope for reversibility. Thus, the impact of new projects on nature and the landscape is usually a very important aspect of a project, and is evaluated by, for example, environmental impact analysis or cost–benefit analysis.

- spatial separation effects/barrier effect (also influenced by utilization of infrastructure);
- reduction in the quality of landscapes and loss of tourist value;
- loss of natural land area (loss of biotypes, endangering rare species).
(2) Effects which are caused by the utilization of infrastructure:
- contamination of soil and surface/groundwater systems;
- pollution caused by accidents.

Separation in urban areas

Transport infrastructure in urban areas, such as expressways, can cause separation effects insofar as they cut across existing social interrelationships. This effect has been neglected for a long time in urban planning, but is now becoming an issue in some contexts. Urban life, it is argued, needs the coherence of social structures, and their disturbance leads to a decrease in social welfare. From this it follows that when performing cost–benefit analysis and similar calculations, not only have the general cost savings to the users of the infrastructure to be considered but also the negative impact on social groups in areas that will be separated by the infrastructure project.

Scarcity of space in urban areas

Space in urban areas is a scarce resource, and is needed for a variety of different purposes. Thus, use of urban space for transport will lead to a scarcity of space for other uses. If the space needed for competing activities is not shared equally, the pattern of land use could change substantially, with detrimental social and economic consequences (e.g. dead areas between transport routes). Because of planning controls this negative impact on the urban environment is not reflected in land prices, and has therefore to be quantified and evaluated through a simulation of land-use development following an infrastructure project.

Reduction in natural visibility

Air pollution can have a number of adverse effects on health, buildings, agriculture, and forests as well as on water and soil quality, as described above. In addition, air pollution can have a psychosomatic impact through reducing natural visibility, which not only adversely affects the quality of life of residents but can reduce the attractiveness of a region to tourists. As an example, consider the city of Santiago de Chile. In the clean air program of 1997 the National Commission for the Environment identified as a particular challenge the reduced natural visibility caused by smog in the city (Comisión Nacional, 1998). During these episodes of smog the Andes are hidden from view, affecting the well-being of residents and tourists.

Accidents

Traffic accidents also have to be included within the scope of environmental impacts of traffic, as they harm people. Some of the costs arising from accidents are purely monetary and covered by insurance, but some of the costs (loss of production, loss in terms of human suffering value through grief and pain) are societal. Furthermore, accidents cause congestion, leading to increased air pollution and climate change.

Additional effects from upstream/downstream processes

The following can be listed under this heading:

(1) *Energy production (pre-combustion)*. The production of all types of energy causes additional environmental impact resulting from its production, transport, and distribution. The magnitude of this impact depends directly on the amount of energy used. These effects are relevant for all modes of transport – excepting railways, since the impact on the environment of electricity production for rail operation is considered within air pollution and climate change costs, only risk elements (e.g. nuclear risks) have to be considered additionally. These costs are also relevant in the short term.

(2) *Vehicle production and maintenance*. The production of vehicles and rolling stock is important in the long term, considering the life cycles of different modes of transport; however, the short-term marginal costs are zero. Vehicle production and maintenance causes, in particular, increased air pollution and hastened climate change.

(3) *Infrastructure construction and maintenance*. The same arguments hold for the transportation infrastructure. In the long term, the environmental impact of the infrastructure associated with transportation has to be considered in addition to the environmental costs arising directly from modes of transport. These costs have to be treated similarly to the impacts on nature and the landscape discussed above, because they are associated with existing infrastructure and are thus sunk costs. In contrast, up- and downstream impacts occur especially during the construction phase (e.g. surface renewal).

2.2. Physical measurement and the responsibility of the transport sector

After the definition of indicators it is necessary to consider the guidelines needed for measurement. In this context a problem arises in that the transport sector is not the only cause of environmental impacts. This implies that the measurement step has to employ models that describe the complete path of all impacts, beginning with emission at the sources, continuing with transport and accumulation of exhaust emissions, and ending with the concentrations in environment. Figure 3 illustrates the impact chain of environmental disturbance. For every part of the chain sophisticated models have been developed for each type of effect. For some effects, such as noise or SO_2, the impact mechanism is well explored. For others, such as particulate matter or NO_x, the main mechanism is understood but there are still significant gray areas. As examples, consider noise, ozone, and particulates.

Example 1: noise

Noise can be measured accurately at its source. The distribution of noise in space can be modeled by using digital space models, that can simulate the dampening or echoing effects of buildings and vegetation as well as the effects of wind (Figure 4). Modern noise impact models combine the transport network and noise simulation in such a way that the contribution from transport can be identified accurately.

Example 2: ozone

Ozone is produced near the Earth's surface by chemical reactions between NO_x, hydrocarbons, and other pollutants under particular conditions of sunlight and wind. Although the chemical process is well understood, it is still impossible to predict the ozone concentrations produced by increasing transport emissions. Therefore, ozone production is usually measured by using the concentrations of the chemical precursors as proxies.

Example 3: particulate matter

According to the studies carried out by the World Health Organisation (1999) and others there is clear evidence that the presence of particulates in the air causes cancer. The relationships between emissions, transport, concentrations, and dose–response effects can be modeled with sufficient accuracy to establish a validated impact chain. Furthermore, black carbon particulates also contribute to the greenhouse effect. This also implies that local policies aimed toward reducing emissions of particulate matter could be an effective means to fight global warming.

Figure 5 shows the forecast for the emission/concentration of soot and particulate matter along a main arterial road in Berlin for the year 2010. This underlines the fact that emission/concentration analysis can be matched to the spatial distribution of a population to obtain the basis for a detailed impact analysis for every relevant type of pollutant.

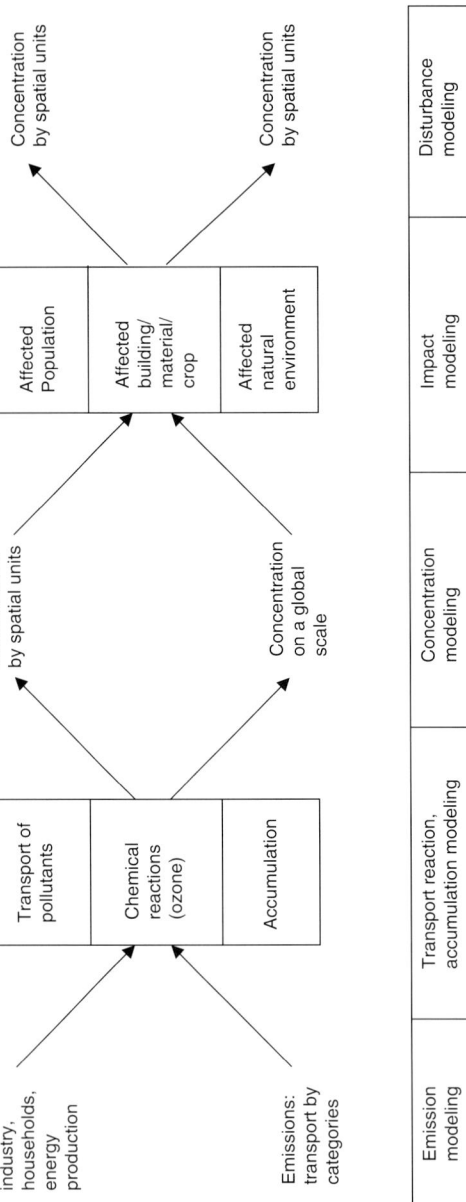

Figure 3. The impact chain for environmental disturbance.

Ch. 2: Environmental Concepts – Physical and Economic

Figure 4. Raster map of noise emission in an urban area. (Source: MOSCA – Project for the European Commission.)

Figure 5. Forecast for the concentration of soot and particulate matter along an arterial road in Berlin. (Source: IVU, 2002.)

3. Treatment of environmental risk by physical (hard) constraints

3.1. The principles of ecological economics

Ecological economics have been developed by Costanza, Boulding, Daly, and others (see Costanza, 1991; Hampicke, 1992) to focus on the fact that the environment needs a special kind of economic treatment. It is based on the following principles:

(1) The *complementarity* of nature and economics. Nature cannot be held servile to economic advantage in the long run.

(2) *Irreversibility*. It is not possible to exploit nature temporarily and then switch to an environmentally more friendly economic behavior later. Destruction of nature can never be completely repaired.
(3) A *holistic approach*. As the ecological/economic system is very complex it is not possible to improve the system by piece-meal policies. The Descartes-type scientific approach of dividing a complex reality into smaller units and then to model/optimize these pieces separately by partial analysis will not work.
(4) *Dynamic feedback*. Looking at systems can never be done successfully through static or comparative static approaches. The progression of a system can only be identified by means of feedback analysis of the dynamic drivers of the ecological/economic system.

Starting from these principles, nature cannot be regarded purely as a means of production or as a source of raw materials, as in the neoclassical theory. More than that, it is a necessary precondition for the continued survival of mankind in the long run. As such, nature can never be traded off against economic wealth. A natural environment with functioning recycling processes, compatible with economic growth and social harmony, is the basis of long-term sustainability.

3.2. Safe minimum standards

Against the background of the four principles above, environmental policy has to protect society against serious losses of unknown probability. An insurance company would in such a situation try to control the behavior of the client in such a way that risk-enhancing activities are reduced by setting safe minimum standards. This precautionary policy is superior to paying premiums and receiving a damage indemnity in the case of loss, because the magnitude of the loss can be much higher than the indemnity payment.

The definition of safe minimum standards has to be treated with utmost responsibility because setting the standards too high would suppress economic activities and jeopardize the material wealth of people while setting the standards too low would lead to a high risk of environmental collapse. The problem of suggesting appropriate safe minimum standards has been tackled in the past by groups of experts such as the WHO or the IPCC. Some examples of standards suggested by international and national organizations are given in Table 4.

3.3. Environmental legacy

The European case is interesting insofar as environmental legacy goes beyond national borders and European law dominates national law. Current EU law is first set in the form of a general treaty (the first treaty was decided in Rome in

Table 4
Examples of international and national (German) safe minimum values and reduction targets

Protects	Safe minimum value/reduction target	From	To	Source
Climate	80% for CO_2 emissions	1990	2040	IPCC
	25% for CO_2 emissions	1990	2005	German federal government
Human health (water, soil, woodlands)	2.5 µg/m^3 for benzene			WHO, UBA
	1.5 µg/m^3 for particulates			
	Reduce risk of cancer by 1: 2500		2005	SRU
	90% benzene, particulates	1988	2005	SRU, LAI
	99% benzene, particulates		2010	UBA
	80% NO_x, VOCs	1987	2005	SRU
	40% NO_x, VOCs		2000	BImSchG
Human health (noise)	65 dB(A) day		2005	UBA
	55 dB(A) night			
	59 dB(A) day		2010	UBA, SRU
	49 dB(A) night			
	50 dB(A) day		2030	UBA
	40 dB(A) night			
Nature and the landscape	Compensation principle for land use in resource areas		2000	BNG
	No construction of new links in protected areas			UBA
	No extension of the length of the federal transport network in future planning			UBA

Key: VOC, volatile organic compounds; BImSchG, Federal Law for Emission Reduction (German); LAI, State Committee for the Reduction of Pollutant Emissions (German); SRU, Advisory Council for Environmental Issues (German); UBA, German Federal Environmental Agency (German).

1956, and the last amendments to the treaty were decided on in Maastricht in 1994). On the basis of the treaty, Directives are enacted, which are monitored by the European Commission.

Directive 85/3850 EG, for instance, makes an environmental impact analysis for all transport investments obligatory, and for projects of the TransEuropean Networks (TENs) an extended environmental risk analysis on a corridor or even network scale is necessary. Figure 6 gives an overview of Directives concerning air pollution and noise.[a]

---

[a]Examples of EU Directives that cover air pollution by transport are 1996/62, 1999/30, 2000/69, and 2001/27, and Directives on noise emissions are 70/157 and 99/101 (these can be read on the EU's website).

National, state/province, and community laws are much more detailed. At the bottom of the pyramid shown the administrative units receive Directives for planning and operation. For instance, Directive RLS 90 in Germany gives detailed guidelines for the design of roads to avoid exceeding noise limits.

4. Economic concepts for the evaluation of environmental impacts

Two different approaches to the evaluation of the costs of environment damage can be identified (Figure 7).

4.1. The welfare maximization approach

The traditional approach of neoclassical welfare theory is based on the assumption that all the required data is complete and available. This implies that environmental damage can be predicted with a high degree of certainty or that probabilities are given. The essential properties of the neoclassical welfare model are:

- Material production and environmental, human, resources are regarded as interchangeable – a reduction in the latter can be compensated for by an increase in the former.
- The societal value system is reflected by market prices – if a market price does not exist for a particular environmental cost it should be approximated by a market analogy.

Figure 6. EU law and the environment.

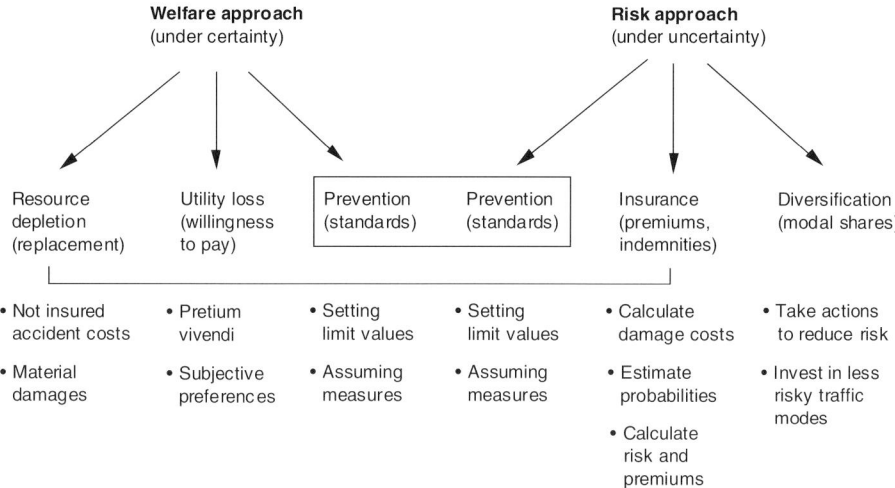

Figure 7. Approaches to the evaluation of the impact of transport on the environment.

- All changes to environmental resources can be expressed in monetary terms.

Usually the replacement cost of depleted resources is calculated (the resource approach), or the willingness to pay (the utility approach) is used to estimate the value of environmental impacts through a market analogy. The resource cost and utility approaches are generally treated as discrete alternatives for the evaluation of the consequences of accidents and environmental impact. But, using the instruments of dynamic welfare theory, it can be shown that both the cost and utility approaches coincide when a complete formulation of a dynamic welfare maximization problem under environmental constraints is given (Kotz et al., 1984).

The resource approach

In the resource approach, all losses caused by environmental impacts are regarded as depletions of resources, that are evaluated either on the basis of the costs of replacement or on the basis on loss of future returns. Thus, if building facades or historical monuments are destroyed by air pollution their economic value can be estimated by the cost of restoration. Humans, animals, and plants are conceptually treated in the same way and viewed as resources, so that their value in terms of replacement (purchase or manufacturing costs) or income (monetary value of future returns) can be determined. The societal value of a human life will thus also be assigned an economic value.

The utility approach

The utility approach is founded on the estimate of the cost of an environmental impact to an individual. The theory is based on hypotheses of individual behavior of the type used in general equilibrium economic theory. The most important part of this approach is the homo oeconomicus hypothesis. This consists of two elements. First, the information premise assumes that all parties are fully aware of the economically relevant data or can treat risk by contingent claims. Second, an individual is able to perform consistent evaluation (order of preferences, utility function) and, in particular, trade-offs between protecting the environment and consumption of resources.

A third strand of this approach requires individuals to respond to changes in their economic situation by a monetary willingness to pay or to sell. This willingness can be measured by stated or revealed-preference techniques. In the first case people are questioned and express the magnitude of their response to an external effect by virtual payments or contingent claims. Revealed-preference approaches try to derive the economic value of an external effect by observing the behavior of affected people.

A distinctive approach for revealing preferences is the hedonic pricing method. Here a demand function is constructed and estimated econometrically. This function includes – beside other market parameters – the environmental quality as an additional argument. The values of the parameters of the demand function are estimated on the basis of field surveys. As the demand function also includes the market prices of manufactured goods as explanatory variables, it is possible to calculate the monetary value of environmental resources by considering the elasticity of substitution between manufactured goods and environmental resources.

The prevention approach

Some environmental damage is impossible to evaluate in monetary terms based on the cost of the damage or willingness to pay because the impact path of the mechanisms from the emission source to the impact on people cannot be constructed (e.g. emission of carbon dioxide). In these cases a prevention approach is often applied that basically estimates the cost of avoiding the harm by prevention measures. Prevention measures are related to standard settings, with their magnitude depending on the level of prevention defined by specified limit values and the preventive technology used.

Note that the prevention approach is only used in neoclassical welfare economics as an auxiliary or second-best method in the scenario when no best method can be applied.

The social rate of discount

It is well known that private investors will discount future earnings and costs in an investment calculation, and that society also has a short-term view of consumption. When it comes to the evaluation of external diseconomies it is assumed that there is some sort of social discount that has to be applied to allow comparability of effects occurring at different periods. The method for estimating a social rate of discount is different from that used for commercial investments. In general terms the social rate of discount equals the value of the societal time preference and of the opportunistic costs of production. It can be derived from a long-term equilibrium growth model with the result that is not necessarily unique. For environmental damage that can be repaired or entirely compensated for, the social rate of discount will equal the commercial investment cost. This is close to the capital market rate of interest. In the case of risk to human health or for mankind to survive (non-reproducible resource losses) the rate of discount can be very low and approach zero.

4.2. Risk approach

The foundation of this approach is the theory of ecological economics. Risk and uncertainty about causation and impacts are basic phenomena associated with deteriorating environmental quality. The main issue of the risk approach is thus risk management according to the precaution principle, instead of cost allocation according to the polluter pays principle. Risk can be managed through a strategy mix consisting of diversification, insurance and prevention.

Diversification

An example for the diversification strategy is the provision of loss-making public transport facilities. The deficits of public passenger services may be seen as the price of risk diversification (they are often referred to as "survival precautions").

Insurance

In the area of safety, insurance contracts can be a means of placing future risks into economic categories. Reinsurance companies that are particularly involved in insuring natural catastrophes have developed calculation schemes to estimate the premiums to cover future expected payments in loss compensation. Such an approach is founded on the assumption that it is possible to crudely estimate expected values and variances of losses such that the problem can be turned into a stochastic resource approach with yearly premiums corresponding to the expected annuities of future payouts.

Prevention

In the context of a risk approach, the prevention cost estimation is no longer an auxiliary method that is applied only if direct measurements of damage costs or of willingness to pay fail. Instead, it has a theoretical underpinning through economic ecology. The theory is based on the hypothesis that "safe minimum standards" describe the long-term sustainability of the economic and social system.

Hirshleifer and Riley (1979) give an example for the decision problem. In the case of a child's life, taking out an insurance policy would be economically irrational, because the family concerned would need less income in the loss state (i.e. without the child) compared with the non-loss state. In a case like this it would be socially rational for an outside agency to transfer income from the "state with loss" to the "state without loss," i.e. to practice a kind of reverse insurance by doing everything to prevent the occurrence of the loss. Where preferences are distorted or where social risks occur, it is up to the state to take action to prevent loss. The costs of these actions are a well-based proxy for a cost evaluation of environmental quality.

Opportunity costs (shadow prices)

The correct economic way to calculate the costs to the environment in the case of hard constraints set by a safe minimum standard is to formulate the welfare problem explicitly and derive the opportunity costs of the environmental factors. A general formulation of the welfare problem, written in a static way for simplicity, can be based on

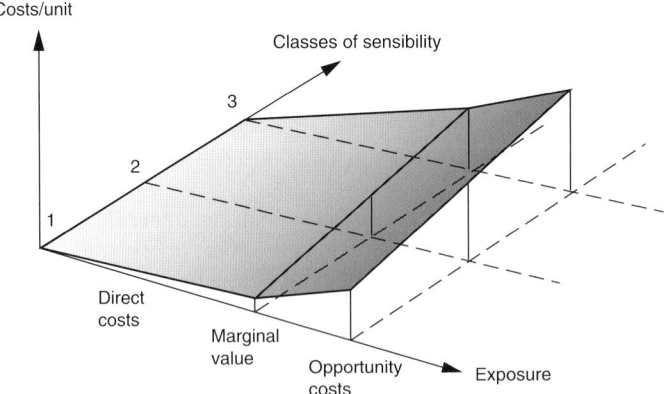

Figure 8. Dual-cost function for evaluation of environmental factors. (Source: IWW et al., 1999.)

Table 5
Results of direct and indirect cost estimations for environmental impacts

Environmental impact	Unit	Direct cost estimation	Shadow price estimation
CO_2	Euros/tonne of emissions	135	70
NO_x	Euros/tonne of emissions	5900	8950
Particulates	Euros/tonne of emissions and millions of inhabitants	880	1180
Benzene	Euros/tonne of emissions and millions of inhabitants	50	950

$$\max\{C(x)\} \quad \text{s.t.} \quad g(x) \leq R,$$

where C is material consumption (or utility from material consumption), R is a vector of safe minimum standards for environmental factors, and x is a vector of production/consumption activities.

In the Lagrange formulation we get

$$\text{Max}\{C(x) - \mu(g(x) - R)\}.$$

The multiplier μ denotes the shadow prices of the environment, i.e. the reduction of material consumption if an environmental standard is tightened by one unit. For practical applications one can construct linear or non-linear programming formulations or complex dynamic simulation models to derive the shadow prices. According to the logic of shadow prices, these only have a positive value if a constraint is binding, or zero, to avoid the result that potential disturbances below the safe minimum standards are not evaluated economically. This concerns the disamenities of affected people that can be traded against monetary compensation. For this reason, IWW et al. (1999) developed a dual-cost approach, evaluating the environmental impacts as resource costs, or as willingness to pay below the safe minimum standards, and switching to the shadow prices if the safe minimum standards are violated (Figure 8).

Taking the values for the direct costs from the INFRAS/IWW study and comparing them with the shadow prices yields the results shown in Table 5. The expectation was that the shadow price method would in general lead to higher cost estimates. This is in general not true. The evaluation of the effects of CO_2 on the environment was lower than in previous estimations that were influenced by the high value of direct damage cost estimations presented by Hohmeyer and Gärtner (1992). (It should be mentioned that direct damage estimations from the USA lead to lower results (Nordhaus, 1991).) The outcome of the shadow price approach indicates that the cost of reducing the risk is much lower than the cost of the damage arising from pessimistic damage expectations. While the differences between the approaches for estimations of the costs of the impact of NO_x and particulate matter are not dramatic, there is a significant deviation for benzene. This indicates that either the limit values assumed for benzene are too rigid or the estimated direct damage costs are too low.

The values listed in Table 5 are average figures. In the case of the indirect shadow pricing method the values can be differentiated according to local situations. This is done by calculating the concentrations of exhaust emissions and noise levels by a simulation model (a combined traffic/geographical information systems model) and assigning the limit values for maximum concentration and noise levels to the regional units.

5. A sustainable development of the transport system

The scientific approach to the evaluation of the environmental impact of human activity can be incorporated in an integrated environmental policy.

First, safe minimum values of environmental quality need to be defined so that major risks to health, of destroying biodiversity, or of jeopardizing rare species are minimized. The measures to achieve a future transportation system which is less damaging to the environment comprise:

- An investment policy based on cost–benefit analysis in which environmental impacts are evaluated as opportunity costs (derived as shadow prices from the safe minimum constraints).
- A pricing policy based on the polluter pays principle, using prices derived from opportunity costs.
- A regulation policy that aims to meet safe minimum values by imposing restrictions on travel behavior.
- Standards setting for technical processes (e.g. pollution from combustion of engines), to incentivize industry to develop cleaner technology.
- Education and behavioral training to make environmentally friendly behavior routine, concentrating on areas in which safe minimum standards are often exceeded.

Simulation models that bring the information from transport models and environmental impact models together can help evaluate environmental policy scenarios. Figure 9 illustrates this concept for urban concentrations of particulate matter. The study area is the German state of Baden-Württemberg, which for purposes of analysis has been modeled by 5 km raster cells. The analysis followed the impact chain presented earlier, i.e. for every element of the impact chain specific transport and environmental models were developed, and appropriate data inventories established. The base case situation in 1992 shows many sensitive environmental areas where the safe minimum standard of 1.5 $\mu g/m^3$ is seriously

Ch. 2: Environmental Concepts – Physical and Economic   31

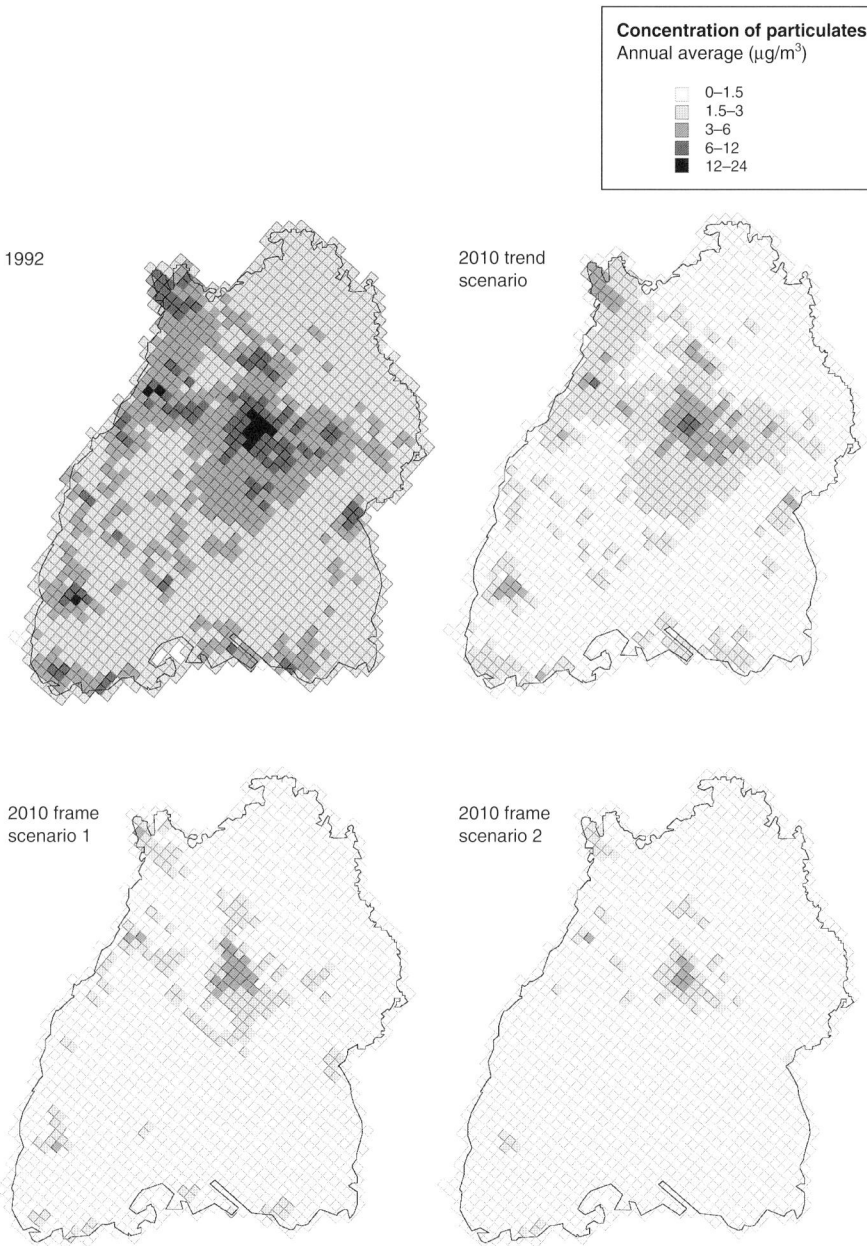

Figure 9. Models for particulate concentrations in the German state of Baden-Württemberg (5 km raster cells). The base case is 1992, and is extrapolated to 2010. The two lower models show the effects of two transport policy approaches. (Source: IWW et al., 1999.)

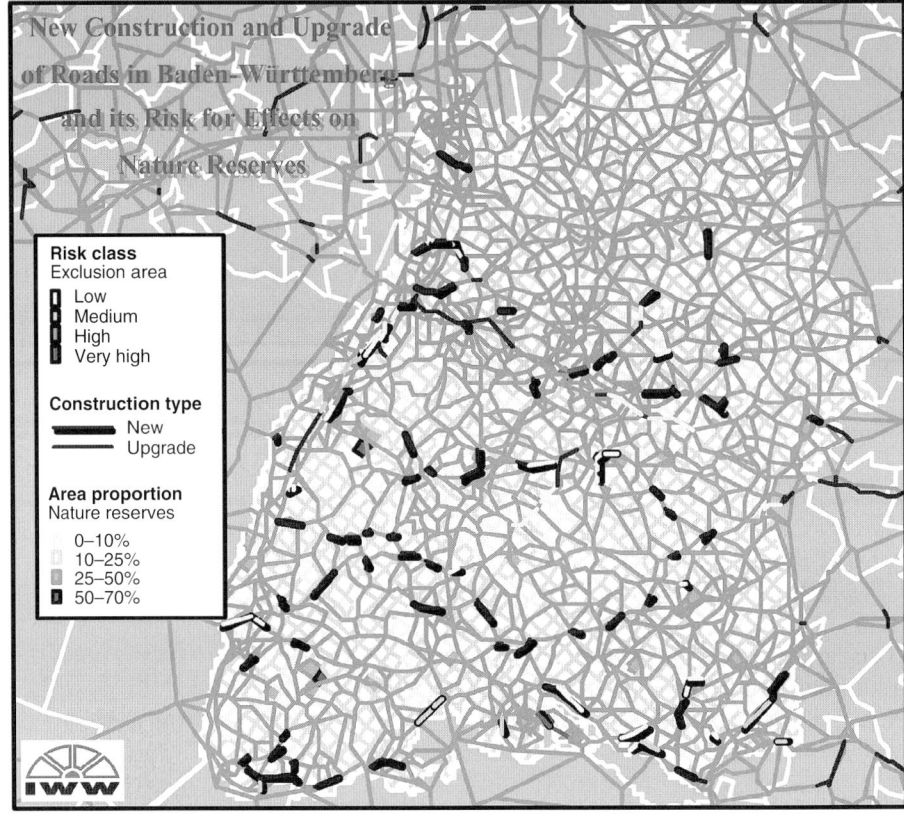

Figure 10. Risk to nature and the landscape from transport links and traffic in the German state of Baden-Württemberg. (Source: IWW et al., 1999.)

exceeded. To investigate trends, air quality is plotted against the effects of expected technical progress in 2010. The picture that develops indicates that technical progress will lead to a significant reduction in particulate matter concentrations, but insufficient to reach the safe minimum standard. Two transport policy approaches were investigated. Scenario 2 is the best approach because it minimizes the violations of environmental standards. The figure shows that only in the densely populated capital city of Baden-Württemberg, Stuttgart, do a few critical spots remain.

For other environmental indicators such as noise or biodiversity, similar models and databases can be constructed. For the effects on nature and landscape conservation a risk classification has been derived, which differentiates between low, medium, high, and very high environmental risk. This risk cluster has been matched with information on the construction of new transport links or the upgrade of existing links. Figure 10 shows the result. It follows from the philosophy of safe minimum standards that investment planning for new and upgraded transport links should try to reduce the identified trouble spots as much as possible.

The second approach to environmental policy consists of measures to treat disamenities and annoyance produced by environmental externalities. For this, a valuation using neoclassical welfare economics is feasible because material goods and environmental quality can be regarded as substitutes. In particular, approaches based on individual preferences such as willingness to pay, contingents, and hedonic pricing methods can be used to derive economic values for environmental impacts. The measures to treat such effects are in principle the same as those listed earlier. The major difference is that the hard constraints of safe minimum values now play no role in the quantification of economic values.

The values for environmental impacts are used in cost–benefit analysis and pricing. Hayashi and Morisugi (2000) provide accounts of a number of international procedures that have been developed as mandatory and standard evaluation procedures.

Regarding pricing, the neoclassical standard evaluation approach for environmental impacts often underpins social marginal cost pricing. Environmental marginal costs are part of the social marginal cost when the latter is defined as the additional cost of operation, time, accident losses, environmental damage, and congestion caused by an additional transport unit. The European Commission (1998) has suggested use of the social marginal cost-pricing scheme for the transport infrastructure of the EU.

While the principle of social marginal cost pricing is heavily debated, in part because it may not lead to a full recovery of infrastructure and environmental costs, the idea of creating economic incentives for a better use of environmental resources is sound. Pricing instruments are in many respects more flexible and effective than command and control instruments. Nevertheless, pricing policies may not be acceptable to society, and there are transaction costs (costs of implementation and enforcement).

6. Conclusions

The quality of measurement and evaluation of environmental impacts is crucially dependent on reliable forecasts of the impact chain, beginning with the emissions at the source and ending with clear results for affected areas and populations. The development of standard evaluation methods, as done in many countries in the form of cost–benefit analysis for transport investment projects, can be useful for consistency because many projects can be evaluated using a single methodological platform. But there are risks to be considered. Standardized approaches generally abstract from detailed impact chain analysis and suggest average figures for evaluating environmental impacts. This can result in misleading evaluations of ecological risk with respect to affected regions and groups within populations. Therefore, there may be a need to explore the impact chain more deeply in physical terms and to adjust the economic calculations to the specifics of the case. This can be important for noise, and for exhaust emissions that are relevant for ozone production. There is a high variance of impacts over space for such factors.

Even in the case of climate effects a regional classification might be necessary if the work of Jacobson (2002) is confirmed. This indicates that local pollution of particulate matter influences the greenhouse effect, a possibility that has not been considered previously.

A second point concerns evaluating environmental impacts. First, safe minimum values for environmental quality can be significantly exceeded. In this case the economic valuation is based on an opportunity cost calculation, measuring the shadow price of the violated environmental constraint. This approach can lead to different prices for regions, affected groups, and producers of the emissions. Second, environmental disturbance can produce less serious disamenities and annoyance. In this case environmental quality can be traded off against material goods, enabling market-type valuation of environmental quality.

References

Babisch, W., H. Ising, P.C. Elwood, D.S. Sharp and D. Bainton (1993) "Traffic noise and cardiovascular risk: the Caerphilly and Speedwell Studies, second phase. Risk estimation, prevalence, and incidence of ischemic heart disease," *Archives of Environmental Health,* 48:406–413.

Babisch W., H. Ising, B. Kruppa and D. Wiens (1994) "The incidence of myocardial infarction and its relation to road traffic noise – the Berlin case control studies," *Environmental International,* 20:469–474.

Comisión Nacional del Mdeio Ambiente (1998) *Plan de Prevencion y Descontaminacion Atmosferica de la Region Metropolitana. Conama.* Santiago: Comisión Nacional del Mdeio Ambiente.

Costanza, R. (1991) *Ecological economics. The science and management of sustainability.* New York: Columbia University Press.

European Commission (1998) *Fair payment for infrastructure use: a phased approach to a common transport infrastructure charging framework for the EU, white paper,* COM(98)466/FIN. Brussels: EC.

Hampicke, U. (1992) *Ökologische ökonomie.* Opladen: Westdeutscher Verlag.

Hayashi, Y. and H. Morisugi (2000) "International comparison of background concept and methodology of transportation project appraisal," *Transport Policy,* 7:73–88.

Hirshleifer, J. and J.G. Riley (1979) "The analytics of uncertainty and information – an expository survey," *Journal of Economic Literature,* 27:1375–1421.

Hohmeyer, O. and M. Gärtner (1992) *The social costs of climate change – a rough estimate of orders of magnitude.* Karlsruhe: EC.

INFRAS (1992) *Gebäudeschäden durch verkehrsbedingte Luftverschmutzung im Auftrag des Dienstes.* Zürich: GVF.

INFRAS and IWW (2000) *External effects of transport.* Paris: UIC.

Intergovernmental Panel for Climate Change (2001) *Climate change 2001: the scientific basis. Summary for policymakers and technical summary of the Working Group I report.* Cambridge: IPCC.

Ising, H., W. Barbisch and B. Kruppa (1998) "Ergebnisse epidemiologischer Forschung im Bereich Lärm," in: *Bundesumweltministerium: Gesundheitsrisiken durch Lärm*. Bonn: Tagung im Wissenschaftszentrum.

IVU (2002) Internet download (http://www.ivu-umwelt.de/refer4.htm)

IWW, IFEU, P. Kessel, PÖU and PTV (1999) *Entwicklung eines Verfahrens zur Aufstellungumweltorientierter Fernverkehrskonzepte als Beitrag zur Bundesverkehrswegeplanung*. Karlsruhe: German Federal Environmental Agency.

Jacobson, M.Z. (2002) "Control of fossil-fuel particulate black carbon and organic matter, possibly the most effective method of slowing global warming," *Journal of Geophysical Research – Atmospheres*, 107 (electronic journal).

Kotz, R., P. Müller and W. Rothengatter (1984) *Entwicklung eines Verfahrens für dynamische Investitionsplanung und Ermittlung des bei der Fortschreibung der BVWP anzuwendenden Zinssatzes*. Expert report commissioned by the Federal Minister of Transport. Ulm: Ulm University.

NEA, INRETS and IWW (1999) *Traffic forecast for the Helsinki Corridors*. Rijswijk: EC.

Nordhaus, W.D. (1991) "To slow or not to slow? The economics of the greenhouse effect," *Economic Journal*, 101:920–937.

Maschke, C. and H. Ising, (1997) *Beeinträchtigung der Gesundheit durch Verkehrslärm*. Bonn: German Federal Ministry for Health.

World Health Organisation (1999) *Health costs due to road traffic-related air pollution, an impact assessment project of Austria, France, Switzerland, economic evaluation*, technical report. London: WHO.

Chapter 3

CLIMATE CHANGE

MANFRED LENZEN and CHRISTOPHER DEY
The University of Sydney

CLIVE HAMILTON
Australian National University, Canberra

1. Introduction

In 1995 the Intergovernmental Panel on Climate Change (IPCC) acknowledged that "the balance of evidence suggests a discernible human influence on the global climate" (Intergovernmental Panel on Climate Change, 1995). This landmark statement confirmed that climate change is now considered to be one of the most serious threats to the environment (Watson et al., 1996). In the third assessment report of the IPCC (IPCC, 2001a), the summarizing statements are stronger: "the warming over the last 100 years is very unlikely to be due to internal variability alone," and "most of the observed warming over the last 50 years is likely to have been due to the increase in greenhouse gas concentrations."

Observations of climate change (with a low degree of scientific uncertainty) include (IPCC, 2001a):

- a global average surface temperature increase over the twentieth century of $0.6 \pm 0.2°C$;
- in the past four decades, an overall global temperature increase in the lower 8 km of the atmosphere of $\sim 0.1°C$ per decade;
- a reduction of snow cover of about 10% since the late 1960s and widespread retreat of mountain glaciers in non-polar regions during the twentieth century;
- an increase in global average sea level of between 0.1 and 0.2 m during the twentieth century;
- an increase in the global ocean heat content since the late 1950s;
- statistically significant changes in the distribution and magnitude of precipitation.

A significant part of the international effort to understand climate change relates to predicting the distribution and magnitude of climate change impacts. Estimating long-term impacts has the dual source of uncertainty of, first, the

Handbook of Transport and the Environment, Edited by D.A. Hensher and K.J. Button
© 2003, Elsevier Ltd

prediction of the levels and types of emissions, and, secondly, the response of the global climate to these emissions. Despite this uncertainty, to give an introduction to the importance of climate change it is worth considering that physical models of the climate system suggest that a stabilization of atmospheric carbon dioxide (CO_2) concentrations at today's level requires a reduction in net emissions of approximately 50% within the next 40 years, and further reductions thereafter. Even with this magnitude of change in greenhouse gas emission trends, a global sea level rise of more than 25 cm must be expected over the next 100 years (Houghton et al., 1997).

In this chapter we give an overview of the causes and mechanisms of climate change, the relationship between climate change and energy use in general and transport operations in particular, a background to international activity addressing climate change, and conclusions about the role of transport in the response to climate change.

1.1. The greenhouse effect and the radiative forcing of climate

The greenhouse effect is a natural phenomenon that refers to the response of the Earth's atmosphere to different wavelengths of electromagnetic radiation. The atmosphere is largely transparent to incoming radiation at solar wavelengths, and largely opaque to outgoing radiation at substantially longer thermal wavelengths. The equilibrium temperature of the Earth, the temperature at which there is a balance between these incoming and outgoing energy flows, is consequently about 30°C higher than it would be in the absence of an atmosphere. This is the (natural) greenhouse effect. Water vapor is by far the most dominant greenhouse gas. Human activities have little direct influence on its atmospheric concentration. CO_2 is also an important greenhouse gas, even though it represents only ~0.03% of the atmosphere. The main natural factors which can alter the equilibrium temperature substantially in decadal time-frames are changes in solar irradiance and large volcanic eruptions.

Since about the mid-eighteenth century, when significant fossil fuel combustion began, human activity has steadily changed the composition of the atmosphere. The concentration of CO_2, released from combustion processes, has increased from a pre-industrial concentration of ~280 ppm to ~365 ppm in 1998. There have also been significant anthropogenic increases in the atmospheric concentrations of two other important greenhouse gases, methane (CH_4) and nitrous oxide (N_2O). The radiative balance consequences of the increases in the concentrations of these gases, as well as several others discussed below, are termed the enhanced greenhouse effect. The efficacy of anthropogenic factors in influencing the Earth's energy balance and hence the climate is described by their radiative forcing in units of watts per meter squared (W/m^2). Positive radiative forcing implies a warming of the Earth's surface, such as that induced by increases in greenhouse gas concentrations. Atmospheric aerosols, a collective term for small airborne particles, are in general an example of a negative radiative forcing agent, and tend to cool the surface.

Figure 1 shows the concentrations of CO_2, CH_4, and N_2O and their approximate radiative forcing over the last millennium. There is in general good consistency between measurements of concentration made from actual air samples (last ~45 years) and air samples extracted from ice cores, leading to a high degree of certainty for these concentrations. Seasonal effects, such as increases in CH_4 and increased uptake of CO_2, can be easily distinguished in air samples. Measurements over the last 20 years indicate a decline in the annual increase of CH_4 in the atmosphere, though the reasons for this and for large observed annual variations in CH_4 concentrations, are not well known (IPCC, 2001a). Once emitted, CO_2, CH_4, and N_2O molecules remain in the atmosphere long enough (>10 years) for them to be termed well-mixed gases with generally globally averaged effects. The halocarbons are the fourth class of well-mixed greenhouse gases. These are carbon compounds containing fluorine, bromine, chlorine, or iodine, and most are anthropogenic in origin. Halocarbons containing chlorine (e.g. the chlorofluorocarbons – CFCs) and bromine participate in reactions which deplete stratospheric ozone. The release of these gases has reduced substantially since the early 1990s due to the effectiveness of international controls mandated by the Montreal Protocol, and their atmospheric concentrations are now falling. However, concentrations of their replacements, which are also long lived and powerful greenhouse gases, are increasing. Perfluorocarbons (e.g. CF_4 and C_2F_6) and silicon tetraflouride (SF_6) together form a fifth class of gases emitted in small quantities but which are also are extremely long lived and radiatively effective. Their contribution to the enhanced greenhouse effect is small, but their longevity and increasing concentrations may increase their importance. A summary of the atmospheric characteristics of the main well-mixed greenhouse gases is given in Table 1.

In addition to the gases described above, there are other important contributions to radiative forcing of the atmosphere which are generally short lived. Ozone (O_3), the gas which in the stratosphere naturally screens the Earth's surface from ultraviolet radiation, is also present lower down in the troposphere. The radiative forcing of ozone in the troposphere (positive forcing) and the stratosphere (negative) is different and complex. It is formed by photochemical processes (not directly emitted), and has lifetimes of weeks to months, so its distribution is not uniform (IPCC, 2001a). There are gases with indirect radiative influences due to their effect on ozone and CH_4 via chemical reactions. These include oxides of nitrogen (general term NO_x), carbon monoxide (CO), and volatile organic compounds (VOCs). The scientific understanding of these agents is low.

Aerosols are the final important known contributor to radiative forcing. They can have direct effects such as scattering and absorption of solar and/or thermal radiation, and indirect effects through their influence on the radiative properties of clouds. There are both natural and anthropogenic sources of aerosols, but in

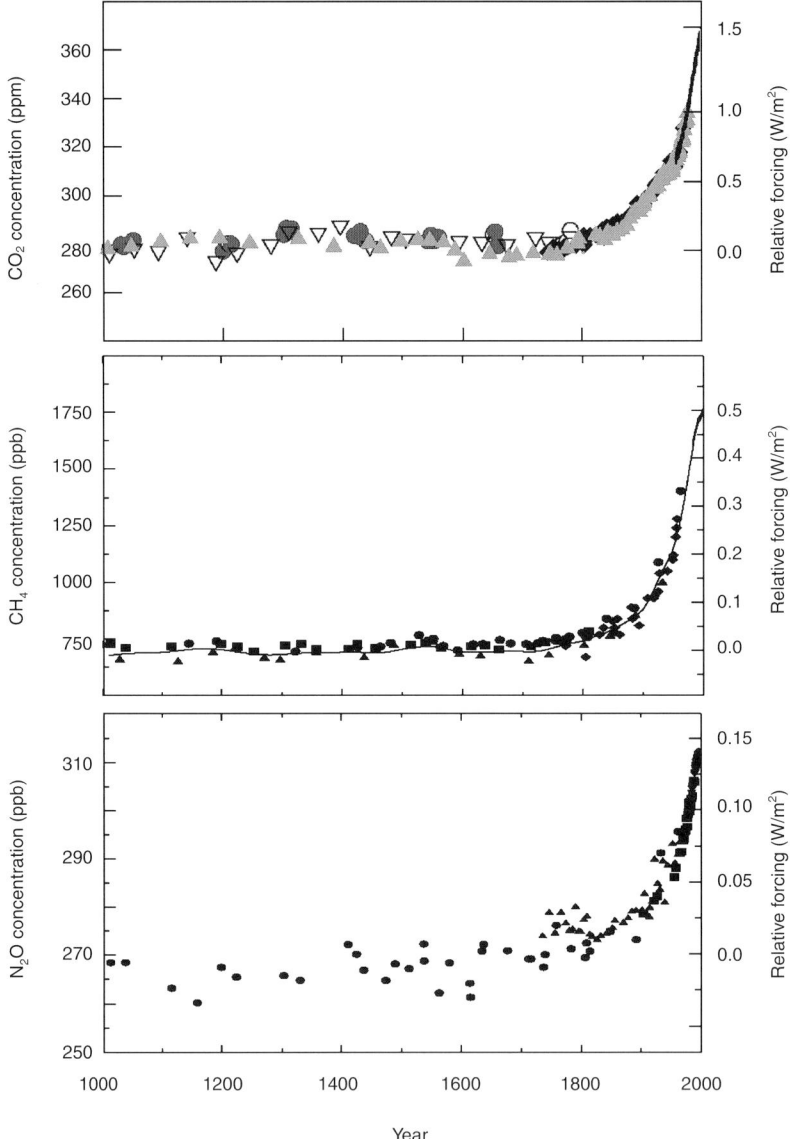

Figure 1. Historic global atmospheric concentrations and approximate radiative forcing contributions of three well-mixed greenhouse gases (IPCC 2001c). Different symbols indicate different measurement methods.

Table 1
Characteristics of the four well-mixed anthropogenic greenhouse gases

	Pre-industrial concentration	Concentration in 1998	Average annual increase last 20 years	Approximate relative importance of the well-mixed greenhouse gases
CO_2	~280 ppm	365 ppm	1.5 ppm (0.4%)	~60%
CH_4	~700 ppb	1745 ppb	~5 ppb (~0.3%)	~20%
N_2O	~270 ppb	314 ppb	0.8 ppb (0.25%)	~5%
Halocarbons	0 ppb	Various	Various	~15%

Source: after IPCC (2001c).

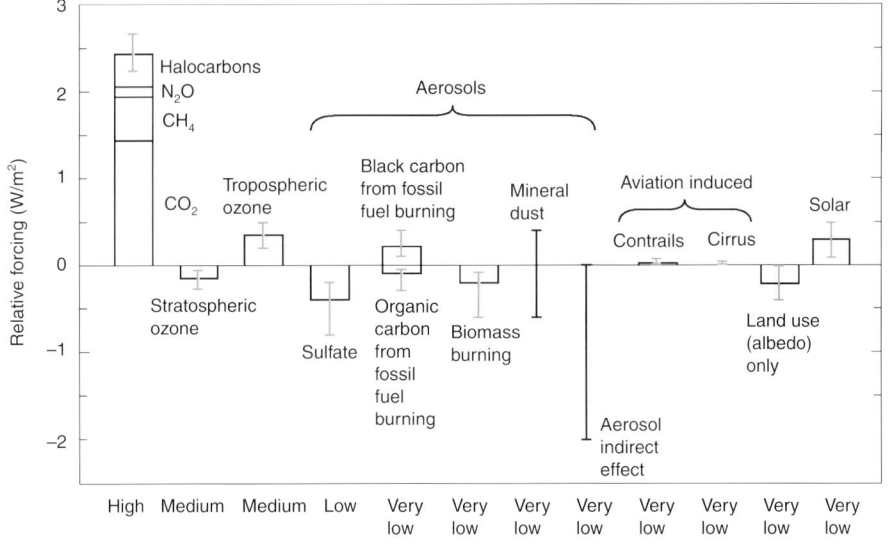

Figure 2. Global mean radiative forcing for the year 2000, relative to 1750, in terms of the known factors, together with an indication of the scientific knowledge of the factors.

general their abundance, predominantly in the lower troposphere, is increasing. Direct aerosol forcing, primarily from sulfates, biomass burning, and solid carbon emissions, is mainly negative. Our understanding of the indirect radiative forcing of aerosols is also limited.

The total effects of all known radiative forcing agents are summarized in Figure 2. No sound estimates can be made for the radiative forcing of mineral dust and the magnitude of the indirect aerosol effect. A further possible source of indirect radiative forcing, aviation, is estimated to be small, though again the level of understanding is very low. Negative land use (albedo) forcing refers to an increase in the average reflectivity of the surface to incoming sunlight. The best estimate of the net radiative forcing from quantifiable contributions is ~2.2 W/m^2.

For simplicity, the net greenhouse effectiveness by mass of a gas over a given time-frame is often stated relative to that of a reference gas (usually CO_2). Known as global warming potentials (GWPs), these factors are useful for estimating the *relative* impacts of per kilogram of emissions of different gases. GWPs by mass relative to 1 kg of CO_2 are given in Table 2 for several gases, incorporating direct and indirect effects.

1.2. Sources of greenhouse gas emissions

About half of the total CO_2 equivalent (CO_2-e) greenhouse gas emissions (figures obtained using the 100 year GWPs given in Table 2) are from CO_2 emissions from fossil energy sources (Table 3). The remainder are due mainly to agriculture, land use change, and petroleum refining, gas flaring, and fuel conversion. These last three sources are perhaps more correctly allocated to their end use categories, rather than listed separately. There are large uncertainties (up to ±50%) with estimates for agriculture and land use change, the figures in Table 3 being typically mid-range. During the last 20 years, about three-quarters of the anthropogenic emissions of CO_2 have been due to fossil fuel burning, and the remainder mainly from deforestation (IPCC, 2001a). About half of these emissions are taken up by land and ocean processes, with the remainder accumulating in the atmosphere. Anthropogenic CH_4 emissions (e.g. from fossil fuel use, agriculture, and landfills) represent about 60% of total CH_4 emissions. For N_2O emissions, about one-third are anthropogenic (e.g. agricultural soils, cattle feedlots, and the chemical industry).

1.3. Equity and sustainability in the context of climate change

The wealthier 10% of the world's population creates about two-thirds of global greenhouse gas emissions. Average per capita CO_2 emissions in North America,

Table 2
Global warming potentials for some of the main greenhouse gases

	CO_2	CH_4	N_2O	CO	NO_x (surface)	NO_x (aviation)
GWP (20 years)	1	62	275	2–10		
GWP (100 years)	1	23	296	1–3	5	450
GWP (500 years)	1	7	156	0.3–1		

Source: after IPCC (2001a).

Table 3
Sectoral breakdown of anthropogenic greenhouse gas emissions in 1995 as CO_2 from energy use, and CO_2 equivalent from all activities.

Sector	CO_2 emissions from energy use ($\times 10^6$ t CO_2 1995)	Equivalent emissions – all activities ($\times 10^6$ t CO_2-e 1995)
Buildings	6 400 (32%)	6 600 (17%)
Transport	4 500 (22%)	4 800 (12%)
Industry	8 600 (42%)	9 500 (24%)
Agriculture	800 (4%)	8 000 (20%)
Land use change	–	3 500 (9%)
Waste	–	1 400 (4%)
Emissions from petroleum refining, gas flaring, and fuel conversion	–	5 900 (15%)
Total	20 300	39 700

Derived from various IPCC documents (IPCC, 1996, 1999, 2000, 2001a,b).

Australia, Europe, or Japan are about ten times higher than those in South Asia or China (Figure 3). Each column represents one of the regions noted below the horizontal axis. The column width is proportional to the population, while the height shows the annual per capita emissions of CO_2 in a region. Hence, the column area represents the total amount of CO_2 emitted annually from each region. Furthermore, each column contains contributions from four sources, as explained in the figure caption.

Per capita emissions vary over a wide range, between 1 t CO_2/year in poor regions of South Asia and more than 20 t CO_2/year in affluent North America. The CO_2 emitted from a region is not necessarily identical to the CO_2 emissions associated with the regional consumption, because some emissions are associated with traded commodities (Proops et al., 1993; Machado et al., 2001). A major part of the CO_2 emissions due to land use changes in South America and Southeast Asia, for example, is associated with land clearing for timber exports. If the per capita responsibility (rather than the territorial emission) of CO_2 was to be assessed, these emissions would have to be added to those of industrialized countries, thus increasing the gap between rich and poor. There are disparities, which are not shown in Figure 3. These are due to the fact that, in general, developing countries are less able to adapt to climate change, and therefore are likely to suffer from more severe environmental damage than industrialized countries (IPCC, 1995).

Apportioning the same right to emit to everybody on the planet and at the same time reducing emissions by 50% (stabilization of atmospheric CO_2 concentrations) yields an equitable and sustainable greenhouse gas level of about 3 t CO_2-e/person (Lenzen, 1997; Byrne et al., 1998). In order to achieve international equity and sustainability, industrialized nations would need to reduce emissions by about

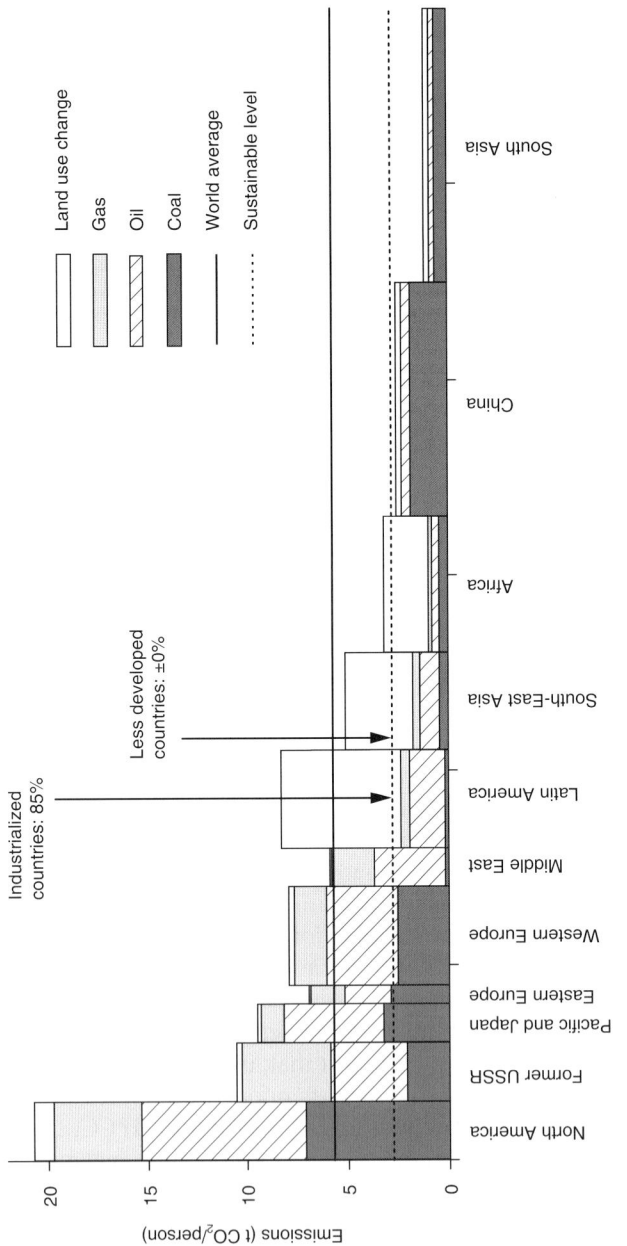

Figure 3. 1998 per capita CO_2 emissions by world region and source.

85%, while developing nations can, more or less, remain at present levels (Figure 3). Even more drastic reductions would be required under intergenerational equity, where industrialized nations are held accountable for cumulative historical emissions (Neumayer, 2000).

Wealth is the main indicator for emissions worldwide (Figure 4). Most countries show CO_2 intensities of between 0.4 kg CO_2/US \$ and 0.8 kg CO_2/US \$. Countries above the upper boundary need a particularly large amount of CO_2 in order to generate US \$1 of gross domestic product (GDP), such as the former USSR (resource waste and inefficient technology) and the USA (low energy prices). Countries below the lower boundary show below-average CO_2 intensities such as France (large proportion of nuclear power), Switzerland (service-oriented economy), and Brazil (large proportion of hydroelectricity). Developing countries accumulate in the lower left corner of the diagram. At an average CO_2 intensity of 0.6 kg CO_2/US \$, the sustainable level corresponds to a per capita GDP (and hence per capita annual expenditure) of US \$3300.

1.4. History of greenhouse gas emissions

Regional CO_2 emissions from fossil fuel burning, cement manufacture, and gas flaring (compiled by Marland et al., 2001) are plotted in Figure 5. The logarithmic scale emphasizes the fact that North America, Western Europe, and centrally planned Europe have dominated production of historical greenhouse gas emissions.

During the past three decades, global greenhouse gas emissions have been increasing at an average of 1.7% per year. This trend has slowed down somewhat during the 1990s (Table 4). Moreover, a strong growth in per-capita GDP in non-OECD countries is observed, accompanied by an even stronger decrease in CO_2/GDP, so that per-capita CO_2 emissions in non-OECD countries have actually decreased, population growth notwithstanding. Still, per-capita GDP and CO_2 emissions are still much lower in non-OECD countries than in the OECD.

Breaking down the total increase in global greenhouse gas emissions (+0.8%/year) into contributions from carbon intensity of GDP (CO_2/GDP), wealth (GDP/person), and population shows that increasing wealth is the main driving factor for recent emissions trends, followed by population growth (Table 5). The main driving forces behind the per capita GDP growth are the increasing demand for electricity in developing countries and the growing transport sector in OECD countries (International Energy Agency, 2000b). These increases are partly offset by the "de-carbonization of GDP," especially in non-OECD countries.

Owing to the low per capita emissions level in much of the poorer part of the developing world (see Figure 3), the influence of population growth in these regions on global emissions is thus at present considerably lower than that of GDP growth in the industrialized world (World Commission on Environment and

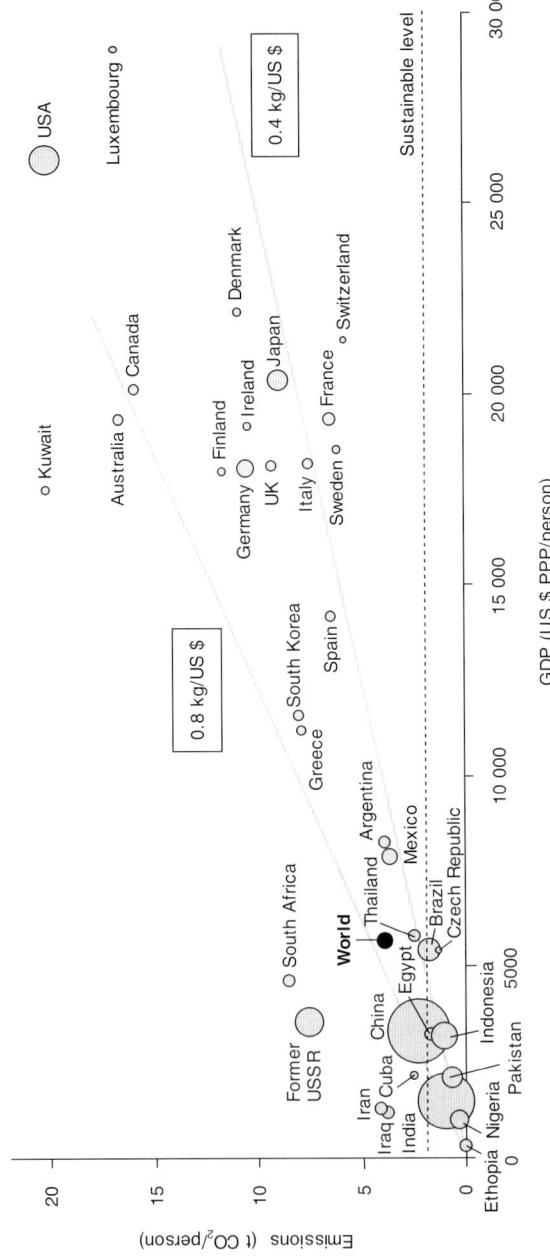

Figure 4. 1998 per capita CO_2 emissions and GDP in purchasing power parity (PPP). The sizes of the circles are proportional to the respective population.

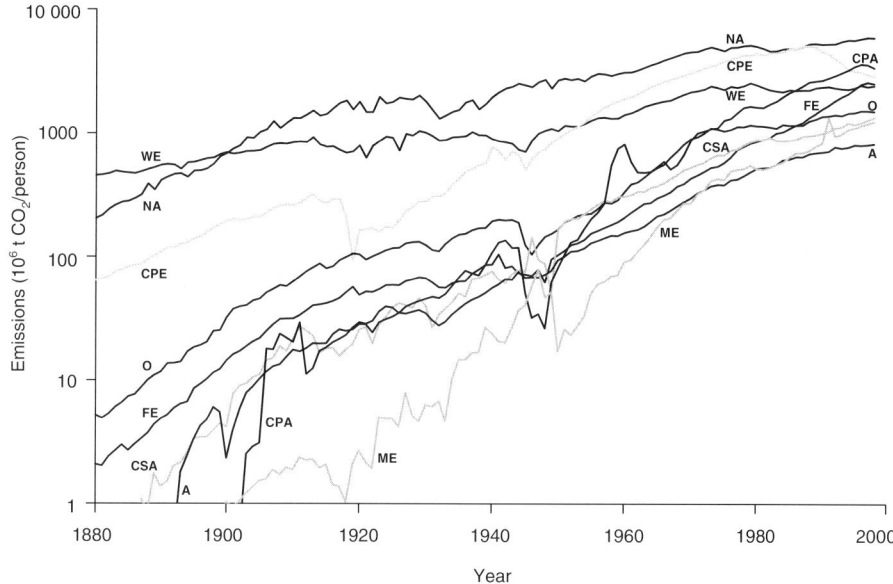

Figure 5. Historical CO_2 emissions by region. Key: A, Africa; CPA, centrally planned Asia; CPE, centrally planned Europe; CSE, Central and South America; FE, Far East; ME, Middle East; NA, North America; O, Oceania; WE, western Europe. (After Marland et al., 2001.)

Table 4
Factors determining CO_2 emissions from fuel combustion in OECD and non-OECD countries in 1998 (1990–1998 annual trends in parentheses)

	OECD	Non-OECD	World
CO_2 (10^6 t)	12 096 (+1.0%)	9 288 (+0.5%)	21 384 (+0.8%)
CO_2/GDP (kg/US $)	0.61 (−1.2%)	0.67 (−3.5%)	0.64 (−2.2%)
GDP/person (US $)	17 957 (+1.5%)	2 918 (+2.4%)	5 739 (+1.6%)
Population (10^6)	1 100 (+0.7%)	4 764 (+1.6%)	5 864 (+1.4%)
GDP (10^9 US $)	19 753 (+2.4%)	13 900 (+4.1%)	33 653 (+3.0%)
CO_2/person (t)	11.0 (+0.3%)	1.9 (−1.1%)	3.6 (−0.6%)

Source: after International Energy Agency (2000a).

Development, 1987; Parikh, 1996). Paradoxically, while the population issues of developing countries have been the subject of international negotiations on climate change, the unsustainable consumption of the industrialized nations has never been adequately acknowledged (Parikh and Painuly, 1994). Moreover, participation in climate change research and discussions is heavily skewed in favor of "Northern" institutions, resulting in "Southern" participants perceiving negotiations to revolve around the interests and policy positions of the developed world (Kandlikar and Sagar, 1999). It is therefore not surprising that the wealthy industrialized nations are being accused of appropriating yet another global area and thus exercising environmental colonialism (Agarwal and Narain, 1991).

"Many in the South feel that climate change is an issue of lifestyles" (Kandlikar and Sagar, 1999). In order to support the life of an average Australian, for example, about 25 t CO_2-e are emitted annually, which is more than seven times the equitable and sustainable level (Lenzen and Smith, 2000). About 20% of these emissions are caused by household energy and private car use, while the remaining 80% are required for the provision of consumer goods, and commercial and public services.

In most industrialized countries, emissions are mainly driven by income growth (Common and Salma, 1992; Proops et al., 1993; Wilson et al., 1994; Schipper et al., 1997; Hamilton and Turton, 1999; Heil and Selden, 2001; Hamilton and Turton, 2002) (see Figure 6). This, along with increasing women's participation in the workforce, influences lifestyle choices such as family size, home type, floor space and location, comfort through appliance ownership, mobility through car ownership, out-of-home leisure, and holiday travel. These choices affect greenhouse gas emissions from households as well as from the transportation, manufacturing, and commercial services sectors to a greater extent than energy efficiency measures or fuel mixture changes (Schipper, 1998). Carbon intensities have decreased in general over the past three decades, but markedly only in countries that have undergone significant fuel changes in their energy supply system (mostly towards hydroelectric and nuclear power), such as Sweden, Norway, and France.

1.5. International negotiations

Climate change emerged as a major public issue in 1988, about 3 years after a conference at Villach, Austria, which provided the first authoritative scientific evaluation of the expected magnitude of climate change. In June 1988 a meeting

Table 5
Break down of global greenhouse gas emissions trends

	Contribution (%)
GDP/person (non-OECD)	1.0
GDP/person (OECD)	0.9
Population (non-OECD)	0.7
Population OECD	0.4
CO_2/GDP (OECD)	–0.7
CO_2/GDP (non-OECD)	–1.5
Total	0.8

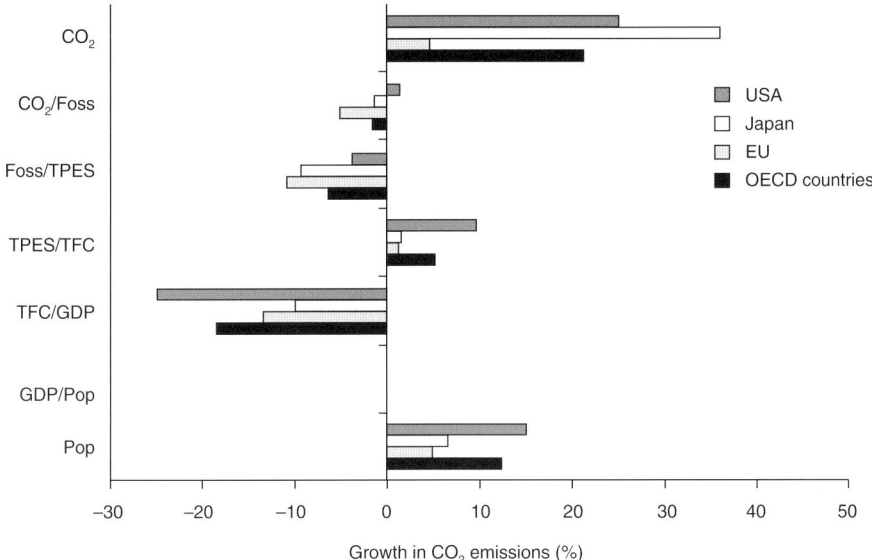

Figure 6. Contributions to growth in CO_2 emissions from energy use in the USA, Japan, EU, and OECD countries (1982–1997) (after Hamilton and Turton, 2002). This analysis relates emissions (CO_2) to ratios of fossil fuel consumption (Foss), total primary energy supply (TPES), total final consumption of energy (TFC), GDP, and population (Pop).

of more than 300 scientists and policy makers from 48 countries was held in Toronto. Although the meeting had no special status, it quickly became famous for its "call for action," which urged the adoption of an initial global goal to reduce CO_2 emissions by about 20% below 1988 levels by the year 2005. This "Toronto target" was not based on any analysis of the reductions necessary to decrease the risk of catastrophic change to an acceptable level, but it provided a focus for the magnitude and urgency of the international task at hand.

In November 1988 the IPCC was established under the auspices of the UN Environment Program and the World Meteorological Organization. Its purpose was to report to the Second World Climate Conference (scheduled for Geneva in October 1990) on the science and impacts of global warming, and strategies to forestall, delay, or adapt to the possibility of climate change.

The next milestone in the evolution of the issue occurred in June 1992. At the UN Conference on Environment and Development in Rio – the famous Earth Summit – 155 nations signed the UN Framework Convention on Climate Change (UNFCCC), the basic international instrument to deal with climate change which came into force in March 1994. The convention designated the year 2000 as the year by which signatories would return greenhouse gas emissions to their 1990

Table 6
Kyoto Protocol targets for selected Annex B countries

Country	Target (percentage of base year or period)
Australia	108
Canada	94
Denmark	92
European Community	92
Iceland	110
Japan	94
New Zealand	100
Russian Federation	100
Sweden	92
Ukraine	100
USA	93

levels. Although this was not an obligation on signatory nations, the issue of binding obligations was raised at the First Conference of the Parties (COP1), held in Berlin in March 1995. COP1 led to the Berlin Mandate, the instrument that set in train the events leading to the Kyoto Protocol, agreed in December 1997.

The Kyoto Protocol was a landmark agreement that would require signatory industrialized countries (inscribed in Annex B of the protocol) to reduce their greenhouse gas emissions by an average of 5.2% below 1990 levels in the first commitment period of 2008–2012. The targets agreed for selected countries are shown in Table 6. In addition to assigning emission targets to industrialized countries, the protocol specified a number of "flexibility mechanisms" that influence how and where countries can meet their targets.

Several aspects of the protocol deserve comment. First, the targets set for the USA, Japan, and the EU, which together account for 70% of total Annex B emissions, differ by only 2%, a very small variation for countries with markedly different emissions profiles. Each country in the EU was assigned a target of 92% of 1990 levels, but Article 4 allows parties to reach an agreement to fulfil their commitments jointly, a provision that allows the EU to establish a "bubble" in which targets vary by agreement as long as the overall target of 92% is met.

The target for the Russian Federation was especially contentious. Russia has experienced severe deindustrialization since 1990 so that without any interventions its emissions are expected to be only about 90% of 1990 levels by around 2010. The difference between its expected actual emissions of 90% and its assigned amount of 100% became known as "hot air." This gap provides for a large tranche of emission permits that can be sold to other Annex B countries so that, in the words of one commentator, "American Cadillacs will be fuelled by Russian depression" (Hamilton, 1998).

The primary flexibility mechanisms built into the protocol was the provision for emissions trading. The protocol authorizes the establishment of an international system of emissions trading that allows for the transfer and acquisition of "assigned amounts" among Annex B parties for the purposes of meeting their obligations in the first commitment period (2008–2012). The rationale for emissions trading is simple. In each country there is a range of emission reduction possibilities. The economic cost of cutting emissions by a given amount will vary between these possibilities, and it makes sense to adopt a system that allows the required level of emission reductions to be concentrated in those activities where it is cheapest.

The protocol also included a provision to take account of changes in the emissions from industrialized countries resulting from sequestration of carbon in forest sinks, so that the evaluation of emissions in the commitment period accounts for both greenhouse gases and carbon sinks. The generation of emission credits from new forest plantations is another means for Annex B countries to meet their targets.

The protocol also established the Clean Development Mechanism (CDM) that allows Annex B parties, and private entities within them, to acquire tradable emission credits by investing in projects that reduce emissions in developing countries. These credits can be used by Annex B parties to meet their emission obligations under the protocol.

The agreement at Kyoto initiated further rounds of negotiation to clarify the rules, and these negotiations provided the opportunity for reluctant nations such as the USA and Australia to water down the emission cuts that would be mandated by the agreement. Negotiations broke down severely at a conference in The Hague in November 2000 with the "umbrella" group of countries (USA, Japan, Russia, Australia, and Canada) attempting to open up large loopholes in the protocol and the EU resisting. Shortly afterwards, the new US president, George Bush, finally repudiated the protocol, claiming that it would be too costly and that it would be "unfair" without participation by developing countries. But the momentum of the negotiations led to a conference at Marrakech in November 2001, where an agreement was finally struck on nearly all of the outstanding issues, including highly contentious questions relating to carbon sinks and penalties for non-compliance.

By the time of the Marrakech conference, the IPCC had brought down its Third Assessment Report, an exhaustive treatment of the science of climate change that rang the warning bells more loudly than before. At the time of writing it appears likely that enough countries will ratify the Kyoto Protocol for it to come into force in 2003, without the participation of the USA. The future beyond that is very uncertain. If European and Japanese companies suffer any trade disadvantages as a result of their governments' decisions to reduce emissions, it is likely that retaliatory action will be taken against US companies. In addition, the strengthening of the science of climate change and the increasingly apparent impacts of a warming world will renew the pressure for more far-reaching action to reduce global greenhouse gas emissions.

2. Transport and greenhouse gas emissions

As seen in Table 3, transport accounts for 22% of global CO_2 emissions from fuel combustion, and ~12% of total equivalent greenhouse gas emissions. In contrast to other sectors, transport is almost completely reliant (95%) upon petroleum products, the remainder being mostly natural gas (IPCC, 2001b). The breakdown by mode of global CO_2 emissions from transport energy use is as follows: road transport, 74%; air transport, including aviation bunkers, 12%; shipping, including marine bunkers, 10%; and rail, 4% (International Energy Agency, 1993, 2000a).

2.1. Mobile sources

Fuel emission factors are used to convert the energy content of fuels to emissions of CO_2. Representative values are given in Table 7. For most fuels, 99% is assumed to be oxidized upon combustion (National Greenhouse Gas Inventory Committee, 1996). In addition to greenhouse gas emissions in the form of CO_2 from fuel combustion, there are other radiative forcing consequences of transport use such as atmospheric CH_4 production from photochemical processes with CO emissions, effects of aerosols from ground transport, and high- atmospheric effects of aviation. Since road sources dominate total transport emissions, a summary of non-CO_2 emission is provided in Table 8 for these sources only (representative figures for Australia). Further details on the emissions from the different transport sectors are given elsewhere in this handbook. For alternative fuel options, see Chapter 9, and, for details on the emissions from new, cleaner vehicles, see Chapter 10.

As with total CO_2 emissions, the industrialized world is responsible for more than two-thirds of transport-related CO_2 emissions, with ~60% occurring in the road transport sector alone (Figure 7). Per capita emissions from transport in the USA are about three times higher than in Europe and Japan, and about 20 times higher than in Africa and Asia (Scholl et al., 1996). Americans pay the least in fuel and vehicle taxes, drive the most fuel-inefficient cars, own the most cars, and travel twice as far by car as Europeans, and five times as much by air (Schipper et al., 1997).

A closer look at OECD countries reveals that road transport covers the bulk of passenger and freight movements (Table 9). Nevertheless, air transport shows by far the highest growth rates amongst all modes (road ~2%, rail ~1%, air 2–5%).

The impact on climate change by the transport sector is not restricted to greenhouse gases produced directly from combustion of fuels in vehicles but also includes indirect requirements necessary for the provision of transport infrastructure (Fels, 1975, 1978; US Congressional Budget Office, 1977; Rose, 1979; Kulash, 1982; Delucchi, 1996, 1997; Marheineke et al., 1999; Matsuhashi et al., 2000; Nansai et al., 2001). In 1994–1995, Australian passenger and freight transport produced about 90 million t CO_2-e directly, but an additional 75 million t CO_2-e is linked to the

Table 7
Fuel emission factors and energy contents

Fuel	Emission factor (g CO_2/MJ)	Energy content (MJ/kg)
Gasoline	69.4	44.8
Diesel oil	74.1	43.3
Jet kerosene	71.6	44.6
Liquefied petroleum gas	63.1	47.3
Residual fuel oil	77.4	40.2

Source: after National Greenhouse Gas Inventory Committee (1996) and International Energy Agency (2000a).

Table 8
Road sector non-CO_2 emissions

| Category | Subcategory | Emission (g/km) | | | |
		CH_4	N_2O	NO_x	CO
Passenger cars and light trucks	Gasoline	0.05	0.05	0.9	5.5
	Diesel oil	0.01	0.012	1.1	1.1
	LPG	0.09	0.008	2.0	22
Medium trucks	Diesel oil	0.02	0.017	3.1	1.8
Heavy trucks	Diesel oil	0.07	0.025	15.3	7.9
Buses	Diesel oil	0.03	0.025	4.9	2.9

Source: after National Greenhouse Gas Inventory Committee (1996).

manufacture of vehicles, the construction and maintenance of roads, railways, stations, ports, and airports, the provision of street lighting, the extraction and refining of crude oil, the distribution of fuels, the generation of electricity, the disposal and recycling of vehicles and structures, and the administration of transport businesses (Lenzen, 1999). Hence, in a comprehensive assessment of the impact on climate change by transportation systems over their full life cycle, indirect requirements have to be taken into account.

2.2. History of emissions

Transport use parallels (and in fact sometimes overtakes) economic growth. At present, the OECD countries' transport sectors are responsible for about a quarter of the increase in global greenhouse gas emissions (International Energy

Agency, 2000b). In fact, in the past three decades the share of transport in total CO_2 emissions has increased more in OECD countries than in any other region (Table 10). While transport use is still increasing in Europe and Japan (around 3% annual growth in CO_2 emissions in 1992), this trend has slowed somewhat in the USA (0.6%) (Scholl et al., 1996). Except for the USA, the predominant trend has been toward greater per capita emissions. (Schipper et al., 1997). However, motorization is increasing rapidly also in developing Asian countries, facilitated by increasing GDP and therefore car ownership (Schipper et al., 2001).

While in the OECD countries the move to larger and more powerful vehicles, and travel at lower occupancies, has partly offset fuel efficiency improvements, especially in the 1990s (Figure 8a), the most important driving factor for the increase in transport-related emissions is the growth in GDP, which in turn positively correlates with car ownership and travel activity (Figure 8b). The latter is also growing rapidly in some non-OECD countries such as South Korea, Indonesia, and China, and could cause a 10% addition to their total emissions during the next decade (Schipper et al., 2001). However, for the majority of the developing world, car ownership is still much lower than in the industrialized world (< 1 car/100 people).

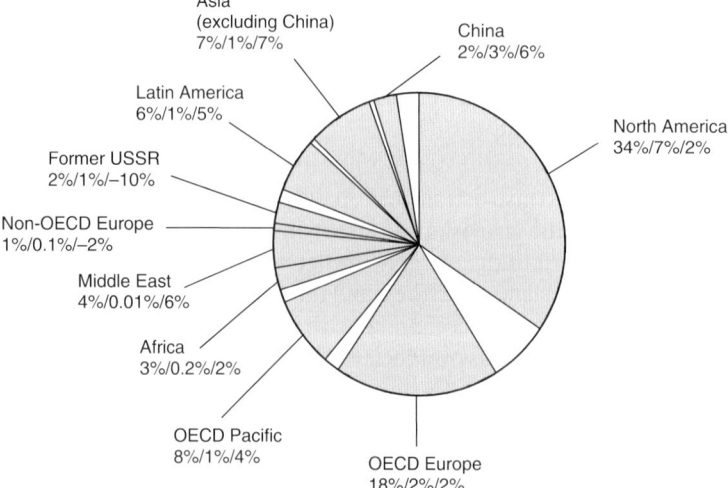

Figure 7. Contributions to 1998 transport-related CO_2 emissions (4.6 Gt), by region and mode (after International Energy Agency, 2000a). Labels show the percentage of emissions from road transport, the percentage of emissions from non-road transport, and the 1990–1997 growth rate. The lines link the labels to the segment representing road transport; the adjacent clockwise white segment represents all other modes for that country.

Table 9
Modal split by of transport energy consumption in OECD countries (projected annual growth rates in parentheses)

Transport mode	Energy consumption (%)		
	North America	OECD countries (Europe)	OECD countries (Pacific)
Passenger			
Cars	57 (+1.4)	54 (+1.7)	57 (+1.2)
Railways	1 (+0.4)	1 (+1.0)	3 (+0.9)
Buses	1 (+1.5)	3 (+1.3)	1 (+0.8)
Aviation	8 (+2.3)	8 (+4.5)	5 (+3.3)
Freight			
Trucks	24 (+2.0)	30 (+2.2)	25 (+1.9)
Railways	7 (+1.6)	3 (+0.1)	3 (+1.8)
Shipping	2 (−0.7)	1 (+0.1)	5 (+0.2)

Source: data from International Energy Agency (2000b) and Scholl et al. (1996).

Furthermore, a shift toward air travel has increased emissions in almost all OECD countries (Schipper et al., 1997). The most important factor driving up emissions for freight is once again activity, or tonne kilometers hauled, closely followed by modal shifts from rail and shipping to trucks, which are particularly marked in Germany, France, and Japan.

3. Conclusions: the role of transport in future abatement efforts

In almost every part of the world, transport-related emissions are rising in absolute and per capita terms, as is their share of the total emissions. The discrepancy between the extraordinary growth rates of the transport sectors and the reduction targets under the Kyoto Protocol pose major problems for decision-makers in OECD countries. The main challenges are growing car ownership, the rapid expansion of aviation, and the increase in road freight, particularly in Europe. In contrast, projected emissions of Eastern European countries and the former USSR are well below their commitments, due mainly to the severe economic downturn in that region in the 1990s. The effect that globalization and liberalization of trade will have on emissions, however, remains unclear, due to competing scales, and structural, technological, and product effects (van Veen-Groot and Nijkamp, 1999).

It is now widely accepted that a doubling of the concentration of greenhouse gases in the atmosphere would be dangerous, although a doubling appears unavoidable

(IPCC, 2001c). According to the IPCC, stabilizing concentrations at double pre-industrial levels will require severe cuts in annual global emissions, eventually by 60% or more, so the Kyoto Protocol is only a first small step. Given the wide variation in national levels of emissions per capita and income per capita, it would be unfeasible and unfair to require all nations to cut their emissions by 60% of current levels. Developing countries might be expected to reduce their emissions by less than this amount whereas wealthy countries with high per capita emissions should expect to cut their emissions by more than 60% in the longer term.

Like the climate system itself, energy, transport, and urban systems have great inertia. Transport systems, buildings, urban layouts and electric power plants have long life spans or take decades to change. This means that, to achieve significant reductions in annual global emissions and avoid the worst effects of climate change, early planning and immediate action are needed.

In 2000 the UK Royal Commission on Environmental Pollution published a report examining the feasibility of achieving a 60% reduction in Britain's emissions by 2050. The UK government has responded with a detailed discussion of how such a reduction might be achieved. Noting that the UK "is likely to face increasingly demanding carbon reduction targets," it concludes (UK Cabinet Office, 2002):

Table 10
Share of transport in total CO_2 emissions. Latin America's high transport share can be explained by a relatively small contribution of the electricity sector to CO_2 emissions due to widespread use of hydroelectric power. Similarly, other non-OECD-country transport shares are influenced in absolute terms by the degree of electrification and manufacturing.

	Total CO_2 emission (%)		
	1971	1990	1998
OECD			
North America	25	29	30
Europe	14	20	23
Pacific	16	20	22
Non-OECD			
Africa	20	18	17
Middle East	14	20	18
Europe	10	9	13
Former USSR	9	9	8
Latin America	31	33	34
Asia (excluding China)	14	16	18
China	4	6	8
World	19	22	24

Source: after International Energy Agency (1998, 2000a).

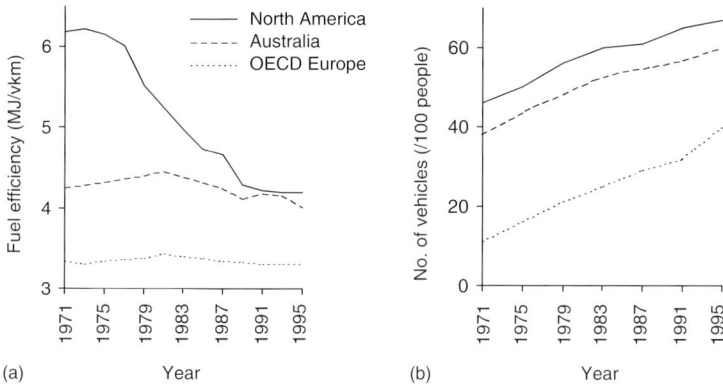

Figure 8. (a) Fuel efficiency and (b) vehicle ownership of new passenger cars in OECD countries. (After Schipper et al., 2001; for actual fuel efficiencies of on-road fleets, see Schipper, 1993.)

Credible scenarios for 2050 can deliver a 60% cut in CO_2 emissions, but large changes would be needed both in the energy system and in society. ... Given the strong chance that future, legally binding, international targets will become more stringent beyond 2012, a precautionary approach suggests that the UK should be setting about creating a range of future options by which low carbon futures could be delivered, as, and when, the time comes.

Growth in demand for transport will be driven by increased economic activity, higher incomes and population growth. However, major technology improvements are expected in transport, and a faster turnover of the vehicle fleet would facilitate a rapid uptake of these technologies. Adoption of hybrid vehicles could saturate the vehicle market well before 2050, dramatically cutting the fuel consumption of road vehicles. In addition, lighter materials, improved aerodynamics and less rolling resistance will further improve the efficiency of all vehicles, while increased average load weight and improved logistics will drive heavy vehicle efficiency improvements. Fuel cell technology could feasibly achieve 50% penetration of the road transport market by 2050, enabling a similar proportion of transport fuel to be sourced from renewable electricity (used to produce hydrogen) with zero greenhouse gas emissions (Turton et al., 2002).

A substantial increase in public transport patronage is expected to have a small but noticeable impact on overall emissions. Improvements in rail operations and efficiency could result in a substantial shift of some freight from road to rail in countries such as the USA, Canada, and Australia, while very fast train technology could curtail the growth of air travel. Improvements in marine, air, and rail efficiency, combined with electrification of entire rail systems, could reduce energy use and emissions further.

Liquid biofuels have the potential to replace petroleum fuels in most transport applications (and in other applications, such as in agricultural and construction equipment). However, there may be limits on the use of biofuels in air transport, particularly international travel where planes must be able to operate on the fuels available in the countries of destination.

In the medium term, alternative, low-carbon fuels are being considered predominantly in the USA, and fuel efficiency improvements are being pursued throughout OECD countries. A key element of CO_2 abatement strategies in Europe and Japan is to address demand restraint and demand shift (fuel taxation, road pricing, and urban access restrictions) in order to reduce overall traffic levels (International Energy Agency, 2000b). Developing countries face both the opportunity and the challenge to combine rapid transportation growth and environmental objectives in future planning decisions, while their transport systems are only beginning to grow (Schipper et al., 2000). Role models, such as the case of Curitiba, Brazil, may lead the way to developing mobility with lower car dependence (Smith and Raemaekers, 1998).

References

Agarwal, A. and S. Narain (1991) *Global warming in an unequal world*. New Delhi: Centre for Science and Environment.

Byrne, J., Y.-D. Wang, H. Lee and J.-d. Kim (1998) "An equity- and sustainability-based policy response to global climate change," *Energy Policy,* 26:335–343.

Delucchi, M. (1996) *Emissions of criteria pollutants, toxic air pollutants, and greenhouse gases, from the use of alternative transportation modes and fuels*, Report No. UCD-ITS-RR-96-12. University of California, Davis: Institute of Transportation Studies.

Delucchi, M.A. (1997) *A revised model of emissions of greenhouse gases from the use of transportation fuels and electricity*, Report No. UCD-ITS-RR-97-22. University of California, Davis: Institute of Transportation Studies.

Fels, M.F. (1975) "Comparative energy costs of urban transportation systems," *Transportation Research*, 9:297–308.

Fels, M.F. (1978) "Breakdown of rapid rail energy costs: a study of three systems," *Energy*, 3:507–522.

Hamilton, C. and H. Turton (1999) Population policy and environmental degradation: sources and trends in greenhouse gas emissions, *People and Place*, 7:42–62.

Hamilton, C. and H. Turton (2002) "Determinants of emissions growth in OECD countries," *Energy Policy*, 30:63–71.

Hamilton, G. (1998) "Quotation of Farhana Yamin, Foundation for International Law and Development," *Vancouver Sun*, 18 March.

Heil, M.T. and T.M. Selden (2001) "International trade intensity and carbon emissions: a cross-country econometric analysis," *Journal of Environment and Development*, 10:35–49.

Houghton, J.T., L.G. Meira Filho, D.J. Griggs and K. Maskell, eds (1997) *Stabilization of atmospheric greenhouse gases: physical, biological and socio-economic implications*. Cambridge: Intergovernmental Panel on Climate Change.

Intergovernmental Panel on Climate Change (1995) *IPCC second assessment synthesis of scientific-technical information relevant to interpreting Article 2 of the UN Framework Convention on Climate Change*. Bracknell: IPCC.

Intergovernmental Panel on Climate Change (1996) *Climate change 1995: impacts, adaptations and mitigation of climate change: scientific-technical analyses* (R.T. Watson et al., eds). Cambridge: Cambridge University Press/IPCC.

Intergovernmental Panel on Climate Change (1999) *Aviation and the global atmosphere – IPCC special report* (J.E. Penner et al., eds). Cambridge: Cambridge University Press/IPCC.

Intergovernmental Panel on Climate Change (2000) *Land Use, Land Use Changes and Forestry – IPCC Special Report* (R.T. Watson et al., eds). Cambridge: Cambridge University Press/IPCC.

Intergovernmental Panel on Climate Change (2001a) *Climate change 2001: the scientific basis. Contributions of Working Group I to the Third Assessment Report of the Intergovernmental Panel on Climate Change* (J.T. Houghton et al., eds). Cambridge: Cambridge University Press.

Intergovernmental Panel on Climate Change (2001b) *Climate change 2001: mitigation. Contributions of Working Group III to the Third Assessment Report of the Intergovernmental Panel on Climate Change*. Cambridge: Cambridge University Press.

Intergovernmental Panel on Climate Change (2001c) *Climate change 2001: synthesis report. Synthesis of the third assessment report*. Cambridge: Cambridge University Press/IPCC/UN Environment Programme/World Meteorological Organisation.

International Energy Agency (1993) *Cars and climate change*. Paris: OECD/IEA.

International Energy Agency (1998) *World energy outlook 1998*. Paris: OECD/IEA.

International Energy Agency (2000a) CO_2 *emissions from fuel combustion 1971–1998*. Paris: OECD/IEA.

International Energy Agency (2000b) *World energy outlook 2000*. Paris: OECD/IEA.

International Energy Agency (2001) *Key world energy statistics*. Paris: International Energy Agency (http://www.iea.org).

Kandlikar, M. and A. Sagar (1999) "Climate change research and analysis in India: an integrated assessment of a South-North divide," *Global Environmental Change*, 9:119–138.

Kulash, D.J. (1982) "Energy efficiency: which modes, which programs?" in: H.S. Levinson, and R.A. Weant, eds, *Urban transportation, perspectives and prospects*, pp. 86–95. Westport: Eno Foundation for Transportation.

Lenzen, M. (1997) "International equity and greenhouse gas emissions," in: N. Low, ed., *Environmental justice, papers from the Melbourne Conference*. Melbourne: Faculty of Architecture, Building and Planning, The University of Melbourne.

Lenzen, M. (1999) "Total requirements of energy and greenhouse gases for Australian transport," *Transportation Research D*, 4:265–290.

Lenzen, M. and S. Smith (2000) "Teaching responsibility for climate change: three neglected issues," *Australian Journal of Environmental Education*, 15/16:69–78.

Machado, G., R. Schaeffer and E. Worrell (2001) "Energy and carbon embodied in the international trade of Brazil: an input-output approach," *Ecological Economics*, 36:409–424.

Marheineke, T., R. Friedrich and W. Krewitt (1999) "Application of a hybrid-approach to the life cycle inventory analysis of a freight transport task," in: Society of Automotive Engineers, ed., *SAE 1998 Transactions – Journal of Passenger Cars*. Warrendale: Society of Automotive Engineers.

Marland, G., T.A. Boden and R.J. Andres (2001) "Global, regional, and national CO_2 emissions," in: *Trends: a compendium of data on global change*. Oak Ridge: Carbon Dioxide Information Analysis Center, Oak Ridge National Laboratory, US Department of Energy.

Matsuhashi, R., Y. Kudoh, Y. Yoshida, H. Ishitani, M. Yoshioka and K. Yoshioka (2000) "Life cycle of CO_2-emissions from electric vehicles and gasoline vehicles utilizing a process-relational model," *International Journal of Life Cycle Assessment*, 5:306–312.

Nansai, K., S. Tohno, M. Kono, M. Kasahara and Y. Moriguchi (2001) "Life-cycle analysis of charging infrastructure for electric vehicles," *Applied Energy*, 70:251–265.

National Greenhouse Gas Inventory Committee (1996) *Australian methodology for the estimation of greenhouse gas emissions and sinks. Workbook for Transport (mobile sources) 3.1*. Canberra: Department of the Environment, Sport and Territories.

Neumayer, E. (2000) "In defence of historical accountability for greenhouse gas emissions," *Ecological Economics*, 33:185–192.

Parikh, J. (1996) "Consumption patterns: the driving force of environmental stress," in: P.H. May and R. Serôa da Motta, eds, *Pricing the Planet*, pp. 39–48. New York: Columbia University Press.

Parikh, J.K. and J.P. Painuly (1994) "Population, consumption patterns and climate change: a socioeconomic perspective from the south," *Ambio*, 23:434–437.

Proops, J.L.R., M. Faber and G. Wagenhals (1993) *Reducing CO_2 emissions*. Berlin: Springer-Verlag.

Rose, A.B. (1979) *Energy intensity and related parameters of selected transportation modes: freight movements*, Report No. ORNL-5554. Oak Ridge: Oak Ridge National Laboratory.

Schipper, L. (1993) "Global climate change: linking energy, energy efficiency, human activities and climate change," *Environmental Science Research*, 45:37–44.

Schipper, L. (1998) "Life-styles and the environment: the case of energy," *IEEE Engineering Management Review*, 26:3–14.

Schipper, L., M. Ting, M. Khrushch and W. Golove (1997) "The evolution of CO_2 emissions from energy use in industrialized countries: an end-use analysis," *Energy Policy*, 25:651–672.

Schipper, L., C. Marie-Lilliu and R. Gorham (2000) *Flexing the link between transport and greenhouse gas emissions*. Paris: International Energy Agency.

Schipper, L., C. Marie-Lilliu and G. Lewis-Davis (2001) *Asia Pacific Journal of Energy* (http://www.iea.org/pubs/free/articles/schipper/rapmot.htm).

Scholl, L., L. Schipper and N. Kiang (1996) "CO_2 Emissions from passenger transport: a comparison of international trends from 1973 to 1992," *Energy Policy*, 24:17–30.

Smith, H. and J. Raemaekers (1998) "Land use pattern and transport in Curitiba," *Land Use Policy*, 15:233–251.

Turton, H., M. Jinlong, H. Saddler and C. Hamilton (2002) *Long-term greenhouse gas scenarios: a pilot study of how Australia can achieve deep cuts in emissions*, Discussion Paper No. 48. Canberra: The Australia Institute (http://www.tai.org.au).

UK Cabinet Office (2002) *The energy review*. Report by the Performance and Innovation Unit of the British Cabinet Office, February (http://www.piu.gov.uk/2002/energy/report/).

Common, M.S. and U. Salma (1992) "Accounting for changes in Australian carbon dioxide emissions," *Energy Economics*, 14:217–225.

US Congressional Budget Office (1977) *Urban transportation and energy: the potential savings of different modes*, Background Paper. Washington, DC: US Congress.

van Veen-Groot, D. and P. Nijkamp (1999) "Globalisation, transport and the environment: new perspectives for ecological economics," *Ecological Economics*, 31:331–346.

Watson, R.T., M.C. Zinyowera and R.H. Moss, eds (1996) *Climate change 1995: impacts, adaptations and mitigation of climate change: scientific-technical analyses*. Cambridge: Intergovernmental Panel on Climate Change.

Wilson, B., L. Ho Trieu and B. Brown (1994) "Energy efficiency trends in Australia," *Energy Policy*, 22:287–296.

World Commission on Environment and Development (1987) *Our common future*. Oxford: Oxford University Press.

Chapter 4

AIR QUALITY

BRITT A. HOLMÉN
University of Connecticut, Storrs, CT

DEBBIE A. NIEMEIER
University of California, Davis, CA

1. Introduction

The Los Angeles smog motivated the promulgation of the first US regulatory standard for control of automotive emissions, while European emission control regulations, such as requiring three-way catalytic converters, were driven primarily by a need to reduce acid rain (Colvile et al., 2001). The effects of implementing tailpipe emission controls and national air quality standards have been significant. In a recent study documenting EU-15 emissions trends from 1981 through 1998 (Ntziachristos et al., 2002), steady increases of nitrogen oxides emissions were observed during the 1980s, with an estimated 20% of these increases attributed to on-road transportation activity. With the introduction of the three-way catalyst for new passenger vehicles in the early 1990s, emissions of nitrogen oxides (NO_x) by Europe declined by more than 20% between 1991 and 1998, essentially returning NO_x emission levels to those of the late 1980s. These gains, however, have been at least partially offset by increases in other pollutants, which are largely attributable to expanding travel activity. For example, carbon dioxide (CO_2) emissions for the EU-15 have steadily risen since the early 1980s; this trend is consistent with increases in vehicle-kilometers of travel during the same period across all vehicle type categories. Projections to 2010–2020 indicate that CO_2 emissions are likely to continue increasing as the projected total number of vehicle-kilometers, particularly by passenger cars, continues to rise (Ntziachristos et al., 2002).

Air quality trends in the USA have been similar. According to the latest US Environmental Protection Agency (EPA) *Trends Report* (Environmental Protection Agency, 2001a), although vehicle-miles of travel increased by 143%, total emissions for nitrogen monoxide (NO) decreased by 11%, ozone (O_3, 1 h average) decreased by 21%, and carbon monoxide (CO) decreased by 61% between 1981 and 2000. However, total green house gas emissions (CO_2, NO, methane (CH_4), and fluorinated compounds) rose by 11% between 1990 and 1998. Transportation sources were estimated to account for approximately 31% of CO_2 emissions related to combustion, approximately 1% of CH_4 emissions, and approximately 20% of NO emissions (an increase of over 30% from 1990) in 1997 (Environmental Protection Agency, 2001a).

In the USA, air quality is regulated through the Federal Clean Air Act (CAA) and associated amendments (CAAA) (Environmental Protection Agency, 1990), which confers responsibility for creating and enforcing air quality regulations to the EPA (Environmental Protection Agency, 1990). The CAAA required the EPA to establish primary standards (to protect public health) and secondary standards (to protect public welfare) for six pollutants considered harmful to public health, the environment, and social welfare. The standards, known as the National Ambient Air Quality Standards (NAAQS), set the maximum allowable concentration limits for CO, nitrogen dioxide (NO_2), O_3, particulate matter (PM), lead (Pb), and sulfur dioxide (SO_2).

These six pollutants are commonly referred to as criteria pollutants. All criteria pollutants have primary standards, some of which are primarily aimed at long-term exposure and some that are designed to limit short-term exposure levels. Motor vehicles are considered a major source for four of the criteria pollutants: CO, NO_2, O_3, and PM. CO is a colorless, odorless gas formed as a result of incomplete combustion (when the carbon in fuel is not completely burned). Motor vehicle exhaust accounts for about 60% of all CO emissions nationwide and as much as 95% in urban areas (Environmental Protection Agency, 2001a). CO enters the bloodstream through inhalation, and reduces the availability of oxygen in the blood. Inhalation of high amounts of CO can cause visual impairment, confusion, loss of dexterity, and reduced work capacity; prolonged exposure can result in coma and death (Koenig, 2000).

NO_2 is a highly reactive gas that plays an important role in the formation of ozone (Seinfeld and Pandis, 1998). NO_x emissions, which are the sum of NO and NO_2, are produced predominantly by high-temperature combustion processes. It has been estimated that roughly 45% of all NO_x emissions are derived from transportation sources (Seinfeld and Pandis, 1998). NO_2 is the most common of the nitrogen oxides, and has both acute and chronic adverse health effects (Koenig, 2000). NO_2 inhibits respiratory immune defenses and increases the risk of contracting viral and bacterial respiratory illnesses (Environmental Protection Agency, 1991a). Chronic exposure to ambient NO_2 for healthy adults has also been shown to reduce lung function (Schindler et al., 1998) and result in bronchial inflammation, coughing, wheezing, and shortness of breath (Hasselbad et al., 1992).

Ground level O_3 is created when volatile organic compounds (VOCs) and NO_x react in sunlight. In most urban areas, vehicle emissions are the major sources of VOCs and NO_x (National Research Council, 2000). Both short- and long-term

Table 1
Transportation-relevant NAAQS

Pollutant	Primary standard		Secondary standard
	Averaging	Concentration	
CO	8 h	9 ppm	None
	1 h	35 ppm	None
NO_2	Annual mean	0.053 ppm	Same as primary
O_3	Maximum daily 1 h average	0.12 ppm	Same as primary
	4th maximum daily 8 h average	0.08 ppm	
PM_{10}	Annual mean	50 µg/m³	Same as primary
	24 h	150 µg/m³	
$PM_{2.5}$	Annual mean	15 µg/m³	Same as primary
	24 h	65 µg/m³	

Source: adapted from Environmental Protection Agency (2001a).

exposure to O_3 has been shown to be harmful to human health (Environmental Protection Agency, 2000a). For example, increases in hospital emergency room visits (American Lung Association, 2001), admissions for respiratory causes, (Burnett et al., 1997), and daily mortality rates (Tuolomi et al., 1997; Samet et al., 2000) have all been shown to be associated with high levels of ambient O_3 exposure. Reduced lung function and increased respiratory illnesses in children (Frischer et al., 1999) and in sensitive populations, such as the elderly and asthmatic (MacNee and Donaldson, 1999), have also been associated with ozone exposure.

PM refers to particles that can be directly emitted from sources or can be formed in the atmosphere. The chemical properties of particles are influenced by time of year, the types of surrounding sources, and meteorology. Both fine particles ($PM_{2.5}$; particles less than 2.5 µm in aerodynamic diameter) and coarse particles (PM_{10}; particles less than 10 µm in aerodynamic diameter) have been associated with health risks such as pulmonary inflammation, respiratory infections, stunted respiratory development, inhibited cardiopulmonary function, blood clotting, and premature death (Holgate et al., 1999; American Lung Association, 2001). Ambient concentrations of PM_{10} have been shown to increase respiratory and cardiac disease symptoms in the elderly and children (Zanobetti et al., 2000). Pulmonary inflammation and increased risk of blood clotting have been shown to occur even in healthy individuals after exposure to concentrated airborne particulates (Ghio et al., 2000).

Each year, measurements of pollutant concentrations, known as ambient concentrations, are taken across a monitoring network of air samplers. These concentrations are then compared with the NAAQS contained in Table 1 to determine if a state is in attainment or non-attainment. To safeguard human health, states with regions that do not meet the NAAQS for criteria pollutants, known as non-attainment areas, must prepare State Implementation Plans (SIPs). A SIP describes the collection of regulations a state will use to bring air quality regions into attainment with the NAAQS. In terms of transportation, the SIPs define the regional mobile emission budgets. These budgets represent the total allowable emissions that can be produced by a particular region's transportation plan (RTP) and transportation improvement program (TIP), which is a multi-year prioritized list of federally funded or approved transportation improvements.

This chapter will provide an overview of all transportation-related sources of air pollution in terms of regulatory requirements, data and methods for emissions modeling and estimation, and some of the scientific issues associated with current mobile source certification and enforcement.

2. Mobile source emissions overview

Total emissions inventories are composed of both on-road and off-road mobile sources as well as non-mobile sources (Figure 1). The mobile sources, both on-road and non-road combined, account for less than 30% of the $PM_{2.5}$ emissions, approximately 55% of the NO_x, 78% of the CO, and 45% of the hydrocarbon (HC) total emissions (Environmental Protection Agency, 2001a). With the exception of $PM_{2.5}$, on-road emissions exceed that of off-road mobile emissions. The primary sources of on- and off-road mobile source emissions are transportation related. For on-road emissions, major sources include light duty passenger cars and trucks and heavy-duty gasoline and diesel trucks (Figure 2).

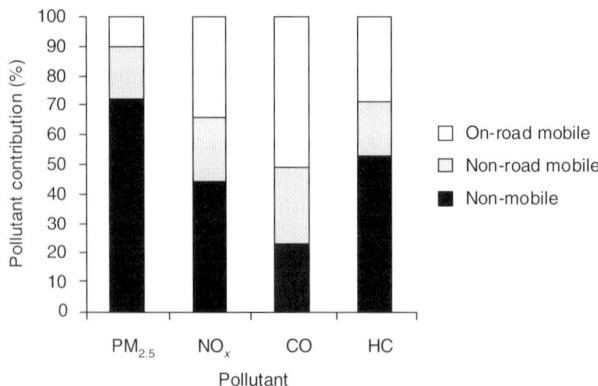

Figure 1. Sources of transportation air pollutants (Environmental Protection Agency, 2001a).

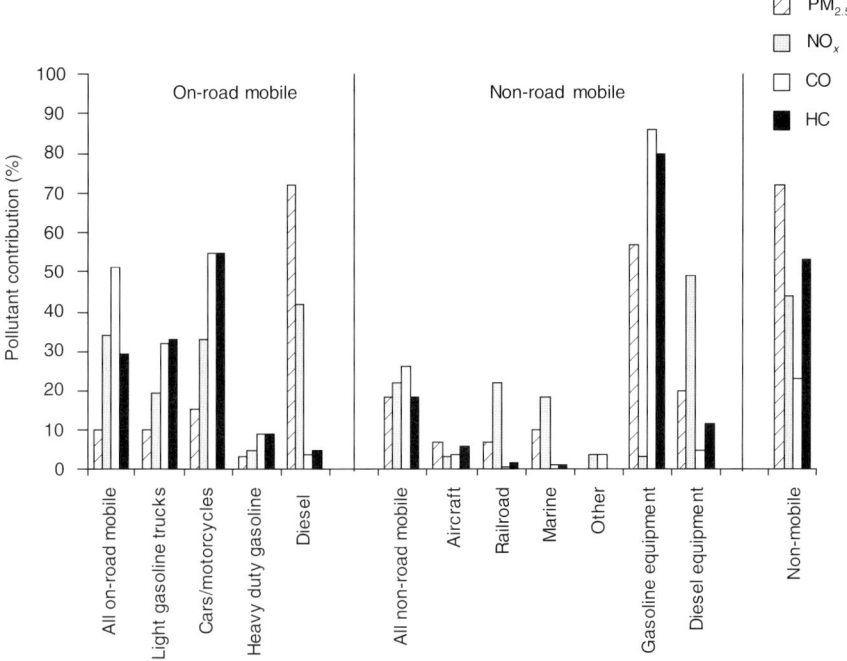

Figure 2. Categories of vehicles contributing to mobile source emissions of four pollutants. (Based on Environmental Protection Agency, 2001a.)

2.1. On-road sources

Automobile emissions are created from two sources: exhaust emissions and evaporative processes. Gasoline (and diesel) fuel contains compounds that comprise hydrogen and carbon atoms. In perfect combustion, oxygen converts all the hydrogen in the fuel to water and all the carbon to CO_2. But internal combustion engines are not 100% efficient. When fuel is only partially burned or partially oxidized under high pressure and temperature, like the conditions in engines, tailpipe emissions of HCs, CO, and NO_x result. Evaporative emissions are created when HCs escape during refueling, when gasoline vapors are vented during typical hot engine operation, and when a hot engine is turned off and the vehicle is stationary.

Tailpipe emissions and emission inventories

Most developed countries control vehicle emissions through the use of tailpipe certification standards and, in the USA, through transportation conformity, a regulatory process that relies on the preparation of mobile emissions inventories. For gasoline-powered vehicle certification, new vehicles are mounted on a chassis dynamometer and tested over several regulatory driving cycles (i.e. the Federal Test Procedure) that are intended to simulate the range of vehicle operating conditions encountered during real-world driving. Vehicle exhaust, diluted by use of a federally legislated constant volume sampler (CVS), is collected in a bag over the course of the driving cycle and analyzed for its gas species composition (HC, CO, NO_x, CO_2). Particulate matter is collected on a filter and quantified by total mass collected over the driving cycle. The measured concentrations are compared with certification standards that are defined by vehicle model year, and expressed in terms of grams per mile. For example, Tier 0 standards include model years 1981 through 1992, while Tier 1 standards begin with model year 1994 (for an excellent synthesis of the vehicle certification standards see National Research Council (2000)).

For diesel vehicles, new diesel engines are tested on engine dynamometers over a transient Federal Test Procedure to ensure compliance with exhaust emission standards. Diesel vehicles are significant sources of NO_x and PM compared with automobiles, which have relatively higher CO and HC emissions than trucks.

The CAA ensured that air quality improvements would be achieved by requiring development of state implementation plans that prescribed how each state would meet the NAAQS. For mobile emissions, rules and procedures by which the CAA provisions are interpreted are known as the transportation conformity rule (40 CFR Parts 51 and 93, as amended by 62 FR 43780, August 1997). The transportation conformity rule requires that all federally funded or approved transportation projects must be consistent with statewide air quality goals. Under conformity, regions must demonstrate that all federally funded transportation plans, programs, and projects are consistent with the mobile source emissions budgets established in the SIPs (Environmental Protection Agency, 1993a).

Inventories of on-road mobile emissions are typically estimated by multiplying an emission factor, generated from tailpipe measurements of a vehicle on a chassis dynamometer, by an estimate of associated travel activity for each type of vehicle on the road. In most emission calculations, there are three types of emissions computed: running exhaust emissions, start emissions, and evaporative emissions. Running exhaust emissions occur when vehicles are operating in a hot stabilized mode. Start emissions are the emissions generated during the first few minutes of vehicle operation, and are a function of how long the vehicle has been sitting prior to a key-on activity. Evaporative emissions result from the fact that gasoline components are volatile, that is, they evaporate more readily when temperatures are higher.

Evaporative emissions include hot soak, diurnal, resting loss, and running loss emissions. Hot soak emissions are HC vapors that are emitted within 1 h after the engine has been turned off. Diurnal emissions are created when the ambient temperature increases during a parking event. If the ambient temperature is constant or declining, resting loss emissions occur when a vehicle is at rest. Both diurnal emissions and resting loss emissions have two components: partial-day emissions, created when vehicles park for less than one day; and multiple-day emissions, when vehicles park for more than one day. Running loss emissions occur when vehicle gasoline vapors are created while vehicles are operating.

Emission factors for each type of emission are combined with various types of travel activity to estimate total emissions. For example, vehicle miles of travel (VMT) and speed data generated by travel demand models are used to compute running emissions. Trip end information taken from both the travel demand models and travel surveys are used to estimate the number of vehicle starts and vehicle "soak" times. Emission inventories represent the sum of running exhaust, start, and evaporative emissions for HCs, CO, NO_x, and PM.

In the USA, both conformity and SIP mobile emission budgets are currently prepared using emission factors from one of two models: the MOBILE series developed by the EPA, or the Motor Vehicle Emission Inventory model series developed for California by the California Air Resources Board (CARB). The latest releases of these models are MOBILE6 and EMFAC2000, respectively. In Europe, the COPERT model is often used to prepare mobile emission inventories; the latest release of this model is version 3, which was used to prepare recent national estimates of emissions from roadway sources (Ntziachristos et al., 2002).

Control measures

Both the USA and Europe have implemented various inspection and maintenance and emission control programs. Perhaps one of the most well-known programs is the use of oxygenated fuels. In 1998 the EU adopted Directive 98/69/EC and Directive 98/70/EC; the former sets stringent emission standards for cars and light vans that applies to all new vehicles sold from 1 January 2001 (known as Euro III standards), and the latter sets tighter fuel quality specifications that apply to petrol and diesel from 1 January 2000 and 2005. In addition to these measures, vehicles will be required to have on-board diagnostics and pass vehicle emission tests at lower temperatures.

In the USA, state and local governmental bodies can use inspection and maintenance programs and local transportation demand measures to reduce vehicles emissions. The CAA of 1990 also mandated the use of clean fuels in a number of regions during winter months. The clean fuels regulated the minimum oxygen content to enable better fuel combustion. The two primary fuel oxygenates used are MTBE (methyl t-butyl ether), which has since been found to present certain groundwater contaminant risks, and ethanol.

2.2. Off-road sources

As on-road mobile sources, faced with increasingly stringent emissions requirements, are controlled, the contributions from non-road sources such as agricultural equipment, off-highway construction vehicles, recreational equipment, locomotives, marine engines, and aircraft become increasingly important. The EPA acted upon its mandate in Section 213 of the CAA in 1991 by conducting an investigation to quantify "non-road" (or "off-road") engine and vehicle emissions. A non-road engine is defined by Section 216 of the CAA as an internal combustion engine that is not in a motor vehicle or a vehicle used solely for competition.

The *Nonroad Engine and Vehicle Emission Study* (Environmental Protection Agency, 1991b) chiefly examined the CO, VOC, and NO_x emissions from all major non-road sources except locomotives and aircraft, which are covered under separate sections of the CAA. The non-road engine study also examined the emissions of PM, oxides of sulfur (SO_x), and five pollutants considered at the time to be toxic air contaminants (benzene, 1,3-butadiene, aldehydes, gasoline vapors, and nitrosamines). Over 800 types of non-road engines and vehicles were classified into ten non-road equipment categories (Table 2), many of which can be considered transportation-related sources of air pollution.

The non-road engine study quantified emissions of a given pollutant i using an emission factor scheme similar to that used for on-road sources:

$$M_i = NHP\,LF\,EF_i \tag{1}$$

where M_i is the mass of pollutant (i typically expressed in tons per year), N is the number of equipment units being operated in the area over the period of time being modeled (year or season), H is the annual (or seasonal) use in hours, P is the average rated power of the equipment in horsepower (hp), LF is the load factor that describes typical operating conditions, and EF_i is the average emission factor of i per unit of work (g/hp-h). Each of these factors was estimated for 24 O_3 and/or

Table 2
Non-road source categories as categorized by the EPA (a)

Lawn and garden equipment	Industrial equipment
(chain saws, lawn mowers)	*(forklifts, loaders)*
Recreational marine equipment	Construction equipment
(boats, jet skis)	*(excavators, graders)*
Recreational equipment	**Agricultural equipment**
(snowmobile, off-road motorcycle)	*(tractors, combines)*
Light commercial equipment	Logging equipment
Airport service equipment	**Commercial marine vessels**

Note: (a) categories in **bold** are mainly transportation-related.

Table 3
Contribution of non-road sources to total emission inventory (a)

VOC	NO_x	CO	PM
7–12%	14–17%	5–9%	1–2%

Note: (a) based on data for 24 non-attainment areas (Environmental Protection Agency, 1991b).

CO non-attainment areas across the USA using data obtained by the EPA either from contractors, the states, or equipment manufacturers (Environmental Protection Agency, 1991b). Table 3 summarizes the estimated median contributions by non-road sources for the 24 non-attainment areas studied, and indicates that non-road sources are the most significant for VOC and NO_x, the two pollutant precursors to ground-level O_3. It should be kept in mind that the emission estimates in the 1991 EPA report were based on data that may not have been representative of real-world non-road engine use, chiefly due to the lack of extensive emissions measurements on in-use equipment and the lack of representative cycles for testing such equipment.

As a result of the 1991 study, the EPA set initial emission standards for new large (>50 hp or 37 kW) non-road diesel engines in 1994, with the goal of achieving NO_x emission reductions of 30%. The 1994 standards, called "Tier I," were phased in over the model years 1996–2000 (59 FR 31306, 17 June 1994). Subsequently, a 1998 Final Rule set more stringent Tier 2 and Tier 3 standards for large non-road diesel engines, and established Tier 1 and Tier 2 standards for smaller (<50 hp) non-road engines (63 FR 56968, 23 October 1998). Recently, in October 2001, the EPA published a staff technical paper, *Nonroad Diesel Emission Standards* (Environmental Protection Agency, 2001b) to address the issue of the technological feasibility of implementing the Tier 3 large diesel and Tier 2 small diesel engine emission standards promulgated in 1998. In this most recent assessment, the EPA reports that progress made in the development of new technologies to control diesel engine emissions since 1998 indicates that implementation of both the Tier 3 and Tier 2 standards is feasible (Environmental Protection Agency, 2001b).

The only remaining issue related to non-road diesel engine emissions is the development of a transient test cycle for reliable sampling of PM. This issue is discussed in more detail in Section 3.1. It is important because volatile and semi-volatile gaseous species can condense on existing particles and/or nucleate as new particles depending on the dilution conditions used to sample the hot exhaust (Kittelson, 1998), and ultrafine PM has recently come under intense scrutiny as a result of health studies linking particulates with adverse respiratory illness, asthma, and even death (Dockery et al., 1993; Donaldson et al., 2000).

Marine engines

Marine engines are thought to be a significant source of air pollutants, but few studies have quantified emissions to both water and air. The pollutants of concern are reactive organic gases (ROGs), CO, and NO_x and therefore outboard motors and personal watercraft are sources of O_3 precursors. To facilitate emissions testing, the EPA certification test procedure for outboard engines and personal watercraft involves sampling exhaust without immersion in water, and therefore overestimates air emissions of water-soluble species such as MTBE (Gabele and Pyle, 2000) because the exhaust port is located on the propeller unit, which is immersed in water during engine operation. Emissions depend on engine type, with two-stroke HC emissions being an order of magnitude higher than for four-stroke engines (Environmental Protection Agency, 1991b; Kado et al., 2000).

Commercial marine engines using diesel engines >30 liters/cylinder propel ocean-going cruise ships, container ships, and tankers, and were not included in the EPA's 1999 rule-making for new marine diesel engines because it was expected that international emission standards would be adopted. To date, the international standards have not been ratified, so the EPA proposed new emission standards for these very large marine diesel engines on 29 May 2002 (US Government, 2002).

Of primary concern are the NO_x emissions from these vessels, which although estimated to account for only 1.5% of US mobile-source NO_x, increases to 37% of emissions in some port areas (US Government, 2002). Currently, ships have insignificant HC and CO emissions relative to on-road sources, but the relative contribution is expected to increase as a result of recently implemented highway and diesel vehicle standards and the relatively slow turnover of large vessels. For these reasons, the 2002 proposed rule includes HC emission limits of 0.4 g/kW-h and CO standards of 3.0 g/kW-h (US Government, 2002). The proposed Tier 1 standards will apply to new engines in 2004, and stricter Tier 2 standards intended to reduce NO_x emissions by an additional 30% will come into effect in 2006. The recent commercial vessel proposal also includes a voluntary "blue cruise" program to encourage the installation of air pollution control equipment (US Government, 2002).

Locomotives

Rail transport of goods represents 41% of intercity ton-miles, compared with 27% for trucks, and locomotives are more fuel-efficient than diesel trucks (Environmental Protection Agency, 1998). In fact, rail transport doubled from 0.6 billion to 1.3 billion ton-miles between 1955 and 1995 while the total annual fuel consumption remained constant at ~3500 billion gallons per year (Environmental Protection Agency, 1998). Furthermore, locomotives are approximately three times cleaner than trucks on a ton-mile basis (Environmental Protection Agency, 1998). The main reason for the difference in emissions, despite the fact that locomotives and trucks are both diesel vehicles, is that the engine is mechanically decoupled from the drive motor in a locomotive, whereas it is not in a truck. This allows the locomotive engine to operate at discrete steady-state modes of operation with only short periods of acceleration between the eight available throttle notches (plus idle and dynamic brake); conditions that reduce fuel consumption and concomitant emissions. Highway vehicles, on the other hand, experience highly transient operating conditions that consume more fuel and lead to higher emissions.

Newly manufactured and remanufactured locomotives and locomotive engines have been regulated since the EPA issued final emissions standards in 1998 (US Government, 1998). The major pollutants of interest from locomotives are NO_x, the only pollutant for which locomotives contribute over 1% to the national emissions inventory, as well as HC, CO, PM, and smoke. The regulations were phased in, starting in 2000, with different tiers of regulation depending on the year of manufacturer. Tier 0 standards are for NO_x only, and later tiers are intended to reduce NO_x emissions further as well as control HC, CO, PM, and smoke. Locomotives originally manufactured before 1973 are not regulated, but remanufactured locomotives, regardless of year of original manufacturer, are regulated (US Government, 1998). This is important, and unique to mobile source emissions standards, and is based on the fact that locomotives are initially built to be remanufactured every 5–10 years of their ~40 year useful life. Remanufacturing also has important implications for emissions control because engine replacement will typically result in better emissions performance.

The federal test procedure for locomotives involves chassis testing with timed periods of operation at idle, the dynamic brake and each of the eight throttle notch positions. The test sequence does not include a cold start because locomotives are rarely allowed to cool to ambient temperature during use because difficulty of starting a cold engine, especially in winter, and loss of coolant can result in engine damage (Environmental Protection Agency, 1998).

Air transport sources

Worldwide, airline revenue from passenger-kilometers grew by nearly 9% per year between 1960 and the mid-1990s, slowing to about 5% per year in 1997 (Penner et al., 1999). Consequently, because emissions from ground-based mobile sources are generally decreasing, commercial aircraft emissions represent a fast-growing segment of the transportation sector's emission inventory. In 1995, aircraft represented about 2% of the total US NO_x and CO ground-level mobile source emissions inventory, with commercial aircraft emissions accounting for between 70 and 30%, respectively, of total aircraft emissions (US Government, 1997).

Airport operations comprise a number of emission sources, including aircraft main engines and auxiliary power units, ground support equipment, and ground access vehicles. Aircraft engines are estimated to comprise approximately 45% of total air pollutant emissions from airport operations, with ground access vehicles, including passenger pick-up and drop-off, accounting for 45%, and auxiliary ground units and ground support equipment comprising the remaining 10% (US Government, 1997).

Aircraft emissions, which are released directly into the upper troposphere and lower stratosphere, include CO_2 and water vapor, with lesser quantities of NO and NO_2, SO_x, and soot. The emitted gases and particles have been shown to contribute to climate change by changing the concentration of atmospheric greenhouse gases, including CO_2, O_3, and CH_4. Other possible effects of aircraft emissions include the formation of condensation trails (contrails), which possibly leads to increased production of cirrus clouds (Penner et al., 1999). A recent report suggests that aviation's potential impact on climate change was about 3.5% of all human activities (Environmental Protection Agency, 2000b).

The International Civil Aviation Organization (ICAO) is an agency within the United Nations that is charged with establishing international aircraft engine emission standards. The ICAO was established in 1944 by the United Nations to ensure that international aviation was developed in a responsible and equitable basis (Penner et al., 1999); this responsibility was extended to include establishing standards and developing regulations to minimize impacts on the environment in 1972 at the United Nations Conference on the Human Environment (International Civil Aviation Organization, 1993). There are more than 150 participating member states of the ICAO, and, although voluntary, the participating nations have agreed to adopt the ICAO standards when possible.

The ICAO aircraft emission standards use a reference landing and take-off cycle to establish emission limits for NO_x, CO, and HCs. The ICAO maintains a comprehensive database of aircraft jet engine emissions certification data known as the *Engine Exhaust Emissions Data Bank*, first issued in 1995. There are currently no standards or required control measures for emissions generated from ground support equipment or vehicles.

3. Important issues facing us

3.1. Fine particles

Fine particles in the atmosphere derive from three major processes: primary emission, condensation of gas phase species, and via secondary chemical reactions between gaseous precursors to form liquid or solid particles (Seinfeld and Pandis,

1998). All combustion sources (vehicles, power plants, incinerators, residential furnaces, biomass burning) emit significant numbers of submicrometer-sized particles and therefore contribute to $PM_{2.5}$ levels. Motor vehicles, especially diesel vehicles, account for the majority of fine particles in urban areas, and these particles are the focus of increased environmental regulatory interest (Scientific Review Panel, 1998; Lloyd and Cackette, 2001) owing to recent epidemiological evidence linking ambient fine particle concentrations to respiratory illnesses, morbidity, and mortality (Pope et al., 2002).

Ambient $PM_{2.5}$ is now regulated in the USA as a national ambient air quality criteria pollutant on the basis of mass of fine PM collected on a filter (Environmental Protection Agency, 2002c). This measurement contrasts with vehicle exhaust emission standards that are based on total particulate matter collected after exhaust dilution and are expressed as mass per kilometer driven. However, since the majority of particles emitted from vehicles are in the submicrometer size range, assuming that no dilution tunnel artifacts are sampled, the total PM mass measured during a vehicle emissions test is essentially a measure of the submicrometer particles that comprise $PM_{2.5}$. Recently, however, concerns have been raised that particle number concentration or surface area, rather than mass concentration, may have a more direct relationship with adverse human health effects because ultrafine particles (diameter <100 nm) are more toxic to lung tissue than fine particles of identical composition (Donaldson et al., 2000). Nanoparticles (<50 nm) from motor vehicle exhaust form by gas-to-particle reactions induced during dilution in the atmosphere (Kittelson, 1998). Therefore, laboratory certification tests must be developed to avoid the creation of nanoparticle artifacts that would not be produced under real-world dilution conditions. This is an active area of research because various laboratories, employing different dilution techniques and sampling methods, have documented that sampling conditions such as relative humidity, temperature, dilution ratio, and dilution rate can all significantly affect measured size distributions and may create nanoparticle artifacts (Abdul-Khalek et al., 1999; Kittelson et al., 1999). Despite these hurdles, laboratory dynamometer tests continue to be used to compare particle emissions from different types of vehicles because of the benefits of relatively controlled sampling conditions in the laboratory environment.

Currently, no reliable models exist to predict the ultrafine particle size distributions from vehicles, especially under various modes of vehicle operation (speed, acceleration rate) and the wide range of atmospheric meteorological conditions (temperature, relative humidity) that occur under real-world driving conditions. Furthermore, the composition of these particles on a time-resolved basis is difficult to assess because their small total mass demands collection over long sampling times in order to perform reliable chemical analyses by standard techniques. Future research efforts that examine both the size distribution and composition of these finest particles emitted by vehicles on a time-resolved basis are needed to assess ultrafine particle formation mechanisms and human exposure levels.

Diesel engines produce significantly more (~100-fold) PM than gasoline engines, and diesel PM is considered an air toxic (Environmental Protection Agency, 2000c). Further, considering the important role diesel vehicles play in the US economy for low-cost, long-distance transportation of goods, these vehicles will have a significant impact on air quality for the foreseeable future (Lloyd and Cackette, 2001). Laboratory and epidemiological studies are needed to determine whether number-based air quality criteria are more appropriate measures of the adverse health effects of PM than mass-based standards.

How alternative fuels and engine technologies affect particulate matter and NO_x emissions is not well understood. In many urban areas, transit buses are a significant source of heavy duty vehicle traffic, and many municipalities, including Los Angeles, Sacramento, Cleveland, New York, and Atlanta, have recently modified their fleets to use compressed natural gas as the "clean" alternative to conventional uncontrolled diesel vehicles to meet increasingly strict PM air quality regulations. The emissions from these vehicles need to be studied in order to understand how air quality in urban areas will change as heavy duty fleets transition to new technologies.

The mandated use of ultra-low sulfur diesel fuel (<15 ppm of sulfur) and the effect this change will have on total particle mass and number emissions also needs to be investigated. Preliminary data show significant reductions in number emissions, but, surprisingly, nanoparticle modes were generated under some vehicle operating conditions. The composition and source of nanoparticles under these conditions needs to be evaluated. Because HC species are not thought to nucleate during exhaust dilution, sulfates have been identified as the key component of nanoparticles (Shi and Harrison, 1999). Attention has recently turned to the high sulfur content of lubricating oils (~0.5 wt%) as a potential source of the nanoparticle mode generated in vehicles operating on ultra-low sulfur fuel (Tobias et al., 2001). Thus, as diesel fuel sulfur levels are reduced starting in 2006, sulfur in lubricating oil may become a more important source of vehicle-derived nanoparticles.

3.2. Toxics

An important category of emissions are known as air toxics (or hazardous air pollutants); these are toxic air pollutants that are known or probable carcinogens or linked to other serious health problems such as cancer, neurological, cardiovascular, and respiratory diseases, and birth and reproductive defects (Environmental Protection Agency, 1993b, 2000c). Sources of toxic air pollutants include, for example, electrical power plants, fast food restaurants, vehicles, and cleaning

Table 4
Mobile source air toxics

Toxic	Total emissions by mobile source (%)	Mobile emissions (%)	
		On-road sources	Non-road sources
(1) Benzene	76	48	28
(2) 1,3-Butadiene	60	42	18
(3) Acetaldehyde	70	29	41
(4) Diesel PM (a)	~100	~1/3	~2/3
(5) Formaldehyde	49	24	25
(6) Acrolein	39	16	23

Source: adapted from US Government (2001).
Note: (a) although industrial sources often utilize diesel equipment, such as generators, these are considered to produce relatively minor contributions to the total diesel emissions.

solvents. These pollutants can remain in the atmosphere for a long time and contribute to air and water contamination at considerable distances from the original sources.

In the USA the EPA is responsible for regulating 189 air toxics that have been identified for regulatory purposes based on their environmental and health risks (Environmental Protection Agency, 1993b, 2000c). In March 2001, the EPA published a final rule-making that identified 21 air toxic pollutants specifically associated with on-road and non-road mobile sources (US Government, 2001). These pollutants are acrolein, acetaldehyde, arsenic compounds, benzene, 1,3-butadiene, chromium compounds, diesel PM and diesel exhaust gases, dioxins and furans, ethylbenzene, formaldehyde, n-hexane, lead compounds, manganese compounds, mercury compounds, MTBE, naphthalene, nickel compounds, polycyclic organic matter, styrene, toluene, and xylene. The EPA has stated that compounds on the toxics list do not necessarily signify a risk to public health or welfare but will be evaluated further by the EPA.

Although all of the pollutants identified above are produced in some amount by mobile sources, the EPA has identified six for which mobile sources can be considered a major contributor and that present the greatest public health risk: diesel exhaust (which includes both diesel exhaust PM and organic gases), benzene, 1,3-butadiene, formaldehyde, acetaldehyde, and acrolein. Using 1996 emissions estimates, the percentage of total emissions accounted for by the mobile source portion of these pollutants ranged between approximately 39% (acrolein) to 76% (benzene) (Table 4).

Relatively little is known about the on-road contributions of air toxics. In May 2001 the EPA announced the release of MOBILE6.2, which can be used to estimate mobile source toxic and particulate emissions. To estimate the particulate emissions, PART5 was integrated into MOBILE6. The MOBILE6.2 particulate emission estimates will not be the same as the PART5 estimates because of changes in vehicle registration and technology distributions and the updating of some of the basic particulate emission rates for future vehicle model years (Environmental Protection Agency, 2002a,b).

For the toxics estimates, MOBILE6.2 includes default emission factor values, in units of grams per mile, for six mobile source air toxics (Environmental Protection Agency, 2002b): acetaldehyde, formaldehyde, 1,3-butadiene, benzene, MTBE, and acrolein. Of the six pollutants, benzene and MTBE are produced in both exhaust and evaporative emissions; acetaldehyde, formaldehyde, 1,3-butadiene, and acrolein are components of exhaust emissions only (Environmental Protection Agency, 2002b). MOBILE6.2 reports emission factors for 28 vehicle types by exhaust, crankcase, diurnal, hot soak, running loss, resting loss, or refueling loss emissions.

For the new model the EPA has consolidated pre-existing modeling and spreadsheet tools into the MOBILE6 modeling platform rather than significantly updating the modeling platform. Consequently, there are a number of important outstanding transportation air quality research questions related to its implementation. There are currently no specific certification standards for air toxics emissions from motor vehicles. Toxics can be regulated indirectly through emissions standards for HCs and for diesel PM. There is a need to better understand the concentrations of air toxics emitted by vehicles operating on the road because emissions may be related to vehicle age and maintenance.

A major research thrust in the transportation–mobile emissions interface over the next few years will be directed toward producing highly resolved spatial and temporal models for both transportation activities and mobile emissions. Recent regulatory changes in mandated fuel composition will affect vehicle emissions and mobile source emissions inventories; new methodologies for incorporating these changes quickly into models is important because it affects transportation planning. As off-road sources become increasingly important in the emissions inventory budgets, new transportation activity models will be needed in this sector to enable development without exceeding SIP limits.

The future for air quality is bright; a remaining challenge is to develop more highly resolved estimation tools so the links between air quality and human exposure can be examined in a more robust manner. Further, vehicle sampling methodologies for fine PM and air toxics need to be critically examined and compared with real-world concentrations of these important pollutants.

References

Abdul-Khalek, I.S., D.B. Kittelson and F. Brear (1999) *The influence of dilution conditions on diesel exhaust particle size distribution measurements*. SAE Technical Paper 1999-01-1142:1-9. Washington, DC: Society of Automotive Engineers.

American Lung Association (2001) *Selected key studies on particulate matter and health: 1997–2001*. New York: ALA.
Burnett, R.T., J.R. Brook, W.T. Yung, R.E. Dales and D. Krewski (1997) "Association between ozone and hospitalization for respiratory diseases in 16 Canadian cities," *Environmental Research,* 72:24–31.
Colvile, R.N., E.J. Hutchinson, J.S. Mindell and R.F. Warren (2001) "The transport sector as a source of air pollution," *Atmospheric Environment* 35:1537–1565.
Dockery, D.W., C.A. Pope, X.P. Xu, J.D. Spengler, J.H. Ware, M.E. Fay, B.G. Ferris and F.E. Speizer. (1993) "An association between air pollution and mortality in six United States cities," *New England Journal of Medicine*, 329:1753–1759.
Donaldson, K., V. Stone, P.S. Gilmour, D.M. Brown and W. MacNee (2000) "Ultrafine particles: mechanisms of lung injury," *Philosophical Transactions of the Royal Society of London, Series A*, 358:2741–2749.
Environmental Protection Agency (1990) *Clean Air Act Amendments (CAAA), Vol. Title 40 of the Code of Federal Regulations Parts 50–99 (40 CFR 50–99)*. Washington, DC: EPA.
Environmental Protection Agency (1991a) "Air quality criteria for oxides of nitrogen," in: *EPA-/600/ 8–01/049*. Washington, DC: EPA.
Environmental Protection Agency (1991b) *Nonroad engine and vehicle emission study*, EPA 460/3-91-02; NTIS PB92-126960. Ann Arbor: Office of Transportation and Air Quality, EPA.
Environmental Protection Agency (1993a) As amended August 1995, November 1995, and August 1997. Criteria and procedures for determining conformity to State or Federal Implementation Plans of transportation plans, programs, and projects funded or approved under Title 23 U.S.C. or the Federal Transit Act., pp. 62188 Federal Register 58(225).
Environmental Protection Agency (1993b) *Motor vehicle-related air toxics study*, EPA 454/R-01-004. Washington, DC: Technical Support Branch, Emissions Planning and Strategies Division, Office of Mobile Sources, Office of Air and Radiation, EPA.
Environmental Protection Agency (1998) *Locomotive emission standards: regulatory support document*. Washington, DC: Office of Mobile Sources, EPA.
Environmental Protection Agency (2000a) *National air quality and emissions trends report*, 1999 EPA 454/R-01-04. Office of Air Quality, Planning and Standards, EPA, Research Triangle Park.
Environmental Protection Agency (2000b) *Aircraft contrails fact sheet*, EPA 430-F-00-005. Washington, DC: Air and Radiation Office, EPA.
Environmental Protection Agency (2000c) *Technical support document: control of emissions of hazardous air pollutants from motor vehicles and motor vehicle fuels*, EPA 420-R-00-023. Washington, DC: Office of Transportation and Air Quality, EPA:
Environmental Protection Agency (2001a) *National air quality and emissions trends report, 2000*, EPA 454/R-01-004. Research Triangle Park: Office of Air Quality Planning and Standards, Emissions Monitoring and Analysis Division, EPA.
Environmental Protection Agency (2001b) *Emission standards for new nonroad engines. Environmental fact sheet*, EPA 420-F-01–026. Office of Transportation and Air Quality, Ann Arbor.
Environmental Protection Agency (2002a) *Particulate emission factor model, technical description*, EPA 420-R-02-012. Washington, DC: Assessment and Standards Division, Office of Transportation and Air Quality, EPA.
Environmental Protection Agency (2002b) *Technical description of MOBILE6.2 and guidance on its use for emission inventory preparation*, EPA 420-R-02–011. Washington, DC: Assessment and Standards Division, Office of Transportation and Air Quality, EPA.
Environmental Protection Agency (2002c) *D.C. circuit court upholds clean air standards*, Headquarters Press Release. EPA, Washington, DC.
Frischer, T., M. Studnicka, C. Gartner, E. Tauber, F. Horak, A. Veiter, J.l. Spengler and R. Urbanek (1999) "Lung function growth and ambient ozone: a three-year population study in school children," *American Journal of Respiratory and Critical Care Medicine*, 160:390–396.
Gabele, P.A. and S.M. Pyle (2000) "Emissions from two outboard engines operating on reformulated gasoline containing MTBE," *Environmental Science and Technology*, 34:368–372.
Ghio, A.J., C. Kim and R.B. Devlin (2000) "Concentrated ambient air particles induce mild pulmonary inflammation in healthy human volunteers," *American Journal of Respiratory and Critical Care Medicine*, 162:981–988.

Hasselbad, V., D.M. Eddy and D.J. Kotchmar (1992) "Synthesis of environmental evidence: nitrogen dioxide epidemiology studies," *Journal of Air and Waste Management Association*, 42:662–671.

Holgate, S.T., J.M. Samet, H.S. Koren and R.L. Maynard, eds (1999) *Air pollution and health*. New York: Academic Press.

International Civil Aviation Organization (1993) *Aircraft engine emissions*. New York: United Nations.

Kado, N.Y., R.A. Okamoto, J. Karim and P.A. Kuzmicky (2000) "Airborne particle emissions from 2- and 4-stroke outboard marine engines: polycyclic aromatic hydrocarbon and bioassay analyses," *Environmental Science and Technology*, 34:2714–2720.

Kittelson, D.B (1998) "Engines and nanoparticles: a review," *Journal of Aerosol Science* 29:575–588.

Kittelson, D.B., M. Arnold and W.F. Watts Jr (1999) *Review of diesel particulate matter sampling methods, final report*. Minneapolis: University of Minnesota.

Koenig, J.Q. (2000) *Health effects of ambient air pollution*. Boston: Kluwer.

Lloyd, A.C. and T.A. Cackette (2001) "Diesel engines: environmental impact and control," *Journal of the Air Waste Management Association*, 51:809–847.

MacNee, W. and K. Donaldson (1999) "Particulate air pollution: injurious and protective mechanisms in the lungs," in: S.T. Holgate, J.M. Samet, H.S. Koren and R.L. Maynard, eds, *Air pollution and health*. New York: Academic Press.

National Research Council (2000) *Modeling mobile source emissions*. Washington, DC: National Academy Press.

Ntziachristos, L., P.M. Tourlou, Z. Samaras, S. Geivanidis and A. Andrias (2002) *National and central estimates for air emissions from road transport*, Technical Report 74. Copenhagen: European Environmental Agency.

Penner, J., D. Lister, D. Griggs, D. Dokken and M. McFarland (1999) *Aviation and the global atmosphere: summary for policymakers*. Geneva: Intergovernmental Panel on Climate Change, UNEP, WMO.

Pope, C.A., R.T. Burnett, M.J. Thun, E.E. Calle, D. Krewsi, K. Ito and G.D. Thurston (2002) "Lung cancer, cardiopulmonary mortality, and long-term exposure to fine particulate air pollution," *Journal of the American Medical Association*, 287:1132–1141.

Samet, J.M., F. Dominici, F.C. Curriero, I. Coursac and S.L. Zeger (2000) "Fine particulate air pollution and mortality in 20 U.S. cities," *New England Journal of Medicine*, 343:1742–1749.

Schindler, C., U. Ackermann-Liebrich, P. Leuenberger, C. Monn, R. Rapp, G. Bolognini, J.P. Bongard, O. Brandli, G. Domenighetti, W. Karrer, R. Keller, T.G. Medici, A.P. Perruchoud, M.H. Schoni, J.M. Tschopp, B. Villiger and J.P. Zellweger (1998) "Associations between lung function and estimated average exposure to NO_2 in eight areas of Switzerland," *Epidemiology*, 9:405–411.

Scientific Review Panel (1998) *Findings on the report on diesel exhaust*. Sacramento: Scientific Review Panel.

Seinfeld, J.H. and S.N. Pandis (1998) *Atmospheric chemistry and physics*. New York: Wiley.

Shi, J.P., and R.M. Harrison (1999) "Investigation of ultrafine particle formation during diesel exhaust dilution," *Environmental Science and Technology*, 33:3730–3736.

Tobias, H.J., D.E. Beving, P.J. Ziemann, H. Sakurai, M. Zuk, P.H. McMurry, D. Zarling, R. Waytulonis and D.B. Kittelson (2001) "Chemical analysis of diesel engine nanoparticle using a nano-DMA thermal desorption particle beam mass spectrometer," *Environmental Science and Technology*, 35:2233–2243.

Tuolomi, G., K. Katsouyanni, D. Zmirou, J. Schwartz, C. Spix, A.P. de Leon, A. Tobias, P. Quennel, D. Rabczenko, L. Bacharova, L. Bisanti, J.M. Vonk and A. Ponka. (1997) "Short-term effects of ambient oxidant exposure on mortality: a combined analysis within the APHEA project," *American Journal of Epidemiology*, 146:177–185.

US Government (1997) "Control of air pollution from aircraft and aircraft engines, emission standards and test procedures, final and proposed rule," pp. 25355–25367. *Federal register*, 40 CFR Part 87. Washington, DC: US Government Printing Office.

US Government (1998) "Emission standards for locomotives and locomotive engines; final rule," in: *Federal register*, 40 CFR Parts 85, 89 and 92. Washington, DC: US Government Printing Office.

US Government (2001) "Control of emissions of hazardous air pollutants from mobile sources; final rule," in: *Federal register*, 40 CFR Parts 80 and 86. Washington, DC: US Government Printing Office.

US Government (2002) "Control of emissions of air pollution from new marine compression-ignition engines at or above 30 liters/cylinder; proposed rule," in: *Federal register*, 40 CFR Part 94. Washington, DC: US Government Printing Office.

Zanobetti, A., J. Schwartz and D. Gold (2000) "Are there sensitive subgroups for the effects of airborne particles?" *Environmental Health Perspectives*, 108:481–845.

Chapter 5

THE ECONOMICS OF NOISE

DAVID GILLEN
Wilfrid Laurier University, Waterloo

1. Introduction

In this chapter we examine the economics of noise, using airport noise as an illustration.

Airport noise is an example of an externality. An externality is a by-product of production or consumption that benefits or costs someone who has no direct control over its presence. When your neighbors cut their lawns you are a beneficiary if the appearance of the neighborhood matters to you. Passive cigarette smoking on airplanes imposes a costly spillover on its recipients. When an airport's neighbors awaken to aircraft noise, they incur a similar cost without any direct control over how large it will be.

Externalities create a strategic problem for an airport's manager because the recipients can retaliate. For example, the decision to reschedule movements to one runway while another undergoes repair typically produces increased public complaints about noise. The strategic significance of the externality problem depends directly on the seriousness of the retaliation that might arise. An assessment of the needs and potential for retaliation of the "players" in an airport's environment represents a crucial step in the development of a noise strategy.

At issue in the dispute between an airport's neighbors and its customers is the level of use of a common property resource – the surrounding physical environment. Demands of landowners who face expropriation, complaints about noise, and political opposition to expansion plans influence the feasibility of increasing airport services. Expropriation costs reduce the profitability of expansion investment. Political forces can reduce the probability that regulators allow expansion at all. Both demands, then, are expressions of a "supply price" for a resource that the airport needs.

An airport's customers similarly value the use of the surrounding environment but for different reasons. Their "demand price" is the maximum that they would be willing to pay to use the resources of the airport as a transportation facility. In the absence of a market in which both sides can agree about how noisy airport activity will be, the airport's owners and managers must provide strategies that coordinate the demands of its neighbors and its customers. Otherwise they will face the obstacles and constraints that arise when one side acts on its dissatisfaction.[a]

An airport's neighbors have gained increasing strategic power for several reasons. Many airports' interest in capacity expansion has never been higher. Congestion and unabated growth in demand for air transportation have increased the potential costs of failing to implement successful capacity expansion plans. This makes the threat posed by dissatisfied airport neighbors considerably more important than it would be if the industry were experiencing no growth.

A common response to noise complaints in the past denied that noise generates costs, and focused instead on progress and economic benefits derived from more intensive use of airport resources. Nevertheless, noise is costly, and not just as it negatively affects an airport's neighbors. To the extent that these neighbors have any strategic leverage, they can delay or block indefinitely socially efficient increases in airport capacity. There can also be restrictions placed on airport operations, which will affect the efficiency and effectiveness of the utilization of airport capital.

Growing public awareness and acknowledgement of negative externalities like air and water pollution have moved the resolution of externality problems to the front of the political agenda. It is easier today for opponents of airport expansion to use the political system by participating in environmental impact hearings and electoral politics. Even if an airport's managers are not under pressure to expand, they face a greater strategic challenge based on their environmental roles.

The political response to airport noise may also create a moral hazard problem. Moral hazard describes selfish behavior that a contract cannot prevent and arises in this case because it is always in the interest of current residents to lobby for policies that reduce the current noise profile. If that happens, housing prices/rents will rise and people who are more sensitive to noise will move into the area. This will start the whole cycle again. Increasing noise levels has the opposite effect, a combination of rents falling and replacing noise sensitive existing residents with those who have less sensitivity. Therefore, the moral hazard can arise from either current residents or airport users.

---

[a]Airports in North America, Europe, and Asia are experiencing extraordinary pressures to accommodate increased traffic by adding more slots and runways. Simultaneously, a general demand for more environmental responsibility is forcing airports to listen to and deal with groups affected adversely by airport externalities. The urgency of the congestion problem coupled with this environmental awareness is increasing the public's strategic leverage in approval processes. This leverage could have a significant negative impact on the rationalization of the worldwide air transportation system. Airport managers must respond by adopting comprehensive noise strategies that balance the demands of their customers and their neighbors.

2. The economics of noise

A number of strategies have been developed to reduce noise. Each of these strategies has associated costs and benefits that are borne by different groups. Costs have not been seriously considered nor systematically assessed when choosing from among the various noise strategies available. These costs can be significant, and we suspect that the magnitude and incidence varies across the alternative strategies. Among the costs are land use controls that may limit the productive use of land as well as tax revenues to municipalities, and operating procedures which may have an impact upon operating and scheduling costs or result in flight delays (due to special routing or corridors). The move to quieter aircraft will impose significant capital costs upon the carriers.[a] Airport closures, night curfews, etc., impose costs on the airport in terms of lost revenue, and reduce available capacity at a time of already significant congestion. The procedures can also result in under-utilization of aircraft, particularly in the case of airfreight companies. In some cases noise fees are established with no real economic basis.

However, noise management strategies will have some impact on the magnitude of the noise externality that airport neighbors are faced with. But what management strategy will have the most effect in reducing the "noise problem"? This will depend on a number of factors, two of which are:

(1) Which features or characteristics of the noise problem does the management strategy affect?
(2) How important is each feature to the noise recipients?

In order to develop an efficient and effective noise management program the magnitude and distribution of the benefits and costs of the strategies must be considered. Which strategies are more efficient? To what extent should a particular strategy be implemented? Where do diminishing returns set in and where do marginal costs and benefits equalize? Without such estimates not only will airport and air carrier resources be wasted but more harm than good may result from well-intentioned but ill-based strategies aimed at mitigating the noise problem.

3. Externalities and social cost

Making investment decisions or deciding which management strategies to pursue is, in principle, a straightforward process. The gains from the investment or

---

[a] In the USA, aircraft are described under Federal Aviation Agency (FAA) regulations as fitting into particular "stages." A stage 1 aircraft would be an old Boeing 707; a stage 2 aircraft would be represented by a Boeing 727 or early model Boeing 737. A stage 3 aircraft would be a modern Airbus as well as newer Boeing products such as the 767, 757, or 777.

strategy are compared with the costs. Investments and strategies are ranked according to their return, and with the objective of maximizing the rate of return the decision is self-evident. A similar picture could be developed with respect to a consumer making decisions with regard to purchases: the consumer would rank choices on the basis of costs and gains and select the bundle of goods that maximizes the net gains.

These seemingly simple propositions of conventional economics are based upon the notion that prices reflect consumer desires and in the long run will direct resources where they are most productive. The examples above also mask simplifying characteristics: there is a common goal, profit or utility; costs and benefits accrue to the same economic agent or the weights to be attached to different groups who may be the recipients of benefits or costs can be identified; prices reflect all the costs and gains; and markets are well defined.

Noise is an excellent example of an economic good that is "bad" or undesired. It is a product for which there is no well-defined market and hence no well-defined price. The producers of noise are generally not the consumers of noise; thus, the price of goods for which noise is an undesirable by-product do not reflect the full "social costs" of their production.[a]

How should decisions with respect to noise reduction strategies or investments, such as engine redesign be made in order to mitigate noise? The economics of such a decision demands that, first, measures of the gains and losses be made and then an objective standard formulated; then, a decision as to which strategy or set of strategies to use can be made. In order to accomplish this, both costs and benefits must be measured in some commensurate units. This requires "monetizing" noise or valuing noise in terms of a currency metric or at minimum being able to rate the relative values of different strategies. Costs of particular strategies or investments are relatively straightforward and can be appraised. However, the benefits of noise reduction or the valuation of quiet are not easily evaluated.[b]

4. Social cost and strategy choice

One way of viewing the effects of various noise management strategies is to consider how they affect costs and benefits. Noise from an aircraft operation is a by-product, or externality, of the output of the aviation industry.[a] Figure 1

---

[a]Air fares do not in most cases contain a price for quietness. However, this is gradually changing in some parts of the world; for example, a number of European airports have introduced a noise charge for flights that exceed a specified noise level when landing or taking off.

[b]The Roskill Study (1970) in the UK was the first to use formal analysis in assessing noise impacts and is credited with getting formal analysis integrated with airport planning.

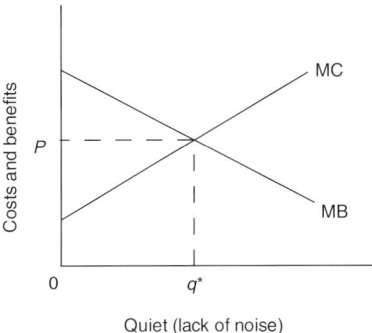

Figure 1. The optimal amount of noise.

illustrates the "optimal" amount of noise. The notion of an optimal amount of any good is that amount which is worth what it costs and in most all cases the optimal amount is not zero.[b] In effect there has to be a balancing of benefits and costs.

In Figure 1, q^* is the optimal level of noise (or quiet), and it illustrates that the optimal level occurs where the incremental benefits (MB) of additional noise reduction just equals the incremental costs (MC) of reducing noise. The total benefits of a level of quiet, q^*, are measured by the area under the MB function between 0 and q^*. The total costs of reducing noise to the level indicated by q^* is given by the area under the MC function between 0 and q^*.[c]

The efficient level of quiet, q^*, is achievable in a number of different ways. Furthermore, q^* can be valued in different ways as well because it has multiple dimensions. By this we mean that the noise externality may be described by the cumulative amount of noise, the average amount of noise, the maximum amount of noise at a given moment in time, and the frequency of exposure to noise. The benefit function is a simple linear combination of these characteristics. Each may have a different value. It is even possible that a particular characteristic has a very low or zero value. Two points are worth noting. First, if the valuation of any one characteristic increases, the MB function rises. Thus, if airport neighbors become more noise-sensitive, MB shifts upward. Second, if a noise strategy is put in place,

---

[a]The following analysis treats noise as a one-dimensional output yet it can have multiple attributes or dimensions. However, this would not change the main point. Operationalizing multiple dimensions could be accomplished using hedonic approaches to characterizing products.

[b]To eliminate or have zero noise from aircraft would require shutting down an airfield. This could be very costly in terms of employment, generated economic activity and development, and loss of investment in capital and land.

[c]The benefit and cost functions are presented as linear in the analysis. However, there is no reason they need be, and in fact there is debate in the literature that the damages rise non-linearly with increases in certain noise attributes.

Figure 2. Benefits and costs of noise management strategies.

which affects a noise characteristic that has little or no value, MC will most likely exceed MB. Such a situation is illustrated in Figure 1 at q^*. Therefore, Figure 1 can be thought to apply to any one-noise strategy as well as to the aggregate noise problem. Each noise strategy has costs and benefits. To select the "best" one requires that for each strategy all costs and benefits be measured and compared.

Once benefits and costs of the alternative strategies have been determined, the relative value of a strategy can be assessed. To illustrate how even a coarse classification of cost and benefit impacts can assist in sorting noise management strategies, suppose that each noise management strategy is ranked in terms of noise reduction versus noise redistribution with reduction being preferred to redistribution. A strategy that reduced noise could be rated, as "high benefit," and redistribution would be "low benefit."

As more precision is added to the values of the costs and benefits, the alternative strategies can be ranked more thoroughly. In effect, with finer valuations, the analysis moves from a coarse assessment to Figure 2, which is based on a full information cost and benefit analysis. Figure 2 illustrates the application of this framework to the assessment of four alternative noise management strategies. Any strategy that is on or above the 45° line is one which yields a positive return; the monetary value of benefits per unit cost is >1. In the illustration, strategy 4 is one that should be rejected since it costs more than the benefits received.

The economically efficient strategy is strategy 1 since it yields the greatest benefits per unit cost. However, all of strategies 1 through 3 yield positive net benefits.

In order to select the most efficient and effective strategy it is necessary to:

(1) identify the costs of each strategy;
(2) assess whether a strategy alters the characteristics of noise that are annoying;
(3) determine how a reduction in the noise externality is valued;
(4) determine the population impact of a strategy.

4.1. Property rights for noise

As with any externality the person or firm who owns the right to create the externality, such as make noise or have quiet, will affect the outcome of how much of an externality is generated and the costs of achieving the final level of the externality. In some parts of the world the airport has the right to create noise, and nearby residents must tolerate it or move. In other cases, most notably in the USA, the right to quiet rests with residents, and should the airport create noise that is deemed undesirable, the residents can resort to legal action to either reduce the noise or be compensated in some way. In Europe, Australia, and Canada, political rather than legal action by nearby airport residents has resulted in lower noise exposure.

5. Airport noise measures

Noise is simultaneously two phenomena. The acoustician characterizes noise technically in terms of physically measured sound pressure levels. In the noise management context, noise also describes the physiological, psychological, and behavioral responses of the listener to the physical phenomenon. Differential weighting of day and night noise events in the calculation of cumulative noise measures recognizes this dual nature of noise. For instance, the NEF (noise exposure forecast) weights night noise 16.67 times more heavily than day events. However, time of day weighting does not reflect the complex nature of noise completely, and this has affected previous noise management strategies.

An official group of noise metrics has been established for measuring and technically evaluating noise for land-use planning and environmental impact assessment. To control aircraft noise at the source, the FAA employs a second system of metrics for aircraft certification. The noise metrics utilized most often in North America can be separated into four general categories (Federal Aviation Administration, 1985; DWG Research Associates, 1990):

(1) single-event maximum sound levels (ALm, PNL, PNLT);
(2) single-event energy dose (SENEL, EPNL);
(3) cumulative energy average metrics (Leq, Ldn, CNEL, NEF);
(4) cumulative time metrics (TA).

Within and between categories there is some bridging of the noise metrics either by definition or mathematics. The two most common measures seen in Canada and the USA are NEF and, to a lesser degree, Ldn.[a] The day–night sound level (Ldn) is a single-number measure of community noise. The Ldn value, which has been A-weighted, is employed as a predictor of the effects of cumulative aircraft noise to the airport environs. In the Ldn process of measuring, the noise generated from each aircraft take-off or landing at ground level is calculated and accumulated for a 24 h period. Due to increased sensitivity to noise during night-time hours, daytime and night-time exposures are treated separately, with night-time (22:00–07:00) allocated a 10 dB penalty. The Ldn has been reassessed frequently during its 30 years of use.

The noise exposure forecast (NEF), used in Canada, Europe, and Australia, is an index that uses individual aircraft source noise expressed in EPNL (EPNdB) over a 24 h period weighted for the time of day. To calculate the NEF at a specific location, the noise contribution from each aircraft operating from each runway is assessed by considering the distance from the point in question to the aircraft and then obtaining EPNdB (the decibel rating in the EPN scale) values from the appropriate SPNdB (the decibel rating in the SPN scale) versus distance curve. The noise contributions of all aircraft operating on all runways are summed on an antilog basis to obtain the total noise exposure at that one location. Noise contours of surrounding airport environs can be calculated by joining points of equal NEF value. Calculations of these values requires information on the number of operating aircraft, the type of aircraft, the individual noise characteristics of the aircraft, flight path data, time of day of flight and the flight operating procedures of the pilot.

5.1. Assessing the costs of noise management strategies

Eventually, a complete noise strategy assessment involves estimates of the size of the cost impact associated with a noise management strategy. If aircraft restrictions increase airline operating costs, a cost analysis of the magnitude of these effects is required. The preparation for this level of detail requires some understanding of where to look for cost impacts and an understanding of underlying cost drivers. This knowledge of the "technology" of noise management strategy provides a framework for the manager trying to understand the relative merits of different approaches. Costs can also arise because an airport might be under-utilized because of the choice of noise strategies.

As illustrated in Table 1, noise management strategies can be placed into three groups: airport and airspace use strategies, aircraft operations strategies, and aircraft restrictions strategies. It is assumed that these groups of strategies share common cost and benefit impacts (although the magnitudes may differ depending on the specific strategy).

---

[a]Ldn is approximately equal to NEF-35. Both are highly responsive to changes in noise energy level and change relatively little with small to moderate changes in frequency of flights.

Table 1
Airport noise strategy impacts

	Costs	Benefits
Airport and airspace use	Airline operating costs, fuel crew time, flight time, capital depreciation Reduced airport capacity Higher air traffic control costs and lower productivity Pilot load Airline scheduling and aircraft positioning Passenger time: timing of flights and frequency of flights affects desired versus actual travel time	Noise concentrated in corridor – more noise but affecting fewer people Reduced noise concentration, broadly shared over community Reduced noise for SENEL and flight frequency Reduction noise at sensitive times
Aircraft operations	Increased pilot workload Reduced airport productivity Reduced airport capacity Airline less flexible in use of fleet Reduced productivity of airline fleet	Reduced noise Reduced noise for small section of community Small noise reduction over broad community
Aircraft restrictions	Cost to airline of reduced capital use and scheduling Reduced system efficiency Reduced air traffic control productivity to position aircraft Increased cargo/courier costs with increase in rate of depreciation of stage II aircraft Affects competitive advantage between different carriers	Significant reduction in noise everywhere (even where it has a low marginal benefit)

5.2. Assessing the benefits of noise management strategies

The other half of the noise management strategy calculation concerns the benefits that flow to airport neighbors from the different strategies. To measure the benefits requires that a value be placed on a reduction in noise exposure as well as a measure of the amount by which noise exposure has changed. It is a relatively straightforward task, using one of the noise metrics described earlier, to measure the change in noise exposure.[a] However, there is no market in which noise is bought and sold, and thus a market price cannot be directly measured. A number of techniques have been proposed, and used, to estimate a value for quiet to measure and understand how it impacts people. The "value" could be an index of disturbance or amount of disturbance. Another approach advocated by economists, as well as others, is to place a monetary value on noise. These can be measures of willingness to pay to avoid noise exposure or willingness to accept noise if compensated.

The literature on noise annoyance documents a variety of activities that neighbors of airports find are negatively affected by airport noise. Bullen and Hede (1982) find that conversation, sleep, television watching, entertaining, and outdoor leisure are named by those affected by airport noise as activities that are disturbed. Noise disturbance depends on several factors. Personal characteristics affect an individual's overall reaction to noise; an individual's previous experience with noise, their expectations about noise, and their attitudes toward the airport all play a role. These differences mean that the tendency to be disturbed by a given amount of noise will be a distributed variable.

Analysts interested in measuring the value (or cost) of noise exposure rely on a number of statistical and non-statistical techniques. These include hedonic price analysis, choice models, and appraisals. The last is a non-statistical technique while the first two use regression technique. A popular method is "hedonic price analysis." This technique treats products or services as having multiple attributes or characteristics. The demand is not for the product but for characteristics. Products are considered nothing more than bundles of characteristics. Characteristics bundled in different ways or proportions yield different products. In the case of noise it becomes one more characteristic associated with a house along with lot size, number of rooms, and square footage, for example.[b] The noise variable can measure the characteristics of noise, how loud it is on average, how frequently it arises, and how variable the events are. These are all properties of noise at a particular location. Collecting information on housing characteristics, including noise and other location attributes and the selling prices of these homes, will provide a data set that can be used in a regression to develop a measure of noise impact or noise depreciation.

Choice models are designed to examine an individual's selection of housing location, which may then be seen as depending partially on the noise characteristics at that location and other locations. These ideas are familiar because they also form the theoretical underpinnings of hedonic price analysis. The theory of consumer discrete choice shows how to model the probability that a consumer will choose a particular alternative from among a finite set. In particular, it models the connection between the probability and the individual's utility for the alternative, which in turn is related to the alternative's characteristics. When this model of choice is combined with an appropriate

---

[a]In any measurement, assumptions have to be made regarding the number and type of aircraft using the airport or overflying a particular location. This may cause some variance between locations. As with any application there is a tempering of principle with practicality.

[b]Hedonic analysis was introduced by Rosen (1974).

error theory for the observed choices of consumers, the result is an empirical model that can reveal information about the individual's utility function. The individual's "value" of noise can be estimated in principle from a sample of observed choices.

To estimate individuals' values of noise, which are expected to differ depending on personal traits, requires several observations. If it is possible to assemble enough observed choices, and there is information on the attributes of the rejected choices, it is possible to use regression techniques to develop a measure of noise valuation. This is termed a revealed-preference technique because the observed choice by the individual "reveals" that person's preferences for the bundle of house and location attributes.

There are also experimental methods that can be used to generate data regarding people's choices. This approach is called stated-preference analysis, because presented with a set of alternatives, people state their selection.[a] This experimental method, using either conjoint analysis or contingent valuation techniques, uses a sample of individuals who state what they would do in a variety of hypothetical choice situations that are designed to reveal information about the value of noise. Respondents' information about the alternatives from which they can choose is experimentally manipulated to force them to make trade-offs between the price of a house and the amount of noise they can expect to experience. In principle, their stated choices in the experiment can reveal information about the respondents' willingness to pay a higher price for a quieter location.

The non-statistical approach is to use appraisal methods. In this case, experienced real estate appraisers familiar with a location or community are used to assess what their experience has provided. These techniques are also termed Delphi methods or expert assessments. There have been a relatively few such studies published using this technique.

The vast majority of studies of valuing noise have used hedonic analysis of housing prices, which is an indirect method that rests on decomposing the price of housing into the quality contribution associated with noise or its components. The intuition behind the application of the hedonic approach to housing markets is relatively straightforward. Each house can be viewed as a basket of attributes. The price of each basket will be determined by the particular combination of attributes it displays. Naturally, it would be expected that properties with more desirable attributes would command a higher price, and those with a greater number of less attractive attributes to command a lower price. The price of the house will be determined by the supply of houses with differing attributes and the preferences of consumers. By being able to control for differences in the housing attributes

---

[a] Stated-preference techniques have been around for a long time, and are used particularly in marketing.

and neighborhood characteristics, the separate impact of noise exposure on house prices (value) can be established.

The connection between cumulative measures of airport noise and real estate prices has been explored for a number of North American and European airports. The relationship between noise exposure and house price is generally expressed in terms of a noise depreciation index (NDI). The NDI measures the percentage depreciation for each unit increase in noise exposure. In a 1991 study of the housing market around Pearson International Airport in Toronto Canada, Gillen and Levesque (1992) found for single-family housing, a 1% increase in the NEF measure reduces housing values all else held constant by an average 0.26%. There have been a large number of hedonic studies around the world. A sample of the numerous hedonic studies with their measured NDI are provided in Tables 2 and 3.

Aviation noise appears to reduce prices of otherwise similar houses between 0.4 and 0.9% for each NEF decibel. In order to apply these values to measure the value of quiet, information on housing, location, and resident characteristics would be needed. The macro conditions affecting the housing market would also need to be taken into account. Another consideration is that the NEF measure is a

Table 2
Example US hedonic studies

Study	Location	Type of noise	Means of valuation	Results (NDI)
Gamble et al. (1974)	Bogota	Road traffic	Hedonic house pricing	2.22
	Rosendale			0.24
	North Springfield			0.21
	All three areas			0.26
Price (1974)	Boston	Aircraft	Hedonic house pricing	0.83
Maser et al. (1977)	Rochester, NY:	Aircraft	Hedonic house pricing	
	City			0.88
	Suburban			0.61
Nelson (1979)	San Francisco	Aircraft	Hedonic house pricing	0.58
	St Louis			0.51
	Cleveland			0.29
	New Orleans			0.4
	San Diego			0.75
	Buffalo			0.52
Nelson (1980)	Review of existing studies	Aircraft	Hedonic house pricing	0.62
Palmquist (1984)	Kingsgate	Aircraft	Hedonic house pricing	0.48
	North King County			0.30
	Spokane			0.08
Nelson (1980)	Review of existing studies	Road traffic	Hedonic house pricing	0.40
O'Byrne et al. (1985)	Atlanta (1980)	Aircraft	Hedonic house pricing	0.69
	Atlanta (1970)			0.64

Table 3
Example non-US hedonic studies

Study	Location	Type of noise	Means of valuation	Results (NDI)
Mieskowski and Saper (1978)	Toronto, Canada	Aircraft	Hedonic house pricing	0.52
Abelson (1979)	Marrickville, Australia Rockdale, Australia	Aircraft	Hedonic house pricing	0.40 0.50
McMillan et al. (1979)	Edmonton, Canada	Aircraft	Hedonic house pricing	0.51

Hall et al. (1982)	Toronto, Canada:
	  Arterial
	  Expressway
		Road traffic	Hedonic house pricing	
				0.42
				0.52

Quinet (1969)	Review of existing studies	Road traffic	Productivity loss and annoyance	0.1% of GDP
Hidano et al. (2002)	Tokyo, Japan	Road traffic	Hedonic house pricing	0.70

Uyeno et al. (1993)	Vancouver, Canada:
	  Detached houses
	  Condominiums
	  Vacant land
		Aircraft	Hedonic house pricing	
				0.65
				0.90
				1.66

cumulative metric, and thus these results do not reveal anything directly about the individual effects of loudness and number of events, information that would be useful in examining the benefits of alternative noise management strategies. A better approach to investigate the loudness and frequency effects involves allowing the two to be estimated independently. The results can then be compared with those based on the NEF to determine which is the statistically superior model of noise effects in housing markets.

6. Summary

Aircraft or road traffic noise represents an externality since it may impose a cost on members of society who do not generate it: residents located near airports are forced to consume noise while passengers who use the "quiet" pay nothing for it. Because noise is not priced in any market, there may be too much of it, just as there may be too much air pollution because the atmosphere is not priced. Whenever a resource has no price, it is considered not to be scarce and hence is used intensively.[a] Quiet, like air and water, is a scarce resource, and too much may be lost if noise has no price; we may have too many flights or too much highway traffic.

The solution to the noise problem is to manage it, as with any scarce resource. The amount of noise to be accepted, the supply of noise, is a community decision based on community values and economics. The idea of noise capacity is central to the solution of the noise problem. It is the measure of the total amount of noise that the community is willing to accept. It depends on the solution to two problems: the development of a behavioral noise index that establishes the community valuation of quiet, the costs of changing the amount of quiet, and the community's willingness to accept such change; and the development of a market device that results in a negotiated definition of the noise capacity of the community and a mechanism to allocate that capacity efficiently.

Legal actions to reduce noise often focus on its economic consequences. The question of value arises when compensation is sought. But noise management has largely ignored the question of value as a basis of policy. How much is a householder willing to pay to avoid the annoyance associated with noise? How is this value relevant to the practical concerns of establishing noise management strategies? Research shows that the economic cost of noise from the viewpoint of households and housing markets can be quantified.

The development of workable noise management strategies should consider the following points. First, provide benefits in reasonable proportion to the costs households incur. Although aircraft noise in residential areas is an economic cost, the noise management process must recognize that steps to abate noise also involve economic costs. Steps to manage aircraft noise in urban areas should aim to balance the benefits derived from noise abatement with the costs of abatement initiatives. Spending $10 on noise management for every $1 in benefits is no more justifiable than devoting insufficient effort to managing the problem. Abatement by means of reducing aviation or traffic activity also carries an economic cost, and these must be included in any economic assessment. Second, target solutions appropriately. For example, some neighborhoods may be more seriously affected by the frequency of overflights than by cumulative noise energy. Such communities would realize benefit more from flight restriction than from insulation. In other communities the reverse may be true. Noise management should measure the source of noise problems, and target programs accordingly. Third, distinguish short-term from long-term initiatives. Measures to reduce noise exposure may be effective in the short term. They are likely to be less effective in the long term, as growth leads event frequency to emerge as a dominant source of property depreciation, annoyance, and other costs.

A final consideration is the issue of property rights for quiet. In some jurisdictions a failure to manage the noise problem has implicitly placed the right to make noise with the airport and airlines. However, the quiet of a community is a public asset, like air and water, just as much as the airport is. The benefits of

---

[a]An economist would argue it would be used until the marginal benefit was zero.

airport capacity usually exceed associated noise costs. The recipients of these benefits should finance the costs of reducing any negative externalities.

References

Abelson, P.W. (1979) *Cost benefit analysis and environmental problems*. Farnborough: Saxon house.
Bullen, R.B. and A.J. Hede (1986) "Reaction to aircraft noise in residential areas around Australian airports," *Journal of Sound and Vibration*, 108:86–112.
DWG Research Associates (1990) *The management of airport noise. Report to Transportation Development Centre*. Montreal: DWG Research Associates.
Federal Aviation Administration (1985) *Aviation noise effects*. Washington, DC: Federal Aviation Administration, Department of Transportation.
Gamble, H.B., O.H. Sauerlender and C.J. Langley (1974) "Adverse and beneficial effects of highways on property values," *Transport Research Record*, 508:37–48.
Gillen, D.W. and T.J. Levesque (1992) *Alternative methodologies for determining the impact and valuation of aviation noise: a survey of the applications*, Technical Report 89/02.
Hall, F., B. Breston and S.M. Taylor (1978) The effects of highway noise on residential property values. Hamilton: Department of Civil Engineering, McMaster University.
Hidano, N. (2002) *The economic value of the environment and public policy: a hedonic approach*. Cheltenham: Edward Elgar.
McMillan, M., B. Reid and D. Gillen (1980) "An extension of the hedonic approach for estimating the value of quiet," *Land Economics*, 56:315–328.
Maser, S.M., W.H. Riker and R.N. Rosett (1977) "The effects of zoning and externalities on the price of land: an empirical analysis of Monroe County," *Journal of Law and Economics*, 20:111–132.
Mieszkowski, P. and A. Saper (1978) "An estimate of the effects of airport noise on property values," *Journal of urban Economics*, 3:425–440.
Nelson, J.P. (1980) "Airport noise and property values: a survey of recent evidence," *Journal of Transport Economics and Policy*, 14:37–52.
Nelson, J.P. (1982) "Highway noise and property values: a survey of recent evidence," *Journal of Transport Economics and Policy*, 16:117–138.
O'Byrne, P.H., J.P. Nelson and J.J. Seneca (1985) "Housing values, census estimates, disequilibrium and the environmental cost of airport noise: a case study of Atlanta," *Journal of Environmental Economics and Management*, 12:169–178.
Palmquist, R.B. (1984) "Estimating the demand for characteristics of housing," *Review of Economics and Statistics*, 66:394–404.
Price, I. (1974) "The social cost of airport noise as measured by rental changes: the case of Logan Airport." Unpublished PhD dissertation. Boston: Boston University.
Quinet, E. (1989) *The social cost of transport*. Paris: OECD Directorate.
Roskill, The Honorable Mr Justice, chairman (1970) *Commission on the Third London Airport: papers and proceedings*. London: HMSO.
Uyeno, D., S.W. Hamilton, A.J.G. Biggs (1993) "Density of residential land use and the impact of airport noise," *Journal of Transport Economics and Policy*, 27:3–18.

Chapter 6

SAFETY

IAN SAVAGE
Northwestern University, IL

1. Introduction

The vast majority of lapses in safety in transport provision cause injury and property damage, but have negligible effects on the environment. However, there are occasions when the release of harmful freight pollutes the environment, and poses a health risk to bystanders. While the official terminology varies, these types of freight are usually referred to as "hazardous materials and wastes" or "dangerous goods." In the USA, the name is commonly shortened to "hazmats," which is the term used in this chapter. In addition, the term "release" will be used rather than "spill," as it more generically covers incidents involving solids, liquids, or gasses, as well as incidents involving fire or explosion.

Some of these releases occur after collisions or other types of crashes. (Note that safety professionals prefer the word "crash" rather than "accident.") However, many occur due to safety lapses that do not involve crashes and often are associated with loading and unloading of transport vehicles. These include ruptures of hoses, overfilling of tanks, valves that are not properly closed, and structural failure of tanks or other packaging. The foundation for the analysis of hazmat releases is understanding the incentives for firms to provide safe transportation. These issues are considered in a companion chapter in the *Handbook of Transport Systems and Traffic Control* (Savage, 2001). The current chapter provides a more detailed analysis of the subset of crashes or operational errors that cause negative spillover effects, called "externalities," on third parties.

2. Estimating the risks

2.1. The big picture

It is almost impossible to make risk comparisons across modes or across time. Data on the number and magnitude of releases are not reported in a consistent format across modes. In particular, for some modes, releases that occur during loading and unloading at customers' premises or occur due to leaks that are not related to crashes are not reported. Unlike passenger transport, where a common metric such as fatalities can be used, it is difficult to compare incidents when the magnitude and the nature of the damage to the environment varies depending on the material involved. Moreover, it is very difficult to obtain data on the amount of various materials shipped each year, making calculation of release rates unreliable.

However, some information is available from government reports. US rail statistics report that in 2000 in the USA there were 7000 cars containing hazmats involved in crashes. Just less than 15% of these cars sustained damage, and 75 released some or all of their cargo. These crashes, primarily derailments, led to 13 occasions when a total of 5,000 people had to be evacuated from the surrounding area. However, no fatalities were recorded and only one employee suffered a non-fatal injury due to hazmat exposure following a collision or derailment.

On US highways, federal data only relate to trucks engaged in interstate commerce. Crashes involving firms that only provide local transport are not recorded in a central database. In 1999, 2500 interstate trucks carrying hazmats were involved in crashes that were serious enough that an injury occurred or that a tow-truck was required. In 20% of cases there was a release of the hazmat, and on 45 occasions there were some fatalities, mostly when flammable liquids were involved (although it is not clear what proportion were caused by exposure to the hazmat *vis-à-vis* injuries from the initial crash).

The US Coast Guard reports that five incidents in 2000 resulted in 90% of the total accidental release of oil into US coastal waters. Two-thirds of the spillage came from pipeline leaks or storage tank ruptures on the shore. There were two vessel-based spills, one resulting from a barge being overfilled at a dock, and the other from the sinking of a large luxury yacht. Pipelines carrying liquids, primarily crude oil and oil products, suffered 147 incidents in 2000 leading to the release of 4.5 million gallons, or seven times that spilled into the sea. Gas pipelines were associated with 234 incidents, causing 37 fatalities as compared with only one fatality for oil pipelines.

The number of fatal injuries in the USA, totaling about 80, is a relatively small proportion of the 43 000 annual transport fatalities in that country. However, the number can vary markedly from year to year owing to a small number of rare but catastrophic incidents. High-fatality events in recent years in the USA include the 1996 crash of a commercial airliner near Miami with the loss of all 110 aboard, which was partly attributable to improperly packaged hazmats in the aircraft's hold. There have been other horrendous incidents elsewhere in the world in the past few decades, including the deaths of more than 200 in the explosion of a road tanker of propylene at a holiday camp in Spain in 1978, and the deaths by burning of more than 500 Nigerians in 1998 after thieves ruptured an oil pipeline. The same is true for the amount of environmental damage. The grounding of the

Table 1
Categorization, with examples, of hazmats (with cost per major rail incident from Dennis (1996) in parentheses)

Health hazard	Environmental hazard		
	High	Medium	Low
Poison inhalation	Anhydrous ammonia, chlorine (typically the environmental hazard is low, but this is not always the case) (US $1.6 million)		
Flammable/combustible	Phosphorus, styrene (US $4.5 million)	Acetaldehyde, fuel oil, gasoline (US $1.9 million)	Liquid petroleum gas (LPG), methanol (US $0.9 million)
Explosive			Ammonium nitrate, armaments
Radiological	Nuclear wastes		
Other hazard (e.g. corrosive)	Perchloroethylene, chloroform (US $17.2 million)	Acrylic acid, caustic soda (US $0.8 million)	Acetic acid, molten sulfur (US $0.7 million)
Not normally a health hazard		Crude oil	Asphalt

tanker *Exxon Valdez* in Alaska in 1989 led to the release of 15 times more oil than was spilled in US waters in the whole of the year 2000.

2.2. Health risks versus environmental risks

The risks posed by hazmats are very heterogeneous. It is useful to think in terms of a matrix that plots the risk to the environment on one axis, and the risk to the health of humans on the other. Such a matrix, with examples, is shown in Table 1. This table is an expansion of a table in Dennis (1996), where the health risk is based on standard US Department of Transportation classification, and the environmental risk is based on work by consulting engineers for a US railroad. (More detail on classification of materials is given in Chapter 39.) The extent of the environmental damage depends on whether the material evaporates with little damage, is a solid or pooling liquid (e.g. fuel oil) that is relatively easy to clean up, or is a liquid such as styrene that soaks into the soil and could possibly contaminate the ground water. The table is only a rough guide. The environmental impact depends on the precise chemical formulation of the product, the circumstances and location of the release, and whether after the release the product reacts with other materials or with naturally occurring substances such as water. Likewise, the health risks to bystanders vary. Incidents involving fire, explosion, or the release of poisonous fumes can cause a high level of localized health risk. In contrast, release of crude oil into the sea from a grounded oil tanker does not normally pose a significant threat to human health, albeit that the environmental damage can be severe.

2.3. Quantitative risk assessment

There is a large literature in which government agencies, consulting firms and academics have tried to quantify the risks. Because the environmental and health consequences vary so much, these quantitative risk assessment (QRA) estimates tend to be very specific, and often relate to the movement of a given quantity of a certain material between two points. Analyses of this type have practical relevance when shipments can be made by different modes with a variety of routes. QRA models follow the principles of "event trees" which build submodels and assign probabilities to different stages in the chain of events by which a relatively routine crash or operational error can turn into a major disaster (Rhyne, 1994; Nicolet-Monnier and Gheorge, 1996) (see also Chapter 39). Typically a QRA model will include some or all of the following branches in the event tree:

(1) the probability that a crash or an operational error occurs;
(2) the probability that in the incident there is a loss of containment of the hazmat;
(3) the rate of release of the hazmat from its container;
(4) the probability that an external ignition source exists or a fire occurs simultaneously with the release, which might lead to explosive or flammable products igniting or a "boiling liquid–expanding vapor explosion" (BLEVE) occurring;
(5) the physical properties of the material, and models of how it disperses;
(6) the geography, wind speed and direction, or currents at the time of release;
(7) a model of individual health impacts that depends on the land use around the site of the release;
(8) a model of environmental impacts.

In theory, QRA should be able to produce estimates of both health impacts (steps 1 to 7) and the environmental impact (step 8). However, full application of QRA to environmental impacts is relatively new. It is perhaps not surprising that the severe health consequences of some hazmats have attracted the most attention in a field that is only about 20 years old.

QRA has so many steps, assumptions, and submodels that there is plenty of opportunity for competing models to produce differing answers. The University of Waterloo in Canada held a conference in 1992 that included an exercise where rival teams used their own models to estimate the risks of transporting three different hazmats (chlorine, LPG, and gasoline) by both rail and truck in a given 100 km corridor (Saccomanno and Cassidy, 1993). The purpose of the conference was to try to identify best practice for the various parts of the QRA model. When measured in terms of expected annual fatalities, the results from the various models varied by orders of magnitude. The ratio of the highest to the lowest estimate for each hazmat/mode pair varied between 10 and 300! Moreover, in the transport of chlorine, the teams disagreed about the relative safety of rail and truck.

Yet the variability in results is to be expected. Analysts really cannot predict precisely where a release will occur, nor its magnitude and impacts. Therefore, unlike a QRA of a fixed facility such as a chemical plant, it is difficult to generalize on the number of people exposed and the physical characteristics of the site of the release. A release on a bridge or in wetlands can have considerable effects on water supply. A fire in a tunnel or other enclosed location is more serious than in an open, easily accessible, location. The effects of a maritime oil spill will depend on the proximity of the coast, direction of currents, presence of flora and fauna, the strength of the waves, which will break up the oil, and the amount of sunlight, which affects evaporation.

QRA is based on an event tree which can have multiple outcomes, with different probabilities. Consequently it provides information on the full range of possible outcomes, along with their associated probabilities, and not just a single most-likely outcome. The former information is usually displayed using an "FN" curve. This curve is plotted on a graph where the vertical axis shows the probability (or the frequency per period of time) and the horizontal axis is the magnitude of the consequences. The latter axis is usually denominated as the number of people killed, but in principle it could be the amount of material released. Both axes are plotted on a logarithmic scale to accommodate the large range for both variables. The FN curve shows the probability that an incident of a certain magnitude or greater occurring. Consequently, the curve will always be downward-sloping (or possibly flat for limited ranges), as illustrated in Figure 1. The precise intercept, slope, and shape will vary depending on the nature of the risk.

The FN curve reflects the fact that while most hazmat incidents involve few, if any, fatalities and limited environmental damage, there are "doomsday" predictions of low-probability incidents that could cause mass destruction and a high number of fatalities. It is not difficult to point to at least one example of a major disaster for each hazmat type somewhere in the world during the past century. While large disasters invoke morbid curiosity, not to mention public fear, one should not ignore the relatively numerous smaller incidents. A good example is maritime oil spills. While the legacies of the *Torrey Canyon* and the *Exxon Valdez* persist decades after the last bird or sea otter has been rehabilitated and the seashore cleaned, a closer look reveals a different story. A 2002 report by the US National Research Council revealed that 7.7% of the oil in the sea originates from

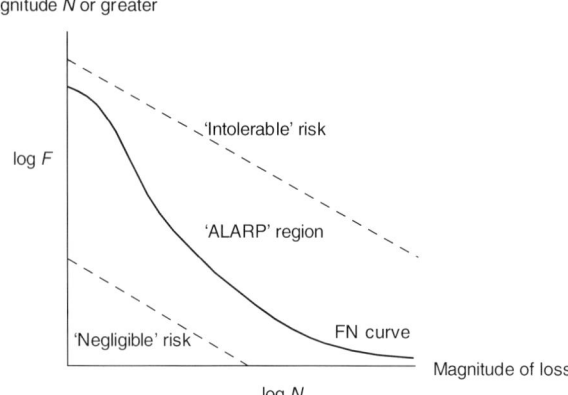

Figure 1. Example of an FN curve.

spills from tankers. However, three times that amount originates from discharge of bilge water, tank cleaning, and loss of ships' fuel oil (none of which are usually included in annual accident reports), spills in port associated with the rupture of hoses during loading and unloading, and failures of dockside tanks and pipes. The pattern carries over to other modes of transport. The probability of a hazmat release is far greater during the loading and unloading of a transport vehicle than it is *en route*, albeit that the quantities released are usually relatively small.

3. Risk assessment

3.1. Intolerable and negligible risks

How should an FN curve be interpreted? A 1983 report by the British Royal Society suggested some guidelines on the acceptability of health risks. There are some risks that are so "negligible" that they do not merit study and no remedial actions are necessary. Typically, this is thought of as risks that are more unlikely than the probability of being hit by lightning, which is an annual risk of about one in 3 million. At the other extreme are risks that are so large that they are "intolerable" and should be eliminated even at great cost. The definition of these risks is open to some controversy. For employees of transport firms the often-quoted intolerable annual risk is one in 1000, equivalent to some of the most hazardous occupations such as deep-sea fishing. The boundary for other parties is often quoted as an annual risk of one in 10 000. But there is a body of professional opinion that considers that this figure may be appropriate for customers or other people with some economic interest in the activity, but the risk for bystanders should be one in 100 000 or one in a million. To my knowledge, there are no equivalent metrics that deal with hazards that pose environmental rather than health risks. The dashed lines in Figure 1 illustrate how these boundaries may be represented in an FN diagram. The Royal Society report argues that if the FN curve falls beneath the lower dashed line then no further study is warranted. But if all, or parts, of it fall above the upper line then the risk (or at least certain aspects of it) should be ameliorated without regard to cost.

3.2. ALARP risks

The area between the dashed lines in Figure 1 is called the "as low as reasonably practical" or ALARP region. ALARP risks should only be reduced after society has balanced the risks and the benefits that the product confers. The fact that most risks fall in the ALARP region has prompted some critics to conclude that QRA by itself is not a particularly helpful public policy tool. Benefit–cost analysis is the tool of choice in the ALARP region, to provide insight and guidance in situations such as when hazmats could be shipped by a safer alternative mode or routing but at a higher cost, or when risk-reducing, but costly, regulations are proposed.

In an analysis, one side of the balance sheet is derived from the additional operational or capital expenses resulting from the proposed regulation or the alternative routing. Economists assume that these additional expenses will be passed along in higher prices to the ultimate consumer of the hazmat. Most consumers will therefore suffer reduced consumer surplus (the difference between what they are willing to pay and what they actually have to pay), and a few consumers will be priced out of the market. The other side of the balance sheet represents a valuation of the reduced risk of health and environment damage. The change in some types of damage can be measured relatively easily. These pecuniary losses include: the value of lost cargo; the costs of repairing transport vehicles and infrastructure; costs incurred in the clean-up of property proximate to the release; expenses incurred by emergency services; and compensation paid to third parties for damage to their health or property. (As with expenses, these financial items should be translated into their effect on the surplus of the ultimate user of the hazmat.) There are other categories of damages that are not normally measured in monetary terms, such as the pain and suffering from health problems, and environmental damage above and beyond that captured by the clean-up costs, and compensation paid to affected parties such as farmers and the fishing industry.

There is a small literature on the magnitude of the damages that are measured in monetary terms (see Chapter 39). Perhaps the most comprehensive is Dennis (1996), who collected data on financial payments by railroads after major releases of hazmats in the USA from 1982 to 1992. About a third of the payments were for environmental clean-up costs. Legal settlements with property owners and for personal injuries represented 56%, with the remaining 10% representing equipment damage, loss of cargo, and miscellaneous items such as evacuating neighboring residents. He found that the payments varied widely depending on the nature of the hazmat. The average payment, in current prices, for each of groups of materials that he investigated are shown in parentheses in the various cells of the matrix in Table 1. It is clear that payments escalate quickly for products with high environmental damage. Dennis notes that in his study the most damaging products are halogenated organic compounds (HOCs), which are commonly used as degreasing agents. These products "are denser than water and penetrate deeply into aquifers. In addition, the standards for remediation are stringent, since some HOCs are suspected carcinogens." Data are also available, from a consultant's report, on payments made following major oil tanker spills in the 1980s. The average cost, at current prices, of the environmental clean-up was US $22 per US gallon spilt, and legal settlements averaged US $125 per US gallon. Of course, the cost will vary depending on the circumstances of individual spills. The clean-up cost of the *Exxon Valdez* disaster is estimated to have been of the order of US $270 per US gallon spilled.

Transport economics has been at the forefront of benefit–cost analysis involving non-pecuniary losses. There is an extensive literature on the value that should be placed on averting a statistical death in excess of purely financial considerations such as medical and funeral expenses and lost wages. There is somewhat less of a consensus on the valuation of the pain and suffering from non-fatal physical injuries and adverse health consequences. Both of these issues are investigated in other chapters in this handbook and will not be elaborated on here. In much of the hazmat literature, the extent of the environmental damage is taken to be equivalent to the costs of the clean-up, site remediation, and the compensation paid to parties whose livelihood depends on natural resources. This has the limitation that animals, plants, or fish that are not cash crops appear to have no value. Moreover, there is a perverse implication that a sea otter only has value if it survives and requires time and effort to clean its fur. There is also the assumption that remediation is sufficient to restore the environment to the condition it was before the hazmat release. Clearly in some circumstances this will be true, but it is not always the case. Part of the outcry over the *Exxon Valdez* was motivated by the despoiling of pristine Prince William Sound and its ecosystem.

There has been a long history of economists trying to attach a value to places of natural beauty or to specific species of animals or plants (see Hanley et al. (2001) for a textbook introduction). Calculations are complicated by the fact that scientists are unclear about the long-term environmental impacts of the release of some substances. The early literature used a "revealed-preference" approach by arguing that the value of places of natural beauty was at least as much as the expense and time costs that individuals incur to visit these places. More recently, "stated-preference" questionnaire surveys have been used to obtain "contingent valuations" from samples of the population. The latter allow for the possibility that some respondents derive pleasure from the knowledge that a particular location or species exists, even if they have no plans to actually visit or to witness the species first hand. This is known as "passive use." Contingent valuation studies are controversial because of the difficulty in asking appropriate questions and the risk of inflated valuation.

4. Market forces and failures

The preceding sections have clearly identified that the environmental and health risks are not trivial. But do they constitute "a problem?" After all, society has come to depend on products and manufacturing strategies that require shipment of oil and other hazmats. Where does the balance lie between the benefits and costs? The market forces that combine to provide suitable levels of safety, and the possible reasons why markets may fail to perform properly, are discussed in a previous handbook in this series (Savage, 2001).

In an ideal world shippers would be knowledgeable about the safety of the transport companies that they contract with, and the shipper ultimately bears both the costs of providing safety and the damages resulting from crashes and releases of hazmats. In such a world, shippers of hazmats are given the correct incentives to choose the level of safety that is not only the best from their point of view, but is also socially optimal. As discussed in Savage (2001), several different safety levels may prevail in the marketplace. There are incentives for shippers of particularly hazardous materials to select transport firms that offer a high level of safety. Shippers of less-hazardous substances may prefer to choose somewhat less safe, but less expensive, transport. Whatever level of safety they choose, it will probably be less than the maximum level of safety that would be technically possible. This is because it is commonly assumed that beyond a certain level of safety, the marginal costs of further ameliorating risk will be larger than the environmental and health damages averted. While society has chosen not to avert some releases, this is a socially optimal decision because society prefers to bear these residual risks rather pay higher prices for the hazmat and the products that it might constitute.

4.1. Market failures

The power of market forces to determine levels of safety that society desires should not be underestimated. However, the power of the market will be lessened by one or more of the following six market failures:

- shippers are not aware of the safety performance of the carriers that they use;
- shippers have cognitive problems interpreting safety data on carriers;
- carriers make myopic safety decisions in order to "cheat" poorly informed shippers by posing as superior safety firms when in reality they provide poor safety;
- crashes or hazmat releases impose externality costs on innocent bystanders, which do not figure in the decision-making by shippers and carriers;
- the probability of a crash or hazmat release depends on the amount of care taken by the carrier and another party, such as collisions between trucks and automobiles, and the initiating parties may not consider the externality impacts on others;
- there is limited competition in the marketplace, which reduces the choice of safety levels available to shippers.

Failure 4 is the most germane to this chapter, and will be discussed in detail in the following sections. That is not to say that some of the other failures are not present. Pipelines are characterized by imperfect competition, and trucks carrying hazmats collide with other road users. Imperfect information (failures 1 and 2) is probably less prevalent in freight markets than it is in passenger transport. Hazmat shippers tend to be large corporations who make repeat purchases of transport services. Therefore, they tend to be informed purchasers who can act in a dispassionate way in trading off between the price and safety performance of individual carriers. Moreover, because of their "deep pockets" as large corporations as compared with, say, relatively small trucking firms, hazmat shippers have even more incentive to select carriers in which they have confidence, so as to avoid being a co-defendant in a lawsuit resulting from a release. Firms such as DuPont, the chemical manufacturer, were pioneers in establishing programs to vet the safety practices of trucking firms that they use. Nonetheless, there is always the possibility that an unscrupulous carrier may misrepresent itself to shippers and provide a lower level of safety than desired, yet be willing to do so because they can declare bankruptcy if a large release occurs.

4.2. The law and economics of externalities

Elementary economics suggests that a two-part market failure will result if the externality effects on bystanders are not incorporated (or "internalized") into the decision-making of carriers and shippers (Shavell, 1987). First, carriers do not take into account the losses incurred by bystanders when deciding on the level of safety to provide to shippers. Therefore they offer a lower level of safety than they would if they had to compensate the injured bystanders because there is now less incentive to provide higher levels of safety. Moreover, there is a second failure in that because carriers do not have to pay compensation they can offer a lower price to shippers. As a result, shippers will purchase "too much" output. Bystanders consequently suffer double harm. Carriers provide less-safe service, increasing the probability of a release, and also increase the amount of exposure to the risk.

This market failure has been recognized for centuries, leading to long-standing legal requirements that carriers pay compensation to bystanders. The analytical rationale for such payments was discussed by the Nobel prize winner Ronald Coase in a 1960 paper. His famous theorem indicated that provided the carriers and bystanders can bargain at negligible costs then the market failure could be removed irrespective of whether the carriers or the bystanders have the "property right." By property right he meant whether the bystanders have the right not to have their health or property injured, or whether the carriers have a right to conduct their business. In the former case, the carriers have to compensate injured bystanders, and in the latter case bystanders have to make payment to carriers to convince them to provide a higher level of safety. The distribution of costs and benefits between the parties differs in the two circumstances, but both are a market resolution of the underlying problem.

In reality, legal precedent has come down in favor of the property right residing with the bystanders. This is because the carrier of hazmats determines the probability of a release and can influence this probability in the most cost-effective way. While it is conceivable that bystanders might take precautions to protect themselves, say by building a barrier next to their property, the law does not normally look for this. (Albeit that in one famous opinion in a complex appeals court case the judge observed that the best use of land in a particular neighborhood was for a rail switching yard rather than for residential use, implying that the affected bystanders had exercised insufficient care by purchasing property next to the railroad.)

To claim legal damages for losses, bystanders have to file a "tort" law suit under the common law of negligence. The bystander has the burden of proof to show negligence on the part of the carrier. In the eyes of some courts, the bystanders have an even stronger position in that "strict liability" exists. This means that the carrier must pay for losses irrespective of whether negligence can be demonstrated. The legal precedent is an 1868 case in England where the water from a reservoir of a mill flooded a nearby mine. The current Restatement of Torts used in the USA provides for strict liability for "abnormal or ultrahazardous activities." It is unclear whether this applies to shipments of hazmats. In the USA the case law that supports the application of strict liability is a 1972 case involving the crash of a road gasoline tanker. Yet, there are other courts and jurisdictions that have held that bystanders have to demonstrate negligence by the carrier.

With a regime of strict liability, the market failure is removed (Shavell, 1987). The carriers now internalize the externality costs and use it in calculating the level of safety that they offer to shippers. Also, the expected costs of paying damages are incorporated into the price paid by shippers. Consequently, shippers are given appropriate incentives to act in a socially optimal way. For example, faced with high prices due to elevated externality risks, shippers can choose to use a safer mode or route, or decide to relocate their manufacturing plants and warehouses.

This optimal result need not necessarily apply under a regime of negligence. In these situations, the carrier only has to pay damages if it can be shown that they were negligent in providing less than "due care." One would hope that the courts would be able to define "due care" consistent with the levels of safety that society would wish a carrier of hazmats to provide. In this case, Shavell demonstrates that carriers have every incentive to provide the socially optimal level of safety. Unfortunately, by doing so they escape liability and will not have to incorporate the costs of externalities into their pricing to shippers. Therefore, a market failure exists because shippers will purchase too much transport, and bystanders will face increased exposure to possible harm.

This distinction may have limited practical effect if, in practice, legal settlements approximate strict liability. The standards of proof of negligence may be quite low. Evidence that a train derailed and spilled cargo on neighboring property may be sufficient to prove negligence on the basis of the legal principle of *res ipsa loquitur* ("the facts speak for themselves"). Even if injured bystanders are required to show evidence of negligence, this should be relatively easy to obtain. Most releases are "caused" because someone has done something wrong: an employee has deviated from operating rules; a piece of equipment was not inspected properly; or a particular safety device had not been installed or was not working.

5. Is liability sufficient?

It would seem that under legal standards of strict liability, or those that in practice approximate it, that carriers internalize most of the externality. They have to compensate bystanders for losses, and generally pay directly for the costs of clean-up and remediation. In theory, the market failure should be ameliorated. Yet, the considerable public unease with hazmat transport seems to suggest otherwise. Why is this? It is a combination of seven limitations of a liability regime.

5.1. Some types of financial harm are ineligible for compensation

Not all types of harm are recoverable. For many years, plaintiffs were unable to recover purely economic losses such as increased business expenses or lost revenue. However, there is a trend to allow such claims. Experienced lawyers suggest that carriers will typically offer to pay for costs incurred by businesses such as clean-up and damage to inventory, but will probably not pay for profits foregone due to the interruption of business. Individuals will be offered compensation, based on their actual hourly wages, if they are unable to go to work due to evacuation of their homes or workplace. People displaced from their homes are usually offered compensation for actual out-of-pocket expenses, but not for any emotional costs they may incur.

Moreover, claims are only permissible if the bystander is both proximate to the site of the release, and is also a foreseeable victim of the accident. Juries have to find an uninterrupted sequence of events from the carrier's actions to the bystander's harm. Major disputes occur when an intermediate event occurs between the initial negligent act by the carrier and the bystander. In a well-known US case, the owners of a barge that had spilled oil were found not liable to compensate a sailor on another barge many kilometers downstream who, several days later, slipped on the oil that had been washed onto his deck.

5.2. Emergency response costs are borne by the public

Hazmat releases usually require the attendance of emergency services. At the very least, ambulances and the fire department will attend. If an evacuation is necessary, police will be called to help in the evacuation and provide security for the affected area. Local schools may have to be opened to provide temporary accommodations for those displaced, and the Red Cross may be called to provide bedding and food service for the residents and emergency workers. Typically there is no legal liability for carriers to compensate the emergency services. Some US fire departments do have schemes whereby industrial concerns contribute after a major incident, while other fire departments take pride in the fact that no charge is made for their services. The trend in the USA is for more local authorities to charge for attendance by emergency services.

5.3. Non-pecuniary losses

Earlier in the chapter, several types of non-pecuniary losses were identified, comprising pain and suffering from health risks and the despoiling of places of natural beauty and injury to flora and fauna that are not cash crops. Plaintiffs are often able to collect compensation for the former, especially in the case of fatal injuries or long-term disablement. For the latter, there is often not an appropriate party who can file a law suit on behalf of deceased frogs or sea otters. The only legal remedy is for the courts to award punitive damages over and above compensatory damages. These can only be assessed when the court finds that the carrier has engaged in "willful or wanton conduct." It can be argued that uncompensated non-pecuniary losses loom large in the public's view of hazmat transport.

5.4. Liability is not accurately reflected in pricing

Shippers play a vital role in determining the risk to bystanders because they determine the quantity of transport produced, and hence the number of releases that occur. For them to make correct decisions, the prices charged by carriers should reflect the costs of clean-up and liability payments for the specific commodity. Some carriers may specialize in the carriage of only one type of hazmat (gasoline road tankers for example) and can easily build these costs into their pricing. However, most carry many different commodities. For an optimal market solution, carriers should charge different prices depending on the externalities associated with that particular product.

The differences in price may be large. Dennis (1996) extended his analysis of the cost of the clean-up of rail crashes to estimate the cost per car-mile. Products such as LPG that pose a low environmental hazard would only incur a risk premium of 0.6% on the basic cost of transport. But products that pose high environmental risks, such as phosphorus, would incur a premium of 5.2%, and chloroform a substantial 13.6%. If a carrier cannot or does not differentiate in this way, and charges a standard price mark-up to recoup total release costs and liability claims, then shippers are sent the wrong signal. Such a pricing scheme will result in the transport of too much extremely hazardous materials, and too little less-hazardous or non-hazardous materials. At the time of Dennis' study, some railroads had tried to incorporate specific costs into their rate structure, but the practice was not widespread or particularly refined.

5.5. Bystanders prefer zero risk

Bystanders rationally prefer zero risk of externalities, because they believe that the costs of risk reduction are borne solely by the carrier. Consequently they will always lobby for further risk reductions. Of course, it is not strictly true that bystanders do not bear the cost of risk reduction. These costs are passed onto shippers, and will be reflected in the prices paid by consumers of goods that directly or indirectly utilize hazmats. In many cases the consumers and the bystanders may be one and the same, and thus rationally they should trade off the risks and the benefits. However, in practice they may not recognize this connection. In some circumstances there may be concern that the benefits are widespread but the risks are disproportionately imposed on one group of people. This "environmental justice" argument has particular application to manufacturing

Ch. 6: Safety
111

plants or toxic waste dumps that may be located in poorer neighborhoods, but can also arise in transport applications such as the location of terminal facilities or the concentration of traffic on certain routes.

5.6. Risk perceptions may differ from reality

There is a school of thought that suggests that bystanders are intolerant of risks even if they are fully compensated for any losses, and are aware that as consumers they will ultimately pay for any risk reduction. This is because they perceive that the risks occur more frequently, and have more severe consequences than is really the case. Carriers and shippers make decisions on safety based on the amount of compensation that is paid for actual harm. But bystanders use other metrics to determine their attitudes to various risk, and these need not be in line with the pecuniary harms.

There is a large literature in which psychometric researchers have asked respondents to rate risks based on various characteristics (Slovic, 1993). Because most of these characteristics are collinear with each other, factor analysis has been used to boil these down to two major factors. The first is whether the probability and consequences of a risk are known in advance and generally understood. This is referred to as the "unknown factor." The second is that certain types of risk engender "dread." The dread factor is an amalgam of various risk attributes including whether the victim is exposed involuntarily, whether the risk involves a nasty drawn-out form of death, and whether the consequences can be mitigated by the diligence or skill of the victim when a risky situation occurs. Researchers have found that the higher the unknown or dread rating of a risk, the more that society is intolerant of it. In particular, there is a literature dating from the 1960s that suggests that people are far more intolerant of risks to which they were exposed involuntarily compared with risks that they had, in some sense, voluntarily decided to assume.

The perceptions of various risks can be plotted as points on a two-axis diagram, such as Figure 2. The empirical literature seems to suggest that the relevant hazmat risks fall in the shaded area. The exception is the risk perception of nuclear wastes, which appears in the top right-hand corner. The perceptions of conventional explosives appear at the bottom of the graph because the consequences of the risk are well understood. Many chemicals are toward the top of the graph because people doubt that even scientists fully understand the long-term consequences of exposure after a release. Because most respondents are involuntary bystanders to these risks, they tend to have high dread factor scores. This effect is heightened because the dispersion of poisonous fumes can endanger people who live or work in places that are distant from obvious sources of danger such as rail lines, manufacturing plants or major highways. Some high fatality scenarios such as

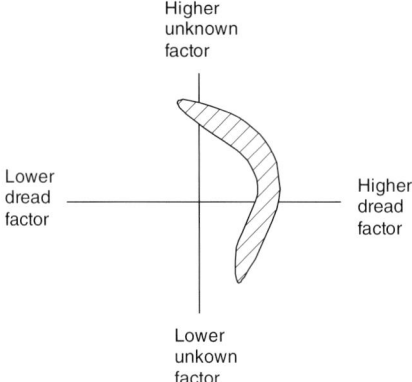

Figure 2. Location of hazmats in unknown-dread factor space.

explosions of road tankers engender very high levels of dread even though the nature of the risk might be reasonably well known.

The intolerance of hazmat risks is compounded by misjudgements of the frequency of risky events (Lichtenstein et al., 1978). The literature indicates two effects. The first is called "primary bias" and is the tendency to overestimate infrequent causes of death such as botulism, floods, and tornadoes and underestimate more frequent causes such as heart disease and cancer. The cross-over point where reality was closest to perception was for risks with an annual probability of one in 225 000 such as appendicitis. All hazmat risks are much smaller than this level. A second effect known as "secondary bias" suggests that people overestimate the frequency of dramatic and sensational events that claim multiple victims at one time, and downplay unspectacular events that claim one victim at a time. Hazmat releases would appear to suffer from an overestimation of frequency on both counts.

The overall effect is that society tends to regard hazmat risks as occurring more frequently and are of a more intolerable nature than would be warranted by an analysis of the actual probabilities and losses incurred. This means that society regards the expected externalities posed by hazmats to be larger than the actual legal settlements, and consequently views liability as providing insufficient incentives.

5.7. Liability is an "after the fact" remedy

Liability is inherently an after-the-fact, *ex-post*, form of risk control. Carriers only have to bear the externality cost after a release has occurred, is detected, and damages are paid for losses. There is an inherent assumption that rational carriers will take into account the frequency and magnitude of possible losses when deciding on their safety precautions and their pricing. Hazmat releases are rare events, and most carriers will not have direct experience of the consequences of releases. It is easy to argue that many carriers will be myopic in their decisions. Some will do so for avaricious reasons, hoping that a release will not occur, and seeking bankruptcy protection in the event of large adverse legal judgements. Other carriers may act in good faith, but not anticipate the possible environmental costs. After all, evidence earlier in this chapter demonstrates that experts differ by orders of magnitude in quantifying the risks. The implication of this and the other limitations of liability is that society may justifiably demand proactive regulations and controls on hazmat transport rather than passively accept that the problem will be taken care of by the operation of a legal liability regime.

6. Public policy

Even legal scholars argue that liability often has to be complemented by before-the-fact, *ex-ante*, safety regulation (Shavell, 1987). There has been a long history of public policy intervention in hazmat transport, dating back to early legislation dealing with the movement of explosives by, or for, the military. A convenient way to catalog the various possible public policy responses is to work sequentially through the various stages in the event tree of a QRA. That is to say, first look at policies that may affect the probability of a crash or operational error occurring, then those that reduce the probability of the loss of containment or slow the rate of release, and finally those that minimize the effects on the surrounding environment.

Clearly the hazmat problem will be mitigated by more general public policy on safety, which is discussed in a previous handbook in this series (Savage, 2001). If crashes or errors in general are reduced then externalities will fall. Sometimes the relationship is reversed. The presence of externalities motivates the promulgation of general safety regulation. For many freight modes, potential externalities are the primary market failure. If a freight train of non-hazardous materials has a wreck on a private right-of-way, it is certainly an important issue for the railroad, its customers, employees, and insurance company, but the public concern is less clear. The same is probably true if a ship carrying lumber breaks up in open ocean. But as soon as a plume of chlorine gas envelopes a small town or oil reaches the coastline, public policy is invoked. The implementing of comprehensive safety regulation of US railroads by the Federal Railroad Safety Act of 1970, while a response to generally deteriorating safety, was given impetus by a string of wrecks in 1969 involving ruptures of tank cars containing hazmats in the center of small towns.

While general safety regulation will affect the probability of a crash or operational error, the remainder of the QRA event tree is influenced by specific hazmat regulations. One strand of these regulations deals with ensuring that hazmats are contained following a crash or operational error. This is a design issue. The requirement by the US Congress following the wreck of the *Exxon Valdez* that oil tankers must be built with double hulls is supposed to reduce the probability of a release if there is a collision or a grounding. For many years a major factor in releases from rail tank cars was the tendency in a wreck for couplers of neighboring cars to ride up and puncture the tank. This risk can be mitigated by mandating the installation of "head shields" that protect the ends of tanks, and by designing the coupler so that its puncturing ability is reduced. Inlet and outlet valves can be designed to reduce the possibility that they are torn away in a crash. Other hazmats are carried in smaller packages or cylinders, and there are design issues regarding the robustness of these packages. The consensus is that packaging standards have been generally non-controversial as they typically specify the performance characteristics for the packaging and the specific design is left up to the industry and its suppliers. Finally, there are requirements to reduce risk by placing hazmat vehicles in the center of trains and by ensuring that products that would produce a particularly lethal combination if mixed, are not coupled next to each other.

For some hazmats the main danger is a post-crash fire. Even if the hazmat itself remains contained during the crash, there is the risk of a BLEVE if there is external heating. One solution is to require thermal insulation of tank cars and trucks. This ensures that the internal temperature does not rise above a certain point for a specified period of time despite the presence of external fire. Prompt attendance by fire departments can complement the insulation by extinguishing the fire or applying foam to undamaged tanks to keep the temperature in check.

Discussion of the fire department leads to the next mitigating intervention: the equipping and location of response teams such as fire departments to respond to hazmat incidents. Aside from the suppression of fire, these response teams can contain the rate of release and dispersion of liquid or solid hazmats, and apply some initial remediation. In addition, they work with police authorities to recommend evacuating parties who are in danger. The effectiveness of emergency response depends on the ability to quickly determine the nature of the hazmat involved and applying the proper procedures and precautions. Public policy has required the placarding of hazmat vehicles with information on the specific cargo and the hazards posed. There have also been requirements that vehicles contain detailed manifests and carriers provide a 24 h telephone service that emergency services can call to obtain information. Governments have also worked with industry to produce emergency response information that is provided to fire departments.

Fire departments are usually the first responders to hazmat releases. In locations such as large industrial cities, the departments are well trained and

Ch. 6: Safety   115

equipped to deal with chemical and other industrial fires. However, many serious truck and rail releases occur in small towns and rural areas where the fire department usually only responds to domestic and agricultural fires and routine highway crashes. In many cases the departments are staffed by volunteers. The extent to which additional training, protective clothing, special equipment, and remediation agents are provided to these departments is a costly public policy issue.

In some cases, a limited number of specialized hazmat response teams are formed. Some large shippers or industry associations may support hazmat response teams. An analytical issue is where these teams should be located so as to minimize average response times. There is a large literature on this subject, a literature that is interwoven with that on a related issue: the choice of routes for hazmats. Road transport obviously provides considerable flexibility, but rail often has several possible routes. Trade-offs exist between longer routes that increase the time that hazmats are in transport, and use lower quality roads, yet pass through less-populated areas. Public policy might use these analyses to mandate that hazmat travel be concentrated on a limited number of less-populated or less environmentally sensitive corridors to facilitate provision of emergency response teams. Models of this type are typically based on QRAs (for an introduction, with examples, see Abkowitz (1993) or Turnquist and List (1993) (see also Chapter 39). Such models can also be used for modal choice decisions. Sometimes it may be more desirable to move certain hazmats by road rather than rail because, while trucks might have a higher crash rate, they can be routed around populated areas whereas the railroad has traditionally operated through the center of towns.

7. Summary

Movement of hazardous materials is a fact of modern industrial society, and transport has an inherent risk of crashes and operational errors. While the probability of a loss of containment of hazmats is small, some materials pose considerable dangers both to humans and the environment. Because of the nature of some of these risks, psychologists have found that people tend to overestimate the probability and consequences. Owing to this and other factors, legal mechanisms that require victims to be compensated for actual losses are seen as inadequate to provide for the level of safety demanded by society. Public policy has intervened by working with transport firms on the packaging of hazmats, routes to reduce public exposure, and the provision, equipping, and training of emergency response teams. Analytically, the desirability of these policies can be determined using QRA models. These models are multifaceted and dependent on many submodels and assumptions. Rival models can provide very different results and divergent conclusions. They also tend to focus exclusively on the effects on humans. There is thus much work still be done on evaluating the probability and the consequences of hazmat releases on the environment.

References

Abkowitz, M. (1993) "Multiobjective policy analysis of hazardous materials routing," in: L.N. Moses and D. Lindstrom, eds, *Transportation of hazardous materials*. Boston: Kluwer.
Coase, R.H. (1960) "The problem of social costs," *Journal of Law and Economics*, 3:1–44.
Dennis, S.M. (1996) "Estimating risk costs per unit of exposure for hazardous materials transported by rail," *Logistics and Transportation Review*, 32:351–375.
Hanley N., J.F. Shogren, and B. White (2001) *Introduction to environmental economics*. Oxford: Oxford University Press.
Lichtenstein, S., P Slovic, B. Fischhoff, M. Layman and M. Coombs (1978) "Judged frequency of lethal events," *Journal of Experimental Psychology: Human Memory and Learning*, 4:551–578.
National Research Council (2002) *Oil in the sea III: inputs, fates and effects*. Washington, DC: National Academy Press.
Nicolet-Monnier, M., and A.V. Gheorge (1996) *Quantitative risk assessment of hazardous materials transport systems: rail, road, pipelines, and ship*. Dordrecht: Kluwer.
Rhyne, W.R. (1994) *Hazardous materials transportation risk analysis: quantitative approaches for truck and train*. New York: Van Nostrand Reinhold.
Royal Society (1983) *Risk assessment: a group study report*. London: Royal Society.
Saccomanno, F.F., and K. Cassidy, eds (1993) *Transportation of hazardous goods: assessing the risks*. Waterloo: Institute for Risk Research.
Savage, I. (2001) "Transport safety," in: K.J. Button and D.A. Henscher, eds, *Handbook of transport systems and traffic control*. Oxford: Elsevier Science.
Shavell, S. (1987) *Economic analysis of accident law*. Cambridge: Harvard University Press.
Slovic, P. (1993) "Communication, recreancy, and organizational effectiveness," in: L.N. Moses and D. Lindstrom, eds, *Transportation of hazardous materials*. Boston: Kluwer.
Turnquist, M.A. and G.F. List (1993) "Sitting emergency response teams; tradeoffs among response time, risk, risk equity and cost," in: L.N. Moses and D. Lindstrom, eds, *Transportation of hazardous materials*. Boston: Kluwer.

Chapter 7

AMENITY AND SEVERANCE

SUSAN HANDY
University of California, Davis, CA

1. Introduction

In 1998 the US Department of Transportation for the State of Texas, better known as TxDOT, won a court case that allowed the department to move forward with plans for an extension to State Highway 161 through Grand Prairie, a small city located about halfway between Dallas and Fort Worth and just south of the Dallas-Fort Worth International Airport. A neighborhood group had been battling this freeway in the courts for more than decade. At the core of the battle was the environmental impact statement (EIS), required for this project under the National Environmental Policy Act of 1969, and the adequacy of its assessment of the impacts of the proposed freeway on the surrounding community. The preferred alignment for the freeway as recommended by the EIS would take 9.9 acres from a well-used, 24.7 acre city park. The freeway structure, elevated as it passed next to the neighborhood and through the park, would project noise and shadows into the adjacent areas and create a barrier between the neighborhood and the park. Although it was clear that the proposal would reduce amenity in the community and increase severance between different parts of the community, the EIS provided little in the way of analysis of these issues. Nevertheless, the judge in the case concluded that the EIS reflected standard practice in transportation planning.

Techniques for assessing the impacts of transportation projects on amenity and severance in a community are neither well developed nor widely used. Interest in developing such techniques first emerged in the 1960s and 1970s in the wake of concerns over the impacts of freeway building on existing communities, but the challenge of defining these concepts, let alone measuring them, contributed to a lack of progress. In the absence of standardized techniques, amenity and severance are often ignored or at least underplayed in environmental impact assessments and transportation planning processes. As an appreciation of the importance of these concepts grows, however, the tools available for measuring and evaluating them have improved and examples of efforts to enhance amenity and reduce severance have proliferated. Although more basic research on the

Handbook of Transport and the Environment, Edited by D.A. Hensher and K.J. Button
© 2003, Elsevier Ltd

concepts of amenity and severance is needed, planners can find effective ways to address these concerns. This chapter defines amenity and severance, reviews the tools available to planners for assessing these characteristics, and presents examples of policies and projects designed to enhance amenity and reduce severance.

2. Defining the concepts

Both amenity and severance are characteristics of a community that are determined by the physical environment yet depend on the human response to that environment. Most people can tell you to what degree a community has amenity or whether it has experienced severance, but the assessments of degree and explanations of why will vary from person to person. Amenity is perhaps the more subjective of the two characteristics, but severance involves a significant perceptual component as well.

2.1. Amenity

Amenity refers to the quality of a place, the way it looks, sounds, smells, and feels, and it affects the way people experience a place. The aesthetic qualities of a place are an important part of amenity, but amenity is broader in concept. Amenity is determined both by the physical design of a place and the human activity that takes place there. A place that has amenity is pleasant, attractive, and agreeable, as well as convenient and comfortable. Transportation amenity comes in three forms: the amenity of the transportation system for its users, the impact of the community on the amenity of the transportation system, and the impact of the transportation system on the amenity of a community. In addition, amenity will vary for each transportation mode within the same community.

The amenity of the transportation system for its users depends on the qualities of vehicle interiors, stopping places, and pathways. For automobile users, the shape and upholstery of seats, the quality of the sound system, the smoothness of the ride, the lack of noise from the road, and the aesthetics of the car interior all contribute to the amenity of the experience. The design of the road also affects amenity, as does the availability of rest stops, gas stations, and other needed services along the way, and the design of parking facilities at the destination. For transit users the qualities of the bus or rail car and the design of bus stops or rail stations contribute to the amenity of the experience. For bicyclists and pedestrians the design of the pathway, including pathway widths, separation from vehicle traffic, the availability of shade, and the adequacy of lighting, is most important to amenity. In all cases, other users may also impact amenity. Drivers who cut in and out of traffic, bus riders who talk loudly, and bicyclists or pedestrians who hog the path all reduce the amenity of the experience for others, for example.

The design of the community also affects the amenity of the transportation system by influencing the view from the road, bus, train, bikeway, or walkway. The size, design, and placement of buildings, signs, and other structures relative to the pathway and the amount and type of landscaping found alongside the pathway contribute to a more or less pleasant experience. A train ride through an industrial area of a city does not offer the same amenity as a train ride through a forest, and a ride on a subway offers little in the way of a view of any sort at all. Human activity within view of the road may make the experience more interesting, though the refuse of human activity – graffiti, garbage, vandalism – tends to reduce amenity. These two forms of transportation amenity – the amenity of the transportation system as shaped by the design of the system and the design of the community – are of interest to planners because of their impact on travel behavior.

The transportation system also affects the amenity of a community in many ways. Transportation facilities represent a significant element of the built environment, accounting for a substantial share of land in urban areas, especially where abundant surface parking is provided. The pavement associated with these facilities impacts the appearance of the community and may help to increase ambient temperatures. Elevated structures, whether for roads or rail, also impact the appearance of the community and may cast shadows on surrounding areas and increase noise levels. When designed solely from the standpoint of function, these facilities tend to detract from the amenity of a community. When attention is paid to aesthetics in design, these facilities may add to the amenity of a community. The use of these facilities also affects the amenity of a community. Vehicle traffic, including cars, buses, and trains, adds to noise levels, reduces air quality, and threatens safety for the surrounding community, thereby reducing amenity. Pedestrian and bicycle traffic can increase the appeal of a place, thereby increasing amenity, or, depending on the nature of that traffic, decrease the appeal of a place, thereby decreasing amenity. This form of transportation amenity – the impact of the transportation system on the amenity of the community – should be a part of community impact assessments for proposed transportation projects and policies.

These connections between transportation and amenity are, of course, highly subjective. What for one person adds to amenity may for another person detract from amenity. Finding lots of other people out walking, for example, may add to the enjoyment of a walk for some but detract from the enjoyment for others by increasing the opportunity for or necessity of social interaction. What adds to amenity in one place may detract from amenity in another. An elevated train in downtown Chicago has a certain charm, for example, but would seem a noisy intrusion through an otherwise quiet park. This subjectivity makes an assessment of amenity challenging but no less important than the assessment of more objective characteristics of a community.

2.2. Severance

Severance refers to separation or partitions between people, between people and places, or between two places. The purpose of the transportation system is the opposite of severance: its purpose is to join, link, or connect one place to another, people to places, and people to each other. But sometimes the transportation system serves to sever rather than connect. Human communities are severed when a new facility, such as a freeway or a rail system, is built through an existing community, and local streets are lost to accommodate the new facility. Natural communities may be severed when a new highway is built along a new alignment through an undeveloped area. Such impacts are often referred to as the "barrier effect," and may be as much psychological as physical, as much perceived as real. However, the barrier effect and severance are not quite the same thing. In a community that grows up around an existing highway or rail line the transportation facility may serve as a barrier that impedes the creation of connections between people and places but it did not sever connections because none existed at the time it was built. Transportation projects can also contribute to severance by displacing residents and businesses, thus eliminating connections without necessarily creating a barrier.

Severance can also be understood through its converse, at both a physical and a social level. Connectivity is a physical quality of transportation networks that takes into account the number and directness of the connections between places served by a network. Good connectivity means that travelers have multiple, relatively direct routes to their destinations (Figure 1). Poor connectivity means few, relatively indirect routes to their destinations (Figure 2). Drivers have some level of connectivity via the road system to practically all destinations, at least within metropolitan areas. Transit riders, on the other hand, might find significant gaps in connectivity to parts of the region that are not served by the transit system. Pedestrians and bicyclists may also have connectivity to practically all destinations via the road system, though the poor quality of travel on the road system for these users often creates an effective barrier. As a physical concept, connectivity reflects the potential for movement through the transportation system but does not describe the way that residents actually choose to move through that system.

Community cohesion also represents the converse of severance but takes into account the social implications of physical changes. This concept is often defined as comprising the broader notions of shared values and common goals among members of a community. In a cohesive community, residents have a sense of belonging and feel a strong attachment to the community and their neighbors, and they make use of local facilities and engage in community activities. Although usually defined in social and economic terms, the physical environment plays a role in either fostering or hindering community cohesion in three important ways: by creating borders that help to define the community, by creating barriers that divide

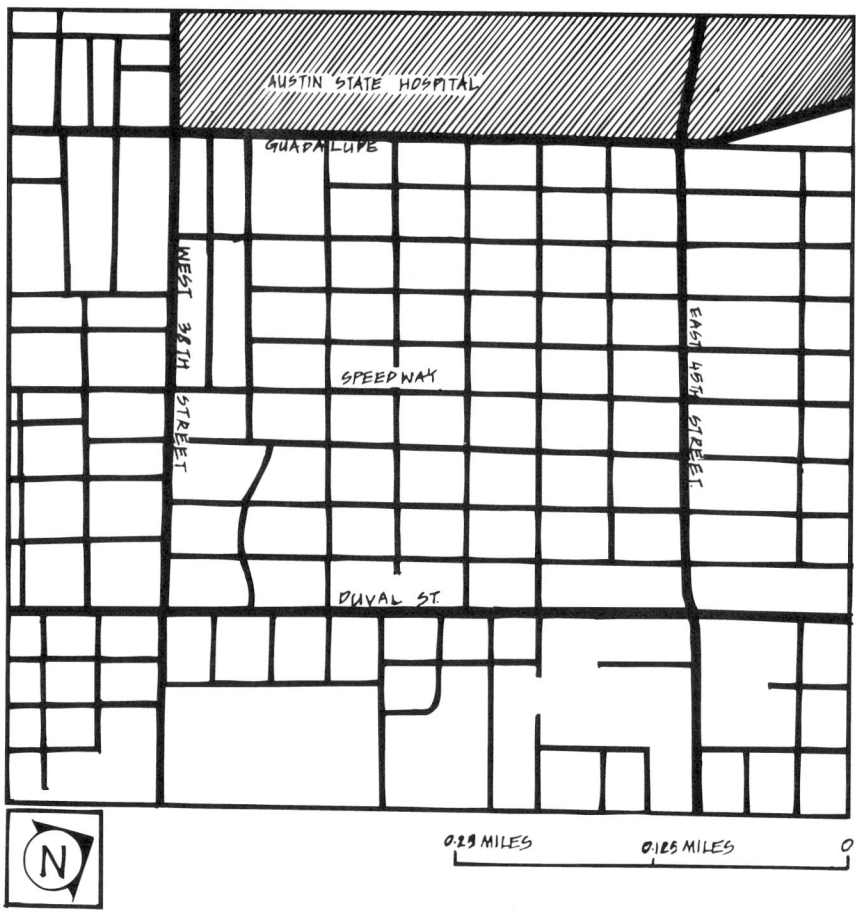

Figure 1. High-connectivity street network: Hyde Park neighborhood, Austin, Texas.

a community, and by creating gathering spots that foster community interaction. In these ways, transportation facilities affect the network of social interactions within the community. Roadways can serve as borders or barriers. Major arterials often help to define the boundaries of a neighborhood, for example, but projects to widen a road through an existing community or upgrade a surface street to a controlled-access freeway can create a barrier between two halves of a previously cohesive community. Streets within the community are also an important public space and can provide a place for residents to gather and interact. Boulevards and traditional main streets, for example, have long played this role in urban settings. Rail lines also can serve as borders or barriers, and rail stations as well as bus stops may serve to foster interaction in the community. Bicycle and pedestrian facilities also tend to foster interaction, and by doing so are less likely to create a barrier in the community. Whether transportation facilities will serve as borders, barriers, or gathering spots depends in part on how residents perceive and react to these facilities.

2.3. The connection between amenity and severance

Amenity and severance are relatively distinct characteristics of a community, yet one influences the other in important ways. First, a lack of amenity can help to

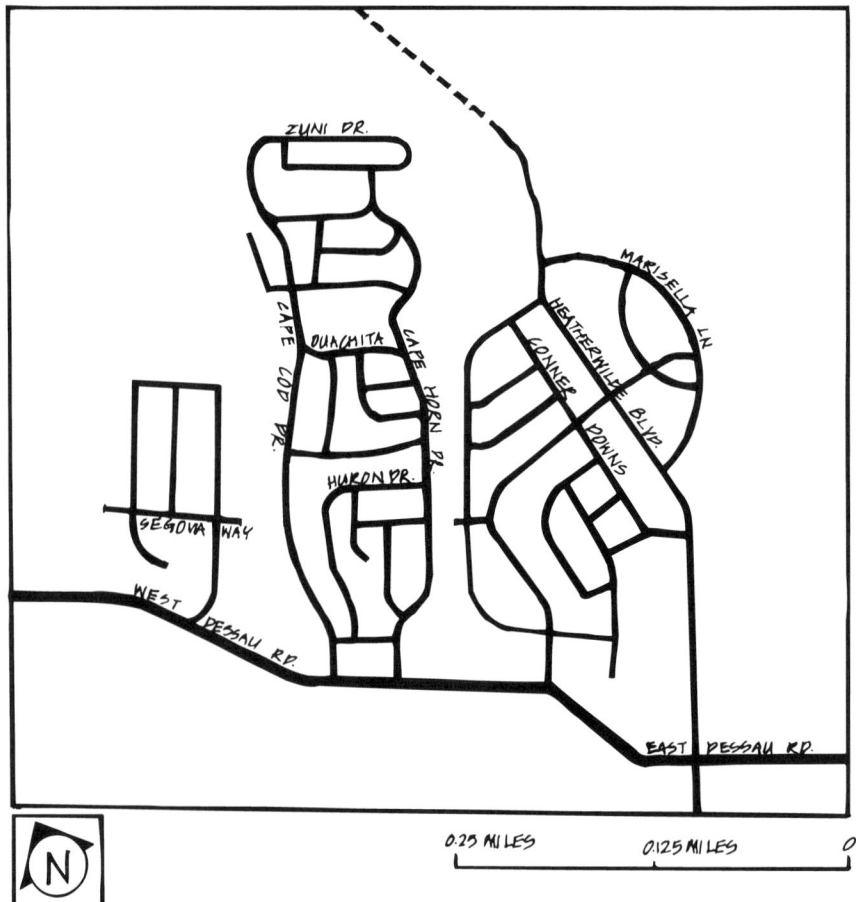

Figure 2. Low-connectivity network: Dessau Road neighborhoods, Austin, Texas.

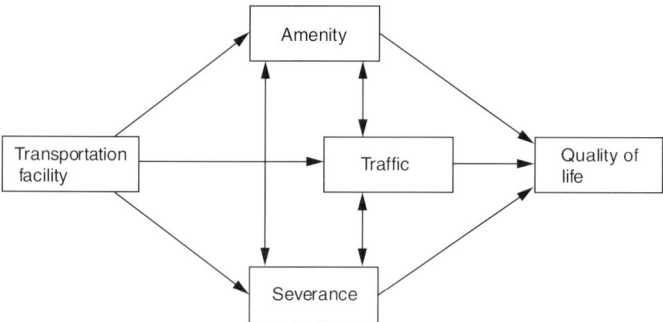

Figure 3. The relationships between amenity, severance, and traffic.

sever a community. A six-lane arterial street with no landscaping and poorly designed pedestrian crossings, for example, might serve as an effective barrier between two sides of a community, while a four-lane arterial street with mature landscaping, wide sidewalks, and pedestrian signals might help to link the two sides. Second, a project that increases severance often reduces amenity in a community. An elevated freeway that creates a barrier through a community, for example, increases noise levels, creates visual blight, and may make it harder for residents to get to community facilities, thereby reducing amenity from the standpoint of both aesthetics and convenience. In addition, both amenity and severance are closely tied to levels of traffic. High levels of traffic, for example, both reduce the amenity of a place and create an effective barrier. Appleyard's (1981) classic study of patterns of social interaction on three streets in San Francisco carrying low, medium, and high levels of traffic elegantly documents this effect. At the same time, amenity and severance both influence the travel experience and thus the choices that individuals make about travel and the traffic they generate. Amenity and severance thus shape the quality of life in a community both directly and indirectly through their impact on traffic (Figure 3). Although assessments of transportation projects are generally limited to the direct impacts of the projects on amenity and severance, a more thorough approach would trace these interdependencies to evaluate the overall implications for quality of life in the community.

3. Techniques for assessing amenity and severance

In order to consider amenity and severance within the transportation planning process, techniques for assessing these rather abstract concepts must be available to planners. The assessment of amenity and severance as a part of the transportation planning process generally involves three steps. First, the current level of amenity or severance must be determined. Second, the impact of a proposed project or policy on amenity or severance must be estimated. Third, the value of that impact to the community must be calculated, particularly if amenity and severance are to be incorporated into traditional cost–benefit analyses. All three steps can be challenging, although the third step is generally the most controversial. Some techniques skip right to the third step, making the first two steps implicit to the analysis.

Three important considerations guide the development of techniques for assessing amenity and severance: validity, practicality, and understandability. First, the measures used to represent amenity and severance must accurately reflect the concepts of amenity and severance. When the concepts themselves are vague, as is the case for amenity and severance, establishing validity is especially challenging. Second, the measures must be relatively easy to calculate with available data or data that are easy to obtain. Otherwise, the measures will not be practical for use in the transportation planning process. Finally, the measures must be relatively easy for the general public to understand, given the importance of public involvement in the planning process. Although most measures rate well on practicality and understandability, the validity of these measures rests more on intuition than on empirical testing. Publications on community impact assessment (e.g. Florida Department of Transport, 2000) and social impact assessment (e.g. US Department of Commerce et al., 1994) provide important guidance on techniques for evaluating impacts on characteristics such as amenity and severance.

3.1. Assessing amenity

Determining the level of amenity in a particular community is not a straightforward task. Amenity is an inherently subjective and multidimensional concept, and standard measures of amenity simply do not exist. The most obvious approach is to ask residents what they think of a place, how they would rate its amenity – a stated-preference approach. Another approach is to observe the choices that residents make and infer from their choices their evaluations of amenity – a revealed-preference approach. Both approaches offer the potential for determining the level of amenity and valuing a change in amenity in a particular community, but neither necessarily provides an accurate picture of actual preferences. In general, the techniques for valuing amenity are better developed than techniques for measuring amenity but they are also more complex.

A simple measure of amenity might take the form

$$A = w_1 C_1 + w_2 C_2 + w_3 C_3 + \ldots$$

where A is the overall amenity, C_i is a characteristic of a place that contributes to amenity, and w_i is a weight representing the relative importance of that characteristic

Planners must first calibrate this measure by determining what characteristics to include and what weights to assign them. A list of characteristics that may contribute to the amenity of a place is relatively easy to generate. The relative importance of these characteristics is not so easy to determine, however, and may vary significantly from person to person. One way to tackle this problem is to survey residents of the community or communities where amenity is to be evaluated. In the survey, residents can be asked to rate the importance of each characteristic, for example on a scale from 1 (not important) to 5 (very important). The average ratings can then be used as weights for the characteristics in a simple model for determining the overall amenity of a place based on its characteristics. A more sophisticated approach is to have residents rate the amenity of a sample of places representing a wide range of characteristics. These ratings are then used as dependent variables in a regression model, with various characteristics of each place as the independent, or explanatory, variables. The regression analysis indicates which characteristics are significantly correlated with amenity, and the coefficients estimated in the analysis indicate their relative importance. Factor analysis can be used to condense a long list of characteristics that potentially influence amenity into a smaller set of composite factors. This approach often improves the efficiency of the analysis when a large number of interrelated variables are involved. The model that results from the regression analysis can be used to generate measures of amenity in different places, at different times, under different conditions. In addition, the coefficients of the model can be transformed into elasticities that show the change in amenity that results from a given change in one characteristic or factor.

Two approaches to surveying residents about their ratings of amenity are now frequently used. In walk-around surveys, residents walk through the community, rating the amenity of different places within the community and identifying positive and negative characteristics. Community image surveys are an increasingly popular technique for eliciting preferences for different types of development from residents of a community using a slide show of images of different places. Although both approaches are often used as a public involvement tool rather than a measurement tool, they provide a way of systematically evaluating amenity. The version of the community image survey developed by the Local Government Commission (2002) involves a slide show of 40 different images. Survey participants are asked to rate each image on a scale of −10 to +10 depending on how much they like or dislike each image (such as those in Figures 4 and 5). The scores are then averaged for each image, to represent the collective evaluation of that image. The images are shown again along with the average scores, and participants are given a chance to discuss their responses. Both the community image survey and the walk-around survey approaches can be used to identify characteristics of places that contribute in positive or negative ways to amenity and for evaluating the overall level of amenity in a community.

A more rigorous form of stated-preference survey is increasingly used in transportation planning to assess the probable response to proposed policies or projects. In this technique, a series of scenarios are defined that vary with respect to a few key variables. Participants are given two scenarios and asked how they would respond. By systematically structuring the scenarios and the comparisons offered, researchers can determine the relative value participants place on different variables and the trade-offs they are willing to make between different variables. This technique can be used both to develop a model for measuring amenity and to assess the response to changes in amenity. In the first application, participants might be shown two images of places and asked which has higher amenity. Visual simulation can be used to create a series of images for use in the survey that vary systematically on only one or two characteristics at a time so that the effect of different characteristics on amenity can be isolated. In the second application,

Figure 4. How would you rate the amenity of this place on a scale of –10 to +10?

Figure 5. How would you rate the amenity of this place on a scale of −10 to +10?

participants might be given descriptions that include amenity characteristics of two mode or route options, for example, and asked which one they would pick. Again, the descriptions would vary systematically on only one or two characteristics at a time. In both applications, statistical analysis techniques are used to determine the relative importance of different characteristics in explaining amenity or responses to amenity.

In the planning process, it is often necessary to put a value on amenity, to measure the benefit of an improvement in amenity or the cost of a decline in amenity. Contingent valuation is another sophisticated stated-preference technique useful in estimating the value of amenity and is described in more detail in Chapter 19. This technique, which ascribes a monetary value to a public asset that is not sold on the market, is frequently used in environmental planning, though rarely in transportation planning. Although many different versions of contingent valuation have been developed, it commonly involves questionnaires that ask participants about their willingness to pay for a public asset, such as a healthy wetland, a beautifully designed bridge, or a traffic-free park. In this way, the cost of providing the asset can be weighed against the estimated monetary benefit to the community. The methodological issues associated with contingent valuation are complex, however, and the validity of the results is often questionable.

In revealed-preference approaches the value of amenity is inferred from observed or reported behavior. Mode choice models used in transportation planning are one form of this approach. These models, using data from travel surveys, estimate the probability of choosing one mode over others based on the characteristics of the different modes. Amenity is rarely incorporated into these models because data on characteristics that influence amenity are not generally available. If such data were available, mode choice models could provide an important tool for assessing the relative importance of amenity. Hedonic pricing models are another important form of the revealed-preference approach. These models estimate housing prices based on the characteristics of the housing unit and its location, and have been used to estimate the value of proximity to a transit station or to a freeway, variables that represent access to transportation but also the impact of transportation on amenity. The development of both mode choice models and hedonic pricing models requires a level of statistical expertise beyond that found in many planning agencies, however.

3.2. Measuring severance

Severance can be measured at two levels: the physical environment, and the social response to the physical environment. Measures at the level of the physical environment are considerably more straightforward and objective than measures at the level of the social response to that physical environment. Measures of the converse of severance are more common than measures of severance itself.

Physical barriers such as freeways or rivers that create discontinuities in the transportation network are easy to identify. Barriers created by high levels of traffic or by low amenity or other perceptual factors can be more subtle. One indication of such barriers is relatively low volumes of traffic – pedestrian, bicycle, or vehicular – crossing a particular street or passing through a certain area. The key to this approach is to find a suitable benchmark against which to compare the volume of crossing traffic, such as the volume of traffic within the areas on either side of the suspected barrier. Another approach is to survey residents about their usual destinations and travel routes. By mapping their responses, it may be possible to identify streets that effectively serve as barriers. These techniques work well for before-and-after studies of the impact of a transportation project, but are not easily used to predict the impact of a project.

Several different approaches have been used to measure the connectivity of the street network (Handy et al., 2003). Simple ratios of the number of intersections per mile of street in the network or of streets per square mile of area can give a basic indication of the connectivity of the network. The ratio of the distance between two points via the street network to the straight-line distance between the two points is perhaps a more valid measure of connectivity but also one that is hard to implement in practice. Geographic information systems can facilitate the calculation of both network and straight-line distances, but a rationale for the selection of a sample of points in the network must be devised. In the USA, two other measures of connectivity have been used by cities to establish connectivity requirements for new development. The first is simply the average block length or the distance between streets: shorter block lengths are correlated with a greater number of intersections, which generally leads to greater connectivity. The second is a "connectivity index," calculated as the ratio between "links" (street sections between intersections) and "nodes" (intersections and cul-de-sacs). The higher the index, the higher the assumed connectivity. Using any one of these connectivity measures, the impact of a transportation project on severance can be calculated as the difference in connectivity with and without the project.

The value of connectivity for drivers can be estimated in a variety of ways. One approach is to estimate the change in average travel distance that the change in connectivity will produce. For a small area, the change in travel distance can be estimated manually or using the network analysis capabilities of a geographic information system for a sample of points in the network. The sample must be carefully selected, however, so as to accurately represent the range of impacts on travel distance. The overall estimated change in travel distance can then be converted to a monetary value using standard cost-per-distance assumptions. For large-scale changes in connectivity, such as the construction of a freeway, the impact on travel distances for freeway users and for local traffic can be estimated directly using a regional travel demand forecasting model. However, the model must reflect enough detail in the local street network that increases in travel distances for local traffic are accurately estimated. Again, the changes in distance can be converted into monetary values using standard cost-per-distance assumptions. The impact of connectivity on travel time rather than distance can also be used in these calculations, although assumptions about the value of time can be problematic. The value of connectivity for bicyclists and pedestrians is less easily measured, not only because the cost-per-mile is not readily quantifiable but also because decreased connectivity may lead bicyclists and pedestrians to forego trips altogether. For these users, willingness-to-pay approaches, described above, may prove more useful.

Community cohesion has been measured in a wide variety of ways by researchers, but not all of these measures are useful for planning practice. Data on the use of community facilities, membership in local organizations, the tenure of community residents, the homogeneity of the population, the share of households that are families, and residential and commercial vacancy rates can be used as indicators of community cohesion. Surveys of community residents can be used to determine the degree of identity with the community, desire to stay in the community, and satisfaction with the community. Observations of activity within the community can also be used to assess community cohesion. None of these indicators on its own is likely to produce a complete assessment of community cohesion, so a multifaceted approach must be used. Estimates of the impact of a project or a policy on community cohesion are trickier than estimates of the impact on connectivity, as they require a prediction of how these social indicators will change in response to the project or policy. Surveys or focus groups with residents and interviews with community leaders can serve this purpose, but residents and leaders may find it hard to say how they will respond to the project in terms of these indicators.

Placing a value on community cohesion is even trickier. Contingent valuation techniques, such as the willingness-to-pay approach, described earlier, are hard to apply to community cohesion. According to some researchers, community cohesion fosters economic opportunity and may thus have measurable economic value. Still, determining just what share of the local economy can be attributed to community cohesion is not easy.

3.3. Incorporating amenity and severance into composite measures

Planners often use what might be called composite measures that reflect a variety of characteristics of a place. Aspects of amenity and severance are not always included in these measures but they often could be. Two types of composite measures in particular offer a promising opportunity to bring concerns about amenity and severance into the planning process: accessibility measures and measures of the pedestrian or bicycle environment.

Accessibility can be defined as the ease of reaching needed or desired activities. Measures of accessibility generally incorporate both an "attractiveness" element and an "impedance" element. The attractiveness element reflects the qualities of the activities and the destinations where they are found and is often measured in terms of the amount of activity at a particular destination. The impedance element reflects the qualities of the transportation system that connects the traveler to potential destinations and is often measured in terms of travel cost. Amenity and severance both play an important role in determining accessibility, yet are rarely incorporated into such measures because the data needed to do so are rarely available (Handy and Clifton, 2001a). Amenity affects both attractiveness and impedance, the former by influencing the appeal and convenience of potential destinations and the latter by influencing the experience of travel and thus the perceived travel cost. Severance affects impedance more directly than amenity and may work to increase impedance or to eliminate potential destinations altogether. The use of accessibility measures in transportation planning is growing.

Measures of the quality of pedestrian and bicycle environments are also increasingly used in transportation planning. These measures are generally developed using relatively simple techniques, such as professional judgment or simple stated-preference surveys, to determine what factors to include and what weights to give them in the measure. For example, the advocacy group 1000 Friends of Oregon developed a "pedestrian environment factor," or "PEF," for the Portland area that combined ratings of sidewalk continuity, topography, ease of street crossings, and the type of local street network (grid versus cul-de-sac) using equal weights (Parsons Brinckerhoff Quade & Douglas, 1993). The US Federal Highway Administration developed a "bicycle compatability index" by asking a sample of bicyclists to rate videotaped images of different bicycle routes. Regression analysis was used to create an equation that incorporates nine different variables, weighted by their regression coefficients, that reflect the design of the street, the nature of vehicle traffic on the street, and the type of development along the street (US Federal Highway Administration, 1999). More recently, the US Department of Transportation published a "bikeability checklist" that residents can use to assess the quality of the bicycle environment in their community. This checklist includes numerous amenity factors, including debris, lighting, and traffic, as well as severance factors, such as the abrupt ending of a bike path (US Department of Transportation, 2002). Measures like these provide planners with a tool for evaluating the overall quality of a place as determined by elements of amenity and severance.

4. Policies to improve amenity and reduce severance

4.1. Improving amenity

Amenity has long held an important place in transportation planning. Aesthetic concerns were given a high priority in the design of the mass transit and highway systems built in the first half of the twentieth century, and although function was often given greater weight over form in the decades following World War II, aesthetics and convenience were not ignored in the design of the new rapid transit and freeway systems. For example, in 1963, California established a scenic highway program with the goal of adding to the pleasure of the traveling experience and boosting the tourist economy (California Department of Transportation, 1996). In the same year, the state department of transportation hired the architect Mario Ciampi to design aesthetic structures for the new Junipero Serra Freeway (Interstate 280) along the San Francisco peninsula. Officially labeled by the state as "the world's most beautiful freeway," this split-level facility was designed to follow the contours of the hills through which it winds and is often cited as a model

Figure 6. The Junipero Serra Freeway, California.

for freeway design (Figure 6). However, such examples are more the exception than the rule, and transportation agencies have often argued that the additional cost of aesthetic features cannot be justified when transportation funding is already stretched thin. Nevertheless, in response to growing concerns over the social and environmental impacts of the transportation system, amenity has been given greater weight in official policy in the USA in recent years, and the public has been given a greater role in defining and creating amenity. Examples at the federal, state, and local levels illustrate the broad range of policies that now support improved amenity.

The Intermodal Surface Transportation Efficiency Act created new programs that put amenity at the forefront. The National Scenic Byways Program has designated 72 roads in the USA as scenic byways or "all-American roads" based on their archaeological, cultural, historic, natural, recreational, and scenic qualities. The purpose of the program is to provide resources to help local communities create "a unique travel experience and enhanced local quality of life through efforts to preserve, protect, interpret, and promote the intrinsic qualities of designated byways" (US Federal Highway Administration, 2002a). The transportation enhancements program provides federal funds for projects that enhance the amenity of the transportation system, including projects to convert railroad rights-of-way to pedestrian and bicycle trails, restore historic train stations, renovate streetscapes, and build visitor centers or transportation museums. As of 2002, the program had poured US $2.4 billion into over 12 000 projects (Federal Highway Administration, 2002b). Since the early 1990s, the Federal Highway Administration has worked with the American Association of State Highway Officials to promote "context-sensitive design," defined as "a collaborative, interdisciplinary approach that involves all stakeholders to develop a transportation facility that fits its physical setting and preserves scenic, aesthetic, historic, and environmental resources, while maintaining safety and mobility" (US Federal Highway Administration, 2002c). This effort has lead to changes in official guidelines for the design of highways in the USA.

This increased attention to amenity in transportation can be found in projects throughout the USA. In El Paso, the Texas Department of Transportation decorated existing freeways with a colorful design motif reflective of the local culture and developed through a broad public involvement program. This project also involved extensive landscaping with native species, and the construction of dramatic marker at the entrance to the city along Interstate 10. Transit agencies have focused on creating amenity through the design of bus shelters, rail stations, and even vehicles as a way of promoting transit use. Art, landscaping, and architecture were used in Dallas, Texas, to create a unique identity for each station in its light rail system, which opened in 1996. The Valley Transportation Authority in Santa Clara County, California, built a childcare center at its Tamien light rail station using federal transportation funding in 1994, and contracts with a national daycare operator to run the center. The goal of the project, which includes a variety of additional incentives to use transit, is to make it easier for parents of small children to use transit. At the local level, traffic-calming programs have enhanced the amenity of the street environment for pedestrians and bicyclists by slowing traffic and providing attractive landscaping. Other local policies, such as sign ordinances and design guidelines, help to improve the amenity of transportation corridors.

Improved amenity is important as an end in itself but has added importance for transportation planning through its impact on travel behavior and thus levels of traffic. Choices about travel clearly depend on the experience of travel, not just how long it takes to get somewhere but also how enjoyable the experience is. The findings from studies that have looked at the experience of travel are intriguing. For example:

- Commuting increases stress levels, and unpleasant commutes increase stress even more (Novaco et al., 1990). The kind of visual blight found along major arterials in metropolitan areas – parking lots, signs, billboards, power lines, etc. – does little to reduce stress in comparison with natural environments (Ulrich et al., 1991). Low-amenity environments thus add to the cost of driving, although it is not clear that they discourage driving.

- Many drivers actually like driving, and value the time they spend in the car, both for the things they can do while driving, including watching the scenery, and for the sake of driving itself (Mokhtarian et al., 2001). High-amenity environments, both internal and external to the car, may thus encourage more driving by increasing the enjoyment of driving.
- Graffiti, litter, empty lots, vacant buildings, and other negative qualities around bus stops are associated with higher levels of crime and thus lower safety for bus passengers (Loukaitou-Sideris, 1999). The amenity of bus stops may thus discourage transit use, and undoubtedly affects the quality of the experience for those who must ride the bus.
- The quality of the pedestrian environment, as influenced by traffic levels, shade, scenery, and other characteristics, is tied to the frequency with which residents choose to stroll around the block or walk to a local store (Handy and Clifton, 2001b). High-amenity environments may thus encourage walking.

Findings like these are important in understanding how amenity – or the lack thereof – impacts travel behavior. Theory suggests that travel choices depend on the relative utility, or value, of the different possible choices. In selecting a mode, travelers consider factors such as travel times in deciding which mode best suits their needs. Although amenity is not likely to be the primary factor in most mode decisions, it may have enough impact to tip the balance from one mode to another and it may be the primary factor on at least some occasions. For transit, walking, and biking to have a chance of competing with driving for those who have a choice, they must offer high levels of amenity. Of course, as the amenity within cars increases, the amenity of the alternatives may not matter, and as driving increases, the amenity of the alternatives declines.

4.2. Reducing severance

The issue of severance came to the fore in the USA with the "freeway revolts" of the 1960s. At that time, the realization that freeway projects throughout the country were dividing and thus helping to destroy low-income and minority communities led to changes in the planning process and helped to shape the requirements for environmental impact assessment. The importance of avoiding severance and of reconnecting communities is increasingly recognized in official policy.

In 1994, President Clinton signed Executive Order 12898, Federal Actions to Address Environmental Justice in Minority Populations and Low-Income Populations. This order was related to Title VI of the Civil Rights Act of 1964, and required federal agencies "to achieve environmental justice by identifying and addressing disproportionately high and adverse human health and environmental effects, including the interrelated social and economic effects of their programs,

Figure 7. Pedestrian/bicycle bridge over Interstate 80 in Berkeley, California.

policies, and activities on minority populations and low-income populations in the United States." As interpreted by the US Federal Highway Administration, environmental justice includes not just the minimization of adverse effects but also the prevention of "the denial of, reduction in, or significant delay in the receipt of benefits by minority and low-income populations" (US Federal Highway Administration, 1998). The environmental justice requirement has put new attention on the impacts of transportation projects on severance and forced transportation planning agencies to assess community impacts in low-income and minority areas. In addition, the requirement establishes the need for efforts to remedy past impacts on these communities.

With the help of the federal transportation enhancements program, described above, local communities are reconnecting communities previously severed by freeways, particularly for bicyclists and pedestrians, for whom the extra travel distance can be a significant impediment. Berkeley and Davis, California, have recently completed bicycle/pedestrian bridges over Interstate Highway 80 (Figure 7). San Antonio, Texas, recently renovated an abandoned rail bridge under Interstate Highway 35 for use by bicyclists and pedestrians. Up the highway in

Austin, Texas, the city is working with the Texas Department of Transportation (TxDOT) to redesign the interstate through downtown to physically reconnect local streets across the freeway. The goal of the proposed design is to repair the psychological rift between the historically minority and low-income east side of Austin and downtown that was created when the freeway was built in the late 1950s (Figures 8 and 9). Even farther up the highway, the city of Dallas is working

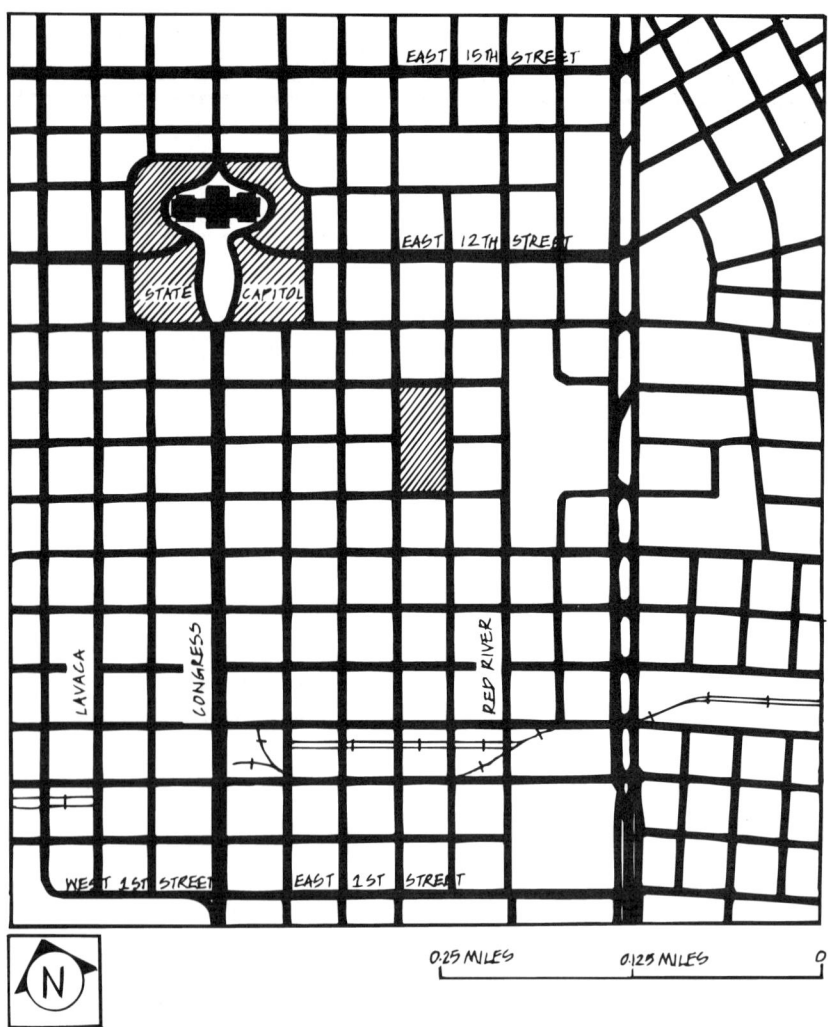

Figure 8. Downtown Austin, Texas, before construction of IH 35.

Ch. 7: Amenity and Severance   137

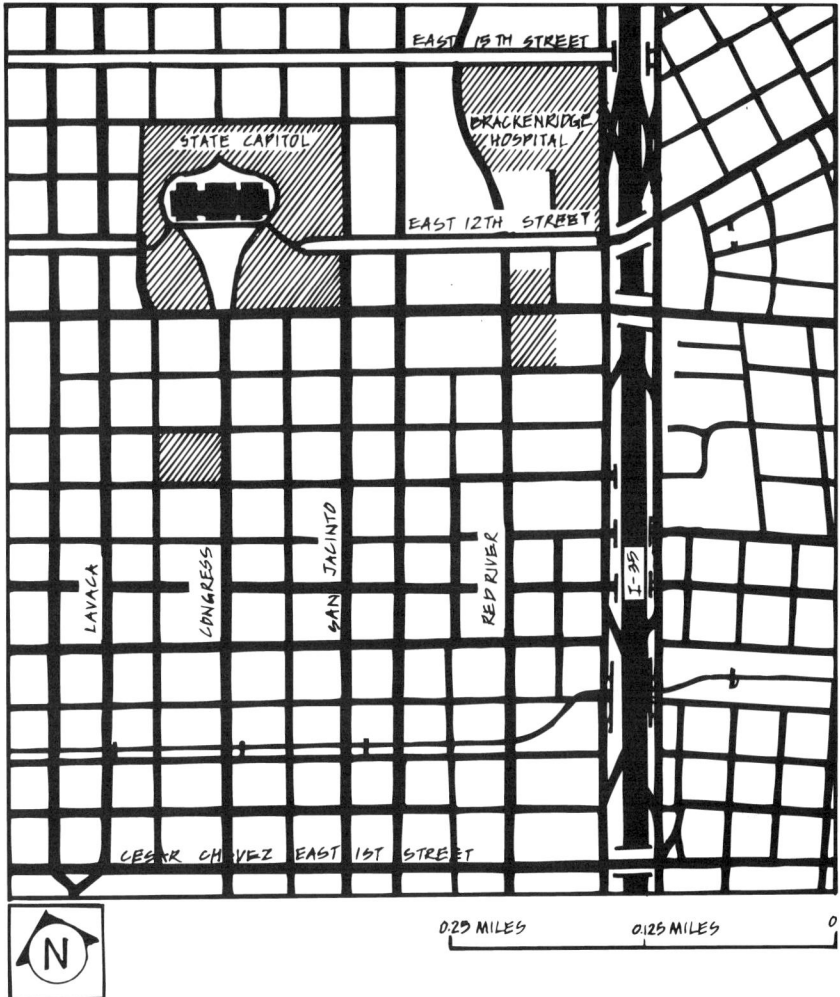

Figure 9. Downtown Austin after construction of IH 35.

with TxDOT on a proposal to cover an existing freeway to re-establish local connections within the community. San Francisco tore down a waterfront freeway in the 1990s, and Milwaukee, Wisconsin, will soon tear down an aging downtown freeway. Both removals were intended in part to reconnect severed parts of the city. A growing number of cities in the USA, from Portland, Oregon, to Cary, North Carolina, have adopted "connectivity ordinances," designed to increase the degree of connectivity in new residential subdivisions.

The impact of such changes on travel behavior is largely untested. Most obviously, traffic on reconnected streets should increase, but traffic elsewhere should decrease. More uncertain is the impact on total travel – whether increased connectivity might lead to a net decrease in total travel by decreasing travel distances or to a net increase in total travel by encouraging new trips. For drivers, increased connectivity has the potential to reduce travel distances and times, but by doing so may increase the frequency of trips by drivers and may lead them to choose more distant destinations than they otherwise would. The impact on total vehicle travel is thus uncertain. For bicyclists and pedestrians, increased connectivity should reduce travel distances and may also expand the number of destinations they can reach within the limits of their own physical capabilities. Improved bicycle and pedestrian connectivity may also encourage more people to use these modes. An increase in walking and bicycling does not necessarily reduce driving, however, as bicycling and walking trips are often made in addition to rather than in place of driving trips. Clearly, the impacts of connectivity changes on travel behavior will depend on the particular context in which those changes take place and the ways in which residents choose to respond. The uncertainty of the impacts points to the need for strategic planning of projects designed to increase connectivity.

A continued demand for severance provides an interesting counter force to the trend towards increased connectivity. The most blatant example of this demand is the growth in gated communities in the USA and elsewhere. In these communities, residents choose to erect barriers between themselves and others as a way of enhancing amenity as well as safety. In the typical suburban residential subdivision in the USA the barrier is created not through walls and gates but through the design of the street network to eliminate through streets and limit the connections between the subdivision and surrounding communities. Houses on cul-de-sacs sell for premiums, and residents vigorously fight efforts to extend dead-end streets as the surrounding area grows. Although some of the demand for severance can surely be attributed to a desire for racial and, perhaps even more so, economic segregation, concerns over traffic and its impacts on amenity and safety are most widely voiced. But local governments sometimes promote severance as well. In the 1970s, Berkeley, California, became one of the first cities to implement an extensive street closure program to reduce traffic in residential areas. In the 1990s, several cities in the USA, including Houston and Los Angeles, closed off streets in older residential areas as a way of combating crime. Traffic-calming programs, now popular throughout the USA, often include full or partial street closures.

5. Conclusions

Factoring the intangible concepts of amenity and severance into environmental impact assessment, cost–benefit analysis, and other planning processes presents a significant challenge to planners. Without well-tested, widely used techniques for evaluating these qualities of a place, planners tend to downplay their importance, even if unintentionally. Yet amenity and severance are important to quality of life in our communities, and the impacts of transportation projects and policies on amenity and severance and, in turn, the impacts of amenity and severance on travel need to be assessed. This need combined with the lack of proven tools creates a problem for planners, for which two approaches to a solution seem possible. One approach is to work to improve the techniques available to planners for quantifying these concepts and their value. The academic community needs to work with the planning community on the development of such techniques. The other approach is to accept that these intangible qualities of a place and their value can't truly be quantified and so maybe planners should not try. The challenge of the latter approach is to ensure that amenity and severance are given appropriate weight in planning discussions and are not ignored because they are not quantified, as is often the case. In the immortal words of Albert Einstein, "Not everything that counts can be counted, and not everything that can be counted counts."

References

Appleyard, D. (1981) *Livable streets*. Berkeley: University of California Press.

California Department of Transportation (1996) *Guidelines for the official designation of scenic highways*. Sacramento: Caltrans (http://www.dot.ca.gov/hq/LandArch/scenic/shpg2.htm#b).

Florida Department of Transportation (2000) *Community impact assessment: a handbook for transportation professionals*. Tampa: Center for Urban Transportation Research, University of South Florida (http://www.lib.usf.edu/cgi-bin/Ebind2h3.pl/cutr0198).

Handy, S. and K. Clifton (2001a) "Evaluating neighborhood accessibility: possibilities and practicalities," *Journal of Transportation and Statistics*, 4:67–78.

Handy, S. and K. Clifton (2001b) "Local shopping as a strategy for reducing automobile travel," *Transportation*, 28:317–346.

Handy, S., R. Paterson and K. Scanlan (2003) *Can't get there from here: planning for street connectivity*, Planning Advisory Service Report. Washington, DC: American Planning Association.

Local Government Commission (2002) *The community image survey*. Sacramento: Local Government Commission (http://www.lgc.org/ps/cis/).

Loukaitou-Sideris, A. (1999) "Hot spots of bus stop crime: the importance of environmental attributes," *Journal of the American Planning Association*, 6:395–411.

Mokhtarian, P.L., I. Salomon and L.S. Redmond (2001) "Understanding the demand for travel: it's not purely derived," *Innovation*, 14:355–380.

Novaco, R.W., D. Stokols and L. Milanesi (1990) "Objective and subjective dimensions of travel impedance as determinants of commuting stress," *American Journal of Community Psychology*, 18:231–256.

Parsons Brinckerhoff Quade & Douglas (1993) *Making land use transportation air quality connections: the pedestrian environment*, Vol. 4A. Portland: 1000 Friends of Oregon (http://ntl.bts.gov/DOCS/tped.html).

Ulrich, R.S., R.F. Simons, B.D. Losito, E. Fiorito, M.A. Miles and M. Zelson (1991) "Stress recovery during exposure to natural and urban environments," *Journal of Environmental Psychology*, 11:201–230.

US Department of Commerce, National Oceanic and Atmospheric Administration, and National Marine Fisheries Service (1994) *Guidelines and principles for social impact assessment*. Belhaven:

Interorganizational Committee on Guidelines and Principles for Social Impact Assessment (http://www.nmfs.noaa.gov/sfa/social_impact_guide.htm).

US Department of Transportation (2002) *Bikeability checklist*. Washington, DC: National Highway Traffic Safety Administration and Pedestrian and Bicycle Information Center (http://www.bicyclinginfo.org/pdf/bikabilitychecklist.pdf).

US Federal Highway Administration (1998) *FHWA actions to address environmental justice in minority populations and low-income populations*, Order 6620.23.. Washington, DC: FHWA (http://www.fhwa.dot.gov/legsregs/directives/orders/6640_23.htm).

US Federal Highway Administration (1999) *The bicycle compatability index: a level-of-service concept*. Washington, DC: FHWA (http://safety.fhwa.dot.gov/fourthlevel/pdf/TechBriefJul99.pdf).

US Federal Highway Administration (2002a) *National scenic byways program: program information*. Washington, DC: FHWA (http://www.byways.org/community/program/program_info.html).

US Federal Highway Administration (2002b) *Transportation enhancements overview*. Washington, DC: FHWA (http://www.fhwa.dot.gov/environment/tea2.htm).

US Federal Highway Administration (2002c) *Context-sensitive design: thinking beyond the pavement*. Washington, DC: FHWA (http://www.fhwa.dot.gov/csd/).

Chapter 8

TRANSPORTATION FUELS – A SYSTEM PERSPECTIVE

BENGT JOHANSSON
Lund University

1. Introduction

The transport sector depends almost totally on the use of petroleum fuels. There has long been widespread concern that almost two thirds of our oil resources are concentrated to the Middle East, and energy security is still a central issue for many countries. An even more serious problem is perhaps the contribution to the greenhouse effect from the use of petroleum. The fact that transportation carbon dioxide emission is increasing at a higher rate than the emission from other sectors is a cause of special concern. Moreover, motor vehicles constitute the most significant source of local and regional emissions such as nitrogen oxides (NO_x), various hydrocarbons, sulfur, and particulate matter. The choice of fuel may, to a greater or lesser extent, influence all the emissions from transportation.

In the coming sections various fuel options will be analyzed from a system perspective, with the focus on their potential role in environmental strategies. Factors of importance are the emission of greenhouse gases, the emission of pollutants with local and regional environmental impact, land use issues (mostly in connection with renewable energy sources), and cost-effectiveness of the different strategies. Many different fuels are discussed. Assuming that the issue of climate change will increase in importance in the future, fuels based on renewable energy (especially biomass) will be dealt with in greater detail.

It is recognized that transportation fuel strategies should be regarded in the context of the energy sector as a whole as different areas of consumption may be competitors for the same limited energy resources. Transportation fuel strategies should also be developed in connection with other options for reducing the environmental impact of transportation, such as fuel efficiency improvement, the development of exhaust reduction technology, transport management, etc. The focus in this text will be placed on fuels for road transport, which today is responsible for the dominating fraction of energy use in the transportation sector.

Handbook of Transport and the Environment, Edited by D.A. Hensher and K.J. Button
© *2003, Elsevier Ltd*

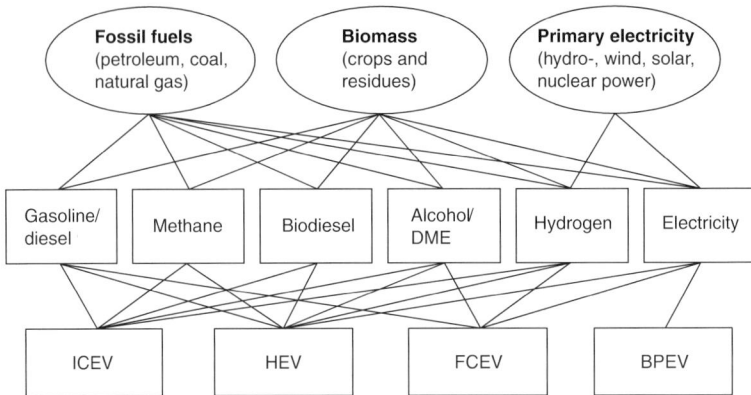

Figure 1. Possible pathways for energy from primary resource to final end use. Key: ICEV, internal combustion engine vehicle; HEV, hybrid electric vehicle; FCEV, fuel cell electric vehicle; BPEV, battery powered electric vehicle.

2. Fuel chains – an introduction

A wide variety of potential combinations of transportation fuels and vehicle technologies can be conceived for use in future transport systems (Figure 1). The environmental effect of various transportation fuel options depends on the primary energy source, the energy carrier and vehicle type. The primary energy source (e.g. oil, coal, or biomass) used to produce the transportation fuel will be especially important in relation to the emission of greenhouse gases. The chosen energy carrier (e.g. gasoline, methanol, or electricity), together with vehicle technology will, on the other hand, be the most important factors with regard to local and regional environmental effects (air quality, acidification, eutrophication, and ozone formation). Emissions arise not only at the vehicle end-use stage but also from fuel extraction, the machinery used for biomass production, methane leakage from natural gas distribution, etc.

Most vehicles today are ICEVs, and comparative environmental evaluations of different fuel alternatives are usually made for this vehicle type. BPEVs, HEVs, and FCEVs all have potential for significantly lower emissions and higher primary energy efficiencies (calculated from "well to wheel") than ICEVs, and the compatibility of fuels with these vehicle alternatives may therefore be a key factor when evaluating the fuels in a longer perspective.

Transportation fuels can be produced, in principle, from any available primary energy source. The current dominance of petroleum fuels is a result of the relative simplicity with which it can be used to produce liquid fuels. Liquid fuels have the advantage of being both easily stored in the vehicle and being relatively efficiently used in the currently dominating ICEVs.

Natural gas and biogas can be used directly as transportation fuels in ICEVs but require a more complicated storage system in the vehicle.

Solid fuels such as coal and biomass are not directly applicable as transportation fuels in ICEVs but must be converted, preferably, to liquid fuels such as alcohols. They can also be converted to hydrogen or electricity, which can both be used in vehicles. An important issue for both these energy carriers is the possibility of storing them in the vehicle.

Electricity produced from thermal power stations (based on fossil fuels, nuclear energy, or biomass) or intermittent sources such as hydro-, wind, and solar power could be used directly as an energy carrier in electric vehicles or could be transformed to hydrogen. Transforming electricity into hydrogen and back to power in the vehicles leads to significant energy losses, but reduces the problem of storage. Although the storage of hydrogen in vehicles has still not economically been solved, the technical problem of energy storage in electric vehicles seems even more problematic than for hydrogen, and the prospects for developing battery-powered electric vehicles with a driving range comparable to those of current vehicles seem bleak.

3. Primary energy sources for transportation fuels

The shift away from oil as the dominant primary source of transportation fuels is not likely to be driven by physical resource constraints, at least not in the short or medium term. A reserve-to-consumption ratio of about 45 years is often cited, but if the total resource base is taken into account, including oil shale, tar sands, and heavy crude oil, and divided by the present rate of consumption, the ratio is about 240 years (Table 1). It should, however, be acknowledged that the statistics for fossil fuel reserves are very uncertain, partly for technical reasons, and partly for political reasons, as many countries have reasons to overestimate their reserves. Although oil is the primary resource for nearly all transportation fuels today, natural gas and coal can also be used. The total resource base divided by the present rate of consumption is close to 450 years for gas and more than 1500 years for coal.

It is, however, probable that the price of petroleum transportation fuels will increase in the longer run as more costly resources have to be utilized in response to an increasing demand for these fuels. The size of such a price increase might be affected by technology development, which may reduce the production costs of conventional and unconventional oil and fuel substitution in other sectors where oil might be replaced by other fossil or renewable fuels. As the cost of alternative energy sources to petroleum are, relatively speaking, higher in the transportation sector than in the heat and electricity sectors, it seems that petroleum-based transportation fuels will maintain their competitive advantage longer than oil used in other sectors.

Renewable energy sources supplied 11–16% of world energy use in 1998. Traditional use of biomass, often in inefficient and polluting ways, accounts for about three-quarters of the total use. The available flow of renewable energy is several thousand times greater than present global energy use. Thus, there is no primary resource constraint on increasing its use.

The most promising renewable source of primary energy for fluid transportation fuels is biomass. The potential long-term contribution of biomass to world energy supply is high: of the order of 300 EJ per year, corresponding to 75% or more of the present global energy use (World Energy Council, 2000).

The physical potential for wind and solar power is significantly larger than the global energy consumption, and the main obstacles for exploiting this potential are connected with land-use conflicts, energy storage issues, and cost.

4. Conventional fuels in ICEVs

During recent decades there has been a continuous development of less-polluting transportation fuels and better combustion technologies. Some of the more important developments have been:

- The reduction and, in many cases, elimination of lead in fuels.
- Major reductions in fuel sulfur content. This has resulted in both a direct reduction of sulfur dioxide emission and the possibility of utilizing more sophisticated technologies to reduce other emissions and improve efficiency.

Table 1
Global resource base for fossil fuels and uranium (EJ unless otherwise indicated)

	World Energy Council estimates		International Institute for Applied Energy Systems Analysis estimates			
	Proven reserves	Ultimately recoverable	Reserves	Resources	Resource base	Consumption (1988)
Conventional oil	6 300	8 400	6 300	6 090	12 390	143
Unconventional oil	–	23 100	8 190	13 944	22 050	–
Conventional gas	5 586	9 240	5 922	11 718	17 640	85
Unconventional gas	–	–	8 064	10 836	18 900	–
Coal and lignite	18 060	142 800	25 452	117 348	142 800	93
Uranium (tonnes)	3.4×10^9	17×10^9	–	–	–	64 000

Source: Estimates are based on World Energy Council (1998) and International Institute for Applied Energy Systems Analysis and World Energy Council (1998).

Table 2
Emissions (g/km) from passenger cars and heavy duty trucks in Sweden in 1988 and 1996, and estimates of the technological potential for 2010. The emissions are estimated real-world averages for the whole vehicle life-cycle (taking into account emission increase as a result of temperature, humidity and technology ageing)

	Passenger cars						Heavy duty vehicles					
	Hydrocarbons			NO_x			Particulates			NO_x		
	1988	1996	2010	1988	1996	2010	1988	1996	2010	1988	1996	2010
Petrol	2.5	0.89	0.08	1.5	0.26	0.04	NA	NA	NA	NA	NA	NA
Diesel	0.67	0.13	0.02	1.1	0.63	0.04	0.58	0.3	0.10	16.6	11.5	4.1
Biogas/ natural gas	2.1	0.05	0.01	2.3	0.14	0.02	–	0.01	0.005	–	4.5	0.8
Alcohol	4.2	0.82	0.03	1.4	0.07	0.01	–	0.01	0.005	–	6	1

Source: Egebäck et al. (1997).
Key: NA, not applicable – no data available.

- The reformulation of gasoline, which has reduced the content of the most harmful hydrocarbons (e.g. benzene).

Simultaneously, technologies such as the three-way catalytic converter, lean-burn diesel technology, and particulate traps have reduced the emissions of many pollutants connected with the combustion of fossil fuels. Other technologies, such as exhaust gas recirculation and methods of reducing cold-start emissions, could lead to further emission reductions in the coming decade. Table 2 gives the estimated average emission levels for vehicles sold in Sweden in 1988 and 1996, and technical potentials for 2010. The estimates indicate the potential of reducing the emission levels of several pollutants to levels that are only a fraction of those at the end of the 1980s.

Currently, the reduction of local air pollution is the main driving force behind alternative fuels around the world. The potential for technical development expressed in Table 2 indicates that this driving force for alternative fuels may become less important as emissions from ICEVs using conventional fuels are continuously reduced. The issue of CO_2 emission will, however, still be a problem for conventional fossil fuels. For vehicles using fossil fuels, energy efficiency improvements will remain the main option for reducing greenhouse gases.

It should be emphasized that the figures given in Table 2 are based on well-functioning exhaust gas treatment (although some loss of efficiency due to catalyst ageing is included in the estimates). In situations where the risk of malfunctioning is higher (e.g. if efficient systems for inspection and technology maintenance are lacking) the use of inherently less-polluting alternative fuels may provide significant advantages for local air quality.

5. Alternative fuels – technologies and emissions

5.1. Methane gas

Methane gas can be produced both from fossil and renewable energy sources. The fossil alternative, natural gas, is currently widely used in the energy sector, but so far only to a minor extent in the transportation sector. The development of biogas systems has so far been pursued as an integral part of solving waste treatment problems, either by collecting gas from landfills or by fermenting organic waste and manure in dedicated biogas plants. Biogas plants can also utilize dedicated energy crops, but the cost of the gas produced will be significantly higher with this feedstock.

Studies show that the emissions from biogas- and natural-gas-fueled vehicles can be very low (Table 2). There will be almost no particulate emission, and the emission of other pollutants, such as hydrocarbons and NO_x, can be kept at levels similar to those for gasoline.

5.2. Biodiesel

Perhaps the simplest way to produce transportation fuels from biomass is to extract oil from oliferous plants such as rapeseed, soybeans, or sunflowers. Esters such as rape methyl ester (RME) can be produced through transesterification with methanol. These fuels can be used directly in diesel engines. Emission measurements indicate that replacing diesel with RME would result an increase in NO_x emissions whereas the emissions of hydrocarbons and particulates could be reduced. These differences in emission might possibly be the effect of using engines not designed for such fuels (leading to high NO_x emissions) and the use of emission measurement methods that are designed in a way that they cannot detect all the emissions from the new fuel (which may lead to an underestimation of the emission of hydrocarbons and particulates) (Egebäck, 1997).

5.3. Ethanol

Ethanol is today widely used as a biofuel in Brazil, the USA, and Europe. The feedstock for ethanol production is sugar cane, maize, or cereals. The production is based on biological processes using yeast and bacteria. New processes for producing ethanol from low-cost cellulose feedstock are under development, but no such production is today operating on a commercial scale. Ethanol is a fuel particularly suitable for Otto engines. It could also be used efficiently in diesel engines with ignition additives. Experience from the extensive Swedish biofuel program indicates a potential for lower emission levels of all the regulated pollutants compared with gasoline and diesel (e.g. see Table 2). The only exception may be aldehydes, but modern catalytic converter technology seems to be able to reduce the emission of these substances to levels similar to those from gasoline and diesel (Egebäck et al., 1997).

5.4. Methanol and dimethyl ether (DME)

The feedstock for the methanol produced today is almost exclusively natural gas. DME can also be produced effectively from natural gas. Both methanol and DME can be produced from coal or biomass through thermal gasification. Methanol has properties similar to those of ethanol and is a suitable fuel for Otto engines but is also usable in diesel engines with additives. The emission levels are also similar to those of ethanol. DME, in contrast, is a typical diesel fuel but has the potential for significantly lower emissions than diesel.

5.5. Hydrogen

Hydrogen is often proposed as the fuel of the future. It can be produced from many different kinds of feedstock. A general advantage, irrespective of feedstock, is the possibility of almost eliminating the emission of hydrocarbons, carbon monoxide, and particulates. The potential use of hydrogen in future, highly efficient FCEVs is, however, perhaps the most important factor causing attention to be directed toward this fuel during recent years. The currently dominating method of hydrogen production is steam reforming of natural gas. Hydrogen can be produced from biomass and coal with a similar gasification technology to that used for methanol and DME, but with even higher efficiency.

If carbon dioxide recovery and sequestration proves to be a feasible option in the future, hydrogen may be of special interest as carbon can be removed from fossil fuels (e.g. natural gas) at central plants where carbon sequestration is competitive. Carbon dioxide recovery and sequestration has attracted increasing attention during the past decade as a carbon mitigation alternative. The idea is to prevent the carbon from fossil fuels from reaching the atmosphere, either by removing it from the flue gases of large heat or power plants, or during fuel processing when producing hydrogen from fossil fuels. It would then be deposited in depleted oil or natural gas fields, deep aquifers, or in deep oceans. Deep ocean sequestration offers the greatest potential for carbon dioxide deposition, but more research is needed to better understand the security, costs, and environmental impact of various deposition schemes (World Energy Council, 2000). Existing studies indicate that this is a relatively cost-effective method compared with other methods of mitigating carbon dioxide.

Finally, hydrogen can be produced through electrolysis using electricity which can be produced from almost any primary energy source, ranging from less available, low-cost electricity produced in existing plants during periods of low demand to potentially abundant but costly electricity from solar cells.

The main barriers to the development of a hydrogen-based energy system are the need for new distribution systems and, especially, the need to develop efficient and cheap hydrogen storage systems. With current technology, the least costly storage alternative is as compressed gas. Another alternative is storage as metal hydrides. Metal hydride storage requires less space but is heavy, and costs much more than storage as compressed gas. Storage of liquid hydrogen is energy-consuming and wasteful for private cars. Hydrogen storage using carbon nanofibers is under development and offers the potential for dramatically improving hydrogen storage (World Energy Council, 2000).

5.6. Electricity

Electricity is an energy carrier that can be used for many purposes in a very energy-efficient way. This is also true for vehicle propulsion. Local zero emissions is another important advantage of electric vehicles (although emissions may arise from thermal plants used for electricity production). The main problem associated with electric vehicles is that of energy storage. So far, there are no storage systems capable of providing driving ranges comparable to those of conventional vehicles.

5.7. The use of alternative fuels in HEVs and FCEVs

Both HEVs (a combination of electric and mechanical drive systems) and FCEVs (which use a fuel cell to produce the electricity necessary for the electric drive system) provide opportunities to combine the high efficiency of electric drivetrains with the advantage of using a fuel instead of electricity, allowing for a longer driving range.

6. Fuel cycle emissions

To obtain a comprehensive picture of the emissions resulting from fuel use a fuel cycle perspective is valuable. In Figure 2 the fuel cycle emissions of carbon dioxide for some fossil- and biomass-based transportation fuels are shown. A significant difference can be seen between the fuel cycle emissions from biomass-based fuels

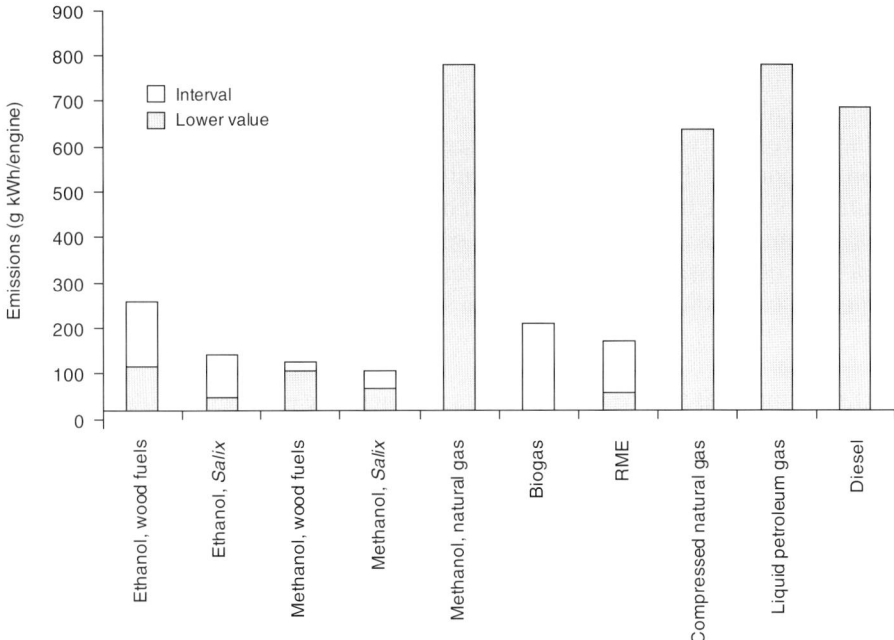

Figure 2. Fuel-cycle emission of carbon dioxide for some fuels used in heavy duty vehicles based on Swedish conditions (Blinge et al., 1997). *Salix* is the most widely used species for short-rotation forestry in Sweden. Key: CNG, compressed natural gas; LPG, liquid petroleum gas.

and fossil fuels. Not all the fuel alternatives discussed above are included in this figure. Neither biomass-based DME nor hydrogen are included, but would have similar emission levels to biomass-based methanol. Emission estimates for ethanol produced from sugar or starch vary significantly depending on the technology assumed from, in the best case, being close to the emissions of fuels based on cellulose feedstock, to in the worst case, being as high as for gasoline or diesel (Intergovernmental Panel on Climate Change, 1996). The results shown in Figure 2 are based on assumptions that best technologies are used in the different stages of the fuel cycle. When long-term strategic choices are made it is reasonable to make such assumptions. Other life-cycle analyses are based on other technological assumptions, which might have significant effect on emissions. This is illustrated in Table 3.

The results from fuel cycle studies for other pollutants are less easy to interpret. In contrast to carbon dioxide emissions, the damage caused by other pollutants usually depends largely on the location of the emission. Road vehicle exhaust could be expected to be more harmful than emissions from agricultural machinery or central power plants as more people are exposed to vehicle exhaust. Estimates could often vary significantly depending on technological assumptions, as the emission of, for example, hydrocarbons, NO_x, and particulates seems to be easier to control than carbon dioxide.

Historically, vehicle emissions have dominated fuel cycle emissions. As road vehicles are faced with more stringent regulations, other emission sources become more important. For example, agricultural machinery may be an important contributor to the fuel cycle emission of biomass-based transportation fuels as the specific emissions are higher than the specific emissions from road vehicles due to a lack of emission regulation (Johansson, 1995). This effect illustrates the importance of reducing emissions at all stages of the fuel chain.

7. Environmental and resource aspects of renewable energy technologies

Fuel cycle emission is not the only aspect that determines the environmental performance of a transportation fuel. The potential for biomass production is limited by physical restrictions; competition with other land use such as food production, and environmental restrictions, for example concerning biodiversity conservation. The possibility of using biomass as a substitute for fossil fuels depends on feedstock productivity and conversion efficiencies. The productivity of different biomass alternatives differs significantly between crops and geographic location (Table 4). It also depends on the plant materials and cultivation method employed.

Table 3
Life cycle greenhouse gas emissions for alternative fuels

Fuel	Life-cycle greenhouse gas emission (g/km CO_2 equivalent)
Gasoline	222–282
Reformulated gasoline	222–283
Diesel	173–266
Liquefied petroleum gas	180–203
Compressed natural gas	164–253
Methanol from coal	424–426
Methanol from natural gas	250–252
Methanol from wood	65–81
Ethanol from sugar cane	70–123
Ethanol from corn	90–263
Ethanol from wood	65–81
Liquid hydrogen	29–88

Source: Intergovernmental Panel on Climate Change (1996).

Table 4
Net energy yields of agricultural feedstock suitable for transportation fuel production. Net energy yields are calculated as energy yields minus energy input

Biomass resource	Net energy yields (GJ/ha) (a)	Driving distances obtainable for passenger cars (1000 km/ha)
Sweden		
Rapeseed (including straw)	60 (today)	11
	70 (2015, estimate)	14
Wheat (including straw)	70 (today)	12
	120 (2015, estimate)	23
Lucerne	110 (today)	26
	210 (2015, estimate)	48
Salix (short rotation forest)	145 (today)	20–48
	270 (2015, estimate)	36–88
Tropical plants (e.g. eucalyptus)		
No genetic improvement, no fertiliser, and no irrigation	30–180	–
Genetic improvement, fertiliser, and irrigation	340–550	–
Sugar cane (Brazil, Zambia)	400–500	–

Source: Gustavsson et al. (1995), Johansson (1996), and World Energy Council (2000).
Note: (a) Year indicated in parentheses.
Key: –, not estimated.

In a comprehensive assessment of biomass system efficiency, biomass conversion efficiencies and the potential to utilize by-products should also be accounted for. In Table 4 some estimates of the potential production of transportation services from biomass on Swedish agricultural land are indicated. Due to its high productivity, the use of fuels produced from *Salix* (willow) would result in a greater transportation potential than the use of fuels from annual agricultural crops with lower productivity. The production of transportation fuels from both rapeseed and wheat would, however, provide by-products that could be used as fodder. Production technologies for ethanol from cellulosic biomass may provide energy by-products useful for heating purposes. In both these cases the by-products improve the total environmental performance but will not be able to eliminate the economic problems associated with these technologies, see below.

It should also be realized that the use of biomass to replace fossil fuels for heat and power production is more resource- and cost-efficient than using biomass for transportation fuel production (Gustavsson et al., 1995). If global biomass resources are not sufficiently large for both these sectors this would suggest that priority should be given to the use of biomass for heat and power production. If biomass strategies are combined with concerted energy efficiency measures, and other renewable energy sources are developed for heat and electricity production, biomass resources might, however, be sufficient for transportation fuel purposes.

Current agricultural practices are often not benign and exert pressure on the land. An increased use of perennial crops at the expense of annual crops could result in a reduction in this environmental pressure. Studies show that increased cultivation of perennial crops can reduce nutrient leaching, and soil erosion, and is expected to maintain or increase the organic matter in soil.

Other potential sources of feedstock for biomass-based transportation fuels are logging residues and waste from forest industries. Extensive research indicates that extraction of logging residues is compatible with ecologically sustainable forestry on condition that stumps and a fraction of other residues are left on the site, and that the forest is compensated for nutrient losses through, for example ash recirculation to the forest.

The environmental impact of hydro-, solar, and wind power is of another character to that of biomass extraction. The impact of hydropower is largely connected with the building of dams, which constitutes severe intrusion into the natural environment. Wind power has an enormous global physical potential, but the location of wind power plants often meets resistance in the industrial world due to perceived negative effects on the landscape, noise, and uncertain effects on flora and fauna. Solar cells used for transportation fuel production could probably be located in areas where the negative environmental impact is negligible (e.g. unpopulated desert areas), and the main concern in this case is the demand for rare earth metals such as tellurium, indium, selenium, and ruthenium, which are elements used in some of the most interesting solar cells.

8. Economic issues – a focus on alternatives

In this section, key economic factors in the introduction of alternative fuels will be discussed. Methodological problems arise when technologies at different levels of development are compared. There are many estimates of the future production costs of different transportation fuels, but they are all heavily dependent on the assumptions that have been made regarding future technical development.

In a comparison of different alternatives it is important to distinguish between costs and prices. Prices are determined in the marketplace by the balance between supply and demand. The local price of gasoline and diesel depends on international market prices and domestic tax levels. Such prices are also affected by the cost of local and regional distribution and the existence (or non-existence) of real market competition. The market price is, to a large extent, determined by the political decisions made by the OPEC countries. The production costs of petroleum also differ significantly between the Middle East, where crude oil can be produced for

Table 5
Current gasoline and diesel prices, production costs of different biomass-based transportation fuels, and estimated costs for natural gas and natural-gas-based methanol

Fuel	Price/cost (US $/GJ)	
	Short-term	Long-term
Gasoline (Rotterdam price)	4.5–6.5	–
Diesel (Rotterdam price)	4.2–5.5	–
RME, cost	15–25	–
Ethanol from sugar crops	15–25 (sugar beet) 8–10 (sugar cane)	–
Ethanol from lignocellulosic biomass	10–15	6–7
Hydrogen from lignocellulosic biomass	8–10	6–8
Methanol from lignocellulosic biomass	11–13	7–10
Natural gas	1.5–3	–
Methanol from natural gas	5	–

Source: Johansson (1996, 1999), International Energy Agency (1999), and World Energy Council (2000). Fuel distribution cost is not included.
Key: –, not estimated.

only a few US dollars per barrel, and in a new Arctic oil field where the production cost may be around US $15–20 per barrel (International Energy Agency, 1999).

Alternative fuels must be able to compete with these fuels, and will in the long term face a pressure to be produced at costs competitive with those of conventional fuels. "Competitive" in this sense does not necessarily mean "the same cost," but the cost difference should at least not be higher than that which can be motivated by environmental or energy security reasons.

For all transportation fuels the cost of the feedstock is central to the total cost of production. The cost of the feedstock is affected not only by the "real" production cost, determined mainly by the input of labor and capital, but also by existing subsidies. Subsidies are frequently used in both fossil fuel and biomass markets. For example, in the EU, agricultural subsidies form a major fraction of a farmer's income, and a producer of transportation fuel can acquire feedstock at lower prices than would be motivated by the production cost.

In Table 5 the production costs for some biomass-based fuels are compared with current gasoline and diesel prices and estimated costs for competing fossil alternatives, such as natural gas and fossil-based methanol. The cost estimates are all very uncertain. One important conclusion, however, is that production costs for fuels from conventional agricultural crops will have difficulty in competing with fuels derived from cellulose biomass (logging residues, forest industry residues, biomass from short rotation forests).

The production cost of hydrogen via electrolysis depends on the cost of electricity (Table 6). Generally, the production of hydrogen through electrolysis cannot compete economically with the production of hydrogen from biomass or from fossil fuels with carbon sequestration.

The distribution of alternative fuels might pose extra costs compared with the distribution of conventional fuels, especially in the initial stage as the need for other fuels at gasoline stations would require new investments. Similar distribution systems can be used for alternative liquid fuels as for gasoline and diesel, although the lower energy density of alcohol fuels would impose extra costs on the system. The large-scale distribution of gaseous fuels such as natural gas and hydrogen would probably be based on a pipeline distribution system. The cost will be extremely sensitive to the overall local conditions and the demand for transportation fuels. Biogas production plants are small-scale systems, and the gas would probably be mainly used locally. The use of existing natural gas systems can also provide a natural means of distributing biogas. In Table 7 indicative distribution cost estimates are shown.

Table 6
Estimated production cost of hydrogen via electrolysis at different electricity prices. The values indicate typical values. The cost estimates are based on large-scale hydrolysis with the utilization times indicated

Electricity cost (US $/kWh)	Hydrogen cost (US $/GJ)	Method of production
0.020	12	Low-cost electricity (8000 h full load)
0.03–0.04	27–29	Wind power (2000 h full load)
0.06–0.09	36–43	Potential future solar electricity in sunny areas (1500 h full load)

Source: Gröndalen (1998) and World Energy Council (2000).

Table 7
Indicative costs for fuel distribution

Fuel	Distribution cost (US $/GJ)
Petroleum fuels	3.5–4
Alcohol fuels	5–6
RME	3.4
Hydrogen	6–11

Sources: International Energy Agency (1999) and Ogden (1999).

Ch. 8: Transportation Fuels – a System Perspective   155

Table 8
Factors involved in the evaluation of different transportation fuels

Technical factors	Environmental factors	Economic factors
Technological development level Functionality Safety	Fuel cycle emissions Environmental impact of land use (mainly for renewable energy sources) Resource efficiency (feedstock productivity, conversion efficiency, etc.)	Feedstock cost Fuel conversion cost Distribution cost Cost of vehicles using the studied fuels

Alternative liquid fuels can be used in conventional vehicles with only minor additions to the cost. For gaseous fuels, especially hydrogen, gas storage might be the issue determining its success.

A conclusion that can be drawn from the discussion above is that one would not expect fuels based on renewable energy sources to be competitive with petroleum fuels before the latter rise in price, either as a result of shrinking reserves in the future, or through some kind of tax differentiation between the fuels. This differentiation could be based on high economic valuation of carbon dioxide emission or emissions with local and regional effects. The advantages to the local and regional environment from using alternative fuels are greatest in heavy duty vehicles, which would motivate the use of alternative transportation fuels primarily in buses and trucks.

9. Discussion

The intention of this chapter was to describe the potentially available fuels for the transportation sector with the focus on alternatives to the currently dominating petroleum fuels. The choice of fuel depends on several different factors. Various factors that could have an effect on the choice of fuel and therefore should be evaluated are summarized in Table 8.

From a policy perspective it is important to analyze the competitiveness of the alternatives both in the short and long term. Long-term potentials are often not achievable unless the technologies (fuels and vehicles) are developed, produced, and used on a large enough scale to gain scale advantages and learning effects, and to develop the market. On the other hand, an understanding of the short-term competitiveness of the fuels is crucial to devise incentives that are suitable for the introduction of a chosen fuel. In the short-term perspective the environmental advantages of alternative fuels are often not worth the extra cost of their implementation. A transition to alternative fuels must instead be motivated by a long-term need to redirect the transportation sector to more sustainable energy sources. It is, however, extremely difficult to forecast which fuels would be preferable in the long-term perspective. Backing the wrong horse might prove to be very costly, while making no bet at all might also be costly in the long run.

As has been shown, several alternative fuels could be used to reduce the environmental impact of the transportation sector. Some alternatives are restricted in various ways as a result of land use limitations. The future development of alternative transportation fuels will largely be governed by ambitions related to carbon dioxide reduction. In the first place, fossil fuels should probably be replaced where they are used for heat and electricity production. If the ambition is to drastically reduce carbon dioxide emission, cost-efficient strategies will have to include dedicated efforts towards energy efficiency. In this case, renewable energy sources might suffice for more than one purpose. Energy efficiency should in any case be given high priority in relation to alternative transportation fuels as energy efficiency improvements seem to be more cost effective the fuel substitution.

The choice between alternative fuels based on renewable sources cannot be made with our current level of knowledge. Hydrogen shows many advantageous characteristics, but requires the development of a less expensive storage technology. In the short run, fuels based on biomass are the most competitive of the renewable alternatives. Significantly increasing fossil fuel prices, either as a result of increased scarcity or as a result of more stringent restrictions on carbon dioxide emissions, would make renewable energy sources more competitive in general. Biomass prices may increase with demand, and hydrogen based on other sources, such as wind or solar power, could then become competitive. The relative abundance of these sources may, in this case, be important and may compensate for their relatively higher production costs.

References

Blinge, M., P.-O. Arnäs, S. Bäckström, Å. Furnander and K. Hovelius (1997) *Livscykelanalys (LCA) av drivmedel*. Stockholm: The Swedish Transport and Communications Research Board.

Egebäck, K.-E., P. Ahlvik and R. Westerholm (1997) *Emissionsfaktorer för fordon drivna med fossila respektive alternativa bränslen*. Stockholm: The Swedish Transport and Communications Research Board.

Gröndalen, O. (1998) *Väte – framtidens energibärare?* Elforsk Report 98:19. Stockholm: Elforsk.

Gustavsson, L., P. Börjesson, B. Johansson and P. Svenningsson (1995) "Reducing CO_2 emissions by substituting biomass for fossil fuels," *Energy – The International Journal*, 20:1097–1113.

Intergovernmental Panel on Climate Change (1996) *Climate change 1995 – impacts, adaptation and mitigation of climate change: scientific technical analysis. Second assessment report of the IPCC,* Vol. II. Cambridge: Cambridge University Press.

International Energy Agency (1999) *Automotive fuels for the future. The search for alternatives*. Paris: IEA.

International Institute for Applied Energy Systems Analysis and World Energy Council (1998) *Global energy perspectives*. Cambridge: Cambridge University Press.

Johansson, B. (1995) "Strategies for reducing emissions of air pollutants from the Swedish transporation sector," *Transportation Research A*, 29:371–385.

Johansson, B. (1996) "Transportation fuels from Swedish biomass – environmental and cost aspects," *Transportation Research D*, 1:47–62

Johansson, B. (1999) "The economy of alternative fuels when including the cost of air pollution *Transportation Research D*, 4:91–108.

Ogden, J.M. (1999) Prospects for building a hydrogen energy infrastructure," *Annual Review of Energy and the Environment*, 24:227–279.

World Energy Assessement (2000) *Energy and the challenge of sustainability*. New York: UNDP.

World Energy Council (1998) *Survey of energy resources*. London: WEA.

Chapter 9

FUEL OPTIONS

MUKESH KHARE
Indian Institute of Technology, Delhi

PRATEEK SHARMA
GGS Indraprastha University, Delhi

1. Introduction

Transport is an essential human activity and it has played an important role in the development of many societies. However, the environmental costs of this energy-intensive sector are also critical: e.g. it produces 20% of all anthropogenic greenhouse gas emissions. While all modes of transport have an environmental impact, the major impact is from road transport. Since the early part of the twentieth century the primary automotive fuels have been gasoline and diesel; however, a few countries such as Brazil, Italy, and New Zealand have developed a vehicle transportation system based on alternative fuels (AFs).

Fuel composition and characteristics play an important role in emissions, and standards for gasoline and diesel were established to ensure that they meet minimum requirements. Changes in one fuel characteristics may lower emissions of one pollutant but increase those of another. For example, a decrease in the aromatic content of gasoline may lower carbon monoxide (CO) and hydrocarbon (HC) emissions but may increase nitrogen oxide (NO_x) emissions. However, a major advantage of fuel modification is that it often can take effect quickly and begin reducing pollutant emissions immediately.

The substitution of cleaner burning AFs for conventional gasoline and diesel fuels has attracted significant attention during the past two decades. The outlook for AFs over the next decade will be influenced by the effectiveness of efforts to reduce emissions from gasoline and diesel. However, to improve and sustain air quality as well as to conserve oil reserves and preserve energy sources, AFs are being considered as effective substitutes for conventional fuels.

Handbook of Transport and the Environment, Edited by D.A. Hensher and K.J. Button
© 2003, Elsevier Ltd

2. Types of fuels

2.1. Gasoline

Gasoline is a mixture of 200–300 HCs that evaporates between ambient temperature and 200°C. Various chemicals and blending agents are also added to improve its properties, for example lead compounds. Various types of gasoline can be delineated.

Low-lead gasoline

A low-lead gasoline contains 26.4–39.6 g lead per cubic meter. The addition of lead is one of the cheapest means of producing high-octane gasoline; the lead also protects exhaust valves against wear, and serves as a lubricant. However, lead adversely affects health once it enters the environment as a lead aerosol. A number of countries have eliminated the use of leaded gasoline.

Unleaded gasoline

The USA and Canada banned the use of lead in gasoline in 1990. Austria was the first European country to ban the addition of lead to gasoline in 1993. Now, almost all nations have stopped adding lead to gasoline.

Oxygenated gasoline

Oxygenated supplements substitute for lead additives in gasoline. Oxygenates are produced from a variety of feedstocks. For example, ethanol is derived mostly from agricultural feedstocks, and methanol is derived primarily from natural gas. The commonly used oxygenate in gasoline blends are methanol, ethanol, t-butyl alcohol (TBA), methyl t-butyl ether (MTBE), and ethyl t-butyl ether (ETBA). The volume of oxygenates in gasoline blends varies from 3 to 22%; while commonly used blends have 10–15% of oxygenates. The oxygen content is 1–2% by weight. The advantages of oxygenated gasoline over HC-only fuel are:

- reduced CO and HC emissions;
- lower emissions from older vehicles, especially of benzene;
- higher octane rating.

MTBE and other ethers are the preferred oxygenates as they produce high octane ratings and are less water-sensitive than alcohols. The cost of using ethers is also relatively moderate (about US $0.01–0.03 per liter – 1993 prices) (Faiz et al., 1996).

Reformulated gasoline

The reformulation of gasoline is primarily carried out to reduce volatility (evaporative emissions) and sulfur (catalyst efficiency). Research has shown that reformulated gasoline reduces non-methane HCs (NMHCs) emissions by 12–27% compared with HC-only fuels. CO emissions are also reduced by 21–28%, and NO_x emissions by 7–16%. Formaldehyde emissions are also 13% lower (Air Quality Improvement Research Program, 1993).

2.2. Gasoline fuel properties and their effects on emissions

Fuel volatility

Fuel volatility is measured by the Reid vapor pressure (RVP) – the vapor pressure at a fixed temperature (100°F or 37.8°C). Increasing the RVP from 9 to 11.9 psi roughly doubles the evaporative emissions; lowering the RVP from 9 to 8 psi decreases total evaporative emissions by 34% with no significant effect on fuel economy; it also reduces HC emissions by 4% and CO by 9%, but NO_x emissions are unaffected.

Olefins

Olefins (also called alkenes) are a class of HCs that have one or more double bonds in their carbon structure, e.g. ethylene, propylene, and butene. A reduction of the olefin content in gasoline reduces NO_x emissions by 6%. However, volatile organic compound (VOC) emissions are increased by 6%.

Aromatic HCs

Aromatic HCs have one or more benzene rings in their molecular structure. Aromatic HCs in engine exhaust increase the reactivity of VOCs. A reduction of the content of aromatic HCs in gasoline reduces NO_x and benzene emissions (Air Quality Improvement Research Program, 1993).

2.3. Diesel

High thermal efficiency is the primary reason why almost all commercial vehicles in the medium to heavy range are powered by diesel engines. Despite their low output both per liter and per kilogram, which translates into higher initial cost, diesel engines still offer a lower overall operational cost. Automotive gas oil or high-speed diesel (HSD) is used for road vehicles, while low-speed diesel (LSD) is used for ships.

The quality and composition of diesel fuel both have important effects on pollutant emissions. The fuel variables that have the most significant effects on emissions are sulfur content, cetane number, and the fraction of aromatic HCs in the fuel.

Sulfur content

Sulfur in diesel fuel is released in exhaust mostly as sulfur dioxide; that which is not emitted as sulfur dioxide is converted to various metal sulfates and sulfuric acid in particulate form. In heavy-duty diesel engines, particulate emissions account for about 1-3% of the fuel sulfur, whereas it is 3–5% for light-duty diesel engines (Faiz et al., 1996). These sulfate particles are hygroscopic in nature, i.e. they tend to absorb significant quantities of water from air.

HSD is classified on the basis of sulfur content. Low-sulfur HSD contains between 0.1 to 0.5% sulfur by weight; extra-low-sulfur HSD contains 0.25% sulfur; and ultra-low-sulfur HSD contains 0.05% sulfur. The presence of significant amounts of sulfur (>0.05%) limits the potential use of catalytic converters or catalytic traps – oxidizers for oxidation, controlling particulate, CO, and HC emissions from diesel vehicles. If only particulate emissions are considered, the level from one new diesel car equals that from 24 new gasoline cars or 81 compressed natural gas (CNG) cars; if gas emissions are considered, diesel gases from one new diesel car equals the output from two gasoline cars (Down to Earth, 2000). Studies indicate that diesel engines emit 10–100 times more nano- and ultrafine particles than modern gasoline vehicles equipped with catalytic converters (Conservation of Clean Air and Water in Europe, 1994). Figure 1 provides a simple illustration of the complex structure and the composition of diesel particulates (Mark and Morey, 1999). In order to reduce sulfur dioxide and particulate emissions, many countries, including the USA, have agreed to limit the fuel sulfur content to 0.05%, with a future reduction to 0.03%. One of the control technologies to reduce particulates is the use of diesel oxidation catalysts (DOCs). DOCs target the soluble organic fraction of particulates and oxidizes HCs to carbon dioxide and water, thus reducing particulate mass emissions.

Cetane number

The cetane number is a measure of the ignition quality of a fuel in the combustion chamber. It is determined by comparing the ignition quality of a fuel under standard operating conditions with a blend of two reference fuels – the straight-chain paraffin n-cetane (with a value of 100 by definition) and a branched paraffin, heptamethylnonane (with an assigned value of 15). The higher the cetane number,

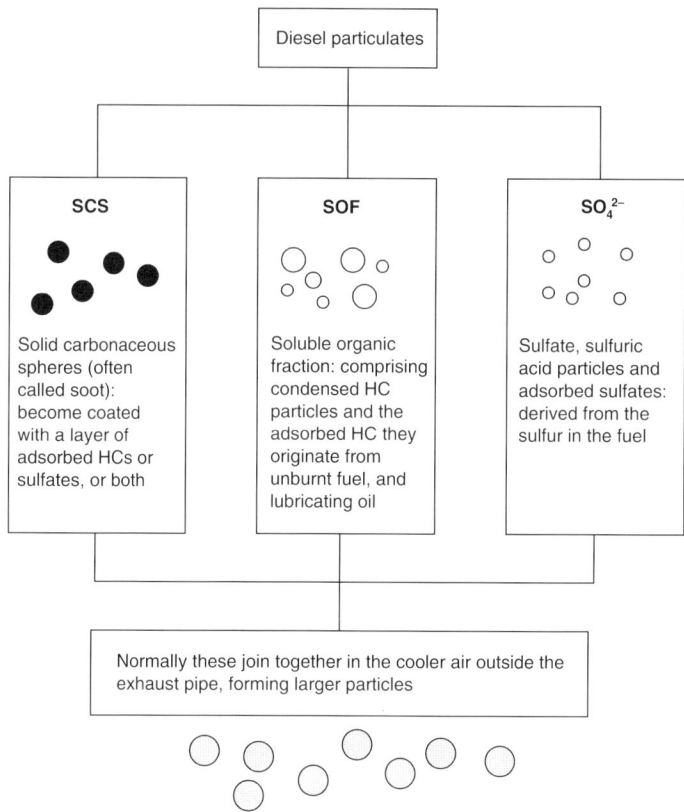

Figure 1. Composition and structure of diesel particulates.

the shorter the delay between the injection and the ignition, and the better the ignition quality. High-cetane fuel is also associated with improved cold starting, reduced white smoke, less noise, and reduced HC, CO, and particulate emissions. There is a trade-off between cetane number and emission benefits: a cetane number above 50 may increase NO_x emissions by 2% and particulate emissions by up to 6%. There is thus little evidence that emissions would improve with fuel cetane numbers above current European levels (43–57 with an average of 50).

Hydrocarbons

Aromatic HCs have poor self-ignition properties. Diesel fuels with a high fraction of aromatics tend to have a low cetane number, typically in the range 40–45, or even lower. This results in more combustion noise, and increased HC and NO_x

emissions. A high aromatic content is also correlated with higher carbonaceous particulate emissions with an increased content of soluble organic fraction (SOF) emissions.

Diesel reformulation

Changing the basic formulation of diesel fuel to reduce emissions is expensive. For this reason, the most cost-effective way of achieving significant emission reductions is through diesel fuel additives. These additives are organic compounds of calcium, barium, or magnesium, which greatly reduce the visible smoke. Cetane enhancers, generally organic nitrates, are used to improve the self-ignition properties of diesel fuel.

Effect of diesel fuel properties on emissions

A generalized assessment of individual diesel fuel properties on emissions is shown in Table 1.

2.4. Type and effect of emissions from conventional fuel-driven vehicles

The major pollutants emitted from gasoline-fueled vehicles are CO, HC, NO_x, lead (only for leaded gasoline fuel), and sulfur dioxide. The pollutants emanating from the exhaust of diesel-fueled vehicles are particulates, NO_x, sulfur dioxide, CO, and HC. Table 2 lists the types of emission and their relative harmful environmental effects (see also Romieu, 1992).

Table 1
Influence of diesel fuel properties on exhaust emissions

Fuel property		Smoke		Gases			Particulates
		White	Black	HC	CO	NO_x	
Density	Higher	+	+				+
	Lower	–	–				–
Viscosity	Higher		+		+		+
	Lower		–		–		–
Cetane number	Higher	–		–	–	–	–
	Lower	+		+	+	+	+

Source: Faiz et al. (1996).
Key: +, increased; –, decreased.

Table 2
Major pollutants from conventionally fuelled vehicles and their harmful effects

Pollutant	Physiological effects	Comments
CO	Reduces the blood's capacity to transport available oxygen to the tissues owing to the formation of carboxyhemoglobin	Extremely dangerous and problematic for short-term high-dose exposures. CO uptake impairs perception and thinking, slows reflexes, and causes drowsiness, angina, unconsciousness, and ultimately death
NO_x	Increases susceptibility to respiratory infection, increases airway resistance in asthmatics, and decreases pulmonary function	Dangerous and problematic for long-term continuous exposure, causing chronic diseases related to respiratory and pulmonary functions
HC (a)	Toxic and carcinogenic effects. Irritation of eye, nose, and mucus membranes, coughing, nausea, and shortness of breath	Dangerous and problematic for long-term continuous exposure, causing chronic diseases of the nervous, hematological, immunological, and respiratory systems
Pb	Perception, short-term memory loss, and impaired reaction time (US States Environmental Protection Agency, 1990). The chronic effect in adults is predominantly high blood pressure	Constitutes a significant hazard to children less than 6 years old and to adult women of reproductive age, causing acute effects
Particulates	Respiratory, pulmonary, and cardiovascular damage	Short-term exposure effects are reversible and diminish after a few days without exposure. Long-term exposure increases the risk of respiratory and cardiorespiratory mortality and morbidity
SO_2	Affects upper respiratory tract causing reduced lung function	Long-term continuous exposure causes respiratory diseases, increasing risk of mortality and morbidity

Note: (a) toxic HC emissions from gasoline and AFs are listed in Table 4.

3. Alternative fuels

The possibility of substituting cleaner-burning AFs for gasoline and diesel has drawn increasing attention over the past decade. A vast array of scientific and popular literature is available on the subject of AFs (Air Quality Improvement Research Program, 1992; Hutcheson, 1995; Office of Technology Assessment, 1995; Organisation for Economic Development and Co-operation, 1995; Delucchi, 1996, 1997).

3.1. What are AFs?

AFs are derived from non-crude oil resources. In general, AFs include all vehicular fuels other than gasoline and diesel fuels. These are natural gas (methane, CH_4), propane (C_3H_8), methanol (CH_3OH), ethanol (C_2H_5OH), hydrogen (H_2) and electricity. Although electricity is not actually a fuel, it is a source of energy that can be used to propel vehicles.

3.2. Why are AFs important?

AFs provide three distinct advantages over conventional fuels (Table 3).

Some AFs have the potential for significant cost-effective reductions in emissions of CO, HCs, and NO_x but may cause sharp increases in emissions of other toxic pollutants (Table 4). In many cases the same or even greater emission reductions could be achieved using a conventional fuel with an advanced emission control system. Care is thus needed when evaluating air quality claims for AFs.

In many parts of the world, CNG and LPG compete with gasoline or diesel fuels, and may therefore be attractive from an economic as well as environmental

Table 3
Advantages of AFs over conventional fuels

Advantage	Comments
Energy independence	AFs are more likely to be produced from domestic resources
Reduced emissions	AFs generally reduce vehicular emissions
Lower costs	Some AFs offer the potential to lower fleet operating costs

Table 4
Emissions of toxic organic compounds from gasoline and AFs (mg/km)

Compound	Gasoline	RFG	M85	M100	E85	CNG	LPG
Benzene	7.95	4.88	4.38	0.32	1.21	0.242	0.242
Toluene	33.66	3.45	8.66	2.11	0.75	0.695	0.695
1,3-Butadiene	0.50	0.24	0.44	2.05	0.12	0.40	–
Formaldehyde	4.78	0.60	13.87	21.76	3.15	2.712	4.870
Acrolein	1.12	–	4.44	0.09	–	0.330	0.118

Source: Organisation for Economic Development and Co-operation (1995).
Key: RFG, reformulated gasoline; M85, 85% methanol blend; M100, pure methanol; E85, 85% ethanol blend (15% ordinary gasoline); CNG, compressed natural gas; LPG, liquefied petroleum gas.

Table 5
Retail (1992) prices of conventional and AFs in the USA (US $/liter)

Gasoline	Methanol	Ethanol	LPG	CNG	H_2
0.25–0.96	0.58–0.67	NA	0.69–0.80	0.29–0.65	6.96–11.6

Source: Seisler et al. (1993).

perspective. Table 5 compares the historic cost of AFs in the USA with that of gasoline.

The cost of transportation comprises two components: capital and operating costs paid by the users; all other external costs resulting from the use of transportation and which are not paid for directly by users (e.g. the health effects of air pollution from combustion of vehicle fuels, damage to ecosystems from fuel leakages/spills, and climatic changes due to greenhouse gas emissions). Delucchi et al. (1994) and Delucchi (1996) have undertaken preliminary analyses of the social cost of transportation, and have concluded that the monetary value of the health effects of air pollution is one of the largest external costs of transportation.

3.3. AF characteristics

The characteristics of fuels – both favorable and unfavorable – must be considered when making long-term decisions about alternatives to gasoline. The basic properties of AFs are given in Table 6 and compared with conventional fuels.

It is evident from the table that AFs have a lower energy density and therefore require a greater volume of on-board storage than gasoline or diesel. CNG, H_2, and LPG, on the other hand, provide more energy per kilogram than does gasoline, which indicates that vehicle operation with AFs should be more efficient than with gasoline. However, a vehicle using "clean" AFs will not necessarily have low pollutant emissions. Much depends on the level of pollution control technology employed. While strict "technology-forcing" emission standards have produced advances in gasoline and diesel engine emissions control technologies, AFs have not been subjected to similar regulations until recently. This is particularly true of retrofit equipment for converting existing vehicles to run on AFs. Very few countries have promulgated regulations requiring emissions certification for such retrofitted engines using AFs. Because of the absence of such regulations, many vehicle conversion kits are sold with relatively poor air:fuel ratio control, resulting in high emissions. Table 7 shows the maintenance failure rates for vehicles in Canada using gasoline, LPG, and CNG (B.C. Ministry of Energy, Mines, and Petroleum Resources, 1994).

Regulatory pressure may result in the incorporation of well-designed emission control systems in retrofit kits. But the lowest emissions and most efficient operation will naturally be obtained with engines designed solely to use AFs.

4. Types of AFs

4.1. Compressed natural gas

CNG is a gaseous mixture of HCs consisting of approximately 80–90% methane. Natural gas is colorless, odorless, non-toxic, and highly flammable. Owing to its low energy density, it is compressed to a pressure of 200–250 kg/cm^3 and stored in a cylinder to maximize the amount that can be carried by a vehicle. CNG is not a liquid fuel and is not the same as LPG, which consists of propane and butane in liquid form.

There are over 1 million vehicles running on CNG in the world. CNG as a fuel has a long and established record in Europe, Canada, New Zealand, Australia,

Table 6
Fuel properties

Fuel	Heating value (MJ/kg)	Air:fuel ratio ($\lambda = 1$)	Heat of vaporization (MJ/Kg)	Cetane rating	Octane rating	Energy density (MJ/l)
Gasoline	42.66	14.6	0.36	–	83–90	33.00
Diesel	43.20	14.5	0.286	40–65	–	36.50
CNG	49.91	17.2	0.507	–	130	21.13
LPG	45.95	15.8	0.428	–	89	23.60
Methanol	19.86	6.5	1.186	3	91	15.84
Ethanol	26.85	9.0	0.842	8	92	21.12
Hydrogen	119.44	34.3	–	–	–	–

Source: Maxwell and Jones (1993).

Table 7
Inspection and maintenance failure rates for light duty vehicles in British Columbia, Canada, using gasoline, LPG, and CNG fuels

Model year	Gasoline (%)	LPG (%)	CNG (%)
1974 or older	31	19	11
1975–1981	37	42	24
1982–1987	25	47	23
1988–1993	6	44	34

Table 8
A comparison of CNG with gasoline in terms of emissions

Emissions	CNG emission characteristics compared with gasoline
CO	70% lower
CO_2	Low
Non-methane organic gas	89% lower
NO_x	87% lower
Evaporative emissions during fuelling	Nil (for gasoline, evaporative emissions are around 50% of the total HCs)
Formaldehyde	50% lower
Acetaldehyde	80% lower
Benzene	Nil
1,3-Butadiene	Nil
Cold-start emissions	Low
Particulates	Negligible

and the USA. Other countries, such as Japan, Mexico, Malaysia, Pakistan, Bangladesh, and India, are recognizing the benefits of CNG and plan to expand its use.

Its main drawback is the lack of refueling facilities. High-flow-rate, high-pressure CNG compressors are expensive and require a large capital investment. Another drawback is the water content of CNG, which can cause corrosion problems in gas cylinders; this water must be efficiently removed from the system by dryers (Maxwell and Jones, 1993).

Most of the CNG vehicles in operation worldwide are retrofits, converted from gasoline and diesel vehicles.

Emissions

CNG is an inherently clean-burning fuel. It contains less carbon than any other fossil fuel and thus produces lower carbon dioxide emissions per vehicle-km traveled. While CNG emits more methane than gasoline does, this is offset by a substantial reduction in carbon dioxide emissions compared with other fuels. Table 8 provides a comparison of CNG with gasoline in terms of exhaust emissions.

A study conducted by the Commonwealth Scientific and Industrial Research Organisation in Australia (Beer, 2000) graded CNG as the cleanest fuel when compared with the conventional fuels (Table 9).

Energy release

In terms of energy, 1 kg of CNG is equivalent to about 1.349 liters of gasoline or 1.18 liters of diesel. On a volumetric basis, 1 m^3 of CNG is equivalent to about 1.10 liters of gasoline or 1.0 liter of diesel. In addition, its high octane value makes it possible to attain higher efficiency.

Table 9
The cleanest fuels

Fuel	Emissions (g/km)				Particulate emissions compared with CNG emissions
	CO	Non-methane VOCs	NO_x	Particulates	
Low-sulfur diesel (500 ppm sulphur)	1.32	0.50	14.72	0.22	340% higher than CNG emissions
Ultra-low-sulfur diesel (50 ppm sulphur)	1.41	0.52	14.32	0.16	220% higher than CNG emission
CNG	0.66	2.75	9.87	0.05	–

Source: Beer (2000).

Price

CNG costs vary greatly from country to country, and even within countries, due to infrastructure and transport cost; for example, in India, CNG currently costs approximately 68% less than gasoline and 32% less than diesel (Indraprastha Gas, 2000). Where gas is available by pipeline from the field, its price is normally set in competition with residual fuel oil or coal. The market-clearing price under these conditions is typically about US $2.84 per million kilojoules (equivalent to about US $0.108 per liter of diesel fuel value). Natural gas compression costs can add another US $0.47–1.09 per million kilojoules, depending on the facility's size and the natural gas supply pressure.

Safety

CNG is lighter than air. In the event of leak, it will rise and disperse in the atmosphere, rather than remain on the ground like gasoline or LPG. The ignition temperature of CNG is much higher than gasoline, making it more difficult to ignite. CNG will not burn when its concentration in air is below 5% or above 15%. Thus, a high concentration of gas in the air is needed for CNG to ignite, which is not easy to achieve in the event of a leak.

4.2. Liquefied petroleum gas

LPG is a mixture of several gases in varying proportions that is liquefied by compression or refrigeration and stored in thick-walled containers. The major constituents are propane (C_3H_8) and n-butane (C_4H_{10}), with minor quantities of propene (C_3H_6), butene (C_4H_8), isobutane, and, to a lesser extent, ethane (C_2H_6). In cold climates, LPG has a higher proportion of propane and propene to provide adequate vapor pressure in winter; in warm climates, LPG consists mostly of n-butane and butene. LPG is non-toxic.

LPG can be stored at a pressure of 250 psi, much lower than that used for CNG; thus, it is possible to carry more fuel on-board than is the case with CNG.

A major disadvantage of LPG is its limited supply, which rules out any large scale conversion to LPG fuel.

LPG, at present, powers an estimated 4 million vehicles in several countries, including Australia, Canada, Italy, Japan, Korea, the Netherlands, New Zealand, Thailand, and the USA.

Emissions

LPG is similar to CNG in many of its emission characteristics. It produces nearly zero particulates, very little CO and moderate HC emissions. Evaporative emissions are negligible. The CO_2 emissions are lower than that of gasoline owing to a lower carbon:energy ratio and a higher octane rating. Cold start emissions are negligible. NO_x emissions are similar to those of gasoline. Overall, LPG provides less air quality benefits than CNG, mainly because the HC emissions are photochemically more reactive and emissions of CO are higher (Faiz et al., 1996).

Energy release

The volumetric energy content of LPG is less than that of gasoline (0.73:1). LPG-fueled heavy-duty vehicles consume 20–30% (v/v) more fuel than similar vehicles using gasoline. In comparison with diesel, LPG has a higher energy content per kilogram (Faiz et al., 1996).

Price

The price of LPG is low in most countries compared with that of other HC fuels. For consumer-grade LPG in the USA the wholesale price has been about US $0.018–0.021 per liter for several years (or about 30% less than the wholesale cost of diesel on an energy basis). Depending on the location, however, the additional costs of storing and transporting LPG may affect this advantage.

Safety

LPG poses a greater safety risk than CNG. Unlike CNG, LPG vapor is heavier than air, so leaks in the fuel system will cause pooling of gas at ground level, where it can easily be ignited. The flammability limits of LPG vapor are 97–85% to 90.4% in air. LPG vehicles may be subjected to restrictions on parking in enclosed spaces.

4.3. Methanol

Methanol (CH_3OH) is an alcohol. Most of the world's methanol is produced by a process that uses natural gas as a feedstock. However, the ability to produce methanol from feedstocks such as coal or biomass is of interest for reducing petroleum imports. Production of methanol from coal does have potential for long-term usage owing to the large world reserves of coal; a major disadvantage to this method of production is the generation of CO_2, which is higher than that for refining gasoline. The best alternative production technique of methanol as an AF is from urban waste and refuse. Methanol, processed from biomass and urban waste, will produce a significant amount of energy without consuming fossil energy. Production ratios (energy available from methanol divided by the non-renewable energy input) as high as 2.3 can be achieved for the conversion of biomass to methanol (Maxwell and Jones, 1993).

Methanol is an excellent internal combustion engine fuel in terms of its octane number, density, and heating value (stoichiometric mixture) (American Petroleum Institute, 1988). The high octane rating allows the use of a high compression ratio (up to 15:10) (Maxwell and Jones, 1993). Methane is used either as M85 (a mixture of 85% methanol and 15% HCs) or M100 (100% methanol).

The use of methanol as an AF is widely promoted in the USA. However, any large-scale use of methanol as a vehicle fuel will require substantial investments in fuel storage, transportation, and dispensing facilities.

Emissions

Some of the disadvantages of M85 methanol are similar to those of gasoline. Although M85 results in reduced emissions of formaldehyde, the acetaldehyde emissions approach the levels of ethanol–gasoline blends (Faiz et al., 1996). M100 methanol generates about five times more formaldehyde than gasoline does. In cold climates, the use of methanol as a fuel in vehicles may cause cold-starting problems and can result in higher cold-start exhaust emissions, i.e. unburnt fuel (HCs and formaldehyde) and CO emissions. The emissions of CO and formaldehyde can, though, be controlled by the use of catalytic converters.

Energy

Methanol has a lower heating value than other fuels (19.86 MJ/kg, see Table 6). Since the heating value is a measure of the energy that can be delivered by the fuel, it determines the distance that the vehicle can be driven on a given amount (volume) of fuel. Compared with gasoline, about twice as much methanol is required to drive a vehicle an equivalent distance.

Price

The world methanol production capacity is limited to about 7 billion gallons per annum. M85 is costlier than gasoline (Air Quality Improvement Research Program, 1993).

Safety

Unlike HC fuels, methanol burns with a nearly non-luminous flame that is impossible to see in daylight. The vapor pressure of methanol is also such that it can form a flammable mixture in the headspace of a fuel tank at ambient temperatures. It is also toxic. Hence, issues of safety and handling are much greater for methanol than for gasoline.

4.4. Ethanol

Ethanol is an alcohol, and its chemical and physical properties are very similar to those of methanol except that it is considerably cleaner, less toxic, and less corrosive. In addition, ethanol has a higher volumetric energy content. Ethanol can be produced by the fermentation of sugar cane or corn ("grain alcohol"), but it is more expensive to produce than methanol and requires large harvests of these crops and large amounts of energy for its production, which may lead to "upstream" environmental problems, particularly soil degradation (Organisation for Economic Development and Co-operation, 1995). Ethanol can also be made from cellulose obtained from agriculture residue and waste paper. Ethanol is available in two main forms, as hydrous ethanol (95% mixture with water) or anhydrous ethanol (99.5% mixture with benzene). Fuel-grade ethanol is produced in Brazil, where one-third of its 12 million cars are powered by ethanol.

When ethanol is blended with ordinary gasoline in proportions up to 22%, the resulting mixture is known as "gasohol." In addition to the perceived environmental benefits of using ethanol as a fuel, when ethanol is added to gasoline the octane rating is increased, thus eliminating the need for anti-knock additives such as lead compounds. Gasohol is extensively used in Brazil, South Africa, and the USA.

Emissions

Emissions from ethanol-powered vehicles are not well characterized, but they are high in unburnt ethanol, acetaldehyde (more than 12 times higher than for gasoline), and formaldehyde. Compared with gasoline-fueled vehicles, CO is

20–30% lower, and NO_x is 15% lower. Evaporative emissions are also lower than for gasoline. The low vapor pressure of ethanol causes "cold start" problems, resulting in high cold-start emissions. Emissions of benzene and particulates are also substantially lower for ethanol-powered vehicles. Table 10 shows average emissions from gasohol and ethanol light-duty vehicles in Brazil (Faiz et al., 1996).

Energy

As shown in Table 6, ethanol has a lower heat value when compared with other AFs (26.85 MJ/kg). This means that about 1.5 times as much ethanol is required to drive a vehicle an equivalent distance using gasoline.

Safety

Ethanol is highly inflammable. Although it is less volatile than gasoline, it is more explosive. As an intoxicant, ethanol presents special supervisory challenges.

Price

The cost of ethanol is higher than gasoline, except where it is heavily subsidized (as in Brazil). In the USA the price ranges from US $0.26–0.41 per liter equivalent to US $0.40–0.65 per liter of gasoline on an energy basis.

4.5. Biodiesel

Biodiesel is produced by reacting vegetable or animal fats with methanol or ethanol to produce a lower viscosity fuel that is similar in physical characteristics to diesel. Table 11 compares the properties of biodiesel with those of diesel.

Emissions

CO and HC emissions are low in comparison with diesel fuel. However, studies have shown that biodiesel emits more NO_x than conventional diesel. This is due to

Table 10
Average emissions from gasohol and ethanol (g/km)

Fuel	CO	HCs	NO_x
Gasohol	40.5	3.8	1.4
Ethanol	18.8	1.6	1.1

Source: Faiz et al. (1996).

Table 11
A comparison of biodiesel and diesel

Property	Biodiesel	Diesel
Viscosity (kg/m s)	4.1–4.5	2.3–2.8
Heat of combustion (MJ/kg)	37.1–37.7	42.8
Cetane number	46–52	47–51
Carbon (% wt)	77–78	86
Hydrogen (% wt)	11–12	13
Oxygen (% wt)	10–11	0
Water (mg/kg)	500	50
Nitrogen (ppm)	29	0
Density (kg/m^3)	882–885	850–860

Source: Faiz et al. (1996).

the higher cetane number of biodiesel and its higher nitrogen content. There is controversy regarding particulate emissions (Alfuso et al., 1993; Hutcheson, 1995), and Alfuso et al. (1993) in particular have reported higher particulate emissions in comparison with conventional diesel fuel.

Price

The cost of biodiesel fuel is US $0.66–0.92 per liter, which is substantially higher than conventional diesel, which makes it less attractive as an AF.

4.6. Hydrogen

Hydrogen has the potential to be the cleanest fuel. However, it suffers from two major problems: production and storage. Hydrogen is not a fossil fuel and therefore not found in significant quantities in nature. As a result, it must be manufactured. The most common methods are electrolysis of water, reforming natural gas, or partial oxidation and steam reforming other fossil fuels. The most economical method is from reforming natural gas. Significant investments are needed in the infrastructure for the delivery, storage, and dispensing of hydrogen if it is used as a vehicle fuel.

Emissions

The combustion of hydrogen produces mainly water vapor. In vehicles, the only pollutant produced in the course of hydrogen combustion is NO_x, with small amounts of HCs, CO, and particulates from lubricating oil. NO_x emissions from

Table 12
Hydrogen-fuelled vehicle emissions

Vehicle	Emissions (g/mile)		
	HCs	CO	NO_x
1972 Gremlin bus (1587.3 kg)	0.000	0.000	0.205
Rosa bus (4031.7 kg)	0.015	0.043	1.393
Rosa car (997.7 kg) (a)	0.004	0.011	0.345
Eimco H_2 car (997.7 kg) (a)	0.004	0.011	0.040

Source: TOPTEC (1991).
Note: (a) estimated emission values (concept vehicle designs).

existing prototype hydrogen vehicles are similar to those from gasoline vehicles (Kukkonen and Shelef, 1994). Hydrogen combustion produces no direct emissions of CO_2; however, indirect CO_2 emissions depend on the nature of the energy source used to produce the hydrogen. Mackenzie (1994) provides an excellent review of the prospects and potential of hydrogen fuel-driven vehicles. Table 12 gives emissions for some hydrogen-fueled vehicles, such as a 1972 Mitsubishi passenger bus converted for operation with hydrogen.

Energy

The heat value of hydrogen is 119.4 MJ/kg (see Table 6), which is almost three times that of gasoline. Consequently, a hydrogen engine will be more efficient than a gasoline or diesel engine.

Safety

Hydrogen is a highly flammable gas and thus potentially dangerous. It is lighter than air, and mixes readily with air to form an explosive mixture. Hydrogen is also difficult to store because its molecules are very small.

Price

Owing to the high cost of producing hydrogen and lack of storage reserves, it is unlikely that hydrogen will be a cost-effective AF. One of the most promising developments is a prototype 60 – passenger hydrogen bus produced by Canada's Ballard power systems. However, the Ballard prototype costs three times as much to operate as a comparable diesel bus. Economies of scale and improved hydrogen fuel cells might make hydrogen-powered vehicles competitive with conventional diesel vehicles in the long term (American Association of State Highway and Transportation Officials, 1996).

4.7. Electricity

Electricity has long been used as an alternative to petroleum fuels: the first electric cars were built in the nineteenth century, and initially outnumbered gasoline-fueled vehicles. However, owing to their poor range and low speed, interest in battery electric vehicles (BEVs) soon waned.

In recent years there has been renewed interest in BEVs, and many countries in Europe and Asia are funding research on the development of a viable, economic BEV. A number of battery electric cars have been put on the market, and BEVs are used in noise-sensitive situations, e.g. milk deliveries to homes in UK cities. The performance of commercially available battery electric cars remains poor, however, despite advances in battery and other technologies: a typical modern electric car has a range of about 75 km, and the batteries require 4–8 h to recharge.

Because batteries can supply only enough energy for short trips, hybrid electric vehicles (HEVs) are being developed, which combine a battery-driven electric motor with an internal combustion engine (which may use an AF). The internal combustion engine may drive a generator, to produce electricity, or it might power the drive train in a conventional manner. HEVs using gas turbines instead of traditional spark ignition or diesel engines to generate electricity have been investigated. The first of these hybrids to be marketed was the Toyota Prius, launched in 1997.

There is also intensive research on electric vehicles using fuel cells. A fuel cell converts chemical energy directly into electrical energy. In a fuel cell, the electricity-producing reactants are continually supplied from an external source, such as a hydrogen storage tank. There are four types of fuel cells: phosphoric acid, alkaline, solid oxides, and proton exchange membrane (PEM) fuel cells. PEM fuel cells are best suited for use in highway vehicles (Organisation for Economic Development and Co-operation/International Energy Agency, 1993). Fuel cells are efficient, quiet, and reliable, and are predicted to demonstrate energy conversion efficiencies up to 50%, compared with the 20–25% efficiency of a typical gasoline engine.

Another method for powering electric vehicles is to provide a permanent supply of electricity. For example, trolley buses or trams using overhead wires have been used for public transport since the nineteenth century, and are still common in many countries, especially in Latin America, Asia, and Eastern Europe. Globally, there are over 370 trolley bus systems. The largest system is in Brazil, with 480 trolley buses. Electric train systems and metros using either overhead wires or surface rails are also common technologies.

Emissions

Conventional electric vehicles such as BEVs produce virtually no emissions; however, the indirect emissions from the production of electricity by power plants can be attributed to electric vehicles.

Emissions from HEVs using fuel cells are very much lower than those generated by a power station to produce an equivalent amount of electricity. The reforming of natural gas to produce the hydrogen required for the fuel cell would generate small but measurable amounts of NO_x and CO (Faiz et al., 1996).

A gas turbine engine can use any combustible fuel that can be injected into the airstream. Thus, to minimize emissions, a fuel which burns completely and cleanly can theoretically be chosen.

Safety

The primary safety concern is the need for proper maintenance of fuel cells against leakage and the safe disposal of batteries and fuel cells.

Electric vehicles such as trolley buses often use high-voltage overhead wires, which are vulnerable to accidents and sabotage.

Price

Conventional electric vehicles have high operating and capital costs compared with diesel-fueled ones. However, they are economical for "shuttle" services. The cost of a BEV in the US is about US $35 000. HEVs are significantly more expensive than conventionally fueled vehicles. However, this additional cost has a substantial payoff in near-zero emissions (Office of Technology Assessment, US Congress, 1995).

5. Greenhouse gas emissions

DeLuchi (1993) has developed a greenhouse-gas emission model to estimate emissions of greenhouse gases from automobiles, buses, power plants, and other activities. The model includes "fuel cycle" emissions – emissions from the recovery and transport of primary energy feedstocks, the production of fuels from feedstocks, the distribution of fuels to end users, the end use of fuels in vehicles, the servicing and maintenance of transport modes, the building of major energy facilities, and the manufacture of materials for motor vehicles and their assembly. Table 13 shows the greenhouse gas emission factors for the DeLuchi model.

Table 13
Greenhouse gas emission factors, in grams of CO_2-equivalent emissions from fuel production and transport per million joules of energy delivered to end users (except where noted) (a)

Fuel	Factor (g/10^6 J)
Coal	6.01
Reformulated gasoline	21.61
Conventional gasoline	19.28
Low-sulfur diesel	13.99
Residual fuel oil	13.11
Refinery gas	5.21
Petroleum coke	7.69
Natural gas for heat, CNG (b)	9.01
Nuclear power (c)	12.46
Methanol from natural gas	34.01
Methanol from coal	116.31
Methanol from wood	20.85
Ethanol from corn	112.37
Ethanol from wood (d)	–0.88
Synthetic natural gas from wood	13.43
Hydrogen from solar power	0.095
LPG from a mix of NG and oil (e)	9.47
LPG from natural-gas liquids	7.42
84LPG from petroleum	12.74
Wood for power production	5.23

Notes:
(a) Updated version of model documented in DeLuchi (1993).
(b) Emissions from the generation of electricity used to compress natural gas are calculated separately (as emissions from activities at service stations) and included in the final totals.
(c) Units are grams of CO_2 equivalents per million joules of power generated.
(d) The negative value is due to emissions credit from the sale of excess power generated by burning portions of feedstock not converted to fuel.

6. Factors influencing the large-scale use of AFs

6.1. Cost

The high cost of production is the primary factor influencing the large-scale use of AFs. The additional cost of fuel storage and distribution also affect the use of AFs. Gasoline and diesel substitutes require relatively small changes to the existing distribution system, while CNG, LPG, and alcohol fuels require more extensive changes. The cost of production of the fuels is also a consideration, as is the technology needed to produce them. CNG and LPG are economically as competitive as gasoline to produce; methanol and ethanol are only marginally so. Methanol from coal or biomass, and ethanol from biomass, are estimated to cost twice as much as gasoline to produce (International Energy Agency, 1990). Compared with gasoline or diesel, the cost of biodiesel is 3–4 times higher.

6.2. End use considerations

AFs require changes to the ways in which they are distributed and marketed: an inadequate supply and unreliable distribution systems may inhibit consumer acceptance of AFs. Experience with ethanol in Brazil and CNG in New Zealand suggests that the main factors influencing large-scale introduction of CNG and alcohol fuels are price competitiveness, availability, safety and quality standards, reliability of the distribution system, and technological reliabilty of vehicles.

6.3. Life cycle emissions

Automotive life cycle emissions may be divided into three major stages: vehicle production, fuel production, and vehicle use. The life-cycle emissions from fuel production and end use have received considerable attention in recent years with the emergence of a variety of AFs for which the end use emissions are considerably lower. Tables 14 and 15 give life cycle emissions for conventional and AFs (Lewis and Gover, 1996).

Table 14
Life cycle emissions for gasoline-fueled cars with respect to fuel production, vehicle production, and in-service use

Life cycle stage	Emissions (g/km)					
	CO_2	CO	NO_x	HCs from paint	SO_2	Particulates
Fuel production	47.0	0.061	0.174	0.388	0.185	0.011
Vehicle production	54.5	0.021	0.160	0.105	0.493	0.016
Vehicle use	186.3	3.371	0.224	0.299	0.020	0.005
Total	287.8	3.453	0.558	0.792	0.699	0.032

Table 15
Life cycle emissions from cars for conventional fuels and AFs

Fuel	Emissions(g/km)					
	CO_2	CO	NO_x	HCs	SO_2	Particulates
Gasoline	287.8	3.453	0.558	0.792	0.699	0.032
Diesel	227.1	0.489	0.981	0.384	0702	0.131
LPG	239.0	3.889	0.482	0.443	0.649	0.027
CNG	242.0	0.863	0.457	1.137	0.575	0.022
Methanol	233.7	3.292	0.729	0.914	0.549	0.023
Biodiesel (a)	292.0	3.419	0.784	0.597	0.640	0.039
Electricity	228.1	0.068	0.520	0.451	1.005	0.040

Note: (a) The aggregate life cycle emissions for biodiesel fuel are as high as those from conventional diesel fuels. This is owing to the non-direct emissions arising from various processes in the production of biodiesel such as tilling, planting the crops (rapeseed, soybean, sunflower), fertilizing, and harvesting. These processes require the use of motorized farm equipment, which produce exhaust emissions and use fossil fuel energy. In addition, the production of biodiesel needs methanol in the "transesterification" process, which also produces emissions.

7. Conclusions

Among the AFs, the greatest emission reductions are obtained with hydrogen, followed by CNG and LPG. Conventional electric vehicles such as BEVs have zero emissions, although emissions of NO_x and sulfur dioxide associated with the generation of electricity by power stations can exceed those from conventional gasoline and diesel vehicles on an energy equivalence basis.

CNG may capture a major share of the market in developing countries as an AF for commercial vehicle fleets. However, the inconvenience of storage and slow refueling may limit its appeal in the consumer vehicle market.

In the developing world, after-market conversion to LPG or CNG will remain the primary mode of AF use. The strength of the market will depend upon the retail cost of AFs.

A potential market in the developing world is for additives or reformulated gasoline. MTBE and ETBE are the preferred additives in most cases as they require no changes in vehicle technology. With reasonable fiscal incentives, appropriate fuel pricing, and technical support, electric two and three wheelers could substitute for their petroleum-fueled counterparts in many highly congested urban areas in the developing world.

In theory, a policy-maker in transportation may evaluate a wide range of alternatives (from expanding highway capacity to managing existing demand) using cost–benefit analysis. This involves one quantifying and monetizing all of the costs and benefits to the society of the alternatives, and picking the alternative that yields the greatest net benefit. Following this approach, past experiences with the use of ethanol in Brazil, and CNG in New Zealand and India, suggest that the main factors which affect the large-scale introduction of CNG and alcohol fuels are price competitiveness, feed stock availability, and cost. In the case of India, the main factor influencing the widespread use of CNG is the monetary value of the health effects arising from air pollutants. Thus, Brazil's use of ethanol, and New Zealand's and India's use of CNG, demonstrate that it is possible to develop large AF markets within a reasonable time-frame if the financial incentives are favorable and adequate efforts are made to overcome consumer uncertainty. But, in both instances, it appeared important that substantial subsidies were offered to persuade consumers to switch to AFs.

Acknowledgments

The authors are grateful to Niraj Sharma, Shiva Nagendra, and Shaily Mahendra for their help and assistance.

References

Air Quality Improvement Research Program (1992) *A study of fuel effects on emissions from high emitting vehicles*. Technical Bulletin No. 11. Atlanta: Auto/Oil Coordinating Research Council.

Air Quality Improvement Research Program (1993) *Auto/oil air quality improvement research program phase I final report*. Atlanta: Auto/Oil Coordinating Research Council.

Alfuso, S., M. Aurlemma, G. Police and M.V. Prati (1993) *The effect of methyl-ester of rapeseed oil on combustion and emissions of DI diesel engines*. SAE Paper 932801. Warrendale: Society of Automotive Engineers.

American Association of State Highway and Transportation Officials (1996) *Energy alternative – the bus that sheds water*. Washington, DC: International Transportation Observer.

American Petroleum Institute (1988) *Alcohols and ethers*. Publication No. 4261, 2nd edn. Washimgton, DC: API.

B.C. Ministry of Energy, Mines, and Petroleum Resources (1994) *Cleaner fuels for cleaner air: the role of alternative transportation fuels in British Columbia*. Victoria: B.C. Ministry of Energy, Mines, and Petroleum Resources.

Beer, T. (2000) *Lifecycle emissions analysis of alternative fuels for heavy vehicles*. CSIRO Atmospheric Research Report. Canberra: Commonwealth Scientific and Research Organisation.

Conservation of Clean Air and Water in Europe (1994) *Motor vehicle emissions regulations and fuel specifications*. Report 4/94. Brussels: CONCAWE

Delucchi, M.A. (1993) *Emissions of greenhouse gases from the use of transportation fuels and electricity*, Vol. I, ANL/ESD/TM-22. Argonne: Center for Transportation Research, Argonne National Laboratory.

Delucchi, M.A. (1996) *Emissions of criteria pollutants, toxic air pollutants, and greenhouse gases, from the use of alternative transportation modes and fuels*. Davis: Institute of Transportation Studies, University of California.

Delucchi, M.A. (1997) *A revised model of emissions of greenhouse gases from the use of transportation fuels and electricity*. Davis: Institute of Transportation Studies, University of California.

Delucchi, M.A., K. McCubbin, J. Murphy and S. Hsu (1994) *The annualized social cost of motor-vehicle use in the U.S., based on 1990–1991 data*. Davis: Institute of Transportation Studies, University of California.

Down to Earth (2000) "Of cars that kill," *Down to Earth*, 15 May:28–30.

Faiz, A., C.S. Weaves and M.P. Walsh (1996) *Air pollution from motor vehicles, standards and technologies for controlling emissions*. Washington, DC: The World Bank.

Hutcheson, R.C. (1995) *Alternative fuels in the automotive market*. CONCAWE Report No. 2/95. Brussels: CONCAWE.

Indraprastha Gas Limited (2000) *CNG, the wonder fuel for cars*. New Delhi: IGL.

International Energy Agency (1990) *Substitute fuels for road transport: a technology assessment*. Paris: OECD.

Kukkonen, C.A. and M. Shelef (1994) *Hydrogen as an alternative automotive fuel: 1993 update*. SAE Paper 940766. Warrendale: Society of Automotive Engineers.

Lewis, C.A. and M.P. Gover, (1996) "Life-cycle analysis of motor fuel emissions. Estimation of pollutant emissions from transport," in: *COST 319, interim report and proceedings workshop Nov 27–28, 1995*, CEC/DGVII. Brussels: European Commission.

Mackenzie, J.J. (1994) *The keys to the car: electric and hydrogen vehicles for the 21st century*. Washington, DC: World Research Institute.

Mark, J. and C. Morey, (1999) *Diesel passenger vehicles and the environment*. Berkeley: Union of Concerned Scientists.

Maxwell, T.T. and J.C. Jones, (1993) *Alternative fuels: emissions, economies and performance*. Warrendale: Society of Automotive Engineers.

Office of Technology Assessment, US Congress (1995) *Advanced automotive technology: visions of a super-efficient family car*, OTA-ETI-638. Washington, DC: US Government Printing Office.

Organisation for Economic Development and Co-operation (1995) *Motor vehicle pollution reduction strategies beyond 2010*. Paris: OECD.

Organisation for Economic Development and Co-operation/International Energy Association (1993) *Cars and climate change*. Paris: OECD.

Romieu, I. (1992) "Epidemiologic studies of the health effects of air pollution due to motor vehicles," in: D.E. Mage and O. Zali, eds, *Motor vehicle pollution: public health impact and control measures*. Geneva: World Health Organization and Department of Public Health.

Seisler, J., G. Sperling, C.S. Weaver and S.H. Turner (1993) "Alternative fuels," in: *Energy law and transactions*. Oakland: Bender.

TOPTEC (1991) *Emissions from alternative fuelled vehicles*. San Antonio: Society of Automotive Engineers.

US Environmental Protection Agency (1990) *Air quality criteria for lead: supplement to the 1986 addendum*. Washington, DC: Office of Research and Development, US Environmental Protection Agency.

Chapter 10

CLEANER VEHICLES

DANIEL SPERLING
University of California, Davis, CA

1. Introduction

As populations and economies expand, increasing quantities of natural resources are extracted and processed, more goods are moved, more people travel, more energy is used, and more wastes are generated. One outcome is over 800 million motor vehicles operating in the world today, consuming around 40 million barrels of petroleum per day, producing about a half of the urban pollution, and emitting over a tenth of the world's anthropogenic greenhouse gases (International Energy Agency, 2000). This is not sustainable unless energy and environmental performance is improved. In this chapter, we focus on the energy and environmental performance of land-based vehicles, especially those operating on roads. We examine internal combustion engine vehicles, electric-drive vehicles, and alternative fuels.

2. Recent history of alternative fuels

History is littered with efforts to replace petroleum fuels and improve upon petroleum-powered internal combustion engines. Initiatives and investments have largely come and gone, succumbing to unanticipated successes in finding and extracting petroleum and reducing emissions from petroleum-fueled engines. A common theme throughout this long history is the growing importance of environmental impacts as a determining factor in energy production and use.

The modern history of alternative fuels begins in the mid-1970s, just after the 1973 Arab oil embargo (Sperling, 1988, 1995). Nations began searching for ways to attain energy independence. They began to investigate the use of alternative resources – mostly coal, oil shale, oil sands, and biomass. Natural gas was virtually ignored in most countries since it was considered even scarcer than petroleum. By the late 1970s, a number of countries were beginning to invest vast sums in pursuit of energy independence. The USA was investing tens of billions of dollars in synthetic fuel plants that converted mostly coal and oil shale into petroleum-like

Handbook of Transport and the Environment, Edited by D.A. Hensher and K.J. Button
© 2003, Elsevier Ltd

fuels. Brazil began a massive program to convert sugar cane into ethanol, and South Africa increased its coal-to-fuels investments.

By the early 1980s, perceptions began to shift. The costs of manufacturing petroleum-like fuels from coal and oil shale were greater than anticipated, and petroleum-like synthetic fuels did not help reduce persistent urban air pollution. After tens of billions of dollars of wasted investment in expensive synthetic fuel plants, the USA shifted its focus to the use of methanol and natural gas in internal combustion engines. South Africa, however, expanded its commitment to coal-to-liquids technology as a means of resisting international sanctions over apartheid, while Brazil increased its commitment to ethanol produced from sugar cane.

In the mid- and late 1980s, with the drop in oil prices (from about US $30 per barrel to under $15), the most capital-intensive alternative fuel investments evaporated, and environmental issues began coming to the forefront. Attention began to shift toward natural gas fuels, and in the USA to methanol made from natural gas. Both were cleaner burning than gasoline and diesel fuels, and natural gas was being found in increasing quantities around the world. Methanol never gained widespread acceptance, largely because it could not compete with dropping oil prices, while less expensive natural gas remained a minor option in many countries around the world.

Natural gas vehicles continue to have a small but expanding presence in many countries around the world. They may be seen as a small incremental enhancement, but they also require substantial investments in fuel stations. These vehicles mostly use conventional internal combustion (spark ignition) engines. They burn fuel that is compressed at local fuel stations and then placed in high-pressure tanks on board the vehicles. The tanks add some extra cost, but the fuel is usually somewhat less expensive than gasoline. Greenhouse gas emissions are about 20% less than gasoline on an energy cycle basis (taking into account emissions upstream at the production site), and air pollutant emissions tend to be somewhat lower (Organisation for Economic Development and Co-operation, 1993). Natural gas has gained widespread use in urban transit buses in many cities, including in the USA – replacing diesel engines – largely because they are much cleaner burning than twentieth-century diesel engines. (In Delhi, India, the Supreme Court required all buses to switch from diesel to natural gas in 2000 (Bose and Sperling, 2002).) As emissions of diesel engines are reduced in the first decade of the twenty-first century, it is likely that the switch to natural gas buses will be slowed or even reversed.

Other alternative fuel efforts persisted through the 1990s and early twenty-first century, but remain of modest scale. Brazil scaled back its ethanol program, from virtually all new cars running on ethanol in the late 1980s to ethanol currently being used only as a blending component with gasoline. The USA has slowly expanded its heavily subsidized corn-to-ethanol program (scheduled to amount to about 3% of gasoline sales by about 2005), Canada is slowly expanding its modest investment in synthetic fuel plants that convert oil sands into petroleum-like fuels (about 10% of Canadian oil production in 2000, with plans to expand to 25%, equivalent to about 400,000 barrels per day), and South Africa continues its coal-to-fuels program (supplying about 40% of domestic transport fuel consumption) (Prozzi et al., 2002). Most recently, a number of major energy companies have been building processing plants in remote areas of the world to convert natural gas into petroleum-like fuels. These gas-to-liquid processes remain uncompetitive with gasoline and diesel fuels, but produce zero-sulfur clean fuels that are becoming increasingly attractive as governments impose low-sulfur requirements on fuel suppliers.

In all these cases, the internal combustion engine remained dominant, and alternative fuels were being burned as gasoline and, sometimes, diesel fuel substitutes.

In 1990, a dramatic event marked the beginning of a new era. California adopted a new rule that required all major automakers to sell a certain percentage of zero-emission vehicles (ZEVs), beginning in 1998. The mandate had two effects (Williams and Sperling, 2002). First, automakers accelerated their already intensive efforts to reduce emissions from internal combustion engines – in part as a defensive measure against mandates for electric vehicles. And second, it accelerated the development of inherently cleaner-burning electric-drive vehicle technologies. The ZEV mandate has been delayed and greatly transformed over the years. But its effect has been revolutionary.

3. Internal combustion engines

Internal combustion engines power virtually all motor vehicles. While the technology has been commercially available for over 100 years, it continues to undergo substantial improvement, especially in terms of its environmental performance. Mostly two types are used. Spark ignition engines are used in most cars and light trucks, usually powered by gasoline, and compression ignition engines are used in most trucks and buses, usually powered by diesel fuel.

3.1. Spark ignition (gasoline) engines

Since the 1960s, huge improvements have been made in reducing pollution from gasoline engines. Emissions of conventional air pollutants have been reduced by 90% and more compared with their uncontrolled state. Further emissions improvements are expected, facilitated by reformulation of petroleum fuels, especially by reducing sulfur levels. The lower sulfur facilitates the use of even more effective pollution control devices. Modern gasoline cars have emissions that approach zero; they are barely measurable.

Energy improvements have been more difficult and elusive, not because of technology but mostly because of consumer preferences. In the USA the average gasoline-powered light-duty vehicle sold in year 2000 had a slightly worse fuel economy than the average vehicle sold in 1980 – but weighed 21% more, had 79% more horsepower, and accelerated from 0 to 60 miles per hour in 26% less time, and also offered many more energy-consuming accessories and capabilities, including four-wheel drive and air conditioning (National Research Council, 2002). From a technical engineering energy efficiency perspective, the modern US car is therefore about 30% more efficient than it was 20 years earlier, even though fuel economy is no better. Further efficiency improvements are continuing to be made – in engine combustion, use of light-weight materials, and conversion of mechanical and hydraulic subsystems to electric control. In countries with more aggressive fuel economy (and greenhouse gas) policies, including Europe and Japan, fuel economy improvements are more likely to accompany fuel efficiency improvements. In the EU, automakers have agreed to a 25% reduction in carbon dioxide emissions per vehicle kilometer between 1995 and 2008, and Japan adopted rules in 1998 requiring a 20–25% reduction in fuel consumption for most vehicle classes by 2010 (Plotkin, 2001). Of the major car-buying regions, only the USA did not adopt more stringent fuel consumption rules during the 1990s.

3.2. Diesel engines

Diesel engines are considerably more controversial, especially in the USA and Japan (Walsh, 2001). The governor of Tokyo and the air quality regulators in southern California launched campaigns in the late 1990s to ban diesel engines. Diesel engines are often viewed as inherently dirty and noisy, belching clouds of black soot. Indeed, older diesel technology fitted that image well. But there is another story.

Diesel engines are commonplace. Freight companies and bus operators rely almost exclusively on diesel engines for their trucks and buses. Indeed, diesel engines continue to increase their market share worldwide, now accounting for about 40% of all roadway fuel consumed. In Europe, diesel cars account for about one-third of sales – compared with less than 1% of cars and 4% of light trucks in the USA, and about 10% of cars in Japan – and the share continues to increase. (Diesel cars are increasing their market share in Europe in part because diesel fuel is taxed less than gasoline, and in part because automakers are pursuing diesel engines as the primary strategy to meet the 25% reduction in carbon dioxide emission rates.)

New diesel engines are vastly enhanced and nearly as clean and quiet as a gasoline engine. Diesel engines tend to produce much lower levels of carbon monoxide and hydrocarbons than gasoline engines, but much higher levels of nitrogen oxides (NO_x) and particulate matter. Newer engines are being outfitted with particulate filters that greatly reduce soot emissions, and are expected to bring particulate levels close to those of gasoline engines. However, even with continuing improvements, diesel engines are expected to continue emitting higher levels of NO_x (precursors to photochemical ozone).

The controversy over diesel engines is likely to continue and even intensify. In the USA, stronger pollution control rules are hindering the introduction of diesel engines in cars and light trucks, and disrupting heavy-duty engine manufacturing. But diesel engines are considerably more energy-efficient than gasoline engines. Advanced direct-injection diesel engines are up to 45% more efficient than current gasoline engines, and about 20% more efficient than advanced gasoline engines. European regulators have set less stringent NO_x and particulate emission standards for diesel cars relative to gasoline cars, in order to allow their rapid introduction. The USA has not done so, insisting that diesel cars must meet the same emission standards as gasoline cars.

In summary, internal combustion engine technology is still evolving, especially diesel engines. Future engines will be even cleaner and more efficient – with improved aftertreatment devices, improved engine design and operation, and improved low-sulfur fuels. Internal combustion engines are here to stay for a very long time, operating mostly on petroleum fuels. They have compelling advantages that are difficult to replicate with other propulsion technologies and fuels.

4. Toward electric-drive vehicle technology

Two factors suggest that even with improving internal combustion engine technology, a transition is about to occur to electric-drive technology. The first is intensifying calls for even cleaner, more energy efficient, and lower greenhouse-gas-emitting vehicles. The second is rapid innovation in light-weight materials, energy storage and conversion, power electronics, and computing. Indeed, the transition process is already underway.

Electric-drive vehicles are defined as those vehicles whose wheels are turned in part or entirely by electric motors, rather than by a mechanical drive train powered by an internal combustion engine. Electric-drive vehicles include not only those powered by batteries charged using the domestic electricity supply but also vehicles that generate electricity onboard or store it in devices other than batteries. Their common denominator is in the efficient electric motors that drive the wheels and extract energy from the car's motion when it slows down. Internal combustion vehicles, in contrast, employ a constantly running engine whose power is diverted through a series of gears and clutches to drive the wheels and to turn a generator for the electrically powered accessories in the car.

Although electrically driven vehicles have a history as old as that of the internal combustion engine, a number of recent technology developments provide promise that this form of transportation will eventually be efficient and inexpensive enough to compete with internal combustion engine vehicles. Overcoming the entrenched advantages of petroleum-powered vehicles will, however, take time and resources, and the transformation may occur in unpredictable ways.

Electric-drive vehicles are more efficient – and thus less polluting – than internal combustion vehicles for a variety of reasons. First, because the electric motor is directly connected to the wheels it consumes no energy while the car is at rest or coasting, increasing the effective efficiency by as much as 20%. Regenerative braking schemes – which employ the motor as a generator when the car is slowing down – can return as much as a half of an electric vehicle's kinetic energy to the storage cells, giving it a major advantage in stop-and-go urban traffic. Most important, the motor converts more than 90% of the energy in its storage cells to motive force, whereas internal combustion drives utilize less than 25% of the energy in a gallon of gasoline.

The question is: how and from where will the electricity be delivered in ways that preserve the inherent advantages of the electric motor and its controls? The most attractive choices appear to be batteries, fuel cells, and hybridized systems of internal combustion engines and batteries. Each has a different set of positive and negative attributes relative to internal combustion engines – for both consumers and vehicle manufacturers.

4.1. Battery electric vehicles

Battery-powered electric vehicles have a long history, dating to the nineteenth century. Initially they competed successfully with early gasoline cars, but the high cost and large bulk of batteries eventually gave way to the more energy-dense and portable petroleum fuels, even though they were safer, quieter, and more energy efficient.

Battery electric vehicles have many positive attributes. They are quiet, provide an appealing driving feel, reduce energy use and greenhouse emissions, and are zero emitting. Even including pollution generated at the power plant source, the pollution benefits are large in most cases. Regardless of how the electricity is generated, battery electric vehicles would practically eliminate emissions of carbon monoxide and volatile unburned hydrocarbons, and greatly diminish NO_x emissions (Wang et al., 1990). In areas served by dirty coal-fired power plants, they might marginally increase the emissions of sulfur oxides and particulate matter. The impact of electric vehicles on air pollution would be largest, of course, where electricity is produced from solar, nuclear, wind, or hydroelectric power. The pollution benefits would be greatest in places such as California, where most of the electricity comes from tightly controlled natural gas plants and zero-emitting hydroelectric and nuclear plants, and France, where most electricity comes from nuclear power, but also in very polluted cities where reductions in tailpipe emissions are greatly valued – such as Mexico City, Beijing, Bangkok, and Katmandu.

Other advantages include home recharging and the driving feel. In all drive clinics and surveys, the majority of electric vehicle drivers affirm that they prefer the smooth, hard acceleration associated with the high torque of electric motors (the effect is especially noticeable at low speeds) (e.g. Turrentine et al., 1992). Many people also see home recharging as desirable (Kurani et al., 1994). Most people prefer not to patronize retail fuel stations, some strongly so (Sperling and Kitamura, 1986).

The key problem is the battery. Battery technology has improved dramatically since the nineteenth century, and continues to improve. Through the 1990s, entirely new battery technologies were commercialized that store more energy in less volume at less cost. The proliferation of portable consumer products, including laptop computers and camcorders, spurred the development of these improved batteries – resulting in nickel cadmium, nickel–metal hydride, and, more recently, lithium batteries. But scaling up these battery technologies has proved formidable, and even with the improvements, cost and bulk remain high.

Indeed, into the foreseeable future, batteries will not be cheap nor compact enough for battery-powered electric vehicles to be cost competitive with internal combustion engine vehicles – unless used in smaller vehicles with reduced performance expectation. In other words, the only attractive opportunity for battery electric vehicles appear to be small neighborhood and city electric vehicles, and perhaps electric scooters – vehicles with top speeds less than 100 kph and ranges less than 100 km (Sperling, 1994). More important markets for battery-powered vehicles to date have been off-road equipment, where noise and pollution are especially offensive (especially within enclosed spaces). For these vehicles, not much energy is needed, and thus a relatively small battery can be used. The additional cost of the battery in these cases can potentially be offset by the longer life of the electric power train, reduced maintenance, and lower energy costs – as well as by noise and pollution benefits.

4.2. Hybrid electric vehicles

Hybrid electric vehicles combine an electric motor with a combustion engine. By severing the direct connection between engine and wheels, the engine can operate at steady load near its maximum efficiency, as with stationary engines. The engine is downsized, with onboard energy storage devices such as batteries or ultracapacitors providing the power surges needed for hill climbing and passing.

In some sense, hybrids are a middling technology (Sperling, 1995). Compared with internal combustion engine vehicles, hybrids have better energy efficiency, easier-to-control emissions (since engines are operating at a steady load) and, like all electric-drive vehicles, a superior driving feel (the result of high torque and smoother acceleration at lower speeds). But due to redundant powerplants, they are inherently more expensive and possibly less reliable than combustion vehicles. Hybrids have longer range and fewer batteries than battery EVs, but are technologically more complex, generally lack home recharging (which appears to be highly valued in the US market), and present a less pure environmental image.

The first mass-produced hybrid electric vehicle was put on sale in Japan in December 1997: the Toyota Prius. This model was updated for sale in North America and Europe in 2000. Honda unveiled a hybrid electric car in 2000 as well, and added a hybrid version of its popular Civic model in 2002. These early hybrid electric cars are priced about US $1500–3500 more than comparable gasoline models. They have 25–50% better fuel economy. By mid-2002, Toyota had sold almost 100 000 Prius cars, and was claiming that they were not losing money on them (with the higher price). Most major automakers plan to unveil hybrid electric models during the first decade of the twenty-first century.

Hybrid vehicles are not a single uniform technology (An et al., 2001). They encompass a wide range of designs and technologies. Like fuel cells, they build upon electric-drive technology developed for battery electric vehicles. They can use a variety of combustion engines, including spark ignition, diesel compression ignition, and gas turbine types, and may store electricity in a variety of devices, though batteries and perhaps ultracapacitors are the preferred technologies.

These various components may be combined in a variety of ways to achieve a variety of goals. Hybrid electric vehicle may be designed to:

- minimize emissions by incorporating large battery packs and operating mostly in a zero-emissions mode (and also providing home recharging capability);
- minimize energy consumption by operating a small combustion engine full time;
- minimize changes in conventional petroleum-powered hybrid electric vehicles by using a very small battery pack mostly just to gain the energy benefits of regenerative braking;
- achieve a variety of other cost and performance goals.

In practice, a variety of hybrid designs will likely be manufactured, each responding to different government rules and subsidies, and targeted at different market segments. Initially, smaller battery packs will be used, since this will restrain costs.

Despite the early successes of Toyota and Honda, automakers are reluctant to make major commitments to hybrid electric technology. They are less risky and less expensive than battery electric vehicles, but still more expensive to produce than conventional gasoline and diesel vehicles. They provide improved fuel economy, but unless fuel costs are high and the vehicle is driven intensively, the fuel savings do not offset the higher purchase price.

Will others follow Toyota and Honda? If fuel economy standards were toughened, or incentives provided to automakers and consumers, then demand would undoubtedly strengthen. But short of those conditions, and especially in the USA, where long-term fuel prices are near historical lows (adjusted for inflation), automakers will likely proceed cautiously.

4.3. Fuel cell vehicles and hydrogen

Perhaps the most promising option is fuel cells (Lipman and Sperling, 2002; DeCicco, 2001). Fuel cells have unique attributes that are attractive to both consumers and automotive suppliers. Though at an early stage of development, they are widely viewed as the most likely successor to the internal combustion engine, since they will dramatically reduce energy and environmental impacts while providing equal or better performance than internal combustion engines. Indeed, fuel cell vehicles provide the opportunity to shift from today's hydrocarbon-based energy system to a more sustainable hydrogen economy. It is this vision that explains much of the interest in fuel cells.

Fuel cells convert fuels directly into electricity, with no by-products other than water. It is an electrochemical process so there is no combustion, and therefore no combustion byproducts. There are a number of different fuel cell technologies. At this time, the most attractive for vehicle applications is the proton exchange membrane (PEM) system. In a PEM fuel cell, hydrogen is the fuel: the two inputs are hydrogen, delivered to the anode of the fuel cell, and air (containing oxygen), delivered to the cathode. Electrons travel from the anode through a wire, and the positively charged ions (protons) that have made the same trip through the electrolyte (the "proton exchange membrane") react simply and elegantly, with the help of a catalyst, to form pure water and nothing more. The induced movement of electrons creates an electric current. And thus, fuel cells oxidize hydrogen to water vapor, emitting essentially no other effluents as they generate electricity.

Other fuel cell technologies also exist, but they operate at much higher temperatures or require pure oxygen. Neither case is suited to widespread vehicle use. Pure oxygen is expensive and difficult to supply, and vehicles are expected to power up in a matter of seconds. Fuel cells operating at high temperatures (such as solid oxide fuel cells) require up to an hour to power up. One other fuel cell type that may have promise is a variation of PEM fuel cells in which methanol is input directly into the fuel cell (instead of hydrogen). Direct methanol fuel cells are potentially attractive because methanol is more energy dense than hydrogen and can be stored more easily on the vehicle, and because it is less expensive to create a fuel distribution system for methanol than hydrogen.

The concept of the fuel cell traces its roots back to William Grove's experiments on water electrolysis in 1839, but the commercial history of fuel cell technologies remains rather limited over 150 years later.

Fuel cell development received a boost in the late 1950s, when the US National Aeronautic and Space Administration (NASA) determined that fuel cell technology was the most promising option for producing electricity in space in a compact, efficient, and safe fashion. NASA used PEM and alkaline fuel cells, the latter requiring pure oxygen, in the Apollo, Gemini, and Space Shuttle programs. The first motor vehicle application was an experimental farm tractor in 1959. In the 1960s, General Motors began experimenting with fuel cell technology, demonstrating the world's first drivable fuel cell passenger vehicle in 1966. Interest in fuel cells subsequently lagged through the 1970s and 1980s.

Interest in fuel cell vehicles revived in the early 1990s, motivated by California's ZEV mandate. The mandate had attracted attention to zero-emission technology. Battery electric vehicles were the initial target. But it soon became apparent that the high cost and low energy density of batteries rendered battery electric vehicles unfeasible as a mainstream option. Interest quickly shifted to other means of achieving inherently low emissions. Most attention is focused on the use of PEM fuel cells, running on either pure hydrogen or coupled with an on-board reformer device that could convert methanol or gasoline-like fuels into hydrogen. Other efforts include development of direct methanol fuel cells, and use of high-temperature solid oxide fuel cells as auxiliary power units dedicated to powering accessories (such as refrigeration units in trucks and to heat truck cabins overnight while the driver sleeps).

Great strides have been made in reducing size and cost, and increasing performance. Ballard Power Systems, the early leader in fuel cell development, was able to increase the power density of their fuel cell stacks 11-fold between 1989 and 1996, and their 2001 commercially available fuel cell doubles that. General Motors and Toyota, two of the other leading developers, have demonstrated similar progress.

Despite rapid progress, significant challenges remain for the commercialization of fuel cell vehicles. The principal challenges are:

- development of a hydrogen refueling infrastructure;
- compact, low cost on-board fuel reformers, if hydrogen is not available;
- onboard hydrogen storage systems that are safe, compact, lightweight, inexpensive, and quick to refuel;
- further cost reductions in fuel cell systems.

Fuel cells are attractive in part because they are potentially applicable to most types of vehicles – including not only light-duty passenger vehicles, but also urban buses, delivery vehicles, fork lift trucks, airport baggage handling vehicles, mining vehicles, golf carts, scooters, boats, and even airplanes, as well as auxiliary power units for heavy-duty trucks. Of these, the urban bus market segment has received the most attention initially, with fuel cell bus demonstration projects conducted in the late 1990s in Vancouver, Chicago, Sacramento, Palm Desert, and Washington, DC. Ballard Power Systems and DaimlerChrysler are delivering 30 fuel cell-powered fuel cell buses to European cities beginning in 2002.

As of 2002, all major automakers had substantial fuel cell development programs. Test programs for light-duty vehicles were underway in the USA (under the California Fuel Cell Partnership), Germany, the UK, and Japan.

Two principal concerns are hindering fuel cell vehicle commercialization. One is cost. Fuel cells are revolutionary new products. Their cost in mass production is not known, though there are no fundamental reasons, such as high material costs, that make them inherently more expensive than internal combustion engine systems. Indeed, they may eventually prove less expensive, especially on a life-cycle cost basis. Only with time, experience, and money will the cost question be answered.

The second concern is fuel. Fuel cells are simpler, less expensive, and more energy efficient when operating on hydrogen. But hydrogen is not readily available, and is difficult to store (it is the lightest element known). An alternative is to use methanol or a gasoline-like fuel, which can be provided much more easily, especially gasoline. A reformer device would be installed on the vehicle to convert those liquid fuels to hydrogen for use in the fuel cell, or methanol could be input directly. Prototype fuel cell vehicles have been built that run on hydrogen, methanol, or gasoline, and that store hydrogen as a cryogenic liquid, compressed gas, in metal hydrides, or as sodium borohydrate. In general, automakers agree that hydrogen is the ultimate fuel for fuel cell vehicles, and that future fuel cell vehicles are likely to operate directly on hydrogen. But there are significant differences of opinion with regard to the preferred and likely evolution of vehicles and refueling systems over time.

Fuel cells are superior to internal combustion engines in several important ways, and it is for these reasons that automakers expect fuel cells to dominate eventually. They offer better environmental performance, better energy efficiency, quiet (but not silent) operation, rapid acceleration from a standstill owing to the torque characteristics of electric motors, and potentially low maintenance requirements. Furthermore, fuel cell vehicles have the potential to perform functions for which conventional vehicles are poorly suited, such as providing remote electrical power (for construction sites, recreational uses, etc.) and possibly even acting as distributed electricity generators when parked at homes and offices and connected to a supplemental fuel supply. They also provide automotive designers with much more leeway in the design of vehicles, since they facilitate the elimination of mechanical and hydraulic devices and subsystems. Because of these attributes, fuel cell vehicles could provide additional value to the consumer and automaker, and therefore be perceived as superior to internal combustion engines. Even if they prove more expensive, these added attractions could make them more appealing to both consumers and automotive suppliers.

The potential energy and environmental benefits are large, especially when operating on hydrogen, enhancing their societal benefits. Hydrogen-powered fuel cell vehicles would emit essentially no air pollution, consume less than half as much energy as comparable gasoline vehicles, eliminate petroleum use, and sharply reduce greenhouse gas emissions. The quantity of greenhouse gas emissions would depend on how the hydrogen is produced and stored. If made from water using solar energy, the ultimate dream, greenhouse gas emissions are essentially zero. If made from natural gas, the expected production pathway into the foreseeable future, emissions would be reduced to about 40% of those of gasoline vehicles. If made from petroleum, reductions would be small relative to gasoline vehicles, and about the same as diesel vehicles.

The process of introducing a revolutionary product such as fuel cells, where many of the attractions are outside the marketplace, is fraught with uncertainty. Fuel cells, like all nascent technologies, are characterized by high manufacturing costs, uncertain long-term performance and durability, and lack of a clear technological consensus or "dominant design" for the individual niches for which they are being considered. As commercialization of fuel cell technology proceeds, manufacturing volumes will increase, costs will fall, and long-term product performance and durability will be better understood. However, fuel cell systems will not easily or "automatically" penetrate automotive markets, despite their attractive qualities. This is due not only to the uncertain durability of fuel cells and potential cost differences between fuel cell systems and competing systems but also because the incumbent technologies are typically "locked in" and have a series of network relationships that reinforce their continued use.

The barriers are perhaps more forbidding in the transportation arena (compared for instance with the electricity market) because the motor vehicle system in place has evolved for over a century to support gasoline-powered, internal combustion engine vehicles. In most places of the world, the vehicle refueling infrastructure and vehicle service industries that support the use of motor vehicles are entrenched in a way that will make changes to the *status quo* inevitably difficult. Furthermore, owing to environmental pressures and partly in response to progress in fuel cell development, other more conventional technology is a "moving target." Such options as hybrid electric vehicles, with a small gasoline or diesel engine coupled with a battery-powered electric driveline, are capable of achieving impressive levels of efficiency and environmental performance at cost levels that fuel cell vehicles will be challenged to meet, especially initially.

Thus, a key aspect of the early commercialization of fuel cell systems is to develop market niches in which they have competitive advantages, and then to expand to other broader niches and segments as production volumes expand and costs drop. Almost all successful technologies move through this "virtuous cycle." A key aspect of the virtuous cycle is the cost reduction that occurs through a combination of scale economies in production, and also learning that takes place with regard to both product and manufacturing process design. Using the concepts of "learning curves" and "experience curves," one finds that many different products have shown a consistent pattern of cost reduction with increases in cumulative production volume. In essence, manufactured products tend to decline in cost by 10–30% with each doubling of cumulative production volume. Thus, if a product can gain an initial foothold in the market due to some competitive advantage, this can trigger the virtuous cycle and ultimately allow a new technology to break into a market that is dominated by an incumbent technology.

The desire to achieve zero tailpipe emissions for vehicles that operate in dense urban areas is a motivating force that could give fuel cell vehicles an important niche. The only zero-emission vehicle type other than direct-hydrogen fuel cell vehicles that is practical at the present time is the battery electric vehicle, and this vehicle type is characterized by short driving ranges, long recharge times, and potentially high life-cycle costs. To the extent that zero-emission vehicles are encouraged or even mandated in certain areas, direct-hydrogen fuel cell vehicles may have to compete only with battery electric vehicles and not the entire suite of vehicle technology options. This could give them a much firmer foothold to break into motor vehicle markets.

The exact commercialization plans for fuel cell vehicles have not been disclosed by automakers, but they have suggested initial plans for introducing these vehicles. In general, introduction of fuel cell vehicles into limited fleet applications (hundreds of vehicles) is expected in the 2003–2005 time-frame with broader introduction to private consumers expected in about 2008–2010. As costs come down and products are enhanced, companies and governments will realign their polices and business strategies to accommodate fuel cell attributes and opportunities.

One can envision various scenarios and pathways by which fuel cells can expand their presence. Shell International, well known for its sophisticated scenario planning, posits two energy scenarios for 2050 (Shell, 2001). One of them is centered around and motivated by fuel cell advances. In this scenario, fuel cell sales start with stationary applications for businesses willing to pay a premium for highly reliable power without voltage fluctuations or outages. They then spread to vehicles. By 2025, in this scenario, half of all vehicle sales in OECD countries, and one-quarter worldwide, are fuel cell vehicles. It is entirely plausible, though far from certain, that fuel cells will eventually become the dominant energy conversion device across all sectors, fueled by hydrogen.

5. Conclusions

The transition to cleaner and more energy-efficient vehicle technologies continues. Internal combustion engine vehicles, burning gasoline and diesel fuels, will dominate into the foreseeable future. These vehicles will be cleaner burning and more energy-efficient (though not necessarily with better fuel economy). In some parts of the world, alternative fuels will be used as niche fuels and complements to petroleum fuels, but they are not likely to displace petroleum in the foreseeable future.

The more momentous transition underway is toward electric-drive propulsion technology. Battery electric vehicles will increasingly be used in niche applications. The technologies more likely to play a major role are hybrid electric and fuel cell propulsion technologies. Fuel cells present more dramatic opportunities for major energy and environmental improvements, and for transforming the automotive and energy industries.

The future is highly uncertain. However, it appears likely that fuel cells will gradually enter niche applications where they offer clear advantages over other options. But when or whether fuel cells will flourish remains unknowable. It is entirely plausible, for instance, that vehicles will follow a more incremental path from today's internal combustion engine systems, first shifting to hybrid electric vehicles with small combustion engines. And it may be that continuing refinements of these hybrid technologies will keep fuel cells at the margin, competitive only in specialized niches. What is virtually certain is that the environmental performance of vehicles will continue to improve.

References

An, A., A. Vyas, J. Anderson and D. Santini (2001) *Evaluating commercial and prototype HEVs*, 2001-01-0951. Warrington: Society of Automotive Engineers.

Bose, R. and D. Sperling (2002) "Transport in Delhi, India: environmental problems and opportunities," *Transportation Research Record* (in press).

DeCicco, J. (2001) *Fuel cell vehicles: technology, market, and policy issues*. Research Report RR-010. Warrington: Society of Automotive Engineers.

International Energy Agency (2000) *CO_2 emissions from fuel combustion: 1971–98*. Paris: IEA.

Kurani, K., T. Turrentine and D. Sperling (1994) "Demand for electric vehicles in hybrid households: an exploratory analysis," *Transport Policy*, 1:244–256.

Lipman, T.E. and D. Sperling (2003) "Fuel cell commercialization perspectives – market concepts, competing technologies, and cost challenges for automotive and stationary applications," in: *Handbook of fuel cells: fundamentals, technology, and applications*. Chichester: Wiley.

National Research Council (2002) *Effectiveness and impact of corporate average fuel economy (CAFE) standards*. Washington, DC: National Academy Press.

Organisation for Economic Development and Co-operation (1993) *Choosing an alternative fuel*. Paris: OECD.

Plotkin, S. (2001) "European and Japanese initiatives to boost automotive fuel economy: what they are, their prospects for success, their usefulness as a guide for U.S. actions," *Energy Policy*, 29:1073–1084.

Prozzi, J., C. Naude, D. Sperling and M.A. Delucchi (2002) *Greenhouse gas scenarios for South Africa*. Arlington: Pew Center on Global Climate Change.

Shell International (2001) *Energy needs, choices and probabilities: scenario to 2050*. London: Global Business Environment.

Sperling, D. (1988) *New transportation fuels: a strategic approach to technological change*. Berkeley: University of California Press.

Sperling, D. (1994) "Prospects for neighborhood vehicles," *Transportation Research Record*, 1444:16–22.

Sperling, D. (1995) *Future drive: electric vehicles and sustainable transportation*. Washington, DC: Island Press.

Sperling, D. and R. Kitamura (1986) "Refueling and new fuels," *Transportation Research A*, 20:15–23.

Turrentine, T., D. Sperling and K. Kurani (1992) *Market potential of electric and natural gas vehicles*. Research Report 92-8. Davis: Institute of Transportation Studies, University of California.

Walsh, M.P. (2001) *Global trends in diesel emissions regulation – a 2001 update,* 2001-01-0183. Warrington: Society of Automotive Engineers.

Wang, Q., M. Delucchi and D. Sperling (1990) "Emission impacts of electric vehicles," *Journal of the Air and Water Management Association*, 40:1275–1284.

Williams, B. and D. Sperling (2003) *Description and assessment of California's zero emission vehicle mandate*. Davis: Institute of Transportation Studies, University of California.

Part 2

SECTORAL OVERVIEWS

Chapter 11

CARBON DIOXIDE EMISSIONS FROM TRANSPORTATION: TRENDS, DRIVING FACTORS, AND FORCES FOR CHANGE[a]

LEE J. SCHIPPER
World Resources Institute/EMBARQ, Washington, DC

LEWIS FULTON
International Energy Agency, Paris

1. The CO_2 problem: the policy imperative after Kyoto

In December 1997, leaders of the world's governments met in Kyoto, Japan, to discuss a protocol for reducing greenhouse gas emissions from number of anthropogenic sources, particularly carbon emission from the use of fossil fuels. While the details of each country's pledges, commitments, or expectations vary greatly among countries, all parties were aware of the key role transportation played in the rise of emissions from fossil fuels.

Figure 1 shows the growing share of World CO_2 emissions contributed by the transportation sector over the past 30 years and projected to 2020 by the IEA (International Energy Agency, 2000). The rise in the share from transport to 1999 stagnates. Yet increasingly the share from transport is seen as difficult to throttle back. This chapter explores some of the basic forces behind the growth in absolute emissions from transport.

Figure 2 shows how per capita CO_2 emissions from passenger and freight transport combined have risen with per capita GDP for each world region. While there are differences in the slope of the rise in emissions versus income by country, and differences in the level at a given income, there is little sign of any break in the connection between increased income and increased emission. The only exception occurred in the North American data, which occurred during a period of much higher fuel prices and rapid improvements in automobile fuel economy.

---

[a]The opinions expressed herein are those of the authors and not necessarily those of WRI, IEA, or other organizations that sponsored the original work reviewed in this chapter.

Handbook of Transport and the Environment, Edited by D.A. Hensher and K.J. Button
© 2003, Elsevier Ltd

For travel, higher incomes mean more travel, increasingly by private vehicle and air; for freight, higher incomes mean higher volumes of freight, increasingly by trucking. These modes are the most carbon-intensive, i.e. they have the greatest emissions per passenger – or tonne-kilometer of activity. The ratio of emissions to activity depends on vehicle characteristics, traffic, load factors, and other elements we review next. All of these components of emissions taken together yield emissions, hence reductions in emissions can arise if one (emissions/unit of activity) drops faster than activity rises – or if activity falls. On the surface, then, the coupling between per capita income and per capita emissions from transport appears strong if no other forces intervene. This seems to give a clear message: reducing or even restraining emissions from transportation may be difficult compared with other sectors. This is both a technical and a political issue. Confronting this issue depends on a good understanding of the forces driving energy use and emissions related to transportation. We focus on these for much of this chapter, returning at the end to indicate what consequences the trends have for policies. We shall illustrate these using data from a selection of IEA countries, then interpret the trends in Figure 2 for other parts of the world.

2. Underlying factors affecting CO_2 emissions for travel and freight

In order to systematically consider various factors affecting CO_2 emissions in transport, a framework is needed to understand and separate these factors (for decomposition in other sectors, see Schipper (1995) and Schipper et al. (1993)). The IEA has carried out numerous index decompositions of the factors underlying changes in CO_2 emissions from both freight and travel, as well as from other sectors (e.g. see Schipper et al., 1996, 1997; Scholl et al., 1996). We begin with the following basic formula:

$$G = AS_i I_i F_{i,j}, \qquad (1)$$

where G is the greenhouse gas (carbon) emissions from, A is total travel activity, S is a vector of the modal shares I, and I is the modal energy intensity of each mode i. The last term, $F_{i,j}$, represents the sum of each of the fuels j in mode i, using standard IPCC coefficients to convert fuel (or electricity) used back to carbon emissions. Emissions from the electric power sector are allocated to end use electricity (rail, tram, etc.) at the countrywide average ratio of total sectoral emissions to electricity produced in the economy.[a]

---

[a]Net of power station own-use and transmission losses. More detailed analysis could explore the full fuel cycle emissions from obtaining and refining the fuels, but the present analysis is limited to combustion.

Ch. 11: Carbon Dioxide Emissions from Transportation

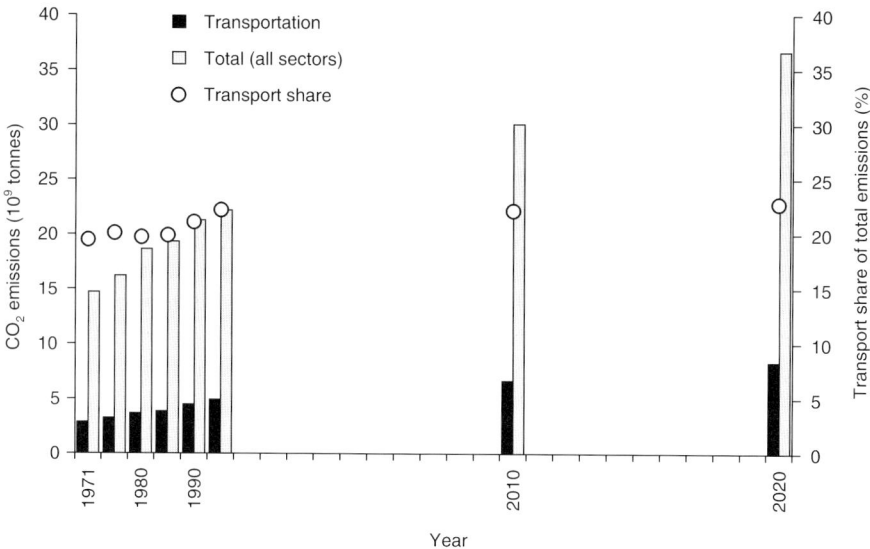

Figure 1. World carbon dioxide (CO_2) emissions, total and transport sector. (Source: IEA.)

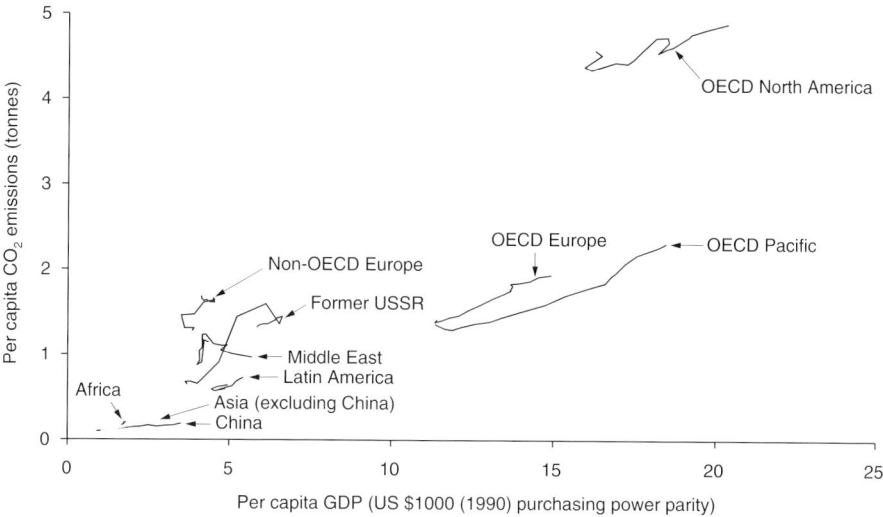

Figure 2. CO_2 emissions from transport and GDP, 1980–1997. Note that GDP is measured in real, 1990, local currencies and converted to US dollars at 1990 purchasing power parity. (Source: IEA.)

The modal energy intensity term itself is composed of several components:[a]

$$I_j = E_i \text{VC}_i \text{CU}_i, \qquad (2)$$

where E is technical efficiency, VC is vehicle characteristics, and CU is capacity utilization for each mode I. Taking only E and VC yields what we call vehicle intensity (fuel used per kilometer).

Technical efficiency is the energy required to propel a vehicle of a given set of characteristics a given distance, and is affected by the motor, drive train, frictional terms (including drag), etc. For cars, characteristics could be represented by car power, and technical efficiency by energy use per kilometer per unit of power. Capacity utilization would be measured as the number of people per vehicle. Driving conditions and driver behavior (accelerations, etc.) affect technical efficiency.

Thus, some terms in this decomposition that are nominally "technical" actually have important behavioral components. Total travel and modal choice are obviously behavioral factors, too. The same is true for changes in the types of vehicle people choose to buy, and changes in traffic and driver behavior. All of these affect how technology turns energy into mobility.

Fuel coefficients track the carbon intensity of fuels. Other greenhouse gases are emitted from transportation, including carbon monoxide (CO), nitrogen dioxide (N_2O), and methane (CH_4). Methane could become important if the use of compressed natural gas, currently less than 1% of global transport fuel, grows. For alternative fuels (even renewable fuels, such as the heavily processed corn-derived ethanol in the USA), a full fuel cycle analysis of feedstock production, conversion, fuel distribution, and vehicle refueling must be made to ascertain the full emissions of those fuels, not simply those occurring during driving. Most alternatives to gasoline and diesel have higher greenhouse gas losses associated with bringing the fuel to the tank ("well-to-tank," or WTT). But several have lower vehicle emissions, and a few, such as hydrogen, are expected to have no vehicle emissions. Thus, the entire "well-to-wheels" (WTW) pathway must be addressed. However, CO_2 is still the dominant greenhouse gas in this pathway, and petroleum-based fuels account for about 98% of all energy in motorized transport in almost every country.

2.1. Passenger transport

Passenger transport typically accounts for 60–70% of energy use and emissions from transportation.[b] Travel activity (A) is typically measured in passenger-kilometers over

---

[a]Real drive cycles and routing also influence modal energy intensity.

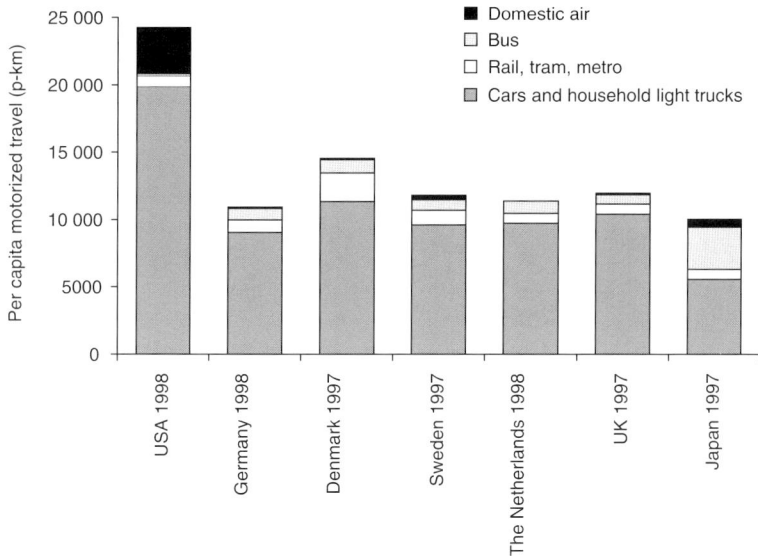

Figure 3. Per capita motorized travel by mode. (Source: national data compiled by the IEA.)

each mode (S_j). Figure 3 shows per capita domestic travel by motorized mode for a number of IEA countries in the late 1990s. Were walking and cycling to be included, the totals would rise a little, most notably in Germany and the UK (about 5%), and in Denmark and the Netherlands (about 10%).

The dominant mode in Figure 3 is automobile travel. This is driven in part by automobile ownership. Ownership has risen with income, although it is showing some saturation in the most motorized countries, as the figure suggests. Distance traveled per vehicle (vehicle-kilometers or v-kilometer) is rising slowly with income too, and continues to rise in most countries, even as car ownership stabilizes (Figure 4). In countries where both car ownership and travel per vehicle are rising, travel per capita is rising quite rapidly.

Closer examination of trends in vehicle fuel use links activity to emissions. We defined the vehicle energy intensity as energy use per vehicle-kilometer, and the modal energy intensity as energy use per tonne-kilometer or passenger-kilometer (cf. equations (1) and (2)). Vehicle energy intensity (for a given size and power) is

---

[b]To understand how all the figures are derived, see Schipper et al. (1992a) for the first decomposition study, Schipper (1995) for a review of trends in automobile energy use, Scholl et al. (1996) for the analysis of CO_2 from travel, Kiang and Schipper (1996) for the analysis of Japan, Schipper et al. (1997) for the analysis of freight, and Schippers et al. (1992b) for information on how these splits (and original data) were obtained. Data for Canada, the Netherlands, and Australia were gathered during IEA studies of these countries.

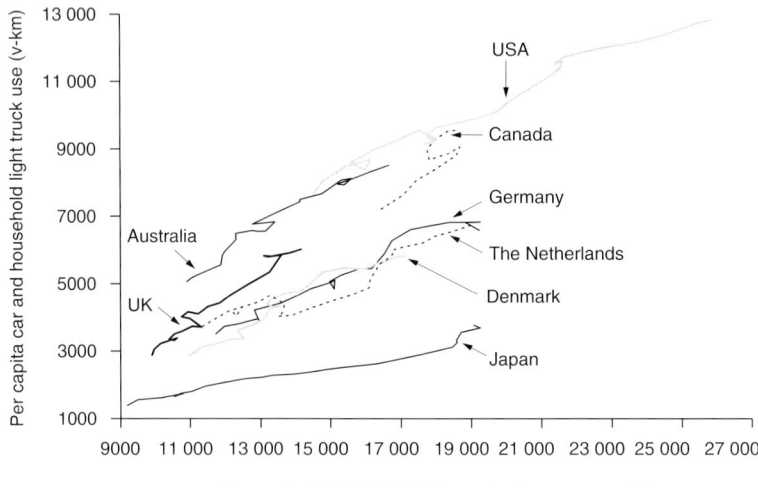

Figure 4. Car use per capita versus GDP per capita. Note: "Germany" in Figures 5–7, 9 and 11 excludes the former East German region. (Source: national data compiled by the IEA.)

related to the efficiency of the vehicle, while modal intensity depends also on the number of passengers or amount of freight carried. Since cars account for most of the energy use, we will focus on trends in their intensities.

Figure 5 shows the average vehicle fuel intensity, or fuel use per 100 km, for car fleets. Personal light trucks are taken into account in the USA, as they account for nearly 30% of household vehicles.[a] Fuel intensity fell dramatically in the USA (and Canada, not shown), but barely changed in most European countries (and in Japan). The values for the early 1990s reflect car fleets that have been almost completely renewed since the early 1970s. Because of the near equivalence of diesel, gasoline, and LPG fuels counted here, the curves also represent approximate carbon intensity.

As shown in Figure 5, throughout the 1970s and 1980s, stock-average fuel intensity changed in most countries, with the most dramatic improvements in the USA. However, by 1990, the rate of improvement in the USA and elsewhere declined to near zero, due to a flattening in new car fuel economy. New vehicle fuel economy did not improve significantly during the 1990s, in part due to a trend

---

[a]These figures are assembled from national data and count the energy content of each kind of fuel, which is higher for diesel than for gasoline or liquefied petroleum gas. Results are then converted to "gasoline equivalents" at the lower heat content of gasoline of 31.4 MJ/l. Carbon values are approximate, since fuel changes affects them slightly differently than fuel.

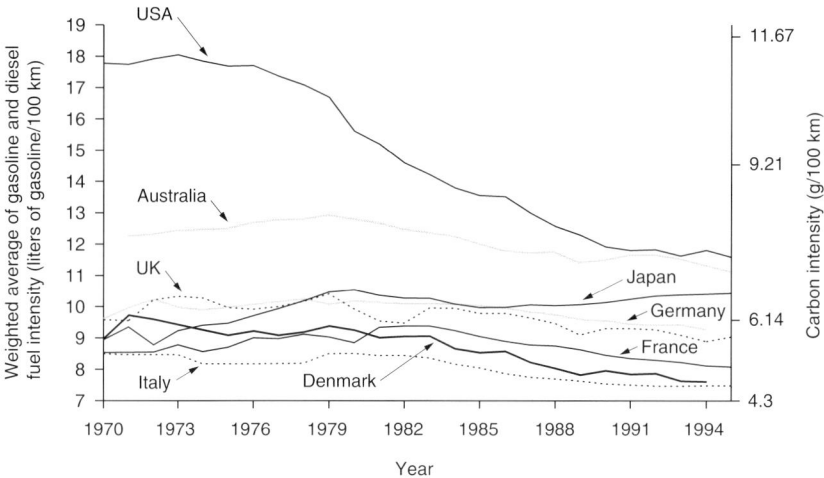

Figure 5. Fuel intensity (left axis) and approximate carbon intensity (right axis) of car and passenger light truck fleets. (Source: national data compiled by the IEA.)

toward increased vehicle size, weight, and power that offset technical efficiency improvements. In the USA there was a general shift toward larger vehicles; the share of minivans, SUVs, and light-duty trucks (for personal use) rose from only a few percent in 1985 to over 30% by 1995. More recently (since about 1998), new vehicle fuel intensity (often called fuel economy) in most European countries has begun improving again, in line with the targeted improvements in the voluntary commitments by European car manufacturers. By contrast, new vehicle fuel economy in the USA has continued to deteriorate. But since new vehicles represent less than ten of the stock in any given year, the effect of these latest trends on stock averages may take several years to become significant.

Carbon intensities of other modes

Outside of the USA the energy and carbon intensities, per passenger-kilometer, of rail and bus travel are significantly below those of cars. In the USA, city buses and, in some cases, commuter rail have, on average, higher carbon intensities than cars (although lower than light-duty trucks and SUVs). This is because the transit vehicles themselves are mostly empty throughout much of the day, loaded only in one direction in the rush hour. Since their mode share and travel share is usually so low, bus and rail modes contribute very little to any nation's carbon emissions from travel.

Air travel is different. Carbon intensities for domestic air travel are difficult to measure in many countries because fuel use for domestic travel alone is not recorded separately from that of national airlines flying abroad (Krueger, 2001). Additionally the fuel used for air freight is not often subtracted from that for travel. For countries with reliable data (e.g. the USA, Canada, Australia, Sweden, and Italy) the results are surprising. In the large countries, carbon intensity tends to be about equal to that of private cars, or even lower in the case of the USA. In the relatively smaller countries of Europe, the carbon intensities of air travel are higher than for cars because of factors forcing up fuel intensities: shorter average flight distances, greater congestion at airports, and the use of smaller aircraft. In international travel outside of Europe, however, carbon intensities converge, since the overall patterns resemble those of the first three (larger) countries. The average flight distance in the USA is over 700 km. This is longer than any flight possible in many countries.

Overall, domestic air travel emissions represent 5–10% of the total for the large countries but under 5% for western Europe. However, this mode was growing the most rapidly until the terrorist attacks on the USA of 11 September 2001. While that growth may pick up again, some traffic in Europe will probably be deflected to the growing number of rapid rail connections, which in addition to their competitive

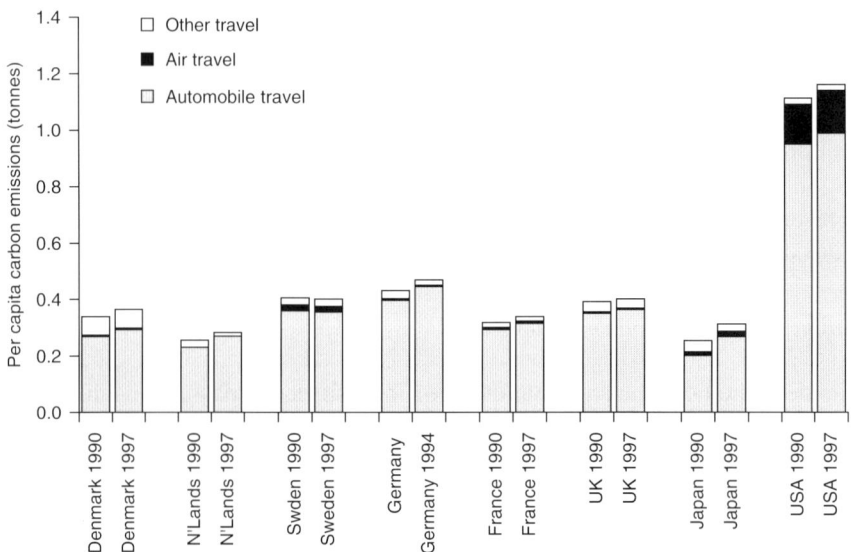

Figure 6. Per capita carbon emissions from travel. (Source: IEA calculations based on national data for fuel use.)

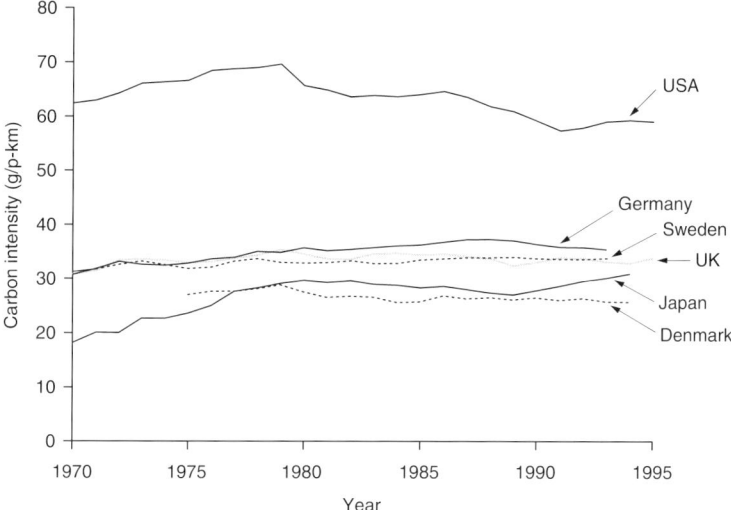

Figure 7. Aggregate carbon intensity of travel, 1970s to 1990s. (Source: IEA calculations based on national data.)

travel times between city centers, offer fewer security problems that have slowed down airport check-in.

When the carbon intensities of each mode are combined with the level of travel in each mode, overall emissions per capita by mode can be portrayed. Figure 6 gives values for the mid-1990s and for 1990 itself. Since automobile driving dominates travel and has among the highest carbon intensities, it dominates overall emissions. And since automobile and domestic air travel are rising, overall emissions in the late 1990s were higher than in 1990, and continue to rise.

Aggregate carbon intensity can be expressed by aggregating and combining the data in Figures 3 and 8. The results, shown in Figure 7, reflect distinct trends. In the USA (and Canada, not shown), the carbon intensity of dominant automobiles and air travel fell enough to affect aggregate intensity by nearly 20% after the mid-1970s. In Europe and Japan, by contrast, the carbon intensities of modes fell less. As the decomposition work shows, modal shifts toward cars and air travel were great enough to raise aggregate intensity by roughly 5%, while in the USA and Canada, these shifts were essentially complete by the mid-1970s. In no country was there any important shift to lower-carbon fuels; in fact, the shift toward diesel fuel in France, Germany, and Italy may have provided little if any reduction in carbon intensity because of diesel's higher carbon content and the much greater driving distances of diesels. More recently, however, carbon intensities of automobiles in Europe have begun to fall, and the impact of modal shifts has lessened.

2.2. Freight transport

With goods movement, or freight carried on the territory of each country by truck, rail, or ship and barge[a], activity is usually measured in tonne-kilometer, the number of kilometres each tonne moves. The level of freight activity (within a country, including the domestic portion of foreign trade but excluding good carried on trucks of a third country[b]) itself is coupled to industrial or total GDP (Schipper et al., 1997). Conspicuous is the wider spread among countries and the different rates of change of freight with changes in GDP.

Figure 8 shows freight levels by mode for the mid-1990s. Large countries have greater haulage per unit of GDP, but a larger share of that haulage is by ship or rail, two modes with lower carbon intensities than trucking. Moreover, the composition of freight drives the modal mix: large bulky commodities and raw materials are more likely to go by rail, and higher-value commodities and finished products by truck or air (Schipper et al., 1997). These characteristics of freight are a key element for understanding the components of CO_2 emissions.

From Figure 8, two factors appear to be significant for the level of freight relative to GDP. One is geography: the USA, as well as Australia and Canada (not shown) have the highest levels of domestic freight for a given GDP. This high level is dominated by rail and shipping (barge or boat), two modes that have very low modal energy intensities. Sweden is intermediate, while Denmark, Germany, and the UK are dominated by trucking, but total domestic freight levels are much lower relative to either population or GDP. The Netherlands is high because of traffic hauled to and from the port of Rotterdam by Dutch trucking, which is counted in domestic statistics and as transit traffic has a far greater impact than does similar traffic omitted from the data for Denmark, Germany, or the UK. Geography appears to work in the other direction here compared with its effect on travel: in small or dense countries, trucks more easily handle the relatively short distances that freight travels.

---

[a]International marine bunkers represent 10% of world-wide CO_2 emissions from transport. Unfortunately, tonne-kilometer data from this branch are not available by country of origin or registry in a way that matches fuel consumption data, nor are either tonne-kilometer or emissions "assigned" to any country. As with international air travel, we have to skip this important sector in our domestic analysis.

[b]At the time of writing we are still unable to separate transit trucking from domestic trucking in the Netherlands, which boosts that country's total freight significantly.

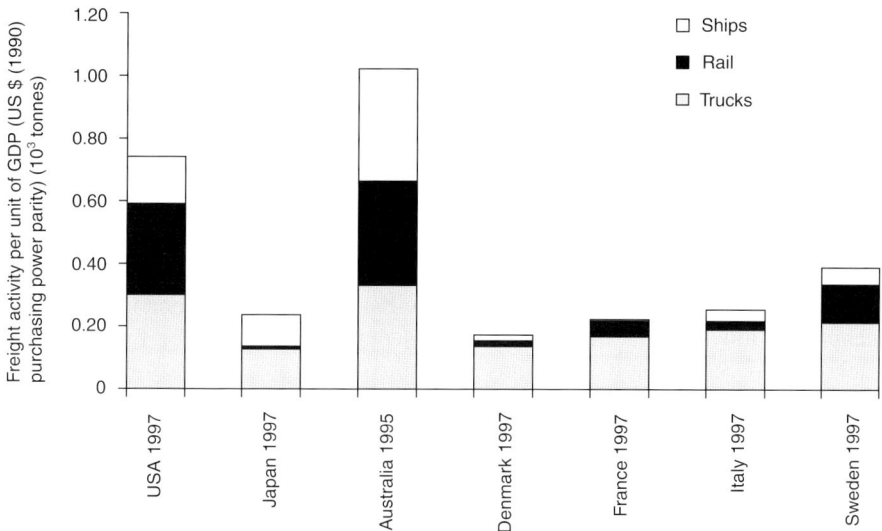

Figure 8. Domestic freight activity per unit of GDP by mode. (Source: national data compiled by the IEA.)

Freight carbon intensities present a somewhat different story to that of geography. Schipper et al. (1997) found that different kinds of commodities were associated with different modes of travel. Bulk materials go most often by rail or barge, but their role is declining compared with that of finished goods, which tend to travel by truck or air. These are factors not likely to be influenced heavily by concerns for CO_2, although fuel prices will have some impact. Thus, technology and utilization predominantly affect trucking, and are the key parameters for understanding CO_2 emissions from freight.

In most countries, the vehicle intensity of trucks of a given size has fallen through time. This is a result of increased penetration of the diesel engine as well as improvements in a given type of diesel or gasoline truck. But the ratio of fuel use to freight hauled continues to vary considerably among countries, as Figure 9 shows. Since trucks are produced by large, international firms, differences between the figures shown cannot be attributed to any extent to actual differences in the energy efficiency of trucks. Instead the differences arise largely because of differences in the fleet mix (between large, medium, and light trucks), differences in traffic, and, above all, differences in the capacity utilization of each kind of truck. These changes and differences in turn have explanations in the need for just-in-time deliveries, the rising value (as opposed to tonnage) of freight, and, above all, the relative unimportance of fuel costs (compared with other costs) in determining the optimal use of trucks.

The carbon intensities of rail freight and inland or coastal shipping are much lower than those for trucking. This reflects three important factors: first, vehicles are much bigger; second, they move more slowly; and, third, they rarely stop. Of course, these factors also cloak the reason why trucking has gained share from other modes: higher speeds and greater flexibility of loading locations.

As Figure 10 shows, the CO_2 emissions from freight relative to GDP are dominated by trucks. But there is greater variation in the ratio of emissions to GDP among countries than there is for travel, because both intensities and modal mix as well as the total level of freight, relative to GDP, vary so much among countries (Schipper et al., 1997). Germany has low emissions per unit of GDP because of low freight and low emissions per tonne-kilometer for dominant trucks. The USA has low emissions per unit of freight but a very high level of freight and consequently much higher emissions than Germany. Denmark has a low amount of freight hauled per unit of GDP but a very high truck share and the highest ratio of emissions to tonne-kilometer hauled, hence high emissions. Policies must consider each of these components to find where CO_2 restraint might be possible.

The carbon intensities can be combined with modal activity and aggregated and combined to reveal the aggregate carbon intensity of freight, whose time development is shown in Figure 11. As with travel, the carbon intensity of freight is dominated by one mode, trucking. Unlike travel, however, there is an important increase in aggregate intensity in most countries. This is a result of the great shift

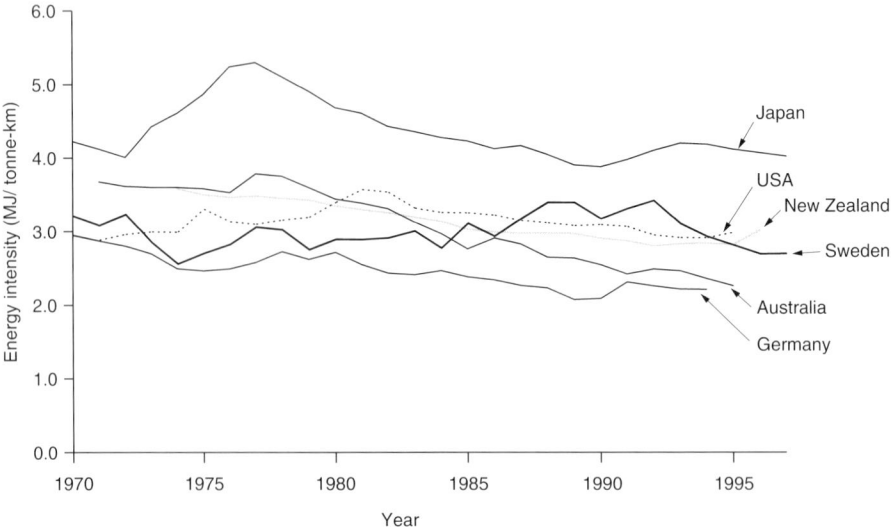

Figure 9. Energy intensity of trucking over time. (Source: national data compiled by the IEA.)

Ch. 11: Carbon Dioxide Emissions from Transportation

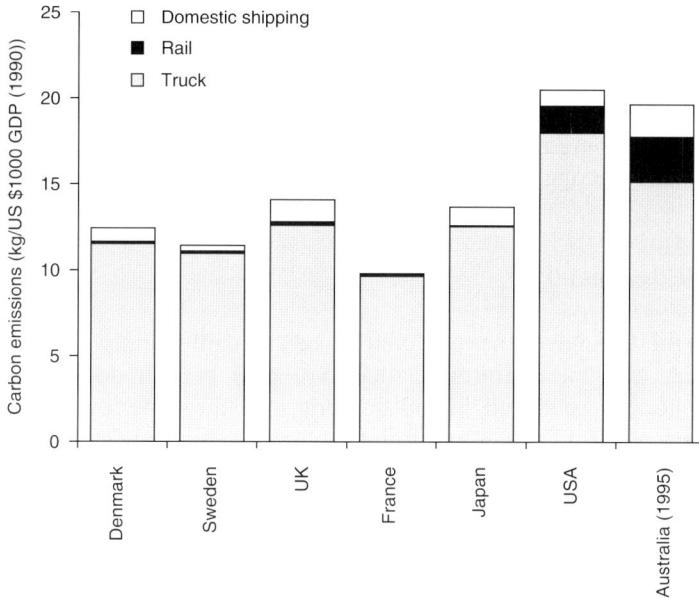

Figure 10. Carbon emissions from domestic freight by mode, per unit of GDP.

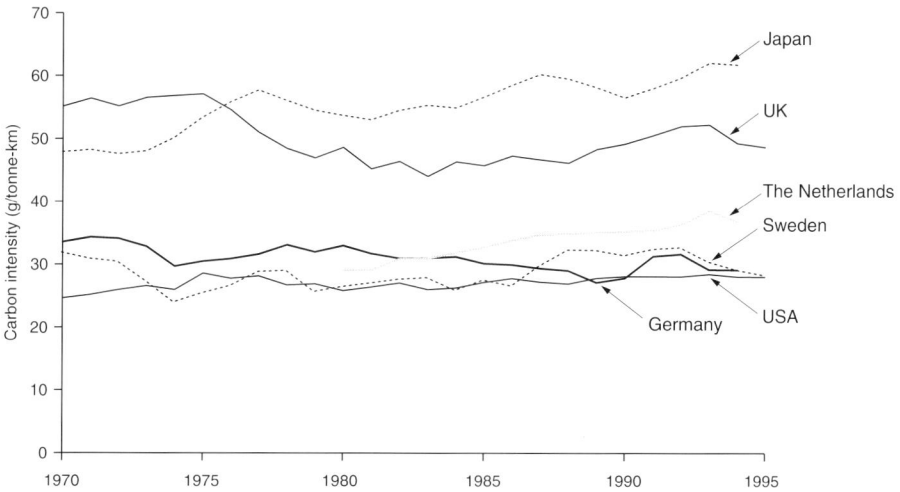

Figure 11. Aggregate carbon intensity for freight over time. (Source: national data compiled by the IEA.)

to trucking in Europe and Japan, which was more important than the modest declines in the energy intensities of most modes. Freight underwent even less fuel shifting than did passenger travel, since diesel already dominated freight by the mid-1970s, and there has been virtually no shift to low-carbon fuels. In the few countries where some rail has switched to nuclear or hydro-based electricity, its role is so small that aggregate carbon intensity has been almost untouched.

2.3. Non-IEA countries

Data from the IEA cover the total energy use and carbon emissions from almost all non-IEA countries. However, these are only broken down by the most aggregate modes – road, rail, inland shipping, and, for some countries, domestic air. Further splits into travel and freight, type of vehicle and fuel, etc., are not available from any reliable international data sources. Some countries have taken occasional surveys of each mode, but generally the only reliable data available cover national railroads, and then the data are rarely divided into passenger and freight operations. Additionally, most developing countries have large numbers of informal transport vehicles (for hire) in urban areas, whose fuel use and activity are poorly known. Finally, fuel use in Asian urban areas includes significant contributions from two- and three-wheelers.

A similar problem plagues activity data. Few countries tabulate vehicle activity or passenger-kilometers in private cars, and only a handful of countries even tabulate passenger- and tonne-kilometers in for-hire road transport. With few accurate data covering informal passenger transport or two- and three-wheelers, the link between transport activity and carbon emissions is poorly understood for these countries.

What can be gleaned from the available data, however, presents a picture not too different from the aggregate view for IEA countries. Figure 2 showed growth in CO_2 emissions from transport and total by world region, 1980 through 1997. The rise in the transport share in the aggregate world trends (Figure 1) is found in all the developing regions. Some data do exist, however, that estimate activity, energy use, and carbon emissions in urban areas of developing countries, and Figure 12 shows the estimated distances driven and carbon emissions from different vehicle and fuel combinations in the Mexico City region. But the input data are poor: vehicles in use, distances, and fuel intensities are generally estimated, and even fuel sales data are unreliable because of vehicles crossing boundaries and the leakage of untaxed fuels into the transport sector, particularly that of diesel.

Although few systematic data exist to break down carbon emissions of road traffic by mode and fuel, the ASIF estimates for large cities (such as those used for Figure 12), which implicitly calculate fuel intensities and therefore emissions,

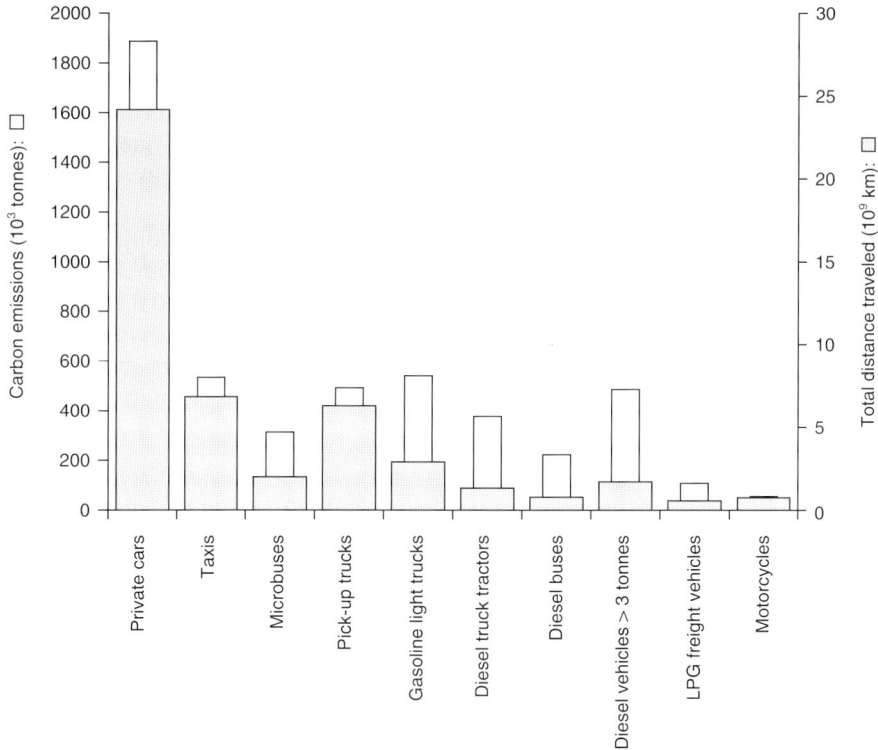

Figure 12. Carbon emissions and vehicle use in the Mexico City metropolitan region. (Data compiled by the Secretaria de Media Ambiente, Districto Federale, Mexico City, and elaborated by the World Resources Institute.)

represent an important first start. Although often these are only rough estimates, they reflect several important assumptions based on knowledge of the technologies used in newer vehicles in developing countries:

- Both cars and trucks in developing countries are less powerful than those in IEA countries. However, the technologies used for engines and drive trains are with few exceptions (notably middle-income countries with large internationally competitive vehicle industries such as Brazil and Mexico) based on old, less-efficient technologies than those in IEA countries. Hence, the average new car or truck in a developing country may use less fuel per kilometer than its IEA country counterpart but actually use more fuel per unit of weight or horsepower. Thus, CO_2 emissions per kilometer are not as low as might be expected.

- The car and truck fleets should, in principle, be younger in developing countries than in IEA countries because the numbers of vehicles have grown much more rapidly in the last two decades. However, in almost every country, older vehicles remain in the fleet for longer than in IEA countries. As older vehicles tend to run less efficiently than newer ones, there are significant numbers of inefficient (and highly polluting) vehicles in developing countries.
- Fuel quality and vehicle maintenance is less reliable in developing countries than in developed countries, also raising emissions per kilometer.
- Finally, and perhaps most important, the quality of roads and the congestion in urban traffic is often much worse in developing countries (especially in larger cities) than in most IEA countries. These factors push up fuel intensities by as much as 50% over the ideal conditions of smooth roads and minor congestion.

As an example of the impacts of these factors, the Mexico City authorities assume that the fuel economy for gasoline cars is 12.5 l/100 km, above the US average of 11 l/100 km for a fleet that is dominated by relatively small cars.

One important factor works in the opposite direction to bring the energy intensities of travel and freight lower than in IEA countries: the average passenger occupancy in cars is typically above two, while in IEA countries it is well below two. This is because there are fewer cars (hence more shared rides) and larger family sizes (including servants for upper-class families) in developing countries. Buses and metros are usually full, trains often dangerously overcrowded, and trucks perilously overloaded.

This largely qualitative picture helps explain the low values of CO_2 emissions per unit of GDP implied by Figure 2 for the lower-income countries. Car and truck use tends to grow faster than GDP only when countries pass through middle-income levels and a worker's annual salary surpasses the price of a car. This point was reached long ago in most IEA countries (and more recently in Eastern Europe), leading to high car ownership and use in these countries, but has been attained by only handful of developing countries (Korea, Brazil, Mexico, and Taiwan). This surge in car use has occurred in developing countries primarily in urban areas where road space is scarce, congestion high, and travel in cars correspondingly suppressed.

The other factor that reduces CO_2 emissions in most developing countries is the important role of non-motorized transport (including animal power and pedicabs) in both urban and rural areas. The enormous popularity of two wheelers, which in India outnumber four wheelers by about six to one, also lowers overall emissions while providing owners with small vehicles that can navigate congested traffic. While these vehicles create pollution and congestion problems of their own, their widespread use may mean lower CO_2 emissions/GDP for the crowded cities of the developing world.

Ch. 11: Carbon Dioxide Emissions from Transportation

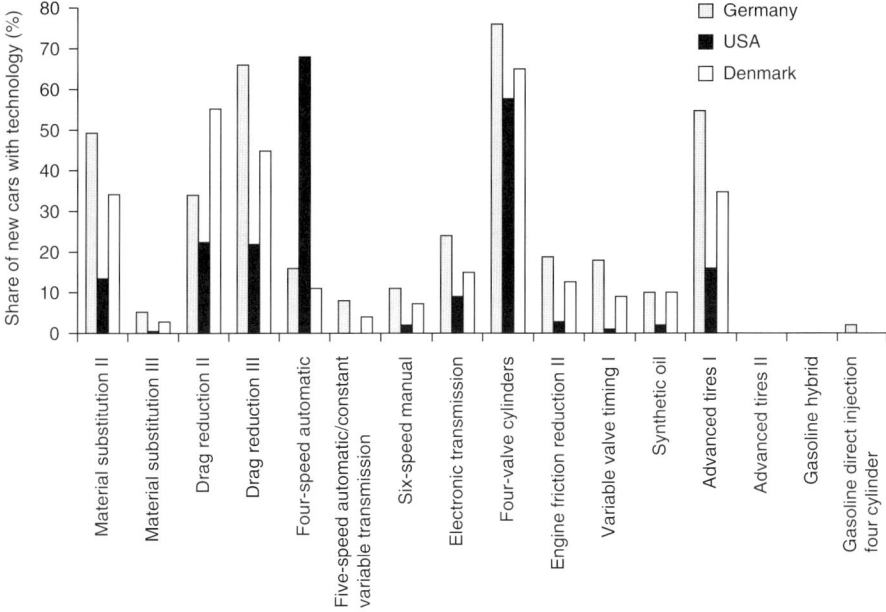

Figure 13. Market penetration of selected technologies in compact cars in Germany and the USA, 1998. (Source: International Energy Agency, 2001.)

3. The future

What could restrain CO_2 emissions in the future? In the closing section of this chapter we discuss what our research suggests.

3.1. Technology

There is no doubt that available technology offers enormous potential for reducing CO_2 and other emissions, and benefiting the environment in other ways (e.g. International Energy Agency, 2001). But in many countries, fuel pricing has not given any strong signals towards emissions reductions; incomes are rising; and people who can are moving away from congestion, noise, and air pollution, even as Japanese, North American, and European authorities move to reduce air pollution. In early reviews we noted the importance of the interaction of technology and behavior (Schipper et al., 1992a). Trends in car size and power are one important measure of current trends in car-buying behavior (Schipper, 1995). A more recent in-depth review (International Energy Agency, 2001) suggests a wide scope for improving fuel economy (Figure 13), as represented by the low penetration of many of the technologies indicated in the figure. Many of these technologies would pay for themselves in fuel savings.

Figure 14 shows that, while implementing a full set of technologies could result in much lower fuel consumption from new cars in the future, much of this improvement is likely to be lost to shifts in consumer purchases to bigger, heavier vehicles. Note that Figure 14, which is for the USA, focuses just on compact cars – further erosion in fuel economy improvement are likely to come from purchase shifts from this car class to bigger, heavier classes – and to minivans, SUVs, and light-duty trucks.

Thus, the problem is that although technology has the potential to reduce emissions, it might not be deployed to save energy and reduce CO_2 without strong market signals in that direction. Examination of automobile advertising in virtually every OECD country in 1997 confirms that CO_2 reduction is not a major marketing theme.

Alternative fuels continue to promise some relief. There are many propulsion sources that offer nearly the same performance as gasoline and diesel but with lower net CO_2 emissions (Sperling and Delucchi, 1989, 1993; Wang and Delucchi, 1992; Sperling, 1994; Ministerie van Volkshuisvesting, Ruimtelijke Ordening en Milieubeheer, 1996). These are making only slow progress in the market place, most likely because of the higher costs of the vehicles, but in some cases because

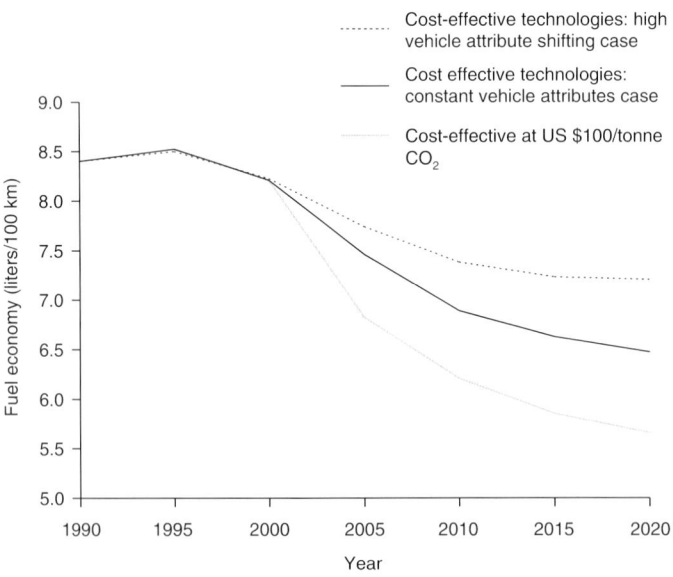

Figure 14. Cost-effective technologies implemented in cars over time in the USA: three scenarios. (Source: International Energy Agency, 2001.)

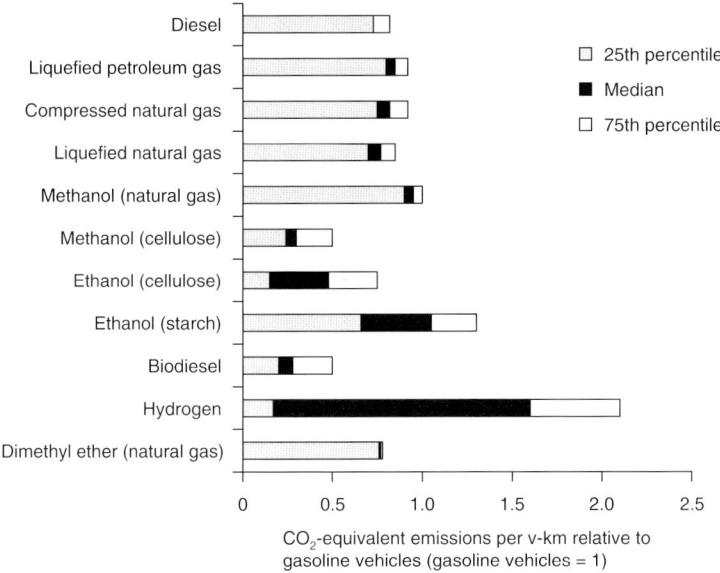

Figure 15. Near-term CO_2-equivalent reductions: alternative-fueled vehicles compared with conventional gasoline vehicles. (Source: International Energy Agency, 2001.)

the fuels themselves are more costly than gasoline or diesel. Or it is possible that "nearly" the same performance is not really correct? Most technologies have one or more drawbacks, such as shorter driving range, longer refueling time, smaller trunk space, or poor acceleration performance. Again, behavior cannot be separated from technology. Without heavy regulations or significant price differences, the alternatives are making little headway.

In any case, many alternative fuels offer only relatively small CO_2 reductions, on a "life-cycle" or "well-to-wheels" basis (Figure 15). Only cellulosic alcohols, biodiesel, and electric- or hydrogen-powered vehicles (if the electricity/hydrogen is obtained from a low-greenhouse-gas source) are capable of providing greater than 50% reductions in CO_2-equivalent emissions per kilometer of driving.

As shown in Figure 15, diesel engines themselves offer significant potential for lower net fuel intensity and CO_2 emissions, and do as well as many alternative fuels, such as compressed natural gas and liquefied petroleum gas. New light- and medium-sized diesel cars in Europe with turbo-direct injection (TDI) offer fuel consumption at a steady 90 kph in the range of 3.9–4.5 l/100 km (Schipper et al., 2002).[a] It must be remembered that diesel fuel is taxed much more lightly than

---

[a] Mitsubushi announced successful development of a TDI gasoline motor in September 1996.

gasoline in some countries; not surprisingly, its consumption is associated with significantly higher car travel. Equally as important, diesel TDI is appearing on heavier American-style vans in Europe, bringing fuel-driving costs down to affordable levels. Again, technology can work both ways when consumer behavior is counted.

Diesel actually releases more CO_2 per unit of energy during combustion than gasoline, although its production may require less energy in refineries. The net impacts of switching to diesel, or indeed any other fuel, should be evaluated using both full-fuel-cycle studies that take into account the marginal release of CO_2 anywhere in the fuel chain and studies of how diesel cars are actually used, as noted above (Schipper et al., 2002). Particulates and oxides of nitrogen are also a concern. And the use of any propulsion source must be evaluated under realistic conditions taking into account human behavior that affects fuel economy, not simply tests. Electric propulsion may offer attractive ways of removing combustion from cars to power plants, often released away from cities, but if that use remains untaxed as a road fuel while incentives are offered to provide easy entry to cities or low-cost parking, then consumers may again find a cheaper way to use cars than before, resulting in more driving. It is clear that alternative propulsion may offer significant CO_2 benefits at little perceived loss of driving amenity, but until we better understand all the costs, all the emissions, and, above all, the real interaction between alternative propulsion as a system and travel behavior, our expectations should be at best guarded.

There are, of course, a wide variety of options for dampening the growth of travel – but few of these have been the source of large CO_2 reductions to date. General categories of options include improving transit systems to encourage modal shifts, pricing mechanisms (fuel or road) to reduce the demand for travel, parking-related measures, promotion of non-motorized modes, land-use planning, and development of telematic systems to increase the travel efficiency for both passengers and freight. Since many of the options are tangled up with the policies used to pursue them, they are addressed in the following section.

3.2. Policies under development

The IEA reviewed greenhouse gas reduction policies in the USA and five European nations through 1999. In each national study the IEA reviewed (International Energy Agency, 2000), there appears to be a combination of technological change (including that driven by research, development, and demonstration projects and pricing policies), higher costs for lower-emitting fuels, and application of transportation measures that could improve transportation and restrain or even reduce CO_2 emissions over the next decade. These could change both emissions per kilometer and total kilometers enough to make a real difference in fuel consumption, as clearly happened in the USA in the 1970s and 1980s. For trucks, technological improvements and low-CO_2 fuels can also make a significant dent in CO_2 emissions, but it appears that there is also a very large potential for changing the way trucks are used. Truck utilization may not change in response to CO_2 pressures alone, but may to policies designed to increase modal competition, reduce congestion, pollution, and noise in built-up areas, lower road damage, and deal with other externalities that are focused on freight than travel. Thus, while CO_2 policies alone may not have a great impact on CO_2, other transport policy measures that affect CO_2 could eventually yield reductions in European, Japanese, and North American transportation CO_2 emissions. Other considerations include:

- Most CO_2 policies must be embedded in larger transport reform measures, as noted at the outset and codified now in the CO_2 plans of a number of European countries. Most of the measures designed to reform transport and make the system more effective will lead to somewhat lower levels of traffic, a modest rise in the role of collective modes, and less air pollution. These will all help to restrain CO_2 emissions.
- Pricing is important to rearranging the various signals that boost the use of cars and trucks over other modes, encourage families to live farther from built-up areas, and permit manufacturers to look far and wide for suppliers and markets. No-one expects price reforms alone to solve problems, but few expect transport problems to solve themselves without pricing reforms. This is particularly important for the possible trade-offs among pollutants, the search for fuels with a lower carbon content, and the encouragement of low-pollution vehicles. So far, some of the Nordic countries have adopted differential pricing of fuels, and (with Germany and the Netherlands) have begun to tax vehicles according to their rated emissions. A new feature of this thrust is that differentiated taxation also drives yearly registration fees.
- Technology offers enormous potential for reducing environmental problems associated with transport. But pricing is also central to both developing and deploying technology. Car companies fear large investments in fuel-saving technology or alternative propulsion without strong market support for the purchase of what they develop. Even with a dramatic breakthrough that reduces fuel consumption spectacularly, taxation reform may be necessary just to keep revenues about constant for maintaining the transport infrastructure. And while very low-consuming vehicles do not necessarily imply significant increases in vehicle use, wise governments will act to make sure that when technology leaps, signals about both CO_2 and other transportation externalities are not muted.
- There are many local policies (not explicitly reviewed here) that take direct aim at daily mobility, such as road pricing and other forms of transport demand management. Introducing such schemes is important for clearing

congestion, but is often politically difficult. Similarly, there is some expectation that careful attention to land use planning and higher density development will reduce the need to travel. But the positive experience with land use planning in Nordic countries and the Netherlands is hard to relate to specific declines in car use or drops in total mobility. These tools may be wise transport planning instruments to keep cities pleasant, but they remain uncertain tools for reducing CO_2 emissions unless employed in conjunction with other measures.

The most important lesson from the IEA review is that packages of measures seem the best way to restrain CO_2 emissions from their historical trends. Whether the present packages in Europe will do this remains to be seen. That there have been no significant new transport CO_2-related polices in the USA since the signing of the Kyoto Protocol in 1997 is regrettable.

We will not speculate here on how much policies might restrain or reduce future CO_2 emissions from travel or freight. However, the likely size of other transport externalities is considerably greater than those from CO_2 emissions alone. This suggests that only a broad framework that integrates concerns for CO_2 with strategies to solve other transport-related problems can be successful. If the externalities of transport are indeed as serious as the literature suggests, then their prompt and thoughtful treatment, together with measures designed to address CO_2, including taxation, could break the links described earlier in this chapter. And if governments are really as concerned both about "sustainable transport" and CO_2 emissions as their prolific reports suggest, then the forces could be mustered for this important integration.

References

International Energy Association (2000) *World energy outlook 2000*. Paris: IEA.
International Energy Association (2001) *Saving oil and reducing CO_2 emissions from transport: options and strategies*. Paris: IEA.
Kiang, N. and L. Schipper (1996) "Energy trends in the japanese transportation sector," *Transport Policy*, 3:21–35.
Schipper, L.J. (1995) "Determinants of automobile use and energy consumption in OECD countries: a review of the period 1970–1992," *Annual Review of Energy and Environment*, 20:325–386.
Schipper, L.J., R. Steiner, P. Duerr, F. An and S. Stroem (1992a) "Energy use in passenger transport in OECD countries: changes between 1970 and 1987," *Transportation*, 19:25–42.
Schipper, L.J., S. Meyers, R. Howarth and R. Steiner (1992b) *Energy efficiency and human activity: past trends, future prospects*. Cambridge: Cambridge University Press.
Schipper, L.J., M.J. Figueroa, L. Price and M. Espey (1993a) "Mind the gap: the vicious circle of measuring automobile fuel use," *Energy Policy*, 21:1173–1190.
Schipper, L.J., R. Steiner, M.J. Figueroa and K. Dolan (1993b) "Fuel prices and economy: factors affecting land travel," *Transport Policy*, 1:6–20.
Schipper, L.J., M.J. Figueroa and R. Gorham (1995) *People on the move: a comparison of travel patterns in OECD countries*. Berkeley: Institute of Urban and Regional Development, University of California.

Schipper, L.J., M. Ting, M. Khrushch, P. Monahan, F. Unander and W. Golove (1996) *The evolution of carbon dioxide emissions from energy use in industrialized countries: an end-use analysis*, LBL-38574. Berkeley: Lawrence Berkeley Laboratory.

Schipper, L.J., L. Scholl and L. Price (1997) "Energy use and carbon from freight in ten industrialised countries: an analysis of trends from 1973 to 1992," *Transportation Research D*, 2:57–76.

Scholl, L., L Schipper and N. Kiang (1996) "CO_2 emissions from passenger transport: a comparison of international trends from 1973–1992," *Energy Policy*, 24:17–30.

Sperling, D. (1994) *Future drive: electric vehicles and sustainable transportation*. Washington, DC: Island Press.

Sperling, D. and M. Delucchi (1989) "Transportation energy futures," *Annual Review of Energy*, 14:375–424.

Sperling, D. and M. Delucchi (1993) "Alternative Transportation Energy," in: R.J. Gilbert, ed., *The environment of oil, studies in industrial organization*. Dordrecht: Kluwer.

Ministerie van Volkshuisvesting, Ruimtelijke Ordening en Milieubeheer [Ministry of Housing, Spatial Planning and Environment] (1996) *Voertuigtechniek en brandstoffen*. The Hague: VROM.

Wang, Q. and M. Delucchi (1992) "Impacts of electric vehicles on primary energy consumption and petroleum displacement," *Energy – The International Journal*, 17:351–356.

Chapter 12

TRANSPORT ENERGY AND EMISSIONS: BUSES

JOHN STANLEY and PAUL WATKISS
Bus Association Of Victoria

1. Scope

The air pollution and climate change implications of motorized transport, deriving essentially from fuel use and the broader circumstances of this use, are major issues in the development of sustainable transport systems. While traffic congestion costs are typically the largest measured external cost of road use, recent research on the economic costs of air pollution and climate change has indicated the significance of these costs, especially air pollution (Maddison et al., 1996; European Conference of Ministers of Transport, 1998; European Commission, 2001a; Sansom et al., 2001).

High air pollution costs from motorized transport are primarily due to the effect of particulate emissions from diesel use. As buses are largely dependent on diesel fuel they have been a focus of attention in efforts to improve air quality, particularly in places such as California where air quality concerns have been marked.

The Kyoto Protocol has highlighted international concern about the climate change implications of greenhouse gas emissions. Motorized transport typically accounts for about one-sixth to one-fifth of total greenhouse gas emissions in western economies, with emission rates projected to increase rather than decrease in future years because of growing private vehicle use. Buses are not a major source of concern with respect to greenhouse gas emissions but they do provide a means of lowering total emissions from motorized transport if their modal share can be increased.

This chapter considers the contribution of buses to air pollution and climate change concerns and outlines ways in which that contribution can be reduced. This involves either or both of the following:

- reducing the relevant emissions from buses;
- increasing the share by buses of the total transport task, when usage levels are such as will achieve reductions in total transport sector emissions.

Handbook of Transport and the Environment, Edited by D.A. Hensher and K.J. Button
© 2003, Elsevier Ltd

The chapter presents separate discussions of air quality and climate change issues associated with buses. It begins with a discussion of air quality concerns associated with motorized transport, then outlines ways in which air pollution from heavy motor vehicles in general, and buses in particular, is being reduced, considering diesel and a range of alternative fuels. The same fuels are then considered with respect to their climate change impacts in bus use.

The chapter presents some estimates of air pollution and climate change impacts in monetary terms, as well as physical estimates (e.g. grams per kilometer). The monetary estimates are to enable broad comparisons of relative magnitude of impact to be made between air pollution and climate change impacts of bus use. Readers interested in exploring the detailed basis for monetary valuation in this context are referred to European Commission (2001a).

2. Air pollution

On average, current urban diesel buses emit more emissions of oxides of nitrogen (NO_x) and PM [particulate matter] than if all bus riders were driving separately.

California Air Resources Board (2001)

2.1. Choice of pollutants and impacts

Studies of air pollution episodes have shown that very high levels of ambient air pollution are associated with marked increases in adverse health effects. Recent studies also reveal smaller increases in adverse health effects at the current levels of ambient air pollution typically present in urban areas. These health effects include a range of end-points, such as premature mortality (deaths brought forward), respiratory and cardiovascular hospital admissions, and possibly exacerbation of asthma, other respiratory symptoms, and loss of lung function. The evidence for these effects is strongest for the pollutants PM_{10} (particulates >10 µm in aerodynamic diameter) and ozone, and the relationships are widely accepted as causal. Recent studies also suggest that long-term exposure to these pollutants, especially particles, may also damage health and that these effects may be substantially greater than the acute effects described above.

Air pollution also impacts on other receptors. The effects of atmospheric pollutants on buildings provide some of the clearest examples of air pollution damage, through building soiling and material erosion. Soiling results from the deposition of particles on external surfaces and leads to discoloration of stone and other materials. Surface erosion occurs as a result of sulfur dioxide and acidic deposition, especially for stone, but also for other materials as well. Ozone is also known to damage polymeric materials such as plastics and rubbers.

Air pollution also can impact on natural and semi-natural ecosystems. Ozone can have harmful effects on many plants at the concentrations commonly found and can lead to reduced crop yields. Impacts on ecosystems ranging from forests to freshwater are also well documented, with acidity, nutrient supply (nitrogen deposition) and ozone playing a role in these impacts. Air pollution also has effects on visibility and, through this, on amenity.

It is now widely accepted that transport-related emissions are associated with short-term health effects at the concentrations found in most cities. There is also a broad consensus that the effects of these pollutants on health can be quantified using exposure–response relationships, based on epidemiological studies that link pollution concentrations or increments to levels of health effects.

A number of studies have recommended sets of exposure–response functions for quantification of health effects from transport (such as the UK Department of Health's COMEAP group, the European Commission's ExternE Study, and US Environmental Protection Agency reviews; e.g. see European Commission, 2001a). In all cases there is a considerable overlap in the main pollutants and end-points identified, although there remain differences in the relationships proposed. It is likely that steps to increase this consistency between studies will be put in place, under the auspices of World Health Organisation, in the coming years. These health effects are usually valued using willingness-to-pay estimates. A summary of the pollutants and impacts typically considered is presented in Table 1.

From a transport policy perspective, the air quality standards of most current relevance are those for PM_{10} and NO_x/NO_2, with buses being a particular concern in relation to PM_{10} because of their reliance on diesel engines. In studies that attempt to place monetary values on air pollution impacts of motorized transport, particulate damage is typically the largest single "external" cost item by a significant margin.

2.2. Criteria emissions from heavy-duty motor vehicles

Emission regulations limit the production of carbon monoxide, hydrocarbons, NO_x, and particulates from motor vehicles. Table 2 sets out the European standards for emissions from heavy-duty vehicles (including buses), showing how these have tightened considerably over time, with US 98 and Japan 2004 standards shown for comparison purposes. In the areas of particulates and NO_x, Euro 2/3 and US 98 standards are broadly similar. Euro 1 to Euro 5 require dramatic reductions in emissions of particulates, by a factor of 18. For NO_x, where reductions are more difficult to achieve, reduction by a factor of 4 is still expected from Euro 1 to Euro 5.

Table 1
The impacts of different pollutants

Pollutant	Health effects	Non-health effects
Particulate matter ($PM_{10}/PM_{2.5}$) (a)	Substantial epidemiological evidence of adverse acute health effects of particulate air pollution in Europe and the USA; and strong, but much less widespread, epidemiological evidence of chronic health effects including life expectancy (USA only)	Dominant cause of building soiling Reduces visual range (i.e. visibility)
	Quantification can include acute mortality (deaths brought forward), chronic mortality (life expectancy), a number of acute morbidity end-points (from respiratory hospital admissions (RHAs) through to minor restricted activity days) and chronic morbidity impacts. Valuation based on willingness to pay. Mortality based on value of statistical life (A $5 million) but usually adjusted to reflect years of life lost	
Sulfur dioxide (SO_2)	European results have established an association of SO_2 with acute mortality, and probably with hospital admissions. However, evidence from epidemiological studies carried out in the USA is less convincing	Material damage (SO_2 and secondary pollutants) Effects on crop yield. Ecosystem damage by SO_2 and secondary pollutants including acidification (although there are potential benefits through fertilization) Sulfates reduce visual range
	SO_2 leads to formation of secondary particles (sulfates) over regional range	
	European studies quantify acute mortality (deaths brought forward), and RHAs from SO_2. Effects of sulfates are quantified using specific relationships or assuming similarity to $PM_{10}/PM_{2.5}$, as identified above	
Carbon monoxide (CO)	Sever health effects at high levels. Relatively little epidemiological evidence concerning ambient CO levels, but a number of (well-conducted) studies report positive associations. Some studies quantify acute hospital admissions (congestive heart failure). Other studies including associations with mortality usually discounted because of the problems separating CO from other components of the air pollution mixture, although information on CO is accumulating and may change in the future	–

Table 1
Contd

Pollutant	Health effects	Non-health effects
Nitrogen dioxide (NO_2)	Health effects at very high concentrations. Some studies report ambient NO_2 health effects; however, most reviews consider NO_2 as not causal but acting as a surrogate for a mixture (e.g. the effects disappear when the data are corrected for secondary particles). Possible relationship with RHAs. Direct effects usually not quantified, although information on NO_2 is accumulating NO_x leads to formation of secondary particles (nitrates) over regional range. Studies quantify nitrates assuming similarity to $PM_{10}/PM_{2.5}$. NO_x is also an ozone precursor	Ecosystem damage through secondary pollutants including nitrogen deposition (eutrophication) and acidification (although there are potential benefits through fertilization) Ozone precursor Reduces visual range
Non-methane volatile organic compounds (NMVOCs)	Ozone precursors (see text)	Ozone precursor
Ozone (O_3)	Strong evidence of a relationship between ambient ozone and acute mortality and RHAs. Evidence of other of acute morbidity end-points (e.g. exacerbation of asthma). Quantification of these effects is usually undertaken	Damage to materials (paints, polymers, and rubbers). Effects on crop yield
Benzene (C_6H_6)	Possible carcinogen. Mortality	–
Polyaromatic hydrocarbons (PAHs)	Possible carcinogen. Mortality	–

Note: (a) $PM_{2.5}$, particulate matter >2.5 μm in aerodynamic diameter.

Table 2
Emission standards (g/kWh) for heavy-duty diesel vehicle engines

Pollutant	Euro 1 (1993)	Euro 2 (1996)	Euro 3 (2000)	Euro 4 (2005)	Euro 5 (2008)	US 98 (1998)	Japan 2004
CO	4.5	4.0	2.1	1.5	1.5	15.5	2.22
Hydrocarbons	1.1	1.1	0.66	0.46	0.46	1.3	0.87
NO_x	8.0	7.0	5.0	3.5	2.0	4.0	3.38
PM_{10}	0.36	0.15	0.1	0.02	0.02	0.1	0.18

The two main paths pursued by bus engine manufacturers and bus operators to meet these tightening emission standards are a diesel path, which involves development of lower-emission diesel engines operating on cleaner diesel fuel, and an alternative fuels path, where fuels such as compressed natural gas (CNG), liquefied petroleum gas (LPG), ethanol and biodiesel are used to deliver lower emission levels. Figure 2 presents some relevant emission estimates for diesel and alternative fuels. A hybrid electric path is another alternative, involving a smaller diesel engine plus one or more electric motors to drive the wheels. Fuel cell technology seems to be widely agreed as the most likely long-term answer to emission problems from buses.

2.3. Diesel

Several fuel parameters affect diesel emissions, such as sulfur, cetane, density, T95 distillation (volatility), and PAHs. Sulfur is widely agreed to be the most significant factor, because of its link to particulate emissions. Fine particles in diesel exhaust are a direct threat to human health, as outlined in Table 1.

To meet the Euro 1 and Euro 2 standards, diesel engines require turbochargers, direct fuel injection and computerized engine management systems. The addition of catalysts and/or particle traps to meet the Euro 4 and Euro 5 standards may be required (although some manufacturers believe they may be able to "tune" engines to meet the legislation), with an associated requirement to lower diesel sulfur levels. European fuel quality specifications limit sulfur to 500 ppm for Euro 2, 350 ppm for Euro 3 and 50 ppm for Euro 4. Fuels with even lower sulfur levels (e.g. 10 ppm) are already on the market in some locations.

Oxidation catalysts have been effective in delivering reductions in particulate emissions on older buses. They are an important ingredient in the USA, for example under the US Environmental Protection Agency's urban bus retrofit program. Under that program, there are five manufacturers with certified oxidation catalysts capable of providing at least a 25% reduction in PM emissions (California Air Resources Board, 2001).

Particulate traps filter fine particles from diesel exhaust, using ceramic, fiber, or metallic filter media. The filters are commonly combined with catalysts that incinerate accumulated PM. Examples of this technology are Johnson Matthey's Continuously Regenerating Technology (CRT) DPF and Engelhard's DPX catalytic particulate filter. The former requires use of diesel with a sulfur content of less than 15 ppm, according to the California Air Resources Board (2001). The devices are very efficient at removing PM, and are conveniently packaged as a direct muffler replacement.

The California Air Resources Board reports on the results of the Clean Diesel Demonstration Program conducted by New York City Transit. That program tested the results of using PM retrofits on urban buses. It concluded that the use of ultra-low-sulfur diesel fuel alone resulted in a 76% average fall in hydrocarbon emissions, 29% average fall in CO and 29% in PM. The CRT resulted in 93–98% reductions in total hydrocarbons, CO, and PM (using the New York Bus Cycle).

Neither oxidation catalysts nor particulate traps have any direct impact on reducing the high emissions of NO_x from diesel engines. The California Air Resources Board (2001) reports that there are five main approaches being pursued to reduce NO_x emissions to levels required by future emission standards: selective catalytic reduction; the lean NO_x ($DeNO_x$) catalyst; adsorber technology (considered one of the most promising options); plasma exhaust technology; and exhaust gas recirculation. In the USA, manufacturers are focusing research and development on finding a solution in the 2007–2010 time period, as required by US Environmental Protection Agency regulations. In Europe, Euro 4 and Euro 5 legislation will require a solution even earlier, and the Euro 5 standard is likely to influence the technology developed for Euro 4. Recent discussion with manufacturers indicates that selective catalytic reduction is the most promising option.

Emissions from buses and heavy goods vehicles vary with speed, technology, and fuel. The effects of cleaner vehicles and cleaner fuels are significant. There have been very large reductions for all pollutants from the introduction of modern vehicles in the fleet (i.e. with Euro standards). The introduction of lower-sulfur diesel also leads to major emissions reductions for PM_{10} and SO_2 (with some reductions for NO_x also).

2.4. Alternative fuels

While the diesel engine has been a high-efficiency, reliable, compact, and economic converter of mechanical energy for heavy-duty vehicles, there is increasing interest in alternative energy sources under pressure to cut emission levels. CNG, LNG (liquefied natural gas), and LPG are major alternatives. These fuels burn very cleanly and have inherent emission levels that are much lower than diesel. After-treatments are needed with diesel to achieve emission rates similar to CNG. There has been a rapid increase in use of CNG in California, in particular, where 31% of route buses are expected to be alternative fuel (mainly CNG) buses by October 2002. The comparable percentage was 22% in January 2001.

The lack of a comprehensive refueling infrastructure presents obstacles to the widespread use of CNG, typically restricting this fuel to larger fleets. Also, the size and weight of CNG tanks can result in reduced passenger loadings, for any given axle mass limit, compared with LPG and diesel.

Modern technology makes natural gas compliant with Euro 5 norms, with the exception of hydrocarbons (which is not a pollutant of concern in most countries at current concentrations). However, the typical CNG bus is about 20% more expensive than its diesel counterpart, consumes more fuel (up to 30%), and may not achieve the same serviceability levels as diesel. Favorable taxation treatment of CNG fuel in some countries (e.g. Australia), however, improves the relative economics of operation. It is arguable whether such taxation incentives are sustainable long term, as the relative environmental performance of diesel and gas continues to narrow. Quieter operation in urban stop–start settings (e.g. route buses or waste collection) is an advantage of gas operation.

It has been relatively rare for LPG to be used in heavy vehicles, although this is now being considered as a heavy fuel, and LPG-fueled buses have been developed and tested. LPG has an environmental performance record that is slightly above that of CNG and also has three times the energy density. The fuel has been successfully used by the Vienna bus fleet since 1963. Modern buses have been tested by DAF. However, as it is heavier than air, some countries are wary of licensing the fuel.

Hybrid electric power trains are another path to reducing emissions from urban buses. Anyon (2002) describes a hybrid power train as a load-leveling system. The electric motor handles the fluctuations in speed and load, which it can do more efficiently than an internal combustion engine. This allows a much smaller diesel engine to be used (e.g. 3 liters rather than 8–10 liters), complemented by one or more electric motors. During travel phases that are energy-intensive, such as during rapid acceleration, the generated power is supplemented by drawing extra current from the batteries. Stop–start bus operation is an ideal application of this technology, the California Air Resources Board (2001) noting a test program improvement in fuel economy of 65% (from 1.4 to 2.3 mpg).

Fuel cells are usually seen as the next step in technological development, after a hybrid electric power train. A fuel cell replaces the internal combustion engine and generator as the source of on-board electricity generation. The fuel cell will continue to produce energy in the form of electricity and heat so long as fuel is supplied. Emissions from this type of system will be lower than from the cleanest fuel combustion processes.

There are several trials of fuel cell buses taking place at present, such as in the USA and Canada, and with a trial to commence in Australia shortly. Costs are currently extremely high, and commercialization dates are argued to be anywhere between 2003 and 2015, indicating the uncertainty surrounding implementation.

Bi-fuel operation is another means of reducing PM and smoke emissions from bus operation. This may involve, for example, the engine running on a mixture of diesel and gaseous fuel (e.g. CNG or LPG). Most relevant test data are confidential to the companies involved, so comparative data are scarce.

Figure 1 sets out some comparative data on emissions of air pollutants from alternative fuels, in comparison with Euro 2 vehicles. This shows the benefits of

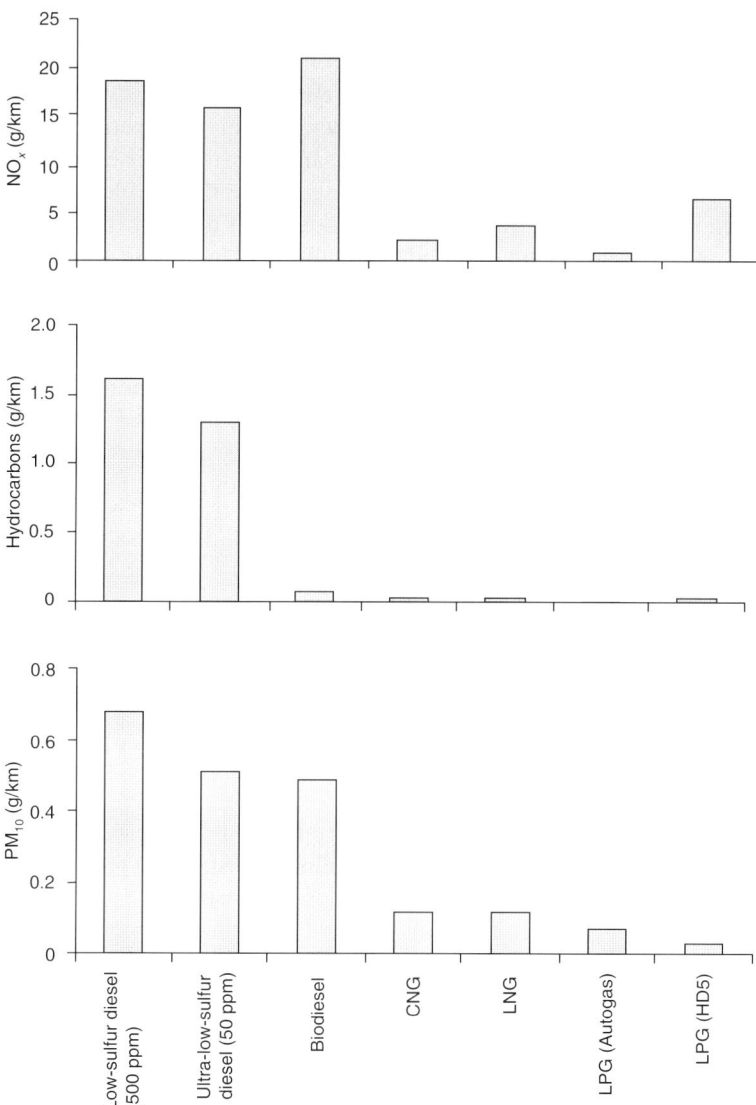

Figure 1. Exhaust pipe emissions from alternative-fueled and Euro 2 diesel buses (Commonwealth Scientific and Industrial Research Organization, 2002.)

alternative fuels. However, as Euro 4 vehicles are introduced that use low-sulfur diesel, this advantage will be lost. For example, test data show there is almost no difference in particle emissions between Euro 4 vehicles with particle traps and CNG or LPG buses (Murray et al., 2000).

When evaluating the emissions from different fuels, it is important to consider all emissions across the fuel and vehicle life-cycle (i.e. from "well to wheel"). However, there is one very important factor when evaluating upstream emissions: these emissions should not be treated in the same way to end use emissions. The key issue is the location of emissions. End-use emissions are released at ground level, often in urban areas, where population densities are very high. In contrast, upstream emissions are often released from tall stacks in remote areas, or, for the majority of crude extraction emissions, from offshore fields. Emissions from such locations will clearly not have local air quality effects and should not be treated equally as exhaust pipe emissions (note this is not the case, however, for greenhouse gas emissions, which can be treated equally irrespective of location). Within this chapter, these upstream effects have not been quantified and included in the results. This may slightly underestimate total effects, as a proportion of upstream emissions will be released close to urban areas, e.g. from refineries.

2.5. Quantifying and valuing air pollution effects

The European Commission has supported extensive work on valuing the air pollution costs of transport. European Commission (2001a) research teams, have used the following method to quantify and value health effects of air pollution:

(1) quantify the emissions from the pollutant source;
(2) assess the resulting air pollution concentrations in the surrounding area from these emissions (e.g. using air pollution dispersion models);
(3) assess the population-weighted pollution increases;
(4) use exposure–response functions that link, for example, population-weighted pollution increments to health end-points;
(5) value these end-points using economic-based estimates.

The illustrative results presented in this chapter are based on values derived from such a "bottom-up" approach to valuing air pollution, using the results of the European Union's ExternE project (European Commission, 1995, 1999, 2001a). This takes account of the effects of speed, location, and technology, and allows a picture to be built of the environmental costs of different vehicles, traveling on different roads, in different locations. It provides the necessary information to look at the environmental costs of the transport sector at a high level.

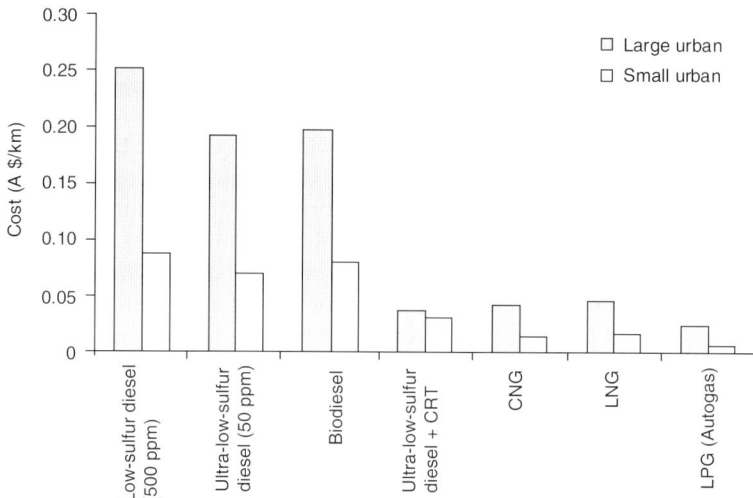

Figure 2. Air pollution damage costs for a number of buses. (Source: CSIRO emissions data, and Bus Industry Confederation (2001) unit cost estimates; the latter are for ultra-low-sulfur diesel with a particulate trap.)

Figure 2 shows air pollution costs for a sample of buses, based on the Commonwealth Scientific and Industrial Research Organization emission factors presented in Figure 1 and applying unit damage costs appropriate in different types of locations (ignoring speed differences). Figure 2 also includes an estimate for a city diesel bus (10 ppm sulfur diesel) using a particulate trap (CRT), based on European emission test data from the UK Cleaner Vehicles Task Force.

Figure 2 shows that a Euro 2 diesel bus (using 500 ppm sulfur diesel) produces air pollution costs of A $0.08–0.25/km, depending on the urban area. Ultra-low-sulfur diesel reduces these costs to A $0.07–0.19/km. CNG damage costs are estimated at about A $0.013–0.042/km for the range of area sizes. This gives a significant benefit over conventional or low-sulfur diesel. However, the benefits of CNG are significantly less for ultra-low-sulfur diesel, and CNG has similar (or even higher) air pollution damage costs to a bus running on "city diesel" with a particulate trap.

Commonwealth Scientific and Industrial Research Organization (2001) emissions estimates suggest that biodiesel produces similar air pollution costs to diesel, because of high particulate and NO_x emissions. LPG has the lowest air pollution costs per kilometer of all those fuels shown in the figure. The relative performance of the fuels is similar to previous studies in Europe.

3. Climate change

The effects of global climate change from greenhouse gas emissions are diverse and potentially very large. They are likely to have very large economic costs, both from adaptation (e.g. coastal protection costs) as well as damage to health and the environment. Carbon dioxide (CO_2), methane (CH_4), and nitrous oxide (N_2O) are the main emissions of concern from transport fuel production and use. The impacts of these emissions are independent of location, and so a tonne of CO_2 released from upstream fuel refinery processing can be treated in an identical manner to a tonne of CO_2 released from a vehicle in an urban area.

Road transport is a major contributor to greenhouse gas emissions, and these emissions are growing with the transport task in many countries. Cars alone, for example, contribute 9% of Australia's greenhouse gas emissions. The road transport sector must thus be a major focus of efforts to contain greenhouse gas emissions.

3.1. Emissions

Greenhouse gas emissions from vehicles vary with speed (non-linearly). There are large differences in emissions between slow and fast moving traffic, with CO_2 emissions being significantly higher, per distance traveled, at low speeds. This has implications for urban traffic congestion.

For buses, fuel efficiency and therefore CO_2 emissions do not vary greatly between older and more modern vehicles (e.g. different Euro standards). There are small efficiency improvements for modern vehicles, and also with the use of

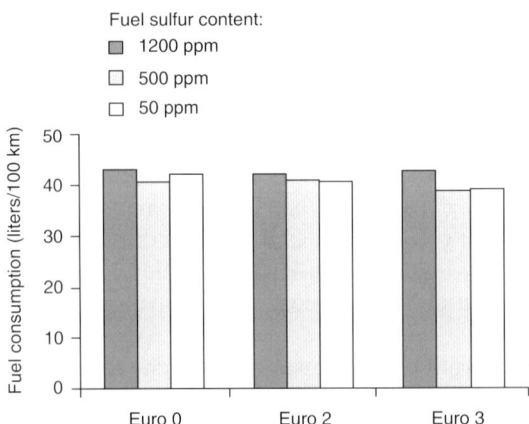

Figure 3. Fuel consumption rates for diesel buses with different fuels and technologies. (Source: Bus Industry Confederation test cycle data on Australian buses.)

different diesel fuels. The effects of these two variables can be seen in Figure 3, which shows fuel consumption (test cycle data) for buses meeting different Euro standards and running on different sulfur content fuels in some Australian tests (Bus Industry Confederation, 2001). The Euro 2 and Euro 3 vehicles generally achieved slightly better fuel economy than the Euro 0 vehicle, and the 500 and 50 ppm sulfur fuels gave better economy than the 1200 ppm fuel, particularly in the Euro 3 vehicle, but the differences are not marked.

The end use emissions of CO_2 from some major alternative fuels are generally similar to those from conventionally fueled vehicles, even when emissions from upstream fuel extraction, processing and distribution are taken into account (Box 1).

3.2. Putting a cost on greenhouse gas emissions

The externalities of greenhouse gas emissions are ideally suited to recovery through fuel taxes (charge), as emissions are directly related to the energy and carbon content of different fuels. The most appropriate instrument is a carbon tax, as this can be set to match the carbon emissions from the combustion of a liter of fuel. However, debate exists on what the appropriate costs per tonne of carbon emitted should be.

The carbon tax should be set at the optimum level, which is the point, at any given time, when the marginal abatement cost and the marginal social damage (or benefit of abatement) are equal. Expressed another way, the incremental social costs of additional abatement (i.e. reducing emissions by 1 tonne) should be equal to the additional social benefits of avoided damage.

Box 1 shows that the differences in the greenhouse gas emissions from diesel and alternative fuels are low, with the exception of biofuels. Gaseous fuels show only limited greenhouse gas benefits over diesel on a life-cycle basis.

A number of studies have quantified the likely future damage costs from climate change, and used these values to derive a marginal cost per tonne of carbon from marginal changes in emission levels. These studies take the predicted changes in global mean temperature, precipitation, and sea level rise, and quantify the likely impacts of these effects, along with impacts on human health, agriculture, water resources, and ecosystems.

One of the more comprehensive studies, the ExternE study (European Commission, 1999), has estimated a central value of around A $40/tonne of CO_2 for current emissions, with a central range of A $20–90/tonne of CO_2. This central value is also similar to recent estimates of the global marginal abatement costs of meeting the Kyoto Protocol. For example, recent analysis (European Commission, 2001b) has indicated that the marginal abatement costs for the EU to meet the Kyoto targets is A $35-70/tonne of CO_2, although it is stressed this value is only relevant for the short-term: the marginal damage costs and the marginal abatement costs will increase dramatically in future years.

The greenhouse values for CH_4 and N_2O emissions from the ExternE study have also been used (these values have been used in recent policy work in Europe, and

Box 1
Life-cycle greenhouse gas emissions from alternative fuel buses

There is generally less information on the emissions from alternative fuel vehicles than on emissions from diesel vehicles. The use of CNG and LPG fuels in heavy vehicles produces similar greenhouse gas emissions to conventional diesel vehicles on a per kilometer basis (although alternative vehicles have greenhouse gas emission benefits relative to gasoline use in light vehicles). For heavy vehicles, although gaseous fuels have a lower carbon content, fuel use (MJ/km) is increased for LPG and CNG vehicles (as engine efficiency is lower for spark ignition engines) and alternative vehicles have a weight penalty. The emissions test programs in the literature generally report that dedicated LPG and CNG heavy vehicles have similar emissions to modern diesel vehicles, but that converted or bi-fuel alternative fuel vehicles often compare less favorably.

When comparing different fuels, emissions from upstream fuel extraction, processing, and distribution should also be taken into account, as well as tailpipe emissions. Diesel and LPG have similar upstream emissions. CNG has lower CO_2 emissions due to the lower levels of processing required with gas, although methane emissions can offset these benefits, especially if gas is supplied from the low-pressure network (e.g. residential). The overall emissions from different fuels (based on the CSIRO Stage 2 study) are shown below. This study gives slightly lower greenhouse gas emissions from CNG and LPG fuels than the European literature. Bio-fuels have significant greenhouse gas emission emissions benefits, as all emissions from the tailpipe are discounted as they are of biomass origin. These fuels tend to have higher greenhouse gas emission emissions from upstream activities relative to conventional or CNG/LPG fuels, but the zero tailpipe emissions more than compensates for this.

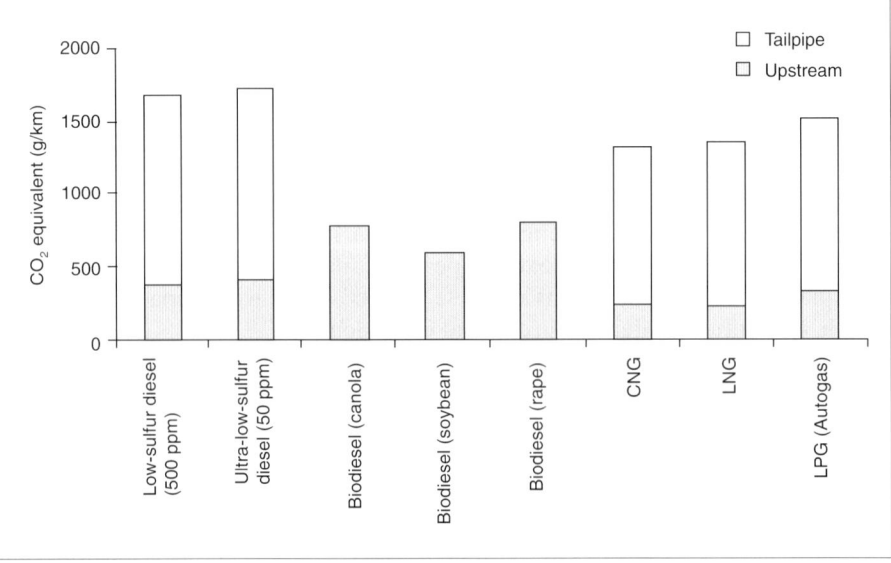

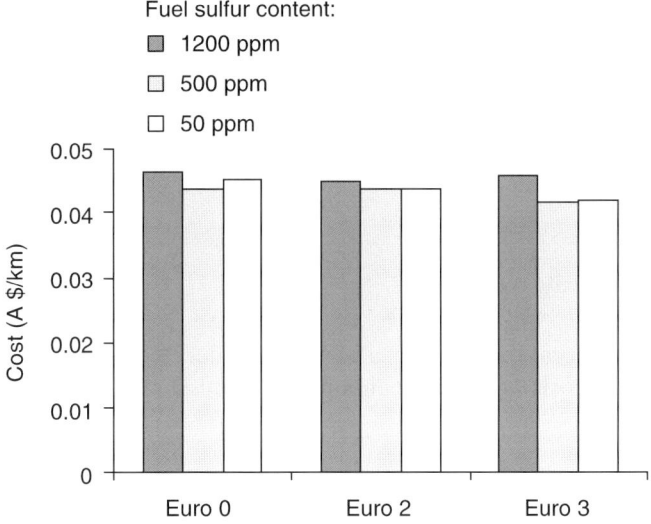

Figure 4. Damage costs per kilometer from exhaust pipe emissions from diesel buses.

have been applied here). Within the per kilometre costs for greenhouse emissions presented in this chapter, the total impact of these latter components is very small (being a maximum of about A $0.005/km for LPG and much less for CNG and diesel).

3.3. Charges per litre

The use of the central value of A $40/tonne of CO_2 can be combined with emission rates to show the relevant external costs per kilometer. The relevant values, based on the bus emission test data derived by the Bus Industry Confederation (2001) are shown in Figure 4 in Australian dollars per kilometer. The costs for large articulated trucks will be similar. The values for cars will be lower, although these differences will be removed when expressed in dollars per liter of fuel. Converting these values to fuel volume gives a relevant duty level (carbon tax) of A $0.107/liter of diesel, based on exhaust pipe emissions. This value is the same irrespective of the type of vehicle using the fuel (with the exception of small fluctuations from combustion efficiency). Large differences can, however, result if different damage costs are applied.

Relevant charges for other fuels (based on exhaust pipe emissions) would be A $0.091/liter for gasoline, approximately A $0.06/liter for LPG, and A $0.107/kg for CNG. On this basis, biofuels would attract a zero duty level, as their exhaust pipe CO_2 emissions are "renewable" in nature (biomass derived).

However, in looking to provide an incentive to switch to lower-carbon fuels, and to ensure benefits at the exhaust pipe are not offset by emissions in fuel extraction and production, life-cycle emissions should be considered (rather than just exhaust pipe emissions). This is particularly important for capturing potential benefits of alternative fuels (Box 2). The gaseous fuels (CNG and LPG) do not offer large benefits over diesel. However, on a whole-of-life basis there may be some benefits.

4. Public and private transport

In metropolitan areas, buses offer a means to reduce congestion and to reduce both congestion costs and the greenhouse gas emissions from urban transport,

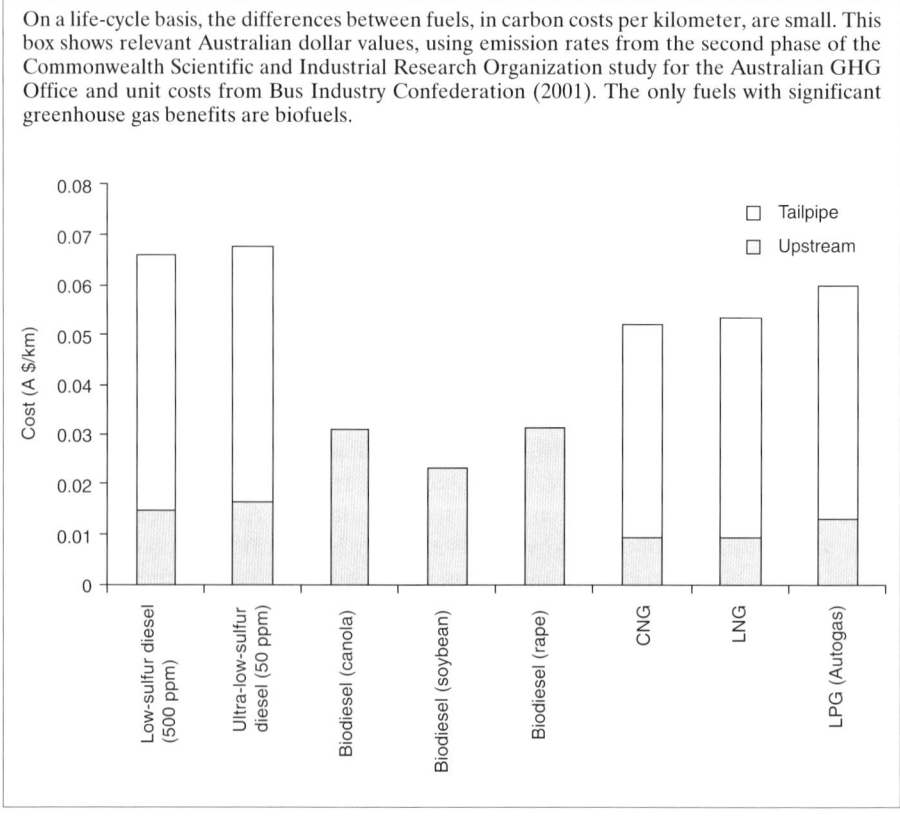

Box 2
Life-cycle greenhouse gas emissions from alternative fuels

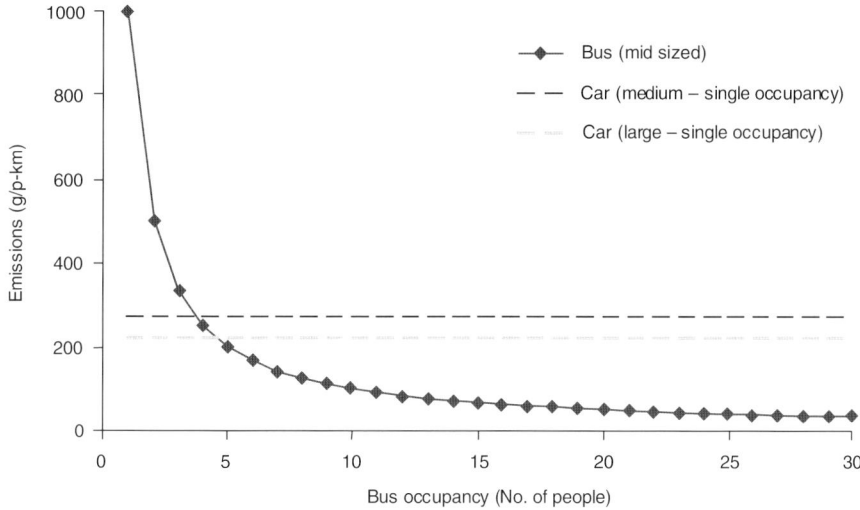

Figure 5. Greenhouse gas emissions per passenger-kilometer. The values for buses are based on central values from the BIC (2001) test data.

especially when that bus use is facilitated by on-road priority. Illustrative greenhouse gas effects are given in Figure 5, showing the relative CO_2 emissions per passenger-kilometer for a bus against medium-sized and large cars. Once bus occupancy exceeds around three people, then the greenhouse gas emissions per passenger-kilometer are lower from buses, and this differential increases sharply with occupancy. The values are based on typical transport flows in urban areas (rather than congested areas). Given the increasing size of many vehicles in Australia and in most Western economies (e.g. toward 4 by 4 or MPVs), this differential is likely to become larger in future years. In rural areas, buses similarly provide an efficient means to transport large numbers of people (e.g. school runs) and avoid larger numbers of vehicle trips by private cars.

In urban areas, the use of modern buses (e.g. meeting the Euro 2, 3, or 4 standard) and alternative fuels also means that increased bus use offers a way to significantly reduce pollutant emissions per passenger km, and this is reflected in the relative environmental costs. There is however, a difference to the pattern seen for greenhouse gas emissions in that the use of older buses can be counter-productive with respect to urban air quality due to the very much higher pollutant emissions from older diesel vehicles.

Bus patronage therefore has the potential to reduce transport sector greenhouse gas emissions, while also contributing to lower air pollution levels and reduced congestion costs in urban areas. These benefits are not currently recognized through pricing signals to motorists, and fiscal incentives need to be provided to users when choosing between private and public transport in urban areas.

5. Conclusions

The growing focus on how motorized transport affects urban air quality in general, and the health effects of particulate emissions more specifically, has underpinned policy measures to significantly reduce emission rates from new buses (and other vehicles). Lower-emission bus engines and cleaner fuels, particularly diesel with lower levels of sulfur but also an increasing range of alternative fuels, have combined to dramatically lower emission rates from individual buses. This improved emission performance at the level of the individual vehicle/fuel, combined with increasing governmental focus on increasing the mode share performed by buses and public transport more generally, provides a platform for continuing improvement in urban air quality as it is affected by motorized transport. As bus emission rates fall with modern emission standards and diesel fuel quality is improved, there is little to choose between diesel and alternative fuels in terms of air quality impacts.

Apart from biofuels, there is also little to choose between diesel and alternative fuels in terms of greenhouse gas emissions. The major way buses can assist the reduction of greenhouse gas emissions is through achieving a higher share of the personal transport task. This is largely dependent on measures to improve service frequency, span and coverage, better on-road priority for bus operation (to deliver faster, more reliable travel times), improved marketing and service integration, and on car users being made more accountable for the social costs of their travel choices.

References

Anyon, P. (2002) "New technologies for bus power sources, smart urban," *Transport*, 1:18–19.

Bus Industry Confederation (2001) "Getting the prices right: policy for more sustainable fuel taxation for road transport in Australia." Submission to the Commonwealth Fuel Taxation Inquiry.

California Air Resources Board (2001) "The public transit bus fleet rule status report." Paper presented to CARB Public Meeting.

Committee on the Medical Effects of Air Pollutants (1998) *Quantification of the effects of air pollution on health in the UK Department of Health*. London: The Stationery Office.

Commonwealth Scientific and Industrial Research Organization (2001) *Comparison of transport fuels. Final report to the Australian Greenhouse Gas Office (EV45A/2/F3C) on the stage 2 study of life cycle emissions analysis of alternative fuels for heavy vehicles*. Canberra: CSIRO.

European Commission (1995) *European Commission, DGXII. Science, research and development, JOULE. Externalities of energy, 'ExternE' project*, Vol. 2. Methodology report (EUR 16521 EN). Luxembourg: EC.

European Commission (1999) *European Commission, Research Directorate General. Externalities of energy, 'ExternE' project*, Vol. 7. Methodology 1998 update (EUR 19083). Luxembourg: EC.

European Commission (2001a) *External costs of energy conversion – improvement of the ExternE methodology and assessment of energy-related transport externalities. Final publishable report of the ExternE core/transport project*. Brussels: EC DEG Research. (Also published as: Friedrich, R. and P. Bickel, eds (2001) *Environmental external costs of transport*. Berlin: Springer-Verlag.)

European Commission (2001b) *Economic evaluation of sectoral emission reduction objectives for climate change*. Luxembourg: EC.

European Conference of Ministers of Transport (1998) *Efficient transport for Europe: policies for internalisation of external costs*. Paris: EMCT.

Maddison, D., O.Johansson and D. Pearce (1996) *Blueprint 5: the true costs of road transport*. London: Earthscan.

Murray, J., B. Lane, K. Lillie and J. McCallum (2000) *The report of the Alternative Fuels Group of the Cleaner Vehicles Task Force*. London: Department of Trade and Industry.

Sansom, T., C.A. Nash, P.J. Mackie, J. Shires and P. Watkiss (2001) *Surface transport costs and charges Great Britain 1998. Final report for the Department of the Environment, Transport and the Regions*. Leeds: Institute for Transport Studies, University of Leeds.

Chapter 13

TRANSPORT ENERGY AND EMISSIONS: URBAN PUBLIC TRANSPORT

STEPHEN POTTER

The Open University, Milton Keynes

1. Urban public transport and energy use

In recent years, transport's use of energy has risen strongly. Forty years ago, in most developed economies, transport's proportion of total energy use was between 15 and 20%. Today it is around 35% of all energy consumption. Most of this energy use is for oil (which supplies 98% of transport energy use), and demand is still rising strongly (UK Department of Trade and Industry, 1999). Urban public transport accounts for very little of this growth in energy use, or of transport's overall energy consumption. It is also less oil-dependent. For example, in the UK, of all fuel used for transport, 76% was consumed by private road transport (cars and lorries) and 18% by air travel. Only 4% of transport energy was used by buses and railways and 2% by water transport (UK Department of Trade and Industry, 2000). The situation is similar in other developed economies. The rise in transport's use of energy has primarily come about by the increased use of the private car for personal transport and the road lorry for freight.

This does not mean that the energy and emissions from urban public transport is not an important issue. As urban policies increasingly seek to transfer travel from the private car to public transport, questions arise about the impact this might have on overall emissions. Studies of transport energy and emissions from passenger transport often concentrate upon individual vehicles, but this is only a part of the vehicle/transport system generating the total amount of energy used and pollutants emitted. This total is a product of a number of factors. As well as the energy used per vehicle, key variables are how well occupied and utilized a vehicle is, patterns of use, and the overall volume of travel undertaken (Potter, 2001). Outside of this vehicle/transport system there are also indirect travel-generating effects, such as long-distance commuter rail contributing to metropolitan decentralization and so leading to increased car use and dependency. An awareness of such wider system effects helps to explain why energy efficiency and emissions improvements to individual vehicles have been accompanied by a substantial increase in energy use and emissions from the transport sector. This chapter explores the nature of energy use and emissions from urban public transport and indicates some of the strategic issues involved. It starts by examining energy and emissions from public transport vehicles themselves and then extends the system boundary to encompass public transport systems, how they are developed for transport and environmental policies, and then indirect effects upon wider travel patterns and behavior.

2. Measuring vehicle energy and emissions

Life cycle analysis studies of the environmental impacts of road vehicles (e.g. Teufel et al., 1993; Organisation for Economic Co-operation and Development (OECD), 1993) have indicated that that the fuel used in running vehicles represents 80–90% of total life cycle energy use. The production and processing of materials, vehicle manufacture, maintenance and disposal stages of the life cycle are relatively insignificant compared with the energy consumed and emissions generated when vehicles are in use. The OECD study, for example, calculated carbon dioxide (CO_2) emissions from an "average" gasoline car, and showed that only 9% was from vehicle manufacturing, with 76% from the fuel at point of use and a further 15% from emissions and losses in the fuel supply system. These life cycle studies were of cars, which are utilized less intensively and have a shorter life than public transport vehicles. Thus, it is probable that an even higher proportion of the energy and emission impacts of buses, trams, and trains are in their use phase.

However, when considering energy and emissions from vehicle operations, it is important to use data on fuel life cycle (or primary energy) consumption. As noted in the OECD study, energy use and emissions in the fuel supply system are important for vehicles powered by internal combustion engines. It is even more so for public transport modes using electricity, where there can be 60% losses in electricity generation. This particularly applies to CO_2 emissions, which are a function of the amount of fossil fuel used. For local urban air quality, emissions at the point of use (delivered energy) become more important.

3. Air quality emissions

Diesel or electricity predominantly powers urban public transport vehicles. Buses and many trains are diesel powered, whereas electrification is widespread for urban railway lines, and is standard for metro and tram systems. Diesel has a reputation as a rather "dirty" fuel, and the adverse health effect of PM_{10} particles (i.e. those with a diameter <10 μm) in diesel bus emissions has attracted considerable attention. However, in recent years there have been significant improvements to both diesel fuel formulations (e.g. low-sulfur "city" diesel) and to engine design and exhaust after-treatments. For electricity, emissions are transferred to power stations, which may use a variety of fuels.

It is useful to separate emissions from urban public transport into those that affect urban air quality and those that contribute to global climate change. For diesel-powered buses and trains, the key emissions that affect air quality are:

- Carbon monoxide (CO) – a highly toxic gas that can impair brain function and, in sufficient concentrations, kill. Transport is the major source of CO, with 90% coming from cars.
- Nitrogen oxides (NO_x) – these cause respiratory problems and contribute to low-level ozone formation and acid rain. Transport produces about half of all NO_x emissions. Diesel vehicles (buses, lorries, diesel trains, and cars) are an important source.
- Hydrocarbons (HCs) – these include known carcinogens.
- Particulate matter (PM) – about half of all particulates come from diesel vehicles. These aggravate respiratory diseases and smaller particles (PM_{10}) may be carcinogenic.

In all cases, urban public transport vehicles are only a minority source, although there can be health concerns in certain specific locations of the health risks associated with PM_{10} emissions from diesel engines. Such locations include where buses operate in busy shopping streets, near bus depots, or large stations served by diesel trains.

Electric vehicles produce no significant emissions in their operations on urban streets, with pollution transferred to the site of power stations. Fossil fuel (particularly coal and oil) power stations are a major source of sulfur dioxide (SO_2) and NO_x. These emissions also have regional air quality impacts as they play a key role in producing acid rain. Natural gas-fueled power stations do not emit any SO_2 as it is removed before the gas is distributed. Nuclear power stations produce no emissions that affect urban air quality (and tend to be located well away from urban areas), but have other important environmental and health issues, including toxic waste disposal and accident risk. Hydroelectricity and other renewable energy sources produce no emissions affecting local air quality, but again there are other environmental impacts (e.g. the environmental and ecosystem effects of large dams).

Carpenter (1994), in his examination of the environmental impact of railways, compiled information from a number of UK and German sources on emissions by a several types of public transport vehicle. Table 1 summarizes the "typical emissions" for urban public transport modes.

As the issue of modal transfer between car and urban public transport is important, Carpenter's "typical" figure for cars is also included. Per passenger-kilometer, NO_x and CO emissions are substantially lower for urban public transport modes than traveling by car. Electric rail (via power stations) does have high SO_2 emissions, but this is counterbalanced by very low emissions of other pollutants.

The information in Table 1 dates from the early/mid-1990s, and since then governments throughout the world have introduced increasingly stringent regulations to cut emissions from new diesel and gasoline vehicles. This was detailed in Chapter 12 on buses, with Table 2 in that chapter detailing the improvement in emission standards in the EU, the USA, and Japan. Of note is the considerable reduction in diesel fuel particle emissions, which addresses the major air quality concern of urban buses. However, as Ford (2002) notes in his review of diesel train engines, in Europe these standards apply only to road vehicles. So, although buses have to meet the increasingly stringent Euro standards, trains do not. This is not the situation in the USA, where the US Environmental Protection Agency has introduced NO_x and particulate limits for diesel trains. However, in Europe, local urban diesel multiple-unit trains are powered by variants of diesel engines designed for lorries and buses. As these meet the Euro emission standards, then the trains they power will also have lower emissions.

The situation is not quite as simple as automotive emission standards automatically reducing emissions from urban passenger diesel trains. The operating regime of trains is different to that of buses and lorries, and engine adjustments to improve the fuel economy of train engines will increase NO_x emissions to above the Euro limits. The International Union of Railways (UIC), in conjunction with rail operators and suppliers, has been developing a new set of emission limits for rail traction diesels. The figures for smaller engines (used in urban diesel multiple-unit trains) are shown in Table 2. Due to the different operating regime and test cycles, these are not directly comparable to the road vehicle Euro standards. The considerable reduction in NO_x is of note, as this is a crucial local air pollutant from diesel engines.

Table 1
Typical emissions from urban public transport

Mode	Emissions (g/p-km)			
	NO_x	SO_2	CO	HCs
Bus	0.8	0.1	1.0	0.1
Diesel rail	1.0	0.2	0.1	0.1
Electric rail	0.4	1.1	0.1	0.002
Tram/metro	0.2	–	0.01	–
Car	2.1	–	11.0	–

Source: summarized from Carpenter (1994).

Table 2
Proposed UIC diesel engine emissions

Date	Emissions (g/kWh)			
	NO_x	HCs	CO	PM
Until 31.12.02	12	0.8	3.0	
1.1.03–31.12.07	9.9	0.8	3.0	0.25
From 1.01.08	4.5	0.5	2.0	0.15

Source: adapted from Ford (2002).

4. Climate change emissions

The principal gas contributing to climate change is CO_2. As noted above, gasses and particulates affecting local air quality can be addressed by technologies that reduce or eliminate them at source, although improvements may be countered by an increase in the amount of travel. Emissions of CO_2 are not amenable to such "technical fixes," as they are simply a function of the carbon content of fossil fuels. Diesel fuel averages 2.7 kg of CO_2 per liter, with gasoline a little lower at 2.4 kg of CO_2 per liter. Liquefied petroleum gas (LPG) and compressed natural gas (CNG) have a lower carbon content (with natural gas having 0.18 kg of CO_2/kWh). The carbon content of fuels is somewhat modified by the technology of diesel, gasoline, and gas engines, which have inherently different efficiencies. The diesel engine is more efficient than the gasoline engine, with gas engines somewhat less efficient than either diesel or gasoline engines.

A number of studies (Wood, 1995; Potter, 2000; Roy et al., 2002) have compiled empirical information on the amount of energy and CO_2 emissions arising from the operations of various transport modes. Table 3 is a compilation from these sources for a range of urban public transport vehicles. These figures are for fuel life cycle, allowing for the different engine efficiencies and fuel production systems and the carbon content of the fuels concerned. Clearly, the energy use depends very much upon the individual designs of vehicles and their operating regimes, and the above studies do note variations. It should be emphasized that Table 3 only contains information on urban public transport vehicles. Larger and faster inter-city trains, for example, have higher energy use and CO_2 emissions.

The figures in Table 3 are largely based on UK data. The information for buses was provided by a number of urban bus companies and that for railways by London suburban rail operators. The light rail figures were provided for the modern tram operations in Manchester and the metro figure is for the London Underground. The data have been compared with other UK and European studies

Table 3
Fuel life cycle energy consumption and CO_2 emissions for urban transport modes

Mode	Seats	Energy consumption (MJ/v-km)	CO_2 emissions (kg/v-km)	Energy consumption (MJ/seat-km)	CO_2 emissions (g/seat-km)
Urban electric train	300	117	11.7	0.39	39
Urban diesel train	146	74	8.8	0.50	60
Light rail	265	47	10.1	0.18	38
Metro	555	122	26.0	0.22	46
Single deck bus	49	14.2	1.6	0.29	33
Double deck bus	74	16.2	1.9	0.22	26
Minibus	20	7.1	0.8	0.36	40
Medium-sized car	5	3.5	0.39	0.70	78

Source: based on Carpenter (1994), Potter (2000), and Roy et al.(2002).

of energy and CO_2 emissions (European Commission, 1992). This comparison suggests that the energy use and CO_2 emissions for buses and diesel trains are broadly similar to those found in other developed countries. For electric trains, light rail, and metros, the energy use is also broadly similar to the UK figures, but CO_2 emissions vary according to the primary fuel mix of the power stations. The UK mix of gas, coal, and nuclear generation was estimated to produce 480 g of CO_2/kWh.[a]

Because of the considerable variation in the size of public transport vehicles, a valid comparison can only be made if a standard unit is used. Hence, Table 3 uses the unit of energy and emissions per passenger seat-kilometer to produce comparable figures. In general, the slower forms of public transport using lighter vehicles consume less energy and produce the least CO_2 emissions. The metro figure is surprisingly high. There are two reasons for this. One is that it involves an older system and vehicles than the other vehicles for which data were gathered. There is also a problem with urban transport vehicles designed to accommodate standing as well as seated passengers, which particularly affects metro services such as the London Underground. Dividing energy and CO_2 emissions by seats thus gives the impression that such vehicles are less efficient than they actually are. For urban and transport policy comparisons, figures for a medium-sized car are

---

[a]Modern coal power stations produce about 950 g of CO_2 per kilowatt-hour of electricity generated, and gas combined cycle stations about 450 g of CO_2 per kilowatt-hour of electricity generated (Everett and Alexander, 2000). The UK average also includes oil, hydro, and nuclear generation.

also included. This shows that, per seat-kilometer, public transport uses less energy and produces less CO_2 emissions than a typical car.

The "per seat-kilometer" measure in Table 3 provides a valid comparison between different public transport modes, but in actual practice there is a further variable that crucially affects the actual emissions per passenger-kilometer. This is how well occupied a vehicle is. If there is only the driver in a private car, then he or she will be consuming 3.5 MJ per passenger-kilometer compared with around 0.2–0.3 MJ for a fully loaded bus or train. In such a situation, driving a car consumes ten times the energy than if the same trip were made by public transport. In the UK, actual peak-hour car occupancy averages 1.17 persons (Potter, 2000) while trains and buses are near fully loaded (with standing in addition to seated passengers), so in such circumstances such a ratio of energy use is likely to be achieved.

In the off-peak period the situation is different. For shopping, leisure, and holiday trips, car occupancy is in the range of 2–3 persons (50–60%), and off-peak loadings of public transport average 40% or less. Taking vehicle occupancy/loadings into account makes it more difficult to produce a comparison between modes, as occupancy varies considerably between systems and time, and is affected by demography and even culture. Table 4 is a reworking of the data from Table 3, with adjustments from other data sources (principally Carpenter, 1994). This estimates the average loading experienced in peak and off-peak trips. Even at peak times, trains and buses are not fully occupied for the whole of a trip. A train may well have a crush loading of 130% (or more) as it arrives at a city-center terminus, and metro systems often have more people standing than sitting (a 200%+ loading based on seats). However, only a proportion of those passengers were on board when the train started its journey, and counter-peak services will be running at much lower levels of occupancy. These figures were obtained from public transport operators in the UK, and some other European sources. For example, in 2000 the Docklands Light Railway in London had an average seat occupancy of 43%, and the Tyne and Wear Metro 30%[a].

Although some of the figures in Table 3 are reported to two decimal places; this should not be taken as a precise level of accuracy. The data sources used contained some variation, although the relative energy use and emissions between modes was in proportion. These are the best comparable figures from the various empirical sources, and show the difference that allowing for occupancy makes. For peak period travel, the ratio of energy and emissions from public transport compared with the car drops from that of 1:10 using the seat-kilometer measure to about 1:7. For off-peak travel the ratio drops even further: it is only around 2:1, and for some

---

[a] Information on passenger-kilometers, loaded vehicle-kilometers, and vehicle seating capacity permits such calculations. Some of this information for the UK can be found on the Internet (www.transtat.dft.gov.uk).

Table 4
Peak and off-peak fuel life cycle energy consumption and CO_2 emissions for urban transport

Mode	Energy consumption (MJ/seat-km)	CO_2 emissions (g/seat-km)	Peak travel			Off-peak travel		
			Assumed occupancy (%)	Energy consumption (MJ/p-km)	CO_2 emissions (g/p-km)	Assumed occupancy (%)	Energy consumption (MJ/p-km)	CO_2 emissions (g/p-km)
Urban electric train	0.39	39	60	0.65	65	25	1.56	156
Urban diesel train	0.50	60	60	0.83	98	25	2.00	240
Light rail	0.18	38	70	0.25	54	40	0.45	95
Metro	0.22	46	70	0.31	66	40	0.55	115
Single-deck bus	0.29	33	50	0.58	66	20	1.45	165
Double-deck bus	0.22	26	50	0.44	52	20	1.10	130
Minibus	0.36	40	70	0.51	57	20	1.80	200
Medium-sized car	0.70	78	23	3.04	339	40	1.75	195

Source: based on Carpenter (1994), Potter (2000), and Roy et al.(2002).

Table 5
Fuel life cycle energy consumption of a single-deck bus and medium-sized car according to occupancy

Loading (%)	Energy consumption (MJ/p-km)	
	Single-deck bus	Medium-sized car
100	0.29	0.7
90	0.32	0.9
80	0.36	0.9
70	0.42	2.1
60	0.49	2.1
50	0.57	2.1
40	0.71	1.8
30	0.91	1.8
20	1.42	3.5
10	2.84	3.5
5	7.10	3.5
2.5	14.2	3.5

types of public transport the average energy used is higher than for a car (although in general CO_2 emissions remain lower for public transport).

This has important implications. It shows that the biggest environmental gain in modal shift from car to public transport is achieved where and when cars are poorly occupied. Once the occupancy level of public transport drops, its energy and emissions performance worsens. Table 5 provides a detailed example of this effect using the example of a single deck bus and a medium-sized car. In a situation when car occupancy averages three people, then the bus would need to average more than a 15% loading (seven people on a single-deck bus) to be more energy-efficient. If car occupancy averaged two people, the bus would need to average more than a 13% loading (six passengers).

However, there is an important practical consideration to be made with regard to such comparisons. If car trips are transferred to off-peak public transport, it can be accommodated by increasing the loads on existing services, so no additional energy and emissions are involved. Indeed, improving public transport occupancy levels by modal transfer from cars will yield very positive energy and emission reduction results. It is important to take into account if a policy measure will affect occupancy levels.

With careful interpretation and use, such figures can be used to evaluate the energy and CO_2 emissions of alternative public transport systems or for policy development. For example, in a recent project for the UK government exploring the modal shift impacts of personal tax concessions on public transport commuting, an estimate was made of the amount of CO_2 reduced by alternative policy options (Potter et al., 2001). This estimated that, given the average UK car fuel consumption of 9 liters per 100 km, and the average commuting distance by car, each single car occupancy commuting trip produces about 1.3 tonnes of CO_2 emissions per annum. Were a tax instrument introduced that resulted in car commuters shifting to public transport, it was assumed that, commuting being at peak times, additional services would have to be provided. The net reduction in CO_2 emissions from cars would therefore be counterbalanced by rises from the new public transport services. Using similar data to that in Tables 3 and 4, it was estimated that public transport in peak hours used less than 20% of the energy consumed by a single-occupancy car. Thus, for every peak-hour car trip diverted to public transport, the net CO_2 saved would be 80% of the gross cut in CO_2 from the car, amounting to a cut of just over 1 tonne per annum for every single car occupancy trip diverted to public transport.

5. Improving energy and emissions from public transport

Overall, both road and rail urban public transport has a good energy efficiency performance – but can this be further improved? Fuel economy has for long been of commercial importance in public transport operations and improvements have been continually achieved. However, there are trends that have counterbalanced this. In particular, higher speeds for trains and the inclusion of air conditioning and other power-hungry on-board equipment means that fuel consumption has recently increased, rather than decreased. This has had a larger effect on inter-urban trains and road coaches rather than urban public transport services, which tend to be slower and where air conditioning is less frequently used. However, some factors, such as achieving high acceleration for local stopping services, have raised energy use for urban trains as well.

For buses, despite the diesel bus's relatively good environmental credentials, the public often perceive diesel buses as polluting. Wood (1996) suggests that:

> a bus perceived to be clean (as well as *being* clean) is more likely to attract passengers from cars and thus contribute to a general environmental improvement. Of course, the cleaner buses actually are, then the greater their environmental advantages over cars. Furthermore, low-emission buses will make bus stations and other centres of their activity more pleasant places.

The latter point is not insignificant. For example, shop owners in city-center streets are becoming antagonistic to bus operations on pollution grounds, particularly in otherwise pedestrianized streets.

As already noted, increasingly stringent Euro and UIC standards are cutting diesel emissions, but the transport agenda contains more than the clean-up of existing fuels and engines. For private cars, alternative fuels to gasoline and diesel have attracted considerable attention. These have included LPG, CNG, biofuels such as ethanol and methanol, electricity from batteries, and (in the longer term) electricity from hydrogen (using fuel cells). For public transport, electric traction is far from being new or innovative. Electric-powered train, tram, and metro systems are well established and commonplace.

For buses, however, diesel is starting to be challenged by a number of new fuels. These fuels and their associated technologies were covered in detail in Chapter 12, on buses. Overall, battery electric traction is not suitable for vehicles above the size of a minibus, and appears not to be viable outside of small niche applications. A number of US cities use small fleets of heavily subsidized battery electric minibuses for city center shuttles. They have also been tried in Europe: Florence and Rome use Italian-built 27-seater electric minibuses for city center services, which have received substantial EU subsidies. Overall the experience of battery electric buses in not encouraging. The operating regime is too demanding, the range too short, and recharging too lengthy. For example, the first UK electric bus scheme started in Oxford in 1993 connecting the city center with the railway station. Each bus needed an 11 h overnight charge and a 15 min boost each hour before commencing the 4 km route. Electric minibuses have been more successful for specialist transport services for the elderly and disabled (Potter, 1999), but their use has practically ceased even in this less operationally demanding role.

For other alternative fuels, application to buses has been considerably more positive. Generally it is easier to apply fuels such as LPG, CNG, or even hydrogen to public transport than to private cars. Fueling infrastructure is a major problem for alternative fuels, but with fueling for public transport vehicles concentrated at train or bus depots, this is relatively easily accommodated. The predictable requirements and limited infrastructure requirements mean that bus operations are a good sector for a new technology's initial application. Owen (1996) notes that buses are the lead market for new fuels followed by vans, taxis, and "city cars" (second cars used for local trips). Indeed, in countries such as New Zealand and Italy, where natural gas has been an important fuel for many years, CNG buses are commonplace. They have been introduced for simple economic reasons, and are an established part of the public transport fleet.

Alternative fuels for buses are largely being promoted to reduce pollutants affecting air quality – particularly NO_x and particulates produced by diesel-powered buses. LPG- and CNG-powered buses can meet the ever-tightening air emission standards with less need for complex exhaust after-treatment. Tests on a Volvo CNG bus achieved the following emission levels: 2.5 g/kWh of NO_x, 0.28 g/kWh of CO, 0.53 g/kWh of HCs, and 0.1 g/kWh of PM. However, as noted in Chapter 12, it appears that there is little to difference between state-of-the-art diesel and CNG technologies. It is possible that the application of new diesel fuel formulations and clean-up technologies (such as the CRT particulate trap) may maintain diesel's dominance of the bus market.

In terms of CO_2 emissions, alternative fuels also present a mixed picture. As was noted in Chapter 12, it is important to consider total life cycle emissions and not just those at the point of use. Research by the OECD (1995) and Energy Technology Support Unit (1996) has documented the life cycle emissions of CO_2 from a variety of alternative fuels. The benchmark is diesel, producing 210 g/km. Compared with this, CNG produces 238 g/km, methanol from natural gas 254 g/km, and ethanol from maize 247 g/km. All of these alternative fuels produce more CO_2 than diesel. LPG is about the same as diesel, with the only fuels that represent a significant improvement being methanol from wood (89 g/km), ethanol from wood (59 g/km), and liquid hydrogen (62 g/km). The biofuels from wood do not involve a large amount of energy in growing and manufacturing processes, but there is a major constraint of limited supply.

Rather than switching fuels, fuels can be used more efficiently. This can apply to both the vehicle and the transport system. Rail electrification is an example of a system approach. Until recently the energy losses in electricity production were roughly similar to the energy losses from a diesel engine. However, the use of gas combined cycle power stations together with regenerative braking returning current to the power supply system means that electrification can cut CO_2 emissions.

At the level of the vehicle, although there have been incremental improvements to diesel engines, it is the use of hybrid engines that offers the greatest improvement in fuel consumption. Hybrid engines were described in Chapter 12. Hybrid cars are now available, but, as Lane (2002) notes, hybrid buses have been given less priority and are still at the development stage. They are expected to be commercially available by 2005 (Atkin and Storey, 1998; UK Department of Trade and Industry, 2000). One advanced example of a hybrid is the Volvo Environmental Concept Bus. This is a gas turbine–electric hybrid, which can run on ethanol or a variety of other cleaner fuels.

In the long term, hydrogen fuel cells are viewed as the ideal clean transport fuel–engine system. A fuel cell involves chemical energy conversion whereby the combination of hydrogen and oxygen produces electricity with water as the only waste product. Vehicles would have hydrogen tanks supplying the fuel cell, with the electricity generated on board being used to power electric drive motors. With an on board "reformer" other fuels can be used, but this results in a loss of efficiency and the production of some emissions. Fuel cells produce energy more efficiently than an internal combustion engine, so, as noted above, CO_2 emissions can be cut by about two-thirds compared with diesel traction. The method of manufacturing the hydrogen, as with electricity, is crucial in achieving this improvement.

There has been rapid progress in the trial automotive use of fuel cells in recent years. As detailed by Lane (2002), DaimlerChrysler built a demonstration fuel cell Nebus in 1997, and a small fleet of these buses saw service in Germany, Chicago, and Vancouver. This was followed in 2000 with a demonstration of the Zebus ("Zero Emissions Bus") in California as part of the California Fuel Cell Partnership Programme. A major European fuel cell bus project is planned for 2002–2005, with 27 DaimlerChrysler "Citaro" buses in nine cities, including London, Reykjavik (linked to the hydrogen being produced with geothermal energy), Stockholm, Amsterdam, and Hamburg. The intention is that this project will lead to commercial fuel cell bus production. There seems to be no interest in applying fuel cell technology to railways, where it would appear to have potential to deliver the benefits of electrification without the cost of electrifying lines.

Overall, the basic technology of public transport vehicles has altered remarkably little in the last 50 years. Within this regime, in the last decade, significant improvements have been achieved that have cut the emission of pollutants. Fuel efficiency of public transport has been historically good compared with car travel, with some incremental improvements. Recently, new technologies and fuels have come to challenge the diesel bus, but it now appears they offer no real energy efficiency or emission improvements over advanced diesel technologies. A diesel–electric hybrid looks the most promising option for the immediate future. In the long term, hydrogen fuel cells represent a significantly cleaner technological regime for urban public transport.

6. Energy and emissions at the systems level

Reference has already been made in this chapter to policies to reduce energy use and emissions from the passenger transport system by transferring trips from car to public transport. Public transport, when adequately utilized, is an inherently more energy efficient system, and electric traction emits fewer pollutants than diesel or gasoline. However, it is necessary to conclude with a warning that the design of an urban public transport system as a whole, and not just the vehicles within it, can have major implications for energy use and emissions. The main danger is if a public transport development, rather than diverting trips from the more environmentally damaging modes of car and air, simply generates more travel, replacing walking and cycling, and contributes toward a generally more transport-intensive society.

In such circumstances, generating more public transport trips will be environmentally degrading in the same way that more car trips are environmentally degrading. However, in policy development little discernment is made about the way in which urban public transport expands and develops. There appears to be an assumption that any growth in public transport must be environmentally beneficial. For example, Adrian Shooter, Managing Director of the Chiltern Railways (Shooter, 1997), said in the early days of rail privatization in the UK that:

> There are opportunities for saving costs, but these are limited; there are bigger opportunities for increasing revenue. As fares are regulated, the surest way to increase revenue is to increase the number of passengers travelling. There is thus a neat alignment of objectives: action taken in the pursuit of profit ... is compatible with the socio-political objective of getting more people to travel by train and thereby easing road congestion.

The juxtaposition of policy aims and commercial interests is not as perfect as Shooter suggests. How expansion occurs is crucial to the net environmental impacts. It is generally more profitable for railways to expand long distance commuting, leisure and business markets rather than short distance urban services. Short-distance urban commuting is also an expensive and loss-making market, even though it may be a priority for urban and environmental policy.

The increasing transport dependency of our economy and society began with public transport 50–100 years ago with the development of trams, suburban railways, and buses, allowing people to live beyond walking distance from their workplace. Subsequently it has been the private car that has accelerated the decentralization of people, workplaces, and services to create our ever more transport-dominated lifestyles. Certain types of public transport developments can contribute toward this situation. For example, work by the International Energy Agency, OECD, and others (reported by the Royal Institute of International Affairs, 1999) viewed long-distance, high-speed rail commuting as inherently environmentally damaging. Long-distance high-speed rail reinforces car-led metropolitan decentralization. People relocate from cities and suburbs, where their trips are relatively short, and walking and public transport viable, to dispersed, city fringe and rural settlements, which are highly travel-intensive and where most of that travel has to be by car. Commuting constitutes fewer than 20% of all trips. A fast rail service may result in the work journey being made by public transport, but if it is doubled in length, emissions and fuel use will be high. Add to that increased car travel and longer trips for the 80% of all other travel that takes place, then long-distance, fast rail services can only be seen as worsening energy consumption and emissions from transport.

Potter and Roy (1996) have documented examples of the tendency toward such environmentally damaging rail developments in the UK, and note similar trends even in the more environmentally conscious Netherlands, where new rail infrastructure was provided as part of the National Environmental Policy Plan, but Dutch Railways, being required to behave in a more commercial manner, used the new capacity to develop long-distance commercially lucrative flows and not short-distance commuter services to effect a shift from car use. The former is more profitable, but far less environmentally relevant.

The final analysis of the environmental impacts of public transport must be whether the net systems effect increases or reduces the overall amount of energy and emissions produced from the transport sector as a whole.

7. Conclusions

Exploring the energy and emissions from public transport is not as straightforward as it may initially seem. There is more to this issue than just documenting the amount of fuel used by a bus or train, and the various emissions that emerge from the exhaust pipe. Vehicle performance is very important. In general, public transport vehicles have a good energy and emissions record, and new technologies have yielded further improvements, with a potential of further improvements yet to come. Some surprises are emerging, including the unexpected matching by diesel of the environmental performance of alternative fuels. It appears that the diesel bus (probably as a diesel–electric hybrid) may well be our mainstay until the fuel cell bus eventually becomes a practical and commercial reality.

But as a wider system boundary is adopted, the energy and emissions picture becomes less clear. Low loadings at some times and in some places are an almost inevitable part of a comprehensive urban public transport system. These crucially reduce energy efficiency and raise emissions per passenger carried. Once the system boundary is extended to cover the transport system as a whole, then more disturbing features emerge. There is a danger that some types of public transport developments, advocated as helping to address transport's environmental impacts, may actually worsen them. A more integrated understanding is needed as urban public transport's energy use and emissions can only be fully evaluated at this highest systems level. And at this level all transport is using unsustainable amounts of energy and generating unacceptable emissions, even if some may not be as bad as others.

References

Atkin, G. and J. Storey (1998) *Electric vehicles, prospects for battery, fuel cell and hybrid powered vehicles*. London: Financial Times.

Carpenter, T.G. (1994) *The environmental impact of railways.* Chichester: Wiley.

European Commission (1992) *Green paper: the impact of transport on the environment: a community strategy for 'sustainable mobility.'* Luxembourg: EC.

Everett, R. and G. Alexander (2000) *Working with our environment: technology for a sustainable future*, T172. *Energy file part 1: energy and its use.* Milton Keynes: The Open University.

Ford, R. (2002) "Diesel engines," *Modern Railways*, June:68–69.

Lane, B. (2002) "Optimising implementation strategies for fuel cell powered road transport systems in the United Kingdom," PhD Thesis. Milton Keynes: The Open University.

Organisation for Economic Co-operation and Development (1993) *Cars and climate change*. Paris: OECD.

Organisation for Economic Co-operation and Development (1995) *Motor vehicle pollution: reduction strategies beyond 2010*. Paris: OECD.

Owen, D. (1996) "Plugging in to EVs," in: *Electric and hybrid vehicle technology '96*, pp. 188–190.

Potter, S. (1999) "Managing the design of an innovative green transport project," *Design Journal*, 2:51–60.

Potter, S. (2000) *Working with our environment: technology for a sustainable future*, T172, Theme 2. *Travelling light*. Milton Keynes:The Open University.
Potter, S. (2001) "Cutting CO_2 emissions from personal transport: a consumption systems approach," in: *7th European Roundtable on Cleaner Production, Institute for Industrial and Environmental Economics*. Lund: Lund University.
Potter, S. and R. Roy (1996) *The environmental implications of rail privatisation*. Report to the ESRC. Milton Keynes: The Open University.
Potter, S., M. Enoch, T. Rye and C. Black (2001) *The potential for further changes to the personal taxation regime to encourage modal shift*. London: Department of the Environment, Transport and the Regions (http://www.dtlr.gov.uk/itwp/modalshift/index.htm).
Roy, R., S. Potter and K. Yarrow (2002) *Towards sustainable higher education: phase 1 final report*. Milton Keynes: Design Innovation Group, The Open University.
Royal Institute of International Affairs (1999) *2010–20 Transport Workshop: Policy Challenges and Technological Options*. London: Royal Institute of International Affairs.
Shooter, A. (1997) "Chiltern Railways goes for growth," *Modern Railways*, Feb.:81–85.
Teufel, D, P. Bauer and K. Scmitt (1993) *Öko-Billanzen von Fahrzeugen*. Heidelberg: Umwelt und Prognose Institut.
UK Department of the Environment, Transport and the Regions (2000) *Transport statistics Great Britain*. London: The Stationery Office.
UK Department of Trade and Industry (1999) *Digest of energy statistics*. London: The Stationery Office.
UK Department of Trade and Industry (2000) *The report of the Alternative Fuels Group of the Cleaner Vehicle Task Force*. London: The Stationery Office (www.roads.detr.gov.uk/cvtf/index.htm).
Energy Technology Support Unit (1996) *Alternative road transport fuels; a preliminary life-cycle study for the UK*. London: The Stationery Office.
Wood, C. (1995) *Energy use by different passenger modes*. Norwich: Transplan.
Wood, C. (1996) "Golden fuels or fuel's Gold?" *Chartered Institute of Logistics and Transport Journal*.

Chapter 14

TRANSPORT ENERGY AND EMISSIONS: AVIATION

HUGH SOMERVILLE
British Airways, Harmondsworth

1. Background

1.1. The industry

Aviation plays an integral part in the world's transport and communication network. In 2001–2002, British Airways, one of the major international airlines, carried 41 million passengers to some 220 destinations in over 90 countries with nearly 1500 flights per day. Through the Oneworld Alliance there is an extended network that covered some 570 destinations in 135 countries. The aviation industry world-wide in 1994 (Intergovernmental Panel on Climate Change, 1999) flew some 1.2 billion passengers using some 15 000 aircraft. The overall routes measured some 15 million km and involved close to 10 000 airports. Some 24 million jobs depend on aviation world-wide, and the annual gross output is more than US $1000 billion. One example is provided by the tourism industry. It is claimed that the tourism industry provides, overall, some ten jobs for every one in airlines. Some 250 million people world-wide depend on the tourism industry, which is, of course, an amalgam of component industries, providing some 10% of the total global gross domestic product reaching around 25% in some regions such as the Caribbean.

While opinions on future growth vary, there seems little doubt that world-wide growth in aviation will be of the order of 5% for the next decade, with lower growth in Europe than in some other parts of the world. These are large figures, and it is self-evident that there is close interaction and, indeed, interdependence on other transport modes. It goes without saying that an industry of this size has an impact on the environment, and over the last few years public interest in the environmental and social impacts of aviation has grown accordingly. Public interest is increasingly centered on growth and the resulting potential increase in energy consumption. At least for the near and medium term this consumption is likely to be in the form of kerosene derived from oil. As the industry grows, combustion of this fuel will lead to generation of increasing amounts of carbon

Handbook of Transport and the Environment, Edited by D.A. Hensher and K.J. Button
© 2003, Elsevier Ltd

dioxide (CO_2), the main greenhouse gas, despite improvements in the efficiency of engines and aerodynamic design. Nitrogen oxides (NO_x) and water vapor, formed during the combustion process in aircraft engines, may also lead to greenhouse effects when emitted at cruise altitudes.

1.2. Aviation and sustainable development

Increasingly, governments, not-for-profit organizations, industry, and other organizations are giving attention to the role of different enterprises in a future sustainable global society. The classical definition of sustainable development is that of the Brundtland Report in 1987: "development that meets the needs of the present without compromising the ability of future generations to meet their own needs." In May 1999 the UK government strategy for sustainable development was published, and provides a useful benchmark against which to examine aviation.

What is sustainable development?

According to the UK government view, it is "a better quality of life for everyone, now and for generations to come." This brief interpretation is relatively easy to support; some might argue that it could be more demanding. There is little denial that aviation can improve the quality of life. Discussion centers on the selective nature of access to aviation and the balance of costs and benefits. While the real cost of aviation has reduced over the years it is still only accessible to a minority of the global population. No one should contest the need for a favorable balance of benefits against undesirable environmental and social effects. Quality of life and sustainability cannot be delivered by individual companies but rather must be met by society as a whole.

The UK government also identified four broad objectives:

(1) *Social progress that recognizes the needs of everyone.* Aviation is an essential part of the world's communication and economic system. Directly and indirectly it provides jobs throughout the world. Leisure and business travel, and air cargo, provide benefits to economies, both of developed and less developed countries. By bringing people together, airlines contribute to business, to political understanding, and to cultural interchange. The International Air Transport Association has reported that many member airlines are publicly reporting on relevant environmental and social issues (e.g. see Lufthansa, 2002; British Airways, 2002). However, business and society still have a long way to go to fully understand the interactions with the environment and people, for example in the area of human rights.

(2) *Effective protection of the environment.* Aviation has invested consistently in clean technology, through acquisition of newer aircraft emitting less noise,

using less fuel, and emitting less of polluting exhaust gases. Many airlines now track progress in minimizing effects on the environment through targets and indicators, which are reported to the public. There is an open and expanding program of reporting and engaging in dialogue with key stakeholder groups.
(3) *Prudent use of natural resources.* Some airlines have been leaders in measuring and reporting the consumption of natural resources and in setting targets for improvement. Although remarkable progress has been made, there is still a long way to go. Efficiency is an essential first step on the route to long-term sustainability.
(4) *Maintenance of high and stable levels of economic growth and employment.* Aviation has shown a consistent pattern of overall growth in economic and employment terms over the last few decades. This pattern will continue, although the rate of growth may slow. There is increasing understanding of the external costs, and benefits, of aviation. However, identification of costs depends on scientific determination of impacts and on development of appropriate costing mechanisms. In the meantime, minimizing the impacts is the best route to reducing these costs.

A fundamental question for transport organizations is whether clean technology, efficiency, and environmental responsibility will be sufficient to attain long-term sustainability in the eyes of society as a whole. There are three elements commonly taken as contributing to sustainability:

(1) *Environmental.* Is the industry committed to reducing harmful impacts of aviation? How can performance be improved on noise, emissions, waste management, and sustainable tourism?
(2) *Economic.* This is the basic requirement; profit is an essential complement to environmental and social programs. What do airlines offer the world in terms of trade flow, jobs, shareholder returns, and communication infrastructure? What benefits do passengers bring to their destinations and points of departure?
(3) *Social.* That is, elationships with staff, customers, and shareholders as well as suppliers, partners, communities, regulators, and other stakeholders. Who is excluded from the prosperity generated, and who are the victims? Are fundamental responsibilities met for employees, and customers in terms of wealth creation, safety, security, and fair play. Are human rights respected?

The industry will only add value in the eyes of stakeholders if its image and supporting activities address all three areas and are relevant, not necessarily equally, to all stakeholder groups. This can only be achieved it there is adequate attention to governance within the company, with clarity on accountability for these areas and transparency in communication on them. Within British Airways the environmental challenge has been divided into five areas:

- noise;
- emissions and fuel efficiency;
- waste;
- congestion and infrastructure;
- tourism and conservation.

While all of these are interrelated to a greater or lesser extent, this discussion concentrates on emissions and fuel efficiency.

2. Emissions

The clean technology of modern aircraft engines has all but eliminated emissions of carbon monoxide and hydrocarbons. Kerosene is low in sulfur. Fuel efficiency has doubled over the last 25 years. The fuel and emission efficiencies of aviation overlap with other transport modes, and are still improving. While it is always difficult to make "apples to apples" comparisons, aviation compares favorably with other transport modes in broader environmental comparisons (Figures 1 and 2).

2.1. Local air quality

There are questions about the effect of aviation on local air quality close to airports, particularly relating to NO_x. Emissions of NO_x have, perversely, tended until recently to increase with the higher pressures and temperatures of more

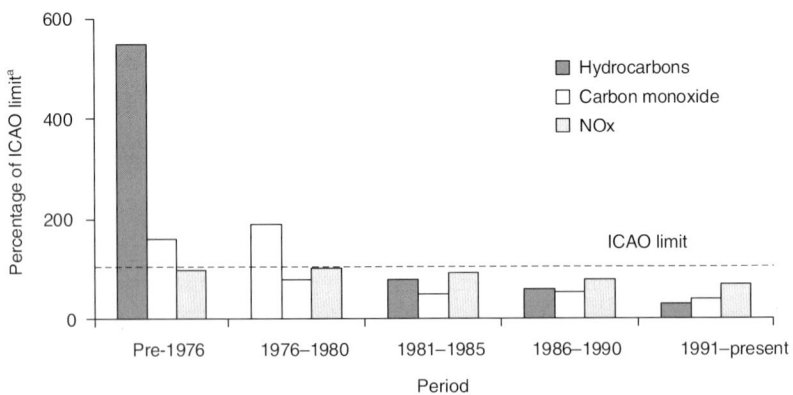

[a]New international standards for gaseous emissions became effective in 1996

Figure 1. Aircraft engine emissions. (Source: Boeing.)

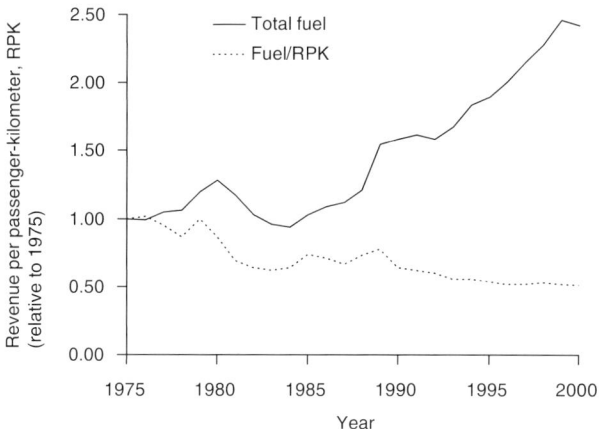

Figure 2. British Airways: fuel consumption and efficiency.

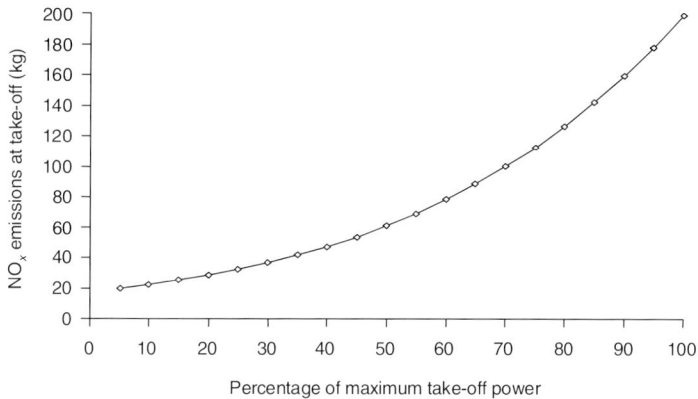

Figure 3. Effect of take-off power on NO_x emissions for a Boeing 747-436.

efficient engines. Most estimates of the aviation contribution to local air quality have been based on the standard International Civil Aviation Organization (ICAO) landing and take-off cycle. This includes all emissions up to 3000 ft. Clearly this does not all relate to the immediate airport environment, and, consequently, the aircraft contribution to the local air burden has been significantly overestimated.

One way to reduce NO_x emissions is to lower thrust levels at take-off (Figure 3). However, this can involve significant trade-offs. For example, while use of reduced thrust is widely practiced, it can make it more difficult to comply with noise requirements, for example departure noise limits at the London airports. Thus, the role of airports in local air quality is likely to be a matter of ongoing discussion. British Airways is currently leading a stakeholder group, working closely with the airport operator BAA plc, looking at better ways of establishing aircraft contributions to the airport emissions inventory, with particular reference to Heathrow airport.

On the ground, surface access to airports is largely dependent on private cars. Airports such as Manchester, Heathrow and Gatwick in the UK have worked hard to achieve reduced car dependence with, at Heathrow and Gatwick, over 30% of passengers arriving by public transport. The emphasis on public transport access is a feature of many airports, in particular other major European hubs such as Frankfurt and Schiphol. Achievement of further improvement will require incentives or other measures to encourage individuals to use public transport. While better rail access to airports is important, buses are more flexible and more immediate and less costly than new rail services, but are clearly vulnerable to road congestion. Particularly in Europe, there are limited opportunities to substitute rail for air. In any event, the net environmental effect of substitution of rail for air is not necessarily beneficial (Air Transport Action Group, 2002; Maibach and Schneider, 2002), as seen in Figures 4 and 5.

2.2. Global impact

The major environmental issue facing transport industries, and probably the world-wide community, is global warming and climate change. Most if not all modes of transport are still increasing their consumption of fossil fuels and as a direct result, their emissions of carbon dioxide – the principal greenhouse gas. Thus, an essential element of any integrated transport policy must be an integrated

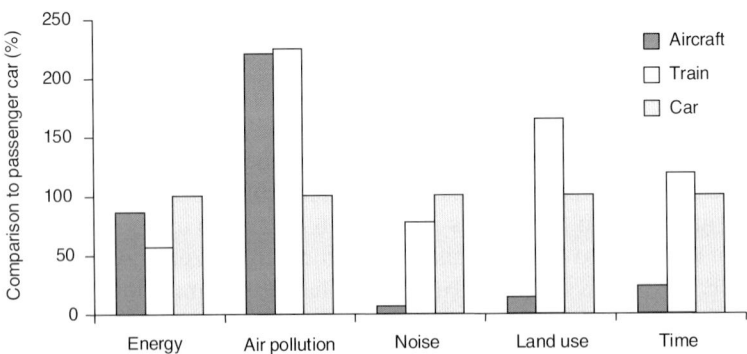

Figure 4. Environmental performance of passenger transport modes (route: Amsterdam to Paris). (Source: Roos et al., 1997.)

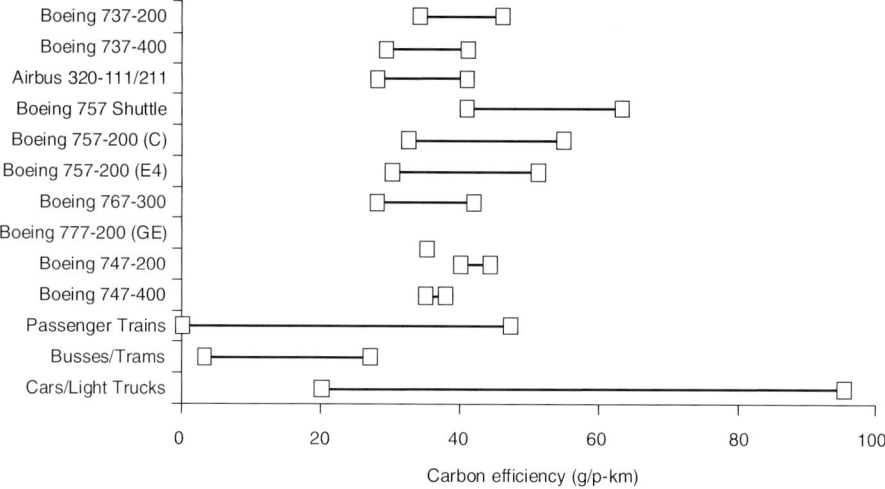

Figure 5. Carbon efficiency. (Source: Whiteleg, 1993; Faiz et al., 1996; British Airways, 1999.)

response to this issue. We must, of course, encourage development of the scientific understanding of the nature, scale, and effects on the climate of greenhouse gas emissions (e.g. see US National Research Council, 2002). We should also encourage healthy assessment of the political dogma that has been adopted widely, that action is necessary and that controls must be put in place to limit man's contribution. However, the chances of there being any reversal of the consensus that action is necessary are small. Thus, aviation must identify possible mechanisms for limiting its contribution and move swiftly towards more concrete action.

2.3. Aviation and global warming

The 1999 report from the UN Intergovernmental Panel on Climate Change (IPCC) provides an accurate assessment of what is known about aviation's input to man-made global warming and mechanisms for possible mitigation (Figure 6). However, the report does not provide all of the knowledge necessary to facilitate solutions. For aviation the "basket" of gases that can contribute to global warming is different from those for ground-based sources, with only carbon dioxide being common. This is one reason why aviation is not included in the agreed targets set under the Kyoto Protocol.

The extent to which the Kyoto Protocol will influence management of aviation emissions is not yet clear. However, statements from several countries at the Johannesburg Summit suggest that sufficient states will ratify the protocol to bring it into force. Article 2.2 of the protocol calls for developed countries to pursue limitation or reduction of greenhouse gases from "aviation bunker fuels," working through the ICAO. Under the protocol, domestic aviation emissions (internal flight sectors and related operations) are assigned to national inventories. These account for around 50% of the global total, with the remaining emissions from international flights being split between developed and less developed countries. Recognizing that the Kyoto Protocol treats international and domestic emissions from the aviation sector differently, ICAO Resolution 14/1 of 2001 notes the potential advantages of harmonizing treatment of the two categories of emissions.

The IPCC report identified three main areas of identified or potential impact from aviation.

- *Carbon dioxide.* Carbon dioxide from aviation is indistinguishable from that from other sources in terms of its effects, and can be regarded as fully mixed in the global atmosphere. Aviation accounts for around 2.5% of total carbon dioxide from burning of fossil fuels (Figure 7). Within Europe, aviation accounts for some 12% of transport carbon dioxide emissions, and thus for some 3% of the total (Figure 8).
- *Water vapor.* Like carbon dioxide, water vapor is directly formed from the fuel, kerosene, by combustion. There is huge uncertainty over the effects of water vapor, which can form condensation trails and cirrus clouds. The possible effect is large. Reduction in carbon dioxide emissions will also lead to reduction in water vapor, as both are derived directly from the fuel. One

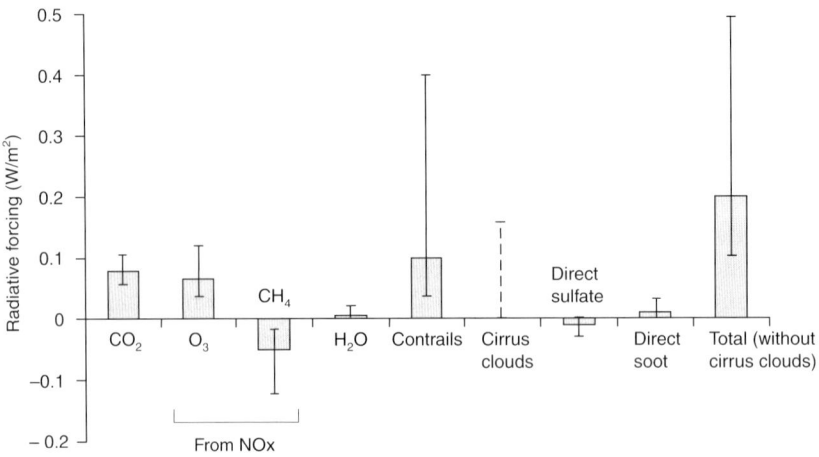

Figure 6. Projected radiative forcing from aircraft in 2050. (Source: Intergovernmental Panel on Climate Change, 1999.)

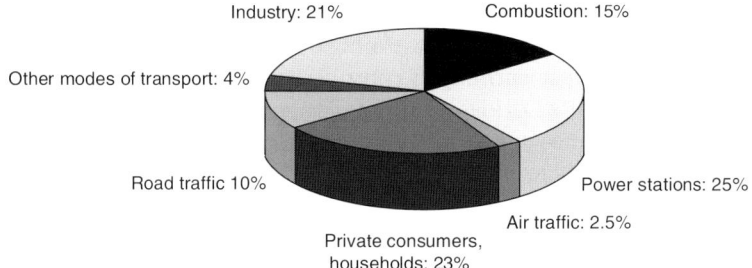

Figure 7. Man-made sources of carbon dioxide (approximate contributions).

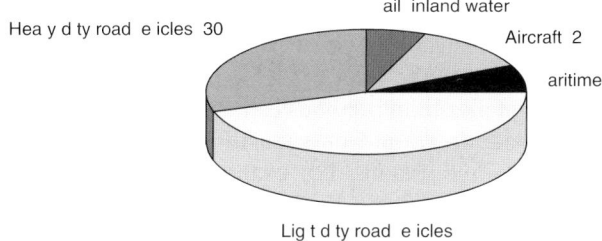

Figure 8. Aviation share of world transport CO_2 emissions.

possible approach to minimizing condensation trails and cloud formation is to change the height of aircraft cruising. However, this would involve a trade-off with fuel efficiency and carbon dioxide emissions.

- *Nitrogen oxides.* The IPCC identified two effects of NO_x, one warming and one cooling, both with a high level of uncertainty. Warming results from ozone formation and an enhanced greenhouse effect; while cooling is caused by removal of methane moving to the upper atmosphere from terrestrial sources. The two effects do not directly cancel each other, partly because of differences in regional impacts. The formation of NO_x in jet engines is dependent on the temperature and pressure of combustion and the residence time in the combustion chamber. The higher temperatures and pressures that have delivered huge improvements in fuel efficiency have led to another trade-off – a trend toward higher NO_x emissions. Advanced combustion technologies are now being incorporated in new engine designs that reduce NO_x emissions with minimal effects on fuel efficiency, although the airworthiness of some of the options remains to be proven.

In addition, aircraft emit small amounts of sulfur emissions and particulates, which have small direct cooling and warming effects, respectively. However, both can be involved in indirect warming by contrails and aviation-induced cirrus cloud. Gases such as NO_x, sulfur oxides, and water vapor, and particulate matter, have relatively short residence times in the atmosphere (hours to months) and are therefore concentrated close to flight routes – thus they may be associated with regional effects.

Together these effects account for some 3.5% of man's current contribution to global warming. This could grow to 4–15% by 2050, with 6–7% generally held as the most likely range. The 2050 estimates are based on incorporation of efficiency improvements from engine and airframe technology, from improvements in air traffic management systems and in other operational aspects. However, the scenarios used in the IPCC report for estimating the 2050 impact are also based on growth unrestricted in the supply of aircraft, of airports, or of fuel with those at the high end clearly being less plausible. Also, work since the IPCC report (European Commission, 2001a) has found the roles of NO_x emissions from aircraft and line-shaped contrails to be smaller than previous estimates.

The challenge for aviation should be seen in context of commitments and proposals for reductions in emissions. For example, the UK is committed to a reduction of 12% in carbon dioxide by 2008–2012 relative to 1990, with an aspirational reduction of 20% in the same time frame. A long-term reduction of some 60% is beginning to feature in some analyses of long-term needs, for example from the UK's Royal Commission on Environmental Pollution (1994, 1997).

2.4. Regulatory controls

In terms of climate change and aviation, the relevant body to set regulatory standards is the ICAO, which is advised by its Committee on Aviation Environmental Protection (CAEP). The most recent ICAO emission standard is for NO_x, dating from 1998. Following establishment of such an ICAO standard, member states may implement the standard on a national basis. Current emission standards for NO_x and other exhaust gas components address only the standard ICAO landing and take-off cycle. No serious attempts have been made as yet to regulate for fuel consumption, although discussions have started within the ICAO on possible approaches to setting standards for emissions at cruise altitudes.

2.5. Market-based measures

Much attention has focused on a kerosene tax. Such taxes already exist in the USA for example, where a domestic tax of some US $0.04 per gallon has been levied for some time. More recently, attempts to implement charges on an international basis, for example by Norway, have run into difficulties because of clauses in the bilateral service level agreements that preclude such taxation. These agreements have their origin in the Chicago Convention of 1944.

A number of studies have been carried out on the cost benefit aspects of a kerosene tax. Perhaps the most detailed and most relevant is the 1999 report for the European Commission (1999). For the scenario that causes minimal distortion of competition, an intra-European tax applying to all carriers, there would be considerable cost to the industry in terms of jobs and revenue, with minimal environmental benefit, even at a doubling of the price of kerosene. Thus, the major drawback to a tax would appear to be that it delivers little if any direct environmental benefit. Nonetheless, there are strident calls from some non-governmental organizations and politicians for the imposition of such taxes.

Tradable permits have been advanced as a realistic option, and here again a number of scenarios are possible: trading within aviation; trading across industry borders; and trading combined with an element of charge or tax. Permits, if administered strictly, can clearly deliver improvements in environmental performance. However, the market is uncertain. Permits have been used successfully within the USA to control emissions of sulfur dioxide. BP and Shell have set up schemes for the internal trading of carbon dioxide emissions, and a UK scheme (UK Department of Environment, Food and Rural Affairs, 2001) has been implemented, in which British Airways is participating based on emissions arising from its internal UK flights, as well as energy consumption in its UK properties. A European trading scheme (European Commission, 2001b) is being developed for 2006; however, transport is excluded at this time.

The general consensus seems to be that emissions trading is the best way forward for aviation, at least in the medium term, albeit the possibility of other measures running alongside trading is not excluded. It would be essential for such a scheme to be open to trading with other parties, for example those managing offsets or with other industries. This view has been generally supported by the work of ICAO's CAEP Working Group 5 (International Civil Aviation Organisation, 2001), the UK's Institute of Public Policy Research (2001), and by internal work within the International Air Transport Association (IATA).

Offsets, direct or through joint implementation and clean development mechanisms, must play a role in the future. Offsets could arise through sequestration, the simplest illustrations of which are forestation or prevention of deforestation. However, there are many other alternatives, for example investment in renewable energy such as wind farms. Fuels from renewable sources such as biomass are not likely to play a direct role – in the long term it seems that hydrocarbons from oil and gas will have preferred uses in chemicals of high added value and in transportation fuels with high specification, such as kerosene, where alternatives such as hydrogen are not realistic. Fuels from biomass and technology such as fuel cells will, probably, be better used for ground-based transportation or to substitute for fossil fuels in other areas. Eventually, radical changes in aviation technology and technology may well be implemented. Clearly, better understanding of the impact of NO_x and water vapor on the global climate will be necessary to drive such long-term changes. The "Greener by Design" group in the UK has published a report covering technology, market, and operational options for improving performance. The technology report does not advocate any particular solutions but rather lays out some of the possibilities.

It is now widely accepted that aviation should meet its external costs, although there is no clear way in which to calculate the costs. Aviation, through airport charges, already pays for its own infrastructure in most developed countries. In the UK, through air passenger duty, airlines are contributing some UK £1 billion per year to the exchequer.

The UK Department for the Environment, Transport and the Regions (2000) has brought together estimates of the marginal damage costs of noise and climate change, excluding damage from local air pollution. The costs per short haul passenger ranged from UK £2.50 to £3.30, depending on aircraft type, and for long haul from UK £18.05 to £20.24. Coincidentally, these costs are very close to air passenger tax, which was brought in as a surrogate kerosene tax. However, the determination of some external costs (and benefits) of aviation is still at an early stage. The first steps must be to improve understanding of what the external costs are and, while there has been some preliminary work, these costs are far from being understood, in particular in areas such as emissions of NO_x and water vapor at cruise altitudes.

2.6. Voluntary measures

These are the obvious starting point for mitigation of adverse effects. Examples include signing up to agreements on efficiency targets, sequestration of carbon dioxide, and investment in renewable resources. British Airways established a target of 30% improvement in efficiency over the period 1990–2010, including improvements in air traffic management (British Airways, 2002). The Association of European Airlines has indicated an improvement of 22.4% improvement over the period 1990–2010, excluding air traffic management, and the IATA has also set a goal of 1.1% annual improvement for the world-wide fleet over a similar period. Given that aviation is already extremely fuel-efficient, these are considerable additional challenges to the industry and not just "business as usual." Voluntary measures are playing an increasing role in addressing environmental and social issues in the tourism industry, led by the UNEP Tour Operators Initiative (UN Environmental Programme, 2002).

2.7. Inefficiencies

There are also inefficiencies in the air (e.g. Intergovernmental Panel on Climate Change, 1999; Dings et al., 2002). It is common knowledge within the industry that many domestic and international routes, particularly in Europe, are significantly longer than the "great circle" point-to-point distances. In 1998 a Eurocontrol Performance Review Commission revealed that, of the 1 560 000 flights handled by air traffic control for London in 1997, 8.7% were delayed compared with 1.2% of the 743 000 flights at Frankfurt, and 10.3% of 1 056 000 handled at Paris. European air traffic control comprised at that time:

- 68 control centers;
- 31 national systems;
- 18 suppliers of hardware;
- 22 operating systems;
- 30 programming languages;

and is still fragmented.

Despite some improvements, airlines continue to press for simplification of the European system. Safety will remain the primary concern. There are considerable environmental benefits to be gained from reduction in flight distances and elimination of delays. Reductions in flight distances, use of closer to optimal operational altitudes, and reductions in delays both on the ground and in the air will be gained through introduction of satellite-based navigational systems, complemented by additional airport infrastructure.

2.8. What are airlines doing

Airlines have invested huge sums in aircraft delivering ever better levels of environmental performance. Many airlines have additional environmental programs. As an illustration, British Airways has undertaken a number of actions that are relevant. These include:

- Open reporting on environmental performance, with public access to data. Performance indicators have been developed as an essential element of reporting in order to identify progress and set targets.
- Participating actively in some of the relevant ICAO working groups and in preparation of the 1999 IPCC report.
- Leading IATA's involvement in publishing opportunities for operational improvements in fuel efficiency through the ICAO.
- Joint sponsorship of a study by the UK's Institute of Public Policy Research (2000) on market options, which has concluded that emissions trading is an appropriate way forward.

- Involvement in the UK emissions trading scheme.
- Donation of some US $0.5 million in value in travel awards to conservation organizations each year, including some involved in climate change issues.
- Investment in the operating arm of the UK's high-speed rail link.
- Sponsoring the only free, to passengers, bus service in the London transport network and introduction of, with the BAA, of a free transport zone at Heathrow for all passengers.
- Participating in the multi-stakeholder Greener by Design (2002) group, looking at the future role of technology and other mechanisms.
- A small project with the UK organization Climate Care on offsetting emissions of carbon dioxide through distribution of low-energy light bulbs in Mauritius.

3. The future

It is possible to create a picture in which aviation is a part of sustainable society; but it is far too early to be definitive on how the impact of emissions will be managed. Advances in technology and improvements in operational and system efficiency will continue to contribute. Offsets, joint implementation, and clean development mechanisms can all play a role. Offsets could arise through sequestration, the simplest illustrations of which are forestation or prevention of deforestation (e.g. Royal Society, 2001). However, there are other alternatives, such as disposal of carbon dioxide in the deep ocean – not an option directly available to aviation. Another form of sequestration would be for an emitter of greenhouse gases to offset these by investing in renewable energy such as wind farms. Fuels from renewable sources such as biomass are not likely to play a direct role – in the long term it seems that hydrocarbons from oil and gas will have preferred uses in chemicals of high added value and in transportation fuels with high specification, such as kerosene, where alternatives, such as hydrogen, are not realistic. Fuels from biomass, and technology such as fuel cells, will be better used for ground-based transportation or to substitute for fossil fuels in other areas.

There is as yet little clarity in the mechanisms for implementing joint implementation and the clean development mechanism. These are under investigation within the conference of parties to the Framework Convention on Climate Change. Likewise, further work is necessary to determine the potential of renewable energy sources to play a direct or indirect part in the future. Other issues that need to be resolved are the allocation of international emissions under the Framework Convention on Climate Change.

4. Conclusion

Governments, industry, and the public all have vital roles to play in promoting sustainable development across society. Transport is an essential element of the world social and economic structure. Inevitably there will be changes in future years (eg. COOL Europe, 2001). Aviation is a global industry, and the issues faced, such as allocation of emissions, require global solutions. Without ratification of the Kyoto Agreement, or introduction of some similar global mechanism, progress is likely to be slow. The ICAO must be involved; the ICAO has also to become more inclusive, although some members and some of those involved as observers have expressed doubt as to the ability of the ICAO to deliver the improvements necessary. The question must be asked – if not through ICAO then is there a better way?

It is only a decade since the Rio Earth Summit in 1992, 6 years since Kyoto in 1997, and 4 years since the IPCC report on aviation in 1999. Much has already happened in a relatively short period. Governments and industry will need to be innovative if they are to work together to continue to develop aviation as a vital component of the global economy. New airports will be required, new runways, and new ways for the public to travel to and from airports. These are major issues facing us all.

Aviation has a long history of environmental innovation, and improvements continue to be made. There is still substantial uncertainty over the effects of engine exhaust emissions, in particular in relation to global warming. Priority should be given to the determination of these effects. Kerosene is likely to remain the fuel for aviation for at least the next few decades. Progress on managing aviation's input to global warming will probably depend on a mix of measures, with emissions trading the most likely measure to make a substantial impact in the medium term. Against a background of addressing the issues, there is no reason why aviation should not continue to grow within the overall context of sustainable development.

References

Air Transport Action Group (2002) Aviation in a sustainable world: partnerships to meet society's growing mobility needs. Geneva: ATAG.
British Airways (2002) *Annual social and environmental report*. London: BA.
COOL Europe (2001) *European dialogue strategic vision on long term climate policies for the European transport sector*. Wageningen: Wageningen University.
Dings, J.M.W., R.C.N. Wit, B.A. Leurs and M.D. Davidson (2002) *External costs of aviation*. Delft: CE Delft.
European Commission (1999) *Analysis of the taxation of aircraft fuel*. Study VII/C/4-33/97 by Resource Analysis, MVA Ltd, The Dutch National Aerospace laboratory and the International Institute of Air and Space Law. Luxembourg: EC.

European Commission (2001a) *European Research in the Stratosphere 1996–2000*, EUR 19867. Brussels: Directorate General for Research, EC.
European Commission (2001b) *Proposal for a Directive of the European parliament and the council establishing a scheme for greenhouse gas emission allowance trading within the Community and amending council Directive 96/61/EC*. Brussels: EC.
Faiz, A., C.S. Weaver and M.P. Walsh (1996) *Air pollution from motor vehicles*. Washington, DC: The World Bank.
Greener by Design (2002) *Improving operations – the technology challenge – market base options*. London: The Society of British Aerospace Companies.
Institute for Public Policy Research (2000) *Plane trading*. London: IPCC.
Institute for Public Policy Research (2001) *Sustainable aviation 2030*. London: IPCC.
Intergovernmental Panel on Climate Change (1999) *Aviation and the global atmosphere*. Cambridge: Cambridge University Press.
International Civil Aviation Organization (2001) *Report of the Fifth Meeting of the Committee for Aviation Environmental Protection*. ICAO, Montreal.
Lufthansa (2002) *Balance*. Frankfurt: Lufthansa.
Maibach, M. and C. Schneider (2002) *External costs of corridors. A comparison between air, road and rail*. Zurich: Infras.
National Research Council (2002) *For greener skies – reducing environmental impacts of aviation*. Washington, DC: Aeronautics and Space Engineering Board.
Roos, J., A. Bleijenberg and W. Dijkstra (1997) *Energy use and emissions drom aviation and other modes for long distance travel in Europe*. Delft: CE Delft.
Royal Commission for Environmental Pollution (1994) *Transport and the environment*, 18th Report. London: RCEP.
Royal Commission for Environmental Pollution (1997) *Transport and the environment – developments since 1994*. London: RCEP.
Royal Society (2001) *The role of land carbon sinks in mitigating global climate change*. London: The Royal Society.
UN Environmental Programme (2002) *Tour operators initiative for sustainable tourism development – work in progress*. Paris: UNEP Division of Technology, Industry and Economy.
UK Department of the Environment, Food and Rural Affairs (2001) *Framework for the UK emissions trading scheme*. London: DEFRA.
UK Department of the Environment, Transport and the Regions (2000) *Valuing the external costs of aviation*. London: DETR.

Chapter 15

ENVIRONMENTAL IMPACTS OF SHIPPING

WAYNE K. TALLEY
Old Dominion University, Norfolk, VA

1. Introduction

Ships interact in many ways with the environment. They accidentally and intentionally release substances into the environment. When tanker vessel accidents spill large quantities of oil, they receive the attention of the world's media, politicians, and the general public. The damage to plants, fisheries, birds, and mammals can be considerable.

This chapter discusses the environmental impacts of shipping, i.e. from the operation of commercial vessels and related activities. Although vessel oil spills are its main focus, other environmental impacts of shipping that are receiving attention are also discussed. Vessel ballast water acquired in one region may contain indigenous aquatic life that will be harmful to the indigenous aquatic life of the region where the water is discharged. Vessels pollute the air when they emit nitrogen and sulfur dioxide.

Anti-fouling chemicals to remove unwanted growth of biological material on the water-immersed surface of a vessel may not only be effective in killing those organisms attached to the vessel hull but other sea life as well. The most toxic of these chemicals is tributyltin. Sea life may also be killed when waterways are dredged to deeper depths. The disposal of dredged sediments that are biologically and chemically active and hazardous materials from scrapped vessels can contaminate disposal sites. The disposal of vessel wastes at sea can pollute waterways.

2. Vessel oil spills

A vessel may spill oil accidentally or intentionally. Accidental spillage may result from a vessel accident or during oil transfers, i.e. during the loading and unloading of oil cargo and fueling. Intentional spillage is typically operational dumping, e.g. after discharging its oil cargo a vessel takes ballast water into its cargo tanks to

Handbook of Transport and the Environment, Edited by D.A. Hensher and K.J. Button
© 2003, Elsevier Ltd

ensure stability on the return trip, but then dumps the dirty ballast, a water-in-oil mixture, on or before arrival at the loading port (Talley et al., 2001).

Vessels may spill oil from oil cargo and fuel tanks. Oil cargo vessels include tankers and tank barges. Tanker vessels are the world's largest man-made moving objects; the largest, so-called super-tankers, exceed 320 000 deadweight tons in size (US tons are used in this chapter; 1 US ton = 0.9 tonne). Unlike the tanker, the tank barge does not have its own propulsion system, but is either pushed or pulled by a tugboat. Non-oil-cargo vessels, e.g. fishing, passenger, solid-bulk, and container vessels, may spill oil from their fuel tanks.

World-wide vessel oil spill statistics are reasonably accurate and available for large accidental spills, but less so for smaller accidental spills, and even less so for intentional spills. With these caveats in mind, the database of the International Tanker Owners Pollution Federation (ITOPF) consists of world-wide vessel accidental oil spills for oil cargo vessels (tankers, tank barges, and combination vessels). An oil spill is defined as oil lost to the environment, including that which is burnt or remains in a sunken vessel. Yearly accidental vessel oil spills for the 1974–2000 period from this database are given in Table 1. The data suggest a declining trend in accidental vessel oil spills since 1991.

The majority of the approximately 10 000 accidental vessel oil spills in the ITOPF database are transfer spills, i.e. 53.0% are transfer spills, 20.6% are vessel accident spills, and the remainder (26.4%) are unknown. Further, the vast majority (85%) of the spills are relatively small, i.e. less than 7 tons. Today, a major tanker spill is a rare event. The number of large spills (greater than 700 tons) have declined over time: 24.1, 8.8, and 7.3 oil spills per year on average for the 1970–1979, 1980–1989, and 1990–1999 periods, respectively. Further, 35, 28, 14, 6, 6, and 11% of the large spills were grounding, collision, hull failure, fire/explosion, loading/unloading, and other/unknown spills, respectively. Although large spills are few in number, they account for a significant percentage of the yearly accidental vessel oil spilt. In 1979 the *Atlantic Empress* tanker spilt 287 000 tons of oil (the largest vessel accident oil spillage on record), 47.2% of the yearly total; in 1983 the *Castillo de Bellver* spilt 252 000 tons, 65.6% of the yearly total; and in 1991 the *ABT Summer* spilt 260 000 tons, 59.8% of the yearly total. Table 2 lists the world's 20 largest tanker accident oil spills.

Hypothesized determinants of the amount of oil spilt from an oil cargo vessel accident (Oil-spilt) include type of accident (TA), cause of accident (CA), operating conditions (OC), vessel characteristics (VC), and vessel damage severity (Vessel-dam), i.e.

$$\text{Oil-spilt} = f(\text{TA, CA, OC, VC, Vessel-dam}). \tag{1}$$

The type of accident may be a collision, a fire/explosion, a material/equipment failure, or a grounding accident. Also, the accident may involve two or more vessels or a single vessel. The cause of an accident may be due to either a human

Table 1
World-wide accidental vessel oil spills

Year	Quantity (10^3 tons)
1974	169
1975	342
1976	369
1977	298
1978	395
1979	608
1980	103
1981	44
1982	11
1983	384
1984	28
1985	88
1986	19
1987	30
1988	198
1889	178
1990	61
1991	435
1992	162
1993	144
1994	105
1995	9
1996	79
1997	67
1998	10
1999	29
2000	12

Source: ITOPF database.

(e.g. operator error and intoxication), a vessel (e.g. corrosion and propulsion failure), or an environmental (e.g. adverse weather) cause. Operating conditions describe the environment in which a vessel was operating at the time of an accident, e.g. type of waterway where the accident occurred, weather/visibility characteristics, and phase of vessel operation. The type of waterway may be an inland (river, harbor, lake, or a bay), a coastal, or an ocean waterway. Weather/visibility characteristics may include the presence of fog, precipitation, wind speed, and whether the accident occurred at nighttime versus daytime. The phase of vessel operation includes whether the vessel was underway, docked/moored, or adrift at the time of the accident. Vessel characteristics include a vessel's age and size.

Estimates of equation (1) for tanker and tank barge vessel accidents are found in Talley (1999, 2000). The studies utilize a unique micro-database of individual

Table 2
The world's 20 largest tanker accident oil spills, 1960–1997

Quantity (10^3 ton)	Vessel	Year
287	*Atlantic Empress*	1979
260	*ABT Summer*	1991
252	*Castillo de Bellver*	1983
223	*Amoco Cadiz*	1978
144	*Haven*	1991
132	*Odyssey*	1988
119	*Torrey Canyon*	1967
115	*Sea Star*	1972
100	*Urquiola*	1976
95	*Hawaiian Patriot*	1977
94.6	*Independenta*	1979
88	*Jakob Maersk*	1975
84.7	*Braer*	1993
80	*Khark 5*	1989
73.5	*Aegean Sea*	1992
72	*Sea Empress*	1996
72	*Katina P.*	1992
70	*Nova*	1985
60	*Epic Colocotronis*	1975
60	*Sinclair Petrolore*	1960

Source: White and Baker (1998).

tanker and tank barge accidents investigated by the US Coast Guard for the 1981–1991 period. It includes non-US flag vessel accidents that occurred in US waters and US flag vessel accidents that occurred anywhere in the world. In the estimation of equation (1) by Talley, Oil-Spilt is the cost of oil lost, and Vessel-Dam is the vessel damage cost, both in US dollars. The vessel damage cost is the cost of restoring the damaged vessel to the service condition that existed prior to its accident.

Statistically significant results in the estimation of equation (1) based upon a sample of 1568 tanker accidents suggest that tanker accident oil spillage (Talley, 1999) is greater for groundings than for collision, fire/explosion, and material/equipment failure accidents; is less for US than for non-US flag tankers; and increases with vessel damage. Statistically significant estimation results for equation (1) based upon a sample of 2472 inland waterway tank barge accidents suggest that tank barge accident oil spillage (Talley, 2000) is less when a tank barge is involved in a multi-vessel accident; is greater for collision and material/equipment failure accidents than for fire/explosions and groundings; increases with tank barge age; and is greater if the accident occurs in a river, as opposed to other inland waterways.

It is difficult to extrapolate the nature and extent of the environmental damage that follows a vessel oil spill. "Because of the interactions of a great number of factors, two spills in the same place will have very different environmental consequences depending, for example, on the time of year, weather conditions and success of the clean-up" (Dicks, 1998). The winter oiling of, for example, a salt marsh may have little effect on above-ground parts of plants that naturally die back at that time of year, as opposed to spring or summer when there is new growth. If the oil spill occurs in the season when birds and mammals are congregating and fish and shellfish are spawning, the damage to these species from an oil spill can be considerable. The weather conditions of high temperatures and wind speeds increase the evaporation of oil, decreasing the toxicity of oil remaining on the water. The clean-up process can decrease as well as increase the environmental damage from an oil spill. The removal of oil from shorelines will decrease its threat to organisms, but the removal process itself can also damage or kill some organisms.

The environmental impact of a vessel oil spill will also depend on the type of oil spilt and the speed of oil recovery. Crude oils and oil products vary widely in their physical and chemical properties. Light oils, e.g. gasoline, are more toxic than heavy oils and thus more likely to penetrate and disrupt cell membranes of organisms; but heavy oils that spill on shorelines may blanket organisms and kill them via the physical effect of smothering rather than through toxic effects. The speed of oil recovery is affected by the type of oil spilt, the climate and season, and the physical and biological characteristics of the area. Environmental damage is likely to be more pronounced when oil is spilt in shallow inlets, where there is less natural dispersion and dilution of oil than in open seas. The sensitivity of species to oil varies. For example, seabirds have high mortality rates from oiling, whereas some seaweed species survive oil pollution because their mucilaginous coating prevents oil penetration.

It does not necessarily follow that the larger the vessel oil spill the greater will be the environmental damage from the spill. A large oil spill that does not impact coastlines may cause little or no environmental damage, whereas a much smaller spill that impacts coastlines may result in major environmental damage. An example of the latter is the *Exxon Valdez* tanker accident. In March 1989 the *Exxon Valdez* ran aground in Prince William Sound, Alaska, a scenic wilderness, spilling nearly 37 000 tons of oil. The spillage ranks 34th in size among world-wide vessel spills, but the response to the spillage was the most expensive in oil spill history (White and Baker, 1998). The spillage, the largest oil spillage in US waters, impacted coastlines, resulting in major environmental damage, e.g. 1000 sea otters and 35 000 seabirds died; major damage to fisheries also resulted; and more than 10 000 workers were employed at the height of the clean-up operations.

Exxon has paid US $2.2 billion for clean-up, US $1 billion to settle state and federal lawsuits, and US $300 million for lost wages to 11 000 fisherman and business firms. The cost to the fisheries of south-central Alaska has been estimated to be US $108.1 million, the largest component being a US $65.4 million reduction in the pink salmon fishery in the first year following the accident (Cohen, 1995). In 1994 an Alaska jury awarded an additional US $5.3 billion in punitive and compensatory damages to those hurt by the *Exxon Valdez* oil spill. Exxon appealed, but its appeal was rejected by an Alaska appeals court in March 2000.

The *Exxon Valdez* accident was also the impetus for the US Congress to pass the Oil Pollution Act of 1990 (OPA-90), which established accountability for vessel oil spills in US waters. The liability of the vessel owner could be as high as US $1200 per vessel gross ton or US $10 million for vessels over 3000 gross tons, whichever is greater. If the vessel owner, or liable party, is found guilty of gross negligence or in violation of laws, the liability would be unlimited, and liable parties could be subject to both criminal and civil sanctions. Further, claims could be filed against parties who have an interest in the ownership or operation of the vessel and fit the OPA-90 definition of a "responsible party."

OPA-90 requires vessels using US waters to carry certificates of financial responsibility (COFRs), proving that the owners have funds that could cover the maximum liability limits of cleaning up an oil spill. As of June 1996, 1839 tankers and 3978 tank barges had complied with this requirement. When a vessel accident spill occurs, the US Coast Guard designates and notifies the party at fault. If the vessel has a COFR, the guarantor or insurer is also notified. The government then takes care of the clean-up and subsequently sends the bill for expenses incurred to the appropriate party.

OPA-90 also mandates double hulls for tankers and tank barges traveling in US waters by the year 2015 – the assumption being that double hulls would reduce the vessel damage severity of an accident, which, in turn, would reduce oil spillage in the accident. The cost-effectiveness of double hulls in reducing vessel accident oil spillage, however, has been questioned. Hopkins (1992) states that "costs appear substantial relative to benefits, and lawmakers' emphasis on design standards deflects attention from alternative risk reduction strategies, e.g. operation and maintenance measures that warrant equal attention." Brown and Savage (1996) found that the expected benefits of reduced tanker spillage from the double-hull requirement are only 20% of the increased construction and operation costs of double-hulled tankers. In addition, Jin et al. (1995) found that electronic charts may be a far more cost-effective approach than double hulls for marine pollution control.

In December 1999 the single-hull tanker vessel, the *Erika*, broke up and sank in the Bay of Biscay, spilling 11 million liters of heavy fuel oil that polluted 400 km of French beaches. In response to the *Erika* spill and as part of their campaign to reduce water pollution, the transport ministers of the EU called for a world-wide phasing out of single-hull tankers by 2012. The phasing-out would be done in steps based upon tanker age and size.

In 1994 the 150 member countries of the International Maritime Organization (IMO) adopted the International Safety Management Code. The code mandated that by 1 July 1998 all liquid- and solid-bulk vessels, passenger vessels, and high-speed vessels of more than 500 gross tons had to have certification of compliance to the code for safe operation and pollution prevention. Any vessel not complying with the code would be unable to obtain insurance and denied access to the world's major ports. Further, the International Association of Classification Societies, whose 13 members inspect 60% of the world fleet, has agreed to undertake more frequent and in-depth vessel inspections.

3. Ballast water disposal

A common and necessary practice to insure vessel stability is for vessels to take on and discharge ballast water. While in port, ballast water may be pumped into vessel cargo, or specially designed tanks to compensate for variance in weight distributions as cargo is removed. When cargo is loaded, the ballast water is released in amounts according to the design of the vessel and the profile of how the vessel is loaded. A large containership, for example, may carry 15 000 tons of ballast water.

When vessels take on ballast water, aquatic life indigenous to that region is often found in the water. When the water is discharged in another region, the discharged aquatic life may then thrive and disrupt the local ecological system. When there are no natural predators, the non-indigenous aquatic life will alter or destroy the natural marine ecosystem. For example, the comb jelly, which was transported in ballast water from the USA to the Black and Azov Seas, almost wiped out the local anchovy fisheries. In 1999 an invasive species, the green crab, was found in the US waters off Washington state. Human health can also be at risk. The Asian strain of the cholera bacterium was likely introduced into Latin American waters through the discharge of ballast water. Invasive species can also cause property damage. The zebra mussel, for example, introduced into the Great Lakes in the mid-1980s by vessels arriving from Europe, has caused US $5 billion in damage to water pipes, boat hulls, and other surfaces in the Great Lakes (Loy, 1999).

One solution for preventing or greatly reducing the discharge of ballast-water non-indigenous aquatic life is mid-ocean ballast water exchange. Ballast water taken onboard when vessels are in ocean water depths of 2000 m or greater are expected to be free of invasive species. The avoidance of non-indigenous species in ballast tanks from this exchange, however, is not total, since not all of the ballast water is replaced. Mid-ocean ballast exchange is a time-consuming process that takes at least 48 h and can cost up to US $25 000 for a large vessel that utilizes its crew for close monitoring. If performed by all ocean vessels calling at US ports, the expected annual cost is US $51 million (Mongelluzzo, 2000). However, since the exchange is done while the vessel remains underway, vessels are not delayed. The IMO considers mid-ocean ballast exchange as the best short-term solution for avoiding the discharge of ballast-water non-indigenous species. Long-term solutions are likely to be innovations in the treatment of ballast water that remove or kill non-indigenous species.

Shipping lines are engaging in mid-ocean ballast exchange at an increasing rate, especially since passage of the 1997 IMO resolution that established a voluntary mid-ocean ballast exchange program. The US National Invasive Species Act of 1996 made mid-ocean ballast exchange mandatory for ocean vessels entering the Great Lakes and the Hudson River, but voluntary for vessels arriving at other US ports. Since 1 March 1997 the Port of Vancouver, British Columbia, requires entering vessels to have performed mid-ocean ballast exchange. And since 1 January 2000 all vessels calling directly from a foreign port and entering the US ports of Los Angeles, Long Beach, and Oakland in California are required to have performed a mid-ocean ballast exchange; further, shipping lines are subject to a US $600 fee per vessel call to fund research into new methods of preventing foreign aquatic species from entering California waters. The California requirements were precipitated by the discovery of more than 200 non-indigenous species in San Francisco Bay and 46 non-indigenous species in the Los Angeles/Long Beach port complexes. The state of Washington also has a mandatory mid-ocean ballast exchange regulation.

All vessels calling at US ports must report to the Coast Guard on their ballast water management practices. Since 21 December 2001, ocean carriers must submit a ballast water management report at least 24 h prior to arrival in the first US port of call rather than after arrival, as in the past. A number of US states also require ballast water management reports. Since 22 September 2000, ocean vessels calling at Washington state ports have been required to send the Washington Fish and Wildlife Commission the same information on ballast water management practices that they send the Coast Guard. The states of Maryland, Oregon, and Virginia have a similar reporting requirements. In addition to reporting, other states have pending legislation for sterilizing ballast water and requiring permits for ballast water discharges. However, the number of disparate state programs has led US ports and shipping lines (that call at these ports) to seek federal legislation that would pre-empt state ballast water regulations.

The US Environmental Protection Agency is seeking to regulate ballast water release as pollution under the Clean Water Act by requiring that ballast water be discharged into shoreside tanks for purification or disposal. Since large amounts of foreign ballast water, 9 million liters per hour, are discharged in US waters, and since large port tank facilities would have to be built, this regulation would be very costly (Tirschwell, 1999).

4. Air pollution

Although commercial vessels account for only 2% of the world's consumption of fossil fuels, they are a significant source of ocean air pollution. Vessel engines are the dirtiest combustion sources per ton of fuel consumed, producing 14% of the world's nitrogen emissions from fossil fuels and 16% of all sulfur emissions from petroleum (Spice, 1999). Gases from vessel power plants account for 60% of the sulfur dioxide found in the air over large areas (with busy shipping lanes) of the North Atlantic and North Pacific oceans (Capaldo et al., 1999).

Commercial vessels are also a significant source (5–30%) of sulfur dioxide pollution in coastal areas; 70% of ocean-going vessel emissions occur within 400 km of land (Capaldo et al, 1999). Proposals to reduce vessel emissions in Southern California, the location of the ports of Los Angeles and Long Beach, include reducing vessel speeds to 12 knots within 25 miles (40 km) of a port, and moving shipping channels further offshore. "Cold ironing," i.e. requiring vessels while in port to shut down their engines and to be powered by shore-side electricity, has been proposed as a means to reduce vessel air pollution while a vessel is in port. However, any benefits to be gained from lower emissions could be negated from the safety hazard of tangled electrical wires.

5. Anti-fouling pollution (tributyltin)

Fouling is the unwanted growth of biological material, e.g. barnacles, algae, or mollusks, on the water-immersed surface of a vessel. When vessel hulls are clean and smooth, i.e. free of fouling, they travel faster through water and consume less fuel. Fouling can be removed when a vessel is dry docked, which occurs every 2–5 years. An alternative approach to reduce fouling is to apply an anti-fouling coating to the vessel's hull. Prior to the 1960s vessel hulls were coated with lime, and later with arsenical and mercurial compounds to reduce fouling. During the 1960s, anti-fouling paints were developed using metallic compounds, in particular the organotin compound tributyltin (TBT). By the 1970s most ocean-going vessels had TBT painted on to their hulls.

While anti-fouling TBT paints have been found to be effective in killing organisms attached to vessel hulls, they have also killed and caused genetic alterations in other sea life, e.g. shell deformations in oysters. In the 1970s TBT contamination was linked to the high mortality of oyster larvae in the Arcachon Bay on the west coast of France. In the 1980s in south-west England, TBT poisoning was linked to the decline of the dog whelk.

TBT is the most toxic substance ever deliberately introduced into the marine environment (Evans et al., 1995). Further, it persists in the marine environment. High concentrations of TBT have been found in the world's coastal waters, especially in ports and harbors where boats and vessels are concentrated. As a consequence, a number of countries have introduced regulations to limit the use of TBT in anti-fouling paints. France, for example, prohibits the use of TBT anti-fouling paints on vessels less than 25 m in length. In 1990 the IMO's Marine Environment Protection Committee (MEPC) adopted Resolution MEPC 46(30), "Measures to Control Potential Adverse Impacts Associated with Use of Tributyltin Compounds in Anti-Fouling Paints," which recommends the elimination of TBT anti-fouling paint on non-aluminum-hulled vessels of less than 25 m in length. While a mandatory phase out of TBT anti-fouling paints for ocean-going vessels is a goal of the IMO, acceptable alternatives are required before the phase out can be adopted.

6. Dredging

Dredging is the process of increasing the water depths of waterways by removing sediments from their bottoms. The environmental effects of dredging include: turbidity, ecosystem, and spoil disposal effects.

Dredging of waterways causes elevated suspended solids (turbidity plumes). The distance a plume moves from its point of origin is dependent upon waterway currents, the nature of the plume, the scope of dredging, and the preventive measures employed by the dredging contractor. Excessive turbidity can affect fish species by abrading sensitive epithelial tissues, clogging gills, and reducing light penetration. Light reduction further reduces the photosynthesis of phytoplankton, kills submerged vegetation, and reduces water oxygen. Also, sediments raised by dredging can bury plants away from the dredged site, thereby reducing their density. The reduction in plant density can, in turn, erode bottom sediments and increase silt.

Dredging not only removes plants but also changes the physical, biological, and chemical structure of the ecosystem. The removal of bottom sediments frequently kills benthic organisms and disrupts their feeding habitat. The noise, turbulence, and obstructions from dredging operations themselves also disrupt organisms and their habitat. In some cases, it may take years for the recolonization of organisms to occur.

Suspended sediments dredged from waterways are generally biologically and chemically active. Dredged spoils from harbor and port waterways that are in proximity to industrial and urban centers are often contaminated with pollutants such as heavy metals, organochlorine compounds, polyaromatic hydrocarbons, and petroleum hydrocarbons. Disposal sites for dredged spoils often have high levels of sediment build-up and oxygen depletion, which create adverse conditions for biotic communities.

In the USA the primary disposal site for dredge spoils of ocean ports is the ocean. Because of environmental contamination concerns, a number of alternative sites are being considered as well as the decontamination of spoils prior to their disposal. A disposal site may not only benefit the depositor of spoils but the site itself. For example, it has been suggested that dredge spoils from the Port of New York and New Jersey be used for coal mine remediation in Pennsylvania. Acidic seepage from abandoned mines poses a threat to the drinkable water supply. It is anticipated that the disposal of dredge spoils in these mines would stop the seepage.

7. Vessel scrapping

The traditional method of scrapping obsolete vessels is to sell the scrapping rights to ship-breaking companies, which then dismantle the vessels and sell the scrap material and reusable equipment. Environmental concerns arise in the disposal of scrapped vessel materials that contain hazardous materials, e.g. polychlorinated biphenyls (PCBs). In the USA, PCBs were commonly used in vessel construction and repair from the 1930s until 1976, when the Toxic Substances Control Act of 1976 was passed by the US Congress. Specifically, PCBs were used as dielectric fluids and coolants in transformers and capacitors and sometimes as a fire retardant in such solid materials as electrical cable insulation and felt gaskets.

In the USA the focus of the regulation on the use of PCBs in vessels has been on dielectric fluids, not PCBs in solid materials. Under the Environmental Protection Agency's 1998 PCB Bulk Product Rule, a municipal or sanitary landfill may accept non-liquid PCBs at certain levels for disposal. However, some scrapping companies have found it difficult to locate landfills that will accept non-liquid PCBs.

Because of stringent environmental and worker safety legislation in major industrialized countries, vessel scrapping has shifted to countries such as India, Bangladesh, and Pakistan, where there are less stringent regulations. Groups such as Greenpeace International and the Basel Action Network have campaigned against vessel scrapping as a violator of the Basel Convention that prohibits the exports of toxic waste from developed to developing countries. Further, vessel-scrapping environmental issues are currently under investigation by the IMO. Greenpeace is also campaigning for ship-owners to remove hazardous materials from vessels prior to their dismantling, and that a complete inventory of all hazardous wastes on board be made.

8. Waste disposal at sea

Vessel waste disposed at sea may include gray water (water waste from galleys, showers, and kitchens) and garbage (food waste and disposable items such as utensils, plastic cups, bottles, and tins). Gray water may contain high levels of bacteria that are harmful to marine ecosystems. Food waste poses fewer environmental concerns than metals and plastics, since organic matter is easier to biodegrade. The disposal of metals and plastics at sea may destroy pristine marine ecosystems. The environmental impact of waste disposal at sea by cruise ships is especially a concern as they dispose of greater amounts of sea waste relative to other types of ship.

Discharges of garbage into US navigable waters is prohibited, unless there is a National Pollutant Discharge Elimination Systems permit. However, this permit is not required for any discharge that is incidental to the normal operation of a vessel; ballast water discharge is considered an incidental discharge.

Ocean dumping of waste is regulated by the IMO Convention on the Prevention of Marine Pollution by Dumping Wastes and Other Materials. The regulations contain provisions that allow ships to dispose of shredded glass and tins, treated food, and human waste by discharging them at sea.

9. Summary

The environmental impact that has received the most attention is that from vessel oil spills, damaging plants, fisheries, birds, and mammals. However, there are other impacts, which, while receiving less attention, can be just as damaging to the environment. Discharged vessel ballast water may contain aquatic life that is harmful to the indigenous aquatic life of the region. Vessels pollute the air when they emit nitrogen and sulfur dioxide. Anti-fouling chemicals, particularly TBT, that are effective in killing organisms attached to the vessel hull also kill other sea life. Sea life may also be killed when waterways are dredged to deeper depths. Biologically and chemically active dredged sediments and hazardous materials from scrapped vessels can contaminate disposal sites. Vessel waste disposal at sea can pollute waterways.

References

Brown, R.S. and I. Savage (1996) "The Economics of double-hulled tankers," *Maritime Policy and Management*, 23:167–175.
Capaldo, K., J. Corbett, P. Kasibhatla, P. Fischbeck and S. Pandis (1999) "Effects of ship emissions on sulphur cycling and radiative climate forcing over the ocean," *Nature*, 400:743–746.
Cohen, M.J. (1995) "Technological disasters and natural resource damage assessment: an evaluation of the *Exxon Valdez* oil spill," *Land Economics*, 71:5–82.
Dicks, B. (1998) "The environmental impact of marine oil spills: effects, recovery and compensation," in: *International Seminar on Tanker Safety, Pollution Prevention, Spill Response and Compensation*, Paper. Rio de Janeiro.
Evans, S.M., T. Leksono and P.D. McKinnell (1995) "Tributyltin pollution: a diminishing problem following legislation limiting the use of TBT-based anti-fouling paints," *Marine Pollution Bulletin*, 30:14–21.

Hopkins, T.D. (1992) "Oil spill reduction and costs of ship design regulation," *Contemporary Policy Issues*, 10:59–70.
Jin, D., H.L. Kite-Powell and J.M. Broadus (1995) "Dynamic economic analysis of marine pollution prevention technologies: an application to double hulls and electronic charts," *International Hydrographic Review*, 72:71–96.
Loy, J.M. (1999) "The coast guard and ballast-water management," *Journal of Commerce*, 27 Oct.:6.
Mongelluzzo, B. (2000) "California law targets foreign species," *Journal of Commerce*, 4 Jan.:1.
Spice, B. (1999) "Ship pollution study: emissions cool earth," *Journal of Commerce*, 23 Aug.:2.
Talley, W.K. (1999) "Determinants of the property damage costs of tanker accidents," *Transportation Research D*, 4:413–426.
Talley, W.K. (2000) "Oil spillage and damage costs: U.S. inland waterway tank barge accidents," *International Journal of Maritime Economics*, II:217–234.
Talley, W.K., D. Jin and H. Kite-Powell (2001) "Vessel accident oil-spillage: post US OPA-90," *Transportation Research D*, 6:405–415.
Tirschwell, P. (1999) "Terminating aliens: EPA's help is sought by environmentalists," *Journal of Commerce*, 27 Sept.: 9.
White, I.C. and J.M. Baker (1998) "The *Sea Empress* oil spill in context," in: *International Conference on the Sea Empress Oil Spill*. Cardiff.

Chapter 16

TRANSPORT ENERGY AND EMISSIONS: RAIL

ALAIN BONNAFOUS and CHARLES RAUX
Laboratoire d'Economie des Transports, Lyon

1. Introduction

While pollutant emissions from transport have only recently become an issue, their energy costs have been a long-standing concern. It can even be said that, historically, from the beginning of railways, there has always been an association between rail and what we today call transport energy efficiency. The next section describes this association.

However, today, other issues are at stake. The first consists of a comparison between rail's environmental performance and that of other transport modes, which we consider in Section 3. On the grounds of sustainable development, the average values used in this assessment may encourage a policy in favor of modal transfer towards rail.

A great deal of caution is required with regard to the parameters that are usually given in order to characterize the relative performance of different modes: the relative values can be considerably modified in real transport situations. It is, for example, vital to consider also the implications of freight terminal costs, feeder journeys in cases that do not involve door-to-door transport, vehicle loading rates, how the driving power is produced, etc.; these are covered in Section 4.

In the light of these factors how can we identify the optimum policy? What we must do is measure, in real situations, the impacts on demand of a given modal transfer policy (for example in the case of increasing the cost of cars, a loss in mobility or user surplus) or the capital costs for rail infrastructure. This is discussed in Section 5.

The conclusion highlights the fact that we arrive at situations where it is necessary to compare the energy savings or pollution reductions with the outlay involved. We therefore need to find monetary equivalents for the physical quantities in question to be able to conduct rigorous case by case evaluations.

2. The historical association between rail and energy efficiency

The historical association between rail transport and energy efficiency has its source in the technological development of contact between wheels and rails that began more than three centuries ago and continued with the steam locomotive revolution. This technology came to dominate vast areas before being severely hit by competition from motorized road transport.

2.1 From the first rails ...

Wooden rails were used from 1670 in England, in the Newcastle upon Tyne region, and iron-clad rails were developed in the middle of the eighteenth century, at the same time as wheel-hooping techniques. These techniques more than doubled the load that a horse, the main source of tractive power at the time, could tow. But it is obviously the steam locomotive that was responsible for the real technological revolution.

The first steam car was invented by the French engineer Joseph Cugnot in 1770. Two English inventors, Vivian and Trevithick, filed the first patent in 1802. Their locomotive inspired an American, Oliver Ewans, to produce a steam engine that ran on rails but which was greeted with only skepticism in 1804. Advances in both the steam engine that produced the energy and the rail track system that consumed it very soon gave birth to the technology responsible for the railway revolution. The first "modern" steam engine was built by George Stephenson, the son of an English miner. Stephenson received the necessary power by improving the tubular boiler invented by a Frenchman, Marc Seguin. In 1829, Stephenson's *Rocket* won the Rainhill competition by towing 13 tonnes at a speed of almost 24 km an hour.

This engine already possessed the essential features of the locomotives that were to be responsible for rail's development, and also demonstrated the economic performance that was to enable rail to be the dominant terrestrial mode for more than a century: the energy efficiency of the system was such that it was able to transport several times more freight or passengers than a stagecoach, which was able to carry barely more than a tonne, at far higher speeds. In addition, as a result of bulking, from the outset rail was able to undercut road transport and operate at prices that were only slightly higher than inland waterway transport.

Even at this early stage of rail's history, we can compare the *Rocket*'s 24 km per hour, which was obviously improved on very soon, to the 2 km an hour achieved by water transport, the 4 km an hour achieved by a standard horse-drawn wagon, and the 8 km an hour of the fastest horse-drawn service.

2.2. ... to spatial expansion

Under these conditions, the only thing that limited rail's market share was the network's spatial expansion. This took place at a spectacular rate during the second half of the nineteenth century in industrial countries. In France, for example, starting in the 1860s, a thousand kilometers of new lines were opened every year, whereas at the end of the twentieth century it took 20 years to construct the first thousand kilometers of new high-speed line!

To put today's energy use and pollution problems into context, we need to look at what happened next, that is to say, the revival of road transport as a consequence of cars and trucks. In terms of the economic processes involved, what happened during the twentieth century was very similar to what had occurred in the nineteenth century, but with very different results. Before the First World War, when road transport was essentially horse-drawn, it had continuously lost market share for freight transport. From the 1920s, the motor vehicle began to play the same role as the train in the previous century and brought fresh life to the road: roads had less than 10% of the freight market in western Europe in 1920; this figure was to reach 50% in 1970, then 80% at the end of the century. Passenger transport underwent a similar change.

In spite of the steady fall in rail's market share, there are some market segments where its position has improved because of favorable trade-offs between price and time. Examples are high-speed rail, daily transport in major conurbations, combined transport in Europe, and long-distance freight transport in North America. However, nothing seems able to halt the growth of car and truck transport, which has serious effects on congestion, energy use, and pollution.

The foregoing arguments suggest that rail may provide a way of overcoming these adverse effects, which are incompatible with international commitments such as the Kyoto Protocol or the imperatives of sustainable development. However, for it to provide an effective solution its theoretical potential must be clearly identified, as must the practicalities of sustainable development.

3. Energy use and pollution: some orders of magnitude

With regard to energy use and pollutant emissions, it is standard practice to compare the relative performance of rail and other modes of transport on the basis of a few very general indicators. While these indicators obviously have a meaning, even just as aggregate statistics, they must be used with caution.

3.1. The energy problem

One way of comparing rail with its main competitor, which is road transport, is to consider the amount of transport that can be produced by a given quantity of energy. Thus, on the basis of the specific consumptions that applied in Europe in the last years of the twentieth century, 1 kg of oil equivalent produces:

- 19 p-km in a car;
- 82.6 p-km in a high-speed train;
- 57.6 tonne-km in a loaded 25 tonne truck;
- 128.2 tonne-km in a full train.

Judging from these raw figures alone, rail is at least four times more efficient for passengers and at least twice as efficient for goods.

These comparisons based on average values are obviously very simple. They are really too simple in the light of the diversity of real situations and the actual problems that arise in a given location. There are two main methodological difficulties.

First, there is a technical difficulty that involves energy efficiency. Energy use for roads is derived from statistics concerning the amount of fuel actually consumed by combustion engines. The energy use for rail is derived from statistics on the number of kilowatt-hours actually consumed by electric traction units. In countries where electrification has not proceeded very far, rail traction using diesel engines must also be considered.

However, in an energy balance sheet of this type, very frequently what is ultimately involved is the amount of fossil energy used for one unit of transport production. It is this use of fossil energy that matters with regard to the non-renewable resources of the planet and greenhouse gas emissions. We cannot just consider the ultimate electrical energy demand of rail if the electricity involved has been produced by a coal- or oil-fired power station. Here, the relevant 1 kg of oil equivalent is that consumed by the power station, and this necessarily depends on the efficiency of the power station (and also the efficiency of the electrical distribution network that transports the electricity to the catenary which supplies the train).

The values of the energy use indicators are therefore very different in a country that favors nuclear energy, where the above indicators are still relevant as "average" values, from those in a country that has abandoned the nuclear industry, where they need substantial correction.

The second difficulty is linked to transport service production. In the case of passenger transport, for example, we can easily see that the average energy efficiency conceals a considerable diversity of situations: a given type of train can carry more than 2000 passengers on major routes in large urban areas, but on regional services it is not unusual for it to carry less than a dozen. The energy efficiency of the two situations in passenger-kilometer terms is obviously not the same.

The same difficulties arise when we tackle the issue of local and global pollution, in particular on the basis of carbon dioxide emissions which are relevant both to global pollution (which contributes to the greenhouse effect) and to energy efficiency.

Table 1
Energy use and emissions per passenger-kilometer for long-distance travel

Mode		Energy use (MJ/p-km)	Emissions (g/p-km)			
			CO_2	NO_x	Volatile organic compounds	SO_2
Aircraft	500 km	2.2	160	0.47	0.06	0.05
	1500 km	1.6	115	0.40	0.03	0.05
Car	Gasoline, 2 occupants	1.5	110	0.08	0.03	0.02
	Diesel, 2 occupants	1.3	100	0.39	0.05	0.03
	Diesel, 1 occupant	3.2	235	0.76	0.09	0.07
Train	High speed	0.7	40	0.24	0.01	0.06
	Conventional	0.8	50	0.28	0.01	0.07
Coach		0.3	20	0.29	0.02	0.01

Source: Roos et al. (1997).

3.2. The problem of negative impacts

It is also possible to compare rail with other transport modes on the basis of the three major negative impacts, namely accidents, noise, and atmospheric pollution. One of the fullest sources of data is a study published by the European Conference of Ministers of Transport (EMCT) (1998), which summarizes a vast amount of data from many previous studies.

Table 1 shows per passenger-kilometer emissions of major pollutants for the different transport modes: these figures take account of average loading rates (65% for planes, high-speed rail, and coaches; 40% for conventional trains), and consider the average mode of electricity production in the north-west of Europe, that is to say, a higher proportion of electricity from nuclear power stations than in the rest of the world.

These figures show that there are large differences in emission levels between modes, and that the relative positions of the modes depend on which pollutant is considered. With a satisfactory loading rate the coach consumes the least energy, followed by the train then the car. However, for nitrogen oxides, a gasoline car with a catalytic converter and two occupants pollutes least (contrasting with the diesel car). For volatile organic compounds, the train is in the best position, followed by the coach, then the car. Lastly, for sulfur dioxide, the gasoline car with a catalytic converter and two occupants again performs best, but the car generally is at the same level as the train.

A similar comparison (Table 2) can be drawn up for goods transport, with a loading rate of 67% for planes, 55 or 45% for heavy trucks, 33% for trains, and

50% for boats. For energy use, the most efficient mode is coastal transport, followed by inland-waterway transport, then the train. However, the electric train is the very clear leader for nitrogen oxides, and is also level with coastal transport for emissions of volatile organic compounds. Finally, trucks are not in such a bad position for sulfur dioxide emissions, occupying the same position as barges used in inland-waterway transport.

These data suggest two things: first, a transfer toward rail may be justified on the grounds of sustainable development; but, on the other hand, it is necessary to consider actual situations or at least situations that are close to reality in order to accurately assess the energy and pollution implications of such a modal transfer.

4. From average values to realities in the field

To illustrate the point we have just made we shall now look at the comparison between rail and road in the case of the market where combined transport operators and road haulage companies are engaged in fierce competition. This market is of particular interest because it is generally recognized as being the segment of the freight market where rail is doing more than simply maintaining its position *vis-à-vis* the road, and also where it is accepted as being less environmentally harmful. However, we shall see that the second hypothesis is only true if certain conditions are met.

Table 2
Energy use and emissions per freight-kilometer for long-distance travel

Mode		Energy use (MJ/tonne-km)	Emissions (g/tonne-km)			
			CO_2	NO_x	Volatile organic compounds	SO_2
Aircraft	500 km	19.5	1420	4.33	0.65	0.42
	1500 km	11.0	800	2.66	0.25	0.23
Truck	35 tonnes gvw	1.34	100	1.20	0.05	0.03
	20 tonnes gvw	2.77	200	2.26	0.10	0.05
Train	Diesel	0.95	69	1.22	0.07	0.08
	Electric	0.83	38	0.07	0.00	0.21
Barge		0.54	40	0.69	0.04	0.04
Coaster	Diesel	0.19	13	0.26	0.01	0.02
	Fuel oil	0.17	12	0.32	0.01	0.24

Source: Dings and Dijkstra (1997).

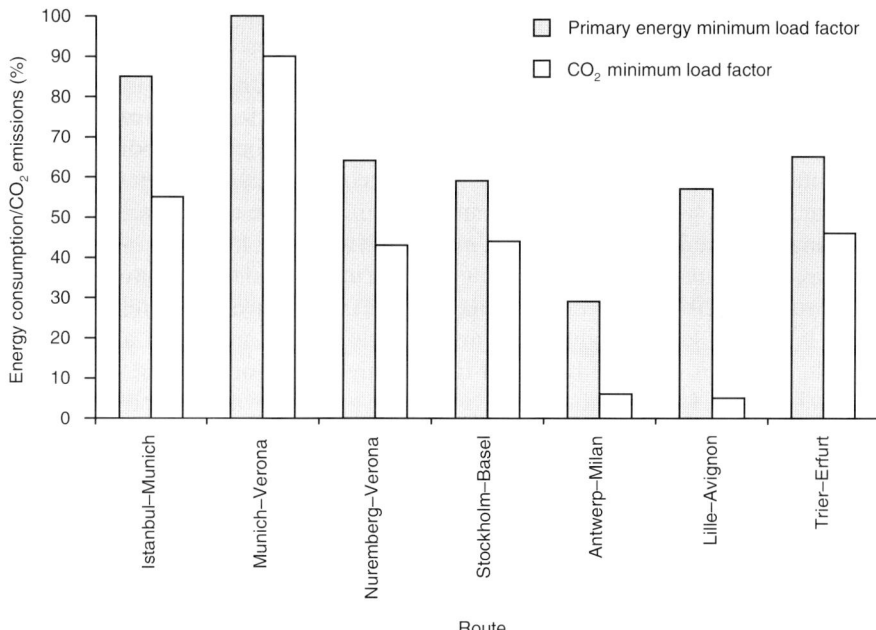

Figure 1. Required train loading rates for primary energy consumption and CO_2 emissions of combined road–rail transport to be lower than those of road transport. (Source: Institut für Energie- und Umweltforschung and Studiengesellschaft für den kombinierten Verkehr, 2002.)

The International Road Union has recently published a study commissioned from two German research institutes (Institut für Energie- und Umweltforschung and Studiengesellschaft für den kombinierten Verkehr, 2002) that consisted of systematic comparisons between primary energy use and carbon dioxide emissions in the case of 19 links. These links comprise services between origins and destinations within Europe on which two transport modes – road and combined road–rail – are available to shippers. In what follows, we will need to refer to just seven of these examples to illustrate our point.

4.1. Varied energy balance sheets

Figure 1 shows the required loading rate for combined transport to outperform road transport in terms of primary energy use and carbon dioxide emissions.

To begin with, let us consider the primary energy consumption of transport services. The diversity of the situations confirms the fact that we must refer to more than just average values if we wish to compare the performance of the two alternatives. On average, it is, however, true that combined transport provides energy savings when the loading rate of trains is at an acceptable level.

But, paradoxically, there are cases where the energy balance sheet is in the favor of road transport. This is the case for the Munich–Verona road–rail link, where all the factors unite to cancel out the advantages of combined transport: first, the road route is relatively short (only 437 km); secondly, this link uses the "rolling road" technique, which involves loading an entire lorry on to the train; lastly, the total length of the journey is 617 km, mainly owing to the fact that a lorry travels 80 km in the wrong direction on leaving Munich in order to reach the rolling road. Under such conditions, the energy balance sheet will always favor the road.

The situation seems slightly less unfavorable for a route such as Istanbul–Munich, as in this case the road–rail link is only 53 km longer than when going entirely by road. However, the rail section of the journey (which is also on a rolling road, with the entire lorry on the train) is relatively short (648 km out of a total length of 2119 km), the traffic levels are not very high, and the average loading rate for trains is only 65%. For the energy balance sheet to be in favor of rail, the average loading rate would need to be 85%.

In the five other examples we have selected, either the semi-trailer or just the container is loaded on to the train. The energy balance sheet is here very much in favor of rail, as the train loading rates are between 75 and 90%. The route that performs the best is that by container combined transport between Antwerp and Milan, which has several factors in its favor: the container train journey is quite long (963 km), the feeder journeys are short (66 km in all), the road route is 273 km longer, and the average loading rate of trains is 80%. This case is very typical of the container shuttle services that serve the very large European ports, and also for the major links in what is known as the Trans-European Network.

These examples show that the four conditions below must all be satisfied in order for combined transport to be more energy efficient than road transport:

- the rail link must be of an adequate length (more than 500 km);
- the entire combined transport route must not be significantly longer than the road route;
- rail transport must involve loading containers only, not entire vehicles;
- the trains must have a high loading rate.

4.2. Negative impacts and carbon dioxide emissions

However, the energy balance sheet is not the only environmental concern in the context of transport, in particular in view of the fact that localized pollution is particularly great when road traffic is concentrated along urbanized corridors. This is a major problem in Alpine valleys that are crossed by four of the seven routes we have described above. The local environmental balance sheet is in this case more important than the energy balance sheet, in particular because all the major Alpine railway lines have been electrified and are responsible for little local pollution other than noise.

With regard to global pollution, in particular comparisons between carbon dioxide emissions, we are again confronted with the problem of electricity production, which is effectively illustrated by Figure 1. For example, in Figure 1 we can see that the performance of the two combined transport links between Stockholm and Basle and Lille and Avignon are very similar in energy terms: the first is more energy-efficient than road alone if the rail occupancy rate is at least 59%; the second achieves this with a rate of at least 57%. However, the loading rates in order for carbon dioxide emissions to be in equilibrium are very different: 44% for the Stockholm–Basle link, and only 5% for Lille–Avignon.

The difference is mainly due to the proportion of the electricity that is produced from fossil fuels in the area where the rail sections of the routes are located. In Germany, where most of the first route is located, this proportion is 64%, whereas the second line is in France, where the proportion is only 8%.

Whether we consider conserving reserves of fossil hydrocarbons or the related objective of limiting greenhouse gas emissions, the benefits of rail are closely correlated with the relative importance of the nuclear electric sector.

Of course, these conclusions are not only valid for this case, but also for passenger transport, in particular with regard to the sensitivity of the energy balance sheets and the relative negative impacts to the loading rate of trains. The microeconomic argument that the transfer of one passenger from the car to the train saves society from some adverse effects is fallacious. If it is necessary to transport a large number of empty seats to bring about the modal transfer of a few users, the social balance sheet ought to be closely examined.

5. So what is the optimum policy?

We do not just need to know if the environmental appraisal of a given action to encourage rail is, in the final analysis, good for the environment. If this is the case and there is an environmental benefit, we still need to find out if the action is globally beneficial for society. We shall look at two examples, one relating to passengers and the other to freight, to illustrate this issue of social benefit and the need for appraisal.

5.1. Should we attract travelers to trains?

We have taken the example of the Paris region because four-fifths of the public transport passenger-kilometers traveled by its inhabitants are by rail, and also

Table 3
Effects of some regulatory measures on transport modal split in the Paris region

Measure	Change (%)					
	Travel by public transport (p-km)	Travel by car (v-km)	Total travel (p-km)	Public transport revenue	Total user expenditure (a)	Total time
Extension of suburban public transport network	+5	−3	+1	+9	0	0
50% reduction in public transport fares	+34	−6	+12	−32	−10	+9
0.8 euros/km road pricing charge in the city of Paris	+4	−6	−1	+5	+7	−2
33% reduction in road speeds	+6	−22	−9	+6	−20	+6

Source: Morellet (2002).
Note: (a) including public transport pricing, tolls, fuel and pay parking; excluding car maintenance and repair costs.

because all the possible ways of encouraging modal transfer toward public transport are currently being explored, with the dual aim of limiting congestion and reducing transport pollution.

In 1999, the Paris region had almost 11 million inhabitants and covered an area of 12 000 km^2: the densely populated inner urban zone has 8.7 million inhabitants in an area of 2100 km^2 (the city of Paris has a population of 2.1 million in an area of 105 km^2). Daily weekday travel in the region totaled approximately 148 million passenger-kilometers in 1996, 52% of which were by car or motorized two-wheeler, 44% were by public transport (bus and rail including metro, tram, and regional trains), and 4% were on foot or by bicycle. Eighty-two percent of the public transport passenger-kilometers were by rail (metro and regional trains). The total amount spent by users (exclusive of vehicle maintenance and depreciation) was 14 million euros per day, and the time spent traveling totaled almost 11 million hours per day.

As the main author of a model known as MATISSE, Morellet has conducted a recent study (Morellet and Marchal, 2001; Morellet, 2002) that estimated the effects of different push and pull measures on car/public transport modal split. The measures involved either an improvement in public transport supply, or an increase in the cost of car use.

Some significant findings from this study are presented in Table 3. These relate to the number of passenger-kilometers traveled (total and for each mode), and, in order to be able to assess the surplus, public transport revenue and monetary and time expenditure by transport users. These calculations have been performed with the socio-economic context (population, income, and jobs) as it stood in 1996. Furthermore, it has been assumed that the road space made available by a reduction in road congestion has been used to benefit other modes. The measures in question have been presented in ascending order on the basis of the number of car vehicle-kilometers they save. The management measures and their outcomes are as follows:

- Extending the public transport network would cut access times to it by a half, and mean that a half of public transport trips could be made without transfers. This measure would lead to a 5% rise in public transport travel demand and a 3% drop in car travel demand; public transport revenue would increase by 9%, but this would not be nearly enough to finance the extension of the network, while there would be a very slight reduction in user expenditure in both money and time. In view of the considerable investment that extending the networks requires in this scenario, we can state that the benefits of the policy are small in relation to its costs.
- A 50% reduction in all urban and regional public transport fares (both single and season tickets) would increase the number of public transport passenger-kilometers by more than a third, but the distances covered by cars would fall by just 6%. The increased amount of travel would therefore mostly benefit public transport users, but would result in a drop in revenue of almost a third, therefore an increase in the subsidy required to make up the deficit and an increase in total user travel time. The poor result for modal transfer suggests that the energy balance sheet and the environmental balance sheet for the measure would not necessarily be positive.
- Applying a road toll of 0.8 euros per kilometer in the city of Paris would lead to a similar reduction in car travel demand and a slight increase in public transport travel demand (4%), leading to a similar increase in public transport revenue (5%). But total user expenditure would rise by 7% as a result of the toll, and there would be some reduction in congestion. It should be noted that increasing the cost of all motor vehicle fuels by a half would have a similar result. There would therefore not be an enormous expansion in rail travel, but the effects would be favorable both to the environment and public finances.[a]
- Lastly, a reduction of one-third in motor vehicle speeds, obtained by regulations and traffic restrictions, would have the most striking effect on demand for car travel, leading to a 22% reduction in vehicle-kilometers.

---

[a] A city-center toll scheme of this nature was implemented in London on 17 February 2003, and is performing well.

This reduction is not compensated for by an equivalent rise in public transport demand, and would result in a 9% reduction in overall travel, a 20% reduction in transport user expenditure, and a 6% rise in travel time. While the environmental effects are positive, they are obviously "paid for" by a very significant loss in surplus for car users.

This example demonstrates that it is not very easy to attract travelers to trains, and that doing so always has a social cost. The simulations also suggest that combining certain measures may provide solutions. For example, the only measure that provides additional revenue, i.e. the toll that generates 1.5 million euros per day, would balance out the 1.4 million euro revenue loss that would result from a halving of public transport fares.

Obviously, the implementation of fuel taxation or road toll scenarios, or scenarios where public transport supply is increased, encounters difficulties with regard to social and political acceptability by motorists and taxpayers, respectively.

5.2. A very topical example for freight

This example involves the Alpine crossing problem, probably one of the most serious transport problems in the EU. The flows that are causing problems now, and which will do so even more in the future, are those that cross a line which extends from the Fréjus pass (between France and Italy) to the Brenner pass (between Austria and Italy): for freight, there are only seven road crossings and four rail crossings over this 430 km line (which can be compared with the 200 or so road passages on the 300 km border between France and Belgium!). All the forecasts agree that these crossings will be saturated in 10–15 years time. We can get some idea of what this saturation means by looking at what happened when the 1999 Mont Blanc tunnel fire led to the closure until 2002 of one of the main road crossings between France and Italy.

Increasing the capacity of existing roads is no longer an available option as there are already high-capacity crossing roads. The governments involved are not considering building motorways in the few suitable valleys, if only just to protect the ecosystems.

The only significant sources of capacity are therefore the rail links, whose capacities and performance can be increased. Switzerland has therefore proposed two major rail crossings from Germany to Italy and has started to construct the first, the Lötschberg–Simplon piggy-back transport link. Construction of the Gothard route is planned to follow this.

Concurrently, a road toll has been introduced for lorries. This should provide both a significant part of the funding for the rail investment and help channel transport demand toward rail. Transport mode decisions involve a trade-off between price and time, and hauliers will have the opportunity to put their lorries on the train across Switzerland and the Alps at a price and a commercial speed that are competitive with the road route.

A similar scheme is being considered for the Lyon–Turin link. This should provide both a high-speed passenger rail link (at 330 km/h) and piggy-back trains, owing to the construction of a wide-base tunnel 54 km long under Mont Cenis. The idea is for the motorway companies who operate the two motorway crossings that pass through the Mont Blanc and the Fréjus tunnels to be involved in the scheme so that the road tolls can play the dual role of funding the system and channeling demand.

This is a striking example of a practical application of the recommendations of economic theory and, more particularly, the two golden rules that should inform both the decision to invest and the setting of prices for using saturated infrastructure (European Conference of Ministers of Transport, 1998):

(1) investment to increase capacity should be continued until its marginal cost is equal to the total economic and social costs that it saves;
(2) the charge for using the infrastructure should cover the long-term marginal social cost.

The second recommendation, which is sometimes disputed if only because of the difficulties involved in measuring the long-term marginal social cost, nevertheless relates to a principle that is relatively simple to implement: when an infrastructure is saturated, the charge made for using it should be increased to a level that is either sufficiently dissuasive to bring demand down to below the capacity or to fund additional investment to increase capacity.

If the option of making the investment is selected it is because it is in principle considered to be profitable for society, which means that appraisal has shown that it has a positive net present value. The schemes described above, which are in fact the largest rail projects in the world, involve considerable capital cost, over 10 billion euros in each case. Evaluation therefore amounts to asking what is virtually a common-sense question: Does going ahead with the scheme create more value than it destroys?

Of course, the value of what is destroyed and the value of what is created must be considered in the broad sense, that is to say not just in terms of financial costs but also aspects such as user safety, comfort, and surplus, and, of course, pollution.

This relates to other chapters in this handbook that are specifically concerned with the problems of assigning monetary values to effects that are outside of the monetary sphere. Suffice it to say here that the future of major rail schemes does not just depend on their financial profitability but is very directly linked to the monetary value ascribed to a tonne of carbon and some other negative impacts of transport.

Table 4
Specific costs of adverse effects and hazards

Mode	Costs (ECU)		
	Air pollution	Noise	Accidents
Car (per 1000 p-km)	5–7	3	33
Rail passenger transport (per 1000 p-km)	0.6–3.5	11	3
Road freight transport (per 1000 t-km)	23	8	21
Rail freight transport (per 1000 t-km)	0.2–1.2	16	1

Source: European Conference of Ministers of Transport (1998) and Institut für Energie- und Umweltforschung and Studiengesellschaft für den kombinierten Verkehr (1995).

5.3. Evaluation still remains to be done

It is clear that we arrive at situations where it is necessary to compare energy savings or pollution reductions with the abatement costs; that is to say with the financial cost (in the case of an investment in rail) or with the reduction in travel or user surplus (if it has been decided to make the car more expensive or slower). It is therefore necessary to find monetary equivalents for the physical quantities involved.

There are, of course, major methodological difficulties involved in monetarizing these effects, but it has been the subject of a great deal of work. Based on a survey of this work, the ECMT has proposed the figures that are set out in Table 4, and which are expressed in ECU (the European monetary unit that preceded the Euro). Like Table 3, which gave physical indicators, this table shows that, overall, rail passenger transport has a considerable advantage over car transport with regard to pollution and safety. This advantage is even greater in the case of freight transport. However, rail is considerably noisier than the road for a similar level of service production.

Of course, the relative positions are changing, first because of progress stimulated by increasingly severe standards for road vehicles, and secondly because of the variable quality of the match between supply and demand, as this alters the loading rate of vehicles which we have seen to be decisive for the environmental efficiency of rail.

6. Conclusion

This all goes to show the extent to which a transport policy that aims to increase rail use requires rigorous socio-economic appraisals that must be conducted on a case-by-case basis. However, these rigorous appraisals involve themselves several prerequisites. These include not only the issue of energy or environmental efficiency but also a good knowledge of passenger or freight demand behavior; optimal pricing for managing this demand and financing investments; and a permanent discussion about the "good" monetary values of external effects. This means that the whole transport economics is concerned by the future of railways.

References

Dings, D. and W. Dijkstra (1997) *Specific energy consumption and emissions of freight transport*. Delft: CE.
European Conference of Ministers of Transport (1998) *Efficient transport for Europe. Policies for internalisation of external costs*. Paris: OECD.
Institut für Energie- und Umweltforschung and Studiengesellschaft für den kombinierten Verkehr (2002) *Comparative analysis of energy consumption and CO_2 emissions of road transport and combined transport road/rail*. Geneva: International Road Union.
Morellet, O. (2002) "Effet de différentes mesures de politique de transport visant à orienter la demande dans une région du type de l'Ile-de-France." Report for the Commissariat Général du Plan, Paris (unpublished).
Morellet, O. and P. Marchal (2001) "Demande de transport de personnes: une théorie unifiée de l'urbain à l'intercontinental," *Recherche Transport Sécurité*, 71:49–100.
Roos, J., A. Bleijenberg and W. Dijkstra (1997) *Energy use and emissions from aviation and other modes for long distance travel in Europe*. Delft: CE.

Chapter 17

ENVIRONMENTAL IMPACT ASSESSMENT FOR SUSTAINABLE TRANSPORT

SUNDER L. DHINGRA, K.V.K. RAO and V.M. TOM
Indian Institute of Technology, Bombay

1. Introduction

Environmental impact analysis (EIA) has been developed as a tool to address environmental issues in decision-making. Over the past few decades EIA systems have been adopted world-wide, and the EIA process has evolved to meet concerns about applying the decision-making process to strategic environment assessment. Humans have always exploited natural resources to achieve better living standards and for technological developments. Historically, human settlers burnt forests, constructed roads, manipulated river courses for navigational and agricultural purposes etc.; the environmental impacts of this activity were limited to the immediate locality. However, the environmental consequences triggered by the industrial revolution had wide and deeper consequences, which has led to a reactionary damage control measures during the middle of the last century. Fortunately, the focus has now shifted to the prediction and mitigation of impacts.

Economic, social, and environmental changes are inherent to development. While development aims to bring about positive changes, it can also lead to conflicts. The need to avoid adverse impacts and to ensure long-term benefits led to the concept of sustainability. This has become accepted as an essential feature of development, if the aim of increased well-being and greater equity in fulfilling basic needs is to be met for the present and future generations. In order to predict the environmental impacts of any development activity and to provide an opportunity to mitigate negative impacts and enhance positive impacts, the EIA procedure was developed. EIA may be defined as a formal process to predict the environmental consequences of human development activities and to plan appropriate measures to eliminate or reduce adverse effects and to augment positive effects. In EIA the environment is viewed as a system comprising human beings, fauna and flora, soil, water, air, the climate, and the landscape; and EIA is also concerned with the interaction between these components. EIA provides a unique opportunity to demonstrate ways in which the environment may be improved as part of the development process. EIA also predicts the conflicts and constraints between a proposed project, program, or sectoral plan and its environment. It indicates whether mitigation measures need to be incorporated to minimize problems. It also enables monitoring programs to be established to assess future impacts and provide data on which managers can take informed decisions to avoid environmental damage.

The impacts of transportation systems on human society and the environment are wide-ranging; they are not only environmental but also social and economic, since transportation systems may be both economically and environmentally inefficient. The major environmental concerns include air pollution, acidification, and climate change; while economic inefficiencies include direct and indirect subsidies and important external costs arising from accidents, congestion, and damage to health.

Any transportation project will have some impact on the environment. In the case of new roads penetrating undisturbed country, its impact could be profound. The general environmental pollution and damage caused by roads is closely associated with the level of economic activity. An increase in gross national product (GNP) is likely to lead to an increase in the environmental cost of transport. In actuality, environmental problems are likely to be ignored unless they are addressed in connection with specific projects. If there is to be any significant environmental impact, it is recommended that specialist advice from environmentalists and conservationists should be sought (United Nations, 1990). Some headway has to be made to consider at the very least the most severe environmental impacts arising from a proposed scheme in qualitative terms, if not quantitatively, by adopting suitable conservation strategies.

A sustainable condition for this planet is one in which there is stability for both social and physical systems, achieved through meeting the needs of the present without compromising the ability of future generations to meet their own needs (World Commission on Environment and Development, 1987). Our transportation decisions and investments today should expand, not limit, the economic, ecological, and social choices available to future generations.

Sustainable economics is usually seen as consisting of three interconnected components: ecological (or environmental), social (or human), and economic (Petts, 1999). The environmental component focuses on preserving the resilience and dynamic ability of biological and physical systems to adapt to change. The economic approach is based on the concept of the maximum flow of income while maintaining the stock of assets or capital that yields these benefits. The sociocultural aspect of sustainability focuses on eliminating poverty and defending the rights of the future generations. The aim is to maintain the stability of social and cultural systems and reducing destructive conflicts.

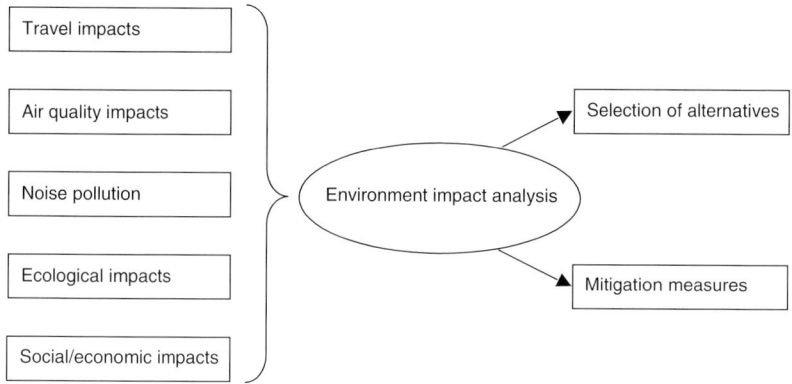

Figure 1. EIA implementation for transport.

2. The environmental impact assessment process

The EIA components and the process that is relevant to transport systems are presented in Figure 1. The various impacts of transportation projects on air quality, society, the economy, the ecology, and travel are considered, and are quantified so that alternative plans can be compared for their relative impact on the environment. The individual indices are converted to a combined environmental index by which different transport options are compared. The individual indices can also be compared with the relevant standards, and if the impact value exceeds a standard, appropriate mitigation measure can be suggested. Each of these components is discussed in detail in the following sections, followed by a case study to illustrate the methodology.

3. The transport model

The environmental impact of a transportation infrastructure project depends on the transport characteristics of the base year and the expected growth. The transport model predicts the traffic volumes and speeds for different vehicle modes for each transportation link under various transportation alternatives for the base year and the horizon year. For the study, the affected area is divided into different zones with identified road links. The model should generate separate networks for private vehicles and public transport modes. The transport model consists of different submodels, which include trip generation, trip distribution, and modal split. The trip generation submodel gives the relationship for trips generated and attracted for every zone. The trip distribution model predicts the trips between zone pairs, and the modal split identifies the proportion of trips for different modes. The underlying assumptions are that an individual selects a transport mode based on the perceived cost of travel by different traffic modes, which also internalizes the value of time. These trips are assigned to each road link based on volume of traffic. Speed–travel time curves are obtained that relate traffic flow to speed for private and public transport modes. Thus, the transport model provides output in the form of cars (or PCUs (passenger car units) in the case of heterogeneous traffic), vehicle speed, and vehicle-kilometers for cars and trucks on each road link of the study area. Transport models are described in more detail by Ortutzar and Willumsen (1996) and Hensher and Button (2000).

4. Air pollution

The most important environmental impact caused by transport is air pollution. The polluting factors include emission of acidifying and greenhouse gases such as carbon dioxide (CO_2) and nitrogen oxides (NO_x); and ambient air pollution caused by the emission of CO, NO_x, suspended particulate matter (SPM), etc. Most transport development activity has some adverse impact on air quality as it invariably increases vehicle mobility and thus emissions. Hence, there is a need to understand the nature of air pollution, and methods to quantify and to mitigate them.

A characteristic of transport-induced air pollution is that its source is linear in nature and has its own distinct emission traits. The impact of air pollution on humans, and on fauna and flora, are well understood. For example, consider the effects of two pollutants on humans: carbon monoxide exposure of 5.0–5.5% causes a significant decrease in maximal oxygen consumption, and the effects include cardiovascular, neurobehavioral and perinatal consequences; and short exposure (10–15 min) to nitrogen dioxide (NO_2) at a level of 3.0–9.4 mg/m^3 causes changes in pulmonary function.

Canter (1996) has identified six generic procedural steps in assessing air quality; identification of the air quality impact of the proposed project; description of the existing air quality; identification of relevant air quality standards; impact prediction; assessment of significant impacts; and identification of appropriate mitigation measures. An air pollution impact assessment procedure is:

(1) establish background air quality levels by conducting surveys;
(2) identify applicable air quality criteria and standards;
(3) forecast future air pollutant emissions from the proposed development;
(4) forecast future ambient air pollutant concentrations from the proposed development;
(5) develop air quality indices for quantitative evaluation and interpretation;

(6) compare the predicted ambient air quality levels with air quality standards;
(7) select alternatives or pollution mitigation measures.

The assessment starts by collection of information on the exiting baseline situation, which includes pollutant source and ambient air pollution concentrations; local climate and meteorological parameters; and local topography and land use characteristics. The lack of any information needs to be supplemented by baseline monitoring. An important issue in the assessment of air quality impact is the air quality standard by which the impacts are compared. Two aspects are important here: ambient air standards and emission standards. The former applies to the general ambient atmosphere, while the latter refers to the pollutant material emitted from a source to the ambient atmosphere. Every government has air quality standards at least as stringent as international standards. If the national standards do not match the international standards, this should be noted clearly in the assessment process.

The third step is predicting the future mode-wise pollutant emission of all vehicles. This involves predicting the traffic volume and modal split of vehicles for each transportation link within the area of influence based on the base year travel pattern and using demand forecasting models (Hensher and Button, 2000) The output of such models gives mode-wise traffic volume on a link. This information can be further processed to obtain the vehicle-kilometers of each mode and thereby the emissions level from vehicles on each link in the study area.

The fourth step is to ascertain the future ambient air pollutant concentration that will be caused by the transport project. This is done by gathering information on the general characteristics of the study area in relation to air dispersion. Different models exist for finding the pollutant dispersion along a stretch of road. The air quality model relates air pollutant emissions to the resulting ambient air pollutant concentrations under different topographical and environmental settings, including meteorological conditions. The output of the model gives the pollutant concentration at specified locations. The most commonly used basis for modeling pollutant dispersion is the Gaussian plume formulation, since this is less complex in nature and has proved to have higher correlation coefficients (Rao et al., 1980). The pollutant concentration C at a point specified by the y and z coordinates near a road is given by Watkins (1984):

$$C = \frac{QT}{2\pi\sigma_y\sigma_z u}\exp\left(-\frac{y^2}{2\sigma_y^2}\right)\left\{\exp\left[-\frac{1}{2}\left(\frac{z+H}{\sigma_z}\right)^2\right]+\exp\left[-\frac{1}{2}\left(\frac{z-H}{\sigma_z}\right)^2\right]\right\}, \quad (1)$$

where Q is the pollutant emission rate, T is the traffic flow in vehicles/hour, σ_y and σ_z are the standard deviations of the plume concentration distribution in the horizontal and vertical directions, u is the wind speed, and H is the emission height. Thus, C is calculated as the sum of contributions from a series of point source representatives of the road. The plume concentration standard deviation (σ_y and σ_z) depends on atmospheric stability, which is categorized according to wind speed, downwind speed, and cross-wind distances between the source and the receptor.

In the fifth step the model determines the values of indicators or indices to reflect the air quality impacts of the transportation alternatives on an area using the estimated pollutant concentrations from the previous step. Since there are a number of pollutants, a combined index considering all of them needs to developed for easy comparisons. Thus, an air pollution index (API) is devised to transform diverse data into a single quantity, and is defined as

$$\mathrm{API} = \frac{1}{4}\left(\frac{C_{SO_2}}{SO_{2\,std}} + \frac{C_{NO_x}}{NO_{x\,std}} + \frac{C_{SPM}}{SPM_{std}} + \frac{C_{CO}}{CO_{std}}\right), \qquad (2)$$

where C_{SO_2}, C_{NO_x}, C_{SPM}, and C_{CO} are the predicted concentrations of SO_2, NO_x, SPM, and CO, respectively, and $SO_{2\,std}$, $NO_{x\,std}$, SPM_{std}, and CO_{std} are the respective standards laid down. These standards are for a 24 h averaging period, except CO_{std}, which is for a 1 h averaging period. C_{SO_2}, C_{NO_x}, C_{SPM}, and C_{CO} are predicted concentration as obtained in the earlier step. It should be noted that all the pollutants are given equal weights in equation (2); however, based on one's experience, different weights can be assigned to the pollutants. The API obtained needs to be modified by considering the population of each of the grids in the study area by defining a population-weighted API, denoted API_{sr} and defined as

$$\mathrm{API}_{sr} = \frac{\sum Pd_i L_i w\, \mathrm{API}_i}{\sum Pd_i L_i w}, \qquad (3)$$

where Pd_i is the population density in the ith grid, L_i is the length of the link intercepting the grid in meters, API_i is the API developed for the ith grid, and W is the width of the impact corridor, taken as 150 m on either sides of the link. A higher value of API_{sr} for a subregion implies higher impacts in terms of exposure to air pollution by the population. The pollution index thus obtained for the study area considering the pollution of different components and the populations in the study area is used to compare different transportation options, and the best alternative can be selected for implementation.

5. Noise impact assessment

Transport development and operation activities are major sources of noise pollution; while the former is limited to the construction period, the latter affects the environment for a prolonged duration. Noise pollution is of two kinds: direct noise from road/rail vehicles, especially in heavily built-up areas; and vibration caused by heavy vehicles and trains. Although noise pollution is primarily just a nuisance, prolonged exposure to noise is harmful to humans, buildings, and underground services.

Noise pollution assessment studies are helpful in determining the noise generated by the use of transportation systems in the community. Akin to air pollution studies, the noise level of a new facility is estimated and compared with competent standards. Typically the study involves the following steps:

(1) identify the noise indicators;
(2) estimate the traffic parameters for each option;
(3) predict traffic-related noise using a transport noise model;
(4) assess the noise impact.

The first step in the noise impact study is the identification of a proper index that reflects the noise pollution level. However, the main difficulty in a noise impact study is the presence of a diverse noise scales and ratings. For example L_{10}, L_{50}, and L_{90} are some commonly used indices (Petts, 1999) which are defined as the weighted average noise levels in excess of 10, 50, and 90% of the time, respectively. The equivalent noise level (L_{eq}) is another indicator, defined as the average sound energy for an observer expressed in decibels. A model to calculate the equivalent sound level (L_{eq}) for an infinitely long roadway has been formulated based on Indian conditions by applying modifications to the model terms developed by the US Federal Highway Administration:

$$L_{eq\,i}(h) = \bar{L}_{OE\,i} + 10\log\left(\frac{N_i}{S_i T}\right) + 10\log\left(\frac{15}{d}\right)^{1+\alpha} + \delta_s - 15, \qquad (4)$$

where $L_{eq\,i}(h)$ is the L_{eq} at hour h for the ith vehicle type (cars, trucks, etc.), $\bar{L}_{OE\,i}$ is the reference mean sound level for the ith vehicle type (e.g. 55 dB for cars, 65 dB for trucks), N_i is the number of class i vehicles passing at time T in the particular road section, S_i is the average speed for the ith vehicle class (km/h) on the particular road section as obtained from survey results, T is the duration for which L_{eq} is desired, and must correspond to N_i ($T = 1$ h), d is the perpendicular distance (m) from the center line of the traffic lane to the location of the observer, α is a factor which relates to the adsorption characteristics of the ground cover between the roadway and the observer, and δ_s is the shielding factor provided by a noise barrier.

Noise generated from transport activity needs to be assessed separately. This is best captured in the traffic noise index (TNI), defined as the weighted sound level sampled at numerous discrete intervals out doors over a 24 h period. It is the weighted combination of L_{10} and L_{90} (Suzuki et al., 1989):

$$\text{TNI} = 4(L_{10} - L_{90}) + L_{90}^{-30} \qquad (5)$$

The TNI (considering noise-related standards) is defined as follows, with day and night defined separately. TNI_d is the percentage of the length of road links in a subregion exceeding the daytime standard ($L_{eq\,d}$) of 65 dBA for average commercial land use. TNI_n is the percentage of the length of road links in a subregion exceeding the nighttime standard ($L_{eq\,n}$) 55 dBA for average commercial land use (AIC Watson, 1996).

The second step is to predict the traffic composition and growth of traffic in the horizon year based on the traffic details of the base year, using the transport model discussed in Section 3.

The third step is to predict the noise level generated by the traffic using an appropriate noise prediction model. The noise prediction model is used to predict traffic noise for heavy and light vehicles for each road link at a distance of 30 m from the center of the road. The modeling exercise is repeated for each transport link in the study area, and the results are processed to calculate TNI values to facilitate comparison of noise impacts across the subregions and different alternatives. The noise impacts from traffic in urban settings with a high density of housing are highly localized, and mainly concentrated along road corridors. Hence, commuters and people living along major traffic corridors are the two population groups likely to be impacted by traffic noise. Traffic noise from the road/rail sections passing through green zones may also affect wildlife in these areas.

6. Ecological impacts

Ecological disturbances are not always well recognized and treated comprehensively because transportation systems and their components are usually planned, built, and operated locally, and on a project-by-project basis. Considered together over time, the individual disturbances emerge as a source of larger ecological perturbations that require innovative approaches to understand and control them. Transportation systems will have grave ecological consequences even if they do not emit any pollutants (Committee for a Study on Transportation, 2001) as they have a vast infrastructure. The pervasive road/rail network is itself a source of many environmental disturbances. The physical imprint of a road or railway line can alter the biological diversity of a region.

Two types of ecological impacts, namely direct and development induced, occur as a result of implementation of rail and road projects. Direct impacts are caused by destruction of flora and fauna owing to the construction of roads or railway lines. Since the introduction of roads and railway lines in a region is known to induce development in the area, hitherto virgin forests and wetlands could experience pressure for development. The severity of direct or development-induced impacts on the ecological resources of an area depends on the extent and

Table 1
Classification of natural ecosystems and their weights

Type of area	Weight
Natural vegetation with high species diversity and tree canopy cover >60%	4
Natural vegetation with moderate species diversity and tree canopy cover >30–60%	4
Natural vegetation with high species diversity and tree canopy cover of 30–60%	3
Natural vegetation with moderate species diversity and tree canopy cover of 30–60%	3
Scattered trees with 60% ground cover of herbs, grasses, and bushes (species diversity moderate to low)	2
Ground cover of natural vegetation less than 60% or the degradation of the area is irreversible	1

Source: AIC Watson (1996).

richness of these resources at the road/rail project site. The ecological impacts of the options for a transportation project are assessed at a qualitative level using the following framework:

(1) describe the location and existing ecological status of the relevant road/rail link for each option;
(2) assess qualitatively the direct and development-induced impacts;
(3) select mitigation measures.

In addition to providing qualitative analysis of ecological impacts, an attempt is also made to quantify these impacts so that a comparison of these impacts can be made across the proposed transport alternatives. The rationale used for quantifying ecological impacts is as follows:

- damage to an area from a road/rail scheme will be proportional to the length of the road/rail segment passing through the area;
- damage will be severe if the ecology of the area or system is of high quality.

Further, because of the difference in the degree of importance attached to natural and man-made ecological systems, the impacts on these two types of systems are considered separately. The ecological impact on each of the systems is measured by adding weights representing the quality of the system. Thus, ecological impact indices for the two systems can be expressed as $\sum Wn_i L_i$ and $\sum Wm_j L_j$, where Wn_i is the weight associated with or importance given to a natural ecological system of class i, Wm_j is the weight associated with or importance given to a man-made ecological system of class j, L_i is the total length of the road/rail link in the natural ecological system classified as category i, and L_j is the total length of road/rail link in the man-made ecological system classified as category j. Classification of ecological systems and the weights assigned to them are given in Tables 1 and 2 for natural and man-made systems, respectively. A higher weight

Table 2
Classification for agricultural land and associated weights

Type of area	Weight
Agricultural land with 2 crops or plantations with ground cover >60%	3
Agricultural land with 1 crop or plantation and ground cover of 30–60%	2
Fallow agricultural land or plantation with ground cover <30%	1

Source: AIC Watson (1996).

value indicates higher quality of an ecological area, which is thus more prone to suffering adverse impacts from a road/rail project. Thus, higher values of EI represent the potential for more adverse impacts on an ecological system.

7. Social and economic impacts

The ultimate aim of any transportation project is to improve the quality of life of people overall, but inevitably some will be adversely affected. The social and economic impacts can be broadly classified into four areas:

- community cohesion;
- economic development;
- traffic noise;
- land-use and visual quality.

The four effects are interrelated, but should be studied separately (Curry and Anderson, 1972).

The term "community cohesion" is used to describe patterns of social networking within a community. The effects of transportation projects on community cohesion "may be beneficial or adverse, and may include splitting neighborhoods, isolating a portion of a neighborhood or an ethnic group, generating new development, changing property values, or separating residents from community facilities" (US Federal Highway Administration, 1987). Table 3 lists the steps involved in community cohesion impact analysis.

One of the major social impacts of transportation projects is the relocation of businesses and housing. An appraisal of the social impacts for a region can be done using

$$\text{SI} = \sum N_{hi} \tag{6}$$

where SI is the social impact index for a subregion, N_{hi} is the number of households displaced owing to the ith project falling in the subregion. SI can be further improved by including other social effects along with their weights.

Table 3
Community cohesion impact analysis

Steps	Methods
(1) Define the study area	Interviews, focus groups, and surveys
(2) Collect information from community leaders and groups active in the community	Site analysis
	Maps and aerial photographs
(3) Spend time in the study area	Databases on structures
(4) Estimate the existing level of community cohesion	
(5) Extrapolate the project's effects in areas of relative cohesiveness	

Source: Forkenbrock and Weisbrod (2001).

Table 4
Economic development impact analysis

Steps	Methods
(1) Measure the transportation factors affecting economic development	Expert interviews
	Market studies
(2) Estimate the direct effect on business competitiveness	Case studies
	Computer models
(3) Estimate the direct effect on business growth or decline	Input-output models
(4) Estimate indirect, induced, and dynamic effects on economic development	

Source: Forkenbrock and Weisbrod (2001).

Economic development is the process through which economic activity in an area is expanded to provide more jobs and income to the residents. Economic development policies are generally designed to improve the quality of life by increasing incomes, job choices, activity choices, stability, and amenities. Table 4 lists the steps involved in economic impact analysis.

Traffic noise is defined as any unwanted sound. Though it does not have serious ill effects on health unless a person is exposed for a very long time, it is a major source of nuisance in a community and severely affects the quality of life. Table 5 lists the steps involved in noise impact analysis.

Transportation projects can drastically alter land-use patterns. Moreover, they have a significant visual effect on the surrounding built environment when they require new structures to be built, older structures to be torn down, or change the view of pleasant settings. It is important to consider the magnitude of the effect that a project has on visual quality by making an assessment regarding its suitability within and compatibility with its particular urban setting. Table 6 lists the steps involved in land-use and visual quality impact analysis.

Table 5
Noise impact analysis and methods

Steps	Methods
(1) Define the impact area and affected land uses and activities	Look-up tables (TNMLOOK)
(2) Do an initial screening analysis	Traffic noise prediction models
(3) Determine the existing noise level	
(4) Predict traffic noise levels resulting from the transportation project	
(5) Identify and evaluate noise effects	
(6) Identify construction noise effects	

Source: Forkenbrock and Weisbrod (2001).

Table 6
Visual quality impact analysis

Steps	Methods
(1) Define the study area	Visual preference surveys
(2) Determine the changes to be considered and possible alternatives	Analogous case studies
	Artist's sketches
(3) Select a medium or media to simulate and present the environment	Photo-realism techniques
	GIS-based approaches
(4) Identify respondents who will observe the environment and assess the likely effects of the project	Virtual metropolitan models
(5) Develop a procedure to record observer responses to the environment	
(6) Analyze the responses and provide feedback	

Source: Forkenbrock and Weisbrod (2001).

8. Travel impacts

The various links in a network are interdependent. The nature of traffic flow in a link affects the flow characteristics in others. Hence, it is necessary to take into consideration the effect of a project on the entire system (Schade and Rothengatter, 2001). The high investment options will obviously be associated with higher levels of adverse environmental impacts. Therefore, comparison of the environmental impacts of options for a transportation project alone is not sufficient to decide the merits of each of the alternatives. The environmental impacts should be considered in conjunction with the transportation and social benefits offered by the alternatives to arrive at an appropriate transport strategy for the region. Two indices used to reflect transportation objectives are the traffic congestion index (TCI) and the transport efficiency index (TEI) (AIC Watson, 1996). These indices are defined in such a manner that they are commensurate with other environmental impact indicators/indices. In other words, if the lowest value of the population-weighted API is a desirable value, then the lowest value of TCI will also be desirable.

8.1. Transport congestion indicator

TCI is defined as the percentage of link length in a subregion exceeding a traffic volume to capacity ratio (V/C) of 0.7 for inter-city areas and 0.87 for downtown areas (0.7 and 0.87 correspond to class C and class D levels of service, respectively), and is obtained directly from the transport model. This is related to the level of service (LOS), which is indicated in terms of V/C. LOS is defined as the TCI of the link length in a subregion exceeding the V/C value of 0.87. TCI measures the congestion level in a region, and needs to be calculated for all options in a transport project.

8.2. Transport efficiency index

This index is important from the viewpoint of representing energy efficiency and reduction in the pollution potential of the transportation alternatives. TEI is well established with respect to optimum vehicle speed. However, it should be borne in mind that vehicular pollution at speeds other than the optimum can also be high. The optimum speed for light and heavy vehicles is 65 and 45 km/h, respectively, based on the fact that road conditions in the study area not allowing higher speeds, and that vehicles should at least be run at the lower end of the optimum speed range. TEI is defined by the following expression:

$$\text{TEI} = 0.5 \left(\frac{\sum \text{PCU}_{li} |1 - S_{li}/65|}{\sum \text{PCU}_{li}} + \frac{\sum \text{PCU}_{hi} |1 - S_{hi}/45|}{\sum \text{PCU}_{hi}} \right), \tag{7}$$

where PCU_{li} is the passenger car unit for light vehicles for road link i. PCU_{hi} is the passenger car unit for heavy vehicles for road link i. S_{li} is the average speed of light vehicles on link i, and S_{hi} is the average speed of heavy vehicles on link i.

TEI encapsulates the concept that vehicles operating close to their optimum speeds will be fuel-efficient and less polluting. However, the index is deliberately defined to reflect efficiency in terms of energy utilization and pollution generation, so that the TEI value is directly proportional to the adverse impact. TEI will be close to zero if vehicles are operating efficiently at near-optimum speeds. Both TSI and TEI need to be calculated for each transportation alternative and subregion. In this way, the various transportation options in a scheme can be evaluated with respect to their environmental impacts as well as their transportation objectives.

9. Implementation of EIA

An approach of disaggregating and computation followed by aggregation is used to obtain EIA for the three possible project types, namely intercity, intracity, and rural. The steps in this process are:

(1) disaggregation, which is done by dividing the project region into subregions followed by division of each subregion into grids;
(2) development of indices to represent the source–impact framework identified earlier for a subregion to calculate the impacts;
(3) aggregation, to arrive at EI.

The procedure for the aggregation of indices in terms of EI is

$$\text{EI} = \frac{\sum W_i I_i}{\sum I_i} \qquad (8)$$

where W_i is the weight attached to the ith index and I_i is the ith value of the index. The formula for EI thus has the feature of normalization to account for the different scale of each index. The weights attached are decided by the opinion of experts in various fields such as transportation, ecology, and the social sciences.

10. A case study

10.1. The Mumbai Urban Transport Project

An environmental impact assessment study of the city of Mumbai, on the west coast of the Indian subcontinent – the Mumbai Urban Transport Project II (MUTP-II; AIC Watson 1996) – is discussed in this section. The study area covers 4164 km^2. The aim of the study was to evaluate the impact of six transportation options/alternatives, which consider different degrees of investment for road and rail projects. Each of these options is aimed at increasing the transport infrastructure in the region. These six options are listed in Table 7.

The environmental resources of the Mumbai region must not be damaged by transport projects. To ensure this goal is achieved, EIA has been done at three levels: sectoral, programmatic, and project 'micro' levels.

Table 7
Summary of transport options for the Mumbai area for EIA comparison

Option	Transport improvement strategy
1	Minimum intervention on road/rail
2	Moderate rail investment: establish new rail link and use extra rolling stock
3	High rail investment: construct rail corridor and enhance existing services
4	Demand management and high rail investment
5	Moderate road investment: improve the highways by road widening and building fly-overs
6	High road investment: development of highway network with new fly-overs, by-passes, etc., as build–operate–transfer projects

Sectoral level environmental assessment is conducted by distinguishing between significant positive and negative impacts, direct and indirect impacts, or immediate and long-term impacts of a proposed transportation strategy. It evaluates the impact quantitatively and, wherever feasible, in terms of environmental costs and benefits by assigning economic value. Programmatic level environmental assessment is conducted for subprojects such as pedestrian subways, road over bridges (ROBs)/road under bridges (RUBs), fly-overs, and traffic management schemes that will be replicated in the project, to identify impacts and develop generic mitigation measures. At the project or micro level, fully fledged EIA is required: various alternatives are examined and compared (which include planning, design, technology selection, construction techniques, and phasing), including a "do nothing" option in terms of potential environmental impacts, incorporating noise and air quality assessment, to quantify the costs and benefits of each alternative considering the cost of mitigation measures. The sectoral level environmental assessment is described below.

10.2. The EIA process

A sectoral level EIA strategy was formulated to evaluate the transport options. The steps involved are summarized below. In the first step, the study area was divided into four sectors, namely Island city, western suburbs, eastern suburbs, and the rest of the MMR (Mumbai Metropolitan Region). The classification is based on the distinct land use and the economic and transportation characteristics of an area. In the second step, to assess the impact of the transportation projects the following areas were studied:

- transport modeling;
- air quality impacts, since each transportation option affects the vehicular composition differently;
- noise impacts, again owing to different vehicular compositions for each option;
- ecological and land use impacts, as the construction of transportation facilities may cause ecological impacts on adjoining areas;
- social and economic impacts.

10.3. Transport modeling

For transport modeling the study area was divided into 110 zones, with about 1200 links and about 500 bus and rail routes covering all sectors. Separate networks for the private and public transport modes were created for the model.

10.4. Air quality impacts

Air quality indices were used to determine the baseline air quality of the study area as a whole and of each sector. A comparison of the ambient air pollutant concentration levels resulting from the transport options with ambient air quality standards provided a measure of the impacts. API is used as the parameter for comparison, since this will give a single index, taking care of all the major pollutant concentrations. The Central Pollution Control Board (CPCB) has established ambient air quality standards against which the API of each sector can be compared.

For calculations of API, each sector was subdivided into square grids, and pollution monitoring carried out for 3 days or more at various locations. These monitored pollutant concentration values were used to estimate baseline concentrations at the center of each grid by using the inverse squares weighted interpolation, incorporating the influence of prevailing wind pattern and topographical features.

A simple air dispersion model was used which relates vehicular emission to the ambient air pollutant concentration under different environmental settings. The roll-back model was used, which is a simple proportionate reduction model based on the assumption that a reduction in pollutant emissions proportionately reduces the resulting ambient air pollutant concentrations.

Vehicular emissions were assigned to a grid, based on the length of links intercepted by the grid and the respective vehicle-kilometers. The modal split and emission levels for each vehicle-kilometer were also used in the model. The base year emission and concentration estimates for grids in each subregion and for each pollutant were related using a simple regression technique. Equations are thus obtained for each pollutant from a different transport option in a sector. The impact on air quality for people living near (defined as 150 m in this study) the major roads was used to weight the API. These population-weighted pollutant indices were computed as follows:

$$\text{API}_w = \frac{\sum \text{Pd}_j L_j w\, \text{API}_j}{\sum \text{Pd}_j L_j w}, \qquad (9)$$

where Pd_j is the population density for grid j, L_j is the total road length in grid j (with an area of 150 × 150 m), and API_j is the API estimated for grid j. This procedure was repeated for each sector. The API results for the Island city sector are given in Table 8.

10.5. Noise impacts

The noise impacts were assessed for all the sectors. As an example, consider the Island city sector, which has 143 major road links. Although the transportation alternatives will not alter the number of these road links or the total road length in the subregion, these options are likely to affect traffic noise levels. The transport model estimates the traffic parameters required to be used in the noise prediction model. The US Federal Highway Administration model (equation (4)) was used to predict noise levels at a distance of 30 m from the road center line for each road link in a sector for both the base year and horizon year. Traffic noise indicators for daytime and nighttime are calculated to represent the noise impacts on populations living adjacent to road corridors for all transport options in a sector. The results for the Island city sector are given in Table 8.

10.6. Ecological impacts

In the Island city sector only two options have the potential to affect the area's ecology. In the first scenario a rail section will need to be constructed, but closer examination indicates that ecological damage will not occur. The other option involves the construction of a freeway, which could affect the marine ecosystem, as the freeway will run close to the coast. A detailed environmental study was conducted for the latter option, and is reported in Table 8. Other sectors were similarly studied.

10.7. Social impacts

The Island city sector has a high commercial activity, mainly in the form of small shops. Obviously traffic improvements will reduce congestion and improve the flow. However, the construction and operation phase may cause adverse effects such as the disruption of traffic and visual obstructions. A similar approach was adopted to investigate societal impacts in the other sectors.

10.8. Travel impacts

The rail and road schemes in the various alternatives aim to achieve certain traffic objectives. TEI and TCI were used to provide an overall comparison of the impacts of the different transport options. Table 8 presents the results for the Iisland city sector.

10.9. EIA evaluation

The purpose of the Mumbai environmental analysis was to assist decision-makers to finalize a transportation strategy for the area. To achieve this it is necessary that the impacts of the alternative transportation schemes are compared. To facilitate the comparison of impacts across the six transport options, various impacts were quantified by using indicators and indices. These indicators and indices were defined in such a way that they are consistent when reflecting the order of impacts. In other words, the higher a value, the greater the adverse impacts on the environment. The various indices were then combined to form a single environmental index by using appropriate weights. The procedures used to determine these weights are described below. About a dozen experts from the disciplines of transportation, planning and environmental management, ecology, town planning, sociology, and environmental engineering were invited to participate in this process. The group members were first asked to allocate 100 points among the four main impact categories, i.e. pollution, ecological, social, and transportation impacts. Each member was requested to provide a rationale for distributing the points, so that other members could have the opportunity to modify their scores with the objective of arriving at a distribution of points satisfactory to all the members. The distribution of points or weights arrived at are shown in Table 9. After determining the first level of weights, the weight associated with each impact type was further distributed among the indices identified under that impact type. The assessment indices obtained earlier were multiplied by the appropriate weights after normalizing them. The normalized values are shown in Table 10, and the product of the weights and normalized values are given in Table 11.

Similarly, the EI for each sector was determined (Table 12). To compare the environmental impacts of the various transport options the consolidated EI was computed for all the options for the horizon year. To achieve this the indices of each transport option were normalized by dividing by an indicator value. The sum

Ch. 17: Environmental Impact Assessment for Sustainable Transport 327

Table 8
The environmental impact values of different indices for the Island city sector

	API_{sr}	TNI_d	TNI_n	EI_1	EI_2	SI	TEI	TCI
Base year	312.8	61.4	91.5	0	0	0	0.56	10.8
Option 1	343.0	65.4	92.07	0	0	0	0.52	12.5
Option 2	338.0	65.4	95.03	0	0	0	0.52	11.0
Option 3	376.0	65.4	95.03	0	0	0	0.52	12.8
Option 4	240.0	63.7	98.73	0	0	0	0.46	6.9
Option 5	352.0	67.7	94.99	0	0	0	0.52	9.6
Option 6	332.0	70.3	95.73	0	0	0	0.50	7.7

Table 9
Weights assigned to various indices for the Island city sector

Index	Weight
API_{sr}	18
TNI_d	2.7
TNI_n	5.3
EI_1	18
EI_2	9
SI	15
TEI	12
TCI	20
Total	100

Table 10
Normalized index values for the Island city sector

	API_{sr}	TNI_d	TNI_n	EI_1	EI_2	SI	TEI	TCI
Option 1	0.17	0.16	0.16	0.00	0.00	0.00	0.17	0.21
Option 2	0.17	0.16	0.17	0.00	0.00	0.00	0.17	0.18
Option 3	0.19	0.16	0.17	0.00	0.00	0.00	0.17	0.21
Option 4	0.12	0.16	0.17	0.00	0.00	0.00	0.15	0.11
Option 5	0.18	0.17	0.17	0.00	0.00	0.00	0.17	0.16
Option 6	0.17	0.18	0.17	1.00	0.00	0.00	0.16	0.13

of the normalized index values for all the transport options is given in Table 12. The normalized values for each transport option are multiplied by their respective weights and added together to compute the EI for that transport option for that sector, as shown in Table 12.

Table 11
Weighted index values for the island city sector

	API_{sr}	TNI_d	TNI_n	EI_1	EI_2	SI	TEI	TCI	EIA score
Option 1	3.12	0.44	0.86	0	0	0	2.1	4.13	10.65
Option 2	3.07	0.44	0.89	0	0	0	2.0	3.64	10.04
Option 3	3.42	0.44	0.89	0	0	0	2.0	4.22	10.97
Option 4	2.18	0.43	0.92	0	0	0	1.8	2.27	7.60
Option 5	3.20	0.45	0.89	0	0	0	2.1	3.19	9.83
Option 6	3.01	0.47	0.89	18	0	0	2.0	2.55	26.92
Weight	18	2.67	5.33	18	9	15	12	20	100

Table 12
EI scores for the study area and the four sectors

Option	Mumbai (study area)	Island city (sector 1)	Western suburbs (sector 2)	Eastern suburbs (sector 3)	Rest of MMR (sector 4)
Option 1	12.40	10.65	11.24	11.16	12.35
Option 2	16.10	10.04	16.73	15.10	13.18
Option 3	16.20	10.97	16.82	14.34	13.97
Option 4	15.78	7.60	17.29	15.33	12.73
Option 5	18.89	9.83	14.07	22.76	22.98
Option 6	20.78	26.92	14.87	21.33	24.82

10.10. Inferences

From the EI score it is obvious that option 1 is the preferred alternative. However, all the options have EI scores within a narrow range; consequently, the financial implications of each option become the deciding factor. Option 6 was selected as the preferred option, considering both EI and the financial aspects.

11. Conclusion

In this chapter an attempt has been made to provide a methodology for environmental impact assessment of any transportation project, thereby leading to a sustainable transportation infrastructure. The contribution of policy decisions based on EIA to achieve the goal of sustainable development has been studied. It can be seen that EIA-based policies and implementation go a long way toward minimizing negative environmental impacts and paving the way for all-round development on environmental, social, and economic fronts. The criteria used to identify critical environmental impacts have been clearly stated. The impacts of transportation on the atmosphere have been examined, and a methodology to quantify the effects of the various pollutants into a single index proposed. Noise pollution caused by traffic has been examined, and its various sources identified, and indices to quantify these have also been proposed. The ecological impacts of transport networks, and an index pertaining to this (EI), have been given. Social and economic impacts of transportation have been listed, and a methodology to gauge their effects provided. The impacts of transportation in terms of travel have been studied, and indices to quantify congestion and efficiency obtained.

A case study has been described that demonstrates the proposed EIA methodology for the city of Mumbai, India. The study illustrates the methodology presented above. In this study, EI has been evaluated for different investment options, and the best option thus identified. However, it is possible that this study may have overlooked certain factors that could have major significance in the future. Future work needs to be done toward deriving a comprehensive sustainability index that incorporates such factors as and when they are recognized.

References

AIC Watson (1996) *MUTP II. Sectoral level environmental assessment.* Mumbai: AIC Watson.
Canter, L.W. (1996) *Environmental impact assessment*, 2nd edn. New York: McGraw Hill.
Committee for a Study on Transportation (2001) *Toward a sustainable future. Transportation Research Board Special Report*, No. 251. Washington, DC: Transportation Research Board.
Curry, D.A. and D.G. Anderson (1972) *Procedures for estimating for highway user costs, air pollution and noise effects. National Cooperative Highway Research Program*, Report 133. Washington, DC: Transportation Research Board.
Forkenbrock, D.J. and G.E. Weisbrod (2001) *Guidebook for assessing the social and economic effects of transportation projects. National Cooperative Highway Research Program*, No. 456. Washington, DC: Transportation Research Board.
Hensher, D.A. and K.J. Button, eds (2000) *Handbook of transport modelling.* Oxford: Pergamon.
Ortuzar, J. de D. and L.G. Willumsen (1996) *Modelling transport*, 2nd edn. Chichester: Wiley.
Petts, J., ed.(1999) *Handbook of environment impact assessment*, Vol. 1. Malden: Blackwell Science.
Rao, S.T., G. Sistla, M.T. Keenan and S.T. Wilson, (1980) "An evaluation of some commonly used Highway dispersion models," *Journal of the Air Pollution Control Association,* 30:239–246.
Schade, W. and W. Rothengatter (2001) *Strategic sustainability analysis: broadening existing assessment approaches for transport policies. Transportation Research Board Record*, No. 1756. Washington, DC: Transportation Research Board.
Suzuki, Y., P.S. Pak and G. Kim (1989) "Impact analysis of construction of Kansai international airport," *Journal of Urban Planning and Development,* 115:33–49.
United Nations (1990) *Environmental impact assessment. Guidelines for transport development.* New York: UN.
Velmurugan, S. (1994) "Environmental Impact Assessment of Highway Projects," PhD Thesis. Bombay: Civil Engineering Department, Indian Institute of Technology.
Watkins, L.H. (1984) *Environmental impact of roads and traffic.* Amsterdam: Applied Science.
World Commission on Environment and Development ("The Brundtland Commission") (1987) *Our common future.* Oxford: Oxford University Press.

Part 3

APPRAISAL AND VALUATION ISSUES

Chapter 18

TRANSPORT INVESTMENT APPRAISAL AND THE ENVIRONMENT

PETER NIJKAMP, BARRY UBBELS and ERIK VERHOEF
Free University, Amsterdam

1. Introduction

Investment appraisal is an important issue in transport planning and policy. The investments are usually long lasted, practically irreversible, and costly, and may at the same time have a great impact on people's lives and the development of communities and regions. Investment decisions should therefore be well thought through, and various alternatives should be compared carefully before making a final choice. The most widely applied appraisal technique in transport is cost–benefit analysis (CBA). CBA essentially compares the projected future stream of benefits from a project with its initial and future costs. It thus allows a ranking of several competing projects or project variants, or a decision not to undertake any of these. Investment decisions on transport investment are usually made by public authorities, often motivated by infrastructure's (sometimes merely perceived) "public good" character[a]. Besides, uncertainty in future patronage and relatively high fixed costs make private parties only rarely interested in investing in transport infrastructure. Consequently, the central criterion employed in practical transport investment appraisal is often related to the project's contribution to social welfare – often operationalized as social surplus – rather than the more narrow criterion of profits that a private enterprise would use.

The evaluation of projects is not straightforward. It should identify key consequences of a proposed project and provide quantitative information about them. The various types of effects should next be made comparable, so that a

---

[a] A good is said to be a "public good" when its consumption satisfies two criteria, namely "non-rivalry" (the consumption by one actor does not reduce availability for other actors) and non-excludability (it is practically or economically impossible to exclude, through prices, an actor from consuming the good). A standard example of a public good concerns protection from floods through dykes. A free market will typically not lead to an efficient supply of public goods. See Varian (1992) for a detailed discussion.

Handbook of Transport and the Environment, Edited by D.A. Hensher and K.J. Button
© *2003, Elsevier Ltd*

Table 1
Some of the principal effects resulting from the construction of a road

Traffic economy and road maintenance	Environmental and land-use effects	Regional development
Traffic safety Travel time Comfort Vehicle costs Maintenance User benefits	Noise Air pollution Barrier effects Water pollution Vibrations Landscape/scenery Nature conservation Land development	Regional economic growth, employment, and trade balance Effects for trade, industry and tourism

Source: adapted from Button (1993a).

choice can be made in the typical case where different project alternatives would score better on different criteria, and no strictly dominant alternative is available. In CBA, the aim is to accomplish this by expressing the effects in the same units (money), so that trade-offs between different types of effects can be made. Transport investments are, however, characterized by a wide variety of effects, most of them long-lasting and sometimes hard to quantify in terms of monetary equivalents. One specific type of effect, which is difficult to measure, is central in this discussion: environmental effects. The construction and subsequent use of infrastructure will have important external effects (such as noise pollution and emissions) that have to be included in a social evaluation as they affect the welfare of society. This contribution will discuss some key issues that will play a role in transport investment appraisal when environmental externalities[a] are present.

2. Transport infrastructure investment and appraisal methods

The main principle of economic investment appraisal is straightforward. A profit-maximizing firm should, in the absence of budget constraints, undertake investments when the projected financial "net present value" – the present value of a discounted stream[b] of current and future net revenues – is positive. For public investments, the main difference would be that instead of profit maximization, social welfare maximization should be the main objective steering investment decisions. While

---

[a] An externality or external effect is said to exist when the behavior of the one actor directly affects the well-being of another actor, while there is no market on which the effect is traded. A standard example of an externality concerns air pollution. A free market will typically not lead to an efficient outcome when external effects exist (see Varian, 1992).

there are many complexities in undertaking commercial investment appraisal (e.g. allowing for risk of unexpected changes in demand), public investment appraisal has attracted most attention in the transport literature. The wide-ranging and long-term effects of most major changes in transport infrastructure necessitate the employment of sophisticated methods of project appraisal and of comprehensive techniques for decision-making. For example, the wide range of effects that have to be taken into account with investment for a road (see Table 1).

This wide range of effects may make it very difficult for policy-makers to decide whether a project is worthwhile to undertake, or to rank competing projects. A skillfully performed project appraisal will thus be helpful in structuring information. The rise in the development of appraisal techniques for transport projects came in the late 1960s and early 1970s (Grant-Muller et al., 2001). Key topics of research in those days included the measurement of the relevant monetary values for time and safety benefits. This work found its application in the appraisal of individual large projects, in the development of standard appraisal methods for smaller projects such as new sections of road, and in the assessment of city and regional transport plans.

CBA is the common basis for most appraisal frameworks. It aims at expressing all relevant effects of a particular project in a common *numéraire*, namely in monetary terms – hence costs and benefits. Despite its appeal, several limitations exist and are well recognized. Two major weaknesses often mentioned include the unavailability of accurate estimates of shadow prices for various effects, and the method's often implicit assumption that different types of effects can be regarded as "additive substitutes," meaning that these effects can be traded off on a dollar-for-dollar basis. As a consequence, several complementary approaches have been employed, such as cost-effectiveness analysis, planning balance sheet methods, and shadow project approaches. An alternative approach may be objectives led, with the goal of maximizing with respect to a set of socially based objectives rather than market values. Multicriteria analysis (MCA) typifies this approach. MCA is often seen as competing with CBA, although there is no fundamental reason why the

---

[b]Discounting of future costs and benefits is a procedure that aims to account for the fact that future costs and benefits at present have a lower value than current costs and benefits of the same size. For instance, with a constant market interest rate of 5%, receiving $100 now and putting it in a bank account is equivalent to receiving $1.05 \times \$100 = \$105$ in 1 year's time, or $1.05 \times 1.05 \times \$100 = \$110.25$ in 2 years' time. Similarly, the obligation to pay $100 in 1 year's time is equivalent to the obligation to pay $\$100/1.05 = \$95.24$ immediately: putting that amount of money in a bank account suffices to pay the $100 1 year later. Time discounting reflects these principles, and the net present value of a project that involves costs C_t and benefits B_t in years t, with a lifetime of T years and a constant interest rate of r can accordingly be calculated as

$$\text{NPV} = \sum_{t=0}^{T} \frac{B_t - C_t}{(1+r)^t}$$

(see also Mackie and Nellthorp, 2001).

two approaches may not be used in an entirely complementary manner within an overall framework. It has been argued that that the efficiency check on transport decisions can most properly be carried out by means of CBA methods, while equity and sustainability checks need broader approaches, based on MCA approaches (SAMI, 2000). For an overview of MCA in the context of environmental evaluation, the reader is referred to Janssen and Munda (1999).

Transport has proved a fruitful area for the application of CBA techniques. Most European national frameworks now have CBA at their core (Grant-Muller et al., 2001). Therefore, we will say more about CBA below, and will consider the role of environmental effects in transport investment appraisal mainly from the perspective of CBA.

3. CBA in transport: some issues relevant for environmental appraisal

The basic philosophy of CBA can be traced back to the writings of Dupuit (1844). It is essentially not a purely accounting system but an evaluation method based on applied welfare theory. It seeks to determine the net social surplus of public investments or of institutional decisions. Prest and Turvey (1965) defined CBA as a practical way of assessing the desirability of projects for which it is important to take a long view (looking at repercussions in the future) and a wide view (allowing for side-effects of many kinds). Since the function of public investment is to advance social welfare, CBA is employed in public investment decisions where market imperfections require that a wider viewpoint is adopted than that of the private profit maximizing investor. This makes CBA very useful to appraise transport investments, where the government is most often the investor. Transport was therefore amongst the first fields in which CBA came into regular application. For instance, in the UK two of the classical seminal applications of the technique were the studies of the M1 motorway and of the Victoria Line – an underground railway line in London (Nash, 1993). Following these studies, techniques were developed for the routine appraisal of road schemes and of public transport schemes where these have a social intent.

Many detailed reviews on CBA in transport are available, including Nash (1993), Small (1999), Mackie and Nellthorp (2001), and Grant-Muller et al. (2001); and Hanley (1999) considers CBA from the perspective of environmental policy and management. It is certainly not our purpose to redo the work in these reviews here, or to provide another overview of the essentials of CBA in transport investment appraisal. Very briefly, the major steps would include, after the determination of a sufficiently broad set of project alternatives to be considered, for every project (alternative): (1) an assessment and quantification of all the alternative's relevant effects – relative to some well-defined "base" scenario – in current and future periods; (2) the expression of these effects in monetary terms;

(3) the discounting of these costs and benefits to make them comparable to costs and benefits in the current period; (4) so that eventually the project's net present value (NPV) can be determined. Instead, we will focus on a few aspects of CBA in transport that are particularly relevant for the appraisal of environmental effects.

3.1. Welfare measurement in applied CBAs: social surplus

CBA typically uses consumer surplus (CS) as the operational measure for benefits. This measure has some well-recognized theoretical properties that make it less attractive than Hicksian welfare measures such as compensating and equivalent compensation (CV and EV; see Varian, 1992) from a theoretical perspective. In particular, CS is not an exact monetary measure for welfare changes, and need not be uniquely defined if multiple prices or quantities change simultaneously. However, these drawbacks are often taken for granted, as a countervailing immediate advantage of CS is that it is based on more or less directly observable market demand functions by taking individuals' willingness to pay as the basis for the determination of benefits. Moreover, Willig (1976) has argued rather convincingly that the discrepancy between CS and the theoretically more correct measures of CV or EV need not be large in applied work, and may often be negligible when compared with other uncertainties inherently present in practical appraisals – especially when income effects due to the projects considered are relatively small. The costs are, when appropriate, measured in market prices. If social values however differ from market prices when the latter do not properly reflect marginal social costs (one instance would be wages under high involuntary unemployment, another concerns environmental pollution for which no market price generally exists), so-called shadow prices are used instead to calculate the social costs involved in the project. A number of techniques that have been used for determining shadow prices of pollution and environmental quality are discussed in Section 4.2, where it will be explained that, consistent with the CBA methodology, these also typically seek to assess society's willingness to pay to prevent pollution.

3.2. CBA under various "second-best" conditions

If transport investments took the form of continuous rather than discrete expansions, and if the transport system and the spatial economic system it serves operated under first-best conditions with all prices reflecting marginal social costs, CBA would be relatively straightforward – at least if the prediction of effects were not too difficult and reliable shadow prices for each of these were available. However, the discreteness of most projects prevents marginal analyses from being appropriate. One implication is that induced demand effects must be taken into good consideration, at the risk of obtaining seriously biased results otherwise (Williams and Moore, 1990; Small, 1992). And second-best conditions prevailing (with non-optimal prices in transport or related markets) will typically mean that induced indirect effects from the investment – be it elsewhere in the network, in other transport modes, or in economic sectors other than transport – may imply substantial indirect welfare effects that ought to be accounted for in CBA.

For instance, an important feature of transport that often complicates applied welfare analyses is that it usually manifests itself on a network. As a result, the benefits and costs associated with the addition of a link (e.g. a road) to an existing network, or the expansion of its capacity under conditions of congestion, will typically not be confined to that link itself. Instead, re-routing, rescheduling, and other behavioral responses will generally occur after an investment, until a new network equilibrium is reached. This means that costs and benefits may change for links and origin–destination pairs throughout the network, and will not be confined to the link where the investment takes place. Especially when the use of the network at these other links is not optimized from the social perspective through optimal pricing (i.e. when second-best conditions apply), these induced changes may constitute substantial welfare effects that ought to be taken into account in a comprehensive CBA.

In applied work, the network-wide welfare effects of an improvement of a single link of that network are often approximated using the so-called rule of half, which would be a precise measure for surplus changes only if all demand and cross-demand functions would be linear (Button, 1993a). This rule estimates the total welfare of an improvement as the sum over all user groups of the average use level for a group (averaged over the situation without and with the project carried out), multiplied by the change in average (per user in that group) generalized costs (e.g. Mackie and Nellthorp, 2001). These generalized costs include all costs experienced by a user of the network, typically encompassing both monetized (e.g. fuel) and non-monetized (e.g. the valuation of travel time) components. The importance of considering such network effects in CBA is illustrated dramatically by the well-known "Braess paradox" (Braess, 1968), according to which the addition of a link to a congested network on which no optimal congestion prices are set can actually increase total travel costs.

Network effects are also important to consider when estimating the environmental impacts of an improvement in a single link. Even when only total emissions, over the entire network, would be relevant for determining the environmental costs, as would for instance seem appropriate for the emission of greenhouse gases, it is important to correct the measured change in emissions on the link itself for induced changes elsewhere on the network. These changes can involve both decreases (e.g. for parallel links) and increases (e.g. for serial links, when expanded capacity generates additional traffic). Calculating these changes requires predicting the new network equilibrium that will arise once the project investigated is completed. Whether induced increases or decreases in traffic elsewhere in the network will lead to additional welfare gains or welfare losses will depend on whether those links are initially underpriced or overpriced. Contrary to popular belief, overpricing need not be exceptional in road transport, given prevailing rates of gasoline taxes; especially not in off-peak travel (e.g. Parry and Bento, 2002). In such cases, induced increases in traffic may lead to net welfare increases, despite the induced increase in emissions.

Things may become further complicated when the marginal environmental costs associated with a given unit of emissions vary over time or place (e.g. over links). For instance, when seen from the environmental perspective, the expansion of a ring road around a city may induce negative environmental effects owing to the generation of additional traffic or perhaps due to the increase in average trip lengths, but may generate positive environmental effects to the extent it succeeds in attracting traffic previously using the inner-city network, where marginal external environmental costs may be significantly higher owing to the greater population density, the closer proximity of recipients of the emissions, or because "stop-and-go" inner-city traffic will typically cause higher emissions per vehicle-kilometer. Likewise, an expansion of capacity may lead to the occurrence of the so-called "return-to-the-peak" phenomenon. In addition to the implied direct benefits (people travel closer to the preferred time) and costs (congestion will not reduce by as much as it would without a return-to-the-peak), this may again affect the marginal environmental external costs of a given user, and thus affect the project's environmental costs. A positive indirect environmental effect of a return to the peak, compared with the situation where people would not adjust their behavior following the capacity expansion, would occur if these marginal costs are lower in the peak than outside it, as may be the case for noise annoyance: an extra car will have a very limited impact on total traffic noise in peak travelling but may be a distinct nuisance outside the peak period. A negative indirect effect occurs in the reverse situation, for instance when the emissions per vehicle-kilometer are higher in stop-and-go peak travel, or at low average speeds in general, than for freely flowing traffic.

These examples show that, just as is the case for the determination of total user benefits and costs following the improvement of one link in a network, it is also important to consider for the determination of environmental (and noise) costs the dynamic network equilibrium effects of the proposed change for a comprehensive CBA. The effects occurring elsewhere than on the link itself may be substantial, and may thus significantly affect a given project's overall cost–benefit ratio, as well as the ranking in welfare terms of competing projects.

Although we have phrased the above discussion in terms of a unimodal network, the same type of arguments would of course apply when taking a multimodal perspective. Put simply: the extra emissions resulting from an additional passenger on a new public transport service would have to be corrected for the emissions this person may have caused prior to the investment, be it smaller, when cycling, or larger, when driving a car, than in the new situation, for a comprehensive assessment. The implied welfare effects will typically be larger in absolute terms when prices on these other modes deviate more strongly from optimal ones.

A second type of complexity in the environmental appraisal of transport infrastructure investments is closely related to the question of whether or not "indirect economic effects" of such investments would exist, which should be added to the "direct effects" as can be identified based on the surplus as measured by the demand function for transport. In defending the case of such indirect effects, often appeal is made to the increased economic activity that may follow a successful infrastructural expansion, and for which it is believed that the associated net benefits, because they arise primarily in a market different from the transportation market, would not be captured in an analysis that derives benefits only as pertaining to the demand for transport. However, a closer examination of these arguments often reveals that these benefits in fact are reflected properly by the demand function for transport after all. The emerging view is that only when market failures exist in the markets "served" by the infrastructure considered, there would be net welfare effects of transport infrastructure investments that are not properly reflected by the demand function for transport (Small, 1999; Standing Advisory Committee on Trunk Road Assessment, 1999). Examples of such market imperfections include market power, which can be reduced by exposing spatial monopolists to greater competition through greater accessibility, and agglomeration externalities (unpriced benefits of clustering in space, which can be exploited to a greater degree when infrastructure investments allow a further growth of an agglomeration). However, it should be emphasized that these types of implied indirect effects are not always positive.

One example of a negative indirect effect that should be accounted for in a transport CBA concerns the case where the investment would lead to a production expansion of a polluting industry that is not currently taxed optimally for its emissions. Again, such indirect environmental effects are by no means negative by definition. This is related to the simple fact that a road usually runs two ways. It may well be the case that the increase in capacity yields a new spatial equilibrium in which the production of relatively efficient and clean producers has increased and that of inefficient and dirty producers has decreased, as a result of intensified spatial competition. The overall environmental effect may then be positive when summing over increased transport emissions, increased emissions from the clean producers, and decreased emissions from the dirty producers. This argument bears clear parallels with the analysis in Verhoef et al. (1997), who consider the effects of environmental transport policies in a spatial equilibrium setting with polluting production sectors; and its exploration too would require the consideration of transport markets in an integrated spatial equilibrium framework.

As a third important type of second-best situation that may complicate CBA in transport, we briefly mention existing distortions in the tax system. When applying the rule of half the generalized costs include taxes, and it is of course appropriate to consider the changes in the regulator's surplus in addition to changes in consumer and, when relevant, producer surpluses: taxes saved or paid constitute no real benefit or cost to society, but involve transfers instead. However, to reflect that existing taxes are typically distortionary, a dollar change in total taxes received from an investment should typically be valued at more than a dollar if the change will in the long run be compensated for by changes in taxes elsewhere. This is equivalent to saying that the "shadow price of public funds," being the social value of an additional dollar of tax revenues, will exceed unity. Of course, a similar correction would have to be made for the valuation of the initial investment costs, when financed directly or indirectly through taxation. Lindsey and Verhoef (2001) discuss this issue in further detail in the context of transport pricing, but the principles discussed there carry over to CBA for transport investments.

We may conclude that the assessment of environmental effects or costs, when monetized in transport infrastructure appraisal, although in terms of principles is straightforward at first sight, may become more complicated once second-best conditions apply either in the transport mode considered, in the transport system in general, or in the spatial economy that is "served" by the infrastructure network in which the investment is to be made. This is not so surprising after all, as the principle mimics one of the central conclusions that was emphasized for transport pricing in Lindsey and Verhoef (2001). An implication is that a solid CBA for a transport investment would ideally require analyses with a transport network model (multimodal when spill-overs between modes are important, and dynamic when the investment considered seeks to reduce peak congestion), and with a multisectoral spatial general equilibrium model when market imperfections in the sectors served by the infrastructure are likely to be important.

3.3. Discounting

One aspect of CBA that continues to attract much attention involves the choice of a discount rate, needed to bring costs and benefits arising at different moments during the project's life time on an equal footing. The choice of a discount rate may strongly affect the desirability and ranking of different projects considered, so it is a potentially decisive choice that deserves careful consideration. The selection of an appropriate social rate of discounting is not straightforward, if anything because capital markets are not perfect and no single stable interest rate applies throughout the economy and over time (Small, 1999).

The reviews of CBA mentioned earlier discuss various issues pertaining to the selection of a social discount rate. One particular issue that we would like to address here concerns the discounting of the distant future in relation to environmental impacts. Various justifications have been given why future environmental degradation should be discounted at a low or even zero rate. Most arguments involve intergenerational equity, and a desire to limit adverse environmental impacts of current choices on future generations. Indeed, future environmental disasters, causing huge social costs, may become practically insignificant in CBA when discounted at market-based interest rates (a $1 loss in 100 years' time is currently worth only $1/$(1.05)^{100}$=0.7 cents when discounted at a 5% rate – and 0.006 cents when incurred in 200 years from now). This implication of discounting of course causes unease if it is considered important to protect the environment in the interest of future generations.

Sympathetic to the purpose of protecting future generations' interests as it may be, it should be realized that the use of different discount rates may easily introduce inconsistencies in a CBA or policies in general. Horowitz (1996), for instance, presents an example where policies under diverging discount rates will become time-inconsistent: future regulators will not want to follow the current regulator's plans. He suggests reflecting environmental concerns for future generations by adjusting future prices, rather than discount rates, to avoid such inconsistencies.

Another potential source of inconsistency is that when a project leads to both future benefits and future environmental costs, the maximization of net present value under diverging discount rates may lead to choices that can be Pareto-improved upon: i.e. welfare at each moment in time can be improved by making a different decision. This can be illustrated using a simple, abstract example, where an infinitely lived current investment induces an endless future stream of time-invariant benefits B and environmental costs E per year. By choosing some irreversible parameter x ($0 \leq x \leq 1$) now, the regulator can reduce E at the expense of reducing B, according to

$$E = 0.5x^2,$$
$$B = x - 0.5x^2.$$

With welfare defined as $W = B - E$, it is easily found that a choice of $x = 0.5$ would maximize W in every period (the first-order condition is $dW/dx = 1 - 2x = 0$), leading to an optimal yearly level of W equal to 0.25 ($B = 0.375$, $E = 0.125$). When, however, x is chosen so as to maximize the net present value with B discounted at an interest rate of 4% and E at a lower environmental one of 1%, the objective function becomes

$$\text{NPV}(B) - \text{NPV}(E) = (x - 0.5x^2)/0.04 - (0.5x^2)/0.01 = 25x - 62.5x^2,$$

which has the first-order condition $25 - 125x = 0$. Hence, x would be set at 0.2, leading to a yearly level of W equal to 0.16 ($B = 0.18$, $E = 0.02$). Clearly, in this example, future generations would be better off if the current regulator discounted the project's benefits and environmental costs at equal rates (independent of whether it is the high or the low one). The current example depends crucially on the assumption that the current choice will affect both future environmental costs and future benefits (as will often be the case for transport investments). A lower discount rate for future environmental costs when benefits would only occur in the current period would not harm but benefit future generations. The example, simple as it may be, warns against a too careless adjustment of discount rates for environmental damages to reflect concerns for future generations.

3.4. Spatial scope of CBAs

Transport infrastructures may affect the well-being of people living nearby, but also of course that of people living further away. Occasional users from different regions or countries may benefit from new or improved roads, and the environmental impacts may vary from emissions with largely local impacts to the emission of greenhouse gases, potentially inflicting costs on regions whose inhabitants are unlikely to ever use that infrastructure. In a similar vein, it is well known that the impacts on economic welfare may include substantial distributive effects (e.g. when the increase in welfare for people living near a facility occurs jointly with an induced decrease in welfare elsewhere) in addition to the generative effects – the generation of additional "total" welfare (Rietveld, 1989). As a result, a project's desirability, as well as the ranking of alternatives, may depend on the definition of the "planning area" and, with that, of the spatial set of individuals whose welfare is assumed to matter in the CBA.

The geographical boundaries for a CBA may in some instances be defined by the jurisdiction that commissions the appraisal, and that would finance the prospective projects. In other cases, official guidelines may exist that for instance stipulate that the appropriate level of spatial aggregation should be the national one, for example motivated by the desire to avoid wasteful investments by lower level authorities that would merely redistribute – rather than generate – national welfare. From an overall efficiency viewpoint, it is rather obvious that everybody would eventually benefit if all CBAs took a global perspective and hence considered welfare impacts world-wide, and – lump-sum – redistributions between and inside jurisdictions were possible. But this is probably a rather theoretical consideration, not viable in the practice of transport policy-making. In any case, the spatial demarcation is an important aspect for the design and the interpretation of CBAs. From the environmental perspective, one could expect that for localized externalities, this demarcation may create a bias in favor of projects running close to the borders of a planning area, given population densities – although a countervailing effect may occur if such routings would reduce the number of residents that would enjoy improved accessibility. Furthermore, to the extent that this occurs, as well as for global environmental externalities, the spatial demarcation may mean that environmental impacts will not get the weight that would be given were global welfare effects to be considered.

3.5. Transport appraisal and environmental sustainability

Hanley (1999) raises the interesting question of whether the instrument of CBA in project appraisal, when applied consistently, would lead to the achievement of environmental sustainability – a popular concept in environmental policy making ever since the publication of the Brundtland Report (World Commission on Environment and Development, 1987). The answer appears to depend on the definition of environmental sustainability used. Indeed, already within 5 years after the Brundtland Report's publication, Pezzey (1993) identified numerous possible definitions and interpretations of the politically popular but scientifically ambiguous concept of sustainability. Hanley (1999) observes that CBA typically does not address intertemporal nor intratemporal equity issues, while distributional considerations are often central to the concept of sustainable development. This points to a first potential inconsistency between CBA and the strive for sustainability, although one might object that different welfare weights could be introduced in the summation of costs and benefits to account for this, at least to some extent.

As an aside, it is useful to consider the parallel question of whether a consistent use of CBA in project appraisal would eventually lead to an economically optimal infrastructural configuration. Does any sequence of improvements, until a point is reached where no further improvements can be realized, necessarily bring the system to its optimum? This question cannot generally be answered in the affirmative. One important reason is that there may be interdependencies between projects – especially, of course, in transport. It may well be the case that a certain project that would not be selected in isolation would become desirable if other investments are also undertaken; or conversely, a project that has been carried out becomes redundant after a time when infrastructure at other places and/or in other modes is developed further, or when optimal pricing is introduced on the network, or major parts of it. More generally, with substitute transport modes being at least potentially available and when economies of scale, scope and density in transportation are important, it is certainly not inconceivable that multiple locally – in a mathematical sense – optimal infrastructure configurations exist. The one being achieved when consistently following CBA appraisals may then depend both on the initial situation and on the sequence in which projects are evaluated and implemented. These considerations would warn against taking too narrow a perspective when defining the set of projects and project variants to be considered in designing CBAs.

Returning to the issue of sustainability, Hanley (1999) observes that if sustainable development were defined as a non-declining stock of natural resources, as some propose (this corresponds to the "strong" definition, as opposed to "weak" definitions that allow for substitution between stocks), CBA-based public decision-making would in general not guarantee sustainability. A CBA framework in which costs and benefits of different types are added and subtracted would instead allow trade-offs between a larger use of environmental resources against increased present or future benefits. One could also argue that this apparent inconsistency need not be fundamental, as CBAs can be imagined in which the use of some environmental resources above some threshold levels, possibly zero, is valued at an infinite shadow price. However, this strategy, in turn, may be problematic if the CBA concerns only one relatively small part of the economy, while the threshold concerns the economy-wide use of resources. It would leave unanswered the question of what the threshold should be when considered at the level of an individual project, and it would create complicated interdependencies between CBAs in different areas of the economy, and between CBAs and the current and future use of environmental resources in other economic sectors in general. If the resource considered is renewable, one option would be to require that a "shadow project," which compensates for the use of the resource in the original project, is actually undertaken and is included in the CBA. But environmental concerns often involve non-renewable resources, or unique environmental goods that cannot be replicated exactly. Shadow projects may thus not always provide a fully satisfactory solution to this dilemma.

It is thus clear that CBAs focus on aggregate social surplus rather than on the distribution of costs and benefits, and that their typical application to individual projects in individual economic sectors, and their related typical application of constant shadow prices for environmental effects, may often be at odds with operational definitions of sustainable development. However, it is worth emphasizing in this context that it has been questioned in the literature whether concepts such as sustainable transport can be defined in a meaningful way in the first place, even if "sustainable development" could be defined unambiguously (e.g. Verhoef et al., 1997). The main concern is that the definition of sustainability of a subsystem with relatively strong interactions with other subsystems (such as one economic sector – e.g. transport – among many, or one region in a larger spatial system) appears meaningless if such interactions are not taken into account explicitly. This consideration becomes particularly relevant due to the focus of sustainability and CBA on long-run impacts. To give a simplistic example: a complete ban on transport may make it look sustainable from a partial perspective (there would be zero emissions from transport), but the induced additional emissions resulting from less-efficient production following spatial de-specialization may make this solution less environmentally sustainable than a configuration with transport. As the same type of concern would apply to an even larger extent to individual investment projects within a sector, one could argue that the observed tension between CBA and the objective of sustainable development need not always point to shortcomings in CBA *per se*, but may also merely reflect the inherent difficulty, or impossibility, of operationalizing all aspects of sustainable development at the disaggregated level of individual projects. When facing the choice between different projects or variants, this would therefore not necessarily create a systematic bias against CBA when compared with alternative project appraisal techniques.

Two final issues deserve brief consideration. First, as mentioned, it is customary to apply constant shadow prices for environmental effects induced by the projects considered in CBAs, which is often motivated by the small size relative to total emissions in an economy or in the sector. However, when damage from pollution depends not only additively on that from different pollutants but also the mix of pollutants is of importance, this simplifying assumption may have to be relaxed. For instance, ozone is formed from the interaction of nitrogen oxides and volatile organic compounds (Delucchi, 2000). The same holds true when the environmental effects considered become damaging only when exceeding some critical level (a classic example being the reversal of ocean streams when global warming exceeds a certain – unknown – level). For reasons comparable to those discussed above, especially when the associated emissions are not solely due to the projects considered, this type of "environmental complexity" (the term used by Hanley, 1999) may lead to complicated interdependencies between CBAs in different sectors, and between CBAs and emissions from other sectors, if these issues are to be given serious treatment in appraisal. However, these complexities may also imply that constant environmental shadow prices are not appropriate within a CBA for a given project. This need not disqualify CBA as an appraisal technique as such, but may make its execution significantly more complicated.

Second, the policy focus on sustainable development has made future environmental impacts more central in the environmental discourse. Apart from difficulties surrounding discounting, this also makes uncertainty more central in the analysis. Uncertainty may concern both future spatio-economic developments – introducing for instance demand uncertainty – but also the future costs of current emissions. The debate on the existence and severity of global warming is illustrative. Uncertainty may create specific problems for CBA, especially when no information is available that would allow the calculation of expected costs and benefits. In cases where expected environmental costs can be calculated, the next question would be whether or not environmental risk spreading is possible to a sufficient degree so that one could set the social risk premium equal to zero – as suggested by the so-called Arrow–Lind theorem – or whether a positive risk premium would be appropriate. The information required to calculate expected costs will in general be harder to obtain if non-linearities and discontinuities characterize the behavior of the ecological system (Hanley, 1999).

In practice, CBAs may partially account for this by deploying scenario and sensitivity analyses, and environmental policy may be based on precautionary principles that on the one hand may prevent huge irreversible future environmental costs, but on the other hand may lead to considerable current costs or forgone benefits. Regrettably, under this type of uncertainty, by definition no optimal degree of precaution can be established. It is evident that the existence of uncertainty – admittedly unavoidable – may substantially reduce the transparency of CBAs.

4. The valuation of environmental effects from transport

Transport investment projects may have many environmental effects, both at the local and global level. The challenge for appraisal has been to find ways of bringing all of these within one framework in a way that allows trade-offs between different types of environmental effects, and between environmental effects and other types of effects. In the following, we first discuss briefly the local, regional, and global environmental effects important when evaluating transport investments. The section starts with a brief discussion of valuation techniques, and concludes with some recent estimates of environmental costs of transport.

4.1. Environmental effects of transport

Various categories of environmental effects from transport and transport infrastructure are usually distinguished. The listing draws heavily on the European Conference of Ministers of Transport (ECMT) (1998).

Transport noise and vibration are, unlike most forms of air pollution, specific in space and, especially, in time. That is, noise causes nuisance only at the time and place it is emitted, although the effects may be longer lasted. Transport is a major source of noise annoyance in most societies, partly due to its concentration in denser areas. Vibration, particularly by heavy vehicles on uneven surfaces, may in addition cause damage to transport infrastructure, buildings, underground pipes and drains, and so on.

Transport emissions include various types of air pollution (local, regional, and global), to which transport is one of the major contributors. While in some respects the environmental damage done by transport is increasing, reductions have also been achieved. Carbon monoxide and dioxide, nitrogen oxide, sulfur dioxide, volatile organic compounds, and particulate matter are examples of emissions that are measured in this context. Particulates are generally identified as the most significant air pollutant in terms of induced health cost (e.g. Delucchi, 2000; Mackie and Nellthorp, 2001). Its damage costs are much higher per unit mass of pollutant emitted in urban areas, owing to the higher density of recipients. The two best known examples of global air pollution are the greenhouse effect, to which transport is a major contributor through emissions of carbon dioxide and other greenhouse gases, and ozone layer depletion, to which transport contributes relatively little (European Conference of Ministers of Transport, 1998).

Visual intrusion may result from the presence of infrastructure and from reduced visibility caused by air pollution. It is very difficult to quantify these effects, let alone to value them. Values can be expected to vary markedly between different projects. A new road in a formerly unspoiled area is likely to be viewed differently from one directly parallel to an existing road.

Comparable measurement problems will hinder the valuation of *severance of human and natural communities*. Here also, difficulties in quantification need not imply unimportance in appraisal. The effects may range from mild hindrance, such as waiting times for crossings, to the complete separation of formerly integrated human communities or ecosystems.

Waste disposal is often ignored in appraisal studies. However, the disposal of used oil, coolant, and hydraulic fluid, used tires and batteries, and scrapped vehicles may cause serious damage to the environment. The damage may occur either in the home country, or abroad if international second-hand markets or ecological dumping are important. Also, infrastructure construction may results in large quantities of waste, in particular spoil from earthworks.

Water contamination may for instance result from leaks in underground storage tanks or from fuel spillage at gas stations; or from salt, chemicals, or lost oil or other fluids on or near the road that will eventually pollute ground water. This has direct environmental impacts, and may in addition impose costs on local authorities responsible for water quality control.

4.2. The valuation of environmental externalities

The consideration of the above types of environmental effects in a CBA requires the identification of the economic value of environmental goods. The difficulty with this is of course that environmental goods are normally not traded, and hence no market price can be observed that would reflect or approximate marginal costs or benefits. Different valuation methods have been developed in the environmental economics literature that aim to identify the shadow prices for these goods. These valuation methods can be identified as belonging to one or more of the various types of "environmental values." One possible classification of environmental values, illustrative in that it includes the most often mentioned types, is provided in Figure 1 (based loosely on Perman et al., 1999).

Regardless of which type of value is considered, valuation methods aim to estimate the individuals' marginal willingness to pay (WTP), in monetary units, for improvements in the quantity or quality of the environmental good concerned, and are therefore consistent with the general philosophy of CBA, in which relevant welfare effects are expressed in monetary units. Economists have developed a number of procedures that, at least in the case of some externalities, provide reasonable guidance to the monetized value of these effects, despite the remaining uncertainty and dispersion in values produced (Button, 1993b). In recent years the level of sophistication used in this process has risen considerably. A brief outline of possibilities to derive estimates of the value of environmental effects is set out here. Figure 2 gives a concise overview of the valuation methods used for environmental externalities, including noise annoyance.

The left-hand side of Figure2 shows actual valuation methods, reviewed in greater detail in, for example, Perman et al. (1999) and in various contributions in Van den Bergh (1999). Among these, behavioral techniques deserve preference from a theoretical perspective, as these techniques assess the receptors' valuation. Mitchell and Carson (1989) observe in this respect that there is little theoretical basis for the use of non-behavioral techniques in welfare economics, since the damage functions are not directly related to the consumers' utility functions. Furthermore, non-behavioral techniques measure "use" values at best (see Figure 1), and cannot infer "non-use" values. Nevertheless, non-behavioral techniques receive much support in practice, in particular since the figures produced appear harder.

Two main categories of behavioral techniques are distinguished. Revealed-preference techniques can be applied when surrogate markets for the environmental good to be valued exist; that is, when consumers' marginal willingness to pay for changes in the effect can be measured by looking at their behavior in other, related markets. Such other markets may be housing markets and labor markets when hedonic techniques are used to statistically infer the value of, for example, noise annoyance as an attribute of housing services, or safety as an attribute of jobs. The travel cost method would typically seek to measure the valuation for natural parks by looking at the expenses that visitors incur in order to see the park. Household production functions can be used to infer how households, in their production of utility, try to defend themselves from the impacts of certain externalities.

When the goal is to value non-use values, or when no surrogate markets exist, stated-preference techniques can be used to infer consumers' willingness to pay by confronting them with hypothetical markets. Contingent valuation studies try to ask for a willingness to pay directly, possibly by confronting respondents with various bids for a certain good. Conjoint analysis techniques typically confront respondents with two or more scenarios in which the quantity or quality of an environmental good and some financial transfer vary, and asks them to indicate the most preferred option.

When time or money is lacking to undertake a genuine valuation study, short-cut approaches, such as those indicated on the right-hand side of Figure 2, are

Use value (related to the "use" of the good as a consumption good or production factor – note that "consumption" need not always deplete the good: enjoying a scenic view is also a form of consumption)				Non-use value (not related to the "use" of the good as a consumption good or production factor)			
Direct use value (the use of the good itself)		Indirect use value (the existence of the good improves the quantity or quality of other consumption goods or production factors – e.g. fresh air)		Option value (related to possible future use of the good)	Quasi-option value (related to possible future information on the importance of the good)	Existence value	
As a consumption good	As a production factor	Affecting consumption goods	Affecting production factors			Philanthropic value (for contemporaries)	Bequest value (for future generations)

Figure 1. A classification of different types of environmental values.

Valuation approaches			Short-cut approaches
Behavioral		Non-behavioral	
Surrogate markets (revealed preference): • Hedonic techniques • Travel cost techniques • Household production functions	Hypothetical markets (stated preference): • Contingent valuation in various forms • Conjoint analysis	• Damage costs (buildings, crops, etc.) • Costs of illness	• Prevention costs: hypothetical defensive, abatement or repair programs • Actual defensive, abatement or repair programs

Figure 2. A classification of different types of environmental values. (Adapted from Verhoef, 1996.)

sometimes used. These can be criticized on many grounds. Important considerations are that circularity may plague the estimates (e.g. an externality that is considered unimportant by the authority would induce small public defensive outlays, which would subsequently produce a low estimate of the external costs); that defensive outlays may not always be possible (it is hard or impossible to protect oneself from global warming or from the extinction of some species); that defensive outlays by private parties are typically carried out up to the point where marginal benefits equal marginal costs so that external costs remain in existence that are not measured using the method; and that hypothetical full defense programs may on the one hand consider too large a reduction of the externality but on the other hand bear no relation to the true external costs if they are not actually carried out.

A technique often looked at as the basis for valuation methods involves the construction of "dose–response" relationships (e.g. Friedriech and Bickel, 2002). In fact, this is not a separate valuation method but rather a means of transforming complex effects into a series of items which can be valued more easily (European Conference of Ministers of Transport, 1998). Dose–response work involves estimating physical or medical relationships linking environmental variables to quantifiable effects. Sometimes, the damage categories will involve marketed goods, such as crop yields, and market prices can be used. Many other categories will still be non-marketed, in which case the effects must be valued using the previous techniques. The so-called value of a statistical life may play an important role in this phase (e.g. see Chapter 24), in particular when concentrations are translated into mortality impacts.

Valuation of non-marketed goods is not an exact science. Uncertainty is inherent in techniques based on statistical inference, and furthermore it is not possible to control for all relevant variables in a diverse population. However, valuation studies do provide an indication of the costs and benefits useful to include in the CBA. To account for these uncertainties, lowest and highest estimates are often provided, along with a central estimate.

4.3. Some recent estimates of environmental external costs of transport

Many estimates of external costs of transport have become available over recent decades (e.g. see Chapter 19). The European Conference of Ministers of Transport (1998), for example, presents values for European countries, whereas Delucchi (2000) summarizes findings for the USA. It would take up too much space to give a detailed account of these and other studies here, bu,t for illustrative reasons, Tables 2 and 3 provide some summary results.

The figures in Table 2 give average estimates over countries, vehicle classes, urban versus non-urban traffic, and the time of day. The dispersion of cost components over these dimensions may be significant. For instance, the air

Table 2
Illustrative environmental external cost estimates (Europe 1990–1995)

	Passenger cars (ECU/ 1000 v-km)	Freight trucks (ECU/ 1000 v-km)	Passenger cars (ECU/ 1000 p-km)	Rail passengers (ECU/ 1000 p-km)	Ttrucks (ECU/ 1000 t-km)	Rail freight (Ecu/ 1000 t-km)
Noise	5	23	3	4	8	6
Air pollution	13	66	7	2	23	1
Climate change	10	28	6	3	10	1

Source: adapted from European Conference of Ministers of Transport (1998).

Table 3
Total environmental external costs of US motor vehicle use 1990–1991

	Low (US $/ billion)	High (US $/ billion)	Low (US $/ 1000 v-mile) (a)	High (US $/ 1000 v-mile) (a)	Low (US $/ 1000 v-km) (b)	High (US $/ 1000 v-km) (b)
Air pollution						
Overall	32.4	493.1	14.9	226.9	24.0	365.2
Human health related	24.3	450.0	11.2	207.1	18.0	333.3
Water contamination	0.4	1.5	0.2	0.7	0.3	1.1
Noise	0.5	15	0.2	6.9	0.4	11.1
Climate change	5.0	37.0	2.3	17.0	3.7	27.4
Total	38.3	546.6	17.6	251.5	28.4	404.8

Source: adapted from Delucchi (2000).
Notes:
(a) Calculated using the total vehicle-miles-traveled figures for 1991 in Delucchi (1997), summing over *all* vehicle types.
(b) Using 1 mile = 1.6093 km.

pollution cost estimates in the table are based on unit prices of 5 ECU per kilogram of nitrogen oxides, plus 5 ECU per kilogram of volatile organic compounds, plus, in cities alone, 70 ECU per kilogram of particulates emitted. As a result, the environmental charges calculated by the ECMT, when combining pollution, noise, and climate change, are 0.015 ECU/v-km in rural areas and 0.025 ECU/v-km in urban areas (note that these figures are lower than what might be gathered from Figure 1; see Appendix D in European Conference of Ministers of Transport (1998)). Both correspond to around 25% of the total optimal charges calculated, which include, for instance, external accident costs, infrastructure costs and congestion. Also, the representation in terms of costs per kilometer may be somewhat misleading. That is, the difference in emissions per vehicle-kilometer may be a factor of 10 or more, depending on whether one considers a cold or hot engine (European Conference of Ministers of Transport, 1998). Likewise, traffic conditions may of course have a great impact on emissions per kilometer.

Table 3 summarizes some main findings by Delucchi (2000), who reports the total environmental costs of motor vehicle use for the USA in 1990–1991. The results for instance illustrate that air pollution is the most important component in the external environmental costs of road transport, and that the uncertainty of estimates, as represented by the difference between the low and high estimates, is substantial.

Only because we suspect that some readers may otherwise make the same "quick-and-dirty" calculations themselves in order to compare the estimates in Tables 2 and 3, we have converted the figures in the latter into per vehicle-kilometer values on a very rough basis (averaged over all vehicle types, including passenger cars and trucks). This suggests that Delucchi's low estimate for air pollution and his high estimate for noise would be of the same order of magnitude as the ECMT figures (note that the ECMT figures are in ECUs, which were later converted into euros on a 1 to 1 basis, while Delucchi's are in US dollars; and also note that we have not attempted to convert the estimates to the same base year). Such differences may be due to a wide number of causes, including local conditions (e.g. population densities), differences in actual consumers' valuation of external effects, valuation methods used, environmental characteristics of vehicles, and vehicle mixes in average traffic conditions.

5. Conclusion

Transport investment appraisal can be seen as a tool to rationalize investment decisions. If the project is analyzed on behalf of a government, then a broad appraisal will be required, considering all relevant economic and social impacts of the scheme. Environmental effects comprise one important category of such impacts. This review considered the inclusion of environmental effects in transport investment appraisal mainly from the perspective of CBA, the most widely adopted appraisal technique.

Although the basic principles of CBA are straightforward, several complications were identified that may play an important role in practical CBAs. These include second-best aspects, difficulties with discounting and with the spatial scope of CBAs, and the relation between CBA and the popular but multifaceted and often ill-defined policy concept of sustainable development.

CBA takes individuals' willingness to pay as the starting point for valuation of effects. Values for time, safety, and environmental impacts can be derived from surrogate or hypothetical markets. Although the environmental effects from transport projects are well recognized and increasingly well understood, it is not always obvious how these should be valued in order to include them in a CBA. One of the challenges for CBA is then to find ways of bringing all the environmental impacts within the CBA framework in a way that does not cause problems arising from inconsistency, and which reflects in an appropriate way the much greater uncertainty associated with many environmental impacts.

Acknowledgments

Erik Verhoef's research has been supported by a fellowship of the Royal Netherlands Academy of Arts and Sciences.

References

Braess, D. (1968) "Über ein Paradoxen des Verkehrsplanung," *Unternehmenforschung*, 12:258–268.
Button, K. (1993a) *Transport economics*, 2 edn. Aldershot: Edward Elgar.
Button, K. (1993b) *Transport, the environment and economic policy*. Aldershot: Edward Elgar.
Delucchi, M.A. (2000) "Environmental externalities of motor-vehicle use in the US," *Journal of Transport Economics and Policy*, 34:135–168.
Delucchi, M.A. (1997) "The annualized social cost of motor-vehicle use in the US based on 1990–1991 data: summary of theory, data, methods and results," in: D.L. Greene, D.W. Jones and M.A. Delucchi, eds, *The full costs and benefits of transportation: contributions to theory, method and measurement*. Heidelberg: Springer-Verlag.
Dupuit, J. (1844) "On the measurement of the utility of public works," in: D. Murphy, ed.,*Transport*. London: Penguin.
European Conference of Ministers of Transport (1998) *Efficient transport for Europe, policies for internalisation of external costs.* Paris: OECD.
Friedriech, R. and P. Bickel (2002) *Environmental external costs of transport*. Berlin: Springer-Verlag.
Grant-Muller, S.M., P. Mackie, J. Nellthorp and A. Pearman (2001) "Economic appraisal of European transport projects: the state of the art revisited," *Transport Reviews*, 2:237–261.
Hanley, N. (1999) "Cost–benefit analysis of environmental policy and management," in: J.C.J.M. van den Bergh, ed., *Handbook of environmental and resource economics*. Aldershot: Edward Elgar.
Horowitz, J.K. (1996) "Environmental policy under a non-market discount rate," *Ecological Economics*, 16:73–78.
Janssen, R. and G. Munda (1999) "Multi-criteria methods for quantitative, qualitative and fuzzy evaluation problems," in: J.C.J.M. van den Bergh, ed., *Handbook of environmental and resource economics*. Aldershot: Edward Elgar.
Lindsey, C.R. and E.T. Verhoef (2001) "Traffic congestion and congestion pricing," In: D.A. Hensher and K.J. Button, eds, *Handbook of transport systems and traffic control*. Oxford: Pergamon.
Mackie, P. and J. Nellthorp (2001) "Cost–benefit analysis in transport," in: D.A. Hensher and K.J. Button, eds, *Handbook of transport systems and traffic control*. Oxford: Pergamon.
Mitchell, R.C. and R.T. Carson (1989) *Using surveys to value public goods: the contingent valuation method*. Washington, DC: Resources for the Future.
Nash, C. A. (1993) "Cost–benefit analysis of transport projects," in: A. Williams and E. Giardina, eds, *Efficiency in the public sector: the theory and practice of cost–benefit analysis*. Aldershot: Edward Elgar.
Parry, I.W.H. and A. Bento (2002) "Estimating the welfare effect of congestion taxes: the critical importance of other distortions within the transport system," *Journal of Urban Economics*, 51:339–365.

Perman, R., Y. Ma, J. McGilvray and M. Common (1999) *Natural resource & environmental economics*, 2nd edn. Harlow: Longman.
Pezzey, J. (1993) "Sustainability: an interdisciplinary guide," *Environmental Values*, 1:321–362.
Prest, A.R., and R. Turvey (1965) *The social appraisal of projects – a text in cost–benefit analysis* London: Macmillan.
Rietveld, P. (1989) "Infrastructure and regional development: a survey of multiregional economic models," *Annals of Regional Science*, 23:255–274.
Small, K.A. (1992) *Urban transportation economics. Fundamentals of pure and applied economics.* Chur: Harwood.
Small, K.A. (1999) "Project evaluation," in: J. Gómez-Ibáñez, W.B. Tye and C. Winston, eds, *Essays in transportation economics and policy*, pp. 137–177. Washington, DC: Brookings Institution Press.
Standing Advisory Committee on Trunk Road Assessment (1999) *Transport and the economy*. London: Department of the Environment, Transport and the Regions (http://www.roads.dft.gov.uk/roadnetwork/sactra/report99/).
Standing Advisory Committee on Trunk Road Assessment (2000) *Strategic assessment for the interaction of CTP-instruments*, Deliverable 4. Brussels: EC.
Van den Bergh, J.C.J.M. (1999) *Handbook of environmental and resource economic policy*. Aldershot: Edward Elgar.
Varian, H. (1992) *Microeconomic analysis*, 2nd edn. New York: Norton.
Verhoef, E.T. (1996) *The economics of regulating road transport*. Cheltenham: Edward Elgar.
Verhoef, E.T., J.C.J.M. van den Bergh and K.J. Button (1997) "Transport, spatial economy and the global environment," *Environment and Planning*, 29A:1195–1213.
Williams, H.C.W.L. and L.A.R. Moore (1990) "Appraisal of highway investments under fixed and variable demand," *Journal of Transport Economics and Policy*, 24:61–81.
Willig, R.D. (1976) "Consumer's surplus without apology," *American Economic Review*, 66:589–597.
World Commission on Environment and Development (1987) *Our common future*. Oxford: Oxford University Press.

Chapter 19

EVALUATION OF ENVIRONMENTAL IMPACTS

EMILE QUINET
Ecole Nationale des Ponts et Chaussées, Paris

1. Introduction

Transport facilities and activities can create a variety of environmental damages, and various techniques can be used to avoid, reduce, or compensate such costs. Transportation planning and policy analysis require suitable methods to evaluate such impacts in order to make optimal trade-offs between environmental protection and other social objectives. For example, just as a consumer must sometimes decide whether to pay extra for a quieter or safer vehicle, a community must decide how much extra it should be willing to pay for noise mitigation, air pollution reduction measures, wildlife preservation, and other strategies that reduce environmental damages from transport. Such decisions require accurate information about the quantity of impacts that will result from specific transport activities, the value to assign such impacts, and the impact reduction that can be expected from particular mitigation measures. This chapter describes various techniques and tools that are suitable for such analysis.

The next section defines the scope of the analysis, that is to say, the list of impacts to consider. Section 3 presents the general methodology for their evaluation. Next, we will show how this methodology applies to each of the impacts on the list. This is followed by a presentation of some of the overall results in Section 5. A concluding section suggests possibilities for improvement whilst at the same time defining the limits.

2. The scope of the analysis

Transportation can have a wide range of environmental impacts. We use a fairly wide perspective, which includes the following:

- aesthetic effects resulting from new infrastructure and vehicle use;
- impacts on ecosystems – a category which includes habitat and community fragmentation, animals and plants, soil and underground water pollution, and sea-water pollution;

- noise and vibration caused by vehicles on land, in the water, and in the air;
- local and regional air pollution from vehicle exhausts;
- global air pollution caused by major emissions of greenhouse gases, especially carbon dioxide (CO_2);
- urban impacts, that is to say the effect transport has on the occupation of space, urban development, and the localization of businesses, the barrier effect, and the consequences for economic development;
- the consequences for non-renewable natural resources – the depletion of fossil fuel resources and the reduction of available space as a result of transport facility development;
- upstream and downstream effects, resulting from activities relating to transport (manufacture of vehicles and infrastructures and the goods needed to operate them).

Traffic congestion and the delay it causes are excluded from this list, as well as unsafety and delinquency because they are primarily economic costs, and so are considered elsewhere: safety is discussed in Chapter 6; traffic congestion is addressed in Volume 3 in this series of handbooks. However, traffic congestion can exacerbate some environmental impacts, such as energy consumption and pollution emissions. As with any classification, there may be points that overlap. For example, water pollution consists, in part, of air pollutants that settle onto surface water.

3. The objectives of the evaluation

Transport environmental impact evaluation can aid in decision-making, including strategic policy analysis, planning and investment decisions, facility design, and pricing. It can help inform decisions that take place at several different levels: that of the master plan where infrastructures are only defined in outline, that of choices concerning route, where it is a question of choosing between two or three possible routes, and that of execution, where the route is defined and where the size of the embankments or the height of the noise-reducing walls must be chosen. It can apply to questions of regulation (should transport noise be regulated, and if so, at what level?) and tariff systems, in such a way as to implement the "polluter pays" principle.

Each of these objectives has a corresponding level of ambition within the evaluation. At the very least, one can describe the phenomenon. For certain impacts, for example landscape aesthetic impacts, this may be the extent of a particular analysis (although we will see later, it is possible to translate impacts such as aesthetic losses into monetary terms, given adequate resources).

The next step is to quantify physical impacts, that is, to measure impacts in units such as hectares of green space converted to pavement, decibels of noise imposed on residents, tonnes of various pollutants released, and changes in energy consumption. These can be presented in various ways, such as total land impacted, annual emissions, or per capita emissions.

It is often useful to monetize such impacts to more easily incorporate them in economic analysis. Impacts that are not monetized (sometimes called intangibles) tend to be overlooked and undervalued in economic evaluation. Monetizing non-market goods is increasingly common for planning and policy analysis, allowing more consistent and equitable decision-making. For example, it could be inefficient and unfair to spend US $1 000 000 per reduced human fatality in one situation (perhaps through investments in a medical treatment) but not spend US $100 000 to provide comparable human health benefits in another sector or location (perhaps by improving roadway safety).

For several decades, transport economists have used monetized values for travel time and crash injuries, and in recent years have begun to incorporate monetized values of environmental and social impacts. There is nothing unusual or mysterious about valuing non-market goods. Individuals and public officials often make decisions that trade non-market goods, such as security and aesthetics against market goods. For example:

- Home-buyers must decide how much extra they will pay (in actual cash or by giving up other amenities) for a residence that is subject to less noise or air pollution.
- Public agencies must decide how much society should spend to achieve goals such as increased travel speeds, health care, and environmental improvements.
- Individuals must choose how much to spend on safety (such as buying optional vehicle safety equipment), or how much compensation they require for dangerous work.
- Similarly, communities must often make decisions that involve trade-offs between various financial and environmental costs. Monetizing environmental costs can help guide such decisions, making the trade-offs more consistent and understandable to decisions-makers and other stakeholders.

We will not dwell any more on monetization problems, as they are dealt with in Chapter 20.

4. Methodological issues

The evaluation of environmental impacts involves a series of stages, from source to target, and from physical to economic impacts. Several types of data and analysis techniques may be required, and each of these can affect the accuracy of the final results. To take the example of air pollution, we must successively:

- Estimate, in kind and in quantity, the gaseous emissions produced by a transport activity.
- Determine how these gases move in the atmosphere, both in time and space, taking into account any chemical transformations they may undergo.
- Calculate the effect they will have on targets such as humans, wildlife, and buildings. If we take effects on health as an example, the result for this stage would be a number of deaths and sick persons, or in the case of wildlife, the number and kinds of animal species killed or suffering morbidity.
- Finally, the monetization stage applies monetary cost values to these damages, including estimates of the value of human morbidity and mortality, plus losses of commodities such as reduced agricultural production.

Let us also mention that the total cost of an impact is the sum of all individual impacts. Many published estimates, especially of air pollution, costs only consider a limited set of impacts (e.g. human deaths and acute health problems that require medical treatment, while ignoring more minor medical problems, reduced agricultural productivity and ecological damages), and so represent only a portion of the total costs of motor vehicle air pollution.

Taken together, these stages, known as the "impact pathway approach," may be represented by a diagram such as that shown in Figure 1, taken from Friedrich and Bickel (2002).

Two different aspects are clearly shown in this diagram:

- A physical aspect, represented by the left side of the diagram, which expresses the relationships between transport activities and impacts on the environment. This is fed by the body of accumulated scientific knowledge that establishes the laws and parameters on which these relationships depend. The laws in question are often expressed by functional relationships between emissions and their effects, known as "dose–response" relationships or the "exposure–response" relationships, which highlight how, and in accordance with which parameters, impacts are related to emissions.
- An economic aspect, described on the right side of the diagram. This aspect takes quantity as its starting point (number of deaths, quantities of crops destroyed, and species disappeared) and applies unitary values to these quantities (value of a death, value of a crop). In the case of commodities (i.e. goods commonly sold in a competitive market), these unitary values are the market prices. For non-market goods they are determined by methods which essentially aim to evaluate what the individuals suffering the impact on the environment would be willing to accept – i.e. the amount of financial compensation that victims would have demanded before they would volunteer to accept such damages (for further details on the determination of these unitary values, see Chapter 20). Methods known as "revealed-preference methods" analyze situations

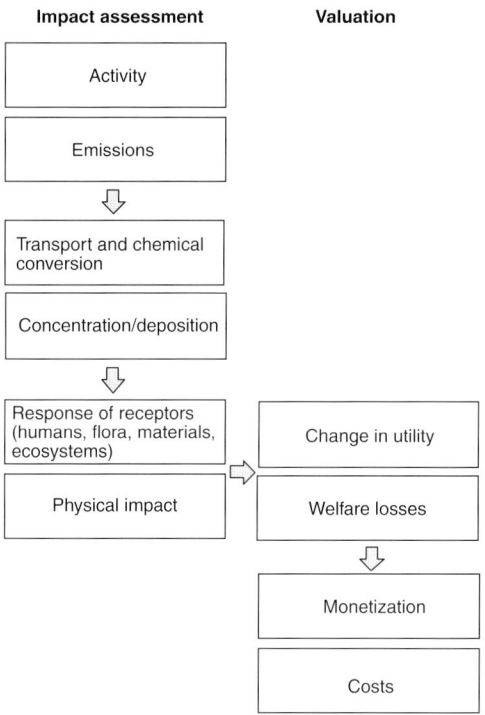

Figure 1. The impact pathway approach for the quantification of marginal external costs caused by air pollution and noise. (Source: Friedrich and Bickel, 2002.)

where the individual has a choice between greater or lesser degrees of pollution or nuisance and more or less of a commodity. Methods known as "declared- or stated-preference methods" are based on surveys where individuals are asked how much they would be prepared to pay to avoid such pollution. Finally, cost of damage methods seek to estimate the monetary cost of repairing the damage caused by the pollution or nuisance in question. These methods enable us to give meaning to, and to measure, concepts such as the cost of a year of human life saved, the cost of a year's illness avoided or the cost of the decibel.

The type of diagram in Figure 1, which has just been explained in the case of air pollution, constitutes an ideal that cannot be applied in its purest form for all impacts. Many factors exist which may make its implementation variable. Each type of impact requires different methods to quantify and monetize, which face various barriers and obstacles:

- First, one may have to skip a stage, or the series may not be completed. It is, for example, obvious that the quantification of effects such as the aesthetic consequences, has no precise meaning. This does not mean that one cannot attribute a monetary value to a landscape, however, as we will see later.
- Monetization is often difficult, at least given the present state of our knowledge. For example, while we agree that biodiversity has significant value, it is difficult to place a value on a particular incremental change in the quantity or quality of wildlife habitat.
- Ideally, we would apply this type of diagram to each unit of transport or for each isolated section of infrastructure, and then, to reply to questions on wider geographical areas, aggregate the elementary information gathered in this way (the "bottom-up" approach). But the implementation of this ideal often runs up against our inadequate knowledge and the difficulty of obtaining the necessary data. So opposite approaches, of the "top-down" type, are also used. In this way, overall results are obtained, but we cannot distinguish with any degree of precision between local situations or the various types of vehicle. The more dependent on local parameters the phenomena are, the more unsuitable "top-down" studies become, and as our knowledge develops, they are being used less and less.
- The implementation of the above-mentioned methods of evaluation runs up against another difficulty, that of synergies between impacts, which makes their separate analysis deceptive. For example, earth and air pollution combine to modify the flora in a particular way. But our knowledge concerning these synergies is still very limited, except in certain particular cases.

5. Evaluation by type of impact

These general considerations will now be developed more specifically for each type of impact mentioned in Section 2. We will tackle them in order of our degree of knowledge concerning their measurement, in ascending order from non-quantifiable impacts to monetizable impacts, via impacts which are merely quantifiable. For each type of impact, we assess the methodology of evaluation, its accuracy and difficulties of implementation, and how it fits to each possible purpose of the evaluation.

5.1. Non-quantifiable impacts

Non-quantifiable impacts are costs and benefits that are considered unsuitable for measurement, given available knowledge and resources. Aesthetic damages are often included in this category. There is no standard way to measure these impacts in order to compare costs between different sites and situations, so they tend to be evaluated qualitatively. Although they are not usually quantified, it is possible to survey individuals to determine their willingness to pay to avoid damage to a particular site, or their willingness to accept compensation for the loss of such resources. This type of evaluation, besides the inherent vagueness of the declared preferences method, is closely linked to the site itself, and therefore tends to be difficult to transpose from one site to another. The accumulation of evaluations does not give us a great deal of information on the value to be bestowed on a site which has not yet been evaluated.

The evaluation of damage to a site requires precise knowledge of its final state, which is often only possible in the advanced stages of project planning and development. In the stages preceding this, that of the master plan or choice of route, the evaluation of the visual effects is carried out through maps which define zones of classification for sites in accordance with their degree of interest and the degree of attention that must be paid to their modification. We therefore obtain not an evaluation of the impact which will be made on a site but an indication of the degree of damage to the site that it is possible to allow. This might be considered an attenuated form of impact evaluation.

5.2. Quantifiable impacts which are non-monetizable or monetizable only with difficulty

We would place impacts on ecosystems, urban effects, and the consequences of impacts on non-renewable natural resources in this category.

Ecosystems

Healthy ecosystems have many functions, such as wildlife habitats, providing fishing and hunting opportunities, sources of clean water, and reducing risks to human health. These functions can be measured in physical terms (e.g. catch rates, water quality, or property damage avoided), or may be the object of quantitative indicators (e.g. topographical maps, soil maps, land use maps, natural resource and habitat maps, and demographic and socio-economic data, coupled with regional surveys of outdoor recreation and of preferences for environmental amenities).

Transportation has many effects on these ecosystems. Transportation infrastructures are a major source of habitat fragmentation, green space and farmland loss, and disruption to underground and surface water flow; they may even lead to the disappearance of species on the site in question when the residual habitats are no longer of the quality or size required. Transport activities can also impact ecosystems through soil and water pollution (leakage from fuel tanks and pipes, water run-off from roads, particles, etc.).

These impacts may first be evaluated by the variation of the indicators defining the qualities of the ecosystem in question and the services it renders. These impacts may be monetized when the services rendered are commodities (agricultural and fishery production), or by one of the general methods, for non-commodity goods. However, the results are specific to a particular location or situation. The transposition to other situations may be difficult, and even the choice of quantitative indicators must be adapted to the local situation.

Special mention must be made of marine pollution. It has two sources: first, non-accidental pollution from waste thrown into the sea by boats, and, secondly, accidental pollution that follows damage or shipwrecks when toxic products such as oil or chemicals are discharged. The most well-known examples are the *Exxon Valdez* and *Amoco Cadiz* accidents. The quantification of the impacts involves the measurement of the levels of toxic products or evaluation of the damage in terms of the destruction of individuals of each species affected, or by the loss of recreation value of the sites affected. In the case of accidental pollution when an oil tanker is shipwrecked, the monetization of the impacts has seen some of the most famous cases of the application of contingent value.

Urban effects

Transportation has many urban effects. Some of these effects are quantifiable and even monetizable, even though their monetization is not yet tried and tested. They impinge on daily life and are the result mainly of infrastructures, the most well known being the "barrier effect": a new linear infrastructure divides the urban habitat in two, forcing the inhabitants to change their daily travel routines (shopping, social life, etc.) The consequences can be quantified in numbers of trips modified, and these can even be evaluated in monetary terms, by estimating the cost of the extra time involved in maintaining old habits.

Other more long-term effects, far more difficult to evaluate, are outside the scope of this handbook. These are the consequences of transport on localization and on the level of economic activities. The transport–land use models which are used to inform us of these consequences certainly provide information on localization changes, new industrial establishments, and urban dynamics, but they are difficult to implement, and depend on the availability of the numerous data needed to feed them. They are used to produce maps showing changes in localizations, or figures giving the rates at which economic activities are increasing as a result of infrastructures whose effect remains to be assessed.

Non-renewable natural resource depletion

A variety of natural resources are non-renewable, and their unnecessary depletion violates principles of sustainability. In particular, some economists consider depletion of fossil fuels to impose ecological and economic costs on future generations. In addition, consumption of these resources can impose economic costs, particularly in regions that import a significant portion of the fuel they consume.

This is the case in the consumption of fossil fuels, especially oil, of which large quantities are used by the main forms of transport, the consumption of which can easily be measured or forecast with great accuracy since the units of consumption are well known and statistics abound on the consumption of oil by country, by region, by mode of transport, etc. This is also the case with the consumption of land brought about by the presence of infrastructure, land which is therefore unavailable for other productive uses, including farm land, and wildlife habitat. We can measure in terms of area, or in monetary terms, by counting each unit of area at its market value or at a value judged to be more representative of its collective rarity.

5.3. Quantifiable and monetizable impacts

Impacts in terms of global, local, and regional pollution, depending on air pollution emissions, and noise may be placed in this category.

Air pollution emissions

Motor vehicles emit a variety of pollutants, which have a variety of negative impacts, as summarized in Table 1. Some of these impacts are local or regional, and therefore sensitive to where emissions occur. Others are global, and so their cost is not significantly affected by geographic location. For example, the costs of emitting nitrogen oxides and hydrocarbons is much greater in cities that have significant ozone problems than if the same pollutants were emitted in a rural area, but carbon dioxide emission costs are virtually the same regardless of where they occur.

Local and regional air pollution

This is the result of motor vehicle emissions, road vehicles in particular. Local air pollution – occurring in the immediate vicinity of the pollution source – is a problem in urban areas. At this level, the effects are above all caused by particles – to which continued exposure increases the risk of cancer – and from aromatic hydrocarbons. Regional pollution covers a wider area, after dispersal of pollutants in the atmosphere, and chemical transformation. The gases most responsible at this level are nitrogen and sulfur oxides, the accumulation of which increases the risk of asthma and cardiovascular illnesses. Certain gases, such as the nitrogen

Table 1
Vehicle pollution emissions

Emission	Description	Source	Harmful effects	Scale
Carbon monoxide (CO)	A toxic gas which undermines the ability of blood to carry oxygen	Internal combustion engines	Human health, climate change	Very local
Fine particulates (PM_{10}, $PM_{2.5}$)	Particles consisting of fuel and carbon	Diesel engines and other sources	Human health, aesthetics	Local and regional
Road dust	Dust particles created by vehicle movement	Vehicle use	Human health, aesthetics	Local
Nitrogen oxides (NO_x)	Various compounds. Some are toxic, all contribute to ozone formation	Internal combustion engines	Human health, ozone precursor	Regional
Hydrocarbons (HCs)	Unburned fuel. Forms ozone	Fuel production and internal combustion engines	Human health, ozone precursor	Regional
Volatile organic hydrocarbons (VOCs)	A variety of organic compounds that form aerosols	Fuel production and internal combustion engines	Human health, ozone precursor	Local and regional
Toxics (e.g. benzene)	VOCs that are toxic and carcinogenic	Fuel production and internal combustion engines	Human health risks	Very local
Ozone (O_3)	Major urban air pollution problem resulting from NO_x and VOCs combined in sunlight	NO_x and VOC	Human health, plants, aesthetics	Regional
Sulfur oxides (SO_x)	Lung irritant, and causes acid rain	Diesel engines	Human health risks, acid rain	Regional
Carbon dioxide (CO_2)	By-product of combustion.	Fuel production and internal combustion engines	Climate change	Global
Methane (CH_4)	A gas with significant greenhouse gas properties	Fuel production and internal combustion engines	Climate change	Global
Chlorofluorocarbons (CFCs)	Durable chemicals formerly widely used, now with use restrictions owing to environmental risks	Vehicles (especially those with older air conditioner units)	Ozone depletion	Global

Source: Litman (2002).

oxides, have an effect at both levels. Finally, a synergy exists between some of these gases, a synergy which we are as yet uncertain how to deal with.

Very many studies have been carried out to evaluate these effects. They use a chain of models which represent first of all vehicle emissions, then follow the movements of the gases emitted into the atmosphere and the chemical transformations resulting from their interaction, and, finally, from epidemiological studies, the effects on human health. We can transform these effects into monetary terms by the intermediary of ideas of the statistical value of a year of human life lost. Statistical studies have also enabled us to evaluate damage to buildings and to wildlife. We therefore have at our disposal, a comprehensive analysis of the causal chain following impact pathway methodology, and can therefore determine the elementary costs of each vehicle.

The results vary significantly, depending on the pollution control standards that existed when the vehicle was brought into service – progress has been fast in recent years – and depending on how well the vehicle has been maintained. At the moment, the principal uncertainties relate to the long-term effects on health, and, in particular, the carcinogenic effects of unburnt particles.

Global air pollution

The two main impacts of transport on global air pollution are the greenhouse effect, to which transport is a major contributor, and ozone layer depletion, to which transport contributes a little through air transport emissions.

The evaluation of the greenhouse effect is carried out in stages: estimation of the effects of human activities and in particular transport, on the warming of the atmosphere, then evaluation of the consequences in terms of climate, and, lastly, consequences on human activities and national GDP. There is considerable uncertainty about some of these factors. Several different gasses contribute to the greenhouse effect, the largest of which is anthropogenic (human emitted) carbon dioxide, a third of which is currently produced by transport-related activities.

It has been estimated that if present trends in the emission of carbon dioxide continue, and the carbon dioxide content increases proportionally, the temperature of the atmosphere is expected to rise by 2–10°C within 100 years (although there is great uncertainty surrounding the exact temperature rise), with very significant consequences for the climate. This temperature rise will have a number of effects. We will probably see a rise in the level of the sea, with the risk of submersion for certain countries. Sea currents would be reversed, bringing temperature changes for the lands they affect. Estimates of the impact on a nation's domestic product have been made, and vary considerably from country to country. For the USA, for which the most thorough studies have been carried out, the result would be a drop of around 1.5% in the GDP, but for others it would be much greater[a]. These evaluations are uncertain, but the situation they try to anticipate would be difficult to reverse, because of cumulative nature of the occurrences in question and of the difficulty in reducing the CO_2 content.

Noise

Noise is one of the most obvious environmental impacts of transport activity. Vehicle traffic noise can have several types of negative impacts. First, it creates a temporary nuisance for those who have to suffer it (such as disruption of conversations and rest), and, secondly, prolonged exposure to traffic noise can lead to physical illnesses associated with stress and inadequate sleep.

Many studies have been dedicated to the first of these effects. They are primarily based on the definition of unit measurements of noise, of which the most commonly used is the decibel, and indicators of the annoyance it causes. We also have at our disposal on-site noise measurement instruments which enable us to draw up noise maps (these maps are, in particular, in common use for incidences of noise of aircraft in the vicinity of airports), and models which help forecast the noise which will be emitted by a given activity. Lastly, studies with similar results, based both on methods of declared preferences and revealed preferences, provide values for the psychological distress caused by each extra decibel an individual receives. The effects on health (stress, loss of sleep, and cardiovascular effects), which are cumulative, have been the subject of fewer studies that consider quantification. The few analyses which have been carried out show that these effects are less marked than the psychological effects, at least in monetary terms. These physiological costs represent only a quarter of the total noise costs.

The chain which enables us to pass from the source of the noise to the monetary evaluation of the nuisance caused has been thoroughly explored. But its implementation in practical decision-making often poses insoluble problems. Noise is very dependent on local conditions. A very precise description of the topography is needed to be able to forecast it, and very many measurements are needed to measure it. In other words, it is impossible to forecast noise for a project which has not yet been fully defined (a stadium at the master plan stage, for example), and costly in other cases. Lastly, for the same reasons, even when the projects have been well defined, estimates or forecasts are unreliable, and the unreliability comes more from the technical conditions under which the offending decibels are evaluated than from their monetary valuation. It is the technical, and not the economic, stage which is the weak link in the evaluation process.

---

[a]It should be noted that these estimates are based on costs of a tonne of carbon – costs of damages – which are different to "optimal" taxes, which represent the taxes which must be implemented to achieve the emission objectives decided upon by public authorities (resulting from the Kyoto Protocol, for example). These taxes depend on the objectives that have been set, and may differ from country to country.

Traffic noise costs can be quantified, in part, by measuring the reduction in residential property values near busy roads and airports compared with otherwise similar properties in quieter locations (called "hedonic pricing" analysis). However, such studies can only reflect a portion of total noise costs: this technique assumes that at the time consumers are purchasing a home, they can accurately predict the degree of traffic noise exposure at each location and the negative impacts it will have on their lives; this technique does not capture non-residential noise costs, such as the discomfort of traffic noise to pedestrians on a sidewalk or visitors to a park.

Upstream and downstream impacts

The indirect consequences of transportation activities linked to the construction and operation of infrastructure and vehicles come under this heading. In principle, these effects are vast since all the types of consequences previously analyzed may be found here (e.g. aesthetic consequences of building refineries, or soil and water pollution caused by automobile manufacturing), and their complete knowledge would imply a life-cycle assessment, but, in fact, the effects which seem the most important and on which most attention has been centered are those linked to global, regional, and local pollution of the air and to the consequences of energy production. The methods of evaluating these impacts are no different in principle to those used in the direct evaluation of transport impacts apart from the fact that certain authors introduce an element of risk into the production of nuclear energy, the effects of which, in terms of air pollution, are nil. This risk is evaluated by an estimation – subject to caution, naturally – of the probabilities of an accident occurring in a nuclear power plant and of the cost of such an accident.

6. The presentation in perspective and results of the studies

After this presentation of the various impacts and the means of evaluating them, one might be tempted to use the results obtained to compare modes of transport, or compare countries, or to estimate changes which may occur over the years. Such syntheses are the purpose of the evaluation, but must be made with caution and prudence, for several reasons:

- First, certain impacts are very dependent on local situations, and results that emerge as an average will be false in each specific situation
- Many evaluations have poor reliability. Results change with progress in emission control techniques.
- Lastly, emission cost studies often focus on just a portion of the total pollutants and impacts. For example, some studies only consider severe human health damages (those requiring medical treatment or causing

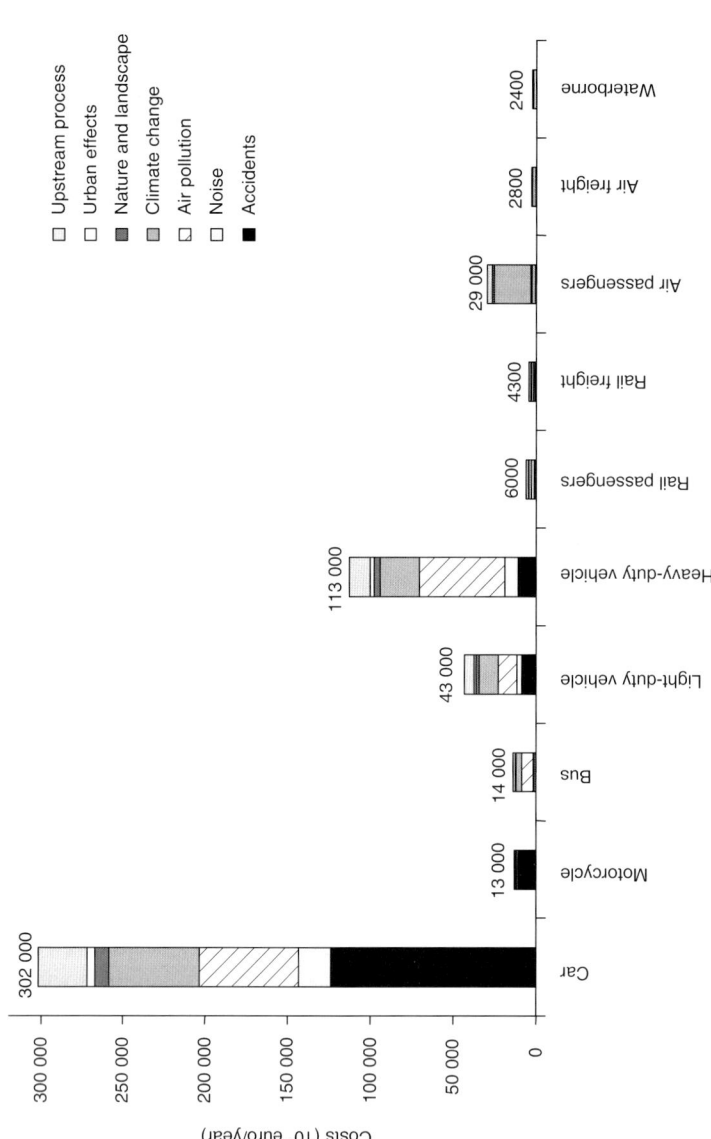

Figure 2. Total external costs of transport for 1995 (EUR 12), by transport mode and cost. (Source: INFRAS/Institut für Wirtschaftspolitik und Wirtschaftsforschung, 2000.)

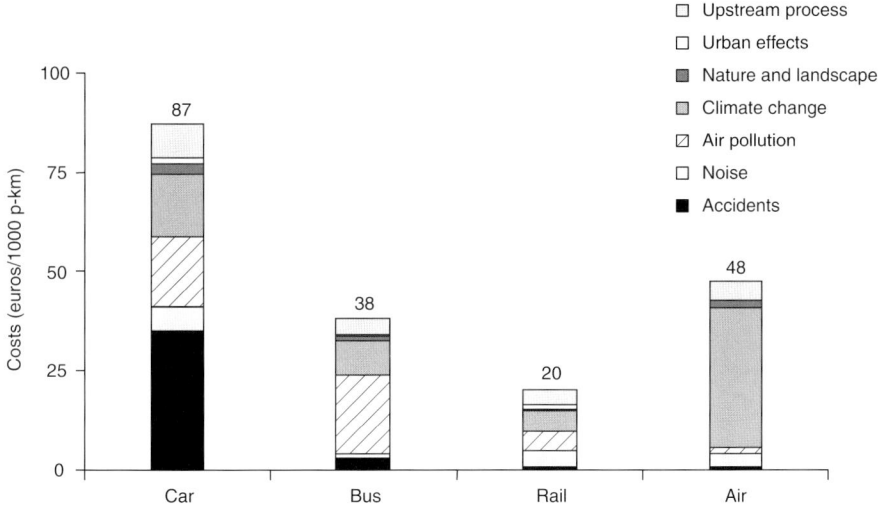

Figure 3. Average external costs for 1995 (EUR 12), by transport mode and cost (passenger transport, without congestion costs). (Source: INFRAS/Institut für Wirtschaftspolitik und Wirtschaftsforschung, 2000.)

disability and death) from ozone or particulates, while excluding the impacts of other emissions, less severe human health impacts, and damages to agricultural production, ecological systems, and aesthetics. As a result, such studies tend to understate the full costs of vehicle air pollution.

Several studies have attempted to quantify and compare the full costs of transport, including environmental costs. Such studies can provide helpful information as to the relative importance of different types of costs and the value of reducing such impacts.

For example, the INFRAS/Institut für Wirtschaftspolitik und Wirtschaftsforschung (2000) study discusses the total transports costs for Europe, for passengers and for goods, and also the costs per passenger-kilometer (Figures 2 and 3).

Litman (2002) provides a comparison for the USA with some non-environmental costs such as travel time, vehicle operating costs, and accident costs (Figures 4 and 5).

7. Conclusions

This overview demonstrates that considerable efforts have been made to evaluate the impacts of transport on the environment, efforts which match the vital importance of the environment for our societies.

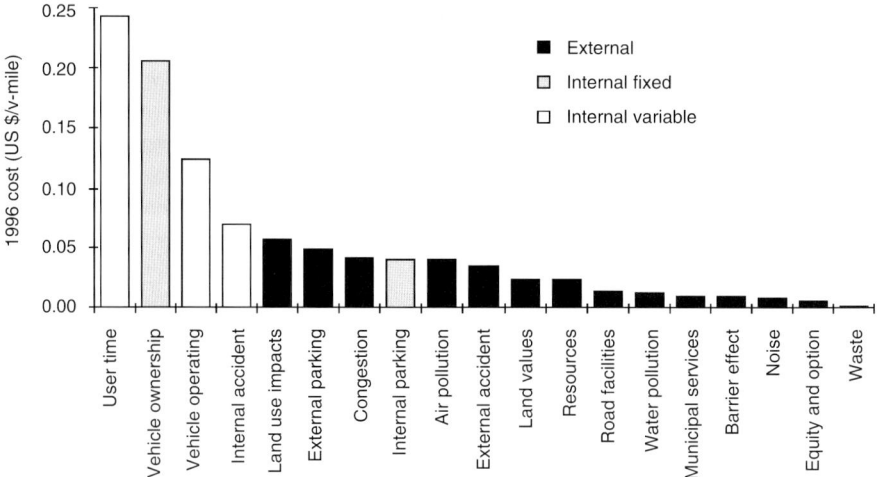

Figure 4. Automobile costs ranked by magnitude. (Source: Litman 2002.)

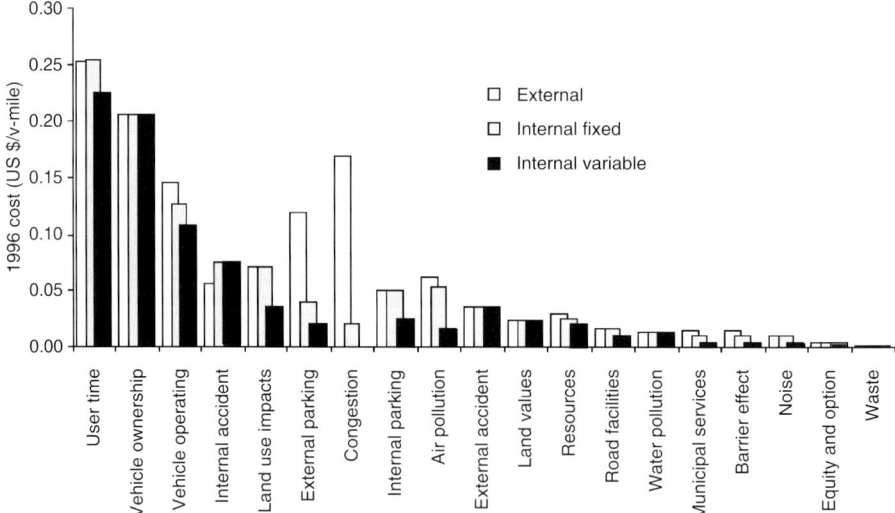

Figure 5. Automobile costs by travel conditions. (Source: Litman 2002.)

These efforts face a variety of obstacles. First, the physical parameters to which impacts are subject are in general complex, little known, in particular with regard to their long-term effects, and beset by the kind of unreliability that always surrounds large-scale models with multiple parameters.

In addition, there are considerable local differences for very many impacts, such as noise, visual impacts, and effects on ecosystems. Consequently, the parameters are not transposable, and scientific studies often have to be re-done, adjusting the parameters in each particular case.

This is a challenge when it comes to offering help in decision-making, where time and financial means are limited. To enable us to take up this challenge, it is important that the pool of studies which allows us to describe the physical parameters in question is developed, and that the available data concerning impacts on the environment are increasingly abundant and varied.

References

European Conference of Ministers of Transport (1998) *Efficient transport for Europe, policies for internalisation of external costs.* Paris: OECD.

Friedrich, R. and P. Bickel, eds (2002) *Environmental external costs of transport.* Berlin: Springer-Verlag.

INFRAS/Institut für Wirtschaftspolitik und Wirtschaftsforschung (2000) *External costs of transport. Accident, environmental and congestion costs in western Europe.* Paris: International Union of Railways.

Litman, T. (1999) *Transportation cost and benefit analysis; techniques, estimates and implications.* Victoria: Victoria Transport Policy Institute.

Organisation for Economic Co-operation and Development (1988) *Transport and the environment.* Paris: OECD.

Chapter 20

VALUATION OF ENVIRONMENTAL EXTERNALITIES

WIKTOR ADAMOWICZ
University of Alberta

1. Introduction

Transportation impacts on the environment are complex and multifaceted. Transportation impacts can arise from emissions, and affect air quality or water quality. Noise is generated by transportation corridors. Land used for transportation could displace habitat for wildlife species or threatened plants. Collisions or accidents can affect humans as well as wildlife. These primary impacts follow complex pathways to generate effects on "end-points" that affect economic well-being. For example, changes in human mortality and morbidity can arise from changes in air quality associated with transportation. These air quality impacts may also have non-health effects (or, more specifically, non-human health effects), such as impacts on agricultural productivity, forest productivity, visibility, or wildlife species. Some of these end-points are clearly linked to economic systems, and have links to market values (agriculture, forestry) while other end-points have economic value that is not captured by the marketplace (human health, ecosystems, wildlife, etc.). These non-market or environmental values are controversial since their value is not apparent in market transactions, yet these values can be very large and can be the major drivers behind environmental policy (e.g. US Environmental Protection Agency, 1999). While the physical relationships between transportation and the environment have been widely studied, the relationship between transportation, environmental impacts, and economic analysis has received less attention. Nevertheless, this linkage is necessary for an analysis of policy options since economic analysis can make measures of environmental impact commensurate with measures of infrastructure costs or investments (Maddison et al., 1996).

In this chapter the focus is on non-human health environmental effects, which are commonly referred to as "non-health effects." Human health effects (mortality and morbidity) are the focus of other chapters in this volume. Furthermore, the focus is on non-health effects that are environmental in nature. This chapter is also concerned with the valuation of these non-health effects. As such, all impacts are examined in terms of their relevance to humans since economic valuation is an assessment of the value that individuals in society would place on changes in prices, quantities, or, of most relevance in our case, environmental quality.

Figure 1 summarizes the linkages between transportation, human health effects and non-health effects. Transportation emissions can result in human health impacts directly (e.g. particulate matter), and they can also affect wildlife and ecosystems. Land use decisions (road construction, etc.) can reduce habitat or can result in increased human access to a region and increased disturbance. Accidents can affect wildlife populations. Note, however, that there may also be indirect linkages between impacts on ecosystems and human health. For example, the dotted line linking wildlife/ecosystems and human mortality/morbidity may be the linkage between pollutant effects on fish or wildlife that are then ingested by humans, resulting in health effects. In this chapter we do not examine such indirect linkages but focus instead on the direct linkages between transportation and non-health impacts.

While Figure 1 summarizes the physical linkages between transportation and the environment, Figure 2 outlines the linkages that are necessary for valuation. In order to develop valuation estimates, the definition of the "goods" must be clear. This is referred to as developing the "end-points" for economic analysis where the end-points are items that have value or can be valued. In the case of emissions affecting fish population, for example, changes in commercial fishing profitability (a market end-point) may arise and/or recreational fishing value (typically a

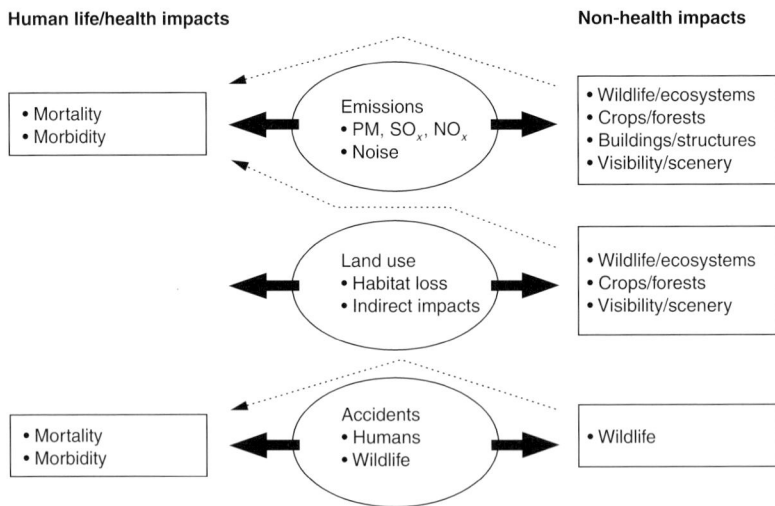

Figure 1. Relationship between transportation externalities and impacts.

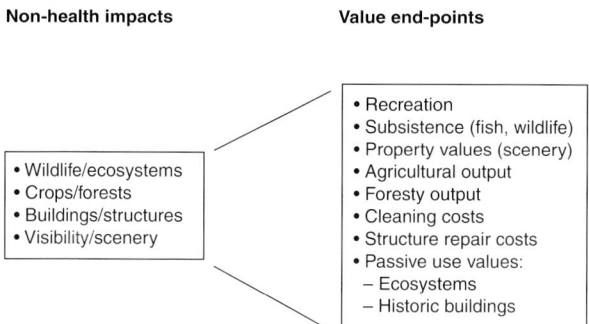

Figure 2. Non-health impacts and value end-points.

non-market end-point) may be affected. Commercial fishing is a market-based end-point because the fish are traded in a market, and the price is reflective of value. Recreational fishing is often not priced in a market, and economic valuation techniques need to be employed to identify the value of a change in fish population on recreational fishing.

Some common end-points are listed in Figure 2. These include end-points that are closely linked to markets such as agricultural crop impacts, forestry impact, repairs required to maintain structures such as bridges, buildings, etc. (material damage), and the value of changes to household cleaning or soiling. Non-market impacts include change in visibility, recreation, and values for the existence of habitats (passive use values or existence values) or the preservation of historical buildings.

2. The damage function approach

The accepted approach for valuing impacts on the environment is a damage function approach. This approach traces the steps of a change in emissions or policy, first to a change in environmental quality (air quality, water quality, etc.), then to a change in value. For example, a change in transportation emissions of particulate matter (PM) arising from a new regulation would be traced through to the changes in air quality (concentration of PM), the change in health and non-health end-points, and, finally, the valuation of these end-points. Note that the exercise always involves the evaluation of changes or marginal analysis. An example of non-health values could be the following: a change in acid deposition resulting from improved regulations would be traced to changes in fish populations; changes in recreational angler behavior arising from these fish population changes would then be examined to reveal measures of value for the population change.

Table 1
Valuation techniques

	Revealed preference (observed behavior)	Stated preference (hypothetical)
Direct valuation	Competitive market	Contingent valuation (open ended) Contingent valuation (bidding game)
Indirect valuation	Travel cost/random utility models Hedonic property models Referenda	Referendum contingent valuation Contingent behavior Choice experiments

Source: based on Mitchell and Carson (1989), Freeman (1993), and Royal Society of Canada (2001).

3. Value and valuation techniques

A common definition of value in economic analysis is the amount an individual would be willing to give up (or be compensated for) in order to be as well off as they were before a change. This is an identification of how much an individual would trade in exchange for a particular good or a service. Individual value estimates (or measures of compensating variation) are aggregated over all relevant individual to generate estimates of social value that are used in policy analysis. Freeman (1993) provides an excellent overview of the theoretical concepts relating to economic welfare analysis.

Various valuation techniques have arisen to attempt to construct measures of value for different goods and services. Table 1 summarizes the most popular valuation techniques. If actual observations of behavior are available for the good in question, the revealed preferences of the individual provide measures of value. Thus, markets for commercially caught fish provide direct value estimates for fish. A stated-preference, or hypothetical, method that produces direct estimates of value is the open-ended contingent valuation method (Mitchell and Carson, 1989). This method asks individuals directly how much they would pay for a change in a quantity or quality of a market or environmental good. Indirect valuation techniques infer value from behavioral choices or hypothetical questions (see also Carson 2000). Since individuals rarely calculate their actual value for a good in market settings; indirect methods are felt to be more realistic. Revealed preferences over housing, for example, can be used to identify a relationship between the amount that individuals would be willing to pay for a house and the air quality, level of noise, or visibility in the neighborhood (Braden and Kolstad, 1991). The individuals are not purchasing the air quality directly, but they are revealing their value for it indirectly. Similarly, stated-preference techniques such as choice experiments ask individuals to choose between alternatives that are described by attributes and prices (Adamowicz, 2000; Louviere et al., 2000). These choices reveal the trade-offs that the individuals are willing to make and implicitly the values associated with attributes. Valuation techniques are summarized below. Note, however, that not all of these techniques are consistent with utility theory or reveal an accurate willingness to pay for environmental quality change.

3.1. Change in consumer and producer surplus

When market-based demand curves are available they can be used to develop estimates of consumer and producer surplus (or measures such as compensating variation). If the environmental impact in question is directly linked to such market-demand curves, it will be possible to use these traditional economic welfare measures to establish the value of the impact (Braden and Kolstad, 1991; Freeman, 1993).

3.2. Avoided costs

If the impacts of an environmental quality change are reversible using some form of market process, then the costs of this process can be used as a measure of avoided cost (in the case of improvements in environmental quality). For example, dirt arising from air pollution can be removed by hiring cleaning services or trading leisure time for cleaning time. The value of reduced cleaning costs following a reduction in air pollution could be measured in this fashion. However, these are not actual willingness to pay estimates and they depend on the assumptions of the labor/leisure trade-offs associated with such activities.

3.3. Averting behavior

In order to avoid the impact of an environmental quality change an individual could choose to invest in defensive activities or averting behaviors. For example, the value of air quality improvements could be examined through assessment of purchases of air conditioners or the value of water quality improvements could be assessed through analysis of the purchase of bottled water. However, it is often difficult to separate the behavior intended to avoid the environmental damage from other joint products. Also, it is often difficult to collect information on many averting behavior purchases (Freeman, 1993).

3.4. Hedonic price methods

Hedonic price methods attempt to decompose the purchase price of market goods into various attributes. The most common example is the examination of the price of housing in terms of the attributes of the house, air quality, noise, school quality, etc. This decomposition provides measures of the value of changes in environmental quality factors. This method has also been employed to examine the value of risk reductions in labor markets and wages as well as the value of environmental quality changes at recreational sites (hedonic travel cost models). Hedonic price methods have been popular in the analysis of housing value; however, increasingly researchers are employing random utility models to assess the value of attributes in housing markets. The latter have several advantages in terms of welfare measurement, and appear to have performed well in comparisons of the two methods (Cropper et al., 1993).

3.5. Contingent valuation

Contingent valuation elicits estimates of value directly from individuals by asking highly structured survey questions. Thus, contingent valuation is a stated-preference method. These questions commonly ask individuals if they would choose to pay a certain amount for an increase in environmental quality of some form. These questions are often structured as a referendum to capture the social institution that is common in providing such public goods and to make the question incentive compatible. A wide variety of contingent valuation mechanisms have been used, including single open-ended questions, single discrete choice (take it or leave it) questions, multiple discrete choice questions, and other formats. A significant research effort has taken place to identify factors affecting contingent valuation responses and to assess the degree to which these responses are reflective of actual consumer welfare. Further details can be found in Carson (2000) and Mitchell and Carson (1989). An exposition of the analysis of contingent valuation surveys can be found in Hanemann and Kanninen (1999).

3.6. Choice experiments

Choice experiments are also stated-preference methods, but they most often involve presenting individuals with choices that are described by attributes of a situation. Choice experiments are often referred to as attribute-based methods or attribute-based stated choice methods. These methods are valuable when the identification of marginal values of attributes is important, when new alternatives with new attributes are being introduced, or when an attribute-based approach provides a better context for the decision. Choice experiment data can be used to identify values/trade-offs, or they can be combined with revealed-preference information on the same decision to enhance the data used for valuation. Choice experiment data are analyzed using a random utility framework, as are many contingent valuation and travel cost models. Thus, these methods are employed in a utility consistent framework. Adamowicz (2000) and Louviere et al. (2000) discuss choice experiments further.

3.7. Travel cost models

Travel cost models arose from the recognition that travel and time costs form an implicit price for accessing recreation resources. Thus, the travel decision (site choice, frequency of trips) reveals the trade-offs between environmental quality and monetary outlay. Simple travel cost models that examine the number of trips to a specific recreation site as a function of price (distance) have been replaced by more complex models that include the substitution between alternatives, the possibility of corner solutions (no trips to some alternatives), the trade-off between frequency of trips and site choice, and the inclusion of environmental quality attributes as explanators of site choice. Overviews of travel cost models are provided in Parsons (2003) and Freeman (1993).

4. Valuation of non-health end-points

The general valuation techniques described above have been applied in various ways to non-health end-points associated with changes in air quality, water quality, land-use, and other effects related to transportation. A summary of the end-points and common valuation approaches is presented in Table 2.

4.1. Valuation of agricultural and forest impacts

Non-health impacts arise from changes to production systems that rely on environmental services for part of their activity (forestry, agriculture). For example, changes in ozone levels are recognized to affect plant growth, and thus may result in economic impacts. Freeman (1993) and Adams and Crocker (1991) provide the conceptual approach to such impacts. There are three main issues associated with the valuation of crop and forest impacts; (1) assessing the impact of the change in environmental quality on production or consumption; (2) assessing the response of input and output market prices to these changes; and (3) examining adaptations made by producers/consumers in response to these changes (changes in management strategies, input mixes, etc.). Several techniques have been used to evaluate the impact of air quality changes on crops. The most common, and simplest, approach is to forecast the change in output (yields, etc.) and multiply these changes in quantity by the current price of the output (Adams and Crocker, 1991).

Table 2
Valuation of non-health end-points

Environmental impact	Valuation estimates available?	Technique
Agricultural and forestry impacts	Yes	Revealed preference: Change in consumer and producer surplus Change in profit/market values Hedonic price methods Stated preference: Contingent valuation Choice experiments
Household soiling/damage to structures	Yes	Revealed preference: Change in consumer and producer surplus, averting behavior Hedonic price methods Stated preference: Contingent valuation Choice experiments Other: Avoided cost
Visibility/aesthetics	Yes	Revealed preference: Hedonic price methods Stated preference: Contingent valuation Choice experiments
Noise	Yes	Revealed preference: Averting behavior Hedonic price methods Stated preference: Contingent valuation Choice experiments
Recreation (impacts on wildlife, visibility, scenery, loss of habitat areas, disturbance from roads, etc.). (See Table 3)	Yes	Revealed preference: Travel cost models (random utility models, demand systems models) Stated preference: Contingent valuation Choice experiments
Ecosystem effects: impacts on passive use values (existence values, threatened species, etc).	Few if any	Stated preference: Contingent valuation Choice experiments
Impacts on historic buildings, cultural landmarks, etc.	Few	Stated preference: Contingent valuation Choice experiments

Source: based on Freeman (1993).

This approach suffers from the fact that no behavioral changes are incorporated into the process and thus could overstate the impact significantly.

A second approach is to construct operations research models (linear programming, etc.) and derive the value of the impact by assessing change in the output from these models. This approach is consistent with economic theory as it examines the behavioral response to changes in environmental quality. However, this approach typically employs representative firms and operates on the notion that the operations research model accurately reflects the actions of the economic agents. Adams and Crocker provide information on a number of studies that employ this approach to assess the impacts of ozone on agricultural productivity (see also Royal Society of Canada, 2001). Most of the models include price changes, output substitution possibilities, and input substitution possibilities.

Adams and Crocker (1991) provide an overview of the empirical findings in studies of impacts to agricultural systems. Their significant observations are:

- Assessing consumer and producer impacts is essential as producers can gain from decreases in environmental quality (because of the structure of the market).
- Consumer losses make up a substantial portion of the impact of environmental quality changes such as air quality changes.
- Impacts will change significantly depending on the region being examined and the biological and economic features of the regions (Adams and Crocker, 1991).

A third approach to valuation of agricultural/forest effects is to employ econometric techniques to examine markets (supply and demand) or profit functions of an industry and their response to changes in environmental quality. The hedonic property value approach is also an example of an econometric approach to assessing materials damage. While these approaches examine changes in market prices, outputs, etc., in response to changes in environmental quality, they also suffer from a number of theoretical and empirical difficulties. Finally, survey approaches (contingent valuation, etc.) can be employed to assess the value of changes in environmental quality on producers. However, these methods have not been used to a large degree, in part because of the challenges in constructing contingent valuation scenarios that can be easily responded to and also because of the availability of other, market based, approaches to valuation.

4.2. Valuation of recreation impacts

Transportation impacts that affect air quality, water quality, or habitat changes may translate into changes in aquatic and terrestrial systems, and thus into changes in the quality of recreational experiences. The most commonly explored pathway involves assessing the impact on fish populations (as a result of acid

Table 3
Approaches for assessing the value of recreation impacts

Approach	Criteria		
	Welfare theoretic (yes/no)	Numbers of studies (many/some/few)	Other limitations
Change in expenditures	No	Some	May not be at all related to welfare impact
Unit day values times change in participation	No	Some	Ignores value changes and only examines participation changes
Random utility/discrete choice models (revealed-preference and/or choice experiments)	Yes	Some	Many examples, but few linked specifically to transportation impacts on environmental quality
Demand systems framework	Yes	Few	Few examples and few linked specifically to transportation impacts on environmental quality
Contingent valuation	Yes	Some	Difficult to construct scenarios
Hedonic travel cost	Yes	Few	Interpretation difficulties
Traditional travel cost	Yes (but not usually when quality changes are involved)	Some	Cannot be easily employed in analysis of quality changes

Source: based on Royal Society of Canada (2001).

deposition, for example), resulting in change in fish catch rates for anglers. A second example involves the decline in recreational experience quality associated with change in visibility. Several approaches have been employed to examine the economic welfare impact of changes in environmental quality on recreation. These include unit day values approaches, analyses of recreation expenditures, contingent valuation, choice experiments/random utility/discrete choice travel cost models, hedonic travel cost models, and traditional travel cost models. These methods are outlined in Table 3. This table provides an assessment about whether these methods are consistent with utility theory, whether there are many studies in the category and whether there are other caveats or considerations about the approach. For an overview of recreation demand models see Parsons (2003) and Freeman (1993).

Of the methods presented in Table 3, random utility/discrete choice models (Parsons, 2002) and the demand systems framework (Phaneuf et al., 2000) are state-of-the-art approaches to evaluate the impacts of changes in environmental quality on recreation. These include impacts on fish/wildlife (damage to fish populations, for example) as well as impacts associated with visibility, habitat quality, etc. Random utility approaches (based on revealed-preference, stated-preference, or combined data) include consideration of substitution possibilities, provide for direct assessment of environmental quality changes on behavior and value, and are theoretically consistent (Holmes and Adamowicz, 2002). The Air Quality Valuation Model (AQVM; Stratus Consulting, 1999), for example, includes recreation demand models in its database for assessing the economic impact of air quality changes. In this model, a 1% change in acid deposition from air quality changes generates between Can. $0.003 and Can. $0.07 (1996 basis) per angler day. The analysis of the US Clean Air Act Amendments (US Environmental Protection Agency, 1999) includes studies that assess the impact of toxics on recreational angling. Summaries of the recreation values and studies can be found at the Environmental Valuation Reference Inventory (http://www.evri.ec.gc.ca/evri/).

A key component in the analysis of impacts on recreation is the degree of substitution between recreational alternatives available to the individual. If many alternatives are available, the economic impact associated with effects on a single alternative will be small. In addition, if a large number of alternatives are affected by the change in environmental quality, the way that non-participation (an alternative that involves not participating in the activity) is modeled is critical to the assessment of value (Parsons, 2003). Therefore, recreation impacts, while possibly affecting large numbers of people, have tended to be relatively small when compared with mortality or morbidity effects.

4.3. Valuation of other non-health impacts

Beyond agricultural, forestry, recreation, and visibility impacts, a number of other potential impacts associated with transportation changes can be examined. Among these are damages to infrastructure (buildings, etc.), noise, property value changes through visibility changes, and household soiling. Infrastructure damages are often valued by examining defensive expenditures (expenditures incurred to prevent damages) or expenditures on repairs. Neither of these approaches is necessarily consistent with economic theory. A novel approach to valuing damages to monuments (historical artifacts) by stated-preference analysis was conducted by Morey et al. (2002).

Visibility impacts in housing markets could be assessed using hedonic price methods or stated-preference methods. A difficulty that arises, however, is that the perceived health benefits of improved visibility may be confounded with aesthetic benefits. Also, there is the potential for the air quality effects to be below the threshold of perceived effects and thus difficulties are introduced in defining and valuing such effects. Policy analyses examining these types of impacts have largely relied on contingent valuation estimates. For example, the US Clean Air Act (US Environmental Protection Agency, 1999) analysis employed a contingent valuation measure. The AQVM (Stratus Consulting, 1999) employs estimates based on increases in particulate matter where a 5% increase in particulate matter generates a welfare loss of Can. $10 (1996 basis) per household per year. These impacts could be assessed (probably more reliably) in a hedonic price or random utility framework.

The value of reductions in household soiling, arising from reduced particulate matter, has been examined using avoided cost approaches. However, it is not clear that the household's response to additional soiling would be to hire labor to address the additional soiling, to re-deploy the household labor in some fashion, or to use other methods to address the issue (e.g. invest in other technologies to reduce damages – defensive expenditures). Thus, the methods that employ estimates of hired labor as a response to soiling may generate significantly biased estimates of value, and may not be consistent with economic theory. Other methods that rely on household production approaches and examine changes in household labor and resource allocation in response to different levels of soiling are more defensible.

4.4. Passive use values

One of the most controversial forms of value is passive use value (often called existence value). This value arises when there are no direct behavioral links between an individual and a value end-point. For example, a transportation route may be planned that goes through endangered species habitat. There is no market for the endangered species component of the land, and their existence is essentially a pure public good. There is not necessarily a behavior such as recreation related to the endangered species habitat. Therefore, the only ways to assess such values are stated-preference methods (Adamowicz, 2000). Passive use value estimates and the change in such values associated with transportation externalities are very rare. Thus, the values of impacts on ecosystems, protected areas, endangered species, monuments, historic buildings, etc., are largely unknown. While significant strides in the development of these techniques have been made, there remain concerns about the validity of these estimates. In most economic analyses they are identified as highly uncertain and potentially large (e.g. US Environmental Protection Agency, 1999).

5. Examples of non-health values

A large number of studies have been conducted to assess the monetary value of non-health values. A repository of these values can be found at (http://www.evri.ec.gc.ca/evri/). In some cases these values have been used in integrated policy analyses, such as the analysis of the US Clean Air Act Amendments (US Environmental Protection Agency, 1999) or the evaluation of particulate matter and ozone standards by the Royal Society of Canada (2001). In these studies the non-health component has comprised a little over 1% of the total benefits estimate. For example, in the US Environmental Protection Agency study, non-health benefits make up 0.04% of the estimated total benefits of air quality regulation. It should be noted that many highly uncertain areas are excluded from current benefits estimates/end-points (e.g. ecosystem impacts), and thus additional research in these areas may reveal a somewhat different pattern in non-health benefits in the future. A second consideration is that there are relatively few studies of non-health benefits specifically applied to externalities arising from transportation. Most recreation studies, for example, are aimed at assessing the impacts associated with natural resource damages (oil spills, toxic wastes, etc.) Transferring benefit estimates from other applications (referred to as benefit transfer) is the only option in these cases, but there are many concerns about the credibility of benefit transfers. Additional examples can be found in Daniels and Adamowicz (2000).

6. Conclusions

A number of methods for measuring the value of non-health-related environmental externalities have been examined. In addition, valuation of some specific end-points (agriculture, recreation, etc.) has been discussed. Some of the key issues arising in the valuation of non-health environmental externalities are:

- In most policy applications non-health values tend to be small relative to health related values associated with environmental quality change. However, some of the non-health value are uncertain and may be quite large. Ecosystem values or passive use values are often cited as being potentially large.
- In many cases, multiple methods are available for the assessment of environmental values for any given end-point. It is best to use methods

that are consistent with economic theory (i.e. willingness-to-pay measures arising from individual based trade-off models). It is also often advisable to combine measures from multiple sources and/or combine data types in deriving value estimates. Most policy models that contain economic value estimates attempt to employ a number of estimates and construct a distribution of value estimates rather than relying on single estimates.

- While health-related values, such as mortality risk values, are based primarily on individuals, non-health values often involve complex interactions between individuals and environmental conditions. Recreation values, for example, are a function of the substitute sites available to an individual. Values for visibility depend on the location of the individual and the scenery being viewed. Thus, non-health environmental values may be less transferable than health related values. Values of mortality risk, for example, may not differ between individuals with similar sociodemographic characteristics living in different regions of a country. Values associated with recreation may differ substantially.
- Both revealed-preference and stated-preference methods have been employed and appear to have performed well as methods of environmental valuation when carefully applied. Increasingly, it is being recognized that stated-preference and revealed-preference data simply arise from different data-generating processes, each of which has its own positive and negative aspects. Future research in valuation will likely involve both types of data as well as combinations of data types.
- Valuation estimates rely on models of choice or demand that illustrate trade-offs made by individuals. Thus, as theories of choice behavior evolve, so will valuation methods. Among the emerging issues in choice behavior are the recognition of the choice context as an important element in modeling choice behavior (Swait et al., 2002) and the need to increase our understanding of variances in choice processes (Louviere et al., 2002).

Acknowledgment

This chapter was completed while I was a Gilbert White Visiting Fellow at Resources for the Future, Washington, DC, and I am grateful for their support.

References

Adamowicz, W.L. (2000) "Environmental valuation," in: J. Louviere, D. Hensher and J. Swait, eds, *Stated choice methods - analysis and application*. Cambridge: Cambridge University Press.
Adams, R.M. and T.D. Crocker (1991) "Materials damages," in: J.B. Braden and C.D. Kolstad, eds, *Measuring the demand for environmental quality*. Amsterdam: North-Holland.

Braden, J.B. and C.D. Kolstad, eds (1991) *Measuring the demand for environmental quality.* Amsterdam: North-Holland.
Carson, R.T. (2000) "Contingent valuation: a users guide," *Environmental Science and Technology*, 34:1413–1418.
Cropper, M.L., L. Deck, N. Kishor and K.E. McConnell (1993) "Valuing product attributes using single market data: a comparison of hedonic and discrete choice approaches," *Review of Economics and Statistics*, 75:225–232.
Daniels, R. and W. Adamowicz (2000) "Environmental valuation," in: D. Hensher and K. Button, eds, *Handbook of transport modelling*, pp. 285–301. Amsterdam: Pergamon.
Freeman, A.M. (1993) *The measurement of environmental and resource values.* Baltimore: Resources for the Future Press.
Hanemann, W.M. and B. Kanninen (1999) "The statistical analysis of discrete response data," in: I. Bateman and K. Willis, eds, *Valuing environmental preferences*. Oxford: Oxford University Press.
Holmes, T. and W. Adamowicz (2003) "Attribute based methods," in: P. Champ, T. Brown and K. Boyle, eds, *A primer on the economic valuation of the environment*. Dordrecht: Kluwer.
Louviere, J.J., D.A. Hensher and J. Swait (2000) *Stated choice analysis and methods*. Cambridge: Cambridge University Press.
Louviere, J., R. Carson, A. Ainslie, T. Cameron, J.R. DeShazo, D. Hensher, R. Kohn, T. Marley and D. Street (2002) Dissecting the random component of utility. *Marketing Letters*, 13:177–193.
Maddison, D., D. Pearce, O. Johansson, E. Calthorp, T. Litman and E. Verhoef (1996) *The true costs of road transport*. London: Earthscan.
Mitchell, R.C., and R.T. Carson (1989) *Using surveys to value public goods: the contingent valuation method.* Baltimore: Resources for the Future.
Morey, E.R., K. Rossmann, L. Chestnut and S. Ragland (2003) "Modeling and estimating WTP for reducing acid deposition injuries to cultural resources: using choice experiments in a group setting to estimate passive-use values," in: S. Narvud and R. Ready, eds, *Valuing cultural resources*. Cheltenham: Edward Elgar.
Parsons, G. (2003) "The travel cost model," in: P. Champ, T. Brown and K. Boyle, eds, *A primer on the economic valuation of the environment*. Dordrecht: Kluwer.
Phaneuf, D.J., C.L. Kling, and J.A. Herriges (2000) "Estimation and welfare calculations in a generalized corner solution model with an application to recreation demand," *Review of Economics and Statistics*, 82: 83–92.
Royal Society of Canada (2001) *Report of the Expert Panel to Review the Socioeconomic Models and Related Components Supporting the Development of Canada-wide Standards for Particulate Matter and Ozone.* Ottawa: Royal Society of Canada.
Swait, J., W. Adamowicz, W.M. Hanemann, A. Diederich, J. Krosnick, D. Layton, W. Provencher, D. Schkade and R. Tourangeau (2002) "Context dependence and aggregation in disaggregate choice analysis," *Marketing Letters*, 13:195–205.
US Environmental Protection Agency (1999) *The benefits and costs of the Clean Air Act 1990 to 2010. EPA Report to Congress*, EPA-410-R-99–001. Washington, DC: Office of Air and Radiation, Office of Policy, EPA.

Chapter 21

VALUATION CASE STUDIES

JUAN DE DIOS ORTÚZAR and LUIS IGNACIO RIZZI
Pontificia Universidad Católica de Chile, Casilla

1. Introduction

Although it is relatively easy in theory, the actual valuation of environmental goods is complex since we need to place a monetary value on a non-traded good. Many studies based on revealed-preference (RP) data, such as hedonic pricing, rest on rather dubious assumptions. For example, it is customary to assume that people are fully aware of the environmental goods being modeled and that they consider these in the same way the modeler does. As an alternative approach, stated-preference (SP) methods allow for a different perspective: a pseudo-market is created in which respondents have to act as they would do if in real life. If respondents agree to "play the game," many of the previous problems should disappear – but do they? In addition, a sound microeconomic foundation is required for an SP technique to be a viable input for cost–benefit analysis.

According to Nash (1997), methods designed to elicit people's preferences about environmental goods should be more successful when attempting to value local and perceived externalities. These constitute adverse effects of transport systems on which most people may have already defined their preferences. Road accidents, local pollution, and noise clearly fall within this category, and are currently deemed to rank among the most negative impacts of road transport on a local scale. Hence, it is believed that appropriate valuation case studies could be designed in order to derive willingness-to-pay (WTP) measures for each of these externalities. Daniels and Adamowicz (2000) consider the most important issues concerning environmental valuation; readers are directed there for additional information on this topic.

In this chapter we present the microeconomic foundations for conducting SP experiments and describe three different case studies on valuing transport externalities, based on what is arguably the most promising SP technique: stated-choice methods. In Section 2, a brief description of the random utility approach is provided in order to guide both experimental design and econometric analysis. Sections 3 and 4 deal with SP applications for the valuation of interurban

Handbook of Transport and the Environment, Edited by D.A. Hensher and K.J. Button
© 2003, Elsevier Ltd

road accidents and atmospheric pollution in a large metropolis, respectively. Interestingly, both experiments were carried out in a developing country: Chile. Section 5 gives an example of a SP application to elicit people's WTP for noise reduction in Portugal. The chapter closes with our conclusions.

2. Random utility and SP methods

In this section we provide guidance to perform an econometric analysis based on sound microeconomic principles. This will make apparent why some rather severe restrictions on preferences are necessary in most SP applications, which, if not followed, may render the whole analysis dubious. Assume an individual has to choose one option out of a given choice set. The utility maximization problem will look like this:

$$\max_m \langle \max_x U(x, q_m)/m \in M \rangle, \tag{1}$$

subject to $px + c_m = I$, where x is a vector of goods, M the discrete choice set (its cardinal is N), m is an element of that set, p is the vector price of goods x, c_m is the cost of alternative m, q_m is the vector of attributes of alternative m, and I is income. This constitutes a discrete maximization problem, which can be decomposed into N differentiable subproblems:

$$\max_x U(x, q_m)/m \in M, \tag{2}$$

subject to $px = I - c_m$.

The individual will choose that option which reports the highest level of U among the N differentiable problems. Thus, we obtain a conditional indirect utility function for each of the N alternatives:

$$V_m = V(p, I - c_m). \tag{3}$$

Assuming an additively conditional indirect utility function, equation (3) yields

$$V_m(p, I - c_m, q_m) = v_m(p) + v_m(I - c_m) + v_m(q_m),$$

and as clearly the first term is the same for each alternative m, it drops out. Next assume a linear-in-income utility function, so that the preceding equation looks like

$$V_m(p, I - c_m, q_m) = \alpha(I - c_m) + v_m(q_m),$$

and now income drops out. Observe that the marginal utility of income is given by minus the parameter of cost. Finally, if we also assume an additive $v_m(q_m)$ term, the following is obtained:

$$V_m(p, I - c_m, q_m) = \alpha^\circ c_m + \sum \beta_l q_{ml}, \tag{4}$$

where α^o and β_l are the parameters associated to cost and each of the l attributes of each option m (α^o accounts for the sign change in α). This result could have been obtained also by a first order Taylor expansion of equation (3). It is important that the reader be fully aware of the restrictions that equation (4) poses on preferences according to how it was derived. Although this model is correct from the consumer's perspective, it is not from the modeler's standpoint. As he does not observe all relevant information to conclude which alternative the consumer will choose, he can just obtain choice probabilities. To that end, equation (4) should read like this:

$$U_m = U(p, I - c_m, q_m \varepsilon_m), \tag{5}$$

where ε represents an error term. Note that these error terms are not just statistical noise that deviate observations from their expected value, but components of preferences themselves from the modeler's perspective; hence, error terms will have an impact on both underlying preferences and welfare measures (Hanemann and Kanninen, 1999). As an analogy to equation (4) we obtain

$$U_m = \alpha^o c_m + \sum_l \beta_l q_{ml} + \varepsilon_m = V_m + \varepsilon_m, \tag{6}$$

and note that errors were introduced in additive form. If they distribute identically and independently (iid) Gumbel between alternatives, the popular multinomial logit model is obtained (e.g. see Ortúzar and Willumsen, 2001). The probability of choosing a specific alternative, say i from M, is

$$\text{Prob}(i) = \text{Prob}(U_i > U_m, i \neq m, \forall m \in M)$$

$$\left(= \frac{\exp(V_i)}{\sum_{m \in M} \exp(V_m)} \quad \text{if a logit model} \right). \tag{7}$$

If the modeler is interested in valuing an specific attribute l, he can consider the ratio β_l/α^o. This gives the maximum monetary value that an individual would pay for a marginal improvement in attribute l, and is simply obtained by fixing the level of the conditional indirect utility and allowing the cost and the level of attribute l to vary only in equation (6). By marginal, it is implied that an improvement in the alternative is currently being chosen and will continue to be chosen. In the case studies presented below we will only compute this type of welfare measure.

For non-marginal improvements and/or improvements in the attributes of not chosen options affecting the probability of choice, the simple ratio above does not work because it fails to take into account that people can switch between alternatives in order to attain the highest level of utility. It can be shown that for the logit model with linear-in-income utility, the appropriate welfare measure is given by the change in the inclusive value (composite utility) before and after the change (Small and Rosen, 1981):

$$-\frac{1}{\alpha}\left[\log\left(\sum_{m\in M}\exp(V_m)\right)^{ac} - \log\left(\sum_{m\in M}\exp(V_m)\right)^{bc}\right]. \tag{8}$$

When the assumption of a linear-in-income utility function does not work, a much more involved formula is needed. For a detailed discussion on the microeconomic foundations of random utility models, its applications to SP surveys, and on how to develop welfare measures, the reader is advised to consult Adamowicz (2000), Freeman (1993), Hanemann (1999), Hanemann and Kanimen (1999), Louviere et al. (2000), and McFadden (1995).

3. First case study: interurban road accidents

An SP survey was designed to estimate the value of a statistical life (VSL) in an interurban road context. When it comes to estimating values for road safety, contingent valuation, standard gamble, or the chain method techniques are typical applications; see Chapter 24 for an account on how to estimate WTP for safety improvements and the application of contingent valuation and the chain method to obtain the VSL. In almost all these cases people are confronted with situations where risks are expressed as tiny probabilities, and in order to come up with a monetary value, a trade-off between risk and money is involved. This kind of context simulation may not bear upon actual choices where individuals have to consider a bundle of attributes of a particular good in a definite choice context. As an alternative approach, Rizzi and Ortúzar (2002) decided to carry out an SP route choice experiment; to the authors' knowledge this is the first ever application of the SP approach to value interurban road safety. A survey was conducted for car trips between the conurbations of Santiago and Viña del Mar/Valparaíso (the two largest in Chile); these are located 120 km apart using Route 68, which carries one of the highest traffic volumes in the country.

After three pilot surveys a robust self-completion questionnaire for the main survey was developed. The survey instrument had three parts. The first asked about the frequency with which the person drove on interurban roads in general, and in particular on Route 68. The second part included the choice experiment itself and questions related to road accident experience and attitudes. Finally, the third part of the survey asked for socio-economic data.

Three variables were considered for the choice experiment: travel time, toll charge, and annual accident rate. After extensive analysis and pilot testing, the last variable was defined as the number of accidents during the year in which at least one car occupant died. Thus, the risk variable was designed to represent the

Table 1
Attribute difference levels

Weekend toll (US $)	Weekday toll (US $)	Accidents per year	Travel time (min)
3.0	2.4	−4	−30
−2.0	−1.6	8	−15
1.0	0.8	−12	−45

Table 2
Block differences after utility balance for weekends and weekdays (latter in parentheses)

Block 1			Block 2			Block 3		
Toll	Accidents	Time	Toll	Accidents	Time	Toll	Accidents	Time
3 (2.4)	−4	−30	2 (1.6)	−4	−15	3 (2.4)	−4	−45
3 (2.4)	8	−45	3 (2.4)	−8	−30	3 (2.4)	−8	−15
3 (2.4)	−12	−15	3 (2.4)	−12	−45	3 (2.4)	−12	−30
2 (1.6)	−4	−45	2 (1.6)	−4	−30	2 (1.6)	−4	−15
−2 (−1.6)	8	15	−2 (−1.6)	8	45	−2 (−1.6)	8	30
2 (1.6)	−12	−30	3 (2.4)	−12	−15	2 (1.6)	12	−45
1 (0.8)	−4	−15	1 (0.8)	4	−45	1 (0.8)	−4	−30
1 (0.8)	8	−30	1 (0.8)	8	−15	1 (0.8)	8	−45
1 (0.8)	−12	−45	1 (0.8)	−12	30	1 (0.8)	−12	15

general level of safety on the route; deaths of pedestrians and deaths caused by vehicles other than cars were excluded. The experimental design was based on attribute differences, which is what matters when estimating discrete choice models (Hensher, 1990). Table 1 shows the levels of the attribute differences.

An experimental design allowing for interactions and quadratic effects was adopted. A complete profile would have implied each respondent having to answer 27 choice situations; but based on previous experience in Chile the authors decided that this would put too much burden upon respondents. Thus, the design was split into three nine-choice blocks (i.e. three respondents would be necessary for a whole replication). In order to improve the statistical design, dominant alternatives were eliminated by inverting the sign difference; also, an increase in utility balance as suggested by Huber and Zwerina (1996) was sought. Thus, there was a pragmatic departure from strict orthogonality that was compensated for by increased realism and the avoidance of dominated (completely uninformative) choice situations. The details of the statistical design may be seen in Rizzi and Ortuzar (2003). Table 2 shows attribute differences for each block. In addition, the order of presentation of choice situations was randomized to avoid inducing a definite pattern of correlation due to the order in which situations appeared (Louviere et al., 2000).

3.1. The choice context

Several scenarios were considered: traveling on a weekend (for social purposes) and traveling during the week (for work or administrative purposes); the latter could also include coming back at night. With respect to trips on working days, the time of day could be either the morning or evening. In every case the trip was assumed to be unavoidable, so a non-purchase option was not a possibility. Finally, all trips were placed in periods of the day that made certain that travel time savings were highly likely (low to moderate congestion).

A problem with the risk variable was that although the figures presented were factual, people might not have been familiar with them; however, people are aware that Route 68 ranks among the safest in Chile (high police control and a reasonably good highway design). The introduction to the choice experiment stated that the actual number of accidents with at least one fatality during the previous two years was 27 on average.

Thus the context was clearly defined: the day, time of day, and trip purpose were all specified. It was also assumed that the person who answered the questionnaire was the driver and she or he paid for the toll. Although road safety is a public good since all drivers benefit from a road safety scheme, it has a private dimension in the sense that interviewees had to answer what route they would choose for a particular trip: there was little room for an altruistic choice.

3.2. Discrete choice modeling

When the survey was completed, 342 responses were considered appropriate for the analysis. As each respondent made nine choices, the potential total number of observations (pseudo-individuals) was 3078, a reasonable sample size. Although the problem of serial correlation between observations coming from the same person was not considered, there is no reason to believe that this shortcoming would seriously affect the results. In all cases binary logit models including interactions and a quadratic effect were estimated using ALOGIT (Daly, 1992). In the most general case tested, the deterministic component of the indirect utility function V_i is

$$V_i = \alpha(r_i - \bar{r}) + \beta(c_i - \bar{c}) + \chi(t_i - \bar{t}) + \delta(r_i - \bar{r})(c_i - \bar{c}) \\ + \gamma(c_i - \bar{c})(t_i - \bar{t}) + \eta(r_i - \bar{r})^2 \tag{9}$$

where r denotes risk, c the toll, t time, and i the route i. All values were mean centered at $\bar{r}$, $\bar{c}$, and $\bar{t}$, to avoid correlation between the linear and quadratic risk variables. The interaction and quadratic terms not considered in equation (9) were not statistically different from zero in their empirical analysis. Interactions and quadratic effects allow the expression of subjective values as functions of the attribute levels, instead of as fixed values independent of the alternatives; however, as others before, it was found that using more flexible forms may lead to some inconsistencies. For example, it is easy to see from equation (10) below that negative values for safety may appear if the numerator and denominator have different signs.

The risk variable was constructed as follows: the total number of trips by car taking place on Route 68 was 3.7 million in 1997, and the average number of deaths by each fatal accident involving car victims was 1.32. The product of the number of fatal accidents by the average number of deaths per accident divided by the number of trips yielded the probability of a car occupant dying on Route 68. As this was a value around 0.096 per 10 000 trips, it is obvious that the SP experiment would not have worked if based on variations of such tiny probabilities.

The formal definition of the VSL is the following. First, the marginal rate of substitution between income and risk for pseudo-individual j is the implicit value of life (IVL):

$$\text{IVL}_j = \frac{\alpha + \delta(c_i - \bar{c}) + 2\eta(r_i - \bar{r})}{\beta + \delta(r_i - \bar{r}) + \gamma(t_i - \bar{t})}. \tag{10}$$

Provided there is no correlation between WTP and risk, averaging IVLs over the whole sample (n pseudo-individuals) yields the VSL:

$$\text{VSL} = \frac{\sum_j \text{IVL}_j}{n} \tag{11}$$

Note that when linear models are considered the IVL and VSL are equal because the non-linear terms disappear; in this case IVL was a constant (α/β) for all individuals. The VSL thus derived has to be interpreted as an annual societal WTP for reducing one statistical death per year for individuals traveling by car on Route 68. To be more explicit, each time a trip is made the driver would be willing to pay an amount equal to $\text{IVL}_j(1/3\ 700\ 000)$ per trip to avoid a statistical death on that route, on an annual basis; aggregating all these values over the total number of trips in a year, the VSL is obtained. By the same procedure, the individual's subjective value of travel time (SVT_j) and the mean value of travel time (VTT) are given by equations (12) and (13), respectively. Note that at mean sample values ($\bar{r}$, $\bar{c}$, and $\bar{t}$) both IVL and SVT reduce to α/β and χ/β, respectively, in this case:

$$\text{SVT}_j = \frac{\chi}{\beta + \delta(r_i - \bar{r}) + \gamma(t_i - \bar{t})}, \tag{12}$$

$$\text{VTT} = \frac{\sum_j \text{VTT}_j}{n}. \tag{13}$$

Table 3 shows the results of the analysis for two sets of models with good fits and indirect utility functions that did not bring about any negative values of time nor negative IVLs for any observation. Models L_1 and L_2 included lexicographic answers (i.e. by individuals who always choose the option that was best in one attribute, see Saelensminde, 2001) and models W_1 and W_2 did not; the first model in each case is a linear specification. However, it was found that 21, 72, and 57 individuals exhibited lexicographic behavior in the toll, risk, and travel time variables, respectively, totaling 150 persons (44% of the sample). Removing these individuals left 192 respondents, amounting to 1721 observations for the second set of models.

It can also be seen from the table that lexicographic answers do have an effect on the estimates: both VSL and VTT are higher for the L_k models but a much better general fit can be observed in the case of the W_k models. Model L_2 shows rather high VTT and VSL due to the nature of the utility function. As reported by Gaudry et al. (1989) and Hensher (1999), different specifications of the deterministic component of the indirect utility function bring about variations in parameter

Table 3
Binary logit route choice models. Coefficient values and t ratios (in parentheses) (a)

	L_1	L_2	W_1	W_2
Risk (α)	-0.288×10^6	-0.288×10^6	-0.246×10^6	-0.253×10^6
	(−14.7)	(−14.6)	(−9.5)	(−9.6)
Time (χ)	−0.0391	−0.0398	−0.0052	−0.0521
	(−14.4)	(−14.5)	(−13.9)	(−9.4)
Toll (β)	-0.745×10^{-3}	-0.748×10^{-3}	-0.125×10^{-2}	-0.126×10^{-2}
	(−7.9)	(−7.7)	(−9.9)	(−9.9)
Risk × toll (δ)	–	92.73	–	109.9
		(3.2)		(2.8)
Toll × time (γ)	–	-0.637×10^{-5}	–	NS
		(−2.3)		
Risk^2 (η)	–	-0.468×10^{11}	–	NS
		(−2.7)		
VTT (US $)	0.105	0.204	0.083	0.083
VSL (US $)	772 721	1 286 064	392 817	381 473
$\rho^2(c)$	0.0765	0.0811	0.1182	0.1216
Sample size	3071	3071	1721	1721

Note: (a) The conversion rate was US $1 = Ch. $500 at the time of the survey. NS, not significantly different from zero. Coefficients are shown only up to the third decimal, thus giving rise to rounding errors if subjective value point estimates are calculated from the table.

Table 4
Confidence intervals at mean sample values

Model	α/β (US $) (confidence interval)	χ/β (US $) (confidence interval)
L_1	772 721 (659 755–947 391)	0.105 (0.092–0.121)
L_2	771 226 (656 226–951 180)	0.106 (0.094–0.128)
W_1	392 817 (337 290–455 860)	0.083 (0.075–0.091)
W_2	400 793 (344 904–464 754)	0.083 (0.075–0.092)

ratios. However, at mean sample values both the IVL and the subjective value of time are very similar to the L_1 model values.

In order to assess the variability of the estimates, confidence intervals for the IVL and VTT at mean sample values (α/β and χ/β) were constructed following Armstrong et al. (2000), as shown in Table 4. Note that for both measures the upper limit of the W models is below the lower range of the L models, confirming once again that lexicographic answers do make a difference.

3.3. Introduction of socio-economic variables

Behavioral modeling can be enriched using individual specific (IS) variables representing in this case both socio-economic and trip-related effects. These factors were introduced in a non-traditional form interacting with level-of-service parameters, so that the linear utility function looks like

$$V_{ij} = \left(\alpha_0 + \sum_l \alpha_l s_{lj}\right) r_{ij} + \left(\chi_0 + \sum_l \chi_l s_{lj}\right) t_{ij} + \beta_0 c_{ij} \qquad (i=1,2). \tag{14}$$

The binary variable s_{lj} represents the IS attribute l (i.e. age, sex, time of day travel) of individual j. Equation (14) states that, given the IS variables, level-of-service coefficients may differ; note that a given IS variable could enter each of the three coefficient expressions. This form of introducing the IS data allows estimating models that are almost unique to each individual in a simple way, helping to reduce the problem of random taste variations.

It would also help to reduce, but only to some extent, the problem of serial correlation since tastes are customized according to the individual. In this case, the IVL is computed through

$$\text{IVL}_j = \frac{\alpha_0 + \sum_l \alpha_l s_{ij}}{\beta}, \tag{15}$$

and the VSL, as before. It is interesting to note how the IS variables are capitalized in the estimation of the IVL: its value now depends on both the socio-economic characteristics of the individual and on the features of the particular trip.

These models had significantly better goodness-of-fit indices than the models in Table 3 and were also superior to random parameter mixed logit specifications (Rizzi and Ortúzar, 2003); the models revealed a higher preference for safety by women than by men; age also plays a role – the older the person the higher was the preference for safety. On the other hand, if a person assumed to have traveled with a companion when she or he was answering the questionnaire, she or he was more aware of risk. Finally, these results implied that there was a higher preference for safety if the trip took place at night (an expected result), and if respondents were from Valparaíso or Viña del Mar (i.e. the smaller, provincial, conurbation), they appeared to be less willing to pay for safety than people from Santiago, the larger metropolis.

4. Second case study: valuation of local air pollution

Ortúzar and Rodriguez (2002) designed an SP ranking experiment to estimate WTP for reduced atmospheric pollution in Santiago. The authors looked for a choice context where each option could be associated with different individual pollutant exposures. It was found that a realistic way of "offering" distinct atmospheric conditions consisted of presenting different residential locations associated with different air quality levels. This context was supported by the notion that when families decide where to live, they consider not only the dwelling characteristics but also the features of its location (Hunt et al., 1994), including air quality and accessibility conditions. As a residential location represents a medium/long-term decision and can be labeled a complex decision process, rank-order data was used. It has been found that this format is particularly appropriate in these cases. In addition, Hunt et al. (1994) and Ortúzar et al. (2000) had used ranking data in a residential choice context with good results. The latter experience is especially meaningful because that survey was carried out in the same geographical area and using a similar survey format.

4.1. Definition of the air quality attribute

The attributes characterizing an option in an SP exercise should have a clearly defined and unique interpretation, so that individuals manifest their preference valuing objectively "the same thing." This was a complex task as it involved identifying an appropriate attribute to represent different air quality conditions, and the analytical measurement units of pollutant concentrations are unknown for a large share of the community. The authors looked for an air quality measure that was part of the daily references of a typical citizen and that had a direct relationship with the concentration of atmospheric pollutants.

After several pilot studies, the current air quality index (ICA) for Santiago was considered an adequate measure. The ICA index converts concentrations of five major air pollutants (carbon monoxide (CO), sulfur dioxide (SO_2), nitrogen dioxide (NO_2), ozone (O_3), and fine particulate matter (PM_{10})) into a single number and a matching description using a linear approximation. These pollutants are continuously monitored at eight different stations in the city, where an index value is calculated daily. Then, the concentration of each pollutant is converted to its ICA equivalence, and the highest number becomes the ICA level for that station. Finally, the station with the highest number yields the global ICA level for the whole city.

This information is disseminated daily through the media. Every television and newspaper meteorological report includes the ICA index, emphasizing the area where the station recording that level is located. The environmental contingence day qualification (alert, pre-emergency, and emergency days) receives special attention. This is directly determined on the basis of ICA levels measured during the year. According to this local profile, it was concluded that an adequate attribute to represent air quality conditions for a particular location was the number of days when the zone index would qualify for a city contingence day status.

4.2. Identification of attributes and selection of measurement units

Although there are many factors influencing housing choice behavior (Hunt et al., 1994) it was considered reasonable to include only a subset of these attributes (emphasizing that any others would stay constant), as the main goal of the study was not to model housing market behavior. So, two attributes belonging to the same category of air quality, accessibility to work and accessibility to study were chosen, both expressed in minutes of travel time for each individual in the household. The last factor considered was the rent paid, which was essential to obtain a monetary valuation for the other attributes, and also gave an important dose of realism to the hypothetical exercise.

The task of choosing appropriate measurement units was straightforward for the accessibility attributes (minutes) and the rent (Chilean dollars), but this was not the case for air quality. It was decided to use the number of days per year with a contingence level as a second-best measurement unit. After conducting a pilot study, the number of days per year with an alert level associated with each residential location was selected, as there were more variations between areas than was the case for pre-emergency and emergency days.

4.3. Data collection strategy

A 3^4 fractional factorial design, leading to nine hypothetical situations (Louviere et al., 2000), was used, adding an option depicting the current situation of the household (in terms of the variables used). This was done in order to test for the existence of an "aversion to change location" effect (i.e. reflecting an overvaluation of the current situation when compared with the alternatives offered), which had been observed by Ortúzar et al. (2000). The survey was customized, ensuring that situations were well within a context familiar to each household. The levels were adjusted if the variations were smaller than thresholds based on absolute differences.

A data collection strategy that had proved successful before involved two stages and the participation of a small group of well-trained interviewers. They made two visits to each family contacted. In the first, the main characteristics of the dwelling and basic information about the family members were sought. Once these data were processed, the interviewer made a second visit, 2 days later, where the customized SP exercise was presented and a few complementary questions were asked.

After the ranking process was completed, the interviewer formulated 12 extra questions to detect how consistently the family had addressed the choice process, and to investigate if the attribute levels had been considered realistic. An important feature of this approach is that the ranking task was carried out by the whole family, trading off good attributes of certain options for some members (say travel time) with worse features for others.

In order to improve the response quality the study focused on families that had occupied their present residence for less than 2 years. Also, only tenants were considered under the assumption that they would have found a hypothetical move (and consequently the SP exercise proposed) more realistic than house-owners.

4.4. Modeling results

A total of 107 households were interviewed. The socio-economic information from the sample was representative of middle- and high-income people in Santiago. The variables used at the modeling stage were: TVW_{hi}, travel time to work by individual h from location i (minutes per trip); TVS_{hi}, travel time to study by individual h from location i (minutes per trip); and f_{Th}, f_{Eh}, frequency of trips to work and study, respectively, by individual h (trips per week). Using these variables, household accessibility variables were defined:

$$TVW_i = \sum_{h \in H_i} f_{Th} TVW_{hi}, \tag{16}$$

Table 5
Estimated models

Attributes		Parameter (*t* test)	
		Standard logit	Mixed logit
TVW	Mean	−0.00417 (−10.6)	−0.00992 (−7.9)
	SD		0.00573 (4.5)
TVS	Mean	−0.00250 (−7.8)	−0.00577 (−8.2)
	SD		0.00266 (2.7)
DA	Mean	−0.27370 (−11.0)	−0.47863 (−6.8)
	SD		0.40567 (4.7)
R	Mean	−0.02641 (−12.5)	−0.0574 (−7.0)
	SD		0.04748 (6.2)
δ_{Actual}	Mean	0.89690 (5.9)	1.05325 (5.5)
Log-likelihood		−849.6	−747.0

Key: SD, standard deviation.

$$\text{TVS}_i = \sum_{h \in H_i} f_{Eh} \text{TVS}_{hi}. \tag{17}$$

Other variables were: DA_i, days of alert associated with residential location i (days per year); R_i, value of the house rental (thousands of Chilean dollars per month); and a dummy δ_{Actual}, which takes the value 1 if option i represents the household's current location, and 0 otherwise. The indirect utility function specification used was linear-in-parameters, and consistent with the proposed microeconomic framework:

$$V_i = \theta_{Actual}\delta_{Actual} + \theta_{TVT}TVW_i + \theta_{TVE}TVS_i + \theta_{DA}DA_i + \theta_R R_i. \tag{18}$$

Models were estimated with and without lexicographic individuals. In the latter case, a much better fit was observed (Ortúzar and Rodriguez, 2002); thus, only results for those models will be considered herein. Table 5 shows results concerning two models: the first is estimated by means of standard binary logit and the second by means of binary mixed logit with normal random taste parameters (Sillano and Ortúzar, 2002). The second specification allows for repeated observations from an individual through a distribution of tastes in the sample.

All parameters have the expected sign, and the coefficients of the dummy variable δ_{Actual} turned out to be significantly positive, implying an inertia effect in the sense of adding a plus to the utility of the current residential location. The mixed logit model presents a better fit, all parameters related to the standard deviation of the taste parameters where significant, thus the null hypothesis of fixed taste parameters across the population was rejected.

Table 6 presents WTP estimates and their 95% confidence intervals following Armstrong et al. (2000). The ratios of parameters tend to be quite stable. When compared, ratios of parameters from the standard and mixed logit specifications lie within each others' confidence intervals, except for the WTP value for days of alert reductions. Unfortunately, it is not possible to say what people are actually valuing when stating a WTP for fewer days of alert. It could be related to health effects or to visibility, or to a combination of both. Research in progress on environmental risk perception should help to clarify this issue.

It is interesting to mention that, as in the previous case, the values of time obtained were consistent with values obtained previously in the country using much simpler set-ups. This could be taken as an indication that respondents both understood the experiment and played the game seriously.

5. Third case study: valuation of noise

Arsenio et al. (2002) designed a computer-based SP choice survey to estimate WTP for noise reductions. During each computer-aided personal interview the household was offered 12 random comparisons of two apartment profiles one at a time. In order to maximize respondent's familiarity with the situations presented, the various flat options were assumed to be located within the same building or lot where the household lived. Each flat profile was described by varying the levels of four attributes found relevant in the Lisbon housing market: view, noise, housing service charge, and sun exposure. Each household was told that the two apartment options were identical in terms of all other attributes.

As part of the survey a wide range of influential variables was also collected, related to the socio-economic profile of the household (income, age, and gender composition, level of education), attitudes and behavior of the household members when indoors (i.e. windows open during spring/summer, averting noise behavior, type of activities usually conducted at home during the day), levels of annoyance,

Table 6
WTP as ratios of population means (a)

Attributes	Willingness-to-pay values (confidence interval)	
	Standard logit	Mixed logit
TVW (Ch. $/min)	36 (29–45)	37 (25–54)
TVS (Ch. $/min)	22 (16–28)	25 (14–40)
DA (Ch. $/DA per year)	124 362 (100 818–152 301)	98 009 (70 127–135 793)

Note: (a) at the time of the survey, US $1 = Ch. $500.

Table 7
Mixed logit models (a)

Variable description	Model 1: perceptions	
	Mean (t)	SD (t)
(1) Increase in noise levels (base)	−0.0473 (−2.54)	–
(2) Decrease in noise levels (base)	−0.0439 (−2.49)	0.0206 (8.61) (d)
(3) Interaction of noise with exposure back/quieter façade (dummy variable)	−0.0673 (−5.93)	0.0548 (6.47) (d)
(4) Interaction of noise with number years living at the site (dummy variable)	0.02346 (2.19)	0.0214 (2.66) (d)
(5) Interaction of noise with familiarity to choice context (lot)	0.01143 (0.83)	0.0531 (5.56) (d)
(6) Interaction of noise with gender (dummy variable)	−0.02698 (−2.977)	0.0472 (4.07) (d)
(7) Interaction of noise with size of noise changes relative to the *status quo* (b)	0.00352 (2.281)	–
(8) Interaction of noise with dummy for floor number ≥ 4	−0.01518 (−1.414)	
(9) Interaction of housing service charge levels with current payment (base HSC/10^6)	0.00596 (3.12)	–
(10) Housing service charge deflated by household income per person (c)	−0.03281 (−3.26)	–
(11) Interaction of housing service charge with missing income	−0.00022 (−3.28)	–
(12) View (e)	−3.527 (−24.9)	0.911 (5.749)
(13) Sun exposure	0.0391 (7.181)	0.0544 (6.415) (d)
Log-likelihood at convergence	−2448.513	

Notes:
(a) Housing service charge: 1999 escudos per month per household (US $1 = 230 escudos (approximately) at the time of the survey).
(b) Functional form: (noise − base level in respondents apartment)^2
(c) Functional form: (housing service charge)/(income per person)$^{0.5}$.
(d) Normal distribution.
(e) Log-normal distribution.

perception of noise indoors, and real physical noise measures taken *in situ*, and building characteristics. Noise was represented by two alternative measures: first, indoor noise perceptions based on a rating scale ranging from 0 to 100, where 100 was very quiet and 0 was very noisy; secondly, the equivalent physical noise measures.

The SP choice experiment generated 4944 observations for econometric modeling corresponding to 412 households. To allow for the effect of repeated observations a mixed logit model specification was used. Table 7 shows only the model based on perceptions, which outperformed the model based on physical noise measures,

Table 8
Subjective values of noise per unit of perceived decrease. Rating scale: 0 (very noisy) to 100 (very quiet)

Adjusted income per person per household	Experienced noise level (QBASE)	Noise level (QIMP)	Change (QIMP–QBASE)	Marginal value of noise: front flat (a)	Marginal value of noise: quieter façade (a)
30 000	60	70	10	254	718
	60	80	20	205	670
	40	50	10	263	732
	40	60	20	224	697

Note: (a) 1999 escudos per month per household (US $1 = 230 escudos (approximately) at the time of the survey).

but both were consistent in detecting the main influential effects on the marginal values of noise. The mixed logit model was also far superior to the equivalent standard multinomial logit model with interaction effects, and its main results can be summarized as follows.

The best specification for the coefficient for noise increase was a fixed one. It had the expected sign, and it was lower than the corresponding coefficient for reductions in noise. The best specification for the coefficient for noise reductions was a random parameters one, with a normal distribution. Households located at the quieter façade (the back) presented a higher value of noise reduction than those fronting the main road. The standard deviation of this coefficient was highly significant.

During the SP experiment, respondents were offered flat options within the same block or lot. Although the respondent's familiarity with those flat options was taken into account, it can be expected that the random variation (e.g. due to less precise ideas or perceptions about the internal noise levels indoors) is higher when choices are within the same lot of the respondent than when choices involve only the same block. Attachment of the respondent to the *status quo* is also expected to be greater. Results show that the value of noise reduction is lower for households who faced a flat choice set within the same lot (negative sign for this coefficient, see variable 5 in Table 7). The best specification for this coefficient was allowing it to vary across individuals following a Normal distribution.

In Lisbon, females tend to spend more time at home than males due to their professions and childcare related activities. Results show lower values of noise reduction for males than females *ceteris paribus*. The best specification for the interaction of this dummy coefficient with noise was allowing it to vary across individuals following a Normal distribution. The standard deviation of the mean coefficient was highly significant, reflecting the importance of unobserved random variation intrinsic to each case/individual.

Table 8 shows the variation of the mean subjective values of (perceived) noise reduction for a male respondent who has lived for less than 5 years in a lower-floor flat (<4). Only one level of income per person was considered, and two conditions of flat exposure (front and back). The base housing service charge takes the value of 7500 (1999 escudos per month). The results in Table 8 are in line with expectations and theoretical plausibility.

The marginal values of noise reduction are around three times higher for households located in the quiet façade. Considering the same size of improvement and flat exposure, the marginal values of noise increase slightly as the noise level in the base case gets better. In addition, as the level of deterioration in noise level (QIMP) increases, *ceteris paribus*, the marginal value for noise compensation decreases.

6. Summary

Random utility models have been discussed in this chapter, hopefully encouraging the practice of environmental valuation. As in most application areas, a sound microeconomic theory is required if the analyst expects his or her research to be an adequate input for cost–benefit analysis. In this sense, it is important that the reader is aware of all the restrictive assumptions that are required to generate useful and/or practical models, consistent with microeconomic principles. Such an "imperfect" analysis is preferable to no evaluation at all, or to an evaluation based on less scientific criteria.

Three case studies were described in this chapter. The aim of each was to elicit the values that people place on three local environmental goods (accidents, air pollution, and noise) for which there does not exist a proper market, but on which preferences are deemed to be well defined. These studies show that SP techniques based on conjoint analysis provide a way forward to derive such monetary values. However, there is still a long way to go to derive values that could be consistently used at governmental level in official cost–benefit analyses. More empirical evidence is needed, and a great deal of external validation of derived values is required.

The most important conclusion with respect to the three case studies is the realism that the SP technique needs to achieve if the experiment is to yield satisfactory and truthful results. Simulated markets should mimic real-life markets in order to provide a sensible input for cost–benefit analysis. Additionally, these experiments should also help us to understand how people would adjust their behavior in the presence of externalities so that behavior can also be forecast when the level of an externality is changed.

The first two studies indicate that these techniques can also be implemented in developing countries. Transferring values from developed countries to developing countries is not warranted, and many caveats should be considered. Hence, it is apparent that there is a need to undertake these kinds of studies in countries at various levels of development.

Acknowledgments

The authors wish to thank Luis Cifuentes and Huw Williams for many useful discussions related to the issues of interest in this paper; we also wish to thank Wictor Adamowicz for his comments. We are grateful to Elisabette Arsenio for having shared her latest findings with us. Finally, we want to acknowledge the support of the Chilean Fund for Scientific and Technological Research (FONDECYT) through Project 1000616.

References

Adamowicz, W.L. (2000) "Environmental valuation case studies," in: J.J. Louviere, D.A. Hensher and J.D. Swait, eds, *Stated choice methods: analysis and application*. Cambridge: Cambridge University Press.
Armstrong, P.M., R.A. Garrido and J. de D. Ortúzar (2000) "Confidence intervals to bound the value of time," *Transportation Research E*, 37:143–161.
Arsenio, E., A. Bristol and M. Wardman (2002) "Values of traffic noise from a SP-choice experiment in Lisbon," in: *The 2002 International Congress and Exposition on Noise Control Engineering*. Deaborn.
Daly, A.J. (1992) *ALOGIT 3.2 users manual*. The Hague: Hague Consulting Group.
Daniels, R. and W.L. Adamowicz (2000) "Environmental valuation," in: D.A. Hensher and K.J. Button, eds, *Handbook of transport modelling*. Oxford: Pergamon.
Freeman, A.M. (1993) *The measurement of environmental and resource values*. Baltimore: Resources for the Future Press.
Gaudry, M.J.I., S.R. Jara-Díaz and J. de D. Ortúzar (1989) "Value of time sensitivity to model specification," *Transportation Research B*, 23:151–158.
Hanemann, W.M. (1999) "Welfare analysis with discrete choice models," in: C. Kling and J. Herriges, eds, *Valuing recreation and the environment: revealed preference methods in theory and practice*. Northampton: Edward Elgar.
Hanemann, W.M. and B. Kanninen (1999) "The statistical analysis of discrete response data," in: I. Bateman and K. Willis, eds, *Valuing environmental preferences*. Oxford: Oxford University Press.
Hensher, D.A. (1990) "The orthogonality issue in stated choice designs," in: M. Fischer, P. Nijkamp and Y. Papageorgiou, eds, *Spatial choices and processes*. Amsterdam: Elsevier.
Hensher, D.A. (1999) *The valuation of time savings for urban car drivers in New Zealand: evaluating alternative model specifications*. Working Paper. Sydney: Institute of Transportation Studies, Sydney University.
Huber, J. and K. Zwerina (1996) "The importance of utility balance in efficient choice designs," *Journal of Marketing Research*, 33:307–317.
Hunt, J.D., J.D.P. McMillan and J.E. Abraham (1994) "Stated preference investigation of influences on attractiveness of residential locations," *Transportation Research Record*, 1466:17–35.
Louviere, J.J., D.A. Hensher and J.D. Swait, (2000) *Stated choice methods: analysis and application*. Cambridge: Cambridge University Press.
McFadden, D. (1995) *Computing willingness to pay in random utility models*. Working Paper. Berkely: Department of Economics, University of California at Berkeley.

Nash, C. (1997) "Transport externalities: does monetary valuation make sense?" in: G. de Rus and C. Nash, eds, *Recent developments in transport economics.* London: Ashgate Press.
Ortúzar, J. de D. and G. Rodríguez (2002) "Valuing reductions in environmental pollution in a residential location context," *Transportation Research D*, 7:407–428.
Ortúzar, J. de D. and L.G. Willumsen (2001) *Modelling transport*, 3rd edn. Chichester: Wiley.
Ortúzar, J. de D., F.J. Martínez and F.J. Varela (2000b) "Stated preference in modelling accessibility," *International Planning Studies*, 5:65–85.
Rizzi, L.I. and J. de D. Ortúzar (2003) "Stated preference in the valuation of interurban road safety," *Accident Analysis and Prevention*, 35:9–22.
Saelensminde, K. (2001) "Inconsistent choices in stated choice data," *Transportation*, 28:269–296.
Sillano, M. and J. de D. Ortúzar (2002) *WTP estimation with random parameter logit models: some new evidence*. Mimeo. Casilla: Department of Transport Engineering, Pontificia Universidad Católica de Chile.
Small, K. and S. Rosen (1981) "Applied welfare economics with discrete choice models," *Econometrica*, 49:105–130.

Chapter 22

THE HEALTH EFFECTS OF MOTOR VEHICLE-RELATED AIR POLLUTION

DONALD R. McCUBBIN
Abt Associates Inc., Bethesda, MD

MARK A. DELUCCHI
University of California, Davis, CA

1. Introduction

Emissions from motor vehicles and related sources, such as petroleum refineries, have a variety of effects on human health. The effects can be as innocuous as itchy eyes, or as serious as chronic lung disease or heart failure. These physical effects] analysts and policy-makers who wish to perform social cost–benefit analyses of transportation investments, prioritize efforts to mitigate damages, or simply examine cost trends. Health costs generally are one of the largest environmental costs of motor vehicle use (Delucchi, 2000).

In this chapter we review recent studies of the health effects of air pollution related to the use of motor vehicles in the USA, and attempt to quantify the impacts (e.g. the number of premature deaths due to motor vehicle air pollution). Although we focus on the physical health effects, we also review how to combine these estimates of physical effects with their estimated monetary cost to produce an estimate of the total social cost of the health effects of motor vehicle pollution.

We begin with a review of motor vehicle emissions and exposure to motor-vehicle-related air pollution (see Chapters 4, 11, and 12 for further discussion of emissions and air quality). The health effects of exposure to motor-vehicle-related air pollution are then discussed. We conclude with a brief discussion of the valuation of health effects (see Chapters 19, 20, 21, and 24 for further discussions of valuation) and a summary of two recent estimates of the total social cost of the health effects of motor vehicle pollution.

Handbook of Transport and the Environment, Edited by D.A. Hensher and K.J. Button
© *2003, Elsevier Ltd*

2. Air emissions from motor vehicle use

The production, distribution, and combustion of gasoline and diesel introduce hundreds of compounds to the air. Typically, however, researchers in the USA and elsewhere focus on the emissions regulated by relevant environmental authorities, such as the US Environmental Protection Agency (EPA). In the case of motor vehicles in the USA, these are: carbon monoxide (CO), nitrogen dioxide (NO_2), non-methane-organic compounds (NMOCs), lead (Pb; the USA regulates the lead content of fuel, rather than lead emissions *per se*), sulfur dioxide (SO_2; the USA regulates the sulfur content of fuel, rather than SO_2 emissions *per se*), and particulate matter (PM). The EPA has also developed a list of 21 pollutants, or "mobile source air toxics," linked to cancer and other serious health effects. These toxic pollutants include acetaldehyde, acrolein, benzene, 1,3-butadiene, formaldehyde, diesel particulates, and diesel exhaust organic gases, among others.

Estimating motor vehicle emissions is the first step in an analysis of the total health impacts of motor vehicle air pollution. Emissions from motor vehicles and motor-vehicle-related sources are estimated using emission factors, which express emissions of each pollutant per unit of some activity (e.g. grams of PM emitted per mile of travel by a bus, or grams of nitrogen oxides (NO_x) emitted per gallon of crude oil processed by a certain area of a petroleum refinery). Emission factors for stationary sources (such as petroleum refineries) and area sources (such as road construction activities) are documented in the EPA's emission factor handbook, known as AP-42 (US Environmental Protection Agency, 1995). Emission factors for volatile organic compounds (VOCs), CO, and NO_x for the various classes of motor vehicles are estimated in grams per mile by an EPA computer model, called MOBILE5 (soon to be superceded by MOBILE6). Emission factors for PM and sulfur oxides (SO_x) are estimated by a separate EPA computer model, similar to the MOBILE model, called PART5. Europe uses a similar motor vehicle emission factor model, called CORINAIR.

These emission factors can be very uncertain. This uncertainty matters greatly in estimates of the total social cost of the health effects of motor vehicle air pollution, which we review at the end of this chapter. Delucchi and McCubbin (1996) analyzed the emission factor models, and concluded that the MOBILE5 model probably underestimated real-world gram per mile emissions of VOCs, CO, and NO_x from light-duty gasoline-powered motor vehicles (MOBILE6 may correct these problems); the PART5 model may underestimate real-world PM emissions from heavy-duty diesel vehicles; and AP-42 probably overestimates emissions of particulate matter greater than 10 μm (PM_{10}) from road dust and substantially overestimates emissions of particulate matter less than 2.5 μm in diameter ($PM_{2.5}$) from road dust.

3. Exposure to ambient air pollution related to motor vehicle use

Because emitted pollutants are dispersed and transformed into the ambient pollutants to which people are exposed, we will follow the practice of most researchers and distinguish between emissions and ambient pollution. Emissions are what come directly from sources, such as motor vehicles, in the units expressed in the emission factor models mentioned above. Ambient pollution is what results from the dispersion and chemical transformation of emitted pollutants. In regulatory terms, the most common ambient pollutants are the so-called "criteria" pollutants – those for which the EPA has established National Ambient Air Quality Standards: CO, NO_2, ozone (O_3), Pb, SO_2, PM_{10}, and, most recently, $PM_{2.5}$. We can see that most regulated emissions also are regulated ambient air pollutants (CO, NO_x, Pb, SO_2, and some PM). However, this is not always the case. The ambient pollutant O_3, for example, is not emitted as such, but rather is formed from a complex series of chemical reactions involving emissions of VOCs, NO_x, CO, and other compounds. And PM, which is not a single compound, but a class of compounds, can be formed from chemical reactions involving emissions NO_x, VOCs, SO_2, ammonia, and other compounds.

Estimating exposure to ambient air pollution due to motor vehicle use is the second step in an analysis of the total health impacts of motor-vehicle-related emissions. Because most general (i.e. non-source-specific) studies of the health effects of pollution relate human physical responses to measures of ambient outdoor pollutant concentrations, air quality and exposure models must start with estimates of motor vehicle emissions and produce estimates of the changes in ambient concentrations of pollutants resulting from those emissions in the areas where people are exposed. To do this, air quality and exposure models must account for the physical dispersion of the emissions from the point of emissions to the point of exposure, and for any chemical transformations of the pollutants along the way. The processes of dispersion and chemical transformation are quite complex. Dispersion depends on characteristics of the emission source, topography, weather, wind, the built environment, and other factors. Chemical transformations depend on the mix of chemicals, weather, wind, dispersion, and other factors. The best models can predict ambient pollutant concentrations resulting from emissions with about 30% accuracy, but in many situations the error can be much greater.

In the analysis of the health effects of motor vehicle air pollution, it is especially important to model exposure accurately because people generally are much closer to motor vehicle emission sources than they are to other major sources of emissions, such as power plants. As a result, pollution from motor vehicles typically accounts for a far greater share of total human exposure to pollution than its share of total regional pollution might suggest. For example, even if only 10% of all PM emitted in a region is from motor vehicle, 30% or more of the ambient PM to which people are exposed may come from motor vehicles. This relatively

Table 1
Adverse health effects due to air pollutants linked to motor vehicles

Emission	Ambient pollutant	Health effect
PM, SO_2, NO_x, VOC	PM	Premature mortality, chronic bronchitis, respiratory and cardiovascular hospital admissions, asthma attacks, minor respiratory symptoms
VOC, NO_x	O_3	Premature mortality, respiratory hospital admissions, asthma attacks
CO	CO	Cardiovascular hospital admissions
NO_x	NO_2	Minor respiratory symptoms (e.g. sore throat, excess phlegm and eye irritation)
SO_2	SO_2	Minor respiratory symptoms (e.g. wheeze and chest tightness)
VOC, PM	Toxics	Cancer (polyaromatic hydrocarbons, dioxins/furans), lung cancer (arsenic, nickel, chromium, diesel particulates), liver and skin cancer (arsenic), leukemia (benzene), respiratory cancer (formaldehyde), cognitive impairment (lead), neurobehavioral effects (mercury)

high human exposure to PM from motor vehicles, combined with the great health damages of PM pollution, makes PM emissions from motor vehicles one of the most damaging forms of air pollution.

4. Health effects of exposure to motor vehicle air pollution

An extensive epidemiological literature indicates that air pollution causes a variety of effects including premature mortality, chronic illness, and hospital admissions for respiratory and cardiovascular illnesses. To quantify the health impacts of the criteria pollutants due to motor vehicles, analysts develop concentration–response functions derived from epidemiological studies. These functions allow the analyst to estimate the change in health effects that would result from a change in exposure to each pollutant.

Table 1 lists the health effects reasonably linked to individual pollutants. Estimating effects by individual pollutant is consistent with the current regulatory structure in the USA and other countries. However, air pollutant concentrations are often correlated, which makes it difficult to identify the effects of individual pollutants, and increases the likelihood of double-counting effects when trying to sum pollutant-specific effects together. To avoid double-counting, we assign effects first to the pollutant with the strongest epidemiological evidence, and assign the same effect to other pollutants only if there is clear evidence that this second pollutant has an effect independent of the first.

4.1. Particulate matter

PM is by far the most damaging pollutant emitted by motor vehicles (Delucchi, 2000). It also is one of the most complex: a heterogeneous mix of solid and liquid compounds, including organic aerosols, sulfates, nitrates, and metals, suspended in the atmosphere. It includes a wide range of chemical constituents, of different structures and sizes, with different physiological and biological effects. Because the size distribution and chemical composition of PM vary from one emissions source to the next (e.g. particles from diesel engines are quite a bit different from particles from road dust), it is likely that some emissions sources contribute more to the estimated overall harm than do others. To correctly attribute the estimated health effects to motor vehicles, one must specify the properties of PM – the sizes and compositions – that are most harmful.

Many epidemiological studies conducted over the last three decades have found a wide variety of adverse health effects linked to total suspended particulate matter (TSP). However, more recent studies have found that particles larger than 10 μm in diameter are not especially harmful, as they are filtered in the upper respiratory tract before reaching the lungs. The literature suggests that $PM_{2.5}$ is most harmful, and that particles with diameters of between 2.5 and 10 μm ("coarse PM_{10}") have a smaller and less serious health impact (Pope et al., 2000), although at least one study has found that $PM_{2.5}$ and coarse PM were equally harmful in causing premature mortality.

There are a number of hypotheses regarding which components of PM are the most harmful. Components under study include transition metals, particle acidity, and ultrafine particles (less than 0.1 μm in diameter), which deposit deeply in the lungs and have a large surface area per unit mass. However, there is not yet a leading contender for "most harmful component." Wichmann et al. (2000) examined the impact of ultrafine particles on premature mortality and did not find a difference between ultrafine particles and other particles in $PM_{2.5}$.

There has been some progress in understanding how PM affects the body. For example, researchers have found that PM exposure leads to an increase in heart attack risk factors such as increased heart rate, higher C-reactive protein in the blood (a marker for cell damage and inflammation), and increased blood viscosity (Dockery, 2001).

A range of approaches to examine the potential impacts of particles from different sources have been employed. Schwartz et al. (1999) looked at health effects during and after dust storms. Their results suggest that fugitive dust particles from agricultural tillage, from construction, and kicked up by vehicles (road dust) are less harmful than other types of particles, but not entirely harmless. In contrast, motor vehicle PM appears especially harmful. For example, using factor analysis to estimate the impacts of different particle sources, Laden et al. (2000) reported that motor vehicles had the strongest effect on premature mortality, followed by coal combustion, and finally by crustal sources, which had no effect. Considering this limited information, we speculate that fugitive dust particles of a given size class could be anywhere from about half as potent as other (mainly combustion) particles to an order of magnitude less potent.

Mortality associated with particulate pollution

Death, of course, is the most serious health effect of air pollution, and PM appears to be the most deadly air pollutant. The mortality impact of particulate pollution can be measured as the number of deaths (lives lost), the number of life-years lost (which is equal to the number of deaths multiplied by the average number of years lost per death), or the number of quality-adjusted life-years lost (QALYs, which are based on the life-years lost). If, as many analysts believe, the cost of each premature death ought to be a function of the number of years of life lost (because, for example, a case in which pollution accelerates the death of an already ill person by a few days is felt to be less costly than a case in which pollution robs a healthy person of many years of life), then the total number of life-years (quality adjusted or not) is a more useful measure in a social cost analysis than is just the total number of deaths.

Mortality owing to air pollution is estimated by either "prospective cohort" studies or "time series" studies. Prospective cohort studies) keep track of individuals over many years, and estimate the relative risk of dying due to long-term exposure to PM using the survival times of people in the cohort. The relative risk from a cohort study reflects the percentage increase in the probability of death for an individual given a long-term increase in PM.

Time series studies link daily mortality with daily ambient pollution concentrations, and, based on the number of deaths each day, estimate the relative risk of dying on days with high versus low PM levels. The relative risk from a time series study reflects the percentage increase in the number of deaths given a short-term increase in PM.

By quantifying the differences in survival probabilities over time, a cohort study can provide an accurate estimate of the change in total life years lost, which as suggested above may be a more useful measure of mortality than is just the total number of deaths. One also can use the relative risk from a cohort study to estimate the total number of deaths, but doing so involves an implicit and potentially inaccurate assumption about the number of years lost per death, and hence is sensible only if one prefers the total number of deaths as the measure of the mortality impact.

By contrast, a time series study provides only an accurate estimate of the number of deaths; it does not provide information on the total number of life-years lost or the number of years lost per death. To estimate the total number of life-years lost from a time series study, one must make an explicit assumption about the number of years lost per death and multiply this by the estimated number of deaths. It turns out to be particularly difficult to estimate the number of years lost per death in a time series study.

Another important difference between cohort studies and time series studies has to do with the lag time between pollution exposure and death. Time series studies capture only those deaths that occur very shortly after exposure to pollution (i.e. within a few days or weeks). These short-term or immediate deaths may involve anywhere from a few days to many years of life lost. (Short-term deaths that involve only a few days of life lost often are called "harvest" deaths.) Cohort studies capture deaths that occur years after exposure as well deaths that occur very shortly after exposure.

Morbidity associated with particulate pollution

Studies have found PM linked to a wide range of adverse health effects apart from mortality, including chronic bronchitis, hospital admissions for respiratory and cardiovascular illnesses, emergency room visits, school-day absences, and asthma attacks.

Chronic illness is perhaps the most difficult health effect to quantify. It may develop gradually, after years of exposure, and hence not be associated with any single year or episode of exposure. Nevertheless, several studies have found that PM is associated with chronic respiratory problems. Dockery et al. (1996) found PM linked to higher incidence of bronchitis symptoms in grade school children, and both Abbey et al. (1995) and Schwartz (1993) found a higher incidence of chronic bronchitis in adults.

Respiratory and cardiovascular hospital admissions are the two broad categories of hospital admissions that have been related to exposure to PM. Perhaps the best study to date is that by Samet et al. (2000a) who estimated the impact of PM_{10} on hospital admissions for pneumonia, chronic obstructive pulmonary disease and cardiovascular illnesses among persons 65 and older in 14 US cities. The study authors concluded that gaseous pollutants other than PM had little effect on the estimated PM effect.

A number of other relatively minor health effects have been linked to PM, including asthma attacks (Ostro et al., 2001) and lower respiratory symptoms and cough (Schwartz and Neas, 2000). In addition, there has been a wide range of laboratory and epidemiological studies examining the effect of PM on cardiopulmonary functioning (e.g. Avol et al., 2001). For the most part, however, minor health effects and cardiopulmonary functioning are not significant components of a benefit–cost analysis because the monetary values for these effects are low or are simply not known. As discussed below, the monetized value of premature mortality and chronic bronchitis dominates the analysis.

4.2. Ozone

O_3 is a strong oxidant associated with a number of adverse health effects, ranging from relatively minor symptoms to hospital admissions, chronic illness, and even premature mortality. However, not all studies have found O_3 linked to these effects. In particular, there is a significant amount of uncertainty about the relationships between O_3 and both mortality and chronic illness.

A link between O_3 and premature mortality is biologically plausible, and is consistent with documented morbidity effects. Some recent studies examining the O_3–mortality relationship include Levy et al. (2001) and Goldberg et al. (2001). While these studies have reported a significant link, some questions remain about its significance because of the sensitivity of the result to the weather specification and the lack of adequate control for fine PM.

There is limited evidence regarding the link between air pollution and the development of chronic illness. A review of research data by the EPA concluded that prolonged O_3 exposure causes structural changes in several regions of the respiratory tract (US Environmental Protection Agency, 1996), and the available epidemiological studies are suggestive of a link between chronic health effects in humans and long-term O_3 exposure. Some evidence points to O_3 and the development of asthma. Using a cohort of Seventh Day Adventists in California, Abbey et al. (1993) and McDonnell et al. (1999) reported a significant link between O_3 and the development of asthma in adults; however, Levy et al. (2001) have questioned this link.

In regards to hospital admissions and relatively minor respiratory symptoms, the evidence of a significant link is more solid. Some studies have reported an association between O_3 and respiratory hospital admissions (Moolgavkar, 2000). Other effects associated with O_3 include asthma symptoms (e.g. Ostro et al., 2001), and a variety of minor respiratory symptoms (e.g. Krupnick et al., 1990). There is little evidence linking O_3 and cardiovascular admissions.

4.3. Carbon monoxide

CO is dangerous because it binds with hemoglobin in the blood to form carboxyhemoglobin, thereby reducing the oxygen-carrying capacity of the blood and limiting the release of oxygen from circulating hemoglobin. As such, the most plausible effect pathway for CO is through the cardiovascular system. Schwartz and Morris (1995) and Schwartz (1997, 1999) provide reasonably compelling evidence of a link between CO and cardiovascular problems, controlling for potential confounding by PM_{10}.

Regarding mortality, the available evidence suggests that CO exposure may increase the risk of premature mortality. Moolgavkar (2000) noted a strong effect for CO, controlling for PM, as did Burnett et al. (1998). However, the weight of evidence still is still too slight to establish a dose–response function that directly links CO with mortality. An indirect link with mortality via the link between CO and hospital admissions for heart failure is a possibility. (For example, McCubbin and Delucchi (1999) assumed that 6% of the estimated cases of hospital admittances for congestive heart failure related to CO result in mortality.)

4.4. Nitrogen dioxide

Some laboratory and epidemiological studies suggest that NO_2 increases respiratory and cardiovascular hospital admissions (e.g. Burnett et al., 1999), minor respiratory symptoms, and eye irritation (e.g. Schwartz and Zeger, 1990). However, study results vary widely. Similarly, there is little convincing evidence linking NO_2 to more serious health effects such as chronic bronchitis, cancer, or premature mortality. McCubbin and Delucchi (1999) used the work by Schwartz and Zeger to estimate a relationship between NO_2 and sore throat, excess phlegm, and eye irritation.

4.5. Sulfur dioxide

There is only weak evidence that SO_2 as an ambient pollutant – as opposed to a precursor to ambient PM – has an effect independent of other pollutants, at least at levels commonly found in the US laboratory studies, suggest that SO_2 can lead to wheeze and chest tightness at relatively high exposure levels (e.g. Balmes et al., 1987). However, these studies are not easily transferable to ambient conditions, and the effects measured are not ones for which we have economic values.

Studies that have examined respiratory ailments and hospital admissions and controlled for more than one air pollutant either could not determine which pollutant was the causative agent (e.g. Moolgavkar et al., 1997), or else could not find an effect for SO_2 independent of fine PM (e.g. Burnett et al., 1999). Similarly, most mortality studies in the USA have failed to find a significant link between mortality and SO_2. There are some exceptions. Moolgavkar (2000) reported significant effects for gaseous pollutants including SO_2, but noted that SO_2 is most likely simply correlated with the true causative agent. Studies in Europe (Zmirou et al., 1998), China (Xu et al., 2000), and Korea (Lee et al., 2000) have reported a significant link between SO_2 and mortality; however, it is not clear that these studies adequately controlled for fine PM (including particulate sulfate). Likewise, the prospective cohort study conducted by Pope et al. (2002) reported a significant effect for both sulfates and SO_2, but the most likely explanation is that SO_2 is acting as a surrogate for another pollutant such as fine PM (Schwartz et al., 2001). For these reasons, Table 2 does not include the health impacts of SO_2 as an ambient pollutant.

4.6. Toxic air pollutants

Motor vehicles emit a wide range of toxic compounds, which can be acutely or chronically poisonous, as well as cause cancer, gene mutations, and abnormal fetal development. The EPA recently listed 21 mobile source air toxics known or suspected to cause cancer or serious health effects (Table 1). However, even within this shortened list, it is difficult to quantify their associated health effects, primarily due to a lack of concentration-response functions. Cancer is commonly quantified from pollutants such as benzene, formaldehyde, acetaldehyde, 1,3-butadiene, and diesel particulates (e.g. US Environmental Protection Agency, 1993). And where lead is still in the gasoline, cognitive disabilities and other non-cancerous effects associated with lead exposure are also measured (US Environmental Protection Agency, 1997).

To translate exposure into estimated cancer cases, researchers typically use the linear cancer model – also termed the "one-hit" model because even very small amounts of toxics cause cancer. This model requires the estimation of a unit-risk number (for details, see US Environmental Protection Agency, 1993). A unit-risk number estimates the excess risk of cancer, to one individual, from 70 years (a lifetime) of continuous exposure to a unit of pollution. To estimate the number of excess cancers in a given year, one determines the number of "exposure-years" to one unit of the pollutant. (For example, the exposure of 70 people to one unit for a year is equal to 70 exposure-years.) Multiplying the number of exposure-years by the unit-risk number then gives the number of cancer cases that will arise from exposure to motor vehicles.

Lead impairs cognitive development in children, causing lower IQs and lower productivity in later life. To reduce this threat, the USA and a number of other countries have phased lead out of gasoline, one of the prime contributors to lead exposure. This phase-out has resulted in substantially lower blood lead levels in these countries (Thomas et al., 1999), and improvements in worker productivity valued in billions of dollars annually (Grosse et al., 2002).

5. Valuing the health effects of motor vehicle air pollution

The final step in an analysis of the social cost of the health effects of motor vehicle air pollution is valuation. In this step, the results from the epidemiological literature, which link air pollution to health effects (discussed in the previous section), are merged with the results from the economics literature, which place a value on short-term illnesses, chronic morbidity, mortality, and cancer. There is an extensive economics literature on the theory, methods, and data used for valuing health effects avoided (see Chapters 19–22 and 24).

5.1. Valuing health effects using damage function approach

Economists use two general methods to estimate the cost of a variety of health effects including the risk of premature mortality, hospital admissions, asthma and other illnesses: the "observed market" approach, and the "constructed market" approach. The "observed market" approach includes "techniques that rely on demand and cost functions, market prices, and observed behavior and choices." Household production functions and cost-of-illness studies that estimate the direct out of pocket expenses of illness are examples. The "constructed market" approach includes techniques that directly ask people's "willingness to pay or accept compensation for a postulated change, how their behavior would change, or how they would rank alternative situations involving different combinations of health and income or consumption." Contingent valuation is an example.

The advantage of the observed-market approach is that it is based on actual behavior; the disadvantage is that the markets being observed value only part of what we wish to value, or else value it only implicitly, as part of a bundle of goods. The constructed-market approach avoids this problem by specifying precisely and explicitly what is to be valued, but it is reliable only insofar as people respond realistically to the constructed market.

Valuing mortality

Mortality is by far the single most costly health effect of air pollution, in large part because the value of a single premature death is orders of magnitude higher than most other health effects. Because of its importance to the analysis and of the uncertainty inherent in its estimation, the valuation of mortality is the subject of intense debate. A common approach is to value premature deaths, each with the value of a statistical life. In addition, one might assign different values depending on the degree of prematurity, as well as the timing of the death. (McCubbin and Delucchi (1999) distinguished between harvest deaths and non-harvest deaths, and discounted to the present the value of future deaths.) Alternatively, one might simply focus on valuing life-years lost (e.g. Friedrich and Bickel, 2001).

A common approach to valuing premature mortality is to estimate the value of a risk reduction using contingent valuation or hedonic methods (e.g. $500 for a 1 in 10 000 risk reduction), and then convert this estimate to the value of a statistical life ($5 million). This value, in turn, can be used to estimate a value per life-year, assuming an estimate of remaining life expectancy. For example, Moore and Viscusi (1988) assumed that a typical respondent in a mortal risk study has a life expectancy of an additional 35 years; dividing $5 million per statistical life, the 35 years gives an estimate of $143 000 per life-year, assuming no discounting. Using a 3% discount rate, the implied value of each life-year lost would rise to just under $300 000 per year. Given assumptions on when the deaths occur over time, it is straightforward to find the discounted value of premature mortality.

A problem with applying risk valuation studies to the valuation of the health effects of air pollution is that the characteristics of air pollution risk – the population affected, the mode of death, the voluntariness of the risk – can differ significantly from the characteristics of the risks in the valuation studies. Only recently have studies attempted to value the specific characteristics of air pollution risk.

Valuing chronic bronchitis

Research indicates that people are willing to pay large amounts of money to avoid chronic illnesses such as asthma, chronic bronchitis, and emphysema. PM-related chronic bronchitis is expected to last from the initial onset of the illness throughout the rest of the individual's life. Willingness to pay (WTP) to avoid chronic bronchitis would therefore be expected to incorporate the present discounted value of a potentially long stream of costs (e.g. medical expenditures and lost earnings) and pain and suffering associated with the illness. Viscusi et al. (1991) and Krupnick and Cropper (1992) provide estimates of WTP to avoid a case of chronic bronchitis, that range from about US $0.5 million to US $2.0 million.

Valuing hospital admissions

The value to society of an individual's avoidance of hospital admission has two components: (1) the cost of illness (COI) to a society, including the total medical costs plus the value of the lost productivity, plus (2) the WTP of the individual and others to avoid the pain and suffering resulting from the illness. In the absence of estimates of social WTP to avoid hospital admissions for specific illnesses or of the value of pain and suffering, estimates of total COI are typically used as lower bound estimates of the total social cost Some analyses adjust COI estimates upward by multiplying by an estimate of the ratio of WTP to COI, to better approximate total WTP.

Valuing cancer

Toxic pollutants such as benzene and diesel particulates increase the risk that people contract cancer. Cancers often have a long latency period, and are expensive and time-consuming to treat. The chance of recovery depends on many factors, including the age of the person and the type of cancer. For fatal cancer cases, one might assign the value of a statistical life at the point at which the cancer is discovered, and ignore costs incurred between the time of discovery and death. The omission of post-discovery costs understates the present value of the cost of cancer, but assigning the value at the point of discovery rather than at the point of death tends to overestimate the present value, so that these two simplifications tend to cancel.

6. Analyses of the social cost of the health effects of motor vehicle air pollution

Estimates of emissions, exposure, impacts, and monetary value can be combined to produce an estimate of the total cost of the health effects of motor vehicle air pollution. Table 2 presents the results of one such analysis of the total cost of air pollution (McCubbin and Delucchi, 1999). The most striking result is the large impact of ambient PM. Direct emissions of PM have the highest cost per kilogram of emissions, followed by NO_x and SO_x. Emissions of NO_x are more costly as precursors to secondary particulate matter than they are as precursors to O_3 or to direct NO_2 formation. On the other hand, emissions of CO are the least costly per kilogram, because they do not affect PM levels or directly affect mortality. Ambient CO, O_3, NO_2, and toxics (not shown) all cause much smaller damages than does ambient PM. PM damages are so high because PM pollution kills or chronically sickens far more people than do the other pollutants, which typically cause relatively mild and far less costly effects such as mild respiratory distress.

The upstream emissions sources contribute only a minor part of the total motor-vehicle-related damage. The damages from road dust have a wide range, on account of uncertainty regarding the emissions and potency of road dust, but could be quite large. The cost per kilogram of exhaust emissions is highest, and the cost per kilogram of combined exhaust, road dust, and upstream emissions is the lowest. This is because upstream sources are more remote, and road dust less potent, than are exhaust emissions.

Recent detailed case studies of the external costs of motor vehicle air pollution in Europe have produced similar results. Friedrich and Bickel (2001) reported that the costs of premature mortality resulting from direct emissions of PM and

Table 2
Health cost per kilogram of motor vehicle emissions in the USA (US dollars, 1991 basis) (a)

Source (b)	Emission	Ambient pollutant	USA		Urban USA		Los Angeles	
			Low	High	Low	High	Low	High
Vehicles	CO	CO	<0.1	0.1	<0.1	0.1	<0.1	0.2
	NO_x	Nitrates–PM_{10}	1.0	16.6	1.4	22.4	6.1	75.8
		NO_2	0.2	0.7	0.2	1.0	0.5	2.6
	Total NO_x		1.2	17.3	1.6	23.3	6.6	78.5
	$PM_{2.5}$	$PM_{2.5}$	10.4	159.2	14.8	225.4	64.0	779.1
	$PM_{2.5}$–PM_{10}	$PM_{2.5}$–PM_{10}	6.7	17.7	9.1	23.9	38.1	78.3
	Total PM_{10}	Total PM_{10}	9.8	133.8	13.7	187.5	58.8	638.3
	SO_x	Sulfates–PM_{10}	6.9	65.5	9.6	90.9	35.0	227.0
	VOC	Organics–PM_{10}	0.1	1.2	0.1	1.5	0.5	4.3
	VOCs, NO_x	O_3	<0.1	0.1	<0.1	0.1	0.1	0.4
Vehicles, upstream, road dust	$PM_{2.5}$	$PM_{2.5}$	3.2	45.2	6.5	88.8	41.9	405.3
	$PM_{2.5}$–PM_{10}	$PM_{2.5}$–PM_{10}	0.3	3.0	0.6	6.2	4.7	29.8
	Total PM_{10}	Total PM_{10}	0.6	15.1	1.5	31.7	12.4	155.6

Notes:
(a) Costs based on a 10% reduction in motor-vehicle-related emissions.
(b) "Vehicles" refers to exhaust emissions. "Vehicles, upstream, road dust" includes vehicle emissions plus simultaneously reduced emissions from motor-vehicle-related upstream sources (such as petroleum refineries producing gasoline) and of dust from paved and unpaved roads.

the secondary formation of sulfates and nitrates dominated the analyses, and that the costs per kilogram were of the same order of magnitude as those reported in Table 2. Perhaps the largest difference between the European work and that by McCubbin and Delucchi, is the assumption that both O_3 and SO_2 cause premature mortality in addition to mortality due to particulate matter. This resulted in somewhat larger benefits associated with reducing ambient SO_2 and O_3 levels, but did not change the conclusion that motor vehicle related particulate matter is especially dangerous.

7. Unanswered questions

The difference between the lower- and upper-bound estimates of damages in Table 2 is considerable – typically a factor of 10–20. This great uncertainty, while unsettling, properly reflects the current gaps in our understanding of the links between emissions, exposure, health effects, and economic value. These gaps point to questions for future researchers.

For many pollutants, the emission inventory is uncertain, primarily because the underlying emission factors (in grams per unit of activity) are not well characterized. However, this uncertainty probably is fairly small compared with the ranges of uncertainties in estimating damages. There is little question that air pollution harms people's health, but questions still remain as to what pollutant or suite of pollutants causes the harm. PM appears to cause most of the estimated damages. As a result, researchers are actively collecting monitoring data for a wide range of particle components to test the impacts of the various PM constituents, and developing models of how particles act on the body.

Many researchers believe that $PM_{2.5}$ is more dangerous than larger PM, but the functional relationship between particle size and health effects has not been quantified. There is some indication that road dust and other soil- and mineral-based PM is less damaging than sulfate PM from combustion, but the evidence is only suggestive, and certainly does not yet demonstrate that mineral-based particulates such as road dust have no adverse health effects at all.

Air pollution probably has different effects on different age groups. These differences, which have not been well quantified, might be important because society might wish to attach different values to damages to different age groups. Future work should determine damage coefficients by age group.

Although further research will help answer these and other questions, and reduce the uncertainty in the valuation step, it is unlikely that society ever will agree on point estimates for damage values, and that we always will have to choose plausible lower and upper bounds.

References

Abbey, D.E., F. Petersen, P.K. Mills and W.C. Beeson. (1993) "Long-term ambient concentrations of total suspended particulates, ozone, and sulfur dioxide and respiratory symptoms in a nonsmoking population," *Archives of Environmental Health,* 48:33–46.

Abbey, D.E., B.E. Ostro, G. Fraser, T. Vancuren and R.J. Burchette(1995) "Estimating fine particulates less than 2.5 microns in aerodynamic diameter ($PM_{2.5}$) from airport visibility data in California," *Journal of Exposure Analysis and Environmental Epidemiology,* 5:161–180.

Avol, E.L., W.J. Gauderman, S.M. Tan, S.J. London and J.M. Peters (2001) "Respiratory effects of relocating to areas of differing air pollution levels," *American Journal of Respiratory and Critical Care Medicine,* 164:2067–72.

Balmes, J.R., J.M. Fine and D. Sheppard (1987) "Symptomatic bronchoconstriction after short-term inhalation of sulfur dioxide," *American Review of Respiratory Diseases,* 136:1117–1121.

Burnett, R.T., S. Cakmak, M.E. Raizenne, D. Stieb, R. Vincent and D. Krewski (1998) "The association between ambient carbon monoxide levels and daily mortality in Toronto Canada," *Journal of the Air and Waste Management Association,* 48:689–700.

Burnett, R.T., M. Smith-Doiron, D. Stieb, D. Calmak and S. Brook (1999) "Effects of particulate and gaseous air pollution on cardiorespiratory hospitalizations," *Archives of Environmental Health,* 54:130–139.

Delucchi, M.A. (2000) "Environmental externalities of motor vehicle use in the U.S.," *Journal of Transport Economics and Policy,* 34:135–168.

Delucchi, M.A. and D.R. McCubbin (1996) *The contribution of motor vehicles and other sources to ambient air pollution.* Davis.

Dockery, D.W. (2001) "Epidemiologic evidence of cardiovascular effects of particulate air pollution," *Environmental Health Perspectives,* 109:483–486.

Dockery, D.W., J. Cunningham, A.I. Damokosh, L.M. Neas, J.D. Spengler, P. Kutrakis, J.H. Ware, M. Raizenne and F.E. Speizer (1996) "Health effects of acid aerosols on North American children – respiratory symptoms," *Environmental Health Perspectives,* 104:500–505.

Friedrich, R. and P. Bickel, eds (2001) *Environmental external costs of transport.* Berlin: Springer-Verlag.

Goldberg, M.S., R.T. Burnett, J. Brook, J.C. Backar, M.-F. Valoirs and R. Vincent (2001) "Associations between daily cause-specific mortality and concentrations of ground-level ozone in Montreal, Quebec," *American Journal of Epidemiology,* 154:817–826.

Grosse, S. D., T. D. Matte, J. Schwartz and R.J. Jackson (2002) Economic gains resulting from the reduction in children's exposure to lead in the United States. *Environmental Health Perspectives,* 110:563–569.

Krupnick, A.J. and M.L. Cropper (1992) "The effect of information on health risk valuations," *Journal of Risk and Uncertainty,* 5:29–48.

Krupnick, A.J., W. Harrington and B. Ostro (1990) "Ambient ozone and acute health effects – evidence from daily data," *Journal of Environmental Economics and Management,* 18:1–18.

Laden, F., L.M. Neas, D.W. Dockery and J. Schwartz (2000) "Association of fine particulate matter from different sources with daily mortality in six US cities," *Environmental Health Perspectives,* 108:941–947.

Lee, J.T., H. Kim, Y.-C. Hong, H.J. Kwon, J. Schwartz and D.C. Christiani (2000) "Air pollution and daily mortality in seven major cities of Korea, 1991–1997," *Environmental Research,* 84:247–254.

McCubbin, D.R. and M.A. Delucchi (1999) "The health costs of motor vehicle-related air pollution," *Journal of Transport Economics and Policy,* 33:253–286.

McDonnell, W.F., D.E. Abbey, N. Nishino and M.D. Lebowitz(1999) "Long-term ambient ozone concentration and the incidence of asthma in nonsmoking adults: the AHSMOG study," *Environmental Research,* 80:110–121.

Moolgavkar, S.H. (2000) "Air pollution and daily mortality in three U.S. counties," *Environmental Health Perspectives,* 108:777–784.

Moolgavkar, S.H., E.G. Luebeck and E.L. Anderson (1997) "Air pollution and hospital admissions for respiratory causes in Minneapolis St. Paul and Birmingham," *Epidemiology,* 8:364–370.

Ostro, B., M. Lipsett, J. Mann, H. Braxten-Owens and M. White (2001) "Air pollution and exacerbation of asthma in African-American children in Los Angeles," *Epidemiology,* 12:200–208.

Pope, C.A., R.T. Burnett, M.J. Thun, E.E. Calle, D. Krewski, K. Ito and G.D. Thurston (2002) "Lung cancer, cardiopulmonary mortality, and long-term exposure to fine particulate air pollution," *Journal of the American Medical Association,* 287:1132–1141.

Samet, J., S. Zeger, F. Dominici, F. Curriero, I Coursac, D. Dockery, J. Swartz and A. Zanobetti (2000a) *The national morbidity, mortality, and air pollution study,* Cambridge.

Samet, J.M., F. Dominici, F.C. Curriero and S.L. Zeger (2000b) "Fine particulate air pollution and mortality in 20 U.S. cities, 1987–1994," *New England Journal of Medicine,* 343:1742–1749.

Schwartz, J. (1993) "Particulate air pollution and chronic respiratory disease," *Environmental Research,* 62:7–13.

Schwartz, J. (1997) "Air pollution and hospital admissions for cardiovascular disease in Tucson," *Epidemiology,* 8:371–377.

Schwartz, J. (1999) "Air pollution and hospital admissions for heart disease in eight U.S. counties," *Epidemiology,* 10:17–22.

Schwartz, J. and R. Morris (1995) "Air pollution and hospital admissions for cardiovascular disease in Detroit, Michigan," *American Journal of Epidemiology,* 142:23–35.

Schwartz, J. and L.M. Neas (2000) "Fine particles are more strongly associated than coarse particles with acute respiratory health effects in schoolchildren," *Epidemiology,* 11:6–10.

Schwartz, J. and S. Zeger (1990) "Passive smoking, air pollution, and acute respiratory symptoms in a diary study of student nurses," *American Review of Respiratory Disease,* 141:62–67.

Schwartz, J., G. Norris, T. Larson, L. Shepherd, C. Claiborne and J. Koenig (1999) "Episodes of high coarse particle concentrations are not associated with increased mortality," *Environmental Health Perspectives,* 107:339–342.

Schwartz, J., F. Ballester, M. Saez et al. (2001) "The concentration-response relation between air pollution and daily deaths," *Environmental Health Perspectives,* 109:1001–1006.
Thomas, V.M., R.H. Socolow, J.J. Fanelli and T. Spiro (1999) "Effects of reducing lead in gasoline: an analysis of the international experience," *Environmental Science and Technology,* 33:3942–3948.
Thurston, G.D. and K. Ito (2001) "Epidemiological studies of acute ozone exposures and mortality," *Journal of Exposure Analysis and Environmental Epidemiology,* 11:286–294.
US Environmental Protection Agency (1993) *Motor vehicle-related air toxics study.* Ann Arbor: EPA.
US Environmental Protection Agency (1995) *Compilation of air pollutant emission factors,* Vol. I. *Stationary sources,* AP-42, 5th edn. Research Triangle Park: EPA.
US Environmental Protection Agency (1996) *Air quality criteria for ozone and related photochemical oxidants,* Vol. III, Washington, DC: EPA.
US Environmental Protection Agency (1997) *The benefits and costs of the Clean Air Act: 1970 to 1990.* Washington, DC: EPA.
Viscusi, W.K., W.A. Magat and J. Huber (1991) "Pricing environmental health risks – survey assessments of risk–risk and risk–dollar trade-offs for chronic bronchitis," *Journal of Environmental Economics and Management,* 21:32–51.
Wichmann, H.E., C. Spix, T. Tuch, G. Wolke, J. Heinrich, W.G. Kregling and J. Heyder (2000) *Daily mortality and fine and ultrafine particles in Erfurt, Germany,* Part I. *Role of particle number and particle mass.* Cambridge.
Xu, Z., D. Yu, L. Jing and X. Xu(2000) "Air pollution and daily mortality in Shenyang, China," *Archives of Environmental Health,* 55:115–120.
Zmirou, D., J. Schwartz, M. Saez, A. Zanobetti, B. Wojtyniak, G. Touloumi, G. Spix, A. Ponce de León, Y. Le Moullec, L. Bacharova, J. Schonten, A. Pönkë and K. Katsouyanni (1998) "Time series analysis of air pollution and cause-specific mortality," *Epidemiology,* 9:495–503.

Chapter 23

ENVIRONMENTAL EXTERNALITIES OF MOTOR VEHICLE USE

MARK A. DELUCCHI
University of California, Davis, CA

1. Introduction

Motor vehicles cause air pollution, noise pollution, water pollution, and other forms of environmental degradation. This pollution affects human health, visibility, agriculture, buildings, terrestrial and aquatic ecosystems, and the global climate. Motor vehicle air pollution kills and injures people, reduces crops yields, and corrodes buildings; motor vehicle noise disturbs hundreds of millions of people who live near busy roads; leaks and spills of petroleum fuels contaminate groundwater and coastal areas; and emissions of carbon dioxide and other so-called "greenhouse gases" from the production and use of motor fuels and vehicles contribute to global climate change. The cost to society of these impacts may amount to hundreds of billions of dollars per year.

Although these costs to society are large and pervasive, they are not actually reflected in the transportation prices paid by the persons whose traveling decisions give rise to the social costs. This divergence between the costs that society bears and the costs that travelers pay is, loosely speaking, an externality. In economic terms, externalities are undesirable because when they are present some people may make economic choices whose costs to society exceed the benefits. From the standpoint of social welfare, such choices should not be made.

One way to address this inefficiency is to estimate the dollar value of the environmental damages and then incorporate the estimates into prices of transportation goods and services or into cost–benefit analyses of transportation investments. In this way, prices and cost–benefit analyses would reflect the full cost to society – the private cost plus the external cost – rather than just the private cost to individuals. Toward this end, this chapter reviews the external environmental costs of motor vehicle use in the USA.

The chapter has three main parts: (1) definitions and scope; (2) reviews of estimates of external costs of air pollution, climate change, water pollution, noise, and other environmental impacts; and (3) examples of applications of estimates of

Handbook of Transport and the Environment, Edited by D.A. Hensher and K.J. Button
© *2003, Elsevier Ltd*

external costs. It is not meant to provide, on the one hand, a comprehensive review of the literature on environmental externalities, or, on the other, an analysis of any particular transportation policy, plan or technology. Rather, it is meant to familiarize a general audience with the methods, data, results, and uses of analyses of the external costs of motor vehicle use in the USA. The estimates presented in this paper can be used in analyses of efficient pricing of motor vehicle goods, services, and infrastructure; in evaluations of the social costs and benefits of transportation investments and plans; and in analyses of trends in costs, for the purpose of prioritizing research.

Baumol and Oates (1988) and Cropper and Oates (1992) present a technical discussion of the general theory of environmental externalities. The volume edited by Greene et al. (1997) contains contributions on the social costs and benefits of transportation. The May 2000 issue of the *Journal of Transport Economics and Policy* is devoted to estimates of the external costs of motor vehicle use, including but not limited to environmental external costs. Friedrich and Bickel (2001) present the results of a multi-year, comprehensive, state-of-the art series of studies of the environmental external costs of transport in Europe.

2. Definitions and scope

2.1. What is an externality?

A widely accepted definition is that an externality is present when one person makes a decision (such as whether or not to drive) that affects the non-monetary welfare of another person (such as the other person's health, via air emissions from driving) without accounting for this welfare effect (i.e. the first person doesn't consider how his driving might affect the health of the other person). By this definition, a negative "externality" is synonymous not with "damage," but with "unaccounted for damage."

Externalities usually are attributed to the absence of ownership rights for the resource in question. For example, air pollution is an externality because individual air molecules are not owned and bought and sold in markets. If air molecules could be owned and bought and sold, then any decision that affected the quality and hence the value of air (e.g. a decision about whether to drive) would include an explicit voluntary transaction in air molecules. By such transactions drivers would pay for the price of their impacts on air quality; there would be no unaccounted-for impacts, and no externalities. It follows from this characterization that the ideal or first-best remedy for externalities, in principle, is to establish micro-level property rights. Of course, in most cases this is practically impossible, which is why the externality exists in the first place.

If it is not possible to establish micro-level property rights, then collective bargaining, with "macro-level" property rights (such as the general right to pollute air) is the next best solution. If negotiation is not possible, then environmental taxes (called "Pigovian" taxes by economists) are warranted. However, if it is very costly to estimate and administer Pigovian taxes, it may be preferable to enforce emission standards. To ensure the maximum gain in social welfare, an environmental tax should be equal to the cost of the environmental damage, and should be levied on the immediate source of damage and not on some proxy. For example, damages from motor vehicle air pollution should be addressed by taxes that vary with the pollutant emitted and the time and place of emission, because the actual damages are a function these. A tax on some proxy, such as gasoline use, would not be ideal because it would not capture the nuances of time, place, and individual pollutants. (In fact, a tax on a proxy can actually make us worse off than no tax at all, because it might reduce beneficial consumption without mitigating any environmental damages.)

2.2. Scope of the chapter

This chapter reviews environmental externalities of motor vehicle use: air pollution, climate change, noise pollution, and water pollution. It does not consider certain related concepts:

(1) *Transportation externalities not related to environmental damage.* There are, of course, external costs of transportation not related to environmental damage: external costs of motor vehicle crashes, traffic congestion, and the use of imported oil. These may be quite large: of the order of US $100–300 billion annually in the USA (Delucchi, 1997). They are excluded to keep the chapter focused on the environmental theme of this volume.

(2) *Market failures other than external costs.* Externalities are but one of several kinds of failure in transportation markets. For example, the world market for oil is subject occasionally to non-competitive quasi-monopolistic behavior by some producers (such as those in OPEC), which leads to a supply of oil that is less than is economically optimal. Virtually all motor vehicle goods and services are subject to many kinds of taxes, which can change prices and in theory lead to losses in social welfare. Information, especially as regards motor vehicle risk and insurance, is not perfect. And a variety of standards and regulations concerning motor vehicles may misallocate resources or cause perverse incentives, as in the case of federal tax policy that favors giving employees free parking at work. The methods for estimating these other market failures, and the prescriptions for addressing them, are

different from those for externalities. None, for example, are best corrected by the sort of taxation discussed above.

(3) *The impact of taxes that might be viewed as implicit charges for environmental damages.* This chapter estimates the external environmental costs of motor vehicle use in the USA. It does not include any environmental damage costs that are optimally taxed (and hence no longer external) because, from our standpoint, properly internalized costs are not relevant to policy analysis: if there is an optimal tax equal to marginal unaccounted-for damage, then damages have been estimated, prices have been set, and the market failure has been corrected.

It turns out that in the US transportation sector there are no such optimal environmental charges (explicitly estimated to be equal to marginal unaccounted-for damage). However, there are, or have been, non-optimal environmental charges, and there are excise taxes (mainly taxes on gasoline) that might be viewed partly as implicit charges for some environmental damages. Even though non-optimal environmental charges and general excise taxes do not function as true Pigovian taxes on environmental damage, they do affect motor vehicle use and hence can affect environmental damages related to motor vehicle use. Estimating the effects of non-optimal taxes on environmental damages and general social welfare is more complicated than estimating external costs, because one must estimate first specifically how the taxes affect motor vehicle use, and then estimate how the specific changes in motor vehicle use affect the environment. This chapter does not discuss the magnitude or potential environmental or welfare impacts of non-optimal taxes related to motor vehicle use. (See Borger et al. (1997) for a related discussion.)

To put environmental externalities of motor vehicle use in perspective, Delucchi (1997) estimates that they are 36–64% of all external costs of motor vehicle use, and 3–16% of the total social cost of motor vehicle use, where the total social cost includes all private costs (such as motor vehicle ownership and operation), time costs, and public-sector costs. My judgment is that environmental externalities probably are of the order of 5% of the total social cost of motor vehicle use in the USA.

3. External environmental costs of motor vehicle use

3.1. General method

The general method for estimating the external cost of environmental damages associated with motor vehicle use is straightforward conceptually:

(1) posit some change in motor vehicle use;
(2) estimate the associated change in air, noise, or water emissions;

(3) estimate the resultant change in air quality, noise exposure, or water quality;
(4) estimate the health, visibility, or agricultural impacts of the change in air quality or water quality;
(5) value the impacts in monetary terms.

Because most environmental damages vary spatially and temporally, it is important, in principle, to specify when and where the change in motor vehicle use and related activities occurs. Generally, this requires sophisticated models with site- or population-specific input parameters.

In the following sections the methods, data, and results of some recent analyses of the environmental external costs of motor vehicle use are reviewed (Murphy and Delucchi (1998) and Quinet (1997) review older studies). Estimates of air pollution damage cost per unit of pollutant emission and of the noise damage cost per mile of travel, for a small change in motor vehicle use are also presented; and for the purpose of establishing a common basis for comparing environmental damages the total dollar costs of environmental externalities of motor vehicle use are estimated – the environmental damage costs that would be saved were motor vehicle use eliminated entirely. This of course is meant only as a convenient point of reference, and is not pertinent to any conceivable policy regarding motor vehicles. Low and high estimates are given, which are based on my judgment, or the judgment of the study authors, as to the likely lower or upper bounds on individual parameter values.

3.2. Air pollution: health effects

Motor vehicles and their related emission sources, such as petroleum refineries, emit many different kinds of air pollutants, which affect human health in a variety of ways. The cost of these health effects is one of the largest external costs of motor vehicle use. Chapter 22 reviews the methods, data, and results of estimates of the health effects of motor vehicle air pollution (see also Rabl and Spadaro, 2000); hence, this chapter provides only an abbreviated discussion. Table 1 shows McCubbin and Delucchi's estimates of the dollar cost of the health impacts of a kilogram of emission from motor vehicles in the USA.

The most important result in McCubbin and Delucchi (1999; see also Chapter 22) – and in all other recent damage–cost analyses of the health cost of air pollution (e.g. Friedrich and Bickel, 2001; Rabl and Spadaro, 2000) – is the high cost of particulate matter pollution (Table 1), and the potentially large contribution of motor vehicles to ambient particulate levels. Particulates appear to cause a number of respiratory ailments, including chronic illness and mortality. Motor vehicles contribute the smaller, more dangerous particulates directly from exhaust emissions and indirectly from the large amounts of "precursor" gases that they emit such as nitrogen dioxide. Motor vehicles also emit large amounts of fairly coarse soil-based particulates from road dust – dust kicked up into the atmosphere from moving vehicles.

CO, NO_x, ozone, and SO_x appear to have much smaller health effects than does particulate matter (Tables 1 and 2). Aside from their contribution to particulate formation, emissions of NO_x, SO_x, and VOCs are relatively unimportant. McCubbin and Delucchi (1999; see also Chapter 22) note that this might be due to a failure to capture all of the health effects of ozone, which is formed from the interaction of NO_x and VOCs.

Of course, at every stage of the modeling process there is considerable uncertainty, which generally McCubbin and Delucchi represent with lower and upper-bound estimates. For several of the emission estimates, the difference between the lower and upper-bound estimates is a roughly a factor of two, and for most of the valuation functions or parameters, the difference is at least a factor of four. All told, the uncertainty compounds into an order-of-magnitude difference between the low and the high estimates of total cost (Table 2).

3.3. Air pollution: reduced visibility

Overview

Particles and gases in the atmosphere scatter and absorb light, and thereby reduce visibility (Watson and Chow, 1994). Although natural sources of particles, such as volcanoes, can significantly degrade visibility, most poor visibility is due to

Table 1
The external cost per kilogram of direct motor vehicle emissions in urban areas of the USA in 1990, for a 10% change in motor vehicle use (US $/kg, 1991 basis)

Emissions source	PM_{10}		NO_x		SO_x		CO		VOCs		VOCs + NO_x	
	Low	High	Low	High	Low	High	Low	High	Low	High	Low	High
Health	13.7	187	1.6	23.3	9.6	90.9	0.0	0.1	0.1	1.5	0.0	0.1
Visibility	0.4	3.9	0.2	1.1	0.9	4.0	0.0	0.0	0.0	0.0	0.0	0.0
Crops	NE	NE	NE	NE	NE	NE	0.0	0.0	0.0	0.0	0.2	0.3
Total	14.1	191	1.8	24.5	10.5	94.9	0.0	0.1	0.1	1.5	0.4	0.7

Source: Delucchi (1998, 2000).
Key: PM_{10}, particulate matter of aerodynamic diameter of 10 μm or less; NO_x, nitrogen oxides; CO, carbon monoxide; SO_x, sulfur oxides; VOCs, volatile organic compounds; VOCs + NO_x, VOCs and NO_x as precursors to ozone; NE, not estimated.

Table 2
Environmental costs of total motor vehicle use in the USA, 1990–1991 (US $ billions, 1991 basis)

Cost item	Low	High
Air pollution		
Human mortality and morbidity from particulates (a)	16.7	266.4
Human mortality and morbidity from other pollutants	2.3	17.1
Human mortality and morbidity from pollutants from upstream processes	2.3	13.0
Human mortality and morbidity from road dust	3.0	153.5
Human health subtotal	24.3	450.0
Loss of visibility	3.6	27.4
Damage to agricultural crops	3.3	5.7
Damage to materials	1.0	8.0
Damage to forests	0.2	2.0
Air pollution subtotal	32.4	493.1
Water pollution		
Health and environmental effects of leaking motor-fuel storage tanks (b)	0.1	0.5
Environmental and economic impacts of large oil spills	0.2	0.5
Urban run-off polluted by oil from motor vehicles	0.1	0.5
Water pollution subtotal	0.4	1.5
Noise from motor vehicles	0.5	15.0
Climate change due to fuel cycle emissions of greenhouse gases (c)	5 (0.3)	37 (8)
Total	38.3	546.6

Source: Delucchi (2000, 1998).
Key: NE, not estimated; NA, not applicable.
Notes:
(a) Includes secondary PM, formed from direct emissions of SO_x, NO_x, and ammonia.
(b) This is my estimate of the cost as of about 2000. The cost probably was several times higher in 1991, because leakage prevention and clean-up programs were less widespread in the USA at that time.
(c) Values in parentheses are US damages only.

anthropogenic sources such as such as power plants, vehicle exhaust, biomass burning, suspended dust, and industrial activities. Poor visibility diminishes the enjoyment of scenic vistas and makes travel hazardous. Statistical analyses of property values reveal that people are willing to pay a premium for houses in areas with good visibility and air quality.

The particles that are most efficient at scattering light are about the same size as the wavelength of visible light – about 0.5 μm. Most particles emitted by the combustion of motor fuel, and some particles of road dust, are between 0.1 and 1.0 μm. Hence, the use of motor vehicles potentially is a significant cause of visibility degradation.

Estimation methods

In the analysis of the visibility cost of motor vehicle emissions, the estimation of emissions and air quality (steps 2 and 3 of the damage function method outlined above) proceeds generally as it does in the analysis of the health cost of motor vehicle emissions (see Chapter 22 on health costs, Chapters 11 and 12 on emissions, and Chapter 4 on air quality). In the impact-modeling step (4) of the analysis, one estimates the impact on visibility of the change in air quality. To do this, one can estimate the change in visual range associated with the change in air quality, or, as Delucchi et al. (2002) do, develop a measure of air quality in which pollutants are weighted by their contribution to light extinction.

The valuation step (5) here is the most uncertain. There are two ways to estimate the value of impaired outdoor visibility: contingent valuation, in which people are asked to value visibility in a hypothetical market, and hedonic price analysis, in which researchers analyze the value of air quality (not necessarily visibility *per se*) that is implicit in the prices that people pay for houses in regions that have different average annual levels of air quality (Cropper and Oates, 1992). In their national analysis, Delucchi et al. (2002) choose a meta-hedonic-price analysis by Smith and Huang (1995), because it is based on a large number of studies in the USA, and includes income as an explanatory variable. On the basis of studies that disaggregate willingness to pay for "air quality" into that for specific effects (health, visibility, soiling, etc.), Delucchi et al. (2002) assume that the value of visibility per se constitutes 15% to 35% of the total value of "air quality" estimated by the Smith and Huang (1995) hedonic model.

Estimates

Chestnut and Dennis (1997) review estimates of the cost of visibility degradation in residential and recreational areas in the USA. However, they do not develop national totals, or estimate the cost attributable to motor vehicle use. Delucchi et al. (2002) use the damage function method to estimate the cost of visibility degradation due to motor vehicle emissions in the USA.

The results of the Delucchi et al. (2002) analysis are summarized in Table 1, which shows the visibility cost per kilogram of pollutant emitted from motor vehicles, and Table 2, which shows the total visibility cost in the USA. Table 1 indicates that, per kilogram of emission, direct PM and SO_x emissions have the largest visibility costs. The cost per kilogram of SO_x exceeds the cost per kilogram of NO_x because the fraction of SO_x that becomes particulate sulfate exceeds the fraction of NO_x that becomes particulate nitrate (and it is the nitrates and sulfates, rather than the SO_x and NO_x precursors, that reduce visibility). The cost per kilogram of VOCs is so small because such a small fraction of VOC emissions becomes the organic aerosol that reduces visibility. Table 2 shows that the total visibility cost in the USA ranges from about US $4 billion to US $30 billion per year.

3.4. Air pollution: crop losses

Overview

The detrimental effects of ambient ozone on crops, even at relatively low concentrations, are well established. Ozone enters plant leaves through openings in the leaf surface and then produces byproducts that reduce the efficiency of photosynthesis. Research summarized in Spash (1997) suggests that ozone, either alone or in combination with NO_x and SO_x, is responsible for virtually all US crop losses resulting from air pollution. In an effort to address this problem, the US Clean Air Act and its amendments include air pollution damages to vegetation as one of the criteria by which secondary national ambient air quality standards are evaluated.

Estimation methods

Over the past 15 years, formal models have been developed to estimate the economic welfare cost of the crop losses caused by air pollution. Virtually all of these estimate the cost of ambient pollution, and not the cost attributable to any particular emission source. However, Murphy et al. (1999) used the damage function method, with a model of agricultural production and demand, to estimate the cost of crop damage caused by emissions related to motor vehicle use.

The estimation of emissions and air quality (steps 2 and 3 of the damage function method outlined on p. 432) proceeds here as with health and visibility costs. In the "impact" step (4), researchers use "yield–response" functions to determine the change in crop yields as a function of the concentration of a pollutant (usually ozone). For these functions, Murphy et al. (1999) and most others draw mainly from the work of the National Crop Loss Assessment Network, an experimental, field-assessment program initiated by the US Environmental Protection Agency (EPA) in order to improve the state of knowledge regarding the impact of air pollution on agricultural production.

Estimates

Table 1 shows the crop damage cost per kilogram of emissions, and Table 2 shows total crop damages due to all motor vehicle related ozone pollution, from the analysis of Murphy et al. (1999).

Table 1 shows costs per kilogram of NO_x and VOCs combined because these pollutants contribute jointly to ozone production. Although the US costs per kilogram of VOCs plus NO_x hold only for the actual proportions of VOCs and NO_x emitted in 1990, they probably are reasonably accurate for moderate deviations from the 1990 proportions.

These results appear to be consistent with results from other similar studies. The estimate implies that pollution attributable to motor vehicle use probably causes agricultural damages costing US $3–6 billion per year, which is much less than the damages to human health. Thus, crop damage probably constitutes a relatively minor portion of the total cost of air pollution from motor vehicles.

3.5. Air pollution: material damage

Overview

Oxidants, PM, and acid air pollution can erode and soil a variety of man-made materials. Damaged materials are unsightly, and sometimes are structurally unsound. This decay has an economic cost.

In principle, the cost of damage to materials from motor vehicle air pollution can be estimated with the damage function approach outlined above. However, although there are suitable air quality models and inventories of materials at risk to acid deposition, there are no up-to-date damage functions and valuation functions for the USA. As a consequence, no-one has performed a recent, original, detailed analysis of the cost of materials damage from air pollution in the USA.

More work has also been done in Europe (e.g. see Friederich and Bickel,(2001).

Estimates

Adams et al. (1996) review seven estimates, all done in the 1970s, of the cost of oxidant damage to materials, and find damage estimates ranging from US $1.6 billion to US $3.8 billion per year (1984 basis). Lee et al. (1995) review old US studies of ozone damages to materials, and then estimate damage costs to materials and paints, and the cost of anti-ozonants added to rubber. Their estimates appear to correspond to about US $0.1–3 billion annually in the USA.

SO_x and PM also damage materials, at least as much as does ozone. These are indicators that these damages could be worth US $5–10 billion per year, or more (Delucchi, 1998).

Finally, according to a study reviewed in Adams et al. (1996), the national cost of materials damage from all pollutants was US $6.8 billion (1984 basis), or US $8.6 billion on a 1991 cost basis. All told, these and other studies indicate that the total damage to materials, including soiling damages, from all sources of pollution in the USA, is at least US $5 billion, and perhaps as high as US $20 billion or more (1991 basis), although I am skeptical of the higher values. Estimating informally that motor vehicles contribute 20–40% of the total, the total damage to materials from motor vehicle pollution is US $ 1.0–8.0 billion (1991 basis) (Table 2).

3.6. Air pollution: forest damage

Overview

Ozone and acid air pollution can injure trees. Although it is difficult to isolate the causes of forest decline, there is reasonably compelling evidence that ozone air pollution and acid deposition is at least partially responsible for some of the damages.

Damaged forests produce less timber than do healthy forests, and are less appealing as recreational sites, and less suitable for wildlife habitat. Unfortunately, there do not appear to be any pollutant damage functions or valuation functions that can be applied to national forest data, as part of a damage function estimate of the cost. This is not surprising: not only it is difficult to isolate the anthropogenic from the natural causes of forest decline, it is difficult to sort out the effects of different pollution burdens: ambient ozone, acid deposition directly on trees, acid deposition on soil, the combined effects of ozone and acid deposition, and excessive nitrogen deposition (Taylor et al., 1994). In light of the scientific uncertainties, the estimates reported below must be regarded as preliminary.

Estimates

An estimate done for the US National Acid Precipitation Assessment Program indicates that acid rain may cause US $0.34–0.71 billion (1984 basis) worth of damage annually to hardwood and softwood forests in the eastern USA. The estimate was based on spatial equilibrium model of stumpage and forest products, and assumed that acid rain reduced forest growth by 10–20%. Work cited in Adams et al. (1996) assumes that acid deposition causes losses of 6–21% in eastern softwood forests, and then applies an econometric model to estimate that these losses are worth US $1.5–7.2 billion (1986 basis) per year.

These estimates, and others mentioned in Delucchi (1998, 2000), suggest that in the US damages to forests from all air pollution are in the range of US $0.5 billion to perhaps as much as US $5 billion per year. The motor vehicle contribution might reasonably be estimated as lying between 30 and 40%, or perhaps US $0.2–2.0 billion in 1991 (Table 2). This is less even than the cost of crop damages due to motor vehicle air pollution (a finding that is consistent with results from the European

"ExternE" study of external costs), and makes forest damages a relatively minor cost of motor vehicle air pollution. This estimate does not include pollution damages to ecosystems other than forests.

3.7. Climate change

Overview

Most atmospheric scientists believe that an increase in the concentration of "greenhouse gases" -- primarily carbon dioxide (CO_2), methane (CH_4), nitrous oxide (N_2O), ozone (O_3), and chlorofluorocarbons (CFCs) – will increase the mean global temperature of the earth. Recently, an international team of scientists, working as the Intergovernmental Panel on Climate Change (2001), has reaffirmed that anthropogenic emissions of so-called "greenhouse gases" do affect the climate of the earth and will continue to do so for hundreds of years. In the long run, this global climate change might affect agriculture, coastal developments, urban infrastructure, human health, and other aspects of life on earth.

Highway vehicles are a major source of the greenhouse gases thought to be responsible for climate change. In the USA, for example, the motor fuel life cycle accounts for as much as 30% of total CO_2 emissions from the use of all fossil fuels (Delucchi, 1999). In the Organisation for Economic Co-operation and Development (OECD) countries, the highway fuel life cycle contributes about one-quarter of all CO_2 emitted from the use of fossil fuels. Worldwide, the highway fuel life cycle contributes less than 20% of total CO_2 emissions from the use of fossil fuels, primarily because outside of the OECD countries relatively few people own and drive cars.

A detailed application of the damage function approach to estimate the climate change cost of motor vehicle emissions would use emission inventory or life cycle emission models, general circulation models of global climate, regional-impact models, and micro- and macro-economic valuation models. (A "life cycle" emissions model includes emissions from the entire production and use life of fuels and vehicles; for example, it includes emissions from the refinery production of gasoline as well as from the end use of gasoline.) Unfortunately, nobody has linked the most detailed of these models to produce correspondingly detailed estimates of the economic cost of climate change attributable to emissions from specific sources, such as transportation. However, several researchers have developed and applied integrated damage cost models with comparatively simplified representations of the processes, impacts, and costs of climate change. These models, which thus combine steps 3, 4, and 5 of the damage function approach, provide estimates of the total climate-change cost of a kilogram of CO_2 emitted anywhere. (See Chapter 3 for additional discussion of climate change and transportation.)

The damage cost of CO_2-equivalent emissions

The global damage cost per unit of CO_2 or CO_2-equivalent emitted depends on the level of emissions, the response of the climate, the scope and magnitude of damages considered (especially impacts on famine and disease), the time horizon, the discount rate, the normative treatment of risk and low-probability/high-cost events, and other factors. None of these are easy to model, and as a result, estimates of the damage cost vary widely.

Delucchi (1998, 2000) and Tol (1999) review estimates of the damage cost of CO_2 emissions. Among the best estimates are those of Cline (1992) and Tol (1999). Most of the estimates of damages tend, very roughly, towards US $10/tonne of CO_2, although estimated damages and control costs can be at least an order of magnitude higher or lower than this. Indeed, if one compounds the uncertainty in key parameters, such as the discount rate, the number of lives lost due to global warming, and the value of those lives, the overall uncertainty can span several orders of magnitude. Nonetheless, one may take as a reasonable range US $3 to US $20 of total global damage per tonne of CO_2 (or its equivalent) emitted anywhere, or US $0.3 to US $4.2 of damages in the USA per tonne of CO_2.

Estimates

Multiplying the US $/tonne damage costs by estimates of total CO_2-equivalent emissions over the life cycle of motor fuels and motor vehicles (Delucchi, 1999), we can estimate that emissions of greenhouse gases from motor vehicle use in 1990 in the USA caused US $5–37 billion in damages globally, and US $0.3–8 billion dollars in damages in the USA (Table 2). Of course even these upper and lower bounds are quite uncertain. More precise estimates await a better understanding of the consequences and costs of global warming. Nonetheless, these rough estimates do suggest that the cost of climate change is on a par with the cost of visibility, and less than the cost of health effects.

3.8. Noise

Overview

In many urban areas, noise can be a serious problem. Noise disturbs sleep, disrupts activities, hinders work, impedes learning, and causes stress. Indeed, surveys often find that noise is the most common disturbance in the home. And motor vehicles generally are the primary source of that noise. (See Chapter 5 for additional discussion of motor vehicle noise.)

Table 3
The marginal cost of noise from a 10% increase in VMT, for different types of vehicles on different types of roads, in urbanized areas (1990 travel, US $/1000 per VMT; 1991 cost basis)

	Interstate	Other freeways	Principal arterials	Minor arterials	Collectors	Local roads
LDAs	2.96	4.25	1.18	0.57	0.07	0.00
MDTs	8.50	13.20	7.02	5.37	1.05	0.00
HDTs	16.69	30.80	20.07	29.93	4.93	0.00
Buses	6.36	9.77	7.18	6.42	1.22	0.00
Motorcycles	17.15	27.03	8.71	4.67	0.56	0.00

Source: Delucchi and Hsu (1998).
Key: VMT, vehicle-miles of travel; LDA, light-duty auto; MDT, medium-duty truck; HDT, heavy-duty truck.

Estimation methods

The total cost of noise can be estimated as a function of the percentage loss of housing value per decibel of noise above a threshold, the average annualized value of a housing unit, the number of housing units exposed to motor vehicle noise, the amount of noise exposure above the threshold, and a scaling factor that accounts for costs in non-residential areas (if these are included in the analysis) (Hailing and Cohen, 1996). The amount of noise above the threshold, in turn, can be modeled as a function of the speed, volume and mix of vehicle traffic; the noise absorption characteristics of ground surfaces; and the extent that objects, such as hills and buildings, shield the receptor from the source, and other factors.

One of the most important parameters is the loss of house value per decibel. Studies of the shadow price of noise in the housing market indicate that each decibel of noise above a threshold (usually 55 dB) reduces the value of a home by 0.2–1.3% (Delucchi and Hsu, 1998).

Estimates

Delucchi and Hsu (1998) apply a detailed noise damage model to actual housing and traffic conditions in every urban area of the USA, and estimate that total motor vehicle noise damages in residential and non-residential areas of the USA are US $0.5–15 billion per year (Table 2). This range is consistent with the results of nearly 20 studies of the cost of traffic noise in Europe and the USA from 1975 to 1991, reviewed by Verhoef (1994). In the Delucchi and Hsu analysis, damages are proportional to the assumed loss of housing value per decibel, which as indicated above is very uncertain. Damages also are sensitive to the assumed damage threshold: if the threshold is 50 dB rather than 55 dB, the total damage roughly triples.

Table 3 shows the cost per mile of travel by five different kinds of vehicles for six different kinds of roads, for a 10% increase in VMT. Heavy trucks cause an order of magnitude more damage per mile than do light-duty vehicles. Roads with high-speed traffic generate more damage than do roads with low-speed traffic, and roads close to houses cause more damage than do roads far from houses, all else being equal. (In the case of LDAs and motorcycles, damages are much more sensitive to vehicle speed than to distance from source to receptor, and as a result, these vehicles produce little or no damage on low-speed local roads.) Others have found similar results. Delucchi and Hsu (1998) also estimate that damages could be at least an order of magnitude lower or higher than the "base case" estimates presented here.

Water pollution: leaking motor-fuel storage tanks

Some motor fuel leaks from underground storage tanks, contaminates groundwater, and causes health problems and property damage. Ideally, one would model these external costs of leaking storage tanks with a damage function approach analogous to that used to model the costs of air pollution: characterize the population of underground tanks; estimate the probability of leaks of various sizes and types as a function of the characteristics of the tanks; model the dispersion and fate of fuel leaks; model the exposure of people and susceptible property to fuel leaks; estimate the effects of exposure to the fuel; and estimate the dollar value of the effects. However, there are not enough data and modeling tools to be able to do this satisfactorily for the entire nation. As a result, existing estimates of damages from leaking fuel storage tanks are little better than guesses.

The estimation problem is made more difficult by the mitigation of the actual environmental problem: in the late 1980s in the USA, the EPA enacted strict regulations on underground storage tanks, which required operators to upgrade storage tanks and maintain financial assurance to cover mitigation and third-party liability costs. These requirements, and the EPA's related clean-up and prevention program, undoubtedly have greatly reduced the frequency, magnitude, and external cost of leaking storage tanks, because the private cost of preventing and cleaning up leaks presumably has been incorporated into current service station margins on the price of gasoline.

Improperly or illegally disposed tanks can cause environmental problems. Unfortunately, it appears that even less is known about the quantitative risk from disposed tanks than about the risk from operating tanks. It is likely that the entire health and environmental cost of underground petroleum storage tanks, including costs of disposed tanks, is significantly less than US $1 billion annually (Table 2).

3.9. Water pollution: large oil spills

Large oil spills can seriously disrupt marine ecosystems and cause substantial economic losses to fisheries and tourist industries. They often attract a great deal of attention, and occasionally engender new or tougher environmental laws, such as the US Oil Pollution Act of 1990, passed in response to the oil spilled from the grounding of the *Exxon Valdez* in Prince William Sound in Alaska.

There have been a number of estimates of the damage cost of large oil spills. However, it is difficult to derive from these an estimate of the external cost attributable to motor vehicle use. In the first place, oil spills are an external cost of motor vehicle use only if a change in motor-fuel use changes the frequency or severity of oil spills, and these changes will occur only if the affected oil comes from producers who ship to or from the USA by international tanker. Furthermore, the problem of modeling the relationship between motor fuel use and the frequency and severity of oil spills is complicated by the aforementioned Oil Pollution Act of 1990, which requires that oil tankers be double-hulled and that tanker owners and operators be financially capable of paying for oil clean-up. These new regulations undoubtedly have decreased the risk of oil spills (and also raised the market cost of oil), and thereby render virtually useless historical data on risk.

Delucchi (1998, 2000) reviews a number of studies, and estimates a present annual-average oil spill cost of something on the order of US $0.10/barrel of oil produced. This results in total damages attributable to motor vehicle use in the USA of less than US $1 billion annually (Table 2).

3.10. Water pollution: other

Urban run-off

Oil, fuel, coolant, and other chemicals leak or are discarded from motor vehicles, and eventually pollute rivers, lakes, wetlands, and oceans.

Several studies have shown that motor vehicles are a major source of pollution in urban run-off (e.g. Latimer et al., 1990). This polluted run-off, in turn, can significantly degrade rivers, lakes, streams, and wetlands. Unfortunately, there is not enough information available yet to get from these general findings to a real model of the monetary cost of urban run-off due to motor vehicles. It is speculated that the cost of this pollution is comparable to the cost of groundwater pollution from leaking underground storage tanks.

Nitrogen deposition

A substantial fraction of the nitrogen emitted from motor vehicles (as NO_x) deposits out of the atmosphere onto soil, plants, man-made structures, and water bodies. This nitrogen deposition can stress plants, corrode materials, and eutrophy bays and lakes by feeding algal blooms that consume oxygen as they decay. In the Chesapeake Bay in the eastern USA, air pollution accounts for some 27% of the total nitrogen load.

Unfortunately, there are insufficient data to estimate either the contribution of motor vehicle NO_x emissions to water degradation nationally, or the cost of that degradation.

3.11. Other external environmental costs of motor vehicle use

There appear to be no credible estimates of pollution damages to ecosystems other than forests, of the environmental and esthetic impacts of motor vehicle waste, or of vibration damages from motor vehicles. Also, there has been little quantification of the environmental and social costs of the highway infrastructure itself. The construction, existence, and even maintenance of the motor vehicle infrastructure, apart from the level of use of the infrastructure, can destroy natural habitat and physically divide human communities. Moreover, the motor vehicle infrastructure usually is unsightly. Studies reviewed by Willis et al. (1998) suggest that the non-market amenity and landscape value of land given over to roads in the USA might be of the order of US $1 billion.

3.12. Summary of environmental external costs of motor vehicle use

Table 2 summarizes the estimates of the non-monetary costs of environmental externalities related to motor vehicles use. Some consider that the upper end of the cost range – over US $500 billion – is too high (see Delucchi et al., 2002), and that the total probably is of the order of US $100 billion (1991 basis). The range is of the order 1–10% of 1991 US GDP, with a best estimate of about 2%. Other studies have results of comparable magnitude (see Quinet, 1997).

4. Some applications

Estimates of the environmental external costs of motor vehicle use can be used in analyses of transportation pricing, taxation, planning, and investment. Several examples follow.

4.1. Evaluating alternative fuels

To reduce the external environmental costs of motor fuel use, policy-makers and regulators around the world have been encouraging and requiring the use of alternatives to gasoline and diesel fuel. Perhaps the most well-known example is California's "zero-emission vehicle" program, which mandated the sale of battery electric vehicles with no exhaust emissions. Because alternative fuels and alternative-fuel vehicles often cost more than conventional fuels and vehicles, it is natural to ask whether the monetary value of the reduction in environmental costs provided by the alternatives justifies their extra private consumer costs. The sorts of estimates summarized above can be used in this kind of evaluation.

Johansson (1999) compares the cost-per-mile of vehicles using alternative fuels (methanol, natural gas, and biogas) with the cost of gasoline and diesel vehicles, counting the cost of fuel, differences in the capital cost of the vehicle, and the cost of emissions of CO_2 (US \$55/tonne), VOCs (US \$4–7/kg, urban areas), NO_x (US \$7/kg, urban areas), and PM (US \$135/kg, urban areas, US \$1256/kg city centers) (cf. similar estimates in Table 1 here). He finds that all of the alternative-fuel vehicles have a higher fuel and vehicle capital cost, but lower pollution costs, than do their gasoline and diesel counterparts. In the year 2015, in almost all cases, the benefit of lower pollution costs does not offset the higher private (fuel plus capital) costs, with the result that the alternative-fuel vehicles have a higher social cost per mile than do their gasoline or diesel counterparts. The exception is diesel vehicles in city centers, where the extremely high cost of particulate emissions (US \$1236/kg), due presumably to very high exposure, results in a higher social cost for diesel vehicles than for alternatives.

Delucchi and Lipman (2001) use estimates of external costs (from Table 1 here and other sources) and private manufacturing and operating costs to compare the social life cycle cost of battery powered electric vehicles and gasoline passenger vehicles, under high volume production. They find that a gasoline vehicle has US \$0.004–0.037/mile greater external costs than does an electric vehicle, but that these differences probably are smaller than the difference in the private ownership and operating cost (US \$0.02–0.20/mile higher for the electric vehicle). The cost-per-mile of the electric vehicle battery, even under high-volume, "learned-out" production, is higher than the relatively small reductions in air pollution and oil use externalities, which are small in part because modern gasoline vehicles are relatively clean and efficient. Others (e.g. Kazimi, 1997) have reached similar conclusions.

4.2. Mode choice

Estimates of external costs can be used to compare the full social costs of different transport modes. For example, Romilly (1999) estimates the changes in the external costs of pollution, fuel consumption, congestion, noise, accidents, and road damage that result from switching 160 people, initially in 100 cars, to buses, at different bus occupancy rates. He finds that at a 50% bus occupancy, pollution damage costs increase by UK £6300 per year, on account of the very high particulate emissions from buses. (However, this probably would not apply to "clean diesel" buses, with particulate traps and low-sulfur fuel.) He estimates that all other external costs except road damage are reduced. The change in congestion cost dominates the change in the other external costs.

4.3. Trade-offs between urban air pollution and climate change

External cost estimates can be used to evaluate trade-offs implied by policies that reduce emissions of greenhouse gases but increase emissions of the most harmful urban air pollutants. For example, Delucchi (1999) uses US dollar per kilogram damage values (from Table 1 here and from other sources) to evaluate the net social cost of switching from gasoline to diesel fuel, and finds that the cost of the increased PM and NO_x emissions from diesel vehicles probably exceeds the benefit of reduced greenhouse gas emissions.

4.4. Motor vehicle pricing, land use, and transit

Estimates of external costs have been applied in models of land use and transportation. Johnston and Rodier (1999) use models of travel demand, emissions, and consumer welfare to estimate the impact of several pricing and transit policies on motor vehicle use, emissions, and traveler welfare, in Sacramento, California. They find that charging motorists for their average external costs had only a minor effect on total driving, especially compared with policies aimed at promoting transit-oriented development, light-rail, and advanced transit.

4.5. Optimal pricing, taxation, and investment

Estimates of the external environmental costs of motor vehicle use have been incorporated into analyses of optimal transportation pricing, taxation, and investment. For example, Borger et al. (1997) use marginal damage cost estimates in an analysis of the efficiency of alternative pricing and regulatory instruments to internalize the external costs. They find that crude instruments like fuel taxes, public transport prices, and technological regulation can achieve only 30% of the maximum potential welfare gain from internalizing external costs. In order to obtain the maximum benefit, the pricing system must discriminate between peak and off-peak and urban and non-urban trips. Forkenbrock (1999) estimates the external costs of intercity truck freight transportation and finds that user fees would have to be increased about threefold to internalize these costs.

5. Conclusion

In the past few years, a number of analysts have attempted to quantify the environmental externalities of motor vehicle use. The best studies use the damage function approach, which starts with an assumed change in motor vehicle use, and then models emissions, exposure to pollution, the impacts of pollution, and the value of the impacts. These studies find that in most cases, and always in urban areas, the cost of air pollution is greater than the cost of water pollution, noise, or climate change. The impact of air pollution on human health – which, mainly, is the impact of particulate pollution on human mortality – is more costly than the impact of air pollution on visibility, crops, materials, or forests. However, for most impacts, there remains considerable uncertainty in all stages of the damage cost analysis.

The recent estimates of the environmental externalities of motor vehicle use have been applied in a number of interesting ways: in comparisons of the social costs and benefits of different transportation fuels, technologies or modes; in evaluation of the trade-offs between different kinds of environmental impacts (e.g. climate change versus urban air pollution); and in analyses of motor vehicle pricing and land-use policies. These recent applications offer policy makers interesting indications of the effects of their policies and plans on economic efficiency and social welfare.

References

Adams, R.M., C. Anderson, J.H.B. Garner, B.A. Hale, W.E. Hogsett, D.F. Kanesky, J. Lawrence, E.H. Lee, A.S. Lefohn, P. Miller, V. Runecles, J.A. Weber and R.D. Yanai (1996) "Environmental effects of ozone and related photochemical oxidants," in *Air quality criteria for ozone and related photochemical oxidants*, Vol. II. Washington, DC: Office of Research and Development, Environmental Protection Agency.

Baumol, W.J. and W.E. Oates (1988) *The theory of environmental policy*, 2nd edn. New York: Cambridge University Press.

Borger, B.D., S. Ochelen, S. Proost and D. Swysen (1997) "Alternative transport pricing and regulation policies: a welfare analysis for Belgium in 2005," *Transportation Research D*, 2:177–198.

Chestnut, L.G. and R.L. Dennis (1997) "Economic benefits of improvements in visibility: acid rain provisions of the 1990 Clean Air Act Amendments," *Journal of the Air and Waste Management Association*, 47:395–402.

Cline, W.R. (1992) *The economics of global warming*. Washington, DC: Institute for International Economics.

Cropper, M.L. and W.E. Oates (1992) "Environmental economics: a survey," *Journal of Economic Literature*, 30:675–740.

Delucchi, M.A. (1997) *The annualized social cost of motor vehicle use, 1990–1991: summary of theory, methods, data, and results*, UCD-ITS-RR-96-3 (1). Davis: Institute of Transportation Studies, University of California.

Delucchi, M.A. (1998) *Summary of the nonmonetary externalities of motor vehicle use*, UCD-ITS-RR-96-3 (9). Davis: Institute of Transportation Studies, University of California.

Delucchi, M.A. (1999) "Transportation and global climate," *Journal of Urban Technology*, 6:25–46.

Delucchi, M.A. (2000) "Environmental externalities of motor vehicle use in the U.S.," *Journal of Transport Economics and Policy,* 34:135–168.
Delucchi, M.A. and S.-L. Hsu (1998) "The external damage cost of noise from motor vehicles," *Journal of Transportation and Statistics,* 1:1–24.
Delucchi, M.A. and T.E. Lipman (2001) "An analysis of the retail and life cycle cost of battery-powered electric vehicles," *Transportation Research,* 6:371–404.
Delucchi, M.A., J.J. Murphy and D.R. McCubbin (2002) "The health and visibility cost of air pollution: comparison of estimation methods," *Journal of Environmental Management,* 64:139–152.
Forkenbrock, D.J. (1999) "External costs of intercity truck freight transportation," *Transportation Research,* 33:505–526.
Friedrich, R. and P. Bickel, eds, (2001) *Environmental external costs of transport.* Stuttgart: Springer-Verlag.
Greene, D.L., D.W. Jones and M.A. Delucchi, eds (1997) *Measuring the full social costs and benefits of transportation.* Heidelberg: Springer-Verlag.
Hailing, D. and H. Cohen (1996) "Residential noise damage costs caused by motor vehicles," *Transportation Research Record,* 1559:84–94.
Intergovernmental Panel on Climate Change (2001) *Climate change 2001: the scientific basis.* Cambridge: Cambridge University Press.
Johansson, B. (1999) "The economy of alternative fuels when including the cost of air pollution," *Transportation Research D,* 4:91–108.
Johnston, R.A. and Rodier, C.J. (1999) "Synergisms among land use, transit, and travel pricing policies," *Transportation Research Record,* 1670:3–7.
Kazimi, C. (1997) "Evaluating the environmental impacts of alternative-fuel vehicles," *Journal of Environmental Economics and Management,* 33:163–185.
Latimer, J.S., E.J. Hoffman, G. Hoffman, J.L. Fasching and J.G. Quinn (1990) "Sources of hydrocarbons in urban runoff," *Water, Air, and Soil Pollution,* 52:1–21.
Lee, D.S., M.R. Holland and N. Falla (1995) "The potential impact of ozone on materials in the U.K.," *Atmospheric Environment,* 30:1053–11065.
McCubbin, D.R. and M.A. Delucchi (1999) "The health cost of motor vehicle related air pollution," *Journal of Transport Economics and Policy,* 33:253–286.
Murphy, J.J. and M.A. Delucchi (1998) "A review of the literature on the social cost of motor vehicle use in the United States," *Journal of Transportation and Statistics,* 1:15–42.
Murphy, J.J., M.A. Delucchi, J. Kim and D.R. McCubbin, (1999) "The cost of crop damage caused by ozone air pollution from motor vehicles," *Journal of Environmental Management,* 55:273–289.
Quinet, E. (1997) "Full social costs of transportation in Europe," in: D.L. Greene, D. Jones and M.A. Delucchi, eds, *Measuring the full social costs and benefits of transportation,* pp. 69–112. Heidelberg: Springer-Verlag.
Rabl, A. and J.V. Spadaro (2000) "Public health impact of air pollution and implications for the energy system," *Annual Review of Energy and the Environment,* 25:601–627.
Romilly, P. (1999) "Substitution of bus for car travel in urban britain: an economic evaluation of bus and car exhaust emission and other cost," *Transportation Research D,* 4:109–125.
Smith, V.K. and J.C. Huang (1995) "Can markets value air quality? A meta-analysis of hedonic property value models," *Journal of Political Economy,* 103:209–227.
Spash, C.L. (1997) "Assessing the economic benefits to agriculture from air pollution control," *Journal of Economic Surveys,* 11:47- 70.
Taylor, G.E. Jr, D.W. Johnson and C.P. Andersen, (1994) "Air pollution and forest ecosystems: a regional to global perspective," *Ecological Applications,* 4:662–689.
Tol, R.S.J. (1999) "The marginal costs of greenhouse gas emissions," *Energy Journal,* 20:61–81.
Verhoef, E. (1994) "External effects and social costs of road transport," *Transportation Research A,* 28:273–287.
Watson, J.G. and J.C. Chow (1994) "Clear sky as a challenge for society," *Annual Review of Energy and Environment,* 19:241–266.
Willis, K.G., G.D. Garrod and D.R. Harvey, (1998) "A review of cost–benefit analysis as applied to the evaluation of new road proposals in the U.K.," *Transportation Research D,* 3:141–156.

Chapter 24

VALUATION OF SAFETY

MICHAEL JONES-LEE
University of Newcastle upon Tyne

GRAHAM LOOMES
University of East Anglia, Norwich

1. Introduction

Two inescapable facts confront those concerned to determine the appropriate level of provision of public safety. First, safety is typically not a free good and, second, society's resources are not limitless. This means that a responsible decision for or against any proposed public safety improvement requires a judgement as to whether or not the reduction in risk afforded by the improvement is sufficient to justify its cost of provision. This then raises the question of how such a judgement might be made.

On the basis of straightforward intuition, most of us would no doubt agree that a safety improvement that would cost just a few thousand pounds, and which could be expected to prevent several premature deaths, would be well warranted. Equally, most people would have little hesitation in deciding against a proposal that would cost several millions of pounds but which would, at best, prevent only one or two non-fatal injuries involving minor cuts and bruises. In less extreme cases, however, matters are not quite so straightforward.

Clearly, were it possible to obtain an acceptable measure of the monetary value of safety, then this would go a long way toward resolving the dilemma inherent in most safety expenditure decisions. In particular, given such a measure, it would be possible to weigh the benefits of safety improvement explicitly against other costs and benefits – such as capital costs and reduced damage to vehicles and property – in the course of the cost–benefit analysis of safety projects.

But how are monetary values of safety to be defined and estimated? And can we expect the value for, say, the prevention of a fatality to remain uniform across different contexts such as roads, rail or air pollution? Or will the value vary from one context to another, reflecting differing degrees of perceived voluntariness, control and the degree of "dread" associated with the risk concerned? These are some of the questions that this chapter will seek to address.

Handbook of Transport and the Environment, Edited by D.A. Hensher and K.J. Button
© *2003, Elsevier Ltd*

2. Valuing safety: issues of principle

While a number of different approaches have been proposed for the definition and estimation of monetary values of safety, only two would seem to deserve serious consideration, namely the "gross output" (or "human capital") approach and the "willingness-to-pay" (WTP) approach.

Under the gross output approach – until recently employed by most of the countries that associate explicit monetary values with safety – the major component of the cost of an accident resulting in one premature fatality, for example, is the sum total of the victim's future output (or income) extinguished as a result of his or her premature demise. In the case of individuals whose services are not marketed, such as housewives, imputations are typically made for such services. An allowance is then added for various other economic effects such as damage to vehicles and property, police and medical costs and so on.

As such, the gross output approach can be viewed as an attempt to measure the impact of death or injury on current and future levels of national output, broadly construed to include various non-marketed services. In some countries a further more or less arbitrary allowance for the "pain, grief, and suffering" of the victim (or the latter's dependants, relatives and friends) is also incorporated in the gross output measure. Values of the prevention of premature death are, in turn, defined in terms of the costs avoided. To give the reader an idea of the magnitude of the costs and values that emerge under the gross output approach, the UK Department of the Environment, Transport and the Regions – now the Department of Transport, Local Government and the Regions (DTLR) – most recent gross output-based cost of a fatality was UK £180 330 in 1985 prices, of which about 28% was an allowance for pain, grief, and suffering. Updated for inflation and the growth of real output per capita, this figure would now stand at some UK £415 000 in 2002 prices.

The major objection to the gross output approach is that most of us almost certainly value safety principally because of our aversion to the prospect of our own and others' death and injury *per se*, rather than because of a concern to preserve current and future levels of output and income. If this is so, then values of safety ought ideally to be defined so as to reflect people's "pure" preferences for safety, as such, rather than in terms of effects on output and income, as in the gross output approach. However, in order to define and estimate values of safety in this way, we clearly require some means of measuring people's preferences for safety and, more particularly their strength of preference. How can this be done? Arguably, the most obvious and natural measure of the extent of a person's preference for anything is the maximum amount that he or she would be willing to pay for it. This amount reflects not only the person's valuation of the desired good or service relative to other potential objects of expenditure, but also the individual's ability to pay – which is itself a manifestation of society's overall resource constraint.

Thus, under what has not surprisingly come to be known as the WTP approach to the valuation of safety, one attempts first to determine the maximum amounts that those affected would individually be willing to pay for (typically small) improvements in their own and others' safety. Given that most public safety improvements constitute what economists would term "public goods" – in the sense that once provided, a safety improvement on a particular facility constitutes a benefit for all of those who use the facility concerned – the overall value of the safety improvement is taken to be reflected in aggregate individual WTP. The amounts that individuals would be willing to pay are therefore simply summed – possibly with distributional weights[a] – across all individuals to arrive at an overall value for the safety improvement concerned. The resultant figure is thus a clear reflection of what the safety improvement is "worth" to the affected group, relative to the alternative ways in which each individual might have spent his or her limited income.[b] Furthermore, defining values of safety in this way effectively "mimics" the operation of market forces – in circumstances in which markets do not exist – insofar as such forces can be seen as vehicles for allowing individual preferences to interact with relative scarcities and production possibilities in determining the allocation of a society's scarce resources.

In order to standardize values of safety that emerge from the WTP approach and render them comparable with values derived under other approaches (such as gross output), the concept of the prevention of a "statistical" fatality or injury or health impairment is employed. To illustrate this concept, suppose that a group of 100 000 people enjoys a safety improvement that reduces the probability of premature death during a forthcoming period by, on average, one in 100 000 for each and every member of the group. The expected number of fatalities within the group during the forthcoming period will thereby be reduced by precisely one and

---

[a]These weights, if inversely related to income or wealth, would reflect the judgement that a marginal pound's worth of benefit to the poor would be socially more valuable than a marginal pound's worth of benefit to the rich. The objection to the use of the weights is that if the distribution of income or wealth is held to be suboptimal, then it would be more appropriately and effectively adjusted by redistributive taxes and transfers, rather than by "tampering" with the inputs to a cost–benefit analysis.

[b]Indeed, in studies that involve asking members of the public more or less directly about WTP for a particular safety improvement it is extremely important to remind respondents to bear in mind the amount they can afford to pay when answering the WTP questions. It is also important to appreciate that the fact that a person indicates that she would be willing to pay, say, UK £20 to effect a one in 100 000 reduction in the risk of premature death during the coming year does not mean that she would be willing to pay UK £20 × 100 000 = £2 million to avoid the certainty of premature death, which for most people is well in excess of lifetime income and therefore not affordable. Rather, the UK £20 is WTP for an essentially marginal reduction in risk and therefore cannot be converted directly into WTP for a non-marginal reduction given that, for most people, the underlying safety valuation function is highly non-linear (e.g. see Jones-Lee, 1976).

the safety improvement is thus described as involving the prevention of one "statistical" fatality.

Now suppose that individuals within this group are, on average, each willing to pay £v for the one in 100 000 reduction in the probability of death afforded by the safety improvement. Aggregate WTP will then be given by £v x 100 000. This figure is naturally referred to as the WTP-based value of preventing one statistical fatality (VPF).[a]

Clearly, in the above example, average individual WTP, £v, for the average individual risk reduction of one in 100 000 is a reflection of the rate at which individuals in the group are willing to trade off wealth against risk "at the margin," in the sense that the trade-offs concerned typically involve small variations in wealth and small variations in risk. Empirical work on the valuation of safety therefore tends to focus upon these individual marginal wealth/risk trade-off rates.

All of this having been said, it is extremely important to appreciate that defined in this way the VPF is not a "value (or price) of life" in the sense of a sum that any given individual would accept in compensation for the certainty of his or her own death – for most of us, no finite sum would suffice for this purpose, so that in this sense life is literally priceless. Rather, the VPF is aggregate WTP for typically very small reductions in individual risk of death (which, realistically, is what most safety improvements actually offer at the individual level).

Before proceeding to consider the various ways in which researchers have attempted to obtain empirical estimates of values of safety using the WTP approach, two further points should be noted. First, so far only passing reference has been made to people's concern – and hence WTP – for others', as well as their own safety. To the extent that people do display such "altruistic" concern then *prima facie* one would expect that it would be appropriate to augment the WTP-based VPF to reflect the amounts that people would be willing to pay for an improvement in others' safety. However, it turns out that under quite plausible assumptions regarding the nature of people's altruistic concern for others' safety on the one hand and their material wellbeing on the other (the latter being reflected by their wealth or consumption), augmenting the VPF to reflect WTP for other's safety would involve a form of double-counting and would therefore ultimately be unwarranted. Thus, the issue of whether and how peoples' concern for others' safety ought to be accommodated within the WTP approach hinges on the essentially empirical question of the relationship between such concern and concern for others' wealth or consumption.[b]

---

[a] An alternative but somewhat less felicitous terminology often used in the literature is the "value of statistical life" (VOSL).

[b] For a further discussion of these and related issues, see, for example, Jones-Lee (1992).

A second important aspect of the WTP approach involves recognition of the fact that safety improvements also have "direct" economic effects, such as avoidance of net output losses[a] material damage, medical and police costs and so on. To the extent that people appear in the main not to take account of such factors in assessing their WTP for improved safety (and there is some evidence that they tend not to; Jones-Lee et al., 1985), then an allowance for these factors should clearly be added to WTP-based values of safety. However, such additions tend to be relatively modest in relation to the typical magnitude of aggregate WTP for safety *per se*, at least in the case of risks of death or serious injury/illness.

3. Empirical estimates of WTP-based values of safety

Having examined the basic principles of the WTP approach, let us now turn to the question of how one might, in practice, obtain empirical estimates of values of prevention of statistical fatalities and non-fatal injuries or illness.

Broadly speaking, three types of empirical estimation procedure have been employed to derive WTP-based values of safety. These are known respectively as the "revealed-preference" (or "implied value"), the "contingent valuation" (or "expressed value"), and "relative valuation" approaches.[b]

Essentially, the revealed-preference approach involves the identification of situations in which people actually do trade off income or wealth against physical risk – for example, in labor markets where riskier jobs can be expected to command clearly identifiable wage premiums. By contrast, the contingent valuation approach involves asking a representative sample of people more or less directly about their individual WTP for improved safety (or, sometimes, their willingness to accept compensation for increased risk).

The problem with the revealed-preference approach when applied to labor market data is that it depends on being able to disentangle risk-related wage differentials from the many other factors that enter into the determination of wage rates. The approach also presupposes that workers are well-informed about the risks that they actually face in the workplace.

Viewed in this light, the great advantage of the contingent valuation approach is that it allows the researcher to go directly and unambiguously to the relevant wealth/risk trade-off – at least, in principle. On the other hand, the contingent valuation approach has the disadvantage of relying upon the assumption that

---

[a] An individual's net output is defined as the excess of his or her gross-of-tax lifetime output over and above lifetime consumption.

[b] For a fuller account of the various empirical estimation procedures employed in the estimation of values for environmental goods including health and safety, see Daniels and Adamowicz (2000).

people are able to give considered, accurate and unbiased answers to hypothetical questions about typically small changes in already very small risks.

Finally, unlike the revealed-preference and contingent valuation approaches, the relative valuation approach does not involve an attempt to estimate wealth/risk trade-offs directly, but rather seeks to determine the value of preventing one kind of physical harm relative *to* another. Thus, for example, the DTLR's current monetary values for the prevention of non-fatal road injuries of various levels of severity were obtained by applying estimates of such relative valuations to an absolute monetary "peg" in the form of the DTLR's existing WTP-based roads VPF.

4. WTP-based values of road safety

WTP-based values of road safety are currently used in road project appraisal in the UK, USA, Canada, Sweden, and New Zealand, with several other countries employing values that have been substantially influenced by the results of WTP studies.[a] More specifically, in the UK the DTLR currently employs a figure of UK £1.14 million in June 2000 prices for the prevention of a statistical fatality in its roads project appraisal. This figure was based on the findings of a study which obtained estimates of the roads VPF using a variant of the contingent valuation approach (Carthy et al., 1999). In turn, the DTLR's values for the prevention of serious and slight non-fatal injuries are UK £128 650 and UK £9920, respectively, again in 2000 prices, these figures having been obtained using the relative valuation approach to estimate non-fatal/fatal valuation relativities (Jones-Lee and Loomes, 1995a).

In the USA, the Department of Transportation currently values the prevention of a statistical road fatality at US $3 million, this being an update of a figure originally recommended in 1991 following a survey of the then existing literature on empirical estimation of WTP-based values of safety (Urban Institute, 1991).

In turn, Transport Canada employs a WTP-based value for the prevention of a statistical fatality of Can. $1.5 million in 1991 prices based on a survey of the literature. Updated for inflation and growth this would be very close to the current DTLR UK value.

Finally, the WTP values used in Sweden and New Zealand were derived under the contingent valuation approach, and in 1999 prices are SEK 14.30 million (roughly UK £1.07 million) and NZ $2.5 million (roughly UK £820 000), though in the latter case it should be noted that the New Zealand Land Transport Safety Authority is considering increasing the figure to NZ $4 million (roughly UK £1.32 million)

---

[a]For a somewhat fuller account of the valuation procedures employed in other countries, see Travén et al. (2002); and for a discussion of the application of stated-preference techniques in the estimation of the value of safety in a less developed country, see Chapter 21.

on the basis of recommendations following an extensive contingent valuation study carried out in New Zealand in 1997–1998 (Guria et al., 1999).

5. WTP-based values of rail safety

Given that WTP-based values of safety are intended to reflect the preferences and attitudes to risk of members of the public, it is clearly possible that these values will vary from one hazard context to another reflecting, *inter alia*, differing degrees of dread at the prospect of death or injury in different circumstances, together with different perceptions of (1) the voluntariness with which risks are assumed, (2) the control that potential victims have over these risks, and (3) who holds responsibility for containing the risks. For example, many people view the risks arising from nuclear power generation as insidious, involuntary, outside their own control, poorly understood and the responsibility of other people. By contrast, the risks associated with sporting and recreational activities are mostly perceived to be essentially voluntary, more controllable, well understood and largely one's own responsibility. It would therefore not be surprising if the WTP-based VPF for nuclear power generation were to be (possibly substantially) larger than its counterpart for sporting and recreational activities.

In view of this, as part of the study that resulted in the DTLR's most recent WTP-based roads VPF, WTP-based values were also estimated for various other contexts, namely rail, domestic fires and fires in public places. For various reasons it was decided to approach the estimation of monetary values of safety in these other contexts using the relative valuation approach, the intention being to treat the roads VPF estimated in the earlier part of the project and discussed in the previous section as the absolute monetary "peg" on which to "hang" these relative valuations.

Denoting the VPF for roads by V_{RD} and for rail by V_{RL}, the valuation relativity, V_{RL}/V_{RD} was estimated to be 0.834 (Chilton et al., 2002). Clearly, this entails that V_{RL} stands at a discount in relation to V_{RD}, a finding that the authors of the study attributed to a number of effects including (1) the fact that some 60% of the study sample reported an annual rail mileage that was below the UK National average and (2) the fact that at the time of the study it had been several years since the occurrence of a rail accident involving in excess of ten fatalities.

In view of this, following the rail accident at Ladbroke Grove in October 1999 in which 29 passengers and two train drivers died, the UK Health and Safety Executive (HSE) decided to commission a "follow-up" relative valuation study to be conducted in the London commuter belt with a quota requirement that at least 40% of the sample should be regular rail users.

As reported in Chilton et al. (2002), for the follow-up study sample as a whole, the rail/roads safety valuation relativity, V_{RL}/V_{RD}, was estimated to be 1.03, which represents a 24% increase on the figure from the earlier study. However, for the subsample of "high" rail users (defined as those who traveled 1000 miles or more per annum by rail) the V_{RL}/V_{RD} relativity was 1.157, which is some 39% higher than the estimate from the earlier study. Interestingly, the follow-up study on high rail users' rail/road relativity is very similar to that which emerged from an earlier study on the valuation of safety on the London Underground metro system if the data from the latter are analyzed using the same estimation procedure as was employed in the follow-up study (Jones-Lee and Loomes, 1995b).

6. The valuation of safety by Railtrack

The company responsible for running most of the UK's railway infrastructure, Railtrack (now taken over by Network Rail), elected to employ WTP-based values of safety in the early 1990s. Currently, Network Rail applies two distinct VPFs in its appraisal of proposed rail safety projects. The first – which is to all intents and purposes the current DTLR roads fatality figure updated for growth and inflation and rounded to UK £1.24 million in June 2002 prices[a] – is applied to situations in which passengers or staff can be taken to have a substantial degree of control, as in the case of single fatality accidents at level crossings or on platforms. However, the second VPF, which is employed in cases in which the risk concerned affects large numbers of people (e.g. a trainload, or population living near to a railway line) and the people concerned have a little or no control, or where risks are near the HSE's upper tolerability limit, is UK £3.46 million in June 2000 prices, i.e. 2.8 times the DTLR roads-based figure (Railtrack, 2000a).

Essentially, the higher VPF was arrived at by applying multipliers – estimated on the basis of judgement and expert opinion – to the "base" DTLR roads figure to reflect (1) the magnitude of rail risk relative to the HSE's "tolerability of risk" range between its lower and upper bounds[b] and (2) six "risk aversion" factors including lack of control, catastrophic potential, benefit to other than the risk taker, unknown nature of the risk, dread of type of death, and blame to the organization.

So, in the light of the rail/road safety valuation relativities reported above in Section 4, is Railtrack's two-tiered WTP-based VPF defensible? As far as the lower figure – applicable to, say, fatal accidents on platforms or at level crossings – is concerned, the answer would seem to be "yes."

However, when one turns to the higher figure of 2.8 times the DTLR roads VPF – applicable in the case of major train accidents – then the situation seems

---

[a]Apparently, Network Rail updates the latest DTLR VPF annually on the basis of estimated growth in real income per capita and forecast inflation.

altogether less clear-cut. Thus, it was argued in Jones-Lee (1998) that this higher figure could, in principle, be justified on the basis of (1) a "context" premium relative to the roads VPF, reflecting considerations of voluntariness, control, responsibility and dread, and (2) a "scale" premium, reflecting the misperception of risk, and consequent misallocation/disruption costs that research reported in Evans and Morrison (1997) suggests may well result from the occurrence of a catastrophic rail accident involving large-scale loss of life. However, it would appear that the rail/road safety valuation relativities reported above in Section 4 comprehensively remove the basis for the context premium argument. In turn, it has to be conceded that the appropriateness of the inclusion of a misallocation/disruption cost scale premium in the rail VPF is, to say the least, debatable and that there is an argument that the avoidance of such costs should be entered in cost–benefit analysis as a component quite separate and distinct from safety-related values.

If these arguments are granted, then the inexorable conclusion is that if a defense is to be found for Railtrack's higher VPF of about 2.8 times the DTLR roads figure then this cannot be found in currently available empirical evidence concerning the preferences of members of the travelling public. In short, strict adherence to the ethical principles typically taken to underpin conventional social cost–benefit analysis would indicate that a VPF equal to 2.8 times the DTLR roads value is a substantial overestimate.

If a defense for Railtrack's higher VPF is to be found it therefore appears that it has to be sought in considerations other than the preferences and wishes of members of the traveling public. A clue as to where such a defense might be found is provided in Railtrack (1997):

[b]The "tolerability of risk" framework employed by the HSE in implementing and enforcing the UK Health and Safety at Work etc. Act 1974, the Management of Health and Safety at Work Regulations 1992, and the Railways (Safety Case) Regulations 1994 essentially consists of three components, namely:

(1) an upper bound, above which risks are deemed to be unacceptable (or "intolerable") and, save in exceptional circumstances, must either be reduced, whatever the cost, or the activity giving rise to the risk discontinued;
(2) a lower bound below which risks are regarded as being "broadly acceptable" and therefore requiring no action to effect further reduction;
(3) a range between the upper and lower bounds in which risks are regarded as being "tolerable" provided that they have been reduced to levels that are "as low as reasonably practicable" (ALARP).

While in its most recent publications the HSE is somewhat equivocal about the precise levels at which the upper and lower bounds of the ALARP region should be set (Health and Safety Executive, 1999), there are indications that, broadly speaking, the HSE continues to endorse its earlier recommendation that for fatality risks the upper bound should be one in 10 000 per annum for individual members of the public and one in 1000 per annum for workplace risks, while the lower bound should generally be treated as being in the region of one in a million.

An example which frequently arises, in considering high-profile risks and measures to reduce them is the value of corporate reputation/public relations (PR)/political goodwill. Considerations in this area are undoubtedly of great practical importance.

Thus, Railtrack's decision to adopt a VPF for higher-profile, large-scale rail accidents equal to 2.8 times the corresponding roads figure seems not entirely unreasonable given the media reaction and political attention that is inevitably generated by a large-scale rail accident such as those which occurred at Clapham Junction and Ladbroke Grove.

Of course it could be argued that another defense for a rail VPF that generally exceeds its roads counterpart might be found in the "societal concerns" referred to in Health and Safety Executive (1999, paras 24, 122–127) and Railtrack (2000b, p. 20). However, it is hard to know what these "societal concerns" really are if other than media reaction and political response. Certainly, it would appear that they are not a reflection of the travelling public's higher degree of aversion to the prospect of large-scale simultaneous loss of life relative to its aversion to the prospect of the same number of lives lost in separate accidents. This is borne out (1) by the rail/road valuation relativities reported above in Section 4 and (2) by the fact that when asked whether the possibility of large-scale loss of life in a rail accident should be an argument in favor of prioritizing rail relative to road safety, the modal response of participants in the two studies referred to in Section 4 was that it should not. Similar findings relating to the London Underground metro system versus road safety are reported in Jones-Lee and Loomes (1995b).

But if "societal concern" really is no more than a shorthand for media reaction and political response, it would seem to give such reaction and response rather more significance than they deserve in the process of allocating society's scarce resources.

7. Summary and conclusion

The fundamental prescriptive premise of conventional social cost–benefit analysis is that decisions concerning the allocation of society's scarce resources should, so far as possible, reflect the preferences – and more particularly the strength of preference – of those members of the public who will be affected by the decision concerned. More specifically, given that members of the public not only stand to benefit from, say, an improved level of public transport safety, but also ultimately pay for it (through, for example, fares on public transport or taxation), in a democracy there is clearly a persuasive case for ensuring that their preferences are taken into account in decisions affecting public safety.

Thus, for example, Railtrack (1997)

Ch. 24: Valuation of Safety
461

aims, first, to capture the value which the general public in Britain would wish put on railway safety, and second, to take account of the corresponding value used in considering safety on the main transport mode, roads.

In order to effect the prescriptive principle underpinning cost–benefit analysis one clearly requires a measure of the value (or "worth") of a desired change, taking account of the inevitable scarcity of resources. Not surprisingly, therefore, the conventional measure of the value of a desired outcome within cost–benefit analysis is people's collective maximum WTP for the outcome taking account of the amount they can afford to pay, given their level of income.

So in the case of a proposed safety improvement, under this so-called WTP approach one would ideally like to discover how much people would be willing to pay for the improvement in their own (and possibly others') safety. The total sum elicited would then be a clear reflection of what the safety improvement was worth to those in the affected group, relative to alternative ways in which they could have spent their limited incomes.

Not surprisingly therefore, there is an increasing tendency for transport safety investment and regulatory decisions throughout the world to be taken on the basis of values that reflect the aggregate WTP for risk reduction of those affected by the decision concerned. These values are typically estimated in one of two ways. The first estimation procedure involves asking a representative sample of the population more or less directly how much each person would be willing to pay for a pre-specified reduction in the risk of premature death on a given transport mode and then aggregating across the number of people for whom the risk reduction could be expected to prevent one premature fatality. The second estimation procedure is based on observation of the rate at which people actually do trade wealth for risk as in, for example, labor markets where riskier jobs typically command clearly identifiable wage premiums.

By now, several countries employ WTP-based values of safety in road project appraisal. Typically, the value for prevention of a premature fatality lies in the UK £1–2 million range, with values for the prevention of serious and slight non-fatal injuries respectively being set at roughly one tenth and one hundredth of the fatality figure. In the case of rail in the UK, Network Rail uses two WTP-based values for the prevention of a premature death. The first, applied to single-fatality accidents on, for example, platforms, is set equal to the roads figure. The second, for use in the case of train crashes involving multiple fatalities and in which victims have little or no control, is set at 2.8 times the roads figure. This having been said, research carried out by the authors and others indicates that even regular rail users do not subscribe to such a wide differential between values of rail and road safety. Finally, it is also worth remarking that the ongoing installation of the Train Protection and Warning System (which prevents trains passing red danger signals up to a speed of 70 mph) on the UK's main line railway system requires a value for the prevention of a rail fatality in excess of UK £5 million if it is to be justified on cost–benefit grounds alone.

References

Carthy, T., S. Chilton, J. Covey, L. Hopkins, M. Jones-Lee, G. Loomes, N. Pidgeon and A. Spencer (1999) "On the contingent valuation of safety and the safety of contingent valuation: part 2 – the CV/SG "chained" approach," *Journal of Risk and Uncertainty,* 17:187–213.

Chilton, S., J. Covey, L. Hopkins., M.W. Jones-Lee, G. Loomes, N. Pidgeon and A. Spencer (2002) "Public perceptions of risk and preference-based values of safety," *Journal of Risk and Uncertainty,* 25:211-232.

Daniels, R. and V. Adamowicz, (2000) "Environmental valuation" in: D.A. Hensher and K. Button (2000) *Handbook of transport modelling.* Oxford: Pergamon.

Evans, A.W. and A.D. Morrison (1997) "Incorporating accident risk disruption in economic models of public transport," *Journal of Transport Economics and Policy,* 31:117–147.

Guria, J., W. Jones, M.W. Jones-Lee, M. Keall, J. Leung and G. Loomes (1999) *The values of statistical life and prevention of injuries in New Zealand.* Report. Wellington: New Zealand Land Transport Safety Authority.

Health and Safety Executive (1999) *Reducing risks, protecting people,* London: HSE Books.

Jones-Lee, M.W. (1976) *The value of life: an economics analysis.* London: Martin Robertson.

Jones-Lee, M.W. (1992) "Paternalistic altruism and the value of statistical life," *Economic Journal,* 102:80–90.

Jones-Lee, M.W. (1998) *The valuation of safety in the appraisal of proposed rail safety projects.* Report. London: Railtrack.

Jones-Lee, M.W. and G. Loomes (1995a) "Valuing the prevention of non-fatal road injuries: contingent valuation vs standard gambles," *Oxford Economic Papers,* 47:676–695.

Jones-Lee, M.W. and G. Loomes (1995b) "Scale and context effects in the valuation of transport safety," *Journal of Risk and Uncertainty,* 11:183–203.

Jones-Lee, M.W., M. Hammerton and P.R. Philips (1985) "The value of safety: results of a national sample survey," *Economic Journal,* 95:49–72.

Railtrack (1997) *Safety decision rules on the main line railways: draft green paper.* London: Railtrack.

Railtrack (2000a) *Railway Group Safety Plan 2000/01.* London: Safety and Standards Directorate, Railtrack.

Railtrack (2000b) *Safety decision making – discussion paper.* London: Safety and Standards Directorate, Railtrack.

Travén, A., P. Maraste and U. Persson (2002) "International comparison of costs of fatal accidents in 1990 and 1999," *Accident Analysis and Prevention,* 34:323–332.

Urban Institute (1991) *The costs of highway crashes, final report.* Report FHWA-RD-91-055. Washington, DC: The Urban Institute.

Chapter 25

LOCATION EXTERNALITIES: EFFECTS ON MODELING, INFRASTRUCTURE PROVISION AND OPTIMAL PLANNING

FRANCISCO MARTÍNEZ
University of Chile, Santiago

1. Introduction

In this chapter we study how the interaction between agents in the urban context affects the location distribution of households and firms in the city. By "interaction" we mean the dependency of one's location choices on other agents' location, or in other words how the location decisions of one agent may affect the location choices of all other agents. These interactions are a form of externality inasmuch as individuals make choices that generate unpremeditated effects on other individuals.

In large cities there are a number of externalities, for example those associated to the transport system, which are well identified by the public eye and the media because of their known harmful effects, such as traffic congestion that increase travel times, or noise and pollution that damage health. In the production of sector, retail and services for example, there are also interactions that generate spatial agglomeration economies, which describe the extra benefit of producing in an area where the land use is advantageous for the economic activity. Similarly the valuation of the neighborhood quality by households and firms generates yet another form of externality, more commonly associated with the location of residences than with other commercial activities.

The importance of externalities is well recognized in urban studies. For example, Fujita (1989) classifies urban externalities into three groups: (1) local public goods, (2) neighborhood and traffic congestion, and (3) external (agglomeration) economies, product variety, and city sizes. Other studies are focused on some specific externalities, for example Arnott and MacKinnon (1978) examined the effects of congestion in the transport network, and Anas (1988) examined the optimal pricing of a natural environment in a general equilibrium economy.

Here we concentrate on the effects of the interaction between agents arising from the fact that neighborhood quality is a valuable attribute for locating agents,

Handbook of Transport and the Environment, Edited by D.A. Hensher and K.J. Button
© 2003, Elsevier Ltd

which we call location externalities. For our purpose, particularly when we evaluate benefits, all other external effects are either ignored or assumed internalized by some mechanism. The reason for this is simple: as for scale economies studied by Fujita et al. (1999), location externalities are fundamental to the dynamic process underpinning the development of a city, and their understanding is crucial in the analysis of city planning.

Like Fujita et al., our aim is to understand how the location distribution of residents and firms in the city can be explained as the result of individual decisions, from the micro- to the macro-level or via a bottom-up approach. Fujita et al. study an economy where interactions between agents are dominated by scale economies in consumption and production and by transport costs, which cause non-linear dynamics where the economic signs are prices – of goods and land – and labor wages. They show that this approach is able to produce multi-center patterns and to describe the agglomeration tendency of economic activities. In our case we focus on agents' valuation of local amenities, which usually reflect strong social and cultural links across society that affect location choices directly. In this sense, these approaches are complementary, with both introducing complexity by incorporating non-linear effects; that of Fujita et al. has a stronger focus on the production–consumption process, for a system of cities where distance plays the main role, while our study focuses on residential and social activities, and concentrates more on intra-city patterns where social interactions are comparatively more important. Fujita et al. develop a spatially continuous and analytically treatable model that simplifies reality at the cost of overly homogeneous and symmetric solutions. In contrast, we consider a discontinuous space (at the cost of arbitrarily defined zones), which allows us to represent heterogeneous location patterns and produce readily applicable models.

Location externalities describe the mutual interaction between agents, which at a micro-level means that the location of one or more households and/or firms in a neighborhood modifies the quality of that neighborhood. Thus, the allocation of one agent affects the location of a number of other agents because it alters the built environment; subsequently, these agents will tend to relocate in order to adjust to new neighborhood advantages and, by so doing, the built environment is modified again. In short, location externalities are generated, which also affect location behavior. This describes a sequence of interactions and interdependencies between location choices that generate a strong urban dynamic.

These externalities may have negative effects, such as overcrowding and racial issues, as well as positive effects, such as the concentration of homogenous groups (defined by ethnic, cultural, or other characteristics) or the local availability of services and amenities, or mixed effects. For example, statistical evidence shows that in Santiago (Chile) the neighborhood socio-economic level is a dominant factor in residential location choice – a characteristic probably shared by many other cities in the region. Although this is perceived by agents as a positive externality, at an aggregate level it induces severe spatial segregation of the population by income class, which can act as a seed for social tension. The study of location externalities allows us to understand and predict such social effects.

In the case of firms, the emphasis in the literature has been on the study of the economic forces that drive firms to move closer to suppliers of inputs, including the labor force, and to consumers of products, both movements generated by the non-linear effects of economies of scale in these interactions (Fujita et al., 1999). However, firms may also consider other social interactions, such as neighborhood prestige for headquarters or personal networking, which, in addition to economies of scale, generate complementary forces that cause a dynamic clustering of firms.

The objective of this chapter is to understand location externalities, specify the interactions mathematically, and present a model able to simulate their complex effects on land use development. This allows us to evaluate public investment, and provides a method for the calculation of efficient land shadow prices. Finally, we discuss the nature of the equilibrium in the urban free market and how regulations and subsidies can move the market toward an optimal land use pattern, subject of course to a definition of the optimal city as identified exogenously.

2. The land use theoretical model

In this section we describe the theoretical microeconomic model of the distribution of activities – households and firms – in the city. Essentially, it is a model of consumers' behavior in a real market, where the urban location pattern emerges out of the agents' interdependent discrete choice process operating under market regulations.

Consumers are represented by households differentiated by socio-economic groups, and by firms segmented by industry types, each group denoted by the index h. Supply is provided in a variety of land and buildings discrete options, which, for the benefit of a simple presentation, we consider to be exogenously defined. This represents a short-run analysis that yields a trade economy, although the model can be expanded for the long term, where suppliers behave as profit maximizers. Space is arbitrarily divided into homogeneous zones (denoted by index i) described by a set of attributes included as elements of a vector z, which provide an explicit representation of the built environment and land use in each zone. Other attributes describing the building and land characteristic of a specific property (denoted by index v) are also included in z. It is worth emphasizing that consumers' utility depends not only on the consumption of goods and services, denoted by the vector x, but also on the set of attributes of the location choice representing the built environment in each zone, which transfers information associated with location externalities across agents in the model. The utility function is then $U_h(x, z)$, with z representing location externalities.

The main market assumptions are that location options are sold by an auction process and that the land market attains equilibrium at each point in time, which simply imposes the condition that every agent is allocated somewhere in the city. Specifying the equilibrium and externalities in this way defines a complex non-linear mathematical equilibrium problem that, considering the dimensions involved, probably explains why location externalities have been largely ignored in applied equilibrium land use models. This approach is explained in more detail in Martínez (1996), and has been utilized in a land use model of Santiago, called MUSSA (Martínez and Donoso, 2001), which provides the empirical examples presented below.

The theoretical background for assuming auctions is based on the observation that a location in the urban context is a very scarce resource because the right to use it, by renting or buying, provides access to the benefits arising from the neighborhood amenities generated by the built and natural environment. This makes each location a quasi-unique or differentiable good, which yields a monopoly power to the landowner who obtains maximum benefit by an auction process that extract the maximum willingness to pay from consumers, as proposed by Alonso (1964). Consumers take part in the auction by making bids for location options, where bids represent their willingness to pay. According to Solow (1973) and Rosen (1974), willingness to pay is a function obtained analytically as the inverse of the land rents of the corresponding indirect utility function conditional on the location choice. Let us denote by V_{hvi} the indirect utility function conditional on the location option vi. Assuming that each agent "consumes" only one location and has fixed income I_h, this function can be expressed as $V_{hvi} = V_h(I_h - r_{vi}, p, z_{vi})$, where p is the price vector for goods and services, excluding the location price (or rent) r_{vi}, and z_{vi} is the vector of the zone and building attributes and accessibility indices.

Then, the willingness-to-pay or bid function, conditional on obtaining a given utility level U_h, is

$$B_{hvi} \equiv I_h - V_h^{-1}(p, z_{vi}, U_h), \tag{1}$$

which represents the maximum value the agent is willing to pay for a location described by z_{vi} to obtain a utility level U_h given the exogenous I_h and p. One can understand this function in the context of choice models by assuming that the agent considers a fixed utility level, which is exogenously defined by market conditions, and assesses her/his monetary value for each available location option in the city using this bid function, which represents the price that would make the agent indifferent to choosing an alternative location since the utility level is assumed fixed across space. An important observation is that from equation (1) we get $e_h = B_{hvi} + V_{hvi}^{-1}$, which represents the expenditure function for all goods plus the location cost if the consumer actually pays B; this will be relevant for the evaluation of different land use patterns. Another observation is that similar bid functions can be derived for firms directly from their profit functions.

For our purpose it is important to observe that bid functions theoretically embed location externalities or interactions between agents by means of vector z in equation (1). Because the allocation of these activities is the result of auctions, it follows that bids depend on bids. This dependency represents a technological externality between agents, defined directly in their utility function, which operates in the urban system in addition to the pecuniary interaction through land prices. Analytically, this interaction generates a non-linear fixed-point problem that describes in the model the dynamics introduced by the explicit representation of location externalities.

Then, in the short run with supply assumed to be exogenous, equilibrium is twofold. First, at each location equilibrium is defined by the auction mechanism[a], where the auctioneer selects the maximum bidder h^*:

$$h^* = \mathrm{argmax}_{h \in H} B_{h'vi}, \qquad (2)$$

where H is the set of bidders including households and firms, but excludes activities forbidden by regulations. This best-bidder rule is sufficient for the simultaneous conditions that suppliers maximize profit and agents maximize their utility or consumers' surplus, as shown in Martínez (1992, 2000). By this property the best-bidder rule simultaneously defines the optimal allocation of agents and rents at each building location supplied.

The second equilibrium condition relates to the whole market. Unlike markets of products where consumers decide how much – if any – they buy of each good, in this market we assume that all agents (or at least residents) consume only one location, but also not less than one. This means that every agent has to be located somewhere at equilibrium, provided that there are sufficient location options. Thus, agents trade each other's location alternatives in auctions up to an equilibrium state that defines the maximum utility level attainable by each consumer in the market, represented by $U_h = U_h^*$ in equation (1).

The above theory leads to a complex model of the economics of a city that is extremely difficult to use for predictions. The fact that supply is discrete (zone system) and differentiable (location externalities) makes it mathematically untreatable for large cities. Moreover, what is more important is to recognize that the introduction of externalities represents in the model a phenomenon that induces inherent instability in the model outcomes. This phenomenon has been widely described in the social sciences (Schelling, 1978), and it is well

---

[a] In the urban land market, buildings usually have known common values, for example provided by real estate agents, so we expect the auctioneer to receive several similar bids; nevertheless, inevitably the final value is only defined by the auction. On the issue of auctions with common values, see, for example, the review by McAffe and McMillan (1987).

recognized that it leads to complex non-linear mathematical formulations, with small changes in initial conditions causing dramatic differences in the location pattern and rents.

3. An operational model

One way in which to tackle the complexity discussed at the end of the previous section is to introduce continuity by transforming the deterministic problem into its probabilistic equivalent, which smoothes discontinuities associated with the agents' choice of process. A second complementary tool is to choose a probability distribution that has some properties that help to solve the location problem. Finally, complexity may, in a real case, be less dramatic than the theoretical extremes, which also helps to reduce the complexity.

Additionally, a probabilistic approach provides the extra benefit of generating a more realistic model because it allow us to represent the idiosyncratic variability of bid functions across agents within a cluster. Then, we can apply the above model to clusters of homogeneous agents rather than to individuals. The idiosyncratic variability on agents' behavior takes into account the usual socio-economic and cultural differences considered in random utility theory but also the variability in information and speculative behavior in auction processes.

Thus, we assume bids are given by

$$B_{hvi} = b_{hvi} + \varepsilon_{hvi}, \tag{3}$$

where h represents a cluster of homogeneous agents, b_{hvi} is the deterministic component of bids, and ε_{hvi} is a random term. From the large number of potential distributions for random terms, the Gumbel distribution is cleverly justified by Ellickson (1981) for clusters of agents taking part in auctions. He argues that for a set of individual random bids of agents within a cluster, each one following any distribution, only the maximum bid in the cluster is relevant for the auction process. Since the maximum of a set of random terms follow an extreme value distribution, such as the Gumbel, choosing this distribution has a sound theoretical basis. For simplicity we also assume random terms as independent and identical with null mode and the scale parameter μ. Applying these assumptions we obtain the following operational model.

First, the expression for the expected maximum bid across all agents' clusters, which directly represents the expected rent at location (v, i), is

$$r_{vi} = E\left(\operatorname*{Max}_{h \in H}(b_{hvi} + \varepsilon_{hi})\right) = \frac{1}{\mu} \ln \sum_{h \in H} \exp(\mu b_{hvi}) + \frac{\gamma}{\mu}, \tag{4}$$

where γ is Euler's constant (approximately 0.577). Second, the probability of consumer h being the best bidder conditional on the availability of option vi is given by the following well-known multinomial logit expression:

$$P_{h/vi} = \frac{\exp(\mu b_{hvi})}{\sum_{h' \in H} \exp(\mu b_{h'vi})} = \exp \mu \left(b_{hvi} - r_{vi} + \frac{\gamma}{\mu} \right), \quad (5)$$

where equation (4) was replaced in the denominator of the first logit formula in equation (5) to obtain the right-hand expression. This equation states that the probability asymptotically tends to 1 – a case of deterministic choice – as the consumer's bid tends to the expected rent.

Equations (3) to (5) represent a discrete location model based on random bidding in an urban auction market, what we call the random bidding model (RBM).

Let us see how this model solves the complexity and eliminates instability. Note that bids in equation (5) are functions of the attribute vector z that depends on the location pattern given by location probabilities (P). Thus, $z = z(P)$ and $P_{h/vi} = f(P)$, which shows that equation (5) reproduces the non-linear fixed-point problem mentioned above. From Brouwer's fixed-point theorem (see Mas-Colell et al., 1995) and because the probability matrix is continuous and defined as a unitary ball, a solution for this fixed-point exists, although there may be multiple solutions. Extensive empirical study indicates that as long as the behavior distribution of agents has a enough variance to be away from the deterministic bidding case ($\mu \ll \infty$ in equations (4) and (5)), a unique and stable solution is obtained, even for non-linear bid functions. Then, we conclude that, despite the complexity of externalities the RBM benefits from the continuity of the probabilistic approach and exploits the structure of the Gumbel distribution to find a solution.

4. Scenarios and benefits

The set of exogenous conditions for the urban market represents a scenario, including population, land regulations, and the transport system, as well as agents' behavior parameters. For each scenario, denoted by t, the equilibrium can be calculated by obtaining the vector of maximum utility levels U^t and the location pattern that defines attributes z^t; additionally, land rents can calculated. Having the foregoing in mind, in this section we define an economic measure for the total social benefit yield by a given scenario, which can be taken as an index of the performance of the regulations and projects included in the scenario.

Economists calculate consumers' benefits from the variation in the consumer's surplus between two different scenarios. Fortunately, these benefits can be calculated directly from willingness-to-pay values, recalling that the bid functions in equation (1) represent consumers' expenditure functions and also recalling that the variation in expenditure holding utility constant is, by definition, the consumers' income – equivalent or compensating – variation, which is a rigorous benefit measure. We can then define the consumers' surplus as

$$\Delta S_{hvi} \equiv \Delta B(U^t) - \Delta r_{vi}, \tag{6}$$

where Δ represents the variation between two equilibrated scenarios (for more details see Martínez, 2000). Suppliers, on the other hand, capture a portion of the benefits equal to the variation in rents. Adding consumers' surplus across population and suppliers' surplus across supply options yields an economic measure of the land use social benefit (B^{LU}). Given that rents are only transferred between consumers and suppliers, they cancel out.

This agent-based benefit index may be aggregated to obtain a social welfare index, calculated by aggregating benefits by cluster across zones and then aggregating across clusters weighted by the number of members located in each zone. We may also introduce a set of equity parameters γ_h that represents a differentiated social valuation of benefits according to who receives them. Then, the difference in total social benefit comparing scenario 1 with a base scenario 0 is

$$B^{LU} = \sum_{h \in H} \gamma_h \left(\sum_{(v,i) \in \Omega} [N^1_{hvi} B_h(z^1_{vi}, I^1_h, U^t_h) - N^0_{hvi} B_h(z^0_{vi}, I^0_h, U^t_h)] \right), \tag{7}$$

where N_{hvi} is the number of agents h located at option vi, and Ω is the set of supply options[a].

Note that equation (7) has complex bid terms of the form $B(z^1, I^1, U^0)$ or $B(z^0, I^0, U^1)$ that require evaluating bids at a non-equilibrium point. Also, the variation in rents is represented by the variation in successful bids:

$$\Delta r_{vi} = \sum_{(v,i) \in \Omega} [N^1_{hvi} B_h(z^1_{vi}, I^1_h, U^1_h) - N^0_{hvi} B_h(z^0_{vi}, I^0_h, U^0_h)], \tag{8}$$

which has different superscripts for utilities to the term in parentheses in equation (7). Thus, the variation in rents does not represent an economic measure of social benefits, and represents only the variation of suppliers' benefits; rents and benefits are equal only if utilities are held constant between the compared scenarios, a very unlikely scenario.

---

[a]For the purpose of our empirical examination, in the rest of this chapter we assume no variation in the total population,

$$\sum_{vi} N^1_{hvi} = \sum_{vi} N^0_{hvi} = N_h,$$

and we take $\gamma_h = 1$.

5. Optimal planning

We have identified location externalities and proposed an operational model that yields equilibrium solutions for the urban market. However, externalities call for a careful social analysis of the free market equilibrium, to verify if the outcome is consistent with social goals (efficiency, equity, environment, etc.) or to define market interventions required (such as regulations or incentives) to attain an optimal city.

Social goals have to be defined somehow by the city, to which a social welfare function may be associated, and the notion of optimality can be defined with regards to such goal. A common welfare function used in the economics literature is the aggregated benefit defined above as B^{LU} less the social cost involved; we take this function with all $\gamma = 1$ as an example in the following analysis. Then, we propose that the planner's problem in modern cities as the need to identify the set and level of planning tools available for the authority that maximize the welfare function under free market equilibrium conditions. This approach allows agents to participate in the urban market freely and competitively, achieving market equilibrium conditions, while the planning agency seeks to improve performance in social goals by defining the optimal set of market regulations.

Let us now specify the planners problem. The market equilibrium at year t can be described by the land use pattern (z^t), the utility level achieved by agents (U^t), and the associated social benefit measure $B^{LU}(z^t, U^t)$. The solution and the associated benefits depend on the regulatory scenario exogenously defined, which can be described by a set of physical zoning regulations and price – subsidy or taxing – policies, denoted by R^t. In addition to the set of regulations, the scenario may include a set of private and public projects and policies (Y^t). Then the corresponding total cost of the scenario is $C^t = C(R^t, Y^t)$ and the net social benefit is $B^t = B^{LU}(R^t, Y^t) - C(R^t, Y^t)$. Then, the optimal planning problem is to find an optimum set (R^*, Y^*) that maximizes the social benefit:

$$(R^*, Y^*) = \underset{R,Y}{\operatorname{argmax}} B(R,Y) \quad \forall t \quad \text{s.t. equilibrium,} \tag{9}$$

where (R^*, Y^*) represents the optimal scenario of planning regulations and projects/policies that maximizes the city welfare function. Significant research is still required before equation (8) can be solved for the general case; however, analyzing a set of scenarios and comparing them will provide some information.

Notice that this approach has the advantage of being free of the Mirelees "unequal treatment of equals" phenomenon (Fujita, 1989), which identifies cases in urban economics where at the optimum identical agents achieve different utility levels. Fujita applies the Herbert–Stevens model to overcome the Mirelees phenomenon, where the objective is to maximize the total surplus subject to a set of exogenously specified target utilities for all households types; the solution is always efficient, and all efficient solutions are generated by varying utility levels. In our approach, the Mireless phenomenon is ruled out by the equilibrium conditions that guarantee intra-cluster identical utility levels[a], but, in contrast to the Herbert–Stevens model, here they are endogenously determined by equilibrium. We recognize, of course, that an unconstrained optimal land use pattern potentially yields higher benefits than one constrained to equilibrium, but while the former is a theoretical optimal city, the latter has the important benefit that it is feasible in a free market.

Additionally, the optimally planned city in our approach complies with the auction Nash equilibrium, not the classical Walras equilibrium for a perfect competitive market. Our model is based on a discrete space, and forecasts an optimal equilibrium dependent on a basal partition of the urban land (zones), and the good traded is defined by a set of endogenously generated zone and dwelling attributes, whereas the Herbert–Stevens model trades empty continuous land. We optimize the urban regulatory system, while in the Herbert–Stevens approach it is implicit in the exogenously given supply that fulfils any absent regulation; as a result, equation (10) below does not collapse into a minimization of the costs C^t as in Fujitas' optimum city models. Additionally, Arnott and MacKinnon (1978) and Anas (1998) ignore location externalities to reach the conclusion that the equilibrium location pattern and rents are optimal for the B^{LU} welfare function; this would not be the case if location externalities were explicit.

In what follows we discuss two specific issues associated with optimal planning.[b] First, how do location externalities affect the social value of land, which is a parameter used for the evaluation of transport and other urban projects? Second, does the free market generate optimum outcomes of location patters or can one find a set of economic incentives that increase social benefits? To generate an empirical test we use the algorithm developed in the MUSSA model, which in addition to the RBM includes a model of the supply side (Martínez and Donoso, 2001).

5.1. Social prices for land expropriation

Consider a transport infrastructure project that requires expropriation of a set of land lots, $\Psi \subset \Omega$, each one with market price p_i and land size q_i. Assuming urban equilibrium prior to the expropriation, the *ex ante* vector of land prices p represents the maximum value that the society attaches to the expropriated land,

---

[a]More rigorously, this argument is only partially true for our model since utilities are stochastic variables, and there is intra-cluster variation in utilities.

[b]The issue of how planning regulations affect urban outcomes is outside the scope of this chapter, but is discussed in Martínez and Donoso (2000).

therefore it represents the social value of this resource. In the long term, the transport project will modify not only accessibility but also the location pattern of activities. Transport evaluation methods do consider the value of the variation in accessibility, but they ignore changes in utilities associated with relocation effects. From our previous discussion we know that location externalities induce relocation in a complex manner, so the change in land use benefits cannot be anticipated without modeling location choices.

For example, a new road project induces location externalities that modify the land use pattern beyond the spatial limits of the expropriated land, because it attracts or discourages the location of agents, which via location externalities changes the location pattern in a wide area. The essence of the social pricing argument is that the price used to value the expropriated land should internalize all these (dis)benefits, which are not incorporated in *ex ante* price signals nor in the usual evaluation methods of transport projects because they use a fixed short-run transport demand curve that ignores how it is displaced (to the right or left) owing to location externalities. This means that the generation or reduction of trips is mispredicted, which may have a significant impact on the evaluation of transport infrastructure. Naturally, a similar argument applies to other urban projects involving land expropriation.

The question we want to address is: what is the social land value that, taking into account location externalities, should be used for transport project appraisals? The answer is, straightforwardly, a price that internalizes the difference between social benefits obtained at the *ex ante* and *ex post* equilibria. The *ex post* equilibrium has to be calculated solving the market equilibrium with the project and then calculating benefits using equation (7). Then, the shadow land price per unit of area expropriated (say per square meter) r^s is simply the market price plus the extra disbenefit induced by the project per area unit:

$$r^s = r - \frac{B^{LU}}{Q} = r - \frac{1}{Q}\left(\sum_{h \in H} \sum_{\substack{(v,i)=\Omega \\ (v,i)=\Psi}} [N^1_{hvi} B^1_{hvi}(U^t) - N^0_{hvi} B^0_{hvi}(U^t)] \right), \quad (10)$$

where r is the *ex ante* market value of land,

$$B^k_{hvi}(U^t) \equiv B_h(z^k_{vi}, I^k_h, U^t_h)$$

and

$$Q = \sum_{k \in \Psi} q_k$$

is the total land take; the index t refers to any reference situation 0 or 1. In the absence of location externalities no impact on the location pattern is expected from expropriation, hence $z^1 = z^0$ and $U^0 = U^1$, then $B^1_{hvi} = B^0_{hvi}$. The amount of expropriated land Q affects the equilibrium, and thus modifies z in every zone and U in every cluster, which explains why the summation in equation (10) is across all locations (except the expropriated land $(v, i) \notin \Psi$)). Notice that a project that generates positive relocation benefits has a reduced shadow price that increases its odds of being implemented; the opposite is true for harmful projects in terms of location impact. Thus, it is plausible for shadow prices to be below the market price; in fact, even negative prices are possible if the project has significant land use benefits, indicating the social need to subsidize the project. For example, in the economic assessment of urban road projects the correct valuation of expropriated land is likely to modify the social priority of infrastructure investment in favor of less land-hungry projects.

Building developers may anticipate, at least partially, potential land use benefits concentrated in some zones and associated with changes in accessibility. In order to capitalize on these changes they may react by investing in the vicinity of the project, inducing further land use effects. These demand–supply interaction effects can only be incorporated in the calculation of equilibrium and land use benefits if location externalities and the reaction of the supply side are contained in the land use equilibrium model, as in our model if we include the supply behavior component.

Using equation (10) in the cost–benefit analysis of road projects requires some fundamental assumptions. First, the demand of the transport system has to be inelastic to changes in land use (short term), otherwise the shift in the transport demand counts for the benefits of location externalities (Martínez and Araya, 2000). Second, every impact from other externalities (i.e. congestion, noise, and pollution) has to be assumed internalized or evaluated; if not, other corrections need to be considered (e.g. Arnott and McKinnon, 1978). Only under these assumptions do the proposed shadow price corrections reflect additional economic land use benefits that have been ignored in the traditional cost–benefit analysis of transport projects. Unfortunately, we know of no correcting methods that can be applied to current practice in transport project appraisal that avoid modeling land use.

To illustrate our arguments, an empirical example was developed for a hypothetical transport plan that involved expropriation of 5% of the total land in some zones of the city of Santiago, Chile. The land use model MUSSA was run for the cases with ($t = 1$) and without ($t = 0$) the plan, obtaining expected bids and rents for each equilibrium situation; no reductions were made to transport operating costs associated with the new infrastructure. Using these outputs, shadow prices were calculated using equation (10), and the results are shown in Table 1. The plan was applied to two different urban areas: high and low density. In both cases the shadow price is higher than the market price, indicating that expropriation induces relocations and price changes that generate disbenefits; this effect is, however, more significant in the more developed urban areas where land is more scarce. The plan induces a shadow price 4.8% above the market price

Table 1
Example of shadow prices in Santiago

		Urban development	
		High level	Low level
Unit benefit (US $/m² month)	B^{LU}/Q	−0.20	−0.08
Market rent (US $/m² month)	r	4.21	4.21
Shadow price (US $/m² month)	r^s	4.41	4.29
Shadow/market price (%)	$(r^s - r)/r$	4.8	1.9
Total project benefit correction (US $/month)	$Q(r^s - r)$	522.283	209.167

in the more developed area, while in the less developed area the shadow price is still larger than the market price but only by 1.9%. It is worth noticing that these figures are high enough to affect the results of the economic assessment of some transport projects.

5.2. Optimal land pricing

Let us now examine the case of optimal pricing policies based on the welfare index B^{LU}, aimed at inducing an optimized land use via the introduction of taxes/subsidies. In contrast to the shadow prices case, where the infrastructure decision is taken exogenous to the market, say by the government, here monetary incentives affect agents' decisions. As in the previous section, equilibrium conditions are imposed to the optimum, so intra-cluster constant utility is preserved across the city.

It is worth explaining the rationale of introducing subsidies/taxes. The issue here is that a space of equilibria can be defined, with each point in this multidimensional space representing a tax/subsidy policy. Each equilibrium point also has an associated land use benefit. Assuming that a tax/subsidy policy is politically feasible, we want to find the optimal set of values of this policy, that is, the level and structure of tax/subsidies that generates the maximum benefit. The optimal solution, however, may not be easy to achieve, because it is likely to require a significant relocation and rebuilding process, and for the optimal city a policy of economic incentives will be required. Even though this optimal solution is far from a real situation, the result has utility as a theoretical reference.

Therefore, the optimal pricing policy requires levying the area with a vector of tax/subsidy (s) that maximizes the net benefit induced by the land use change. This is given by

$$\text{Max}_s [B^{LU}(s) - C(s)] \quad \text{s.t. equilibrium,} \quad (11)$$

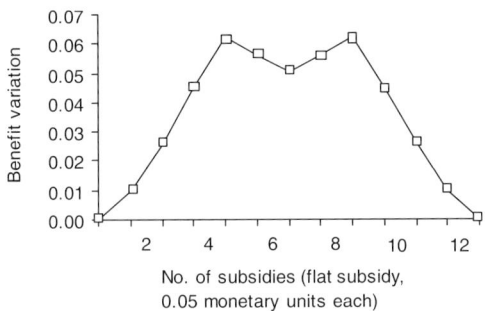

Figure 1. Social benefits by number of subsidies.

where $C(s)$ is the extra social cost associated with the location pattern generated by s. The complexity introduced by the equilibrium in equation (11) makes the solution of this problem a subject for ongoing research. However, the following results from a pilot experiment encourage future investigations.

We have modeled a very simple city, with two zones, two building types, and three types of residents differentiated by income level, yielding 12 combinations of alternative submarkets: an individual cluster (h), a building type (v), or a zone (i), or any combination of these options. The number of submarkets subsidized and the level of subsidies for each of them represent the policy options that a planner can consider when assigning subsidies. The optimization procedure iterates considering all different policy options assuming no extra costs ($C(s) = 0$). In our experiment the subsidy levels were limited to equality in all policies. The model explores all available policy options for each number of subsidies considered and calculates the associated social benefit index $B^{LU}(s)$. The maximum index obtained for each number of subsidies across submarkets is plotted in Figure 1, which shows a global maximum of four subsidies; this result depends on the level of subsidies tested. It also shows that the trivial policies – no subsidy or equal subsidies in all submarkets – yield no social benefits.

Our model reveals the existence of subsidy structures that generate higher social benefits than those obtained from zero subsidy. In our experiment this was the case for any number of subsidies (except for the trivial cases). Also, it proves that there is a non-trivial optimum number of subsidies to be assigned. Of course, these results cannot be taken as a general conclusion, since much more experimentation is required, for example relaxing the condition of equal level of subsidies, but the point has been made that the model can produce pricing policies that alter the free market equilibrium, yielding social benefits. Additionally, in all our experimental cases social benefits do not offset the total amount of subsidies introduced, but it should be recalled that subsidies percolate into rents and are, therefore, capitalized by producers. Thus, for planners to recover the resources used for the subsidies, real state properties should be taxed according to the extra rents obtained by suppliers. These findings provide scope for more theoretical studies and for a wide spectrum of empirical analysis.

6. Summary

In this chapter we have presented a macroeconomic stochastic bid–auction equilibrium model (RBM) that theoretically explains how location externalities induce location effects in the city system as well as changes in property rents and benefits. These externalities make a case for considering pricing policies, such as shadow prices and taxes/subsidies, in order to internalize these effects according to social goals. We have provided some empirical analysis in order to generate social optima decisions under free market equilibrium conditions, but this was limited to a specific city welfare function that maximizes the total unweighted consumer utilities and supplier profits; many other welfare functions can be studied that will yield different and potentially more interesting results.

The method for calculating shadow prices for land expropriation requires the use of a land use model able to predict the impacts of location externalities, thus complementing current practice in transport project appraisals and potentially altering decisions on infrastructure development. The calculation of land shadow prices, however, is complex, since it involves the simulation of the new land use equilibrium induced by the transport project. The increase in the social cost of land expropriation may be high enough, between 1.9 and 4.8% above the private value in our example, to affect the results of project appraisals and development priorities in favor of those that are either less land-demanding or require land in less-developed areas. Conversely, projects that liberate land from transport infrastructure receive a land price premium according to the benefits induced by location externalities. This argument favors reductions in road capacity and increases in investment in public transport in large cities.

Additionally, we have examined the existence of optimal location patterns, again with examples limited to a specific welfare measure. Empirical evidence presented here indicates that a non-zero subsidy policy is likely to produce an optimal location pattern. This opens a vast research area on methods to find optimum city structures, optimum tax/subsidy incentives, and "appropriate" definitions of city welfare functions, which will all require a good deal of investigation.

Acknowledgments

The research was partially funded by Fondecyt and Millenium. The author thanks the Chilean Government (SECTRA) for the financial support to develop the model MUSSA, and P. Manterola and F. Aguila, who contributed to the empirical analysis.

References

Alonso, W. (1964) *Location and land use*. Cambridge: Harvard University Press.
Anas, A. (1988) "Optimal preservation and pricing of natural public lands in general equilibrium," *Journal of Environmental Economics and Management*, 15:158–172.
Arnott, R.J. and J.G. MacKinnon (1978) "Market and shadow land rents with congestion," *American Economic Review*, 68:588–600.
Ellickson, B. (1981) "An alternative test of the hedonic theory of housing markets," *Journal of Urban Economics*, 9:56–79.
Fujita, M. (1989) *Urban economic theory, land use and city size*. Cambridge: Cambridge University Press.
Fujita, M., P. Krugman and A. Venables (1999) *The spatial economy: cities, regions and the international trade*. Cambridge: MIT Press.
McAffe, P.N and J. McMillan (1987) "Auctions and bidding," *Journal of Economic Literature*, 25:699–738.
Martínez, F.J. (1992) "The bid–choice land use model: an integrated economic framework," *Environment and Planing A*, 15:871–885.
Martínez, F.J. (1996) "MUSSA a land use model for Santiago City," *Transportation Research Record*, 1552:126–134.
Martínez, F.J. (2000) "Towards a land-use and transport interaction framework," in: D. Hensher and K. Button, eds, *Transport modelling*. Oxford: Pergamon.
Martínez, F.J. and C. Araya (2000) "Transport and land use benefits under location externalities," *Environment and Planning A*, 32:1521–1709.
Martínez, F.J. and P. Donoso (1996) "MUSSA model: the theoretical framework," in D. Hensher, J. King and T. Oun, eds, *Modelling Transport Systems: Proceedings of the 7th World Conference on Transportation Research*, Vol. 2. Oxford: Pergamon.
Martínez, F.J. and P. Donoso (2000). "Modelling land use planning effects: zone regulations and subsidies," in: *9th International Association for Travel Behavior Conference*. Gold Coast.
Martínez, F.J. and P. Donoso (2001) "MUSSA: a land use equilibrium model with location externalities, planning regulations and pricing policies," in: *7th International Conference on Computers in Urban Planning and Urban Management (CUPUM 2001)*. Hawaii.
Mas-Colell, A., M.D. Whinston and J.R. Green (1995) *Microeconomic theory*. New York: Oxford University Press.
Rosen, S. (1974) "Hedonic prices and implicit markets: product differentiation in pure competition," *Journal of Political Economy*, 62:34–55.
Schelling, T.C. (1978) *Micromotives and macrobehaviour*. New York: Norton.
Solow, R.M. (1973) "On equilibrium models of urban location," in: M. Parkin, ed., *Essays in modern economics*. London: Longman.

Part 4

POLICY ISSUES

Chapter 26

MACROECONOMIC POLICIES AND THE ENVIRONMENT

STEIN HANSEN
Nordic Consulting Group AS, Oslo

1. Introduction

It is increasingly recognized that macroeconomics via its impacts on the level and structure of economic activities in a region, a country, or the world at large, has a multitude of direct and indirect environmental impacts, requiring an understanding of linkages between the ecosystems and the economic systems (e.g. Gandhi, 1996).

At the same time, it is of interest to measure the macroeconomic consequences of different levels of environmental (e.g. transport) externalities, and of measures to reduce and internalize these, whether these measures are of a macroeconomic nature, or, for example, regulatory command and control measures. This raises questions such as: what are the impacts of transport externalities on economic growth? In short, macroeconomic policies can have profound and often unexpected environmental effects, which again can impact on macroeconomic performance, such as growth rates, competitiveness, budgetary balance, balance of payments, and distribution. This is a topic surrounded by much mystique and misunderstanding, and we will seek to clarify on this in the following.

2. Do we need a "green GDP"?

Macroeconomic analyses are based on the "GDP (gross domestic product) family" of concepts, and associated data from national income accounting. These concepts and data have been carefully defined and are internally consistent. There is broad international consensus throughout the UN member countries to adhere to these concepts definitions so as to make possible comparisons along a range of development indicators between countries at a point in time as well as over time for one and more countries.

The GDP family of macroeconomic concepts is frequently used as a means to evaluate macroeconomic policy. However, unconditional use of these concepts

Handbook of Transport and the Environment, Edited by D.A. Hensher and K.J. Button
© *2003, Elsevier Ltd*

may give misleading impressions of welfare development and may suggest a wrong approach toward management of our income and natural resource base. This has become particularly apparent when focusing on the economic impacts on future generations of today's depletion of fossil fuels, of the extermination of numerous species in the flora and fauna, and of the use of nature's sinks to absorb, store, or recycle polluting emissions to the air, water, and soils. To the extent that these economic effects are not incorporated in the prices and costs that the users of these resources are faced with, we can term them environmental economic externalities.

The European Conference of Ministers of Transport (ECMT) has estimated total traffic-related external costs to be between 1.7 and 7% of GDP in the Organisation of Economic Co-operation and Development (OECD) countries. For the European part of the OECD, the estimated external cost interval can be narrowed down to between US $400 and 700 billion per year (1996 prices). Such estimates are uncertain and controversial, but what is clear is that whether the true costs are half or double these amounts, they are huge in absolute monetary terms as well as in terms of conventional macroeconomic indicators such as those of the GDP family.

Because such externality estimates have become so large in absolute and relative terms in a national income accounting statistics setting, many observers claim that the rate of economic growth as measured by GDP is not matched by an equivalent rate of growth in perceived quality of life. Such criticism has led to various proposals to correct the conventional GDP for the adverse changes in quality of life that are not directly reflected in this GDP measure. Such corrections would then lead to a "green GDP," where the loss of, for example, environmental capital not measured in the conventional national income accounts is taken into account. Furthermore, it has been suggested that the conventionally measured GDP is corrected by subtracting the costs associated with preventing or repairing damages due to pollution, traffic accidents, etc. In this way, the "green GDP" is expected to reflect real welfare changes in a better way than the conventional GDP.

Such suggested corrections are by no means new. A measure of economic welfare (MEW) was proposed in 1972 by Nordhaus and Tobin. Cobb and Daly suggested an index for sustainable economic welfare (ISEW) in 1990, and Uno proposed a net national welfare index (NNW) in 1992. The human development index (HDI), adopted by the UN Development Programme in the annual *Human Development Reports* since 1992 (UNDP, 1992), on the other hand, is clearly not an attempt at correcting the GDP. It is simply an alternative welfare indicator.

In order to properly assess the merits and weaknesses of the conventional GDP and the proposed alternatives, a brief overview of what GDP is designed to measure is in place. GDP is one among a series of indicators calculated for each country in accordance with the definitions of the UN System of National Accounts. These accounts are meant to cover all economic transactions in society, including the illegal ones. The main rule is to value all transactions in accordance with market prices, but where such markets do not exist there are established principles for estimating substitute prices. This applies to, for example, farmers' consumption of the food and fodder they grow themselves, and the value of living in your own house.

GDP thus measures the value added from the overall production of goods and services in a society, which in turn is available for consumption, investment, and export. By subtracting what is used to maintain the capital stocks, one derives the net domestic product (NDP). Ideally, one would want to include as much loss of environmental capital and natural resources as possible when calculating the NDP. NDP is thus a direct derivate of the conventional GDP.

Against this background one can assess the proposed alternatives to the conventional GDP and NDP such as the proposal to subtract costs associated with transport externalities (e.g. pollution damages and traffic accidents). The apparent rationale for such correction is that once such an externality has occurred, and the damage is to be repaired (e.g. an injured person is taken to hospital for treatment after being involved in a traffic accident, or an illness caused by vehicular emissions is to be treated in a hospital), then it is argued that GDP or NDP, conventionally measured, increases because the value of the health sector services goes up. It obviously appears paradoxical and illogical that GDP or NDP should grow as a result of, for example, an accident happening, because, clearly, welfare and quality of life is not improved as a result of accidents. This line of reasoning would lead to another set of macro- as well as microeconomic policies, as compared with those that would result if indicators of economic performance (growth, etc.) were based on conventional national income accounting concepts and statistics. Consequently, environmental and social development would also differ in the two cases.

However, we would argue that such corrective proposals are misguided and ill-founded. First of all, it is not all certain that GDP or NDP grows when negative transport externalities resulting in increased hospitalization of victims increases. The doctors who treat these victims could have specialized in and would then have been available for other highly valued medical services if these externalities had been prevented or avoided at the outset, and these services would also contribute to GDP and NDP. In most countries, the waiting lines at hospitals and doctors' offices suggest that there is no lack of challenges and tasks for medical personnel.

Furthermore, if the level of adverse transport externalities in a country is persistently high, the capacity of the hospitals to receive and treat those suffering as a result of these externalities has to be maintained at a high level. Consequently, substantial human and physical capital (sophisticated hospitals are much more capital-intensive than primary health care clinics providing, for the most part, preventive services) has to be locked in to do such tasks. This will naturally be at the expense of other GDP-enhancing tasks, either within the health sector, or – if policy measures were undertaken to permanently reduce the volume and incidence of these transport-related externalities – in completely different sectors of society requiring highly skilled and motivated personnel. With significantly fewer transport externalities, society could afford to train fewer health specialists and support staff, and allow these people to train themselves for production of goods and services in other sectors of society contributing to GDP and NDP growth.

Also, those suffering as a result of transport externalities may have been employed in productive work, and as a result of illness and injury due to the said externality, are prevented from continuing their work temporarily or permanently. This in fact implies a loss of GDP, so that the net GDP and NDP effect of transport externalities may well be negative, even when conventionally measured.

It is also important to stress that once someone has suffered the impact of a transport externality, it is obviously desirable that the ill or injured person is provided with immediate and high-quality treatment so as to save life and/or bring the person back to normal health. This clearly enhances the well-being of those affected compared with a situation where no or poorer-quality treatment is offered. A high level of GDP suggests that a country can afford this. Having an efficient hospital sector is a good welfare sign in itself for those who are so unfortunate as to suffer as a result of such externalities. Therefore, to include the costs of treatment in GDP need not be such a misleading indicator of welfare, let alone output.

This is not to suggest that the conventional GDP and NDP covers all welfare-related aspects of externalities; a lot of suffering is not measured and monetized, for those directly affected, their loved ones, or those whose waiting time for hospital treatment is extended as a result of intra-health sector competition for scarce medical expertise.

In sum, from a macroeconomic perspective, where all available resources and their management should be seen in context, transport policy measures that internalize externalities could free up human and physical capital, operating and maintenance resources for investment, and operating activities in other productive sectors of the economy. Such changes will be absorbed by the conventional GDP and NDP, and thus reflect the output changes and important aspects of the welfare changes that we really want to measure.

This links up to the macroeconomic setting in the following way: if the proposed improvements to reduce and internalize transport externalities were actually implemented, and if that, for example, slowed down traffic, then the costs of goods and services delivered throughout the economy, as well as land values in different locations, would change, but at different rates depending on the transport intensity of the different goods and services. This again would impact on the prices of other goods and services, and as a result the various demands and supplies would be affected. In the end, GDP and NDP themselves would therefore be affected.

To assess and compare these impacts and changes, macroeconomic models have been developed and tailored to reflect the specific circumstances and characteristics of a given country for a given time period and political setting. Depending on the institutional, political, and economic regime, as well as the configuration of the economy in question, a set of structural equations describing this economy and its various interactions is constructed in terms of quantifiable national income accounting concepts (variables) and a series of policy instrument variables that decision-makers can decide on in order to achieve stated political development goals. By means of such models, analysts can compare a large set of dimensions of the developmental outcomes of many alternative policy packages. With well-developed transparency for transmitting and presenting alternative policy outcomes, it becomes possible to establish a high-quality debate on the developmental impacts of different political priorities as a basis for final decision-making. Such models now have the capacity to elaborate the environmental impacts of different macro-policies and the macroeconomic impact of environmental changes resulting from sectoral or macro-policy decisions. Such macro-policy impact models have gradually been expanded in line with the availability of more detailed environmental statistics that can, for example, be used to assess dose–response interactions of, for example, emissions to the environment from transport and stationary users of fossil fuels. It is by means of such macro-impact models – and not by "greening" the GDP – that makes it possible in a realistic way to assess the wider consequences of alternative macro- and environmental policies.

3. Environmental impacts of macroeconomic policies

Macroeconomic policies that enhance conventionally measured economic growth, may do so by stimulating the volume of goods and services output which in turn may stimulate transport activities. Depending on the composition of the transport services demanded and supplied, and what energy efficiency and emission control measures are in place, penetration of unspoiled areas, increased emissions, accidents, and congestion may be a result of such policies. Adverse externalities as described in earlier sections of this chapter may dampen the initial growth effect and certainly reduce the welfare effect of the growth (e.g. see Hansen, 1996).

Examples of such environmental macroeconomic inter-linkages are many. The terms of trade of a country are affected by changes in the exchange rate of the local currency. Devaluation makes exports cheaper and imports more expensive. As a result there will be repercussions throughout the economy both between and within sectors, and there are bound to be environmental impacts from this, some of which are benign, others adverse.

Stabilization and adjustment measures may constitute rational and necessary actions in a distorted economy that has suffered severely (poverty, unemployment, etc.) from lost competitiveness due to, for example, an artificially high exchange rate. However, regardless of how rational and meaningful such exchange rate adjustments may be, it is useful to be aware and take into account from the outset that such policy changes may also have significant environmental impacts. For a natural-resource-dependent economy, devaluation may spur a rapid growth in raw materials exports (logging, fisheries, mining), and if the controls with those having concessions to harvest from the national resource stock are slack, the net result may be severe leakages that end up draining the economy, because short-term rent-seeking concessionaires may run down the natural resource capital base without adequate replanting, repair, or compensation to the economy. This would mean a lower growth-enhancing capital base for future generations. The conclusion is that there is a need for a carefully designed integrated package of well-balanced complementary economy-wide policy measures, so that the adverse environmental effects of devaluation are countered by enforceable legal measures, along with price, tax, and subsidy changes on the use of input factors, goods, and services of relevance in this context.

Other macroeconomic policy changes that are likely to have environmental impacts are interest rate changes, and changes in a country's foreign debt burden (e.g. see Hansen, 1989). The former alters the competitive relations between capital and labor-intensive sectors and production techniques within sectors, and this again can have significant effects on what national natural resources and sinks are mobilized and how this is done. The latter – in particular measures that reduce the debt burden of heavily indebted countries – may on the one hand reduce the political pressures to tap the natural resource base to finance principal and interest payments but on the other hand it has the same effect on resource mobilization as a fresh foreign capital injection, and it is how this additional capital is spent that decides whether the environmental impact of this macroeconomic policy measure will be adverse or benign. Some governments may decide to use such an opportunity to slow down tapping of the country's resource base, and use the fresh capital to strengthen activities and sectors that are less resource-extractive, while other governments may stimulate accelerated extraction with this added capital. Such extraction stimulation may be indirect or direct. Indirectly, this may occur as a result of accelerated investments in the transport network to make natural-resource-endowed parts of the country more accessible to harvesting and possible exploitation.

The opposite is of course also possible. The removal of macroeconomic distortions by means of, for example, devaluation, reduced interest rates, removal of distorting subsidies and taxes, and reduced foreign debt burden, combined with adequate environmental management and monitoring capacity, may reinforce the capacity to sustain economic growth and welfare.

This observation contradicts the oft-quoted myth held, for example, by some non-governmental organizations that improved fiscal discipline is environmentally harmful. This belief is based on the observation that when a fiscal deficit reduction is sought, governments start cutting where resistance is weakest, and environment ministries and agencies are generally the youngest and least established government agencies. Budget reductions for such small and weak agencies, yet to establish their position and identity, can be a hard blow, and is certainly damaging for the environmental awareness work in the country.

However, such fiscal disciplining measures tend to require far larger expenditure reductions than the cuts in environment budgets can offer. Cuts have to be made in other areas as well. Even if the military budget is protected by influential lobby groups, infrastructure sectors will likely be hit hard as well. Typically, during periods of austerity, projects requiring large public transfers are also shelved or postponed. In many cases, such projects have severe adverse environmental and cultural impacts, e.g. power projects, dams, roads, harbors, and transmission lines. The resulting investment inaction could therefore be environmentally benign. Not only that, the environmental damages avoided by not implementing these projects as a result of increased budgetary discipline would likely far exceed any environmental gains that a small, powerless, and probably ineffective and understaffed environment agency/ministry could have achieved. Therefore, while it is sad to see a fragile and enthusiastic environment agency crumble, there could be some comfort in the sobering observation that the much larger (but probably much smaller in terms of percentage points) cuts in other budget components more than compensate for the loss of state-managed environmental protection capability. Suffice it to say that overall sustainability would of course be further enhanced if reallocation secured the survival and strengthening of infant environment agencies.

Criticism of stabilization and structural adjustment programs by environmentally and socially concerned groups should, however, not at all be dismissed as a result of the above conclusion. Much more economic and environmental improvement could be achieved from stabilization and adjustment, provided there is a political will to implement the proposed reforms. The question of incidence is at the core of obstacles to improvement. Asymmetry of political power and information among affected parties tend to prevent the simultaneous implementation of apparent win–win reforms. One could in most cases easily avoid reducing small and fragile environmental and health care budgets, by saving on the substantial budget drains caused by, for example, fertilizer, pesticide, water, and energy subsidies, most of which accrue to the well-to-do, rather than to the poor and vulnerable. The health budget could, for example, be restructured from capital-intensive curative hospitals toward labor-intensive preventive health care, which typically is enhanced by simple pollution prevention in residential and farmland areas. A lot of environment-related health damage is avoided when fewer pesticides are used, and those that are being used applied in accordance with the manufacturer's instructions. Because such broad macroeconomic reform packages are frequently proposed, it is important to trace their economic and environmental repercussions in order to devise compensatory measures to reduce the political obstacles to implementation.

The current professional consensus among economists is that macroeconomic stability is a minimum and necessary (but far from sufficient) condition for preserving the environment (Gandhi, 1996). Environmental degradation is generally caused by market, policy, and institutional failure relating to the use of environmental resources and sinks. At the same time, it should be acknowledged that macroeconomic policies are inefficient and blunt instruments for mitigating environmental degradation, for which appropriate environmental policies are the most efficient and direct instruments. However, one cannot generalize. Each country is a specific case requiring tailor-made policy packages that explicitly take into account the country-specific setting for policy reforms and the environment that it will impact on.

A closer look at how macroeconomic analytic tools can be applied to examine how alternative macroeconomic policy options are expected to contribute to reaching an environmental target specifically focusing on the transport sector is clearly illustrated for the USA in a macroeconomic study commissioned by its Environmental Protection Agency in the 1990s (Brinner et al., 1991). Its task was to examine alternative policy options for reducing gasoline consumption and the resulting carbon dioxide emissions, and the topic and approach is therefore now of less interest and value in today's global environment setting.

The study concentrated on the level of gasoline tax necessary for stabilizing carbon dioxide emissions from a light vehicle fleet over a 20 year period, and the impact of such a tax on a set of macroeconomic indicators. This application of macroeconomic analysis to compare the macroeconomic outcomes of alternative ways of reaching a set environmental target related to the transport sector is particularly interesting because it discusses how different recycling and other fiscal uses for the gasoline tax revenue affect the performance of the US economy. Which macroeconomic policy package will be most benign to the economy while achieving the stated environmental goal?

The analysis focused on a gasoline tax increase which would help raise revenue that could help reduce the federal budget deficit or help finance a simultaneous reduction in personal and corporate income taxes or a reduction in the employer-paid portion of payroll taxes. The first option is revenue raising in the sense that gasoline tax revenues are applied to federal deficit reduction. The other two options are deficit-neutral. In order to define the impact of the proposed environmental policy (i.e. the carbon dioxide-stabilizing gasoline tax), it is necessary to neutralize its impact on federal finances by offsetting it with other fiscal policies. This is done by establishing the difference between government expenditures and revenues that would obtain if the economy operated at full employment.

Not surprisingly, each of the three options would result in a different level of macroeconomic performance. The revenue-raising scenario is shown to have adverse short-term macroeconomic impacts, because the gasoline tax raises inflation and reduces after tax household income. If monetary policies curtail the inflation, the recessionary impulse of the policy would strengthen. After 10 years this recessionary burden eases, however, and benefits begin to appear. The lower budget deficit enhances national savings, implying lower real credit costs and higher investments. After 16 years it is suggested that GDP performance will be back to normal, and, in addition, the underlying strength of the economy developed during this adjustment period will contribute to a faster growth in the following years, in spite of the stabilized carbon dioxide emissions. The political feasibility of such a long adjustment period is of course another question!

The two revenue recycling policies are shown to have quite different impacts on the economy. The income tax cuts replace most of the direct purchasing power drained by the gasoline tax, thus eliminating the short-term recessionary burden. On the other hand, the increased income enhances the inflationary pressure of the overall policy, because neither theory nor empirical experience supports an assumption that personal and corporate income tax cuts lead to lower wages and prices. It is therefore expected that this policy would induce the Federal Reserve to tighten credit policies and raise nominal interest rates. Because the primary short-term determinant of inflation is the level of economic activity under full employment, targeting inflation is nearly equivalent to targeting real GDP during the first 10 years of the simulation. As a consequence, the revenue-raising and tax-cutting scenarios yield very similar growth rates for the first 10 years. As regards sustainability, however, the policy strategies differ fundamentally. The real GDP composition is critically different and this takes effect on GDP growth after 10 years, because personal income tax reductions help support consumption at the expense of lower business investments, which are curtailed by the higher interest rates. After 10 years, this reduces the productive capital stock and the economy's growth potential, so that GDP losses are magnified.

The second revenue-recycling policy (where the gasoline tax revenue is offset by a reduction in the employer-paid portion of payroll taxes) generates a much more favorable development path because it is both deficit- and inflation-neutral. Such a policy has only a slight recessionary impact after 5 years, and national income losses over the long run are virtually eliminated. Prices of gasoline-intensive goods rise (and gasoline consumption falls, as intended), while prices of labor-intensive goods and services decline (and consumption of these goods and services rise). Changes in inflation, interest rates, and the distribution of national income between households and businesses are minimal, and this overall policy package maintains the level of national income while achieving the environmental target. In the case of the USA this study appears to suggest that there is scope for double dividends in the form of improved environmental quality and enhanced demand for labor, while the levels of key macroeconomic indicators remain steady.

The Norwegian Ministry of Finance has since the 1960s used a set of complementary, computable multi-sector macroeconomic models for medium-

and long-term national planning (e.g. see Hansen et al., 2000). When natural resource accounting was introduced in the 1970s as a supplement to conventional national income accounting, work began to gradually modify and expand these macroeconomic models to incorporate an increasing number of environmentally relevant variables in order to facilitate the impact analysis of macroeconomic policy changes on key environment indicators, as well as the macroeconomic impacts of key environmental policy changes.

This approach has made it possible to compare many alternative medium- and long-term scenarios in terms of conventional macroeconomic performance indicators, as well as – in one of the more recent and comprehensive such comparisons – environmental and social performance indicators (Hansen et al., 2000). This governmental planning approach is now routine, and it means that all the line ministries have developed capability to use and interpret the results of these models. Thus, the ministries of transport, energy and environment can carry out specific and relatively detailed impact studies of particular policy changes, and discuss the results based on the same set of exogenous development assumptions as those used by the ministry of finance. In other words, interministry communication and dialogue is much facilitated, and a lot of time and effort is saved in the medium- and long-term planning and budgeting processes.

As an illustration, following the sustainable development focus from the UN Conference on Environment and Development 1992 in Rio de Janeiro, the Friends of the Earth (an influential environmental private organization) lobbied for a broad-based set of drastic environmental restrictions on the Norwegian economy so as to comply with the scientific conclusions at the time regarding climate change threats and biodiversity loss threats. A working group was established to quantify these environmental demands and introduce them as far as possible into these macroeconomic models and simulate what would happen to the economy over the next 40 years as compared with a "business as usual" or a "government base case" scenario. Some 26 such environmental conditions were explicitly incorporated into the models either in the form of goals to be achieved, or as exogenous constraints on the models. A series of scenarios were then simulated, each reflecting a different set of policy actions primarily aimed at curbing climate gas emissions relative to the emissions implied by the base and business as usual cases. The policies that were explicitly tested comprised half a dozen climate change measures in various combinations, so as to identify the vulnerability of and environmental as well as economic impact on various sectors and interest groups to particular policy measures. Since several non-climate environment variables correlate strongly with climate gas emissions, several of these were explicitly modeled as well so that their local health and environmental impacts could be assessed for each scenario.

The main conclusion – perhaps surprisingly – is that the rather open and exposed fossil-fuel-dependent Norwegian economy is quite resilient to even draconian taxes and regulations on fossil fuels and/or climate gas emissions. Obviously, there will significant intersectoral changes and transition burdens imposed on people who will need to seek new employment, but a lot of these changes will occur gradually and many jobs will be phased in and out, in line with the demographic changes of the work force. Overall growth will be just marginally less than that of the base case or the business as usual scenario. The reason for this resilience is that changes take place gradually and in a planned and publicized manner, and the underlying technical assumptions of the production structure of the different sectors allow for factor substitution and technological progress in line with historical experience. The results are presented in such as way that policy-makers can establish cost-efficiency with regard to those parameters that matter most to them, including "no-regret" solutions.

4. Macro-impacts of environmental policies and technological progress

Environment policy reforms include incentive and/or fiscal reforms by means of economic instruments as well as regulatory measures. In both cases one would expect the policy reform to be initiated in response to observed market and institutional distortions that establishe and maintain inefficiencies in the economy that reduce the growth potential compared with a development scenario without such distortions. In addition, the observed distortions may also result in distributional impacts that from, for example, a poverty reduction perspective are unfortunate and unintended.

The contents of such reforms depends on the objective. In some cases there is an observed need to generate revenue to pay for environmental monitoring and controls as well as raise revenue in order to provide financial support to accelerated installation of environmentally more-benign technologies and production methods. From a revenue-generating perspective, the authority should focus on goods and services with inelastic demands, since the users (consumers and producers of inputs) will continue to demand virtually the same volume of the goods when their prices go up. In such cases the immediate environmental changes from the reform is negligible, but it can be assumed that gradually the users will seek to replace the taxed polluting good or extraction of the resource that needs more careful monitoring and management with substitutes that are environmentally more sustainable. At the same time, the fiscal position of the authorities is strengthened so as to provide more freedom and opportunities to enhance environmental monitoring and reform capability and capacity. The authorities may decide to take such a reform opportunity to raise overall government revenue and thus strengthen the budget, or it may seek more popular political support for the reform measures by reducing other taxes and tariffs so that the overall budget impact is zero. In many cases, even when the former outcome would be desirable from a long-term budgetary perspective, the revenue neutral option may be the only feasible one for political reasons.

In other cases the purpose of the policy reform is to reduce polluting or excessively extractive activities by affecting the user incentives that have led to overexploitation and excessive emissions in the first place. These cases are characterized by the total marginal costs due to users' behavior clearly exceeding the prices these users face in the market. There is, in other words, an adverse environmental externality not captured by the prices the users face in the market or in the tax and tariff regime imposed by the authorities. If, in such cases, the polluting goods and services in question are inelastic in demand, there would be the revenue-generating effects described above, and modest immediate environmental impacts. However, aside from the incentives to seek new and alternative solutions that would result in fewer emissions from and reduced consumption of the goods that are being taxed, the increased revenue payments also acts on users as an increased tax burden that reduces their income, and thus the consumption of all goods and services in proportions reflected in the budget shares and income elasticities of these goods.

For goods and services that are demand-elastic in their price, the demand volume could decline significantly as a direct consequence of the policy being implemented. In line with this, emissions and excessive resource extraction would also be curtailed. However, it does not follow that reduced demand for the goods and services in question would leave demand for and use of all other goods and service unaffected. It is therefore important to tailor such price changes (by means of user charges and tariffs) such that the demand for all goods and services that result in excessive emissions and use of the resource in question is reduced to levels that are considered environmentally acceptable. Once this happens, one needs to identify how the income that is no longer used for these environmentally harmful purposes will be reallocated in the economy, and if the expected outcome is environmentally, socially and economically acceptable and desirable.

Environmental technology progress is often portrayed as a benefit when energy consumption grows along with resource extraction. Outcomes are often presented as if the initial effect of innovation – e.g. a doubling or tripling of car fuel efficiency – will result in a corresponding reduction in fuel use and associated emissions. As convincingly shown by Khazzoom (1980, 1987, 1989) and Brookes (1990), and summarized by Saunders (1992), energy efficiency gains in any one sector have energy consumption ramifications extending economy-wide; and economy-wide impacts can have unpredictable results and spread further to non-energy uses of environmental importance as well. At the root of this issue is the notion that energy efficiency gains actually look to the user a lot like price reductions. A doubling of a car's energy efficiency means that its mileage is doubled, which is experienced by users in the same way as a 50% reduction in the fuel price. Consequently, it spurs increased demand either directly through price elasticity effects, or indirectly through released purchasing power redirected to other energy-using and resource-using goods and services.

What is now referred to as the Khazzoom–Brookes postulate states that increases in energy efficiency can lead to increased, not decreased, energy consumption. In the context of neoclassical growth theory it can be shown that, using a Cobb–Douglas production function, this postulate holds unambiguously, and efficiency gains for any factor of production increases energy consumption. With a certain nested constant elasticity of substitution (CES) production function, this holds under most conditions; more specifically, pure energy efficiency gains increase energy consumption if the energy elasticity of substitution is greater than unity, but energy consumption decreases if this elasticity is less than unity. For other types of CES-nesting schemes the elasticity condition does not matter; energy consumption increases irrespective of whether it is larger or smaller than unity. Furthermore, it has been shown to hold when applying a highly general translog production function. Capital, labor, and neutral efficiency gains increase energy consumption whether production is Cobb–Douglas or nested CES, suggesting that any technology improvement that is not strictly an energy efficiency gain may increase energy consumption.

Therefore, both theoretical and empirical studies suggest that one needs to look more closely at such impacts in each concrete case, because unexpected environmental as well as distributional impacts can be either benign or adverse, and could necessitate simultaneous countermeasures so as to achieve the originally intended environmental outcomes with a minimum of undesired side-effects. What is typically required and not easily implemented are purchasing power contracting measures in the form of some sort of tax or tariff that reduces purchasing power to its pre-technological innovation level.

5. Mainstreaming environmental impacts into macroeconomic analyses

Since the ecosystem and the economic system are so closely interlinked, analyses of these linkages, aiming to diagnose the distortions and causes of welfare-damaging adverse externalities, require tools that will simultaneously address the key environmental and economic concerns. Computable general equilibrium (CGE) models have been developed for this purpose, taking advantage of the rapidly growing computing power available even to laptop users. Such models are designed around macroeconomic and environmental variables that are typically collected and monitored as part of a country's national statistics production.

In order to be country-specific and policy-impact relevant for affected stakeholders, such CGE models should be multisectoral, and both the specific sectors to be included and their relative importance will vary from one country to another. Depending on the design of the model's structural equations, it will typically addresses medium- or long-term development issues. Such models are now routinely used by ministries of finance as well as ministries of energy, industry, and the environment world-wide, to test alternative development scenarios and "compare notes" as inputs to the budgetary and long-term planning and programming processes.

The initial focus has been on analysis of the main macroeconomic parameters and the distribution of production and employment by sector, where the growth of total production is mainly decided by technological changes, growth of real capital, and labor supply, and access to commodities and natural resources. However, such models can also give a reasonably detailed description of production and use of energy and other natural resource inputs in the country. In addition, submodels have been developed that compute emissions of different pollutants from fossil fuels and various industrial processes. In this way, CGE models can be used to investigate simultaneously the development of the economy, energy consumption, and some environmental changes. Physical dose–response models reflecting the health and productivity impacts of various emission levels can be used in conjunction with such CGE macro-models as a basis for quantifying adverse environmental and health effects of alternative development paths being examined (e.g. Hansen et al., 2000).

In an increasing number of settings and countries, the same macro-models are applied in planning a budgeting by both line ministries and the ministries of finance and the central banks. This facilitates a consistent data and assumptions basis for the planning and budgetary dialogue, and the general computable macroeconomic planning models can be tailor-made to reflect the prevailing macroeconomic and environmental concerns, by incorporating relevant environment variables (reflecting the state and changes to this for a number of critical pollution and natural resources indicators) that are of particular interest as regards monitoring. Whereas this has gradually become common procedure in many OECD countries, such macroeconomic environment impact assessment is now gradually being mainstreamed in many developing countries via the operational policy directives that apply when they seek multilateral development finance assistance in the form of structural or sector adjustment loans in support of domestic economic reforms.

References

Brinner, R.E., M.G. Shelby, J.M. Yanchar and A. Cristofaro (1991) "Optimising tax strategies to reduce greenhouse gases without curtailing growth," *Energy Journal*, 12:1–14.
Brookes, L. (1990) "Energy efficiency and economic fallacies," *Energy Policy*, March:783–785.
Cobb, J.B. and H. Daly (1990) *For the common good*. London: Green Print.
Gandhi, V.P., ed. (1996) *Macroeconomics and the environment*. Washington, DC: International Monetary Fund.
Hansen, S. (1989) "Debt for nature swaps – overview and discussion of key issues," *Ecological Economics*, 1:77–93.

Hansen, S. (1996) "Macroeconomic policies and the environment," in: V.P. Gandhi, ed., *Macroeconomics and the environment*, pp. 44–64. Washington, DC: International Monetary Fund.

Hansen, S., P.F. Jasperson and I. Rasmussen (2000) *Towards a sustainable economy: the application of ecological premises to long-term planning in Norway.* Basingstoke: Macmillan.

Khazzoom, J.D. (1980) "Economic implications of mandated efficiency standards for household appliances," *Energy Journal*, 11: 21–40.

Khazzoom, J.D. (1987) "Energy savings from more efficient appliances," *Energy Journal*, 8: 85–89.

Khazzoom, J.D. (1989) "Energy savings from efficient appliances: a rejoinder," *Energy Journal*, 10:157–166.

Nordhaus, W. and J. Tobin (1972) "Is growth obsolete?" in: *Economic growth*. National Bureau of Economic Research, General Series, No. 96E. New York: Columbia University Press.

Saunders, H.D. (1992) "The Khazzoom–Brookes postulate and neoclassical growth," *Energy Journal*, 13:130–148.

UN Development Programme (1992) *Human development report 1992*. New York: Oxford University Press.

Uno, K. (1992) "Composite measures of quality of life. Social, economic, and environmental accounting and modelling," in: *22nd General Conference of the International Association for Research in Income and Wealth*. Paper. Flims.

Chapter 27

HISTORY OF ENVIRONMENTAL LEGISLATION

PETER R. STOPHER
The University of Sydney

1. Introduction

Although the general background of environmental legislation is reviewed briefly, the main purpose of this chapter is to trace the history of legislation on the environment that targets transport specifically, particularly transport within and between urban areas and the environmental impacts that such transport typically generates. In addition, it is not feasible within the bounds of this chapter to provide a review of the history of legislation on transport and the environment from around the world. Therefore, environmental legislation in just two countries, the USA and Australia, will be concentrated on, with the aim of using these specific examples to trace the general development of environmental awareness, concerns, and legislation with particular application to transport. To those who may feel slighted by the omission of details on environmental history in their particular countries, the author apologizes, but hopes that this chapter will be considered of value, even with these admitted omissions.

The history of environmental legislation is a long one, but one with many very lengthy gaps within it. Concern over the environment has occurred historically only after a society has reached a certain level of wealth and productivity, or has adopted a philosophy that has engendered environmental awareness. Prior to achieving such levels, it appears to be true that pragmatic societies have been unwilling to pay much attention to the environment, but have rather felt willing to sacrifice environmental concerns for economic growth. At other times during human history, societies have simply been unaware of the environmental effects of their actions, or have been naïve and assumed that such environmental effects will either be of no direct consequence to themselves, or are temporary and will heal themselves. Possibly, the cynic might suggest that some societies have been willing to accept environmental consequences, provided that these will not affect their own generation, and be problems only for a succeeding generation.

Thomas (2001) suggests that another aspect of the historical development of environmental issues has religious connotations. In early civilizations, he contends that abandonment of religious attitudes of oneness with nature, and replacement

Handbook of Transport and the Environment, Edited by D.A. Hensher and K.J. Button
© *2003, Elsevier Ltd*

of these attitudes with one of separateness from nature was one of the most pervasive traits that resulted in environmental degradation. In turn, this environmental degradation frequently gave rise to the collapse of a civilization or society. He cites, as an example, the early civilizations in Mesopotamia, which were among the first to construct cities and engage in extensive agriculture, with irrigation. Unfortunately, a lack of care or understanding of the environmental consequences resulted in salting of the land, flooding, erosion, and destruction of the countryside, eventually resulting in the decline of the society. Failure to maintain a balance between man and his environment is seen as a significant factor in the decline of these societies. Similar problems may be arising today in parts of Africa, South America (particularly in the Amazon Basin), and South-East Asia, as a result of the failure of macroeconomic policies, and introduction of policies that sacrifice the environment for fast economic gains, often with little understanding of, or interest in, the longer-term negative consequences.

Two exceptions among early civilizations to the collapse, as a result of wealth and development leading to environmental degradation, appear to have been the Ancient Greek and the Chinese civilizations. The ancient Chinese revered their environment and stressed the need for balance in life between the various elements and forces in the world and had a strong religious focus. As a result, early Chinese cultures, particularly in the Shang and Chou dynasties (Washington State University, 2002a,b), did not appear to suffer from the problems seen in Mesopotamia. Exploitation of natural resources was limited, and environmental consequences relatively benign, so that environmental damage and a need for legislation to reverse or restrict it, did not appear.

Thomas (2001) points out that the Greeks embraced a religious perspective that recognized "humanity's oneness with nature." As a result, not only did the Greek civilization not undertake developments that were injurious to the environment in major ways but also planted trees and plants around temples, and forbade hunting in sacred groves. In contrast, the Roman civilization embraced a philosophy that the world was here for humans to use and from which they could profit. While religious taboos prevented the earliest Romans from meddling significantly with the natural environment, the ancient Romans in the middle and late Republic and the Empire (Thomas, 2001) proceeded to discover and use a wide variety of natural resources with little concern for any effects this might have on the environment or ecology. The ancient Romans were also profoundly concerned with creating order out of the chaos of the world as they found and perceived it. Probably there has been no civilization prior to the Romans that has attempted to impose such a rigorous and artificial structure on the natural environment. It is, therefore, unsurprising that one of the first pieces of environmental legislation that the author has been able to find dates to 50 BC and is of Roman origin. This legislation related to noise pollution in Rome and prohibited the use of wheeled vehicles between sunrise and 2 hours before sunset. The law fell into disuse by the third century, resulting in a serious increase in noise pollution in Rome (Hughes, 1975). Other civilizations of the ancient world do not appear to have generated any known instances of environmental laws, although many of them appear to have caused a range of environmental problems.

Through the early years of western civilization the concepts of Judeo-Christian ideology dominated, with the notion that man was created to have dominion over the natural world. For many hundreds of years this resulted in agriculture, hunting, felling of trees, mining of ores, and other uses of the natural environment. Western societies were largely blissfully unaware of any environmental consequences, and tended to regard the use of the natural resources around them as a God-given right. With this philosophy firmly in mind, animal species disappeared through over-hunting, forests were denuded, and strip mines and other means of removing the earth's riches were pursued with little concern for alterations to the environment. It was not until the eighteenth and nineteenth centuries that the undesirable changes to the environment caused by these activities began to become sufficiently evident as to alarm people (Thomas, 2001). It was only at about this point in time that soil erosion, floods, disappearance of wildlife through hunting and habitat loss, and other environmental damage began to be recognized as a consequence of the domination of humans over the natural world. Even then, legislation to protect the environment was very slow in appearing.

2. The emergence of modern environmental legislation

Probably the earliest modern instance of environmental legislation, which is also a form of land-use planning, was a decree issued by Napoleon in 1810 that divided noxious occupations into categories: those that could be tolerated close to houses, those that must be no nearer than the outskirts of town, and those that must be removed from areas of habitation. In effect, as well as being a form of town planning, this was a law against odor and air pollution around Paris (Thomas, 2001). It is noteworthy, however, that while this decree limited where certain occupations could be carried out, it did not change the fact that these occupations continued to be carried out, and that the noxious consequences were only to be removed from areas of habitation, rather than prevented, or at least reduced. Following after this, various other instances can be found of legislation that limited or prohibited certain activities that were deemed injurious to the environment. For example, legislation around 1828 in Sydney was aimed at protecting the Tank Stream. However, legislation in the form of national, state-wide, or provincial laws regulating or prohibiting practices on the basis of environmental damage did not appear until the latter half of the twentieth century.

So far as transport is concerned, two things are worth noting as to the long lack of any legislation that affected transport and its environmental impacts. First, the size of settlements was quite limited for many hundreds of years. In the time of the Roman Empire most towns were no more than 20 minutes walking distance across, and a person standing in the middle of the town and shouting an alarm could be heard on the walls of the town. Towns with a population of 10 000 persons represented close to the largest settlements throughout much of western Europe for many centuries of the modern era. Contributing to this limitation in the size of settlements and as a second reason for lack of environmental concerns with transport is that transport evolved extremely slowly over the millennia. In the ancient Roman Empire, transport included walking, riding on various beasts (horses, camels, elephants, etc.), traveling in wheeled vehicles that were pulled by beasts of burden or by humans, and traveling on water either with the use of oars or sails. These same forms of transport were still predominant at the beginning of the eighteenth century in western Europe. While there had been evolution in the shape and structure of wheeled carriages, the motive power largely remained animal, and the same beasts of burden were ridden as in the time of Julius Caesar. These forms of transport limited the size of cities, because of their slow speed, and the difficulties of moving large quantities of freight from production to market. It is of note, however, that congestion is known have existed in towns in the Middle Ages: streets were frequently narrow, and rules of the road were largely nonexistent. Often, travel in these towns was a free for all that could easily become bogged down, literally in mud, or metaphorically in competing movements.

A transport revolution began in the eighteenth century. Late in that century and into the early parts of the nineteenth century, experiments were begun with steam engines, which eventually proved to be the first real competitor to animals for pulling wagons. Stationary steam engines first found service in running mine pumps, following the inventions of Thomas Savery and Thomas Newcomen in the mid-eighteenth century. In 1804, Robert Trevithick first attempted to use a steam engine to pull a wagon, but failed. Within a few years, however, George Stephenson succeeded in using a steam engine to pull a wagon, and shortly thereafter designed and built his *Rocket*, which became the basis of the Stockton and Darlington Railway – the first railway in the world, beginning operation in 1825. Thus commenced a revolution that would see, over the next two centuries, the development of steam engines to power ships, cars, and omnibuses, the internal combustion engine, electric motors, nuclear-powered engines, and a range of engines for aircraft and, eventually, space vehicles. At the start of the twenty-first century we are now developing dual-powered vehicles, fuel cell vehicles, and other new technologies, largely in an attempt to break away from transport that depends on the use of fossil fuels and that produces significant environmental pollutants from the burning of those fuels.

During the days of animal-drawn transport, environmental issues for transport were primarily those of noise (as in the case of the Roman legislation), and solid pollution. However, because of the potential to use animal droppings for fertilizer, which could, in turn, increase the production of hay, grass, and other grains consumed by the same animals, horse- and ox-drawn transport could be regarded in many ways as being a sustainable form of transport, with relatively minor environmental consequences. Added to this, if congestion caused slowing or stopping of the vehicles, little additional environmental impact ensued. Possibly noise levels increased, and there may have been somewhat more of a concentration of solid wastes from transport, but little else arose as a negative environmental consequence of congestion.

In contrast, the transport revolution of the nineteenth and twentieth centuries brought with it a host of new environmental consequences, many of which were not recognized until late in the twentieth century. Steam engines required coal, and produced smoke and ash. The smoke contained certain noxious gases, including oxides of sulfur and nitrogen, and particulate matter. The coal had to be mined, and the coal mines, tailings from the mines, and associated machinery created other forms of pollution – visual, odoriferous, gaseous, and water-based, among others. The internal combustion engine produced less visible, but no less harmful, exhaust products, but also increased concentrations of population, with corresponding concentrations of pollutants. An almost immediate effect of the steam train was a noticeable increase in the size of settlements. Whereas the size of settlements had tended to be limited in the previous several thousand years to the distances that one could walk or ride on an animal in a reasonable time, the steam engine began to create linear extensions into the countryside from eighteenth-century towns that were subsequently linked by bus and then car transport. Only in the twentieth century did it become possible for settlements to contain hundreds of thousands, if not millions, of people, and this was almost entirely as a result of the internal combustion engine, and its application in private cars and buses. Of course, these increased conurbations also produced hitherto unheard of concentrations of waste products from transport and other human activities. Cities began to experience a variety of consequences of this new mobility and ability to congregate, resulting from the change in scale of development, as well as the nearly unseen forms of pollution. Only in the past two centuries have cities experienced serious levels of air pollution, as well as many other environmental consequences. Before this, technology was too primitive and settlements too small for these consequences to arise.

Now, in the early twenty-first century, we not only experience various forms of air, water, and noise pollution in our cities, but also may be experiencing the creation of micro-climates. These micro-climates may give rise to extreme weather conditions that affect large conurbations and that have not been seen before in our occupation of this planet. There have been suggestions that the excessive ground heating of expanses of concrete and bitumen in the vicinity of large cities may result in the formation of thunderstorm cells of particular severity. These, in turn, may result in tornadoes, large damaging hail, other types of severe wind episodes, and torrential rains, not to mention extremes of lightning.

In the first half of the twentieth century the transport revolution continued almost unabated. Two World Wars caused some slowing of the development of civilian transport means, only to accelerate after each war as inventions of improved transport for military purposes during each of the wars found civilian application. Not until the 1950s and 1960s does it appear that modern societies began to recognize and become concerned about the environmental consequences of the transport revolution and the development of much larger settlements than had ever before been known. Before this, and perhaps representing one of the first steps in environmental legislation, was the creation of national parks in, among other countries, the USA and Australia. In the USA these were first legislated in 1916, although Yellowstone Park had been set aside as a national park as early as 1872. National parks now exist in many different countries around the world, many of them having first been legislated in the first half of the twentieth century.

Probably the earliest instance of environmental action against transport occurred in the USA in the 1960s, when the citizens of San Francisco protested against the construction of the Embarcadero Freeway along the waterfront of San Francisco Bay. The protest took the form of a lawsuit against the California Department of Highways and the Federal Highway Administration, and was successful in stopping the construction of the freeway after only a short section had been completed. This came at a time when there was a rising awareness in the USA of the environment and of the damage that man was doing to it. It was further fuelled by the attitude of the US Bureau of Public Roads and its successor, the Federal Highway Administration (FHWA), and state highway departments that had largely ignored public opinion and input over the years. Rather, traffic engineers and transport planners of the 1950s and 1960s felt certain that they knew what the country needed in transport infrastructure, even though recognizing that their efforts would meet with local disapproval from time to time. Both the California Highway Department and the FHWA felt certain that the building of urban freeways in California was the best thing for the state and country, and proceeded with their plans without further consultation. This rather arrogant attitude, together with the obvious undesirability of blocking the views of the San Francisco Bay by the building of the Embarcadero Freeway were all that were required to initiate the first significant protest and lawsuit against highway building, and thereby begin the recent legislative history for the environment, and transport in particular.

3. US legislation on transport and the environment

3.1. The National Environmental Protection Act of 1969

The protest against the Embarcadero Freeway in San Francisco appears to have been the culmination of pressure on the US Department of Transportation that led to the inclusion in the Federal-Aid Highway Act of 1968 (23 USC 128) of requirements for the FHWA to begin a process of public consultation for any highway projects involving expenditure of federal funds. Under the joint authority of this act and the Department of Transportation act of 1966 (49 USC), the Department of Transportation, through the FHWA, issued a Policy and Procedure Memorandum, referenced as PPM 20-8, which set in place the first federally mandated public consultation process for highway projects in the USA. Foreshadowing the legislation that was then passing through the US Congress, PPM 20–8 had two purposes (US Department of Transportation, 1969):

> to ensure to the maximum extent practicable, that highway locations and designs reflect and are consistent with Federal, State, and local goals and objectives. The rules, policies and procedures established by this PPM are intended to afford full opportunity for effective public participation in the consideration of highway location and design proposals

and

> The PPM requires State Highway Departments to consider fully a wide range of factors in determining highway locations and highway designs ... [the PPM] provides for a two-hearing procedure ... to give all interested persons an opportunity ... to express their views ... when the flexibility to respond to these views still exists.

Thus, the principal elements of the PPM were to initiate a public participation effort in designing new highways, and to require the consideration of a wide range of direct and indirect impacts caused by constructing and operating a new highway. The teeth in this policy and procedure memorandum was the withholding of federal approval and federal funds for any project that failed to observe and apply the rules, policies, and procedures contained within it. The two-hearing process was defined as a corridor-level hearing at the outset of the project, where the potential corridors in which a project could be built would be identified, but where the corridor width was expected to be much wider than the eventual project right-of-way, in order to preclude such things as speculative property purchasing and development. A second hearing was required to agree on the alignment of the project in the preferred corridor. Rules and procedures for publicizing these hearings were also included in the PPM.

Further foreshadowing the legislation in the US Congress that would soon replace the PPM, the document listed 20 factors that were to be taken into account in determining highway locations. These were defined in the following terms (US Department of Transportation, 1969):

> 'Social, economic, and environmental effects' means the direct and indirect benefits or losses to the community and to highway users. It includes all such effects that are relevant and applicable to the particular location or design.

The indirect benefits or losses included such items as national defense, economic activity, employment, recreation and parks, aesthetics, residential and neighborhood character and location, natural and historic landmarks, noise, air and water pollution, and property values.

This policy took immediate effect. However, in 1969, the US Congress passed the National Environmental Policy Act (NEPA), whose provisions superseded PPM 20-8. The NEPA broadened the application of the public hearing process and the requirement to consider the direct and indirect benefits and losses to users and communities to apply to all federally funded projects, not just highway projects. In addition, the NEPA introduced a formal document requirement to show that the hearings had taken place, and that consideration of the wide range of direct and indirect effects had been taken into account. This formal document was called the Environmental Impact Statement (EIS). The NEPA further specified several important elements that have become a central part of all succeeding federal legislation and most state laws relating to environmental process.

First, the NEPA specified that the process must be commenced by the publication of a Notice of Intent (NOI) that would forewarn potentially interested parties of the nature of the project to be considered and the commencement of the process to develop an environmental impact assessment. Second, the NEPA specified that, among the alternatives to be considered at the first hearing must be the "do-nothing" or "no-build" alternative. Further, this alternative must be similarly evaluated in terms of environmental impacts, so that it could be established that the impacts of building the project would be less harmful than those of not building anything. This was to be the acid test as to whether a project would move forward at all. The first public hearing thereby became effectively a scoping meeting, in which agreement was sought on what alternatives should be considered, and also on what specific impacts might need to be studied in detail.

Third, the NEPA specified that the second hearing was to consider a draft environmental impact statement, which must be published sufficiently far in advance of the hearing that the public would be able to make comment on the document and its findings. In preparing the final EIS, there was required to be a complete report of all public comments and questions received, together with the responses of the agency responsible for preparing the EIS. Fourth, the NEPA specified that the EIS must not only document the impacts that were expected to result from the preferred project, but must also include details of the mitigation steps that would be undertaken to deal with unavoidable negative impacts. Fifth, the NEPA defined a "locally preferred alternative," which was to be the result sought at the first public hearing, and which would then proceed as the basis of the development of the EIS. However, the EIS was required to document the impacts not only of the locally-preferred alternative, but also of the no-build alternative, and at least one other alternative that was a serious candidate for consideration. Finally, the NEPA defined that the federal agency that was the principal funding agency was to be the agency to which the EIS would be submitted and that would make the decision on whether or not a project could proceed. At the same time, the NEPA reserved an oversight role in ensuring that impacts were adequately addressed and appropriately analyzed.

The NEPA also defined the course of action required to develop an Environmental Impact Analysis (EIA) that might document that there were no significant environmental impacts arising out of a proposed federally funded initiative. In such a case, the EIA, after being reviewed in a public hearing, and assuming that no new evidence was uncovered, could be submitted to the federal agency sponsoring the project for a Finding Of No Significant Impact (FONSI). However, the public participation required under the NEPA still remained in place. Further action, following the declaration of a FONSI, was not required. However, where a FONSI was not obtained, then mitigation programs must be developed and implemented, a final EIS must be developed, and all mitigation activities must be detailed within it.

3.2. Subsequent US federal legislation

In 1970, following the signing into law of the NEPA, the US Congress passed three additional Acts that had significant environmental implications – the Clean Air Act (CAA) of 1970, the Environmental Quality Improvement Act (EQIA) of 1970, and the Federal-Aid Highway Act of 1970 (Stopher and Meyburg, 1976). The CAA of 1970 was not directed specifically toward transport, and it was not specifically in US clean air legislation. However, the CAA of 1970 established compounds, oxides of sulfur, oxides of nitrogen, carbon monoxide, and particulate matter as among the most important air pollutants that would be used to assess air quality and determine whether or not a region met the NAAQS. In many ways, this legislation helped to identify more clearly what should be considered under the air pollution aspect of the NEPA and the subsequent federal legislation on transport and the environment. The CAA also set up the Environmental Protection Agency (EPA), which was charged with administering the provisions of the CAA.

The EQIA set up the Office of Environmental Quality under the Council for Environmental Quality. Subsequently, this was replaced by the EPA, which took over the responsibilities of both the Office of Environmental Quality and the Council for Environmental Quality. The EQIA was a complementary act to the NEPA, charged with assisting in the evaluation process and research. The NEPA and EQIA together required the federal government to make the final determination of the trade-offs between capital improvements and environmental impacts. In other words, it was identified that, in the case of federally funded projects, the federal agency funding the project would make the final determination of whether or not the impacts were worth incurring.

The Federal-Aid Highway Act of 1970 incorporated and made part of the highway funding process the requirements of the NEPA. Further, this act gave rise to the development of PPM 90-4, requiring the development of "Action Plans." These action plans were designed to detail responsibilities and procedures for identifying social, environmental, and economic consequences of transport plans. They also were designed to ensure a high technical quality in the development of EISs, as called for under the NEPA.

Other federal legislation of relevance included the Uniform Relocation Assistance and Real Property Acquisition Policies Act of 1970. This act, for the first time, laid out requirements for appropriate compensation of those whose property was required for a federal construction project, and also detailed how market value was to be obtained for purchasing such properties. Because PPM 20-8 and the NEPA each specified that land taking and relocation were among the factors to be considered in an environmental analysis, this act was of specific relevance to indicate how property should be acquired and what responsibilities existed for relocating households and businesses.

Since the early 1970s, there have been numerous pieces of federal legislation that have some relevance to environmental assessment of transport projects. Probably the most important such legislation in the transport arena have been the CAAA of 1977 and then of 1990, and the Intermodal Surface Transportation Efficiency Act (ISTEA) of 1991. Under the 1977 CAAA, State Improvement Plans (SIPs) were defined. These were plans to be developed by areas not in attainment of the NAAQS that would show how attainment of these air quality standards would be reached within the time frames set out by the CAAA of 1977. The CAAA of 1977 introduced the requirement for "reasonable further progress" (RFP) toward attaining the air quality standards, and required the development of transportation control plans (TCPs) in urban areas that were not in attainment. These TCPs represented the first direct recognition in the clean air legislation of the role that transport plays in creating air pollution, and represented the first direct legislative requirements to be placed on transport in the USA by an act that was not first and foremost a transport act.

The 1977 CAAA resulted in a Memorandum of Understanding (MOU) between the US Department of Transportation and the EPA on air quality and planning. The CAAA also set 1982 as the target year for attainment for all but the most polluted areas, which had until 1987. The CAAA introduced Transportation Control Measures (TCMs) as a means to assist a region to attain air quality standards. The TCMs generally related to such actions as encouraging ride-sharing (carpools, bus riding, etc.), and improvement of traffic flow through traffic management actions, in an effort to reduce pollution from congested traffic.

Additionally, the CAAA introduced the possibility of "sanctions" on an area that did not achieve the NAAQS, where these sanctions included the withholding of federal funds for transport infrastructure investments. Nevertheless, the CAAA of 1977 was not implemented rigorously, and sanctions were never applied. As a result, the targets of 1982 and 1987 were not met, and, indeed, some regions actually recorded worsening not improving air quality.

Congress passed a further set of amendments in 1990 – the CAAA of 1990. These amendments gave teeth to the transportation portions of the CAA: a series of target years were mandated, dependent on the level of non-attainment of the NAAQS. Failure to meet the target date meant automatic reclassification to the next level of non-attainment. The 1990 CAAA also strengthened sanctions, by impounding federal highway funds for areas that do not comply. Further, SIP revisions were again required from non-attainment areas, and maintenance plans required from areas that were, in the past non-attainment areas, but had subsequently improved air quality to the level of attainment. In addition, no new capacity additions could be made for low-occupancy vehicles in non-attainment areas. In other words, the only permitted capacity increases were for high-occupancy vehicles. A final very significant element of the CAAA of 1990 was that the legislation specifically opened the door to citizens to bring lawsuits against agencies involved in attempting to meet air quality standards. These lawsuits could be brought on the basis that appropriate analysis had not been performed, or that relevant issues to cleaning up the air had been neglected or ignored.

The ISTEA of 1991 added strength to requirements in the 1990 CAAA. Planning requirements for non-attainment areas were stipulated in detail in the ISTEA, where they had only been noted in broad terms in the CAAA of 1990. The ISTEA also set up Congestion Management and Air Quality Funds (CMAQ) to be used in non-attainment areas to achieve the goals of the CAAA. It also provided further detail on what must be included in transport plans to meet the requirements of the CAAA and NEPA, and clarified certain circumstances under which the public could bring lawsuits to enforce compliance with these federal laws. The ISTEA was complimentary to, and further extended, the CAAA of 1990. Subsequent transport legislation, such as the Transportation Efficiency Act for the 21st Century (TEA-21), has continued to maintain and even strengthen these requirements.

A direct outcome of the legislation on clean air was the introduction of catalytic converters on passenger cars, which also required the removal of lead from petrol, because the presence of lead in the petrol would disable the catalytic converter. The clean air legislation also led to efforts to reduce the sulfur content of motor fuels, and unleaded petrol brought with it reductions in sulfur content as a by-product of the reformulation of petrol. Clean air legislation also introduced the notion of testing vehicles for emissions. However, in the USA, emissions testing on a regular basis remains a matter of state, rather than federal, legislation, with many states still resisting the introduction of compulsory emissions tests for privately owned vehicles.

In the meantime, in response to the oil crisis of 1973, the US Congress passed the Energy Conservation and Policy Act of 1975, which instituted fuel efficiency requirements for passenger cars and light trucks. From that point until the present, the US Congress has passed legislation setting the "corporate average fuel economy" (CAFE) for newly manufactured vehicles, usually with a goal for the following 5 years. Responsibility for implementing this legislation is placed with the National Highway Traffic Safety Administration (NHTSA), which has recently issued a final rule for model year 2004 light trucks. In addition, the Alternative Motor Fuels Act of 1988 established CAFE incentives for the manufacture of vehicles that used alcohol or natural gas fuels. A recent evaluation of this legislation concluded that it has had mixed effects, and that other actions may be needed to bring about serious efforts to replace petroleum-based fuels in motor vehicles. In a related action, the US Congress enacted a national maximum speed limit of 55 mph in 1974, following establishment of a temporary rule for a maximum speed limit that was enacted in 1973. This national maximum speed limit was enforced through the threat of withdrawal of federal aid funds for highways for states not conforming to the law. All 50 states and territories implemented the measure. Amendments in 1987 and 1991 allowed states to increase speed limits on rural interstates and similar highways. However, in 1995, the national maximum speed limit was repealed, and states were left to set their own maximum speed limits.

Other areas of environmental legislation relate to marine pollution, noise pollution, and other similar impacts associated with non-land-based transport systems. Space does not permit a review of all of these areas of legislation. However, the USA was again one of the first countries to legislate on aircraft noise in the late 1960s, and has also been one of the leaders in tackling various types of marine pollution. Much more recently, the USA introduced regulations on outboard engine emissions, beginning with the 1998 model year. A new standard was introduced, requiring a 75% reduction in outboard motor emissions by the model year 2006 (Graham Barclay Marine, 2002). While other countries do not yet appear to be following this legislation with their own, the dominance of the USA as a market for sales of such engines is likely to impact emissions levels throughout the world.

Overall, the environmental legislation passed by the US Congress in the past 30 years appears to represent not only the first comprehensive legislation on transport and environment by any country, but is probably also the most prescriptive and far-reaching legislation that exists in any nation at this time, particularly at a national level. Furthermore, it appears that only in the USA has legislation on transport specifically embodied and expanded on environmental requirements.

3.3. Other legislation in the USA

The legislation discussed in the preceding sections of this chapter focused on the federal legislation in the USA. All of that legislation is tied to federal funding, and thus does not apply to any project or initiative that involves no federal funds. However, following the passage of the NEPA in 1969, most states have enacted their own legislation that applies to projects that are financed with state and local funds, and even, in some instances, with private funds. For example, the California legislature passed the California Environmental Quality Act (CEQA) in 1970, which requires the preparation of Draft and Final Environmental Impact Reports (EIRs). The CEQA applies to projects that both do and do not have federal funding that are undertaken in the state of California. As with most state legislation, some aspects of the CEQA are more stringent than the NEPA, while others are less stringent. For any project covered by both the CEQA and NEPA, the more stringent requirements of each act apply. A joint document – the *Environmental Impact Statement/Environmental Impact Report* – is to be prepared for such projects, and will satisfy both pieces of relevant legislation, provided that the requirements of the NEPA are augmented, where necessary, so as to meet the requirements of the CEQA. For projects where only the CEQA applies, it becomes the ruling legislation, and an EIR will be required. This pattern is repeated in most US states.

4. Legislation on transport and the environment in other countries

Subsequent to the passage of the NEPA in the USA, the EIA procedures embodied in that legislation have been adapted and adopted in many countries around the world (Harvey, 1998). As noted by Harvey (1998), the major exceptions to this are a number of countries in Africa and the Middle East. Wood (1995) also suggests that the earliest instance of legislation outside the USA on the environment was that of New South Wales, Australia, which introduced a very rudimentary environmental impact policy in 1972, following the announcement of a Commonwealth EIA policy in Australia. In the same year, Singapore formed a Ministry of the Environment, whose purpose was to assess the environmental impacts of development proposals, and Japan adopted EIA procedures for major development projects (Harvey, 1998). Norway also formed a Ministry of Environment in 1972, following legislation (Act No. 63 of 19 June 1970) in 1970 relating to protection of nature and biodiversity that also had implications on how transport infrastructure could be built.

In the following year, Canada introduced a cabinet directive for environmental impact assessment, while Australia and Columbia both introduced specific EIA legislation in 1974. By cabinet minute, New Zealand also introduced EIA procedures in that year. A number of other countries introduced some form of environmental impact assessment procedure over the next few years, although the manner of introduction and the strength of the requirements varied widely. Among the other countries introducing some form of environmental impact assessment guideline or requirement were: Thailand in 1975; France, Ireland, and West Germany in 1976; The Philippines in 1977; and the Netherlands, China, and Taiwan in 1979 (Gilpin, 1995; Wood, 1995; Harvey, 1998). By 1985 there was a directive from the EC on environmental impact assessment, but it was not until 1988 that the UK finally implemented formal legislation calling for environmental impact assessment of major projects (Harvey, 1998). However, the UK has introduced public inquiries to look at the full implications of transport investment decisions much earlier, and partly in response to early pressures against road-building solutions, such as the proposed inner London motorways that were stopped in the 1960s.

Various countries around the world have also followed the USA lead in a number of other areas, including introduction of unleaded gasoline, use of catalytic converters, reduction of sulfur content in motor fuels, and other related actions. In other instances, other countries or international bodies have pioneered legislation or rules relating to environmental concerns in transport. This has included European efforts in developing cleaner diesel engines, particularly for use in buses, and also other efforts relating to the reduction of greenhouse gases from transport sources.

In addition to individual countries, there are a number of international agencies that have also introduced some form of environmental impact assessment procedure. These include the UN Environment Programme, the OECD, the US Agency for International Development, the World Bank, and the Overseas Development Administration (Glasson et al., 1994). The London Convention of 1972 on Prevention of Marine Pollution by Dumping of Wastes and Other Matters is another example of this type of international action (International Maritime Organization, 1996).

It seems that, almost without exception, other countries around the world have been less prescriptive with environmental legislation, and have also not focused on transport to the extent that the USA has done. There are also different triggers for when an environmental assessment is required in the different instances of environmental legislation. As an illustration of some of the differences, this chapter concludes with a look at how environmental impact assessment works in Australia, which, as noted above, was one of the first countries outside the USA to adopt legislation of this type.

5. Australian legislation on transport and the environment

For the most part, Australia has followed the US lead, but with each state passing its own legislation. In each case the legislation is rather similar to that of the NEPA of the USA. This is the reverse of the process that occurred in the USA, where the federal government led the process and the states followed. In Australia, the Commonwealth has taken a somewhat "hands off" attitude to state projects, and has preferred to defer to the states. Commonwealth legislation passed in 1974 in the form of the Environment Protection (Impact of Proposals) Act of 1974 applies to all proposals and projects directly funded by the Commonwealth. Specific elements of the process to which the act applies are:

(1) formulation of proposals;
(2) carrying out of works;
(3) negotiation/operation/enforcement of agreements;
(4) making of decisions;
(5) incurring of expenditure.

The act was originally administered by the Australian EPA in the Department of Environment, Sport, and Tourism, but is now administered by Environment Australia. There were some amendments to the act over the years from 1974 to 1996, but no substantive changes have occurred since 1996. The act requires a similar process to the US NEPA, namely a first stage – preparation of an NOI – followed by a second stage – preparation of a PER or EIS by the responsible agency, which is then submitted to EPA. The third stage is the development and acceptance of the final EIS. The act is discretionary rather than mandatory in its application – the Minister for the Environment makes a determination as to whether or not the act applies to any specific case. In contrast, the US federal legislation always applies if any federal funds are involved, and there is no discretion provided in its application. This is the first sense in which this legislation is more "hands off" than the US legislation. The second area in which this is evidenced is in the type of reporting and analysis required.

In contrast to the US situation, the Australian Commonwealth law defines two thresholds. The first is a threshold of Environmental Significance. An action of government falls below this threshold if impacts are deemed by the sponsoring agency to be indiscernible. In such a case, no reporting is required. In effect, this corresponds to the US situation of a FONSI, but in the USA the FONSI can only be obtained after undertaking a comprehensive environmental impact assessment, while, in Australia, a finding of indiscernible impacts can be developed without a formal study or report. The next threshold is that of acceptability of environmental impacts. If impacts are considered to be acceptable, then only the NOI and the PER are required. Only in the event that impacts are expected or determined to be unacceptable is a full EIS required to be developed.

In the event that both state and commonwealth laws may apply to a project, there is again a difference from the US situation. In the USA, both state and federal law will then apply, and requirements of both must be met. In Australia, only one law will apply, and the decision as to whether state or commonwealth law will be followed is to be determined on a case-by-case basis by the governmental departments concerned. There is an Inter-Governmental Agreement on Environment (IGEA) that specifies how this will be done.

All five Australian states and two territories have enacted their own legislation, and there are distinct differences among these, as in the case of the USA. Different terminology is used and different reports are required, depending on state. For example, the Western Australia Environment Protection Act of 1986 defines the first stage as a Consultative Environmental Review (CER), the second stage as a PER, and the third stage as an Environmental Review and Management Plan (ERMP). The New South Wales Environmental Planning and Assessment Act of 1979 (amended in 1999) calls for an NOI, PER, and EIS, in much the same way as the Commonwealth Act, although certain stipulations about these are different in the New South Wales legislation.

No legislation at Commonwealth or state level specifically incorporates transport-related environment issues, unlike the situation in the USA, where a number of transport and other Acts incorporate elements of the environmental legislation, often making it more detailed and applicable than in the original environmental legislation. State legislation may apply to public projects only, or to all projects if they are of sufficient magnitude. In other words, only large-scale privately funded projects would be required to adhere to the environmental laws, although some provisions may be found in SEPPs, REPs, LEPs, and DCPs. In the USA the federal legislation only affects projects undertaken with some portion of federal funds. On the other hand, state laws often apply to all projects, no matter who is funding them, and often apply to all private sector projects. In Australia, transport fits as a public project in most states and for most projects. However, a loophole may exist. If a toll road is built by the private sector and subsequently is operated and maintained by the private sector, it is not clear that such a project would be required to conform to environmental legislation.

It is perhaps surprising that transport in Australia has not received more attention in the legislative process, with respect to environmental impacts. Transport is frequently a major source of negative environmental effects; increasing demands on the transport system generate congestion, which, in turn, increases the environmental problems created by traffic. In the USA, transport has been singled out as a prime contributor to air pollution and to other types of environmental degradation. As a result, there are, as previously noted, a number of pieces of legislation that address transport-specific impacts, *per se*.

Greenhouse gases, which are now taking a more prominent position in the environmental debate, are produced in significant quantities by transport. In the USA, these gases have received relatively little legislative attention, either in respect of the entire economy, or in the transport sector itself. In Australia, which has tended to be in advance of the USA in concerns about and strategies to counteract greenhouse gases, there is again a lack of legislation or requirements for analysis of these gases, and the impact of various projects on their production. There is also no legislation that is aimed specifically at reducing greenhouse gases by laying requirements on transport options. Australia was also rather late in introducing catalytic converters and unleaded gasoline, with the latter being introduced only in 1986. As of 1993, while Japan, Brazil, South Korea, and Canada had all reached a complete phase out of leaded gasoline, and the USA consumed only 1% of total gasoline sales as leaded gasoline, Australia consumed 45% unleaded gasoline and 55% leaded gasoline (US Bureau of Transportation Statistics, 1996).

6. Conclusions

The modern history of environmental legislation is relatively short, and its beginnings can be traced back only to the late 1960s, less than 40 years ago. Nevertheless, in that time, legislation has been promulgated on a wide variety of environmental elements, and has clearly changed the process by which transport infrastructure investments are planned and implemented. There are also probably few areas of modern society that have received such universal legislation by individual countries, multinational agencies, and regions. Not only that, but the legislation has tended to focus principally on setting in place a similar process in all instances. In most countries, a major project must now be accompanied by an EIA, which must meet similar specifications and analytical standards no matter where it is done.

At the same time, this consistency of concern with the environment and provision of mandated procedures has given rise to another phenomenon – the creation of a variety of environmental disciplines concerned with different aspects of environmental impact. As Harvey (1998) notes, there are now such study programs and qualifications as environmental engineering, environmental law, environmental medicine, and environmental politics. An emerging area of concern, particularly in the USA, is the issue of environmental justice, which concerns itself with who benefits and who loses, particularly in terms of sociodemographic groups. It is probably true to state that there has never before in the history of mankind been such a global awareness of environmental issues, environmental degradation, and a desire for a strong environmental perspective to be adopted in the use of resources and the creation of infrastructure.

References

Gilpin, A. (1995) *Environmental impact assessment (EIA): cutting edge for the 21st century*. Cambridge: Cambridge University Press.

Glasson, J., A. Therivel and A. Chadwick (1994) *Introduction to environmental impact assessment*. London: University College London Press.

Graham Barclay Marine (2002) *The straight story on emission regulations*. Forster: Graham Barclay Marine (http://www.barclaymarine.com.au/emissions.htm).
Harvey, N. (1998) *Environmental impact assessment: procedures, practice, and prospects in Australia*. Melbourne: Oxford University Press.
Hughes, J.D. (1975) *Ecology in ancient civilisations*. Albuquerque: University of New Mexico Press.
International Maritime Organization (1996) *A brief description of the London Convention 1972 and the 1996 Protocol*. London: International Maritime Organization (http://www.londonconvention.org/London_Convention.htm).
Stopher, P.R. and A.H. Meyburg (1976) *Transportation systems evaluation*. Lexington: Lexington Books.
Thomas, I. (2001) *Environmental impact assessment in Australia: theory and practice*. Leichhardt: Federation Press.
US Bureau of Transportation Statistics (1996) "An international comparison of transportation and air pollution," in: *Transportation statistics annual report*. Washington, DC: Department of Transportation, Bureau of Transportation Statistics.
US Department of Transportation (1969) *Policy and Procedure Memorandum 20-8*. Washington, DC: Federal Highway Administration, Department of Transportation.
Washington State University (2002a) *Ancient China: the Shang*. Pullman: Washington State University (http://www.wsu.edu.8080/~dee/ANCCHINA/SHANG.htm).
Washington State University (2002b) *Ancient China: the Chou*. Pullman: Washington State University (http://www.wsu.edu.8080/~dee/ANCCHINA/CHOU.htm).
Wood, C. (1995) *Environmental impact assessment: a comparative review*. London: Longman.

Chapter 28

INTERNATIONAL COORDINATION OF ENVIRONMENTAL POLICIES AND MULTILATERAL ENVIRONMENTAL AGREEMENTS[a]

JEROEN C.J.M. VAN DEN BERGH
Free University, Amsterdam

NURIA CASTELLS
UN Conference on Trade and Development (UNCTAD), Geneva

1. The need for international coordination of environmental policies

Although environmental policies are predominantly designed and implemented at a national level, certain characteristics of environmental problems, in combination with the aim to realize the best public policy response to them, lead to a need for international coordination and cooperation. These characteristics include the presence of transboundary pollution and the environmental impact of international trade. International coordination is not required when the causes and effects of environmental problems are local, falling within the boundaries of national or subnational jurisdictions. The latter is known as the subsidiarity principle.

It is now common practice to conceptualize transboundary environmental pollution as a form of externalities (Pearce and Warford, 1993). The notion of externalities reflects the presence of unintended physical impacts of decisions by one individual or organization – e.g. a firm – on another. Such impacts occur outside any market and remain uncompensated. Transboundary externalities can occur because the global environment is mostly an open access resource, or more generally a public good, i.e. no one's property. The lack of property rights generally stimulates externalities, as it allows the global environment to be regarded as a source of free goods. This readily permits neglect and overuse, which in turn have negative consequences for both the environment and economic welfare.

Among the most important transboundary environmental problems are acid rain, climate change, tropical deforestation, biodiversity loss, pollution of the open seas, and international transport of hazardous waste. These problems are,

---

[a] The opinions expressed do not necessarily reflect those of the UNCTAD.

Handbook of Transport and the Environment, Edited by D.A. Hensher and K.J. Button
© 2003, Elsevier Ltd

moreover, interrelated. This is most noticeable for tropical deforestation and biodiversity loss through habitat destruction, and for climate change and deforestation with regard to the capture of carbon dioxide (CO_2). Stratospheric ozone depletion is no longer on the "critical" list, because the success story of international agreements, the Montreal Protocol, has led to a rapid phasing out of chlorofluorocarbons, the most important cause of ozone depletion. An issue of increasing concern is the use of genetically modified organisms, including living modified organisms, and their potentially uncontrolled propagation by means of international trade. The Biosafety Protocol of Cartagena – within the Convention on Biodiversity – is a response to this concern.

Transportation and international environmental problems have an intricate and complex relationship. The international trade in physical commodities is a cause of much long-distance transport, via road, air, boat or rail. Transport itself is an important contributor to transboundary problems, notably the enhanced greenhouse effect (especially emissions of CO_2), acid rain (emissions of nitrogen oxides (NO_x)), and transport of hazardous waste. The lowering of transport costs through technical progress and organizational change – such as the emergence of smoothly operating multimodal transport systems – has stimulated international trade. Trade and transport are thus mutually supportive, and one reinforces the environmental effects directly related to the other.

An important policy form that coordinates national environmental policies is a multilateral environmental agreement (MEA). An alternative is a structural supranational governance structure, as currently emerging within the EU. However, international agreements are much more common, as will be illustrated in Section 4.

This chapter provides a short introduction to the literature on the international coordination of environmental policies and multilateral environmental agreements. Section 2 discusses some general insights on the economic theory of environmental policy that are useful in studying international policy coordination. Section 3 reviews theories that have been invoked to understand the processes of agreement formation and stability. Section 4 presents an illustrative overview of current international institutions and multilateral environmental agreements. The chapter ends with a conclusion.

2. Environmental policy theory: from a national to an international perspective

For a long time the standard economic theory of environmental policy has been mainly concerned with closed economies, focusing attention on the choice of policy instruments in relation to efficiency (Baumol and Oates, 1988). The archetypal opposition of standards and taxes serves as a benchmark, where normally the efficiency advantages of taxes are emphasized. Many other important instruments can be considered as a combination of "pure" instruments: tradable permits that mix standards with taxes; environmental tax reforms that mix labor and environmental policies; and deposit-refund systems that mix taxes and subsidies. The recent literature extends the evaluation and comparison of instruments to include considerations of uncertainty, imperfect markets, technological innovation, and transaction costs. In addition, other evaluation criteria are taken into account, such as dynamic efficiency, effectiveness, information requirements, ease of monitoring and enforcement, distributional equity, and sustainability (Sterner, 1994).

An important element, both in a national and international context, is the way in which the efficiency–equity trade-off is conceptualized. This is perhaps even more important at an international than at a national level, in view of the extremely skewed income distribution for the world as a whole. Alternative views on this trade-off can be based on utilitarianism, Rawlsian theories of justice, and libertarian thought. Subsequently, principles of equity and efficiency can be derived. At the highest level, a choice between allocation, outcome, and process-based principles needs to be made. Such insights contribute to an understanding of the different positions adopted by countries in the debate on principles for designing international agreements. The relevance of this is currently most visible in the context of a reduction of greenhouse gases (Rose and Kverndokk, 1999).

Awareness of the need for an international dimension to environmental policy has rapidly increased since the mid-1980s. This has given rise to an area of research that is characterized by several overlapping themes: the causes and features of transboundary and global environmental problems; the impact of foreign trade on environmental externalities; the impact of environmental regulation on international trade, including access of developing countries to international markets; the influence of strict national environmental regulation on the international competitive position and location of firms; and the emergence and stability of international policy coordination and trade agreements (van den Bergh, 1999).

The relationship between trade and the environment has been addressed from a variety of theoretical and empirical angles. The questions addressed can be summarized into two strands, whether environmental policy can and should be used as trade policy, and vice versa. Differences in rigor among national environmental policies are considered to lead to distortions in trade. The restriction of trade due to the specific measures pursuant to MEAs has been a point of worry within World Trade Organisation (WTO) circles. Several terms and related ideas have played a dominant role in the discussion about trade and the environment. The following are the most recurrent:

- *Environmental protectionism*: misusing environmental goals to restrict market access. Developing countries want to prevent the use of MEAs to introduce the precautionary principle and other environment-related clauses that would severely restrict market access for their products.

- *Ecological dumping*: a country that tries to improve its international competitive position through relatively lax environmental regulation. Capital flight to "pollution havens," notably developing countries, is a feared consequence. Nevertheless, the empirical evidence for ecological dumping is weak.
- *The Porter hypothesis*: stringent environmental regulations will stimulate innovation to such an extent that the net welfare effect for a country will be strictly positive (Porter and van der Linde, 1995). This seems to reflect a one-sided national context. At an international level, it is likely that there would be losers and winners, depending on the changes in trading markets and the new conditions of competition. Moreover, testing this idea empirically has proved to be very difficult.

A common finding from the economics literature is that environmental impacts of free trade or trade liberalization should not be attributed to trade but to the production sources of trade. This implies that environmental policy should not focus on creating trade barriers, e.g. through import levies, but on charging polluting production sources. This insight, however, needs adaptation for specific circumstances. These depend on whether externalities relate directly to production, transportation, or consumption, whether trading countries are small or large (price taking or setting, having fixed or variable terms of trade), and whether pollution is local or transboundary. Finally, the sharp divide between developed and developing countries creates further concerns, which relate to ethical and legal principles for negotiation, the relation between equity and poverty, and north–south comparative advantages (e.g. Gupta, 1997). The current context for addressing these issues was set out by the Rio Declaration on Environment and Development in 1992, and is currently being revised and possibly strengthened at the forthcoming Rio + 10 Conference, the World Summit for Sustainable Development (WSSD) to be held in Johannesburg in August 2002. Transport has received relatively little attention in the context of trade and environment, and even more generally in trade theory (an exception is Steininger, 2001).

3. Theories of multilateral environmental agreements

An important means of ensuring international cooperation is an international environmental agreement (IEA) or MEA. A range of terms denoting international agreements can be found in the literature: multilateral agreements, international agreements, treaties, conventions, protocols, memoranda of understanding, and "soft law" such as charters and declarations. MEAs are very common in policy circles, notably within the UN and the WTO. The UN Environment Programme (UNEP) has undertaken several international meetings and produced reports concerning the role of MEAs in an international system of good governance (UN Environment Programme, 2001). UNCTAD deals with the trade dimension of MEAs.

The steps to arrive at agreements start with a situation of environmental conflict followed by communication, negotiation and bargaining, signing, and ratification. A subsequent phase concerns the implementation of concrete policy instruments and systems of monitoring and control. The process by which an early environmental concern is with much delay translated into an international agreement has the form of a bottom-up process, starting with certain countries expressing serious environmental concerns. This process is addressed by the literature in different ways, depending on which phase of agreement formation is under examination. Many theories have been applied to the study of international negotiations. Two multi-agent theories have been used to predict and understand the formation and dynamics of international agreements, namely cooperative game theory and negotiation analysis (Castells, 1999). Differences in approaches are mainly due to the assumptions made regarding the behavior of the agents – individuals or countries – involved.

Game theory is the traditional tool in economics for addressing conflicting objectives in relation to free-riding and prisoner dilemma types of situations, which are typical of transboundary environmental problems. Not surprisingly, therefore, it has become the dominant approach in economic analyses of cooperative behavior in environmental conflict situations (Carraro, 1999). Mäler pioneered the acid rain issues by means of game theory, and Barrett the analysis of MEA formation. Attention has been devoted to non-cooperative and cooperative solutions, self-enforcing systems aided by side transfers, and issue linking.

The idea of transfers is very straightforward: a redistribution mechanism assures that countries that lose by signing an MEA are partly or wholly compensated. Transfers thus can assure that the number of signatories is increased. Notably, it can enable developing countries to participate in MEAs, as they often lack means – financial, technological, know-how – to achieve the goals of MEAs. Moreover, transfers can be used as an instrument to enforce cooperation and avoid free-riding. The specific approach used to analyze such issues has been referred to as coalition theory. This studies which coalitions tend to form, i.e. how the total number of potential signatories tends to break up in subgroups. The relevance of coalition theory is that the net benefits of becoming a member of the coalition of signatories depend on the characteristics and "environmental behavior" of non-signatories, as indicated by the level of emissions generated by them. In this context the notion of "leakage" is relevant. It denotes that a country causes extra pollution or damage, or more than its fair share, to the public environment. Note that this is related to, but different from, free-riding. The latter means enjoying the publicly available environmental quality without paying for it.

Analysis of issue linking can identify the conditions that will promote coalitions around combined standpoints (Folmer et al., 1993). Obvious themes for being linked are poverty and development, when negotiating issues of trade and environment. A linking approach resembles the way compromises are made by partners in coalition governments – common in many European countries – so as to meet their objectives. It can in fact be regarded as a step forward in global governance.

Negotiation analysis is a multi-agent theory that addresses the impact of bounded rationality and imperfect information. It has been developed by Sebenius (1992), following the work of Schelling (1960) and Raiffa (1982). The approach can be regarded as a non-equilibrium game theory. Schelling (1960) noted that collective decisions by individuals who do not have identical value systems could create a disorderly and inconsistent value system. As a result, their organizational arrangements and communication systems do not cause them to act like a single rational entity. This evidently holds for the case of MEAs, as they concern cooperation among heterogeneous countries, with different ecosystems and stages of economic development. Negotiation analysis is characterized by the possibility of inefficient outcomes and the replacement of game-theoretic equilibrium solution concepts by "zones of possible agreement."

So far, negotiation analysis has seen only a few applications to MEAs. Sebenius (1995) studied the Law of the Sea, the Montreal Protocol on Ozone, and the Climate Change Convention after the Rio Summit. These analyses focus on potential blocking coalitions that may arise in the search for an agreement. In addition, they show that although linking issues may be a way of reaching an agreement, they can also have the reverse effect of precluding agreement on the main issue. It is found that proposing comprehensive agreements that are too large to be approved by consensus is the surest way to impede an agreement. As an alternative, Sebenius suggests starting with small specific agreements to pave the way for more stringent and larger agreements, through progressive strengthening of the original one.

A number of other theoretical perspectives are possible (Castells, 1999). For reasons of space, we restrict ourselves here to institutional economics as applied to environmental issues (e.g. Swaney, 1987; Opschoor and van der Straaten, 1993). According to Young (1994), all institutions are social artifacts created by human beings – consciously or unconsciously – to cope with problems of coordination and cooperation that arise as a result of interdependencies among the activities of distinct individuals or social groups. This indicates the relevance of institutional economics for the study of MEAs. A specific theory in the context of institutional economics is regime theory, which analyses the formal and informal processes and rules without any restriction on specific types of actors or rules (Rittberger, 1993). It has proved to be valuable in the analysis of MEAs, and has been applied for the study of the Long-Range Transboundary Air Pollution (LRTAP) Convention (Nijkamp and Castells, 2001).

An explicitly historical perspective can be fruitful to explain the pattern of first-comer versus late-comer countries in the emergence of MEAs. This is part of a process of institutional innovation. Such innovation consists of changing social goals and arrangements, and broadening the number of stakeholders involved. Institutional innovation covers phases that are analogous to those in technical innovation: emergence of awareness of an environmental problem in one country (the first comers), followed by diffusion to the international level, and, ultimately, adoption of the concern by late-comer countries. In this context the two-level game approach developed by Putnam (1988) is relevant. This approach recognizes that international negotiations are not only about international relations but also about subnational relations. The latter includes the distribution of costs and benefits among domestic groups, and diversity of opinions on environmental problems and international cooperation. This approach is relevant to the study of MEAs as it can provide an explanation of the different attitudes shown by first comers and late comers.

In practice, none of these theories alone can fully capture the complexity of negotiation and interaction patterns among countries, thereby taking into account the influence of, among others, scientific knowledge and interest groups. This suggests that the various theories and their insights are best be considered as complementary tools for analysis of MEAs.

4. MEAs in practice

International cooperation for environmental policy and nature conservation proceeds along many channels. The UNEP, launched in 1972 after the Stockholm Conference on the Human Environment, fulfils an important coordinating and catalyzing function in the network of environmental cooperation among countries, through monitoring, research, and dissemination of information. Two other important events have had a major impact on international cooperation since then. The first is the report *Our Common Future* in 1987 by the World Commission on Environment and Development (also called the Brundtland Commission), which stimulated the acceptance of sustainable development as a common objective, as well as recognized the intricate links between problems of environment, development, and poverty. The second is the UN Conference on Environment and Development (the "Earth Summit") in 1992 in Rio de Janeiro – the largest conference ever held – where, among other things, two MEAs were initiated: the Framework Convention on Climate Change, and the Convention on Biological Diversity. In 2002, the follow-up meeting in Johannesburg is expected to make a step forward. An important goal is the implementation of Agenda 21, which is a non-binding agreement resulting from the Rio Conference.

Other relevant actors within the realm of the UN system address the issue of the environment specifically related to their own main topic of concern, such as the World Health Organisation (WHO) and the Food and Agricultural Organisation (FAO). In addition, UNCTAD devotes special attention to the integration of environmental considerations with trade rules and development strategies. Next to non-governmental organizations, associations of producers and consumers are increasingly being involved in participatory processes of decision-making, mainly in developed countries. Organizations of scientists that have a direct impact on policy are rare. An important recent exception is the Intergovernmental Panel on Climate Change, which has played an instrumental role in the definition of the UN Framework Convention on Climate Change, and its Kyoto Protocol.

An exhaustive overview of environmental agreements, along with complete legal statements, is available on the Internet (Center for International Earth Science Information Network, 2002). They are categorized into nine areas:

- land use/land cover change and desertification;
- global climate change;
- stratospheric ozone depletion;
- transboundary air pollution;
- conservation of biological diversity;
- deforestation;
- oceans and their living resources;
- trade and the environment;
- population.

The number of international agreements has grown steadily since the 1940s, and has increased markedly since 1970. Some of the most important and best-known environmental agreements are: the Montreal Protocol on Substances that Deplete the Ozone Layer; the Convention on Biological Diversity and its Protocol on Biosafety (usually referred to as the Cartagena Protocol); the Biosphere Reserves Program; the World Heritage Convention; the Basel Convention on Transboundary Movements of Hazardous Wastes; the UN Framework Convention on Climate Change and the Kyoto Protocol, to reduce greenhouses gases emissions; the Ramsar Convention on Wetlands; and one of the oldest MEAs, the Convention on International Trade in Endangered Species of Wild Fauna and Flora (CITES).

In the context of transport, the list of agreements in Box 1 is illustrative. Many agreements are about controlling accidents and pollution spills directly caused by transport, mainly by ships and planes. This is dominated by sea navigation. Other agreements control the movement of waste and toxic substances. In addition, some environmental agreements, such as the Basel Convention and CITES, are relevant, as they have an impact on the regulation, monitoring, and control of freight transport crossing country or regional borders. Agreements on air pollution, with the LRTAP Convention, and the closely related EC Directives and strategies (the NEC Directive and the Clean Air For Europe program), and the Kyoto Protocol, also influence transport. This is because it is one of the sectors

Box 1
A selection of environmental agreements relevant to transport

Agreement Between the Government of the United States of America and the Government of Canada Concerning the Transboundary Movement of Hazardous Wastes
(1986)

Agreement Concerning Cooperation in Taking Measures Against Pollution of the Sea by Oil
(16 September 1971)

Agreement for Cooperation in Dealing with Pollution of the North Sea by Oil and Other Harmful Substances
(13 September 1983)

Agreement to Promote Compliance with International Conservation and Management Measures by Fishing Vessels on the High Seas
(29 November 1993)

Basel Convention on the Control of Transboundary Movements of Hazardous Wastes and Their Disposal
(22 March 1989)

Convention for the Prevention of Marine Pollution by Dumping from Ships and Aircraft (as amended)
(15 February 1972)

Convention for the Protection of the Mediterranean Sea Against Pollution (16 February 1976)

Convention for the Suppression of Unlawful Acts Against the Safety of Maritime Navigation
(10 March 1988)

Convention on International Trade in Endangered Species of Wild Fauna and Flora (CITES)
(3 March 1973)

Convention on Long-Range Transboundary Air Pollution (Geneva) and its 8 protocols on reducing air pollutants emissions (sulfur, nitrogen, ammonia, VOCs POPs, etc.)
(13 November 1979)

Convention on the Ban of the Import into Africa and the Control of Transboundary Movement and Management of Hazardous Wastes Within Africa
(30 January 1991)

Convention on the Prevention of Marine Pollution by Dumping of Wastes and Other Matter
(29 December 1972)

International Convention for the Prevention of Pollution from Ships (MARPOL)
(2 November 1973)

International Convention for the Prevention of Pollution of the Sea by Oil
(12 May 1954; amended 11 April 1962 and 21 October 1969)

International Tropical Timber Agreement
(26 January 1994)

Source: Center for International Earth Science Information Network (2002).

that significantly contribute to certain types of air pollution, notably NO_x, CO_2, and sulfur dioxide (SO_2). The commitments accepted under some of these agreements have, for instance, implied changes in the types of fuels used as well as modifications in the technology of engines.

The practical success of defining, negotiating, signing and implementing MEAs depends on a number of factors that are not all considered in the theoretical literature as discussed in the previous section. Von Moltke (2001) mentions the following critical factors: transparency, participation, reporting, dispute settlement, subsidiarity, implementation review, and technology transfer. An interesting phenomenon in practice that has hardly received any attention in theory is that academic research interacts in a complex way with policy preparation and international treaty negotiations. In particular, the use of Integrated Assessment Models (IAMs) has played a crucial role in transforming the definition of policies on transboundary air pollution – or acid rain – in Europe. The RAINS (regional acidification information simulation) model (Alcamo et al., 1990) has been instrumental in this process (Hordijk, 1995; Castells, 1999). This model, created at the International Institute for Applied Systems Analysis, was a pioneering integrated assessment model designed to provide support to environmental policy-makers. Castells and Ravetz (2001) describe the influence of the RAINS model on the emergence of the LRTAP Convention.

In the debate over climate policy certain modeling approaches have had some influence on the evolution of international policy coordination as well. Economic modeling, for instance, has suggested that a choice between no reduction and reduction is possible, and, moreover, that limited greenhouse gas reduction is sufficient, since the costs of reduction are significant whereas its gains are moderate (Nordhaus, 1994). Whether correct or not, these insights have contributed to a lack of broad ratification and even an outright rejection of the Kyoto Protocol by the US government. An important problem is that scientific and political time-scales are mismatched. This is illustrated by the fact that the expected temperature change during the term of a US president will be at most $0.1°C$, whereas the IPCC predicts that under a "business-as-usual" scenario the mean temperatures world-wide will increase $1.4 - 5.8°C$ by 2100 (Sandalow and Bowles, 2001).

Both cases – acid rain and climate change – illustrate that the role of scientific knowledge in the policy-making process has increased. The availability of information and scientific knowledge on environmental issues, and the improved technical capabilities of processing so much data, have indeed been instrumental in the process of institutional innovation in environmental policy-making. But the advent of powerful models has also introduced the possibility of using them to legitimize particular perspectives on environmental problems and their solution (Castells and Ravetz, 2001).

The previous section discussed the idea that linkage between agreements may be required to move forward in international governance with regard to global environmental problems. The most crucial linking is without any doubt between trade and environmental agreements (Esty, 1994). As a result of the Marrakesh Agreement establishing the General Agreement on Tariffs and Trade (GATT) in

1994, the WTO was born in 1995 as the formal institution to follow-up the original GATT agreement of 1947 and its successive rounds of negotiations. The WTO has the role of verifying and facilitating compliance of the rules of the Multilateral Trading System. Within the Marrakesh Agreement, the Decision on Trade and Environment defines the terms of reference concerning the role of the Committee on Trade and Environment (CTE). The CTE will initially address the use of trade measures for environmental purposes, including those pursuant to MEAs, and environmental measures with significant trade effects (GATT Secretariat, 1994). In terms of instruments, attention will be devoted to charges and taxes for environmental purposes, as well as requirements for environmental purposes relating to products. These include standards and technical regulations, packaging, labeling and recycling.

The main question at stake in this process is the fear from developing countries and some developed countries – notably the USA – that linking MEAs to WTO agreements will mean integrating the precautionary principle with trade rules. Until now, however, no dispute has been submitted for settlement to the WTO concerning MEA issues under the responsibility of the CTE.

According to Biermann (2001), certain MEAs contradict some of the basic obligations under the GATT agreement, notably Articles I, III, and XI. Nonetheless, Article XX, known as the general exception clause, will allow in most cases the parties to justify their action on the basis of the necessity to "protect human, animal or plant life and health" or "relating to the conservation of exhaustible natural resource if such measures are made effective in conjunction with restrictions on domestic production and consumption." An important concept underlying the current WTO rules is non-discrimination of "like products." Public regulations that affect a certain imported product – through a standard or tariff – would be regarded as discriminatory if it is focused on considerations other than concrete characteristics of the respective product. Therefore, an environmental policy creating import barriers against a product, aimed at reducing environmental effects caused by its production process or method, is not allowed within WTO rules (e.g. Patterson, 1992).

Currently, three possible future responses to the need to integrate environmental and trade concerns in the WTO can be identified (UNCTAD, 2002). First, a *"status quo* approach" implies that no steps would be needed to clarify the relationship between trade provisions in MEAs and the WTO rules. The argument is that a country would not challenge in one forum what it has agreed to do in the other one. This probably represents an overly simplistic and incorrect view of governments as consistent, rational agents. Second, an *"ex ante* approach" aims to prevent the WTO rules coming into conflict with necessary trade provisions pursuant to MEAs. Therefore, it suggests an amendment of Article XX of the GATT, which lists the conditions under which exceptions to the rules of the multilateral trading system can be accepted. Finally, an *"ex post* (or waiver) approach" proposes that conflicts will be resolved on a case-by-case basis, through a WTO waiver. However, such an approach would be based on an implicit hierarchy where the last word on any possible protectionist abuse comes from a trade forum that can re-examine and evaluate the trade measures agreed upon within the MEA. This would imply a hierarchy between the WTO and the MEA in question. It is doubtful that this would receive wide acceptance.

5. Conclusions

Since the late 1980s, environmental policy analysis has shifted the attention from national and local to transboundary and global environmental issues. International agreements result from complex processes that depend on the interplay of multiple players with different characteristics, the type of environmental or resource problem, and historical factors. The relationship between global environmental problems, MEAs, and transport is multifaceted. It is based on the direct effect of transport on energy use and related emissions of CO_2, SO_2, and NO_x, as well as on the relationship between transport and international trade. This explains why a variety of insights from different theoretical perspectives can be found. The dominant theory has been cooperative game theory. Other theories are based on considering non-rational behavior, and the institutional context and processes. An important topic of research is linkage of issues to move toward complete international governance. For this purpose, the connection between development, poverty, trade, and environmental agreements is crucial. In practice, this involves, in particular, making WTO rules congruent with MEAs.

Acknowledgment

We would like to thank Joyeeta Gupta for useful comments.

References

Alcamo, J., R. Shaw and L. Hordijk, eds (1990) *The Rains model of acidification: science and strategies in Europe.* Dordrecht: Kluwer.
Barrett, S. (1992) "International environmental agreements as games," in: R. Pethig, ed., *Conflicts and cooperation in managing environmental resources.* Berlin: Springer-Verlag.
Baumol, W.J. and W.E. Oates (1988) *The theory of environmental policy.* Cambridge: Cambridge University Press.
Biermann, F. (2001) "The rising tide of green unilateralism in world trade law. Options for reconciling the emerging north–south conflict," *Journal of World Trade*, 35:421–448.
Carraro, C. (1999) "Environmental conflict, bargaining and cooperation," in: J.C.J.M. van den Bergh, ed., *Handbook of environmental and resource economics.* Cheltenham: Edward Elgar.

Castells, N. (1999) "International Environmental Agreements: Institutional Innovation in European Transboundary Air Pollution Policies," PhD Dissertation. Amsterdam: Free University.
Castells, N. and J. Ravetz (2001) "Science and policy in international environmental agreements. Lessons from the European experience on transboundary air pollution," *International Environmental Agreements: Politics, Law and Economics*, 1:405–425.
Center for International Earth Science Information Network (2002) *Environmental treaties and resource indicators (ENTRI)*. Palisades: CIESIN (http://sedac.ciesin.columbia.edu:9080/entri/index.jsp).
Esty, D.C. (1994) *Greening the GATT: trade, environment, and the future*. Washington, DC: Institute for International Economics.
Folmer, H., P. van Mouche and S. Ragland (1993) "Interconnected games and international environmental problems," *Environmental and Resource Economics*, 3:313–335.
GATT Secretariat (1994) *The results of the Uruguay round of multilateral trade negotiations. The legal texts*. Geneva: GATT Secretariat.
Gupta, J. (1997) *The Climate Change Convention and developing countries – from conflict to consensus?* Dordrecht: Kluwer.
Hordijk, L. (1995) "Integrated assessment models as a basis for air pollution negotiations," *Water, Air and Soil Pollution*, 85:249–60.
Mäler, K.-G. (1990) "International environmental problems," *Oxford Review of Economic Policy*, 6:80–107.
Nijkamp, P. and N. Castells (2001) "Transboundary environmental problems in the European Union: lessons from air pollution policies," *Journal of Environmental Law and Policy*, 4:501–517.
Nordhaus, W.D. (1994) *Managing the global commons: the economics of climate change*. Cambridge: MIT Press.
Opschoor, J.-B. and J. van der Straaten (1993) "Sustainable development: an institutional approach," *Ecological Economics*, 7:203–222.
Patterson, E. (1992) "GATT and the environment: rules changes to minimize adverse trade and environmental effects," *Journal of World Trade Law*, 26:100.
Pearce, D.W. and J.J. Warford (1993) *World without end: economics, environment and sustainable development*. Oxford: Oxford University Press.
Porter, M.E. and C. van der Linde (1995) "Green and competitive: ending the stalemate," *Harvard Business Review*, Sept.-Oct.:120–134.
Putnam, R.D. (1988) "Diplomacy and domestic politics: the logic of two–level games," *International Organization*, 42:427–460.
Raiffa, H. (1982) *The art and science of negotiation*. Cambridge: Harvard University Press.
Rittberger, V., ed. (1993) *Regime theory and international relations*. New York: Oxford University Press.
Rose, A. and S. Kverndokk (1999) "Equity in environmental policy: an application to global warming," in: J.C.J.M. van den Bergh. ed., *Handbook of environmental and resource economics*, pp. 352–379. Cheltenham: Edward Elgar.
Sandalow, D.B., and I.A. Bowles (2001) "Fundamentals of treaty-making on climate change," *Science* 292:1839–1840.
Schelling, T.C. (1960) *The strategy of conflict*. Cambridge: Harvard University Press.
Sebenius, J.K. (1992) "Negotiation analysis: a characterization and review," *Management Science*, 38:18–38.
Sebenius, J.K. (1995) "Dealing with blocking coalitions and related barriers to agreement: lessons from negotiations on the oceans, the ozone and the climate," in: K. Arrow, ed., *Barriers to conflict resolution,* pp. 150–182. New York: Norton.
Steininger, K.W. (2001) *International trade and transport: spatial structure and environmental quality in a global economy*. Cheltenham: Edward Elgar.
Sterner, T., ed. (1994) *Economic policies for sustainable development*. Dordrecht: Kluwer.
Swaney, J.A. (1987) "Elements of neo–institutional environmental economics," *Journal of Economic Issues*, 21:1739–1779.
UNCTAD (2002) *Trade-related multilateral environmental agreements*. Module 5. Geneva: UNCTAD.
UN Environment Programme (2001) International environmental governance: Multilateral Environmental Agreements (MEAs). UNEP/IGM/1/INF/3. Meeting of the open-ended

intergovernmental group of ministers or their representatives on international environmental governance. New York.

van den Bergh, J.C.J.M., ed. (1999). *Handbook of environmental and resource economics.* Cheltenham: Edward Elgar.

von Moltke, K. (2001) *Whither MEAs? The role of international environmental management in the trade and environmental agenda.* Winnipeg: International Institute for Sustainable Development.

Young, O.R. (1994) *International governance.* Ithaca: Cornell University Press.

Chapter 29

ENVIRONMENTAL PRICING IN TRANSPORT

EDWARD CALTHROP and STEF PROOST
Catholic University of Leuven

1. Introduction

Transport activity is inextricably linked with environmental damage. Economists traditionally urge policy-makers to adopt pricing solutions, in particular taxes, to reduce environmental damage rather than quantity restrictions or standards. This chapter examines environmental pricing, defined broadly to include emission taxes, product taxes, and subsidies, and compares it to alternative approaches. We begin with a simple formal model to demonstrate the relative efficiency properties of pricing solutions, before highlighting some of the associated implementation problems. We then extend the scope and realism of the analysis by examining the choice between regulatory instruments in the presence of several market distortions. The basic case for environmental taxes, set at the correct level, is shown to remain.

It is impossible to cover all modes and all real-world case studies of pricing in this discussion. Rather, we illustrate our central point in the context of air pollution from car use. However, as we stress in the concluding section, the essential insight from the model applies to a whole range of environmental problems in the transport sector. A general introduction to the choice of regulatory instruments to tackle environmental damage can be found in Kolstad (1999).

2. Rationale for environmental taxes

Consider air pollution from a transport activity. Emissions can typically be reduced in two ways: through cleaner technology, which is supplied only at a higher resource cost, and through reducing the level of transport activity. As we shall see, one particular pricing instrument, a pollution tax, gives the correct incentive for efficient behavior with respect to both of these margins.

We illustrate ideas with a simple model. Assume a perfectly competitive car market where the cost of supplying a single car-kilometer (without pollution control equipment) is constant. We normalize this cost to zero – and hence all results below can be considered as net of the constant resource cost[a]. In the absence of pollution control, the monetary value of pollution damage per car-kilometer is assumed constant[b], and denoted by $d \in (0, 1)$. The quantity of pollution control per car-kilometer, denoted by $z \in [0, 1]$, is assumed continuous and is supplied at cost $(c/2)z^2$ per kilometer[c]. This parameterization implies that the marginal cost of abatement is rising: more sophisticated and costly techniques are required to further decrease pollution. Abatement can take various forms: catalytic converters, cleaner fuels, lower speed, etc. For ease, we assume $c = 1$. In the presence of pollution abatement, the pollution damage per kilometer is assumed to equal $d(1-z)$. Finally, assume the marginal benefit of a kilometer of car use is given by a linear 45° downward-sloping function: $1-x$, where x is the quantity of car-kilometers. Economists refer to this marginal benefit function as the inverse demand function. The demand function is then $x = 1 - p$, where p is the consumer price: a consumer chooses a level of car use such that the marginal benefit equal the marginal private cost, i.e. the price. This function is illustrated in Figure 1, where the price p^N generates a consumption $x = 1 - p^N \equiv y^N$.

In order to compare environmental pricing with other instruments we first analyze a benchmark solution where a benevolent government can control the amount of pollution control and the quantity of car use directly. This defines the "efficient outcome." Next we allow the car users to choose freely the number of car-kilometers and the degree of pollution abatement. The government can only control pollution indirectly: pricing instruments and technological standards can be used to alter driver behavior, which in turn alters the level of air pollution. An emissions tax – set at the correct level – results in drivers making choices that correspond to the efficient outcome. Other instruments typically fail.

2.1. Efficient outcome

Consider a benevolent government that is able to control directly the choice of pollution abatement, z, and the total number of kilometers driven, y. The objective function for the government is the total net benefit to society, i.e. the benefit of car use minus the costs to society. The total net benefit is the area under the marginal benefit curve in Figure 1 (the benefits of travel) gross of the environmental damage $(d(1-z))$ and the resource cost of using cleaner cars $(z^2/2)$:

---

[a]This assumption simplifies algebraic manipulations.
[b]We abstract from variations according to vehicle model or age, driving speed, cold start-ups, etc.
[c]To keep matters simple, we summarize from issues arising from car ownership and only focus on car use.

$$\int_0^y \left(1 - x - d(1-z) - \frac{z^2}{2}\right) dx. \tag{1}$$

Maximizing this objective with respect to the two control variables, z and y, gives rise to two first-order conditions[a]:

$$y: \quad y = 1 - d(1-z) - \frac{z^2}{2}, \tag{2}$$

$$z: \quad z = d.$$

Investment in pollution abatement equipment is optimal when the marginal cost of abatement, z, per kilometer equals the marginal benefit in reduced air pollution damage, d, per kilometer. Hence:

$$z^* = d. \tag{3}$$

The optimal degree of abatement is not necessarily 100%: the marginal cost of pollution abatement may be too high compared with the marginal damage avoided to justify a high degree of pollution abatement. Substituting equation (3) into the condition for kilometers driven reveals

$$y^* = 1 - d\left(1 - \frac{d}{z}\right). \tag{4}$$

We see that the degree of pollution abatement and the optimal volume of transport interact. Condition (4) states that, at the optimal number of kilometers, y^*, the marginal benefit of an additional kilometer, $1 - y^*$, equals the marginal cost of supplying pollution abatement to society, i.e. a resource cost of $d^2/2$ plus the remaining air pollution damage $d(1-d)$ per kilometer, which in total equals $d(1-d/2)$.

The choice of pollution abatement equipment minimizes the social cost of driving a kilometer. In the absence of any pollution abatement, the cost to society of a kilometer comprises the full air pollution damages d. But this exceeds the cost to society with optimal technology: $d(1-d/2)$. Therefore the optimal number of kilometers driven under optimal abatement technology, given by equation (4), is greater than that under zero abatement, $y(0) = 1 - d$, derived by setting $z = 0$ in condition (2).

2.2. Choice of instruments

In a market economy, the government cannot freely choose the two control variables. However, it may be able to decentralize the efficient outcome by using

---

[a] Given the assumptions made, the objective function is strictly concave, and hence the first-order conditions are also sufficient. We also assume an interior solution.

taxes or standards to alter the behavior of drivers and car producers. We consider three types of pricing instruments – an emissions tax, an emissions reduction subsidy, and a product (or per kilometer) tax – plus a non-pricing instrument (a technological standard). The government returns environmental tax revenues to consumers via a head tax[a] such that tax revenues are merely a transfer to government rather than a resource cost. As a benchmark, however, we begin with the case in which government does not intervene at all.

2.3. No intervention

Competition requires producers to supply at minimum cost. Production cost, given by $z^2/2$, is clearly minimized by setting $z^N = 0$, where the superscript N denotes no intervention. The consumer price per kilometer is equal[b] to $p^N = 0$. In choosing the number of kilometers to drive, a consumer maximises

$$\int_0^y (1 - x - p^N) dx \qquad (5)$$

with respect to y. Kilometers are consumed until the marginal benefit of a unit, $1 - y$, equals the consumer price: $y^N = 1 - p^N = 1 > y^*$.

In the absence of intervention, too many kilometers are consumed ($y^N > y^*$), and emissions per kilometer are too high ($z^N = 0 < z^*$). This corresponds to solution p^N, y^N in Figure 1.

2.4. Emissions tax

An emissions tax set equal to the marginal air pollution damages, d, per kilometer is sufficient to decentralize the efficient outcome, given by equations (3) and (4). First, consider the behavior of producers. We assume that producers pay an emissions tax proportional to the emission rate of the car. In a perfectly competitive market and with constant returns to scale, the additional costs are all passed on to consumers. In choosing a level of pollution abatement equipment to install in a car, a producer must balance the additional resource cost of supplying abatement against the reduction in tax payments. Formally, the problem to be solved is to choose z to minimize unit production cost:

---

[a] This amounts to assuming that there are no other tax distortions in the economy. See Section 4 for some discussion of the case in which this assumption is relaxed.
[b] Recall this is the price net of a fixed resource cost.

$$t(1-z)+\frac{z^2}{2}. \tag{6}$$

Using the superscript T to denote the presence of an emissions tax, the first-order condition requires that

$$z^T = t, \tag{7}$$

and thus, by setting $t = d$, the government ensures that the efficient level of pollution abatement is achieved, as given by equation (3). The producer price of a car-kilometer is therefore given by

$$\begin{aligned} p^T &= d(1-d)+\frac{d^2}{2} \\ &= d\left(1-\frac{d}{2}\right). \end{aligned} \tag{8}$$

Drivers consume kilometers until the marginal benefit equals the price, or

$$\begin{aligned} y^T &= 1 - p^T \\ &= 1 - d\left(1-\frac{d}{2}\right), \end{aligned} \tag{9}$$

where the second line follows from equation (8). Thus, the emissions tax results in the efficient number of kilometers driven, as given in equation (4). The consumer price is equal to the marginal social cost of a kilometer, measured for the optimal technology choice. This solution is illustrated in Figure 1 as solution y^T, p^T. The figure shows two shaded areas: one corresponding to the additional production cost of cars, due to cleaner technology, and the second to the charges for the remaining environmental damage, which equals the collected tax revenue.

2.5. Emissions subsidy

It is sometimes argued that a subsidy for cleaner equipment should be adopted. Clearly a subsidy for cleaner technology creates strong incentives for producers to adopt a higher level of abatement. However, as we now show, a subsidy reduces the price of travel below the marginal social cost, and thus induces consumers to drive too many kilometers.

First, consider the producers' problem. The level of abatement is chosen to minimize unit production costs:

$$\frac{z^2}{2} - sz. \tag{10}$$

Using the superscript S to denote the presence of an emission subsidy, the producer chooses a level of pollution abatement equipment,

$$z^S = s, \tag{11}$$

and hence, by setting $s = d$, the government can induce the efficient level of abatement in equation (3). Now consider the consumers' problem. As with a tax, consumers choose demand such that the marginal benefit of an additional kilometer, $1-y$, is equal to the price, p^S. Crucially, however, the presence of the subsidy reduces the consumer price compared with a tax. Substituting equation (11) into expression (10) gives the consumer price as:

$$p^S = \frac{d^2}{2} - d^2$$
$$= -\frac{d^2}{2}. \tag{12}$$

The consumer price is negative[a] – and hence the optimal number of kilometers is chosen such that

$$y^S = 1 + \frac{d^2}{2} > y^*. \tag{13}$$

While the emissions subsidy induces an efficient level of investment in pollution abatement, it also induces an excessive number of kilometers to be driven. Although a better performing subsidy can be derived[b], the basic inefficiency remains: a subsidy reduces the consumer price of car use and thus gives rise to too high a volume of transport activity.

2.6. A product tax (or kilometer tax)

A product tax is a tax on each unit of the product independent of the production technology. In our setting this corresponds to a tax per car-kilometer independent of the level of pollution abatement. Assume that the government sets the product

---

[a] Recall that this price is net of any reference resource cost. Indeed, in Figure 1, we assume a strictly positive resource cost.

[b] The optimal subsidy is derived by maximizing the net benefit function (1) subject to the constraints on the level of abatement investment given by equation (11) and on the demand for kilometers via the price function (12). Substituting these constraints gives a problem in s only. The solution, however, is not particularly transparent, although clearly the optimal level lies between 0 and d. The same point applies to the product tax and the technology standard: we use arbitrary, though policy-relevant, levels of instruments to illustrate points that also apply to optimized levels.

tax at marginal air pollution damage, i.e. $t = d$. Producers have no incentive to invest in abatement and therefore set $z^P = 0$ – where the superscript P denotes the presence of the product tax. Consumers choose the level of demand such that marginal benefit, $1-y$, equals the consumer price, p^P. But the consumer price is given by $p^P = t = d$, and hence demand is given by

$$y^P = 1 - d < y^*. \tag{14}$$

The product tax can be set to induce drivers to choose the optimal number of kilometers, given a suboptimal level of pollution abatement. This is seen from condition (2), where $y(0) = 1 - d$. A product tax gives poor incentives to adopt efficient technology choices.

2.7. Technological standard

Finally, we consider a non-pricing instrument – a technological standard. Assume that the government decrees that cars must be manufactured with $z = d$. At this level, the marginal cost of pollution control equals the benefit of reduced air pollution. Producers comply, and charge the price $p^{ST} = d^2/2$. Consumers drive until the marginal benefit of a trip equals the consumer price, giving

$$y^{ST} = 1 - \frac{d^2}{2} > y^*. \tag{15}$$

The level of the technological standard is set optimally – and the efficient level of abatement contained in condition (2) is achieved. However, the standard does not achieve the efficient volume of transport: $y^{ST} > y^*$. The consumer price only reflects the resource cost of the standard and not the marginal air pollution damage. As a result, car use remains underpriced, compared with the optimum, and excessive kilometers are driven.

2.8. Comparing instruments

The impact of instruments is compared in Figure 1. Disregarding all implementation costs, an emissions tax (set at marginal external damage, d) is sufficient to decentralize the efficient outcome. All other instruments, both pricing and non-pricing, are inherently inefficient, or second best.

It is natural to rank different policy instruments in terms of their degree of inefficiency. A comparison of instruments can be done on the basis of the benefit function given by expression (1). Indeed, it is clear that the technology standard is

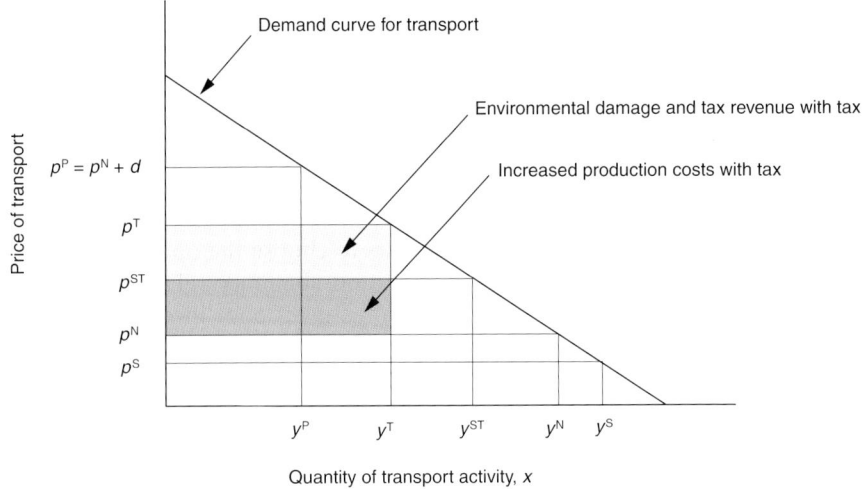

Figure 1. Summary of instruments.

more efficient than an emissions subsidy[a]: both result in the same level of abatement, whilst the technology standard distorts demand less than the subsidy. However, the relative efficiency of the product tax is less straightforward to show, and hence, we provide numerical results in Table 1 based – in a somewhat "back-of-the-envelope" manner – on the European urban car market[b].

We assume that abatement technology is relatively cheap. Under efficient policy, and assuming a central case of $d = 0.1$, nearly 90% of emissions are optimally abated. Therefore, as long as an instrument induces car producers to adopt such a high level of abatement, there is little welfare loss from failing to decentralize the optimal number of kilometers. The technology standard, for instance, requires 90% of emissions to be abated. While the consumer price reflects the resource cost of meeting the standard, it fails to charge for air pollution damage. With a 90% reduction in emissions, and $d = 0.1$, air pollution damage is comparatively small. Thus the technology standard performs very well, almost as efficiently as the emissions tax – indeed, it is clear from Figure 1 that if

---

[a] Again, this refers only to the levels of instruments chosen in our example. Our analysis says nothing about the relative ranking of optimally set second-best instruments.

[b] The welfare assessment is computed from expression (1). In contrast to the text, we take a value of c in the cost function for abatement as 0.11. We vary the value of air pollution damage from 0.05 to 0.15. The optimal quantity of abatement is given by $z = d/c$, which assuming $d = 0.1$ and $c = 0.11$ gives z equal to 0.9. It is thought that EU standards have abated as much as 90% of air pollution, disregarding carbon dioxide (European Conference of Ministers of Transport, 2001).

Table 1
Comparison of the efficiency of instruments

	Relative efficiency of instrument (tax = 100)		
	$d = 0.05$	$d = 0.1$	$d = 0.15$
Emission subsidy	93	89	61
Product tax	11	11	10
Technology standard	97	99	99

environmental damage is small, p^{ST} is only slightly smaller than p^T, and the resulting equilibrium is close to optimal. In these circumstances the subsidy is also relatively efficient: it too results in a 90% reduction in emissions, although, by reducing the consumer price, the final distortion on quantity of kilometers driven is higher than the standard. Indeed, the subsidy becomes relatively less efficient as the magnitude of the air pollution damage increases (compare $d = 0.15$ with $d = 0.05$). The relative efficiency of these instruments stands in stark contrast to a product tax. This instrument gives no incentive for installing pollution abatement equipment. The instrument performs badly in contrast to the others, resulting in only a mere 11% of the efficiency gains of the tax.

Our model is extremely simple and is somewhat biased against the use of pollution taxes. Pollution taxes, in general, perform best when there is a large variation in pollution reduction costs, whereas we analyze the case with homogeneous polluters. A more realistic model would include heterogeneity in the car stock: cars with different ages and odometer readings, different driving styles, etc. In such a model, the advantage of pollution taxes over standards would be increased because taxes reduce pollution at minimal cost by equating the marginal emission reduction costs over polluters. A standard (that does not discriminate over polluters) cannot achieve this. One alternative to a standard is a system of tradable permits, which combines the properties of a pollution tax and a standard. For instance, a cap can be set on the total emissions of pollution, while manufacturers trade for rights to emit. Marginal emission reduction costs are equated between manufacturers.

One final point regarding standards. We have assumed that pollution abatement technology is fixed and known by all parties. But in the transport sector, where there has been rapid technological progress, this is debatable. Governments may be tempted to try to force technology – that is, set standards without knowing the feasibility or the cost of the measure. Examples include the CAFE standards in the USA, the attempt by the European Commission to set fuel consumption at 5 liters per 100 km for all new cars in 2005, the use in California of standards to achieve a market share of 5% for zero-emission cars (by 2002), or the attempt in 1970 by the US government to reduce emissions by 90% by 1975. In each case the regulator had to accept less ambitious targets. This is not surprising. Yao (1988) studies this problem in a two-period setting where the industry being regulated has more information on the effectiveness of research and development efforts. The regulator sets a standard for the first period, observes how difficult it is for the industry to comply, and then sets a further standard in the second period. The industry fears a ratchet effect: if they comply in the first period, they risk even stricter regulation in the second. It is optimal for the industry to under-invest in research and development in the first period in order to keep costs high.

3. Implementation issues

Emissions taxes seems an attractive option for governments. However, our model is in many respects too simplistic. We highlight two issues that may complicate policy advice: first, the technology for taxing on the basis of exhaust pipe emissions is unavailable, and second, even if it were, the damage from emissions is often site- and time-specific.

3.1. Unavailability of emissions tax

Recent technological advances in the measurement of vehicle emissions may justify consideration of an emission tax (Harrington et al., 1994). However, according to Fullerton and West (2002), the technology is currently neither cost-effective nor reliable in the sense that it cannot be tampered with by the owner. Policy-makers must choose between combinations of imperfect instruments in a bid to mimic the efficient but unavailable tax on emissions. In a simple setting, combining instruments may still give the efficient outcome. For instance, in our model, combining a technology standard ($z = d$) with a product tax ($t = d(1 - d)$) perfectly mimics the efficient outcome[a] of the emissions tax. The policy maker may also be able to tax inputs to the production of emissions: for instance, taxing fuels (gasoline, diesel) or vehicles.

Fullerton and West (2000) investigate this issue in a richer model than ours. Drivers choose the size of vehicle to buy, the amount of abatement technology to install, as well as the quantity and environmental quality of the fuel. These authors conclude that combinations of instruments (such as a tax on gasoline, a subsidy to abatement technology, plus a tax on engine size) can only perfectly mimic the

---

[a]To see this, note that condition (3) is directly fulfilled, while the price of car use is given by $p = d(1 - d) + d^2/2$, which, after simple manipulation, gives condition (4).

absent emissions tax in the restrictive case of identical individuals (or with individual-specific tax rates). In the realistic setting of heterogeneous consumers and uniform tax rates, combinations of instruments are less efficient that an emissions tax. In Fullerton and West (2000), the authors use data from the 1994 US Consumer Expenditure Survey to calculate that an optimal combination of taxes on gasoline, car size, and car age can achieve 71% of the welfare gain of the missing emissions tax. A gasoline tax alone attains 62%. Note that the authors assume only one externality – air pollution: see our comments on multiple distortions below.

Our model has abstracted from issues of heterogeneous car stock. Yet given strict standards for new vehicles, emission rates from older vehicles can be some ten times higher than from new ones. Scrapping policies ("cash for clunkers") appear – at least at first sight – an attractive means to tax older vehicles. But to determine the cost-effectiveness of such a policy it is first necessary to construct the supply curve of emission reduction. Hahn (1995) analyzes the various problems surrounding constructing this function. In particular, he highlights a moral hazard problem: only the worst cars get scrapped, which are hardly used anyway. Scrappage policies are likely to be effective only for a short period of time in urban areas, as, over time, the difference between emissions of old and new cars is likely to decrease. Moreover, better inspection and maintenance of cars (e.g. via on-board diagnostics) may strongly reduce the cost-effectiveness of scrappage policies. Alberini et al. (1995) examine empirically the participation rates in a scrappage scheme.

3.2. Variability in air pollution damage

We have assumed a constant marginal damage from air pollution, d. But this damage is likely to be very site- and time-specific, depending strongly on local microclimatic features and population density. For instance, the formation of tropospheric ozone from emissions depends strongly on the presence of sunlight, temperature, and the wind direction. Recent studies have shown that the same weight of particulate matter can be ten times more damaging when emitted in central Paris than in rural France (Bickel et al., 1997).

Kolstad (1987) examines the use of uniform taxes when damage is variable. The optimal uniform tax is shown to depend on the relative slopes of the marginal abatement cost curve and the marginal damage curves. Uniform taxes can, in general, be either more or less efficient than a standard. However, a uniform emission fee does better to the extent that the marginal damage curves are relatively flat and the marginal cost function is relatively steep. There is no particular reason why this should be the case for transport markets. Indeed, applying this general theory to transport markets seems an interesting topic for future research.

4. Comparison with multiple distortions

4.1. Road congestion and air pollution

We have thus far focused on a single type of environmental damage – air pollution. However, most policies designed to tackle air pollution have an additional impact on other distortions within the transport market, such as congestion, noise damage, or accidents. Welfare analysis should therefore measure the impact of policy measures on a range of distortions rather than congestion or air pollution alone.

In the urban car market, congestion is thought to be empirically the most significant external cost, at least in the peak travel period. Table 2 reproduces estimates of the peak-period external cost of car use in Brussels for 2005 under current policies. Diesel cars have significantly higher air pollution costs than gasoline cars: this is due to emissions of small particulate matter, which have been linked to various human health problems.

Our simple model can be extended to show how pricing policy should be adjusted to take account of congestion. Assume that the average time to travel a kilometer depends on total demand (y) in a smoothly convex fashion – to make things easy, assume a functional form, so that the time cost per kilometer is equal to y^2. The net benefit of transport can be adapted from expression (1) to read

$$\int_0^y \left(1 - x - d(1-z) - \frac{z^2}{2} - y^2\right) dx. \tag{16}$$

Maximizing this expression with respect to the two available instruments shows that the efficient outcome is given by $z^* = d$, as in expression (3), while the optimal quantity is given by the implicit expression $y^* = 1 - d(1 - d/2) - 3y^{*2}$. The marginal benefit of a trip, $1 - y$, equals the marginal social cost, namely the resource cost of supplying the abatement technology, the cost of the remaining air pollution damage and the congestion cost. This last element differentiates the optimal quantity with expression (4). A road toll equal to the air pollution damage plus the external congestion cost – in this case $2y^2$ decentralizes the efficient outcome perfectly[a]. Other instruments are less successful – for instance, the technology standard has no impact on congestion levels.

Proost and Van Dender (2001) examine the welfare gains from adopting different types of regulation, including both pricing measures and technology standards. This is done on the basis of a partial equilibrium model (TRENEN) of some 20 transport markets, calibrated to Brussels in 2005. These results are summarized in Table 3.

---

[a]The total time costs equal y^3 and thus the marginal cost of a kilometer equals $3y^2$. The marginal external congestion cost is therefore equal to the marginal cost $3y^2$ minus the private cost per kilometer, y^2, or $2y^2$.

Table 2
External costs (euros/v-km) from urban car use in Brussels

	Gasoline		Diesel	
	Peak	Off-peak	Peak	Off-peak
Congestion	1.856	0.003	1.856	0.003
Air pollution	0.004	0.004	0.042	0.026
Accidents	0.033	0.033	0.033	0.033
Noise	0.002	0.008	0.002	0.008
Total	1.895	0.047	1.932	0.068
Current tax	0.12	0.11	0.08	0.07

Source: Proost and Van Dender (2001).

Table 3
Ranking efficiency of different instruments

Policy-choice	% of possible welfare gain
Time varying cordon-pricing	52
Time invariant parking charges	30
Increased fuel tax	5
Higher technology standard	0
Subsidized abatement equipment	−2

Source: Proost and Van Dender (2001).

A time-varying cordon pricing scheme can – in a somewhat blunt manner – impose both a congestion charge and an emissions tax. It is therefore relatively efficient – achieving some 52% of the welfare gains of a perfect charging system. Parking charges are assumed invariant with time, and thus perform less well. A fuel tax gives some incentive for increasing the fuel efficiency of vehicles, but gives no incentive to alter the time of travel. The authors also consider a number of common policies targeted at air pollution. A higher technology standard (complying with Auto-Oil Scenario III[a]) results in a negligible loss in welfare, while subsidising pollution abatement equipment results in a small loss in welfare.

---

[a]Under this scenario, emissions reductions for gasoline cars in 2005 equal 65% of 1996 levels for nitrogen oxides and volatile organic compounds, and 45% for carbon monoxide. The equivalent figures for diesel cars are 30% and 50%. In addition, particulate matter is reduced by 50%. See Appendix C in Proost and Van Dender (2001) for further details.

The results of Table 3 show that the ranking of instruments in the presence of multiple distortions can differ from that in the presence of a single distortion – air pollution – in Table 2. The fuel tax acts broadly as a product tax. When considering air pollution alone, the product tax performed relatively badly, as it resulted in too few kilometers being driven. In the presence of congestion (or other distortions), this may be beneficial. Hence in Table 3 the fuel tax is more efficient than the technology standard or the emissions subsidy, neither of which help alleviate congestion[a].

Several authors have considered the welfare effect of congestion taxes in the presence of multiple distortions (congestion, air pollution, accidents, etc.). Recent examples include Parry and Bento (2002a) and Verhoef (2002), where the latter considers the spatial impact of various policies.

4.2. Interactions between transport markets and distorted labor markets

Policy reform may have impacts outside the transport sector. For instance, labor taxes distort the economy by subsidizing leisure. Reforming the transport market, for example by introducing a commuting tax, may further exacerbate the labor market distortion. The general point stressed in the literature is that different instruments are likely, *a priori*, to exacerbate labor market distortions to a differing extent. Choices of both the level and type of instrument need to account for these impacts (Goulder et al., 1997, 1999; Fullerton and Metcalf, 2001). In a transport context, Mayeres and Proost (1997, 2001) examine optimal congestion taxes, and the reform of congestion taxes, in the presence of a distorted economy.

This literature also highlights that, in order to evaluate a particular policy, such as an air pollution tax, the analyst needs to consider how the revenue is spent. Intuitively, if the revenue from the tax is used to reduce distortive labor taxes, the net impact on the magnitude of the labor market distortion is smaller than if the revenue is handed back in a lump-sum manner. Parry and Bento (2001b) examine the welfare impact of a marginal increase in the congestion tax on peak-period urban traffic. They find that any positive tax on congestion is welfare reducing if the tax revenue is returned lump-sum. In contrast, a positive tax can increase welfare when used to reduce labor taxes.

---

[a]It is also important to notice that Table 2 compares instruments to reduce air pollution assuming a baseline of zero abatement. In contrast, Table 3 has a baseline of current EU abatement standards for new vehicles, which, as referred to earlier, are thought to have reduced emissions by up to 90%. It is perhaps not surprising, therefore, that further emissions reductions via a higher technological standard in Table 3 reduce welfare.

4.3. Equity impacts and institutional issues

Our simple model in Section 2 abstracts from distributional issues by assuming identical consumers. Our conclusions relate only to the efficiency properties of different instruments. While this is clearly important, efficiency concerns cannot, in general, be separated from equity issues. Indeed, the very presence of a labor market tax in our previous section reflects equity concerns. There are several important distributional aspects to any policy reform. First, how are different groups in society affected by the introduction of the environmental tax or technological standard? Second, who benefits from the cleaner environment? Third, if the reform increases government revenues, who benefits from the recycling of the revenue? Policy evaluation requires detailed general equilibrium modeling to assess these effects.

Mayeres and Proost (1997) use an applied general equilibrium model to analyze optimal road tolls with five types of consumer, differing in labor productivity. The model is calibrated to the Belgian economy. The optimal level of the road toll is shown not to depend strongly on distributional concerns. This is because the initial tax system is assumed to pursue equity objectives in a more or less optimal way. However, the authors do not consider other instruments (subsidies, technological standards, a kilometer tax).

The model of Section 2 also assumes that the government is a benevolent, welfare-maximizing institution. Recent economic literature has relaxed this assumption. Politicians' policy choices may be self-serving: maximizing the probability of being re-elected, the revenues from a policy, or minimizing the workload for the bureaucracy. Alternatively, a transport division may act to meet some *ad hoc* criterion: maximizing the number of trips while keeping the average trip time or emissions below a certain level. Equally, local government may act to maximize welfare of local residents rather than the community as a whole. Environmental taxes may be set without taking into account effects on non-local consumers. However, non-locals may provide an attractive source of tax revenue for the local community. We are not aware of research results on trying to explain government transport policy. However this seems a fruitful line of inquiry.

5. Conclusions

Economic theory makes a compelling case for using taxes to control the environmental side-effects of transportation. We have included this point in the debate over the control of air pollution from vehicles in Europe. Assuming cheap abatement technology and relatively small pollution damage, our numerical illustration stresses that instruments that give correct incentives for adopting pollution control equipment (taxes, subsidies, or technological standards) perform significantly better than those which do not (the kilometer tax). The use of technological standards in Europe may have been a relatively efficient policy. The same theory applies when trying to solve both pollution and congestion problems. Pricing solutions (cordon charges or parking charges) perform better than a kilometer tax or additional abatement standards.

The theory is sufficiently flexible that it applies to many other environmental issues in the transport sector. Take the case of airport noise damage. This can be reduced by installing abatement technology on planes (at higher resource cost) and by reducing the amount of air travel. This mirrors our air pollution problem of Section 2. Simple relabeling of our model allows us to conclude that a noise tax gives correct incentives to invest in quieter aircraft and to reduce air travel. Depending on the costs of abatement and the magnitude of the damage, other pricing solutions (subsidies to abate, product tax on airline travel, or technological standards) may perform relatively well or poorly in comparison with the efficient tax.

We have also stressed limitations in the theory. Taxing emissions may be difficult to implement, while heterogeneity in damages may complicate the choice of instrument. In addition, governments often try to correct several distortions with one instrument (e.g. air pollution and congestion and labor market distortions). Careful analysis is required, often needing to account for effects outside of the transport sector. As is well understood from the theory of the second best, helping matters with respect to one distortion may produce adverse effects elsewhere.

Finally, we stress the need for a positive theory of transport policy. Despite clear efficiency advantages, environmental taxes are rarely adopted in the transport sector. This seems strange: if the efficiency gains are waiting to be enjoyed, why do politicians so rarely seem to pursue them?

Acknowledgements

Edward Calthrop is funded by grant G.0220.01 from the Funds for Scientific Research – Flanders (Belgium).

References

Alberini, A., W. Harrington and V. McConnell (1995) "Determinants of participation in accelerated vehicle retirement programs," *RAND Journal of Economics*, 26:93–112.
Bickel, P., S. Schmid, W. Krewitt and R. Friedrich, eds (1997) *External costs of transport in ExternE*. Final Report. Stuttgart: IER.
European Conference of Ministers of Transport (2001) *Vehicle emission reductions*. Paris: OECD/ECMT.
Fullerton, D. and G. Metcalf (2001) "Environmental controls, scarcity rents, and pre-existing distortions," *Journal of Public Economics*, 80:249–267.

Fullerton, D. and S. West (2000) *Tax and subsidy combinations for the control of car pollution*. NBER Working Paper No. 7774. Cambridge: National Bureau of Economic Research.

Fullerton, D. and S. West (2002) "Can taxes on cars and on gasoline mimic an unavailable tax on emissions?" *Journal of Environmental Economics and Management*, 43:135–157.

Goulder, L.H., I.W.H. Parry and D. Burtraw (1997) "Revenue-raising versus other approaches to environmental protection: the critical significance of pre-existing tax distortions," *RAND Journal of Economics*, 28:708–731.

Goulder, L.H., I.W.H. Parry, R.C. Williams and D. Burtraw (1999) "The cost-effectiveness of alternative instruments for environmental protection in a second-best setting," *Journal of Public Economics*, 72:329–360.

Hahn, R.W. (1995) "An economic analysis of scrappage," *RAND Journal of Economics*, 26:222–242.

Harrington, W., M. Walls and V. McConnell (1994) *Shifting gears: new directions for cars and clean air.* Discussion Paper 94-26-REV. Washington, DC: Resources for the Future.

Kolstad, C. (1987) "Uniformity vs. differentiation in regulation externalities," *Journal of Environmental Economics and Management*, 14:386–399.

Kolstad, C. (1999) *Environmental economics*. Oxford: Oxford University Press.

Parry, I.W.H. and A. Bento (2002a) "Estimating the welfare effects of congestion taxes: the critical importance of other distortions within the transport system," *Journal of Urban Economics*, 51:339–366.

Parry, I.W.H. and A. Bento (2002b) "Revenue-recycling and the welfare effects of road pricing," *Scandinavian Journal of Economics*, 103:645–671.

Mayeres, I. and S. Proost (1997) "Optimal tax and public investment rules for congestion type of externalities," *Scandinavian Journal of Economics*, 99:261–279.

Mayeres, I and S. Proost (2001) "Marginal tax reform, externalities and income distribution," *Journal of Public Economics*, 79:343–363.

Proost, S. and K. Van Dender (2001) "The welfare impacts of alternative policies to address atmospheric pollution in urban road transport," *Regional Science and Urban Economics*, 31:383–411.

Verhoef, E.T. (2002) "Second-best congestion pricing in general static transportation networks with elastic demands," *Regional Science and Urban Economics*, 32:281–310.

Yao, D.A. (1988) "Strategic responses to automobile emissions control: a game-theoretic analysis," *Journal of Environmental Economics and Management*, 15:419–438.

Chapter 30

PLANNING FOR SUSTAINABLE ENVIRONMENTAL FUTURES

DAVID GILLINGWATER and STEPHEN ISON
Loughborough University

1. Introduction

Planning for sustainable environmental futures cannot be treated in isolation from the planning process of which it is a part. Here, the planning process is defined as the statutory system that regulates the development process which brings forward proposals for the use and development of land (Rydin, 1998). The aim of this chapter is to identify the principles under which planners manage the development process, how those principles reflect the adoption of sustainable development, and, through the medium of selected transport-related case studies, explore attempts to deliver sustainable environmental futures.

This form of planning, often referred to as land use or physical planning, is a characteristic of all nation states that claim to pursue principles of liberal democracy through a representative government. In this sense, land use planning is an integral, if contested, feature of advanced capitalist societies where the private ownership of land is just one, albeit important, attribute of property rights and the privatized ownership of socially produced wealth. Although the private ownership of land is a characteristic of advanced capitalist societies, the rights over what an owner can do with it are heavily circumscribed – indeed, the rights to the use and development of land are effectively owned by the state. As a consequence, all proposals for development require the permission of the state. In theory this is a transfer of private property rights to the state; in practice, although the state retains ownership, the requirement to seek permission for development is subject to statutory relaxations that may and do change from time to time.

2. Planning and sustainable development – principles

With regards to the principles that underpin the operation of the planning system, the principles of sustainable development are recent additions (Gibbs et al., 1998;

Royal Commission on Environmental Pollution, 2001). For example, in the UK and elsewhere the statutory planning system has been in operation for well over 50 years, whereas its preoccupation with sustainable development has only been a feature of the last decade (Hall, 1995; UK Department of the Environment, Transport and the Regions, 1998a). This partly explains the initial reluctance of the planning profession to embrace the concept of sustainability: for many, they could see nothing other than a new name and some interesting terminology; for a few, it was seen as a threat to their professional status.

So what are these guiding principles? For as long as the statutory planning system has been in existence the key problem has been urban growth and its containment – how best to reduce the apparently inexorable pressures for suburbanization coupled with how best to protect and renew existing and aging urban centers (Rydin, 1998). In practice, this became translated into a set of trade-offs between the costs and benefits of different types of urban form: should new urban development be concentrated in and around existing urban areas (a concentration strategy) or dispersed to smaller or even new settlements between existing urban areas (a dispersal strategy)? In addition, it raised the question as to who had the right to make the judgment: the private interest of the developer promoting the development or the regulator wanting to control the outcome in the public interest? Whereas the commercial, market-driven pressures for development, particularly new residential development, were essentially for suburban type development, it was long recognized that the social and environmental costs of such an outcome could be significant – no more so than in the implications for travel and transport and the use of and dependence on the car. For the planning system, a more desirable outcome would be for more concentrated forms of development linked to public transport corridors. In others words, two diametrically opposed views of what would be a preferred solution – one reflecting the preferences of private developers, the other the professional preferences of the regulators of land use empowered by statute.

Statutory planning systems are to be found embedded in the very structure of government – at both the central and the local level. The center's primary responsibility is to determine policy nationally, while the local level of government is primarily responsible for implementing that policy, typically through agreed projects and programs. The planning system is thus a clear example of "center-local relations" whereby central government sets the policy ground rules and attaches resources to them for their implementation, and the separately elected local level of government is dependent on those resources for delivering those projects and programs within those agreed ground rules. Transport and environmental policies are an integral part of this delivery process (Banister, 2002).

Within this complex of center-local relations, it is at the local level where the planning system is most visible and where it is seen to wield most power and influence over the outcome of planning applications. At this level the planning system is made up of three separate and contrasting but integrated functions. The first function is the policy function – here, national planning policy is translated into policy at the local level (local here being defined as any level of government that is subnational). It is essentially a proactive and positive function. The aim of this function is to take a long-term view of the future development of an area, to identify a range of appropriate policies for the use and development of land and to suggest where key developments should take place. These policies are enshrined in statutory documents called Development Plans. Once approved, these are legal documents, and carry significant statutory authority. Typically, these Development Plans will be one or more of three main types: (1) policy documents that take a long-term strategic view of an area (typically 15–20 year time horizons over a range of key strategic land uses including housing, industry, commercial activities, transport, and, most importantly, the interactions between them); (2) policy documents that take a shorter-term and more detailed view geographically of an area (typically 5–10 year time horizons with an emphasis on providing a framework to bring forward specific development proposals in a coordinated way); and/or (3) policy documents that combine both strategic policy with shorter-term implementation focused policy.

In addition, there are a range of policy-oriented supporting documents often referred to as "supplementary planning guidance." These are intended to provide either further support for development policies and/or strong guidance in their own right. It is here where planning policy formulated at the center or national level finds its way into local decision-making policy documents such as Development Plans. These typically include, in the UK, case the 25 Planning Policy Guidance Notes (PPGs) produced by central government: for example, PPG1 sets down the basic principles of the statutory planning system whereas PPG13 specifically addresses policy issues on transport and land use. A further example is the requirement for the preparation of annual Local Transport Plans (LTPs), documents that are not specifically part of the Development Plans function but which supplement it and must demonstrate that they integrate with it.

The principal purpose of these policy documents is to provide information to those outside of the planning system on what is likely to be acceptable development in terms of land use, location, scale, and timing. In addition, these Development Plans are intended to help those inside the planning system with responsibility for managing the second function – control.

This control function, often referred to as development control, is responsible for accepting and processing applications for development. It is essentially a reactive function, and is that part of the planning system which more often than not is in the public eye. The aim of this function is to make decisions on applications for development – decisions that can be positive (planning permission is granted), negative (planning permission is refused), or positive/negative (planning permission is granted subject to certain conditions being met prior to, during, and/or after development takes place). All applications need to be determined on what are called "planning grounds" – it must be demonstrated that decisions have been based on policies which can be found in a statutory Development Plan and/or have been supported by supplementary planning guidance and/or reflect the implementation of national planning policy guidance.

The third function is the compensation and betterment function. In terms of compensation, any applicant aggrieved by a decision can seek financial reparation – so long as it can be demonstrated that the decision was made on grounds contrary to sound planning practice or as a result of administrative error. In terms of betterment, the value of land may increase dramatically as a result of a planning decision (e.g. zoning land currently used for agriculture for new housing development in the next 10 years); alternatively, the granting of planning permission may incur large costs for a local authority (e.g. approving an application for a large retail outlet may require major investment in redesigning a road junction). In both cases the owner of the land in question is reaping a potentially large windfall for no investment or without incurring the full cost of their development proposal. Betterment is an attempt to extract for community benefit some of the surplus value created as a result of an administrative decision taken in the "public interest." In the case of land zoned for housing, the scale of development may require a new primary school or a "park-and-ride" facility – in which case the community benefit would require a "planning obligation" from the developer to ensure that facilities were provided in their development; in the case of the need for a redesigned road junction, the developer would agree to a "planning obligation" to pay for all or some of the costs incurred.

It is interesting to note at this stage that this structuring of the statutory planning system is one that has been in place for decades – it is the one that is also currently in place and which will arguably be in place for the foreseeable future (Blowers and Evans, 1997). Note also that there has been no specific reference to the requirements of or need to incorporate the concept or articulation of sustainable development let alone sustainable environmental futures. On reflection, this is not surprising since the account thus far has focused on structures and processes. If we now examine the substance of current planning policy, we can identify what may be a significant change of direction in favor of sustainability-type arguments and their application.

Development Plans have tended to share a common methodology and organization: first, there is an account of the way the locality fits within its regional and national context together with a recognition of the need to work within and embrace current national planning policies and aspirations in planning its future; second, there is an attempt to catalogue the locality's problems and issues based on an in-depth review of empirical evidence and forecasts based on likely "best guess" future trends; third, a statement of generic aims and sectoral objectives for the locality's future will be presented against which future policies should be judged; fourth, a select number of alternative development strategies are presented and evaluated against the aims and objectives and in light of the "best guess" forecasts and likely level of resources to be made available over the period of the plan; fifth, a preferred selection of policies is established and justified together with an accompanying diagrammatic or map-based plan; and, finally, proposals for monitoring and updating the plan will be presented.

Running throughout a Development Plan will be a presumption in favor of applying conventional planning principles, including the containment of urban growth, the need to reduce pressures for suburbanization, and the protection and regeneration of existing and aging urban centers. In recent years, however, there has been a noticeable shift toward more sustainable environmental futures in three directions:

- there is now a clear recognition in the statements of generic aims and sectoral objectives of the need to embrace the principles of sustainable development;
- there is a recognition that Development Plans are no longer designed to meet unconstrained forecasts of future levels of activity, especially in respect of accommodating traffic and transport growth;
- a belated recognition that spatial strategies based on either concentration of land uses or their dispersal are too narrow in conception and need to embrace the incorporation of one or more of new free-standing settlements, brown field developments, and/or conservation strategies.

Underlying all three developments is the recognition that an over-reliance on a "predict-and-provide" approach to the planning process, dependent on public sector-led investment, is no longer appropriate; what is required is to devise development strategies that are predicated on making better use of the resources already in place or which can be anticipated – particularly from the private sector and in partnership with the private sector.

In many of the "best practice" Development Plans currently in place, there has been a distinct shift in emphasis away from the traditional tried-and-tested approach, based on establishing trade-offs between short-run private interests/ benefits and longer-term social consequences/costs through the development of strategic policies for land use change, toward a recognition that a Development Plan should reflect trade-offs between what are seen as short-run quality of life issues (such as the need to increase the number of car-parking spaces) and longer-term global environmental concerns (e.g. energy use and contributions to climate change).

An early and particularly good example of this approach is to be found in the review by one particular local authority in the UK – Nottinghamshire County Council – of its long-term strategic Development Plan. In this statutory document, published in 1993, a whole section is devoted to a discussion of sustainability and strategic planning issues as they pertain to Nottinghamshire (a large and industrially diverse area in the English East Midlands), and a set of five principles developed against which its strategic policies for a sustainable environmental future would need to be assessed. These included: the development of sustainability policies based on the principle of equity or fairness; the prospect of better and healthier lives for local people; protecting the environment, together with the conservation of non-renewable resources; developing a sustainable transport policy so as to reduce the need to travel and encourage travel by means other than the car; and, finally, adoption of the "precautionary principle" – whereby if there are significant risks of damage to the environment from a development proposal, then the benefit of the doubt should be given to the environment.

An interesting and particularly innovative feature of this statutory Development Plan review was the way in which transport and energy use were identified as important criteria to evaluate the location and scale of any new development proposal. It is worth quoting at length from the review (Nottinghamshire County Council, 1993):

> There is no ideal size and shape for an energy-efficient settlement. It is normally identified by a compact development form (ie, moderately high densities) and by a relatively low physical separation of activities (especially a clustering of employment and services) in order to reduce space heating and transport energy requirements. Given this context, it is appropriate for local planning authorities to pursue policies that:
>
> (a) discourage low density development (especially residential);
> (b) promote some degree of concentration of principal employment activities and community facilities (in both central and suburban locations);
> (c) ensure that new development (at moderate or high densities) is well related to established or convenient public transport routes;
> (d) encourage energy-sensitive siting, orientation and layout of new development, particularly in order to allow future energy-saving technologies to be accommodated.
>
> It is anticipated that each policy area can be expanded in local plans to provide a specific framework for development control decisions that would apply not only to green field developments, but also to redevelopment and infilling within existing settlements.

These policy frameworks are light years away from what went before, couched as they were with the aim of promoting economic development while protecting and enhancing the environment. What has brought about this shift in emphasis, and why?

3. Planning sustainable environmental futures

There can be no doubt that for most of the last two decades planning was seen as an encumbrance on an overburdened economy, a major barrier to innovation and market-led solutions to development, a pernicious influence on competition (Blowers and Evans, 1997; Banister, 2002). Throughout the western world there were concerted attempts to reduce the role and influence of the statutory planning system, nowhere more so than in the UK. But as Owens and Cowell (2002) note, much as neo-liberalizing governments such as the UK tried to reduce its significance, it became clear that both government and the development industry needed the statutory planning system as much as the planning system needed the development industry. Three reasons appear to account for this change in political commitment: first, the gradual percolation, recognition, and political impact of the UN's World Commission on Environment and Development report, *Our Common Inheritance*, published in 1987 (the "Brundtland Report") combined with the political commitment this generated for the follow-up UN Conference on Environment and Development in 1992 – the "Rio Earth Summit" – and acceptance of the Rio Declaration's principles; second, although the neo-liberal project of market-led development dominated national agendas, it was not nearly so strongly embraced either at the local level by locally elected local governments (Banister, 2002) or by national independent advisory bodies (Royal Commission on Environmental Pollution, 1994); and, third, the explicit move toward a more positive, future-oriented and proactive (in policy terms) "plan-led" and locally driven planning system promoted at the European level through the EU's 5th Environmental Action Plan, *Towards Sustainability* (European Commission, 1992), and the adoption of the *European Spatial Development Perspective* (ESDP) (UK Department of the Environment, Transport and the Regions, 1999). In fact, it is possible to see a link between these three policy drivers.

Having signed up to the Rio Declaration, the UK government had to demonstrate that they were addressing the issues of sustainable development in practice, if only because the majority of the 27 principles required action at the level of the nation state. As a result it was clear that, in order to deliver on the Rio Declaration, much greater reliance and trust than hitherto would have to be placed on local government and independent advice (Owens and Cowell, 2002). At the same time the UK government was facing pressure from the development industry for stronger guidance on what was deemed acceptable strategic development priorities (most notably in the location and scale of new housing development around Greater London). In order to deliver development projects it was argued that the private sector needed to work in partnership with the planning system at the local level to reflect local requirements through a plan-led approach, where major proposals for development would be identified in and come through the Development Plan process. Finally, in the absence of strong central guidance, many local governments filled what they perceived to be the policy void by devising their own policy guidance, taking Local Agenda 21 (a variant of the Agenda 21 Rio documentation), the EU's 5th Environmental Action Plan and the ESDP as starting points as well as a means to legitimize their activities (Owens and Cowell, 2002). What perhaps also linked these pressures was the fact that responsibility was vested in the same central UK government department – the then Department of the Environment – which managed environmental policy as well as local government and the statutory planning system.

The significance of the impact of these changes can be illustrated through the medium of two transport-related case studies. The first, a case study of the complex interplay between central and local government, focuses on the implementation of national transport policy at the local level; the second, a case study of a proposal for a private sector-led new settlement, focuses on an attempt to win approval based on principles of sustainable development. Although both are UK examples, they have been selected to reflect principles and represent issues that apply universally (Hall, 1995; Royal Commission on Environmental Pollution, 2001).

3.1. Case study – local transport plans and planning policy guidance

In 1998 the UK government – by now a convert to the principles of sustainable development (UK Department of the Environment, Transport and the Regions, 1998a) – published a major and long-awaited policy statement on transport, *A New Deal for Transport: Better for Everyone*, in which it was stated that the main aim of policy would be to increase personal travel choice by improving alternatives to the car and to secure mobility that would be sustainable in the long term (UK Department of the Environment, Transport and the Regions, 1998b). At its center was a new and more embracing concept of "integration": not only integration between modes of transport but integration between transport and other government policies, including environmental policies, and also between transport planning and land use planning. However, what made this concept of integration especially important here is that it was defined essentially in the context of sustainability. As Owens and Cowell (2002) put it:

> recognition that land use, transport and environment were connected across a range of temporal and spatial scales – that local development control decisions, for example, might ultimately have repercussions for the global climate – was an important factor in establishing the 'new remit' for planning.

Part of this "new remit" included a raft of new planning documents, including Local Transport Plans (LTPs).

With this concept of integration in mind, LTPs were introduced as a key feature of central government's proposals, the idea being that it would be up to individual local governments to set out their strategies for transport for their areas over a 5 year period and knowing that in their preparation they would be implementing the center's policy. The incentive for local government to follow national policy was based on their need for central government resources: LTPs not only have to be submitted to and be approved by central government annually but they also take the form of bids for capital funding for local projects. In this form of resource dependency relationship, "bottom-up" priorities are intended to match "top-down" policies.

In terms of central government policy, the primary aim of LTPs is to improve travel choice and reliability of journeys in ways that safeguard both the environment and the health of the nation. LTPs are seen as fulfilling four basic requirements: providing integrated transport strategies for local needs; identifying local targets for improving air quality, road safety, public transport, and road traffic reduction; ensuring a greater certainty of funding from central government; and encouraging greater use of traffic management. What is of particular interest here is that central to the preparation of the LTP is the need to follow the principles of sustainable development – which in this context is defined as "balancing environmental, economic and social considerations" (UK Department of the Environment, Transport and the Regions, 2000).

What is clear is that LTPs are intended to be a means by which national policy can be implemented at the local level, devised in partnership with the community and giving them more discretion, freedom, and responsibility. As such, the key is for them not to be prepared in isolation but to reflect both national and regional policy contexts. At all stages the active involvement of stakeholders – identified as interest groups, businesses, neighboring authorities, and local residents – is seen as essential. For example, health authorities, local education authorities, schools, and environmental organizations are each seen to have an interest and a role to play in terms of the LTP's preparation and eventual implementation. Equally, public participation is identified as a central element in the local planning process and local vision is seen as important in terms of the likely success of a local plan. The view is that local individuals are more aware than anyone of the inherent problems within their community and as such can focus on local priorities.

Throughout central government policy documents, the twin themes of partnership and integration are particularly noticeable. In this context, integration means more than ensuring that train and bus timetables coincide, it means making sure, for example, that local and regional policies are in line with national policies.

In achieving the objectives noted above, the LTP should seek to promote a genuine alternative to car use. Clearly, public transport has a role to play, and in central government's guidance on the preparation of LTPs (UK Department of the Environment, Transport and the Regions, 2000) it is stated that "Policy proposals for buses ... need to be accompanied by effective traffic management measures at local level, which, where possible, reallocate road space to buses and give them priority in congested areas." In addition, the provision for cycling should be of a good quality, in order to both retain and attract users. As such, a local cycling strategy is expected as part of the LTP, as is a local walking strategy.

In order that the needs of all users are addressed, the guidance suggests that local authorities adopt a formal ordering ranging from pedestrians, cyclists, and public transport through to the private car. This would, it is contended, ensure that decisions are consistent with encouraging a change in attitudes and culture consistent with achieving transport and planning objectives.

Land use planning is seen to play an all important role in the overall transport policy package. As such, in addition to the LTP, a further example of statutory planning guidance, Planning Policy Guidance Note 13 (PPG13), on land use and transport, is crucial in placing the emphasis on integrating planning and transport (UK Office of the Deputy Prime Minister, 2001). LTPs are exhorted to complement planning policies designed to promote more sustainable choices of travel in addition to reducing the need to travel, especially by car, which include (UK Department of the Environment, Transport and the Regions, 2000):

- focusing major traffic generators in urban areas near major public transport interchanges;
- locating local and convenience facilities in local centers that are accessible by walking and cycling;
- the accommodation of housing primarily in existing urban areas, highly accessible by public transport, walking, and cycling;
- in rural areas, locating developments for housing, shopping, jobs, leisure, and services in local service centers designed to act as focal points for housing, transport, and other services;
- using parking policies to promote sustainable transport choices and reduce the reliance on the car;
- giving priority to people over traffic, with a mixture of land uses and local neighborhoods and consider giving more road space to pedestrians, cyclists, and public transport in these locations;
- ensuring that the needs of disabled people are taken into account in the implementation of planning policies and traffic management schemes, and in the design of individual developments;
- protecting sites and routes that could be critical in developing infrastructure to widen transport choices for both passenger and freight movements.

As we have seen, land use planning is a long-term strategy that is aimed at shaping the pattern of development through influencing the location, size, density, and mix of land uses. As such, planning can, it is contended, reduce both the need to travel and reduce the length of journeys at the same time as making access to places of work, shops, and leisure facilities more convenient by public transport, walking, and cycling. In terms of managing travel demand, PPG13 also identifies a number of key areas for attention and includes parking, public transport, walking, and cycling (UK Office of the Deputy Prime Minister, 2001).

The availability of car parking spaces is seen to have a major influence on the mode of transport chosen. As such, a reduction in the amount of car parking space available in new developments is viewed as a prerequisite within a package of planning and transport measures if the aim is to promote sustainable travel choices. For example, car-parking charges should be utilized in order to encourage the use of alternative modes. On a more draconian note, local authorities could refuse planning permission for car parks that fail to address policy as stated in the Development Plan. The redevelopment or reuse of existing car parks could also be encouraged.

Both the availability and use of public transport is seen to be all important in reducing reliance on the private car as a main mode of transport. As such, and as part of the LTP process, local authorities should work with public transport operators and use their planning powers to enhance public transport as a means of strengthening the effectiveness of location policies. When considering planning applications in line with the LTP, the aim should include ensuring so far as is practicable that traffic management measures do not impede the effectiveness of public transport services.

Walking is identified as the most important local travel mode offering an opportunity for replacing local car journeys. In assessing planning applications, local authorities should address issues such as: paying attention to the design, location, and access arrangements of any new development in order to promote walking as a prime means of access; promoting high-density, mixed-use development in and around town centers and near to major transport interchanges; promoting and protecting local convenience shops and services that are within easy walking distance of residential areas; and ensuring that the personal security concerns of pedestrians are addressed.

Cycling is seen to have the potential to offer an ideal substitute for short private car trips. In determining planning applications, local authorities should address a number of issues, including the provision of convenient, safe, and secure cycle parking in town centers and influencing the design, location, and access arrangements of development, including restrictions on parking.

As a brief illustration of the ways in which national planning policy guidance on transport and land use (PPG13) and guidance on the preparation of Local Transport Plans interact at the local level, the case of the Greater Nottingham Local Transport Plan is presented here (Nottinghamshire County Council, 2001).

The Greater Nottingham area supports a population of almost 650 000 people, and covers three different local authorities. The LTP is thus a product of joint working between the authorities, and covers a 5 year period, 2001–2006. Based on public consultation exercises, responses "confirmed that an incremental, balanced approach, introducing restraint-based measures coupled with investment in making the alternatives to the car more attractive, was the best means of securing public and business support whilst making progress towards achieving the objectives." As might be expected, the resulting strategy reflected these responses as well as the priority policy areas of central government: in this case, better linking of the use of land with transport planning, managing travel demand, provision of better transport facilities and services, and promoting travel education and awareness. Particular emphasis is placed on managing travel demand through two initiatives: the introduction of on-street parking charges in the city center and the possible implementation of a workplace parking levy on employer commuter car parking. Like all LTPs, this strategy and these initiatives were then translated into a rolling program of costed projects over the 5 year period. For the Greater Nottingham LTP these amounted to a total in excess of UK £135 million of which UK £87 million (or 65%) represented the bid to central government for capital funds (of which 70% was associated with integrated transport measures – including public transport interchanges, "park-and-ride" sites, bus lanes, and real-time travel information systems).

3.2. Case study – new settlement plans

If LTPs attempt to deliver sustainable environmental futures through the complex administrative process of implementing central–local government relations, their primary focus is on local transport issues and personal mobility problems. Although they are required to be prepared within and reflect the wider and more strategic context of Development Plans, they are by definition narrow in their interpretation of sustainability. Attempts to develop wholly new free-standing settlements demonstrate the way in which a market-led approach to sustainable environmental futures is being promoted by the development industry in pursuit of broader sustainability objectives. Of some 40 or so proposals currently under consideration in the UK, the case of the new settlement of Micheldever Station Market Town in the county of Hampshire provides a good example.

Micheldever is a small rural community in southern England within commuting distance of central London. This strategic location is enhanced by its proximity to a major intercity rail line offering direct services to London, as well as access to a major interurban road network. Along with similar strategic corridors, it has been under intense development pressure for many years. Policies of successive statutory Development Plans for the area have been highly restrictive with regards to new housing, preferring to see development pressures accommodated within existing major urban areas (e.g. the cities of Southampton and Portsmouth) and allowing for small-scale infill developments at other locations. The development industry has never accepted that this "concentration" strategy provides a long-term solution to either the location or scale of the pressures they claim to have identified. In 1990, and as a counter to this policy, Eagle Star Estates (a land and property company, and a subsidiary of a major institutional investment and insurance conglomerate with strong pension fund interests), identified Micheldever as a leading contender for a wholly new approach to large-scale development. In 1993 it promoted its strategy for providing sustainable development at Micheldever Station Market Town (Eagle Star, 1993). Based on a point-by-point refutation of the local planning authority's established policy, Eagle Star claimed that its proposals would meet the requirements of sustainable development "in a way and to a degree that is unachievable if the only alternative of piecemeal town and village infilling and expansion is used to make an equivalent housing contribution in Hampshire."

What then were the proposals for this new settlement? In principle they were no different from many of the other schemes that were promoted at that time: development of 5000 new houses for a total population of about 12 000, together with employment, shopping and education facilities. What makes Eagle Star's case of greater interest is the way in which they tried to devise a novel strategy to accommodate this scale of growth in the light of the role that they saw for this new settlement. Their strategy was based on ten core principles, including planning (emphasizing a comprehensive approach), transport (emphasizing energy conservation and pollution reduction), heat and power (also emphasizing energy conservation and pollution reduction), waste (emphasizing its reduction and use of natural resources), water (emphasizing its protection and quality), landscape (emphasizing protection), ecology (emphasizing habitat diversity), and management (emphasizing community control). The key strategic objectives pertaining to planning and transport, and including examples of their justification, comprised (quotations from Eagle Star, 1993):

- To plan to meet most or all daily needs on a local basis.
- To plan for balance on a scale that supports the local provision of essential infrastructure, jobs, and community facilities:

    A planning permission will generate funds, from an increase in land value, that can be invested in essential new infrastructure and community facilities. In addition, land will be made available at nominal or nil cost to provide 1,000 homes for rent and shared ownership for Hampshire people on low incomes.

- To locate homes together with jobs, shops, and social and recreational facilities all within easy walking distance:

    Nowhere will be more than ½ mile from the town centre or a school. No home will be more than 1 mile from local job opportunities.

- To encourage the use of cycleways and footpaths rather than private cars.
- To encourage use of public transport to minimize car usage for inter-urban travel.
- To encourage an integrated public transport system:

Bus services within the market town will link with external rail, bus and coach services. This will reduce the need for car usage and help provide a service to surrounding rural communities.

- To locate development to utilize spare capacity in the existing main road network to minimize congestion.
- To design road access to and from the market town to disperse traffic rather than concentrate it into wasteful traffic jams.
- To design the internal road system to achieve traffic calming and reduce pollution and congestion:

Roads will be designed so the needs of the driver are subordinate to ... road safety.

The proposal for Micheldever Station Market Town is an example of an attempt to design a sustainable environmental future along the lines promoted by Local Agenda 21. It is often held up as an example of what can be achieved in current best practice by the private sector. Indeed, comparison with the previous case study on LTPs shows that many of the principles that were being worked up in the early 1990s are now the basis of current transport planning policy. But a decade on it remains just that – a proposal. Micheldever has yet to obtain planning permission and, despite its impressive credentials, it is unlikely in the foreseeable future to be realized on either the scale or in the way it was originally envisaged. What went wrong? Was it that the principles of sustainable development were not accepted as a sufficiently powerful case to see it through the planning system? Or were other factors at work?

There is little doubt that Micheldever Station Market Town has thus far failed to materialize for three main reasons. First, whatever its merits or credentials with respect to sustainable development, the proposal was essentially speculative and did not emerge through the due processes of the statutory planning system. It originally saw the light of day as a planning application submitted to a local planning authority by a private developer. In other words, it was not "plan-led" – it was not part of nor did it reflect current strategic planning policy for the area as reflected in the agreed statutory Development Plan; rather, it was a reaction against those statutory policies and the Development Plan. In these circumstances it is hardly likely to have generated much in the way of political support. Second, although it was seen as a direct challenge to those agreed planning policies, it was also as much about who should be responsible for setting planning targets – in this case over new housing allocations for Hampshire. The Micheldever Station Market Town proposal thus became embroiled in an intense political struggle between a local authority – Hampshire County Council – and central government, whereby local government was challenging the imposition of a higher proposed allocation given to it by central government under national planning guidance. Finally, the Micheldever proposal was effectively challenging the authority of the local government in Hampshire. In this case they were not assisted by central government's professional advisors. Following a review of new settlement policy, central government advice was to support proposals only if they would result in positive environmental improvements, for example through reclamation of derelict land or upgrading of areas of low landscape value (Rydin, 1998). Whatever its claims for sustainable development, the Micheldever Station Market Town proposal met neither of these criteria.

4. Conclusions

This chapter has focused on sustainable environmental futures from the perspectives of planning principles and practice – in particular, the role that the statutory planning system plays in delivering development proposals and regulating the development process. It has demonstrated the creative tensions that are to be found embedded in any such regulatory system in a society that claims to adhere to the principles of a market-driven liberal democracy. From this perspective the statutory planning system reflects the society of which it is a part – we have the planning system we deserve. The role of the planning system is thus an impossible one – to resolve contradictions and deep-seated conflicts between, on the one hand, competing private interests over the use and development of land and, on the other, private interests and community interests over property rights and development priorities. The tried and tested approach to conflict resolution has been through attempts to generate a broad and general consensus, knowing that the full weight of the legal system is available to those who feel sufficiently aggrieved over the outcome of a decision.

So where do the principles of sustainable development fit into this process? In planning for sustainable environmental futures we have seen how statutory planning handles sustainability, through strategic planning policies and a "plan-led" system. That said, the case of Micheldever Station Market Town has revealed that, whatever the merits of sustainable development, other factors come into play in making decisions – and those other factors have much to do with the consensus-seeking foundations that underpin the statutory planning system. Whatever the merits of the Micheldever Station Market Town proposal they were clearly not sufficient to outweigh its perceived disadvantages of being "too large" in scale and in an "undesirable" location. In this sense, even though the Micheldever proposal can be seen as an example of "weak" sustainability, it was too "strong" for local political consumption (Gibbs et al., 1998). Its time – along with other examples of sustainable environmental futures – has not yet come. And this perhaps is the biggest problem facing the delivery of sustainability principles through a consensus-seeking and politically driven statutory process such as planning: much as planners and politicians like to sign-up to the principles of sustainable development (after all, Hampshire County Council, at the organizational level, has a clearly stated commitment to sustainability), it is at the end of the day only a policy, a statement of principles. Delivering that policy and those principles is, as Owens and Cowell (2002) emphasize, another matter entirely.

In order to deliver policy there has to be a shared understanding (which may or may not mean a consensus) of what sustainability and sustainable development really means in terms that, in a liberal democracy, both the business community and lay people can understand and share. That is the process of securing policy legitimacy (Royal Commission on Environmental Pollution, 2001). At this point in time it is clear that, much as we can find good examples of policies for sustainable environmental futures (such as in the form of LTPs, national planning guidance, and new settlement proposals such as Micheldever Station Market Town), what is missing are good examples of sustainable environmental futures in practice (Owens and Cowell, 2002). Paraphrasing Goodwin (1993), this demonstrates the importance of the political dimension and the responsibility of politicians in generating, securing, and ensuring both the conditions and the political legitimacy necessary for the successful adoption of sustainable development principles in practice. Only that way will we be able to discuss in any meaningful way the concept of sustainable environmental futures.

References

Banister, D. (2002) *Transport planning*, 2nd edn. London: Spon.
Blowers, A. and B. Evans, eds (1997) *Town planning into the 21st century*. London: Routledge.
Eagle Star (1993) *Micheldever Station Market Town: a strategy for the environment – towards a sustainable development*. Winchester: Eagle Star Estates.
European Commission (1992) *Towards sustainability: a new European programme of policy and action in relation to the environment and sustainable development,* COM(92)23. Brussels: Commission of the European Communities.
Gibbs, D., J. Longhurst and C. Braithwaite (1998) "Struggling with sustainability: weak and strong interpretations of sustainable development within local authority practices," *Environment and Planning A*, 30:1351–1366.
Goodwin, P. (1993) "Efficiency and the environment: possibilities of a green-gold coalition," in: D. Banister and K. Button, eds, *Transport, the environment and sustainable development*. London: Spon.
Hall, P. (1995) "A European Perspective on the spatial links between land use, development and transport," in: D. Banister and K. Button, eds, *Transport, the environment and sustainable development*. London: Spon.
Nottinghamshire County Council (1993) *Review of the Nottinghamshire Structure Plan*. West Bridgford: Nottinghamshire County Council.
Nottinghamshire County Council (2001) *Greater Nottingham Local Transport Plan: 2001–2006*. West Bridgford: Nottinghamshire County Council.
Owens, S. and R. Cowell (2002) *Land and limits: interpreting sustainability in the planning process*. London: Routledge.
Royal Commission on Environmental Pollution (1994) *Transport and the environment*, 18th Report, Cmnd 2674. London: The Stationery Office.
Royal Commission on Environmental Pollution (2001) *Environmental planning*, 23rd Report, Cmnd 5459. London: The Stationery Office.

Rydin, Y. (1998) *The British planning system: an introduction*, 2nd edn. Basingstoke: Macmillan.
UK Department of the Environment, Transport and the Regions (1998a) *Planning for sustainable development: towards better practice*. London: The Stationery Office.
UK Department of the Environment, Transport and the Regions (1998b) *A new deal for transport: better for everyone*, Cmnd 3950. *The Government's White Paper on the future of transport*. London: The Stationery Office.
UK Department of the Environment, Transport and the Regions (1999) *European spatial development perspective*. London: The Stationery Office.
UK Department of the Environment, Transport and the Regions (2000) *Guidance on full local transport plans*. London: The Stationery Office.
UK Office of the Deputy Prime Minister (2001) *Planning policy guidance note 13: transport (PPG13)*. London: The Stationery Office.

Chapter 31

ENVIRONMENTAL JUSTICE APPLICATIONS IN TRANSPORT: THE INTERNATIONAL PERSPECTIVE

RAHAF ALSNIH and PETER R. STOPHER
The University of Sydney

1. Introduction

This chapter focuses on the application of environmental justice principles specifically in the transport context. It begins by giving a background of the environmental justice movement and a definition, and proceeds to describe current legislative mandates in the USA. A holistic approach to transport planning is introduced to highlight the importance of the interrelationships between transport and land use planning. Current practices adopted in terms of environmental justice are illustrated from the Mid-Ohio Regional Planning Commission report as well as a description of the data limitations that result from the models used in current analyses. The chapter concludes by providing some recommendations on the areas that need to be developed to address environmental justice principles adequately, and the applicability of these principles internationally.

The environmental justice movement emerged in 1982 in the USA. It was foreshadowed, however, a number of years earlier when, in 1975, the National Cooperative Highway Research Program identified areas that needed to be incorporated in the transport planning process to address the environmental, social, and economic impacts that stemmed from transport developments and policies: a result of the National Environmental Policy Act, introduced in 1969 (Transportation Research Board, 2002). This led to the development of the Policy and Procedure Memorandum (PPM 20-8), issued by the US Department of Transport, soon after (see Chapter 27).

These issues were revisited in 1994 when President Clinton signed Executive Order 12898: Federal Actions to Address Environmental Justice in Minority Populations and Low Income Populations (Blackmon Lane et al., 1998). This in turn led, in 1995, to the following order by the US Department of Transport: Actions to Address Environmental Justice in Minority Populations and Low Income Populations (Chakraborty et al., 1999).

Despite the environmental justice movement originating in the USA, a growing number of countries around the world have begun to investigate the economic,

Handbook of Transport and the Environment, Edited by D.A. Hensher and K.J. Button
© 2003, Elsevier Ltd

social, and environmental impacts of various developments and policy, on disadvantaged and marginalized groups in society. Environmental justice incited many studies to investigate the relationships between the spatial distribution of environmental disamenities and the sociodemographic attributes of communities affected (Baden and Coursey, 2001). To date, the studies conducted found that discrimination against minority and low income groups occurred in terms of the provision of public services, the location of hazardous industry, and the location of waste sites (Transportation Research Board, 2002). However, it is difficult to determine explicitly whether minority and low-income groups reside near environmental hazards due to a lack of housing choice and discriminatory practices in the housing market, or whether discriminatory siting practices have been adopted by policy-makers (Flippen, 2001; Quillian, 2002). It appears that both cases are true. In some instances, people locate near an environmental externality due to a lack of financial resources. In the USA, this is experienced by African Americans and people of Hispanic origin, in particular (Hite, 2000). In other instances, the externality is housed near certain communities (Bass, 1998). This reinforces the need to address environmental justice and why its principles should be adopted, not just in the USA, but also globally, as economic forces polarize societies according to their levels of income, if not also according to their racial origin (Wessel, 2000; Checker, 2001).

2. Background

The environmental justice movement originated in the USA, in 1982, as a result of people opposing the location of a polychlorinated biphenyl (PCB) factory near an African American community in North Carolina (Fritz, 1999; Baden and Coursey, 2001). In many respects, it may be claimed that the beginnings of the movement toward environmental justice occurred as part of the original environmental movement that arose particularly with highway projects in the USA (see Chapter 27). Prior to 1969, highway projects in the USA were decided upon with little or no input from the public. This included decisions on the nature of the highway project (e.g. freeway, expressway, or principal arterial road), the location of the project, and how the project related to the existing road and land infrastructure. In essence, highway projects were determined in the USA on the basis of a definition of need for the project (generally defined from considerations of congestion and levels of service on existing facilities, or provision of links in the interstate system of highways), and were then sited in locations that were least expensive from a strictly engineering viewpoint. There was, and still is, no requirement in the USA for a formal cost–benefit assessment of highway investments, and externalities of highway construction projects were largely ignored.

One result of the cost focus of highway project decisions was that roads were frequently routed through areas with the lowest property acquisition costs. Indeed, this was not restricted to roads alone, but was also true for many other public and private capital investment projects that required land for construction. In the USA, not only have people of low income generally located in close proximity to one another, but so also have various racial and ethnic groups. Because the US population has been made up so extensively from immigration, there has been a tendency to create neighborhoods that are identifiable to specific racial groups. When these groups are also income disadvantaged, they encounter further discrimination in the real estate market. This results in neighborhoods of concentrated disadvantage, where the real estate is characterized by a dilapidated housing stock: these neighborhoods become associated with low property values (Flippen, 2001). It is, therefore, hardly surprising that major new highways (and other projects) were frequently located through neighborhoods that were financially or socially disadvantaged, and often both. Furthermore, there were instances in the 1950s and 1960s in the USA, where road building projects were used as a pretext for slum clearance, or other neighborhood demolition. An example of this was the building of the Dan Ryan Expressway on the south side of the Chicago Central Business District, where a major area of low-income housing was demolished to build this major thoroughfare, and the homes that were taken for this project were subsequently replaced by high-rise apartment blocks. This actually resulted in a new form of urban blight, with the final result being at least no better than the former situation and, in many respects, worse. Consequences stemming from the failure to consider the social and other environmental impacts, and especially failure to look at questions of environmental equity or justice of this project, are clearly evident today.

With the advent of the environmental movement in the 1960s, and the subsequent environmental legislation that was developed, two things changed. First, there was a requirement for public consultation in the construction of major publicly funded projects, and, second, there was a requirement to take into account a wide range of environmental issues. However, these two changes were insufficient of themselves. First, the mandated public hearings were often (and still are, in many cases) ineffective means to engage the public in consultation. Further, these hearings were often seen by low-income persons and those from disadvantaged racial groups as being ineffective or unavailable means for them to express their opinions. These subgroups of the population often see themselves as disenfranchised, or socially excluded, and would assume that the public hearings are for those who are socially included. The perception is often there that these hearings are not for such people and that their opinions, if expressed, would still be ignored or downplayed. Unfortunately, the track record of public hearings in the USA has done little to persuade that the contrary might be true.

Second, while environmental issues now had to be taken into account, there was still no formal cost–benefit procedure required. As a result, simply taking these issues into account did not necessarily involve any consideration of the equity of the impact on different population subgroups. Indeed, on both counts, there have been accusations made quite frequently that both the hearings and the requirements to take into account environmental impacts are treated as little more than a formality, to which lip service must be paid. There are many who would contend that these are frequently undertaken with little intent to change the process.

One thing that did not change in response to the environmental legislation of the 1960s and 1970s was the nature of the travel forecasting and other models used to inform the planning process. These models were not designed to answer the questions of who benefits and who pays, nor to determine directly the incidence of environmental impacts. As a result, with increasing public awareness of the externalities of various construction projects, especially highways, and the partial failure of the environmental legislation to identify who was impacted by the externalities, the notion of environmental justice was born. Indeed, the models have tended to maintain the separation of the user and the non-user, and to lead to considering principally the benefits and costs to the users of the facility that is to be constructed. At the same time, the models fail to identify who the users are, in terms of segments of the population by social or income classes. Environmental impacts, on the other hand, are generally not modeled but are rather assessed in various different qualitative ways, and are also assessed at relatively aggregate levels, making it impossible to distinguish who is impacted, and whether certain impacts will fall more frequently on specific population subgroups.

Still, today, race and income are not usually present in travel demand models, and issues of who is impacted by the externalities of projects are relatively poorly modeled or understood. Land use models, which could potentially help the process, also do not contain information on race or income, and are frequently not part of the planning process. Therefore, the means to identify who benefits and who pays are still largely absent from the planning models. It is with this background, then, that we can consider what environmental justice is, and how and where it applies.

2.1. Definition

Environmental justice refers to the fair treatment[a] and meaningful involvement of all people regardless of race, color, national origin, or income with respect to the

---

[a]Fair treatment is defined in that minority and low-income groups do not bear a disproportionate share of the negative environmental impacts of government actions (Bass, 1998).

development, implementation, and enforcement of environmental laws (Bass, 1998; Quan, 2002). It is also commonly referred to as the equitable distribution of both negative and positive impacts across racial, ethnic, and income groups, with the environment defined to incorporate ecological, economic, and social effects (Transportation Research Board, 2002). In the British context, environmental justice problems arise because environmental problems are a component of social exclusion and therefore an issue of social justice (Agyeman, 2001). In the USA, the Environmental Law Institute's (2002) definition of environmental justice is somewhat problematic because it contains ambiguous terms such as "environmentally burdened communities of color" and refers to environmental impacts as "concerns." It seems to mitigate the significance of the impacts impinged on minority and low-income groups in society. Hence, this definition does not emphasize the importance of environmental justice principles: it does not appear to serve its purpose.

Environmental justice appears to comprise fundamental elements of Rawls's theory of justice, which is based on two principles. The first states that all social primary goods such as liberty, opportunity, income, and wealth are to be distributed equally; the second states that if these goods are not distributed equally, they are to be distributed to favor the disadvantaged (Khisty, 1996; Transportation Research Board, 2002). If environmental justice issues are to be addressed adequately in the USA, and internationally, the definition of environmental justice must be workable and not neutral: it must not divert attention from the adverse impacts on the less powerful in society (Fritz, 1999). This must be acknowledged by governing bodies and agencies internationally.

3. Legislation

Environmental justice issues were revisited in 1994 when President Clinton signed Executive Order 12898: Federal Actions to Address Environmental Justice in Minority Populations and Low Income Populations. This piece of legislation incorporated low-income populations in its investigations of programs, policies, and activities, and hence increased the awareness of the need to address social and community impacts (Blackmon Lane et al., 1998). This in turn led, in 1995, to the following US Department of Transport order, proposed by the Federal Highway Administration: Actions to Address Environmental Justice in Minority Populations and Low Income Populations (Chakraborty et al., 1999).

Executive Order 12898, however, has proved to be problematic because it requires the analyst to know and define disproportionate impacts as well as acknowledge peoples' values and perspectives: this process requires an objective framework by which data can be collected and analyzed (Tonn et al., 2000). To address environmental justice in the USA, and other countries where social–spatial segregation occurs, the forces shaping the urban fabric need to be identified: environmental equality will only result when there is social equality (Agyeman, 2001). This is challenging due to the complexity of issues surrounding environmental justice, such as civil rights, and the fundamental need to address social equality (Blackmon Lane et al., 1998; Purvis, 2001).

In October 1999, the Federal Highway Administration and the Federal Transit Administration issued the memorandum *Implementing Title VI Requirements in Metropolitan and Statewide Planning*, to clarify how metropolitan planning organizations should ensure the consideration of environmental justice in current and future planning certification reviews (Federal Highway Administration, 1999). This memorandum also emphasized the importance of the applicability of environmental justice orders to the processes and products of planning, in addition to the applications of the legislation during project development.

Metropolitan planning organizations were asked to address a set of questions to aid in reviewing and verifying compliance with Title VI requirements. These questions were to concentrate on issues surrounding overall strategies and goals, service equity, and public involvement (Federal Highway Administration, 1999). They are presented in the appendix.

A recognized flaw of this memorandum is that it does not define a specific procedural or analytical approach for demonstrating compliance (Federal Highway Administration, 1999, 2000a). This allows metropolitan planning organizations across the USA to develop their own methods to evaluate planning programs, policies, and processes. The Mid-Ohio Regional Planning Commission developed its own methods when evaluating planning programs, policies and processes in relation to compliance with Title VI and related orders. These are described later in this chapter.

4. The need to address environmental justice in transport planning

In the 1960s and 1970s the US Congress was bombarded with community frustration regarding adverse environmental, social, and economic impacts resulting from transport infrastructure developments and policy. This led to the Policy and Procedure Memorandum (PPM 20–8), issued by the US Department of Transport through the Federal Highway Administration (see Chapter 27). In 1975, the National Cooperative Highway Research Program conducted a project, in relation to the new legislative mandates, and proposed the following to be considered in the transport planning process:

- social, economic, and environmental considerations in transport planning are important because inevitable conflicts among competing interests must be resolved;

- social equity must be explicitly recognized and taken into account in transport decision-making;
- different groups of people can be expected to have different interests and different priorities (Transportation Research Board, 2002).

Environmental justice issues were identified in the transport arena 20 years before they were recognized in the political sphere; however, the concept of community impact has widened over the past 30 years. In the 1960s and 1970s the primary focus was on the direct impacts of transport investments on economic and community development, as well as environmental impacts, such as air and noise pollution. The focus today also encapsulates transport investment effects on urban economic growth and decline, job accessibility, community quality and the disruption to the urban social fabric, and the cost of public transport per capita (Transportation Research Board, 2002).

It is understood that the quality of life[a] in a community is linked to the transport system, and hence it must be understood by transport planners that transport needs differ across population groups (Forkenbrock and Schweitzer, 1999; Transportation Research Board, 2002). This notion is reinforced by the process involved in the dispersal of employment opportunities toward urban fringe areas, which often leads to areas housing a greater concentration of minority groups, such as Atlanta, Georgia (Strait, 2001). Those without a vehicle cannot adequately access jobs that are now predominantly located in fringe areas hence, these individuals may remain unemployed: a characteristic of the spatial mismatch hypothesis (Sanchez, 1999; Federal Highway Administration, 2000a). It has also been documented that low-income households are only one-sixth as likely to own a vehicle as middle- to high-income households, and that car accessibility is greater in non-disadvantaged households than disadvantaged households (Agyeman, 2001; Purvis, 2001). Lack of good public transport systems may lead to "forced car ownership": a phenomenon that eventuated in urban Sydney, Australia, due to an inadequate public transport system, and led to indigenous Australians having to purchase private vehicles. This impacted their lifestyle in a negative manner, because they now had less disposable income owing to car running and maintenance costs (Pollack, 2001).

Also, average employment was found to decrease as the distance from a transit stop increased, and average employment was found to increase as per capita vehicle ownership increased (Sanchez, 1999). Adequate public transport can increase the participation, by part of the low-income group of communities, in employment activities. Hence, today's travel demand models should give more attention to public transport than travel demand models did in the past (Mackett,

---

[a]Quality of life, as defined by Khisty (1996), is the essence of the collective economic, social, and physical conditions of people in a community.

1994; Transportation Research Board, 2002). This directly relates to environmental justice objectives set out in Title VI of the Civil Rights Act introduced by President Clinton in 1994 (Quan, 2002). To address the issue described, new models will have to incorporate better the distribution of benefits and costs in relation to income, race, and ethnicity. Regarding all that has been mentioned thus far, a land use–transport model is likely to be the best option, provided that the land use model also contains information on the location of people by income, race, and any other relevant grouping, a feature that is not present in most current models.

5. Transport and land use interrelationships

In the global context, problems arise when a region has areas that are politically volatile due to growing ethnic tensions such as those witnessed in Belfast in Ireland, Jerusalem in Israel, and Johannesburg in South Africa. Urban and transport planners around the world can best learn from the South African experience. Planners in Johannesburg have approached entrenched social constructs, founded during the apartheid regime, in a proactive way, hence the city has now become a "compact city of opportunity" (Bollens, 2002). What needs to be adopted in the USA, and globally, especially in countries that house different immigrant communities, is multicultural planning. This has increased sensitivity toward the use and perception of urban space by all communities in society, in terms of accommodating their different needs, and does not involve their assimilation into mainstream society. Multicultural or progressive planning will address racial segregation and social issues and, therefore, may help quell the rise of environmental injustice as well as promote more democratic institutions (Wessel, 2000).

There is no doubt that the transport planner must frequently consult the urban planner in order to utilize the correct parameters in travel demand models. These must account for population growth or decline, zoning restrictions, and changing land uses. However, a better approach would be to adopt a land use–transport model that incorporates the nature of the relationship between land use and transport. Land use changes also reflect the changes in the spatial distribution of activities, and this has accessibility implications, particularly for low-income and minority groups. Hence, the importance of land use–transport models is that they can be used to address social inequalities (Mackett, 1994). In addition, land use–transport models will help "bridge the gap" between urban planners and transport planners.

According to Dittmar (1995), the transport system and facilities should be integrated into the community context as well as into both the built and natural environment: the sustainable transport system. He also states that a conservative transport system would be a sustainable transport system, because available financial resources would be used to maintain and rehabilitate the existing urban infrastructure. These improvements may, therefore, enable community groups to revitalize "disintegrating" neighborhoods, which commonly house low-income and minority groups (Flippen, 2001; Quillian, 2002). This provides an example of how a shift in policy focus may result in addressing environmental justice principles, and it also reinforces the importance of land use and transport interrelationships: a more holistic approach to planning (Agyeman, 2001). "Context sensitive design", as defined by the Federal Highway Administration, is the combined interdisciplinary approach that involves all stakeholders in the development of a transport facility whereby the facility preserves the aesthetic, scenic, physical and symbolic resources while maintaining safety and mobility (South, 2002). This new concept also reiterates the importance of a holistic approach to planning.

6. Transport and environmental justice: current practices

Much of the documentation on environmental justice in transport describes a revolution in terms of public involvement in the planning process: public participation in the planning process has increased. This has created a new planning image that has replaced the conventional style of planning, whereby public participation in the decision-making process is not only to promote the welfare of society, but also to increase the welfare of individuals in society (Khisty, 1996). As a result, community groups now devise their own methods and analyses to address environmental justice principles, due to their dissatisfaction with government procedures and findings (Transportation Research Board, 2002). Environmental justice groups such as CAFE (Community Alliance for the Environment) combine environmentalism and social justice. These groups have also brought factionalized communities together, and created a sense of power and unity to minority groups (Checker, 2001).

Social justice requires a democratization of the planning process and this was identified by the Mid-Ohio Regional Planning Commission, in its study, *MPO Environmental Justice Report*, conducted in 1999 (Federal Highway Administration, 2000a; Transportation Research Board, 2002). It has been acknowledged that public involvement should begin in the earliest stages of planning (Blackmon Lane et al., 1998; Federal Highway Administration, 2000a,b). In its study, the Mid-Ohio Regional Planning Commission incorporated land use and transport interrelationships, and utilized a travel demand forecasting model to assess the positive and negative impacts of existing and planned transport investments and infrastructure, on target populations.

The Mid-Ohio Regional Planning Commission identified four key areas of investigation in its report outline:

(1) Obtaining a demographic profile, whereby the location and size of low-income and minority groups were identified.
(2) Acknowledgement of different transport needs by target populations. This was achieved by requiring members of an Environmental Justice Task Force, set up by the Mid-Ohio Regional Planning Commission, to liaise with members of the communities under investigation and retain information on the priorities, values, and needs of these communities in relation to transport. This was used to supplement documentation already available to the Mid-Ohio Regional Planning Commission.
(3) Evaluating public involvement efforts. This began in 1995, and led to the creation of the Citizen Advisory Committee, as well as the Mid-Ohio Regional Planning Commission realizing the need to publicize its activities in order to attract wider public involvement in the planning process.
(4) Assessing the benefits and burdens of the transport system.

This last step was regarded as an analytical development in terms of impact assessment. The Mid-Ohio Regional Planning Commission distinguished between types of measures used to compare the impacts on target and non-target populations:

- Population-based measures that provide information on members of the target population and also take into consideration small pockets of target populations within non-target populations.
- Geographic-based measures that comprise information for a specific geographic area.
- Visual-based measures that are usually presented in map form owing to the lack of comparability. The employment of geographic information systems (GISs) to convey the spatial distribution of impacts. GISs have been acknowledged as a very useful tool in the assessment of environmental justice principles, and aids the analytical procedures for computing demographic attributes of target populations (Blackmon Lane et al., 1998; Chakraborty et al., 1999).

The Mid-Ohio Regional Planning Commission utilized a travel-demand model to assess the benefits and costs of transport system investments. However, results revealed limitations of the data incorporated in the model (Federal Highway Administration, 2000a). Results accruing from this analysis showed that target populations had equal access to jobs. This is unlikely. Analysis was not conducted further to determine what kinds of employment opportunities were available and whether these jobs constituted viable employment opportunities for minority and low-income workers. It must be noted that the model employed was a travel-demand model that integrated land use statistics, not a land use–transport model.

Table 1
Data types useful in environmental analyses

Short-form data	Long-form data	Data on poverty derived from long-form data
Race	Income	Household income
Age	Disability	Household size
	Vehicle availability	Age of the head of household
	Ancestry	

Source: Purvis (2001).

The Mid-Ohio Regional Planning Commission's report identified the need to include land use statistics to address the spatial mismatch issue: the utilization of a land use–transport model was implicitly stated.

Also, the Mid-Ohio Regional Planning Commission's report failed to consider frequency of service of public transport because bus services were assumed to offer a uniform service. This, in itself, failed to give accurate results concerning the access of minority and low-income groups to public transport services. Mackett (1994), in his assessment of land use–transport models, found that the exclusion of land use effects led to the underestimation of the response to changes in public transport policy. This has direct implications for low-income and minority groups. In addition, it stresses the importance of incorporating land use statistics in the modeling stage.

7. Data issues and model estimates

US studies on environmental justice concentrate on distributive, procedural, corrective, and social justice issues. There are two types of models used: income based and race based (Quan, 2002). Table 1 describes data types useful in environmental analyses for both the income- and race-based models. Short-form data come from questions asked of all US citizens in the decennial census, and long-form data come from questions asked of one in eight US citizens in the census. In addition, short-form data are available at the census block group level, and long-form data are available only at coarser levels – the block group and traffic analysis zone levels. What has not been addressed here is the need to collect more culturally sensitive data other than the data types in Table 1 (Pollack, 2001). This may be achieved by employing special project officers, or public involvement professionals, who identify areas of need and, therefore, pass this important information on to the transport planner (South, 2002). This is also a way for communities, unable to voice their needs and concerns for a myriad of reasons, to communicate indirectly with planners and policy-makers.

Another problem encountered by the data described in Table 1 revolves around the definition of poverty and how these data are derived. The US Department of Transport defines a low-income person as an individual whose median household income is less than the US Department of Health and Community Services poverty level (Forkenbrock and Schweitzer, 1999). Poverty level is estimated from a number of socio-economic variables such as age, median home value, housing tenure, household income, and household size. The mix of variables used will depend on the target population investigated. Because poverty data are derived, the results will be influenced by the quality and reliability of the original data. This issue has not been sufficiently addressed in the studies conducted thus far; however, what is mentioned is the need for better methods to improve the quality of information available.

To date, very little research has examined policy implications of observed differences in travel behavior between different racial and ethnic groups and how income constrains activity and travel choices. This contributes to the lack of understanding of why environmental justice issues constantly arise for certain members of society (Transportation Research Board, 2002). As mentioned earlier, the analyst must be aware of the different travel needs of various members of society: communities do not have identical travel patterns and behavior. Improvements are also required for cost and benefit analysis tools, because these instruments usually mask the incidence of impacts on the target population. These issues must be addressed otherwise difficulties and inadequacies associated with the assessment of environmental justice will persist.

It is also known that traditional travel demand models produce aggregate estimates due to simplified computer and mechanical procedures and therefore do not account for differences among the target population, nor capture population dynamics: they treat the population as homogenous. This creates problems for policy-makers, because forecasts are not representative of the target population, hence environmental justice principles will not be addressed (Purvis, 2001).

In addition, it is widely acknowledged that to forecast population growth, information on current and future land uses and past population trends must be obtained. This involves an intensive analytical procedure, usually beyond the scope of the studies investigated. According to Blackmon Lane et al. (1998), this renders all analysis that attempts to quantify likely impacts from proposed transport developments and policy as inaccurate, thus reinforcing the need to adopt a land use–transport model rather than the transport model in isolation.

Land use–transport models are a useful tool that could incorporate social inequality issues in the modeling stage (Mackett, 1994). This is an advance on the current practice whereby social issues are addressed in the decision-making or

Table 2
Land use transportation model usefulness for policy analysis

Policy objective	Degree of usefulness
Reduction of congestion	Very useful
Reduction of energy usage	Very useful
Increase safety	Useful
Improve the environment	Useful
Reduce social inequalities	Useful
Improve the quality of life	Moderately useful
Reduce public expenditure	Moderately useful
Move toward a market economy	Of little use

Source: Mackett (1994).

planning stage. The usefulness of the land use–transport model for policy analysis is described in Table 2. This table also depicts the applicability of the land use–transport model to environmental justice principles.

The incorporation of public involvement is also an area that needs to be developed and widely adopted in order to derive community interests, goals, values and priorities and therefore accommodate environmental justice principles (Blackmon Lane et al., 1998; Agyeman, 2001).

7.1. Data limitations and recommendations

There are obvious data limitations, especially in relation to sensitive data, such as racial origin and culture, and level of income, required to identify the transport needs of low-income and minority groups. In the USA, data of this type are usually only reported at the census tract level – a more aggregate level – to comply with privacy laws (Transportation Research Board, 2002). This creates problems at the data analysis stage, because aggregate estimates mask the transport needs of specific populations and, hence, these are not adequately considered due to a lack of empirical evidence. What is required, therefore, is data collected at a finer geographic resolution to capture the differences in transport needs across the community (Chakraborty et al., 1999).

This leads to conducting research to quantify the variations in mobility, access and travel behavior across different economic, social, and demographic groups, because, presently, insufficient research has been carried out that examines these areas in relation to changes that may occur over time: cross-sectional and longitudinal studies should be employed (Transportation Research Board, 2002). In order to accomplish this, the analyst must be aware of the different transport

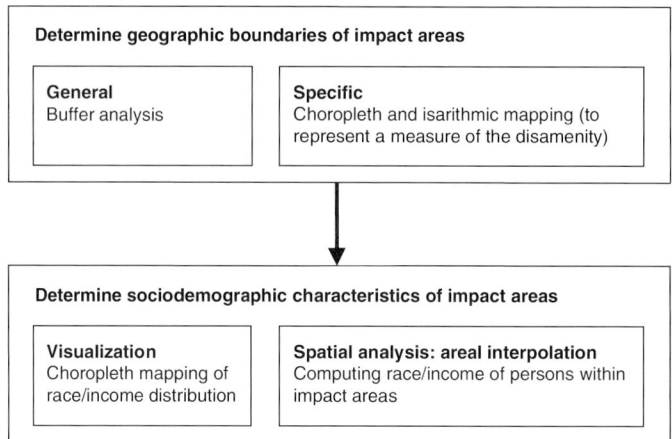

Figure 1. Framework for GIS-based evaluation of environmental justice.

needs of different populations within the community. This may be achieved through greater community consultation, increased community participation in the planning process, and the development of better working definitions and indicators of environmental justice and social equity. It has been previously mentioned that GISs are useful tools to employ in the evaluation of environmental justice principles (Federal Highway Administration, 2000a). Figure 1 provides a conceptual framework for a GIS-based evaluation of environmental justice principles.

However, data limitation problems are encountered with the utilization of GISs for impact analysis. As already discussed, geo-demographic data are often only available at an aggregate level owing to privacy law compliance, while what is required are data at a finer geographic level, because areas likely to be impacted by transport or other projects do not have boundaries identical to those for which data are available (Chakaraborty et al., 1999). In future, this may remain an issue, because people are reluctant to provide personal information from which they can be identified. Hence, models, such as a predictive regression model, may have to be employed to estimate data at a more disaggregate level.

Another problem identified is the requirement of accurate and specific data for GIS-based evaluation to produce useful results. This involves expensive and time-consuming data gathering, unless synthetic data derived from synthetic models are developed.

Research is also needed to recognize, as well as document, ways in which investment policies and innovations in transport affect target populations (Dittmar, 1995). This incorporates analyses of investment policies to highlight the reasons behind the impacts of transport investment on particular communities, and the evaluation of the accessibility levels of low-income, minority, aged, and disabled populations.

As mentioned earlier in this chapter, studies need to be conducted that embark on comparing costs and benefits of transport developments and policy, focusing on the impacts on socially and economically disadvantaged communities (Transportation Research Board, 2002). This area of research needs to identify land use and transport interrelationships and the dynamics of these relationships.

Overall, more research is required into investigating better methods to analyze environmental, social, and economic impacts accruing from transport developments and policy. This may lead to improvement on the current land use–transport models: the models that cater best to addressing environmental justice principles, especially from the urban transport perspective.

8. International applications for environmental justice

Although the environmental justice movement started in the USA and has advanced there far beyond developments in other countries, this relatively new political path has international applications. In China, for example, the formation of new social hierarchies and changes in society will see the establishment of environmental justice as Chinese citizens become more aware of their environment and their rights (Quan, 2002). However, to assess the environmental justice issues adequately in China, new models will have to be devised other than the income- and race-based models utilized in the USA. This is because Chinese society is not fragmented due to race or ethnicity the same way that US society is fragmented: US society is an immigrant-based society with 77% of the population being white non-minority and 12.6% of the population being African American. In China, the Han people comprise 91.6% of the population, and ethnic groups do not comprise such high percentages as ethnic groups in the USA. In addition, China has had no serious racial conflict. Therefore, to assess environmental justice in China, the proposed models are based on occupation and the peasantry worker.

Environmental justice in Canada is viewed as an issue for all members of society: the sustainable environment approach is adopted because communities are not polarized like their US counterparts (Draper and Mitchell, 2001). In the UK the environmental justice movement has began to take more shape through environmental groups; however, it is not yet as influential as in the USA, where the civil rights movement is very powerful (Agyeman, 2001). In central and eastern Europe the collapse of communist regimes has witnessed the development of new legislative frameworks in terms of environmental justice; however, there have not been any practical applications. This is a result of economies in transition, and the priority of governments is economic development, but at the expense of environmental and social justice issues (Costi, 1998). Problems concerning environmental justice will become more evident as these nations exit the transition phase.

It is likely that changing economic conditions around the world will result in greater income disparities between low- and high-income groups, and possibly lead to socio-spatial segregation (Wessel, 2000). With this in mind, and people becoming more aware of their civil rights, environmental justice issues will become more prominent in Canada, the UK, as well as other countries, especially those that house spatially clustered immigrant populations. This emphasizes the increased importance of understanding and incorporating environmental justice principles globally, in all facets of urban and regional planning.

9. Conclusion

With increasing globalization of domestic economies and populations, and, consequently, the development of disadvantaged minority groups in almost every nation in the world, environmental justice concerns are likely to become increasingly an issue world-wide. Thus, while the environmental justice movement began in the USA, it is likely to become increasingly visible in almost every country. This review has shown that current practices, particularly in transport investments, in handling environmental justice issues are not very sophisticated and often lack key detail that would allow a clear determination of impacts on racial and economic minorities.

Among the research and policy issues facing agencies in the USA and around the world that need to comply with environmental justice principles are the following:

- Public involvement[a] should increase and, in the case of the USA, it should be enhanced. Public involvement will become more important because immigrant populations usually grow at a faster rate than white populations, while also often being less able to make use of standard procedures for public involvement. This has been the case for the USA (Weeks, 2002).
- Public involvement professionals should be employed. These individuals are able to deal with conflict management, presentation, problem-solving, negotiation, facilitation, and team-building skills (South, 2002). These individuals should initiate the public involvement process.
- The collection of sensitive data, such as racial origin and income should be conducted more frequently. This may become more viable especially if the

---

[a]Public involvement is meaningfully engaging the public in the decision-making process (Matley, 2002).

public involvement process has been successful. If a bond of trust has been established between the community and agency, it is possible that the collection of sensitive data will not be as problematic as in the past where a high percentage of respondents refused to supply this information. Collection of this type of data has been regarded as controversial. However, according to Matley (2002), successful public involvement usually evokes controversy. Such data need to become a standard part of household travel surveys and other data collection efforts in transport.
- Agencies must correctly identify, and understand, the different transport needs of different groups in society. This will be more achievable if the public involvement process has been successful.
- Better land use and transport models are required. The land use models need to incorporate data on income and racial origin and be able to forecast where different groups of the population will locate, and work. The land use models need to be fully integrated with travel demand models, so as to show the transport implications and to describe better the incidence of transport service levels on different segments of the population.

Most importantly, agencies must understand the concept of environmental justice. This is where governments may have to formulate a definition, to avoid subjective interpretation, and hence introduce tough penalties for agencies that do not comply with all the requirements of environmental justice legislation.

Appendix. Assessing Title VI capability – review questions: an attachment to the Federal Highway Administration and Federal Transit Administration memorandum *Implementing Title VI Requirements in Metropolitan and Statewide Planning***, October 1999**

1. *Overall Strategies and Goals:*

- What strategies and efforts has the planning process developed for ensuring, demonstrating, and substantiating compliance with Title VI? What measures have been used to verify that the multi-modal system access and mobility performance improvements included in the plan and Transportation Improvement Program (TIP) or STIP, and the underlying planning process, comply with Title VI?

- Has the planning process developed a demographic profile of the metropolitan planning area or State that includes identification of the locations of socio-economic groups, including low-income and minority populations as covered by the Executive Order on Environmental Justice and Title VI provisions?

- Does the planning process seek to identify the needs of low-income and minority populations? Does the planning process seek to utilize demographic information to examine the distributions across these groups of the benefits and burdens of the transportation investments included in the plan and TIP (or STIP)? What methods are used to identify imbalances?

2. *Service Equity:*

- Does the planning process have an analytical process in place for assessing the regional benefits and burdens of transportation system investments for different socio-economic groups? Does it have a data collection process to support the analysis effort? Does this analytical process seek to assess the benefit and impact distributions of the investments included in the plan and TIP (or STIP)?

- How does the planning process respond to the analyses produced? Imbalances identified?

3. *Public Involvement:*

- Does the public involvement process have an identified strategy for engaging minority and low-income populations in transportation decision-making? What strategies, if any, have been implemented to reduce participation barriers for such populations? Has their effectiveness been evaluated? Has public involvement in the planning process been routinely evaluated as required by regulation? Have efforts been undertaken to improve performance, especially with regard to low-income and minority populations? Have organizations representing low-income and minority populations been consulted as part of this evaluation? Have their concerns been considered?

- What efforts have been made to engage low-income and minority populations in the certification review public outreach effort? Does the public outreach effort utilize media (such as print, television, radio, etc.) targeted to low-income or minority populations? What issues were raised, how are their concerns documented, and how do they reflect on the performance of the planning process in relation to Title VI requirements?

- What mechanisms are in place to ensure that issues and concerns raised by low-income and minority populations are appropriately considered in the decision-making process? Is there evidence that these concerns have been appropriately considered? Has the metropolitan planning organization (MPO) or State DOT made funds available to local organizations that represent low-income and minority populations to enable their participation in planning processes?

References

Agyeman, J. (2001) "Ethnic minorities in Britain: short change, systematic indifference and sustainable development," *Journal of Environmental Policy and Planning*, 3:15–30.
Baden, B.M. and D.L. Coursey (2002) "The locality of waste sites within the city of Chicago: a demographic, social, and economic analysis," *Resource and Energy Economics*, 24:53–93.
Bollens, S.C. (2002) "Urban planning and intergroup conflict: confronting a fractured public interest," *American Planning Association*, 68:22–42
Bass, R. (1998) "Evaluating environmental justice under the National Environmental Policy Act," *Environmental Impact Assessment Review*, Elsevier Science, 18:83–92.
Blackmon Lane, L., S. Hoffield, and D. Griffin (1998) "Environmental justice evaluation: Wilmington Bypass, Wilmington, North Carolina," *Transportation Research Record*, 1626:131–139.
Chakraborty, J., D.J. Forkenbrock and L.A. Schweitzer (1999) "Using GIS to assess the environmental justice consequences of transportation system changes," *Transactions in GIS*, 3:239–258.
Checker, M. (2001) "Like Nixon coming to China": finding common ground in a multi-ethnic coalition for environmental justice," *Anthropological Quarterly*, 74:135–146.
Costi, A. (1998) "Environmental justice and sustainable development in central and eastern Europe," *European Environment*, 8:107–112.
Dittmar, H. (1995) "A broader context for transportation planning, not just an end in itself," *Journal of the American Planning Association*, 6:7–13.
Draper, D. and B. Mitchell (2001) "Environmental justice considerations in Canada," *Canadian Geographer*, 45:93–98.
Environmental Law Institute (2002) *A citizen's guide to using federal environmental laws to secure environmental justice*. Environmental Law Institute Research Report. Washington, DC: Environmental Law Institute.
Federal Highway Administration (1999) *Implementing Title VI requirements in metropolitan and statewide planning*. Memorandum. Washington, DC: FHWA (http://www.fhwa.dot.gov/environment/ejustice/ej-10–7.htm).
Federal Highway Administration (2000a) *Use of data sources, analytical techniques, and public involvement*. Washington, DC: FHWA (http:// www.fhwa.dot.gov/environment/ejustice/case/morpc.pdf).
Federal Highway Administration (2000b) *Environmental justice: Verona Road/West Beltline needs assessment study*. Washington, DC: FHWA (http://www.fhwa.dot.gov/environment/ejustice/case/case1.htm).
Flippen, C.A. (2001) "Residential segregation and minority home ownership," *Social Science Research*, 30:337–362.
Forkenbrock, D.J. and L.A. Schweitzer (1999) "Environmental justice in transportation planning," *Journal of the American Planning Association*, 65:96–111.
Fritz, J.M. (1999) "Searching for environmental justice: national stories, global possibilities," *Social Justice*, 26:174–189.
Hite, D. (2000) "A random utility model of environmental equity," *Growth and Change*, 31:0–58.
Khisty, C.J. (1996) "Operationalizing concepts of equity for public project investments," *Transportation Research Record*, 1559:94–99.
Mackett, R. (1994) "Land use transportation models for policy analysis," *Planning and Administration Transportation Research Record*, 1466:71–79.
Matley, T.M. (2002) "Effective public involvement in transportation: a primer for practitioners," *Transportation Research News*, 220:4–7.
Pollack, T. (2001) "Transport disadvantage within aboriginal communities in an urban environment," *Urban Policy and Research*, 19:335–346.
Purvis, C.L. (2001) "Data and analysis methods for metropolitan-level environmental justice assessment," *Transportation Research Record* 1756:15–21.

Quan, R. (2002) "Establishing China's environmental justice study models," *Georgetown International Environmental Law Review*, 14:461–487.

Quillian, L. (2002) "Why is black–white residential segregation so persistent? Evidence on three theories from migration data," *Social Science Research*, 31:197–229.

Sanchez, T. (1999) "The connection between public transit and employment: the cases of Portland and Atlanta," *Journal of the American Planning Association*, 65:284–296.

South, L.J. (2002) "Public involvement and the organisational landscape: state departments of transport undergo culture shift," *Transportation Research News*, 220:18–25.

Strait, J.B. (2001) "The impact of compositional and redistributive forces on poverty concentration: the case of the Atlanta, Georgia, metropolitan region: 1980–1990," *Urban Affairs Review*, 37:19–42.

Tonn, B., M. English and C. Travis (2000) "A framework for understanding and improving environmental decision making," *Journal of Environmental Planning and Management*, 43:163-179

Transportation Research Board (2002) "Environmental and social justice surface," in: *Transportation environmental research: a long-term strategy*. Special Report 268. Washington, DC: National Academy Press.

Weeks, J.L. (2002) "Public Involvement by minorities and low-income populations: removing the mystery," *Transportation Research News*, 220:25–34.

Wessel, T. (2000) "Social polarization and socioeconomic segregation in a welfare state: the case of Oslo," *Urban Studies*, 37:1947–1967.

Chapter 32

WINNERS AND LOSERS IN TRANSPORT POLICY: ON EFFICIENCY, EQUITY, AND COMPENSATION

PIET RIETVELD
Vrije Universiteit, Amsterdam

1. Introduction

In many countries equity plays an eminent role in public debates on transport policies. This appears for example from the telling title of an EU green paper *Towards Fair and Efficient Pricing in Transport* (European Commission, 1995*)*. For the USA, Delucchi (1997) notes that "society cares at least as much about equity, opportunity, and justice as it does about efficiency." Another example is a proposal to increase the variable costs of car use and decrease taxes of car ownership in the Netherlands, which was predominantly presented as "fair" (Dutch Ministry of Transport, 2002) because it would mean that "those who travel much have to pay more."

This heavy weight attached to equity in political debates is not reflected by a similar weight on equity in *ex ante* policy studies in transport. The main tool for policy analysis in the transport field is cost–benefit analysis, and this focuses on efficiency rather than on equity aspects. One might argue that this is not problematic since the aim of cost–benefit analysis is modest: to provide information on the overall efficiency of policy proposals. After this information has been produced, it will hopefully play a favorable role in political discussions since it provides those in the political arena with the appropriate arguments. This leads almost inevitably to a gap between the input and output of political processes. But one may wonder whether this gap cannot be reduced. Why cannot one go one step further by addressing equity aspects and compensatory measures in a more explicit manner than is usually done in cost–benefit analysis? For example, when the additional costs implied by compensatory measures are taken into account explicitly, this might lead to an improvement of the outcome of political processes.

These concerns hold true for government policies in general, but in particular for the field of transport policy, which covers fields such as pricing, subsidies, and construction of infrastructure projects. In many countries the transport minister's job tends to be rather difficult compared with that of his colleagues. Problems such as highway congestion, environmental nuisance in aviation, public transport deficits, etc., are not easy to solve since effective policies are usually unpopular among strong interest groups. One might argue that when particular measures have a positive aggregate net welfare, everybody could ultimately be made better off when winners give sufficient compensation to the losers. However, as will be spelled out in this contribution, compensation is not the definitive solution for this issue.

The aim of this chapter is to analyze conflicts between efficiency and equity, and the feasibility of compensation as a tool to solve these conflicts. I start with a discussion of policy processes in transport. This is followed in Section 3 by an investigation of compensation as a tool to solve conflicts of interest in the transport field. Section 4 provides a joint framework for the analysis of equity and efficiency in transport policies. This framework is then used in Section 5 to analyze a number of equity concepts (e.g. "transport users should pay their way," "the polluter pays," and "progressive taxes are better than regressive taxes") sometimes proposed for transport policies. Section 6 concludes.

2. A politico-economic model of transport policy

In the classical Tinbergen approach to government policy (Tinbergen, 1956) the government is an autonomous actor. It is free to choose its targets and the mix of instruments needed to achieve these targets. The mixture of instruments has to be determined in such a way that responses of the private sector are anticipated so that the outcome is as close as possible to the policy goals.

Recent decades have shown that this is not a realistic approach. The social and political arena in which government policies are determined does matter. Therefore, when one wants to understand why governments prefer certain policy instruments above others, the explanation does not only follow from the anticipated impacts they have on the policy targets but also depends on the efforts the actors in the policy arena make to influence government. Figure 1 presents a simple politico-economic model with several actors: government, public bureaucracy, interest groups, voters, and political parties (e.g. Frey, 1983; Dijkstra, 1998).

Figure 1 does not give a complete picture of all elements having an impact on transport policies. For example, it does not include the role of mass media in setting the agenda and raising the interest of voters, and it does not address the point that the government is not a monolith but instead may consist of rival ministries. In addition, differences may be observed between the positions of local, regional, national, and supranational governments. Nevertheless, the figure makes clear that a substantial number of factors have an impact on transport policies:

Ch. 32: Efficiency, Equity, and Compensation

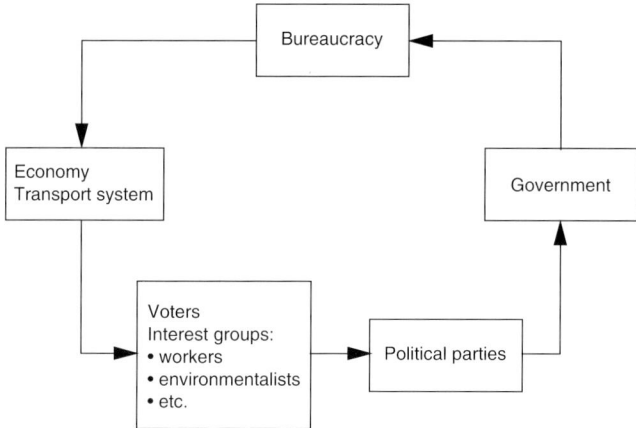

Figure 1. Interrelationships between government, interest groups, and the economy.

- the priority attached to various transport issues by voters;
- the effectiveness of interest groups;
- views of political parties on transport problems;
- government policies with respect to transport;
- bureaucratic routines in dealing with transport problems;
- the effects of government policies;
- the perception of voters with respect to their interests.

In this chapter we will focus on voter's views of transport problems. Let us take as a starting point the main criteria in the context of transport policies: efficiency, equity, and environment. Each voter may impose his or her own weights to these criteria, which can be represented by a point in the triangle in Figure 2. For instance, somebody who focuses entirely on efficiency and ignores environmental or equity considerations will be close to the top angle. This triangle can also be used to describe the position of interest groups according to the weight they attach to the three criteria. An interest group is defined as a group of actors with a joint interest who are prepared to take action to promote their vantage in the social or political arena. For example, environmentalists will put heavy emphasis on environmental aspects and less on equity, whereas labor activists do the reverse. Specific groups relevant in the case of transport are car users, users of public transport, residents living near a railway line, etc. In many cases the relevant actors within interest groups are voters, but sometimes other types of actor may be active such as transport companies and other firms. The importance of the three-dimensional presentation is that it broadens the framework of analysis so that actors do not consider alternatives according to simple dichotomies (e.g. growth versus the environment or equity versus efficiency) but that more dimensions are relevant. This leads to an enriched framework of analysis. For example, in a dichotomous setting a two-party system would lead to the result that parties maximizing the number of votes would both be very near the average opinion of voters (more precisely the median voter – Downs, 1957; Mueller, 1989). Such a simple result no longer holds true in a setting with three main dimensions.

In the figure one can also indicate the position of various political parties such as green, left wing, right wing, or center. These positions follow from the own ideological orientation of parties and of their linkages with the interest groups.

The views of voters with respect to the importance of transport and related problems are not stable but may undergo considerable variation during the course of time. An example is given in Table 1 for the Netherlands. From the table it can be seen that transport is generally not viewed as a problem area. The higher scores at the beginning of the 1970s are most probably related to traffic casualties, which peaked at that time. The increasing scores during the 1990s are likely due to increasing congestion. Environmental problems were considered significant in the early 1970s (the appearance of the *Limits to Growth* report), and in 1989 after the appearance of the Brundland report on sustainability. Equity issues related to the welfare state (e.g. allowances for people who cannot work for health reasons) were important around 1994, when a reform took place of the social welfare state. The high scores for unemployment are closely related to the structural economic

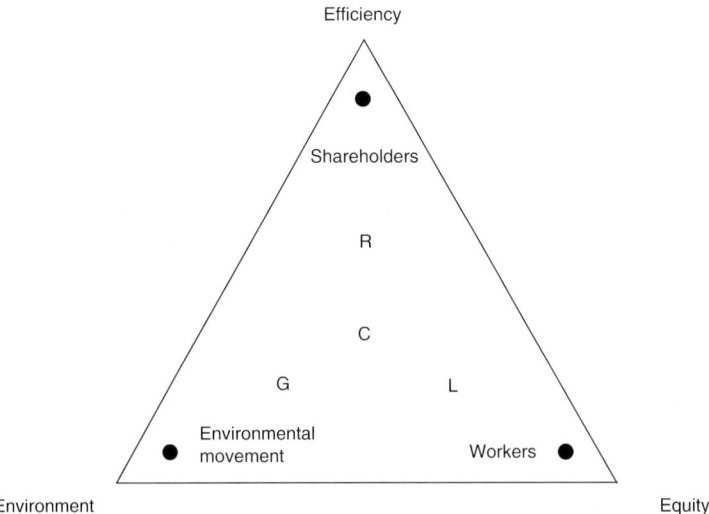

Figure 2. Three-dimensional representation of the priorities of interest groups and political parties (G, green; L, left; R, right; C, center). Any given point in the triangle will indicate the relative weights attached to efficiency, equity, and environmental considerations.

Table 1
The percentage of Dutch citizens, 18 years and older, experiencing particular social problems (1971–1998)

Problem	Year									
	1971	1972	1977	1981	1982	1986	1989	1994	1997	1998
Transport	12	11	3	1	0	1	3	4	12	13
Environment	37	33	16	25	11	13	58	16	13	19
Equity (welfare state)	8	10	12	14	9	16	8	32	8	8
Labor, unemployment	7	21	71	69	74	61	32	41	16	13
Housing	40	27	15	23	7	3	2	6	3	3
Criminality, law, order	8	5	14	13	13	17	16	23	43	43
Minorities, discrimination	6	7	9	9	7	13	9	51	32	42

Source: Central Bureau of Statistics (1998).

problems that became clear after the first and second oil crises. Housing problems gradually disappeared, as residential construction activity was high enough to alleviate structural housing shortages by the end of the 1970s. Criminality and immigration became important issues in the 1990s.

An interesting question is what mechanisms are behind these changes in the perception of social problems and how these relate to changes in government policies. For example, the business cycle will lead to unemployment cycles which in their turn will impact on the sense of urgency of voters so that governments stimulate the economy according to Keynesian principles (Frey, 1983). Also, longer-term economic cycles may eventually call for government initiatives toward structural reform in economies.

Another reason for the existence of cycles is that policy routines of bureaucrats (see Figure 1) do not adjust flexibly to problems when they emerge or disappear, but have a tendency to lag behind. They are late when a problem presents itself, and tend to continue when the urgency of the problem has already disappeared. This may lead to asynchronous patterns in the operational activities of civil servants and the problem perception of voters.

Major accidents are an interesting source of significant changes in public awareness and policy focus. Exceptional events such as major railway accidents or the terrorist attacks on 11 September 2001 may mobilize support for political measures (e.g. in the field of transport safety) that might otherwise never be possible and which may have a lasting effect, for example via legislation.

Within the transport field itself, Hirschman (1958) has identified a reason for cycles. He indicated that due to economies of scale in public infrastructure there will be a tendency that a certain investment program will lead to the creation of excess capacity. This will in its turn have a response from private sector investors

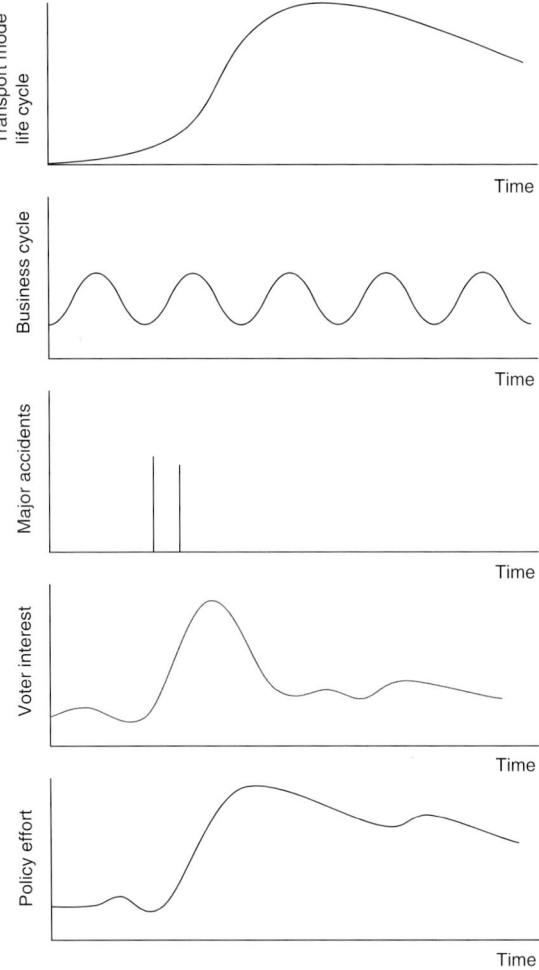

Figure 3. Policy cycles in transport.

after which, gradually, an awareness of bottlenecks will grow (Rietveld and Bruinsma, 1998). Since decision-making procedures for public infrastructure usually take many years, it will take time before the period of bottlenecks is followed by another period of excess capacity.

Another cycle has to do with long-run technological developments in transport. For example, Gruebler and Nakicenovic (1991) have demonstrated that technological developments (e.g. canals, railways, highways, and airport networks) have been characterized by long infrastructure waves. These waves are characterized by a rapid increase in the infrastructure stock during relatively short periods. Evidently, such technology cycles have implications for government policies in terms of regulation, legislation, and infrastructure supply. Figure 3 suggests how the various cycles may be related in time.

After having sketched this broad and long-view perspective on transport policies, we will now discuss in more detail the effects of policies on the various interest groups. Each policy will have its winners and losers, as presented in the triangle of Figure 2. Policy alternatives may be developed to improve the support of interest groups or to satisfy groups that may feel disadvantaged and demand compensation.

3. Compensation in transport policy.

An obvious principle for the evaluation of transport policies is that a policy is attractive when it leads to the situation that nobody loses, and some are better off. This principle is known as "Pareto optimality." In real-world applications, Pareto optimality is not a useful concept, however, because there will always be both winners and losers. For example, taxpayers that contribute to a road in another part of the country do not benefit from it, and hence are among the losers.

In order to arrive at more definite conclusions the Hicks–Kaldor (Hicks, 1939; Kaldor, 1939) concept of hypothetical compensation has been introduced, implying that a policy is welfare-enhancing when the gains of the winners are large enough to compensate the losers. This concept has received wide acceptance. It is at the heart of standard cost–benefit analysis, where the sum of benefits minus costs is the ultimate decision criterion (Button, 1992; Verhoef, 1996). This means that positive net benefits from winners and negative net benefits of losers are added. As long as the sum of these is positive, the implementation of a policy would improve aggregate welfare.

Although the notion of hypothetical compensation sounds attractive, it often leads to practical difficulties. The problem is that the alternative with the highest aggregate net benefits may be one where particular groups are hurt in an extreme way so that they have much reason to resist it and try to influence the political process as outlined in Figure 1. This leads to the idea of replacing hypothetical compensation by actual compensation: when the losers are compensated in reality, everybody will be better off, so that again a Pareto-optimal improvement is obtained.

The problem is that for several reasons actual compensation is not easy, and may even lead to additional costs that have a negative impact on the total performance of a policy:

- The costs of implementation of compensation may be high. This holds true, for example, when specific compensatory measures have to be taken (new vehicles of payment), or when negotiations on compensation can take a long time.

- It is often difficult to determine an adequate level of compensation. The uncertainty relates to, among other problems, the prediction of effects of a policy measure. Another source of uncertainty concerns the valuation of externalities such as noise nuisance. For example, when victims know that they will be compensated, it is tempting for them to overstate the noise problem. Of course, these problems will also be addressed when cost–benefit analysis is carried out and no compensation takes place. Wrong perceptions of winners and losers of their net (positive or negative) benefits may make adequate compensation and skimming hard to accomplish.
- Compensation may have adverse incentives. For example, if drivers who pay road-pricing charges are to be fully compensated, the original incentive to change behavior disappears. And financial compensation for noise nuisance may lead to the situation that victims are not motivated to move residence or take other preventive measures.
- Compensation usually has a lack of focus: it is directed toward broad groups (car drivers, all residents in a certain municipality, etc.) and does not address differences within groups. Since individuals within these groups are usually affected in a different way, this may easily lead to the situation that some individuals are undercompensated while others are overcompensated. Thus, compensation may only partially address the problem it is meant to solve.
- Compensation may be problematic because the resources for compensation cannot easily be mobilized. Note that the counterpart of compensation is skimming the net benefits of winners. Skimming is needed to mobilize the resources for compensation. In the case of infrastructure improvement, users of the infrastructure and landowners will probably be among the winners. For example, a development impact fee or a property tax may serve the skimming purpose, but legal limitations on these tools may make them ineffective. Letting the users pay for infrastructure sounds like a good idea but when there is little or no congestion it would lead to suboptimal use of the infrastructure. An easy solution would seem to be to forget about skimming the benefits and instead cover the compensatory measures by a slight increase in taxes. But this again does not entirely solve the problem since it means that one group of losers (e.g. those suffering from noise nuisance) is replaced by another group of losers: the taxpayers.
- Lack of trust of interest groups *vis-à-vis* the public sector may hamper agreement on compensation. For example, a policy to increase fuel taxes with the promise that car ownership taxes will be reduced may be rejected by the public if it fears that the decrease in the fixed taxes will only be temporary.
- A practice of actual compensation may lead to a culture where everybody is checking whether or not he or she will get a fair share of the pie. This makes citizens alert to distributional issues to such an extent that it becomes difficult to implement transport policies.

In the above discussion on compensation the original distribution of welfare is taken for granted, implying that the *status quo* is the reference point. This may have strange consequences. For example, it would imply that when the losers happen to be high-income households they would nevertheless qualify for compensation. Similarly, when low-income households are winners, their benefits would have to be skimmed. From a broader perspective on equity, such a redistribution would have adverse results, a subject that will be elaborated in the following sections.

A final remark is that even when actual compensation is feasible at zero cost it does not solve all the problems. The point is that the Pareto-optimality concept often does help in evaluating the benefits of one compensation scheme over another. In theory there are many ways to distribute an amount of money such that everybody is better off. But some methods of distribution will be considered fairer than other ways. This calls for a more explicit treatment of equity.

The conclusion is that actual compensation is not a feasible way to realize the highest possible aggregate net benefits while at the same time assuring that nobody is adversely affected. This does not mean that compensation is useless. In many cases it is unavoidable if a transport policy is to be socially acceptable, but the costs involved may be so high that policies that perform excellently according to cost–benefit analysis may nevertheless not be selected. A apt illustration is given for Norway by Fridstrom and Elvik (1997), who carried out a systematic investigation of the lack of correspondence between the cost–benefit analysis of infrastructure projects and the actual projects chosen.

4. A joint framework for equity and efficiency in transport policy

The last section demonstrated that when a policy has a net positive balance between benefits and costs, actual compensation to make everybody better off is usually not feasible: the equity issue cannot be solved simply by a redistribution of benefits. In addition, even if such a redistribution is feasible, the question remains as to which distribution is the fairest. This makes the equity issue important, and we will therefore discuss how equity considerations can be incorporated in cost–benefit analysis.

There is another reason why equity considerations are important. In the above discussion, distributional issues are treated as unintended side-effects of policies that call for correction where feasible. However, distributional issues may also be the prime focus of some transport policies. For example, the construction of infrastructure in peripheral regions may be driven by the desire to promote regional development rather than by efficiency considerations. This calls for an explicit introduction of equity considerations in the evaluation of transport policies and infrastructure projects.

A usual starting point of the analysis of equity is the Dalton principle (Marshall and Olkin, 1979): transfer of income from someone with a high income toward someone with a low income improves equity (and keeps the ranking of individuals according to income unchanged). A consequence is that an equal distribution of income is the most equitable one. This principle is stronger than the Pareto principle mentioned above. For example, when an income distribution between three individuals of (60, 80, 100) changes to (65, 80, 95) the Pareto principle cannot tell whether this is an improvement or not, whereas the Dalton principle can. However, the Dalton principle also has its limitations. For example, it does not tell whether a change from (60, 80, 100) to (69, 69, 102) makes the distribution more equitable or not. Further assumptions are needed in this case to judge whether such a redistribution is fair or not. To this end, a wide range of inequality indicators have been developed such as the Gini index, the Theil coefficient, and the coefficient of variation.

The above approach requires some additional elements to make it really useful. First, differences between households or individuals have to be considered. For example, a large household needs more income than a small one to keep them at the same welfare level. Similarly, a disabled person may need a higher income because he or she is confronted with higher costs (e.g. related to transport). This calls for the use of so-called equivalence scales in order to standardize for the needs of an individual or household (Deaton and Muellbauer, 1980).

A second shortcoming is that the Dalton principle and related inequality indicators are formulated in terms of incomes, whereas in the context of transport and the environment other dimensions also have to be included, such as quality of life and travel time. For example, major welfare consequences of many transport infrastructure projects relate to travel time gains and environmental consequences such as noise nuisance. This calls for a consideration of the welfare position of households rather than income. One way to do this is to use money metric utilities (e.g. Johansson, 1993), where these effects are added to incomes by using valuation methods.

To address the equity issue the government may use a social welfare function to evaluate transport policies. Let $x_1, ..., x_N$ denote the money metric welfare positions of all individuals (income corrected for quality of life indicators). Then, a social welfare function can be formulated to compare various distributions of welfare among individuals (Mueller, 1989):

$$W = W(x_1, ..., x_N). \tag{1}$$

In the simple case where the government ignores distributional aspects, the welfare function would simply be

$$W = (x_1 + ... + x_N)/N, \tag{2}$$

which is essentially the decision rule underlying traditional cost–benefit analysis.

Let $\mu = (x_1 + ... + x_N)/N$ denote the average welfare level. If the government takes into account inequality between citizens we arrive at more refined formulations where both the average welfare μ and its distribution are considered. An interesting candidate is (Rietveld et al., 2002)

$$W(x_1, ..., x_N) = \mu[1 - \text{INEQ}(x_1/\mu, ..., x_N/\mu)], \tag{3}$$

where $\text{INEQ}(x_1/\mu, ..., x_N/\mu)$ is an inequality indicator mentioned above, such as the Gini index or Theil coefficient. Since these inequality indicators are scaled between 0 and 1 the factor [1 − INEQ] represents total equality. Thus, in addition to mean welfare as taken into account in standard cost–benefit analysis, this formulation takes on board the distribution of welfare. This may lead to adjusted rankings where projects with a favorable equity performance may achieve high rankings, even when their contribution to average welfare is not favorable. This approach, called the integrated efficiency–equity (IEE) approach, also provides a good basis for the evaluation of projects that are proposed with an explicit aim of achieving equity.

5. Equity concepts

After having presented a general approach to include equity in policy evaluation, we will now use it to highlight a number of equity concepts as they appear in policy debates and in the literature. The IEE approach developed above will be used where possible to evaluate how convincing these concepts are. We will show that there are several equity concepts that are partly overlapping, and that there is no single concept which can be considered the "right" one. For a balanced transport policy several equity indicators apply, weighted to reflect the needs of a particular situation. A slightly related taxonomy of equity concepts is given by Litman (1999), who also gives a number of useful websites on transport equity issues.

- Consider the fairness concept that comparable individuals should be treated in a comparable way. This is adequately represented by the $\text{INEQ}(x_1/\mu, ..., x_N/\mu)$ function: a policy improving the position of a low-income individual and that leads to an improvement of total welfare would perform even better if expanded to include more individuals in the same category. This concept can also be generalized to relatively homogeneous groups or regions. For example, comparable regions need similar funds for public transport. This concept is termed horizontal equity by Litman (1999).
- A related fairness concept that is sometimes proposed is that all modes should be treated in the same way. This is often meant to imply that it is unfair when road transport has high fuel taxes, whereas no fuel tax is imposed on aviation, and rail transport receives subsidies. Although the

concept has some appeal, it needs to be more specific before it can make sense. For example, a fuel tax to address environmental concerns will affect both road transport and aviation, whereas a tax imposed to cover the costs of construction and maintenance of transport links is relevant only to road transport. A proper starting point will be that costs of public infrastructure and external effects are charged to the users for all modes in a similar way. Subsidies to certain modes might be defended from an equity viewpoint, but note that the equity-based decision criterion mentioned above relates to individuals rather than modes. When certain modes exclusively serve customers from certain lower-income groups it might make sense to provide subsidies to such modes, but in many cases this does not seem to be the case. For example Sociaal Cultureel Planbureau (1994) demonstrates that in the Netherlands there are two main groups of railway users who are over-represented: people from the lowest and highest 10% of the population. As a consequence, a relatively large share of public transport subsidies tends to go to the highest income groups. User side subsidies might be a way to reduce this problem.

- An equity concept with considerable appeal is "transport users should pay their way." As indicated by Gomez Ibañez (1997), this concept is usually interpreted in terms of average costs implying that the collective of all transport users pays for the entire aggregate costs. Since efficiency is characterized by marginal cost pricing, there is a potential gap between efficiency and equity here. For car users this concept would imply that what they pay in terms of car-related taxes should be spent for their benefit in terms of maintenance and construction of roads, surveillance, etc., and possibly also as a compensation for negative externalities. The social welfare function given above indicates that this concept should be evaluated both from its overall efficiency consequences and its distributional implications. The efficiency notion means that negative externalities should be incorporated in the car-related taxes, implying that both marginal congestion costs and environmental costs would be covered. Since for congestion the marginal costs are clearly above average costs, the application of the average cost approach would be at variance with the efficiency concept.
- Progressive taxes are preferred to regressive taxes. This rule follows immediately from the Dalton principle, and is consistent with the social welfare function W as long as equity gains in the $[1 - INEQ]$ part are not offset by a decrease in overall efficiency μ. Income tax usually has a progressive structure, with high-income earners paying a relatively large share of their income in the form of taxes. On the other hand, value-added taxes are proportional to expenditure (as long as there is only one tariff). The incidence of specific taxes such as those on tobacco or gasoline depends strongly on the consumption pattern of households. Those who

drive little will not be affected whereas those who drive a lot will pay more. In some countries there may be a tendency for an increase in the fuel tax or the introduction of road pricing to have a regressive effect because the expenditure share of low-income households is higher in these categories. It should be emphasized that the appropriate way to evaluate the equity implications of a policy is not its effect on disposable income. The impact of a tax increase is often computed as if there is no behavioral response so that the effects on disposable income can indeed be easily computed. However, when transport demand is elastic this is not the appropriate measure. For example, when demand has a price elasticity below -1, disposable income might even improve as a consequence of a price increase. As discussed above, the appropriate dimension is the impact on welfare. This entails the use of consumer surplus to determine the welfare effects of prices. In addition, welfare-improving effects such as time gains and air pollution should be taken into account. This would further aggravate the reverse equity effects of congestion pricing because low-income households tend to have more constraints on their travel times and will thus have lower gains from the introduction of congestion pricing. A countervailing force might be that a shift toward public transport as a consequence of congestion pricing would be equity-enhancing because frequencies would increase leading to lower scheduling costs of all users (Litman, 1999). Finally, note that the mirror image of this equity rule on progressive taxes is "regressive subsidies are preferred to progressive subsidies." This rule has already been discussed in a previous point, in the context of public transport subsidies.

- The well-known polluter pays principle has both efficiency and equity implications. The efficiency element is that it stimulates the polluter to reduce pollution to its optimal level. The equity element is that it is not the victim who has to pay but the polluter: an alternative principle would be that the victim pays, which would mean that the victim compensates the polluter for measures to reduce pollution. The polluter pays principle has gained wide acceptance in environmental policy. It is nevertheless of note that in many negotiations the right to produce external effects is considered a property right, and that the introduction of the polluter pays principle leads to negotiations where the polluters request compensation. For example, an increase in the tax on diesel because of environmental effects will probably lead to claims from transport companies for compensation in the form of tax reductions in other areas. And the introduction of road pricing leads to claims by car drivers for reductions in other taxes on cars (Small, 1992). These are obvious examples of informal property rights related to the *status quo* where the polluter pays principle actually means: "the polluter pays but gets compensation from the government who charges

the tax payers." The limitations of compensation have already been discussed in Section 3.
- Equity should not be considered at an annual level but in a lifetime context. This means that certain measures that appear to affect particular groups of households will have more moderate effects when one considers that household members have different needs and income levels during the various parts of their life-cycle (Poterba, 1989). For example, in many countries, children make extensive use of transport (including school buses), implying that they benefit extensively from subsidies. However, the implied transfers between households with and without children are much smaller when one realizes that those who benefit now will be contributors in the future. It is clear that such calculations are difficult because the variation in life-cycle patterns is large. Nevertheless, it is an important perspective that makes it clear that certain distributional issues are smaller than is often thought.
- A principle that is sometimes used in the evaluation of price measures is that "those affected most by a price measure are those that change their travel behavior," and therefore a policy that affects fewer people is preferred to a policy which affects more. For example, if a tax increase will induce certain consumers to reduce their vehicle ownership, the consequence indeed seems to be greater than when a tax increase does not change travel behavior so that the individual has to solve the budgetary problem by looking at other areas of his or her consumption. A closer look at this principle reveals that it is based on dubious grounds. After a price measure people are free to choose between changing their travel behavior or not changing it. Those that change their travel behavior apparently prefer this choice above doing nothing. Thus, they would be worse off even if they did not change their behavior! The implicit assumption behind this principle seems to be that those who change their travel behavior are among the lower-income brackets because they have less flexibility to absorb the price increase in their overall consumption pattern. But then it would be better to address the position of low-income households explicitly by focusing on the welfare equality factor [1 – INEQ] irrespective of whether the welfare change is the consequence of a change in travel behavior or not.
- "All persons should have equal access to transport services." This extreme concept has little appeal. For example, people living near a airport hub have by definition a higher access to this type of transport services than others. Another objection is that people have different needs, so that it does not make sense to aim at equal access. A more moderate concept is that "all persons should have access above a certain minimum standard." This concept is called "basic mobility" by Litman (1999). It is especially relevant for disabled persons, and in rural areas where public transport services are

spread thinly. An important difference between the two groups is that people living in rural regions might choose to live elsewhere, whereas such a choice does not exist for disabled persons. One might argue that people living in rural areas choose to benefit from low housing costs and a attractive rural environment so that they should solve accessibility problems unaided. Indeed, the integrated efficiency– equity formula is formulated in terms of welfare levels and not in terms of accessibility *per se*. In the case of disabled persons, minimum levels of access are a more serious candidate for the involvement of governments. Three main ways of addressing the equity problem can be distinguished. The first is to subsidize suppliers of dedicated transport services for disabled persons, the second is to give disabled persons an income allowance so that they are in a better position to pay for transport services – however, a general income allowance can be used for any purpose, and there is no guarantee that it will be spent on transport. The third way is a user-side subsidy so that the government can be certain that the money is spent for traveling. Clearly, the third policy has a certain paternalistic aspect, because the government imposes restrictions on the freedom to spend the money.

We can conclude that the integrated efficiency–equity formulation provides a useful framework for discussions on equity issues in transport. An important lessons is that not only is the trade-off between aggregate efficiency and equity important in transport policies but also that equity has many facets so that it is appropriate to use several equity concepts. However, not all concepts used in political debates are equally convincing. The advantage of the IEE formulation is that it helps to distinguish convincing from less convincing equity claims.

6. Conclusion

Equity plays a role in transport policies in two ways. First, equity problems may be an unintended side-effect of policies to address transport problems such as congestion and environmental nuisance. For example, opponents of road pricing may claim that it has adverse equity effects since it will hurt the poor more than the rich. Second, equity may be the explicit aim of certain transport policies such as the construction of infrastructure in underdeveloped regions, subsidies to public transport, or the provision of special facilities for disabled people. In this case, equity is more than a side-effect: it is the main motivation for a policy.

In both cases there is a clear need for a proper definition of equity in a broader context where overall efficiency is also to be considered. The IEE formulation, given in Section 4, is a promising tool to enhance the quality of policy-making. For example, it helps to arrive at a better understanding of a number of frequently used equity concepts such as "transport users should pay their way."

Of course, the IEE approach, which is essentially an extended cost–benefit analysis where equity considerations are explicitly taken into account, will not replace the political processes described in Section 2. It would be naïve for economists to think that they can dictate to policy-makers what they should do. More complete information is certainly no guarantee for a better outcome of political processes. Nevertheless, the information provided via an extended and enriched cost–benefit analysis has the potential to contribute to the transparency and consistency of policy-making processes.

References

Button, K.J. (1992) *Transport economics*. Cheltenham: Edward Elgar.
Central Bureau of Statistics (1998) *Nationaal kiezersonderzoek*, Voorburg: CBS.
Deaton, A.S. and J. Muellbauer (1980) *Economics and consumer behavior*. Cambridge: Cambridge University Press.
Delucchi, M.A. (1997) "The annualized social cost of motor-vehicle use in the U.S. based on 1990–1991 data: summary of theory, data, methods, and results," in: D.L. Green, D.W. Jones and M.A. Delucchi, eds, *The full costs and benefits of transportation*. Berlin: Springer-Verlag.
Dijkstra B.R. (1998) *The political economy of instrument choice in environmental policy*. Groningen: University of Groningen.
Downs, A. (1957) *An economic theory of democracy*. New York: Harper and Row.
Dutch Ministry of Transport (2002) *Wetsvoorstel kilometerheffing*. The Hague: Ministry of Transport.
European Commission (1995) *Towards fair and efficient pricing in transport*. Brussels: EC.
Frey, B.S. (1983) *Democratic economic policy*. Oxford: Martin Robertson.
Fridstrom, L. and R. Elvik (1997) "The barely revealed preference behind road investment policies," *Public Choice*, 92:145–168.
Gomez Ibañez, J.A. (1997) "Estimating whether transport users pay their way: the state of the art," in: D.L. Green, D.W. Jones and M.A. Delucchi, eds, *The full costs and benefits of transportation*. Berlin: Springer-Verlag.
Gruebler, A. and N. Nakicenovic (1991) *Long waves, technology diffusion and substitution*. Research Report 91-17. Laxenburg: International Institute for Applied Systems Analysis.
Hicks, J.R. (1939) "The foundation of welfare economics," *Economic Journal*, 49:696–712.
Hirschman, A.O. (1958) *The strategy of economic development*. New Haven: Yale University Press.
Johansson, P.-O. (1993) *Cost–benefit analysis of environmental change*. Cambridge: Cambridge University Press.
Kaldor, N. (1939) "Welfare propositions of economics and interpersonal comparisons of utility," *Economic Journal*, 49:549–552.
Litman, T. (1999) *Evaluating transportation equity*. Victoria: Victoria Transport Policy Institute (http://www.vtpi.org/tdm/tdm13.htm).
Marshall, A.W. and I. Olkin (1979) *Inequalities: theory of majorization and its applications*. New York: Academic Press.
Mueller, D.C. (1989) *Public choice II*. Cambridge: Cambridge University Press.
Poterba, J. (1989) "Reexamination of tax incidence: lifetime incidence and the distributional burden of excise taxes," *American Economic Review*, 79:325–330.
Rietveld, P and F. Bruinsma (1998) *Is transport infrastructure effective?* Berlin: Springer-Verlag.
Rietveld, P., J. Rouwendal and A. van der Vlist (2002) *Equity issues in the evaluation of transports policies and transport infrastructure projects*. Amsterdam: Faculty of Economics, Vrije Universiteit.
Sociaal Cultureel Planbureau (1994) *Profijt van de overheid III*. The Hague: VUGA.
Small, K.A. (1992) "Using the revenues from congestion pricing," *Transportation*, 19:313–333.

Tinbergen, J. (1956) *Economic policy, principles and design*. Amsterdam: North Holland.
Verhoef, E. (1996) *Economic efficiency and social feasibility in the regulation of road transport externalities*. Cheltenham: Edward Elgar.

Chapter 33

UNINTENDED EFFECTS OF POLICES

PHIL GOODWIN
University College London

1. Background

Most transport policies and substantial projects are implemented with an implied or explicit understanding of what they are intended to achieve – faster travel, or less congestion, or a reduction to environmental damage, fewer accidents, advantages for particular groups, economic regeneration, cost savings, etc. Confidence that the initiative will genuinely contribute to such objectives is usually sought through some sort of formal assessment or appraisal, using a model or set of calculations that estimate how big the effects will be. Such calculations are always simplified in some way or other – it is not remotely possible to calculate all the direct and indirect effects on individual choices and the whole economy, partly because we do not know them all, and partly because even if we did, it would be too big a task. And even those quantities that are calculated may not necessarily be correct, because of faulty assumptions or a biased modeling procedure. The hope is that the main effects will be approximately right, and the omitted effects will be unimportant.

This is not always true. There are many examples where there is much dispute in advance about whether the effects will even go in the desired direction, however carefully the forecasts are made, and in some cases these disputes even continue after the policy is put into effect, because the evidence collected may be ambiguous or cover too small an area, or too short a chain of cause and effect.

Since any intervention is likely to benefit some groups and not others, there will always be room for opposition, and the arguments of that opposition frequently depend on this inherent uncertainty in the appraisal: claims that "this policy will not do what is intended" are inevitable, ubiquitous, and sometimes justified.

There is no established body of research results dealing specifically with this problem in a coherent way, although the author collated some early evidence in Goodwin (1998), which provides more details about some of the examples below. Rather, virtually every major policy initiative in any country produces a mass of written material reflecting the arguments of the different participants, and often controversial policies are implemented only on condition that monitoring is carried out, producing "impact studies," for example before-and-after surveys,

Handbook of Transport and the Environment, Edited by D.A. Hensher and K.J. Button
© 2003, Elsevier Ltd

about what really happened after implementation. This chapter reviews a selection of these – in some cases where the unintended effect was a subject of great concern before implementation and turned out to be less of a problem than feared, and in other cases where there was little or no concern in advance, but a serious problem became apparent later.

2. Examples of problems

The following statements express widespread arguments, showing how broad the unintended effects may be. (They have not all turned out to be true.)

- "Building roads, especially bypasses, is intended to speed up traffic, with beneficial effects on transport and giving the opportunity for environmental improvements in the bypassed area, but the unintended effect is to generate extra traffic giving little or no speed benefit, and worse environmental damage."
- "Traffic bans are intended to improve town center street environments, but the unintended effect is to discourage shoppers and reduce commercial success."
- "Transport investment to reduce transport costs is intended to improve the efficiency and competitiveness of depressed areas, but the unintended effect is to encourage outward investment instead of inward investment."
- "Park-and-ride schemes are intended to attract car users to use public transport for a section of their journey, but the unintended effect is to encourage public transport users to transfer to car instead."
- "Priority schemes giving more road space to public transport, cycles, or pedestrians are intended to encourage environmentally benign travel patterns, but the unintended effect is to cause traffic chaos in the surrounding areas, increasing emissions and congestion overall."

In some cases, experience suggests that the outcome is better than feared, and in other cases worse, though a very common experience is that the initial forecasts did not very accurately predict what would happen.

The evidence on the statements above is now briefly reviewed, though remembering that these are just examples of a very wide class of potential problems.

2.1. Does road building to divert traffic from environmentally sensitive areas result in an overall increase in traffic?

Road building always has environmental consequences, partly due to the construction itself and partly to the long term effects of the traffic using the road.

These latter effects may be positive or negative, depending on the overall effects on the volume and location of traffic. The crucial question is often the balance between these two, i.e. does a new road only affect the location of traffic (in which case a bypass, for example, may reduce the local environmental damage within the bypassed area) or does it affect the total volume of traffic (in which case the environmental effects will be bigger, and more widely spread).

The official assumption in many countries in the past has been that road building affects the location, but not the volume, of traffic, though this assumption is less common than it used to be. It is a growing area of empirical research, of which the starting point was the UK Government's Standing Advisory Committee for Trunk Road Assessment report (SACTRA, 1994). European evidence is reviewed in European Conference of Ministers of Transport (1998) – which also extended the argument of public transport investment – and US evidence by Noland and Lem (2002). The reviews show that the evidence available is eclectic, with no one method or approach being dominant, though the most conclusive findings tend to be based on aggregate time series data, or before-and-after case studies, including traffic counts and travel surveys. There is a wide variety of indirect evidence on travel demand patterns over a very long time period.

Measuring traffic volume in terms of vehicle-kilometers or passenger car unit (pcu) kilometers on a network usually defined by a cordon (though sometimes a specific set of streets or counting points, with appropriate adjustments), the SACTRA conclusion was that a 10% speed increase would lead to a 5–10% increase in the volume of traffic overall. Observed traffic about a year after construction averaged about 10% more than forecast on improved sections, but over 16% more than forecast on "relieved" alternative routes: i.e. the prima facie evidence was that there was a greater percentage of induced traffic on the relieved roads than on the new roads. Of course, not all the forecasting errors are due to induced traffic. Specific improved roads show estimated induced traffic of up to about 40%, the larger figures being in congested urban conditions: in some cases traffic even increased, rather than reduced, on the alternative routes. Induced traffic was greater in the long run (up to 10 years) than the short run. The average results implied a rule of thumb for an average UK road scheme of 10% induced traffic in the short run and 20% in the longer run, though the results were very variable, sensitive to the policy context in studied areas, and large enough to have a significant effect on the economic evaluation of projects. Induced traffic reinforces (but is not the main cause of) the unfeasibility of matching road capacity to unrestricted traffic growth in congested areas.

Studies in many countries since then have reinforced this general pattern of results, albeit with a range of figures. However, it remains a controversial idea, especially in the USA and some other countries where the empirical evidence seems rather similar (e.g. Noland and Lem, 2002), but there has been some difficulty in incorporating them in official assessment procedures, for reasons that do not seem to be connected with either the theoretical or empirical evidence. The pattern is sometimes that countries for which road building forms a larger part of their transport strategy show more resistance to the idea that such building is likely to induce additional traffic – though countries planning to expand public transport infrastructure often treat induced custom as likely, and intended.

A strategic approach to try to completely match road capacity to demand has now been abandoned, *de facto* although not always in principle, in many countries, for reasons not confined to induced traffic. On those occasions where new bypasses are still built, it is suggested that they can be of lower capacity than traditionally assumed, and must in any case be accompanied by simultaneous traffic restriction measures in the bypassed area, and sometimes with demand management (e.g. ramp metering, speed control, capacity allocation, or pricing) on the expanded road to prevent its intended benefits being undermined by induced traffic. Without these conditions (and sometimes even with) it may be taken as very likely that road construction will have an negative environmental impact overall, even if the intention is that it should have a positive one.

2.2. Does town center pedestrianization reduce trade?

Traffic bans or restrictions in town centers are now a quite popular world-wide movement, usually justified in terms of environmental impact, albeit with several different definitions of "environment," ranging from the aesthetic quality and attractiveness of street architecture, through local noise and noxious emissions, to broader questions of air quality and climate change. Effects on retail turnover have been a concern from the beginning (as well as traffic impacts outside the town center). The earliest large-scale applications were led from Germany, with interest in many other European countries and, recently, Australia, the USA, Canada, and other countries. The seminal empirical studies were carried out in Germany, and collated in English by Hass-Klau (1993) together with literature reviews focusing on Germany and the UK; pedestrian counts, on-street surveys, and historical data from 20 towns notably Belfast, Dresden, Schwerin, Munich, Nuremberg, Reading, and Luneburg. Recently, the wider range of cities implementing such policies has resulted in a large number of results from specific towns, from which no consistent evidence has emerged to disprove the early results, but showing quite a wide range that seems to be connected to interactions with other policies in operation.

Hass-Klau's conclusion, broadly followed by others, for example Carley and Donaldson's (1997), is that the unintended effect does exist in reality, as well as being a very strong and recurrent perceived problem among retailers, but typically only for a temporary period, due to problems of disruption of shopping patterns that can last for a year or two. In most cases, well-implemented pedestrianization improved retailing success and was popular among shoppers. As would be expected, after a time retailers become reassured, and sometimes then campaign for an expansion of the restricted area that they had initially opposed. The number of pedestrians has increased by 20–40% in many cases, and may even double. However, part of the increased volume of trade is absorbed in higher rents or local taxes, bringing benefits to other groups besides retailers. There are also problems at the margins of the pedestrianized area, and potential loss of political momentum if implementation is slow or complicated. A study of 31 European cities suggested that towns with light rail systems (which on average are the richer towns, though the direction of cause and effect is not established) tend also to adopt more ambitious pedestrianization schemes than those without. In this sample, towns without light rail schemes had on average 2.7 km of pedestrian-only streets in the town center, and towns with light rail systems averaged 4.9 km of pedestrian-only streets. (Hass-Klau and Crampton, 2002). Hence, it is not entirely possible to distinguish whether it is the better public transport systems or the calmer streets that is most influential in attracting shoppers, and most planners in such cities conclude that both are necessary.

Pedestrianization of large areas, using traditional street patterns, high design standards, and relatively speedy implementation, seems most successful. While political consensus is crucial, this is not necessarily helped by slow and cautious progress.

2.3. Does transport investment discourage economic growth and regeneration?

Although a large number of transport improvement schemes are undertaken with the intention of solving economic difficulties in a local area, or encouraging growth overall, there has been a widespread experience that the optimistic claims of developers are not always converted into reality, and almost never provided with convincing statistical evidence. The UK advisory committee SACTRA (1999) collated international evidence on this, including empirical work in the USA and Germany, case studies in the UK, and developments in economic theory including the "new economic geography" that deals with spatial effects in economies where competition is imperfect. The work has been extended in an international review by European Conference of Ministers of Transport (2001) and in a Dutch study supported by several different government departments (Onderzoek Economische Effecten Infrastructuur, 2002).

These reviews show that the subject remains controversial, with some claims for very large effects that are disputed in quantity and even direction. SACTRA concluded that the statistical evidence was unconvincing and often spurious, and such effects as existed were probably small in mature economies (historical experience of opening up the west of the USA, or Siberia, for example, or the

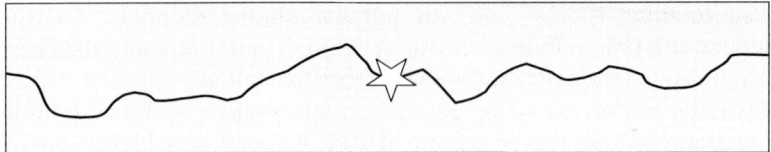

Figure 1. The rectangle represents a country, and the line a very slow road. The star represents a transport enterprise located centrally in the country.

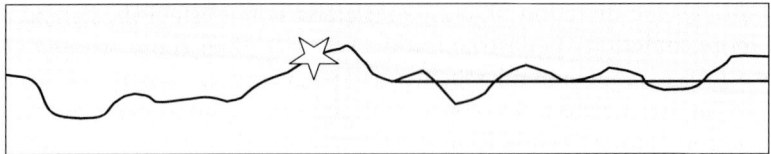

Figure 2. The eastern region has built a fast road, and the transport enterprise has moved west to take advantage of this new road.

economic impacts of the construction of entirely new networks of canals, railways, or motorways, are manifestly connected with transport, but not of relevance to marginal changes in those networks in modern conditions). However, two important theoretical arguments were identified – the "two-way road" and distorted prices.

The "two-way road" was a criticism of the custom of discussing, for example, "roads to ports that encourage exports" without mentioning "roads from ports which encourage imports." An example (drawn from a student exercise devised by the author, adapting a classical proposition knows as the "ice-cream seller problem") is as follows.

Consider a long thin country provided with one very slow east–west road, with one transport enterprise that has sensibly located in the middle, in order to minimize its distances from all destinations (Figure 1). The country has two regions: one in the east and the other in the west.

The central position chosen by the transport enterprise just happens to be on the border between the two regions, each of which wants to attract the company into its own territory for reasons of employment, tax revenue, etc. The region in the east therefore builds a new road, substantially increasing speed (Figure 2). The company decides to relocate to take advantage of this. The question is, which direction should the company move?

The answer is that the best position for the company is now to move away from the improved road, not toward it. The reason for this is that the "middle," in terms of travel time, is still the best position, and the middle is now further west. Of course, in practice this will not always apply because of other factors in the decision, second-round impacts, and the more complicated considerations in real, rather than ideal, space. But it is a strong indication that intention is not the same as outcome, as individuals and companies do not always behave in the way that government bodies would like them to.

Concerning prices, economic theory suggested strongly that whether there were additional wider economic benefits or not depended markedly on whether competition was perfect or imperfect, within which the specific imperfection that was most important related to whether prices – both transport prices and those in the economy as a whole, including wages, etc. – were already well aligned with costs. If prices were too high (e.g. due to local monopoly power), an improved transport link could increase competition, bring prices down, and encourage growth (though not necessarily in the target area, as above). However, if prices were too low – as might be the case especially if external costs of congestion and environmental damage are not included in prices – then transport improvements could perversely have a negative economic effect by increasing the scale of these costs.

This argument remains largely theoretical. There are few, if any, empirical studies whose statistical results have commanded widespread agreement, since there is so much scope for dispute about assumptions and methods. However, the theory is sufficiently strong that potential unintended effects on wider economic efficiency should be taken seriously.

2.4. Do park-and-ride schemes divert people from public transport?

The main work on this was carried out for UK conditions in a series of papers in the mid 1990s, most recently updated by Parkhurst (2000). It is all case study based, comparing the outcomes of park-and-ride schemes mostly in medium to large English cities. Anecdotal evidence suggests that the features found are recognized by transport planners in other countries, though international evidence has not yet been collated in the same way.

Initial surveys were carried out in Oxford and York, together with comparative analysis of available studies from Chester, Bristol, Maidstone, Norwich, Nottingham, Shrewsbury, and Sheffield, with further updating surveys collated from various sources – with varying figures, but broadly similar effects. Questions asked were what users did before the park-and-ride scheme opened, and what they would do if it was not available. The answers showed quite a wide range in the different locations – from 42 to 81% of users of park-and-ride schemes had previously driven all the way into the town center, and from 2 to 12% had previously gone elsewhere. These were the intended effects. But from 5 to 40% had previously traveled all the way by public transport, and had been attracted to use the new park-and-ride facility, therefore using cars more, not less. This was an unintended effect. Further reinforcement was given by asking what users would do if the park-

and-ride scheme was not available: 33–78% said they would use their cars, and park in the city center; between 1 and 21% said they would go somewhere else instead; and 9–35% said they would travel all the way by public transport. Neither of these methods is completely reliable, as what people say is not always accurate, but they both show that there is a significant minority of users of park-and-ride schemes in the "unintended" category.

In the UK this work has led to a widespread recognition at local authority level that while park-and-ride schemes are a useful policy tool, they need to be designed very carefully if they are not going to erode the market for public transport. The main potential solutions relate to locating park-and-ride sites not too close to the town center; seeking improvements to the attractiveness of public transport services outside the town center, including bus priority measures on trunk roads leading to the town (these are not always easy to achieve); and reducing town center parking provision.

2.5. Does reallocating road space for environmental improvements cause traffic chaos in neighboring areas?

There is much interest in reallocating road space between general traffic, favored traffic such as buses or bicycles, new systems such as street-running light rail, other uses such as wider sidewalks for pedestrians or pavement cafes, pedestrian shopping areas, etc. These all involve taking road capacity away from (usually) already congested parts of a network. Concern about the side-effects is ubiquitous, and long-lasting, especially among those traffic engineers who are most familiar with a forecasting technique called a "fixed trip matrix," which assumes the total volume of traffic is fixed, spreading itself among different routes in accordance with ease of use. In that case, any traffic diverted from one route will necessarily be forced to a different one, adding to whatever congestion is already experienced there. In informal terms, this presumption also tends to underpin political disputes between residents or politicians of neighboring areas – who will have to take the traffic?

Evidence on this was reviewed by Cairns et al. (2002), with several updates, and supporting evidence from other authors, since then. Over 70 case studies have been examined, consisting of towns that have implemented one or other of the above policies, or have had road capacity reduced by other causes such as bridge maintenance, or earthquakes or other disasters. The original finding was that some of the traffic diverted from the affected road to other roads "disappeared." This proportion varied widely, according to the specific circumstances, the latest results showing a mean of 22% traffic reduction and a median of 11%. There were a few cases where traffic actually increased (notably where modest reductions in town center capacity were made in connection with increased bypass capacity, the induced traffic from this, in these cases, being bigger than the disappearing traffic from the town center measures). At the other extreme there were cases where the reduction in traffic overall was even greater than the traffic using a closed road, typically because of a build-up of effects from earlier policies.

"Disappearing" traffic is not a good description: the studies suggested that a very wide range of changes in behavior were involved, including the frequency and timing of trips, the method of transport used, the destination chosen, rearrangements in activities by individuals and households, and other changes made over a time-scale of several years.

The effect of these is that while the indirect effects of the policies were wider than had usually been expected, the effects on "traffic chaos" were usually less than had been feared, not more. This is an example where the concern about unintended effects was often overstated, on occasion leading to backing away from initiatives that would have been helpful.

3. Conclusions

Taking the initial list of examples, the author's somewhat judgmental summary of the evidence is shown in Table 1.

Policy instruments serve a wide range of objectives, and we know more about how to predict some of them than others. Similarly, there is a wide range of policy instruments, and we have more experience of some than others. The demand reactions vary widely, as do the contexts. As a result of these factors, unintended effects can occur because the objectives were not fully considered, or because the instrument is not well understood, or the demand and supply effects were not fully understood or were overlooked, or because the specific context had features that were not taken into account.

The problems discussed in this chapter are only examples of unintended effects: the general conclusion is that transport planners should always be aware that the effects forecast in the models they are using will nearly always be more complex than is assumed, and sensible assessment should look outside the modeled effects to evidence in other places, logical argument, and local knowledge. It would be wrong to assume that any claim of unintended effects is always warranted – often it will not be, or will be desirable – but this needs to be argued on its merits rather than by assumption or received wisdom.

The phrase "unintended consequences" is sometimes used as a device to oppose initiatives of any sort: any reasonably imaginative opponent will always be able to think of some plausible chain of cause and effect that would undermine the intended effects. Just as forecasts are often not as reliable as is hoped, so also not all reasons for disbelieving them are equally valid. Therefore, case study experience of similar initiatives in other areas will often be the most decisive evidence.

Table 1
Summary of the evidence for the problems discussed in this chapter

Unintended effect	Evidence
"Building roads, especially bypasses, is intended to speed up traffic, with beneficial effects on transport and giving the opportunity for environmental improvements in the bypassed area, but the unintended effect is to generate extra traffic giving little or no speed benefit, and worse environmental damage"	The balance of the evidence is that induced traffic does exist, and this is now widely but not universally accepted
"Traffic bans are intended to improve town center street environments, but the unintended effect is to discourage shoppers and reduce commercial success"	This is only true in badly designed schemes. Good schemes have the opposite effect, though with some delay of a year or two
"Transport investment to reduce transport costs is intended to improve the efficiency and competitiveness of depressed areas, but the unintended effect is to encourage outward investment instead of inward investment"	There is a strong theoretical argument that this can be true, especially where there are uncharged external costs of congestion or environmental damage, but there is limited empirical evidence either way. Great caution is necessary
"Park-and-ride schemes are intended to attract car users to use public transport for a section of their journey, but the unintended effect is to encourage public transport users to transfer to car instead"	There is much empirical evidence that this is true, but park-and-ride schemes are an environmentally benign policy tool only if accompanied by other supportive measures
"Priority schemes giving more road space to public transport, cycles, or pedestrians are intended to encourage environmentally benign travel patterns, but the unintended effect is to cause traffic chaos in the surrounding areas, increasing emissions and congestion overall"	This is not necessarily true, and the concern is often exaggerated, though supportive other measures can be necessary

References

Cairns, S., S. Atkins and P. Goodwin (2002) "Disappearing traffic? The story so far," *Municipal Engineer*, 151:13–22.
Carley, M. and S. Donaldson (1997) *Sustainable development and retail vitality: state of the art for towns and cities*. London: Historic Burghs Association of Scotland and Transport 2000.
European Conference of Ministers of Transport (1998) *Infrastructure-induced mobility*, Round Table 105. Paris: ECMT.
European Conference of Ministers of Transport (2001) *Assessing the benefits of transport*. Paris: ECMT.
Goodwin, P.B. (1998) "Unintended effects of transport policy," in: D. Banister, ed., *Transport policy and the environment*. London: Spon.

Hass-Klau, C. (1993) "Impact of pedestrianisation and traffic calming on retailing: a review of the evidence from Germany and the UK," *Transport Policy*, 1:21–31.

Hass-Klau, C. and C. Crampton (2002) *Future of urban transport, learning form success and weakness: light rail*. Brighton: Environmental and Transport Planning.

Noland, R.B. and L.L. Lem (2002) "A review of the evidence for induced travel and changes in transportation and environmental policy in the United States and the United Kingdom," *Transportation Research D*, 7:1–26.

Onderzoek Economische Effecten Infrastructuur (2002) Report.The Hague: OEEI.

Parkhurst, G.P. (2000) "Influence of bus-based park and ride facilities on users' car traffic," *Transport Policy*, 7:159–172.

Standing Advisory Committee for Trunk Road Assessment (1994) *Trunk roads and the generation of traffic*. London: The Stationery Office.

Standing Advisory Committee for Trunk Road Assessment (1999) *Transport and the economy*. London: The Stationery Office.

Chapter 34

GLOBAL WARMING AND EMISSION TRADING

TRUONG PHUOC TRUONG
University of New South Wales, Sydney

1. Introduction

The earth's climate is essentially determined by factors that affect the redistribution of energy within the atmosphere, or between the atmosphere, land, and the ocean. The primary source of energy that drives the earth's climate is radiation from the sun. To maintain its long-term equilibrium temperature, the earth must radiate back into space, on average, the same amount of energy that it absorbs from the sun.

Global warming occurs when human activities and natural processes release greenhouse gases (GHGs) such as carbon dioxide (CO_2), methane (CH_4), nitrous oxide (N_2O), hydrofluorocarbons (HFCs), perfluorocarbons (PFCs), and sulfur hexafluoride (SF_6) into the atmosphere. These gases prevent some of the heat radiated from the earth's surface from escaping into outer space, so that the earth's surface will tend to get warmer. It has been estimated that the earth's average surface temperature has increased by about 0.6 ± 0.2°C since the late nineteenth century, and it is very likely that the 1990s was the warmest decade of the millennium in the northern hemisphere, with 1998 being the warmest year in the instrumental record since 1861 (Intergovernmental Panel on Climate Change, 2001). There is strong scientific evidence to suggest that most of the warming observed over the last 50 years is attributable to human activities and is likely to have been due to the increase in GHG concentrations in the earth's atmosphere. Furthermore, if no action is taken now to reduce the current and future levels of GHG emissions into the atmosphere, which will add to these concentrations, current climate models predict that the earth's average surface temperature will rise by about 1.4–5.8°C over the period 1990–2100. This has the potential to cause significant climate change that could result in severe damage to the natural and economic environment and affect the well-being of humans as well as many other species.

International efforts have been made since the early 1970s to try to combat the global warming problem. In 1988, the UN Environment Programme (UNEP) and the World Meteorological Organization (WMO) established the Intergovernmental Panel on Climate Change (IPCC) and gave this body the task of assessing the current state of knowledge about the world climate system, the environmental, economic, and the social impacts of climate change, and also to study possible response strategies. The IPCC released its first assessment report in 1990, which provided a basis for discussion and for international negotiations on issues of climate change. This led to the creation in May 1992 of the UN Framework Convention on Climate Change (UNFCCC, 2003). The framework was signed by 154 states (plus the European Council) at the Rio de Janeiro "Earth Summit" in June 1992. It subsequently came into force in March 1994. The second assessment report of the IPCC was released in December 1995. In this report the IPCC elaborated on the so-called "no-regrets"[a] options and other cost-effective strategies for combating climate change. The IPCC second assessment report provided the foundation for the adoption in 1997 of the Kyoto Protocol, where industrialized countries[b] committed themselves to achieving quantifiable reductions in the levels of GHG emissions. The Kyoto Protocol also specified the mechanisms for achieving these emission reduction targets: the clean development mechanism (CDM), joint implementation (JI), and emissions trading (ET) (Articles 12, 6, and 17 of the protocol, respectively). Through these "flexible" mechanisms it was hoped that countries could share in the burden of adjustments so as to achieve the overall emission reduction target with a minimum level of costs.

GHG emissions have many different sources, but more than 95% of CO_2 emissions in industrialized countries are from fossil fuel combustion. Of this, the transport sector is responsible for 26% of the total CO_2 emissions, the manufacturing sector, 34%, and the energy industries, 19% (UNFCCC, 2003). Of the transport sector, more than half of the total CO_2 emissions are from private road vehicle usage. To reduce CO_2 emissions from the transport sector, a range of policies can be pursued. For example, policies to encourage or mandate improvements in the design of cars to improve on fuel efficiency, policies to encourage reductions in the level of car usage by switching to alternative modes of transport, through improvements in urban design, etc. The third assessment report of the IPCC (IPCC, 2001) estimated the potential for the reduction in CO_2 emissions in the transport sector of between 100 and 300 million tonnes of carbon equivalent per year (C_{eq}/year) in 2010, and between 300 and 700 million C_{eq}/year in 2020. This is about 10% of the total potential emission reductions in all sectors

---

[a]"No regrets" policies are those policies that have no net costs to society even if we assume that the world is not moving toward rapid climate change.

[b]Also called "Annex B" countries because the list was included in Annex B of the Kyoto Protocol, which includes all the countries listed in Annex 1 of the UNFCCC (as amended in 1988) but excluding Turkey and Belarus.

(1900–2600 million C_{eq}/year in 2010 and 3600–5050 million C_{eq}/year in 2020), or about half of the potential in the industrial sector (300–500 million C_{eq}/year in 2010, and 700–900 million C_{eq}/year in 2020). The per unit (direct) costs of CO_2 emission reductions in the transport sector is estimated to be around US $25 to US $50/tonne of carbon (1990 prices). Quite clearly, these costs vary between different countries and also between different sectors of the economy depending on different technologies used as well as different socio-economic conditions. When these costs differ, use of the "flexible" mechanisms of the Kyoto Protocol (such as emission trading) allows the achievement of an overall emission reduction target (for the world as a whole, or for a particular region) to be not only technologically efficient but also economically efficient, with a minimum level of total costs.

2. Global warming as a technological and climate change issue

The earth's climate has remained quite stable during the present interglacial period of about 10 000 years, with mean temperature changes not exceeding 1°C per century (Jepma and Munasinghe, 1998). Increasing energy use since the industrial revolution, however, has led to the rapid accumulation of GHGs – primarily CO_2, CH_4, and N_2O – in the earth's atmosphere at a level well above their naturally occurring or historical levels. Currently, the concentration of CO_2 in the earth's atmosphere is about 360 ppm by volume, compared with pre-industrial levels of around 280 ppm by volume. It is estimated that if no measures are taken to limit GHG emissions into the atmosphere, then, by 2100, carbon levels in the atmosphere will reach about 600 ppm by volume, or more than twice the pre-industrial level. With this doubling in the amount of CO_2 in the atmosphere, it is predicted that the global mean temperature will increase by about 1.2–2.5°C. Such a change is very large by historical standards, and would bring about major climate changes around the world. As a result, being wary of this potential problem, the UNFCCC stated in Article 2 as its ultimate objective, the "stabilisation of greenhouse gas concentrations in the atmosphere at a level that would prevent dangerous anthropogenic interference with the climate system" (UNFCCC, 2003). To ensure that this objective is consistent with the current economic and social policies of all countries, the article also stated: "Such a level should be achieved within a time-frame sufficient to allow ecosystem to adapt naturally to climate change, ... and to enable economic development to proceed in a sustainable manner." Sustainable economic development implies economic efficiency as well as other social and political objectives such as intragenerational and intergenerational equity and popular participation are achieved (Jepma and Munasinghe, 1998). This implies global warming must be considered not only as an environmental and scientific issue but also as an economic and social issue.

3. Global warming as an economic issue

Economists often refer to an environmental problem such as trans-border air pollution, or global warming, as an "externality." This is because the (environmental or economic) costs or damages associated with this type of problem are "external" to the individual decision-makers (consumers or firms, citizens or governments) who carried out the activities that contributed to this type of problem, and the people who bear the costs of these activities typically have no recourse to any action that can help them reduce or control these problems. In the case of global warming, the potential economic and non-economic costs caused by global warming are external to the parties that emit GHGs into the atmosphere, and are borne by the world community as a whole, which has no direct control of these activities.

An externality is said to exist when there is a lack of well-defined property rights (Coase, 1960), especially in relation to the use of a common resource such as the atmosphere. Lack of property rights implies "free" access to the resource, and this will result in the source being overexploited at great costs to all users, but with no user willing to take individual action to correct for these costs. In other words, there is said to be a "coordination failure" in the sense that individual self-interest is not coordinated toward a common goal, such as in the case of a perfectly functioning market, where an "invisible hand" (in the form of a price mechanism) can guide these actions toward a socially optimal market equilibrium. Coordination failure in the case of a common resource can give rise to the so-called "tragedy of the commons," whereby perfectly rational individual actions can lead to socially undesirable outcomes, such as over-fishing of oceans, or pollution of the atmosphere. To avert these problems it is necessary to institute some form of coordinated actions among all or most of the users of the resource.

Coordinated activities do not necessarily have to imply cooperation. Strictly speaking, cooperation requires some degree of willingness to take into account the common interest over and above individual self-interest. Mere coordinated activities, however, do not require this. Thus, for example, in the case of an impersonal market, the activities of the buyers and sellers are coordinated via the market price without any need for individuals to cooperate actively. To fully cooperate, an individual member has to give up the right to unilateral actions, and delegate all these rights to a representative body, which has the authority not only to lay down the initial rules for the distribution of rights and responsibilities among all members but also the power to enforce such rules. In the case of an international problem such as global warming, such full cooperation is difficult to establish. Consequently, non-cooperative but still coordinated activities or agreements, such as the Kyoto Protocol, are important objectives to strive for. The difficult issue is how to determine the scope of such non-cooperative coordinated actions to provide the foundation for voluntary but self-enforcing agreements among groups of countries that will in the end bring about a solution to the problem. This is an important and emerging issue in this area of global warming and emission trading (Carraro and Siniscalco, 1993; Barrett, 1994; Missfeldt, 1999).

4. Emission trading as an instrument for coordinating GHG emission reduction activities

As a first step in the coordination of activities among countries to reduce GHG emissions, some instruments for coordinating these activities must be established. In the area of global warming there are two types of instrument that can be used. The first is the imposition of an internationally coordinated carbon tax, levied on the emission of GHGs into the atmosphere. The second is the establishment of an internationally traded emission permits scheme. When a tax is levied on an emission activity, the cost of the activity is increased. This will tend to decrease the level of the activity. The extent to which a tax will reduce an emission activity is difficult to assess with complete accuracy because this will depend on the nature of the activity, its production processes, and its economic value to different users, and all these factors can vary from country to country. As a result, while the advantage of using the taxation instrument is that its cost is certain (the tax itself), the outcome of the tax policy in terms of a reduction in the level of GHG emissions is uncertain. In contrast, with the use of the emission permit scheme, the outcome is fairly certain with respect to the levels of emission reductions, but the costs of achieving such reductions may not be known with complete accuracy.

A permit is a "right" to emit a certain quantity of GHGs into the atmosphere. If the total volume of permits to be issued to all countries is known and targeted at a certain level (say 5% below the total level of world GHG emissions in 1990 by the year 2010, i.e. the Kyoto Protocol target), then the final outcome in terms of the achieved reductions in the world emission levels of GHGs will also be known with certainty (assuming that the majority of the countries responsible for a significant proportion of GHG emissions in the world agree to participate in the scheme). This is the main advantage of using the emission permits scheme. Furthermore, even if the costs associated with such emission reduction activities are not known with accuracy beforehand, the use of market mechanisms such as emission trading can help to ensure that the total cost to achieve the overall target is minimized. This is because the emission trading market acts as a coordinating instrument to guide emission reduction activities among different individuals and different countries in the world toward the use of the most cost-efficient method for emission reduction. There are, however, many important issues that must be addressed before such a scheme can be established. First, there is the question of what the total level of emission permits (the optimal level of emission reduction) should be. Next is the issue of an "equitable" rule for the initial distribution of these permits. Then, finally, there is also the question of a fair distribution of the gains from emission permit trade. These issues are considered below.

4.1. Determination of the initial volume of permits

As Article 2 of the UNFCCC stipulates, the ultimate objective of the convention is to achieve the "stabilisation of greenhouse gas concentrations in the atmosphere at a level that would prevent dangerous anthropogenic interference with the climate system" (UNFCCC, 2003). How should such a level be determined? First, we note that the stabilization of the GHG concentration level requires some targeting of the GHG emission level. If we then compare this to some "business-as-usual" reference situation, we can define an emission reduction target to be achieved, to stabilize the GHG concentration level. Reducing GHG emissions entails costs as well as generating benefits. The costs can be defined as those related directly to the abatement activities that can help to reduce the level of emission (abatement costs). The benefits, however, are measured in terms of the "avoided damages." If GHG emission reduction leads to a reduction in the level of global warming, and if this can help avoid certain damages that are associated with climate change, then these avoided damages are a measure of the potential benefits of emission reduction. While the costs of abatement can be estimated with some certainty, the benefits as measured in terms of avoidable (economic and non-economic) damages are more difficult to measure or predict with certainty. It can also be hypothesized that while abatement costs increase with increasing abatement (reflecting diminishing returns in these abatement activities), the benefits of avoidable damages will tend to decrease with increasing levels of emission reduction. This is because the reverse of this process – i.e. increasing the level of emissions – will tend to cause damages that increase with increasing levels of emissions. In other words, the risks of global warming and the potential damages caused by climate change are increasing at a faster rate than the rate of increase of the level of emissions.

Given the nature of these costs and benefits, we can then define an "optimal" level for emission (or an optimal level of emission reduction). This is when the net benefits (NB) of GHG emission reduction is maximized, where NB is defined as the difference between the "avoided damages" D (as a measure of the total benefit B) and the actual abatement costs C:

$$NB = B - C = -D - C = -TC,$$

where $TC = D + C$ is defined as the "total costs" of the emission reduction. Maximizing NB is thus equivalent to minimizing TC (Figure 1a), and this is achieved when the marginal abatement cost (MAC) of GHG emission reduction is equal to the marginal avoided damage (MAD). The former is a measure of the

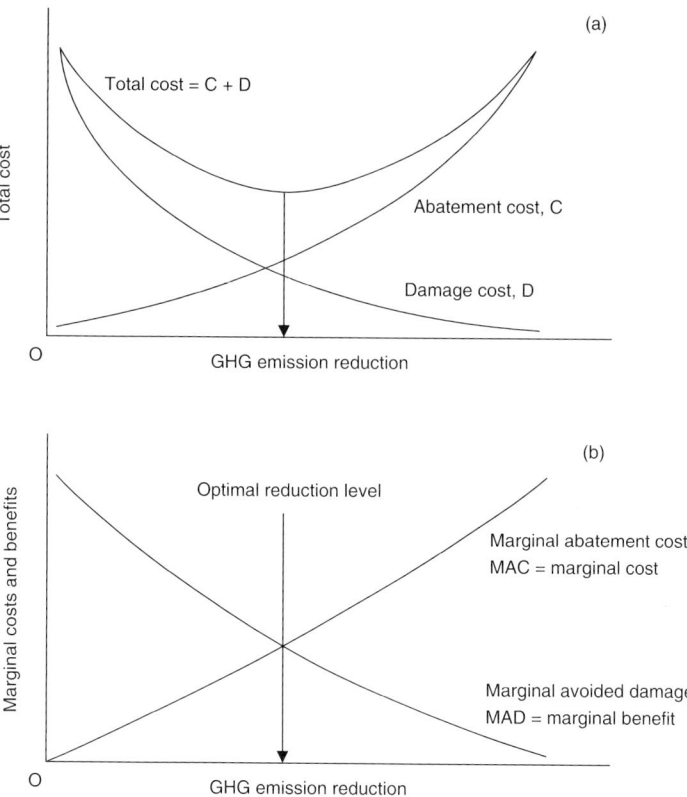

Figure 1. The determination of an optimal level of emission reduction. (Source: Jepma and Munasinghe, 1998.)

"marginal cost," and the latter a measure of the "marginal benefit" of emission reduction activity (Figure 1b).

In practice, the determination of an "optimal" level of emission reduction is made difficult by the fact that, first, the MAC is difficult to measure with accuracy because of the existence of a variety of methods for emission abatement associated with numerous production activities in various sectors of an economy and in different regions of the world. For example, among the many attempts to measure the MAC of CO_2 emission reduction in the USA, using various techniques, from top–down economic models to bottom–up technology-based methods, estimates have ranged from a negative MAC of –2% of the US GNP (a negative MAC implies significant scope for "no-regrets" options in reducing CO_2 emission levels) to a positive MAC of 2% of the US GNP – assuming a target reduction of 20% below a baseline case (Jepma and Munasinghe, 1998). Secondly,

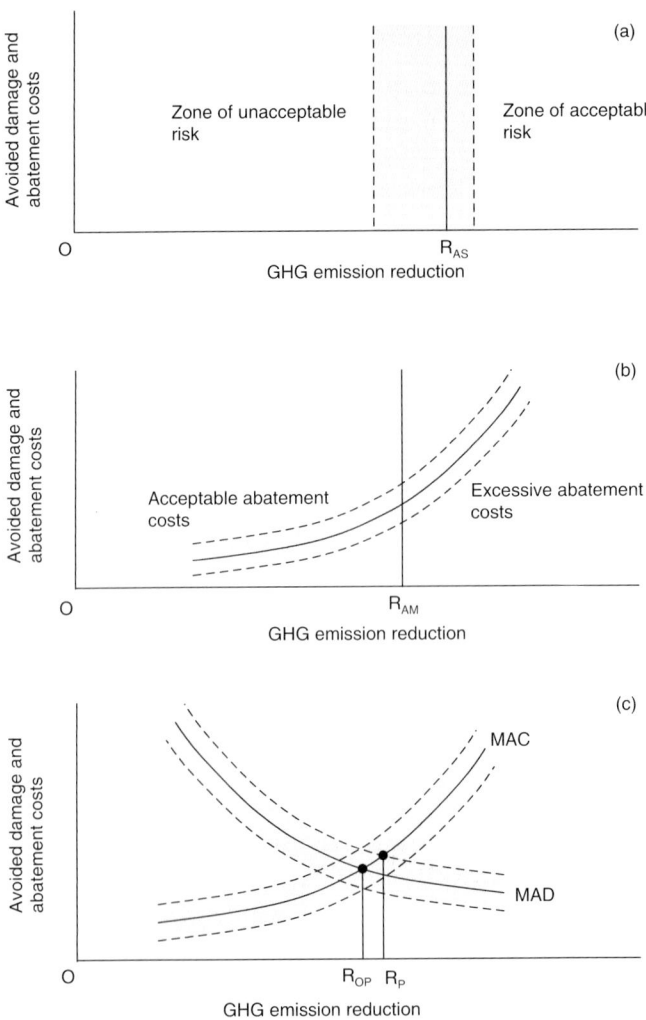

Figure 2. The determination of various standards for target reductions in GHG emissions. (Source: Jepma and Munasinghe, 1998.)

the MAD is also extremely difficult to estimate because of the uncertainty associated with the measurement and prediction of climate change. As a result, the theoretical concept of an "optimal" level of GHG emission reduction is often replaced by a narrower but more practical concept of a "cost-effective" emission reduction standard. For example, there are several standards that can be adopted in relation to the global warming problem: (1) an absolute standard (R_{AS}), based on a scientific determination of the level of unacceptable risk; (2) a less stringent affordable safe minimum standard (R_{AM}), based on an estimate of the MAC but subject to a constraint on the level of an acceptable risk; and, finally, (3) a precautionary standard (R_P), based on an estimate of the affordable MAC but also assuming the worst case scenario for the MAD (Figure 2). This precautionary standard is the standard endorsed by the UNFCCC in Article 3.3.

4.2. Distribution of emission permits

Once the target level of total GHG emissions reduction is defined – which also determines the total volume of emission permits – the next step is to distribute these permits among participating countries. There are different methods for distributing these permits: either by "grandfathering" (i.e. giving them out "free"), or by auctioning, or by a combination of both methods. Auctioning may be the preferred method for distributing the permits within a country because it can sidestep the equity issue of the volume to distribute, for example, among existing and future emitters. However, this option may not be feasible for internationally distributed emission permits because the equity issue in this case stands out as an important problem to be resolved before all signatory countries are willing to participate in the scheme. As a result, the most likely method for distributing the permits internationally would be by way of "grandfathering." However, before these permits can be distributed freely to each country, there must be a rule for allocating the initial volume of permits. There are several rules to choose from:

(1) the rule of equiproportionate reduction in emission levels stipulates that all countries are required to reduce their emission levels by the same proportion relative to the base year to achieve a particular global target;
(2) the equal per capita emission rule requires each human to be assigned the same emission rights;
(3) the equal per GNP emission rule entitles each country to the same emission rights per unit of GNP produced within the country.

The first rule is straightforward and is also easy to use. It has been estimated, for example, that if this rule is to be applied, and if the world as a whole is to meet the Kyoto Protocol target (5% below the total level of world GHG emissions in 1990 by the year 2010), then a uniform reduction of about 10% below the "business-as-usual" situation would be required for all countries (Jepma and Munasinghe, 1998). In effect, this rule was used for the setting of most of the emission reduction targets for Annex 1 countries in the Kyoto Protocol. The rule, however, may be considered inequitable by many countries. For example, a developing country may argue that, historically, industrialized countries have been responsible for most of the current concentration of GHGs in the atmosphere and, therefore, the industrialized countries should bear a greater burden of the emission reductions than developing countries. Industrialized countries, on the other hand, will argue that even though this has been true historically and the current levels of emissions by developing countries are still low compared with those of industrialized countries, in the medium to long term, some developing countries, such as China and India, will have emission levels that will be as high as those of industrialized countries. Therefore, to combat the global emission problem effectively, it is important that developing countries will bear a greater share in reducing their emission levels in the future. An equiproportionate reduction rule for both industrialized countries and developing countries therefore, will not only be inequitable, it is also ineffective in combating the global problem.

On the other hand, if the more equitable and more effective equal per capita or equal per GNP emission rules are to be applied immediately to all countries, this will put a great burden on the developing countries during the initial years when the major concerns in these countries are for social and economic development than environmental protection.

A compromise solution may be to apply these rules gradually, starting with the current levels of emissions as a basis for the distribution of the volume of permits, then, over time, the distribution approaching, for example, the equal per capita rule (Figure 3).

4.3. Emission trading and efficiency gains

Once the emission permits are distributed, an emission trading market can be established to enable countries to reach their emission reduction targets with a

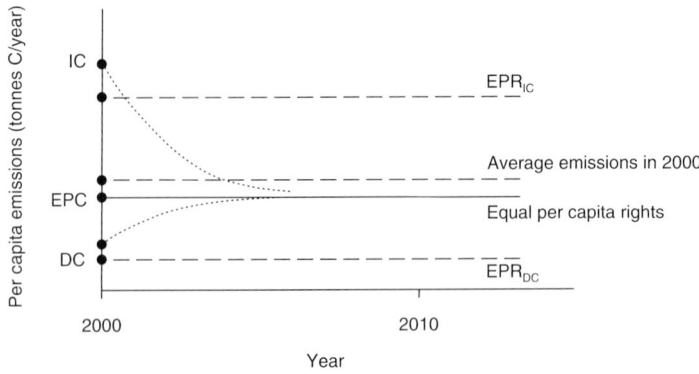

Figure 3. Allocation of initial emission permits. (Source: Jepma and Munasinghe, 1998.)

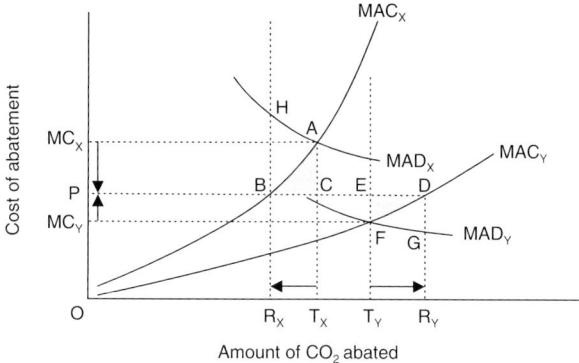

Figure 4. Gains from emission trading.

minimum level of costs. Trading can occur both at a national level within a domestic economy and at an international level between countries.

Consider two trading entities X and Y, which can be firms, or governments. Suppose these entities are allocated emission permits such that their initial targeted emission reduction levels will be R_X and R_Y, respectively (Figure 4). Let MAC_X and MAC_Y be the marginal abatement cost curves for X and Y, respectively. For firms, the MAC indicates the actual marginal costs of installing equipment to capture GHGs before they escape into the atmosphere, or of switching to alternative "cleaner" fuels (such as natural gas instead of coal). For countries, the MAC indicates the shadow price or opportunity cost of the resources used to reduce GHG emissions by one additional unit within the country. The country-specific MAC curve will depend on the nature of the production/emission activities within the country, and also on the characteristics of any emission reduction schemes established within the country (e.g. whether there is a domestic emission trading scheme, or the imposition of a uniform domestic carbon tax).

At the target levels of emission reductions, T_X and T_Y, the marginal abatement costs for X and Y are MC_X and MC_Y, respectively, and the total abatement costs are given by the areas OAT_X and OFT_Y in Figure 4. If these entities are now allowed to trade their emission permits, then X will cut its emission reduction target from T_X to R_X, and Y will increase its emission reduction target from T_Y to R_Y, so that $R_X + R_Y = T_X + T_Y = T$. X will then purchase emission permits from Y by an amount equal to $T_X - R_X$, while Y will sell its emission permits to X by an amount equal to $R_Y - T_Y = T_X - R_X$. The equilibrium price for emission permits in this case will be P. At this price, X gains an amount equal to the area ABC because the total cost of achieving the target T_X is now only $OBCT_X$ compared with OAT_X, and Y will also gain an amount equal to the area EDF because it can now sell the surplus emission permits $R_Y - T_Y$ to X at a price that earns it a revenue of $T_Y EDR_Y$ that is larger than the total emission abatement costs of $T_Y FDR_Y$. The sum of the areas ABC and EDF measures the efficiency gain from emission trading. The size of this gain is clearly dependent on the extent to which MAC_X diverges from MAC_Y. The greater the gap between these two MAC curves, the greater the potential for efficiency gains from emission trading.

4.4. Other issues relating to emission trading

Linking domestic emission trading schemes to international emission trading schemes

As a first step toward the eventual establishment of an international emission trading scheme, perhaps in 2008 according to the Kyoto Protocol schedule, many countries as well as private companies have started to design and experiment with domestic emission trading, to gain experience from these schemes and eventually to link them to the international trading scheme (Haites and Mullins, 2001). The purpose of the establishment and linking together of these different and diverse schemes is to increase the range of MACs for different emission reduction activities, which will then help to bring about greater efficiency gains and lower the total costs of emission reductions (Figure 4). In fact, it can be argued that in many cases the gains from domestic schemes can be as great, or even greater than, the gains from international schemes for some countries (Truong, 2001). This is because of the greater diversity of MACs within a country compared with those between countries.

Essentially, there are two different forms of emission trading: a "cap and trade" system, and a "baseline and credit" system. In the former system, such as that envisaged under the Kyoto Protocol international trading scheme, or under the US SO_2 domestic emission trading scheme, first an overall limit or "cap" is established for the emission level of each participant. Allowances or permits equal to the cap are then distributed, and then these allowances (called "assigned amount units" (AAUs), equalling 1 tonne of CO_2 per unit of AAU in the Kyoto Protocol international emission trading scheme) can be traded. In the "baseline and credit" system, such as that established under the clean development or joint implementation mechanisms of the Kyoto Protocol, a baseline of future emissions is first established for a particular emission entity or source. The baseline can be "business as usual" or "business as usual" with some emission abatement targets included. Credits will then be given (or debits deducted) for the entity if it can subsequently prove that it has reduced the emissions level below this baseline (or has increased the emissions above the baseline). The net credits can then be certified, and the certified emission reduction (CER) units (Kyoto Protocol,

Article 12) can then be traded or used in other ways to achieve compliance with a particular regulatory policy.

The practical as well as theoretical issues associated with designing and linking these diverse emission trading schemes include:

- What will be the most equitable and efficient way for assigning and distributing the initial cap or specifying the baseline for various entities?
- How can the emission allowances (allocated *ex ante*) or emission credits (given *ex post*) of an emission activity be exchanged over time?
- What is the time frame for the exchange, and should there be any limitation put on the exchange? (For example, can an entity borrow ahead or can it only bank the credits it has received?)

These issues form two groups: (1) institutional issues and (2) economic issues. In the former is the question of institutional compatibility (arising from the differences in institutional characteristics of different emission trading systems, which may limit the overall interoperability of the overall system). In the latter is the question of economic efficiency and equity. Efficiency implies a given level of an environmental aggregate target can be achieved at a minimum level of costs. Equity requires that the distribution of the overall burden of adjustments falls fairly among all sources of emissions (Haites and Mullins, 2001).

Market power

Although, in principle, emission trading will deliver efficiency gains to all participating countries, in practice the distribution of these gains depends on the distribution of market power in the permit market. Normally, if permits are distributed by a national government to various production units within the country, then the number of traders in the emission permit market will be large, and the question of market power may not arise. However, if governments hold on to the permits, and if the quantity of permits held by a particular government is large relative to its emission needs, then there is the potential danger for monopolistic behavior by a particular seller of emission permits, who may want to restrict the volume of permits it wishes to sell, to raise the price and earn a greater profit. For example, it has been estimated that under the current emission commitments of the Kyoto Protocol, the eastern European countries forming the Commonwealth of Independent States (CIS) will be in possession of a large volume of emission permits that it will not need to hold on to because the economies of these states are undergoing changes, and during this period the actual level of economic activities – and hence GHG emissions – in these countries will drop significantly below their "business-as-usual" levels even without any efforts to reduce GHG emissions. The CIS can therefore potentially become a monopolistic power with regard to these emission permits, and if it decides to exercise this power, and according to one estimate (Organisation for Economic Co-operation and Development, 2001) the price of an emission permit in the year 2010 could reach a level as high as 20% above its "competitive price." Of course, counteracting this potential monopolistic power is the monopsonistic power of a potentially large permit buyer such as the USA (Organisation for Economic Co-operation and Development, 2001). In practice, however, and with the current outlook, market power is more likely to come from sellers rather than from buyers.

Equity issues and gains from emission trading

Much of the debate about "equity" in emission trading focuses on the initial distribution of emission permits (the initial distribution of emission reduction commitments). For example, the USA cites the lack of initial commitments by developing countries as reasons to justify its withdrawal from the Kyoto Protocol. If we treat emission permits as a natural (and common) resource that can be used as an input into production or consumption activities, then the initial distribution of the permits will give each country an initial "endowment," or initial "rights" to a common resource (the atmosphere), and each country can then use these endowments in their production or consumption activities. The equity issue in relation to the initial distribution of the emission rights is well understood and debated. It is connected to the question of access and usage of a common resource for individual or regional welfare improvement. What is not well understood, however, is the question of equity in relation to the subsequent trade of these rights for "profits." The reason why this becomes an equity issue is that, it has been argued, there is a fundamental difference between the right to use or have access to a common resource for the sole purpose of enjoyment and welfare improvement, and the right to own the resource that can then be traded for "profits" (e.g. Bohringer and Helm, 2002). According to this view, if the resource is by definition a "common" property, then only the first right is justified, not the second. The right to own and trade such a common property for private profit is considered to contradict the definition of "common property." When the right for access is used mainly to facilitate the coordination of emission reduction activities among different regions to reduce the overall emission abatement costs, then it is considered to be justified and beneficial. But when it is used mainly to generate "excessive profit" for one country at the expense of another, then it is considered to be inequitable.

To illustrate this point in detail, consider Figure 4 again. Here, it is argued that if entity Y is selling its emission rights to entity X, then it is fair for Y to expect X to compensate it for the costs (of emission reductions), which is equal to the area $R_Y FDS_Y$. However, it would be unfair for Y to gain from X an amount that reflects not so much the actual costs to Y but rather the willingness to pay (for a general improvement in the common environment), considered from the viewpoint of X. This is perceived as unfair because the problem of emission reduction is a common one, for both X and Y, and, therefore, Y should not take advantage of the greater willingness of X to pay for this common problem, so that Y makes a profit from X.

If we now represent each country's willingness to pay for the common problem by their respective MAD curves, then, to ensure that all countries participate in the scheme, the initial distribution of the permits should be such that they correspond to the points of intersection between the MAD curves and the MAC curves. From Figure 4, the costs to Y for increasing emission reductions from R_Y to S_Y is then given by the area $T_Y FDR_Y$. But Y also derives some benefits from this effort, which is given by the area $T_Y FGR_Y$. The least that Y should be compensated for is thus the area FDG, which represents the net costs. X, on the other hand, enjoys a gross benefit of $R_X HAT_X$ from the emission reduction activity of $(R_Y - T_Y)$ or $(T_X - R_X)$, which can also be used to measure the willingness of X to pay for this emission reduction activity. While emission trading allows both countries to gain from improved efficiency (as measured by the area ABC + DEF), it can also result in an unfair distribution of the gains since there has been an income transfer of $R_X BCT_X = T_Y EDR_Y$ from X to Y, and this transfer largely reflects not so much a "just" compensation for Y for its costs but rather an "unjust" exploitation of X's higher willingness to pay for a common problem.

4.5. Free trade in goods and free trade in emission permits

Free-riding, carbon leakage, and bootstrapping effects

One of the greatest obstacles in encouraging countries to cooperate to deal with a common resource problem such as global warming is the issue of "free-riding." Free-riding implies a country can enjoy the benefit of reduced global warming from another countries' efforts, without having to pay for this in terms of its own efforts to reduce the problem. Free-riding shifts the burden of adjustment from one country to other countries, but, by itself, it does not necessarily aggravate the problem further. This does not mean that, in practical terms, a free-rider will not increase its own GHG emissions in response to other countries' emission reductions. With an increased level of the common resource (clean atmosphere) now available for all to use "freely," the free-rider may decide to use more of this resource on production and/or consumption activities, and, therefore, will increase its own level of GHG emissions over and above the "business-as-usual" situation.

When there is no free trade in goods between countries, free-riding is the only hazard to the common resource problem. When there is a free trade in goods, however, another problem arises – the "carbon leakage" effect. This effect has the following mechanism: the committed countries (i.e. non-free-riders) are now less competitive than the free-rider in the production of carbon-intensive goods (so-called "dirty" goods) because of the higher burden of carbon emission reductions imposed when producing these goods, and the free-rider can take advantage of this and export more of these goods (assuming that the free-rider is a specialized exporter of these "dirty" goods). The carbon emission level in committed countries therefore may be reduced, but this is offset by an increase in the emission levels in non-committed countries.

Carbon leakage is induced by a "pure substitution effect" in producers' activities caused by changing cost structures and hence changing relative prices and terms of trade between committed and non-committed countries. Depending on whether the non-committed countries are predominantly producers or consumers, exporters or importers, of "clean" or "dirty" goods, the carbon leakage effect can range from being inconsequential (perhaps even negative) to quite significant. If positive and significant, the carbon leakage effect will then add to the free-riding effect to offset some of the emission reduction efforts made by committed countries.

There is, however, also a "pure income effect" arising from the changed terms of trade effects between committed and non-committed countries, and this will cause a reduction rather than an increase in the carbon emission levels of non-committed countries. This is because with increased real income levels arising from favorable terms of trade and increased exports of higher-priced "dirty" goods, non-committed countries can now decide to spend some of this increased real income on "environmental goods" (i.e. emission reductions) – assuming that environmental goods are normal goods in these countries. This pure income effect is called "bootstrapping" (Copeland and Taylor, 2000).

Free trade in goods and emission trading

While carbon leakage is seen to reduce the overall effectiveness of unilateral emission reduction activities by committed countries, it acts, however, as a device through which the overall efficiency of such emission reduction activities can be increased. Through this carbon leakage effect the MAC between different countries can be equalized, just as free trade can bring about an equalization of the costs of other factors of production (labor and capital) even though these factors are immobile between countries. If we regard "emission reduction" (clean air) as a factor of production, then free trade in goods can also help to bring about an equalization of MACs for different countries even in the absence of emission trading. This implies that a free trade in goods can be regarded as a strategic substitute for free trade in emission permits. This has an important implication: irrespective of the initial distribution of the emission permits, a free trade in goods (as well as a free trade in emission permits) will help to increase the efficiency of the trading system. Therefore, negotiations on the initial distribution of emission permits can concentrate more fully on the difficult issue of equity.

References

Barrett, S. (1994) "Self-enforcing international environmental agreements," *Oxford Economic Papers*, 46:878–894.
Bohringer, C. and C. Helm (2002) *Fair division with general equilibrium effects and international climate politics.* Working Paper. Magdeburg: University of Magdeburg.
Carraro, C. and D. Siniscalco (1993) "Strategies for the international protection of the environment," *Journal of Public Economics*, 52:309–328.
Coase, R. (1960) "The problem of social costs," *Journal of Law and Economics*, 1:1–45.
Copeland, B.R. and M.S. Taylor (2000) *Free trade and global warming: a trade theory view of the Kyoto Protocol.* NBER Working Paper No. 7657. Cambridge: National Bureau of Economic Research.
Haites, E. and F. Mullins (2001) *Linking domestic and industry greenhouse gas emission trading systems.* Toronto: Margaree Consultants.
Intergovernmental Panel on Climate Change (1995) *Second assessment climate change report.* Geneva: IPCC.
Intergovernmental Panel on Climate Change (2001) *Climate change 2001: synthesis report.* Geneva: IPCC.
Jepma, C. and M. Munasinghe (1998) *Climate change policy.* Cambridge: Cambridge University Press.
Missfeldt, F. (1999) "Game theoretic modelling of transboundary pollution," *Journal of Economic Surveys*, 13:287–321.
Organisation for Economic Co-operation and Development (2001) *Market power and market access in international GHG emission trading.* OECD and IEA Information Paper. Paris: OECD.
Truong, T.P. (2001) "The costs of CO_2 gas emission reductions in major Annex 1 and Non-Annex 1 economies: a comparative study using the GTAP-E model," in: *30th Annual Conference of Economists*. Paper. Perth.
UN Framework Convention on Climate Change (2003) *United Nations Framework Convention on Climate Change* (http://unfccc.int/). Bonn: UNFCCC.

Chapter 35

TRAVEL, TOURISM, AND THE ENVIRONMENT

KENNETH J. BUTTON
George Mason University, Fairfax

1. Introduction

The rising incomes and increased amounts of leisure time enjoyed by many people in industrialized countries has led to an expansion in travel for recreational purposes. Each year there are mass short-term migrations to areas where the climate is more favorable, the scenery more attractive, where there are different cultures to sample, or where there are antiquities to see. Added to this, families are becoming more spatially extended, and as a result family visitations often involve longer trips. As a consequence, tourism is now a major industry that is a significant source of income and employment in many developed and developing economies.[a]

Modern, expansive, and relatively cheap transportation makes much of this possible. Indeed, many charter airline companies, bus companies, and shipping concerns rely on tourism as their main source of business. But this growth in tourism has often been accompanied by increasingly harmful environmental intrusion (Sidhu, 1994).

Here we look at the links between transportation, tourism, and the environment, but there are boundaries to this contribution. It is concerned with the environmental implications of leisure travel but only for longer-distance movements. Individuals travel to nearby sporting, cultural, and other events for leisure purposes, but these local trips are not the main subject here.[b] There is also increasing numbers of references in the transportation literature to "everyday tourism," meaning the enjoyment people get from just driving around, often in cities and sometimes even involving commuting – again this is not considered. The contribution is concerned

---

[a] Although the evidence is that about 55% of the income leaves the host countries in the latter case.

[b] The World Tourism Organization (WTO), an intergovernmental organization, defines tourism as situations where an overnight stay is involved. The WTO also produces regular data sets and forecasts covering most aspects of tourism – see the WTO website (www.world-tourism.org).

Handbook of Transport and the Environment, Edited by D.A. Hensher and K.J. Button
© 2003, Elsevier Ltd

with longer distance non-work travel, often to destinations that have been specifically developed for leisure purposes. In many cases the travel is an integral part of the leisure activity, and may be marketed in conjunction with it, but in others it is purely a necessary cost of reaching the final activity.

The term "tourism" has specific connotations concerning individuals moving from place to place to view and visit. Here it is used in the more general sense of individuals traveling somewhere to enjoy leisure pursuits, including family visits, for a short period of time. Of course, this may embody several movements from place to place and the ability to sight-see as movement takes place, but that is more of a special case. What is important is that tourism very often depends on the environment – both natural and built – for its success. Tourists visit to enjoy an attraction, and the value of any tourist location diminishes if the quality of this attraction significantly deteriorates. This has long been a major dilemma confronting the tourist industry.

2. Background

2.1. The history

Perhaps the earliest tourists were mediaeval monks who moved from monastery to monastery to discuss and to read rare learned manuscripts. This was certainly part work, in the sense of gaining spiritual income, but also had inevitable leisure components associated with it. They actually moved around a lot, some studies suggesting even more than modern academics, but their impacts on the environment were negligible. Pilgrims also traveled great distances and were more numerous, and, although specific routes were established and roads developed, again the associated environmental degradation was minimal except in areas where there were established resting points, and here urban developments of a kind took place.

European courts toured the royal domains in fifteenth and sixteenth centuries, in part so that the monarch could exercise political control and hunt, but also because of the local environmental damage an entourage can do to around a chateau or castle. Sanitation, at the very least, favored mobility. The "grand tours" of the eighteenth century in Europe saw the wealthy beginning to travel for cultural and leisure reasons, and in some cases become involved in the protection of parts of the built environment, most notably when it had links with classical times.

All these activities pale into insignificance, however, when compared with the movements of people and goods for purposes of war and commerce. Until comparatively recently, ordinary people did not move very much from their local town or village unless driven out or conscripted by overlords. The advent of mechanized transport, and most notably the railroads, in the late nineteenth century, combined with rising incomes and industrialization, began to change this. While Thomas Cook is generally seen as the father of modern tourism, when in 1841 he organized a church outing by rail from Leicester in England to Loughborough, about 9 miles away, it took some 30 years or more for the modern idea of "holidaying" or "vacationing" to become common. In many parts of the world this took the form of regional holidays when an entire town or small city would close its factories and communities migrated to the seaside or country retreat for a period. The vacations of this later phase of the Industrial Revolution were not purely a function of higher workers' incomes, or employer generosity, but also reflected a need for periodic wholesale maintenance of industrial plant. Subsequent social legislation and contractual demands of labor unions institutionalized the concept of vacations.

The Post-Fordism phase since World War Two, with its shift to the service industries and expansion of internationalization, has led to greater flexibility in production, and consequently work patterns. This, combined with higher disposable incomes, smaller family sizes, and a broader information base in most developed countries, has led to people taking more, but often shorter, vacations to a wider variety of places. Modern air travel has been a major facilitator of this, as have major institutional changes, such as developments in the EU that have allowed the easier movement of people. The vertical integration of the various elements of the "tourist experiences" through such things as the advent of travel agents and the availability of inclusive tours has also simplified vacationing on the supply side. The Internet is introducing new elements to this.

2.2. The magnitude

The scale of modern tourism is large, and takes a diversity of forms. The World Travel and Tourism Council (WTTC) has argued that the industry is the world's largest, and it is growing rapidly – globally, expenditure on tourism has been rising at an average of about 5% per annum since 1970.[a] Whilst the details of such calculations are open to some debate, it is certainly true that, globally, tourism is a significant employer and generates large amounts of income.

Perhaps of more importance are its roles in particular contexts and locations. Many small islands depend on tourism as their main source of income and their dominant source of foreign exchange. Even in larger economies, tourism can play an important role in generating employment and income (e.g. it accounts for 12% of Spain's GDP) as well as income for transfers elsewhere.

---

[a]The number of tourists fell in 2001, following the terrorist attacks in the USA, but prior to that it had risen every year since 1982.

Table 1
Forecasts of tourist growth (US $ millions) by destination

Destination	1995	2020	Average annual change
Europe	338.4	717	3.0
Americas	108.9	282	3.9
East Asia/Pacific	81.4	397	6.5
Africa	20.2	77	5.5
Middle East	12.4	69	7.1
South Asia	4.2	19	6.2
Intra regional	464.1	1183	3.8
Intercontinental	101.3	378	5.4
Total Trips	565.4	1561	4.1

Source: World Tourism Organization.

At an even more macro-scale, as the costs of long distance travel have declined, and as some of the more traditional tourist locations have become a little passé for seasoned vacationers, so entirely new macro-regions have become more popular destinations. In particular, tourist growth in East Asia and the Pacific was been about four times that of the world average in the 1990s, and is expected to continue as one of the fastest-growing destination regions (Table 1). But on the supply side, the originating regions are still very concentrated, with 58% of international tourists coming from Europe and 18% from the Americas; indeed, 80% of all international travelers originate from only 20 countries. But the traditional destinations still take a large share of the market. For example, while the gap is closing, Europe received some 717 million tourists, and East Asia and the Pacific some 397 million (Table 1). Europe is still likely to retain its position as the main tourist destination in the foreseeable future. Despite the increased demand for longer-distance tourism, intra-regional travel still dominates.

The most popular destinations for international tourists in 2000 were France (75.5 million), USA (50.9 million), and Spain (48.2 million). Changes are taking place, however, and by 2020 it is forecast that China (with 186.6 million visitors) will be by far the world's largest tourist destination.

In financial terms, estimates from the WTTC indicate that tourism in total (including domestic tourism and travel) contributed US $480 billion to the USA's GDP in 2001, with Japan's tourist industry contributing US $135 billion, the UK's US $69 billion and France's US $68 billion.[a] Isolating international tourism, the

[a]WTTC estimates are based on personal consumption, business travel, visitor exports, and government expenditures such as subsidies paid toward cultural attractions, parks, and museums. Annual estimates are posted on their website (www.WTTC.org).

global amount spent was US $476 billion, or about US $680 per international tourist. Some 59 countries belonging to the World Tourist Organization enjoyed receipts amounting to US $1 billion or more in 2000. In terms of gross foreign exchange earnings, the USA earned over US $72 billion in 2001 from international tourism, with Spain gaining US $33 billion and France US $30 billion, although the USA was also the top spending on foreign tourism (US $59 billion). Factors such as political unrest and natural disasters, however, can have serious short-term effects on the monies enjoyed by individual destinations.

2.3. Transportation

The scale and geographical diversity of modern tourism and travel would not be possible without developments in mass transportation. In some cases, such as tourism involving islands, the advent of cheap air travel and cruise liners was a necessary precursor. But even mainland tourist destinations, such as the theme parks in the USA and the beaches of the Mediterranean, only became mass tourist destinations because of air transportation and the growth in motor car ownership. The growth of low-cost airlines ("no-frill carriers" in European markets) has also led to increased numbers of short breaks or weekend holidays in some markets.

In terms of hard numbers, in 1998 air transportation represented 43% of international tourist movements, with road transportation accounting for 42%, and over time the importance of air travel has been growing. There are, however, important regional differences. For example, road and rail account for nearly 60% of international trips in Europe (which consists of many small countries). In contrast, air transportation accounts for about 80% of international tourist movements in South Asia – mainly because of the long-haul traffic coming into the region. Furthermore, East Asia and the Pacific, with their many islands, have a significant amount of sea transportation.

There are increasing concerns about the wider impacts of tourism on the environment and local cultures. However, tourism is a wide-ranging service sector that is highly dependent on other services industries, such as transportation, as well as commodities. The diversity and the complexities of these linkages make it difficult to assess the overall environmental implications of the sector. Consequently, an inevitable degree of simplification and somewhat artificial categorization is employed to tease out the links between travel, tourism, and the environment.

3. Transportation–tourism–environmental linkages

Transportation for travel and tourism has two broad, potentially adverse implications for the environment.

First, there are the direct impacts when transport is actually part of the leisure experience *per se* – this may be seen as the consumption effect. Cruising at sea is perhaps the most obvious example, but there are also many local, national, and regional attractions around the world where people travel as they look at scenic and other attractions. "Truck" tours, for example, have become increasingly popular in Africa and South America, and there are now many luxury train journeys that can be taken, such as the Orient Express and the Blue Train. Indeed, in some cases, such as a space shuttle launch, the viewing of a transportation activity may in itself be the motivation for tourism. In all cases, transportation conveys a positive utility for the tourist.

Second, there are the indirect effects of transport, associated with the derived demands for its use to be able to enjoy the final tourist experience. Most leisure activities involve some form of transportation to access them. In economic terms, transport and leisure activities are often jointly produced. Indeed, in some countries, most notably in Western Europe, the leisure experience is marketed as a joint product in the form of the "inclusive package." This generally includes travel to the leisure site, hotel accommodation, and local tours. But in the majority of countries the products are sold separately. More universal are the short-distance excursions that are taken once the main tourist destination is reached, and here inclusive day-trips are generally available.

The indirect environmental effects can be divided into two distinct components. First, there are the damaging environmental impacts – in economic terms, negative economic externalities, for example noise, atmospheric pollution, and maritime contamination – of travel to and from a tourist destination. Such travel is generally onerous, and seen as one of the costs to be borne to enjoy the facilities at the tourist destination. Some sightseeing *en route* may take place, but that is secondary to the need to reach the destination. The environmental effects take the same diversity of forms as transportation for any other purpose (such as commuting), and, hence, range through from local effects of noise and immediate air pollution to the global implications of greenhouse gas emissions. These types of issue are dealt with elsewhere (see in particular Chapter 3), and are thus given relatively limited treatment here.

More specific are the environmental implications associated with the ways in which a location changes because transportation now makes it accessible to visitors and tourists. The advent of good highways and air transportation contributed to turning central Florida from an orange-growing agricultural region to a theme park center. The same is true of parts of southern California. The Costa Brava in Spain was a basic fishing village before air access made low-cost tourism possible. In economic terms, this shifts the production function for the area, but it also has significant sociological and environmental impacts. In this context, the provision of transportation is not in response to an existing demand but in itself, and with the provision of other inputs and marketing, facilitates the creation of new demands.

Theoretically, this type of long-term effect need not adversely affect the environment provided that the full costs of the production shift are taken into the decisions of tourists. If the overall social costs and benefits (which will involve the widest range of implications over the long term) are reflected in the prices tourists pay, or appropriate adjustments are made in the regulatory regimes imposed, then the environment will be used optimally. Transportation may shift the production activities of an area, but those involved are effectively taking into account any adverse environmental effects in their investment and consumption decisions.

In practice, however, this may not be the case. Where the tourist location involves natural resources it is often difficult to control use at the point of consumption, especially in countries where a shortage of resources makes effective policing difficult. In such circumstances it may be necessary to use restrictions on transportation as a second-best way to conserve the environment. Transportation offering a limited number of access points to a region. Basically, access to the area is restricted by higher fares or limits of transportation supply to keep the number of tourists down to a level consistent with the environmental carrying capacity of the region.

4. The environmental implications

4.1. The consumption effect

Travel is part of the many tourist experiences in the sense that transportation to a tourist destination may actually have positive utility for the tourist – some people enjoy flying or driving to their vacation spot. More germane to the consumption effect, however, is the situation where travel is actually part of the tourist activity. Maritime cruising is a major industry, and is growing. In 2001, about 45% of cruise ships plied in the Caribbean/Bahamas market, with 8% in the European market (notably the Baltic, the Norwegian Coast, and the Spanish and French Riviera), 13% in the Mediterranean, and 8% in Alaska.

Hence, there are many forms a cruise may take – from glacier gazing in Alaska to sun-seeking in the Mediterranean – and each has its own particular set of implications for the environment. The activity of cruising *per se* can result in refuge disposal at sea, local ecological impacts from port visits, and disruptions to maritime life. But even when these are minimized there is an increasing tendency for air travel to ports of embarkation and debarkation, and this has implications for global warming and higher-level ozone depletion.

It is not only maritime cruising that is growing, and the scale of this consumption effect for land-based activities can vary enormously from a few off-road vehicles venturing through the African bush to the mass tourism that occurs in places such as US national parks. For example, Yosemite National Park has 4 million visitors a year that involves 800 000 automobiles and 14 600 buses. The economic benefits to a region from these activities can be significant (Yosemite National Park puts about US $3 billion into the regional economy annually) but such flows would soon begin to dry up if the environmental quality of the tourist experience declined.

The environmental costs of transportation as a pure consumption activity may be declining per tourist, as lead-free gasoline is increasingly used in tourist vehicles, aircraft and ships are becoming more fuel-efficient, and the paths adopted for sight-seeing are more often selected with environmental conservation in mind (Lipman, 1991). The problem is the increase in the total number of people that engage in these activities.

4.2. The access effect

Little will be said specifically on the transportation-induced environmental effects of accessing a tourist location. This is because they are in essence the same as accessing a place of employment. What is often neglected, however, is that a journey to a tourist location does not simply involve the implications of the primary mode (aircraft or ship) but also travel to the point of embarkation and from the point of debarkation to the destination. The car trip to an airport, for example, is part of the tourist trip, and, while the environmental implications are not at the tourist destination, they can still be significant. To take into account the full environmental effects of travel to and from a tourist destination necessitates a full-cost approach, which, in practice, has seldom been attempted to date.

What is clear from the information available of these access affects is that they may be significant. France, for example, is a major transit country for tourists going from northern Europe to the Mediterranean (indeed, one reason that it is recorded as the world's most popular tourist destination is some of this transit traffic stops overnight in France). Some countries, such as Switzerland, have initiated special licensing arrangements that charge transit traffic, in part for infrastructure cost recovery but also to help contain its volume for environmental reasons.

4.3. The tourist effect

Tourists by their nature often destroy the very things that they seek. In other cases, however, tourism can stimulate remediation measures in circumstances where serious environmental degradation was taking place for other reasons. An example of the latter can be the redevelopment of derelict ports and harbors as

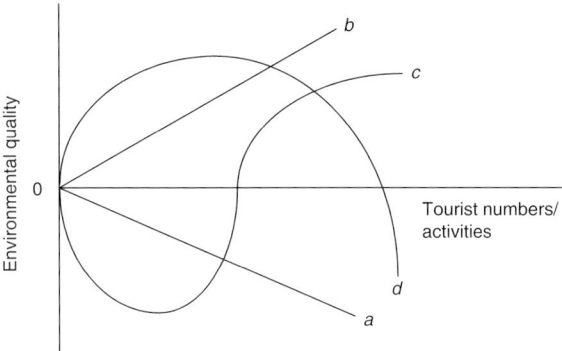

Figure 1. Relationships between changes in tourism levels and environmental quality.

leisure resorts. This often requires not only improving the local built environment but also removing contaminates from the water and cleaning soil pollution.

The relationship between tourism and local environmental quality may change over time as the number of tourists grows, even in the same resort area. Tisdell (1987) suggests that there are a number of possible alternative generalized relationships between changes in tourism levels and environmental quality (Figure 1). There may be straightforward negative effect (relationship *a*), whereby any tourist leaves an adverse environmental imprint – tourism in wilderness areas is the most oft-cited example. But in other cases tourism may have a very positive effect (relationship *b*), where the actual numbers of tourists may in itself be important. The cleaning up of derelict urban locations to be tourist attractions may be an example of this.

In the case of relationship *c*, an initial adverse environmental effect accompanying tourism simply adds to problems created by exiting activities, and is reversed once a threshold number of tourists has been reached. Possibly this is because larger numbers of tourists cause the entire economic structure of the area to shift to activities that are less environmentally damaging, or tourists bring in more resources after some point to provide resources for remediation. Alternatively, in the case of relationship *d*, initial levels of tourism bring about some environmental gains (perhaps in terms of replacing some more environmentally damaging activity), but eventually sheer numbers of tourists cause serious damage to the ecosystem.

There are clearly no hard and solid rules for which of these paths will be followed, it depends on local conditions, the type of tourist activities involved, and the ways in which the revenues from tourism are spent.

It will also depend on the local environmental carrying capacity of the area. This reflects the ability of an area to accept numbers of tourist without any long term

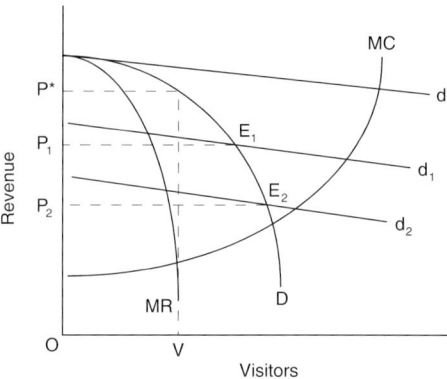

Figure 2. Short- and long-term problems with transportation induced shifts to tourism.

adverse implications for its environment. Activity level *a* in Figure 1 indicates that any visitors would do irretrievable damage, while level *d* gives a clear maximum when the curve crosses the horizontal.

While Figure 1 may, in economic terms, be seen as representing alternative environmental cost curves for tourism, it offers no indication of the optimal level of tourism for any relationship. For this a tourist benefit curve is needed. Such a curve, however, on the assumption that tourists are influenced by local environmental conditions, cannot be drawn independently of the relevant cost curves. What is clear, however, is that there is no automatic mechanism to ensure that the impact of tourism on the environment is optimized. Many of the environmental costs of tourism, such as the release of greenhouse gases, affect the global situation. Even local pollutants are normally associated with individual undertakings (particularly hotels, restaurants, etc.) that without some form of property right allocation or government intervention take no account of the implications for others. These are all standard externality problems.

A major problem, however, is that there may be numerous possible long-term sustainable levels of environmental quality when environmental quality is a function of the number of visitors. What actually materializes can depend on several factors. Some simple economics helps to illustrate some of the issues involved.

In Figure 2, D is drawn to represent the long-run equilibrium levels of tourist demand, assuming that demand for visits to the park or resort at each level of quality remains stationary. In other words, there may be a short-run demand curve for visits, d_1, but because visitors reduce the quality of the facility, there is only one long-run sustainable point on that curve, namely E_1 (which confers P_1 in benefits to each tourist). If the short-run demand curve is d_2, then again there is only one long-run equilibrium point, E_2. These short-run equilibria trace out the long-run demand curve D.

In conventional economic terms, the use of the tourist facility would be maximized when D is equated with the marginal cost (MC) of visits to the facilities borne by the authorities. A difficulty emerges if those responsible for the facility attempt to maximize their income – a not unfamiliar situation in countries where public authorities are short of income or foreign exchange. In simple economic terms this would involve charging prices equal to P* and limiting the number of visitors to V. This would appear to offer a high level of environmental conservation. However, if the short-run demand curve is d* when the initial prices are set, then the profit-maximizing number of tourists would be greater than V, and prices higher (d* being the determining demand curve for the profit-maximizing marginal revenue curve, which is not shown). In this case it would be impossible to return to the long-term profit maximization position. Hence, short-term gains create an unsustainable situation. The situation becomes even more complex and uncertain if one attempts to look at how the revenues from the charges are used. In some scenarios there may be additional environmental costs generated.

Of course, ideally this type of situation should be dealt with through direct actions at the tourist location – monopoly pricing would not be used and prices/access should be set to ensure long-run environmental considerations are included. But this may be impractical because of high transaction costs, political pressures, and enforcement problems. The availability of transportation, and the price being charged for it, influences the number of tourists that enter the area (i.e. the demand for the tourist facility), and consequently can be an important policy tool once the nature of the tourism/environmental impact relationships have been determined. Limiting airport capacity to constrain tourist numbers can, for example, provide a mechanism to ensure that environmental capacities are not exceeded. Indeed, this type of policy is being pursued at a number of island tourist destinations.

4.4. Ecotourism

In recent years the increased interest being shown in the natural environment has resulted in more people seeking to explore and observe a wide range of natural phenomena. The concept of ecotourism has emerged. Steele (1993) defines ecotourism as "an economic process where rare and beautiful eco-systems are marketed internationally to attract tourists." While this awareness of the ecosystem is generally welcomed, it is not clear that it is ecologically sound. Almost by definition, opening access to ecologically sensitive areas can easily lead to environmental damage (Cater, 1994).

In many cases these "rare and beautiful" ecosystems are inevitably located in remote and less accessible places. This leads to the development of transportation infrastructure to support tourist access. In many cases this involves driving track through areas that, although not "rare and beautiful" ecosystems, nevertheless are environmentally sensitive. Hence, while the term "ecotourism" has particular marketing connotations, it often simply entails the same types of transportation-related environmental considerations as conventional forms of tourism.

5. Policy responses

Local concerns have over the years produced a wide range of local policy responses, as it has become recognized that excessive tourism can be counter-productive. On a micro-level, many places are putting a major emphasis on reducing the local environmental intrusion of tourist movements. These initiatives have included the use of biodiesel fuel in Yellowstone Park in the USA (Evanoff, 1999)[a], recycling of waste on cruise ships, limiting movement to specified paths, improved information systems, banning traffic at certain times of the year (e.g. breeding times for fauna) or of the day, and requirements that all goods transported into a tourist location be brought out at the end of a visit (i.e. trash). In the case of Ordesa National Perk in Spain, car traffic has been banned. Physical access has been limited in other cases. For example, only about 15% of Australia's Great Barriers Reef is open to visitors, Stonehenge in England was closed for 15 years, and only a very few visitors are now allowed in to the Lascaux Cave in France. Other cases have seen more direct economic measures being used, with tourists being charged fees for their activities that broadly reflect the full costs of their visits.

Some of the measures are directly aimed at limiting environmental damage irrespective of its cause. This has direct effects on transportation when consumed as part of a consumption activity – the USA, for example, enforces its Clean Water Act, the Clean Air Act, and the Oil Pollution Act for all cruise ships operating in its waters. In many cases, as we have argued, actions are more specific, and have resulted in limiting tourist access to specifically sensitive areas for purely ecological reasons. In other cases, limitations have been more commercially motivated and designed to retain a natural resource purely as a tourist attraction. Essentially, the elasticity of demand for a higher-quality product can result in the restricted number of tourists generating more aggregate revenue.

At the international level, global agencies have sought to ensure that the external costs of transportation, both to the nations involved and more widely, do not become excessive. The tourist industry is competitive, and there are possibilities

---

[a]After ensuring that the fuel fumes, which have the aroma of cooking oil, did not attract bears.

that this can lead to individual countries competing for tourists down to the short-term (including environmental) costs involved. In economic terms, transportation acts to open up tourist markets, and even if the full costs of transportation are internalized – i.e. the fares paid for travel to and from the tourist destination take full cognizance of environmental damage involved – the environmental damage associated with the tourists being at the location are often not.

The UN has sought to ensure that all countries, and smaller island economies in particular, have the opportunity to exploit their tourist potential without excessive strains being put on their environments (Abeyratne, 1999). The difficulty is that much of the focus is on job and income creation. The development of airport and related infrastructure is often preceded by detailed cost–benefit analysis (Mackie and Nellthorp, 2001), if for no other reason than international donor agencies requiring it, that embody environmental elements. What is seldom done, however, is to consider the longer term and wider impact on these countries' environments as a result of a having more tourists. The difficulty is that most impact analysis techniques are only partial, in the sense that they assume that the broad production function of the system will not change and that any development, such as a new or expanded airport, will only have marginal implications.

6. Conclusions

There is a growing understanding of the links between the economic gains from tourism and its associated environmental implications. The role of transportation within this framework is, however, still only partially understood, and the body of explicit literature in this field is small. There are a number of policy initiatives in train to ensure that the immediate environmental implications of the transportation component of tourism are optimized and that environmental carrying capacities are not exceeded. The less direct problems often stem as much from imperfections in the treatment of the environment in the tourist activity as in the treatment of the environment in the transportation activity. Transportation restrictions are often seen as policy tools to partially correct failures to limit the direct environmental impacts of tourists at a resort – rather than reflect the environmental implications of these tourists through prices or regulations, their numbers are limited through actions in the transportation market.

References

Abeyratne, R.I.R. (1999) "Management of the environmental impact of tourism and air transport on small island developing states," *Journal of Air Transport Management*, 5: 31–38.
Cater, E. (1994) "Ecotourism in the Third World – problems and prospects for sustainability," in: E. Cater and G. Lowman, eds, *Ecotourism: a sustainable option?* Chichester: Wiley.

Evanoff, J. (1999) "Alternative fuels at Yellowstone," in: *National parks: transportation alternatives and advanced technology for the 21st century.* Conference Proceedings. Big Sky.

Lipman, G. (1991) "The role of travel and tourism industry – promoting sustainable ecotourism," in: *Royal Geographical Society conference on "ecotourism – a sustainable option."* London: RGS.

Mackie, P.J. and Nellthorp, J. (2001) "Cost–benefit in transport," in: K.J. Button and D.A. Hensher, eds, *Handbook of transport systems and traffic control.* Oxford: Pergamon.

Sidhu, S.S. (1994) *Aviation and sustainable tourism, emerging trends.* New Dehli: Har-Ananad.

Steele, P. (1993) "The economics of ecotourism," *In Focus*, 9:4–6.

Tisdell, C.A. (1987) "Tourism, the environment and profit," *Economic Analysis and Policy*, 17:19–36.

Tisdell, C.A. (1996) "Investment in ecotourism: assessing its economics," *Tourism Economics*, 1:375–87.

Chapter 36

GENDER, TRANSPORTATION, AND THE ENVIRONMENT

AMANDA ROOT
University of Gloucestershire, Cheltenham

LAURIE SCHINTLER
George Mason University, Fairfax, VA

1. Introduction

Women's increased mobility is an important cause for concern for those who wish to limit growth of transport emissions. The distances traveled by women have, over the past 50 years, tended to be different from and less than men's, but in the last 20 years in Europe and the USA, women's mobility patterns have begun to look increasingly like those of men. In the UK, women increased the annual distance they travel by 36% between 1975 and 1995, and as drivers they increased the distance they travel even further, by nearly 200%. Women in the USA are also driving more. Between 1969 and 1995, the average annual distance driven by women increased by 87.4%, which was a rate almost double that experienced by men (Nationwide Personal Transportation Survey, 1995). Demographic change and concerns about personal safety are also contributing to what can be characterized as a trend toward women's mobility becoming more like men's. A similar set of trends is found in developing countries, albeit in the context of women's "travel poverty," that is, inadequate access to choice of travel. In many countries in Asia and Africa, women need to travel more in order to gain greater access to markets (Fernando and Porter, 2002).

There are some important social and environmental issues arising from this increase in transportation. First, transport is a major producer of atmospheric toxins and climate change gases, particularly in urban areas (but also outside these areas as a result of intercity movements, and international travel, particularly by air). Traffic contributes significantly to both fine particulate emissions and the formation of ground-level ozone, and in cities where leaded gasoline is available it can produce up to 80–90% of atmospheric lead. It is responsible in the UK for about a third of carbon dioxide emissions, the major greenhouse gas. The trends for transportation indicate that travel and freight transport will continue to grow for the foreseeable future, ensuring that the environmental damage it causes will continue to increase, unless travel choices change dramatically.

A second consequence of women's greater mobility in developed countries is that there is a process of "individualization" that occurs because of travel (Root, 2000). Travel allows people to become detached from particular social contexts, and this separation can, in turn, generate more desire for movement. This particularly affects women who have traditionally been more involved in close-to-home and local activities (Douglas and Isherwood, 1996). Greater long-distance travel by women will probably add to their growing detachment from more locally based activities, or will be in conflict with locally based commitments.

Third, transport policies need to be "gender proofed" and take into account the specific needs and desires of women in relation to transport and safe, relatively pollution-free living space. Care needs to be taken to ensure that sustainable transport policies reflect women's needs, for decent quality of life in neighborhoods and for mobility.

Women are frequently positioned in gender-specific ways in the labor market and in the domestic sphere. This contributes to a juggling of home with paid work responsibilities, creating gender-specific travel patterns and needs, and, in particular, creating a situation in which women are more likely to be tied to particular localities. This localization of complex journeys and lifestyles could mean that women continue to make more short trips than men, and also value safe streets, relatively clean air, and low levels of traffic noise more than men. They are more likely to be able to relate traffic levels to damage to social relations and community networks. As a consequence, women may be less likely to adopt the dominant attitude of valuing mobility above accessibility. These qualities mean that some women could respond more positively to the challenges of environmentalism in transport, especially in those regions where what can be termed "post-industrial" economic restructuring is most advanced.

2. Women and transport

As concern with sustainability grows so it becomes more important to understand the position of women. While women have traditionally been less mobile than men, this situation is changing, and women are now traveling more, particularly as drivers of personal vehicles. At the same time, the travel patterns of women are still quite different from men's, particularly when viewed according to different age and income categories, and these distinctions as well as the more general motorization trends of women have several implications for sustainability.

Table 1
US daily person-miles traveled and time spent driving by age and gender (1995)

Age (years)	Daily travel (p-miles)		Ratio (female/male) (%)	Daily time spent driving (min)		Ratio (female/male) (%)
	Male	Female		Male	Female	
16–29	34.9	30.6	88	57.7	56.1	97
30–39	38.7	33.1	86	80.7	65.4	81
40–49	39.7	32.4	82	85.5	67.4	79
50–64	34.9	24.5	70	87.7	61.1	70
65–74	26.3	19.4	74	73.2	54.7	75
75+	19.0	10.9	57	81.3	63.3	78

Source: Spain (1997).

2.1. Distance traveled

The increasing motorization of women can be largely attributed to the feminization of the workforce. In the USA, between 1969 and 1995, women's participation in the labor force increased by roughly 122%, which is in sharp contrast to men, whose numbers increased by only 47% (Hu and Young, 1999). Similar trends have been experienced in other nations, including the UK and Sweden. Employment increases the demand for transportation in at least two respects. Most obviously, it generates the need for a commute, but also for women with small children it may also create the demand for additional trips to day care centers, dry-cleaners, and restaurants, as market production is substituted for home production.

While women are increasing the distances they travel, they are still traveling a lesser distance than men, and their average trips are much shorter. In 1998–2000, women in the UK traveled only 71% of the distance that men did, and by car and van the gap was even larger (UK Department of the Environment, Transport and the Regions, 2001). Women in the USA drove only 60–70% as far as men in 1995 (Hu and Young, 1999), and in comparison with the 35.2 p-miles that men drove a day, women traveled only 27.8 p-miles (Nationwide Personal Transportation Survey, 1995). In fact, with the exception of 16–19-year-olds, men in the USA spent approximately 20 min more per day on the road than women (Table 1).

Limitations in women's mobility are in part correlated with child-care, caring for the elderly, and domestic responsibilities. Until the age of 20 years in 1994–1996, women in the UK were typically traveling almost identical distances to men. In 1995–1996 between the ages of 26 and 59 years, the prime years of domestic caring responsibilities, women's travel dropped to just over half of

Table 2
Full car driving license holders in the UK

Age (years)	License holders (%)							
	Male				Female			
	1975–1976	1985–1986	1989–1991	1995–1997	1975–1976	1985–1986	1989–1989	1995–1997
17–20	36	37	52	48	20	29	35	36
21–29	78	73	82	79	43	54	64	67
30–39	85	86	88	89	48	62	67	74
40–49	83	87	89	89	37	56	66	74
50–59	75	81	85	88	24	41	49	61
60–69	58	72	78	83	15	24	33	46
70+	32	51	58	65	4	11	15	22
All ages	69	74	80	81	29	41	49	57
Estimated No. of license holders (millions)	13.3	15.1	15.3	17.6	6	9.1	9.2	13.2

men's, a pattern that was the same 20 years earlier (Root, 2000). In the USA, gender differences in the distance traveled daily and the daily time spend driving in minutes are also lowest for the youngest cohorts. Domestic responsibilities confine women to a particular location, or they have time limiting their travel but also they contribute to shorter commutes.

2.2. Licensing and auto ownership

Licensing and auto ownership trends provide further evidence that women as a whole are becoming increasingly mobile. From 1975 to 1995, the proportion of women in the UK with driver's licenses increased by 90%; while for men the change was only 17%, and as of 1995–1997, 57% of all women in the UK were licensed to drive (Table 2). In the USA, the number of female licensed drivers has also increased significantly. Between 1969 and 1995, licensed women increased by 95%, while for men the change was only 53% (Hu and Young, 1999).

Much of the growth in licensing for women can be attributed to younger females learning to drive, and in fact it is in the 20–34-year-old category where most of the change in the average distance traveled annually occurred. Similarly, the highest licensing rates for women in the UK have been in the younger age groups and, likewise, elderly women still remain under-licensed in comparison with men of the same age. Only 46% of all women in the 60–69-year-old age category and 22% in the over 75-year-old cohort had full licenses in 1995–1997 (Table 2) compared with the 57% for all women. This pattern is likely to change, however, as all of the younger to middle-aged women who currently have licenses move into the older age categories. Similar licensing trends have been experienced in other nations, including, for example, Germany (Zauke and Spitzner, 1997) and Austria (Fürnkranz-Prskawetz et al., 2002).

While more women are learning to drive, they are still more likely than men to be passengers rather than drivers. Of all women in the UK with licenses, only two-thirds are the primary drivers of the household (Hamilton, 2001). In Sweden, 80% of all women are licensed to drive; however, 75% of all those without licenses are women. Women in the USA are passengers for about half of the travel they do, while men are passengers for only one-fourth of the time (Hu and Young, 1999).

There are also disparities in licensing and auto ownership between income groups. In the USA, a majority of the very poor, those on welfare, are women, and car ownership and licensing among them is low. In a study completed by the US Department of Health and Human Services in 1997, only 6% of welfare families reported having a vehicle (General Accounting Office, 1998). This number may be low since welfare eligibility restrictions often prevent many welfare recipients from declaring auto ownership. In addition, it is important to note that while some welfare recipients do own a car, these vehicles in many cases are not dependable. Automobiles owned by such recipients in 1995, for example, had only a reported value of US $619.

2.3. Mode of transportation

Women also tend to travel more by what are generally considered less prestigious modes of transport, i.e. walking and public transit. In 1998–2000, women made fewer trips and traveled greater distances than men in the UK by all modes apart from walking, bus and coach, and as passengers in private cars. Men still traveled more by rail than women. Across different age groups there are distinct differences in the use of the various modes for transportation between men and women. Nearly one-third of all trips made by older women in the over 70-year-old age cohort are as passengers in private vehicles, which is four times that of men in the same age group. Use of bus and coach was also highest for the elderly, and the largest gender gaps in the distance traveled and number of trips made by this mode was for the elderly. Similar patterns in mode choice exist in the USA (Nationwide Personal Transportation Survey, 1995).

2.4. Trip purpose and complexity of trip-making

Women travel for different reasons than men. Whereas the trips made by men tend to center around paid work activities, those of women are more closely associated with their role as family care-takers. Approximately 50% of all person trips made by women in the USA in 1995 were for family and personal business, and two-thirds of the trips women made were to take someone else someplace. In the UK, women make 65% more "escort education" journeys (taking children to school) and approximately 30% more shopping trips. Women in Sweden were twice as likely than men to run household errands and to visit friends and relatives (Hamilton, 2001).

Many of the trips made by women have coupling constraints, or the need to plan travel around someone else's schedule, as well as other time or spatial constraints (e.g. a child has to be dropped off at day care at a particular location at a given time). As a result, women often have to be creative in their trip scheduling, and it is common for women to engage in complex travel behavior such as trip chaining. This is certainly the case in the USA, even when males and females are in employment (Table 3). Women stop more for running household errands than do men on inward and outward commutes, irrespective of the number of persons in a household or its structure. On average, two in three US women make stops on their way home, and 25% make more than one stop. While there are some men who trip chain, the places visited differ, with women tending more often to visit schools, day-care centers and shops. Men are more likely to go to a restaurant or bar. The trend for these more complex commuting patterns is upwards. In the USA the number of intermediate stops on the way to work has grown by about 50% since 1980, and the number on the way home by about 20% (Hu and Young, 1999).

The patterns in women's travel behavior have several implications for sustainable transport. The multiple stops made by women when trip chaining could have adverse implications for atmospheric pollution because of the larger amount of "cold running" entailed. At the same, short trips, if linked together as in a trip chain, may be beneficial to air quality. Trip chaining helps reduce emissions by eliminating the cold start and reducing vehicle distance traveled. The types of diversions undertaken by women also suggest that a larger amount of time is spent in noise-sensitive areas and areas where those most susceptible to the adverse effects of exhaust gas emissions spent a large part of their time. From a transport policy perspective there are also problems that the diversity of variations in trip patterns is greater for females.

Demographic trends indicate further improvements in the mobility of women and continued growth in the number of women drivers on the road. Many of these drivers are likely to fall in the older age cohorts. In the USA, between 1969 and 1995, the highest rates of growth in population were in these cohorts. In 1995, almost 65% of the 75-year-old and over population were female. Elderly women predominantly do not hold a driving license, and consequently have only

Table 3
Stopping for errands during the morning and evening commutes in the USA (1995)

	One stop (%)		Two or more stops (%)	
	Men	Women	Men	Women
Between home and work				
1 adult, no child	11	15	5	5
2 adults, no children	13	14	6	8
1 adult, child (age 0–5 years) (a)	32	41	1	23
2 adult, child (age 0–5 years) (a)	15	38	6	15
1 adult, child (age 6–15 years) (a)	14	32	16	14
2 adult, child (age 6–15 years) (a)	17	25	5	12
Between work and home				
1 adult, no child	32	29	20	31
2 adults, no children	29	30	17	25
1 adult, child (age 0–5 years) (a)	15	31	32	49
2 adult, child (age 0–5 years) (a)	28	42	19	29
1 adult, child (age 6–15 years) (a)	29	38	34	32
2 adult, child (age 6–15 years) (a)	29	33	16	29

Source: Nationwide Personal Transportation Survey (1995).
Note: (a) Age of youngest child.

limited use of cars as passengers. This picture will change dramatically when the current cohorts of younger and middle-aged women begin to enter the older age categories. A far higher proportion of these women, at one-third from German evidence, will have been car owners for the majority of their lives and will expect to use cars for their mobility in their old age (Zauke and Spitzner, 1997). Furthermore, life expectancy figures suggest that because women are out-living men, they will wish to be mobile for longer. Women's life expectancy is greater than that of men's in both North America and the EU. Additionally, if, as demographers suggest, the whole population ages, the proportion of very elderly women who still have mobility requirements will increase further.

3. Women and environmentalism

Women in the developing world have demonstrated that they have different attitudes about the environment and sustainable transportation than men. In this area of the world, women have led environmental campaigns designed to curb the negative impacts of some of the newer transportation technologies, i.e. campaigns to prevent the suburbanization of cities. The environmental campaigns of women in the developing world would appear to be directly associated with their needs for survival.

In many ways, women's struggle in the rural developing world is of necessity an ecological struggle. Because so many women's lives are intimately involved in trying to sustain and conserve water, land, and forests, they understand in an immediate way the costs of technologies that pillage the Earth's natural riches. (Diamond and Orenstein, 1990).

In the developed world, on the other hand, women's attitudes about sustainability are much less apparent, and, in fact, the mobility trends in this part of the world seem to imply that women have no particular concern about the environment. It could be argued though that the specific circumstances and needs of women, coupled with broader societal trends, have limited the transportation options available to them, and while they continue to become increasingly motorized it may not be by choice. In particular, their expanding roles as domestic care-takers and paid workers along with their concerns for security have increasingly placed women in a position of demanding mobility.

3.1. Mobility needs of women

A cluster of changes to cities, such as out of town shopping malls or "villages" and the reallocation of other facilities away from city centers, has meant that home and employment mobility demands and the need to have access to an automobile are often greater for women (Saegert, 1988):

> Documentation of the disadvantages women suffer in environments created through normal market forces and planning practices has begun to accumulate. Two Berkeley geographers provided what they called "a time-geographic perspective on problems in inequality for women" (Palm and Pred, 1974) in which they analysed the spatial location of different facilities and services in relation to residential settlement pattern, time schedules of women's domestic obligations and the availability and accessibility of transportation. More recently Michelson (1984) documented the additional travel time and greater daily stress that working mothers encountered in meeting their childcare needs. He also found that both the burden of taking children to childcare and the personal stress involved were much more likely to be borne by mothers than by fathers.

It has already been shown that in the USA and Europe, women's travel patterns and their employment is often different to men's. Typically, in labor market terms, this involves, with national and regional variations, an increase in temporary jobs often held by women, the polarization of highly skilled and deskilled (often female) workers, and the local state being less well able to meet social welfare objectives. These changes do not only involve transformations in employment, they also affect consumption, rendering leisure journeys ever more important as forms of consumption become, arguably, more distant and more incorporated by market forces.

However, it is also useful to note that access to a car is very useful for many women as it may enable them to fit more paid and unpaid work commitments closer together. The usefulness of cars for women attempting to work the "double shift" of paid employment and household responsibilities can be seen in the following excerpts from a case study report of a woman and her obligations to her husband and children, called "Rosie's day" (Church and Crouch, 1998):

> 'Normally I would work until 2pm and then I don't have time to go home and get out again before Lee gets out of play school. So I stay behind at work and have a sandwich and catch the twenty to three buses. Two times out of four the bus I want doesn't come or they're changing drivers. I sit there and think, 'come on I've got somewhere to be,' I hate the buses! Oh, now Lee [her son who attends play school] won't want to leave and he'll put his shoes on and he'll want to show me things!'
>
> Rosie's husband does not appear to be keen for her work to overlap into his home life. Rural transport is a problem.
>
> 12.25 p.m. Rosie arrives at the childminders. She stops to chat.
>
> 'How was work?...'
>
> 'How's he been?... How are the girls?'
>
> Rosie shepherds both children into the car.
>
> 12.40 p.m. Rosie and the children arrive at play school.
>
> 'We'll wait in the car awhile otherwise we'll be waiting outside for ages.'
>
> [Rosie takes the older children to their Grandma's (Nanny's) house.]
>
> 1.55 p.m. Rosie arrives at Nanny's and waits for five minutes as Nanny is not there yet.
>
> 2.00 p.m. 'I've just got to stop at Rainbow's to pick up a few bits. I don't really want to do much shopping as I may be going away this weekend. Normally I would do my shopping tomorrow. My sister-in-law usually lets me have the car once a week. She's really good like that, if I just call up and say can I have the car.'

Partly because of its mundaneness, this account illustrates how integral access to a car is to many women's lifestyles. Indeed, access to a car is sufficiently important that the Ford motor company used an advertisement in which a young bride proclaimed "I promise to love, honor, obey and spend half my life in a station wagon" (quoted in Shaeffer and Sclar, 1975).

An automobile is also a necessity for the poor, or welfare-dependent, who are seeking to acquire and retain gainful employment. The lack of mobility among welfare recipients often creates economic dependence, as transportation needs interfere in employment opportunities. Mobility is important, as many high-growth areas for entry level employment are in the outer suburbs and well beyond available transit service (US Bureau of Transportation Statistics, 1998). At the same time, there is a substantial gap between existing routes and stations and these growing employment areas. While two-thirds of new employment opportunities are located in the suburbs, few of these jobs are accessible by transit (US General

Accounting Office, 1998). One study estimated that welfare recipients who depend on public transportation, even with extraordinary commutes, are able to access only 40–44% of entry level job openings (Leete and Bania, 1999). Mobility, and in particular employment-related mobility, appears to be a necessary condition for self-sufficiency.

Access to an automobile has also become important for women for safety reasons. Women are generally physically smaller than men and more often travel with vulnerable children. This poses real fears of attack and affects perceptions of the safety of travel. As a result of these concerns, women are often hesitant to use public transportation, particularly when traveling in the evening, with small children or in neighborhoods or areas where crime is perceived to be a problem. A study done in the UK revealed that women's decisions not to use public transportation had little to do with their negative attitudes of the mode and more with concerns they had about security, particularly for children traveling to school (Hamilton, 2001).

The need for women to travel in the evening has increased over the last few decades. "Moonlighting" on the part of women has increased (Spain, 1997) but also for many women who work during the day, household and domestic duties must be completed in the evening hours. In the late 1980s, it was found that 50–70% of women in the UK were frightened of going out after dark in cities (Atkins, 1990). In the mid-1990s, one in eight women said that they felt so unsafe on public transport that they avoided using it (UK Home Office, 1996). Eleven percent of women interviewed never ventured out after dark. Women's experience of traveling at night often makes them feel unsafe when compared with traveling in the day. For example, 10% of women in the UK felt "unsafe" or "very unsafe" waiting on a railway platform in the day, but this figure rose to 53% at night. Similarly heightened fears were experienced in relation to waiting for metro trains, or walking to a car in open or multi-storey car parks. More attacks happen during the day, but, due to fewer numbers traveling at night, the probability of attack at night is higher.

Nevertheless, despite the difficulties of travel, it would appear that women were, in general, less confined to their homes at the end of the twentieth century than in earlier decades. This was largely because of car ownership (Hamilton et al., 1991). There is an irony in that fewer men worry about attacks but are more likely to suffer from them: according to the UK Home Office (1996), 90% of attacks by male strangers are carried out against men.

3.2. Women and traffic management

These constraints, however, cannot operate without resistance. They also position women, with a large degree of congruence, in the role of those categorized above as likely to value accessibility or safe transportation more than mobility (Table 4).

Table 4
Differences in access and background – a comparison

Traffic planners and policy-makers	"Transportation users"
Design of mobility parameters	Mobility needs
Men	Women, children, senior citizens
In the prime of life: 30–60 years of age, largely relieved of work in and for the home, "healthy," not of "foreign" cultural background Engineers or similar professional, power and autonomy undermined by weakening of regulatory state control	
Activities	
Employed full-time	Those involved in so called "reproductive" efforts to keep the breadwinner fit for work; working in the informal sector, part-time and full-time employment, "flexible working hours"
Orientation of acting and thinking	
Questions applicable to the individual, discrete assignments and projects	Questions relating to everyday life, communications, interpersonal relationships, the organization of (daily) life
Orientation toward feasibility, technical options	Orientation towards the limits of what can be coped with
Efficient categories for the various rationalizations	
… of feasibility	… of utility
Speed	Slowness, less acceleration
Longer distances	Reference to room and nearby sites
(home, neighborhood, district)	
Large projects	Incremental improvements
Specialization of functions	General utilization; multiple utility (of space)
Standardization of "solutions"	
Technical optimization by increasing technical effort	Minimum (transportation) cost and effort
The automobile as an "absolute necessity"	Freedom of choice of transportation means
Being "on the road"	Accessibility, freedom of local movement, community orientation.
Structural traffic generation	Structural traffic avoidance

Source: adapted from Zauke and Spitzner (1997).

The characteristics are associated with social trends where the primary orientation is toward the user's set of characteristics. This means that women are likely to be in a position to understand the values of traffic management and restraint better than those whose professional and personal lifestyles are geared toward mobility. The argument is that changes in the economy and cultural sphere have, and are, leading to qualitatively new situations or conjunctures in which women are most appropriately positioned to develop new cultural patterns and to participate critically in constructing in new ways in what Castells (1997) calls the space of flows.

Women's need to juggle home with paid work responsibilities has created gender-specific travel patterns, and a situation in which women are more likely to be tied to particular localities. This localization of complex journeys and lifestyles could mean that women continue to make more short trips than men and that they value safe local streets, relatively clean air, and low levels of traffic noise more than men. They are also more likely to be able to relate traffic levels to damage to social relations and community networks. As a consequence, women are less likely to adopt the dominant attitude of valuing mobility above accessibility. These qualities mean that some groups of women could respond more positively to the challenges of environmentalism in transport.

The concerns and mobility needs of women are not well met through current transportation policies and provisions largely because men are generally in the position of defining mobility parameters (Table 4). Men continue to dominate the transportation planning and engineering fields, although the situation appears to be changing somewhat. At the end of the twentieth century, less than 10% of all civil and architectural engineers in the USA were women (National Science Board, 1998), and women represented only 40% of the field of planning. Men seem to have a different orientation in thinking than women, and their concerns regarding transportation appear to center less around issues such as accessibility and security and more on speed and the ability to drive longer distances. Because they tend to hold full-time jobs during typical work hours during the working week they are also more likely to focus on the transportation needs of the typical commuter. Consequently, they may overlook the needs of many women who may be traveling for non-work purposes or during the off-peak hours.

4. Transportation planning and modeling

An understanding and appreciation of the differences between men and women is important for the design and implementation of equitable and efficient transportation programs. Despite a growing awareness of this need, the ability to actually implement this in practice is still quite limited. This stems in large part from the nature of existing transportation planning models, which fail to capture the unique travel values, needs, circumstances, and decision-making processes of women.

Travel demand models fall into two categories: aggregate or disaggregate. Aggregate models, introduced in the 1950s and now more or less institutionalized, are inherently limited in their ability to capture the details of individual travel behavior, such as those unique to women. Disaggregate models, on the other hand, do characterize individual behavior, but are still limited in a number of respects. Based on neoclassical consumption theory and the postulates and assumptions governing the decision-making behavior of the "economic man," these models assume travelers select between alternatives based on utility maximization. Within this framework, an individual's choice is influenced directly by choice set, utility function, level of knowledge, and rules for decision-making. Although men and women differ significantly in terms of these factors, these distinctions are rarely made in the modeling of travel behavior.

Travel demand models also assume that all travelers face the same choice sets, yet it has been shown that the options available to women are less than those of men. Security concerns, coupling constraints, and the need to carry out both paid and non-paid responsibilities often preclude traditional transit, walking, and bicycling as feasible or desirable modes of transportation. The general dispersion of population has also placed limits on the destinations available to women travelers, particularly those in the lower-income brackets.

Traditional travel demand models also assume that each traveler's primary concern is to minimize travel time or maximize speed, and, furthermore, that men and women are generally uniform in their valuation of travel time. Given the unique travel needs, circumstances, and patterns of women, these assumptions are highly questionable. The value of travel time, or shadow price, is the monetary value placed on a unit of time. In theory, this parameter is derived from the consumer welfare maximization problem and the Lagrange multipliers resulting from this optimization. Individuals or households seek to maximize welfare, or the consumption of market goods and services, leisure time, and time for other non-work-related activities (e.g. travel) subject to some set of constraints. These constraints typically relate to the household or individual's budget, and limits on the time available for various activities (Small, 1992). In the simplest formulation, the disutility of time is equivalent to the value of foregone leisure time (Becker, 1965). In this example, consumers seek to maximize their consumption of market goods and services and leisure time subject to budget and time constraints. Commuting reduces the amount of time available for leisure. Becker's full price is equivalent to the generalized cost function used in transportation analysis.

With some variations in this problem, more complex and alternative expressions for value of time can also be derived. For example, Groneau (1977) examines how value of time is affected by differentiation between leisure and home production and the presence of children. In theory, the value of time for an individual depends on his or her wages or income level, the number and variety of activities in his or her consumption set (e.g. shopping, recreation, childcare), and any time constraints relating to these activities (Small, 1992). Since men and women differ in terms of all of these factors, it is reasonable to believe that their value of time would vary as well.

Transportation planning models also assume that travelers are rational utility maximizers, and are similar in terms of their psychology and the rules used for decision-making. There is some evidence that men and women differ in these respects, and these distinctions are not incorporated in most travel demand models. Women tend to be more risk-averse than men. Although not studied conclusively, there is some evidence to suggest that women are more risk-averse than men when it comes to making travel-related decisions. In studies of traveler information services, women are often less prone to switch routes after receiving travel information on alternative routes (Abdel-Aty et al., 1996). In a stated preference survey of Los Angeles travelers, women tended to be more conservative in their selection of travel alternatives. When given the hypothetical choice between two routes, one that is relatively long but predictable in terms of travel time and another that is less predictable but potentially shorter in terms of travel time, women tended to select the former and men the latter. In addition, risk aversion may affect women's travel decisions, when security and safety are a concern.

The propensity for risk may lead to cognitive anomalies, or departures from rationality, on the part of women. For example, in selecting a route between work and day-care on any given day, a women may show risk aversion for alternatives that in comparison with her normal route (i.e. the reference point), save time and risk preference for losses. Losses may be weighted more heavily owing to the disutility of arriving late to day-care. These points imply that the shape of women's utility functions are likely to be different to those of men owing to differences in risk propensity, and that multiple functions may be necessary to capture risk propensity under different circumstances.

Lastly, the four-step model is designed for large-scale analyses of major highway and transit projects and not for the analysis of smaller projects that have more of a local orientation. Intrazonal travel, and the more localized travel of women, is not effectively captured.

5. Policy implications and conclusions

Environmental issues and gender perspectives need to be better incorporated into the transportation planning and policy-making process. First, women's perspectives are needed, particularly to develop alternative definitions of mobility that reflect transportation needs tied to the multiple paid and non-paid responsibilities of women, including their role as escorts of children and senior citizens. This could help to ensure the design and implementation of transportation systems that are most appropriate for the needs of women but that are also environmentally sensitive. Women's participation in the planning and policy-making process might be facilitated by implementing policies and procedures that encourage women to enter into the engineering or planning field, or, more simply, by hiring women as consultants or experts on transportation projects.

Second, there is a need to reconsider the type of data that is collected for transportation planning analyses and modeling. The travel behavior of passengers, localized travel by non-mechanized forms of transportation, travel demands relating to leisure activities, and the decision-making rules of women are examples of the type of data that should be collected on a regular basis. Further, alternative methods for collecting data such as stated-preference surveying should be explored. A stated-preference survey entails posing hypothetical situations to an individual to elicit information on their preferences, in contrast to revealed preference techniques that use actual observations to draw conclusions about preferences. The primary advantage of a stated-preference survey is that, if designed and executed properly, it shows how individuals will respond to new alternatives or alternatives whose attributes have changed as a result of policy actions.

Third, existing transportation planning models do not reflect the needs, circumstances, attitudes, and cognitive processes of women, and there is a need to reformulate these so that they better capture gender differences in these attributes. It would also be useful for example to explore the decision-making process of women in terms of the way choice sets are formulated and how alternatives are selected. This information might be incorporated into newly emerging modeling frameworks that assume travelers to be boundedly rational and satisficers. Non-linear utility functions that reflect women's attitudes toward risk could also be explored. Given the complexities of claims upon women's time, many of which cannot be "read" via socio-economic class distinctions, it would be useful to include "weights" that reflect women's needs. Additionally, there is a need to explore the differences between men and women in terms of the activities they conduct and the types of trips they make, and to incorporate these distinctions in activity-based modeling frameworks.

Fourth, the economic underpinnings of transportation systems need to be reviewed if we are to move in the direction of greater inclusion of women's mobility needs and environmental protection through more sustainable transport systems. One of the factors that militates against such considerations is the dominance of the idea that transportation should be financed through, and operate according to the dictates of, market forces. The idea that market forces should dictate the shape of transport promulgates the risk and uncertainty that follows market forces and environmental degradation (Beck, 1996), and also runs counter to the actions of various pressure groups and lobbies which seek to make transport accountable to communities and non-governmental organizations. The strength of argument for the utility of market forces has been expressed in another context (Bauman, 1999) as:

> Instead of joining ranks in the war against uncertainty, virtually all effective institutionalized agencies of collective action join in the neo-liberal chorus singing the praise of unbound 'market forces' and free trade, the prime sources of existential uncertainty, as the 'natural state of mankind'; and unite in hammering home the message that letting capital and finances free and giving up all attempts to slow down or regulate erratic movements, is not one political choice among many, but a verdict of reason as well as a political necessity.

The market will not always foster environmental or gender-specific transport solutions. Rather, it will continue to support the implementation of projects that are based on the economic principles and cost minimization. Perhaps the more local orientation of many trips made by women needs to be addressed through regulatory mechanisms and through changed transport planning methodologies that recognize the diverse social and environmental objectives that transport systems address.

Sustainability – environmental and feminist – perspectives need to be applied to transport and transport policy. Women's differing goals and experiences should be more adequately recognized and recorded in transport methodologies. By gendering the recording of journeys, their purposes and the values of those who undertake them, their goals, and the resources these modes involve – environmental, economic, or social – there is scope to develop more democratically accountable and equitable transportation systems. There is also the hypothesis that pure market solutions are linked to increasingly dominant car use. It is possible that women and the groups that they are part of might be best able to articulate the need for more sustainable transport systems.

References

Abdel-Aty, M.A., R. Kitamura, and P.P. Jovanis (1996) "Investigating effect of advanced traveler information on commuter tendency to use transit," *Transportation Research Record*, 1550:66.

Atkins, S. (1990) "Personal security as a transport issue: a state of the art review," *Transport Reviews*, 10:111–26.

Bauman, Z. (1999) *In search of politics*. Cambridge: Polity Press.

Beck, U. (1996) *Risk society: towards a new modernity*. London: Sage.

Becker, G.S. (1965) "A theory of the allocation of time," *Economic Journal*, 75:493–517.

Castells, M. (1997) *The rise of the network society*. Oxford: Blackwell.

Church, W. and S. Crouch (1998) *So, you're a working mother. How is it for you?* London: Minerva Press.

Diamond, I. and G. Orenstein (1990) *Reweaving the world: the emergence of ecofeminism*. San Francisco: Sierra Club Books.

Douglas, M. and B. Isherwood (1996) *The world of goods: towards an anthropology of consumption*. London: Routledge.

Fernando, P. and G. Porter, eds (2002) *Balancing the load: women, gender and transport*, London: Zed.

Fürnkranz-Prskawetz, A., L. Jiang and B.C. O'Neill (2002) *Demographic composition and projections of car use in Austria*. MPIDR Working Paper WP-2002-034. Rostock: Max Planck Institute for Demographic Research (http://www.demogr.mpg.de).

Groneau, R. (1977) "Leisure, home production: a survey," in: O. Ashenfelter and R. Layard, eds, *Handbook of labor economics*, Vol. I. Amsterdam: North-Holland.

Hamilton, K. (2001) "Gender and transport in developed countries," in: *Expert Workshop "Gender Perspectives for Earth Summit 2002: Energy, Transport, Information for Decision-Making."* Paper. London: Stakeholder Forum for Our Common Future (http://www.earthsummit2002.org/workshop/Gender%20Transport%20N%20KH.pdf).

Hamilton, K., L. Jenkins and A. Gregory, (1991) *Women and transport: bus deregulation in West Yorkshire*. Bradford: University of Bradford.

Hu, P.S. and J. Young (1999) *Summary of travel trends: 1995 nationwide personal transportation survey*. Washington, DC: Federal Highway Administration, US Department of Transportation.

Leete, L. and N. Bania (1999) "The impact of welfare reform on local labor markets," *Journal of Policy Analysis and Management*, 18:50–56.

Michelson, W. (1984) *Working mothers and stress, 1980*. Cambridge, MA: Henry A. Murray Research Center of Radcliffe, harvard University.

Nationwide Personal Transportation Survey (1995) *Summary of travel trends*. Washington, DC: Federal Highway Administration, US Department of Transportation.

Pred, A. and R. Palm (1974) *A time–geographic perspective on problems of inequality of women*. Research paper 236. Berkeley: Institute of Urban and Regional Develpment, University of California.

Root, A. (2000) "Transport and communications," in: A.H. Halsey, ed., *Twentieth century british social trends*. London: Macmillan.

Saegert, S. (1988) "The androgynous city: from critique to practice," in: W. Van Vliet, ed., *Women, housing and community*. Aldershot: Avebury.

Schaeffer, K.H. and E. Sclar (1975) *Access for all: transportation and urban growth*. Harmondsworth: Penguin.

Small, K. (1992) *Urban transportation economics*. Char: Harwood.

Spain, D. (1997) *Societal trends: the aging baby boom and women's increased dependence*. Order No. DTFH61-97-P-00314. Washington, DC: Federal Highway Administration, US Department of Transportation.

UK Department of the Environment, Transport and the Regions (2001) *Transport statistics focus on personal travel: 2001 edition*. London: DOT (http://www.transtat.dft.gov.uk/tables/2001/fperson/fpers01.htm)

UK Home Office (1996) *British crime survey*. London: Home Office.

US Bureau of Transportation Statistics (1998) *Welfare reform and access to jobs in boston*, 98-A-0. Washington, DC: Bureau of Transportation Statistics, US Department of Transportation.

US Bureau of Transportation Statistics (1999) *Transportation statistics annual report 1999*, BTS99-03. Washington, DC: Bureau of Transportation Statistics, US Department of Transportation.

US General Accounting Office (1998) *Welfare reform: transportation's role in moving from welfare to work*. Washington, DC: GAO.

US National Science Board (1998) *Science and Engineering Indicators – 1998*, NSB 98-1. Feb. Arlington: National Science Foundation.

Zauke, G. and M. Spitzner, (1997) "Freedom of movement for women: feminist approaches to traffic reduction and a more ecological transport science," *World Transport Policy and Practice*, 3:17–23.

Chapter 37

LOGISTICS AND THE ENVIRONMENT

ALAN C. McKINNON
Heriot-Watt University, Edinburgh

1. Introduction

Many companies now plan and manage their freight transport operations as part of a broader logistical strategy. This allows them to coordinate transport more effectively with related activities such as inventory management, production scheduling, warehousing, order processing, and materials handling. In assessing the environmental impact of freight movement, it is therefore important to take account of logistical trends and the trade-offs that companies make between transport and other elements in the logistical system.

Over the past decade, companies have come under mounting pressure to "green" their logistics. Much of this pressure has come from tightening government regulation. There have also been numerous campaigns by trade bodies (e.g. International Road Transport Union, 2000), environmental groups (Holman, 1996), and governments (e.g. UK Department of the Environment, Transport and the Regions, 1999a) to encourage companies, voluntarily, to adopt environmental best practice in their logistical operations. Benchmarking of freight transport operations has revealed wide variations in efficiency and energy intensity, suggesting that wider adoption of best practice measures would yield significant economic and environmental benefits. These so-called "green–gold" measures, which are largely if not entirely self-financing, now command wide support. They include backloading initiatives, the application of computerized vehicle routing and shared-user distribution. Much less popular are environmental measures that carry a logistical cost penalty. A small minority of companies are prepared to implement these measures to portray themselves as "green" logistics operators. In some sectors, this can bring rewards in higher sales and greater customer loyalty. It can also minimize the risk of a company's reputation being tarnished by the "counter-marketing" campaigns of environmental pressure groups (McKinnon, 1995).

In surveys undertaken in the early 1990s, logistics managers identified their two main environmental concerns as vehicle emissions and the return of packaging waste (PE International, 1993; Wu and Dunn, 1995). Since then, both of these

Handbook of Transport and the Environment, Edited by D.A. Hensher and K.J. Button
© 2003, Elsevier Ltd

areas of concern have been subject to new government controls. Within the EU, for example, emission standards for new trucks and vans have been steadily rising from Euro I in 1992 to the current Euro III specification, which sets the permitted levels of nitrogen oxides and particulate emissions from new vehicles at, respectively, 63% and 16% of their Euro I levels. The 1994 EC Directive on Packaging and Packaging Waste has forced companies to economize in their use of packaging, and led to the creation across Europe of new systems for the collection and recycling of packaging material. Since 1996, there has also been a sharp increase in the number of companies obtaining ISO 14001 accreditation for the environmental management of their logistical systems. To gain this accreditation they must install an environmental management system, undertake regular environmental audits and demonstrate a commitment to continually improve their environmental performance. Standardized auditing procedures have been developed comprising checklists of external effects and guidance on how their impact on surrounding areas can be measured (Worsford, 1994).

While this system of accreditation has been beneficial in raising awareness of environmental issues and promoting the adoption of a range of "green" measures, it can be criticized for not exerting much influence on the broader corporate framework within which logistics operates. Key decisions on, *inter alia*, product design, procurement, production, distribution channels, and sales promotion are generally taken as given, and logistics managers expected to reduce the level of environmental damage within this set of higher level constraints. Decisions affecting freight transport operations, for instance, can be divided into four categories (McKinnon and Woodburn, 1996):

(1) Strategic decisions relating to numbers, locations, and capacity of factories, warehouses, shops, and terminals. These determine the physical "infrastructure" of the business.
(2) Commercial decisions on product sourcing, the subcontracting of the production process, and distribution of finished products. These establish the pattern of trading links between the company and its suppliers, distributors, and customers.
(3) Operational decisions on the scheduling of production and distribution that translate the trading links into discrete freight flows.
(4) Tactical decisions relating to the management of transport resources. Within the framework defined by decisions at the previous three levels, transport managers still have discretion over the choice, routing, and loading of vehicles.

A company's demand for freight transport is the result of a complex interaction between decisions made at these different levels. Many "green logistics" measures have been introduced at the lowest level in this hierarchy, cutting externalities per vehicle-kilometer. Often the beneficial effects of these measures, however, have been offset or negated by higher-level decisions to centralize warehousing, source products from more distant suppliers, and/or move to just-in-time (JIT) replenishment, which often increase total vehicle-kilometers. There is a need therefore for companies to take a more holistic view of the effects of their activities on freight transport and related externalities. This will be the perspective adopted in the remainder of this chapter. It will examine the opportunities for reducing the environmental impact of freight transport "at source" by altering three critical ratios:

(1) Total tonne-kilometers:output – transport intensity. In this context, output can be defined in different ways. Several studies have expressed it in monetary terms, such as GDP or the level of retail sales, whereas others have used weight-based measures. Most of the discussion in this chapter relates to the weight of goods produced and distributed.

(2) Road tonne-kilometers:total tonne-kilometers – modal split. As road transport accounts for the vast majority of freight-related external costs in most countries, this ratio is expressed here in terms of the split between road and alternative, less environmentally damaging modes.

(3) Vehicle-kilometers:tonne-kilometers – vehicle utilization. This ratio determines the amount of vehicle traffic required to handle a given volume of freight movement (measured in tonne-kilometers). It is influenced by three factors: the capacity of the vehicle (in weight and volume terms), the average payload carried on loaded trips, and the proportion of vehicle-kilometers run empty.

(The environmental impact of freight movement is also affected by the ratio of vehicle-kilometers to emissions.)

Numerous studies have explored the opportunities for reducing the environmental impact of road freight transport by manipulating one or more of these ratios (e.g. Whitelegg, 1995; Pastowski, 1997). Some have modeled the impact of changes in these ratios on future freight traffic levels, energy consumption and externalities. Table 1, for example, presents the results of future energy projections for freight transport in the Netherlands, Germany, and the UK based on "business-as-usual" and "green" scenarios. In the following sections, we will assess the scope for altering the three key ratios and the resulting environmental benefits.

2. Reducing transport intensity

The transport intensity of a supply chain is determined both by the number of links and their average length. The number of links can be crudely measured by dividing the tonnes-lifted statistic by the actual weight of goods produced or consumed (i.e. at either end of the supply chain). This index, known as the handling factor,

Table 1
Effects of logistical rationalization measures on energy consumption

Country (study)	Time period	Main measures	Change in energy consumption (%)	
			Business as usual	With rationalization
The Netherlands (Werkgroep 2000, 1993)	1990–2015	Increased fuel efficiency Consolidation of loads Reduced empty running Large modal shift to rail	+47	–46
Germany (DIW, ifeu and IVU/HACON, 1994) (a)	1988–2010	Improved fuel efficiency Large modal shift to rail Higher vehicle utilization Shorter distances traveled	+55	+28
UK (Royal Commission on Environmental Pollution, 1994) (b)	1995–2020	Halving of the rate of tonne-km growth to 10% per decade Large modal shift to rail and water	+56	–4.4

Notes:
(a) Relates to long-distance transport.
(b) Energy calculations based on RCEP modal split targets and estimates of specific energy consumption by mode. Freight traffic forecasts based on UK Department of the Environment, Transport and the Regions (1997).

effectively measures the number of separate freight journeys that a consignment makes in moving from raw material source to final point of sale. As limited data are available on the weight of products produced and consumed, handling factor calculations are inevitably highly approximate. An attempt was made in the EU REDEFINE project to analyze the trend in handling factors in five European countries (France, Germany, the Netherlands, Sweden, and the UK) (Netherlands Economic Institute et al., 1997). This suggested that over the period 1980–1995, handling factors had fluctuated and shown no consistent trend.

Some industrial trends are likely to have been increasing the number of links in the supply chain. In some manufacturing sectors, for instance, a process of vertical disintegration has been occurring, with non-core activities being increasingly subcontracted to outside agencies. Extra tiers have also been added to some supply chains to consolidate inbound flows to factories and distribution centers or to localize the final customization of products. In many retail markets, on the other hand, distribution channels have become more streamlined, with products passing through fewer stockholding points *en route* to shop. The counteracting effects of these processes on the structure of the supply chain may partly explain the absence of any clear trend in handling factor values.

In contrast, the average length of links in the supply chain, known as the average length of haul, has been rising steadily, in most countries, for several decades. Within Europe it has been increasing at an average rate of 1.5–2.0% per annum (European Conference of Ministers of Transport, 2000). Increasing haul lengths have been the main cause of road freight growth. Over the past 30 years, they have been responsible for approximately two-thirds of the increase in road tonne-kilometers within Europe. This increase in average length of haul has been attributed primarily to three developments:

- Wider sourcing of supplies and expansion of market areas. In their search for suppliers capable of offering a superior mix of product quality, service and price, manufacturers and retailers have been sourcing products over greater distances. Surveys undertaken by A.T. Kearney (1999) for the European Logistics Association between 1987 and 1998 revealed a significant decline in the proportion of industrial purchases and sales made within countries and sharp increase in the proportion traded internationally at both European and global levels.
- Centralization of production, warehousing and terminal capacity. This enables companies to exploit economies of scale in the construction and operation of these facilities. By reducing the number of stockholding points in their logistical systems, firms can also take advantage of the so-called "square root law," cutting the amount of safety stock required to provide a given level of customer service (Maister, 1976). For example, according to this law, moving from a decentralized system of ten warehouses to a completely centralized system should, *ceteris paribus*, cut the amount of safety stock by two-thirds. By increasing the average distance from the supply point to the customer, centralization usually generates more freight movement per tonne of product distributed.
- Development of hub-satellite systems. A large and increasing proportion of freight, mainly in the form of parcels or pallet loads, is now assembled at local "satellite" depots trunked to a centralized "hub" for sorting, and distributed via other satellite depots to their final destinations. Indirect routing of freight flows through hubs generates more tonne-kilometers of freight movement than direct inter-depot trunking, though this system offers the advantage or improving vehicle utilization and cutting total traffic levels.

At a macro-economic level, transport intensity can be defined as the ratio of road freight tonne-kilometers to the level of economic activity measured by GDP. In many countries this ratio has been relatively stable, suggesting that it may be difficult to "decouple" these two variables (Pastowski, 1997). A recent EU White

Paper on transport, nevertheless, acknowledges that "we have to consider the option of gradually breaking the link between economic growth and transport growth" (European Commission, 2001). Although not explicitly stated in this policy document, this would entail reducing the number and/or length of links in the supply chain by means of what Bleijenberg (1996) calls "spatio-economic changes."

The number of links in the chain could be cut by increasing the degree of vertical integration in manufacturing, expanding the range of activities carried out on a single site. In some sectors, this would involve fundamental re-engineering of the production process and require very strong inducements. Distribution channels might be further streamlined to reduce the number of intermediate storage and handling points. In many developed countries, however, this streamlining process is well advanced, leaving little opportunity for further rationalization. Moreover, eliminating from the supply chain nodes at which loads are consolidated could be counterproductive as it might reduce vehicle load factors.

In theory it would be possible to reduce the average length of haul, or at least moderate its rate of increase, by reconfiguring production and distribution systems, sourcing products from local suppliers, and finding shorter routes between collection and delivery points.

2.1. Reconfiguring production and distribution systems

These systems, which are shaped by decisions at level 1 in the logistics management hierarchy, are relatively fixed in the short to medium term. It would be very difficult to reverse the geographical concentration of production, given the magnitude of the scale economies that firms have achieved. The logistical cost trade-offs that they make between transport, inventory, and warehousing costs are also very robust. This was confirmed by a computer simulation exercise that modeled the effect of increasing road transport costs on the distribution of products of differing value density (McKinnon, 1998). This analysis established the transport cost levels at which firms would have an economic incentive to decentralize their stockholding/distribution operations. It found that even in the case of products with a relatively low value density, transport costs would have to rise by over 100% to make it economically beneficial to move to a more decentralized structure. It is likely too that this modeling exercise will have underestimated the transport cost threshold as it failed to incorporate all the benefits that firms claim to derive from centralization and took no account of restructuring costs.

A proposal to double freight transport costs would command very little political support. To put it into perspective, the UK's "fuel duty escalator" policy, which increased fuel taxes by 5–6% per annum in real terms between 1994 and 1999, raised road haulage costs by around 10% over this period. This largely precipitated the UK "fuel crisis" of September 2000 in which blockades by hauliers and farmers seriously disrupted the economic and social life of the nation (Whiteing et al., 2002).

In the absence of high "eco-taxes," increasing traffic congestion might force a return to less transport-intensive logistics. Theoretical modeling by Eberhard (2000), however, suggests that this too will be unlikely to cause much logistical restructuring. He simulated the effects on a hypothetical European distribution system of a 50% increase in road traffic levels between 1995 and 2015. It was assumed that road capacity would remain fixed and there would thus be a substantial increase in traffic congestion. By comparing the optimal structures of the distribution systems in 1995 and 2015, he found that the number of warehouses would remain the same (at four) and only marginal changes would have to be made to the locations of two warehouses. The main impact of the growth of congestion would be on the size and shape of the "hinterlands" served by the warehouses.

2.2. Pattern of sourcing

This pattern, which is created by decisions at level 2 in the management hierarchy, is becoming more transport-intensive through time, as products are sourced and marketed over wider areas. The geographical expansion of trade areas appears so fundamental to the process of economic development that it is difficult to see how it can be contained. On the contrary, the development of B2B e-commerce is currently reinforcing the lengthening of supply lines as it enables companies to extend their search for suitable suppliers. Advances in information and communication technology are also making it easier for companies to manage the global supply chains through which remotely sourced products are channeled.

In many industries, factor cost differentials are very wide relative to transport costs, making it economic to move products long distances for intermediate processing that may only add marginally to their value. For most product groups, only a very steep increase in transport costs and/or transit times would be likely to offset these production cost differentials and promote a return to more localized sourcing.

Holzapfel (1995) favors the development of "regional supply structures" within which firms would source as much as possible from local suppliers. Using data collected by Böge (1994) on the "transport logistics" of a pot of strawberry yogurt, he calculated that if, in the production and distribution of this product, the nearest suppliers had been used, total lorry-kilometers could have been reduced by 67%.

If widely applied, this practice would dramatically reverse the recent growth in "food-miles" (Sustain, 1999), but at the expense of customer choice and, possibly, higher prices. Paxton (1994) suggests that the distance food products are transported should be printed on the labeling to allow consumers to take this into account when deciding what to buy. This would be very difficult to implement in practice and be unlikely to have much impact on the buying behavior of the majority of consumers.

In the realms of industrial logistics, Strutyniski (1994) has shown how rationalization of the supply networks of large car assembly plants, with greater "vertical integration" at the regional level, could reduce freight transport requirements by 70%. He concedes, however, that huge increases in transport costs (at least five-fold) would be needed to induce this process of rationalization.

2.3. Vehicle routing

The efficiency with which vehicles are routed around collection and delivery points influences the tonne-kilometer figure. It has been estimated that the use of computerized vehicle routing and scheduling (CVRS) packages can, on average, reduce the distance traveled by around 5–10%, though instances of 20% distance savings are quoted in the literature (Freight Transport Association, 2000). Minimizing the distance traveled need not minimize environmental impact, as the shortest route may involve traversing sensitive urban areas or congested sections of the road network. In theory, it should be possible to calibrate routes in terms of fuel efficiency, emissions, or total external costs, and use the CVRS packages to minimize one of these environmental metrics. No examples have yet been found of this being applied in practice, though some companies, such as the German logistics operator Schenker and the Swedish paper products firm Stora Enso, have developed systems to estimate the level of atmospheric emissions for different modal and routing options.

The development of vehicle tracking and in-cab mobile data communication systems has created the opportunity to replan vehicle schedules and routes in real time while the vehicle is on the road in response to short-term changes in customer requirements and traffic conditions. This dynamic form of CVRS can further reduce freight traffic levels. In an early application of mobile data satellite communications equipment in 25 trucks operated by three haulage companies operating mainly in Belgium, the Netherlands, and the UK, vehicle-kilometers were cut by 1.12% (Anderson et al., 1996). A more recent installation of tracking and monitoring equipment in a fleet of 50 trucks operated by the UK logistics provider Exel has cut engine idling time by 80%, significantly improving the energy efficiency of the distribution operation.

3. Transferring freight to less environmentally damaging modes

Several studies have identified modal shift as the most promising method of reducing energy consumption and emissions in the freight sector (e.g. Plowden and Buchan, 1995). When expressed in terms of kilojoules per tonne-kilometer, the specific primary energy consumption of road freight transport is 4.3 times higher than that of rail and 6.8 times greater than that of waterborne transport (Royal Commission on Environmental Pollution, 1994). These differences in energy intensity are reflected in variations in atmospheric emissions per tonne-kilometer (Dings and Dijkstra, 1997). A major transfer of freight to these alternative modes could, therefore, substantially reduce the overall energy intensity and environmental impact of the freight transport system.

Other studies are more pessimistic about the potential contribution of a modal shift to energy conservation and environmental improvement in the freight sector, for several reasons:

- In those countries where the modal split is heavily skewed toward road, total externalities would be relatively insensitive to even quite large increases in rail and/or water-based transport. Whitelegg (1995), for instance, assesses the effect in the UK of a large modal shift from road to rail and water (50–90% of all motorway truck traffic transferred to rail) on future road freight volumes and concludes that, while such a shift would be feasible and environmentally desirable, it would not arrest the growth in road traffic and related externalities.
- As the accessibility of the alternative modal networks is relatively low, road feeder movements are often required at one or both ends of the trunk haul, and the routing of the flows made more circuitous. The integration of rail and water-based trunk hauls into intermodal services therefore reduces their relative environmental advantage.
- In capturing traffic from road, particularly manufactured products of relatively low density and high time-sensitivity, the utilization of railfreight capacity would be likely to decline, with consequent reductions in average fuel efficiency (TNO-INRO, 1998).
- Doubts have been expressed about the ability of the operators of rail and water-based services to improve their competitiveness sufficiently to secure a much larger share of the freight market (NERA et al., 1997).

Even if the most optimistic projections of a freight modal shift were to materialize, road would remain by the far the dominant mode in most developed countries. The vast majority of road freight journeys are short and between premises that are not rail connected. It is important, therefore, to investigate the opportunities for rationalizing the road freight system by making more efficient use of vehicle capacity.

4. Improving vehicle utilization

4.1. Empty running

Empty running is the most obvious form of vehicle under-utilization. Typically around a third of trunk-kilometers are run empty, though there are significant international variations in the average figure (Netherlands Economic Institute et al., 1997). In larger countries with longer average haul lengths, operators have a greater incentive to find back loads and this is reflected in lower levels of empty running. In countries with a more even geographical distribution of population and economic activity it is easier for operators to achieve balanced loading of their vehicles. Regulatory controls, particularly on the activities of own-account operators, have restricted opportunities for backloading, though in most developed countries these have now been relaxed.

In some countries the proportion of truck-kilometers run empty has been gradually declining. In the UK, for example, the proportion of lorry kilometers run empty dropped from 32.6% in 1980 to 26.4% in 2001 (UK Department of the Environment, Transport and the Regions, 2002). This has yielded large environmental and economic benefits. Had the empty running proportion remained at its 1980 level, CO_2 emissions in 2001 would have been 1.6 million tonnes greater and annual road haulage costs UK £1.5 billion higher. This decline in empty running is partly a consequence of longer-term changes in the nature of freight journeys. These journeys have been lengthening, increasing the economic benefits of backloading, while the proportion of trips with multiple collections/drops, on which empty running usually confined to first or last leg, has been growing (McKinnon, 1996).

These trends have been reinforced by a series of company and industry-wide initiatives to improve backloading. For example, supermarket chains have been implementing both supplier collection and onward delivery schemes. In the case of supplier collection, a returning shop delivery vehicle collects goods from a supplier's premises and carries them to the retailer's distribution center. Onward delivery occurs where a supplier's vehicle offloads goods at the distribution center and backloads with supplies destined for one of the retailer's shops. This is delivered on the way back to the factory, usually with minimal deviation from the direct route. Tesco, the UK's largest supermarket chain, has estimated that over a 5 year period, its supplier collection scheme increased the annual volume of goods carried per trailer by 26.5% and the average annual distance traveled per vehicle by 19.9%. Over this period, there was a total saving in vehicle-kilometers of around 4.8 million, cutting fuel expenditure by UK £750 000 and carbon dioxide emissions by 23 000 tonnes (UK Department of the Environment, Transport and the Regions, 1997).

The development of load matching services has helped operators to extend their search for available backloads. Much of this load matching now occurs on the

Internet, with on-line freight exchanges, such as NTE in the USA and Freight-Traders in Europe, providing a trading platform for carriers and shippers. In addition to running an electronic auction for freight services, these companies can also provide crediting referencing, factoring, and escrow services, creating a much more secure system for the trading of backhaul capacity. The net effect of this form of B2B e-commerce on the environment is difficult to predict, however (James and Hopkinson, 2001). On the one hand, it is likely to improve the utilization of vehicle capacity, cutting the ratio of vehicle-kilometers to tonne-kilometers. On the other hand, by exerting a downward pressure on freight rates, it may stimulate a further increase in the demand for freight movement (i.e. tonne-kilometers). The potential cost savings are exemplified by the Dutch baby food manufacturer Numico NV, which estimates that it was able to cut its European road transport costs by 12% by using an online exchange.

The decline in empty running has also been associated with the growth in the return of packaging waste and reusable handling equipment for recycling and reuse. Environmental pressures on companies to maximize recycling and re-use of materials have created new opportunities for backloading, though not all of the additional return flows are accommodated within the available backhaul capacity. It was estimated in the UK, for example, that the 1997 packaging waste regulations would "lead to a 14% increase in freight vehicle-kilometers attributable to packaging waste" (Anderson et al., 1999).

It is uncertain how long the virtuous trend in empty running can continue. There is general agreement that there will remain a substantial volume of "structural" empty running that will be virtually impossible to eliminate. This is the result of several factors (McKinnon, 1996), including:

- geographical imbalances – in traffic flows at inter-urban, inter-regional and international levels;
- scheduling constraints – which limit the time available for vehicles to pick up a return load;
- vehicle incompatibility – where the consignments available for backloading are unsuited to the type of vehicle making the return journey;
- risk aversion – given the high priority attached to outbound distribution, transport managers are reluctant to take the risk of vehicles not returning in time for the outward journey.

4.2. Load factors on laden trips

On many laden trips, vehicles are only partially loaded. By consolidating loads, and thus raising vehicle load factors, it is possible to cut vehicle-kilometers (relative to tonne-kilometers), with resulting environmental and economic benefits. It is difficult to assess the potential for improving vehicle load factors on the basis of available statistics. Most of the official statistics on vehicle loading are weight based and do not measure the extent to which either the vehicle floor area or cubic capacity is occupied by a load. Since 1998, EU member states have been required to collect data on the proportion of loads constrained by weight or volume. However, only weight-based utilization estimates are available for loads that do not fill the vehicle. In the UK, the average "weight-based" leading factor for trucks of over 3.5 tonnes gross weight was 59% in 2001 (UK Department of the Environment, Transport and the Regions, 2002).

For loads of lower-density products, only volumetric measures of "vehicle fill" can give a true indication of the scope for improved loading. Volumetric data are hard to collect on a consistent basis, however, and as a consequence very little research has been done on the space utilization of vehicles. In a study conducted in the Netherlands and Sweden, Samuelson and Tilanus (1997) asked a panel of industry experts to estimate the average space-utilization of vehicles carrying less than truckload consignments. This revealed that cube utilization was typically very low, at around 28%. On average, however, just over 80% of the deck area would be occupied and 70% of the available pallet positions filled. It was therefore mainly in the vertical dimension that space was being wasted, with average load heights reaching only 47% of the maximum. A survey of road transport operations in the UK food supply chain found that, on average, roughly 78% of vehicle deck area was covered by a load and 66% of the available height occupied, yielding an overall cube utilization index of 50% (McKinnon, 1999). Low average load height was also identified as a major source of inefficiency by consultants A.T. Kearney (1997), in a study of European grocery distribution, calculated that there were "15% extra grocery trucks on European roads as a result of failure to optimize available height." In a more broadly based follow-up study on "transport optimization" for ECR Europe, a research team concluded that it would be possible to "reduce vehicle movements by up to 30% or to absorb up to 30% growth in business freight tonne-kilometers carried without any increase in current levels of goods vehicle movements" (University of St. Gallen, 2000).

A range of measures can be used to improve vehicle loading. These can be classified under four headings: order fulfillment, shared distribution, vehicle design, and the space efficiency of handling equipment and transit packaging.

Order fulfillment

As explained above, operational decisions on the scheduling of production and distribution operations translate business transactions into discrete vehicle movements. Ideally, these schedules should be sufficiently flexible to allow full loads to accumulate before a vehicle is despatched. In practice, companies must trade off the benefits of improved vehicle loading against associated costs, mainly of higher inventory and inferior customer service (Jackson, 1985).

In some sectors, companies have been giving greater priority to inventory reduction and customer service than to the efficient utilization of transport capacity. It is often argued that by sourcing supplies on a JIT or "quick response" basis, demanding more frequent deliveries of smaller quantities within narrower time windows, companies trade off more transport for less inventory (e.g. Whitelegg, 1995; Bleijenberg, 1996). The conventional view is that savings in inventory, and related productivity benefits, can more than offset the additional transport costs.

The negative effects of JIT on vehicle utilization may have been exaggerated, however. A crude indicator of the effect of JIT on the road transport sector is average payload weight. If JIT has been causing a pronounced "de-consolidation" of loads, one would expect to see this reflected in a decline in the average payload weight. Analysis of official freight data for the UK, the Netherlands, and Sweden revealed significant net increases in this index across these countries' truck fleets (McKinnon, 2000). Furthermore, studies of companies operating JIT systems have found that only in a minority of cases does JIT inflate transport costs (Garreau et al., 1991; Tracey et al., 1995). Many of the firms supplying or receiving products on a JIT basis have taken measures that, directly or indirectly, minimize the downward pressure on vehicle load factors. These include the insertion of an additional consolidation point into the supply chain, the "milk-round" collection of orders, and the single sourcing of supplies. The benefits of the first two measures have been illustrated by Nissan UK, which employs the logistics firm Ryder to collect components from suppliers and consolidate them at a "cross-dock" for "line haul" delivery to its assembly plant (UK Department of the Environment, Transport and the Regions, 1999b). It has been estimated that if these suppliers delivered directly to the plant, the inbound vehicle-kilometers would be around 80% higher. Furthermore, as larger, more-fuel efficient vehicles can be used for supplier collection and line haul operations than would be possible with JIT delivery directly from supplier, fuel savings are proportionally greater than this reduction in vehicle-kilometers. Altogether, around 870 000 liters of fuel are saved annually.

Where the order fulfillment process does not have to adhere to the disciplines of JIT manufacturing or "quick response" retailing, other measures can be adopted to improve vehicle utilization (McKinnon, 2000). The nominated day delivery system enables companies to attain higher levels of load consolidation, drop density, and vehicle utilization by concentrating deliveries in particular areas on nominated days. To obtain deliveries on these days, customers must place their orders a minimum number of days in advance. Sales and marketing departments often resist the introduction of this system, however, fearing that the imposition of ordering constraints will reduce competitiveness and jeopardize sales.

The activities of sales and finance departments can also frustrate efforts to improve vehicle utilization in other ways. By operating monthly sales and order–payment cycles they cause delivery volumes to fluctuate making it difficult to manage transport capacity effectively. By abandoning the monthly payment cycle and moving to a system of "rolling credit," which computerized financial accounting systems now facilitate, firms can increase the average level of vehicle loading and reduce traffic levels. Anecdotal evidence suggests that this can cut truck-kilometers by 10–20%.

Shared distribution

In outsourcing their logistics, many companies have demanded dedicated services, with vehicles bearing their livery and allowed to carry only their products. Other firms continue to run in-house fleets for their own exclusive use. Both practices limit the opportunities for multi-company (or "horizontal") consolidation. There is, nevertheless, increasing evidence of major users of dedicated services granting contractors the freedom to transport other firms' traffic in their vehicles, and of own-account operators "carrying for others." There has also been a growth of shared-user (or "network") services in recent years, particularly handling pallet loads and parcels. Several company-sponsored studies in the UK of the potential benefits of shared-user services in the automotive, consumer electrical, and clothing sectors, in each case replacing four or five separate dedicated services, have indicated that this can reduce transport costs and vehicle-kilometers by around 20%.

Vehicle design

The use of drawbar–trailer combinations and double-deck trailers allows firms to increase carrying capacity within vehicle "construction and use" regulations. In the UK, where overhead clearances are relative high because of the heavy reliance on double-deck buses, there has been a steep increase in the number of companies operating double-deck trucks. It was estimated in 1997 that the double-decking of articulated vehicles carrying low-density loads could cut total articulated vehicle traffic in the UK by approximately 5%, reducing carbon dioxide emissions by just over half a million tonnes per annum, and cutting road haulage costs by UK £340 million annually (McKinnon and Campbell, 1997). The economic and environmental case for double-, and in some cases triple-, decking vehicles is strengthening as the average density and "stackability" of freight is declining and as increases in legal limits on truck weight are raising the proportion of loads subject solely to a volume constraint.

Vehicles can also be redesigned in other ways to permit greater load consolidation (Holman, 1996). The compartmentalization of lorries has enabled grocery retailers and their contractors to combine the movement of products at different temperatures on a single journey. This form of "composite distribution," for example, enabled the UK retailer Safeway to reduce the average number of vehicle trips required to deliver 1000 cases from five in 1985 to one in 1995 (Freight Transport Association, 1995)

Space efficiency of handling equipment and transit packaging

The utilization of vehicle deck area and cube is partly determined by the nature of the handling equipment and packaging. Average deck area utilization can vary between 52 and 78%, depending on the dimensions of wooden pallets (A.T. Kearney, 1997). Cube utilization can be raised by around 13% by replacing pallets (in this case Euro-pallets) with thin "slip sheets" (University of St. Gallen, 2000). If a company's sole aim were to pack as much product as possible into a vehicle and thereby minimize vehicle-kilometers, it would probably dispense with handling equipment and transit packaging completely and have all freight "hand-balled" on and off the vehicle. This would maximize vehicle fill, but at the expense of handling efficiency and an increase in the amount of damage to products in transit. Optimizing the trade-off between transport, handling, and damage costs usually involves some under-utilization of vehicle space. Many companies could, nevertheless, use more space-efficient forms of handling equipment and transit packaging without seriously compromising handling efficiency or product integrity. One French food manufacturer, for example, was able to improve vehicle fill by between 35 and 41% by using modules of varying height that permitted more flexible stacking (Holman, 1996). Opportunities for varying the dimensions of handling units are often limited, however, by the configuration of warehouse racking. For example, the racking in many distribution centers handling fast-moving consumer goods can only accommodate pallet loads up to a maximum height of 1.7 m, despite the fact that most articulated vehicles have internal height clearances of 2.4 m.

4.3. Legal limits on vehicle size and weight

A significant proportion of loads are weight or volume constrained. In the UK, for example, approximately two-thirds of road tonne-kilometers are carried in vehicles constrained by either the weight limit or available cubic capacity. Twenty-nine percent of tonne-kilometers is constrained by weight, 26% by volume, and 8% limited by both volume and weight (UK Department of the Environment, Transport and the Regions, 2002). Significant potential therefore exists for increasing load consolidation and cutting vehicle-kilometers by raising legal limits on vehicle weights and sizes. Truck dimensions are clearly constrained by the geometry of road layouts, bridge heights, and reception facilities at industrial and retail premises, as well as public opinion. Opportunities for increasing these dimensions are therefore limited, particularly in more densely developed countries. There has been greater pressure on regulators to increase the maximum weight of vehicles.

The case for increasing the maximum weight of trucks was recently investigated by the author for the UK Commission for Integrated Transport (2000). This study evaluated the benefits and costs of raising maximum truck weight from 40–41 to 44 tonnes. This indicated that there would be significant economic and environmental benefits in approving the weight increase, even after allowance had been made for some erosion of freight traffic from rail and a small traffic-generating effect. It was estimated that the net consolidation of loads in the heavier vehicles would remove 100 million vehicle-kilometers of articulated vehicle traffic from the road network, yielding annual savings in haulage costs worth UK £60–80 million and carbon dioxide reductions of 80 000–100 000 tonnes.

5. City logistics

The environmental problems posed by the movement of freight are at their most acute in urban areas, where traffic densities are high and large populations are exposed to truck exhaust emissions and noise. Over the past couple of decades some logistical trends have exacerbated these environmental problems while others have helped to relieve them. Reductions in inventory levels and back-storeroom space in shops have created the need for more frequent and rapid delivery. Using the Tokyo Metropolitan Area as a case study, Shiomi et al. (1994) illustrate how the move to JIT delivery exacerbated traffic congestion and pollution problems. The application of the JIT principle at the retail level had the potential to generate a large increase in lorry and van traffic. In many sectors of the European and US retail markets, however, multiple retailers have increased their control of shop delivery operations, consolidating loads at distribution centers and sharply reducing the number of vehicle movements required to supply a given of quantity of product. This has yielded significant reductions in the emission of carbon dioxide and other noxious gases by the UK grocery market (McKinnon and Woodburn, 1994). Concern has, nevertheless, been expressed about their use of large articulated vehicles for deliveries in sensitive inner urban environments.

City planners have had to address the issue of whether, in environmental terms, it is better to have a few large vehicles or many small ones. In the 1970s the emphasis in Europe was on limiting the size of trucks allowed into urban areas. It was proposed that trans-shipment centers be established on the outskirts of town and cities at which large inbound loads could be disaggregated for delivery in smaller vehicles. Numerous studies were conducted to assess the feasibility of this concept, most of which concluded that it would dislocate existing distribution systems at significant cost to business and be of limited benefit to the environment (Button and Pearman, 1981). In many US cities in the 1970s and 1980s, where the urban freight problem was defined more in economic than environmental terms, priority was given to consolidating loads, if necessary in larger vehicles (Ogden, 1992).

The "many small, few large" dilemma was complicated by the fact that some environmental effects (such as air pollution, accident levels, and traffic congestion) correlate mainly with vehicle numbers, while others (such as noise, vibration, and accident severity) are largely a function of vehicle size and weight. As concern about air pollution, climate change, and traffic congestion has mounted, and as technical advances in vehicle design have cut engine noise and vibration, the case for consolidating loads in fewer larger vehicles has greatly strengthened. During the 1990s there was a revival of interest in the development of urban freight depots (or "logistical platforms") to act as local load consolidation points. The experience of these facilities has been mixed, however. A freight platform set up in the Dutch city of Maastricht in the early 1990s failed to attract sufficient business, and as a consequence did not meet its economic and environmental goals. On the other hand, several "city logistics" schemes in German cities, such as Bremen and Bielefeld, involving the use of local consolidation depots have proved more successful. The EU Cost 321 program of research on "urban good transport" assessed the effects of a broad range of measures on "ecology, traffic, economy and safety" in 28 cities in 11 European countries (European Commission, 1998). The most effective measures were found to be "in the realms of logistics." Of 13 logistical measures tested, the most promising included "transport co-ordination and co-operation of retailers, reduction in packing volume, common use of vehicle fleets, information systems and telematics applications, [use of] goods distribution centers, consolidation by means of urban containers." Taniguchi and van der Heijden (2000) employed a dynamic simulation model with optimized routing and schedule to assess the impact of three city logistics initiatives on transport costs and carbon dioxide emissions. The largest carbon dioxide reductions accrued from the introduction of a "co-operative freight transport system" (i.e. shared-user transport service), though there were also significant environmental gains from the use of "advanced information systems" by urban delivery vehicles and from the imposition of controls on vehicle load factors in urban areas. Such controls have been trialed in Copenhagen and Amsterdam, where vehicles were only granted access to public freight terminals or inner urban areas if their load factors exceeded a threshold value (60% in Copenhagen and 80% in Amsterdam).

The UK government has encouraged the creation of "quality partnerships for urban distribution," involving local authorities, the freight industry, the business community, residents, and environmental groups, to develop local solutions to urban freight problems (UK Department of the Environment, Transport and the Regions, 1999a). To date, around 25 of these partnerships have been established, reviewing a broad mix of planning, infrastructural, and operational measures, including vehicle routing schemes, the rescheduling of deliveries, priority for freight vehicles on urban roads, and modal interchange facilities.

In devising "city logistics" policies, it is necessary not only to balance economic and environmental objectives but also to trade-off different environmental costs. This is illustrated by the proposal to reschedule urban deliveries to the evening or night when traffic is relatively free-flowing and fewer people are outdoors to experience its effects. This can help companies cut the energy intensity of their distribution operations by running vehicles at more fuel-efficient speeds. A dairy company in London, for example, managed to improve the fuel efficiency of its delivery operations by 13% by switching from daytime to night deliveries (Cooper and Tweddle, 1994). As congestion levels rise on urban roads, the potential savings in fuel and emissions will increase. Night-time running, however, exacerbates the problem of noise irritation both from moving traffic and at collection and delivery points. As a consequence, many municipal authorities impose night curfews on freight deliveries. With greater use now being made of quieter vehicles, often electrically operated or running on alternative fuels such as compressed natural gas, the justification for curfews is weakening. It has been estimated that if half the local night curfews in the UK were lifted, ten major grocery retailers could collectively cut total annual delivery distances by 63 million km and carbon dioxide emissions by 96 000 tonnes (Anon., 2002).

6. Conclusion

One of the central paradoxes in the field of green logistics has been that as vehicles have become more fuel-efficient, cleaner and quieter, reducing externalities per kilometer traveled, major business trends, such as globalization, centralization, and, to a lesser extent, JIT, have been sharply increasing total vehicle-kilometers. Many of the environmental benefits accruing from improvements in vehicle technology are therefore being sacrificed as logistical systems become ever more transport-intensive.

This chapter has examined the opportunities for slowing, and possibly reversing, the growth of truck traffic by reducing three critical ratios: road's share of total freight movement (the modal split), transport intensity, and vehicle utilization. The rationalization of road freight transport has been the subject of numerous studies during the 1990s. These studies have placed differing emphasis on the three key ratios and recommended different sets of corrective measures. There is a general consensus, however, that concerted action to promote alternative modes, encourage more localized sourcing, and raise vehicle load factors would yield substantial savings in vehicle-kilometers and corresponding reductions in environmental costs. The most promising measures are likely to be those targeted on vehicle utilization, as they tend to be largely self-financing.

The ability of logistics managers to economize on their use of freight transport is, nevertheless, inhibited in two respects. First, they are constrained by decisions made at a higher strategic level within the corporate hierarchy, where the objectives of marketing and production are typically given priority and can increase the overall transport intensity of the business. Future increases in transport costs, tightening environmental controls, and worsening traffic congestion will help to redress the balance and force a reassessment of logistical options. Second, the opportunity for an individual company to act unilaterally to cut freight traffic volumes is limited by the activities of customers, distributors, and suppliers with which its logistical system must interface. The rationalization of freight transport operations often requires close cooperation by firms at different levels in the supply chain. There is a need, therefore, for industry-wide initiatives and strong government support for the diffusion of sustainable logistics practices.

References

Dings, J. and W.J. Dijkstra (1997) *Specific energy consumption and emissions of freight transport*. Delft: Centrum voor Energiebesparing en Schone Technologie.

DIW, ifeu and IVU/HACON (1994) *Reduction of air pollution and noise from long distance freight transport by the year 2010*. Research Project No. 104 04 962. Berlin: Federal Environment Agency (Umweltbundesamt).

Eberhard, C. (2000) "Implication of traffic growth for the design of sustainable European distribution systems," in: *Proceedings of the Logistics Research Network Conference*. Cardiff.

European Commission (1998) *COST 321: urban goods transport – final report of the Action*. Brussels: Directorate General Transport, EC.

European Commission (2001) *White Paper: European transport policy for 2010: time to decide* Brussels: EC.

European Conference of Ministers of Transport (2000) *Trends in the transport sector: 1970–1998*. Paris: OECD.

Freight Transport Association (1995) "JIT: time sensitive distribution," *Freight Matters*, 1/95.

Freight Transport Association (2000) *Computerised routing and scheduling for efficient logistics. Good practice guide 273*. Harwell: ETSU.

Garreau, A., R.C. Lieb and R. Millen (1991) "JIT and corporate transport: an international comparison," *International Journal of Physical Distribution and Logistics Management*, 21:42–47.

Holman, C. (1996) *The greening of freight transport in Europe*. Report 96/12. Brussels: European Federation of Transport and Environment.

Holzapfel, H. (1995) "Potential focus of regional economic co-operation to reduce goods transport," *World Transport Problems and Practice* (http://ecoplan.org/wtpp/general/vol1-2.htm).

International Road Transport Union (2000) *Guide to sustainable development*. Geneva: International Road Transport Union.

Jackson, G.C. (1985) A survey of freight consolidation practices *Journal of Business Logistics*, 6:1, 13–34.

James, P. and P. Hopkinson, (2001) "Virtual traffic: ecommerce, transport and distribution," in: J. Wilsdon, ed., *Digital futures: living in a dot-com world*. London: Earthscan.

McKinnon, A.C. (1995) "Logistics and the environment," *Logistics Europe*, 3:16–22.

McKinnon, A.C. (1996) "The empty running and return loading of road goods vehicles," *Transport Logistics*, 1:1–19.

McKinnon, A.C. (1998) "Logistical restructuring, road freight traffic growth and the environment," in: D. Banister, ed., *Transport policy and the environment*. London: Spon.

McKinnon, A.C. (2000) "Sustainable distribution: opportunities to improve vehicle loading," *Industry and Environment*, 23:26–30.

McKinnon, A.C. and J. Campbell (1997) *Opportunities for consolidating volume-constrained loads in double-deck and high-cube vehicles*. Christian Salvesen Logistics Research Paper No. 1. Edinburgh: School of Management, Heriot-Watt University.

McKinnon, A.C. and A. Woodburn (1994) "The consolidation of retail deliveries: its effect on CO_2 emissions," *Transport Policy*, 1:125–136.

McKinnon, A.C. and A. Woodburn (1996) "Logistical restructuring and freight traffic growth: an empirical assessment," *Transportation*, 23:141–152.

Maister, D.H. (1976) "Centralisation of inventories and the square root law," *International Journal of Physical Distribution*, 6:124–134.

NERA, MVA, Travers Morgan and ITS Leeds (1997) *The potential for rail freight*. London: NERA.

Netherlands Economic Institute, Heriot-Watt University, TFK and Service Economiques et Statistique (1997) *Analysis of Collected Data and Selection of Goods Flows*. Deliverables 1 and 2, REDEFINE project. Brussels: European Commission.

Ogden, K.W. (1992) *Urban goods movement: a guide to policy and planning*. Aldershot: Ashgate.

Pastowski, A. (1997) *Decoupling economic development and freight for reducing its negative impacts*. Wuppertal paper No. 78. Wuppertal: Wuppertal Institute for Climate, Environment and Energy.

Paxton, A. (1994) *The food miles report: the dangers of long distance transport of food*. London: Safe Alliance.

PE International (1993) *Going green: the logistics dilemma*. Corby: Institute of Logistics and Distribution Management.

Plowden, S. and K. Buchan (1995) *A new framework for freight transport*. London: Civic Trust.

Royal Commission on Environmental Pollution (1994) *Transport and the environment*. London: The Stationery Office.

Samuelsson, A. and B. Tilanus (1997) "A framework efficiency model for goods transportation, with an application to regional less-than-truckload distribution," *Transport Logistics*, 1:85–152.

Shiomi, E., H. Nomura, G. Chow and N. Katuhiro (1994) "Physical distribution and freight transportation in the Tokyo Metropolitan Area," *Logistics and Transportation Review*, 29:335–253.

Strutyniski, P. (1994) "Reduction of freight transport through lean production," *World Transport Problems and Practice* (http://ecoplan.org/wtpp/general/vol1-2.htm).

Sustain (1999) *Food miles – still on the road to ruin?* London: Sustain.

Taniguchi, E. and R.E.C.M. van der Heijden (2000) "An evaluation methodology for city logistics," *Transport Reviews*, 20: 65–90.

TNO-INRO (1998) *Eufranet survey report: inventorisation of customer needs of freight rail in Europe*. Delft: TNO.

Tracey, M., C.L. Tan, M. Vonderembse and E.J. Bardi (1995) "Re-examination of the effects of just in time on inbound logistics," *International Journal of Logistics Management*, 6:25–37.

UK Department of the Environment, Transport and the Regions (1997) *National road traffic forecasts (Great Britain) 1997*. London: The Stationery Office.

UK Department of the Environment, Transport and the Regions (1999a) *Sustainable distribution: a strategy*. London: DETR.

UK Department of the Environment, Transport and the Regions (1999b) *Efficient JIT supply chain management: Nissan Motor Manufacturing (UK) Ltd*. Good Practice Case Study 374. Energy Efficiency Best Practice Programme. Harwell: ETSU.

UK Department of the Environment, Transport and the Regions (2002) *Transport of goods by road in Great Britain 2001*. London: DETR.

University of St. Gallen (2000) *The transport optimisation report*. Brussels: ECR-Europe.

Whiteing, T., M. Coyle and C. Bamford (2002) "Effective fuel management in road transport fleets," in: G. Lyons, and K. Chatterjee, eds, *Transport lessons from the fuel tax protests of 2000*. Abingdon: Ashgate.

Whitelegg, J. (1995) *Freight transport, logistics and sustainable development*. London: World Wide Fund for Nature.

Worsford, F. (1994) *Best environmental practice: a manager's guide for transport distribution centre.* London: The Stationery Office.

Wu, H.-J. and S.C. Dunn (1995) "Environmentally-responsible logistics systems," *International Journal of Physical Distribution and Logistics Management,* 25:20–38.

Chapter 38

REVERSE LOGISTICS: AN OVERVIEW AND A CAUSAL MODEL

SHAMS RAHMAN
The University of Sydney

1. Introduction

The recovery of used products or parts is receiving much attention as a result of growing environmental concern, increased landfill cost, and increased economic benefits. In recent years, several European nations have enforced legislation charging manufacturers with the responsibility to take back their used products (Boks et al., 1998). These include product categories such as packaging materials, electronics, and cars. These laws and regulations are likely to increase during the next decade, and their impact will not be restricted to developed nations. For instance, three-quarters of the South African leading companies now view environmental issues as strategically important to their business (Stock, 1998).

On one hand environmental-related laws and legislation are forcing companies to be responsible for their waste, but on the other hand, waste disposal costs are increasing rapidly. As a result of depleted landfill and incineration capacities, the cost of landfill activities has increased considerably, and continues to rise (Rogers and Tibben-Lembke, 1998). Considering this evolving business environment, many world class companies have realized that reverse logistics practices, combined with source reduction processes, can be used to gain competitive advantage. Companies such as Xerox (Europe), Hewlett-Packard, Eastman Kodak, and Sears have successfully implemented reuse, remanufacturing, and recycling programs (Kopicki et al., 1993; Maslennikova and Foley, 2000). These initiatives not only have reduced waste and its adverse effect on the environment but have also lowered operating costs and improved the profitability and public image of these companies (Minahan, 1998).

Logistics management focuses primarily on the movement of material from the point of origin to the point of consumption, whereas reverse logistics concentrates on the flow of material from the point of consumption toward the point of origin. Using this notion, Rogers and Tibben-Lembke (1999) defined reverse logistics as:

Handbook of Transport and the Environment, Edited by D.A. Hensher and K.J. Button
© 2003, Elsevier Ltd

> The process of planning, implementing, and controlling the efficient, cost effective flow of raw materials, in-process inventory, finished goods, and related information from the point of consumption to the point of origin for the purpose of recapturing or creating value or proper disposal.

A more comprehensive definition is given by Stock (1998):

> from a business logistics perspective, the term (reverse logistics) refers to the role of logistics in product returns, source reduction, recycling, materials substitution, reuse of materials, waste disposal, and refurbishing, repair, and remanufacturing ... and is a systematic business model that applies best logistics engineering and management methodologies across the enterprise in order to profitably close the loop on the supply chain.

This definition reflects a more holistic view of logistics management that includes both forward and reverse flows. Logistics management incorporating both forward and reverse logistics can be termed integrated logistics management.

This chapter examines key issues in reverse logistics, focusing on motivating factors, characteristics, and types of recovery processes used in reverse logistics networks. Quantitative models that are often employed to design reverse logistics systems are discussed, and areas for future research are also highlighted. The final section of the chapter develops a causal model for successful implementation of reverse logistics programs.

2. Motivation for reverse logistics

It is difficult to estimate the exact amount of reverse logistics activities currently being practiced, since most companies do not track reverse logistics costs in sufficient detail. In a study of several hundred multinational companies, Blumburg (1999) estimated that the 1996 worldwide expenditure on reverse logistics activities (i.e., collection and sorting, transportation, storage and warehousing, repair, recertification, and disposal) was US $15.3 billion. According to Rogers and Tibben-Lembke (1999), reverse logistics accounts for approximately 4% of the total logistics costs, which in turn is about 10% of US GDP. By any estimate the overall amount of reverse logistics activities in OECD countries is large and growing.

However, there appears to be growing interest in reverse logistics. Organizations that once had little interest in reverse logistics are now devoting more resources to the understanding and management of return flows. Many high-profile global companies such as Xerox, Hewlett-Packard, and Motorola now consider the management of return flows as part of their strategic agenda. There appear to be four main factors facilitating this development: environmental considerations, government policy and legislation, economic considerations, and the shift toward services

2.1. Environmental considerations

Manufacturers can no longer ignore public concern about sustainable development. These concerns have imposed significant pressures on companies to consider environmental issues, and have forced many to set up recovery management systems. Successful design and implementation of reverse logistics will benefit a company in two ways. First, it will help companies to comply with environmental legislation. Second, consideration of environmental issues creates an opportunity for firms to project themselves as "green" companies (concern for the environment now being recognized as an important marketing element).

2.2. Government policy and legislation

Several countries, especially in Europe, have enacted legislation and policies that requires manufacturers to take back their products after they have been used. These laws are related to the collection, transportation, recovery, and disposal of used products. As of January 1999, manufacturers and importers of white-and-brown goods in the Netherlands are required to recover their products after use. Similar legislation was adopted for the local automotive industry back in January 1995.

In 1991, Germany introduced the Packaging Ordinance Act, under which companies are required to collect all sales packaging materials. In addition, the German Recycling and Waste Control Act requires manufacturers to actively seek techniques and technologies that avoid waste and promote the recovery processes of unavoidable wastes. Other countries in the EU are now following these German initiatives (Rembert, 1997).

Take-back programs are not prevalent in the USA, however, although some are now being developed. In early 1990s, the state of Maryland passed legislation requiring manufacturers and retailers to take back mercury oxide batteries after use, and at least 15 US states now have law requiring retailers to take back vehicle batteries. As of 2000, Japanese manufacturers of electrical devices are required to recycle their own products. In 1998, the European Commission has adopted a proposal for a directive on Waste Electrical and Electronic Equipment (WEEE) to increase recycling, reduce hazardous substances, and to properly dispose of the left over waste (Rogers and Tibben-Lembke, 1999).

Government legislation is having a positive impact on corporate strategy. Several firms have responded by creating "green" alliances to improve their environmental performance. A major focus of the environmental programs in these firms is life cycle analysis. Life cycle analysis measures the economic and environmental impacts of a product through its manufacture (remanufacture), use (reuse), recycle, and disposal (Kopicki et al., 1993).

2.3. Economic considerations

Landfill space is depleting rapidly, and as a consequence landfill usage costs have increased substantially. For example, the US national average tipping fee (the standard cost to dispose of a ton of waste) increased from US $8 to US $31.50 between 1985 and 1996, a rise of approximately 300% (Rogers and Tibben-Lembke, 1999). Although disposal costs are escalating rapidly, implementation of recoverable manufacturing systems (Figure 1) have been reported to increase companies' efficiency, and hence their profitability; for example, Xerox has recently reported an annual saving of US $3.5 million through its reverse logistics activities in Europe (Maslennikova and Foley, 2000). This is not restricted to copier manufacturing companies only: increased profitability through the use of reverse logistics recovery processes has also been reported for a number of other products such as automobile parts, computers, tires, and aviation equipment (Thierry et al., 1995; Guide, 1996; Ayres et al., 1997; Ferrer, 1997).

2.4. Shift toward buying sets of services

Instead of buying physical products, consumers are gradually moving towards buying a set of services along with products which may include maintenance contracts covering repairs and parts deliveries. Such contracts facilitate the take back of end-of-life products. One such example is Xerox's business strategy.

3. Characteristics of reverse logistics

The operational characteristics of reverse logistics are more complex to manage than traditional logistics activities. These unique characteristics of reverse logistics are outlined in the following section. Discussion is based on research by Guide (2000), Guide et al. (2000) and Veerakamolmal and Gupta (2000). Table 1 shows the differences between recoverable (includes both forward and backward flows of materials) and traditional (includes only forward flows of materials) manufacturing systems.

Since reverse logistics processes are more complex and uncertain compared with forward logistics, effective coordination among the supply chain partnerships

Table 1
A comparison of recoverable and traditional manufacturing environment

Factors	Recoverable manufacturing environment	Traditional manufacturing environment
Environmental focus	Seeks to prevent postproduction waste	Focus on preproduction, environmentally conscious design and manufacturing Pollution prevention and remediation
Logistics	Forward and reverse flows Uncertainty in timing and quantity of returns Supply-driven flows	Open forward flow No returns Demand-driven flows
Production planning and control	Need to balance demands with returns Material recovery uncertainty Stochastic routing and processing time Manufacturing system has three major components: disassembly, remanufacturing, and reassembly	No such need Certainty in planning materials Fixed routings and more stable processing times Manufacturing system has two major components: fabrication and assembly
Forecasting	Forecast both core availability and end-product demand Must forecast part requirements because material recovery rates are uncertain	Forecast only end products No parts forecasting needed
Purchasing	Highly uncertain material requirements owing to variable recovery rates Cores and parts and components, replacement parts/components	Material requirements deterministic Raw materials, new parts, and components
Inventory control and management	Types: cores, remanufactured parts, new parts, new and remanufactured substitute parts, original equipment manufacturer parts Must track and provide accounting for all part types	Types: raw materials, work in process, finished goods Must track and provide accounting for work in process and finished goods

Source: Guide et al. (2000).

and more information and communication technology (ICT) support is required. However, ICT vendors have not yet given a high priority to the integration of reverse logistics functionality into their exiting enterprise resource planning and application service provider systems.

3.1. Supply–demand balance

One of the most difficult variables to control for in a remanufacturing environment is the distribution of returns of end-of-life products, which is a function of products' expected life and rate of technical innovation (Guide and Srivastava, 1997). Mismatch between demand and returns can lead to excess stocks of unwanted parts and components and shortages of required parts and components. This makes inventory management and purchasing difficult to plan and control.

3.2. Accumulation and shortage of parts

There are two main reasons why the distribution of returns and end-of-life products can be hard to predict: uncertainty in timing and quantity of returns; and stochastic routings and processing times.

Uncertainty in timing and quantity of returns

Uncertainty in the timing and quantity of returns affects inventory control decisions. Early in a product's life cycle, when few units are in the field, one can expect a low return rate. As the product matures, a higher rate of return can be expected. Since recovered products might be damaged during servicing or while disassembling, or customers may fail to return the products, the recovery rate of cores (items that will be used to repair and remanufacture) will never be 100% of the sales of a product. The uncertainty in the timing and quantity of returns makes materials requirement planning difficult.

Stochastic routings and processing times

Firms involved in remanufacturing need to assess the condition of parts disassembled from return products, and schedule the work stations. Because the parts recovered for disassembly vary from unit to unit, processing times vary, and thus the routings will vary too. These additional forms of uncertainty make production planning and control and inventory control more difficult than in a traditional manufacturing environment.

3.3. Logistical network

A recoverable manufacturing system has three major components (assembly plant, disassembly plant, and recycling/remanufacturing plant) compared with two components (fabrication and assembly) in a traditional logistics system.

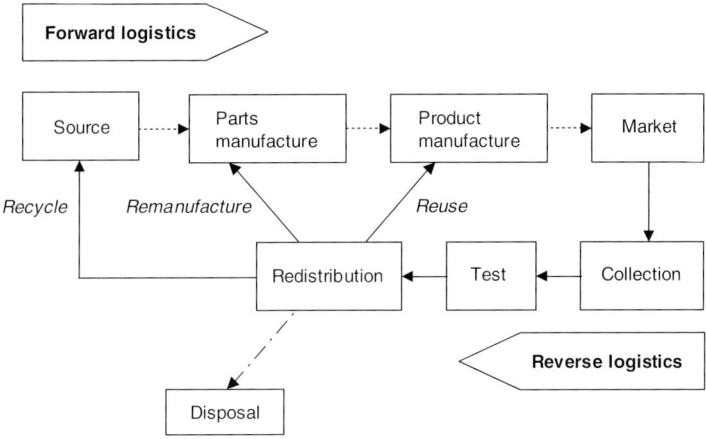

Figure 1. Recovery options in an integrated logistics management.

Reverse logistics networks typically have a convergent structure. Whereas, forward logistics networks most often assume a divergent structure.

3.4. Transportation

Plant location decisions are generally driven by the transportation costs of raw materials. In a recoverable manufacturing system, location decisions will be influenced by the location costs of assembly, disassembly, and remanufacturing plants.

4. Recovery processes and its hierarchy

A reverse logistics system incorporates a logistics system designed to manage the flow of products and parts destined for reuse, recycling, remanufacturing, or disposal with or without energy recovery (Thierry et al., 1995). Figure 1 shows these recovery options. The test phase helps to identify at which phase a particular recovery option may enter the forward logistics chain. Reuse refers to a process in which the recovered product is used again for a purpose similar to the one for which it was designed (Rogers and Tibben-Lembke, 1998). This provides an alternative to new parts and products, and is a common practice for many manufacturers. For example, reusable packages and products are often recovered for direct reuse, after simple operations such as inspection and cleaning. Kroon and Vrijens (1994) have examined the design of a closed-loop deposit-based reverse logistics network for reusable transportation packages in the Netherlands.

In this reverse logistics network system, reusable containers move from the distribution depot to the customer, the customer to the collection depot, and the collection depot to the distribution depot. A detailed discussion of this study is given in the next section. Other examples of reusable items include bottles, pallets, containers, and furniture.

Remanufacturing involves a product being reduced to its constituent parts. Compared with reuse, this requires more extensive work, and often involves completely disassembling the product. Recovered parts can then be reused in the assembly of new products. Some examples of products that are remanufactured are copiers, printers, computers, and car engines. Remanufacturing seeks to bring products to a "good as new" level of quality. Thus, remanufacturing focuses on value-added recovery, rather than just materials recovery (e.g. recycling). The design of a multi-echelon logistics network for a particular model of photocopier studied by Krikke et al. (1999) is a good example of remanufacturing. The reverse logistics system consisted of three main recovery processes: dismantling, preparation, and reassembly, where new and repaired components were reassembled together into new products. Remanufacturing provides customers with an opportunity to acquire products that meet the original product standards at a lower price than a new product. There is evidence to suggest that remanufacturing is not only environmentally sound but also economically profitable (Nasr et al., 1998). A recent study by Lund (1998) estimated that there are over 73 000 firms engaged in remanufacturing in the USA alone.

Sending cartons back to a paper mill or metal scraps to a foundry are examples of recycling. A wide variety of industries are involved in recycling operations. These include consumer electronics, carpet, plastics, automotive, metals, and paper industries. Recycling is considered as the least value-added recovery process compared with the other two options discussed above since it does reuse parts and the products do not retain the functionality of the original items. Despite this, increasingly restrictive environmental regulations and a potential economic benefit has encouraged firms and municipalities to recycle glass, paper, and plastics. Approximately 2 million tonnes of carpet is disposed in the USA each year (Realff et al., 1999). In western Europe the amount is estimated to be 1.6 million tonnes per year (Bohnhoff, 1996). Valued at about US \$1/kg, recyclable carpet can be considered to be an untapped resource.

Recently, Carter and Ellram (1998) proposed a conceptual framework for understanding the reverse logistics hierarchy. Based on the work of Rogers and Tibben-Lembke (1999) and Stock (1998), Figure 2 suggests an extension to Carter and Ellram's (1998) model. The difference between the suggested model and that proposed by Carter and Ellram is that the remanufacturing aspect of reverse logistics has been isolated from the reuse, recycling, and resource reduction options of the recovery process. It is of note that the remanufacturing option of reverse logistics has been the focus of recent research in this field (Guide, 1996;

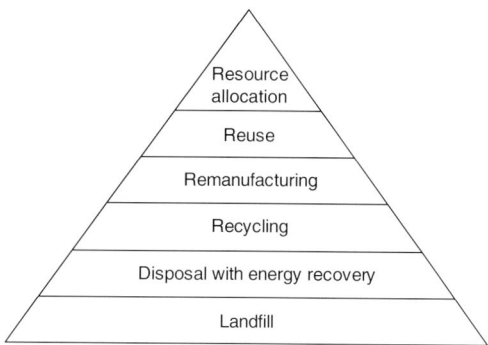

Figure 2. A conceptual framework for reverse logistics hierarchy. (Adapted from Carter and Ellram, 1998.)

Guide and Srivastava, 1998; Jayaraman et al., 1999). The hierarchy in the model proposes that the resource reduction option is at the top and disposal in landfill at the bottom. Other recovery options are located in between these two options.

The hierarchy is based on the concept of value adding. This states that the overriding objective of any reverse logistics system is to maximize value from the recovery process. Resource reduction, which refers to the "minimisation of materials used in products and minimisation of waste and energy achieved through the design of more environmentally efficient products" (Carter and Ellram, 1998), should be the main objective of any supply chain. Development and utilization of resource reduction strategies can help firms minimize flows of materials both in the forward and reverse directions of supply chains. This is consistent with the concept of the lean supply chain (Christopher, 1998; Hines et al., 2000). The next most favorable option is reuse, followed by remanufacturing and recycling. Remanufacturing focuses on higher value-added recovery compared with recycling, which concentrates just on materials recovery. Disposal with or without energy recovery are the last options. The recovery options are not mutually exclusive, and must be considered within the context of the total supply chain cost.

5. Modeling reverse logistics systems

While forward logistics systems in transportation and distribution management have been well researched, reverse logistics networks have received little attention. Through a review of eight recent case studies, this section discusses reverse logistics network design. Three different types of return flow are considered, namely reuse, recycling, and remanufacturing (Figure 2). The case studies are summarized in Tables 2 and 3. A reverse logistics network can occur in one of two contexts: either as a closed-loop or open-loop system. In a closed logistics system, sources and sinks coincide so that flows cycle in the system. Companies adopting this system collect their used products and either refurbish and resell, or remanufacture or recycle them. In an open-loop system, on the other hand, flows enter at one point of the logistics system and leave at another. Companies using this system might assume responsibility for collecting and finding markets for their products, but do not use the recovered materials themselves (Kopicki et al., 1993).

5.1. Network models for reuse

Only one of the eight studies addressed the network design for reuse (Kroon and Vrijens, 1994). This case study examined a closed-loop deposit-based logistics network for reusable transportation packages in the Netherlands. Within this system, the reusable containers move from the distribution depot to the sender,

Table 2
Summary of case studies on reverse logistics networks

Reverse network type	Study	Product	Objective function	Problem formulation	Solution method
Reuse	Kroon and Vrigens (1994)	Reusable containers	Minimum cost for the logistic system	MILP	Heuristics
Recycle	Barros et al. (1998)	Sand	Minimum cost for the logistic system	MILP	Heuristics
	Louwers et al. (1999)	Carpet	Minimum cost for the logistic system	MILP	Fortran 90
	Realff et al. (1999)	Carpet	Maximum achievable income	MILP	AIMMS
	Spengler et al. (1997)	Demolition waste	Maximum achievable income	MILP	LINDO
	Spengler et al. (1997)	Steel	Minimum cost for the logistic system	MILP	
Remanufacturing	Jayaraman et al. (1999)	Cell phone	Minimum cost for the logistic system	0-1 MILP	GAMS
	Kikkle et al. (1999)	Photocopier	Minimum cost for the logistic system	MILP	LINDO

Table 3
Reverse logistics network types

Reverse logistics type	Study	Reverse logistics network	
		Open loop	Closed loop
Reuse	Kroon and Vrigens (1994)		✓
Recycle	Barros et al. (1998)	✓	
	Louwers et al. (1999)	✓	
	Realff et al. (1999)	✓	
	Spengler et al. (1997)	✓	
	Spengler et al. (1997)	✓	
Remanufacturing	Jayaraman et al. (1999)		✓
	Kikkle et al. (1999)		✓

the sender to the receiver, the receiver back to the collection depot, and the collection depot to the distribution depot. There are five groups participating in the system: a central agency owning a pool of reusable plastic containers; senders and recipients of full containers; a logistics service provider, responsible for storing, delivering, and collecting the empty containers; and carriers that transport full containers from senders to recipients. The study focused on the role of the logistics service provider, and its aims were to determine the number of containers required to run the distribution system, where to locate depots for empty containers, and an appropriate fee per shipment. The problem was formulated as a mixed-integer linear programming (MILP) model, which is quite similar to the classical uncapacited plant location problem. The model was solved using a heuristic procedure. The objective function of the problem included transport costs and the fixed cost of having a container depot in a distribution center. The model was used to evaluate several alternative scenarios.

5.2. Network models for remanufacturing

There is evidence to suggest that remanufacturing is not only environmentally sound but also economically profitable (Nasr et al., 1998), since this activity focuses on value-added recovery rather than just materials recovery. We have identified two studies which deal with the analysis of logistics networks for remanufacturing (Krikke et al., 1999; Jayaraman et al., 1999). Krikke et al. (1999) considered the design of a multi-echelon logistics network for a particular photocopier model in Oce, the Netherlands. The reverse logistics system consisted of three main recovery processes: dismantling, in which products are disassembled to a certain level; preparation, in which critical parts are inspected, and, if required, replaced; and reassembly, where new and repaired components are assembled into new products. While the location of dismantling processes was fixed, the objective of the study was to identify the optimal location of the preparation and reassembly facilities. A choice between two predetermined locations (Venlo, the Netherlands and Prague, Czech Republic) was to be made, subject to several managerial constraints. The problem was modeled as a MILP, and solved using the LINDO software package. The results indicated that there were no substantial differences in economic costs among three feasible scenarios. The motivation to install recovery facilities in Prague from a strategic point of view was therefore well justified by the findings.

Jayaraman et al. (1999) developed a closed-loop logistics system for a recoverable product environment. The flow of materials and products in this environment occurs both from the remanufacturer to the customer (forward flow) and from the customer to the remanufacturer (reverse flow). The aim of the study was to determine the optimal number of remanufacturing/distribution facilities that would minimize the production, transportation, and storage costs. Jayaraman et al. present a MILP model similar to a capacited plant location model called REVLOG. The model was solved optimally using the Generalised Algebraic Modelling System (GAMS) software, and presented alternative scenarios.

5.3. Network models for recycling

Increasingly restrictive environmental regulations in Europe and the potential for economic gain has encouraged the European carpet industry to establish a joint reverse logistics network for recycling carpet waste. Louwers et al. (1999) described a case of carpet recycling involving activities such as collection and sorting of waste carpet from various sources (such as households, office buildings, and carpet retailers), shredding, palletizing, and transportation to chemical companies for further processing. The preprocessing activities were to be carried out in regional recovery facilities. The aim of the study was to identify appropriate locations and capacities for the regional facilities. The problem was formulated as a continuous location model. The results suggested that it was economically feasible to recycle carpet waste. Realff et al. (1999) also examined a case study of carpet recycling process in the USA. A key limiting factor to recycling carpet is the lack of an efficient system to collect and process this material. The problem of collecting, transporting, and processing waste carpet was developed as a MILP model and applied to the US carpet industry data. The purpose of the model was to aid in decision-making at the strategic level of recycling infrastructure design and not, as the authors cautioned, to coordinate the actually operation of recycling system, as the logistics component was not detailed enough.

In the mid-1990s, 70% of construction waste in the Netherlands was already being recycled, but the government aimed to increase this to 90%. Approximately 1 million tonnes of sand was being placed in landfills annually. Recycling of sand therefore represented a method for meeting the country's environmental legislation in a way that made economic sense. Waste sand can be grouped into three categories, namely clean sand, which may be reused without further processing; half-clean sand, which can be reused for selected applications; and polluted sand, which must be cleaned before reuse. Barros et al. (1998) reported on the design of a reverse logistics network for recycling sand. The problem was modeled as a multi-level capacitated MILP problem, and was solved using heuristics procedures. Spengler et al. (1997) described two case studies: one regarding demolition waste recycling, the other steel material recycling. These studies were examined in the context of a recent tightening of waste disposal regulation in Germany. Each year, Germany produces 23 million tonnes of demolition waste. At the time of the study, the recycling rate of demolition waste was low, at only 16%. The aim of the German government was to increase this rate up to 60% for building rubble and 40% for construction waste. Spengler et al. suggested that recycling of demolition waste is not always cost-effective, and that only high-quality recycled material can compete with traditional materials. For the first case, they attempted to develop an integrated dismantling and recycling planning system that would provide a maximum net profit. Unlike other studies discussed in this section, this particular case study did not deal with the location problem but instead attempted to delineate how best (in terms of maximizing the net profit) to process demolition waste. For the second case study examining the steel industry, Spengler et al. (1997) developed an MILP model as a modified version of a multi-level plant location model.

Within each type of reverse logistics system, the case studies were compared in terms of product material, problem formulation, solution method, objective function (Table 2), and type of network (Table 3). In all the cases the design of reverse logistics systems were formulated as MILP location–allocation models, which closely resemble multi-stage plant/warehouse location models. Although uncertainty (in the timing and quantity of returns) is a critical characteristic in a recoverable manufacturing environment, this issue has not been included explicitly in the modeling of reverse logistics systems. Rather, the issue of uncertainty was dealt with through the use of parametric analysis (e.g., Jayaraman et al., 1999). Further research in modeling needs to be undertaken to address this issue. Over all, the findings of the case studies suggest that environmental concern, legislative constraints affecting operation of industries, and economic and strategic benefits are the driving forces behind research and development of reverse logistics systems.

6. An effective reverse logistics system

One of the most comprehensive studies in the field of reverse logistics was conducted by Kopicki et al. in 1993. In this study, it was suggested that companies typically evolve through three phases during the implementation of an environmentally conscious program: reactive, proactive, and value-seeking. The common practices of companies belonging to these phases are summarized in Table 4. Newly introduced environmental standards usually force reactive organizations to meet environmental standards. Although they examine environmental issues from time to time, they do not actively pursue competitive advantage through environmental practices. Unlike reactive companies, proactive companies often implement reverse logistics programs such as reuse and recycling, and attempt to develop a competitive advantage by designing effective environmental programs. They tend to produce products that satisfy customers' environmental concerns. Value-seeking companies, by contrast, integrate environmental programs into their business strategy. Most companies in this phase have advanced environmental programs with extremely efficient reverse logistics systems.

Recently, several conceptual models have been developed that suggest ways to design and implement reverse logistics systems. The model developed by Carter and Ellram (1998) identified two sets of factors: internal and external. Jointly, these factors determine whether a company is reactive, proactive, or value-seeking in implementing a reverse logistics system. The two external factors of government regulations and customer demands, and the internal factor of policy innovation, were considered by Carter and Ellram to be the main drivers of reverse logistics systems. As government regulatory and customer demands for "green products" increase, a company is more likely to become involved in advanced environmental programs and institute an efficient and effective reverse logistics system. The principal internal driver is the existence of a policy innovator (or "policy entrepreneur," to use the term coined by Carter and Ellram) within the company who will take personal responsibility for reverse logistics activities. Other factors which may facilitate the implementation of reverse logistics systems include the support of top management, stakeholder commitment, incentive systems, quality of inputs, and vertical integration.

Stock (1998) suggested that factors related to management and control, measurement, and finance determine the success of a reverse logistics program. In this model, the commitment of the top management is considered to be the key driver in reverse logistics activities. As allocation of resources toward environmental and educational programs increases, it is more likely that a company will institute a system of environmental management, which would determine the direction to reverse logistics and environmental activities. It is critical that companies adopt life cycle costing approaches to reverse logistics activities and monitor the performance.

Table 4
Goals and practices of reactive, proactive, and value-seeking companies

	Primary goals of the environmental program	Primary activities used to support the environmental program
Reactive firms	Comply with existing law Fulfil individual environmental commitments Achieve a cost saving	Recycle corrugated cardboard, office paper, and beverage containers Procure products with recycled content Label products that are recyclable, contain recycled material, or have environmental benefits
Proactive firms	Attempt to prevent new environmental laws by voluntarily starting environmental programs Develop competitive advantage through more efficient compliance Sell products that satisfy customers' environmental concerns	Prepare a corporate environmental policy statement, define goals of environment program, and conduct environmental audit Purchase more recycled materials and design products to be environmentally friendly Recycle (and/or reuse) pallets, plastics, and defective products and process or use wastes when possible Assume responsibility for product reuse and recycling through industry alliances and reverse logistics systems
Value-seeking firms	Put environmental activities into a business strategy Operate the firm to reduce its impact on the environmental	Use environmental life cycle analysis to evaluate products and packaging, using the results to help design products to be reused, recycled, and disassembled Create a competitive advantage in reverse logistics programs, including the use of third parties if advantageous Critically review existing processes and products/services asking suppliers to commit to waste reduction goals Develop internal company incentives and enforcement procedures

Source: Kopicki et al. (1993).

Dowlatshahi (2000) proposed a conceptual framework to study the implementation of reverse logistics using 11 factors. These factors can be broadly categorized as strategic and operational issues. Strategic factors include legislative concerns, environmental concerns, customer service, quality, and strategic costs. Some of these factors are the same as those identified by Carter and Ellram (1998). A company must first consider and address these strategic issues and then focus on operational factors at the tactical level of reverse logistics. Operational factors include cost–benefit analysis, transportation, warehousing, supply management, remanufacturing/recycling, and packaging.

We have discussed three conceptual models of reverse logistics. Although described from different perspectives, many factors are common to all three models. Using these models and other literature we identified 10 factors that provide a holistic view of reverse logistics (Table 5).

Based on these factors, a causal model has been developed that shows the cause–effect–cause relationships between these factors (Figure 3). A number of important issues can be seen in the model. Two factors that drive reverse logistics activities are government regulations and customer demand. Carter and Ellram identified these factors as the principal external drivers of reverse logistics. As government regulatory authority and customer demand for environmentally friendly products and services increase, an organization is more likely to develop a reverse logistics system. Since the reactive firms do not actively pursue competitive advantage through environmental practices and reverse logistics programs, they simply comply with exiting laws in order to save costs. Proactive and value-seeking firms, on the other hand, attempt to prevent new environmental laws by voluntarily starting environmental programs and incorporating environmental policies into their business strategies (Kopicki et al., 1993).

Table 5
Critical success factors required for reverse logistics to succeed

Factor	Reference
Government regulations	Carter and Ellram (1998), Dowlatshahi (2000)
Customers	Carter and Ellram (1998), Dowlatshahi (2000)
Top management support	Carter and Ellram (1998), Stock (1998)
Stakeholder commitment	Carter and Ellram (1998)
Policy innovators	Carter and Ellram (1998)
Environmental management system and policy	Dowlatshahi (2000), Stock (1998)
Quality and quantity of inputs	Carter and Ellram (1998), Dowlatshahi (2000), Stock (1998)
Strategic alliances and partnerships	Stock (1998)
Information and communication technology	Daugherty et al. (2002)
Strategic costs	Dowlatshahi (2002), Stock (1998)

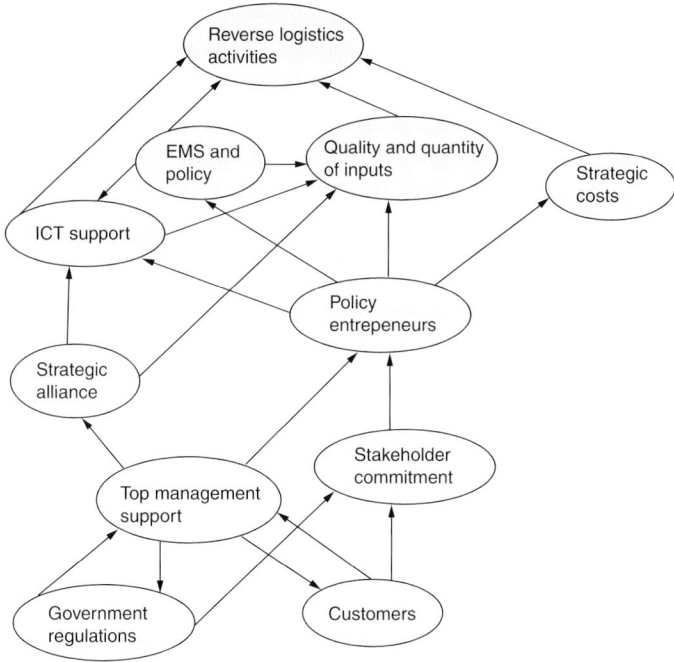

Figure 3. A causal model of reverse logistics.

Governmental regulations and customer demand force top management and stakeholders to establish an internal environmental committee ("policy entrepreneur" – Carter and Ellram (1998)) and allocate resources to environmental programs. In turn, the policy entrepreneur will institute environmental management systems and reverse logistics processes, secure ICT support, ensure the quality and quantity of inputs, and develop measurement systems, such as strategic costing, to monitor the performance of reverse logistics systems. In a reactive firm, the policy entrepreneur will act as a primary internal driver of reverse logistics and top management support may constrain the implementation of a reverse logistics system. On the other hand, top management support and policy entrepreneur are key drivers in proactive and value-seeking firms.

Both internal and external factors are important for successful implementation of reverse logistics activities. External factors may force companies to meet environmental standards. However, without the internal commitment and support, Carter and Ellram (1998, p.99) assert that "the company may very well respond to external pressures by making only minor, cosmetic changes to its (reverse logistics/environmental) systems rather than by implementing programs that are truly environmentally friendly".

7. Conclusion

There are many ways to minimize the environmental costs of business activities, but the reduction of resources and minimization of waste products through reverse logistics activities such as reuse, remanufacturing, and recycling prevents many environmental externalities. In spite of its strategic importance, very little research has been done to develop a holistic view of this field. Most research to date has examined only relatively narrow aspects of reserve logistics such as recycling. Moreover, much of the research is exploratory, which suggests that there is a need for large-scale empirical studies based on conceptual models. In this chapter we have discussed what motivates a firm to initiate reverse logistics activities. We have also discussed different recovery processes and highlighted the differences between traditional manufacturing systems and manufacturing systems using recovery processes. Finally, we have described a causal model for successful implementation of reverse logistics systems.

References

Ayres, R., G. Ferrer and T. van Leynseele (1997) "Eco-efficiency, asset recovery and remanufacturing," *European Management Journal*, 15:557–574.
Barros, A.I., R. Dekker and V. Scholten (1998) "A two-level network for recycling sand: a case study," *European Journal of Operational Research*, 110:199–214.
Blumberg, D.F. (1999) "Strategic examination of reverse logistics and repair service requirements, needs, market size, and opportunities," *Journal of Business Logistics*, 20:141–159.
Bohnhoff, A. (1996) "Recycling of textile floor coverings," in: *Proceedings of Globec'96/Recycle'96*. Davos.
Boks, C., J. Nilsson, K. Masui, K. Suzuki, C. Rose and B.H. Lee (1998) "An international comparison of product end-of-life scenarios and legislation for consumer electronics," in: *Proceedings of the IEEE International Symposium on Electronics and the Environment.* Oak Brook.
Carter, C.R. and L.M. Ellram (1998) "Reverse logistics: a review of the literature and framework for future investigation," *Journal of Business Logistics*, 19:85–102.
Christopher, M. (1998) *Logistics and supply chain management: strategies for reducing cost and improving services*. Englewood Cliffs: Prentice-Hall.
Daugherty, P.J., M.B. Myers and R.G. Richey (2002) "Information support for reverse logistics: the influence of relationship commitment," *Journal of Business Logistics*, 23:85–106.
Dowlatshahi, S. (2000) "Developing a theory of reverse logistics," *Interfaces*, 30:143–155.
Ferrer, G. (1997) "The economics of personal computer remanufacturing," *Resources, Conservation and Recycling*, 21:79–108.
Guide, Jr, V.D.R. (1996) "Scheduling using drum-buffer-rope in a remanufacturing environment," *International Journal of Production Research*, 34:1082–1091.
Guide, Jr, V.D.R. (2000) "Production planning and control for remanufacturing: industry practice and research needs," *Journal of Operations Management*, 18:467–483.
Guide, Jr, V.D.R. and R. Srivastava (1997) "Inventory buffers in recoverable manufacturing," *Journal of Operations Management*, 16:551–568.
Guide, Jr, V.D.R., V. Jayaraman, R. Srivastava and W.C. Benton (2000) "Supply chain management for recoverable manufacturing systems," *Interfaces*, 30:125–142.
Hines, P., R. Laming, D. Jones, P. Cousins and N. Rich (2000) *Value stream management – strategy and excellence in the supply chain*. London: Prentice-Hall.

Jayaraman, V., V.D.R. Guide, R. Srivastava (1999) "A closed-loop logistics model for remanufacturing," *Journal of the Operational Research Society*, 50:497–508.

Kopicki, R.J., M.J. Berg, L. Legg, V. Dasappa and C. Maggioni (1993) *Reuse and recycling: reverse logistics opportunities*. Oak Brook: Council of Logistics Management.

Krikke, H.R., A. von Harten and P.C. Schuur (1999). "Business case Oce: reverse logistics network-design for copiers," *OR Spektrum*, 21:381–409.

Kroon, L. and G. Vrijens (1994) "Returnable containers: an example of reverse logistics," *International Journal of Physical Distribution and Logistics Management*, 25:56–68.

Louwers, D., B.J. Kip, E. Peters, F. Souren and S.D.P. Flapper (1999) "A facility location–allocation model for reusing carpet materials," *Computers and Industrial Engineering*, 36:855–869.

Lund, R. (1998) "Remanufacturing: an American resource," in: *Proceedings of the Fifth International Congress on Environmentally Conscious Design and Manufacturing*. Rochester: Rochester Institute of Technology.

Maslennikova, I. and D. Foley (2000) "Xerox's approach to sustainability," *Interfaces*, 30:226- 233.

Minahan, T. (1998) "Manufacturing takes aim at the end of the supply chain," *Purchasing*, 124:111–112.

Nasr, N., C. Hughson, E. Varel and R. Bauer (1998) *State-of-the-art assessment of remanufacturing technology – draft document*. Rochester: Rochester Institute of Technology.

Realff, M.J., J.C. Ammons and D. Newton (1999) "Carpet recycling: determining the reverse production system design," *Polymer–Plastics Technology and Engineering*, 38:547–567.

Rembert, T.C. (1997) "Package deal: the European war on waste," *Environmental Magazine*, 8:38.

Rogers, D.S. and R.S. Tibben-Lembke, (1999) *Going backwards: reverse logistics trends and practices*. Pittsburg: Reverse Logistics Executive Council.

Spengler, T., H. Puchert, T. Penkuhn and O. Rentz (1997) "Environmental integrated production and recycling management," *European Journal of Operational Research*, 97:308–326.

Stock, J.R. (1998) *Development and implementation of reverse logistics program*. Oak Brook: Council of Logistics Management.

Thierry, M., M. Saloman, J. van Nuen and L.N.V. van Wassenhove (1995) "Strategic issues in product recovery management," *California Management Review*, 37:114–135.

Veerakamolmal, P. and S.M. Gupta (2000) "Optimising the supply chain in reverse logistics," in: *Environmentally Conscious Manufacturing Conference*. Paper. Boston.

Chapter 39

TRANSPORTATION OF HAZARDOUS GOODS AND MATERIALS

WILLIAM G. WATERS II
The University of British Columbia, Vancouver

1. Introduction

It is inevitable that some materials or products have risks associated with their transport; classic examples would be explosives, gasoline, toxic materials, radioactive wastes, and many others. These commodities are identified as "dangerous goods," "dangerous materials," "hazardous materials" (or "hazmats"), or similar in various countries. We adopt the popular US abbreviation of "hazmats" for this chapter.

Hazmats need to be transported, but doing so imposes risks on drivers, handlers or on the public at large. Harm can arise through incidental leaks or spillage through routine handling and transport, or through more severe spillages in crashes. In some cases the consequences could be catastrophic.

In nearly every country, various regulations have emerged to govern the transport of hazmats in an attempt to avoid impacts on operators and, especially, the general public and/or environment. Chapter 6 provides an overview of the rationales for public intervention in transportation markets that involve risks. This chapter complements Chapter 6 by focusing more specifically on the tools and techniques used in analyzing hazmat transportation risks.

2. Hazardous materials and transportation

There are many different materials or substances that could be labeled "hazardous," for different reasons. Various countries have devised classification schemes. The UN places hazmats in nine categories (with some subcategories, and some with packaging performance requirements):

- class 1 – explosives and pyrotechnics;
- class 2 – compressed and liquified gases;
- class 3 – flammable liquids;
- class 4 – flammable solids;

- class 5 – oxidizers and peroxides;
- class 6 – toxic and infectious materials;
- class 7 – Radioactive materials;
- class 8 – corrosive materials;
- class 9 – miscellaneous dangerous substances and articles.

There can be a variety of hazmats with differences in characteristics within these categories. Regulations about the transport of hazmats may differ across the classifications, and in some cases will differ for subcategories or even specific hazmats. Regulations and related issues are available from government departments (e.g. the Research and Special Programs Administration for the USA (http://hazmat.dot.gov/hazhome.htm)).

The dangers associated with hazmats can and will differ significantly. The first complication is that the degree of harm is not solely a function of the physical properties of the hazmat but also of the amount that is released and, especially, the circumstances associated with a spill.

> A hazardous material released in a populated versus unpopulated area, or discharged onto dry land versus into a lake or stream, generates large random variations in the risk costs of an individual release that cannot be predicted based solely on the characteristics of the commodity. The risk costs attendant to any one release may be either much higher or much lower than the average cost of all releases for a given commodity over time.
>
> Dennis (1996)

2.1. Regulatory obligations and incident reporting

Virtually all countries have hazmat regulations in place, but details differ. Generally they require that a shipper be aware of hazards associated with products shipped, and inform carriers and any other relevant agencies of the hazmat and why it is labeled as such. Vehicles may be required to have an external label or placard to identify the hazmat. The USA (and many other countries) requires that the shipper supply a 24 h phone number to be contacted in emergency, and that location must be able to provide details about the hazards associated with the particular shipment along with instructions on how to deal with spills or other emergencies. In some cases, large shippers may have emergency response teams available. In most cases, hazmat emergencies must be dealt with by local community resources such as by fire departments.

There are issues of financial and legal liability that accompany whatever regulatory regime. Chapter 6 reviews the prospect of relying primarily on legal liability concepts to settle hazmat controversies. For various reasons, including market failures, there is public demand for more specific regulations of hazmat transportation rather than sole reliance on legal liability. The extent and type of regulatory frameworks differ among countries and government jurisdictions, and also differ among hazmats.

Generally there are requirements for companies to report the volumes of hazmat movements and any spills or incidents. Although statistics have been compiled for many years, there are always complaints about gaps or weaknesses in the data. Must all spills be reported, or only those above some threshold amount? Because most spills are small, the number of recorded incidents can differ considerably depending on the criteria. Spills in terminals when loading or unloading might not be considered in-transit and thus not included in transport statistics. Intrastate transportation may be under different jurisdiction and regulations than interstate or international traffic. Even where reporting requirements are clear, there are issues of accuracy and enforcement of the reporting regulations. Significant improvements to databases have been made over the years, but inadequacy of data is an ongoing complaint. There is an insatiable appetite for data to enable more thorough evaluation of hazmat transportation risks.

> A major issue that will be addressed in hazardous materials transportation over the next 10 years is the need for more comprehensive and accurate data to support the development of regulations and to conduct risk assessments. Better data are critical to the implementation of effective and equitable regulations.
>
> Allen (2000)

Even if statistics are accurately compiled, there are unavoidable challenges in developing predictions about low-probability high-consequence events. Incident statistics for any year (or even a series of years) may be distorted by the presence or absence of infrequent high-consequence crashes and spills. Combining several years' data may conceal changes in the underlying probabilities.

2.2. Rationales for regulation

Even if accurate data on hazmat incidents are available, there are issues of how much government intervention is warranted. Chapter 6 provides an overview of the economic rationale for government intervention concerning hazmat transportation. The most important rationale for hazmat regulations and policies is correcting for structural failures in a market economy, such as problems of externalities or common property resources. These are situations where the actions of buyers and sellers may impose costs or benefits on others but these are not taken into account in market decisions. In the absence of market failures, laws of property and liability may be sufficient to foster an efficient economic system, providing the transaction costs to access the legal system are not excessive. However, in the presence of externalities or systematic market failure, private contract and its enforcement are insufficient to achieve an efficient outcome. Here there is a case for public intervention such as hazmat regulation to improve the economic performance of a market economy.

The foregoing is the pure economic rationale for government regulation of hazmats. But government policies are driven by more than economic efficiency considerations. Some regulations and policy actions might be explained as paternalism, i.e. public regulation and controls to protect people from their own poor judgment. There is always debate over the appropriate role of government on paternalistic grounds, but there is no doubt that paternalism lies behind some safety regulations. Then there are the actions of individuals and groups who lobby governments to further their particular aims and not necessarily that of society at large.

In sum, formulating public policy is a mix of altruism, rational analysis, and the pushing and pulling of special interests. This is inevitable. But over the longer term, we engage in debate and conduct analysis with the intention of improving economic and social well-being. This includes learning more about the real risks associated with hazmat consumption and transport, relative to the costs and benefits of reducing or alleviating these risks. This is the motivation behind the analysis of hazmat transportation. However, establishing a broad rationale for public regulation of hazmats in a market economy is one thing; identifying and implementing the appropriate policy action is quite another. We turn to the types of studies and analysis to bring this about.

3. Hazmat studies

There are two broad approaches to the analysis of hazmat movements: (1) aggregate or macro studies, and (2) micro studies that evaluate specific hazmat shipments or proposed regulatory changes (i.e. decision analysis). Aggregate studies focus on aggregate statistics of hazmat movements to calculate the frequency of incidents, and to measure the total exposure of the population to hazmat movements of different types. This could refer to the aggregate of all hazmat movements (e.g. Dennis' analysis of total rail hazmat movements and costs, 1996) or the aggregate of a particular type of hazmat. In contrast, the micro approach is for decision-making, to assess the risks associated with a specific hazmat movement and/or the evaluation of regulations.

3.1. Aggregate studies of hazmat incidents and their costs

These studies can encompass all hazmats or the aggregate of a particular category. Their broad purpose is to measure the risk exposure of the population and,

Table 1
Hazardous materials commodity group, rail transportation (sample commodities listed)

Safety hazard	Environmental hazard		
	High	Medium	Low
Poison inhalation hazard	←	Anhydrous ammonia Chlorine Ethylene oxide	→
Flammable/combustible	Phosphorus Styrene Toluene	Acetaldehyde Fuel oil Hexane	Butadiene Liquefied petroleum gas Methanol
All other	Chloroform Metam sodium Perchloroethylene	Acrylic Acid Caustic soda Sulfuric acid	Acetic acid Asphalt Molten sulfur

Source: Dennis (1996).

Table 2
Composition of risk costs, average 1982–1992

Risk cost	Contribution (%)
Legal settlement expenses	55.9
Environmental costs (e.g. clean-up)	32.7
Property loss	3.2
W&S, signals, wrecking	1.3
Equipment damage	0.3
Other	6.6

Source: Dennis (1996).

possibly, the cost consequences associated with the hazmat incidents. Such studies provide part of the background for micro studies to modify hazmat regulations and operations.

A first illustration is Dennis' (1996) estimate of aggregate hazmat movements by rail in the USA. He compiled rail statistics on hazmat traffic, grouping them according to their environmental and safety hazards, shown in Table 1. He compiled data from railroads on expenditures incurred in connection with hazmat spills. He combined various operating statistics to obtain measures of per unit exposure, and estimated the total private and public financial costs associated with the various hazmat categories, both in total and on a per unit basis. The components of total costs are shown in Table 2, the estimated average cost per incident in Table 3, and the risk cost per unit of exposure (per loaded car-mile) in Table 4. These results show the substantial variation in risk costs across the hazmat categories, especially when expressed on a per unit of exposure basis as shown in Table 4. For the most dangerous of the hazmats, the risk costs are substantial, averaging 13% of the costs of transporting the hazmat. The study was limited to "major" hazmat spills. They show how infrequent major events are, but how costly they are to deal with. The per unit table (Table 4) shows the substantial variation in his measure of risk costs per rail car shipment. Table 2 indicates that the largest cost component was legal settlement expenses; insofar as there are uncompensated damages, these figures are likely to be an underestimate of the total costs.

These figures provide one perspective on the frequency and costs associated with rail hazmat spills. The major expenses associated with a spill show how serious these incidents can be, and the per unit risk costs suggest that different degrees of regulatory control may be appropriate for different hazmats. Of course, these figures by themselves do not indicate whether the current

Table 3
Average risk cost of major releases (1994, US $)

Safety hazard	Environmental hazard		
	High	Medium	Low
Poison inhalation hazard	←	1 240 000 No. = 8	→
Flammable/combustible	3 430 000 No. = 16	1 440 000 No. = 39	677.000 No. = 25
All others	13 200 000 No. = 14	644 000 No. = 29	519 000 No. = 14

Source: Dennis (1996).

Table 4
Risk cost per unit of exposure (US cents per loaded car-mile)

Safety hazard	Environmental hazard		
	High	Medium	Low
Poison inhalation hazard	←	1.03	→
Flammable/combustible	10.88	2.61	1.33
All other	28.25	0.69	0.17

Source: Dennis (1996).

Table 5
Estimated number of class 3 hazmat incidents for US trucking, in 1996

Type of incident	No. of occurrences
Accidents en route	
With spill	490
No spill	953
Non-accident incidents, *en route* and at terminal	
Leak *en route*	362
Leak loading/unloading	1961

Source: Abkowitz et al. (2001).

regulations and risk exposure are appropriate or not; this would require extensive additional micro studies.

A second illustration of aggregate cost analysis of hazmats is for trucking of a specific hazmat category (Abkowitz et al., 2001). Abkowitz et al. estimated the aggregate economic costs of class 3 hazmats (flammable liquids) transported by truck in 1996. Their study is also useful for distinguishing spills or leaks that occur in handling, loading, or unloading, in contrast to spills during the actual transport. The latter arise primarily from crashes. They relied on the HMIS (the US Hazardous Materials Information System) database, but supplemented it with data from a few states (extrapolated to all) to adjust for various limitations in the data such as non-reported incidents (some intrastate travel) and information on loading/unloading spills. Table 5 summarizes their estimated number of incidents in 1996; this is presented as an illustration, and not necessarily a predictive guide for other hazmat categories.

Not surprisingly, the majority of spills were associated with loading and unloading, but these summary statistics do not indicate the size of spills nor the cost consequences. These can vary considerably with individual circumstances. They estimate the average costs associated with these incidents.

Table 6 reports their estimated (or, in some cases, assumed) unit costs. Note that there could be debates about specific values chosen, with corresponding implications for the total cost estimates. Table 7 shows their estimated total costs associated with class 3 hazmat incidents for trucks in 1996. The "accident" column includes both spill and non-spill crashes; the "non-accident incidents" category includes both loading/unloading spills as well as leakages *en route* not caused by a crash. Not surprisingly, the economic costs of crash incidents are much higher than spills from handling. Injuries and fatalities are the highest economic cost (US $191 million and $134 million, respectively); carrier damage and estimated delay costs are next (at over US $50 million each). Environmental damage is very small. These figures could change dramatically depending on

Table 6
Unit cost (US $) components for economic analysis of class 3 accidents

Impact	Spill in accident	No-spill accident
Clean up (a)	34 000	
Product loss (a)	3 800	
Carrier damage (a)	36 000	36 000
Property damage (a)	5 900	5 900
Environmental damage (a)	1 800	
Injury (b)	200 000	200 000
Death (b)	2 million	2 million
Evacuation (b)	1 000	
Incident delay (c)	15	15

Source: Abkowitz et al. (2001).
Notes:
(a) Different, typically smaller, figures for non-accident spills, *en route* or loading/unloading.
(b) Cost per person.
(c) Cost per person-hour.

Table 7
Estimated economic effects (US $) of class 3 hazmat incidents in 1996

Impact	Non-accident incidents	Accidents
Clean-up	1 692 460	16 660 000
Product loss	203 940	1 862 000
Carrier damage	301 990	51 948 000
Property damage	365 950	8 513 000
Environmental damage	7 240	882 000
Injury	96 000	190 600 000
Death	6 000 000	134 000 000
Evacuation	5 75 000	1 950 000
Incident delay	13 264 393	52 874 357
Total	22 506 928	459 290 057

Source: Abkowitz et al. (2001).

specific incidents, e.g. the costs of evacuation, which is a rarity. They also note that their estimate of total economic costs of "accidents" of US $459 million is an order of magnitude higher than would be estimated using the HMIS database without augmenting it. That is, the major database relied upon for these analyses was seriously incomplete, and additional data compilation and analysis was necessary to develop a more reliable measure of total economic costs. This serves as a reminder that one of the major ongoing directions for refining and improving analysis of hazmat transportation is the improvement of reporting and databases (noted by Allen, 2000, and cited above).

Note that an aggregate calculation of the costs associated with one or more hazmats includes a great deal of averaging. In some cases it is an assumed constant per unit figure (such as US $200 000 per injury). Common in aggregate studies, all spills are treated as an average, i.e. there is no recognition of the distribution of different size spills that might entail costs not strictly proportional to the size of the spill.

The estimate of the economic costs associated with hazmat incidents is useful to illustrate how serious the problem is, but by itself it does not provide a justification or guide to policy actions to reduce these costs. This requires a formal assessment of the risks which underlie the hazmat handling and transportation, and analysis of the costs of responding to or modifying these risks, i.e. quantitative risk assessment (QRA).

3.2. QRA of hazmat shipments and regulations

QRA refers to the framework employed to evaluate the risks associated with various human activities that have a probability of causing harm to members of society and/or the environment, particularly those with low probability but potentially highly harmful outcomes. It is a process of analysis rather than a specific analytical technique; various techniques can be employed in conducting QRA. QRA can be applied to the analysis of any risky event (e.g. the probability of an asteroid hitting the earth), but the interest here is limited to the analysis of risks associated with hazmat transportation. (A concise and useful overview of QRA for hazmat transportation is Saccomanno and Cassidy (1994); more comprehensive references are Nicolet-Monnier and Gheorge (1996) and Rhyne (1994).)

Although QRA can be applied to aggregate data, for example to estimate the total risk exposure of the population to a hazmat, QRA studies usually have a micro or decision orientation to them: an analysis of the risks associated with a particular hazmat movement and what can be done to reduce these risks, or analysis of the risks associated with a class of hazmats and an evaluation of possible changes to the regulations affecting these movements. The latter studies may work with aggregated data, but it is the decision orientation that is the key feature of QRA.

The basic steps of QRA begin with identifying what events could take place (e.g. the magnitude spills), the probability of their occurrence, and the consequence or harm associated with the event, including as affected by various environmental conditions. The measure of harm may be in physical terms (deaths or injuries) or expressed in a currency such as dollars. In most applications, the next step is evaluation of alternate measures that can be taken to reduce the risk and/or reduce the damage that would be caused by the incident, comparing the cost of interventions with the reduction in risk.

Two useful graphical or flow-chart techniques are "fault trees" and "event trees." Fault trees are a "graphical presentation of the systematic, logical development of the many causes of an undesirable event" such as a leak of a hazmat. They can be thought of as identifying all the various ways that a hazmat leak could occur, e.g. failure of a tank seam, failure of a valve, rupture of a tank, human error in loading or unloading, etc. Or it could be a line graph linking all the ways in which a crash could lead to a hazmat release, linking sequential failures of equipment in some cases. (A step by step fault tree analysis applied to rail chlorine tanks cars is outlined by Rhyne (1994).)

An event tree is a graphical analysis to identify the possible outcomes of the undesirable event. A liquefied petroleum gas (LPG) tanker crash is illustrated in Figure 1 (from Nicolet-Monnier and Gheorge, 1996). Figure 1 incorporates two stages of analysis: first, it identifies all the possible outcomes including sequential linkages, and, second, the analyst determines the probability of the various outcomes and paths taking place. In Figure 1, the most likely outcome of an LPG tanker crash is a small release of gas or no damage (in practice, an event tree would be more explicit on the nature of the crash and have crashes of various severity or circumstances to be included as well). More serious leaks are of lower probability but lead to more serious consequences. Constructing an event tree imposes a discipline to think through all possible outcomes. In Figure 1, a range of possible outcomes from the trivial to the severe are shown, along with their respective probabilities of occurring. The event tree in Figure 1 does not incorporate the factors that identify the further consequences such as the probability of populations being present at the crash scene.

An integrated schematic of risk analysis is Figure 2 (from Saccomanno and Cassidy, 1994). Risk is presented as two broad components: frequency or likelihood of occurrence, and the consequences or severity of outcome. Figure 2 is an abbreviated schematic but useful for drawing attention to concepts and information required to conduct a full analysis: (1) there are the background circumstances (such as traffic volume) that give rise to the possibility of a crash; (2) the fault tree analysis of how a hazmat release takes place; (3) the event tree that identifies the type and size of release; and (4) the environmental factors that affect the severity of consequences of the spill.

A crucial step in the quantification of the events is establishing the probabilities of various events taking place. Providing data exist, historical records can be used to develop probability estimates. Alternatively, engineering analysis, simulation models or simply judgement may be necessary to develop these estimates. Obviously the reliability of the estimates can differ and hence confidence in the final result.

Given the probability estimates of various outcomes, it is necessary to establish the consequences associated with these spills. In most cases, the nature of the

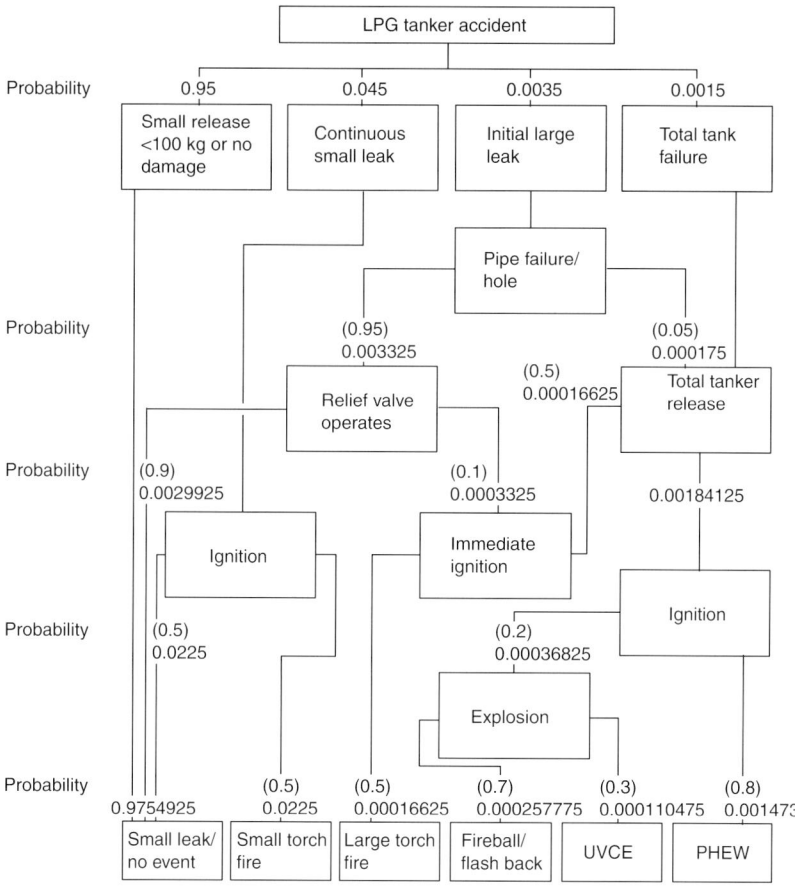

Figure 1. Event tree for a liquid petroleum gas tanker crash. (Source: Nicolet-Monnier and Gheorghe, 1996.)

hazmat is well known, although controversies linger about the severity of various levels of exposure to some substances. If the hazmat is some new substance or its potential harm is not yet known, background research must be done to establish whether or not, and to what degree, exposure to the substance poses harm.

Next, there are a variety of environmental factors that affect the outcome. For example, suppose it is a chlorine gas release. What are the possible wind conditions and directions, where is population located, and what is the density? The last may be affected by the time of day, e.g. are residents away from home at work or at home sleeping? It is necessary to identify the various environmental factors and probabilities of different combinations being present. (An instructive

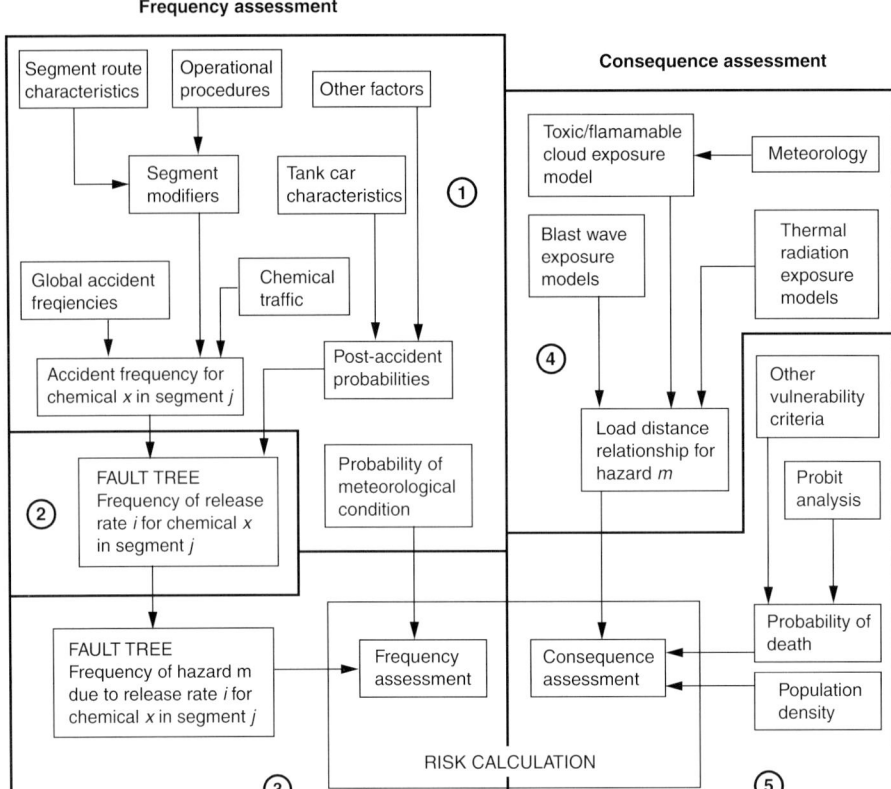

Key:
1 Involvement of hazmat-carrying vehicle in accident
2 Occurrence of breach in containmemt
3 Occurrence of release by type and size
4 Hazard area for different classes of damage
5 Number of people killed and/or injured along route

Figure 2. Risk assessment components. (Source: Saccamanno and Cassidy, 1994.)

fully worked example of QRA applied to a hypothetical chlorine gas shipment involving two modes, one with two routes, is given in Chapter 8 of Rhyne (1994).)

Finally, there are issues in the valuation or measurement of the costs associated with the outcomes. In some cases, this is relatively straightforward such as clean-up costs, and damage to equipment and adjacent property. In other cases, even if the consequences might be predicted with confidence (e.g. the number of fatalities associated with hazmat releases of a specified magnitude and under specified conditions), there are still issues of valuation in monetary terms. The valuation of human life and injury are contentious, but there are a number of conventions that are used in valuing the invaluable. This at least enables relative evaluations to take place in comparing alternate actions that might be taken to prevent or reduce the risks of hazmat transportation; often this is sufficient to assist in decisions.

Risk can be summarized from an individual or social perspective. One can assess the risk exposure of a person at a particular location for example. Isopleths can be constructed; these are contour lines that show the geographic pattern of equal risk probabilities at various locations. Overlaying these with population densities or other land use features provides a visual display risk levels by location. For most hazmat analyses, the focus is on societal risk, the risks borne by all persons potentially affected.

One common way to portray the exposure of a population to hazmat risk is a frequency–number or F–N diagram. It is intended to portray the cumulative probability of risk exposures of various magnitudes. The standard illustration is to plot the frequency (F) of occurrence (a spill) along with the number (N) of injuries or fatalities associated with the spill. There are likely to be several small spills with fewer injuries or deaths, compared with more serious incidents. One can plot this from historical data or as the output of a model estimating probabilities of occurrence. One illustration regarding the transport of chlorine is in Figure 3). Leeming and Saccommano (2001) develop estimates of the risk exposure associated with two modes of transport, road and rail. Figure 3 plots probabilistic estimates of various numbers of fatalities (horizontal axis; note that logarithmic scales are used) plotted against the expected frequency of their occurrence (a higher point indicates a greater probability of occurrence). They compute "upper" "lower," and "best" estimates. In Figure 3, the F–N curve for the "best" estimates are fairly similar for the two modes in this illustration. The upper and lower bound estimates differ noticeably, indicating that the variance of outcomes is higher for road transport, that is, the potential harm from an incident could be greater or smaller for road transport compared with rail. Both show a low frequency of high fatalities and a greater number or probability of incidents with few fatalities. The curvature of the F–N plot indicates the relative frequency of severe and less severe incidents.

The terms "upper," "lower," and "best" do not have standardized meanings. A best estimate usually is the mean or mode of a number of estimates, or determined by particular values for underlying assumptions that are deemed to be the most likely values. The "upper" and "lower" estimates may be one or two standard deviations from the mean estimate, or sometimes an arbitrary choice of a magnitude above or below the mean estimate, such as 25 or 50%. In the illustration by

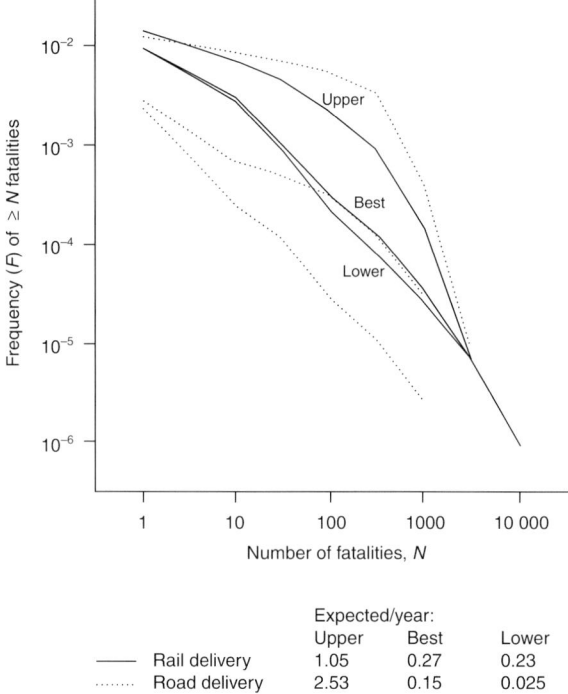

Figure 3. Societal risk estimates for combined site and delivery system: F–N curves. (Source: Leeming and Saccomanno, 2001.)

Leeming and Saccommano, the upper and lower estimates are boundary figures, reflecting the likely upper and lower limits of harm that could come about in the event of an incident. Note the order of magnitude difference between the upper and lower estimates of potential harm from a road transport spill.

The F–N curves are a widely used and useful tool, although as they are two-dimensional they can only plot a relationship between two measures. For example, one must choose either fatalities or injuries for the lower axis, although one could construct a composite index that would be a weighted combination of various outcomes of concerns. One approach is to estimate the total costs associated with a hazmat spill of a certain size, assigning monetary values to life, injuries, and environmental impacts.

Once estimates of risk exposure probabilities are established, combining these with measures of harm provides a measure of the risk exposure to society. Then one can explore different actions that can be taken to reduce the risks or mitigate the consequences of any spill.

3.3. Reducing risks or their consequences

Risk exposure can be reduced by various operational or equipment changes. Vehicles or containers could be designed more strongly to prevent the escape of hazmats in crashes. For example, containers for the transport of nuclear materials are built to be exceptionally strong, to resist leakage even under extreme conditions. Rail tank car designs have been extensively modified and standardized to reduce the danger of damage in derailments. Changes in operations or procedures may reduce risks. Simply modifying loading/unloading procedures might reduce the danger of spills; having clean-up equipment nearby can reduce the damage if a spill should occur. A common procedure in rail operations is to place restrictions on the location of rail cars on a train (cars toward the middle of a train are less likely to derail). Another more complicated restriction is to avoid placing hazmats that would react adjacent to one another on a train.

A variety of models and modeling techniques are used in analysis of hazmat transportation. There are statistical models and computational techniques for estimating probabilistic occurrences based on historical data and/or causal models of factors affecting incident probabilities and environmental factors. Simulation models may be used to explore the implications of alternative assumptions and to generate a range of predictions associated with various probabilistic outcomes and alternative operating procedures.

Various operations-research-optimizing models may be used for devising actions to analyze and mitigate risk exposure. Among the most common analytical models are routing and scheduling models.

Routing models choose a path through a network. Usually the objective is to minimize the transport cost from an origin to a destination by finding the shortest distance (or quickest transit time or lowest transportation cost) through a network. But different routes may entail different probabilities of a crash occurring, and pass through lower- and higher-density population areas. Routing models can choose the path that minimizes population exposure and/or minimizes a combination of population exposure and risks of spills. These can be used for any transportation mode, but are most widely done for truck and rail transportation. An example of a practical multi-objective routing analysis for trucking hazardous waste is Turnquist and List (1993).

Scheduling models take routing models one step further by recognizing that transit times on links (and costs of operation) differ by time of day because of the presence of other vehicles (e.g. other trains on the same track) and congestion. A combination of time slots and routing is needed to identify the cost-minimizing versus risk-minimizing solution. For a concise review of routing and scheduling models for hazmat transportation see List et al. (1991).

Another family of analytical models are location models. These calculate the optimal location of facilities, such as the number and location of response teams to respond to spills within a specified time period. These are adaptations of models used to locate ambulances, fire houses, and similar emergency response depots. List (1993) is an instructive illustration of this type of modeling, including recognition of factors to be considered that go beyond the modeling process. A more thorough discussion of location models and hazmats is in List et al. (1991).

4. Challenges in risk analysis of hazmat transportation

QRA is an attractive, even indispensable, tool for the analysis of risks associated with hazmat transportation. But it is important to recognize that there can be many sources of error or imprecision in doing these analyses. (See Saccomanno et al. (1991) for a summary of various uncertainties in QRA). Shortcomings in data remain the most cited weakness for QRA. Significant advances in data compilation and reliability have been made, but good quantitative analysis has a ravenous appetite for more data. Risky events have probabilistic outcomes, hence a large number of quantitative explorations can be carried out but there may still be additional iterations that are desirable.

Even more difficult than predicting probabilities is predicting the magnitude of the consequences of a hazmat spill. Hazmats have known physical properties, but the human and environmental consequences of a particular spill depend on a great many factors. Simplifications are unavoidable to produce workable estimates of the risk costs associated with hazmat transportation.

Even if the probability of a spill is settled, as well as the physical consequences, there are issues with the monetization of these effects, e.g. what values to assign to life, injuries, and damages to the environment. Cost estimates are needed and produced, but they are not precise figures. Common practice, recognized as a simplification but at least a starting point, is calculation of an average or expected value such as the clean-up cost of a specified size of spill, and to assume that a spill twice the size will entail twice the clean-up cost and cause twice the injuries and environmental damage. That is, there is a linearity or proportionality assumption built in to most cost analyses of hazmat spills. As noted, these probably are a good first approximation, but they are also a source of error in conducting quantitative evaluations.

There are some more general concerns about QRA, regarding the nature of risk taking and how to evaluate it. One is the issue of risk neutrality. We can measure the probabilities and risks associated with an event such as a hazmat spill, but decision-making must reflect the preferences of the decision makers. Should we assume people are risk-neutral or willing to accept higher degrees of risk? It is an important, even critical, first step to calculate the risks, but it is another step to choose a specific course of action and accept or reject various risks in the process. It seems ironic but we regularly see situations where people are prepared to engage in relatively risky activities on their own volition (e.g. various "extreme" sports) yet they may demand extraordinarily low risks for other activities such as the transport of hazmats. One distinction is between risks borne voluntarily versus involuntarily; people might act differently for the former than for the latter. But is this a valid and rational distinction, or something that people have not thought much about?

Another important issue about risk perception (or misperception) is: does it matter if the public accurately recognizes the risks involved or if they hold misperceptions about the level of risk? If people have fears, even if unjustified scientifically, there may still be a public demand for action restricting the hazmat. What is the role of technical analysis such as QRA if there are political pressures for actions that are not warranted by scientific evidence? Many argue that there is an important role for "risk communication" in such circumstances, to inform the public of the best estimates of the risks involved. This would improve the level of debate and facilitate better decisions. That said, there is no denying that QRA and related techniques are still an evolving science. Estimates of quantitative models can be no better than the quality of the data supplied and accuracy of the relationships specified within the model. And despite existing data and experience, we sometimes discover consequences of a hazmat that had gone unrecognized. There is a long history of substances at first considered to be benign or low risk only for us to later discover that they were more dangerous than first thought.

There is a final issue to consider: do people have different feelings or preferences about death or injury by some means compared with others, that is, are there "dread factors" associated with particular hazmats? Chapter 6 outlines some of these extensions to QRA. For whatever reasons, the public may demand levels of protection that differ among hazmats or background circumstances, with no analytical basis for the distinction. This is the public's prerogative in a democracy; in such circumstances, QRA or equivalent analysis remains important for enlightening the debate.

5. Conclusions

There is an unavoidable need for the transportation of hazmats with their attendant risks. Further, the number of substances is increasing over time, and population growth concentrating in urban areas means the prospects of exposure to hazmat risks are increasing. Counterbalancing this are regulations, extensive experience in the handling and transport of hazmats, and analytical methods such as QRA. The nature of hazmat risks is that spills and tragedies will occur. But they are rare enough that they are newsworthy events rather than commonplace. Diligence by shippers and transport operators, governmental oversight, and the refinement of data and analysis can make hazmat emergencies even more rare than they already are.

Acknowledgements

The author wishes to acknowledge helpful comments from Garland Chow, Scott Dennis, and Ian Savage.

References

Abkowitz, M.D., J.P. DeLorenzo, R. Duych, A. Greenberg and T. McSweeney (2001) "Assessing the economic effect of incidents involving truck transport of hazardous materials," *Transportation Research Record*, 1763:125–129.

Allen, J.C. (2001) "What does the new millennium offer for hazardous materials transportation?" Report from the Transportation Research Board Committee on Transportation of Hazardous Materials A1B14, in: "Transportation in the new millennium: state of the art and future directions," Annual Meeting, Transportation Research Board, Washington, DC.

Dennis, S.M. (1996) "Estimating risk costs per unit of exposure for hazardous materials transported by rail," *Logistics and Transportation Review*, 32:351–375.

Leeming, D.G. and F.F. Saccamanno (2001) "Use of quantified risk assessment in evaluating the risks of transporting chlorine by road and rail," *Transportation Research Record*, 1430:27–35.

List, G.F. (1993) "Siting emergency response teams: tradeoffs among response time, risk, risk equity and cost," in: L. Moses and D. Lindstrom, eds, *Transportation of hazardous materials: issues in law, social science and engineering*. Dordrecht: Kluwer.

List, G.F., P.B. Mirchandani, M.A. Turnquist and K.G. Zografos (1991) "Modeling and analysis for hazardous materials transportation: risk analysis, routing/scheduling and facility location," *Transportation Science*, 25:100–114.

Turnquist, M.A. and G.F. List (1993) "Multiobjective policy analysis of hazardous materials routing," in: L. Moses and D. Lindstrom (eds), *Transportation of hazardous materials: issues in law, social science and engineering*. Dordrecht: Kluwer.

Nicolet-Monnier, M. and A.V. Gheorge (1996) *Quantitative risk assessment of hazardous materials transport systems: rail, road, pipelines, and ship*. Dordrecht: Kluwer.

Rhyne, W.R. (1994) *Hazardous materials transportation risk analysis: quantitative approaches for truck and train*. New York: Van Nostrand Reinhold.

Saccomanno, F.F. and K. Cassidy (1994) "QRA and decision making in the transportation of dangerous goods," *Transportation Research Record*, 1430:19–26.

Saccomanno, F.F., A. Stewart, and J. Shortreed (1993) "Uncertainty in the estimation of risks for the transport of hazardous materials," in: L. Moses, and D. Lindstrom, eds, *Transportation of hazardous materials: issues in law, social science and engineering*. Dordrecht: Kluwer.

Chapter 40

PUBLIC ATTITUDES

TOMMY GÄRLING and PETER LOUKOPOULOS
Göteborg University

MARTIN LEE-GOSSELIN
Université Laval, Québec

1. Introduction

In many countries the general public is concerned about the deterioration of the environment. It is also understood by most citizens that present-day transportation of people and goods contributes substantially to this deterioration (Jones, 1995). The former is a public attitude. The latter is the public perception that, in conjunction with the perception that transportation is essential for well-being, forms the basis for an ambivalent public attitude toward transportation. This ambivalent attitude held by the general public is probably an obstacle to powerful political initiatives that implement policies targeting sustainable transportation.

This chapter has three main purposes: (1) to offer a basic guide to the theoretical underpinnings of our understanding of public attitudes toward transport and the environment; (2) to explore the relationships between "attitudes" and "values" – terms that are used in many different ways in the transport field, but here are not synonymous with "preference" or "utility"; (3) to identify empirical findings from psychological research that can aid the design of programs aimed at transport/environmental benefits and enhance their potential success. The chapter first reviews basic attitude concepts in current social psychological research. A review of research on environmental values then follows. The final section analyzes principles of changing public attitudes related to travel behavior.

2. Attitude concepts

"Attitude" refers to a relatively stable evaluative response to a particular entity – the attitude object (Eagly and Chaiken, 1993, 1998). An attitude is less influenced by situational factors than are preferences, but is less stable than personality traits

(Ajzen, 1987). The evaluative response may be affective (e.g. measured as changes in heart rate), cognitive (e.g. evaluative judgments expressed on rating scales), or behavioral (e.g. observations of actual behavior or stated intentions expressing approach–avoidance tendencies).

An attitude object can be anything that is discriminated or held in mind by people. It may be abstract (e.g. a value) or concrete (e.g. an activity), personal (e.g. a particular person one knows), or collective (e.g. public transportation or the environment). Examples of common objects of public attitudes are values such as freedom, equity, or healthiness; social policies; social or ethnic groups; public figures such as politicians; activities such as working, watching TV, and vacationing; and patterns of activities over time such as a healthy lifestyle or environmentally friendly actions.

Attitudes can be formed in different ways. One distinction is between direct and indirect experience (Fazio, 1990): some attitudes are formed on the basis of direct personal experience, others indirectly on the basis of word-of-mouth or mass-media information. Another distinction concerns the role played by affect. According to one view (Zajonc, 1984), attitudes are formed because the attitude object, whether directly or indirectly experienced, evokes immediate positive or negative feelings. An alternative view posits that beliefs or opinions acquired about the attitude object form the basis of the attitude (Fishbein and Ajzen, 1975). In both these classes of theories, attitude is a determinant of behavior. Behavior may also affect attitudes: self-perception theory (Bem, 1972) assumes that people infer their attitude from observations of their behavior.

A substantial amount of research has been devoted to the study of attitude change, including the evaluation of different techniques of changing attitudes (for reviews, see Petty et al., 1997; Petty and Wegener, 1998). In this research the most influential view is that attitudes are based on perceptions. Therefore, providing information about the attitude object is the favored approach to changing attitudes.

A dominant role in applications of attitude research continues to be played by the theory of reasoned action (TRA) and its successor, the theory of planned behavior (TPB). Applications include voting behavior, health behavior, and consumer choice (Sheppard et al., 1988). Two other application areas of TRA and TPB relevant to this chapter are travel behavior (Gärling et al., 1998) and environmental attitudes (Eagly and Kulesa, 1997; Fransson and Gärling, 1999).

TRA and TPB are examples of expectancy–value models of attitudes. Such models posit that attitude is the sum of the product of expectancy and value, where expectancy is the strength of salient beliefs held by people that the attitude object possesses specified levels of attributes, and value is an evaluative judgment of these attribute levels. Beliefs are propositions (true–false statements about the world) linked to each other in network structures stored in memory (e.g. Anderson, 1983).

In applications of expectancy–value types of attitude theories, the aim is frequently to understand the attitudinal determinants of a targeted behavior so that it can later be influenced. Since behavior (e.g. protest actions by the general public) may be of primary interest, the question is raised concerning how well attitude corresponds to behavior. A long history of research (see Eagly and Chaiken, 1993) has identified several boundary conditions. For instance, it is known that the correspondence is improved if attitude is measured at the same level of specificity as the behavior. An example is that a positive attitude toward the environment will not closely correspond to the use of public transport, whereas a positive attitude toward public transport may. A general positive (environmental) attitude may, however, be related to the frequency of a class of behavior (e.g. pro-environmental), even if it is not related to the frequency of specific behaviors in the class (e.g. use of public transport).

Behavior has several determinants in addition to attitude. An important contribution of Fishbein and Ajzen (1975) was to show that intention (i.e. how likely one is to perform the behavior) corresponds to behavior if it is measured relatively close in time at the same level of specificity as the behavior. Although the product–moment correlation between an attitude and a corresponding behavior usually does not exceed 0.40 (meaning that attitude accounts for 16% of the variance in the behavior) (Sheppard et al., 1988; Kraus, 1995), this number may increase to 0.50 (25% explained variance, corresponding to a hit rate of 75% if the variables are dichotomized at the median) if the behavior is related to a stated intention. The intention is in turn positively related to attitude, but also to normative beliefs (the perception that the behavior is desirable by different social groups or society) and to perceived behavioral control (the perception that there are no insurmountable obstacles to performing the behavior) (Ajzen, 1991).

A behavior that is repeated over and over again is normally called a habit. It has frequently been shown that measures of habit correspond more closely to future behavior than do measures of attitude or intention (Ouellette and Wood, 1998). However, a distinction needs to be made between a repeated behavior reflecting a positive attitude or intention and a repeated behavior whose performance is not preceded by the formation of an intention. In the latter case, attempts at changing the attitude toward the behavior are likely to be fruitless because the behavior is predominantly controlled by situational cues rather than by attitude or intention. Observing the frequency with which a behavior is performed is, however, not in itself sufficient to empirically identify these different determinants of repeated behaviors. With the aim of developing a measure that does, Verplanken and collaborators (1997) proposed the response–frequency measure for use in interviews. Illustrations of its application to travel mode choice are found in Gärling et al. (2001). Another application is Garvill et al. (2003), who showed that the measure is related to resistance to changing of car use.

3. Environmental values

Value orientations have been examined in interdisciplinary research on environmental attitudes and pro-environmental behavior (Stern, 1992; Fransson and Gärling, 1999). The basic tenet in this research is that people differ in their deeper sentiments for the environment. Extensive cross-cultural studies of the structure of human values (e.g. Schwartz, 1992) have identified universal value types ordered along two orthogonal dimensions labeled self-transcendence versus self-focusing, and openness versus closedness to change. In this research, values are defined as desirable trans-situational goals (cognitive representations of motivational and affective states) that serve as guiding principles in people's lives. Although values vary in importance (priority) among individuals, groups, and cultures, the value structure is universal, reflecting basic human self-interest needs, needs to belong to groups, and needs for institutions.

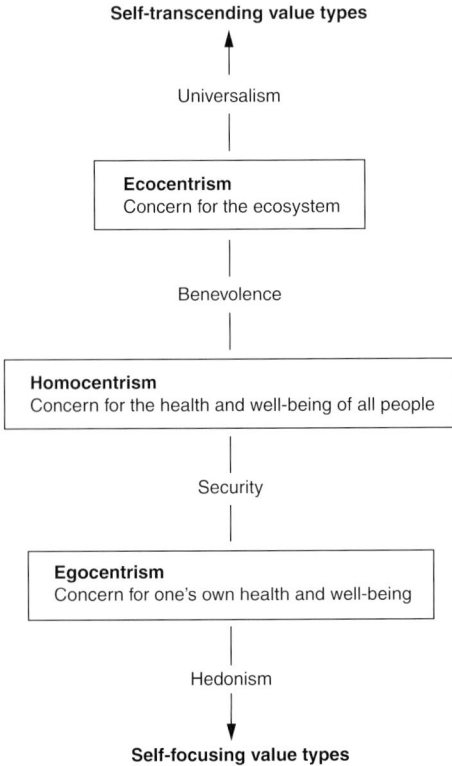

Figure 1. Environmental value orientations positioned on the continuum from self-focusing to self-transcending value types.

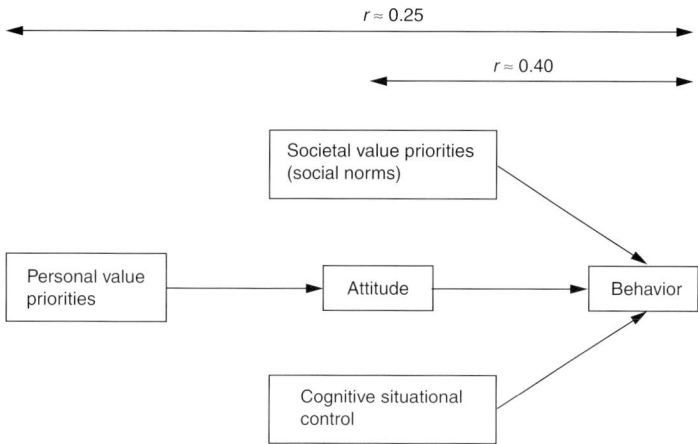

Figure 2. The correspondence between value, attitude, and behavior (r denotes estimated product–moment correlations with behavior; if squared, r is a measure of the proportion of common variance).

Stern and collaborators (e.g. Stern and Dietz 1994) have identified three related environmental value orientations referred to as egocentrism, homocentrism, and ecocentrism. These value orientations differ with respect to how inclusive the threats of the deterioration of the environment are perceived to be, i.e. whether the threat is to one's own well-being, to the well-being of all people, or to the well-being of all people, animals, and plants. Figure 1 shows how the different environmental value orientations are related to the general value types, ordered from self-focused to self-transcendent.

Some research has linked environmental value orientations to sociodemographic factors (Dietz et al., 1998). Although not always conclusively, pro-environmental value orientations tend to be more frequent among the higher educated, political liberals, women, and urban residents. Such value orientations are also more frequent in younger age groups. A relationship has furthermore been established demonstrating that a pro-social value orientation, in contrast to a pro-self-value orientation, disposes people to cooperate in the interest of preserving or contributing to a common resource (Van Lange et al., 2000).

In attitude research (Eagly and Chaiken, 1993), values are conceived of as general attitudes representing one of several factors that influence more specific attitudes, which in turn are one of several determinants of behavior. As may be expected, the correspondence between values and behavior is not strong, as is shown Figure 2, which is based on a meta-analysis of results from thousands of subjects in a diversity of domains. Whereas the product–moment correlation between attitude and behavior may be of the order of 0.40, the correlation between value and behavior barely exceeds 0.25.

A distinction can also be made between personal and social value systems. The latter is dominated by moral norms (Thøgersen, 1996). Personal values are partly internalized general social norms, and partly subcultural or idiosyncratic norms. Social and personal norms are important determinants of pro-environmental behavior. In many cases performing pro-environmental behavior is inconvenient, thus people need to have other than hedonic motives for making the sacrifices they must frequently make. A potential impediment is the so-called "commons dilemma": people may require assurance that a personal sacrifice will not simply be canceled out by a corresponding increase in the selfishness of others. For example, a motorist may approve of fuel-efficient cars, but may hesitate to buy one if he is convinced that other motorists will "take up the slack" he creates by buying powerful sport utility vehicles. An important distinction should also be made between social movement behavior (citizenship actions, policy acceptance and support) in the interest of protecting the environment, and personal-sphere behavior (Stern et al., 1999). The former is more closely related to homocentric and ecocentric values, the latter to egocentric values.

4. Changing public attitudes related to travel behavior

A conceptualization of different influences on travel behavior is provided by Gärling et al. (2002). Figure 3 analyzes the effects of travel demand management (TDM) measures on household travel behavior, as mediated through trip chain attributes, goal setting, the effects on other users, and the effects of public information. The choice of travel options is seen as dependent upon bundles of attributes describing trip chains (e.g. purposes, departure times, costs, travel times), and upon the goals and implementation intentions of households. TDM measures the influence of the bundles of attributes that characterize travel options. These trip chain attributes can directly influence travel choice, as may be the case when a TDM measure results in the closure of certain roads or central city districts. Alternatively, an indirect way in which TDM measures may influence trip chain attributes, and thus travel behavior, is through the effect on other users. That is, other users of the transportation system respond to TDM measures so that the travel options change for other users (e.g. the more people who refrain from car use when congestion pricing is introduced or when public transport is improved, the better it is for those who continue to drive). TDM measures may also indirectly affect people's travel behavior by encouraging the setting of a goal to adjust to the attribute changes. For example, if road pricing is introduced, the result will be increased travel cost. If these travel cost increases are perceived as something that must be reduced, which is dependent on a range of individual factors including income, then the person will set the goal of reducing them.

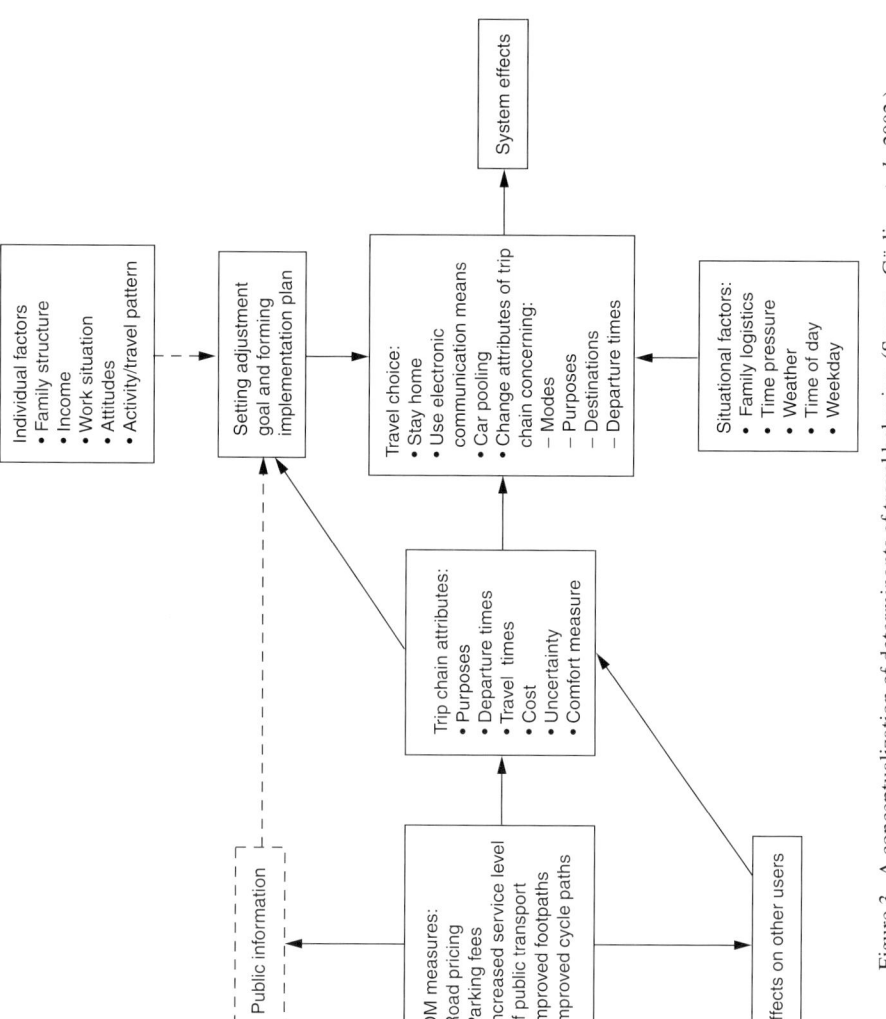

Figure 3. A conceptualization of determinants of travel behavior. (Source: Gärling et al., 2002.)

Setting the adjustment goal, however, does not guarantee achievement, which is dependent on a variety of other factors.

Attitude has played a role in travel behavior research on a par with preference and utility as a proximal determinant of travel mode choice. A breakthrough is the work by Ben-Akiva et al. (1999) in their latent class type of approach to structural equation modeling of travel behavior. Here, attitude is conceptualized as a determinant of the importance of attributes affecting choices. Examples of similar current research on how environmental attitudes influence travel behavior are Golob (2001) and Golob and Hensher (1998). In the following we limit ourselves, however, to discussing the process of changing public attitudes, disregarding how these attitudes may impact on travel behavior. Because of a lack of extensive empirical research in transportation on changes in public attitudes, we are able to provide only illustrative examples

Although encouraged by changing trip chain attributes through TDM measures, goal setting may also be achieved through public information campaigns. Such information campaigns may be thought of as another TDM measure. However, they do not change the objective characteristics of trip chain attributes. Instead, information campaigns rely entirely on changing attitudes and, in turn, on encouraging the setting of goals to reduce unwanted travel.

According to Eagly and Kulesa (1997), an attitude can be strengthened in two ways: it can be supported by many associations arising from either direct or indirect experience (intra-attitudinal structure), or it may be linked to other, more abstract attitudes and values (inter-attitudinal structure). Intra-attitudinal structure is derived from experience (i.e. cognitive, affective, or behavioral evaluative responses to the attitude object), whereas inter-attitudinal structure is the result of linking a target attitude with attitudes that are already acquired (e.g. if one wants to protect the environment and minimize air pollution, then one may support gasoline taxes that minimize car use and limit air pollution).

Attitudes that have an extensive intra-attitudinal structure are more difficult to change because the new information in the persuasive message must compete with the beliefs and knowledge that people already hold. Furthermore, knowledgeable message recipients process new information in a way that maintains their attitudes. This does not necessarily mean that people with attitudes that have an extensive intra-attitudinal structure are closed minded, but rather that they are able to be more critical of new information than less knowledgeable message recipients with weaker attitudes. Attitudes that are strong because of their inter-attitudinal structure allow for effective persuasion through messages containing arguments that highlight the value to which the attitude is linked. If people are somewhat knowledgeable about an issue (e.g. environmental effects of transportation), then persuasive messages need to contain well-formulated arguments that reinforce intra-attitudinal structures consistent with the attitude one wishes to instill in the target audience. Similarly, given the variety of values to which attitudes can be linked, a persuasive message should take advantage of possible inconsistencies and formulate appeals supporting the values one wishes others to endorse.

Contemporary research into attitude change examines the multiple roles of persuasion variables. That is, the focus is no longer on the role a particular variable plays but on the variable when it takes on one of many roles. This is to be expected given research showing that the same variable that may enhance message elaboration or systematic processing (i.e. scrutiny of a persuasive message) in one setting may reduce it in another (Petty et al., 1997). Attitudes that are changed in a less-demanding manner (i.e. where scrutiny of a message is avoided because, for example, the message comes from an expert who is assumed to be knowledgeable) tend to be weaker.

These low-effort and high-effort processes form the basis of the two major models of attitude change in contemporary research (Petty and Wegener, 1998). The elaboration likelihood model of persuasion posits the existence of an elaboration continuum: high elaboration, resulting in attitude change through a central route (where object-relevant information is assessed with respect to already existing knowledge, and the resulting attitude is well articulated and supported by evidence and information); and low elaboration, resulting in attitude change through a peripheral route (where laborious processes are avoided and the resulting attitude is arrived at through a rule of thumb). The central and peripheral routes of attitude change can be equated with attitude resulting from systematic and heuristic processing in the heuristic–systematic model of persuasion. The models are generally similar but use different explanatory language.

Thus, with respect to public information campaigns, a relevant question is: which factors are likely to contribute to the laborious processing of information? This is important because attitude change arising from thorough processing, in contrast to shallow, heuristic processing, is more persistent as it produces a structure of beliefs supporting the changed attitude. Making persuasive messages personally relevant is one method. Others include presenting messages to the target audience in a context where there are few distractions and little time pressure, and using a source that is credible and trustworthy. A wide variety of source, message, recipient, and context variables are discussed by Petty and Wegener (1998), all of which influence whether or not a message is processed systematically (i.e. by the central route). Given the wide variety of variables, the implication is that public information should define the target audience well if the attitude change is to be successful.

How then, for example, could public information campaigns targeting car use reduction take advantage of research into attitude change? Most people may have some knowledge of the adverse environmental effects of private car use, and, therefore, persuasive messages are needed that reinforce attitude-consistent intra-attitudinal structures. Thus, factual knowledge of an improved public transport network with better service may work as a form of indirect experience. If the public transport is truly improved, then word of mouth could function as a form of indirect experience. If the target audience is encouraged to use the public transport system, then direct experience could also achieve the attitude change. Making appeals personally relevant may work for some problems associated with travel behavior but be limited in effectiveness with others. Consider information campaigns about inner-city noise and congestion. If such problems arise from commuters from suburbs or satellite towns, then appeals based on making the city more livable may not be very successful on the grounds of personal relevance. If, however, the message is changed to making arriving at work less stressful, then personal relevance may be increased. Furthermore, taking advantage of the inter-attitudinal structure of attitudes by making appeals to ecocentric environmental values could result in goals being set to decrease commuting by car.

A well-researched topic within the field of attitude change concerns the use of fear or threat appeals. Conclusions regarding the effectiveness of such persuasive messages have been mixed, once again emphasizing the multiple roles of persuasion variables. While certain studies show that higher levels of threat lead to greater persuasion by resulting in central-route processing, other studies show reduced systematic processing, because many fearful participants are so scared that they are unable to critically evaluate the message (i.e. peripheral route processing). In the past, fear appeals with respect to travel behavior have been mostly confined to the individual consequences of unsafe driving such as speeding, or the collective effects of individual actions on acute air pollution episodes. However, evidence is building up that respiratory and other diseases result from the cumulative (chronic) exposure of both road users and nearby dwellers to vehicle emissions (Transportation Research Board, 2002). Research on fear and threat from domains such as smoking and cancer thus provides some useful insights for transport and environment. It turns out that fear appeals often leave the target audience with feelings of powerlessness and lack of control, and to the extent that recipients believe that they cannot do anything about the problem, the message will not be persuasive.

The aim behind any public information campaign seeking to change attitudes is to ultimately change behavior. In travel behavior perhaps the most important impediment is the demonstration that as strength of habit increases, the thoroughness of information processing decreases (Verplanken et al., 1997). It is for this reason that it is recommended that public information campaigns be used in conjunction with other TDM measures, which change trip chain characteristics and thereby change the context so that the existing habit is potentially no longer relevant or applicable. Once this is achieved, public information campaigns designed with attention paid to the multiple roles of persuasion variables, as outlined above, should have a greater chance of changing travel behavior and of potentially beginning the creation of new travel habits. As noted earlier, when discussing how attitudes are formed, experienced positive outcomes of a new travel habit will strengthen a positive attitude whereas the reverse will occur for experienced negative outcomes. This phenomenon may be important in any application.

Campaigns can also work in concert with external forces that impel people to experience novel behaviors that they had previously imagined but never implemented. Individuals or households undergoing a transition such as relocation, job change, or the loss or gain of household members, may undergo shifts in whole sets of travel habits. More dramatic external forces are major supply perturbations such as earthquakes, bridge failures, or fuel shortages. The effective use of such major "opportunities" requires a combination of organized and timely information sources on public attitudes (Lee-Gosselin and Clinton, 1987). In such circumstances, it may be possible to engender radical shifts toward pro-environmental behaviors, even among those who express skepticism about the need to conserve resources, provided that they believe that an emergency is "real" (Lee-Gosselin, 1989).

5. Summary and conclusions

This chapter has summarized basic concepts developed in current research on attitudes and environmental values, and presented some insights from this research on how public attitudes and behavior in the public and private spheres may be changed. It may be concluded that skillfully designed and conducted public information campaigns may have beneficial effects on travel behavior, for instance on car use reduction, but probably only if combined with TDM measures or external forces that break car use habits so that new habits can be developed. The outcomes of new travel habits will also have effects on attitudes, either strengthening a positive attitude or changing it back to a negative attitude. Conversely, TDM measures may cause negative psychological reactions if not accompanied by public information campaigns. Although not highly correlated with specific behaviors, public attitudes related to basic environmental and cooperative value orientations still play important roles in any attempt to change travel behavior.

References

Ajzen, I. (1987) "Attitudes, traits, and actions: dispositional prediction of behaviour in personality and social psychology," in: L. Berkowitz, ed., *Advances in experimental social psychology*, vol. 20. San Diego: Academic Press.

Ajzen, I. (1991) "The theory of planned behaviour," *Organisation Behavaviour and Human Decision Processes*, 50:179–211.

Anderson, J.R. (1983) *The architecture of cognition*. Cambridge: MIT Press.
Bem, D.J. (1972) "Self-perception theory," in: L. Berkowitz, ed., *Advances in experimental social psychology*, vol. 6. New York: Academic Press.
Ben-Akiva, M., D. McFadden, T. Gärling, D. Gopinath, J. Walker, D. Bolduc, A. Borsch-Supan, P. Delquie, O. Larichev, T. Morikawa, A. Polydoropoulou and V. Rao (1999) "Extended framework for modeling choice behaviour," *Marketing Letters*, 10:187–203.
Dietz, T., P.C. Stern, and G.A. Guagnano (1998) "Social structural and social psychological bases of environmental concern," *Environment and Behavavior*, 30:450–471.
Eagly, A.H. and S. Chaiken (1993) *The psychology of attitudes*. Fort Worth: Harcourt Brace Jovanovich.
Eagly, A.H. and S. Chaiken (1998) "Attitude structure and function," in: D.T. Gilbert, S.T. Fiske and G. Lindzey, eds, *The handbook of social psychology*, 4th edn, vol. 1. Englewood Cliffs: McGraw-Hill.
Eagly, A.H. and P. Kulesa (1997) "Attitudes, attitude structure, and resistance to change: implications for persuasion on environmental issues," in: M.H. Bazerman, D.M. Messick, A.E. Tenbrunsel and K.A. Wade-Benzoni, eds, *Environment, ethics, and behaviour: the psychology of environmental valuation and degradation*, pp. 122 – 153. San Francisco: Lexington.
Fazio, R.H. (1990) "Multiple processes by which attitudes guide behaviour: the MODE model as an integrative framework," in: M.P. Zanna, ed., *Advances in experimental social psychology*, vol. 23,. Orlando: Academic Press.
Fishbein, M. and I. Ajzen (1975) *Belief, attitude, intention, and behaviour: an introduction to theory and research*. Reading: Addison-Wesley.
Fransson, N. and T. Gärling (1999) "Environmental concern: conceptual definitions, measurement methods, and research findings," *Journal of Environmental Psychology*, 19:369–382.
Gärling, T., R. Gillholm and A. Gärling (1998) "Reintroducing attitude theory in travel behaviour research: the validity of an interactive interview procedure to predict car use," *Transportation*, 25:129–146.
Gärling, T., S. Fujii and O. Boe (2001) "Empirical tests of a model of determinants of script-based driving choice," *Transportation Research F*, 4: 89–102.
Gärling, T., D. Eek, P. Loukopoulos, S. Fujii, O. Johansson-Stenman, R. Kitamura, R. Pendyala and B. Vilhelmson (2002) "A conceptual analysis of the impact of travel demand management on private car use," *Transport Policy*, 9:59–70.
Garvill J., A. Marell and A. Nordlund (2003) "Effects of increased awareness on choice of travel mode," *Transportation*, 30:63–79.
Golob, T.F. (2001) "Joint models of attitudes and behaviour in evaluation of the San Diego I-15 Congestion Pricing Project," *Transportation Research A*, 35:495–514.
Golob, T.F. and D.A. Hensher (1998) "Greenhouse gas emissions and Australian commuters' attitudes and behaviour concerning abatement policies and personal involvement," *Transportation Research D*, 3:1–18.
Jones, P. (1995) "Road pricing: the public viewpoint," in: B. Johansson and L.-G. Mattson, eds, *Road pricing: theory, empirical assessment and policy*. Boston: Kluwer.
Kraus, S.J. (1995) "Attitudes and the prediction of behaviour: a meta-analysis of the empirical literature," *Personal and Social Psychology B*, 21:58–75.
Lee-Gosselin, M.E.H. (1989) "Research on car-use and lifestyle under future conditions in Canada," in: International Association for Travel Behaviour, ed., *Travel behaviour research*. Aldershot: Avebury, Gower Press.
Lee-Gosselin, M.E.H. and K.M. Clinton (1987) "Integrating research on public attitudes and behaviour into energy contingency planning," *Transportation Research Record*, 1155:37–45.
Ouellette, J.A. and W. Wood (1998) "Habit and intention in everyday life: the multiple processes by which past behaviour predicts future behaviour," *Psychology Bulletin*, 124:54–74.
Petty, R.E. and D.T. Wegener (1998) "Attitude change: multiple roles for persuasion variables," in: D.T. Gilbert, S.T. Fiske and G. Lindzey, eds, *The handbook of social psychology*, 4th edn, vol. 1, pp. 323–390. Englewood Cliffs: McGraw-Hill.
Petty, R.E., D.T. Wegener and L.T. Fabrigar (1997) "Attitudes and attitude change," *Annual Review of Psychology*, 48:609–647.
Schwartz, S. (1992) "Universals in the content and structures of values: theoretical advances and empirical tests in 20 countries," in: M.P. Zanna, ed., *Advances in experimental social psychology*, vol. 25. Orlando: Academic Press.

Sheppard, B.H., J. Hartwick and P.R. Warshaw (1988) "The theory of reasoned action: a meta-analysis of past research with recommendations for modifications and future research," *Journal of Consumer Reserach*, 15:325–343.

Stern, P.C. (1992) "Psychological dimensions of global environmental change," *Annual Review of Psychology*, 43:269–302.

Stern, P.C. and T. Dietz (1994) "The value basis of environmental concern," *Journal Social Issues*, 50:55–84.

Stern, P.C., T. Dietz, T. Abel, G.A. Guagnano and L. Kalof (1999) "A value-belief-norm theory of support for social movements: the case of environmentalism," *Human Ecological Review*, 6:81–97.

Thøgersen, J. (1996) "Recycling and morality: A critical review of the literature," *Environmental Behavavior*, 28:536–558.

Transportation Research Board (2002) *Surface transportation environmental research: a long-term strategy*. Special Report 268. Washington, DC: National Academy Press.

Van Lange, P.A.M., M. Van Vugt and D. De Cremer (2000) "Choosing between personal comfort and the environment: solutions to transportation dilemmas," in: M. Van Vugt, M. Snyder, T.R. Tyler and A. Biel, eds, *Cooperation in modern society*. London: Routledge.

Verplanken B., H. Aarts and A. Van Knippenberg (1997) "Habit, information acquisition, and the process of making travel mode choices," *European Journal of Social Psychology*, 27:539–560.

Zajonc, R.B. (1984) "On the primacy of affect," *American Psychology*, 39:117–123.

Chapter 41

TRAVEL BEHAVIOR CHANGE THROUGH INDIVIDUAL ENGAGEMENT

GEOFF ROSE
Monash University

ELIZABETH AMPT
Steer Davies Gleave, Adelaide

1. Introduction

Many actions taken in relation to the transport system, including both adoption of policies and creation of infrastructure, result in travel behavior change. For example, extending a rail line results in a change in travel behavior with some people taking the new service instead of driving and maybe other people who were not making a trip before now choosing to drive (due to reduced congestion). Viewed in this light, travel behavior change is not something new – it has been an implicit outcome of many, if not all, initiatives designed to address transport problems or challenges. The focus of this chapter is on public campaigns designed to produce travel behavior change. This does represent a relatively new frontier in the transport field, one where what we do not know probably outweighs what we do know. In this chapter we identify the state of knowledge and practice in this field and also point out areas where improved understanding is needed.

An appropriate first step is to define what is meant by a "travel behavior change program." Here we define it as a "public engagement campaign designed to enable individuals to become more aware of their travel options and where possible exercise choices which reduce use of the private motor vehicle." There are certainly elements of marketing in this definition, although the programs considered here include some element of active engagement with the participants rather than relying on passive publicity/advertising, which would usually form a key part of a marketing campaign. In the UK, the term "personalized journey planning techniques" is also applied. Personalized journey planning is

> a set of techniques or approaches that provide individualised analysis or advice to people based on their journey making characteristics. It therefore does not include marketing campaigns such as awareness raising, general exhortations to use particular modes of travel, or the general provision of information about particular forms of transport.
>
> UK Department of Transport, Local Government and the Regions (2002)

Handbook of Transport and the Environment, Edited by D.A. Hensher and K.J. Button
© 2003, Elsevier Science Ltd

Behavioral change occurs when people move from having awareness and knowledge to taking action. The behavioral change approaches considered here rely on a voluntary or "bottom-up" behavioral change as opposed to a regulatory or "top-down" approach. Volition, the exercise of choice to determine action, has strong links to personality (Kuhl and Beckmann, 1994), and so, perhaps not surprisingly then, some of the programs to be described here assess predisposition to change, or core values, prior to determining the nature of the information or initiatives provided to support that process of change.

Travel behavior change programs fit within the context of "travel demand management" (TDM) or "mobility management," meaning that they are one of a set of measures, excluding provision of major infrastructure, which aim to modify travel decisions. The emphasis is therefore on "demand"-side measures rather than "supply"-side measures. Wayte (1991) developed a useful characterization of the range of TDM strategies which can be grouped into strategy areas focused on improving asset utilization, physical restraint, pricing, and urban and social changes. In Wayte's framework, travel behavior change programs come into the last of these strategy areas, namely in the realm of urban and social changes. Travel behavior change programs can take a variety of forms, and the priorities can vary in different cities/applications. High-level objectives usually relate to improving the sustainability of the transport system or improving air quality. One of the common specific aims is to decrease the use of the car, or at least increase the efficiency of car use (e.g. through trip chaining or car pooling). Other aims may be to increase public transport use or the use of active transport modes (walking and cycling).

The following section describes the evolution of travel behavior change programs from travel awareness initiatives to the current forms that rely on a high degree of individual engagement. From that historical base, the nature of existing travel behavior change programs is considered through examination of the two programs which have seen greatest international application, namely, IndiMark and Travel Blending. The nature of those programs is considered, and then the impacts of travel behavior change programs are reviewed. Reflecting the comment made in the opening paragraph of this chapter, it is recognized that this field of travel behavior change is still in its infancy and so consideration is given in the final section to what is still to be learned in this field.

2. Evolution of travel behavior change programs

In the UK, several initiatives, broadly termed "travel awareness," were undertaken in the early 1990s to encourage people to reduce car use. Their prime objective was to make people aware of the need for the reduction in car use, and ways in which this could be achieved. The first stage, and generally the key component of these initiatives, was an advertising campaign assisted by a set of brochures, posters, bumper stickers, and logos to show people the problems of congestion and pollution and to point out the alternatives (e.g. car sharing or pooling, use of public transport, trip chaining, and so on). Later stages often included more targeted efforts such as "walk to school" weeks or "ride to work" campaigns, and facilitated discussions with community groups to get them to understand the issues more thoroughly than can be done with an advertising campaign.

The two initial examples of these which were initiated by local authorities in the UK are TravelWise, begun in Hertfordshire (Hertfordshire County Council, 1993), and HeadStart (Hampshire County Council, 1993). The major thrust of TravelWise tends to be publicity, with an emphasis on advertising on the outside of buses, leaflets, and radio advertising. However, TravelWise is not merely a publicity campaign because it has been promoted through the logo appearing on official council documents such as transport strategy documents and public transport timetables. In addition to the publicity campaign and branding of documents, particular events have been organized under the banner of TravelWise. These include "walk to school weeks" and "bike to work days." HeadStart was launched by Hampshire County Council shortly after Hertfordshire County Council introduced TravelWise. However, Hampshire County Council describes its approach as being a "bottom-up" approach, in contrast to the TravelWise "top-down" approach. The distinction is that TravelWise is aimed at everyone; trying to influence them to a greater or lesser extent by recognition of a name, logo, and concept via a mass media campaign. In contrast, HeadStart focuses on taking the message to community groups and trying to significantly affect the ways these groups think about transport (Steer Davies Gleave, 1996). The main thrust of the HeadStart campaign is the conduct of workshops with community groups. Target groups include parish councils, parent and toddler groups, and fitness groups. In addition, business conferences have been held with the aim of getting commitments to the development of commuter plans, and on another front a "safe routes to schools" campaign was developed.

Each of these programs has its own merits, and certainly raising awareness of the issues is a critical first step in changing behavior. A key Australian project provided an opportunity to develop a new generation of travel behavior change tools that relied on greater engagement with the program participants. The Travel Blending program was initially developed for the National Roads and Motorists' Association (NRMA), Australia's largest motoring membership organization, by Monash University and Steer Davies Gleave (SDG). The NRMA funded a major public initiative called "Clean Air 2000," which aimed to reduce pollution caused by car travel in Sydney prior to the year 2000 Olympics. Clean Air 2000 was a twofold initiative (Gollner, 1996), focusing on encouraging behavioral change in the way people use their cars, and progressing solutions to vehicle-induced air pollution and increasing traffic congestion. The Travel Blending program, was developed to primarily focus on the first of these aims, specifically by reducing car use. The Travel Blending approach was designed to incorporate two important components that most of the earlier travel awareness initiatives lacked. First, an objective and a method to ensure that there are behavior changes as well as awareness and attitude changes (i.e. people actually use the car less); and, second, an in-built monitoring system, to measure whether and what type of changes are actually occurring.

After the pilot study had been completed in Sydney, the Department of Transport in South Australia (Transport SA) engaged SDG to undertake a trial in Adelaide, the capital of South Australia. As the program delivery methods were further refined, SDG undertook other applications of Travel Blending in the UK (Leeds), the USA (New Jersey), and Chile. In South Australia the method has evolved to play a key component in a community development program known as Living Neighbourhoods.

In parallel with the work being undertaken in Australia, Socialdata (a German consultancy firm) was pioneering the direct marketing of public transport. That work has seen the development of a program for direct marketing of travel behavior change known as IndiMark (short for Individualized Marketing). While IndiMark originally focused on marketing of public transport, it has now evolved to encourage use of walking and cycling. IndiMark has seen application in a number of cities in Europe, and is the cornerstone of a major travel behavior change program run in Perth, Western Australia, under the banner of TravelSmart.

Australia continues to be fertile ground for the development of travel behavior change programs. The Australian Capital Territory Department of Urban Services in Canberra is currently finalizing a 300-household pilot of a behavior change program called "Way to Go." The Department of Infrastructure in Melbourne (Victoria) is in 2003 trailing an approach that builds on the strengths of both IndiMark and Travel Blending. In this program, a wide range of options for behavioral change will be offered to households, ranging from the highly detailed level of Travel Blending, specifically customized journey planners for bicycling, walking, or public transport, information on local activities for those people who would find it simplest to reduce trip length, rather than trips, and general information where no other information is applicable. Results will be available by 2004.

One other international initiative worthy of mention has developed over a similar time-frame to those mentioned above. Founded in 1989, the Global Action Plan for the Earth (www.globalactionplan.org) is a non-profit organization that promotes and supports the development of sustainable lifestyles and livable neighborhoods in communities in the USA and elsewhere through service contracts with local, state, and federal government agencies. The US program is part of a larger international effort that is operating in 17 countries with the combined participation of 150 000 people. Over the past 12 years, the Global Action Plan has developed a highly effective set of tools for behavior change and neighborhood-based community organizing. These empowerment tools have produced measurable results defined as behavior change and neighbor-to-neighbor recruitment in a wide diversity of communities – small, medium, and large, urban, suburban, and rural, in over 30 states with 30 000 people. The tools have been continually refined, and at this point could be considered state-of-the-art in community empowerment. While the Global Action Plan offers programs in saving energy and reducing waste, there is also a component for reducing the negative impacts of the car. It uses what is termed The Household EcoTeam Program, which is simple and strategic. Five or six neighborhood households – an EcoTeam – meet eight times over a 4 month period, with the help of a step-by-step workbook and a trained volunteer coach. Choosing from a series of practical actions, the team members support each other to reduce waste, use less water and energy, buy "eco-wise" products, reduce air and water pollution, and encourage other neighbors to get involved. More than increasing awareness, The Household EcoTeam Program enables people to change the way they live – measurably – and has achieved reductions of between 16 and 20% in fuel use (the measure of change in this case).

3. The nature of existing travel behavior change programs

The two best known travel behavior change programs are IndiMark and Travel Blending. Here we outline what is involved in each of these programs. Readers interested in a more comprehensive discussion of the techniques, and where they have been applied, are referred to the recent study of personal journey planning techniques released by the UK Department of Transport, Local Government and the Regions (2002).

3.1. IndiMark

IndiMark is a method for conducting direct marketing of travel behavior change. It involves targeted personal approaches to people identified as potential mode switchers with personalized information, advice, and incentives provided to encourage change (UK Department of Transport, Local Government and the Regions, 2002). IndiMark is generally used for direct marketing of public transport, but has also been applied to encourage use of walking and cycling. The method involves four stages, as summarized as in Table 1.

Table 1
Summary of the IndiMark method

Stage	Description
Contact	All households are contacted by mail and phone, and a short survey is used to determine if they are regular/extensive users of environmentally friendly modes (R), are not at all interested in changing (N), or are interested (I)
Motivation	Problems and requests from the R and I groups are responded to
Information	Information (timetables, maps etc.) is posted to the R and I participants. The R and I participants select the information they want, which is (generally) hand delivered to them within a couple of days
Convincing	Consultation phone calls and home visits on request are made, with selected households in group I receiving tickets to use on public transport for a limited period

Source: Brög and Schadler (1998).

A key step is the initial contact of all households in the target area, with that approach being made by telephone in the current program. Once the predisposition to change is assessed (via a short survey), those households that are initially assessed as being not interested in changing (the N group) are not pursued further. The focus shifts to those who are regular/extensive users of public transport, cycle, or walk (the R group), and those assessed as being interested in using those modes more (the I group). The R and I groups are either rewarded for current behavior or provided with information to assist them to change their travel behavior.

Brög and Schadler (1998) emphasize that IndiMark is built upon the belief that there is a gap between public perception of public transport and the reality, with a large proportion of the population believing it to be worse than it really is. While the processes of targeting and approaching people are generally carried out in a similar way in IndiMark demonstrations, the information, encouragement, and incentives can vary quite widely, and include:

- maps and timetables for public transport routes that are of direct relevance to an individual's needs (e.g. timetables that provide service times at individual public transport stops);
- general maps and timetables, with guidance as to the routes that are of relevance to the individual;
- free travel tickets (usually for up to 1 month) to encourage people to try out the system;
- information on other environmentally friendly modes (walking and cycling), usually in the form of general walking and cycling route maps for the area.

IndiMark has been applied in 12 European countries and in Australia, with projects ranging in size from tens to thousands of people. Its highest profile current application is linked to the TravelSmart initiative, which forms part of The Metropolitan Transport Strategy (MTS) for the Perth Metropolitan Region in Western Australia. The MTS has set a range of targets for modal shift, and TravelSmart has a key role to play in achieving those targets for reducing vehicle use while increasing the use of public transport, and walking and cycling modes. Two of the key features of TravelSmart include:

- centralized or individualized marketing, which informs people of their travel choices and encourages self-help;
- empowerment via the use of local travel surveys to inform local communities about their own travel behavior and, via community learning, to stimulate cultural change processes within the community.

The IndiMark program is the delivery mechanism for the community-based component of Western Australia's TravelSmart initiative, which is based on a number of key principles (UK Department of Transport, Local Government and the Regions, 2002):

- the aim is to inform, motivate, facilitate, and empower rather than tell or advise;
- there is an emphasis on looking at the transport system from a user's perspective rather than a transport systems/planning/logistics viewpoint;
- evaluation is based on actual behavior change rather than just raising community awareness.

3.2. Travel Blending

Travel Blending involves an in-depth analysis of people's travel behavior followed by detailed suggestions on how behavior could be modified, with follow-up monitoring and feedback (Rose and Ampt, 1997; Ampt and Rooney, 1999). The term "Travel Blending" is derived from the way individuals can reduce the use of the car by blending, or mixing, their travel choices over time. This could be through thinking about activities and travel in advance (i.e. in what order can activities be done, who should do them, where should they be done), blending modes (i.e. sometimes using the car, sometimes walking, sometimes taking public transport), or blending activities (i.e. doing as many things as possible in the same place, or on the same journey), or finally blending over time (i.e. making small sustainable changes over time on a weekly or fortnightly basis).

The Travel Blending program involves participants completing 7 day travel diaries to gain an understanding of their personal and household travel patterns.

The diaries are analyzed, and participants are provided with suggestions or tips (reflecting the types of Travel Blending options outlined above), on how individuals or households might reduce their motor vehicle use and increase the overall efficiency of their travel. These suggestions are supported by customized information (e.g. personalized bus/train or cycle journey planners – focusing on the actual journeys for which the alternative might be used, guides to local services, etc.) that assists participants in implementing the suggestions. Participants are encouraged to complete a second 7 day travel diary approximately a month after starting to make the changes so that changes can be measured and presented to them and further feedback can be provided. After the initial recruitment/engagement with the household, the program is delivered through a series of four kits, as detailed in Table 2.

Recruitment of households is usually undertaken via a face to face approach. The completion of the program requires a reasonable commitment from participants, since each diary records all travel over a 7 day period. Perhaps not surprisingly there is a drop out rate, although about two-thirds of those recruited continue to the stage of receiving feedback from the first diary. That feedback is important because it is the main mechanism to encourage behavioral change. The second diary is primarily to measure the magnitude of the changes in travel behavior. Apart from highlighting where changes have occurred, the respondents do not receive further travel change tips based on their travel activity reported in the second diary. In general, about 40% of those recruited remain in the program through to completion of the second diary (UK Department of Transport, Local Government and the Regions, 2002).

Travel Blending has seen application in 10 studies in Australia, the UK, the USA, and Chile. More recently it has evolved to play a key part in a broader community development program known as a "Living Neighbourhood." A Living Neighbourhood is one in which everyone who lives, works, plays, and goes to school in the area is offered a way to save time, money, and create a healthier, more vibrant community (Steer Davies Gleave, 1999). This is done by presenting the opportunity for everyone in the neighborhood to take part in Travel Blending.

The Travel Blending program is applied in a Living Neighbourhood project along with other complementary measures that are aimed at enabling and facilitating travel related and other community development changes in the neighborhood. The common form of these "additional measures" is to employ a person to work in the area to act as a broker, or facilitator of change. The idea behind this is that many barriers may exist to people changing their behavior, and many of these may be overcome by changes within the neighborhood, such as re-routing of bus routes. In addition to responding to resident suggestions, other measures may be introduced – depending on the initiatives of the residents. These range from "green prescriptions," where local GPs will suggest walking or cycling to improve fitness and health for those for whom it is suitable, to quite major

Table 2
Summary of the Travel Blending method

Stage	Description
Engagement and background data	Individuals, preferably all members of a household, are engaged or recruited door to door, or through schools or workplaces. Basic data on both participating and non-participating households is collected, and kit 1 is handed out
Kit 1: Getting started	The "Getting started" kit includes a letter of introduction, a "how and why" booklet (explaining negatives associated with vehicle use and introducing the Travel Blending concept), and a "before" travel diary for each household member plus aids to assist in its completion
Kit 2: Help make a difference	"Before" diaries are analyzed, and a feedback kit is provided that includes numerical details of each person's week of travel (number of trips, trips by mode, time spent travelling, number of cold starts and an indication of car emissions produced). Positive steps that people are already making are highlighted, and suggestions for reducing car travel are proposed (e.g. trip chaining for particular activities, change of mode for a particular destination). Kit 2 also includes the booklet *Thinking about Travel*
Kit 3: Are you on track?	The 3rd kit includes the "after" 7 day travel diary plus the booklet *Track Your Travel 2*, explaining the importance of completing the second set of diaries
Kit 4: Continuing to make a difference	The "after" diaries are analyzed, and a final kit is delivered that includes a summary of the travel behavior revealed in the second diary, identifies the differences between the travel behavior reported in the first and second diaries, and includes a log book to allow people to continue to monitor weekly car travel

initiatives such as the community raising money and building a community playground (to avoid traveling to a more distant one) or converting a church hall to a medical center (to allow local access to a key necessity).

4. Impacts of travel behavior change programs

The growing worldwide experience with the application of travel behavior change programs is providing valuable insight into their impacts. In this section, we consider those impacts from a variety of perspectives. At the level of the individual, it is possible to consider the types of travel behavior changes which they produce. At a macroscopic level, it is possible to measure the aggregate impacts on travel behavior. Extending that macroscopic view, the financial and economic evaluation of the programs is important.

4.1. At the level of the individual

The climate for change is produced through a variety of factors that relate to the manner in which travel behavior change programs engage individuals. This is in part because people are choosing the changes that best suit their lifestyles, rather than having them imposed by someone else (e.g. through regulatory changes). By presenting a range of options that are much broader than a simple mode change this maximizes the opportunities to change since the simple mode change option may not be a convenient or feasible option in parts of many cities or in regional areas. By broadening the context to include other aspects of individual's lives, and reflect their priorities for saving time, money, or improving the environment, people may find the motivation to change even if they are not necessarily interested in improving the environment through reducing car use. Finally, by highlighting many other benefits to the individual and society in terms of health (ranging from increased opportunities for physical activity to a reduction in social isolation), personal safety, road safety, local economic development benefits arising from greater trade through local businesses, and other benefits for an improved quality of life, the motivation for change can extend well beyond a narrow transport context.

The experience with IndiMark is that it results in increases in public transport use as well as increases in levels of cycling and walking. Travel Blending has primarily resulted in changes in the way in which individual's use their car. For example, by increasing the level of trip chaining or car pooling (sometimes related to children's weekend sporting activities) to reduce the vehicle-kilometers of travel by car. At the individual level these changes result in a reduced overall distance traveled by car, less time in the vehicle, increased public transport trips, and increases in the number of trips and travel time by active transport modes (walking and cycling).

4.2. Aggregate changes

We draw on example applications of the travel change programs to illustrate the magnitude of their aggregate impacts. While there is a good deal of variability across the methods employed and the application sites, it is fair to say that the

Table 3
Results from IndiMark application in South Perth

Performance measure		Change (%)
Trips	Car driver	−9.6
	Car passenger	+3.9
	Walking trips	+15.8
	Public transport trips	+21.4
	Bicycle trips	+91.3
	Annual total trips	0
Distance	Car travel distance	−14
Time	Total travel time	+6.9
	Time in car	−11.1

Source: Modified from UK Department of Transport, Local Government and the Regions (2002).

results are positive, with these travel behavior change programs consistently resulting in reductions in vehicle use, improvements in public transport use, and increased walking and cycling. We consider results for IndiMark first, and then turn to Travel Blending.

The South Perth application of IndiMark is the largest and most recent application of the method reported in the literature. Table 3 summarizes the results across a range of performance measures for the South Perth pilot project, which involved approaches to 383 households. The overall distance traveled by car was reduced by 14%, while trips by public transport, walking, and cycling all showed strong increases.

Another source of information in Perth was the bus patronage data collected via the electronic ticketing system. When IndiMark was rolled out in March 2000, the first month's patronage increased 21% over the same month the year before. Over the 7 months for which data are available (March to September), use increased by 26% from 1999 to 2000 (UK Department of Transport, Local Government and the Regions, 2002), with this increase attributed to IndiMark since no substantial changes were made to the bus services during that period.

In Europe, IndiMark has been applied in a variety of case studies. Overall, the increase in public transport trips averaged about 18% across 32 case study sites (UK Department of Transport, Local Government and the Regions, 2002). This figure is comparable with that for the South Perth application, although it is worth noting that the effect varied widely across the European case study sites. The UK Department of Transport, Local Government and the Regions (2002) notes that specifically in relation to the European experience:

- the responses in the Italian and German cases seemed better than in others;
- face-to-face approaches led to a 23% increase in public transport use while postal information lead to a 10% increase;
- there seemed little relationship between the level of public transport use and the degree of the change, although it was noted that the level and quality of public transport services varies across the countries, as did the general perceptions and image of the status of public transport as opposed to the car.

These results suggest that the cultural context is likely to influence the effectiveness of the technique, although another important factor is likely to be the attitudes and enthusiasm of the individuals responsible for delivering the program (UK Department of Transport, Local Government and the Regions, 2002).

Quantitative results from the first Adelaide study of Travel Blending (involving about 100 households) are summarized in Table 4. Results are reported for three key variables relating to vehicle use: the number of car driver trips per person, car driver kilometers per person, and total hours spent in the car per person. In each case, the reductions were found to be statistically significant (Rose and Ampt, 2001).

Aggregate changes in vehicle use are reported in Table 5. The reduction in car use, measured in terms of car driver trips or kilometers, is slightly over 20% for participants, compared with slightly over 10% for the population as a whole. The reductions in time spent in the car tend to be greater, at just over 25% for participants and nearly 20% for the population as a whole. While there are statistically significant reductions in all the variables directly related to total car use, there were no corresponding statistically significant increases in trips by public transport, bicycle, or walking. This suggests that respondents were using their cars more efficiently through increases in trip chaining rather than mode switching.

Similar positive results have been obtained in other applications of Travel Blending, although the reductions in car use are not always as high as those observed in the Australian applications. In the USA (New Jersey), for example, the distance traveled by car only reduced 3.1%, while it was reduced by 5% in the

Table 4
Estimates of reductions in car use for Travel Blending program participants in the Adelaide study

	Diary 1	Diary 2	Change
Car driver trips/person	14	10.80	−3.2
Car driver kilometers/person	146	114.8	−31.2
Total hours in car/person	7.2	5.3	−1.9

Table 5
Estimates of aggregate reductions in car use in the Adelaide Travel Blending study

	Change (%)
All participants	
Car driver trips	−22.7
Car driver kilometers	−21.3
Total hours in car	−26.2
Total people approached	
Car driver trips	−13.6
Car driver kilometers	−11.2
Total hours in car	−19.3

UK (Nottingham) trial (UK Department of Transport, Local Government and the Regions, 2002). A range of factors could be responsible for the variability in results achieved across countries including the underlying efficiency of car use, prevailing congestion levels, quality and extent of public transport provision, and cultural status associated with different travel modes.

4.3. Financial and economic evaluation

It is appropriate to begin the discussion of the financial and economic evaluation of these initiatives by placing their implementation costs into perspective. The implementation costs of IndiMark and Travel Blending are of a similar order of magnitude. The UK Department of Transport, Local Government and the Regions (2002) notes per household delivery costs of the order of A $75 for IndiMark and A $110 for Travel Blending. However, economies of scale exist due to fixed design and printing costs, so actual costs will depend on the scale of the application.

Financial evaluation focuses on the extent to which travel behavior change programs are able to pay for themselves through increased revenue from higher public transport use. Brög and Schadler (1999) indicate that the European experience with IndiMark translates into sufficient additional revenue in the first year to cover the costs of the program, with a surplus after 5 years exceeding two times the original costs. An analysis in Perth (Ker and James, 1999) found that the costs of applying IndiMark throughout the metropolitan area could be recovered over a 30 year time-frame under a high-benefit scenario but not under a low-benefit scenario. Ker and James do note, however, that under both scenarios, the fare revenue would be higher than that which would be obtained without IndiMark.

Beyond the issue of whether travel behavior change programs are able to cover their short-term financial costs, it is also appropriate to consider their long-term benefits and costs. Economic evaluations have been conducted for both IndiMark and Travel Blending. This work has involved quantifying both the costs of delivering these initiatives and the impacts they produce. A range of impacts were included in the analyses and quantified in monetary terms. Those positive or negative impacts, which make up the benefits of the initiatives, included changes in:

- travel time (savings or increases) for individuals or the network (congestion changes);
- vehicle-operating costs;
- fleet or staff cost or expenditures for public transport operations;
- accident and road trauma costs;
- health and fitness;
- emissions and pollution costs (air, noise, greenhouse gas emissions).

An important issue in any economic evaluation is the long-term impacts of travel behavior change programs. In the German pilot studies of IndiMark the longer-term effects were about 75% of those observed in the first year that IndiMark was rolled out (UK Department of Transport, Local Government and the Regions, 2002). Ongoing monitoring in South Perth has indicated that the changes were maintained, and in some cases improved, more than a year after the program was introduced (UK Department of Transport, Local Government and the Regions, 2002). A small-scale follow-up study of the longer-term impacts of Travel Blending, involving 21 households, was reported by Ampt and Rooney (1999). Contrary to expectations, there was a further reduction in car use, of just over a 5% decrease in distance traveled, 6 months after the initial Travel Blending program had been run. The sustainability of the vehicle use reductions was most often attributed by participants to the travel time savings which they experienced. In-depth interviews identified a number of reasons for the higher long-term reductions in vehicle use:

- The need to plan or the inertia in their previous travel behavior meant that some people could not implement the feedback suggestions within the time-frame of the original Travel Blending program; however, over a longer period they were able to implement changes that resulted in a reduction in vehicle use. The awareness generated by the program motivated people to develop other own time-saving measures that reduced car use.
- Changes in school, job, or home locations along with changes in activities reduced vehicle use.

The economic evaluation of the IndiMark program yielded a benefit:cost ratio in excess of 10:1 (Ker and James, 1999), a figure which exceeds those of investment in metropolitan road infrastructure in an Australian context. The benefit:cost ratio for Travel Blending was of the order of 6:1 (Tisato and Robinson, 1999), from which Tisato and Robinson concluded that "besides being intuitively attractive, Travel Blending appears to be economically justified, promising to deliver both private and community benefits, and potentially significant increases in social welfare." These separate economic evaluations of the IndiMark and Travel Blending initiatives suggest that investment in these travel behavior change programs yields a net community benefit.

5. What remains to be learned

One could argue that this section should be longer than the proceeding ones since there is probably more we do not know about this field than what we do know. While travel behavior change programs have been operating in different countries for a number of years, there is still much to be learned. To a large extent this is an emerging area for research rather than a mature area. Here we identify some of the unresolved issues about travel behavior change programs.

While the impacts of these programs have generally been positive in terms of reducing car use, there is also a wide range in the results across applications. This can be reflected in differences in initial uptake rates and the extent to which those recruited complete the entire program (in the case of Travel Blending). A variety of cultural factors relevant to the application context are likely to influence uptake rates as much as the manner in which the first contact is make (in person, via phone, or via mail). A better understanding of these issues would help in attempts to tailor applications to new contexts.

There is clearly a need for at least some minimum service levels to be offered by public transport, or minimum infrastructure to support walking and cycling, to ensure that participants have genuine options to driving the car. The extent to which the competitiveness of those options is influential in determining the uptake rates of the programs, and the final impacts, needs to be better understood. In part this may help to explore new application contexts where infrastructure or services are to be expanded, and a travel behavior change program may have a useful role to play in maximizing the return on that investment.

There is also scope to enhance understanding about the nature and form of the feedback that is provided in the context of Travel Blending. Some researchers have tried initiatives where respondents were provided with feedback on their travel patterns (in a manner similar in concept to Travel Blending), but the results have not all been encouraging, as highlighted by Rose's review of projects in the Netherlands (Rose, 1997) and a recent trial of feedback from an electronic diary in Newcastle in the UK (Thorpe et al., 2001). Further research on the nature of feedback, how it is delivered, and the impacts that it produces would be valuable.

Finally, a critical area for further research is the longer-term impacts of these programs. While initial indications are that the extent and form of behavioral change are maintained, the scale of follow-up studies conducted to date has been limited. There is also a need for better understanding of the nature of interventions required in subsequent years to maintain the changes in behavior. While the economic evaluations conducted to date have included assumptions about annual or regular follow-up activities, the extent and nature of that maintenance activity remains largely undefined.

6. Conclusions

The field of travel behavior change is clearly one that is generating growing international interest. Two major travel behavior change programs, IndiMark and Travel Blending, have now been applied in a number of international contexts. The results to date are encouraging, and suggest that these programs have a valuable role to play in addressing urban transport challenges.

Well-designed travel behavior change programs have demonstrated a capacity to reduce car travel distances by 10–15 percent while increasing public transport use by over 20% in the case of IndiMark in South Perth. While the impacts of these programs have generally been positive in terms of reducing car use, there is also a wide range in the results across applications. This highlights the need for further research to better understand the impact of local or cultural factors as well as to enhance understanding about the nature and form of the feedback that is provided and its impacts on the results that are achieved. Since this is still an emerging area, it is clear that the next decade is sure to see further innovation and increased understanding about the design, delivery, and impacts of travel behavior change programs.

References

Ampt, E.S. and A. Rooney (1999) *Reducing the impact of the car – a sustainable approach.* Modified version of a paper originally presented at the 1998 ATRF. Adelaide: Steer Davies Gleave.

Brög, W. and M. Schadler (1998) "Marketing in public transport is an investment, not a cost," in: *Proceedings of the 22nd Australian Transport Research Forum*. Sydney.

Brög, W. and M. Schadler (1999) "More passengers, higher profits for public transport – (im)possible expectation!?" in: *Proceedings of the 53rd UITP Congress*. Toronto.

Gollner, A. (1996) "Talking reform – shaping Sydney's transport for clean air," in: *Proceedings of the ITE Regional Conference*. Melbourne.

Hampshire County Council (1993) *HeadStart*. Winchester: Hampshire County Council.

Hertfordshire County Council (1993) *TravelWise Campaign*. Hertford: Hertfordshire County Council.

Ker, I. and B. James (1999) "Evaluating behavioural change in transport – a case study of individualised marketing in South Perth, Western Australia," in: *Proceedings of the 23rd Australasian Transport Research Forum*. ATRF.

Kuhl, J. and J. Beckmann (1994) *Volition and personality: action versus state orientation.* Gottingen: Hogrefe and Huber.

Rose, G. (1997) "Attitude and travel behaviour change using survey feedback: insight from Dutch and Australian experience," *Journal of the Eastern Asia Society for Transportation Studies*, 2:1083–1097.

Rose, G. and E.S. Ampt (1997) "Reducing car travel through an 'individual action' programme," in: *1997 Transportation Research Board Conference.* Paper. Washington, DC.

Rose, G. and E. Ampt (2001) "Travel Blending: an Australian travel awareness initiative," *Transportation Research D*, 6:95–110.

Steer Davies Gleave (1996) "A strategy for TravelWise in Leeds." Unpublished report for Leeds City Council and Metro, London.

Steer Davies Gleave (1999) *The Living Neighbourhood – final report.* Walkerville: Transport SA and Environment Australia.

Thorpe, N., J. Nelson and M. Law (2001) "Raising transport and travel awareness through feedback from an electronic travel diary," in: *Proceedings of the IATBR International Conference.* Sydney: Institute of Transport Studies.

Tisato, P. and T. Robinson (1999) "A cost benefit analysis of Travel Blending," in: *Proceedings of the 23rd Australasian Transport Research Forum*, pp. 687–701.

UK Department of Transport, Local Government and the Regions (2002) *A review of the effectiveness of personalised journey planning techniques.* London: DTLR (http://www.local-transport.dtlr.gov.uk/travelplans/pjourney/index.htm).

Wayte, A. (1991) "Road demand management," in: *Travel Demand Management Seminar.* Paper. Perth: PPK Consultants.

Chapter 42

PACKAGING POLICIES TO ADDRESS ENVIRONMENTAL CONCERNS

ERAN FEITELSON
The Hebrew University of Jerusalem

1. Introduction

Many policy measures have been advanced to address the multiple environmental externalities of transport. Almost invariably they are presented as a response to one or more of these externalities. However, as no single measure is able to address all, or even most, of them, it is clear that any strategy intended to address multiple transport externalities will need to employ many different measures. Some of these may either have synergetic effects or contradict each other. Yet, all too often policy measures are advanced and discussed in isolation.

One of the focal points of transport policy research has been on the effectiveness of various policy tools in mitigating negative transport externalities. While some of this research analyzes and compares different policy approaches, such as regulations (command and control), incentives, land use measures, or the introduction of new technologies, other studies scrutinize specific tools – such as road pricing, shared rights of way, light-rail systems, or noise barriers. Almost invariably this research shows that only rarely can a single measure address satisfactorily even a single externality. A common conclusion is thus that ancillary measures are needed.

In some cases ancillary measures are essential if the strategy is to have any effect at all. One of the most notable examples is the need to introduce unleaded fuel in lieu of the introduction of catalytic converters. In other cases, ancillary measures may not be technical requisites, but are still necessary complements. Indeed, most accounts of successes, such as Cervero's (1998) analysis of cities that have implemented successful transit systems, are accounts of successful combinations of measures. That is, combinations that address well the spatial, economic, and political particularities of the city.

However, ancillary measures are needed not only to enhance the effectiveness of the strategies proposed to address transport environmental externalities. As virtually all measures have some distributional effects, which may adversely affect

Handbook of Transport and the Environment, Edited by D.A. Hensher and K.J. Button
© 2003, Elsevier Ltd

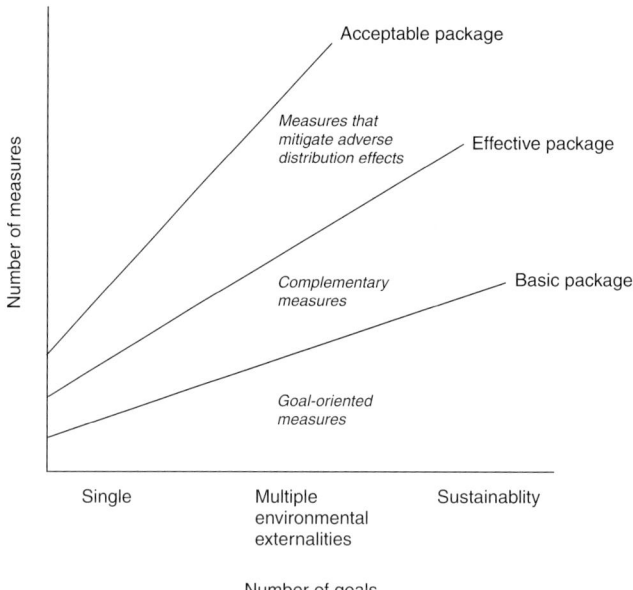

Figure 1. The number of policy measures needed to implement strategies that address transport externalities.

certain population or interest groups, successful implementation of such a strategy may be contingent upon the ability to overcome or mitigate the opposition of those adversely affected. To this end it may be necessary to introduce yet additional measures that will either mitigate the adverse effects of the strategy, or compensate those adversely affected.

Figure 1 depicts schematically the implications of the general observations made so far. It shows that in order to achieve any goal it may be necessary in practice to add to the basic measures geared to achieve this goal two complementary sets of measures, one to enhance the effectiveness of the strategy and the second to increase its acceptability. Hence, any strategy, even one aimed at achieving a single goal, requires that a number of tools be used if it is to be both effective and acceptable.

Clearly, as the number of goals or targets increases so will the number of instruments needed to address the goals effectively (though not necessarily on a one-to-one ratio). However, a larger number of instruments may also increase the number of parties and interests affected, thereby increasing the number of mitigation measures that will be needed to make the complete package acceptable. We can expect, therefore, that effective, acceptable strategies with wide and ambitious goals will comprise relatively large policy packages.

This begs the question as to how such packages can be structured in a rational way, and which considerations have to be taken into account in the delineation of such packages. The remainder of this chapter tackles these questions. In the next section the ways to identify measures that enhance effectiveness are reviewed. As the number of goals affects the complexity of the task, the section differentiates between single-goal efforts and multiple-goal strategies. This is followed by a discussion of the considerations in identification of mitigation measures that may enhance the political acceptability of policy packages. Then, timing, scale, and institutional considerations are raised in the next section. Thus, each of the sections adds to the considerations in the previous section that should be taken into account when formulating strategies to address transport externalities. The chapter ends with a brief overview of the questions that should be addressed when packaging policies into coherent strategies.

2. Generating effective packages

The primary objective of any policy is to achieve certain goals, although in some cases certain measures are advanced for their own sake (often for a private gain). In the case of negative transport externalities, the primary goal is usually to reduce these externalities. The first question facing analysts is how to do so in the most cost-effective manner.

2.1. Single-goal packages

If the strategy targets a single externality a relatively straightforward success criterion can be used. For example, if the stated goal is to reduce carbon dioxide emissions, the optional measures can be evaluated according to their likely contribution to the reduction of carbon dioxide emissions, relative to the cost of implementing them. Essentially, the greater the reduction in emissions per dollar the more a measure is seen as cost-effective.

The first two questions that any analyst proposing a strategy to reduce such an externality should ask are "Which instruments should be included?" and "How many measures should the policy package include?" Clearly, there is no single answer to these questions, as the answers will be a function of context, legal and institutional set-up, available budget, time-frame etc. However, several considerations that should be taken into account in answering these questions can be outlined.

The starting point for delineating a strategy to address a specific negative externality is a review of the measures that are deemed to be the most effective. Regrettably, there are only scant rigorous empirical analyses of many measures, and in many cases the evidence is inconclusive. A notable example is the inconclusive evidence regarding the effects of land use densities on emissions (for reviews, see Breheny, 1992; Anderson et al., 1996). Modeling studies can be used to examine the effects of policies alone or in combinations at various at city and regional levels (Wegener, 1996). They lack, however, the realism of empirical studies. Moreover, as the use of different models may lead to significant variations in results, Rodier et al. (2002) recommend that more than one model be used. However, as a modeling study can be a major undertaking, this may not be feasible in many cases, unless more than one model is readily available. The measures seen as most promising after the initial screening (regardless of the way it was conducted) constitutes the basic package noted in Figure 1.

Once the initial set of measures has been determined, the requisites for the effective use of each measure included in this basic package should be identified. The complementary measures thus identified can then to be added to the basic package. The potential impacts of the resulting more extensive package can then be assessed by running it as a full-simulation or micro-simulation model. An example of this approach the work of Wegener (1996), who identified the most effective package for the Dortmund region by running different packages of this sort as a micro-simulation model, and showed that such combinations are indeed more effective than any single measure.

However, as it is likely that many measures may increase the effectiveness of a basic package, in terms of emission reduction, it is still necessary to address the second question – "How many of these measures should be added?" To address this question it is necessary to assess the marginal cost imposed by each measure, as the criterion to add any measure is whether the total marginal benefit from its addition exceeds the total marginal cost.

The total marginal benefit is a function of its net effects on reduction of emissions (or exposure). These will be the difference between the total reduction in emissions with and without this measure. Ideally, these differences will be valued in monetary terms. As there are synergetic effects between measures it is indeed necessary to assess the difference in total reductions and not only the direct contribution of the additional measure.

The costs of adding a measure are the sum of its direct, indirect, and transaction costs. The direct cost includes the outlays that are needed to implement the measure. These costs are likely to be a function of the extent and cost of the physical infrastructure needed to implement the measure. However, revenues that some measures may generate can mitigate these costs. Examples of the diverse possible revenue-generating measures include new public transport services and various fees or taxes. The indirect costs are the external costs that the measure may impose on other sectors of the economy. For example, development restrictions intended to enhance the attractiveness of public transport are likely to raise land values and reduce the location options for firms and households, thus potentially adversely affecting their profitability or households' utility. Yet, these are not usually captured in analyses of such measures. Transaction costs are a function of the potential opposition to the measure and institutional setup, issues picked up in later sections.

In practice it may be possible in many cases to assess only the net direct costs in monetary terms. Even these are often subject to uncertainty, due to the stochasticity of the revenues (where they are expected to offset costs) and the inaccuracy of outlay forecasts. Benefits may be even more uncertain, as they are often derived from scenario analyses, where there is substantial uncertainty regarding the elements of these scenarios. Thus, sensitivity analyses to test for the implications of these uncertainties are recommended.

2.2. Multiple-goal policy packages

All modes of transportation generate multiple externalities, as is obvious from this volume. Hence, in many cases strategies are designed to address several externalities concurrently. In some cases the same tool can address several externalities. For example, electric cars reduce emissions of air pollutants, carbon dioxide, and noise. Yet, once the single-scenario objective is abandoned, it is necessary also to consider the externalities generated by use of the measures proposed. To continue the electric car example – an increase in battery replacements is likely to create a hazardous waste problem (Lave et al., 2000). Hence, once the analyst considers the multiple-goal scenario the complexity of the task rises exponentially.

In considering the potential of a specific measure when formulating a multiple-measure strategy it is necessary to differentiate between two situations. The first is when the measure may advance one of the goals but will not detract from any of the other goals. This potential pareto-optimal improvement indicates that the policy package being considered is unlikely to be implemented (commensurate with the production likelihood curve of a firm). In such a situation the analysis of the measure is no different than in the single-goal case. That is, its marginal net benefit (reduction of an externality) needs to be compared only with its marginal cost.

The second situation is when a measure being considered to address one or more externalities will have adverse external effects on another goal. In such a situation the advancement of one or more goals by incorporating this measure may thus detract from another goal. Hence, it is necessary to evaluate the measure considered according to its contribution to or detraction from several goals. To do so it is necessary to assess not only the effects of the measure but also the relative importance that is attributed to the different goals. Moreover, as the different goals may have different distribution effects the identity of those affected in each case has to be identified too.

There are two basic approaches to analyses of multiple-goal problems. The first strives to find an index that will allow for a comparison of the goals along a single dimension. Many techniques have been advanced to assess the relative importance of goals that cannot be valued in monetary terms along a single non-monetary dimension. The most straightforward techniques simply require stakeholders to rate the different goals on an ordinal scale. These are often used as a basis for weighting the evaluation criteria in the evaluation stage in the planning process. Other techniques require stakeholders to rank or compare different goals. Saaty (1980), for example, advances a widely used method to systematically prioritize goals through pairwise comparisons. Essentially, a survey is conducted among relevant stakeholders in which they are asked to compare on a scale each set of two goals. Using an eigenvalue approach (not detailed here) to these pairwise comparisons permits calibration of a numerical scale, and hence allows us to prioritize the goals, even when quantitative comparisons of the goals are very problematic. The resulting hierarchy of goals can then be used to weight the different goals. However, all these techniques are limited by their reliance on the participation of stakeholders, which requires all stakeholders to be identified, and by their underlying assumptions regarding the stability of stakeholders' preferences and the ability of stakeholders to obtain, comprehend, and assess all the necessary information (Glasser, 1998).

The second approach does not attempt to reduce all goals and effects into a single dimension. Rather, it argues, that as the choice of any strategy is a political decision, analysts should only identify the implications of various measures for the different goals and different groups of stakeholders, and leave the value-driven weighting of the various considerations to decision-makers. This approach is, perhaps, best exemplified by Lichfield's (1996) community impact evaluation, where all likely effects are meticulously recorded and assessed but are presented as an input to public debate.

3. Politically acceptable packages

In democratic societies the decision to undertake action to mitigate the environmental externalities of transport, at any level (local, regional, or national), is ultimately a political one. Essentially, policies are molded within organizational and institutional constraints, and have to be deemed by those making the decisions as being politically feasible (Majone, 1989). It is for this reason that recent texts regarding transport policy formulation emphasize the need to take political and institutional factors into consideration at an early stage (e.g. Vigar, 2002).

In order to identify the set of potential measures that are deemed to be politically feasible (the political feasibility set) it is necessary to identify the institutional and political constraints on policies. Many of these can be viewed as self-imposed, and hence can arguably be overcome in time (Majone, 1989). In other words, the political feasibility set may shift over time, not least if there is an explicit effort to do so. Yet, such a shift requires a relatively long period of time, as Vigar (2002) shows for the UK case. Thus, institutional structures and perceptions regarding the support or opposition to a measure should be viewed as a constraint, at least in the short and medium term.

Most decisions are not made at one point in time, by a single coherent set of "decision-makers." Rather, they are an outcome of protracted processes that involve many groups. Failure to recognize the multiplicity of actors and the complex interplay between technical rationality and power may often lead to a policy impasse, delays, and fundamental restructuring of the strategy, as Flybjerg (1998) vividly describes for the highly regarded Aalborg project – an award-winning scheme promoted by the Organisation for Economic Development and Co-operation as a model on how to deal with the cars in cities by integrating environmental and social concerns in city plans. Hence, in order for a strategy to be seen as politically feasible it has to address the concerns of not only those with formal decision-making power but also those of various interest and citizen groups.

Feitelson and Salomon (2003) advance a political economy framework for analyzing the adoption of transport innovations. They suggest that any transport innovation (including a policy innovation) is likely to be adopted only if it is perceived to be technically, economically, socially, and politically feasible. That is, in addition to the strategy being technically and economically viable it has to be able to garner the support of, or at least avoid the opposition of, voters (social feasibility), and of the pertinent interest groups. The likelihood that a policy or strategy will be implemented is thus a function of the composition and strength of the supporting and opposing coalitions to it.

The implication of these insights for formulating strategies to address transport externalities is that it is insufficient to simply advance a technically viable cost-effective policy package. Rather, it is necessary to analyze the distributional implications of the various policy tools included in the package, and particularly the interest groups adversely affected. These issues have been widely discussed for the case of road pricing (Jones, 1998; Rietveld and Verhoef, 1998). However, the need to recognize and address the distributional implications is pertinent to other measures as well.

Once the distributional effects are recognized, it is advisable to identify steps that may ameliorate the effects that generate the opposition. These may be in several non-exclusive directions. The first option is to eliminate certain measures from the proposed package, if these measures are seen to generate widespread powerful opposition, and to substitute for these measures with other actions that are likely to induce lesser opposition. The second option is to introduce additional measures that will essentially compensate the adversely affected parties (or part of them), so as to weaken the likely opposition. These are the measures noted in Figure 1 as the measures intended to mitigate adverse distribution effects. The resulting policy package is the "acceptable package" shown in the figure. It should be noted, however, that different measures aimed to address the same distributional effect may be perceived differently. Specifically, Oberholzer-Gee and Weck-Hannemann (2002) suggest that measures that are seen to compensate those affected along the same dimension of the effect, or seen to compensate for environmentally friendly behavior (such as using public transport or non-motorized means), are more favorably received than measures that are seen to "bribe" those adversely affected. A third direction may be to undertake actions that will affect public opinion so as to modify the perceived feasibility set either by modifying the institutional constraints or by changing public and decision-makers' attitudes toward specific measures. Yet, this direction is likely to require a longer time-frame than the previous two, and thus can be considered only as a long-term addendum to the previous approaches, and not as an alternative to them.

Clearly, the actual measures that will be needed in any particular case are context specific, as they will need to address the concerns of particular players – those who have a stake in the specific measure in a specific context. Thus, the formulation of acceptable policy packages, by necessity, will always retain the nature of a craft, whereby there is a need to combine specific knowledge regarding the local power structures, perceptions, and desires of the various pertinent advocacy groups with analyses and forecasts regarding the efficiency and distributional effects of the various measures considered. Only by combining these two types of information can the appropriate ameliorative measures be identified and added to the policy package, or the most offensive measures be detracted and substituted for.

4. Institutional, temporal and spatial considerations

The various negative environmental externalities of transport are apparent at different scales, and have differential implications over time. While some externalities are largely local and ephemeral (noise being the most obvious case), others are widespread and have long-term effects (carbon dioxide being a widely discussed case). Moreover, the contribution to the different externalities varies across mode and the severity of most externalities (carbon dioxide excepted) varies across space. Not surprisingly, the instruments that may be used to mitigate such diverse externalities have different time horizons and spatial scope, and are likely to be within the purview of different jurisdictions or agencies. This has important implications for policy packaging.

4.1. Spatial scale and time horizons

The measures that can be used to address transport environmental externalities differ not only in terms of the activities they target, and hence the externalities they affect, and their perceived effectiveness, but also in terms of the time that is likely to pass before they have an effect, and the spatial scale at which they are pertinent.

The time-frame for considering the use of any measure is actually composed of three elements: the time needed to enact the measure, the time needed for the implementation of the measure once it has been decreed, and the time needed for the relevant market segments to react to the measure.

The time needed to enact a measure is a function of the legal processes that have to be undertaken before a measure is promulgated. In some cases a simple administrative decision may suffice. In many cases the enactment of a measure is contingent upon the completion and ratification of plans. In other cases by-laws or existing legislation have to be modified, requiring the approval of legislatures. More rarely, new major legislation will have to be implemented. Obviously, procedures requiring legislation can be expected to take a substantially longer period of time to be enacted than those that can be adopted under existing procedures and rules. Clearly, the actual time such procedures would take is a function of the political acceptability of the measures proposed.

For some measures the time needed to implement them, once they have been adopted, can be very short. Raising gasoline tax rates is an example of such a case. However, in many other cases this time can be substantial. In certain cases, such as when a new rail system is decided upon, this time period may last for many years. Overall, this time period is expected to be a function of transaction costs, which in turn are a function of the inter-agency coordination required, the extent to which new infrastructure is needed, the level of funds needed, and the ability of the agency promoting the measure to secure these funds. This, in turn, is a function of the importance of this issue in the national agenda, and the extent to which there is opposition to the implementation of the proposed measure.

The time necessary for a measure to have an effect, once implemented, is a function of the time necessary for the affected players to react. Thus, while drivers can react relatively fast to changes in parking availability or fees, the reaction of developers to growth controls is measured in years, and thus a significant effect on urban densities or development patterns may be measured in decades (this time period is affected by the rate of development relative to the existing built stock,

Table 1
Minimal time-scales necessary and spatial levels for enactment of selected measures

Spatial level	Short-term measures (up to 5 years)	Medium-term measures	Long-term measures
Local and urban	Parking fees or limitation; shifts of bases to alternative fuels; traffic calming; cycling paths	Quiet pavements pedestrianization schemes; light rail	
Metropolitan areas	Car and van pooling; Improved information systems	Coordination of public transport systems	Change in urban form coordinate and use with public transport systems; metro systems
National/state level	Gasoline taxes Company car tax	Improved vehicle anti-pollution technology	Introduction of alternative-fuel vehicles

and thus will be slower in developed countries with a stable population than in fast-growing areas).

Measures also differ according to the spatial scale at which they are effective. Some measures, such as gasoline taxes or requirements for low-emission vehicles, can only be effective at the state level. Other measures, such as parking policies or traffic calming, can be implemented at the local level in a relatively wide variety of settings.

Feitelson et al. (2001) suggest, therefore, that comprehensive policy packages for addressing transport environmental externalities should explicitly define the spatial scale for which they are advanced, and include measures with different time horizons. To this end they identify the likely time horizon of different measures and the minimal spatial scale at which they are likely to be effective, as summarized in Table 1.

4.2. Institutional aspects

The ability to implement measures is constrained by legal and institutional structures, as these determine who has the authority to implement different measures and the procedures that are necessary to do so. Thus, in formulating a strategy to address negative transport externalities it is necessary to recognize the procedures needed to enact the different measures that are proposed as part of the strategy, and the actors that need to be involved.

Given the multiple number of modes and externalities, transport–environment interfaces are usually governed by many agencies. In reviewing transport policies in seven western European and North American countries, as well as in Eastern Europe, Pucher and Lefevre (1996) conclude that one of the main impediments to improvements is the institutional fragmentation of transport policy issues, particularly in metropolitan areas. Yet, even if comprehensive metropolitan transport agencies are established with authority over all modes, it is likely that many of the environmental externalities will be governed by additional agencies (such as environmental agencies at different levels). The agencies that affect transport–environment interfaces can, generally, be divided into two groups. The first are those agencies for which these interfaces are an integral part of their mission. These agencies are likely to take an active interest in any strategy geared to address such issues. However, their readiness to cooperate over these issues may be affected by the institutional culture and the history of inter-agency relations. The second group consists of agencies that have the authority to enact relevant measures, but whose main mission does not include transport–environment interfaces. In this case, the agencies may affect these interfaces by the way, using Dery's (1999) terminology. For example, the Israeli treasury determines the level of vehicle taxes on the basis of macro-economic considerations, without any regard to their implications for transport–environment interfaces (Cohen, 1998). In this case, incorporating such measures into a policy package may prove useless, unless these agencies are somehow convinced to widen their scope of considerations to include such interfaces.

A second type of institutional constraints pertains to level of governance. The authority to enact various measures is given in different countries to different levels of government, not least as a function of the degree to which state governance is centralized. This division of power does affect the potential effectiveness of various measures, as many measures may prove ineffectual if enacted over a limited area, such as the area contained within the boundaries of a local jurisdiction. Unless the authority for enactment of the various measures, such as those noted in Table 1, conforms more or less to the spatial level at which they are likely to be effective, their use may not assure the desired outcome.

Most of the discussion regarding level of governance pertains to the intra-national sphere. However, the supra-national sphere is becoming increasingly relevant in this case. This is obvious for international traffic, and particularly for modes where this traffic is a large proportion of the total traffic (such as in air transport). In such cases, international agreements may both constrain the use of various measures, or make the enactment of them an imperative. For example, international agreements may constrain the ability to enact certain restrictions, while requiring that other actions be undertaken.

A third type of institutional constraint pertains to the role of private enterprises. In recent years one of the main issues in transport policy analyses has been that of privatization. Privatization, essentially, consists of agreements that allow private enterprises to operate parts of a transport system. These agreements impose certain obligations both on the operators and on the state. While in such agreements the operators may be required to meet certain environmental criteria, the agreements may also limit the ability of the state to impose new or different restrictions over time, thus effectively limiting the scope of measures that can be included in a policy package.

5. Conclusions

The need to formulate long-range comprehensive strategies to address the multiple environmental externalities of transport is widely recognized. However, the question of how coherent strategies should be formulated from individual measures has received only scant attention to date. In this chapter an attempt has made to highlight the issues involved.

It is suggested that after identifying the goals a strategy will want to achieve analysts should ask several leading questions at the outset. These are:

- Which measures are the most promising for achieving the stated goals?
- What are the prerequisites and necessary complements to these promising measures?
- What are the distributional implications of the measures considered? Who is likely to be adversely affected? Are there citizen or interest groups that are likely to oppose any measure?
- Should any measures be dropped in order to reduce the opposition to the strategy? Can they be substituted for?
- Are there additional measures that may help reduce the opposition to the proposed strategy?
- Who has the authority to enact the different measures considered? Are they party to the strategy? If not, what can be done to bring them on board?
- What is the expected time-frame for reaching decisions? And for acting upon them? And for results to be apparent?

Answering these questions will clearly not provide a blueprint for policy packaging. However, answering these questions can assist in packaging policies into coherent strategies. While using this background to package policies will not assure that the strategy will be accepted and implemented, it can be hoped that advancing a strategy with implementation in mind, on the basis of the answers to these questions, will increase the likelihood that it will indeed be implemented. Yet, the tailoring of the answers received in any local circumstance requires significant knowledge of local power structures and concerns, and hence the real test will be to what extent can analysts address the issues raised in this chapter in different contexts.

References

Anderson, W.P., P.S. Kanaroglou and E.J. Miller (1996) "Urban form energy and the environment: a review of issues evidence and policy," *Urban Studies*, 33:7–35.
Breheny, M.J. (1992) "The contradictions of the compact cities: a review," in: M.J. Breheny, ed., *Sustainable development and urban form*. London: Pion.
Cervero, R. (1998) *The transit metropolis*. Washington, DC: Island Press.
Cohen, G. (1998) "Transport policy as a residual policy: the impact of the Ministry of Finance on ownership and use of private vehicles," Unpublished MA Thesis. Jerusalem: The Hebrew University of Jerusalem.
Dery, D. (1999) "Policy 'by the way': or when policy is incidental to making other policies," *Journal of Public Policy*, 18:163–176.
Feitelson, E. and I. Salomon (2003) "The political economy of transport innovations," in: M. Beuthe, V. Himanen and A. Reggiani, eds, *Transport demand and organisation in an evolving world*. Berlin: Springer-Verlag.
Feitelson, E., I. Salomon and G. Cohen (2001) "From policy measures to policy packages: a spatially, temporally and institutionally differentiated approach," in: E. Feitelson and E. Verhoef, eds, *Transport and environment: in search of sustainable solutions*. Cheltenham: Edward Elgar.
Flyvbjerg, B. (1998) *Rationality and power: democracy in practice*. Chicago: The University of Chicago Press.
Glasser, H. (1998) "On the evaluation of "wicked problems"," in: N. Lichfield, A. Barbanente, D. Bori, A. Khakee and A. Prat, eds, *Evaluation in planning: facing the challenge of complexity*. Dordrecht: Kluwer.
Jones, P. (1998) "Urban road pricing: public acceptability and barriers to implementation," in: K.J. Button and E.T. Verhoef, eds, *Road pricing, traffic congestion and the environment*. Cheltenham: Edward Elgar.
Lave, L., H. Maclean, C. Hendrickson and R. Lankey (2000) "Life-cycle analysis of alternative fuel/propulsion technologies," *Environmental Science and Technology*, 34:3598–3605.
Lichfield, N. (1996) *Community impact evaluation*. London: UCL Press.
Majone, G. (1989) *Evidence, argument and persuasion in the policy process*. New Haven: Yale University Press.
Oberholzer-Gee, F. and H. Weck-Hannemann (2002) "Pricing road use: politico-economic and fairness considerations," *Transportation Research D*, 7:357–371.
Pucher, J. and C. Lefevre (1996) *The urban transport crisis in Europe and North America*. London: Macmillan.
Rietveld, P. and E. Verhoef (1998) "Social feasibility of policies to reduce externalities in transport," in: K.J. Button and E.T. Verhoef, eds, *Road pricing, traffic congestion and the environment*. Cheltenham: Edward Elgar.
Rodier, C.J., R.A. Johnston and J.E. Abrahams (2002) "Heuristic policy analysis of regional land use, transit, and travel pricing scenarios using two urban models," *Transportation Research D*, 7:243–254.
Saaty, T. (1980) *The analytic hierarchy process*. New York: McGraw-Hill.
Vigar, G. (2002) *The politics of mobility: transport, the environment and public policy*. London: Spon.
Wegener, M. (1996) "Reducing CO_2 emissions of transport by reorganisation of urban activities," in: Y. Hayashi and J. Roy, eds, *Transport, land-use and the environment*. Dordrecht: Kluwer.

Chapter 43

THE STREET: INTEGRATING TRANSPORT AND URBAN ENVIRONMENT

STEPHEN MARSHALL
University College London

1. Introduction

The street is much more than an urban road. The street essentially embodies three dimensions in a single package: the street as a transport route, or artery for through movement; the street as a public space, where a variety of human activities take place; and the street as a built frontage. The street therefore combines the linear sense of the "link" in a traffic network diagram, the planar "place" or "square" of civic life, and the sense of the three-dimensional "building block" of urban form. Therefore, although the traffic engineer or transport planner may often loosely equate a street with being a road in an urban context – with certain connotations of access function, pedestrian presence, congestion and so on – the street does have these other urban dimensions that both affect the character and performance of the transport dimension of the street, and which ultimately give the street its purpose.

As a combined transport and urban package, the street has sometimes been considered at best a messy compromise, or at worst, a dysfunctional or even obsolete form. The more extreme functionalist versions of modernist urban and transport planning envisaged cities without streets – the circulation, public space, and buildings could be more or less designed and optimized as separate systems, with discrete buildings or building complexes set in open space served by free-flowing highways (Gold, 1998; Dunnett, 2000).

However, in recent decades there has been a progressive rehabilitation and renaissance of the street, both in principle and in practice. Streets are now recognized as forming part of the essential connective fabric of public space in settlements from rural villages to cities. The street is an important integrating component, acting not only as a physical movement channel and built form but also as a public space, a place of cultural identity, setting for social and economic activity, and indeed contributor to urban equity and sustainability. In turn, street management and design have emerged as a multidisciplinary pursuits, cutting

Handbook of Transport and the Environment, Edited by D.A. Hensher and K.J. Button
© 2003, Elsevier Ltd

across a range of urban transport and environmental issues. Streets may be analyzed from a variety of historical, anthropological, sociological, and cultural perspectives (Anderson, 1978; Moudon, 1987; Fyfe, 1998; Gehl, 1998), from urban design perspectives (Moughtin, 1992; Jacobs, 1993; Southworth and Ben Joseph, 1997; Jacobs et al., 2002), and from the perspective of sustainability (Jefferson et al., 2001).

Yet the street is fundamentally a means of organizing activities around a pattern of circulation. Besides all else, a street is a transport-oriented urban form. Therefore, although a wide variety of professions and people will have an interest and stake in the design and management of streets, the transport planner and engineer will play a central role.

This chapter discusses streets as multifunctional urban spaces that provide for a variety of modes of movement, access, and other urban uses. It "unpacks" the activities of the street, and discusses the implications for management of streets in terms of provision and prioritization of different street users and street types, and suggests an interpretation of the "sustainable street." This is intended to assist consideration of how the transport role of the street may be integrated within its wider urban and environmental context.

2. The street as a microcosm

Starting with its role as an urban road, the street can be regarded as a multi-modal traffic and transport package, catering for a diversity of kinds of movement. The street accommodates through trips and terminating trips, parking and servicing activities, and a variety of transport modes from street-running trams through to vehicular traffic to pedestrians.

Dominant among these forms of movement are motor vehicles of many varieties – cars, buses, and goods vehicles of various kinds, all of which have to be considered and provided for. If we look more closely, we may also recognize a range of types of non-motorized traffic that may, to a greater or lesser extent, use streets. This may include a variety of forms of human-powered locomotion – notably bicycles, but also anything from rollerblades to rickshaws, and to which we might also add children's buggies and scooters. A further class present in some cities is that of vehicles drawn by animals of various kinds. All these vehicular forms of movement vie for space and priority on the street. Some will be more significant than others in terms of demand, and some will be more "recognized" and "provided for" than others.

In addition to vehicular movement, walking has become more recognized and promoted as a mode of transport (Hillman and Whalley, 1979). Of course, walking is much more than a mode of transport. People on the street are more than just pedestrians – units of movement in transit. We can "unpack" the pedestrian mode into a variety of categories of people: window shoppers, sightseers, idlers, strollers, joggers, demonstrators, to name but a few, all of whom have a "journey purpose" that is slightly wider than simply getting from A to B.

Indeed, consideration of the pedestrian opens up a whole new dimension of uses of the street by people. The street is a microcosm of society – perhaps more so even than it is a microcosm of the transport sphere. The street is an urban place, and in different contexts may be the locus for many "land uses": cooking, eating, sleeping, selling, soliciting, making and mending, meeting, demonstrating, observing, entertaining, playing games, etc. The street is a social space, a place for interaction and communication, a political forum, a place of urban "theatre" or spectacle. The street may be an escape from home, or become "home for the homeless." The street has been interpreted as a smellscape, soundscape, and foodscape, a place of desire and dread (Fyfe, 1998).

Much more than an urban road, then, the street can be seen as a vessel for communal and cultural life. A resource space where all sorts of people eke out a livelihood (and even where street animals forage for food), the street can be seen as an "environment" in its own right – a human-wrought habitat – in which transport is at the same time but a single component and yet an integral, formative part.

The street can also be seen as a microcosm of "the" environment, in which a number of ecological and societal issues are played out. The sight and smell of exhaust fumes pumping out of vehicles into the breathing space of pedestrians is a very tangible reminder of what is happening on a wider scale. It reminds us of the need to tackle the issue of who is doing the polluting and who is getting polluted (see Chapter 32). The contrast of the enabled motorist and the beleaguered pedestrian reminds us of the trade-off between the convenience of the affluent and those with access to technology, and the health and welfare of those without. The allocation of space to the one rather than the other is not a trivial nor merely a technical task.

The need for and rights to the use of space is also seen in the trade-off between the needs of individuals who are dependent on a specific locality for their livelihood, and the footloose who are just passing through. This applies whether we are referring to contested street space in a city or the control or consumption of land and resources in the wider or global context. On the other hand, the local versus the general is also manifested in the trade-off between individual needs attached to a specific locale and the common good of everyone else. Without collective investment in through routes that allow communication of people, goods, and ideas, everyone would be worse off.

3. Recognition and prioritization of street users

All these people, activities, and issues can be seen to pertain to the environment of the street. The street is used and shared by "everyone," and so is only "owned" by a planning or highway authority in a limited sense. Therefore, although management of the street is typically entrusted to engineers and other transport professionals, street management is not just about the "hardware" – of infrastructure, of vehicles, or even of pedestrians as physical units of movement. It must also take account of the "software" – of people and their social, cultural, political, and economic activities.

In general, design and planning will tend to prioritize those classes of traffic, people, or uses that are officially recognized and recorded in surveys and data sets. If a particular mode of movement is not recognized, it is unlikely to be catered for; it may be ignored, marginalized, or even discriminated against.

A problem with street management in the past has been the lack of recognition and lack of priority to certain uses and users of the street. Conventionally, there has perhaps been something of a bias toward the transport function, and in particular to motorized traffic. That is, space would be given over to motor traffic in the interests of efficiency and safety. Other uses and users would be marginalized – often literally, as slower modes such pedestrians would be discouraged or physically prevented from using the major central portion of the street space.

Many kinds of movement and other activities would be ignored in conventional transportation surveys, because they did not fit with the perceived overriding function of streets as channels for traffic. For example, a variety of awkward or unconventional modes, and in some cases any kind of pedestrian activity, might be ignored altogether. Yet, if we only see transport in terms of vehicles, or people on the streets as "pedestrians" (without recognizing other activities or behavior), the street will not fulfil its full potential.

Street management effectively involves, first, recognition of street uses and users and, secondly, prioritization of certain uses or users, followed by provision for them. Here, it is suggested that a holistic form of street management would recognize uses and users both in terms of movement (vehicles and pedestrians) and people undertaking other activities.

3.1. Recognition

The more types of vehicle, people, and activities that are recognized, the more they may be assessed in terms of priority and provision. This recognition applies from initial planning and surveying through to final design and management. What and whom are surveyed will be important in this respect.

As far as transport modes are concerned, this means having to consider two-wheeled, non-motorized, and any unconventional modes of transport. For example, Table 1 gives a suggestion for the recognition of a variety of types of movement. This is deliberately weighted toward non-motorized modes to demonstrate how the impression of importance of categories may be reflected in

Table 1
Possible spectrum for recognition of street modes/users

Class	Mode or user
Pedestrians	Pedestrian
Vehicles ridden and/or propelled by people	Pram/baby buggy
	Child's pedal car
	Child's scooter
	Shopping trolley
	Handcart
	Rickshaw
	Skateboard
	Roller skates
	Roller blades
	Wheelchair
	Bicycle
Vehicles propelled by animal traction	Horse-drawn vehicle
	Donkey cart
	Ox cart
Motor vehicles	Public transport vehicles
	Goods vehicles
	Others

the way these are recorded. In a sense, the degree of resolution of the classification system tells us something of the priority. Conventional systems may differentiate several classes of goods vehicle by axle weight and formation – important for design and construction of roads – but conventionally many have lumped all non-motor traffic together or left those modes out altogether.

Therefore, while provision for pedestrians and cyclists and wheelchair users is typically accounted for, there are still a variety of modes that in any particular context may be ignored or penalized. For example, roller bladers, skateboarders, or animal-hauled vehicles may not fit in the scheme of things and may have "nowhere to go," squeezed out of both vehicular and pedestrian-designated spaces. Whatever their merits, their viability may effectively be ruled out from the outset, if they are not even recognized as potential transport modes. To the extent that they do exist as transport modes, they effectively do so despite the system.

Having recognized walking as a mode of transport, we may further open up the pedestrian dimension. For the pedestrian, a variety of activities will take place that are not simply through movement from A to B. People themselves may be "classified" and differentiated according to recognizable types or behaviors (Figure 1). All of these activities might have to be considered in terms of possible design and planning.

Figure 1 is arranged loosely as a "transport" axis (typically the sphere of influence of transport planners and traffic engineers) and a "people" axis (typically

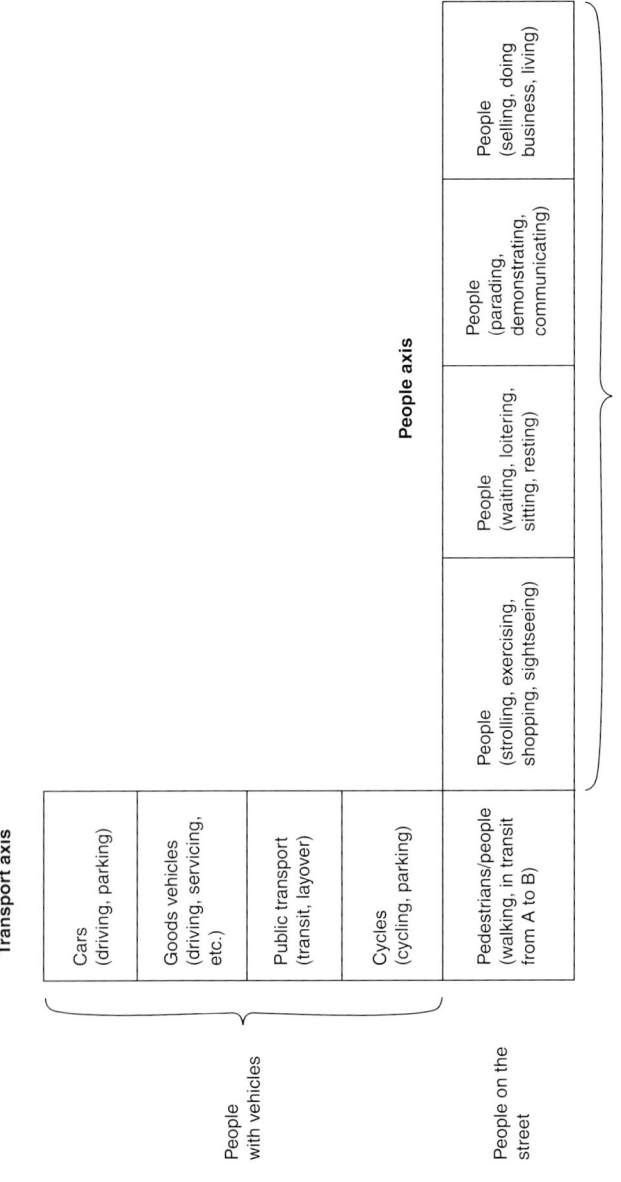

Figure 1. Competing users and uses: transport modes and people activities.

the activities of interest to urban planners and designers, also social scientists and economists). While some activities of "people on the street" have their vehicular equivalents (e.g. vehicular passage for demonstration or "cruising"), these are primarily activities undertaken on foot. The significance of the pedestrian at the conjunction of both "transport" and "people" axes is apparent.

Recognition of the pedestrian will involve consideration at the survey and data collection stages of planning for streets. This will imply different kinds of surveys of activities. Also, while conventional traffic surveys may focus on peak periods, critical conditions for design for street activities may include lunchtime periods and night-time periods. Some environments may be hostile and deter walking or use of public transport (requiring walking and waiting on-street) – their attractiveness will depend on the activities that take place there, often related to adjoining land uses, and not just the infrastructure provision.

3.2. Prioritization

It has been observed that there may be a "natural" priority of user where the largest, fastest or most numerous road user takes priority over other road users (Transport Research Laboratory, 1997). This point has been made in the context of streets in developing cities, but could apply to some extent in any street situation, at least in the absence of some distinct form of management or formal prioritization.

A hierarchy of users can be set out to identify and target reallocation of road space toward "deserving" users. In the context of streets we can distinguish types of user not by class of person as such, but by activities or specifically by mode of movement. The more "deserving" cases would typically be decided according to criteria such as basic need, equity, efficiency, or environmental friendliness.

A variety of kinds of user hierarchy are possible; for example (Institution of Highways and Transportation, 1997):

- emergency services;
- pedestrians;
- disabled people;
- cyclists;
- public transport users;
- drivers of delivery vehicles;
- public utility operators;
- taxis;
- private cars.

Having a set or hierarchy of users explicitly in mind may be a useful starting point in principle, but needs to be backed by effective organization and measures on the ground to make it work.

The significance of a hierarchy nominally promoting the pedestrian over the car must be interpreted in the context of the default convention that vehicles have (or take) priority over pedestrians. That is, in general and unless specifically directed by signage or physical construction, the assumption is that vehicles have right of way, and pedestrians are not at liberty to use the full carriageway width as they please. (The existence of the term "jaywalking" – in some circumstances a punishable offence – demonstrates the inherent presumption of priority to vehicles over pedestrians, unless otherwise directed.)

Therefore, the user hierarchy above may only really be applicable in limited circumstances, such as particular streets or parts of streets. In other words, in some streets, pedestrians will have priority over vehicles, or in some parts of the carriageway, buses may have priority to exclusion of other motor vehicles. These measures may be complemented elsewhere by having separate routes reserved for vehicular or motor vehicular traffic (although these imply urban roads rather than streets). In effect, although streets may be multifunctional in principle, not every street is suitable for accommodating all types of function.

3.3. Provision of road space

There are a number of trade-offs in terms of different competing uses and users of streets. These are often played out in terms of provision of space, for example:

- space for through movement of people and vehicles;
- allocation of carriageway space between different kinds of vehicles;
- space for stationary vehicles (parking and loading);
- space (and time allocation) for crossing traffic and pedestrians;
- circulation and occupation space for pedestrians;
- space for street furniture, planting, etc.

Allocation of road space provision to favor specific modes of movement might include:

- bus lanes;
- cycle lanes;
- reclaiming part of the carriageway as a footway (build-outs, footway widening) or for pedestrian priority (shared surface areas, footway cross-overs).

Provision of road space for different users is a well-established practice, and comprehensive guidance is available. For example, in the UK, a range of transport and street provision issues are brought together in the manual *Transport in the Urban Environment* (Institution of Highways and Transportation, 1997). Guidance is also available on specific issues such as traffic calming (e.g. Devon County Council, 1992; Hass-Klau et al., 1992; County Surveyors Society et al.,

1994) and other approaches to traffic and street management (e.g. Westerman, 1993; Brindle, 1996a; Button and Hensher, 2001).

3.4. Provision for people

Rapoport (1987) has asserted that "cultural variables are primary for any activity, including walking and others, occurring in streets .... *Thus, the use of streets by pedestrians is primarily culturally based*" [emphasis added]. This is quite a remarkable statement, at least for transport planners, more familiar with dealing with walking in terms of trip generation and the value of time.

In conventional urban road design, the pedestrian has often been considered, certainly, but often in terms of being just another transport mode to be accommodated. Just as engineering would deal with "design loads" and "design vehicles," so the pedestrian would just become another design unit. The pedestrian became the "human vehicle" – a physical unit of movement with certain characteristics of size, weight, speed, acceleration, and maneuverability that could all be "designed for" (perhaps with a built-in time-cost-minimizing algorithm, to help explain their pattern of travel).

The very flexibility of this "human vehicle" – at least in locomotive terms – may even have turned out to be a disadvantage, as it allowed the pedestrian to be squeezed: into small, narrow confines, with steep gradients or steps, sharp changes in direction, and constricted sightlines. The "functional" design for the "human vehicle" could enable the creation of the very cramped pavements, blind passages, and tiring, and tiresome, ramps that would act as deterrent to use by real pedestrians in practice.

This deficiency arises because regarding the pedestrian in purely locomotive terms misses out a great breadth of factors that influence the use and attractiveness of walking, including walking as a means of transport but also the wider human experience of being a pedestrian. To design and cater adequately for the pedestrian is therefore not merely an issue of widths and movements traditionally dealt with in engineering design, but must take into account the wider context of an amenable environmental experience (Lang, 1994; see Chapter 7).

Dealing with the pedestrian means dealing with people – with "human" desires and psychological needs for shelter, stimulation, security, beauty, and conviviality – and not just the human-locomotive properties of widths and gradients. Indeed, the conviviality of pedestrian presence can in itself boost the attractiveness of a location as a "people place." In other words, there is a feedback effect, where the more popular places attract more people. This may usefully be borne in mind when prioritizing where pedestrian activity might be promoted.

Provision for the "whole pedestrian" can therefore include design of buildings, providing shelter and visual interest, provisions of stalls and kiosks, and many other features that can help to enhance the environmental experience and encourage pedestrian activity. These include:

- spatial enclosure (lateral and overhead);
- a variety of form, color, material, and textures;
- the use of vegetation and hard landscaping;
- the use of street furniture, places to sit and to congregate;
- provision for complementary uses (e.g. stalls);
- the provision of frontage activity (avoiding blank walls);
- the ability to look into buildings (shop windows) and out of buildings (surveillance).

Urban design approaches that are implicitly or explicitly supportive of pedestrian-friendly environments include those of "townscape" (Cullen, 1961; McCluskey, 1992), urban villages (Aldous, 1992), and pedestrian pockets (Calthorpe, 1989). We should also note the community dimension, since streets are community spaces. In this respect, community participation has become increasingly important, and the recognition that "streets are for people." In this context, issues such as traffic calming are seen not only as exercises in engineering or environmental provision, but as part of "community empowerment," or at least pro-active instigation and intervention by local people (e.g. Engwicht, 1993, 1999; Ernish et al., 1998).

4. Street typology and road hierarchy

The kinds of provision and prioritization discussed in the preceding section can be packaged into particular street types.

In practice, the terms typology and hierarchy are sometimes used interchangeably. Here, we may distinguish between a typology, in which a series of types is recognized, and a hierarchy, in which those types are arranged in an ordered system of relationships. Traditionally, street typologies have been recognized in a variety of urban, transport, and architectural contexts, whereas hierarchy – specifically road hierarchy – is usually associated with transport and highway engineering.

4.1. Conventional road hierarchy

Road hierarchy has been an influential lens, or filter, through which the issue of street typology has been viewed for many years. Hierarchy is a system of network design and management that identifies different types of road according to their functional roles. Road hierarchy is basically set up to avoid conflicts between different road users, their speeds, and their paths of movements, thereby promoting safe, efficient traffic flows. Road hierarchy guides relationships between different types of route, and between those route types and adjacent frontage development (Brindle, 1996b; Institution of Highways and Transportation, 1997).

Conventional road hierarchy has traditionally allocated frontage development and access to certain road types – basically the road types "lower" in the hierarchy – such as those termed "access roads" and "development roads." Conversely, the roads higher in the hierarchy – main roads forming the strategic road network, plus some intermediate roads – are traditionally designated as "distributor roads," which prioritize motor traffic and may not be intended for pedestrians (e.g. footways may not be provided alongside).

The effect of this system in principle was to create a "superstructure" of main roads for through traffic, within which would be sited "environmental areas" or "cells" where the interactions between traffic, pedestrians, and buildings would take place. In the UK, the influential Buchanan Report, among others, promoted a strict separation of routes for movement and local routes within environmental areas (UK Ministry of Transport, 1963). While this recognized the multifunctional role of streets as "urban rooms," this was effectively limited to the role of access road within the environmental areas, in denial of the "urban corridor" function that streets traditionally served.

In practice, the strict distinction between distributor roads for traffic movement and access roads within environmental areas has typically only been achieved for new development (post-1950s housing estates, new towns, and some comprehensively replanned redevelopment areas in inner cities), and has only had limited, piecemeal application to the retrofitting of traditional urban street networks.

4.2. Contemporary evolution

Over the last few decades, there has been a realization that not only is it difficult to apply the "idealized" conventional hierarchy in practice but that it may not even be desirable in theory, given the contemporary drive toward reconciling issues of movement with those of local amenity, environment, and sustainability.

Conventional hierarchy was originally devised as a means of providing for motor traffic, and explicit accommodation of public transport and pedestrians was often missing. In its strictest form, streets (i.e. roads with access to frontages) were restricted to the lowest rungs of the hierarchy – there was no place for the traditional multifunctional high street or arterial street.

There has been a need for road hierarchy to evolve further to explicitly promote types of streets with combinations of "more sustainable" modes and other non-transport urban uses. New or evolving forms of hierarchy might seek to:

- explicitly address not just roads but the wider functions of streets;
- accommodate explicitly pedestrians and public transport;
- allow for different street types based not only on functional transport criteria;
- acknowledge the role of street as a locale/pedestrian "habitat" as well as a transport channel.

Progressive approaches addressing some or all of these include, for example the system in Portland, USA, which explicitly accommodates public transport and pedestrians separately from traffic (Dotterer, 1987); approaches in Australia that revise or develop new kinds of urban street type (Westerman, 1993; Brindle, 1996a; State of Western Australia, 1997); the "living space" model (*Livsrumsmodellen*) that separately recognizes living areas, mixed priority areas, and traffic areas (Gunnarsson, 1993); and the development of a street classification system that can explicitly accommodate arterial streets, that is, major streets combining frontage function and more strategic traffic function (Marshall, 2002).

These cases attempt to accommodate different modes and users. In the case of arterial streets in particular, there is also a need to reconcile the street as a key continuous component in a wider (e.g. citywide) functional system, versus its immediate specific role as a local place. This is partly a trade-off between the strategic and the local, and partly a trade-off between circulation (along an artery) and occupation (of a locale). It is also partly geometric, in that the arterial role is linear (at a certain scale) whereas the locale implies a planar space such as a "cell." Conventionally, the "neighborhood cell" has been interpreted as an area divided or bounded by arterial routes; here, the street space of the arterial street itself is considered as part of the environmental cell (Marshall, 2002).

Overall, we can see that the issue of hierarchy is not only to do with trade-offs between modes (vehicles versus pedestrians) or uses (transport versus urban functions) *per se*, but may also include trade-offs between strategic and local roles and between "arterial" and "cellular" interpretations of urban street space. A systematic approach to street management therefore requires not only "promoting" the pedestrian to a nominal position at the top of the hierarchy, but addressing the spatial organization of the street system to support such a hierarchy.

5. Toward the sustainable street

Sustainability is a broad field open to many interpretations, and accordingly a variety of interpretations of what constitutes a "sustainable street" are possible. This section aims to briefly sum up some of the possible contributions of the street to urban sustainability.

From a transport point of view, a "sustainable street" would accommodate a relatively high proportion of use by "more sustainable" modes – walking, cycling, and public transport (Tolley, 1997). As a physical form, the street allows a combination of these often complementary modes to be accommodated together in a natural linear interchange space – rather than segregating public transport (vehicles) from pedestrians (passengers) – and with an interface with buildings (origins and destinations).

The street can also be seen as part of a compact urban "package." The street is a convenient urban device for arranging medium- to high-density development whether in "brown field" or "green field" sites. This is in contrast to sprawling open-plan layouts, typical of new town and outer urban area developments, which are less sustainable to the extent that they consume more land and have increased distances between buildings and other centers of activity.

From an urban planning point of view, the provision of local shops and clusters of facilities in close proximity can potentially encourage a reduction in the number of trips (if journey purposes can be combined at a single destination), encourage shorter trips (since these facilities are distributed locally), and encourage trips using more environmentally friendly modes of movement (i.e. if the trip becomes sufficiently short that it may be made by cycle or on foot) (Banister and Marshall, 2000).

As an exercise in environmental design, the provision of trees and other planting can help to mitigate or minimize the effects of traffic, both in the sense of the "compensatory" effect on the perception of the street and in the direct sense of absorbing pollutants. The "sustainable street" can also be seen to have a social dimension – regarding factors such as accessibility and equity, and perhaps more intangible factors such as "sense of place" – and an economic dimension – regarding factors relating to the "vitality and viability" of urban areas.

Table 2 presents in summary form a possible view of what might be regarded as basic associations of "sustainable" streets.

6. Conclusions

The design and management of streets is a multifaceted activity that cuts across a multitude of different specialisms even within the transport field – traffic management, geometric design, traffic regulation, and traffic control, to name but a few. This is in addition to the various roles of urban designers and planners, and other disciplines. This chapter has necessarily been limited to a few selected issues, but has attempted to keep in mind the role of the street as transport artery in the context of wider urban and environmental considerations.

We have seen that street management and design involves a trade-off between different uses and users of space. Recognizing the claims of the different users and acknowledging the existence of all modes and users is a step toward arriving at an

Table 2
Interpretation of "sustainable" aspects of streets

Topic	Issues
Green modes	Promotion of "more sustainable" modes: • walking • cycling • public transport • combinations Achieved through: • traffic management – reallocation of road space; signal timings; traffic calming • convenient and attractive interchange space (public transport/pedestrian interface) • provision of a people-friendly "human habitat" to encourage walking
Urban form	The street can be part of a compact urban package
Planning for travel reduction	Streets as "local destinations" with walk-in accessibility: reduced travel through urban facilities, mixed-use frontages and minimization of distances
Environment/ecology	Physical design of street to mitigate environmental consequences of traffic – e.g. planting of trees to absorb pollutants
Social dimension	The street as "social space" or "people place," of social, cultural and political activity
Economic dimension	The street as "market place," vital and viable town centers

appropriate trade-off, in terms of provision and prioritization of space – whether such provision or prioritization implies integration or some degree of segregation.

In particular, this chapter has argued the need to recognize all modes of movement, and not just the main/conventional/vehicular modes. Also, there is a need for recognition of people on the streets not just as "pedestrians," recognizing other activities that require different kinds of design from simple provision for movement. Street management is about catering for people on the street whether in terms of transport or a wider range of social, cultural, political, and economic activities.

Nevertheless, although a variety of disciplines will be involved in the design of the streetscape and the planning of streets in their wider urban context, the transport professional will remain an essential and central player. The transport professional will have a direct influence on the central organizing feature of streets – their circulation role – and on influencing what types of street are provided in the first place. Overall, in a variety of roles, the street can hence be designed and managed to contribute toward a variety of urban objectives including accessibility and sustainability.

The idea of the street as a microcosm of the environment has been suggested: the street is effectively an urban environment in itself, within which a variety of physical resources or capacities and human needs are traded off. However, this idea eventually runs out, in a sense, since with streets we can always add extra capacity to accommodate demand – whether by adding more streets, or building new roads outside the urban street system. Clearly, this does not apply on the global scale: there is no "other" or "outside" environment to draw on. Environmentalists rightly point out that the environment is finite – we are in danger of "running out of" environment. If the world were completely paved over with streets, we would have no option but to treat our streets as carefully tended environments. After all, there is no viable alternative outside our own global "environmental area."

References

Aldous, T. (1992) *Urban villages*. London: Urban Villages Group.
Anderson, S., ed. (1978) *On streets*. Cambridg: MIT Press.
Banister, D. and S. Marshall (2000) *Encouraging transport alternatives: good practice in reducing travel*. London: The Stationery Office.
Brindle, R. (1996a) *Living with traffic*. ARRB Special Report 53. Vermont South: ARRB Transport Research.
Brindle, R. (1996b) "Road hierarchy and functional classification," in: K.W. Ogden and S. Taylor, eds, *Traffic engineering and management*. Melbourne: Institute of Transport Studies, Department of Civil Engineering, Monash University.
Button, K.J. and D.A. Hensher, eds (2001) *Handbook of transport systems and traffic control*. Oxford: Pergamon.
Calthorpe, P. (1989) "The pedestrian pocket," in: D. Kelbaugh, ed., *The pedestrian pocket book*. New York: Princeton Architectural Press.
County Surveyors Society, Department of Transport, Association of Metropolitan District Engineers, Association of London Borough Engineers and Surveyors, and Association of Chief Technical Officers (1994) *Traffic calming in practice*. London: Landor.
Cullen, G. (1961) *Townscape*. London: Architectural Press.
Devon County Council Engineering and Planning Department (1992) *Traffic calming guidelines*. Exeter: Devon County Council.
Dotterer, S. (1987) "Portland's arterial streets classification policy," in: A.V. Moudon, ed., *Public streets for public use*. New York: Van Nostrand.
Dunnett, J. (2000) "Le Corbusier and the city without streets," in: T. Deckker, ed., *The modern city revisited*. London: Spon.
Engwicht, D. (1993) *Reclaiming our cities and towns. Better living with less traffic*. Philadelphia: New Society.
Engwicht, D. (1999) *Street reclaiming. Creating livable streets and vibrant communities*. Gabriola Island: New Society.
Ernish, E., P. Harrison and J. Yuvan, (1998) *Streets for people. traffic calming in your neighborhood. A primer for people who want quieter, safer, friendlier neighborhood streets*. New York: Neighborhood Streets Network.
Fyfe, N., ed. (1998) *Images of the street*. London: Routledge.
Gehl, J. (1998) "The form and use of public space," in: *PTRC European Transport Conference Proceedings of Seminar B, Policy Planning and Sustainability*, vol. 1. PTRC.
Gold, J.R. (1998) "The death of the boulevard," in: N. Fyfe, ed., *Images of the street*. London: Routledge.

Gunnarsson, S.O. (1993) "Traffic planning," in: Institute of Transportation Engineers, ed., *The traffic safety toolbox: a primer on road safety*. Washington, DC: Institute of Transportation Engineers.

Hass-Klau, C., I. Nold, G. Bocker and G. Crampton (1992) *Civilised streets: a guide to traffic calming*. Brighton: Environment and Transport Planning.

Hillman, M. and A. Whalley (1979) *Walking is transport*. London: Policy Studies Institute.

Institution of Highways and Transportation (1997) *Transport in the urban environment*. London: IHT.

Jacobs, A. (1993) *Great streets*. Cambridge: MIT Press.

Jacobs, A., E. Macdonald and Y. Rofé (2002) *The boulevard book. History, evolution, design of multiway boulevards*. Cambridge: MIT Press.

Jefferson, C., J. Rowe and C. Brebbia (2001) *The sustainable street. The environment, human and economic aspects of street design and management*. Southampton: Wessex Institute of Technology.

Lang, J. (1994) *Urban design: the American experience*. New York: Van Nostrand Reinhold.

Marshall, S. (2002) *A first theoretical approach to classification of streets*. ARTISTS Project Deliverable D1.1. London: University of Westminster.

McCluskey, J. (1992) *Road form and townscape*, 2nd edn. Oxford: Butterworth.

Moudon, A.V., ed. (1987) *Public streets for public use*. New York: Van Nostrand Reinhold.

Moughtin, J.C. (1992) *Urban design: street and square*. Oxford: Butterworth.

Rapoport, A. (1987) "Pedestrian street use: culture and perception," in: A.V. Moudon, ed., *Public streets for public use*. New York: Van Nostrand Reinhold.

Southworth, M. and E. Ben Joseph (1997) *Streets and the shaping of towns and cities*. New York: McGraw-Hill.

State of Western Australia (1997) *Liveable neighbourhoods. Community design code*. Perth: State of Western Australia.

Tolley, R., ed. (1997) *The greening of urban transport*. Chichester: Wiley.

Transport Research Laboratory (1997) *Urban design considerations in transport planning. A guide for planners and engineers*. Crowthorne: TRL.

UK Ministry of Transport (1963) *Traffic in towns*. London: HMSO.

Westerman, H. (1993) *Sharing the main street: practitioners' guide to managing the road environment of traffic routes through commercial centres*. Consultants' Report CR 132. Canberra: Australian Transport Safety Bureau.

Chapter 44

INTEGRATED TRANSPORT MODELS FOR ENVIRONMENTAL ASSESSMENT

DAVID A. HENSHER
University of Sydney

1. Introduction

Large-scale urban transportation planning models are recognized as an essential input into the decision-making processes of the great majority of urban planning agencies. The heritage of integrated land use and transport model systems dates back to the late 1950s (see Hensher and Button, 2000). Despite the richness of 45 years of development in statistical modeling, transport networks, equilibration procedures, and data development, there is a sense in the profession that we have not progressed as far as might be expected. It is true that we now have much more sophisticated tools for capturing, representing and managing data (e.g. geographical information systems (GIS) and global positioning systems (GPS)), as well as advanced econometric tools for parameterizing the full gamut of choices made by individuals, households and businesses (e.g. the family of discrete choice models ranging from the multinomial logit through to nested logit and mixed logit – see Hensher and Button, 2000), and hardware allowing the processing of large amounts of data in detailed networks. What we still struggle with is finding ways of utilizing this array of sophisticated technical tools to provide a relevant policy and timely set of meaningful outputs that can accommodate the diverse set of stakeholder needs.

Some of the key themes that have evolved out of the history of integrated land use and transport modeling systems (ILUTMSs) relate to the inadequacy of past efforts to represent the widening set of transport-related choices that are available to individuals in responding to changing circumstances that impact on the travel environment. There is also a growing recognition that populations are extremely heterogeneous in their tastes, and that failure to allow for this in the parameterization of models (as is common when synthetic network data and averages of zonal characteristics are used) is a real source of predictive error in behavioral response. Models with a greater focus on micro-simulation in the transport sector have evolved in large measure as a response to this challenge of representing behavioral response at a more disaggregate (and hence realistic) level. Essentially, it is a call to acknowledge the extent and nature of variance and to represent it explicitly in modeling and application rather than "average it away" as is the tradition in most ILUTMSs.

The long-term aim of modelers is to commit fully to the development of an integrated micro-simulation model (IMSM) system in which decision units (individuals, households, organizations), transport networks (links, etc.), and decision-making processes involving information acquisition, search and choice, etc., embedded in a range of rules all improve on the explanatory and predictive performance of ILUTMSs. The case for micro-simulation as a popular focus for future frameworks for modeling transport systems is well documented (e.g. Miller and Salvini, 2001; Nagel and Auxhausen, 2001). The key research question, however, is the extent to which the promise of the integrated micro-simulation approach can be realized within a practical, operational model. For the immediate future we might expect a mixture of micro-simulation and more aggregate specifications of the relationships representing ILUTMSs.

Integrated models have broad relevance in the transport sector (Axhausen, 1990; Nagel and Axhausen, 2001). The spurt of development activity in recent years has been in part a response to the growing interest in the assessment of policy instruments that can reduce the negative impact of the transport sector on the environment, especially global warming (essentially enhanced greenhouse gas emissions such as carbon dioxide (CO_2) – see Chapter 3) and air pollution (see Chapter 4). Policy instruments that have been shown to contribute in a significant positive way to cleaning up the environment include a gamut of vehicle technology changes, distributed work options (e.g. telecommuting) and relocation of travel activity (via residential and workplace relocations). Traditional ILUTMSs have been noticeably barren in their capability to evaluate improvements in vehicle technology (via vehicle-type choice models – see Hensher and Greene, 2001) and alternative work practice choices. The neglect of a treatment of daily activity travel patterns is also recognized and is an opportunity for richer micro-simulation frameworks (Veldhuisen et al., 2000).

The chapter will focus on the specific environmental aspects of integrated models. However, this will require an initial overview of the main features of model systems that are generic in their relevance. This also serves to remind readers of the importance of assessing environmental policy within the broader framework within which all transport-related policy should be studied, reflecting recognition of the complex interactions between all policy instruments and the full set of measures of the performance of the transport system. Within the limits of one chapter, we cannot do justice to the many variants of currently available integrated models that are introducing new developments including micro-simulation. Rather, we limit our focus to two illustrative systems for passenger travel – TRESIS (Hensher, 2002) and IRPUD (Wegener, 2000). A selection of other contributions is presented in Dörnemann (2000), Esser and Nagel (2001), Martínez and Donoso (2001a), Miller and Salvini (2001), Waddell (2000, 2001), and Veldhuisen et al. (2000). These IMSM systems have been applied at the urban area-wide level (alternatively referred to as intraregional, regional, metropolitan levels).

2. Some key building blocks for ILUTMSs and IMSM systems for passenger travel

The development of integrated systems of any form must reflect the needs of the context within which they will be applied. There appear to be a number of dominating considerations:

- diversity in breadth and coverage of policy instruments (or strategies) (policy relevance);
- inclusion of a range of behavioral models that capture the set of choice responses of the decision-making population (behavioral response relevance);
- sufficient detail in the spatial supply system through transport networks to capture the level of detail used by decision-makers in their behavioral responses (spatial detail relevance);
- sufficient detail in the representation of decision-makers to capture the heterogeneity descriptors that influence behavioral response (decision-maker relevance);
- the capture of sufficient diversity of output indicators to be useful to the full set of stakeholders (output relevance).

ILUTMSs and micro-simulation as a construct promote a view that real systems are extremely complex but that we can approximate reality, to varying degrees, by focusing on the components that are the main drivers of behavioral response at a sufficient level of detail to be useful in implementing policies and plans. The five relevance criteria provide useful signposts for ILUTMS/IMSM systems.

2.1. Policy relevance

There is a growing recognition that many traditional transport policy instruments are relatively blunt over a range that is politically acceptable and within tolerable budgetary limits in respect of delivering on environmental criteria. For example, of the policy instruments available to bus operators in Sydney (e.g. service frequency, travel times), a decrease of bus fares by 40% (which is unlikely to occur for political reasons) has the most significant abatement in greenhouse gas emission, reducing CO_2 by (only) 1.26%. A carbon tax of, say, A $0.20/kg imposed on petrol-based automobiles reduces CO_2 by 2.39%. These are not sizeable impacts, even though welcomed. The message for ILUTMS/IMSM systems is to ensure that there is sufficient diversity in eligible policy evaluation embedded in the suite of behavioral models to provide sufficient leverage for evaluating mixtures of policy instruments that cumulatively have a noticeable impact on the output indicators of interest. A good example of this for environmental impacts often excluded from ILUTMSs is the inclusion of a vehicle-type choice model as an explicit treatment of environmental impacts due to vehicle technology and performance (Hensher and Greene, 2001). Another good example of policy exclusion is ability to analyze the environmental impact of the large number and variety of land use regulations that directly affect the number and distribution of trips (Martínez and Donoso, 2001b).

2.2. Behavioral response relevance

The engine of any ILUTMS/IMSM system is the set of behavioral models defined by choice outcomes and explanatory sources of variability in choice responses of individuals and households. The recognition that individuals or groups of individuals (e.g. a household) make decisions on travel activity and not traffic zones has spawned a huge body of literature experimenting with ways to represent the complex nature of decision-making that leads to activity in the transportation system. Progress is substantial, with two major emphases: the development of an extended set of travel and non-travel choice models that are integrated with feedback; and the use of data to estimate parameters that are drawn from the decision-making unit and preserved at that level rather than some synthetic source or aggregated across decision units.

The recognition of the need to preserve the true behavioral variability in data for model estimation rather than remove it through aggregation is key. While it is always possible to reproduce base circumstances with aggregated data (firstly estimating a model and then calibrating it to a known population profile), the fallacy of this strategy is revealed when one varies a parameterized attribute in policy application since the behavioral response sensitivity preserved through the use of data pertinent to the distribution is non-existent. Another way of stating this is: "One can always improve the statistical fit of a model through data aggregation. With less variability in the data there is less to explain and hence it is easier to explain the residual." Behaviorally this is not progress.

2.3. Spatial detail relevance

It is common practice to use geographical units called traffic zones to represent the locations between and within which travel takes place. The detail varies from a geo-coded x, y coordinate to various degrees of spatial aggregation of zones. In establishing the appropriate level of spatial aggregation, one must distinguish spatial appropriateness for model estimation, system application and output reporting. There is strong support for the position that parameterization of travel choice models should use data that are specific to the decision-making unit, be it an individual, a household, or an organization. Spatial aggregation of data for estimation is to be discouraged since it typically removes significant variability in data across a sampled population used in model estimation. It has been known for many years that there is significant within-zone variability (or heterogeneity) in socio-economic characteristics and network levels of service that is important in establishing precision in parameter estimates. Applications ideally should preserve this level of variability through the use of individual observations and equivalent network detail, although as outlined below we have progressed this desire for individuals and households (with the concept of synthetic or prototypical households), but have not been as successful for network levels of service where zonal representation still dominates. Reporting of outputs is usually provided at a sufficiently high spatial resolution to be meaningful to absorb. As Miller and Salvini (2001) state:

> While zones will play no role in the behavioural processes being modelled, they are essential and unavoidable elements of model's spatial data management system, for at least two reasons. First, much of the base, input data to the model is only available at the zone level (traffic zone, census tract, etc.). Disaggregated lists of individual persons, households, firms, etc. must be synthesised for input into the micro-simulator. Second, zones are often a very convenient and practical means by which to summarise and display model results, as well as to compare these results with observed data for validation purposes.

The ability to preserve behavioral responsiveness associated with relatively homogeneous response groupings is the key to the richness of an ILUTMS/IMSM system. The TRESIS system for example, estimates all the behavioral choice models at the individual or household level using survey data, and implements the model system using synthetic data for individuals and households, vehicle-class data for automobiles, and zonal and network level data for levels of service (e.g. travel times) and location characteristics (e.g. median house prices).

2.4. Decision-maker relevance

A central feature of many ILUTMS/IMSM systems is the concept of synthetic (or prototypical) individuals and associated households. The idea is to preserve the one-to-one mapping of the decision-making unit and the unit of analysis and to utilize sampling as a way of capturing the essential variability of the population through a set of representative (i.e. synthetic) observations that carry weights to indicate their contribution to the overall behavioral response of the population to which they belong.

To motivate the value and power of the synthetic construct and its locational generality, the application process is likened to "dropping" a sample of households into an urban area, each such household being described by a bundle of socio-economic and demographic characteristics for each member and the household in total. These characteristics include all the influences in the suite of utility expressions representing the set of behavioral choice models. Together with other data such as the predefined transport network, dwelling type prices, automobile attributes, and the physical zone system, the characteristics of each synthetic household are used to derive the full set of behavioral choice probabilities for the set of travel, location and vehicle choices and predictions of vehicle use. Each synthetic household carries a weight that represents its contribution to the total population of households. Through time one carries forward the base year weights or, alternatively, modifies the weights to represent the changing composition of households in the population. Details of the process of generating synthetic households is presented in Ton and Hensher (2001). Synthetic households are increasingly being included into ILUTMS/IMSM systems, adding a large amount of behavioral variability within and between households. This is a major improvement over the use of zonal averages for socio-economic characterization.

2.5. Output relevance

A successful ILUTMS/IMSM system must be responsive to the interests of stakeholders. This requires at least sufficient output indicators that satisfy the policy interests of those who focus on the key global dimensions of urban management – efficiency, equity and environmental sustainability. Each should have a set of practical translators of performance including indicators of greenhouse gas emissions, air pollution emissions, revenue sources, transport accessibility and mobility, patronage activity, energy consumption, end-use costs (time and money), and consumer surplus. With a diversified set of high-quality outputs an integrated micro-simulation model system provides a decision support tool for debate and formulation of strategic, tactical, and operational plans and policies. An ILUTMS/IMSM system offers more than forecasts of outcomes; importantly, it is an auxiliary support system for planners and decision-makers who often want to get a feel for implications of the "what if …?" questions. The outputs should be available in quick time so as to feed into the planning process almost continuously. Relevance of output includes timeliness as well as substance.

3. The profile of two ILUTMSs

Two integrated micro-simulation model systems have been selected to illustrate the way in which relevance is designed into their structures. These are the Transport and Environment Strategy Impact Simulator (TRESIS) from Australia (Hensher 2002) and the Intra-regional and Mobility Decision Model (IRPUD) from Germany (Wegener 2000).

3.1. TRESIS

TRESIS is implemented at two levels of spatial detail, 904 zones and 14 zones, for the Sydney metropolitan area. The 14-zone system provides sufficient detail for broad-based policy analysis. We refer to the 14-zone version as a strategy prioritizer. Where a particularly effective policy instrument (or mix of instruments) is identified on a set of performance criteria that requires spatial fine tuning, then the more spatially detailed zonal system can be harnessed. It has, however, been our experience that the majority of policy inquiries can determine the impact of specific policy instruments with a simulation tool that has a relatively coarse network structure, and associated zones, accompanied by the rich detail and diversity of the behavioral choice models and the synthetic representation of individuals and households (currently 3000 synthetic households). Another way of saying this is that much of the variability in behavioral response is attributed to the composition of the decision units and the behavioral choices on offer rather than in the detail of transport networks. The latter has been over-emphasized (in a relative sense) to the detriment of the other features of ILUTMS/IMSM systems in the past.

The modular structure has been designed to facilitate the import of local data such as networks, travel, location and vehicle demand model utility expressions, household profiles and GIS platforms, but has its own GIS and traffic assignment capability. The key components include:

- The behavioral system of choice models for individuals and households estimated using mixtures of revealed and stated preference data for commuter mode and departure time choice, revealed preference data for workplace location, residential location, dwelling type, vehicle type and fleet size choice, and automobile use by location. The model system is a hierarchical set of multinomial models, estimated as nested logits with a full set of inclusive values (for details of choice models, see Hensher and Button, 2000). There are six modes (car drive alone, ride share, train, bus, light rail, and busway system) and six times of day (up to 7.00 am, 7.00–9.00 am, 9.00 am–3.00 pm, 3.00–5.00 pm, 5.00 pm and later).

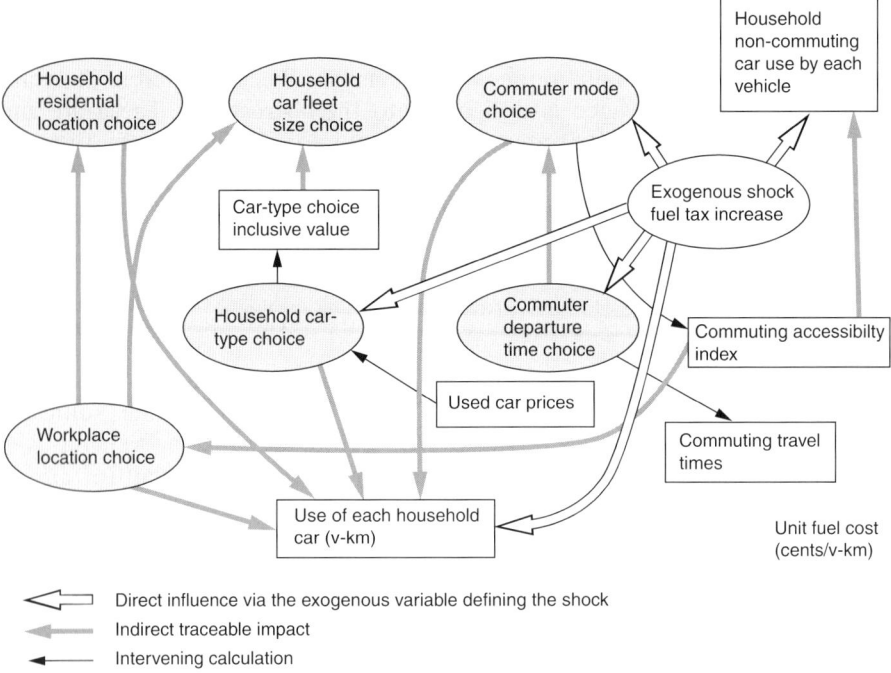

Figure 1. An example of interactions in the TRESIS behavioral system from a policy shock.

Enhancements in progress include a full suite on non-work travel choice models and alternative algorithms and behavioral criteria for equilibration.
- The highway and public transport (rail, bus, light rail, ferry, busway) networks and associated levels of service by time of day.
- The equilibration capability in the travel and automobile markets and disequilibrium in residential location markets.
- The automobile scrappage and price determination models.
- The generation of synthetic households used in application, including the interrelationships between workers in a household (Ton and Hensher, 2001).
- The in-built GIS interface for data and application processing and presentation.
- The extensive databases of primary and secondary data for input into the calibration and implementation of estimated and behavioral models (currently updated to 1998).
- The supply-side system of networks and zone locations.
- The sample generation facility for implementation of a complex system of either 14 or 904 zones and synthetic households.

To illustrate how TRESIS as a system operates, let us introduce an exogenous policy shock such as a fuel tax increase (Figure 1). The process of evaluation starts with adjustments to the relevant attribute(s) that house the cost of travel that is initially directly affected by a fuel tax. This is the operating cost of automobiles (assuming that this tax is not passed on to public transport uses through higher fares). The operating cost of automobiles is parameterized in the utility expressions for car drive-alone and ride-share in the joint commuter mode and departure time choice models as well as the auto-type choice models for each of one-, two-, and three-plus-vehicle households. Having modified these utility expressions (precalibrated to each years base), each synthetic household "passes" through each and every utility expression for worker level and household level choice models and vehicle use models, the latter distinguishing trip purpose (commuting, travel as part of work, other urban and non-urban vehicle kilometers) and number of vehicles in a household. Each synthetic household (and associated workers) carries a weight to define the representation of all households in the sampled population for a specified year.

For each choice model and vehicle use model, choice probabilities are calculated beginning from the bottom of the nested structure (i.e. work practice choice), and moving up through joint mode and departure time choice to workplace location and then residential location choice. Auto-type choice is linked into fleet size choice, and fed through the mode choice model as well as the residential location choice. Dwelling-type choice is linked directly into residential location choice. An iterative equilibration takes place (currently sequentially), starting with the travel market and clearing on travel time in the transport network. Once equilibrium is achieved, the residential location market is disequilibrated on house prices (as best empirical proxies for location rents) with a minimum stock reserved for future occupancy. Finally, the automobile market is cleared up to equilibrium using new and used vehicle prices and a vehicle scrappage model in which vehicles leave the market due to economic influences (i.e. price expectations) and technological obsolescence. New stock is exogenously added in.

Once all markets are adjusted to their particular clearance level (with extensive feedback through all the utility expressions), we have to take into account dynamics. The model system is static and hence produces an instantaneous fully adjusted response to a policy application. In reality choice responses take time to fully adjust, with the amount of time varying by specific decision. We expect that it would take longer for the full effect of the change in residential location to occur and much less time for departure time and even mode choice. Two heuristics were considered – a dynamic incremental approach and a block period approach. The former involves the imposition of a discount factor that establishes the amount of a change in choice probability that is likely to be taken up in the first year of a policy. It removes the rest of the change and uses the new 1 year adjustment as the starting position for the next year. Intuitively we are saying that if we had a fully

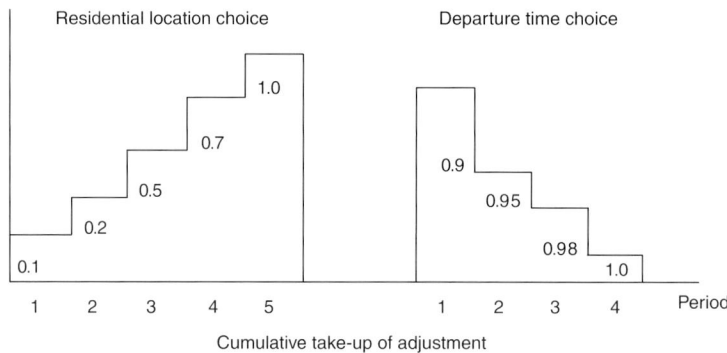

Figure 2. The temporal structure for a block period approach.

dynamic choice model system, we would only observe the discounted impact after each year. The latter approach adopts a longer period such as 5 years as the block of time over which the full effect of a policy will occur. This is a maximum period since some decisions such as departure time choice will be fully adjusted over a short period, in contrast to the residential location decision that we might assume would take the full 5 years to adjust. A set of (default) discount factors would be specified for each of the 5 years as illustrated in Figure 2. Our preference is for the dynamic incremental approach based on the following procedure (Ton, 2002). The choice probabilites evaluated from any choice model at any time t will be adjusted by the differences between the probabilities calculated at (current) time t and time $t - 1$ when the policy is introduced:

$$\text{Adjusted\_Prob}_t = \text{Prob}_t - (\text{Prob}_t - \text{Prob}_{t-1}) * (1 - \text{Dfactor}) \qquad (1)$$

where Adjusted_Prob$_t$ are the adjusted probabilities at time t, Prob$_t$ are probabilities evaluated from a choice model at time t, Prob$_{t-1}$ are probabilities evaluated from a choice model at time $t - 1$, and Dfactor is the discount factor in the range 0 to 1.

Equation (1) should be applied across all alternatives to preserve the important constraint that is the sum of all adjusted probabilities at time t must be equal to 1.0.

TRESIS case study: evaluation of a carbon tax

TRESIS produces aggregate outputs (at a city level) and various disaggregate output options by zone, zone pair, household type, income group, etc. The selection of output indicators of interest is generally determined by the objectives of the study. For example, in an environmental evaluation, greenhouse gas emission (i.e. CO_2) is one appropriate indicator. In an economic analysis, net consumer surplus, vehicle operating cost, and government revenue impacts also provide useful indicators. From a transport planning perspective, we may be interested in indicators such as modal share, total vehicle-kilometers, and trips between each origin–destination pair. We will use a carbon tax to illustrate the TRESIS outputs, focusing on a few of the many performance indicators that represent efficiency, equity, and environmental sustainability (for more details, see Hensher, 2002). The selected indicators are summarized below.

Automobile operating cost. A carbon tax is expected to increase vehicle-operating costs. There are two indicators: average operating cost of automobiles in cents per kilometer (AvOpCost) and total annual auto operating costs in dollars (VehOpCost).

Government revenue. A carbon tax would increase the retail price of gasoline. Auto drivers might react to higher gasoline prices by reducing car use and possibly automobile ownership over a longer time period, and possibly switching to public transport. We expect that a carbon tax would create additional revenue for the government, and increase the revenue from public transport use, but would reduce revenue from fuel excise, parking charges, and vehicle registration due to the impacts on vehicle use and ownership. The six indicators of interest are the total government revenue from a carbon tax (TgovtCarbT), the total government revenue from fuel excise (TgovtExcise), the total government revenue from a parking charge (TgovtPark), the total government revenue from public transport use (TgovtPT), the total government revenue from sales tax (TgovtSales), and the total government revenue from vehicle registration (TgovtVehReg).

End-user cost. A carbon tax is likely to increase end-user cost by increasing vehicle operating costs. Useful indicators of this impact are total annual end-user money cost in present-value dollars (TEUCPV.MC), total annual end-user generalized cost (time and money) (TEUC.TC), and total annual end-user generalized cost in present value dollars (TEUCPV.TC).

Modal share. A carbon tax is likely to decrease car driving-alone and ride-share, but increase public transport share. Four useful indicators are the commuter modal share for car driving-alone (TDA), the commuter modal share for riding-share (TRS), the commuter modal share for train (Ttrain), and the commuter modal share for bus (Tbus).

Greenhouse gas emission. A carbon tax is likely to reduce greenhouse gas emissions due to reduced automobile use. The selected indicator is total annual carbon dioxide in kilograms (TCO2).

Automobile use. A carbon tax is expected to reduce automobile use. The selected indicator is total annual passenger vehicle-kilometers (TVKM).

TRESIS provides the results of these selected indicators for the base case (business as usual) and policy case for each application year. TRESIS provides outputs year by year. Table 1 shows the selected indicators in 2004. If a carbon tax of 20 cents/kg were implemented, the average vehicle operating cost after equilibration would increase by 18.18%. Total government revenue would increase by 14.82%. The total end-user money cost would increase by 7.34%, while total end-user generalized cost would be reduced by 0.344%. Modal commuter shares for automobile trips would decrease, while those for public transport would increase. Total annual vehicle kilometers would reduce by 2.309%, and total greenhouse gas emissions would reduce by 2.392%. One can obtain these indicators for each application year in the evaluation period, and calculate the accumulated impact of the policy over a given period. Figure 3 graphically shows selected policy impacts.

Table 1
Summary results for 20 cents/kg carbon tax: 2004 (A $93)

Indicator	Base case	Carbon tax	Difference (%)
Automobile operating cost			
AvOpCost (cents/km)	6.553	7.744	18.18%
VehOpCost (A $)	6.35×10^8	7.3335×10^8	15.451%
Government revenue			
TGovtCarbT (A $)	0	1.1285×10^8	–
TGovtExcise (A $)	3.7995×10^8	3.7085×10^8	−2.391%
TGovtPark (A $)	9.8675×10^7	9.8475×10^7	−0.207%
TgovtPT (A $)	7.1375×10^7	7.4175×10^7	3.95%
TGovtSales (A $)	5.5885×10^7	5.6315×10^7	0.772%
TGovtVehRe.g. (A $)	1.1425×10^8	1.1425×10^8	−0.132%
Subtotal	7.2005×10^8	8.2685×10^8	14.823%
Total end user cost			
TEUC.MC	1.3715×10^9	1.4725×10^9	7.341%
TEUC.TC	7.755×10^8	7.7245×10^8	−0.344%
Commuter mode share			
TDA (share/No.)	69.90%/1.4895×10^8	69.63%/1.4835×10^8	−0.387%
TRS (share/No.)	19.98%/2.0275×10^7	19.90%/2.0195×10^7	−0.387%
TTain (share/No.)	1.99%/4.245×10^6	2.06%/4.3925×10^6	3.603%
TBus (share/No.)	8.13%/1.7335×10^7	8.41%/1.7915×10^7	3.399%
Greenhouse gas emissions			
TCO2 (kg)	2.5245×10^9	2.4645×10^9	−2.392%
Passenger vehicle-kilometers			
TVKM (km)	9.6935×10^9	9.4695×10^9	−2.309%

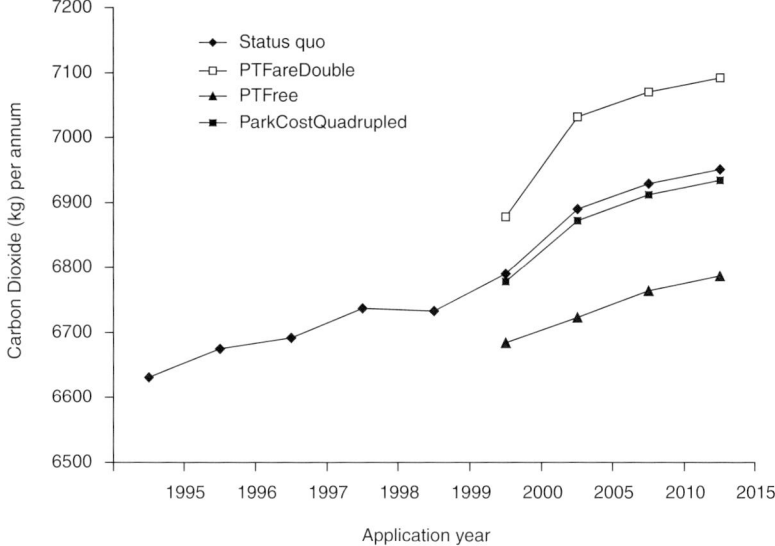

Figure 3. Impact of fares and parking costs on emissions of CO_2.

3.2. IRPUD

IRPUD predicts for each simulation period intra-regional location decisions of industry, residential developers, and households, the resulting migration and travel patterns, construction activity and land-use development and the impacts of public policies in the fields of industrial development, housing, public facilities and transport. Figure 4 is a schematic diagram of the major subsystems considered in the model and their interactions and of the most important policy instruments.

The four square boxes in the corners of the diagram show the major stock variables of the model: population, employment, residential buildings, and non-residential buildings (industrial and commercial workplaces and public facilities). The actors representing these stocks are individuals or households, workers, housing investors, and firms. They interact on five submarkets of urban development. The five sub-markets treated in the model and the market transactions occurring in them are the labor market (new jobs and redundancies); the market for non-residential buildings (new firms and firm relocations); the housing market (immigration, out-migration, new households, and moves); the land and construction market (changes of land use through new construction, modernization, or demolition); and the transport market (trips).

For each submarket the diagram shows supply and demand and the resulting market transactions. Choice in the submarkets is constrained by supply (jobs,

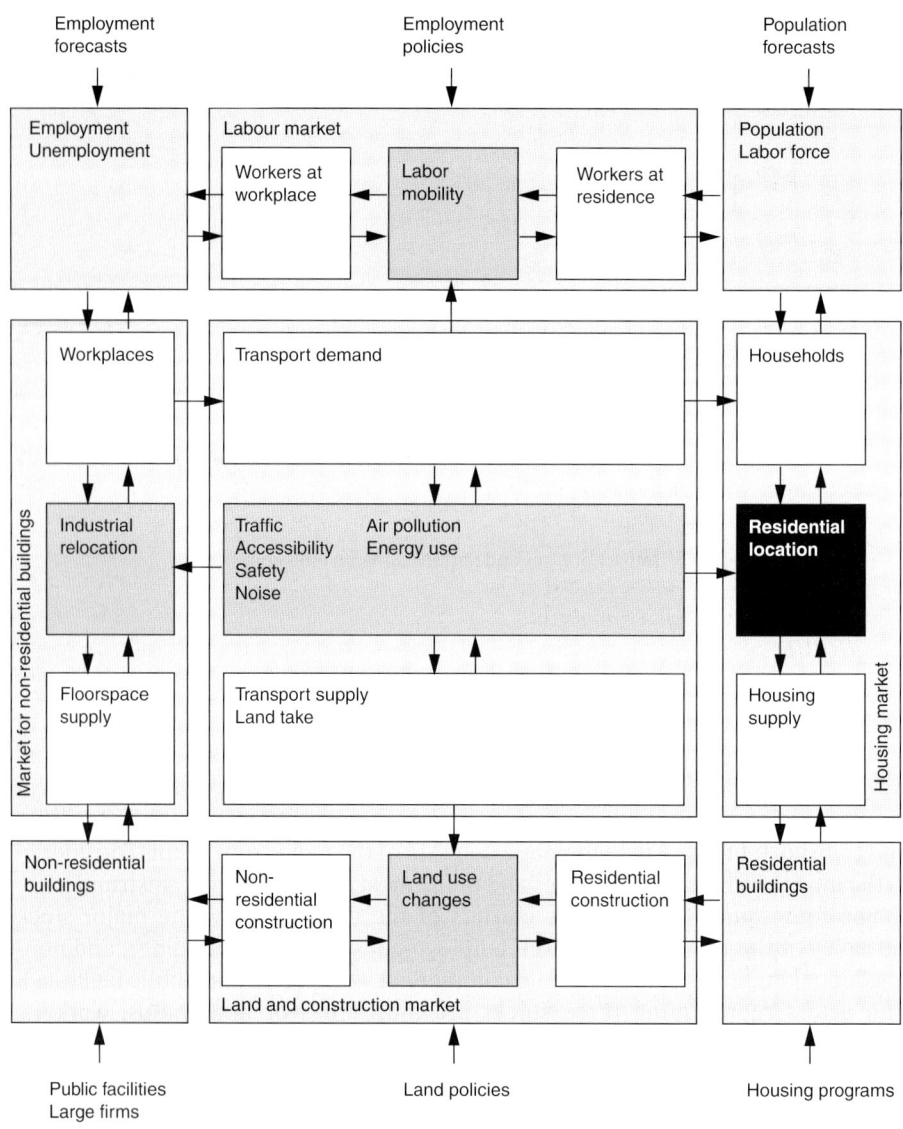

Figure 4. The IRPUD model structure (Wegener, 2000).

vacant housing, vacant land, vacant industrial or commercial floor-space) and guided by attractiveness, defined by an actor-specific aggregate of neighborhood quality, accessibility, and price. The arrows in the diagram indicate exogenous inputs: these are either forecasts of regional employment and population subject to long-term economic and demographic trends or policies in the fields of industrial development, housing, public facilities, and transport.

Like TRESIS, the IRPUD model has a modular structure and consists of six interlinked submodels operating in a recursive fashion on a common spatial-temporal database:

(1) The transport submodel calculates work, shopping, service, and education trips for four socio-economic groups, and three modes, walking/cycling, public transport, and car. The model determines a user-optimum set of flows, where car ownership, trip rates, modal split, and route choice are in equilibrium subject to congestion in the network.
(2) The aging submodel computes all changes of the stock variables of the model which are assumed to result from biological, technological or long-term socio-economic trends originating outside the model. These changes are effected in the model by probabilistic aging or updating models of the Markov type with dynamic transition rates. There are three such models, for employment, population, and households/housing.
(3) The public programs submodel processes a large variety of public programs specified by the model user in the fields of employment, housing, health, welfare, education, recreation, and transport.
(4) The private construction submodel considers investment and location decisions of private developers, i.e. of enterprises erecting new industrial or commercial buildings, and of residential developers who build flats or houses for sale or rent or for their own use. Thus, the submodel is a model of the regional land and construction market.
(5) The labor market submodel models intra-regional labor mobility as decisions of workers to change their job location in the regional labor market.
(6) The housing market submodel simulates intra-regional migration decisions of households as search processes in the regional housing market. Housing search is modeled in a stochastic micro-simulation framework. The results of the housing market submodel are intra-regional migration flows by household category between housing by category in the zones.

The transport submodel is an equilibrium model referring to a point in time. All other submodels are incremental, and refer to a period of time. Submodels (2) to (6) are executed once in each simulation period, while the transport submodel (1) is processed at the beginning and the end of each simulation period. Each submodel passes information to the next submodel in the same period and to its own next iteration in the following period.

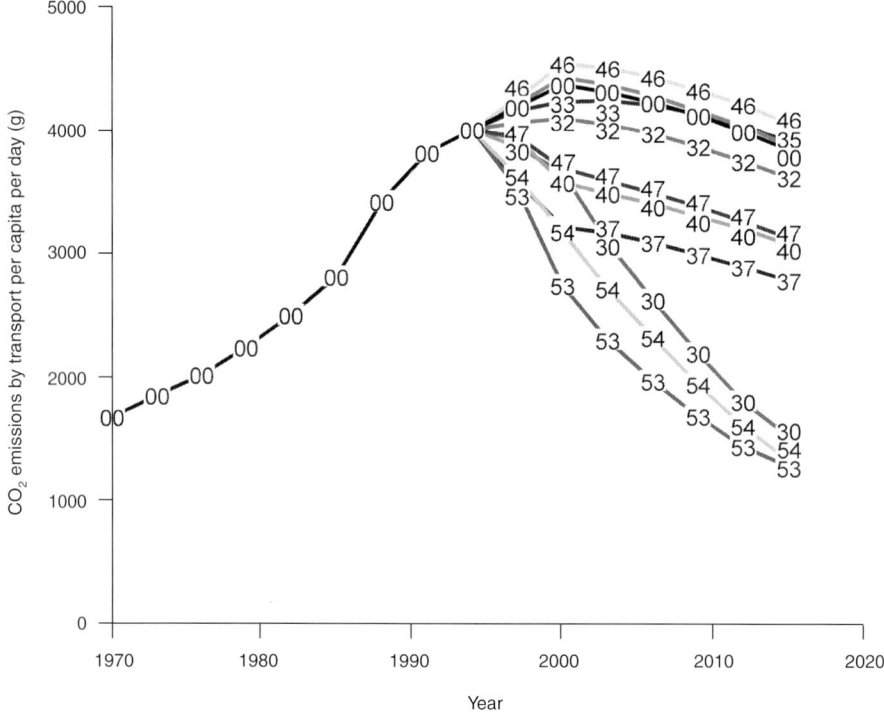

Figure 5. CO_2 emissions in transport (Wegener, 2000).

IRPUD case study: evaluation of transport policies on CO_2 emissions

IRPUD was applied to forecast the impacts of policies to reduce the number of car trips and transport-related emissions of CO_2 in the Dortmund (Germany) metropolitan region by transport demand management. The region is relatively compact: most residents lie within the 30 minute travel time isochrone by car from central Dortmund. The study area has a population of approximately 2.3 million.

Four types of transport policies are evaluated: separate scenarios for travel cost and speed changes and combined scenarios. A base scenario is defined as the trend scenario without policy changes (referred to as scenario 00). The travel cost scenarios are (scenario reference number in parentheses):

- increase petrol price to 12 DM/liter by 2015 and reduce average petrol consumption of cars to 5 l per 100 km by 2015 (30)[a];

[a] 1.95583 DM = 1 euro; 0.8893 euro ~ US $1).

- increase inner-city parking charges, after 2000 quintupled (32);
- reduce public transport fares, after 2000 free (33);
- increase public transport fares, after 2000 doubled (35);
- increase all transport costs, after 2000 doubled (37).

The Travel speed scenarios are:

- make public transport faster (25%) and reduce headways (50%) and make cars slower (40%) (40);
- make public transport and cars faster (25%) (46);
- make public transport and cars slower (40%) (47).

Combination scenarios are:

- promotion of public transport: scenarios 30 + 32 + 40 (53);
- reduction of mobility: scenarios 30 + 32 + 35 + 47 (54).

Figure 5 shows the savings in energy use and CO_2 emissions by all transport, including the additional busses and trains necessary for the growing number of passengers. Despite continued growth in car ownership and travel distances, CO_2 emissions per capita are likely to decrease after 2000 because of the greater energy efficiency of cars. However, without intervention the goal to reduce CO_2 emissions by 25% compared with 1990 cannot be achieved. None of the policies meet this target, except those in which car travel is made significantly more expensive. Scenario 53 implies the smallest sacrifice in mobility.

4. Conclusions

This chapter has presented an overview of the role that integrated land use and transport model systems can play in aiding the assessment of the impact on the environment of transport-related policy instruments and other non-transport instruments that impact on the performance of the transport sector. While the literature is extensive, a set of well-defined perspectives on modeling, data, and software architecture are evolving that highlight the features of integrated model systems that add substantial value to the policy debate. While models are no more than an aid to the debate, they do define a setting within which, as a minimum, we can appreciate where the big gains in policy and investment are most likely to be achieved in respect of positive impacts on the environment (as well as sending warning signals on what instruments detract from environmental progress).

Acknowledgments

I am indebted to colleagues involved in the development of TRESIS (especially Tu Ton, Cam Ng, and Freddy Susanto). Michael Wegener is thanked for permission to reproduce Figure 3 and to draw on his research papers to illustrate the application of IRPUD, as is Francisco Martinez for reading the first draft and checking the key references.

References

Axhausen, K.W. (1990) "A simultaneous simulation of activity chains," in: P.M. Jones, ed., *New approaches in dynamic and activity-based approaches to travel analysis*. Aldershot: Avebury.

Dörnemann, M. (2000) "Micro-simulation of travel behaviour in a congested urban area – MOVER," in: D.A. Hensher, ed., *Travel behaviour research: the leading edge*. Oxford: Pergamon.

Esser, J. and K. Nagel (2001) "Iterative demand generation for transportation simulations," in: D.A. Hensher, ed., *Travel behaviour research: the leading edge*. Oxford: Pergamon.

Hensher, D.A. (2002) "A systematic assessment of the environmental impacts of transport policy: an end use perspective," *Environmental and Resource Economics* (special issue on "Tools of the Trade for Environmental Economists").

Hensher, D.A. and K.J. Button, eds (2000) *Handbook of transport modelling*. Oxford: Pergamon.

Hensher, D.A. and W.H. Greene (2001) "Choosing between conventional, electric and LPG/CNG vehicles in single-vehicle households," in: D.A. Hensher, ed., *Travel behaviour research: the leading edge*. Oxford: Pergamon.

Martínez, F and P. Donoso (2001a) "MUSSA: a land use equilibrium model with location externalities, planning regulations and pricing policies," in: *7th International Conference on Computers in Urban Planning and Urban Management (CUPUM 2001)*. Hawaii.

Martínez, F. and P. Donoso (2001b) "Modeling land use planning effects: zone regulations and subsidies," in: D.A. Hensher, ed., *Travel behaviour research: the leading edge*. Oxford: Pergamon.

Miller, E. and P. Salvini (2001) "The integrated land use, transportation, environment (ILUTE) micro-simulation modelling system: description and current status," in: D.A. Hensher, ed., *Travel behaviour research: the leading edge*. Oxford: Pergamon.

Nagel, K. and K.W. Auxhausen (2001) "Microsimulation," in: D.A. Hensher, ed., *Travel behaviour research: the leading edge*. Oxford: Pergamon.

Ton, T. (2002) *Heuristics to accommodate the temporal adjustment process used in TRESIS V1.3*. Mimeo. Sydney: Institute of Transport Studies, The University of Sydney.

Ton, T. and D.A. Hensher (2001) "Synthesising population data: the specification and generation of synthetic households in TRESIS," in: *World Conference on Transport Research*. Paper. Seoul.

Veldhuisen, J., H. Timmermans and L. Kapoen (2000) "RAMBLAS: a regional planning model based on the microsimulation of daily activity travel patterns," *Environment and Planning A*, 32:427–443.

Waddell, P. (2000) "A behavioral simulation model for metropolitan policy analysis and planning: residential location and housing market components of UrbanSim," *Environment and Planning B*, 27:247–263.

Waddell, P. (2001) "Towards a behavioural integration of land use and transportation modelling," in: D.A. Hensher, ed., *Travel behaviour research: the leading edge*. Oxford: Pergamon.

Wegener, M. (2000) *IRPUD: the IRPUD model: overview*. Dortmund: Institut für Raumplanung.

Chapter 45

TRANSPORTATION DEMAND MANAGEMENT AND "WIN–WIN" TRANSPORTATION SOLUTIONS

TODD A. LITMAN
Victoria Transport Policy Institute, Melbourne

1. What is transportation demand management?

There are two general ways to reduce the economic, social, and environmental costs of transportation activities. One is to improve vehicle and facility design to reduce impacts per unit of vehicle travel. This involves a variety of engineering strategies, such as creating more efficient and less polluting vehicles, and mitigation strategies to minimize the negative impacts of transportation facilities such as roads and parking lots.

The other approach is to reduce total vehicle travel and in other ways change travel behavior in ways that result in more efficient use of transportation resources. The general term for this is transportation demand management (TDM; also called mobility management). There are many different TDM strategies with a variety of impacts, as summarized in Table 1. Some improve the transport options available to users, others provide incentives to choose more efficient travel patterns. Some reduce the need for physical travel through mobility substitutes or more efficient land use. TDM strategies can change travel timing, route, destination, or mode. TDM is an increasingly common response to transport problems. In fact, many transportation problems are virtually unsolvable without some TDM applications (Goodwin, 1997).

TDM can provide multiple benefits, including congestion reduction, road and parking facility cost savings, consumer savings, improved consumer choice, road safety, environmental quality, community livability, efficient land use, and equity. As a result, total benefits are often much greater than solutions that only address one or two problems. TDM can expand the range of solutions considered for addressing transport problems, and allows solutions to be tailored to a particular situation. It can be implemented more quickly than facility capacity expansion.

TDM does not eliminate automobile travel, since cars are efficient for certain types of trips, but if properly applied it can significantly reduce the amount of automobile travel that would otherwise occur, particularly in urban conditions, while benefiting consumers overall, and increasing economic productivity (Litman, 2001).

Handbook of Transport and the Environment, Edited by D.A. Hensher and K.J. Button
© 2003, Elsevier Ltd

2. Consumer impacts of TDM

Some people are skeptical that TDM solutions are feasible, because they require consumers to change their travel habits. Although changing consumer behavior may seem difficult, there are examples of successes, including recycling, smoking reductions, and seat belt use. In each case, a combination of public education, policy changes, and support services have had a dramatic impact on behavior patterns, indicating that a sufficient number of consumers can support such programs politically, and respond to them individually, that they can be effective.

Although they reduce their vehicle travel, consumers can benefit overall. Many TDM strategies use positive incentives, so consumers only reduce their driving when they consider themselves better off. Motorists who continue driving at current levels are no worse off, and they benefit from reduced congestion, crash

Table 1
Examples of TDM strategies. TDM includes more than three dozen strategies that improve travel options, encourage use of efficient modes, and create more accessible land use patterns.

Improve transportation options	Incentives to reduce driving	Parking and land use management	Policy reforms and program
Alternative work schedules	Walking and cycling encouragement	Bicycle parking	Access management
Bicycle improvements	Commuter financial incentives	Car-free districts and pedestrianized streets	Campus transport management
Bike/transit integration	Congestion pricing	Clustered land use	Car-free planning
Car sharing	Distance-based pricing	Location-efficient development	Commute trip reduction programs
Flextime	Fuel taxes	New urbanism	Comprehensive market reforms
Guaranteed ride home	HOV (high-occupancy vehicle) priority	Parking management	Context sensitive design
Individual actions for efficient transport	Parking pricing	Parking solutions	Freight transport management
Park and ride	Pay-as-you-drive vehicle insurance	Parking evaluation	
Pedestrian improvements	Road pricing	Shared parking	Institutional reforms
Ride sharing	Speed reductions	Smart growth	Least-cost planning
Shuttle services	Street reclaiming	Smart growth planning and policy reforms	Regulatory reform
Small-wheeled transport	Vehicle use restrictions	Transit-oriented development (TOD)	School transport management
Taxi service improvements			Special event management
Telework			TDM marketing
Traffic calming			Tourist transport management
Transit improvements			
Universal design			Transportation management associations

Source: Victoria Transport Policy Institute (2002).

Table 2
Conventional and comprehensive transport planning. A summary of the differences between conventional and comprehensive transport evaluation.

	Conventional	Comprehensive
Selection of options	Often ignores TDM options	Includes TDM options
Measuring transportation	Measures vehicle traffic	Measures access
Generated traffic	Ignores many components	Includes all components
Consumer impacts	Travel time changes	Consumer surplus analysis
Downstream congestion	Ignores when evaluating individual projects	Includes
Vehicle costs	Only considers short-term operating costs	Includes all affected vehicle costs
Parking costs	Only if paid by motorist	Includes
Construction impacts	Ignores	Includes
Impacts on non-motorized travel	Ignores	Includes
Impacts on transportation choice	Limited analysis	Comprehensive analysis
Environmental impacts	Limited analysis	Comprehensive analysis
Impacts on land use	Ignores	Includes
Equity impacts	Limited analysis	Comprehensive analysis
Safety and health impacts	Per vehicle-kilometer crash risks	Per capita health risks

risk, and pollution. Some TDM strategies increase user prices, but these can provide offsetting consumer savings and economic benefits. For example, charging motorists directly rather than indirectly for roads and parking can reduce taxes and product costs otherwise needed to subsidize such facilities.

3. TDM evaluation and planning

TDM evaluation requires more comprehensive analysis than normally used for transport planning. Conventional transportation planning tends to use a reductionist approach, in which each problem is treated separately, assigned to a specific government agency with a limited mandate. For example, one agency is responsible for solving traffic congestion, another is responsible for traffic safety, another for environmental quality, and yet another for providing mobility for people who are transportation disadvantaged. This approach tends to undervalue strategies that provide modest but multiple benefits, and can result in solutions to one problem that exacerbates others.

For example, adding roadway capacity can help reduce traffic congestion, but wider roads and the increased vehicle traffic speeds and volumes that result tend to contradict other economic, social, and environmental objectives. Fuel efficiency standards help achieve environmental objectives, but by reducing vehicle-operating costs they can increase congestion, crashes, and urban sprawl. Only a comprehensive analysis framework that accounts for all of these impacts (Table 2) can identify which combination of strategies is overall optimal.

Most individual TDM strategies have modest impacts and benefits, affecting just a few percent of total vehicle travel. As a result, they are seldom considered the most effective solution to a transportation problem. But TDM strategies can have cumulative and synergetic impacts (i.e. their total impacts are greater than the sum of their individual impacts), so it is important to evaluate a TDM program as a package, rather than as individual strategies. A well-planned TDM program can have a significant effect on travel and make a significant contribution toward solving transportation problems.

The most effective TDM program involves a variety of complementary strategies. For example, just improving transit service, perhaps by building a metro system or creating busways, may by itself reduce just 5% of urban-peak automobile travel; and just implementing parking management and parking pricing programs may by itself reduce just 5% of a city's automobile travel. But if implemented together, these strategies may produce a 15% reduction in urban-peak automobile travel, because they provide a combination of positive and negative incentives for discretionary commuters (those who have the option of driving) to use alternative modes.

As much as possible, TDM strategies should give consumers choices. Inefficient and poorly implemented programs can have negative, unintended consequences. For example, some cities have implemented "no drive days," in which motorists are not allowed to use their automobiles on a particular day (e.g. vehicles with license numbers ending in 1 or 2 cannot drive Mondays, those with numbers ending in 3 or 4 cannot drive on Tuesdays, etc.). This is inefficient because it does not allow consumers to choose which trips to forego. It may cause a modest reduction in vehicle traffic if implemented for a week or two, but if implemented frequently it motivates wealthier households to purchase more cars, so they will always have one that can be driven, resulting in an overall increase in automobile travel and pollution emissions. It is far better to give motorists a financial incentive to reduce their driving, and let them forego their least valuable automobile trips.

Similarly, regulations may be ineffective if they are not well designed or enforced. An increase in fuel taxes may do little to reduce automobile travel if a large portion of motorists can purchase cheaper fuel illegally or by driving to another jurisdiction nearby. Taxes on commercial parking fees may simply encourage more employers to provide free parking to employees, in order to avoid the tax. Reducing roadway speed limits is important for improving non-motorized travel, but will do little without strong enforcement.

4. Market distortions and reforms

To understand why TDM can provide such large benefits, it is useful to consider some basic market principles. Efficient markets have certain requirements, including consumer choice, competition, cost-based pricing, and economic neutrality in public policies. Most markets reflect these principles. Consumers have many choices when purchasing food, housing, and clothing, and directly bear most costs associated with their production. But transport markets often violate these principles. TDM strategies can help correct these market distortions, creating a more efficient and equitable transport system (Table 3).

This is not to suggest that driving is bad, or that it provides no benefits. But in a more efficient and neutral transport market consumers would choose to drive less than they do now and be better off as a result. As an analogy, food is essential for life, and therefore provides tremendous benefits. However, this does not mean that more eating is necessarily better, that current diets are optimal, or that society should subsidize all food. At the margin (relative to current consumption), many people would benefit from eating less. If taxes subsidize food, we eat more but have less of things that are taxed, such as jobs, housing, and clothes. Food subsidies may be justified for undernourished people, but since overeating can be as unhealthy as undereating it is both economically and medically harmful to subsidize all food for everybody.

Similarly, that mobility provides benefits does not necessarily mean that more driving is better, that current levels of driving are optimal, or that driving should be subsidized. Transport underpricing is harmful because it requires subsidies from other economic sectors and results in excessive travel that increases many problems. Public policies that favor roadway investments, and automobile-oriented land use patterns are also harmful overall because they reduce travel choices and result in inefficient use of resources.

These inefficiencies are cumulative, so analysis of just one impact underestimates the total harm that results from price distortions, and the potential benefits from market reforms. For example, underpriced parking not only encourages inefficient use of parking facilities, it also exacerbates traffic congestion, roadway costs, crashes, and pollution. Similarly, underpricing parking increases not only congestion and roadway costs but also parking costs, traffic accidents, and pollution.

5. Win–win transportation solutions

Win–win transportation solutions are TDM strategies that are justified for their economic benefits (congestion reductions, road and parking cost savings, consumer cost savings, reduced crash damages, economic development benefits,

Table 3
TDM strategies support market efficiency by correcting market distortions, resulting in a more efficient and equitable transport system.

Market requirements	Current market distortions	TDM impacts
Choice Consumers need viable transport and location options to choose from	Consumers often have few viable alternatives to driving for transportation	TDM strategies often improve transport options and increase demand for travel alternatives.
Competition Producers must face competition to encourage innovation and efficient pricing	Most roads and transit services are public monopolies. There is often little competition or incentive for innovation	TDM strategies can remove barriers, and encourage competition and innovation
Cost-based pricing Prices should reflect costs as much as possible. There should be no significant external costs unless specifically justified	Transportation in general, and driving in particular, is significantly underpriced: most costs are either fixed or external. This results in economically excessive levels of driving and automobile dependency	Many TDM strategies involve more efficient pricing. Some require subsidies, but these are often less than current subsidies for driving, or justified on equity grounds
Economic neutrality Public policies (taxes, subsidies, and investment policies) should apply equally to comparable goods and users	Tax policies, and many transportation planning and funding practices favor automobile traffic over demand management alternatives	Many TDM strategies help correct existing biases in transportation planning and investment practices
Land use Land use policies should not favor automobile-oriented development	Zoning laws, development practices and utility pricing tend to encourage lower-density, automobile-dependent land use patterns	TDM strategies help create more efficient land use patterns and discourage automobile-dependent development

etc.) while also providing environmental and social benefits (Litman, 2000). As a result, they help achieve environmental and social objectives with little or no incremental cost. They consist of technically feasible changes to current policies and practices that use market principles to help solve transportation problems by removing distortions, increasing consumer choice, and encouraging more efficient travel behavior. Most win–win solutions require no new institutions or organizations.

Win–win solutions are "no regrets" measures that minimize such conflicts. They are justified regardless of the value placed on non-market environmental and social objectives. Although their individual impacts may appear modest, their combined benefits can be substantial. If fully implemented to the degree that they are economically justified win–win solutions could reduce motor vehicle impacts by 15–30%, or more if coordinated with other TDM policies. They could meet the Kyoto Protocol emission reduction targets while increasing consumer benefits and economic development. They are particularly important to help achieve more sustainable transportation.

Win–win solutions can be likened to a type of preventive medicine, equivalent to putting the transportation system on a healthier diet. This can avert more difficult and expensive measures that would otherwise be required to address the various problems resulting from increased motor vehicle traffic.

6. Examples of win–win solutions

6.1. Federal

Remove subsidies to oil production and internalize costs. The petroleum industry benefits from a number of subsidies and tax exemptions. These include petroleum research and development program funding, deductions on drilling costs and on oil wells, and royalty waivers on deep-water offshore drilling leases. Removing these creates a more neutral market for petroleum products, such as vehicle fuel.

Revenue-neutral tax shifting. Since governments must tax something to raise revenue, many economists recommend shifting taxes away from socially desirable activities to those that are harmful or risky. For example, a revenue-neutral shift from employment and general sales taxes to resource consumption taxes could reduce pollution while increasing economic productivity and employment. Such tax shifts provide economic benefits because higher fuel prices encourage energy efficiency and technological innovation, reduce the economic costs of imported petroleum, and encourage employment and investment, which stimulates economic development.

Pay-as-you-drive vehicle insurance and other distance-based fees. Converting vehicle insurance and registration fees from fixed charges to a distance-traveled basis approximately doubles variable vehicle expenses (e.g. a motorist who now pays A $1000 per year for insurance and registration would pay 8 cents per mile). This provides a significant financial incentive to reduce driving, while making these charges more fair and affordable. This is predicted to reduce vehicle travel by approximately 12%, reduce crash rates by a greater amount, increase equity, and save consumers money.

Least-cost transportation planning. Least-cost planning means that programs to reduce demand are considered equally with programs to increase capacity, that all significant impacts are included in the analysis, and that the public is involved in developing and evaluating alternatives. This allows demand management strategies to receive appropriate consideration and investment.

Road pricing. Road pricing can be used to reduce traffic congestion, and to charge motorists directly for their roadway costs, which is fairer than current practices that result in substantial cross-subsidies.

Reform motor carrier regulations. Many jurisdictions limit transportation service competition and innovation. Private bus, shuttle, and shared taxi services are often prohibited or restricted in order to maintain monopolies for existing service providers. Regulations should be minimized and focused to address specific problems while encouraging competition, consumer choice and innovation.

6.2. Regional and local

Local and regional TDM programs. TDM programs include a wide variety of services, including ride share matching, transit improvements, bicycle and pedestrian facility improvements, parking management, and promotion of alternative modes. These can provide significant financial savings to governments, businesses and consumers, as well as environmental benefits.

More efficient land use. Current development and land use practices tend to create dispersed, automobile-dependent land use patterns that reduce accessibility and are poorly suited for travel by other modes. "Smart growth" can help create more efficient land use patterns that improve transportation choice and provide other benefits.

More flexible zoning requirements. Parking and road requirements are often inflexible and overgenerous. There are many ways to reduce the amount of land devoted to roads and parking without constraining mobility. Local governments can reduce parking requirements for businesses that have travel management programs or that are located in areas with good transit service. Shared parking allows significant reductions in parking requirements. Parking pricing tends to reduce demand by 10–30%. Location efficient development policies allow households to avoid paying for residential parking spaces they do not need. These strategies provide direct economic and environmental benefits.

Parking cash out. "Cashing out" means that commuters who receive free parking are also offered a cash alternative if they use other modes. This typically reduces driving by 10–30%, and provides non-drivers with a benefit comparable in value to what drivers receive.

Commute trip reduction. Commute trip reduction (also called employee trip reduction or vehicle trip reduction) programs give commuters resources and incentives to reduce their automobile trips. These programs typically include improved transportation options, such as ride sharing, flextime, telecommuting and guaranteed ride home programs; and incentives such a parking management, commuter financial incentives and TDM marketing programs. Commute trip reduction programs often reduce automobile commutes by 20–40% at a particular work site.

Transportation management associations. Transportation management associations provide services such as ride share matching, transit information, and parking coordination in a particular area, such as a commercial district or mall. This achieves more efficient use of resources and allows businesses of all sizes to participate in commute trip reduction programs.

Location-efficient development. Location-efficient development consists of residential and commercial development in areas with mixed land use and good transportation choices (walking and cycling conditions, transit and car sharing services). These features result in reduced automobile ownership and use (10–30% reductions are typical), which provides transportation and parking cost savings to consumers.

School and campus transport management. These programs help overcome barriers to the use of alternative modes, and provide positive incentives for reduced driving to schools and college or university campuses. School trip management usually involves improving pedestrian and cycling access, promoting ride sharing, and encouraging parents to use alternatives when possible. Campus trip management programs often include discounted transit fares, ride share promotion, improved pedestrian and cycling facilities, and increased parking fees. These programs give students, parents, and staff more travel choices, encourage exercise, and reduce parking and congestion problems. They often reduce car trips by 15–30%.

Car sharing. Car sharing provides affordable, short-term (hourly and daily rate) motor vehicle rentals in residential areas. This gives consumers a convenient and affordable alternative to private ownership. Because it has lower fixed costs and higher variable costs than private vehicle ownership, car sharing encourages users to limit their vehicle use to those trips in which driving is truly the best option, and use alternative modes as much as possible. Drivers who join such organizations typically reduce the distance they drive by 30–50%.

Non-motorized transport improvements. Pedestrian and bicycle improvements are important for developing a more balanced transportation system. Residents of communities with good walking and cycling conditions drive less and use transit and ride share more. There are many specific methods for accommodating and encouraging non-motorized transport, including improvements to sidewalks, trails and paths, street crossings, and bicycle-parking facilities.

Traffic calming. Traffic calming includes various strategies to reduce traffic speeds and volumes on specific roads. Typical strategies include traffic circles at intersections, sidewalk bulbs that reduce intersection crossing distances, raised cross-walks, and partial street closures to discourage short-cut traffic through residential neighborhoods. This increases road safety and community livability, creates a more pedestrian- and bicycle-friendly environment, and can reduce vehicle travel, particularly when matched with other TDM measures.

7. Conclusions

TDM strategies can help achieve a variety of economic, social and environmental objectives. A properly planned TDM program can help reduce the environmental impacts of transportation while also supporting economic and social objectives.

Because most TDM strategies provide modest but multiple benefits, they tend to be overlooked and undervalued by conventional, reductionist planning. Conventional transportation planning often implements solutions to one problem that exacerbate others. More comprehensive planning tends to place a higher value on TDM solutions. Transportation professionals increasingly recognize the potential of TDM strategies to help solve problems, but they often treat them as measures of last resort, used to address specific congestion and air pollution problems where conventional solutions are ineffective or infeasible. When all impacts are considered, TDM strategies are often the most cost-effective way to improve transportation, and so should be broadly implemented.

References

Goodwin, P. (1997) *Solving congestion.* Inaugural lecture for the Professorship of Transport Policy. London: University College.
Litman, T. (2000) *Win–win transportation solutions.* Melbourne: Victoria Transport Policy Institute.
Litman, T. (2001) *Socially optimal transport prices and markets.* Melbourne: Victoria Transport Policy Institute.
Victoria Transport Policy Institute (2002) *Online TDM encyclopedia.* Melbourne: Victoria Transport Policy Institute.

AUTHOR INDEX

Abbey, E., 417, 418
Abdel-Aty, M.A., 659
Abdul-Khalek, I.S., 73
Abelson, P.W., 93
Abeyratne, R.I.R., 645
Abkowitz, M.D., 15, 713, 714
Adamowicz, V., 455
Adamowicz, W.L., 378, 381, 385, 386, 387, 391, 394
Adams, R.M., 381, 383, 438, 439
Agarwal, A., 48
Agyeman, J., 569, 570, 571, 573, 577, 579
Ajzen, I., 726, 727
Albernini, A., 539
Alcamo, J., 524
Aldous, T., 780
Alexander, G., 252
Alfuso, S.M., 175
Allen, J.C., 709
Alonso, W., 466
Ampt, E.S., 745, 750, 752
An, A., 192
Anas, A., 472
Anderson, D.G., 318
Anderson, J.R., 726
Anderson, S., 672, 675, 772
Anderson, W.P., 760
Anyon, P., 234
Appleyard, D., 123
Araya, C., 474
Armstrong, P.M., 399, 404
Arnott, R., 463, 472
Arsenio, E., 404
Atkin, G., 258
Atkins, S., 656
Avol, E.L., 418
Axhausen, K.W., 788
Ayres, R., 690

Babisch, W., 14
Baden, B.M., 566
Baker, J.M., 282
Balmes, J.R., 419
Bania, N., 656
Banister, D., 548, 783
Barrett, S., 519, 619
Barros, A.I., 696, 697, 699
Bass, R., 566, 568, 569
Bauman, Z., 661

Baumol, W.J., 430, 516
Beck, U., 661
Becker, G.S., 659
Beckmann, J., 740
Beer, T., 169, 170
Bem, D.J., 726
Ben Joseph, E., 772
Ben-Akiva, M., 732
Bento, A., 339, 542
Bickel, P., 351, 360, 361, 422, 430, 433, 438, 539
Blackmon Lane, L., 566, 569, 570, 573, 574, 577
Bleijenberg, A., 670, 677
Blinge, M., 149
Blowers, A., 550
Blumberg, D.F., 688
Böge, S., 671
Bohnhoff, A., 694
Bohringer, C., 628
Boks, C., 687
Bollens, S.C., 572
Borger, B.D., 432, 447
Bose, R., 186
Bowles, I.A., 524
Braden, J.B., 378, 379, 381
Braess, D., 338
Breheny, M.J., 760
Brindle, R., 779, 781, 782
Brinner, R.E., 488
Brög, W., 744, 751
Brookes, L., 492
Brown, R.S., 284
Bruinsma, F., 590
Buchan, K., 673
Bullen, R.B., 90
Burnett, R.T., 63, 419
Button, K.J., 313, 334, 338, 349, 591, 681, 779, 787, 793
Byrne, J., 43

Cackette, T.A., 73, 74
Cairns, S., 610
Calthorpe, P., 780
Campbell, J., 678
Canter, L.W., 312
Capaldo, K., 287
Carley, M., 606
Carpenter, T.G., 249, 250, 252, 253, 254
Carraro, C., 519, 619
Carson, R.T., 349, 378, 380

Carter, C.R., 694, 695, 700, 702, 703
Carthy, T., 456
Cassidy, K., 101, 715, 716
Castells, N., 520, 524, 657
Cater, E., 643
Cervero, R., 757
Chaiken, S., 725, 727, 729
Chakraborty, J., 569, 574, 577, 578
Checker, M., 566, 573
Chestnut, L.G., 436
Chilton, S., 457
Chow, J.C., 434
Christopher, M., 695
Church, W., 655
Clifton, K., 128, 134
Cline, W.R., 441
Clinton, K.M., 735
Coase, R.H., 107, 618
Cobb, J.B., 482
Cohen, G., 767
Cohen, H., 442
Cohen, M.J., 284
Colvile, R.N., 61
Common, M.S., 49
Cooper, J., 682
Copeland, B.R., 630
Costanza, R., 21
Costi, A., 580
Coursey, D.L., 566
Cowell, R., 554, 562
Crampton, C., 607
Crocker, T.D., 380, 381, 383
Cropper, M.L., 380, 422, 430, 436
Crouch, S., 655
Cullen, G., 780
Curry, D.A., 318

Daly, A.J., 396
Daly, H., 482
Daniels, R., 387, 391, 455
Daugherty, P.J., 702
Deaton, A.S., 594
DeCicco, J., 193
Delucchi, M.A., 54, 165, 167, 178, 179, 220, 411, 412, 415, 419, 422, 423, 424, 432, 433, 434, 435, 436, 440, 441, 442, 443, 444, 446, 447, 585
Dennis, R.L., 436
Dennis, S.M., 99, 103, 110, 708, 710, 711, 712
Dery, D., 767
Diamond, I., 654
Dicks, B., 283
Dietz, T., 729
Dijkstra, B.R., 586
Dijkstra.W.J., 298, 673
Dings, J.M.W., 275, 298, 673

Dittmar, H., 572, 578
Dockery, D.W., 69, 73, 417
Donaldson, K., 63, 69
Donaldson, S., 606
Donoso, P., 466, 472, 789, 790
Dörnemann, M., 789
Dotterer, S., 782
Douglas, M., 648
Dowlatshahi, S., 702
Downs, A., 588
Draper, D., 579
Dunn, S.C., 666
Dunnett, J., 771
Dupuit, J., 336, 346, 348, 351, 352, 353

Eagly, A.H., 725, 726, 727, 729, 732
Eberhard, C., 671
Egebäck, K.-E., 145, 146, 147
Ellickson, B., 468
Ellram, L.M., 694, 695, 700, 702, 703
Elvik, R., 593
Engwicht, D., 780
Ernish, E., 780
Esser, J., 789
Esty, D.C., 524
Evanoff, J., 644
Evans, A.W., 459
Evans, B., 550
Evans, S.M., 287
Everett, R., 252

Faiz, A., 160, 171, 172, 174, 175, 178, 269
Fazio, R.H., 726
Feitelson, E., 763, 766
Fels, M.F., 54
Fernando, P., 647
Ferrer, G., 690
Fishbein, M., 726, 727
Flippen, C.A., 566, 567, 573
Flybjerg, B., 763
Foley, D., 687
Folmer, H., 519
Ford, R., 250, 251
Forkenbrock, D.J., 319, 447, 571, 576
Fransson, N., 726, 728
Freeman, A.M., 378, 379, 381, 382, 385, 394
Frey, B.S., 586, 589
Fridstrom, L., 593
Friedrich, R., 351, 360, 361, 422430, 433, 438
Frischer, T., 63
Fritz, J.M., 566, 569
Fujita, M., 463, 464, 645, 471
Fullerton, D., 538, 539, 542
Fürnkrantz-Prskawetz, A., 651
Fyfe, N., 772, 773

Gabele, P.A., 70
Gamble, H.B., 92
Gandhi, V.P., 481
Gärling, T., 726, 727, 728, 730, 731
Garreau, A., 677
Gärtner, M., 29
Garvill, J., 727
Gaudry, M.J.I., 398
Gehl, J., 772
Gheorge, A.V., 100, 715, 717, 719
Ghio, A.J., 63
Gibbs, D., 547, 561
Gillen, D.W., 92
Gilmour, P.S.,
Gilpin, A., 510
Glasser, H., 762
Glasson, J., 510
Gold, J.R., 771
Goldberg, M.S., 418
Gollner, A., 741
Golob, T.F., 732
Gomez Ibañez, J.A., 596
Goodwin, P.B., 562, 603, 805
Goulder, L.H., 542
Gover, M.P., 180
Grant-Muller, S.M., 335, 336
Greene, D.L., 430
Greene, W.H., 788, 790
Gröndalen, O., 154
Groneau, R., 659
Grosse, S.D., 420
Gruebler, A., 590
Guide, V.D.R.Jr., 690, 691, 692, 695
Gunnarsson, S.O., 782
Gupta, J., 518
Gupta, S.M., 690
Guria, J., 457
Gustavsson, L., 151

Hahn, R.W., 539
Hailing, D., 442
Haites, E., 626, 627
Hall, F., 93
Hall, P., 548, 554
Hamilton, C., 49., 50
Hamilton, K., 652, 656
Hampicke, U., 21
Handy, S., 128, 134
Hanemann, W.M., 380, 393, 394
Hanley, N., 104, 336, 244, 345, 347
Hansen, S., 485, 486, 490, 494
Harrington, W., 538
Harrison, R.M., 74
Harvey, N., 509, 510
Hasselbad, V., 62
Hass-Klau, C., 606, 607, 778

Hayashi, Y., 33
Hede, A.J., 90
Hefflin, B.J., 415
Heil, M.T., 49
Helm, C., 628
Hensher, D.A., 313, 395, 398, 732, 779, 787, 788, 790, 792, 793, 794, 797
Hicks, J.R., 591
Hidano, N., 93
Hillman, M., 772
Hines, P., 695
Hirschman, A.O., 589
Hirshleifer, J., 28
Hite, D., 566
Hohmeyer, O., 29
Holgate, S.T., 63
Holman, C., 665, 678, 679
Holmes, T., 385
Holzapfel, H., 671
Hopkins, T.D., 284
Hopkinson, P., 675
Hordijk, L., 524
Horowitz, J.K., 342
Houghton, J.T., 38
Hsu.S.-L., 442, 443
Hu, P.S., 649, 650, 651, 652
Huang, J.C., 436
Huber, J., 395
Hughes, J.D., 499
Hunt, J.D., 400, 401
Hutcheson, R.C., 165

Isherwood, B., 648
Ising, H., 13., 14
Ito, K., 418

Jackson, G.C., 677
Jacobs, A., 772
Jacobson, M.Z., 16, 34
James, B., 751, 752
James, P., 675
Janssen, R., 336
Jayaraman, V., 695, 696, 697, 698, 699
Jefferson, C., 772
Jepma, C., 617, 621, 622, 623, 624
Jin, D., 284
Johansson, B., 150, 151, 153, 446
Johansson, P.-O., 594
Johnston, R.A., 447
Jones, J.C., 168, 169, 172
Jones, P., 725, 763
Jones-Lee, M.W., 453, 454, 455, 456, 457, 458, 460

Kado, N.Y., 70
Kaldor, N., 591
Kandlikar, M., 48

Kanninen, B., 293, 380, 394
Kazimi, C., 446
Ker, I., 751, 752
Khazzoom, J.D., 492
Khisty, C.J., 569, 573
Kinang, N., 207
Kitamura, R., 191
Kittelson, D.B., 69, 73
Koenig, J.Q., 62, 63
Kolstad, C.D., 378, 379, 381, 530, 539
Kopicki, R.J., 687, 690, 696, 700, 701, 702
Kotz, R., 25
Kraus, S.J., 727
Krikke, H.R., 694, 696, 697
Kroon, L., 696, 697
Krupnick, A.J., 418, 422
Kuhl, J., 740
Kukkonen, C.A., 176
Kulash, D.J., 54
Kulesa, P., 726, 732
Kurani, K., 191
Kverndokk, S., 517

Laden, F., 516
Lane, B., 258
Lang, J., 779
Latimer, J.S., 444
Lave, L., 761
Lee, D.S., 438
Lee, J.T., 420
Lee-Gosselin, 735
Leeming, D.G., 719, 720
Leete, L., 656
Lefevre, C., 767
Lenzen, M., 43, 48, 54
Levesque, T.J., 92
Lewis, C.A., 180
Lichfield, N., 762
Lichtenstein, S., 112
Lim, L.L., 605
Linde, C.van der., 518
Lindsey, C.R., 341
Lipman, G., 640
Lipman, T.E., 193
List, G.F., 115
List, G.F., 721, 722
Litman, T., 366, 372, 595, 597, 598, 805, 810
Lloyd, A.C., 73, 74
Loomes, G., 456, 457, 460
Loukaitou-Sideris, A., 134
Louviere, J.J., 378, 381, 394
Louwers, D., 696, 697, 698
Loy, J.M., 285
Lund, R., 694

Machado, G., 43
Mackenzie, J.J., 176

Mackett, R., 571, 572, 575, 576, 577
Mackie, P.J., 335, 336, 338, 348, 645
MacKinnon, J.G., 463, 472
MacNee, W., 63
Maddison, D., 227, 376,
Maibach, M, 268
Maister, D.H., 669
Majone, G., 762, 763
Mäler, K.-G., 519
Marchal, P., 302
Marheineke, T., 54
Mark, J., 162
Marland, G., 46
Marshall, A.W., 594
Marshall, S., 782, 783
Martínez, F.J., 466, 467, 472, 474, 789, 790
Masche, C., 13
Mas-Colell, A., 469
Maser, S.M., 92
Maslennikova, I., 687
Matley, T.M., 580, 581
Matsuhashi, R., 54
Maxwell, T.T., 168, 169, 172
Mayeres, I., 542, 543
McAffe, P., 467
McCluskey, J., 780
McCubbin, D.R., 412, 419, 422, 423, 424, 433, 434
McDonnell, W.F., 418
McFadden, D., 394
McKinnon, A.C., 665, 666, 670, 675, 676, 677, 678, 680
Mcmillan, J., 467
McMillan, M., 93
Metcalf, G., 542
Meyburg, A.H., 505
Mieszkowski, P., 93
Miller, E., 788, 789, 791
Miller, T.R.
Minahan, T., 687
Missfeldt, F., 619
Mitchell, B., 579
Mitchell, R.C., 349, 378, 380
Mokhtarian, P.L., 134
Moltke, K.von, 524
Mongelluzzo, B., 286
Moolgavkar, S.H., 418, 419
Moore, L.A.R., 338
Morellet, O., 302
Morey, C., 162
Morisugi, H., 33
Morley, E.R., 385
Morris, R., 419
Morrison, A.D., 459
Moudon, A.V., 772
Moughtin, J.C., 772
Muellbauer, J., 594

Author Index

Mueller.D.C., 588, 594
Mullins, F., 626, 627
Munasinghe, M., 617, 621, 622, 623, 624
Munda, G., 336
Murphy, J.J., 437, 438
Murray, J., 236

Nagel, K., 788, 789
Nakicenovic, N., 590
Nansai, K., 54
Narain, S., 48
Nash, C.A., 336, 391
Nasr, N., 694, 697
Neas, L.M., 417
Nellthorp, J., 335, 336, 338, 348, 645
Nelson, J.P., 92
Neumayer, E., 43
Nicolet-Monnier, M., 100, 715, 717
Nijkamp, P., 56, 520
Noland, R.B., 605
Nordhaus, W.D., 29, 482, 524
Novaco, R.W., 133
Ntziachristos, L., 61, 67

O'Byrne, 95
Oates, W.E., 430, 436, 516
Oberholzer-Gee, F., 764
Ogden, J.M., 154
Ogden, K.W., 681
Olkin, I., 594
Opschoor, J.-B., 520
Orenstein, G., 654
Ortúzar, J. de D., 312, 395, 400, 402, 403
Ostro, B., 417, 418
Ouellette, J.A., 727
Owen, D., 257
Owens, S., 554, 562

Painuly, J.P., 48
Palm, R., 654
Palmquist, R.B., 92
Pandis.S.N., 62, 72
Parikh, J.K., 48
Parkhurst, G.P., 609
Parry, I.W.H., 339, 542
Parsons, G., 381, 385
Pastowski, A., 667, 670
Patterson, E., 524
Paxton, A., 672
Pearce, D.W., 515,
Pearman, A.D., 681
Penner, J., 71, 72
Perman, R., 349
Petts, J., 310, 315
Petty, R.E., 726, 733
Pezzey, J., 344

Phaneuf, D.J., 385
Plotkin, S., 188
Plowden, S., 673
Pollack, T., 571, 575
Pope, C.A., 63, 73, 415, 420
Porter, G., 647
Porter, M.E., 518
Poterba, J., 598
Potter, S., 247, 251, 252, 254, 256, 260
Pred, A., 654
Prest, A.R., 336
Price, I., 92
Proops, J.L.R., 43., 49
Proost, S., 540, 541, 542, 543
Prozzi, J., 187
Pucher, J., 767
Purvis, C.L., 570, 571, 575, 576
Putnam, R.D., 520
Pyle, S.M., 70

Quan, R., 569, 575, 579
Quillian, L., 566, 573
Quinet, E., 93, 445

Rabl, A., 433
Raiffa, H., 520
Rao, S.T., 313
Rapoport, A., 779
Ravetz, J., 524
Realff, M.J., 694, 696, 697, 698
Rembert, T.C., 689
Rhyne, W.R., 100, 715, 716, 718
Rietveld, P., 343, 590, 595, 763
Riley, J.C., 28
Rittberger, V., 520
Rizzi, L.I., 395, 400
Robinson, T., 753
Rodier, C.J., 447, 760
Rodríguez, G., 400
Rogers, D.S., 687, 688, 690, 694
Romilly, P., 446
Rooney, A., 745, 752
Roos, D., 297
Roos, J., 268
Root, A., 517, 648, 650
Rose, A.B., 54
Rose, G., 745, 750, 753
Rosen, S., 90, 394, 466
Rothengatter, W., 320
Roy, R., 251, 252, 260
Rydin, Y., 547, 548, 561

Saaty, T., 762
Saccamanno, F.F., 101, 715, 716, 718, 719, 720, 722
Saegert, S., 654
Saelensminde, K.
Sagar, A., 48

Salma, U., 49
Salomon, I, 763
Salvini, P., 788, 789, 791
Samet, J.M., 63, 417
Samuelsson, A., 676
Sanchez, T., 571
Sandalow, D.B., 524
Sansom, T., 227
Saper, A., 93
Saunders, H.D., 492
Savage, I., 98, 105, 113, 284
Schade, W., 32
Schadler, M., 744, 751
Schaeffer, K.H., 655
Schelling, T.C, 468, 520
Schindler, C., 62
Schipper, L., 49, 54, 55, 56, 58, 204, 207, 212, 213, 214, 219, 222
Schneider, C., 268
Scholl, L., 55, 204, 207
Schwartz, J., 415, 417, 419
Schwartz, S., 728
Schweitzer, L.A., 571, 576
Sclar, E., 655
Sebenius, J.K., 520
Seinfeld, J.H., 62, 72
Seisler, J., 167
Selden, T.M., 49
Shavell, S., 106, 107, 113
Shelef, M., 176
Sheppard, B.H., 726, 727
Shi, J.P., 74
Shiomi, E., 680
Shooter, A., 260
Sidhu, S.S., 633
Sillano, M., 403
Siniscalco, D., 619
Slovic, P., 111
Small, K.A., 336, 338, 340, 341, 393, 597, 659
Smith, H., 58
Smith, S., 48
Smith, V.K., 436
Solow, R., 466
South, L.J., 573, 576, 580
Southworth, M., 772
Spadaro, J.V., 433
Spain, D., 649, 656
Spash, C.L., 437
Spengler, T., 696, 697, 699
Sperling, D., 185, 186, 187, 191, 193, 220, 221
Spice, B., 287
Spitzner, M., 651, 653, 657
Srivastava, R., 692, 695
Steele, P., 643
Steininger, K.W., 518
Stern, P.C., 728, 729, 730

Sterner, T., 517
Stock, J.R., 687, 688, 694, 700, 702
Stopher, P.R., 505
Storey, J., 258
Straaten, J.van der., 520
Strait, J.B., 571
Strutyniski, P., 672
Suzuki, Y., 315
Swait, J., 388
Swaney, J.A., 520

Talley, W.K., 280, 281, 282
Taniguchi, E., 681
Taylor, G.E., 439
Taylor, M.S., 630
Teufel, D., 248
Thierry, M., 690
Thøgersen, J., 730
Thomas, I., 497, 498, 499
Thomas, V.M., 420
Thorpe, N, 753
Thurston, G.D., 418
Tibben-Lembke, R.S., 687, 688, 690, 694
Tilanus, B., 676
Tinbergen, J., 586
Tirschwell, P., 286
Tisato, P., 753
Tisdell, C.A., 641
Tobin, J., 482
Tol, R.S.J., 441
Tolley, R., 783
Ton, T., 792, 794, 796
Tonn, B., 569
Tracey, M., 677
Trawén, A., 456
Truong, T.P., 626
Tuolomi, G., 63
Turnquist, M.A., 115, 721
Turrentine, T., 191
Turton, H., 49, 57
Turvey, R., 336
Tweddle, G., 682

Ulrich, R.S., 133
Uno, K., 482
Uyeno, D., 93

Van den Bergh, J.C.J.M., 349, 517
Van Dender, K., 540, 541
van der Heijden, R.E.C.M., 681
Van Lange, P.A.M., 729
van Veen-Groot, D., 56
Varian, H., 333, 334, 337
Veerakamolmal, P., 690
Veldhuisen, J., 788, 789
Verhoef, E.T., 341, 345, 350, 442, 542, 591763
Verplanken, B., 727, 734

Vigar, G., 762, 763
Viscusi, W.K., 422
Vrijens, G., 696, 697

Waddell, P., 789
Walsh, M.P., 188
Wang, Q., 190, 220
Warford, J.J., 515
Watkins, L.H., 313
Watson, J.G., 434
Watson, R.T., 37
Wayte, A., 740
Weck-Hannemann, H., 764
Weeks, J.L., 580
Wegener, D.T., 726, 733
Wegener, M., 760, 788, 793, 800, 802
Weisbrod, G.E., 319
Wessel, T., 566, 572, 580
West, S., 538, 539
Westerman, H., 779, 782
Whalley, A., 772
White, I.C., 282
Whiteing, T., 671
Whitelegg, J., 667, 673, 677

Wichmann, H.E., 415
Williams, B., 187
Williams, H.C.W.L., 338
Willig, R.D., 337
Willis, K.G., 445
Willumsen, L.G., 312
Wilson, B., 49
Wood, C., 251, 256, 510
Wood, W., 727
Woodburn, A., 666, 680
Worsford, F., 666
Wu, H.-J., 666

Xu, Z., 420

Yao, D.A., 538
Young, J., 649, 650, 651, 652
Young, O.R., 520

Zajonc, R.B., 726
Zanobetti, A., 63
Zauke, G., 651, 653, 657
Zeger, S., 419
Zmirou, D., 420
Zwerina, K., 395

SUBJECT INDEX

accessibility, 2, 117–40, 265
accidents, *see* safety
acid rain, 437–9
 see also agriculture
Acts
 Australian Environmental Protection (Impact of Proposals) Act (1974), 411
 California Environmental Quality Act (1970), 509
 German Packaging Ordinance Act, 689
 German Recycling and waste Control Act, 689
 US Alternative Motor Fuels Act, 508
 US Civil Rights Act (1964), 134, 572
 US Clean Air Act Amendment (1977), 505–7
 US Clean Air Act Amendment (1990), 507
 US Clean Water Act, 286, 644
 US Department of Transportation Act (1966), 503
 US Energy Conservation and Policy Act (1975), 508
 US Environmental Quality Improvement Act (1970), 505
 US Federal Clean Air Act (1970), 62, 386, 505, 644
 US Federal Railroad Safety Act (1970), 113
 US Federal-Aid Highway Act (1968), 503, 505
 US Federal-Aid Highway Act (1970), 505, 506
 US Intermodal Surface Efficiency Transportation Act (1991), 132, 506
 US National Environmental Policy Act (1969), 117, 502–5
 US National Invasive Species Act (1996), 286
 US Oil Pollution Act, 644
 US toxic Substances Act (1976), 289
aesthetic effects, 357–8, 362–3, 382
 see also visual intrusion
agriculture, 15, 41, 68, 318, 364, 381–5, 435
 crop loss, 437–8
Air Quality Improvement Research Program, 161, 165, 173
air transport, 9, 10, 15, 53, 54, 55, 57, 71–2, 204, 207, 210, 263–77, 380–1, 596, 633, 637, 640
 air freight, 83, 212, 298
 air traffic control, 275
 aircraft, 1, 68, 71, 72, 83, 84, 88, 89, 93, 94, 98, 363–77, 297
 airports, 14, 16, 68, 72, 81–95, 267–8, 369, 590
Air Transport Action Group, 286
ALOGIT, 396

amenity, 117–40
American Association of State Highway and Transportation Officials, 133, 177
American Lung Association, 63
Arrow–Lind theorem, 346
asthma, 63, 69, 414, 417
auctions, 467, 477
Australian Department of Environment, Sport and Tourism, 511
automobiles, *see* cars

barges, 98, 212, 282–3
benefit–cost analysis, *see* cost–benefit analysis
benzene, 68, 76, 145, 160, 166, 169, 173, 231
bio-diversity, 3, 4, 23, 16, 17, 30, 283–6, 386
bio-fuels, 57, 142, 143, 145–9, 150–1, 153, 174–5, 179, 181, 186, 206, 221, 234–5, 240–2, 244, 273, 446
Braess paradox, 338
bridges, 16, 127, 133
British Columbia Ministry of Energy, Mines, and Petroleum Resources, 167
Bus Industry Confederation, 237, 238, 239
buses, 10, 15, 52, 54, 118, 122, 134, 176–8, 207, 217–8, 227–44, 247–61, 276, 297, 370–1, 633, 640, 651
 depots, 249, 446–7
 lanes, 556, 778, 794

California Air Resources Board, 67, 228, 232
California Department of Transportation, 131
canals, *see* inland waterways
cancer, 74, 112, 365, 412–4, 419, 423
car sharing, 218, 766, 806, 813
cars, 1–3, 13, 15, 52, 64, 118, 176, 185–98, 203–12, 217, 218–20, 237, 247, 253, 255–6, 295, 297, 302–3, 306, 340, 352, 370–2, 397, 411–25, 430–48, 492, 530–46, 559–60, 571, 596–7, 640, 560–2, 654, 750, 766, 792, 795, 802, 807–12
catalytic converters, 61, 145, 162, 172, 233, 530
Cleaner Vehicle Task Force, 237
climate change, *see* global warming
cold starts, 71, 145, 169, 171–2
combined transport, 300
Commission of the EU, 23, 33
Commonwealth of Independent States, 627–8
Commonwealth Scientific and Industrial Research Organization, 235, 237

community severance, 17, 117–40, 318–9, 348, 357
commuting, 133, 259, 558, 797–8
competitive general equilibrium model, 494
congestion, 3, 181, 210, 223–4, 227, 266, 310, 320–1, 325, 339, 372, 446, 454, 485, 540–2, 544, 577, 586, 597, 671, 806, 813–4
connectivity, 117–40
Conservation of Clean Air and Water in Europe, 162
containers, 300
contingent valuations, 105, 127, 128, 130, 378, *see also* stated preference modeling
Convention on the Prevention of maritime Pollution by Dumping of Waste and Other Materials at Sea, 290
COPERT, 67
cost–benefit analysis, 16, 17, 30, 33, 104, 124, 138, 181, 333–54, 429, 451, 462, 566, 568, 586, 591–9, 645
cost-effectiveness analysis, 107, 141, 147, 151, 156, 284, 539, 662
costs
    clean-up, 103–4, 620
    marginal, 85, 86, 105, 339, 348, 362
    marginal abatement, 239
    operating, 88
    sunk, 18
    see also externalities
cycling, 118, 120, 122, 128–9, 131, 135, 138, 302, 340, 604, 775–7, 783–3
    lanes, 778

Dalton principle, 594–9
damage function, 377–8
diesel fuel, 16, 52, 64, 67, 69, 70, 74, 142, 145–7, 150, 153, 159, 161–2, 164, 167–70, 174–5, 178, 181, 187–8, 194, 211, 213, 216–7, 220–1, 230–3, 237, 239, 240–1, 248–9, 250–1, 258, 367, 412, 446
discrete choice models, 91, 392, 395–400
dredging, 288–9, 290
Dutch Ministry of Transport, 585
DWG Research Associates, 87

ecological economics, 21
ecosystems, 4, 316–8, 357, 363–4, 373, 376, 382
    see also bio-diversity
elderly, 63
electric power, 142, 147, 154, 166, 177–9, 185, 189–91, 193–7, 204, 216, 219, 232–4, 248, 250, 257–8, 296, 446
emergency response services, 115, 777
emission standards, 31, 250, 251, 266, 272, 313, 532–6
    CAFE standards, 537, 573
    minimum, 22, 28, 30–1, 578

Energy Technology Support Unit, 258
energy use, 5, 141, 143–4, 255, 293–307, 577
enforcement policies, 33
environmental impact statement, 117, 504
    assessment, 309–29, 509–10, 513
environmental justice, 565–83
Environmental law Institute, 569
environmental pricing, 529–44
equity, 585–60
ethanol, 67, 146, 150, 153, 160, 166–8, 173–4, 179, 180–2, 186–7, 206, 221, 258
European Commission, *see* European Union
European Conference of Ministers of Transport, 297, 305, 306, 347, 348, 351, 352, 482, 536, 605, 607, 668
European Union, 10, 22–4, 33, 48, 50, 51, 61, 67, 229, 236, 239, 252, 257, 273, 304, 537, 553, 585, 653, 666, 670, 681, 689
    Environmental Action Plan, 553
EUROSTAT, 9
Extern E Study, 229, 236, 239, 240, 440
externalities, 10, 82, 83, 93, 95, 97, 106–8, 229, 334, 343, 349, 353, 362, 429–48, 463–78, 481, 568–9, 597, 672, 709, 757–8, 763–4

Food and Agricultural Organization, 521–2
forests, 15, 439–40, 448, 486
free riders, 629–30
Freight Transport association, 672
fuel alternatives, 142–57, 159–83
fuel cells, 142, 192–8, 232, 258–9
fuel efficiency, 70, 185–99, 640, 730–1

gasoline engines, 16, 52, 64, 67, 74, 101, 110, 142, 145, 150, 153–4, 159–61, 167–68, 170, 179, 181, 185, 187–90, 195, 213, 220, 538, 765
gender issues, 5, 648–62
geographical information systems, 129, 320, 574, 578–9
global warming, 5, 16, 37–58, 238–40, 277, 346, 352, 366, 447, 615–31
green accounts, 482–94
greenhouse gases, 3, 13, 16, 37–58, 142, 145, 150, 167, 178, 185–6, 203–24, 243, 268–9, 271, 296, 358, 367–8, 512, 516, 615–31, 648, 797
Greenpeace, 283

hazardous materials, 97, 110, 111–2, 113, 114–5, 219, 707–24
health effects, 3, 13, 17, 26–7, 62–3, 99–100, 141, 165, 166, 228, 230, 236–7, 249, 285, 352, 359–60, 368, 376, 411–25, 433–4
    valuation of life, 25, 361–2, 394–400, 451–62, 711–4
hedonic prices, 90, 128, 369, 379–80, 384
hybrid engines, 142, 148, 177, 191–3, 219, 234, 258, 261

Subject Index

hydrogen fuels, 147–8, 150, 153–4, 156, 166, 175–7, 193–5, 19, 221, 257

INFRAS, 13, 15, 29, 371
infrastructure, 1, 2, 4, 16, 17, 33, 103, 266, 305, 316, 341, 357–8, 365, 385, 585, 590
  construction, 18, 644
inland waterways, 9, 10, 15, 98, 213–4, 282, 298, 371, 590, 607
input–output analysis, 319
Institute for Public Policy Research, 273, 275
Institution of Highways and Transportation, 777
insurance, 811
Intergovernmental Panel on Climate Change, 16, 22, 37, 39, 40, 41, 42, 43, 49, 51, 52, 54, 55, 56, 149, 264, 269, 270–2, 275, 615, 616
International Air Transport association, 264, 273
International Civil Aviation Organization, 72, 267, 270, 273, 275, 277
International Energy Agency, 47, 52, 53, 54, 58, 152, 153, 180, 185, 203, 204, 205, 207, 208, 210, 211, 213, 215, 217, 218, 219, 220, 222, 224, 260
International Maritime Organization, 285, 288, 289, 290
International Road Transport Union, 665
International Road Union, 299
International Tanker Owners Pollution Federation, 280, 281
International Union of Railways, 250
Internet, 635
investment, 27, 83, 84, 322, 483, 534, 578, 604, 807
  appraisal, 333–54
  see also cost–benefit analysis
IRPUD, 788, 793, 799–803
IVU, 22, 668
IWW, 13, 28, 29, 30, 31

Johannesburg Summit, 270
just-in-time production, 667, 677, 680, 682

Keynesian economics, 586
Kyoto Protocol, 16, 50, 51, 56, 203, 224, 227, 239, 269–70, 277, 295, 368, 616–9, 621, 626–8

land-use, 3, 4, 41, 117–40, 141, 222, 317–9, 364, 372, 376, 463–78, 547–62, 566–7, 574–6, 787–804
  compact cities, 572
lead, 3, 14, 75, 144, 160, 165, 412, 751
leakage, see spillage
liability, 108–13
liquid petroleum gas, 110, 149, 150, 179, 180, 181, 208, 217, 221, 235–7, 239–42, 251, 257
logistics, 3, 665–83, 687–704

reverse logistics, 687–704
lorries, see trucks

MATISSE, 302
methane, 16, 38–9, 41–2, 53, 62, 142, 146–7, 150, 153, 166–8, 172, 179, 181, 186, 194–5, 206, 221, 257–8, 446
metro, see transit and subways
Ministerie van Volkshuisvesting, Ruimtelijke Ordening en Milieubeheer, 220
MOBILE, 67, 75
Montreal Protocol, 39
motorcycles, 68, 217, 370
multi-criteria analysis, 335–6
multilateral environmental agreements, 515–26
Mumbai Urban Transport Project, 322–8

National Ambient Air Quality Standards (US), 62, 63, 64, 66, 413, 505
National Greenhouse Gas Inventory Committee, 52–3
National Personal Transportation Survey, 648–9, 651, 653
National Roads and Motorists' Association, 741
Netherlands Economic Institute, 674
noise, 1, 3, 5, 13–4, 19, 81–95, 162, 223, 253, 264, 266, 314–6, 320, 325, 334, 358–9, 368–9, 372, 382, 385, 541, 571
  contours, 88
  measures, 87–8, 442
  traffic noise index, 315–6
  valuation, 89–93, 347, 349, 352, 404–7, 441–3
noise depreciation index, 92
non-renewable resources, 3
nuclear energy, 143, 179
  risk, 18

on-board diagnostics, 67
Organisation for Economic Co-operation and Development, 47, 53, 165–6, 173, 177, 186, 197, 220, 248, 258, 260, 440, 482, 494, 510, 628, 763
Organization of the Petroleum Exporting countries, 152, 431
ozone, 16, 19, 61, 62, 69–70, 72, 239, 346, 348, 383, 413, 418

packaging, 115, 665–6, 678–9
Pareto optimality, 591–3, 594
parking, 133, 372, 541, 544, 778, 807
  park-and-ride, 550, 558, 604, 609–10, 612, 806
peak demand, 253, 255, 339, 341, 447, 808
  see also congestion
pedestrians, 118, 120, 122, 128, 129, 134, 135, 138, 256, 302, 604, 606–7, 651, 745, 772–8, 806
perfluorocarbons, 39
pipelines, 98, 102

polluter-pays principle, 12, 358
precautionary principle, 552, 622–3
prevention policies, 26, 28
prices
　fuel, 170
　marginal cost, 33
　shadow, 28–31
profits, 81, 260, 382, 628, 643
propane, 166, 170
property rights, 87, 95, 107–8, 618
public goods, 323, 396, 464

quantitative risk assessment, 100–2, 103, 113, 114, 115
quantitative risk assessment, 715–6, 722–3

Railtrack, 458–61
railways, 2, 9–10, 15, 16, 53–4, 57, 68, 70–1, 9–99, 101, 113–5, 118–9, 121, 177, 207, 210, 212–5, 248–51, 260, 293–307, 316, 323, 352, 370, 451, 590, 607
　high speed, 276, 297
　light, 794
　piggy back trains, 304–5
　safety, 457–8
RAINS, 524
random bidding model, 469
recycling, 644
　see also scrapping and reverse logistics
Red Cross, 109
REDEFINE, 668
revealed preference methods, 26, 91–2, 104–5, 124, 127, 128, 349, 360, 377–8, 375–88
REVLOG, 698
Rio Earth Summit, 277, 490, 518, 520–1, 553
risk, 12, 27, 32, 346–7, 451, 661, 715–7, 722
　perception, 111–12
road pricing, 58, 223, 302, 597, 599, 730, 763, 764, 806, 812
roads, 1, 3, 9, 16, 53- 4, 56, 61, 64–6, 68, 71, 76, 93, 98, 115, 119, 123, 131–2, 141, 181, 222, 227, 304–5, 316, 323, 338, 343, 359, 363, 376, 391–2, 446, 451, 566–8, 586, 590, 596, 604–12, 638, 657, 667, 670, 771–85
　safety, 456–62
Roskill Commission on the Third London Airport, 84
Royal Institute for International Affairs, 260
Royal Society, 102–3
Royal Society of Canada, 383–4
rule-of-half, 338

safety
　of fuel, 170–4, 178
　of travel 1-5, 18, 97–116, 310, 353, 358, 369, 371, 376, 394–6, 451–62, 483, 541, 577
　see also hazardous materials
school transport, 243, 813
Scientific Review Panel, 73
scrapping, 539
seaports, 1, 4, 288–9, 608, 640
second-best options, 26, 401–2
security, 265
shadow prices, 335, 337, 341, 345–6
shipping, 2, 54, 68, 70, 101–2, 212–5, 279–90, 298
shopping, 249, 253, 659, 773, 775–6
smog, 17, 61
smoke, 164, 234
social rate of discount, 27
soil contamination, 17, 641
solar cells, 148, 152, 179
solar energy, 152, 154
speed limits, 530, 606, 806, 809
spillage, 99, 167, 170, 279, 363, 443–4, 707–24
　see also hazardous materials
Standing Advisory Committee on Trunk Road Assessment, 340, 605, 607
stated preference methods, 91, 105, 124, 349, 361, 375–88, 391–408
Stockholm Conference on the Human Environment, 521
storage tanks, 98
stress, 133
subsidies, 257, 475–6, 486, 533–7, 541, 543, 595, 809, 811
subways, 119, 250
　London Underground, 253, 336, 458–60
surveys, 125–6, 762
sustainable development, 3, 4, 224, 264–6, 277, 295, 561–2, 588, 595–8, 617
　lifestyles, 742
　streets, 771–7, 782–3
　transport, 309–29, 573, 683

taxes, 83, 155, 188, 234, 239, 255, 273, 304, 341, 368, 431–2, 475, 486, 488, 491, 532–44, 592, 619, 765–6, 796–8, 806, 809, 811
taxicabs, 217, 257, 777, 806
teleworking, 806
theory of planned behavior, 726
theory of real outcomes, 726
tolls, 4, 303–4, 395
tourism, 5, 17, 266, 633–45
traffic bans, 604, 606–7, 612
traffic calming, 606–7, 814
traffic free zones, 127
trains, see railways
trams, 177, 207, 248, 250
TransEuropean Networks, 23, 300
transit, 120, 207, 209, 218, 571, 609–10, 651, 775, 776, 783, 803
transition economies, 10–12

Subject Index 827

transport efficiency index, 321–2
transport planning, 123–4, 127, 130, 547–62, 565–93, 680–1
Transport Research Laboratory, 777
Transportation Research Board, 566, 569, 571, 572, 573, 576, 577, 734
travel blending, 736–54
travel time values, 394, 402, 659
TRENEN, 540
TRESIS, 788, 793–6, 801
trip chaining, 652–3, 732
trucks, 1, 2, 3, 10, 52, 54, 64, 98, 101, 110, 188, 195, 204, 207–8, 212–5, 217, 223, 247, 250, 295, 297–8, 306, 315, 352, 442, 665–83
tunnels, 101

UK Cabinet Office, 57
UK Commission for Integrated Transport, 680
UK Department of the Environment, 554
UK Department of Health, 229
UK Department of the Environment, Transport and the Regions, 274, 452, 548, 553, 554, 555, 556, 649, 665, 668, 674, 676, 677, 679, 682
UK Department of Trade and Industry, 248, 258
UK Department of Transport, Local Government and the Regions, 452, 456, 457, 458, 740, 743, 745, 746, 749, 750, 751, 752
UK Home Office, 656
UK Ministry of Transport, 781
UK Office of the Deputy Prime Minister, 649
UK Royal Commission for Environmental Pollution, 57, 272, 548, 553, 554, 562, 673, 743
UN Conference on the Human Environment, 72
UN Development Program, 482
UN Environmental Program, 49, 274, 510, 518–9, 615
UN Framework Convention on Climate Change, 49, 521–2, 616, 617, 620, 623
UN System of National Accounts, 482
UN Trade and Development Agency, 515, 519
uncertainty, 27, 38, 346, 351
Urban Institute, 456
US Agency for Industrial Development, 510
US Bureau of Public Roads, 502
US Bureau of Transportation Statistics, 513, 655
US Coast Guard, 98
US Congressional Budget Office, 54
US Consumer Expenditure Survey, 539
US Department of Commerce, 124
US Department of Health and Community Services, 576
US Department of Transportation, 99, 117, 131, 456, 503, 506, 565, 569, 570
US Environmental Protection Agency, 61, 62, 63, 64, 65, 66, 67, 68, 69, 70, 71, 72, 73, 74, 75, 165, 229, 233, 286, 376, 386–7, 412, 413, 418, 437, 443, 488, 505
US Federal Aviation Administration, 87
US Federal Highways Administration, 131, 132, 133, 315, 318, 325, 502–3, 569, 570, 571, 573, 574, 578
US Federal Reserve Bank, 489
US Federal Transit Administration, 570
US General Accounting Office, 655
US National Acid Precipitation Assessment Program, 439
US National Aeronautic and Space Administration, 194
US National Highway Traffic Safety Administration, 508
US National Research Council, 66, 101, 188, 267
US National Science Board, 658
US Office of Technology Assessment, 165, 178
US Overseas Development Administration, 510
US Research and Special Programs Administration, 708

valuation methods, *see* revealed preference methods *and* stated preference methods
vandalism, 119
vehicle maintenance, 18, 145, 167
vibrations, 347, 358
   benefits transfers, 387
visibility, 434–6
visual intrusion, 16–7, 348
volatile organic compounds, 3, 14, 39, 62, 63, 68, 69, 161, 231, 412–3

walking, *see* pedestrians
waste disposal, 285–6, 348, 372
waste, *see* hazardous materials
water contamination, 13, 16–7, 67, 277–90, 348, 352, 357, 444–5
weight limits, 679
willingness to pay, 13, 25, 33, 229, 337, 349, 378, 388, 391, 392, 404, 422, 436, 451–62, 469–70, 678
wind power, 152, 154
World Bank, 510
World Commission on Environment and Development, 47–8, 264, 310, 553
World Energy Council, 144, 147, 148, 152
World Health Organization, 15, 19, 22, 229, 521
World Meteorological Organization, 49, 616
World Summit for Sustainable Development, 518
World Tourism Organization, 636
World Trade Organisation, 517, 525, 526
World Travel and Tourist Council, 635

zero-emissions vehicles, 187, 197
zoning, 550